P 372
specialized body

CAPITAL
VOLUME ONE

A Critique of Political Economy

KARL MARX

Translated by Samuel Moore and
Edward Aveling

Edited by Friedrich Engels

Dover Publications, Inc.
Mineola, New York

Bibliographical Note

This Dover edition, first published in 2011, is an unabridged republication of *Capital*, as published by The Modern Library, New York, in 1906.

Library of Congress Cataloging-in-Publication Data

Marx, Karl, 1818-1883.
   [Kapital. English]
   Capital / Karl Marx.
      p. cm.
   "This Dover edition, first published in 2011, is an unabridged republication
of Capital, as published by The Modern Library, New York, in 1906."
   ISBN-13: 978-0-486-47748-0
   ISBN-10: 0-486-47748-7
   1. Capital. 2. Economics. I. Title.

HB501.M36 2011
335.4'12—dc22

2010038540

Manufactured in the United States by Courier Corporation
47748701
www.doverpublications.com

CONTENTS.

PAGE

EDITOR'S NOTE TO THE FIRST AMERICAN EDITION, ... 7
AUTHOR'S PREFACES—I. To the First Edition, ... 11
             II. To the Second Edition, ... 16
EDITOR'S PREFACE—To the First English Translation, ... 27
EDITOR'S PREFACE—To the Fourth German Edition, ... 32

PART I.

COMMODITIES AND MONEY.

CHAPTER I.—Commodities, ...41
Section 1.—The two Factors of a Commodity; Use Value and Value (the
     Substance of Value and the Magnitude of Value), ... 41
Section 2.—The Twofold Character of the Labour embodied in Commodities, 48
Section 3.—The Form of Value, or Exchange Value, ... 54
   A. Elementary or Accidental Form o` Value, ... 56
       1. The two Poles of the Expression of Value: Relative Form and
         Equivalent Form, ... 56
       The Relative Form of Value, ... 57
          (a.) The Nature and Import of this Form, ... 57
          (b.) Quantitative Determination of Relative Value, ... 61
       3. The Equivalent Form of Value, ... 64
       4. The Elementary Form of Value considered as a Whole, . . . 69
   B. Total or Expanded Form of Value, ... 72
       1. The Expanded Relative Form of Value, ...72
       2. The Particular Equivalent Form, ... 73
       3. Defects of the Total or Expanded Form of Value, ... 74
   C. The General Form of Value, ... 75
       1. The altered Character of the Form of Value, ... 75
       2. The interdependent Development of the Relative Form of Value,
         and of the Equivalent Form, ... 78
       3. Transition from the General Form to the Money Form, ... 79
   D. The Money Form, ... 80
Section 4.—The Fetishism of Commodities and the Secret thereof, ... 81
CHAPTER II.—Exchange 96
CHAPTER III.—Money, or the Circulation of Commodities, ... 106
Section 1.—The Measure of Value, ... 106
Section 2.—The Medium of Circulation, ... 116
      a. The Metamorphosis of Commodities, ... 116
      b. The Currency of Money, ... 128
      c. Coin, and Symbols of Value, ... 140
Section 3.—Money, ... 146
      a. Hoarding, ... 146
      b. Means of Payment, ... 151
      c. Universal Money, ... 159

PART II.

THE TRANSFORMATION OF MONEY INTO CAPITAL.

CHAPTER IV.—The General Formula for Capital, ... 163
CHAPTER V.—Contradictions in the General Formula of Capital, ... 173
CHAPTER VI.—The Buying and Selling of Labour-Power, ... 185

PART III.

THE PRODUCTION OF ABSOLUTE SURPLUS-VALUE.

PAGE

CHAPTER VII.—The Labour Process and the Process of producing Surplus-Value, ... 197
Section 1.—The Labour Process or the Production of Use-Value, ... 197
Section 2.—The Production of Surplus-Value, ... 207
CHAPTER VIII.—Constant Capital and Variable Capital, ... 221
CHAPTER IX.—The Rate of Surplus-Value, ... 235
Section 1.—The Degree of Exploitation of Labour-Power, ... 235
Section 2.—The Representation of the Components of the Value of the Product by corresponding proportional Parts of the Product itself, . . . 244
Section 3.—Senior's " Last Hour," 248
Section 4.—Surplus-Produce, ... 254
CHAPTER X.—The Working-Day, ... 255
Section 1.—The Limits of the Working-Day, ... 255
Section 2.—The Greed for Surplus-Labour. Manufacturer and Boyard, . . 259
Section 3.—Branches of English Industry without Legal Limits to Exploitation, 268
Section 4.—Day and Night Work. The Relay System, ... 282
Section 5.—The Struggle for a Normal Working-Day. Compulsory Laws for the Extension of the Working-Day from the Middle of the 14th to the End of the 17th Century, ... 290
Section 6.—The Struggle for a Normal Working-Day. Compulsory Limitation by Law of the Working-Time. The English Factory Acts, 1833 to 1864, 304
Section 7.—The Struggle for a Normal Working-Day. Re-action of the English Factory Acts on Other Countries, ... 326
CHAPTER XI.—Rate and Mass of Surplus-Value, ... 331

PART IV.

PRODUCTION OF RELATIVE SURPLUS-VALUE.

CHAPTER XII.—The Concept of Relative Surplus-Value, ... 342
CHAPTER XIII.—Co-Operation, ... 353
CHAPTER XIV.—Division of Labour and Manufacture, ... 368
Section 1.—Twofold Origin of Manufacture, ... 368
Section 2.—The Detail Labourer and his Implements, ... 372
Section 3.—The two Fundamental Forms of Manufacture: Heterogeneous Manufacture, Serial Manufacture, ... 375
Section 4.—Division of Labour in Manufacture, and Division of Labour in Society, ... 385
Section 5.—The Capitalistic Character of Manufacture, ... 395
CHAPTER XV.—Machinery and Modern Industry, ... 405
Section 1.—The Development of Machinery, ... 405
Section 2.—The Value transferred by Machinery to the Product, ... 422
Section 3.—The Proximate Effects of Machinery on the Workman, . . . 430
  a. Appropriation of Supplementary Labour-Power by Capital. The Employment of Women and Children, ... 431
  b. Prolongation of the Working-Day, ... 440
  c. Intensification of Labour, ... 447
Section 4.—The Factory, ... 457
Section 5.—The Strife between Workman and Machinery, ... 466
Section 6.—The Theory of Compensation as regards the Workpeople displaced by Machinery, ... 478
Section 7.—Repulsion and Attraction of Workpeople by the Factory System. Crises of the Cotton Trade, ... 488

Contents.   5

PAGE

Section 8.—Revolution effected in Manufacture, Handicrafts, and Domestic
   Industry by Modern Industry, ... 502
        a. Overthrow of Co-Operation based on Handicraft and on Divi-
         sion of Labour, ... 502
        b. Re-action of the Factory System on Manufacture and Domes-
         tic Industries, ... 504
        c. Modern Manufacture, ... 506
        d. Modern Domestic Industry, ... 509
        e. Passage of Modern Manufacture and Domestic Industry into
         Modern Mechanical Industry. The Hastening of this Revo-
         lution by the Application of the Factory Acts to those In-
         dustries, ... 514
Section 9.—The Factory Acts. Sanitary and Educational Clauses of the same.
   Their general Extension in England, ... 526
Section 10.—Modern Industry and Agriculture, ... 553

PART V.

THE PRODUCTION OF ABSOLUTE AND RELATIVE SURPLUS-VALUE.

CHAPTER XVI.—Absolute and Relative Surplus-Value, ... 557
CHAPTER XVII.—Changes of Magnitude in the Price of Labour-Power and in
   Surplus-Value, ... 568
   I. Length of the Working Day and Intensity of Labour constant. Pro-
     ductiveness of Labour variable, ... 569
   II. Working Day constant. Productiveness of Labour constant. Intensity
     of Labor variable, ... 574
   III. Productiveness and Intensity of Labour constant. Length of the Work-
     ing Day variable, ... 576
   IV. Simultaneous Variations in the Duration, Productiveness and In-
     tensity of Labour, ... 578
      (1.) Diminishing Productiveness of Labour with a simultaneous Length-
       ening of the Working Day, ... 578
      (2.) Increasing Intensity and Productiveness of Labour with simul-
       taneous Shortening of the Working Day, ... 580
CHAPTER XVIII.—Various Formlæ for the Rate of Surplus-Value, ... 582

PART VI.

WAGES.

CHAPTER XIX.—The Transformation of the Value (and respectively the Price)
   of Labour-Power into Wages, ... 586
CHAPTER XX.—Time-wages, ... 594
CHAPTER XXI.—Piece-Wages, ... 602
CHAPTER XXII.—National Differences of Wages, ... 611

PART VII.

THE ACCUMULATION OF CAPITAL.

CHAPTER XXIII.—Simple Reproduction, ... 619
CHAPTER XXIV.—Conversion of Surplus-Value into Capital, ... 634
Section 1.—Capitalist Production on a progressively increasing Scale. Transition of the Laws of Property that characterise Production of Commodities into Laws of Capitalist Appropriation, ... 634
Section 2.—Erroneous Conception, by Political Economy, of Reproduction on
   a progressively increasing Scale, ... 644

Contents.

PAGE

Section 3.—Separation of Surplus-Value into Capital and Revenue. The Abstinence Theory, ... 648

Section 4.—Circumstances that, independently of the proportional Division of Surplus-Value into Capital and Revenue, determine the Amount of Accumulation. Degree of Exploitation of Labour-Power. Productivity of Labour. Growing Difference in Amount between Capital employed and Capital consumed. Magnitude of Capital advanced, ... 656

Section 5.—The so-called Labour Fund, ... 667

CHAPTER XXV.—The General Law of Capitalist Accumulation, ... 671

Section 1.—The increased Demand for Labour-Power that accompanies Accumulation, the Composition of Capital remaining the same, ... 671

Section 2.—Relative Diminution of the Variable Part of Capital simultaneously with the Progress of Accumulation and of the Concentration that accompanies it, ... 681

Section 3.—Progressive Production of a Relative Surplus-Population, or Industrial Reserve Army, ... 689

Section 4.—Different Forms of the Relative Surplus-Population. The General Law of Capitalistic Accumulation, ... 703

Section 5.—Illustrations of the General Law of Capitalist Accumulation, . . 711

    a. England from 1846 to 1866, ... 711

    b. The badly paid Strata of the British Industrial Class, . . . 718

    c. The Nomad Population, ... 728

    d. Effect of Crises on the best paid Part of the Working Class, . 733

    e. The British Agricultural Proletariat, ... 739

    f. Ireland, ... 767

PART VIII.

THE SO-CALLED PRIMITIVE ACCUMULATION.

CHAPTER XXVI.—The Secret of Primitive Accumulation, ... 784

CHAPTER XXVII.—Expropriation of the Agricultural Population from the Land, 788

CHAPTER XXVIII.—Bloody Legislation against the Expropriated from the End of the 15th Century. Forcing down of Wages by Acts of Parliament, . 805

CHAPTER XXIX.—Genesis of the Capitalist Farmer, ... 814

CHAPTER XXX.—Reaction of the Agricultural Revolution on Industry. Creation of the Home Market for Industrial Capital, ... 817

CHAPTER XXXI.—Genesis of the Industrial Capitalist, ... 822

CHAPTER XXXII.—Historical Tendency of Capitalistic Accumulation, . . . 834

CHAPTER XXXIII.—The Modern Theory of Colonization, ... 838

Works and Authors quoted in " Capital," 850

Index. 866

EDITOR'S NOTE TO THE FIRST AMERICAN EDITION.

The original plan of Marx, as outlined in his preface to the first German edition of *Capital,* in 1867, was to divide his work into three volumes. Volume I was to contain Book I, The Process of Capitalist Production. Volume II was scheduled to comprise both Book II, The Process of Capitalist Circulation, and Book III, The Process of Capitalist Production as a Whole. The work was to close with volume III, containing Book IV, A History of Theories of Surplus-Value.

When Marx proceeded to elaborate his work for publication, he had the essential portions of all three volumes, with a few exceptions, worked out in their main analyses and conclusions, but in a very loose and unfinished form. Owing to ill health, he completed only volume I. He died on March 14, 1883, just when a third German edition of this volume was being prepared for the printer.

Frederick Engels, the intimate friend and co-operator of Marx, stepped into the place of his dead comrade and proceeded to complete the work. In the course of the elaboration of volume II it was found that it would be wholly taken up with Book II, The Process of Capitalist Circulation. Its first German edition did not appear until May, 1885, almost 18 years after the first volume.

The publication of the third volume was delayed still longer. When the second German edition of volume II appeared, in July, 1893, Engels was still working on volume

7

III. It was not until October, 1894, that the first German edition of volume III was published, in two separate parts, containing the subject matter of what had been originally planned as Book III of volume II, and treating of The Capitalist Process of Production as a whole.

The reasons for the delay in the publication of volumes II and III, and the difficulties encountered in solving the problem of elaborating the copious notes of Marx into a finished and connected presentation of his theories, have been fully explained by Engels in his various prefaces to these two volumes. His great modesty led him to belittle his own share in this fundamental work. As a matter of fact, a large portion of the contents of *Capital* is as much a creation of Engels as though he had written it independently of Marx.

Engels intended to issue the contents of the manuscripts for Book IV, originally planned as volume III, in the form of a fourth volume of *Capital*. But on the 6th of August, 1895, less than one year after the publication of volume III, he followed his co-worker into the grave, still leaving this work incompleted.

However, some years previous to his demise, and in anticipation of such an eventuality, he had appointed Karl Kautsky, the editor of *Die Neue Zeit,* the scientific organ of the German Socialist Party, as his successor and familiarized him personally with the subject matter intended for volume IV of this work. The material proved to be so voluminous, that Kautsky, instead of making a fourth volume of *Capital* out of it, abandoned the original plan and issued his elaboration as a separate work in three volumes under the title *Theories of Surplus-value.*

The first English translation of the first volume of *Capital* was edited by Engels and published in 1886. Marx had in the meantime made some changes in the text of the second

German edition and of the French translation, both of which appeared in 1873, and he had intended to superintend personally the edition of an English version. But the state of his health interfered with this plan. Engels utilised his notes and the text of the French edition of 1873 in the preparation of a third German edition, and this served as a basis for the first edition of the English translation.

Owing to the fact that the title page of this English translation (published by Swan Sonnenschein & Co.) did not distinctly specify that this was but volume I, it has often been mistaken for the complete work, in spite of the fact that the prefaces of Marx and Engels clearly pointed to the actual condition of the matter.

In 1890, four years after the publication of the first English edition, Engels edited the proofs for a fourth German edition of volume I and enlarged it still more after a repeated comparison with the French edition and with manuscript notes of Marx. But the Swan Sonnenschein edition did not adopt this new version in its subsequent English issues.

This first American edition will be the first complete English edition of the entire Marxian theories of Capitalist Production. It will contain all three volumes of *Capital* in full. The present volume, I, deals with The Process of Capitalist Production in the strict meaning of the term " production." Volume II will treat of The Process of Capitalist Circulation in the strict meaning of the term " circulation." Volume III will contain the final analysis of The Process of Capitalist Production as a Whole, that is of Production and Circulation in their mutual interrelations.

The *Theories of Surplus-Value,* Kautsky's elaboration of the posthumous notes of Marx and Engels, will in due time be published in an English translation as a separate work.

This first American edition of volume I is based on the revised fourth German edition. The text of the English version of the Swan Sonnenschein edition has been compared page for page with this improved German edition, and about ten pages of new text hitherto not rendered in English are thus presented to American readers. All the footnotes have likewise been revised and brought up to date.

For all further information concerning the technical particulars of this work I refer the reader to the prefaces of Marx and Engels.

ERNEST UNTERMANN.

Orlando, Fla., July 18, 1906.

AUTHOR'S PREFACES.

I.—TO THE FIRST EDITION.

THE work, the first volume of which I now submit to the public, forms the continuation of my "Zur Kritik der Politischen Oekonomie" (A Contribution to the Critique of Political Economy) published in 1859. The long pause between the first part and the continuation is due to an illness of many years' duration that again and again interrupted my work.

The substance of that earlier work is summarised in the first three chapters of this volume. This is done not merely for the sake of connection and completeness. The presentation of the subject-matter is improved. As far as circumstances in any way permit, many points only hinted at in the earlier book are here worked out more fully, whilst, conversely, points worked out fully there are only touched upon in this volume. The sections on the history of the theories of value and of money are now, of course, left out altogether. The reader of the earlier work will find, however, in the notes to the first chapter additional sources of reference relative to the history of those theories.

Every beginning is difficult, holds in all sciences. To understand the first chapter, especially the section that contains the analysis of commodities, will, therefore, present the greatest difficulty. That which concerns more especially the analysis of the substance of value and the magnitude of value,

I have, as much as it was possible, popularised.[1] The value-
form, whose fully developed shape is the money-form, is very
elementary and simple. Nevertheless, the human mind has
for more than 2000 years sought in vain to get to the bottom
of it, whilst on the other hand, to the successful analysis of
much more composite and complex forms, there has been at
least an approximation. Why? Because the body, as an organic whole, is more easy of study than are the cells of that
body. In the analysis of economic forms, moreover, neither
microscopes nor chemical reagents are of use. The force of
abstraction must replace both. But in bourgeois society the
commodity-form of the product of labor—or the value-form
of the commodity—is the economic cell-form. To the superficial observer, the analysis of these forms seems to turn upon
minutiæ. It does in fact deal with minutiæ, but they are of
the same order as those dealt with in microscopic anatomy.

With the exception of the section on value-form, therefore,
this volume cannot stand accused on the score of difficulty. I
pre-suppose, of course, a reader who is willing to learn something new and therefore to think for himself.

The physicist either observes physical phenomena where
they occur in their most typical form and most free from
disturbing influence, or, wherever possible, he makes experiments under conditions that assure the occurrence of the phe-

---

[1] This is the more necessary, as even the section of Ferdinand Lassalle's
work against Schulze-Delitzsch, in which he professes to give "the intellectual quintessence" of my explanations on these subjects, contains important mistakes. If Ferdinand Lassalle has borrowed almost literally
from my writings, and without any acknowledgment, all the general
theoretical propositions in his economic works, e.g., those on the historical character of capital, on the connection between the conditions of
production and the mode of production, &c., &c., even to the terminology
created by me, this may perhaps be due to purposes of propaganda. I
am here, of course, not speaking of his detailed working out and application of these propositions, with which I have nothing to do.

nomenon in its normality. In this work I have to examine the capitalist mode of production, and the conditions of production and exchange corresponding to that mode. Up to the present time, their classic ground is England. That is the reason why England is used as the chief illustration in the development of my theoretical ideas. If, however, the German reader shrugs his shoulders at the condition of the English industrial and agricultural laborers, or in optimist fashion comforts himself with the thought that in Germany things are not nearly so bad, I must plainly tell him, *"De to fabula narratur!"*

Intrinsically, it is not a question of the higher or lower degree of development of the social antagonisms that result from the natural laws of capitalist production. It is a question of these laws themselves, of these tendencies working with iron necessity towards inevitable results. The country that is more developed industrially only shows, to the less developed, the image of its own future.

But apart from this. Where capitalist production is fully naturalised among the Germans (for instance, in the factories proper) the condition of things is much worse than in England, because the counterpoise of the Factory Acts is wanting. In all other spheres, we, like all the rest of Continental Western Europe, suffer not only from the development of capitalist production, but also from the incompleteness of that development. Alongside of modern evils, a whole series of inherited evils oppress us, arising from the passive survival of antiquated modes of production, with their inevitable train of social and political anachronisms. We suffer not only from the living, but from the dead. *Le mort saisit le vif!*

The social statistics of Germany and the rest of Continental Western Europe are, in comparison with those of England, wretchedly compiled. But they raise the veil just enough to let us catch a glimpse of the Medusa head behind it. We should be appalled at the state of things at home, if, as in England, our governments and parliaments appointed periodically commissions of enquiry into economic conditions; if these commissions were armed with the same plenary powers to get at the truth; if it was possible to find for this purpose men as competent, as free from partisanship and respect of persons as are the English factory-inspectors, her medical reporters on public health, her commissioners of enquiry into the exploitation of women and children, into housing and food. Perseus wore a magic cap that the monsters he hunted down might not see him. We draw the magic cap down over eyes and ears as a make-believe that there are no monsters. Le us not deceive ourselves on this. As in the 18th century, the American war of independence sounded the tocsin for the European middle-class, so in the 19th century, the American civil war sounded it for the European working-class. In England the progress of social disintegration is palpable. When it has reached a certain point, it must re-act on the continent. There it will take a form more brutal or more humane, according to the degree of development of the working-class itself. Apart from higher motives, therefore, their own most important interests dictate to the classes that are for the nonce the ruling ones, the removal of all legally removable hindrances to the free development of the working-class. For this reason, as well as others, I have given so large a space in this volume to the history, the details, and the results of English factory legislation. One nation can and should learn from others. And even when a society has got upon the right track for the discovery of the natural laws of its movement—and it is the ultimate aim of this work, to lay bare the economic law of motion of modern society—it can neither clear by bold leaps, nor remove by legal enactments, the obstacles offered by the successive phases of its normal development. But it can shorten and lessen the birth-pangs.

To prevent possible misunderstanding, a word. I paint the capitalist and the landlord in no sense *couleur de rose.* But here individuals are dealt with only in so far as they are th personifications of economic categories, embodiments of particular class-relations and class-interests. My stand-point, from which the evolution of the economic formation of society is viewed as a process of natural history, can less than any other make the individual responsible for relations whose creature he socially remains, however much he may subjectively raise himself above them.

In the domain of Political Economy, free scientific enquiry meets not merely the same enemies as in all other domains. The peculiar nature of the material it deals with, summons as foes into the field of battle the most violent, mean and malignant passions of the human breast, the Furies of private interest. The English Established Church, *e.g.,* will more readily pardon an attack on 38 of its 39 articles than on $\frac{1}{39}$ of its income. Now-a-days atheism itself is *culpa levis,* as compared with criticism of existing property relations. Nevertheless, there is an unmistakable advance. I refer, *e.g.,* to the bluebook published within the last few weeks: " Correspondence with Her Majesty's Missions Abroad, regarding Industrial Questions and Trades' Unions." The representatives of the English Crown in foreign countries there declare in so many words that in Germany, in France, to be brief, in all the civilised states of the European continent, a radical change in the existing relations between capital and labor is as evident and inevitable as in England. At the same time, on the other side of the Atlantic Ocean, Mr. Wade, vice-president of the United States, declared in public meetings that, after the abolition of slavery, a radical change of the relations of capital and of property in land is next upon the order of the day. These are signs of the times, not to be hidden by purple mantles or black cassocks. They do not signify that to-morrow a miracle will happen. They show that, within the ruling-classes themselves, a foreboding is dawning, that the present society is no solid crystal, but an organism capable of change, and is constantly changing.

The second volume of this work will treat of the process of the circulation of capital[1] (Book II.), and of the varied forms assumed by capital in the course of its development (Book III.), the third and last volume (Book IV.), the history of the theory.

Every opinion based on scientific criticism I welcome. As to the prejudices of so-called public opinion, to which I have never made concessions, now as aforetime the maxim of the great Florentine is mine:

"Segui il tuo corso, e lascia dir le genti."

KARL MARX.

LONDON, *July* 25, 1867.

II.—TO THE SECOND EDITION.

To the present moment Political Economy, in Germany, is a foreign science. Gustav von Gülich in his "Historical description of Commerce, Industry," &c.,[2] especially in the two first volumes published in 1830, has examined at length the historical circumstances that prevented, in Germany, the development of the capitalist mode of production, and consequently the development, in that country, of modern bourgeois society. Thus the soil whence Political Economy springs was

[1] On p. 618 the author explains what he comprises under this head.
[2] Geschichtliche Darstellung des Handels, der Gewerbe und des Ackerbaus, &c., von Gustav von Gülich. 5 vols., Jena, 1830–45.

wanting. This "science" had to be imported from England and France as a ready-made article; its German professors remained schoolboys. The theoretical expression of a foreign reality was turned, in their hands, into a collection of dogmas, interpreted by them in terms of the petty trading world around them, and therefore misinterpreted. The feeling of scientific impotence, a feeling not wholly to be repressed, and the uneasy consciousness of having to touch a subject in reality foreign to them, was but imperfectly concealed, either under a parade of literary and historical erudition, or by an admixture of extraneous material, borrowed from the so-called "Kameral" sciences, a medley of smatterings, through whose purgatory the hopeless candidate for the German bureaucracy has to pass.

Since 1848 capitalist production has developed rapidly in Germany, and at the present time it is in the full bloom of speculation and swindling. But fate is still unpropitious to our professional economists. At the time when they were able to deal with Political Economy in a straightforward fashion, modern economic conditions did not actually exist in Germany. And as soon as these conditions did come into existence, they did so under circumstances that no longer allowed of their being really and impartially investigated within the bounds of the bourgeois horizon. In so far as Political Economy remains within that horizon, in so far, *i.e.,* as the capitalist régime is looked upon as the absolutely final form of social production, instead of as a passing historical phase of its evolution, Political Economy can remain a science only so long as the class-struggle is latent or manifests itself only in isolated and sporadic phenomena.

Let us take England. Its political economy belongs to the period in which the class-struggle was as yet undeveloped. Its last great representative, Ricardo, in the end, consciously makes the antagonism of class-interests, of wages and profits, of profits and rent, the starting-point of his investigations, naïvely taking this antagonism for a social law of nature. But by this start the science of bourgeois economy had reached the limits beyond which it could not pass. Already in the lifetime of Ricardo, and in opposition to him, it was met by criticism, in the person of Sismondi.[1]

The succeeding period, from 1820 to 1830, was notable in England for scientific activity in the domain of Political Economy. It was the time as well of the vulgarising and extending of Ricardo's theory, as of the contest of that theory with the old school. Splendid tournaments were held. What was done then, is little known to the Continent generally, because the polemic is for the most part scattered through articles in reviews, occasional literature and pamphlets. The unprejudiced character of this polemic—although the theory of Ricardo already serves, in exceptional cases, as a weapon of attack upon bourgeois economy—is explained by the circumstances of the time. On the one hand, modern industry itself was only just emerging from the age of childhood, as is shown by the fact that with the crisis of 1825 it for the first time opens the periodic cycle of its modern life. On the other hand, the class-struggle between capital and labor is forced into the background, politically by the discord between the governments and the feudal aristocracy gathered around the Holy Alliance on the one hand, and the popular masses, led by the bourgeoisie on the other; economically by the quarrel between industrial capital and aristocratic landed property—a quarrel that in France was concealed by the opposition between small and large landed property, and that in England broke out openly after the Corn Laws. The literature of Political Economy in England at this time calls to mind the stormy forward movement in France after Dr. Quesnay's death, but

[1] See my work "Critique, &c.," p. 70.

only as a Saint Martin's summer reminds us of spring. With the year 1830 came the decisive crisis.

In France and in England the bourgeoisie had conquered political power. Thenceforth, the class-struggle, practically as well as theoretically, took on more and more outspoken and threatening forms. It sounded the knell of scientific bourgeois economy. It was thenceforth no longer a question, whether this theorem or that was true, but whether it was useful to capital or harmful, expedient or inexpedient, politically dangerous or not. In place of disinterested enquirers, there were hired prize-fighters; in place of genuine scientific research, the bad conscience and the evil intent of apologetic. Still, even the obtrusive pamphlets with which the Anti-Corn Law League, led by the manufacturers Cobden and Bright, deluged the world, have a historic interest, if no scientific one, on account of their polemic against the landed aristocracy. But since then the Free Trade legislation, inaugurated by Sir Robert Peel, has deprived vulgar economy of this its last sting.

The Continental revolution of 1848-9 also had its reaction in England. Men who still claimed some scientific standing and aspired to be something more than mere sophists and sycophants of the ruling-classes, tried to harmonise the Political Economy of capital with the claims, no longer to be ignored, of the proletariat. Hence a shallow syncretism, of which John Stuart Mill is the best representative. It is a declaration of bankruptcy by bourgeois economy, an event on which the great Russian scholar and critic, N. Tschernyschewsky, has thrown the light of a master mind in his "Outlines of Political Economy according to Mill."

In Germany, therefore, the capitalist mode of production came to a head, after its antagonistic character had already, in France and England, shown itself in a fierce strife of classes. And meanwhile, moreover, the German proletariat had attained a much more clear class-consciousness than the German bourgeoisie. Thus, at the very moment when a bourgeois science of political economy seemed at last possible in Germany, it had in reality again become impossible.

Under these circumstances its professors fell into two groups. The one set, prudent, practical business folk, flocked to the banner of Bastiat, the most superficial and therefore the most adequate representative of the apologetic of vulgar economy; the other, proud of the professorial dignity of their science, followed John Stuart Mill in his attempt to reconcile irreconcilables. Just as in the classical time of bourgeois economy, so also in the time of its decline, the Germans remained mere schoolboys, imitators and followers, petty retailers and hawkers in the service of the great foreign wholesale concern.

The peculiar historic development of German society therefore forbids, in that country, all original work in bourgeois economy; but not the criticism of that economy. So far as such criticism represents a class, it can only represent the class whose vocation in history is the overthrow of the capitalist mode of production and the final abolition of all classes—the proletariat.

The learned and unlearned spokesmen of the German bourgeoisie tried at first to kill "Das-Kapital" by silence, as they had managed to do with my earlier writings. As soon as they found that these tactics no longer fitted in with the conditions of the time, they wrote, under pretence of criticising my book, prescriptions "for the tranquillisation of the bourgeois mind." But they found in the workers' press—see, e.g., Joseph Dietzgen's articles in the "Volksstaat"— antagonists stronger than themselves, to whom (down to this very day) they owe a reply.[1]

[1] The mealy-mouthed babblers of German vulgar economy fell foul of

An excellent Russian translation of "Das Kapital" appeared in the spring of 1872. The edition of 3000 copies is already nearly exhausted. As early as 1871, A. Sieber, Professor of Political Economy in the University of Kiev, in his work "David Ricardo's Theory of Value and of Capital," referred to my theory of value, of money and of capital, as in its fundamentals a necessary sequel to the teaching of Smith and Ricardo. That which astonishes the Western European in the reading of this excellent work, is the author's consistent and firm grasp of the purely theoretical position.

That the method employed in "Das Kapital" has been little understood, is shown by the various conceptions, contradictory one to another, that have been formed of it.

Thus the Paris *Revue Positiviste* reproaches me in that, on the one hand, I treat economics metaphysically, and on the other hand—imagine!—confine myself to the mere critical analysis of actual facts, instead of writing recipes (Comtist ones?) for the cook-shops of the future. In answer to the reproach *in re* metaphysics, Professor Sieber has it: "In so far as it deals with actual theory, the method of Marx is the deductive method of the whole English school, a school whose failings and virtues are common to the best theoretic econ-

the style of my book. No one can feel the literary shortcomings in "Das Kapital" more strongly than I myself. Yet I will for the benefit and the enjoyment of these gentlemen and their public quote in this connection one English and one Russian notice. The "Saturday Review," always hostile to my views, said in its notice of the first edition: "The presentation of the subject invests the driest economic questions with a certain peculiar charm." The "St. Petersburg Journal" (Sankt-Peterburgskie Viedomosti), in its issue of April 20, 1872, says: "The presentation of the subject, with the exception of one or two exceptionally special parts, is distinguished by its comprehensibility by the general reader, its clearness, and in spite of the scientific intricacy of the subject, by an unusual liveliness. In this respect the author in no way resembles . . . the majority of German scholars who . . . write their books in a language so dry and obscure that the heads of ordinary mortals are cracked by it."

omists." M. Block—"Les théoriciens du socialisme en Allemagne, Extrait du Journal des Economistes, Juillet et Aout
1872"—makes the discovery that my method is analytic and
says: "Par cet ouvrage M. Marx se classe parmi les esprits
analytiques les plus éminents." German reviews, of course,
shriek out at "Hegelian sophistics." The *European Messenger*
of St. Petersburg, in an article dealing exclusively with the
method of "Das Kapital" (May number, 1872, pp. 427-436),
finds my method of inquiry severely realistic, but my method
of presentation, unfortunately, German-dialectical. It says:
"At first sight, if the judgment is based on the external form
of the presentation of the subject, Marx is the most ideal of
ideal philosophers, always in the German, *i.e.,* the bad sense
of the word. But in point of fact he is infinitely more realistic than all his fore-runners in the work of economic criticism.
He can in no sense be called an idealist." I cannot answer
the writer better than by aid of a few extracts from his own
criticism, which may interest some of my readers to whom
the Russian original is inaccessible.

After a quotation from the preface to my "Critique of
Political Economy," Berlin, 1859, pp. 11–13, where I discuss
the materialistic basis of my method, the writer goes on:
"The one thing which is of moment to Marx is to find the law
of the phenomena with whose investigation he is concerned;
and not only is that law of moment to him, which governs
these phenomena, in so far as they have a definite form and
mutual connection within a given historical period. Of still
greater moment to him is the law of their variation, of their
development, *i.e.,* of their transition from one form into
another, from one series of connections into a different one.
This law once discovered, he investigates in detail the effects
in which it manifests itself in social life. Consequently, Marx
only troubles himself about one thing; to show, by rigid scien-

tific investigation, the necessity of successive determinate orders of social conditions, and to establish, as impartially as possible, the facts that serve him for fundamental starting points. For this it is quite enough, if he proves, at the same time, both the necessity of the present order of things, and the necessity of another order into which the first must inevitably pass over; and this all the same, whether men believe or do not believe it, whether they are conscious or unconscious of it. Marx treats the social movement as a process of natural history, governed by laws not only independent of human will, consciousness and intelligence, but rather, on the contrary, determining that will, consciousness and intelligence. . . . If in the history of civilisation the conscious element plays a part so subordinate, then it is self-evident that a critical inquiry whose subject-matter is civilisation, can, less than anything else, have for its basis any form of, or any result of, consciousness. That is to say, that not the idea, but the material phenomenon alone can serve as its starting-point. Such an inquiry will confine itself to the confrontation and the comparison of a fact, not with ideas, but with another fact. For this inquiry, the one thing of moment is, that both facts be investigated as accurately as possible, and that they actually form, each with respect to the other, different momenta of an evolution; but most important of all is the rigid analysis of the series of successions, of the sequences and concatenations in which the different stages of such an evolution present themselves. But it will be said, the general laws of economic life are one and the same, no matter whether they are applied to the present or the past. This Marx directly denies. According to him, such abstract laws do not exist. On the contrary, in his opinion every historical period has laws of its own. . . . As soon as society has outlived a given period of development, and is passing over from one given stage to another, it begins to be subject also to other laws. In a word, economic life offers us a phenomenon analogous to the history of evolution in other branches of biology. The old economists misunderstood the nature of economic laws when they likened them to the laws of physics and chemistry. A more thorough analysis of phenomena shows that social organisms differ among themselves as fundamentally as plants or animals. Nay, one and the same phenomenon falls under quite different laws in consequence of the different structure of those organisms as a whole, of the variations of their individual organs, of the different conditions in which those organs function, &c. Marx, *e.g.,* denies that the law of population is the same at all times and in all places. He asserts, on the contrary, that every stage of development has its own law of population. . . . With the varying degree of development of productive power, social conditions and the laws governing them vary too. Whilst Marx sets himself the task of following and explaining from this point of view the economic system established by the sway of capital, he is only formulating, in a strictly scientific manner, the aim that every accurate investigation into economic life must have. The scientific value of such an inquiry lies in the disclosing of the special laws that regulate the origin, existence, development, and death of a given social organism and its replacement by another and higher one. And it is this value that, in point of fact, Marx's book has."

Whilst the writer pictures what he takes to be actually my method, in this striking and [as far as concerns my own application of it] generous way, what else is he picturing but the dialectic method?

Of course the method of presentation must differ in form from that of inquiry. The latter has to appropriate the material in detail, to analyse its different forms of development, to trace out their inner connection. Only after this work is done, can the actual movement be adequately described. If this is done successfully, if the life of the subject-matter is ideally reflected as in a mirror, then it may appear as if we had before us a mere a priori construction.

My dialectic method is not only different from the Hegelian, but is its direct opposite. To Hegel, the life-process of the human brain, *i.e.*, the process of thinking, which, under the name of "the Idea," he even transforms into an independent subject, is the demiurgos of the real world, and the real world is only the external, phenomenal form of "the Idea." With me, on the contrary, the ideal is nothing else than the material world reflected by the human mind, and translated into forms of thought.

The mystifying side of Hegelian dialectic I criticised nearly thirty years ago, at a time when it was still the fashion. But just as I was working at the first volume of "Das Kapital," it was the good pleasure of the peevish, arrogant, mediocre Ἐπίγονοι who now talk large in cultured Germany, to treat Hegel in the same way as the brave Moses Mendelssohn in Lessing's time treated Spinoza, *i.e.*, as a "dead dog." I therefore openly avowed myself the pupil of that mighty thinker, and even here and there, in the chapter on the theory of value, coquetted with the modes of expression peculiar to him. The mystification which dialectic suffers in Hegel's hands, by no means prevents him from being the first to present its general form of working in a comprehensive and conscious manner. With him it is standing on its head. It must be turned right side up again, if you would discover the rational kernel within the mystical shell.

In its mystified form, dialectic became the fashion in Germany, because it seemed to transfigure and to glorify the existing state of things. In its rational form it is a scandal and abomination to bourgeoisdom and its doctrinaire professors, because it includes in its comprehension and affirmative recognition of the existing state of things, at the same time also, the recognition of the negation of that state, of its inevitable breaking up; because it regards every historically developed social form as in fluid movement, and therefore takes into account its transient nature not less than its momentary existence; because it lets nothing impose upon it, and is in its essence critical and revolutionary.

The contradictions inherent in the movement of capitalist society impress themselves upon the practical bourgeois most strikingly in the changes of the periodic cycle, through which modern industry runs, and whose crowning point is the universal crisis. That crisis is once again approaching, although as yet but in its preliminary stage; and by the universality of its theatre and the intensity of its action it will drum dialectics even into the heads of the mushroom-upstarts of the new, holy Prusso-German empire.

KARL MARX.

London, *January 24, 1873.*

EDITOR'S PREFACE TO THE FIRST ENGLISH TRANSLATION.

THE publication of an English version of "Das Kapital" needs no apology. On the contrary, an explanation might be expected why this English version has been delayed until now, seeing that for some years past the theories advocated in this book have been constantly referred to, attacked and defended, interpreted and mis-interpreted, in the periodical press and the current literature of both England and America.

When, soon after the author's death in 1883, it became evident that an English edition of the work was really required, Mr. Samuel Moore, for many years a friend of Marx and of the present writer, and than whom, perhaps, no one is more conversant with the book itself, consented to undertake the translation which the literary executors of Marx were anxious to lay before the public. It was understood that I should compare the MS. with the original work, and suggest such alterations as I might deem advisable. When, by and by, it was found that Mr. Moore's professional occupations prevented him from finishing the translation as quickly as we all desired, we gladly accepted Dr. Aveling's offer to undertake a portion of the work; at the same time Mrs. Aveling, Marx's youngest daughter, offered to check the quotations and to restore the original text of the numerous passages taken from English authors and Bluebooks and translated by Marx into German. This has been done throughout, with but a few unavoidable exceptions.

The following portions of the book have been translated by Dr. Aveling: (1) Chapters X. (The Working Day), and XI. (Rate and Mass of Surplus-Value); (2) Part VI. (Wages, comprising Chapters XIX. to XXII.); (3) from Chapter XXIV., Section 4 (Circumstances that &c.) to the end of the book, comprising the latter part of Chapter XXIV., Chapter XXV., and the whole of Part VIII. (Chapters XXVI. to XXXIII.); (4) the two Author's prefaces. All the rest of the book has been done by Mr. Moore. While, thus, each of the translators is responsible for his share of the work only, I bear a joint responsibility for the whole.

The third German edition, which has been made the basis of our work throughout, was prepared by me, in 1883, with the assistance of notes left by the author, indicating the passages of the second edition to be replaced by designated passages, from the French text published in 1873.[1] The alterations thus effected in the text of the second edition generally coincided with changes prescribed by Marx in a set of MS. instructions for an English translation that was planned, about ten years ago, in America, but abandoned chiefly for want of a fit and proper translator. This MS. was placed at our disposal by our old friend Mr. F. A. Sorge of Hoboken N.J. It designates some further interpolations from the French edition; but, being so many years older than the final instructions for the third edition, I did not consider myself at liberty to make use of it otherwise than sparingly, and chiefly in cases where it helped us over difficulties. In the same way, the French text has been referred to in most of the difficult passages, as an indicator of what the author himself was prepared to sacrifice wherever something of the full

[1] "Le Capital," par Karl Marx. Traduction de M. J. Roy, entièrement revisée par l'auteur. Paris. Lachâtre." This translation, especially in the latter part of the book, contains considerable alterations in and additions to the text of the second German edition.

import of the original had to be sacrificed in the rendering.

There is, however, one difficulty we could not spare the reader: the use of certain terms in a sense different from what they have, not only in common life, but in ordinary political economy. But this was unavoidable. Every new aspect of a science involves a revolution in the technical terms of that science. This is best shown by chemistry, where the whole of the terminology is radically changed about once in twenty years, and where you will hardly find a single organic compound that has not gone through a whole series of different names. Political Economy has generally been content to take, just as they were, the terms of commercial and industrial life, and to operate with them, entirely failing to see that by so doing, it confined itself within the narrow circle of ideas expressed by those terms. Thus, though perfectly aware that both profits and rent are but sub-divisions, fragments of that unpaid part of the product which the laborer has to supply to his employer (its first appropriator, though not its ultimate exclusive owner), yet even classical Political Economy never went beyond the received notions of profits and rent never examined this unpaid part of the product (called by Marx surplus-product) in its integrity as a whole, and therefore never arrived at a clear comprehension, either of it origin and nature, or of the laws that regulate the subsequent distribution of its value. Similarly all industry, not agricultural or handicraft, is indiscriminately comprised in the term of manufacture, and thereby the distinction is obliterated betwee. two great and essentially different periods of economic history: the period of manufacture proper, based on the division of manual labor, and the period of modern industry based o machinery. It is, however, self-evident that theory which views modern capitalist production as a mere passing stage in the economic history of mankind, must make use of terms different from those habitual to writers who look upon that form of production as imperishable and final.

A word respecting the author's method of quoting may not be out of place. In the majority of cases, the quotations serve, in the usual way, as documentary evidence in support of assertions made in the text. But in many instances, passages from economic writers are quoted in order to indicate when, where, and by whom a certain proposition was for the first time clearly enunciated. This is done in cases where the proposition quoted is of importance as being a more or less adequate expression of the conditions of social production and exchange prevalent at the time, and quite irrespective of Marx's recognition, or otherwise, of its general validity. These quotations, therefore, supplement the text by a running commentary taken from the history of the science.

Our translation comprises the first book of the work only. But this first book is in a great measure a whole in itself, and has for twenty years ranked as an independent work. The second book, edited in German by me, in 1885, is decidedly incomplete without the third, which cannot be published before the end of 1887. When Book III. has been brought out in the original German, it will then be soon enough to think about preparing an English edition of both.

"Das Kapital" is often called, on the Continent, "the Bible of the working class." That the conclusions arrived at in this work are daily more and more becoming the fundamental principles of the great working class movement, not only in Germany and Switzerland, but in France, in Holland and Belgium, in America, and even in Italy and Spain; that everywhere the working class more and more recognises, in these conclusions, the most adequate expression of its condition and of its aspirations, nobody acquainted with that movement will deny. And in England, too, the theories of Marx, even at this

moment, exercise a powerful influence upon the socialist movement which is spreading in the ranks of "cultured" people
no less than in those of the working class. But that is not
all. ˗ The time is rapidly approaching when a thorough examination of England's economic position will impose itself
as an irresistible national necessity. The working of the industrial system of this country, impossible without a constant
and rapid extension of production, and therefore of markets,
is coming to ˗ dead stop. Free trade has exhausted its resources; even Manchester doubts this its quondam economic
gospel.[1] Foreign industry, rapidly developing, stares English production in the face everywhere, not only in protected,
but also in neutral markets, and even on this side of the
Channel. While the productive power increases in a geomet-
ric, the extension of ˑnarkets proceeds at best in an arithmetic
ratio. The decennial cycle of stagnation, prosperity, over-
production and crisis, ever recurrent from 1825 to 1867,
seems indeed to have run its course; but only to land us in the
slough of despond of a permanent and chronic depression.
The sighed-for period of prosperity will not come; as often
as we seem to perceive its heralding symptoms, so often do
they again vanish into air. Meanwhile, each succeeding winter
brings up afresh the great question, "what to do with the
unemployed;" but while the number of the unemployed keeps
swelling from year to year, there is nobody to answer that
question; and we can almost calculate the moment when the
unemployed, losing patience, will take their own fate into

---

[1] At the quarterly meeting of the Manchester Chamber of Commerce,
held this afternoon, a warm discussion took place on the subject of Free
Trade. A resolution was moved to the effect that "having waited in vain
40 years for other nations to follow the Free Trade example of England,
this Chamber thinks the time has now arrived to reconsider that position." The resolution was rejected by a majority of one only, the
figures being 21 for, and 22 against.—*Evening Standard,* Nov. 1, 1886.

their own hands. Surely, at such a moment, the voice ought to be heard of a man whose whole theory is the result of a life-long study of the economic history and condition of England, and whom that study led to the conclusion that, at least in Europe, England is the only country where the inevitable social revolution might be effected entirely by peaceful and legal means. He certainly never forgot to add that he hardly expected the English ruling classes to submit, without a "pro-slavery rebellion," to this peaceful and legal revolution.

FREDERICK ENGELS.

November 5, 1886.

EDITOR'S PREFACE TO THE FOURTH GERMAN EDITION.

The fourth edition of this work required of me a revision, which should give to the text and foot notes their final form, so far as possible. The following brief hints will indicate the way in which I performed this task.

After referring once more to the French edition and to the manuscript notes of Marx, I transferred a few additional passages from the French to the German text.[1]

I have also placed the long foot note concerning the mine workers, on pages 461-67, into the text, just as had already been done in the French and English editions. Other small changes are merely of a technical nature.

Furthermore I added a few explanatory notes, especially in places where changed historical conditions seemed to require it. All these additional notes are placed between brackets and marked with my initials.[2]

---

[1] These were inserted by me in the English text of the Swan Sonnenschein edition, and will be found on pages 539, 640-644, 687-689, and 892 of this American edition.—E. U.

[2] These were ten new notes, which I inserted in the respective places of the Swan Sonnenschein edition.—E. U.

A complete revision of the numerous quotations had become necessary, because the English edition had been published in the mean time. Marx's youngest daughter, Eleanor, had undertaken the tedious task of comparing, for this edition, all the quotations with the original works, so that the quotations from English authors, which are the overwhelming majority, are not retranslated from the German, but taken from the original texts. I had to consult the English edition for this fourth German edition. In so doing I found many small inaccuracies. There were references to wrong pages, due either to mistakes in copying, or to accumulated typographical errors of three editions. There were quotation marks, or periods indicating omissions, in wrong places, such as would easily occur in making copious quotations from notes. Now and then I came across a somewhat inappropriate choice of terms made in translating. Some passages were taken from Marx's old manuscripts written in Paris, 1843-45, when he did not yet understand English and read the works of English economists in French translations. This twofold translation carried with it a slight change of expression, for instance in the case of Steuart, Ure, and others. Now I used the English text. Such and similar little inaccuracies and inadvertences were corrected. And if this fourth edition is now compared with former editions, it will be found that this whole tedious process of verification did not change in the least any essential statement of this work. There is but one single quotation which could not be located, namely that from Richard Jones, in section 3 of chapter XXIV. Marx probably made a mistake in the title of the book. All other quotations retain their corroborative power, or even increase it in their present exact form.

In this connection I must revert to an old story.

I have heard of only one case, in which the genuineness of

a quotation by Marx was questioned. Since this case was continued beyond Marx's death, I cannot well afford to ignore it.

The Berlin *Concordia,* the organ of the German Manufacturer's Association, published on March 7, 1872, an anonymous article, entitled: "How Marx Quotes." In it the writer asserted with a superabundant display of moral indignation and unparliamentarian expressions that the quotation from Gladstone's budget speech of April 16, 1863, (cited in the Inaugural Address of the International Workingmen's Association, 1864, and republished in *Capital,* volume I, chapter XXV, section 5 a) was a falsification. It was denied that the statement: "This intoxicating augmentation of wealth and power . . . entirely confined to classes of property," was contained in the stenographical report of Hansard, which was as good as an official report. "This statement is not found anywhere in Gladstone's speech. It says just the reverse. *Marx has formally and materially lied in adding that sentence."*

Marx, who received this issue of the *Concordia* in May of the same year, replied to the anonymous writer in the *Volksstaat* of June 1. As he did not remember the particular newspaper from which he had clipped this report, he contented himself with pointing out that the same quotation was contained in two English papers. Then he quoted the report of the *Times,* according to which Gladstone had said: "That is the state of the case as regards the wealth of this country. I must say for one, I should look almost with apprehension and with pain upon this intoxicating augmentation of wealth and power, if it were my belief that it was confined to classes who are in easy circumstances. This takes no cognizance at all of the condition of the labouring population. The augmentation I have described and which is founded, I think, upon accurate terms, is an augmentation entirely confined to classes of property."

In other words, Gladstone says here that he would be sorry if things were that way, but they *are*. This intoxicating augmentation of wealth and power *is* entirely confined to classes of property. And so far as the *quasi* official Hansard is concerned, Marx continues: "In the subsequent manipulation of his speech for publication Mr. Gladstone was wise enough to eliminate a passage, which was so compromising in the mouth of an English Lord of the Exchequer as that one. By the way, this is an established custom in English parliament, and not by any means a discovery made by Lasker to cheat Bebel."

The anonymous writer then became still madder. Pushing aside his second-hand sources in his reply in the *Concordia*, July 4, he modestly hints, that it is the "custom" to quote parliamentarian speeches from the official reports; that the report of the *Times* (which contained the *added lie*) "was materially identical" with that of Hansard (which did not contain it); that the report of the *Times* even said "just the reverse of what that notorious passage of the Inaugural Address implied." Of course, our anonymous friend keeps still about the fact that the report of the *Times* does not only contain "just the reverse," but also "that notorious passage"! Nevertheless he feels that he has been nailed down, and that only a new trick can save him. Hence he decorates his article, full of "insolent mendacity," until it bristles with pretty epithets, such as "bad faith," "dishonesty," "mendacious assertion," "that lying quotation," "insolent mendacity," "a completely spurious quotation," "this falsification," "simply infamous," etc., and he finds himself compelled to shift the discussion to another ground, promising "to explain in a second article, what interpretation we [the "veracious" anonymous] place upon the meaning of Gladstone's words." As though his individual opinion had anything to do with the matter! This second article is published in the *Concordia* of July 11.

Marx replied once more in the *Volksstaat* of August 7, quoting also the reports of this passage in the *Morning Star* and *Morning Advertiser* of April 17, 1863. Both of them agree in quoting Gladstone to the effect that he would look with apprehension, etc., upon this intoxicating augmentation of wealth and power, if it were confined to classes in easy circumstances. But this augmentation *was* entirely confined to classes possessed of property. Both of these papers also contain the "added lie" word for word. Marx furthermore showed, by comparing these three independent, yet identical reports of newspapers, all of them containing the actually spoken words of Gladstone, with Hansard's report, that Gladstone, in keeping with the "established custom," had "subsequently eliminated" this sentence, as Marx had said. And Marx closes with the statement, that he has no time for further controversy with the anonymous writer. It seems that this worthy had gotten all he wanted, for Marx received no more issues of the *Concordia*.

Thus the matter seemed to be settled. It is true, people who were in touch with the university at Cambridge once or twice dropped hints as to mysterious rumors about some unspeakable literary crime, which Marx was supposed to have committed in *Capital.* But nothing definite could be ascertained in spite of all inquiries. Suddenly, on November 29, 1883, eight months after the death of Marx, a letter appeared in the *Times,* dated at Trinity College, Cambridge, and signed by Sedley Taylor, in which this mannikin, a dabbler in the tamest of coöperative enterprises, at last took occasion to give us some light, not only on the gossip of Cambridge, but also on the anonymous of the *Concordia.*

"What seems very queer," says the mannikin of Trinity College, "is that it remained for professor *Brentano* (then in Breslau, now in Strasburg) . . . to lay bare the bad faith, which had apparently dictated that quotation from Gladstone's speech in the Inaugural Address. Mr. Karl Marx, who . . . tried to justify his quotation, had the temerity, in the deadly shifts to which Brentano's masterly attacks quickly reduced him, to claim that Mr. Gladstone tampered with the report of his speech in the *Times* of April 17, 1863, before it was published in Hansard, in order to eliminate a passage which was, indeed, compromising for the British Chancellor of the Exchequer. When Brentano demonstrated by a detailed comparison of the texts, that the reports of the *Times* and of Hansard agreed to the absolute exclusion of the meaning, impugned to Gladstone's words by a craftily isolated quotation, Marx retreated under the excuse of having no time."

This, then, was the kernel of the walnut! And such was the glorious reflex of Brentano's anonymous campaign, in the *Concordia,* in the coöperative imagination of Cambridge! Thus he lay, and thus he handled his blade in his "masterly attack," this Saint George of the German Manufacturers' Association, while the fiery dragon Marx quickly expired under his feet "in deadly shifts!"

However, this Ariostian description of the struggle serves only to cover up the shifts of our Saint George. There is no longer any mention of "added lies," of "falsification," but merely of "a craftily isolated quotation." The whole question had been shifted, and Saint George and his Cambridge Knight knew very well the reason.

Eleanor Marx replied in the monthly magazine *To-Day,* February, 1884, because the *Times* refused to print her statements. She reduced the discussion to the only point, which was in question, namely: Was that sentence a lie added by

Marx, or not? Whereupon Mr. Sedley Taylor retorted: "The question whether a certain sentence had occurred in Mr. Gladstone's speech or not" was, in his opinion, "of a very inferior importance" in the controversy between Marx and Brentano, "compared with the question, whether the quotation had been made with the intention of reproducing the meaning of Mr. Gladstone or distorting it." And then he admits that the report of the *Times* "contains indeed a contradiction in words"; but, interpreting the context correctly, that is, in a liberal Gladstonian sense, it is evident what Mr. Gladstone *intended* to say. (*To-Day,* March, 1884.) The comic thing about this retort is that our mannikin of Cambridge now insists on *not* quoting this speech from Hansard, as is the "custom" according to the anonymous Mr. Brentano, but from the report of the *Times,* which the same Brentano had designated as "necessarily bungling." Of course, Hansard does not contain that fatal sentence!

It was easy for Eleanor Marx to dissolve this argumentation into thin air in the same number of *To-Day.* Either Mr. Taylor had read the controversy of 1872. In that case he had now "lied," not only "adding," but also "subtracting." Or, he had not read it. Then it was his business to keep his mouth shut. At any rate, it was evident that he did not dare for a moment to maintain the charge of his friend Brentano to the effect that Marx had "added a lie." On the contrary, it was now claimed, that Marx, instead of adding a lie, had suppressed an important sentence. But this same sentence is quoted on page 5 of the Inaugural Address, a few lines before the alleged "added lie." And as for the "contradiction" in Gladstone's speech, isn't it precisely Marx who speaks in another foot note of that chapter in *Capital* of the "continual crying contradictions in Gladstone's budget speeches of 1863 and 1864"? Of course, he does not undertake to reconcile them by liberal hot air, like Sedley Taylor. And the final summing up in Eleanor Marx's reply is this: "On the contrary, Marx has neither suppressed anything essential nor added any lies. He rather has restored and rescued from oblivion a certain sentence of a Gladstonian speech, which had undoubtedly been pronounced, but which somehow found its way out of Hansard."

This was enough for Mr. Sedley Taylor. The result of this whole professorial gossip during ten years and in two great countries was that no one dared henceforth to question Marx's literary conscientiousness. In the future Mr. Sedley Taylor will probably have as little confidence in the literary fighting bulletins of Mr. Brentano, as Mr. Brentano in the papal infallibility of Hansard.

FREDERICK ENGELS.

LONDON, *June* 25, 1890.

(Translated by Ernest Untermann.)

BOOK I.

CAPITALIST PRODUCTION.

PART I.

COMMODITIES AND MONEY.

CHAPTER I.

COMMODITIES.

SECTION 1.—THE TWO FACTORS OF A COMMODITY: USE-VALUE
AND VALUE (THE SUBSTANCE OF VALUE AND THE
MAGNITUDE OF VALUE).

THE wealth of those societies in which the capitalist mode of production prevails, presents itself as "an immense accumulation of commodities," [1] its unit being a single commodity. Our investigation must therefore begin with the analysis of a commodity.

A commodity is, in the first place, an object outside us, a thing that by its properties satisfies human wants of some sort or another. The nature of such wants, whether, for instance, they spring from the stomach or from fancy, makes no differ-

---

[1] Karl Marx "A Contribution to the Critique of Political Economy," 1859, London, p. 19.

ence.[1] Neither are we here concerned to know how the object satisfies these wants, whether directly as means of subsistence, or indirectly as means of production.

Every useful thing, as iron, paper, &c., may be looked at from the two points of view of quality and quantity. It is an assemblage of many properties, and may therefore be of use in various ways. To discover the various use of things is the work of history.[2] So also is the establishment of socially-recognised standards of measure for the quantities of these useful objects. The diversity of these measures has its origin partly in the diverse nature of the objects to be measured, partly in convention.

The utility of a thing makes it a use-value.[3] But this utility is not a thing of air. Being limited by the physical properties of the commodity, it has no existence apart from that commodity. A commodity, such as iron, corn, or a diamond, is therefore, so far as it is a material thing, a use-value, something useful. This property of a commodity is independent of the amount of labour required to appropriate its useful qualities. When treating of use-value, we always assume to be dealing with definite quantities, such as dozens of watches, yards of linen, or tons of iron. The use-values of commodities furnish the material for a special study, that of the commercial knowledge of commodities.[4] Use-values become a reality only by use or consumption: they also con-

---

[1] "Desire implies want; it is the appetite of the mind, and as natural as hunger to the body. . . . The greatest number (of things) have their value from supplying the wants of the mind." Nicolas Barbon: "A Discourse on coining the new money lighter, in answer to Mr. Locke's Considerations," &c. London, 1696. p. 2, 3.

[2] "Things have an intrinsick virtue" (this is Barbon's special term for value in use) "which in all places have the same virtue; as the loadstone to attract iron" (l. c., p. 6). The property which the magnet possesses of attracting iron, became of use only after by means of that property the polarity of the magnet had been discovered.

[3] "The natural worth of anything consists in its fitness to supply the necessities, or serve the conveniences of human life." (John Locke, "Some considerations on the consequences of the lowering of interest, 1691," in Works Edit. London, 1777, Vol. II., p. 28.) In English writers of the 17th century we frequently find "worth" in the sense of value in use, and "value" in the sense of exchange value. This is quite in accordance with the spirit of a language that likes to use a Teutonic word for the actual thing, and a Romance word for its reflexion.

[4] In bourgeois societies the economical fictio juris prevails, that every one, as a buyer, possesses an encyclopædic knowledge of commodities.

stitute the substance of all wealth, whatever may be the social form of that wealth. In the form of society we are about to consider, they are, in addition, the material depositories of exchange value.

Exchange value, at first sight, presents itself as a quantitative relation, as the proportion in which values in use of one sort are exchanged for those of another sort,[1] a relation constantly changing with time and place. Hence exchange value appears to be something accidental and purely relative, and consequently an intrinsic value, *i. e.*, an exchange value that is inseparably connected with, inherent in commodities, seems a contradiction in terms.[2] Let us consider the matter a little more closely.

A given commodity, *e. g.*, a quarter of wheat is exchanged for x blacking, y silk, or z gold, &c.—in short, for other commodities in the most different proportions. Instead of one exchange value, the wheat has, therefore, a great many. But since x blacking, y silk, or z gold, &c., each represent the exchange value of one quarter of wheat, x blacking, y silk, z gold, &c., must as exchange values be replaceable by each other, or equal to each other. Therefore, first: the valid exchange values of a given commodity express something equal; secondly, exchange value, generally, is only the mode of expression, the phenomenal form, of something contained in it, yet distinguishable from it.

Let us take two commodities, *e. g.*, corn and iron. The proportions in which they are exchangeable, whatever those proportions may be, can always be represented by an equation in which a given quantity of corn is equated to some quantity of iron: *e. g.*, 1 quarter corn=x cwt. iron. What does this equation tell us? It tells us that in two different things—in 1 quarter of corn and x cwt. of iron, there exists in equal quantities something common to both. The two things must there-

---

[1] "La valeur consiste dans le rapport d'échange qui se trouve entre telle chose et telle autre, entre telle mesure d'une production, et telle mesure d'une autre." (Le Trosne: De l' Intérêt Social. Physiocrates, Ed. Daire. Paris, 1845. P. 889.)

[2] "Nothing can have an intrinsick value." (N. Barbon, l. c., p. 6); or as Butler says—

> " The value of a thing
> Is just as much at it will bring."

fore be equal to a third, which in itself is neither the one nor the other. Each of them, so far as it is exchange value, must therefore be reducible to this third.

A simple geometrical illustration will make this clear. In order to calculate and compare the areas of rectilinear figures, we decompose them into triangles. But the area of the triangle itself is expressed by something totally different from its visible figure, namely, by half the product of the base into the altitude. In the same way the exchange values of commodities must be capable of being expressed in terms of something common to them all, of which thing they represent a greater or less quantity.

This common "something" cannot be either a geometrical, a chemical, or any other natural property of commodities. Such properties claim our attention only in so far as they affect the utility of those commodities, make them use-values. But the exchange of commodities is evidently an act characterised by a total abstraction from use-value. Then ͵ne use-value is just as good as another, provided only it be present in sufficient quantity. Or, as old Barbon says, "one sort of wares are as good as another, if the values be equal. There is no difference or distinction in things of equal value . . . . An hundred pounds' worth of lead or iron, is of as great value as one hundred pounds' worth of silver or gold." [1] As use-values, commodities are, above all, of different qualities, but as exchange values they are merely different quantities, and consequently do not contain an atom of use-value.

If then we leave out of consideration the use-value of commodities, they have only one common property left, that of being products of labour. But even the product of labour itself has undergone a change in our hands. If we make abstraction from its use-value, we make abstraction at the same time from the material elements and shapes that make the product a use-value; we see in it no longer a table, a house, yarn, or any other useful thing. Its existence as a material thing is put out of sight. Neither can it any longer be regarded as the product of the labour of the joiner, the mason,

[1] N. Barbon, l. c. p. 53 and 7.

the spinner, or of any other definite kind of productive labour. Along with the useful qualities of the products themselves, we put out of sight both the useful character of the various kinds of labour embodied in them, and the concrete forms of that labour; there is nothing left but what is common to them all; all are reduced to one and the same sort of labour, human labour in the abstract.

Let us now consider the residue of each of these products; it consists of the same unsubstantial reality in each, a mere congelation of homogeneous human labour, of labour-power expended withou : regard to the mode of its expenditure. All that these things now tell us is, that human labour-power has been expended in their production, that human labor is embodied in them. When looked at as crystals of this social substance, common to them all, they are—Values.

We have seen that when commodities are exchanged, their exchange value manifests itself as something totally independent of their use-value. But if we abstract from their use-value, there remains their Value as defined above. Therefore, the common substance that manifests itself in the exchange value of commodities, whenever they are exchanged, is their value. The progress of our investigation will show that exchange value is the only form in which the value of commodities can manifest itself or be expressed. For the present, however, we have to consider the nature of value independently of this, its form.

A use-value, or useful article, therefore, has value only because human labour in the abstract has been embodied or materialised in it. How, then, is the magnitude of this value to be measured? Plainly, by the quantity of the value-creating substance, the labour, contained in the article. The quantity of labour, however, is measured by its duration, and labour-time in its turn finds its standard in weeks, days, and hours.

Some people might think that if the value of a commodity is determined by the quantity of labour spent on it, the more idle and unskilful the labourer, the more valuable would his commodity be, because more time would be required in its production. The labour, however, that forms the substance of value, is homogeneous human labour, expenditure of one uniform labour-power. The total labour-power of society, which is embodied in the sum total of the values of all commodities produced by that society, counts here as one homogeneous mass of human labour-power, composed though it be of innumerable individual units. Each of these units is the same as any other, so far as it has the character of the average labour-power of society, and takes effect as such; that is, so far as it requires for producing a commodity, no more time than is needed on an average, no more than is socially necessary. The labour-time socially necessary is that required to produce an article under the normal conditions of production, and with the average degree of skill and intensity prevalent at the time. The introduction of power looms into England probably reduced by one half the labour required to weave a given quantity of yarn into cloth. The hand-loom weavers, as a matter of fact, continued to require the same time as before; but for all that, the product of one hour of their labour represented after the change only half an hour's social labour, and consequently fell to one-half its former value.

We see then that that which determines the magnitude of the value of any article is the amount of labour socially necessary, or the labour-time socially necessary for its production.[1] Each individual commodity, in this connexion, is to be considered as an average sample of its class.[2] Commodities, therefore, in which equal quantities of labour are embodied, or which can be produced in the same time, have the same value. The value of one commodity is to the value of any other, as the labour-time necessary for the production of the one is to that necessary for the production of the other. "As values, all commodities are only definite masses of congealed labour-time."[3]

---

[1] The value of them (the necessaries of life), when they are exchanged the one for another, is regulated by the quantity of labour necessarily required, and commonly taken in producing them." (Some Thoughts on the Interest of Money in general, and particularly in the Publick Funds, &c., Lond., p. 36.) This remarkable anonymous work, written in the last century, bears no date. It is clear, however, from internal evidence, that it appeared in the reign of George II. about 1739 or 1740.

[2] " Toutes les productions d'un même genre ne forment proprement qu'une masse, dont le prix se détermine en général et sans égard aux circonstances particulières." (Le Trosne, l. c. p. 893.)   [3] K. Marx, l. c. p. 24.

The value of a commodity would therefore remain constant, if the labour-time required for its production also remained constant. But the latter changes with every variation in the productiveness of labour. This productiveness is determined by various circumstances, amongst others, by the average amount of skill of the workmen, the state of science, and the degree of its practical application, the social organisation of production, the extent and capabilities of the means of production, and by physical conditions. For example, the same amount of labour in favourable seasons is embodied in 8 bushels of corn, and in unfavourable, only in four. The same labour extracts from rich mines more metal than from poor mines. Diamonds are of very rare occurrence on the earth's surface, and hence their discovery costs, on an average, a great deal of labour-time. Consequently much labour is represented in a small compass. Jacob doubts whether gold has ever been paid for at its full value. This applies still more to diamonds. According to Eschwege, the total produce of the Brazilian diamond mines for the eighty years, ending in 1823, had not realised the price of one-and-a-half years' average produce of the sugar and coffee plantations of the same country, although the diamonds cost much more labour, and therefore represented more value. With richer mines, the same quantity of labour would embody itself in more diamonds and their value would fall. If we could succeed at a small expenditure of labour, in converting carbon into diamonds, their value might fall below that of bricks. In general, the greater the productiveness of labour, the less is the labour-time required for the production of an article, the less is the amount of labour crystallised in that article, and the less is its value; and *vise versâ,* the less the productiveness of labour, the greater is the labour-time required for the production of an article, and the greater is its value. The value of a commodity, therefore, varies directly as the quantity, and inversely as the productiveness, of the labour incorporated in it.

A thing can be a use-value, without having value. This is the case whenever its utility to man is not due to labour. Such are air, virgin soil, natural meadows, &c. A thing can be useful, and the product of human labour, without being a commodity. Whoever directly satisfies his wants ·with the produce of his own labour, creates, indeed, use-values, but not commodities. In order to produce the latter, he must not only produce use-values, but use-values for others, social use-values. Lastly, nothing can have value, without being an object of utility. If the thing is useless, so is the labour contained in it; the labour does not count as labour, and therefore creates no value.

SECTION 2.—THE TWOFOLD CHARACTER OF THE LABOUR EM-
BODIED IN COMMODITIES.

At first sight a commodity presented itself to us as a complex of two things—use-value and exchange-value. Later on, we saw also that labour, too, possesses the same two-fold nature; for, so far as it finds expression in value, it does not possess the same characteristics that belong to it as a creator of use-values. I was the first to point out and to examine critically this two-fold nature of the labour contained in commodities. As this point is the pivot on which a clear comprehension of political economy turns, we must go more into detail.

Let us take two commodities such as a coat and 10 yards of linen, and let the former be double the value of the latter, so that, if 10 yards of linen$=$W, the coat$=$2W.

The coat is a use-value that satisfies a particular want. Its existence is the result of a special sort of productive activity, the nature of which is determined by its aim, mode of operation, subject, means, and result. The labour, whose utility is thus represented by the value in use of its product, or which manifests itself by making its product a use-value, we call useful labour. In this connexion we consider only its useful effect.

As the coat and the linen are two qualitatively different use-values, so also are the two forms of labour that produce them, tailoring and weaving. Were these two objects not qualitatively different, not produced respectively by⌐ labour of different quality, they could not stand to each other in the relation of commodities. Coats are not exchanged for coats, one use-value is not exchanged for another of the same kind.

To all the different varieties of values in use there correspond as many different kinds of useful labour, classified according to the order, genus, species, and variety to which they belong in the social division of labour. This division of labour is a necessary condition for the production of commodities, but it does not follow conversely, that the production of commodities is a necessary condition for the division of labour. In the primitive Indian community there is social division of labour, without production of commodities. Or, to take an example nearer home, in every factory the labour is divided according to a system, but this division is not brought about by the operatives mutually exchanging their individual products. Only such products can become commodities with regard to each other, as result from different kinds of labour, each kind being carried on independently and for the account of private individuals.

To resume, then: In the use-value of each commodity there is contained useful labour, *i. e.,* productive activity of a definite kind and exercised with a definite aim. Use-values cannot confront each other as commodities, unless the useful labour embodied in them is qualitatively different in each of them. In a community, the produce of which in general takes the form of commodities, *i. e.,* in a community of commodity producers, this qualitative difference between the useful forms of labour that are carried on independently by individual producers, each on their own account, develops into a complex system, a social division of labour.

Anyhow, whether the coat be worn by the tailor or by his customer, in either case it operates as a use-value. Nor is the relation between the coat and the labour that produced it altered by the circumstance that tailoring may have become a special trade, an independent branch of the social division of labour. Wherever the want of clothing forced them to it, the human race made clothes for thousands of years, without a single man becoming a tailor. But coats and linen, like every other element of material wealth that is not the spontaneous produce of nature, must invariably owe their existence to a special productive activity, exercised with a definite aim, an activity that appropriates particular nature-given materials to particular human wants. So far therefore as labour is a creator of use-value, is useful labour, it is a necessary condition, independent of all forms of society, for the existence of the human race; it is an eternal nature-imposed necessity, without which there can be no material exchanges between man and Nature, and therefore no life.

The use-values, coat, linen, &c., *i. e.,* the bodies of commodities, are combinations of two elements—matter and labour. If we take away the useful labour expended upon them, a material substratum is always left, which is furnished by Nature without the help of man. The latter can work only as Nature does, that is by changing the form of matter.[1] Nay more, in this work of changing the form he is constantly helped by natural forces. We see, then, that labour is not the only source of material wealth, of use-values produced by labour. As William Petty puts it, labour is its father and the earth its mother.

Let us now pass from the commodity considered as a use-value to the value of commodities.

By our assumption, the coat is worth twice as much as the linen. But this is a mere quantitative difference, which for the present does not concern us. We bear in mind, however, that if the value of the coat is double that of 10 yds. of linen, 20 yds. of linen must have the same value as one coat. So far as they are values, the coat and the linen are things of a like substance, objective expressions of essentially identical labour. But tailoring and weaving are, qualitatively, different kinds of labour. There are, however, states of society in which one and

---

[1] Tutti i fenomeni dell' universo, sieno essi prodotti della mano, dell' uomo, ovvero delle universali leggi della fisica, non ci danno idea di attuale creazione, ma unicamente di una modificazione della materia. Accostare e separare sono gli unici elementi che l'ingegno umano ritrova analizzando l'idea della riproduzione: e tanto è riproduzione di valore (value in use, although Verri in this passage of his controversy with the Physiocrats is not himself quite certain of the kind of value he is speaking of) e di ricchezze se la terra l'aria e l'acqua ne' campi si trasmutino in grano, come se colla mano dell' uomo il glutine di un insetto si trasmuti in velluto ovvero alcuni pezzetti di metallo si organizzino a formare una ripetizione."— Pietro Verri. "Meditazioni sulla Economia Politica" [first printed in 1773] in Custodi's edition of the Italian Economists, Parte Moderna, t. xv. p. 22.

the same man does tailoring and weaving alternately, in which case these two forms of labour are mere modifications of the labour of the same individual, and not special and fixed functions of different persons; just as the coat which our tailor makes one day, and the trousers which he makes another day, imply only a variation in the labour of one and the same individual. Moreover, we see at a glance that, in our capitalist society, a given portion of human labour is, in accordance with the varying demand, at one time supplied in the form of tailoring, at another in the form of weaving. This change may possibly not take place without friction, but take place it must.

Productive activity, if we leave out of sight its special form, viz., the useful character of the labour, is nothing but the expenditure of human labour-power. Tailoring and weaving, though qualitatively different productive activities, are each a productive expenditure of human brains, nerves, and muscles, and in this sense are human labour. They are but two different modes of expending human labour-power. Of course, this labour-power, which remains the same under all its modifications, must have attained a certain pitch of development before it can be expended in a multiplicity of modes. But the value of a commodity represents human labour in the abstract, the expenditure of human labour in general. And just as in society, a general or a banker plays a great part, but mere man, on the other hand, a very shabby part,[1] so here with mere human labour. It is the expenditure of simple labour-power, *i.e.,* of the labour-power which, on an average, apart from any special development, exists in the organism of every ordinary individual. Simple average labour, it is true, varies in character in different countries and at different times, but in a particular society it is given. Skilled labour counts only as simple labour intensified, or rather, as multiplied simple labour, a given quantity of skilled being considered equal to a greater quantity of simple labour. Experience shows that this reduction is constantly being made. A commodity may be the product of the most skilled labour, but its value, by equating it to the product of simple unskilled labour, represents a

[1] Comp. Hegel, Philosophie des Rechts. Berlin, 1840, p. 250 § 190.

definite quantity of the latter labour alone.[1] The different proportions in which different sorts of labour are reduced to unskilled labour as their standard, are established by a social process that goes on behind the backs of the producers, and, consequently, appear to be fixed by custom. For simplicity's sake we shall henceforth account every kind of labour to be unskilled, simple labour; by this we do no more than save ourselves the trouble of making the reduction.

Just as, therefore, in viewing the coat and linen as values, we abstract from their different use-values, so it is with the labour represented by those values: we disregard the difference between its useful forms, weaving and tailoring. As the use-values, coat and linen, are combinations of special productive activities with cloth and yarn, while the values, coat and linen, are, on the other hand, mere homogeneous congelations of indifferentiated labour, so the labour embodied in these latter values does not count by virtue of its productive relation to cloth and yarn, but only as being expenditure of human labour-power. Tailoring and weaving are necessary factors in the creation of the use-values, coat and linen, precisely because these two kinds of labour are of different qualities; but only in so far as abstraction is made from their special qualities, only in so far as both possess the same quality of being human labour, do tailoring and weaving form the substance of the values of the same articles.

Coats and linen, however, are not merely values, but values of definite magnitude, and according to our assumption, the coat is worth twice as much as the ten yards of linen. Whence this difference in their values? It is owing to the fact that the linen contains only half as much labour as the coat, and consequently, that in the production of the latter, labour-power must have been expended during twice the time necessary for the production of the former.

While, therefore, with reference to use-value, the labour contained in a commodity counts only qualitatively, with refer-

---

[1] The reader must note that we are not speaking here of the wages or value that the labourer gets for a given labour time, but of the value of the commodity in which that labour time is materialised. Wages is a category that, as yet, has no existence at the present stage of our investigation.

ence to value it counts only quantitatively, and must first be reduced to human labour pure and simple. In the former case, it is a question of How and What, in the latter of How much? How long a time? Since the magnitude of the value of a commodity represents only the quantity of labour embodied in it, it follows that all commodities, when taken in certain proportions, must be equal in value.

If the productive power of all the different sorts of useful labour required for the production of a coat remains unchanged, the sum of the values of the coat produced increases with their number. If one coat represents x days' labour, two coats represent 2x days' labour, and so on. But assume that the duration of the labour necessary for the production of a coat becomes doubled or halved. In the first case, one coat is worth as much as two coats were before; in the second case, two coats are only worth as much as one was before, although in both cases one coat renders the same service as before, and the useful labour embodied in it remains of the same quality. But the quantity of labour spent on its production has altered.

An increase in the quantity of use-values is an increase of material wealth. With two coats two men can be clothed, with one coat only one man. Nevertheless, an increased quantity of material wealth may correspond to a simultaneous fall in the magnitude of its value. This antagonistic movement has its origin in the two-fold character of labour. Productive power has reference, of course, only to labour of some useful concrete form; the efficacy of any special productive activity during a given time being dependent on its productiveness. Useful labour becomes, therefore, a more or less abundant source of products, in proportion to the rise or fall of its productiveness. On the other hand, no change in this productiveness affects the labour represented by value. Since productive power is an attribute of the concrete useful forms of labour, of course it can no longer have any bearing on that labour, so soon as we make abstraction from those concrete useful forms. However then productive power may vary, the same labour, exercised during equal periods of time, always yields equal amounts of value. But it will yield, during equal periods of time, different quantities of values in use; more, if the productive power rise, fewer, if it fall. The same change in productive power, which increases the fruitfulness of labour, and, in consequence, the quantity of use-values produced by that labour, will diminish the total value of this increased quantity of use-values, provided such change shorten the total labour-time necessary for their production; and *vice versâ.*

On the one hand all labour is, speaking physiologically, an expenditure of human labour-power, and in its character of identical abstract human labour, it creates and forms the value of commodities. On the other hand, all labour is the expenditure of human labour-power in a special form and with a definite aim, and in this, its character of concrete useful labour, it produces use-values.[1]

SECTION 3.—THE FORM OF VALUE OR EXCHANGE VALUE.

Commodities come into the world in the shape of use-values, articles, or goods, such as iron, linen, corn, &c. This is their plain, homely, bodily form. They are, however, commodities,

[1] In order to prove that labour alone is that all-sufficient and real measure, by which at all times the value of all commodities can be estimated and compared, Adam Smith says, "Equal quantities of labour must at all times and in all places have the same value for the labourer. In his normal state of health, strength and activity, and with the average degree of skill that he may possess, he must always give up the same portion of his rest, his freedom, and his happiness." (Wealth of Nations, b. I. ch. v.) On the one hand, Adam Smith here (but not everywhere) confuses the determination of value by means of the quantity of labour expended in the production of commodities, with the determination of the values of commodities by means of the value of labour, and seeks in consequence to prove that equal quantities of labour have always the same value. On the other hand, he has a presentiment, that labour, so far as it manifests itself in the value of commodities, counts only as expenditure of labour power, but he treats this expenditure as the mere sacrifice of rest, freedom, and happiness, not as the same time the normal activity of living beings. But then, he has the modern wage-labourer in his eye. Much more aptly, the anonymous predecessor of Adam Smith, quoted above in Note [1], p. 6, says, "one man has employed himself a week in providing this necessary of life . . . and he that gives him some other in exchange, cannot make a better estimate of what is a proper equivalent, than by computing what cost him just as much labour and time; which in effect is no more than exchanging one man's labour in one thing for a time certain, for another man's labour in another thing for the same time." (l. c. p. 39.) [The English language has the advantage of possessing different words for the two aspects of labour here considered. The labour which creates Use-Value, and counts qualitatively, is *Work*, as distinguished from Labour; that which creates Value and counts quantitatively, is *Labour* as distingiushed from Work. — ED.]

only because they are something twofold, both objects of utility, and, at the same time, depositories of value. They manifest themselves therefore as commodities, or have the form of commodities, only in so far as they have two forms, a physical or natural form, and a value form.

The reality of the value of commodities differs in this respect from Dame Quickly, that we don't know "where to have it." The value of commodities is the very opposite of the coarse materiality of their substance, not an atom of matter enters into its composition. Turn and examine a single commodity, by itself, as we will. Yet in so far as it remains an object of value, it seems impossible to grasp it. If, however, we bear in mind that the value of commodities has a purely social reality, and that they acquire this reality only in so far as they are expressions or embodiments of one identical social substance, viz., human labour, it follows as a matter of course, that value can only manifest itself in the social relation of commodity to commodity. In fact we started from exchange value, or the exchange relation of commodities, in order to get at the value that lies hidden behind it. We must now return to this form under which value first appeared to us.

Every one knows, if he knows nothing else, that commodities have a value form common to them all, and presenting a marked contrast with the varied bodily forms of their use values. I mean their money form. Here, however, a task is set us, the performance of which has never yet even been attempted by *bourgeois* economy, the task of tracing the genesis of this money form, of developing the expression of value implied in the value relation of commodities, from its simplest, almost imperceptible outline, to the dazzling money form. By doing this we shall, at the same time, solve the riddle presented by money.

The simplest value relation is evidently that of one commodity to some one other commodity of a different kind. Hence the relation between the values of two commodities supplies us with the simplest expression of the value of a single commodity.

A. *Elementary or Accidental Form of Value.*

x commodity A=y commodity B, or

x commodity A is worth y commodity B.

20 yards of linen=1 coat, or

20 yards of linen are worth 1 coat.

1. *The two poles of the expression of value: Relative form and Equivalent form.*

The whole mystery of the form of value lies hidden in this elementary form. Its analysis, therefore, is our real difficulty.

Here two different kinds of commodities (in our example the linen and the coat), evidently play two different parts. The linen expresses its value in the coat; the coat serves as the material in which that value is expressed. The former plays an active, the latter a passive, part. The value of the linen is represented as relative value, or appears in relative form. The coat officiates as equivalent, or appears in equivalent form.

The relative form and the equivalent form are two intimately connected, mutually dependent and inseparable elements of the expression of value; but, at the same time, are mutually exclusive, antagonistic extremes—*i.e.,* poles of the same expression. They are allotted respectively to the two different commodities brought into relation by that expression. It is not possible to express the value of linen in linen. 20 yards of linen=20 yards of linen is no expression of value. On the contrary, such an equation merely says that 20 yards of linen are nothing else than 20 yards of linen, a definite quantity of the use-value linen. The value of the linen can therefore be expressed only relatively—*i.e.,* in some other commodity. The relative form of the value of the linen pre-supposes, therefore, the presence of some other commodity—here the coat—under the form of an equivalent. On the other hand, the commodity that figures as the equivalent cannot at the same time assume the relative form. That second commodity is not the one whose value is expressed. Its function is merely to serve as the material in which the value of the first commodity is expressed.

No doubt, the expression 20 yards of linen=1 coat, or 20 yards of linen are worth 1 coat, implies the opposite relation: 1 coat=20 yards of linen, or 1 coat is worth 20 yards of linen. But, in that case, I must reverse the equation, in order to express the value of the coat relatively; and, so soon as I do that the linen becomes the equivalent instead of the coat. A single commodity cannot, therefore, simultaneously assume, in the same expression of value, both forms. The very polarity of these forms makes them mutually exclusive.

Whether, then, a commodity assumes the relative form, or the opposite equivalent form, depends entirely upon its accidental position in the expression of value—that is, upon whether it is the commodity whose value is being expressed or the commodity in which value is being expressed.

2. *The Relative form of value.*
(a.) *The nature and import of this form.*

In order to discover how the elementary expression of the value of a commodity lies hidden in the value relation of two commodities, we must, in the first place, consider the latter entirely apart from its quantitative aspect. The usual mode of procedure is generally the reverse, and in the value relation nothing is seen but the proportion between definite quantities of two different sorts of commodities that are considered equal to each other. It is apt to be forgotten that the magnitudes of different things can be compared quantitatively, only when those magnitudes are expressed in terms of the same unit. It is only as expressions of such a unit that they are of the same denomination, and therefore commensurable.[1]

Whether 20 yards of linen=1 coat or=20 coats or=x

---

[1] The few economists, amongst whom is S. Bailey, who have occupied themselves with the analysis of the form of value, have been unable to arrive at any result, first, because they confuse the form of value with value itself; and second, because, under the coarse influence of the practical bourgeois, they exclusively give their attention to the quantitative aspect of the question. "The command of quantity . . . constitutes value." ("Money and its Vicissitudes." London, 1837, p. 11. By S. Bailey.

coats—that is, whether a given quantity of linen is worth few or many coats, every such statement implies that the linen and coats, as magnitudes of value, are expressions of the same unit, things of the same kind. Linen=coat is the basis of the equation.

But the two commodities whose identity of quality is thus assumed, do not play the same part. It is only the value of the linen that is expressed. And how? By its reference to the coat as its equivalent, as something that can be exchanged for it. In this relation the coat is the mode of existence of value, is value embodied, for only as such is it the same as the linen. On the other hand, the linen's own value comes to the front, receives independent expression, for it is only as being value that it is comparable with the coat as a thing of equal value, or exchangeable with the coat. To borrow an illustration from chemistry, butyric acid is a different substance from propyl formate. Yet both are made up of the same chemical substances, carbon (C), hydrogen (H), and oxygen (O), and that, too, in like proportions—namely, $C_4H_8O_2$. If now we equate butyric acid to propyl formate, then, in the first place, propyl formate would be, in this relation, merely a form of existence of $C_4H_8O_2$; and in the second place, we should be stating that butyric acid also consists of $C_4H_8O_2$. Therefore, by thus equating the two substances, expression would be given to their chemical composition, while their different physical forms would be neglected.

If we say that, as values, commodities are mere congelations of human labour, we reduce them by our analysis, it is true, to the abstraction, value; but we ascribe to this value no form apart from their bodily form. It is otherwise in the value relation of one commodity to another. Here, the one stands forth in its character of value by reason of its relation to the other.

By making the coat the equivalent of the linen, we equate the labour embodied in the former to that in the latter. Now, it is true that the tailoring, which makes the coat, is concrete labour of a different sort from the weaving which makes the linen. But the act of equating it to the weaving, reduces the tailoring to that which is really equal in the two kinds of labour, to their common character of human labour. In this roundabout way, then, the fact is expressed, that weaving also, in so far as it weaves value, has nothing to distinguish it from tailoring, and, consequently, is abstract human labour. It is the expression of equivalence between different sorts of commodities that alone brings into relief the specific character of value-creating labour, and this it does by actually reducing the different varieties of labour embodied in the different kinds of commodities to their common quality of human labour in the abstract.[1]

There is, however, something else required beyond the expression of the specific character of the labour of which the value of the linen consists. Human labour-power in motion, or human labour, creates value, but is not itself value. It becomes value only in its congealed state, when embodied in the form of some object. In order to express the value of the linen as a congelation of human labour, that value must be expressed as having objective existence, as being a something materially different from the linen itself, and yet a something common to the linen and all other commodities. The problem is already solved.

When occupying the position of equivalent in the equation of value, the coat ranks qualitatively as the equal of the linen, as something of the same kind, because it is value. In this position it is a thing in which we see nothing but value, or whose palpable bodily form represents value. Yet the coat itself, the body of the commodity, coat, is a mere use-value. A coat as such no more tells us it is value, than does the first piece of linen we take hold of. This shows that when placed in value

---

[1] The celebrated Franklin, one of the first economists, after Wm. Petty, who saw through the nature of value, says: "Trade in general being nothing else but the exchange of labour for labour, the value of all things is . . . most justly measured by labour." (The works of B. Franklin, &c., edited by Sparks, Boston, 1836, Vol. II., p. 267.) Franklin is unconscious that by estimating the value of everything in labour, he makes abstraction from any difference in the sorts of labour exchanged, and thus reduces them all to equal human labour. But although ignorant of this, yet he says it. He speaks first of "the one labour," then of "the other labour," and finally of "labour," without further qualification, as the substance of the value of everything.

relation to the linen, the coat signifies more than when out of that relation, just as many a man strutting about in a gorgeous uniform counts for more than when in mufti.

In the production of the coat, human labour-power, in the shape of tailoring, must have been actually expended. Human labour is therefore accumulated in it. In this aspect the coat is a depository of value, but though worn to a thread, it does not let this fact show through. And as equivalent of the linen in the value equation, it exists under this aspect alone, counts therefore as embodied value, as a body that is value. A, for instance, cannot be "your majesty" to B, unless at the same time majesty in B's eyes assumes the bodily form of A, and, what is more, with every new father of the people, changes its features, hair, and many other things besides.

Hence, in the value equation, in which the coat is the equivalent of the linen, the coat officiates as the form of value. The value of the commodity linen is expressed by the bodily form of the commodity coat, the value of one by the use-value of the other. As a use-value, the linen is something palpably different from the coat; as value, it is the same as the coat, and now has the appearance of a coat. Thus the linen acquires a value form different from its physical form. The fact that it is value, is made manifest by its equality with the coat, just as the sheep's nature of a Christian is shown in his resemblance to the Lamb of God.

We see, then, all that our analysis of the value of commodities has already told us, is told us by the linen itself, so soon as it comes into communication with another commodity, the coat. Only it betrays its thoughts in that language with which alone it is familiar, the language of commodities. In order to tell us that its own value is created by labour in its abstract character of human labour, it says that the coat, in so far as it is worth as much as the linen, and therefore is value, consists of the same labour as the linen. In order to inform us that its sublime reality as value is not the same as its buckram body, it says that value has the appearance of a coat, and consequently that so far as the linen is value, it and the coat are as like as two peas. We may here remark, that the lan-

guage of commodities has, besides Hebrew, many other more or
less correct dialects. The German "werthsein," to be worth,
for instance, expresses in a less striking manner than the
Romance verbs "valere," "valer," "valoir," that the equating of
commodity B to commodity A, is commodity A's own mode of
expressing its value. Paris vaut bien une messe.

By means, therefore, of the value relation expressed in our
equation, the bodily form of commodity B becomes the value
form of commodity A, or the body of commodity B acts as a
mirror to the value of commodity A.[1] By putting itself in relation with commodity B, as value in *propriâ personâ,* as the
matter of which human labour is made up, the commodity A
converts the value in use, B, into the substance in which to
express its, A's, own value. The value of A, thus expressed in
the use-value of B, has taken the form of relative value.

(b.) *Quantitative determination of Relative value.*

Every commodity, whose value it is intended to express, is a
useful object of given quantity, as 15 bushels of corn, or 100
lbs. of coffee. And a given quantity of any commodity contains a definite quantity of human labor. The value-form
must therefore not only express value generally, but also value
in definite quantity. Therefore, in the value relation of commodity A to commodity B, of the linen to the coat, not only is
the latter, as value in general, made the equal in quality of the
linen, but a definite quantity of coat (1 coat) is made the
equivalent of a definite quantity (20 yards) of linen.

The equation, 20 yards of linen=1 coat, or 20 yards of linen
are worth one coat, implies that the same quantity of value-
substance (congealed labour) is embodied in both; that the
two commodities have each cost the same amount of labour or
the same quantity of labour time. But the labour time
necessary for the production of 20 yards of linen or 1 coat

---

[1] In a sort of way, it is with man as with commodities. Since he comes into
the world neither with a looking glass in his hand, nor as a Fichtian philosopher,
to whom "I am I" is sufficient, man first sees and/recognises himself in other
men. Peter only establishes his own identity as a man by first comparing himself with Paul as being of like kind. And thereby Paul, just as he stands in his
Pauline personality, becomes to Peter the type of the genus homo.

varies with every change in the productiveness of weaving or tailoring. We have now to consider the influence of such changes on the quantitative aspect of the relative expression of value.

I. Let the value of the linen vary,[1] that of the coat remaining constant. If, say in consequence of the exhaustion of flax-growing soil, the labour time necessary for the production of the linen be doubled, the value of the linen will also be doubled. Instead of the equation, 20 yards of linen=1 coat, we should have 20 yards of linen=2 coats, since 1 coat would now contain only half the labour time embodied in 20 yards of linen. If, on the other hand, in consequence, say, of improved looms, this labour time be reduced by one half, the value of the linen would fall by one half. Consequently, we should have 20 yards of linen=½ coat. The relative value of commodity A, *i.e.*, its value expressed in commodity B, rises and falls directly as the value of A, the value of B being supposed constant.

II. Let the value of the linen remain constant, while the value of the coat varies. If, under these circumstances, in consequence, for instance, of a poor crop of wool, the labour time necessary for the production of a coat becomes doubled, we have instead of 20 yards of linen=1 coat, 20 yards of linen =½ coat. If, on the other hand, the value of the coat sinks by one half, then 20 yards of linen=2 coats. Hence, if the value of commodity A remain constant, its relative value expressed in commodity B rises and falls inversely as the value of B.

If we compare the different cases in I. and II., we see that the same change of magnitude in relative value may arise from totally opposite causes. Thus, the equation, 20 yards of linen =1 coat, becomes 20 yards of linen=2 coats, either, because, the value of the linen has doubled, or because the value of the coat has fallen by one half; and it becomes 20 yards of linen =½ coat, either, because the value of the linen has fallen by one half, or because the value of the coat has doubled.

III. Let the quantities of labour time respectively neces-

---

[1] Value is here, as occasionally in the preceding pages, used in the sense of value determined as to quantity, or of magnitude of value.

sary for the production of the linen and the coat vary simultaneously in the same direction and in the same proportion. In this case 20 yards of linen continue equal to 1 coat, however much their values may have altered. Their change of value is seen as soon as they are compared with a third commodity, whose value has remained constant. If the values of all commodities rose or fell simultaneously, and in the same proportion, their relative values would remain unaltered. Their real change of value would appear from the diminished or increased quantity of commodities produced in a given time.

IV. The labour time respectively necessary for the production of the linen and the coat, and therefore the value of these commodities may simultaneously vary in the same direction, but at unequal rates, or in opposite directions, or in other ways. The effect of all these possible different variations, on the relative value of a commodity, may be deduced from the results of I., II., and III.

Thus real changes in the magnitude of value are neither unequivocally nor exhaustively reflected in their relative expression, that is, in the equation expressing the magnitude of relative value. The relative value of a commodity may vary, although its value remains constant. Its relative value may remain constant, although its value varies; and finally, simultaneous variations in the magnitude of value and in that of its relative expression by no means necessarily correspond in amount.[1]

---

[1] This incongruity between the magnitude of value and its relative expression has, with customary ingenuity, been exploited by vulgar economists. For example —"Once admit that A falls, because B, with which it is exchanged, rises. while no less labour is bestowed in the meantime on A, and your general principle of value falls to the ground. . . . If he [Ricardo] allowed that when A rises in value relatively to B, B falls in value relatively to A, he cut away the ground on which he rested his grand proposition, that the value of a commodity is ever determined by the labour embodied in it; for if a change in the cost of A alters not only its own value in relation to B, for which it is exchanged, but also the value of B relatively to that of A, though no change has taken place in the quantity of labour to produce B, then not only the doctrine falls to the ground which asserts that the quantity of labour bestowed on an article regulates its value, but also that which affirms the cost of an article to regulate its value." (J. Broadhurst: Political Economy, London, 1842, p. 11 and 14.

Mr. Broadhurst might just as well say: consider the fractions $\frac{10}{20}$, $\frac{10}{50}$, $\frac{10}{100}$, &c., the number 10 remains unchanged, and yet its proportional magnitude, its magni-

3. *The Equivalent form of value.*

We have seen that commodity A (the linen), by expressing its value in the use-value of a commodity differing in kind (the coat), at the same time impresses upon the latter a specific form of value, namely that of the equivalent. The commodity linen manifests its quality of having a value by the fact that the coat, without having assumed a value form different from its bodily form, is equated to the linen. The fact that the latter therefore has a value is expressed by saying that the coat is directly exchangeable with it. Therefore, when we say that a commodity is in the equivalent form, we express the fact that it is directly exchangeable with other commodities.

When one commodity, such as a coat, serves as the equivalent of another, such as linen, and coats consequently acquire the characteristic property of being directly exchangeable with linen, we are far from knowing in what proportion the two are exchangeable. The value of the linen being given in magnitude, that proportion depends on the value of the coat. Whether the coat serves as the equivalent and the linen as relative value, or the linen as the equivalent and the coat as relative value, the magnitude of the coat's value is determined, independently of its value form, by the labour time necessary for its production. But whenever the coat assumes in the equation of value, the position of equivalent, its value acquires no quantitative expression; on the contrary, the commodity coat now figures only as a definite quantity of some article.

For instance, 40 yards of linen are worth—what? 2 coats. Because the commodity coat here plays the part of equivalent, because the use-value coat, as opposed to the linen, figures as an embodiment of value, therefore a definite number of coats suffices to express the definite quantity of value in the linen. Two coats may therefore express the quantity of value of 40 yards of linen, but they can never express the quantity of their own value. A superficial observation of this fact, namely, that

tude relatively to the numbers 20, 50, 100, &c., continually diminishes. Therefore the great principle that the magnitude of a whole number, such as 10, is "regulated" by the number of times unity is contained in it, falls to the ground. — [The author explains in section 4 of this chapter, p. 93, note 1, what he understands by "Vulgar Economy." — Ed.]

in the equation of value, the equivalent figures exclusively as a simple quantity of some article, of some use-value, has misled Bailey, as also many others, both before and after him, into seeing, in the expression of value, merely a quantitative relation. The truth being, that when a commodity acts as equivalent, no quantitative determination of its value is expressed.

The first peculiarity that strikes us, in considering the form of the equivalent, is this: use-value becomes the form of manifestation, the phenomenal form of its opposite, value.

The bodily form of the commodity becomes its value form. But, mark well, that this quid pro quo exists in the case of any commodity B, only when some other commodity A enters into a value relation with it, and then only within the limits of this relation. Since no commodity can stand in the relation of equivalent to itself, and thus turn its own bodily shape into the expression of its own value, every commodity is compelled to choose some other commodity for its equivalent, and to accept the use-value, that is to say, the bodily shape of that other commodity as the form of its own value.

One of the measures that we apply to commodities as material substances, as use-values, will serve to illustrate this point. A sugar-loaf being a body, is heavy, and therefore has weight: but we can neither see nor touch this weight. We then take various pieces of iron, whose weight has been determined beforehand. The iron, as iron, is no more the form of manifestation of weight, than is the sugar-loaf. Nevertheless, in order to express the sugar-loaf as so much weight, we put it into a weight-relation with the iron. In this relation, the iron officiates as a body representing nothing but weight. A certain quantity of iron therefore serves as the measure of the weight of the sugar, and represents, in relation to the sugar-loaf, weight embodied, the form of manifestation of weight. This part is played by the iron only within this relation, into which the sugar or any other body, whose weight has to be determined, enters with the iron. Were they not both heavy, they could not enter into this relation, and the one could therefore not serve as the expression of the weight of the other. When we throw both into the scales, we see in reality, that as weight they are both the same, and that, therefore, when taken in proper proportions, they have the same weight. Just as the substance iron, as a measure of weight, represents in relation to the sugar-loaf weight alone, so, in our expression of value, the material object, coat, in relation to the linen, represents value alone.

Here, however, the analogy ceases. The iron, in the expression of the weight of the sugar-loaf, represents a natural property common to both bodies, namely their weight; but the coat in the expression of value of the linen, represents a non-natural property of both, something purely social, namely, their value.

Since the relative form of value of a commodity—the linen, for example—expresses the value of that commodity, as being something wholly different from its substance and properties, as being, for instance, coat-like, we see that this expression itself indicates that some social relation lies at the bottom of it. With the equivalent form it is just the contrary. The very essence of this form is that the material commodity itself—the coat—just as it is, expresses value, and is endowed with the form of value by Nature itself. Of course this holds good only so long as the value relation exists, in which the coat stands in the position of equivalent to the linen.[1] Since, however, the properties of a thing are not the result of its relations to other things, but only manifest themselves in such relations, the coat seems to be endowed with its equivalent form, its property of being directly exchangeable, just as much by Nature as it is endowed with the property of being heavy, or the capacity to keep us warm. Hence the enigmatical character of the equivalent form which escapes the notice of the bourgeois political economist, until this form, completely developed, confronts him in the shape of money. He then seeks to explain away the mystical character of gold and silver, by substituting for them less dazzling commodities, and by reciting, with ever renewed satisfaction, the catalogue of_all possible commodities which at one time or another have played the part of equivalent. He

---

[1] Such expressions of relations in general, called by Hegel reflex-categories, form a very curious class. For instance, one man is king only because other men stand in the relation of subjects to him. They, on the contrary, imagine that they are subjects because he is king.

has not the least suspicion that the most simple expression of value, such as 20 yds. of linen=1 coat, already propounds the riddle of the equivalent form for our solution.

The body of the commodity that serves as the equivalent, figures as the materialization of human labour in the abstract and is at the same time the product of some specifically useful concrete labour. This concrete labour becomes, therefore, the medium for expressing abstract human labour. If on the one hand the coat ranks as nothing but the embodiment of abstract human labour, so, on the other hand, the tailoring which is actually embodied in it, counts as nothing but the form under which that abstract labour is realised. In the expression of value of the linen, the utility of the tailoring consists, not in making clothes, but in making an object, which we at once recognise to be Value, and therefore to be a congelation of labour, but of labour indistinguishable from that realised in the value of the linen. In order to act as such a mirror of value, the labour of tailoring must reflect nothing besides its own abstract quality of being human labour generally.

In tailoring, as well as in weaving, human labour-power is expended. Both, therefore, possess the general property of being human labour, and may, therefore, in certain cases, such as in the production of value, have to be considered under this aspect alone. There is nothing mysterious in this. But in the expression of value there is a complete turn of the tables. For instance, how is the fact to be expressed that weaving creates the value of the linen, not by virtue of being weaving, as such, but by reason of its general property of being human labour? Simply by opposing to weaving that other particular form of concrete labour (in this instance tailoring), which produces the equivalent of the product of weaving. Just as the coat in its bodily form became a direct expression of value, so now does tailoring, a concrete form of labour, appear as the direct and palpable embodiment of human labour generally.

Hence, the second peculiarity of the equivalent form is, that concrete labour becomes the form under which its opposite, abstract human labour, manifests itself.

But because this concrete labour, tailoring in our case, ranks as, and is directly indentified with, undifferentiated human labour, it also ranks as identical with any other sort of labor, and therefore with that embodied in linen. Consequently, although, like all other commodity-producing labour, it is the labour of private individuals, yet, at the same time, it ranks as labour directly social in its character. This is the reason why it results in a product directly exchangeable with other commodities. We have then a third peculiarity of the Equivalent form, namely, that the labour of private individuals takes the form of its opposite, labour directly social in its form.

The two latter peculiarities of the Equivalent form will become more intelligible if we go back to the great thinker who was the first to analyse so many forms, whether of thought, society, or nature, and amongst them also the form of value. I mean Aristotle.

In the first place, he clearly enunciates that the money form of commodities is only the further development of the simple form of value—*i. e.,* of the expression of the value of one commodity in some other commodity taken at random; for he says

5 beds=1 house (κλίναι πέντε ἀντὶ οἰκίας) is not to be
  distinguished from
5 beds=so much money.

(κλίναι πέντε ἀντὶ . . . ὅσον αἱ πέντε κλίναι)

He further sees that the value relation which gives rise to this expression makes it necessary that the house should qualitatively be made the equal of the bed, and that, without such an equalization, these two clearly different things could not be compared with each other as commensurable quantities. "Exchange," he says, "cannot take place without equality, and equality not without commensurability" (οὔτ᾽ ἰσότης μὴ οὔσης συμμετρίας). Here, however, he comes to a stop, and gives up the further analysis of the form of value. "It is, however, in reality, impossible (τῇ μὲν οὖν ἀληθείᾳ ἀδύνατον), that such unlike things can be commensurable"—*i. e.,* qualitatively equal. Such an equalisation can only be something foreign to their real nature, consequently only "a make-shift for practical purposes."

Aristotle therefore, himself, tells us, what barred the way to his further analysis; it was the absence of any concept of value. What is that equal something, that common substance, which admits of the value of the beds being expressed by a house? Such a thing, in truth, cannot exist, says Aristotle. And why not? Compared with the beds, the house does represent something equal to them, in so far as it represents what is really equal, both in the beds and the house. And that is— human labour.

There was, however, an important fact which prevented Aristotle from seeing that, to attribute value to commodities, is merely a mode of expressing all labour as equal human labour, and consequently as labour of equal quality. Greek society was founded upon slavery, and had, therefore, for its natural basis, the inequality of men and of their labour powers. The secret of the expression of value, namely, that all kinds of labour are equal and equivalent, because, and so far as they are human labour in general, cannot be deciphered, until the notion of human equality has already acquired the fixity of a popular prejudice. This, however, is possible only in a society in which the great mass of the produce of labour takes the form of commodities, in which, consequently, the dominant relation between man and man, is that of owners of commodities. The brilliancy of Aristotle's genius is shown by this alone, that he discovered, in the expression of the value of commodities, a relation of equality. The peculiar conditions of the society in which he lived, alone prevented him from discovering what, "in truth," was at the bottom of this equality.

4. *The Elementary form of value considered as a whole.*

The elementary form of value of a commodity is contained in the equation, expressing its value relation to another commodity of a different kind, or in its exchange relation to the same. The value of commodity A is qualitatively expressed by the fact that commodity B is directly exchangeable with it. Its value is quantitively expressed by the fact, that a definite quantity of B is exchangeable with a definite quantity of A. In other words, the value of a commodity obtains independent and definite expression, by taking the form of exchange value. When, at the beginning of this chapter, we said, in common parlance, that a commodity is both a use-value and an exchange value, we were, accurately speaking, wrong. A commodity is a use-value or object of utility, and a value. It manifests itself as this two-fold thing, that it is, as soon as its value assumes an independent form—viz., the form exchange value. It never assumes this form when isolated, but only when placed in a value or exchange relation with another commodity of a different kind. When once we know this, such a mode of expression does no harm; it simply serves as an abbreviation.

Our analysis has shown, that the form or expression of the value of a commodity originates in the nature of value, and not that value and its magnitude originate in the mode of their expression as exchange value. This, however, is the delusion as well of the mercantilists and their recent revivors, Ferrier, Ganilh,[1] and others, as also of their antipodes, the modern bagmen of Free Trade, such as Bastiat. The mercantilists lay special stress on the qualitative aspect of the expression of value, and consequently on the equivalent form of commodities, which attains its full perfection in money. The modern hawkers of Free Trade, who must get rid of their article at any price, on the other hand, lay most stress on the quantitative aspect of the relative form of value. For them there consequently exists neither value, nor magnitude of value, anywhere except in its expression by means of the exchange relation of commodities, that is, in the daily list of prices current. MacLeod, who has taken upon himself to dress up the confused ideas of Lombard Street in the most learned finery, is a successful cross between the superstitious mercantilists, and the enlightened Free Trade bagmen.

A close scrutiny of the expression of the value of A in terms of B, contained in the equation expressing the value relation of A to B, has shown us that, within that relation, the bodily form

---

[1] F. L. Ferrier, sous-inspecteur des douanes, "Du gouvernement considerè dans ses rapports avec le commerce," Paris, 1805; and Charles Ganilh, "Des Systèmes d'Economie politique," 2nd ed., Paris, 1821.

of A figures only as a use-value, the bodily form of B only as the form or aspect of value. The opposition or contrast existing internally in each commodity between use-value and value, is, therefore, made evident externally by two commodities being placed in such relation to each other, that the commodity whose value it is sought to express, figures directly as a mere use-value, while the commodity in which that value is to be expressed, figures directly as mere exchange value. Hence the elementary form of value of a commodity is the elementary form in which the contrast contained in that commodity, between use-value and value, becomes apparent.

Every product of labour is, in all states of society, a use-value; but it is only at a definite historical epoch in a society's development that such product becomes a commodity, viz., at the epoch when the labour spent on the production of a useful article becomes expressed as one of the objective qualities of that article, *i.e.,* as its value. It therefore follows that the elementary value-form is also the primitive form under which a product of labour appears historically as a commodity, and that the gradual transformation of such products into commodities, proceeds *pari passu* with the development of the value-form.

We perceive, at first sight, the deficiencies of the elementary form of value: it is a mere germ, which must undergo a series of metamorphoses before it can ripen into the Price-form.

The expression of the value of commodity A in terms of any other commodity B, merely distinguishes the value from the use-value of A, and therefore places A merely in a relation of exchange with a single different commodity, B; but it is still far from expressing A's qualitative equality, and quantitative proportionality, to all commodities. To the elementary relative value-form of a commodity, there corresponds the single equivalent form of one other commodity. Thus, in the relative expression of value of the linen, the coat assumes the form of equivalent, or of being directly exchangeable, only in relation to a single commodity, the linen.

Nevertheless, the elementary form of value passes by an easy transition into a more complete form. It is true that by means of the elementary form, the value of a commodity A, becomes expressed in terms of one, and only one, other commodity. But that one may be a commodity of any kind, coat, iron, corn, or anything else. Therefore, according as A is placed in relation with one or the other, we get for one and the same commodity, different elementary expressions of value.[1] The number of such possible expressions is limited only by the number of the different kinds of commodities distinct from it. The isolated expression of A's value, is therefore convertible into a series, prolonged to any length, of the different elementary expressions of that value.

B. Total or Expanded form of value.

z Com. A=u Com. B or=v Com. C or=w Com. D or=x Com. E or=&c.
(20 yards of linen=1 coat or=10 ℔ tea or=40 ℔ coffee or= 1 quarter corn or=2 ounces gold or=½ ton iron or=&c.)

1. The Expanded Relative form of value.

The value of a single commodity, the linen, for example, is now expressed in terms of numberless other elements of the world of commodities. Every other commodity now becomes a mirror of the linen's value.[2] It is thus, that for the first time

---

[1] In Homer, for instance, the value of an article is expressed in a series of different things. Il. VII., 472-475.

[2] For this reason, we can speak of the coat-value of the linen when its value is expressed in coats, or of its corn-value when expressed in corn, and so on. Every such expression tells us, that what appears in the use-values, coat, corn, &c., is the value of the linen. " The value of any commodity denoting its relation in exchange, we may speak of it as . . . corn-value, cloth-value, according to the commodity with which it is compared; and hence there are a thousand different kinds of value, as many kinds of value as there are commodities in existence, and all are equally real and equally nominal." (A Critical Dissertation on the Nature, Measure and Causes of Value; chiefly in reference to the writings of Mr. Ricardo and his followers. By the author of " Essays on the Formation, &c., of Opinions." London, 1825, p. 39.) S. Bailey, the author of this anonymous work, a work which in its day created much stir in England, fancied that, by thus pointing out the various relative expressions of one and the same value, he proved the impossibility of any determination of the concept of value. However narrow his own views may have been, yet, that he laid his finger on some serious defects in the Ricardian Theory, is proved by the animosity with which he was attacked by Ricardo's followers. See the *Westminster Review* for example.

this value shows itself in its true light as a congelation of undifferentiated human labour. For the labour that creates it, now stands expressly revealed, as labour that ranks equally with every other sort of human labour, no matter what its form, whether tailoring, ploughing, mining, &c. and no matter, therefore, whether it is realised in coats, corn, iron, or gold. The linen, by virtue of the form of its value, now stands in a social relation, no longer with only one other kind of commodity, but with the whole world of commodities. As a commodity, it is a citizen of that world. At the same time, the interminable series of value equations implies, that as regards the value of a commodity, it is a matter of indifference under what particular form, or kind, of use-value it appears.

In the first form, 20 yds. of linen=1 coat, it might for ought that otherwise appears be pure accident, that these two commodities are exchangeable in definite quantities. In the second form, on the contrary, we perceive at once the background that determines, and is essentially different from, this accidental appearance. The value of the linen remains unaltered in magnitude, whether expressed in coats, coffee, or iron, or in numberless different commodities, the property of as many different owners. The accidental relation between two individual commodity-owners disappears. It becomes plain, that it is not the exchange of commodities which regulates the magnitude of their value; but, on the contrary, that it is the magnitude of their value which controls their exchange proportions.

2. *The particular Equivalent form.*

Each commodity, such as coat, tea, corn, iron, &c., figures in the expression of value of the linen, as an equivalent, and consequently as a thing that is value. The bodily form of each of these commodities figures now as a particular equivalent form, one out of many. In the same way the manifold concrete useful kinds of labour, embodied in these different commodities, rank now as so many different forms of the realisation, or manifestation, of undifferentiated human labour.

3. *Defects of the Total or Expanded form of value.*

In the first place, the relative expression of value is incomplete because the series representing it is interminable. The chain of which each equation of value is a link, is liable at any moment to be lengthened by each new kind of commodity that comes into existence and furnishes the material for a fresh expression of value. In the second place, it is a many-coloured mosaic of disparate and independent expressions of value. And lastly, if, as must be the case, the relative value of each commodity in turn, becomes expressed in this expanded form, we get for each of them a relative value-form, different in every case, and consisting of an interminable series of expressions of value. The defects of the expanded relative-value form are reflected in the corresponding equivalent form. Since the bodily form of each single commodity is one particular equivalent form amongst numberless others, we have, on the whole, nothing but fragmentary equivalent forms, each excluding the others. In the same way, also, the special, concrete, useful kind of labour embodied in each particular equivalent, is presented only as a particular kind of labour, and therefore not as an exhaustive representative of human labour generally. The latter, indeed, gains adequate manifestation in the totality of its manifold, particular, concrete forms. But, in that case, its expression in an infinite series is ever incomplete and deficient in unity.

The expanded relative value form is, however, nothing but the sum of the elementary relative expressions or equations of the first kind, such as

$$20 \text{ yards of linen} = 1 \text{ coat}$$
$$20 \text{ yards of linen} = 10 \text{ lbs. of tea, etc.}$$

Each of these implies the corresponding inverted equation,

$$1 \text{ coat} = 20 \text{ yards of linen}$$
$$10 \text{ lbs. of tea} = 20 \text{ yards of linen, etc.}$$

In fact, when a person exchanges his linen for many other commodities, and thus expresses its value in a series of other commodities, it necessarily follows, that the various owners of the latter exchange them for the linen, and consequently express the value of their various commodities in one and the same third commodity, the linen. If then, we reverse the series, 20 yards of linen=1 coat or=10 lbs. of tea, etc., that is to say, if we give expression to the converse relation already implied in the series, we get,

C. The General form of value.

$$
\left.
\begin{array}{l}
\text{1 coat} \\
\text{10 lbs. of tea} \\
\text{40 lbs. of coffee} \\
\text{1 quarter of corn} \\
\text{2 ounces of gold} \\
\text{$\frac{1}{2}$ a ton of iron} \\
\text{x com. A., etc.}
\end{array}
\right\} = \text{20 yards of linen}
$$

1. The altered character of the form of value.

All commodities now express their value (1) in an elementary form, because in a single commodity; (2) with unity, because in one and the same commodity. This form of value is elementary and the same for all, therefore general.

The forms A and B were fit only to express the value of a commodity as something distinct from its use-value or material form.

The first form, A, furnishes such equations as the following:—1 coat=20 yards of linen, 10 lbs. of tea=$\frac{1}{2}$ ton of iron. The value of the coat is equated to linen, that of the tea to iron. But to be equated to linen, and again to iron, is to be as different as are linen and iron. This form, it is plain, occurs practically only in the first beginning, when the products of labour are converted into commodities by accidental and occasional exchanges.

The second form, B, distinguishes, in a more adequate manner than the first, the value of a commodity from its use-value; for the value of the coat is there placed in contrast under all possible shapes with the bodily form of the coat; it is equated to linen, to iron, to tea, in short, to everything else, only not to itself, the coat.   On the other hand, any general expression of value common to all is directly excluded; for, in the equation of value of each commodity, all other commodities now appear only under the form of equivalents.   The expanded form of value comes into actual existence for the first time so soon as a particular product of labour, such as cattle, is no longer exceptionally, but habitually, exchanged for various other commodities.

The third and lastly developed form expresses the values of the whole world of commodities in terms of a single commodity set apart for the purpose, namely, the linen, and thus represents to us their values by means of their equality with linen.   The value of every commodity is now, by being equated to linen, not only differentiated from its own use-value, but from all other use-values generally, and is, by that very fact, expressed as that which is common to all commodities.   By this form, commodities are, for the first time, effectively brought into relation with one another as values, or made to appear as exchange values.

The two earlier forms either express the value of each commodity in terms of a single commodity of a different kind, or in a series of many such commodities.   In both cases, it is, so to say, the special business of each single commodity to find an expression for its value, and this it does without the help of the others.   These others, with respect to the former, play the passive parts of equivalents.   The general form of value C, results from the joint action of the whole world of commodities, and from that alone.   A commodity can acquire a general expression of its value only by all other commodities, simultaneously with it, expressing their values in the same equivalent; and every new commodity must follow suit.   It thus becomes evident that, since the existence of commodities as values is purely social, this social existence can be expressed by the totality of their social relations alone, and consequently that the form of their value must be a socially recognised form.

All commodities being equated to linen now appear not only

as qualitatively equal as values generally, but also as values whose magnitudes are capable of comparison. By expressing the magnitudes of their values in one and the same material, the linen, those magnitudes are also compared with each other. For instance, 10 lbs. of tea=20 yards of linen, and 40 lbs. of coffee=20 yards of linen. Therefore, 10 lbs. of tea=40 lbs. of coffee. In other words, there is contained in 1 lb. of coffee only one-fourth as much substance of value—labour—as is contained in 1 lb. of tea.

The general form of relative value, embracing the whole world of commodities, converts the single commodity that is excluded from the rest, and made to play the part of equivalent —here the linen—into the universal equivalent. The bodily form of the linen is now the form assumed in common by the value of all commodities; it therefore becomes directly exchangeable with all and every of them. The substance linen becomes the visible incarnation, the social chrysalis state of every kind of human labour. Weaving, which is the labour of certain private individuals producing a particular article, linen, acquires in consequence a social character, the character of equality with all other kinds of labour. The innumerable equations of which the general form of value is composed, equate in turn the labour embodied in the linen to that embodied in every other commodity, and they thus convert weaving into the general form of manifestation of undifferentiated human labour. In this manner the labour realised in the values of commodities is presented not only under its negative aspect, under which abstraction is made from every concrete form and useful property of actual work, but its own positive nature is made to reveal itself expressly. The general value-form is the reduction of all kinds of actual labour to their common character of being human labour generally, of being the expenditure of human labour power.

The general value form, which represents all products of labour as mere congelations of undifferentiated human labour, shows by its very structure that it is the social resumé of the world of commodities. That form consequently makes it indisputably evident that in the world of commodities the character possessed by all labour of being *human* labour constitutes its specific social character.

2. *The interdependent development of the Relative form of value, and of the Equivalent form.*

The degree of development of the relative form of value corresponds to that of the equivalent form. But we must bear in mind that the development of the latter is only the expression and result of the development of the former.

The primary or isolated relative form of value of one commodity converts some other commodity into an isolated equivalent. The expanded form of relative value, which is the expression of the value of one commodity in terms of all other commodities, endows those other commodities with the character of particular equivalents differing in kind. And lastly, a particular kind of commodity acquires the character of universal equivalent, because all other commodities make it the material in which they uniformly express their value.

The antagonism between the relative form of value and the equivalent form, the two poles of the value form, is developed concurrently with that form itself.

The first form, 20 yds. of linen=one coat, already contains this antagonism, without as yet fixing it. According as we read this equation forwards or backwards, the parts played by the linen and the coat are different. In the one case the relative value of the linen is expressed in the coat, in the other case the relative value of the coat is expressed in the linen. In this first form of value, therefore, it is difficult to grasp the polar contrast.

Form B shows that only one single commodity at a time can completely expand its relative value, and that it acquires this expanded form only because, and in so far as, all other commodities are, with respect to it, equivalents. Here we cannot reverse the equation, as we can the equation 20 yds. of linen= 1 coat, without altering its general character, and converting it from the expanded form of value into the general form of value.

Finally, the form C gives to the world of commodities a general social relative form of value, because, and in so far as, thereby all commodities, with the exception of one, are excluded from the equivalent form. A single commodity, the linen, appears therefore to have acquired the character of direct exchangeability with every other commodity because, and in so far as, this character is denied to every other commodity.[1]

The commodity that figures as universal equivalent, is, on the other hand, excluded from the relative value form. If the linen, or any other commodity serving as universal equivalent, were, at the same time, to share in the relative form of value, it would have to serve as its own equivalent. We should then have 20 yds. of linen=20 yds. of linen; this tautology expresses neither value, nor magnitude of value. In order to express the relative value of the universal equivalent, we must rather reverse the form C. This equivalent has no relative form of value in common with other commodities, but its value is relatively expressed by a never ending series of other commodities. Thus, the expanded form of relative value, or form B, now shows itself as the specific form of relative value for the equivalent commodity.

3. *Transition from the General form of value to the Money form.*

The universal equivalent form is a form of value in general. It can, therefore, be assumed by any commodity. On the

[1] It is by no means self-evident that this character of direct and universal exchangeability is, so to speak, a polar one, and as intimately connected with its opposite pole, the absence of direct exchangeability, as the positive pole of the magnet is with its negative counterpart. It may therefore be imagined that all commodities can simultaneously have this character impressed upon them, just as it can be imagined that all Catholics can be popes together. It is, of course, highly desirable in the eyes of the petit bourgeois, for whom the production of commodities is the ne plus ultra of human freedom and individual independence, that the inconveniences resulting from this character of commodities not being directly exchangeable, should be removed. Proudhon's socialism is a working out of this Philistine Utopia, a form of socialism which, as I have elsewhere shown, does not possess even the merit of originality. Long before his time, the task was attempted with much better success by Gray, Bray, and others. But, for all that, wisdom of this kind flourishes even now in certain circles under the name of "science." Never has any school played more tricks with the word science, than that of Proudhon, for

"wo Begriffe fehlen
Da stellt zur rechten Zeit ein Wort sich ein."

other hand, if a commodity be found to have assumed the universal equivalent form (form C), this is only because and in so far as it has been excluded from the rest of all other commodities as their equivalent, and that by their own act. And from the moment that this exclusion becomes finally restricted to one particular commodity, from that moment only, the general form of relative value of the world of commodities obtains real consistence and general social validity.

The particular commodity, with whose bodily form the equivalent form is thus socially identified, now becomes the money commodity, or serves as money. It becomes the special social function of that commodity, and consequently its social monopoly, to play within the world of commodities the part of the universal equivalent. Amongst the commodities which, in form B, figure as particular equivalents of the linen, and in form C, express in common their relative values in linen, this foremost place has been attained by one in particular—namely, gold. If, then, in form C we replace the linen by gold, we get,

D. *The Money form.*

$$
\left.
\begin{array}{l}
\text{20 yards of linen} \quad = \\
\text{1 coat} \quad = \\
\text{10 ℔ of tea} \quad = \\
\text{40 ℔ of coffee} \quad = \\
\text{1 qr. of corn} \quad = \\
\text{½ a ton of iron} \quad = \\
\text{x commodity A} \quad =
\end{array}
\right\} \quad \text{2 ounces of gold.}
$$

In passing from form A to form B, and from the latter to form C, the changes are fundamental. On the other hand, there is no difference between forms C and D, except that, in the latter, gold has assumed the equivalent form in the place of linen. Gold is in form D, what linen was in form C—the universal equivalent. The progress consists in this alone, that the character of direct and universal exchangeability—in other words, that the universal equivalent form—has now, by social custom, become finally identified with the substance, gold.

Gold is now money with reference to all other commodities only because it was previously, with reference to them, a simple commodity. Like all other commodities, it was also capable of serving as an equivalent, either as simple equivalent in isolated exchanges, or as particular equivalent by the side of others. Gradually it began to serve, within varying limits, as universal equivalent. So soon as it monopolises this position in the expression of value for the world of commodities, it becomes the money commodity, and then, and not till then, does form D become distinct from form C, and the general form of value become changed into the money form.

The elementary expression of the relative value of a single commodity, such as linen, in terms of the commodity, such as gold, that plays the part of money, is the price form of that commodity. The price form of the linen is therefore
20 yards of linen=2 ounces of gold, or, if 2 ounces of gold
    when coined are £2, 20 yards of linen=£2.

The difficulty in forming a concept of the money form, consists in clearly comprehending the universal equivalent form, and as a necessary corollary, the general form of value, form C. The latter is deducible from form B, the expanded form of value, the essential component element of which, we saw, is form A, 20 yards of linen=1 coat or x commodity A=y commodity B. The simple commodity form is therefore the germ of the money form.

SECTION 4.—THE FETISHISM OF COMMODITIES AND THE SECRET THEREOF.

A commodity appears, at first sight, a very trivial thing, and easily understood. Its analysis shows that it is, in reality, a very queer thing, abounding in metaphysical subtleties and theological niceties. So far as it is a value in use, there is nothing mysterious about it, whether we consider it from the point of view that by its properties it is capable of satisfying human wants, or from the point that those properties are the product of human labour. It is as clear as noon-day, that man, by his industry, changes the forms of the materials furnished by nature, in such a way as to make them useful to him. The form of wood, for instance, is altered, by making a table out of it. Yet, for all that the table continues to be that common, every-day thing, wood. But, so soon as it steps forth as a commodity, it is changed into something transcendent. It not only stands with its feet on the ground, but, in relation to all other commodities, it stands on its head, and evolves out of its wooden brain grotesque ideas, far more wonderful than "table-turning" ever was.

The mystical character of commodities does not originate, therefore, in their use-value. Just as little does it proceed from the nature of the determining factors of value. For, in the first place, however varied the useful kinds of labour, or productive activities, may be, it is a physiological fact, that they are functions of the human organism, and that each such function, whatever may be its nature or form, is essentially the expenditure of human brain, nerves, muscles, &c. Secondly, with regard to that which forms the ground-work for the quantitative determination of value, namely, the duration of that expenditure, or the quantity of labour, it is quite clear that there is a palpable difference between its quantity and quality. In all states of society, the labour-time that it costs to produce the means of subsistence must necessarily be an object of interest to mankind, though not of equal interest in different stages of development.[1]   And lastly, from the moment that men in any way work for one another, their labour assumes a social form.

Whence, then, arises the enigmatical character of the product of labour, so soon as it assumes the form of commodities? Clearly from this form itself. The equality of all sorts of human labour is expressed objectively by their products all being equally values; the measure of the expenditure of labour-power by the duration of that expenditure, takes the form of the quantity of value of the products of labour; and finally, the mutual relations of the producers, within which the social

---

[1] Among the ancient Germans the unit for measuring land was what could be harvested in a day, and was called Tagwerk, Tagwanne (jurnale, or terra jurnalis, or diornalis), Mannsmaad, &c. (See G. L. von Maurer Einleitung zur Geschichte der Mark —, &c. Verfassung, München, 1859, p. 129-59.)

character of their labour affirms itself, take the form of a social relation between the products.

A commodity is therefore a mysterious thing, simply because in it the social character of men's labour appears to them as an objective character stamped upon the product of that labour; because the relation of the producers to the sum total of their own labour is presented to them as a social relation, existing not between themselves, but between the products of their labour. This is the reason why the products of labour become commodities, social things whose qualities are at the same time perceptible and imperceptible by the senses. In the same way the light from an object is perceived by us not as the subjective excitation of our optic nerve, but as the objective form of something outside the eye itself. But, in the act of seeing, there is at all events, an actual passage of light from one thing to another, from the external object to the eye. There is a physical relation between physical things. But it is different with commodities. There, the existence of the things *quâ* commodities, and the value relation between the products of labour which stamps them as commodities, have absolutely no connection with their physical properties and with the material relations arising therefrom. There it is a definite social relation between men, that assumes, in their eyes, the fantastic form of a relation between things. In order, therefore, to find an analogy, we must have recourse to the mist-enveloped regions of the religious world. In that world the productions of the human brain appear as independent beings endowed with life, and entering into relation both with one another and the human race. So it is in the world of commodities with the products of men's hands. This I call the Fetishism which attaches itself to the products of labour, so soon as they are produced as commodities, and which is therefore inseparable from the production of commodities.

This Fetishism of commodities has its origin, as the foregoing analysis has already shown, in the peculiar social character of the labour that produces them.

As a general rule, articles of utility become commodities, only because they are products of the labour of private individ-

úals or groups of individuals who carry on their work independently of each other. The sum total of the labour of all
these private individuals forms the aggregate labour of society.
Since the producers do not come into social contact with each
other until they exchange their products, the specific social
character of each producer's labour does not show itself except
in the act of exchange. In other words, the labour of the individual asserts itself as a part of the labour of society, only
by means of the relations which the act of exchange establishes
directly between the products, and indirectly, through them,
between the producers. To the latter, therefore, the relations
connecting the labour of one individual with that of the rest appear, not as direct social relations between individuals at work,
but as what they really are, material relations between persons
and social relations between things. It is only by being exchanged that the products of labour acquire, as values, one uniform social status, distinct from their varied forms of existence
as objects of utility. This division of a product into a useful
thing and a value becomes practically important, only when exchange has acquired such an extension that useful articles are
produced for the purpose of being exchanged, and their character as values has therefore to be taken into account, beforehand, during production. From this moment the labour of the
individual producer acquires socially a two-fold character.
On the one hand, it must, as a definite useful kind of labour,
satisfy a definite social want, and thus hold its place as part
and parcel of the collective labour of all, as a branch of a social
division of labour that has sprung up spontaneously. On the
other hand, it can satisfy the manifold wants of the individual
producer himself, only in so far as the mutual exchangeability
of all kinds of useful private labour is an established social
fact, and therefore the private useful labour of each producer
ranks on an equality with that of all others. The equalization
of the most different kinds of labour can be the result only of
an abstraction from their inequalities, or of reducing them to
their common denominator, viz., expenditure of human labour
power or human labour in the abstract. The two-fold social
character of the labour of the individual appears to him, when

reflected in his brain, only under those forms which are impressed upon that labour in everyday practice by the exchange of products. In this way, the character that his own labour possesses of being socially useful takes the form of the condition, that the product must be not only useful, but useful for others, and the social character that his particular labour has of being the equal of all other particular kinds of labour, takes the form that all the physically different articles that are the products of labour, have one common quality, viz, that of having value.

Hence, when we bring the products of our labour into relation with each other as values, it is not because we see in these articles the material receptacles of homogeneous human labour. Quite the contrary; whenever, by an exchange, we equate as values our different products, by that very act, we also equate, as human labour, the different kinds of labour expended upon them. We are not aware of this, nevertheless we do it.[1] Value, therefore, does not stalk about with a label describing what it is. It is value, rather, that converts every product into a social hieroglyphic. Later on, we try to decipher the hieroglyphic, to get behind the secret of our own social products; for to stamp an object of utility as a value, is just as much a social product as language. The recent scientific discovery, that the products of labour, so far as they are values, are but material expressions of the human labour spent in their production, marks, indeed, an epoch in the history of the development of the human race, but, by no means, dissipates the mist through which the social character of labour appears to us to be an objective character of the products themselves. The fact, that in the particular form of production with which we are dealing, viz., the production of commodities, the specific social character of private labour carried on independently, consists in the equality of every kind of that labour, by virtue of its being human labour, which character, therefore, assumes

[1]When, therefore, Galiani says: Value is a relation between persons—"La Ricchezza è una ragione tra due persone,"—he ought to have added: a relation between persons expressed as a relation between things. (Galiani: Della Moneta, p. 221, V. III. of Custodi's collection of "Scrittori Classici Italiani di Economia Politicia." Parte Moderna, Milano, 1803.)

in the product the form of value—this fact appears to the producers, notwithstanding the discovery above referred to, to be just as real and final, as the fact, that, after the discovery by science of the component gases of air, the atmosphere itself remained unaltered.

What, first of all, practically concerns producers when they make an exchange, is the question, how much of some other product they get for their own? in what proportions the products are exchangeable? When these proportions have, by custom, attained a certain stability, they appear to result from the nature of the products, so that, for instance, one ton of iron and two ounces of gold appear as naturally to be of equal value as a pound of gold and a pound of iron in spite of their different physical and chemical qualities appear to be of equal weight. The character of having value, when once impressed upon products, obtains fixity only by reason of their acting and re-acting upon each other as quantities of value. These quantities vary continually, independently of the will, foresight and action of the producers. To them, their own social action takes the form of the action of objects, which rule the producers instead of being ruled by them. It requires a fully developed production of commodities before, from accumulated experience alone, the scientific conviction springs up, that all the different kinds of private labour, which are carried on independently of each other, and yet as spontaneously developed branches of the social division of labour, are continually being reduced to the quantitive proportions in which society requires them. And why? Because, in the midst of all the accidental and ever fluctuating exchange-relations between the products, the labour-time socially necessary for their production forcibly asserts itself like an over-riding law of nature. The law of gravity thus asserts itself when a house falls about our ears.[1] The determination of the magnitude of value by labour-time is therefore a secret, hidden under the apparent

---

[1] " What are we to think of a law that asserts itself only by periodical revolutions? It is just nothing but a law of Nature, founded on the want of knowledge of those whose action is the subject of it." (Friedrich Engels: Umrisse zu einer Kritik der Nationa lökonomie," in the "Deutsch-französische Jahrbücher," edited by Arnold Ruge and Karl Marx. Paris, 1844.

fluctuations in the relative values of commodities. Its discovery, while removing all appearance of mere accidentality from the determination of the magnitude of the values of products, yet in no way alters the mode in which that determination takes place.

Man's reflections on the forms of social life, and consequently, also, his scientific analysis of those forms, take a course directly opposite to that of their actual historical development. He begins, post festum, with the results of the process of development ready to hand before him. The characters that stamp products as commodities, and whose establishment is a necessary preliminary to the circulation of commodities, have already acquired the stability of natural, self-understood forms of social life, before man seeks to decipher, not their historical character, for in his eyes they are immutable, but their meaning. Consequently it was the analysis of the prices of commodities that alone led to the determination of the magnitude of value, and it was the common expression of all commodities in money that alone led to the establishment of their characters as values. It is, however, just this ulimate money form of the world of commodities that actually conceals, instead of disclosing, the social character of private labour, and the social relations between the individual producers. When I state that coats or boots stand in a relation to linen, because it is the universal incarnation of abstract human labour, the absurdity of the statement is self-evident. Nevertheless, when the producers of coats and boots compare those articles with linen, or, what is the same thing with gold or silver, as the universal equivalent, they express the relation between their own private labour and the collective labour of society in the same absurd form.

The categories of bourgeois economy consist of such like forms. They are forms of thought expressing with social validity the conditions and relations of a definite, historically determined mode of production, viz., the production of commodities. The whole mystery of commodities, all the magic and necromancy that surrounds the products of labour as long as they take the form of commodities, vanishes therefore, so soon as we come to other forms of production.

Since Robinson Crusoe's experiences are a favorite theme with political economists,[1] let us take a look at him on his island. Moderate though he be, yet some few wants he has to satisfy, and must therefore do a little useful work of various sorts, such as making tools and furniture, taming goats, fishing and hunting. Of his prayers and the like we take no account, since they are a source of pleasure to him, and he looks upon them as so much recreation. In spite of the variety of his work, he knows that his labour, whatever its form, is but the activity of one and the same Robinson, and consequently, that it consists of nothing but different modes of human labour. Necessity itself compels him to apportion his time accurately between his different kinds of work. Whether one kind occupies a greater space in his general activity than another, depends on the difficulties, greater or less as the case may be, to be overcome in attaining the useful effect aimed at. This our friend Robinson soon learns by experience, and having rescued a watch, ledger, and pen and ink from the wreck, commences, like a true-born Briton, to keep a set of books. His stock-book contains a list of the objects of utility that belong to him, of the operations necessary for their production; and lastly, of the labour time that definite quantities of those objects have, on an average, cost him. All the relations between Robinson and the objects that form this wealth of his own creation, are here so simple and clear as to be intelligible without exertion, even to Mr. Sedley Taylor. And yet those relations contain all that is essential to the determination of value.

Let us now transport ourselves from Robinson's island bathed in light to the European middle ages shrouded in darkness. Here, instead of the independent man, we find every-

---

[1] Even Ricardo has his stories à la Robinson. "He makes the primitive hunter and the primitive fisher straightway, as owners of commodities, exchange fish and game in the proportion in which labour-time is incorporated in these exchange values. On this occasion he commits the anachronism of making these men apply to the calculation, so far as their implements have to be taken into account, the annuity tables in current use on the London Exchange in the year 1817. 'The parallelograms of Mr. Owen' appear to be the only form of society, besides the bourgeois form, with which he was acquainted." (Karl Marx: "Critique," &c., p. 69—70.)

one dependent, serfs and lords, vassals and suzerains, laymen and clergy. Personal dependence here characterises the social relations of production just as much as it does the other spheres of life organized on the basis of that production. But for the very reason that personal dependence forms the groundwork of society, there is no necessity for labour and its products to assume a fantastic form different from their reality. They take the shape, in the transactions of society, of services in kind and payments in kind. Here the particular and natural form of labour, and not, as in a society based on production of commodities, its general abstract form is the immediate social form of labour. Compulsory labour is just as properly measured by time, as commodity-producing labour; but every serf knows that what he expends in the service of his lord, is a definite quantity of his own personal labour-power. The tithe to be rendered to the priest is more matter of fact than his blessing. No matter, then, what we may think of the parts played by the different classes of people themselves in this society, the social relations between individuals in the performance of their labour, appear at all events as their own mutual personal relations, and are not disguised under the shape of social relations between the products of labour.

For an example of labour in common or directly associated labour, we have no occasion to go back to that spontaneously developed form which we find on the threshold of the history of all civilized races.[1] We have one close at hand in the patriarchal industries of a peasant family, that produces corn, cattle, yarn, linen, and clothing for home use. These different articles are, as regards the family, so many products of its labour, but as between themselves, they are not commodities. The different kinds of labour, such as tillage, cattle tending,

[1] "A ridiculous presumption has latterly got abroad that common property in its primitive form is specifically a Slavonian, or even exclusively Russian form. It is the primitive form that we can prove to have existed amongst Romans, Teutons, and Celts, and even to this day we find numerous examples, ruins though they be, in India. A more exhaustive study of Asiatic, and especially of Indian forms of common property, would show how from the different forms of primitive common property, different forms of its dissolution have been developed. Thus, for instance, the various original types of Roman and Teutonic private property are deducible from different forms of Indian common property." (Karl Marx. "Critique," &c., p. 29, footnote.)

spinning, weaving and making clothes, which result in the various products, are in themselves, and such as they are, direct social functions, because functions of the family, which just as much as a society based on the production of commodities, possesses a spontaneously developed system of division of labour. The distribution of the work within the family, and the regulation of the labour-time of the several members, depend as well upon differences of age and sex as upon natural conditions varying with the seasons. The labour-power of each individual, by its very nature, operates in this case merely as a definite portion of the whole labour-power of the family, and therefore, the measure of the expenditure of individual labour-power by its duration, appears here by its very nature as a social character of their labour.

Let us now picture to ourselves, by way of change, a community of free individuals, carrying on their work with the means of production in common, in which the labour-power of all the different individuals is consciously applied as the combined labour-power of the community. All the characteristics of Robinson's labour are here repeated, but with this difference, that they are social, instead of individual. Everything produced by him was exclusively the result of his own personal labour, and therefore simply an object of use for himself. The total product of our community is a social product. One portion serves as fresh means of production and remains social. But another portion is consumed by the members as means of subsistence. A distribution of this portion amongst them is consequently necessary. The mode of this distribution will vary with the productive organization of the community, and the degree of historical development attained by the producers. We will assume, but merely for the sake of a parallel with the production of commodities, that the share of each individual producer in the means of subsistence is determined by his labour-time. Labour-time would, in that case, play a double part. Its apportionment in accordance with a definite social plan maintains the proper proportion between the different kinds of work to be done and the various wants of the community. On the other hand, it also

serves as a measure of the portion of the common labour borne
by each individual and of his share in the part of the total
product destined for individual consumption. The social relations of the individual producers, with regard both to their
labour and to its products, are in this case perfectly simple
and intelligible, and that with regard not only to production
but also to distribution.

The religious world is but the reflex of the real world. And
for a society based upon the production of commodities, in
which the producers in general enter into social relations with
one another by treating their products as commodities and
values, whereby they reduce their individual private labour to
the standard of homogeneous human labour—for such a society, Christianity with its *cultus* of abstract man, more especially in its bourgeois developments, Protestantism, Deism, &c.,
is the most fitting form of religion. In the ancient Asiatic
and other ancient modes of production, we find that the conversion of products into commodities, and therefore the conversion of men into producers of commodities, holds a subordinate place, which, however, increases in importance as the
primitive communities approach nearer and nearer to their
dissolution. Trading nations, properly so called, exist in the
ancient world only in its interstices, like the gods of Epicurus
in the Intermundia, or like Jews in the pores of Polish society. Those ancient social organisms of production are, as
compared with bourgeois society, extremely simple and trans-
parent. But they are founded either on the immature development of man individually, who has not yet severed the um-
bilical cord that unites him with his fellow men in a primitive tribal community, or upon direct relations of subjection. They can arise and exist only when the development of
the productive power of labour has not risen beyond a low
stage, and when, therefore, the social relations within the
sphere of material life, between man and man, and between
man and Nature, are correspondingly narrow. This narrow-
ness is reflected in the ancient worship of Nature, and in the
other elements of the popular religions. The religious reflex
of the real world can, in any case, only then finally vanish,

when the practical relations of everyday life offer to man none
but perfectly intelligible and reasonable relations with regard to his fellowmen and to nature.

The life-process of society, which is based on the process of
material production, does not strip off its mystical veil until it
is treated as production by freely associated men, and is consciously regulated by them in accordance with a settled plan.
This, however, demands for society a certain material ground-
work or set of conditions of existence which in their turn are
the spontaneous product of a long and painful process of
development.

Political economy has indeed analysed, however incompletely,[1] value and its magnitude, and has discovered what
lies beneath these forms. But it has never once asked the
question why labour is represented by the value of its product

[1] The insufficiency of Ricardo's analysis of the magnitude of value, and his analysis is by far the best, will appear from the 3rd and 4th book of this work. As
regards values in general, it is the weak point of the classical school of political
economy that it nowhere, expressly and with full consciousness, distinguishes between labour, as it appears in the value of a product and the same labour, as it appears in the use-value of that product. Of course the distinction is practically made
since this school treats labour, at one time under its quantitative aspect, at another
under its qualitative aspect. But it has not the least idea, that when the
difference between various kinds of labour is treated as purely quantitative,
their qualitative unity or equality, and therefore their reduction to abstract human
labour, is implied. For instance, Ricardo declares that he agrees with Destutt
de Tracy in this proposition: "As it is certain that our physical and moral
faculties are alone our original riches, the employment of those faculties, labour
of some kind, is our only original treasure, and it is always from this employment
that all those things are created, which we call riches. . . . It is certain, too,
that all those things only represent the labour which has created them, and if they
have a value, or even two distinct values, they can only derive them from that
(the value) of the labour from which they emanate." (Ricardo, The Principles
of Pol. Econ. 3 Ed. Lond. 1821, p. 334.) We would here only point out that
Ricardo puts his own more profound interpretation upon the words of Destutt.
What the latter really says is, that on the one hand all things which constitute
wealth represent the labour that creates them, but that on the other hand, they
acquire their "two different values" (use-value and exchange-value) from "the
value of labour." He thus falls into the commonplace error of the vulgar economists, who assume the value of one commodity (in this case labour) in order to determine the values of the rest. But Ricardo reads him as if he had said, that labour
(not the value of labour) is embodied both in use-value and exchange-value.
Nevertheless, Ricardo himself pays so little attention to the two-fold character
of the labour which has a two-fold embodiment, that he devotes the whole of his
chapter on " Value and Riches, Their Distinctive Properties," to a laborious examination of the trivialities of a J. B. Say. And at the finish he is quite
astonished to find that Destutt on the one hand agrees with him as to labour being
the source of value, and on the other hand with J. B. Say as to the notion of
value.

and labour time by the magnitude of that value.[1] These formulæ, which bear stamped upon them in unmistakable letters, that they belong to a state of society, in which the process of production has the mastery over man, instead of being controlled by him, such formulæ appear to the bourgeois intellect to be as much a self-evident necessity imposed by nature as productive labour itself. Hence forms of social production that preceded the bourgeois form, are treated by the bourgeoisie in much the same way as the Fathers of the Church treated pre-Christian religions.[2]

[1] It is one of the chief failings of classical economy that it has never succeeded, by means of its analysis of commodities, and, in particular, of their value, in discovering that form under which value becomes exchange-value. Even Adam Smith and Ricardo, the best representatives of the school, treat the form of value as a thing of no importance, as having no connection with the inherent nature of commodities. The reason for this is not solely because their attention is entirely absorbed in the analysis of the magnitude of value. It lies deeper. The value form of the product of labour is not only the most abstract, but is also the most universal form, taken by the product in bourgeois production, and stamps that production as a particular species of social production, and thereby gives it its special historical character. If then we treat this mode of production as one eternally fixed by nature for every state of society, we necessarily overlook that which is the differentia specifica of the value-form, and consequently of the commodity-form, and of its further developments, money-form, capital-form, &c. We consequently find that economists, who are thoroughly agreed as to labour time being the measure of the magnitude of value, have the most strange and contradictory ideas of money, the perfected form of the general equivalent. This is seen in a striking manner when they treat of banking, where the commonplace definitions of money will no longer hold water. This led to the rise of a restored mercantile system (Ganilh, &c.), which sees in value nothing but a social form, or rather the unsubstantial ghost of that form. Once for all I may here state, that by classical political economy, I understand that economy which, since the time of W. Petty, has investigated the real relations of production in bourgeois society, in contradistinction to vulgar economy, which deals with appearances only, ruminates without ceasing on the materials long since provided by scientific economy, and there seeks plausible explanations of the most obtrusive phenomena, for bourgeois daily use, but for the rest, confines itself to systematizing in a pedantic way, and proclaiming for everlasting truths, the trite ideas held by the self-complacent bourgeoisie with regard to their own world, to them the best of all possible worlds.

[2] "The economists have a singular manner of proceeding. There are for them only two kinds of institutions, those of art and those of nature. Feudal institutions are artificial institutions, those of the bourgeoisie are natural institutions. In this they resemble the theologians, who also establish two kinds of religion Every religion but their own is an invention of men, while their own religion is an emanation from God. . . . Thus there has been history, but there is no longer any." Karl Marx, The Poverty of Philosophy, A Reply to 'La Philosophie de la Misère' by Mr. Proudhon. 1847, p. 100. Truly comical is M. Bastiat, who imagines that the ancient Greeks and Romans lived by plunder alone. But when people plunder for centuries, there must always be something at hand for them to seize; the objects of plunder must be continually reproduced. It would thus appear

To what extent some economists are misled by the Fetishism inherent in commodities, or by the objective appearance of the social characteristics of labour, is shown, amongst other ways, by the dull and tedious quarrel over the part played by Nature in the formation of exchange value. Since exchange value is a definite social manner of expressing the amount of labour bestowed upon an object, Nature has no more to do with it, than it has in fixing the course of exchange.

The mode of production in which the product takes the form of a commodity, or is produced directly for exchange, is the most general and most embryonic form of bourgeois production. It therefore makes its appearance at an early date in history, though not in the same predominating and characteristic manner as now-a-days. Hence its Fetish character is comparatively easy to be seen through. But when we come to more concrete forms, even this appearance of simplicity vanishes. Whence arose the illusions of the monetary system? To it gold and silver, when serving as money, did not represent a social relation between producers, but were nat-

that even Greeks and Romans had some process of production, consequently, an economy, which just as much constituted the material basis of their world, as bourgeois economy constitutes that of our modern world. Or perhaps Bastiat means, that a mode of production based on slavery is based on a system of plunder. In that case he treads on dangerous ground. If a giant thinker like Aristotle-erred in his appreciation of slave labour, why should a dwarf economist like Bastiat be right in his appreciation of wage labour? — I seize this opportunity of shortly answering an objection taken by a German paper in America, to my work, "Critique of Political Economy, 1859." In the estimation of that paper, my view that each special mode of production and the social relations corresponding to it, in short, that the economic structure of society, is the real basis on which the juridical and political superstructure is raised, and to which definite social forms of thought correspond; that the mode of production determines the character of the social, political, and intellectual life generally, all this is very true for our own times, in which material interests preponderate, but not for the middle ages, in which Catholicism, nor for Athens and Rome, where politics, reigned supreme. In the first place it strikes one as an odd thing for any one to suppose that these well-worn phrases about the middle ages and the ancient world are unknown to anyone else. This much, however, is clear, that the middle ages could not live on Catholicism, nor the ancient world on politics. On the contrary, it is the mode in which they gained a livelihood that explains why here politics, and there Catholicism, played the chief part. For the rest, it requires but a slight acquaintance with the history of the Roman republic, for example, to be aware that its secret history is the history of its landed property. On the other hand, Don Quixote long ago paid the penalty for wrongly imagining that knight errantry was compatible with all economical forms of society.

ural objects with strange social properties. And modern economy, which looks down with such disdain on the monetary system, does not its superstition come out as clear as noon-day, whenever it treats of capital? How long is it since economy discarded the physiocratic illusion, that rents grow out of the soil and not out of society?

But not to anticipate, we will content ourselves with yet another example relating to the commodity form. Could commodities themselves speak, they would say: Our use-value may be a thing that interests men. It is no part of us as objects. What, however, does belong to us as objects, is our value. Our natural intercourse as commodities proves it. In the eyes of each other we are nothing but exchange values. Now listen how those commodities speak through the mouth of the economist. "Value"—(*i.e.*, exchange value) "is a property of things, riches"—(*i.e.*, use-value) "of man. Value, in this sense, necessarily implies exchanges, riches do not." [1] "Riches" (use-value) "are the attribute of men, value is the attribute of commodities. A man or a community is rich, a pearl or a diamond is valuable. . . A pearl or a diamond is valuable" as a pearl or diamond. [2] So far no chemist has ever discovered exchange value either in a pearl or a diamond. The economical discoverers of this chemical element, who by-the-bye lay special claim to critical acumen, find however that the use-value of objects belongs to them independently of their material properties, while their value, on the other hand, forms a part of them as objects. What confirms them in this view, is the peculiar circumstances that the use-value of objects is realised without exchange, by means of a direct relation between the

[1] Observations on certain verbal disputes in Pol. Econ., particularly relating to value and to demand and supply. Lond., 1821, p. 16.

[2] S. Bailey, l. c., p. 165.

[3] The author of "Observations" and S. Bailey accuse Ricardo of converting exchange value from something relative into something absolute. The opposite is the fact. He has explained the apparent relation between objects, such as diamonds and pearls, in which relation they appear as exchange values, and disclosed the true relation hidden behind the appearances, namely, their relation. to each other as mere expressions of human labour. If the followers of Ricardo answer Bailey somewhat rudely, and by no means convincingly, the reason is to be sought in this, that they were unable to find in Ricardo's own works any key to the hidden relations existing between value and its form, exchange value.

objects and man, while, on the other hand, their value is realised only by exchange, that is, by means of a social process. Who fails here to call to mind our good friend, Dogberry, who informs neighbour Seacoal, that, "To be a well-favoured man is the gift of fortune; but reading and writing comes by nature."

CHAPTER II.

EXCHANGE.

It is plain that commodities cannot go to market and make exchanges of their own account. We must, therefore, have recourse to their guardians, who are also their owners. Commodities are things, and therefore without power of resistance against man. If they are wanting in docility he can use force; in other words, he can take possession of them.[1] In order that these objects may enter into relation with each other as commodities, their guardians must place themselves in relation to one another, as persons whose will resides in those objects, and must behave in such a way that each does not appropriate the commodity of the other, and part with his own, except by means of an act done by mutual consent. They must, therefore, mutually recognise in each other the right of private proprietors. This juridical relation, which thus expresses itself in a contract, whether such contract be part of a developed legal system or not, is a relation between two wills, and is but the reflex of the real economical relation between the two. It is this economical relation that determines the subject matter comprised in each such juridical act.[2] The persons exist for

[1] In the 12th century, so renowned for its piety, they included amongst commodities some very delicate things. Thus a French poet of the period enumerates amongst the goods to be fund in the market of Landit, not only clothing, shoes, leather, agricultural implements, &c., but also "femmes folles de leur corps."

[2] Proudhon begins by taking his ideal of justice, of "justice éternelle," from the juridical relations that correspond to the production of commodities: thereby, it may be noted, he proves, to the consolation of all good citizens, that the production of commodities is a form of production as everlasting as justice. Then he turns round and seeks to reform the actual production of commodities, and the actual legal system corresponding thereto, in accordance with this ideal.

one another merely as representatives of, and, therefore, as owners of, commodities. In the course of our investigation we shall find, in general, that the characters who appear on the economic stage are but the personifications of the economical relations that exist between them.

What chiefly distinguishes a commodity from its owner is the fact, that it looks upon every other commodity as but the form of appearance of its own value. A born leveller and a cynic, it is always ready to exchange not only soul, but body, with any and every other commodity, be the same more repulsive than Maritornes herself. The owner makes up for this lack in the commodity of a sense of the concrete, by his own five and more senses. His commodity possesses for himself no immediate use-value. Otherwise, he would not bring it to the market. It has use-value for others; but for himself its only direct use-value is that of being a depository of exchange value, and consequently, a means of exchange.[1] Therefore, he makes up his mind to part with it for commodities whose value in use is of service to him. All commodities are non-use-values for their owners, and use-values for their non-owners. Consequently, they must all change hands. But this change of hands is what constitutes their exchange, and the latter puts them in relation with each other as values, and realises them as values. Hence commodities must be realised as values before they can be realised as use-values.

On the other hand, they must show that they are use-values before they can be realised as values. For the labour spent upon them counts effectively, only in so far as it is spent

What opinion should we have of a chemist, who, instead of studying the actual laws of the molecular changes in the composition and decomposition of matter, and on that foundation solving definite problems, claimed to regulate the composition and decomposition of matter by means of the "eternal ideas," of "naturalité" and "affinité?" Do we really know any more about "usury," when we say it contradicts "justice éternelle," "équité éternelle," "mutualité éternelle," and other "vérités éternelles" than the fathers of the church did when they said it was incompatible with "grâce éternelle," "foi éternelle," and "la volonté éternelle de Dieu?"

[1] " For two-fold is the use of every object. . . . The one is peculiar to the object as such, the other is not, as a sandal which may be worn, and is also exchangeable. Both are uses of the sandal, for even he who exchanges the sandal for the money or food he is in want of, makes use of the sandal as a sandal. But not in its natural way. For it has not been made for the sake of being exchanged." (Aristoteles, de Rep., 1. i. c. 9.)

in a form that is useful for others. Whether that labour is useful for others and its product consequently capable of satisfying the wants of others, can be proved only by the act of exchange.

Every owner of a commodity wishes to part with it in exchange only for those commodities whose use-value satisfies some want of his. Looked at in this way, exchange is for him simply a private transaction. On the other hand, he desires to realise the value of his commodity, to convert it into any other suitable commodity of equal value, irrespective of whether his own commodity has or has not any use-value for the owner of the other. From this point of view, exchange is for him a social transaction of a general character. But one and the same set of transactions cannot be simultaneously for all owners of commodities both exclusively private and exclusively social and general.

Let us look at the matter a little closer. To the owner of a commodity, every other commodity is, in regard to his own, a particular equivalent, and consequently his own commodity is the universal equivalent for all the others. But since this applies to every owner, there is, in fact, no commodity acting as universal equivalent, and the relative value of commodities possesses no general form under which they can be equated as values and have the magnitude of their values compared. So far, therefore, they do not confront each other as commodities, but only as products or use-values. In their difficulties our commodity-owners think like Faust: "Im Anfang war die That." They therefore acted and transacted before they thought. Instinctively they conform to the laws imposed by the nature of commodities. They cannot bring their commodities into relation as values, and therefore as commodities, except by comparing them with some one other commodity as the universal equivalent. That we saw from the analysis of a commodity. But a particular commodity cannot become the universal equivalent except by a social act. The social action therefore of all other commodities, sets apart the particular commodity in which they all represent their values. Thereby the bodily form of this commodity becomes the form of the socially recognised universal equivalent. To be the universal equivalent, becomes, by this social process, the specific function of the commodity thus excluded by the rest. Thus it becomes—money. "Illi unum consilium habent et virtutem et potestatem suam bestiæ tradunt. Et ne quis possit emere aut vendere, nisi qui habet characterem aut nomen bestiæ, aut numerum nominis ejus." (*Apocalypse.*)

Money is a crystal formed of necessity in the course of the exchanges, whereby different products of labour are practically equated to one another and thus by practice converted into commodities. The historical progress and extension of exchanges develops the contrast, latent in commodities, between use-value and value. The necessity for giving an external expression to this contrast for the purposes of commercial intercourse, urges on the establishment of an independent form of value, and finds no rest until it is once for all satisfied by the differentiation of commodities into commodities and money. At the same rate, then, as the conversion of products into commodities is being accomplished, so also is the conversion of one special commodity into money.[1]

The direct barter of products attains the elementary form of the relative expression of value in one respect, but not in another. That form is x Commodity A=y Commodity B. The form of direct barter is x use-value A=y use-value B.[2] The articles A and B in this case are not as yet commodities, but become so only by the act of barter. The first step made by an object of utility towards acquiring exchange-value is when it forms a non-use-value for its owner, and that happens when it forms a superfluous portion of some article required for his immediate wants. Objects in themselves are external to man, and consequently alienable by him. In order that this alienation may be reciprocal, it is only necessary for

---

[1] From this we may form an estimate of the shrewdness of the petit-bourgeois socialism, which, while perpetuating the production of commodities, aims at abolishing the "antagonism" between money and commodities, and consequently, since money exists only by virtue of this antagonism, at abolishing money itself. We might just as well try to retain Catholicism without the Pope. For more on this point see my work, "Critique of Political Economy," p. 73, ff.

[2] So long as, instead of two distinct use-values being exchanged, a chaotic mass of articles are offered as the equivalent of a single article, which is often the case with savages, even the direct barter of products is in its first infancy.

men, by a tacit understanding, to treat each other as private owners of those alienable objects, and by implication as independent individuals. But such a state of reciprocal independence has no existence in a primitive society based on property in common, whether such a society takes the form of a patriarchal family, an ancient Indian community, or a Peruvian Inca State. The exchange of commodities, therefore, first begins on the boundaries of such communities, at their points of contact with other similar communities, or with members of the latter. So soon, however, as products once become commodities in the external relations of a community, they also, by reaction, become so in its internal intercourse. The proportions in which they are exchangeable are at first quite a matter of chance. What makes them exchangeable is the mutual desire of their owners to alienate them. Meantime the need for foreign objects of utility gradually establishes itself. The constant repetition of exchange makes it a normal social act. In the course of time, therefore, some portion at least of the products of labour must be produced with a special view to exchange. From that moment the distinction becomes firmly established between the utility of an object for the purposes of consumption, and its utility for the purposes of exchange. Its use-value becomes distinguished from its exchange value. On the other hand, the quantitative proportion in which the articles are exchangeable, becomes dependent on their production itself. Custom stamps them as values with definite magnitudes.

In the direct barter of products, each commodity is directly a means of exchange to its owner, and to all other persons an equivalent, but that only in so far as it has use-value for them. At this stage, therefore, the articles exchanged do not acquire a value-form independent of their own use-value, or of the individual needs of the exchangers. The necessity for a value-form grows with the increasing number and variety of the commodities exchanged. The problem and the means of solution arise simultaneously. Commodity-owners never equate their own commodities to those of others, and exchange them on a large scale, without different kinds of commodities belonging to different owners being exchangeable for, and equated as values to, one and the same special article. Such last-mentioned article, by becoming the equivalent of various other commodities, acquires at once, though within narrow limits, the character of a general social equivalent. This character comes and goes with the momentary social acts that called it into life. In turns and transiently it attaches itself first to this and then to that commodity. But with the development of exchange it fixes itself firmly and exclusively to particular sorts of commodities, and becomes crystallised by assuming the money-form. The particular kind of commodity to which it sticks is at first a matter of accident. Nevertheless there are two circumstances whose influence is decisive. The money-form attaches itself either to the most important articles of exchange from outside, and these in fact are primitive and natural forms in which the exchange-value of home products finds expression; or else it attaches itself to the object of utility that forms, like cattle, the chief portion of indigenous alienable wealth. Nomad races are the first to develop the money-form, because all their worldly goods consist of movable objects and are therefore directly alienable; and because their mode of life, by continually bringing them into contact with foreign communities, solicits the exchange of products. Man has often made man himself, under the form of slaves, serve as the primitive material of money, but has never used land for that purpose. Such an idea could only spring up in a bourgeois society already well developed. It dates from the last third of the 17th century, and the first attempt to put it in practice on a national scale was made a century afterwards, during the French bourgeois revolution.

In proportion as exchange bursts its local bonds, and the value of commodities more and more expands into an embodiment of human labour in the abstract, in the same proportion the character of money attaches itself to commodities that are by nature fitted to perform the social function of a universal equivalent. Those commodities are the precious metals.

The truth of the proposition that, "although gold and silver are not by nature money, money is by nature gold and silver," [1] is shown by the fitness of the physical properties of these metals for the functions of money.[2] Up to this point, however, we are acquainted only with one function of money, namely, to serve as the form of manifestation of the value of commodities, or as the material in which the magnitudes of their values are socially expressed. An adequate form of manifestation of value, a fit embodiment of abstract, undifferentiated, and therefore equal human labour, that material alone can be whose every sample exhibits the same uniform qualities. On the other hand, since the difference between the magnitudes of value is purely quantitative, the money commodity must be susceptible of merely quantitative differences, must therefore be divisible at will, and equally capable of being re-united. Gold and silver possess these properties by nature.

The use-value of the money commodity becomes twofold. In addition to its special use-value as a commodity (gold, for instance, serving to stop teeth, to form the raw material of articles of luxury, &c.), it acquires a formal use-value, originating in its specific social function.

Since all commodities are merely particular equivalents of money, the latter being their universal equivalent, they, with regard to the latter as the universal commodity, play the parts of particular commodities.[3]

We have seen that the money-form is but the reflex, thrown upon one single commodity, of the value relations between all the rest. That money is a commodity [4] is therefore a new dis-

---

[1] Karl Marx, l. c. p. 212. "I metalli. . . naturalmente moneta," (Galiani. "Della moneta" in Custodi's Collection: Parte Moderna t. iii.).

[2] For further details on this subject see in my work cited above, the chapter on "The precious metals."

[3] "Il danaro é la merce universale (Verri, l. c., p. 16).

[4] "Silver and gold themselves (which we may call by the general name of bullion), are . . . commodities . . . rising and falling in . . . value. . . Bullion, then, may be reckoned to be of higher value where the smaller weight will purchase the greatest quantity of the product or manufacture of the countrey," &c. ("A Discourse of the General Notions of Money, Trade, and Exchange, as they stand in relations to each other." By a Merchant. Lond., 1695, p. 7.) "Silver and gold, coined or uncoined, though they are used for a measure of all other things, are no less a commodity than wine, oyl, tobacco, cloth, or stuffs." (" A Discourse concerning Trade, and that in particular of the East Indies," &c. London, 1689, p. 2.) "The stock and riches of the kingdom cannot properly be confined to money, nor ought gold and silver to be excluded from being merchandize." ("A

covery only for those who, when they anaiyse it, start from its fully developed shape. The act of exchange gives to the commodity converted into money, not its value, but its specific value-form. By confounding these two distinct things some writers have been led to hold that the value of gold and silver is imaginary.[1] The fact that money can, in certain functions, be replaced by mere symbols of itself, gave rise to that other mistaken notion, that it is itself a mere symbol. Nevertheless under this error lurked a presentiment that the money-form of an object is not an inseparable part of that object, but is simply the form under which certain social relations manifest themselves. In this sense every commodity is a symbol, since, in so far as it is value, it is only the material envelope of the human labour spent upon it.[2] But if it be declared that the social characters assumed by objects, or the material forms assumed by the social qualities of labour under the régime of a definite mode of production, are mere symbols, it is in the same breath also declared that these characteristics are arbitrary fictions sanctioned by the so-called universal consent of mankind. This

Treatise concerning the East India Trade being a most profitable Trade." London, 1680, Reprint 1696, p. 4.)

[1] "L'oro e l'argento hanno valore come metalli anteriore all' esser moneta." (Galiani, l.c.). Locke says, " The universal consent of mankind gave to silver, on account of its qualities which made it suitable for money, an imaginary value." Law, on the other hand, " How could different nations give an imaginary value to any single thing . . . or how could this imaginary value have maintained itself?" But the following shows how little he himself understood about the matter: " Silver was exchanged in proportion to the value in use it possessed, consequently in proportion to its real value. By its adoption as money it received an additional value (une valeur additionelle)" (Jean Law: "Considérations sur le numéraire et le commerce" in E. Daire's Edit. of "Economistes Financiers du XVIII. siècle.," p. 470).

[2] L'Argent en (des denrées) est le signe." (V. de Forbonnais: "Eléments du Commerce, Nouv. Edit. Leyde, 1776," t. II., p. 143.) "Comme signe il est attiré par les denrées." (l.c., p. 155). " L'argent un signe d'une chose et la représente." (Montesquieu: "Esprit des Lois," Oeuvres, Lond. 1767, t. II., p. 2.) "L'argent n'est pas simple signe, car il est lui-même richesse; il ne représente pas les valeurs, il les équivaut." (Le Trosne, l.c., p. 910.) "The notion of value contemplates the valuable article as a mere symbol; the article counts not for what it is, but for what it is worth." (Hegel, l.c., p. 100.) Lawyers started long before economists the idea that money is a mere symbol, and that the value of the precious metals is purely imaginary. This they did in the sycophantic service of the crowned heads, supporting the right of the latter to debase the coinage, during the whole of the middle ages, by the traditions of the Roman Empire and the conceptions of money to be found in the Pandects. "Qu' aucun puisse ni doive faire doute," says an apt scholar of theirs, Philip of Valois, in a decree of 1346, " que à nous et à notre majesté royale n' appartiennent seulement. . . le

suited the mode of explanation in favour during the 18th century. Unable to account for the origin of the puzzling forms assumed by social relations between man and man, people sought to denude them of their strange appearance by ascribing to them a conventional origin.

It has already been remarked above that the equivalent form of a commodity does not imply the determination of the magnitude of its value. Therefore, although we may be aware that gold is money, and consequently directly exchangeable for all other commodities, yet that fact by no means tells how much 10 lbs., for instance, of gold is worth. Money, like every other commodity, cannot express the magnitude of its value except relatively in other commodities. This value is determined by the labour-time required for its production, and is expressed by the quantity of any other commodity that costs the same amount of labour-time.[1] Such quantitative determination of its relative value takes place at the source of its production by means of barter. When it steps into circulation as money, its value is already given. In the last decades of the 17th century it had already been shown that money is a commodity, but this step marks only the infancy of the analysis. The difficulty lies, not in comprehending that money is a commodity, but in discovering how, why and by what means a commodity becomes money.[2]

mestier, le fait, l'état, la provision et toute l'ordonnance des monnaies, de donner tel cours, et pour tel prix comme il nous plait et bon nous semble." It was a maxim of the Roman Law that the value of money was fixed by decree of the emperor. It was expressly forbidden to treat money as a commodity. " Pecunias vero nulli emere fas erit, nam in usu publico constitutas oportet non esse mercem." Some good work on this question has been done by G. F. Pagnini: "Saggio sopra il giusto pregio delle cose, 1751"; Custodi "Parte Moderna," t. II. In the second part of his work Pagnini directs his polemics especially against the lawyers.

[1] " If a man can bring to London an ounce of Silver out of the Earth in .Peru, in the same time that he can produce a bushel of Corn, then the one is the natural price of the other; now, if by reason of new or more easie mines a man can procure two ounces of silver as easily as he formerly did one, the corn will be as cheap at ten shillings the bushel as it was before at five shillings, cæteris paribus." William Petty: "A Treatise on Taxes and Contributions." Lond., 1662, p. 32.

[2] The learned Professor Roscher, after first informing us that " the false definitions of money may be divided into two main groups: those which make it more, and those which make it less, than a commodity," gives us a long and very mixed catalogue of works on the nature of money, from which it appears that he has

We have already seen, from the most elementary expression of value, x commodity A=y commodity B, that the object in which the magnitude of the value of another object is represented, appears to have the equivalent form independently of this relation, as a social property given to it by Nature. We followed up this false appearance to its final establishment, which is complete so soon as the universal equivalent form becomes identified with the bodily form of a particular commodity, and thus crystallised into the money-form. What appears to happen is, not that gold becomes money, in consequence of all other commodities expressing their values in it, but, on the contrary, that all other commodities universally express their values in gold, because it is money. The intermediate steps of the process vanish in the result and leave no trace behind. Commodities find their own value already completely represented, without any initiative on their part, in another commodity existing in company with them. These objects, gold and silver, just as they come out of the bowels of the earth, are forthwith the direct incarnation of all human labour. Hence the magic of money. In the form of society now under consideration, the behaviour of men in the social process of production is purely atomic. Hence their relations to each other in production assume a material character independent of their control and conscious individual action. These facts manifest themselves at first by products as a general rule taking the form of commodities. We have seen how the progressive development of a society of commodity-producers stamps one privileged commodity with the character of money. Hence the riddle presented by money is but the riddle

not the remotest idea of the real history of the theory; and then he moralises thus: " For the rest, it is not to be denied that most of the later economists do not bear sufficiently in mind the peculiarities that distinguish money from other commodities" (it is then, after all, either more or less than a commodity!) . . . "So far, the semi-mercantilist reaction of Ganilh is not altogether without foundation." (Wilhelm Roscher: " Die Grundlagen der Nationaloekonomie," 3rd Edn., 1858, pp. 277-210) More! less! not sufficiently! so far! not altogether! What clearness and precision of ideas and language! And such eclectic professorial twaddle is modestly baptised by Mr. Roscher, " the anatomico-physiological method " of political economy! One discovery however, he must have credit for, namely, that money is "a pleasant commodity."

presented by commodities; only it now strikes us in its most glaring form.

CHAPTER III.
MONEY, OR THE CIRCULATION OF COMMODITIES.

SECTION 1.   THE MEASURE OF VALUES.

THROUGHOUT this work, I assume, for the sake of simplicity, gold as the money-commodity.

The first chief function of money is to supply commodities with the material for the expression of their values, or to represent their values as magnitudes of the same denomination, qualitatively equal, and quantitatively comparable. It thus serves as a *universal measure of value.* And only by virtue of this function does gold, the equivalent commodity *par excellence,* become money.

It is not money that renders commodities commensurable. Just the contrary. It is because all commodities, as values, are realised human labour, and therefore commensurable, that their values can be measured by one and the same special commodity, and the latter be converted into the common measure of their values, *i.e.,* into money. Money as a measure of value, is the phenomenal form that must of necessity be assumed by that measure of value which is immanent in commodities, labour-time.[1]

The expression of the value of a commodity in gold—x

---

[1] The question — Why does not money directly represent labour-time, so that a piece of paper may represent, for instance, x hour's labour, is at bottom the same as the question why, given the production of commodities, must products take the form of commodities? This is evident, since their taking the form of commodities implies their differentiation into commodities and money. Or, why cannot private labour—labour for the account of private individuals—be treated as its opposite, immediate social labour? I have elsewhere examined thoroughly the Utopian idea of "labour-money" in a society founded on the production of commodities (l. c., p. 61, seq.). On this point I will only say further, that Owen's " labour-money," for instance, is no more "money" than a ticket for the theatre. Owen presupposes directly associated labour, a form of production that is entirely inconsistent with the production of commodities. The certificate of labour is merely evidence of the part taken by the individual in the common labour, and of his right to a certain portion of the common produce destined for consumption. But it never enters into Owen's head to presuppose the production of commodities, and at the same time, by juggling with money, to try to evade the necessary conditions of that production.

commodity A=y money-commodity—is its money-form or price. A single equation, such as 1 ton of iron=2 ounces of gold, now suffices to express the value of the iron in a socially valid manner. There is no longer any need for this equation to figure as a link in the chain of equations that express the values of all other commodities, because the equivalent commodity, gold, now has the character of money. The general form of relative value has resumed its original shape of simple or isolated relative value. On the other hand, the expanded expression of relative value, the endless series of equations, has now become the form peculiar to the relative value of the money-commodity. The series itself, too, is now given, and has social recognition in the prices of actual commodities. We have only to read the quotations of a price-list backwards, to find the magnitude of the value of money expressed in all sorts of commodities. But money itself has no price. In order to put it on an equal footing with all other commodities in this respect, we should be obliged to equate it to itself as its own equivalent.

The price or money-form of commodities is, like their form of value generally, a form quite distinct from their palpable bodily form; it is, therefore, a purely ideal or mental form. Although invisible, the value of iron, linen and corn has actual existence in these very articles: it is ideally made perceptible by their equality with gold, a relation that, so to say, exists only in their own heads. Their owner must, therefore, lend them his tongue, or hang a ticket on them, before their prices can be communicated to the outside world.[1] Since the expression of the value of commodities in gold is a merely ideal

---

[1] Savages and half-civilised races use the tong differently. Captain Parry says of the inhabitants on the west coast of Baffin's Bay: "In this case (he refers to barter) they licked it (the thing represented to them) twice to their tongues, after which they seemed to consider the bargain satisfactorily concluded." In the same way, the Eastern Esquimaux licked the articles they received in exchange. If the tongue is thus used in the North as the organ of appropriation, no wonder that, in the South, the stomach serves as the organ of accumulated property, and that a Kaffir estimates the wealth of a man by the size of his belly. That the Kaffirs know what they are about is shown by the following: at the same time that the official British Health Report of 1864 disclosed the deficiency of fat-forming food among a large part of the working class, a certain Dr. Harvey (not, however, the celebrated discoverer of the circulation of the blood), made a good thing by advertising recipes for reducing the superfluous fat of the bourgeoisie and aristocracy.

act, we may use for this purpose imaginary or ideal money. Every trader knows, that he is far from having turned his goods into money, when he has expressed their value in a price or in imaginary money, and that it does not require the least bit of real gold, to estimate in that metal millions of pounds' worth of goods. When, therefore, money serves as a measure of value, it is employed only as imaginary or ideal money. This circumstance has given rise to the wildest theories.[1] But, although the money that performs the functions of a measure of value is only ideal money, price depends entirely upon the actual substance that is money. The value, or in other words, the quantity of human labour contained in a ton of iron, is expressed in imagination by such a quantity of the money-commodity as contains the same amount of labour as the iron. According, therefore, as the measure of value is gold, silver, or copper, the value of the ton of iron will be expressed by very different prices, or will be represented by very different quantities of those metals respectively.

If, therefore, two different commodities, such as gold and silver, are simultaneously measures of value, all commodities have two prices—one a gold-price, the other a silver-price. These exist quietly side by side, so long as the ratio of the value of silver to that of gold remains unchanged, say, at 15 : 1. Every change in their ratio disturbs the ratio which exists between the gold-prices and the silver-prices of commodities, and thus proves, by facts, that a double standard of value is inconsistent with the functions of a standard.[2]

[1] See Karl Marx: "Critique, etc., chapter II. B., Theories of the Unit of Measure of Money," p. 91, ff.

[2] "Wherever gold and silver have by law been made to perform the function of money or of a measure of value side by side, it has always been tried, but in vain, to treat them as one and the same material. To assume that there is an invariable ratio between the quantities of gold and silver in which a given quantity of labour-time is incorporated, is to assume, in fact, that gold and silver are of one and the same material, and that a given mass of the less valuable metal, silver, is a constant fraction of a given mass of gold. From the reign of Edward III. to the time of George II., the history of money in England consists of one long series of perturbations caused by the clashing of the legally fixed ratio between the values of gold and silver, with the fluctuations in their real values. At one time gold was too high, at another, silver. The metal that for the time being was estimated below its value, was withdrawn from circulation, melted and exported. The ratio between the two metals was then again altered by law, but the new nominal ratio soon came into conflict again with the real one. In our own

Commodities with definite prices present themselves under the form: a commodity A=x gold; b commodity B=z gold; c commodity C=y gold, &c., where a, b, c, represent definite quantities of the commodities A, B, C and x, z, y, definite quantities of gold. The values of these commodities are, therefore, changed in imagination into so many different quantities of gold. Hence, in spite of the confusing variety of the commodities themselves, their values become magnitudes of the same denomination, gold-magnitudes. They are now capable of being compared with each other and measured, and the want becomes technically felt of comparing them with some fixed quantity of gold as a unit measure. This unit, by subsequent division into aliquot parts, becomes itself the standard or scale. Before they become money, gold, silver, and copper already possess such standard measures in their standards of weight, so that, for example, a pound weight, while serving as the unit, is, on the one hand, divisible into ounces, and, on the other, may be combined to make up hundredweights.[1] It is owing to this that, in all metallic currencies, the names given to the standards of money or of price were originally taken from the pre-existing names of the standards of weight.

As *measure of value* and as *standard of price,* money has two

times, the slight and transient fall in the value of gold compared with silver, which was a consequence of the Indo-Chinese demand for silver, produced on a far more extended scale in France the same phenomena, export of silver, and its expulsion from circulation by gold. During the years 1855, 1856 and 1857, the excess in France of gold-imports over gold exports amounted to £41,580,000, while the excess of silver-exports over silver-imports was £14,704,000. In fact, in those countries in which both metals are legally measures of value, and therefore both legal tender, so that everyone has the option of paying in either metal, the metal that rises in value is at a premium, and, like every other commodity, measures its price in the over-estimated metal which alone serves in reality as the standard of value. The result of all experience and history with regard to this question is simply that, where two commodities perform by law the functions of a measure of value, in practice one alone maintains that position." (Karl Marx, l. c. pp. 90—91.)

[1] The peculiar circumstance, that while the ounce of gold serves in England as the unit of the standard of money, the pound sterling does not form an aliquot part of it, has been explained as follows: "Our coinage was originally adapted to the employment of silver only, hence, an ounce of silver can always be divided into a certain adequate number of pieces of coin; but as gold was introduced at a later period into a coinage adapted only to silver, an ounce of gold cannot be coined into an aliquot number of pieces." Maclaren, "A Sketch of the History of the Currency." London, 1858, p. 16.

entirely distinct functions to perform. It is the measure of value inasmuch as it is the socially recognised incarnation of human labour; it is the standard of price inasmuch as it is a fixed weight of metal. As the measure of value it serves to convert the values of all the manifold commodities into prices, into imaginary quantities of gold; as the standard of price it measures those quantities of gold. The measure of values measures commodities considered as values; the standard of price measures, on the contrary, quantities of gold by a unit quantity of gold, not the value of one quantity of gold by the weight of another. In order to make gold a standard of price, a certain weight must be fixed upon as the unit. In this case, as in all cases of measuring quantities of the same denomination, the establishment of an unvarying unit of measure is all-important. Hence, the less the unit is subject to variation, so much the better does the standard of price fulfill its office. But only in so far as it is itself a product of labour, and, therefore, potentially variable in value, can gold serve as a measure of value.[1]

It is, in the first place, quite clear that a change in the value of gold does not, in any way, affect its function as a standard of price. No matter how this value varies, the proportions between the values of different quantities of the metal remain constant. However great the fall in its value, 12 ounces of gold still have 12 times the value of 1 ounce; and in prices, the only thing considered is the relation between different quantities of gold. Since, on the other hand, no rise or fall in the value of an ounce of gold can alter its weight, no alteration can take place in the weight of its aliquot parts. Thus gold always renders the same service as an invariable standard of price, however much its value may vary.

In the second place, a change in the value of gold does not interfere with its functions as a measure of value. The change affects all commodities simultaneously, and, therefore, *cæteris paribus,* leaves their relative values *inter se,* unaltered,

---

[1] With English writers the confusion between measure of value and standard of price (standard of value) is indescribable. Their functions, as well as their names, are constantly interchanged.

although those values are now expressed in higher or lower gold-prices.

Just as when we estimate the value of any commodity by a definite quantity of the use-value of some other commodity, so in estimating the value of the former in gold, we assume nothing more than that the production of a given quantity of gold costs, at the given period, a given amount of labour. As regards the fluctuations of prices generally, they are subject to the laws of elementary relative value investigated in a former chapter.

A general rise in the prices of commodities can result only, either from a rise in their values—the value of money remaining constant—or from a fall in the value of money, the values of commodities remaining constant. On the other hand, a general fall in prices can result only, either from a fall in the values of commodities—the value of money remaining constant—or from a rise in the value of money, the values of commodities remaining constant. It therefore by no means follows, that a rise in the value of money necessarily implies a proportional fall in the prices of commodities; or that a fall in the value of money implies a proportional rise in prices. Such change of price holds good only in the case of commodities whose value remains constant. With those, for example whose value rises, simultaneously with, and proportionally to, that of money, there is no alteration in price. And if their value rise either slower or faster than that of money, the fall or rise in their prices will be determined by the difference between the change in their value and that of money; and so on.

Let us now go back to the consideration of the price-form.

By degrees there arises a discrepancy between the current money names of the various weights of the precious metal figuring as money, and the actual weights which those names originally represented. This discrepancy is the result of historical causes, among which the chief are:— (1) The importation of foreign money into an imperfectly developed community. This happened in Rome in its early days, where gold and silver coins circulated at first as foreign commodities.

The names of these foreign coins never coincide with those of the indigenous weights. (2) As wealth increases, the less precious metal is thrust out by the more precious from its place as a measure of value, copper by silver, silver by gold, however much this order of sequence may be in contradiction with poetical chronology.[1] The word pound, for instance, was the money-name given to an actual pound weight of silver. When gold replaced silver as a measure of value, the same name was applied according to the ratio between the values of silver and gold, to perhaps 1-15th of a pound of gold. The word pound, as a money-name, thus becomes differentiated from the same word as a weight-name.[2] (3) The debasing of money carried on for centuries by kings and princes to such an extent that, of the original weights of the coins, nothing in fact remained but the names.

These historical causes convert the separation of the money-name from the weight-name into an established habit with the community.[3] Since the standard of money is on the one hand purely conventional, and must on the other hand find general acceptance, it is in the end regulated by law. A given weight of one of the precious metals, an ounce of gold, for instance, becomes officially divided into aliquot parts, with legally bestowed names, such as pound, dollar, &c. These aliquot parts, which henceforth serve as units of money, are then subdivided into other aliquot parts with legal names, such as shilling, penny, &c.[4] But, both before and after these divisions are made, a definite weight of metal is the standard of metallic money. The sole alteration consists in the subdivision and denomination.

[1] Moreover, it has not general historical validity.

[2] It is thus that the pound sterling in English denotes less than one-third of its original weight; the pound Scot, before the union, only 1-36th; the French livre, 1-74th; the Spanish maravedi, less than 1-1000th; and the Portuguese rei a still smaller fraction.

[3] "Le monete le quali oggi sono ideali sono le più antiche d'ogni nazione, e tutte furono un tempo reali, e perchè erano reali con esse si contava." (Galiani: Della moneta, l. c., p. 153.)

[4] David Urquhart remarks in his "Familiar Words" on the monstrosity (!) that now-a-days a pound (sterling), which is the unit of the English standard of money, is equal to about a quarter of an ounce of gold. "This is falsifying a measure, not establishing a standard." He sees in this "false denomination" of the weight of gold, as in everything else, the falsifying hand of civilisation.

The prices, or quantities of gold, into which the values of commodities are ideally changed, are therefore now expressed in the names of coins, or in the legally valid names of the subdivisions of the gold standard. Hence, instead of saying: A quarter of wheat is worth an ounce of gold; we say, it is worth £3 17s. 10½d. In this way commodities express by their prices how much they are worth, and money serves as *money of account* whenever it is a question of fixing the value of an article in its money-form.[1]

The name of a thing is something distinct from the qualities of that thing. I know nothing of a man, by knowing that his name is Jacob. In the same way with regard to money, every trace of a value-relation disappears in the names pound, dollar, franc, ducat, &c. The confusion caused by attributing a hidden meaning to these cabalistic signs is all the greater, because these money-names express both the values of commodities, and, at the same time, aliquot parts of the weight of the metal that is the standard of money.[2] On the other hand, it is absolutely necessary that value, in order that it may be distinguished from the varied bodily forms of commodities, should assume this material and unmeaning, but, at the same time, purely social form.[3]

[1] When Anacharsis was asked for what purposes the Greeks used money, he replied, "For reckoning." (Athen. Deipn. l. 1v. 49 v. 2. ed Schweighäuser, 1802.)

[2] "Owing to the fact that money, when serving as the standard of price, appears under the same reckoning names as do the prices of commodities, and that therefore the sum of £3 17s. 10¼d. may signify on the one hand an ounce weight of gold, and on the other, the value of a ton of iron, this reckoning name of money has been called its mint-price. Hence there sprang up the extraordinary notion, that the value of gold is estimated in its own material, and that, in contra-distinction to all other commodities, its price is fixed by the State. It was erroneously thought that the giving of reckoning names to definite weights of gold, is the same thing as fixing the value of those weights." (Karl Marx. l. c., p. 89.)

[3] See "Theories of the Unit of Measure of Money" in "Critique of Political Economy," p. 91, ff. The fantastic notions about raising or lowering the mint-price of money by transferring to greater or smaller weights of gold or silver the names already legally appropriated to fixed weights of those metals; such notions, at least in those cases in which they aim, not at clumsy financial operations against creditors, both public and private, but at economical quack remedies have been so exhaustively treated by Wm. Petty in his "Quantulumcunque concerning money: To the Lord Marquis of Halifax, 1682," that even his immediate followers, Sir Dudley North and John Locke, not to mention later ones, could only dilute him. "If the wealth of a nation," he remarks, "could be decupled by a proclamation, it were strange that such proclamations have not long since been made by our Governors." (l. c., p. 36.)

Price is the money-name of the labour realised in a commodity. Hence the expression of the equivalence of a commodity with the sum of money constituting its price, is a tautology,[1] just as in general the expression of the relative value of a commodity is a statement of the equivalence of two commodities. But although price, being the exponent of the magnitude of a commodity's value, is the exponent of its exchange-ratio with money, it does not follow that the exponent of this exchange-ratio is necessarily the exponent of the magnitude of the commodity's value. Suppose two equal quantities of socially necessary labour to be respectively represented by 1 quarter of wheat and £2 (nearly ½ oz. of gold), £2 is the expression in money of the magnitude of the value of the quarter of wheat, or is its price. If now circumstances allow of this price being raised to £3, or compel it to be reduced to £1, then although £1 and £3 may be too small or too great properly to express the magnitude of the wheat's value, nevertheless they are its prices, for they are, in the first place, the form under which its value appears, *i.e.,* money; and in the second place, the exponents of its exchange-ratio with money. If the conditions of production, in other words, if the productive power of labour remain constant, the same amount of social labour-time must, both before and after the change in price, be expended in the reproduction of a quarter of wheat. This circumstance depends, neither on the will of the wheat producer, nor on that of the owners of other commodities.

Magnitude of value expresses a relation of social production, it expresses the connection that necessarily exists between a certain article and the portion of the total labour-time of society required to produce it. As soon as magnitude of value is converted into price, the above necessary relation takes the shape of a more or less accidental exchange-ratio between a single commodity and another, the money-commodity. But this exchange-ratio may express either the real magnitude of that commodity's value, or the quantity of gold deviating from that value, for which, according to circumstances, it may be parted

---

[1] "Ou bien, il faut consentir à dire qu'une valeur d'un million en argent vaut plus qu'une valeur égale en marchandises." (Le Trosne l. c. p. 919), which amounts to saying, "qu'une valeur vaut plus qu'une valeur égale."

with. The possibility, therefore, of quantitative incongruity between price and magnitude of value, or the deviation of the former from the latter, is inherent in the price-form itself. This is no defect, but, on the contrary, admirably adapts the price-form to a mode of production whose inherent laws impose themselves only as the mean of apparently lawless irregularities that compensate one another.

The price-form, however, is not only compatible with the possibility of a quantitative incongruity between magnitude of value and price, *i.e.*, between the former and its expression in money, but it may also conceal a qualitative inconsistency, so much so, that, although money is nothing but the value-form of commodities, price ceases altogether to express value. Objects that in themselves are no commodities, such as conscience, honour, &c., are capable of being offered for sale by their holders, and of thus acquiring, through their price, the form of commodities. Hence an object may have a price without having value. The price in that case is imaginary, like certain quantities in mathematics. On the other hand, the imaginary price-form may sometimes conceal either a direct or indirect real value-relation; for instance, the price of uncultivated land, which is without value, because no human labour has been incorporated in it.

Price, like relative value in general, expresses the value of a commodity (*e.g.*, a ton of iron), by stating that a given quantity of the equivalent (*e.g.*, an ounce of gold), is directly exchangeable for iron. But it by no means states the converse, that iron is directly exchangeable for gold. In order, therefore, that a commodity may in practice act effectively as exchange value, it must quit its bodily shape, must transform itself from mere imaginary into real gold, although to the commodity such transubstantiation may be more difficult than to the Hegelian "concept," the transition from "necessity" to "freedom," or to a lobster the casting of his shell, or to Saint Jerome the putting off of the old Adam.[1] Though a commod-

[1] Jerome had to wrestle hard, not only in his youth with the bodily flesh, as is shown by his fight in the desert with the handsome women of his imagination, but also in his old age with the spiritual flesh. "I thought," he says, "I was in the spirit before the Judge of the Universe." "Who art thou?" asked a voice. "I am

ity may, side by side with its actual form (iron, for instance), take in our imagination the form of gold, yet it cannot at one and the same time actually be both iron and gold. To fix its price, it suffices to equate it to gold in imagination. But to enable it to render to its owner the service of a universal equivalent, it must be actually replaced by gold. If the owner of the iron were to go to the owner of some other commodity offered for exchange, and were to refer him to the price of the iron as proof that it was already money, he would get the same answer as St. Peter gave in heaven to Dante, when the latter recited the creed—

> " Assai bene è trascorsa
> D'esta moneta già la lega e'l peso,
> Ma dimmi se tu l'hai nella tua borsa."

A price therefore implies both that a commodity is exchangeable for money, and also that it must be so exchanged. On the other hand, gold serves as an ideal measure of value, only because it has already, in the process of exchange, established itself as the money-commodity. Under the ideal measure of values there lurks the hard cash.

SECTION 2.—THE MEDIUM OF CIRCULATION.

a. The Metamorphosis of Commodities.

We saw in a former chapter that the exchange of commodities implies contradictory and mutually exclusive conditions. The differentiation of commodities into commodities and money does not sweep away these inconsistencies, but develops a *modus vivendi,* a form in which they can exist side by side. This is generally the way in which real contradictions are reconciled. For instance, it is a contradiction to depict one body as constantly falling towards another, and as, at the same time, constantly flying away from it. The ellipse is a form of motion which, while allowing this contradiction to go on, at the same time reconciles it.

In so far as exchange is a process, by which commodities are transferred from hands in which they are non-use-values, to

a Christian." "Thou liest," thundered back the great Judge, "thou art nought but a Ciceronian."

hands in which they become use-values, it is a social circulation of matter. The product of one form of useful labour replaces that of another. When once a commodity has found a resting-place, where it can serve as a use-value, it falls out of the sphere of exchange into that of consumption. But the former sphere alone interests us at present. We have, therefore, now to consider exchange from a formal point of view; to investigate the change of form or metamorphosis of commodities which effectuates the social circulation of matter.

The comprehension of this change of form is, as a rule, very imperfect. The cause of this imperfection is, apart from indistinct notions of value itself, that every change of form in a commodity results from the exchange of two commodities, an ordinary one and the money-commodity. If we keep in view the material fact alone that a commodity has been exchanged for gold we overlook the very thing that we ought to observe—namely, what has happened to the form of the commodity. We overlook the facts that gold, when a mere commodity, is not money, and that when other commodities express their prices in gold, this gold is but the money-form of those commodities themselves.

Commodities, first of all, enter into the process of exchange just as they are. The process then differentiates them into commodities and money, and thus produces an external opposition corresponding to the internal opposition inherent in them, as being at once use-values and values. Commodities as use-values now stand opposed to money as exchange value. On the other hand, both opposing sides are commodities, unities of use-value and value. But this unity of differences manifests itself at two opposite poles, and at each pole in an opposite way. Being poles they are as necessarily opposite as they are connected. On the one side of the equation we have an ordinary commodity, which is in reality a use-value. Its value is expressed only ideally in its price, by which it is equated to its opponent, the gold, as to the real embodiment of its value. On the other hand, the gold, in its metallic reality ranks as the embodiment of value, as money. Gold, as gold, is exchange value itself. As to its use-value, that has only an ideal existence, represented by the series of expressions of relative value in which it stands face to face with all other commodities, the sum of whose uses makes up the sum of the various uses of gold. These antagonistic forms of commodities are the real forms in which the process of their exchange moves and takes place.

Let us now accompany the owner of some commodity—say, our old friend the weaver of linen—to the scene of action, the market. His 20 yards of linen has a definite price, £2. He exchanges it for the £2, and then, like a man of the good old stamp that he is, he parts with the £2 for a family Bible of the same price. The linen, which in his eyes is a mere commodity, a depository of value, he alienates in exchange for gold, which is the linen's value-form, and this form he again parts with for another commodity, the Bible, which is destined to enter his house as an object of utility and of edification to its inmates. The exchange becomes an accomplished fact by two metamorphoses of opposite yet supplementary character—the conversion of the commodity into money, and the re-conversion of the money into a commodity.[1] The two phases of this metamorphosis are both of them distinct transactions of the weaver—selling, or the exchange of the commodity for money; buying, or the exchange of the money for a commodity; and, the unity of the two acts, selling in order to buy.

The result of the whole transaction, as regards the weaver, is this, that instead of being in possession of the linen, he now has the Bible; instead of his original commodity, he now possesses another of the same value but of different utility. In like manner he procures his other means of subsistence and means of production. From his point of view, the whole process effectuates nothing more than the exchange of the product of his labour for the product of some one else's, nothing more than an exchange of products.

The exchange of commodities is therefore accompanied by the following changes in their form.

---

[1] " ἐκ δὲ τοῦ . . . . . . πυρὸς ἀνταμείβεσθαι πάντα, φησὶν, ὁ ʿΗράκλειτος, καὶ πῦρ ἁπάντων, ὥσπερ χρυσοῦ χρήματα καὶ χρημάτων χρυσός." (F. Lassalle: Die Philosophie Herakleitos des Dunkeln. Berlin, 1845. Vol. I, p. 222.) Lassalle, in his note on this passage, p. 224, n. 3, erroneously makes gold a mere symbol of value.

Commodity—Money—Commodity.

C———M——C.

The result of the whole process is; so far as concerns the objects themselves, C—C, the exchange of one commodity for another, the circulation of materialised social labour. When this result is attained, the process is at an end.

C—M. First metamorphosis, or sale.

The leap taken by value from the body of the commodity, into the body of the gold, is, as I have elsewhere called it, the salto mortale of the commodity. If it falls short, then, although the commodity itself is not harmed, its owner decidedly is. The social division of labour causes his labour to be as one-sided as his wants are many-sided. This is precisely the reason why the product of his labour serves him solely as exchange value. But it cannot acquire the properties of a socially recognised universal equivalent, except by being converted into money. That money, however, is in some one else's pocket. In order to entice the money out of that pocket, our friend's commodity must, above all things, be a use-value to the owner of the money. For this, it is necessary that the labour expended upon it, be of a kind that is socially useful, of a kind that constitutes a branch of the social division of labour. But division of labour is a system of production which has grown up spontaneously and continues to grow behind the backs of the producers. The commodity to be exchanged may possibly be the product of some new kind of labour, that pretends to satisfy newly arisen requirements, or even to give rise itself to new requirements. A particular operation, though yesterday, perhaps, forming one out of the many operations conducted by one producer in creating a given commodity, may to-day separate itself from this connection, may establish itself as an independent branch of labour and send its incomplete product to market as an independent commodity. The circumstances may or may not be ripe for such a separation. To-day the product satisfies a social want. To-morrow the article may, either altogether or partially, be superseded by some other appropriate product. Moreover, although our weaver's labour may be a recognised branch of

the social division of labour, yet that fact is by no means sufficient to guarantee the utility of his 20 yards of linen.   If the
community's want of linen, and such a want has a limit like
every other want, should already be saturated by the products
of rival weavers, our friend's product is superfluous, redundant,
and consequently useless.   Although people do not look a gift-
horse in the mouth, our friend does not frequent the market for
the purpose of making presents.   But suppose his product turn
out a real use-value, and thereby attracts money?   The question
arises, how much will it attract?   No doubt the answer is already anticipated in the price of the article, in the exponent of
the magnitude of its value.   We leave out of consideration here
any accidental miscalculation of value by our friend, a mistake
that is soon rectified in the market.   We suppose him to have
spent on his product only that amount of labour-time that is on
an average socially necessary   The price then, is merely the
money-name of the quantity of social labour realised in his
commodity.   But without the leave, and behind the back, of our
weaver, the old fashioned mode of weaving undergoes a change.
The labour-time that yesterday was without doubt socially necessary to the production of a yard of linen, ceases to be so to-
day, a fact which the owner of the money is only too eager to
prove from the prices quoted by our friend's competitors.   Un-
luckily for him, weavers are not few and far between.   Lastly,
suppose that every piece of linen in the market contains no
more labour-time than is socially necessary.   In spite of this,
all these pieces taken as a whole, may have had superfluous
labour-time spent upon them.   If the market cannot stomach
the whole quantity at the normal price of 2 shillings a yard,
this proves that too great a portion of the total labour of the
community has been expended in the form of weaving.   The
effect is the same as if each individual weaver had expended
more labour-time upon his particular product than is socially
necessary.   Here we may say, with the German proverb:
caught together, hung together.   All the linen in the market
counts but as one article of commerce, of which each piece is
only an aliquot part.   And as a matter of fact, the value also of
each single yard is but the materialised form of the same def-

inite and socially fixed quantity of homogeneous human labour.

We see then, commodities are in love with money, but "the course of true love never did run smooth." The quantitative division of labour is brought about in exactly the same spontaneous and accidental manner as its qualitative division. The owners of commodities therefore find out, that the same division of labour that turns them into independent private producers, also frees the social process of production and the relations of the individual producers to each other within that process, from all dependence on the will of those producers, and that the seeming mutual independence of the individuals is supplemented by a system of general and mutual dependence through or by means of the products.

The division of labour converts the product of labour into a commodity, and thereby makes necessary its further conversion into money. At the same time it also makes the accomplishment of this trans-substantiation quite accidental. Here, however, we are only concerned with the phenomenon in its integrity, and we therefore assume its progress to be normal. Moreover, if the conversion take place at all, that is, if the commodity be not absolutely unsaleable, its metamorphosis does take place although the price realised may be abnormally above or below the value.

The seller has his commodity replaced by gold, the buyer has his gold replaced by a commodity. The fact which here stares us in the face is, that a commodity and gold, 20 yards of linen and £2, have changed hands and places, in other words, that they have been exchanged. But for what is the commodity exchanged? For the shape assumed by its own value, for the universal equivalent. And for what is the gold exchanged? For a particular form of its own use-value. Why does gold take the form of money face to face with the linen? Because the linen's price of £2, its denomination in money, has already equated the linen to gold in its character of money. A commodity strips off its original commodity-form on being alienated, *i.e.,* on the instant its use-value actually attracts the gold, that before existed only ideally in its price. The realisation of a commodity's price, or of its ideal value-

form, is therefore at the same time the realisation of the ideal
use-value of money; the conversion of a commodity into
money, is the simultaneous conversion of money into a commodity. The apparently single process is in reality a double
one. From the pole of the commodity owner it is a sale, from
the opposite pole of the money owner, it is a purchase. In
other words, a sale is a purchase, C—M is also M—C.[1]

Up to this point we have considered men in only one economical capacity, that of owners of commodities, a capacity in
which they appropriate the produce of the labour of others, by
alienating that of their own labour. Hence, for one commodity
owner to meet with another who has money, it is necessary,
either, that the product of the labour of the latter person, the
buyer, should be in itself money, should be gold, the material
of which money consists, or that his product should already
have changed its skin and have stripped off its original form
of a useful object. In order that it may play the part of
money, gold must of course enter the market at some point or
other. This point is to be found at the source of production
of the metal, at which place gold is bartered, as the immediate
product of labour, for some other product of equal value.
From that moment it always represents the realised price of
some commodity.[2] Apart from its exchange for other commodities at the source of its production, gold, in whose-so-ever
hands it may be, is the transformed shape of some commodity
alienated by its owner; it is the product of a sale or of the first
metamorphosis C—M.[3] Gold, as we saw, became ideal money,
or a measure of values, in consequence of all commodities
measuring their values by it, and thus contrasting it ideally
with their natural shape as useful objects, and making it the
shape of their value. It became real money, by the general
alienation of commodities, by actually changing places with
their natural forms as useful objects, and thus becoming in

[1] " Toute vente est achat." (Dr. Quesnay: " Dialogues sur le Commerce et les
Travaux des Artisans." Physiocrates ed. Daire I. Partie, Paris, 1846, p. 170), or
as Quesnay in his "Maximes générales" puts it, "Vendre est acheter."

[2] "Le prix d'une marchandise ne pouvant être payé que par le prix d'une autre
marchandise." (Mercier de la Rivière: "L'Ordre natural et essentiel des sociétés
politiques." Physiocrates, ed. Daire II. Partie, p. 554.)

[3] "Pour avoir cet argent, il faut avoir vendu," l. c., p. 543.

reality the embodiment of their values. When they assume this money-shape, commodities strip off every trace of their natural use-value, and of the particular kind of labour to which they owe their creation, in order to transform themselves into the uniform, socially recognised incarnation of homogeneous human labour. We cannot tell from the mere look of a piece of money, for what particular commodity it has been exchanged. Under their money-form all commodities look alike. Hence, money may be dirt, although dirt is not money. We will assume that the two gold pieces, in consideration of which our weaver has parted with his linen, are the metamorphosed shape of a quarter of wheat. The sale of the linen, C—M, is at the same time its purchase, M—C. But the sale is the first act of a process that ends with a transaction of an opposite nature, namely, the purchase of a Bible; the purchase of the linen, on the other hand, ends a movement that began with a transaction of an opposite nature, namely, with the sale of the wheat. C—M (linen—money), which is the first phase of C—M—C (linen—money—Bible), is also M—C (money—linen), the last phase of another movement C—M—C (wheat—money—linen). The first metamorphosis of one commodity, its transformation from a commodity into money, is therefore also invariably the second metamorphosis of some other commodity, the retransformation of the latter from money into a commodity.[1]

M—C, or purchase. The second and concluding metamorphosis of a commodity.

Because money is the metamorphosed shape of all other commodities, the result of their general alienation, for this reason it is alienable itself without restriction or condition. It reads all prices backwards, and thus, so to say, depicts itself in the bodies of all other commodities, which offer to it the material for the realisation of its own use-value. At the same time the prices, wooing glances cast at money by commodities,

---

[1] As before remarked, the actual producer of gold or silver forms an exception. He exchanges his product directly for another commodity, without having first sold it.

define the limits of its convertibility, by pointing to its quantity. Since every commodity, on becoming money, disappears as a commodity, it is impossible to tell from the money itself, how it got into the hands of its possessor, or what article has been changed into it. Non olet, from whatever source it may come. Representing on the one hand a sold commodity, it represents on the other hand a commodity to be bought.[1]

M—C, a purchase, is, at the same time, C—M, a sale; the concluding metamorphosis of one commodity is the first metamorphosis of another. With regard to our weaver, the life of his commodity ends with the Bible, into which he has reconverted his £2. But suppose the seller of the Bible turns the £2 set free by the weaver into brandy. M—C, the concluding phase of C—M—C (linen, money, Bible), is also C—M, the first phase of C—M—C (Bible, money, brandy). The producer of a particular commodity has that one article alone to offer; this he sells very often in large quantities, but his many and various wants compel him to split up the price realised, the sum of money set free, into numerous purchases. Hence a sale leads to many purchases of various articles. The concluding metamorphosis of a commodity thus constitutes an aggregation of first metamorphoses of various other commodities.

If we now consider the completed metamorphosis of a commodity, as a whole, it appears in the first place, that it is made up of two opposite and complementary movements, C—M and M—C. These two antithetical transmutations of a commodity are brought about by two antithetical social acts on the part of the owner, and these acts in their turn stamp the character of the economical parts played by him. As the person who makes a sale, he is a seller; as the person who makes a purchase, he is a buyer. But just as, upon every such transmutation of a commodity, its two forms, commodity-form and money-form, exist simultaneously but at opposite poles, so every seller has a buyer opposed to him, and every buyer a seller. While one particular commodity is going through its

---

[1] " Si l'argent représente, dans nos mains, les choses que nous pouvons désirer d'acheter, il y représente aussi les choses que nous avons vendues pour cet argent." (Mercier de la Rivière l. c.)

two transmutations in succession, from a commodity into money and from money into another commodity, the owner of the commodity changes in succession his part from that of seller to that of buyer. These characters of seller and buyer are therefore not permanent, but attach themselves in turns to the various persons engaged in the circulation of commodities.

The complete metamorphosis of a commodity, in its simplest form, implies four extremes, and three dramatis personæ. First, a commodity comes face to face with money; the latter is the form taken by the value of the former, and exists in all its hard reality, in the pocket of the buyer. A commodity-owner is thus brought into contact with a possessor of money. So soon, now, as the commodity has been changed into money, the money becomes its transient equivalent-form, the use-value of which equivalent-form is to be found in the bodies of other commodities. Money, the final term of the first transmutation, is at the same time the starting point for the second. The person who is a seller in the first transaction thus becomes a buyer in the second, in which a third commodity-owner appears on the scene as a seller.[1]

The two phases, each inverse to the other, that make up the metamorphosis of a commodity constitute together a circular movement, a circuit: commodity-form, stripping off of this form, and return to the commodity-form. No doubt, the commodity appears here under two different aspects. At the starting point it is not a use-value to its owner; at the finishing point it is. So, too, the money appears in the first phase as a solid crystal of value, a crystal into which the commodity eagerly solidifies, and in the second, dissolves into the mere transient equivalent-form destined to be replaced by a use-value.

The two metamorphoses constituting the circuit are at the same time two inverse partial metamorphoses of two other commodities. One and the same commodity, the linen, opens the series of its own metamorphoses, and completes the metamorphosis of another (the wheat). In the first phase or sale,

[1] "Il y a donc . . . quatre termes et trois contractants, dont l'un intervient deux fois." (Le Trosne l. c. p. 909.)

the linen plays these two parts in its own person. But, then, changed into gold, it completes its own second and final metamorphosis, and helps at the same time to accomplish the first metamorphosis of a third commodity. Hence the circuit made by one commodity in the course of its metamorphoses is inextricably mixed up with the circuits of other commodities. The total of all the different circuits constitutes *the circulation of commodities.*

The circulation of commodities differs from the direct exchange of products (barter), not only in form, but in substance. Only consider the course of events. The weaver has, as a matter of fact, exchanged his linen for a Bible, his own commodity for that of some one else. But this is true only so far as he himself is concerned. The seller of the Bible, who prefers something to warm his inside, no more thought of exchanging his Bible for linen than our weaver knew that wheat had been exchanged for his linen. B's commodity replaces that of A, but A and B do not mutually exchange those commodities. It may, of course, happen that A and B make simultaneous purchases, the one from the other; but such exceptional transactions are by no means the necessary result of the general conditions of the circulation of commodities. We see here, on the one hand, how the exchange of commodities breaks through all local and personal bounds inseparable from direct barter, and develops the circulation of the products of social labor; and on the other hand, how it develops a whole network of social relations spontaneous in their growth and entirely beyond the control of the actors. It is only because the farmer has sold his wheat that the weaver is enabled to sell his linen, only because the weaver has sold his linen that our Hotspur is enabled to sell his Bible, and only because the latter has sold the water of everlasting life that the distiller is enabled to sell his *eau-de-vie,* and so on.

The process of circulation, therefore, does not, like direct barter of products, become extinguished upon the use values changing places and hands. The money does not vanish on dropping out of the circuit of the metamorphosis of a given commodity. It is constantly being precipitated into new places in the arena of circulation vacated by other commodities. In the complete metamorphosis of the linen, for example, linen —money—Bible, the linen first falls out of circulation, and money steps into its place. Then the Bible falls out of circulation, and again money takes its place. When one commodity replaces another, the money commodity always sticks to the hands of some third person.[1] Circulation sweats money from every pore.

Nothing can be more childish than the dogma, that because every sale is a purchase, and every purchase a sale, therefore the circulation of commodities necessarily implies an equilibrium of sales and purchases. If this means that the number of actual sales is equal to the number of purchases, it is mere tautology. But its real purport is to prove that every seller brings his buyer to market with him. Nothing of the kind. The sale and the purchase constitute one identical act, an exchange between a commodity-owner and an owner of money, between two persons as opposed to each other as the two poles of a magnet. They form two distinct acts, of polar and opposite characters, when performed by one single person. Hence the identity of sale and purchase implies that the commodity is useless, if, on being thrown into the alchemistical retort of circulation, it does not come out again in the shape of money; if, in other words, it cannot be sold by its owner, and therefore be bought by the owner of the money That identity further implies that the exchange, if it does take place, constitutes a period of rest, an interval, long or short, in the life of the commodity. Since the first metamorphosis of a commodity is at once a sale and a purchase, it is also an independent process in itself. The purchaser has the commodity, the seller has the money, *i.e.*, a commodity ready to go into circulation at any time. No one can sell unless some one else purchases. But no one is forthwith bound to purchase, because he has just sold. Circulation bursts through all restrictions as to time, place, and individuals, imposed by direct barter, and this it effects by splitting up, into the antithesis of a sale and a purchase, the

---

[1] Self-evident as this may be, it is nevertheless for the most part unobserved by political economists, and especially by the " Freetrader Vulgaris."

direct identity that in barter does exist between the alienation of one's own and the acquisition of some other man's product. To say that these two independent and antithetical acts have an intrinsic unity, are essentially one, is the same as to say that this intrinsic oneness expresses itself in an external antithesis. If the interval in time between the two complementary phases of the complete metamorphosis of a commodity becomes too great, if the split between the sale and the purchase becomes too pronounced, the intimate connexion between them, their oneness, asserts itself by producing—a crisis. The antithesis, use-value and value; the contradictions that private labour is bound to manifest itself as direct social labour, that a particularized concrete kind of labour has to pass for abstract human labour; the contradiction between the personification of objects and the representation of persons by things; all these antitheses and contradictions, which are immanent in commodities, assert themselves, and develop their modes of motion, in the antithetical phases of the metamorphosis of a commodity. These modes therefore imply the possibility, and no more than the possibility, of crisis. The conversion of this mere possibility into a reality is the result of a long series of relations, that, from our present standpoint of simple circulation, have as yet no existence.[1]

b. The currency [2] of money.

The change of form, C—M—C, by which the circulation of the material products of labour is brought about, requires that

---

[1] See my observations on James Mill in "Critique, &c.," p. 123–125. With regard to this subject, we may notice two methods characteristic of apologetic economy. The first is the identification of the circulation of commodities with the direct barter of products, by simple abstraction from their points of difference; the second is, the attempt to explain away the contradictions of capitalist production, by reducing the relations between the persons engaged in that mode of production, to the simple relations arising out of the circulation of commodities. The production and circulation of commodities are, however, phenomena that occur to a greater or less extent in modes of production the most diverse. If we are acquainted with nothing but the abstract categories of circulation, which are common to all these modes of production, we cannot possibly know anything of the specific points of difference of those modes, nor pronounce any judgment upon them. In no science is such a big fuss made with commonplace truisms as in political economy. For instance, J. B. Say sets himself up as a judge of crises, because, forsooth, he knows that a commodity is a product.

[2] *Translator's note.* — This word is here used in its original signification of the

a given value in the shape of a commodity shall begin the process, and shall, also in the shape of a commodity, end it. The movement of the commodity is therefore a circuit. On the other hand, the form of this movement precludes a circuit from being made by the money. The result is not the return of the money, but its continued removal further and further away from its starting-point. So long as the seller sticks fast to his money, which is the transformed shape of his commodity, that commodity is still in the first phase of its metamorphosis, and has completed only half its course. But so soon as he completes the process, so soon as he supplements his sale by a purchase, the money again leaves the hands of its possessor. It is true that if the weaver, after buying the Bible, sells more linen, money comes back into his hands. But this return is not owing to the circulation of the first 20 yards of linen; that circulation resulted in the money getting into the hands of the seller of the Bible. The return of money into the hands of the weaver is brought about only by the renewal or repetition of the process of circulation with a fresh commodity, which renewed process ends with the same result as its predecessor did. Hence the movement directly imparted to money by the circulation of commodities takes the form of a constant motion away from its starting point, of course from the hands of one commodity owner into those of another. This course constitutes its currency (cours de la monnaie).

The currency of money is the constant and monotonous repetition of the same process. The commodity is always in the hands of the seller; the money, as a means of purchase, always in the hands of the buyer. And money serves as a means of purchase by realising the price of the commodity. This realisation transfers the commodity from the seller to the buyer, and removes the money from the hands of the buyer into those of the seller, where it again goes through the same process with another commodity That this one-sided character of the moneys motion arises out of the two-sided character of the commodity's motion, is a circumstance that is veiled over.

course or track pursued by money as it changes from hand to hand, a course which essentially differs from circulation.

The very nature of the circulation of commodities begets the opposite appearance. The first metamorphosis of a commodity is visibly, not only the money's movement, but also that of the commodity itself; in the second metamorphosis, on the contrary, the movement appears to us as the movement of the money alone. In the first phase of its circulation the commodity changes place with the money. Thereupon the commodity, under its aspect of a useful object, falls out of circulation into consumption.[1] In its stead we have its value-shape—the money. It then goes through the second phase of its circulation, not under its own natural shape, but under the shape of money. The continuity of the movement is therefore kept up by the money alone, and the same movement that as regards the commodity consists of two processes of an antithetical character, is, when considered as the movement of the money, always one and the same process, a continued change of places with ever fresh commodities. Hence the result brought about by the circulation of commodities, namely, the replacing of one commodity by another, takes the appearance of having been effected not by means of the change of form of the commodities, but rather by the money acting as a medium of circulation, by an action that circulates commodities, to all appearance motionless in themselves, and transfers them from hands in which they are non-use-values, to hands in which they are use-values; and that in a direction constantly opposed to the direction of the money. The latter is continually withdrawing commodities from circulation and stepping into their places, and in this way continually moving further and further from its starting-point. Hence, although the movement of the money is merely the expression of the circulation of commodities, yet the contrary appears to be the actual fact, and the circulation of commodities seems to be the result of the movement of the money.[2]

---

[1] Even when the commodity is sold over and over again, a phenomenon that at present has no existence for us, it falls, when definitely sold for the last time, out of the sphere of circulation into that of consumption, where it serves either as means of subsistence or means of production.

[2] " Il (l'argent) n'a d'autre mouvement que celui qui lui est imprimé par les productions." (Le Trosne l.c.p. 885.)

Again, money functions as a means of circulation, only because in it the values of commodities have independent reality. Hence its movement, as the medium of circulation, is, in fact, merely the movement of commodities while changing their forms. This fact must therefore make itself plainly visible in the currency of money. The twofold change of form in a commodity is reflected in the twice repeated change of place of the same piece of money during the complete metamorphosis of a commodity, and in its constantly repeated change of place, as metamorphosis follows metamorphosis, and each becomes interlaced with the others.

The linen, for instance, first of all exchanges its commodity-form for its money-form. The last term of its first metamorphosis (C—M), or the money-form, is the first term of its final metamorphosis (M—C), of its re-conversion into a useful commodity, the Bible. But each of these changes of form is accomplished by an exchange between commodity and money, by their reciprocal displacement. The same pieces of coin, in the first act, changed places with the linen, in the second, with the Bible. They are displaced twice. The first metamorphosis puts them into the weaver's pocket, the second draws them out of it. The two inverse changes undergone by the same commodity are reflected in the displacement, twice repeated, but in opposite directions, of the same pieces of coin.

If, on the contrary, only one phase of the metamorphosis is gone through, if there are only sales or only purchases, then a given piece of money changes its place only once. Its second change corresponds to and expresses the second metamorphosis of the commodity, its re-conversion from money into another commodity intended for use. It is a matter of course, that all this is applicable to the simple circulation of commodities alone, the only form that we are now considering.

Every commodity, when it first steps into circulation, and undergoes its first change of form, does so only to fall out of circulation again and to be replaced by other commodities. Money, on the contrary, as the medium of circulation, keeps continually within the sphere of circulation, and moves about in it. The question therefore arises, how much money this sphere constantly absorbs?

In a given country there take place every day at the same time, but in different localities, numerous one-sided metamorphoses of commodities, or, in other words, numerous sales and numerous purchases. The commodities are equated beforehand in imagination, by their prices, to definite quantities of money. And since, in the form of circulation now under consideration, money and commodities always come bodily face to face, one at the positive pole of purchase, the other at the negative pole of sale, it is clear that the amount of the means of circulation required, is determined beforehand by the sum of the prices of all these commodities. As a matter of fact, the money in reality represents the quantity or sum of gold ideally expressed beforehand by the sum of the prices of the commodities. The equality of these two sums is therefore self-evident. We know, however, that, the values of commodities remaining constant, their prices vary with the value of gold (the material of money), rising in proportion as it falls, and falling in proportion as it rises. Now if, in consequence of such a rise or fall in the value of gold, the sum of the prices of commodities fall or rise, the quantity of money in currency must fall or rise to the same extent. The change in the quantity of the circulating medium is, in this case, it is true, caused by money itself, yet not in virtue of its function as a medium of circulation, but of its function as a measure of value. First, the price of the commodities varies inversely as the value of the money, and then the quantity of the medium of circulation varies directly as the price of the commodities. Exactly the same thing would happen if, for instance, instead of the value of gold falling, gold were replaced by silver as the measure of value, or if, instead of the value of silver rising, gold were to thrust silver out from being the measure of value. In the one case, more silver would be current than gold was before; in the other case, less gold would be current than silver was before. In each case the value of the material of money, *i.e.*, the value of the commodity that serves as the measure of value, would have under-

gone a change, and therefore, so, too, would the prices of commodities which express their values in money, and so, too,
would the quantity of money current whose function it is to
realise those prices. We have already seen, that the sphere of
circulation has an opening through which gold (or the material
of money generally) enters into it as a commodity with a given
value. Hence, when money enters on its functions as a
measure of value, when it expresses prices, its value is already
determined. If now its value fall, this fact is first evidenced
by a change in the prices of those commodities that are
directly bartered for the precious metals at the sources of
their production. The greater part of all other commodities,
especially in the imperfectly developed stages of civil society,
will continue for a long time to be estimated by the former
antiquated and illusory value of the measure of value.
Nevertheless, one commodity infects another through their
common value-relation, so that their prices, expressed in gold
or in silver, gradually settle down into the proportions determined by their comparative values, until finally the values of
all commodities are estimated in terms of the new value of the
metal that constitutes money. This process is accompanied by
the continued increase in the quantity of the precious metals,
an increase caused by their streaming in to replace the articles
directly bartered for them at their sources of production. In
proportion therefore as commodities in general acquire their
true prices, in proportion as their values become estimated
according to the fallen value of the precious metal, in the
same proportion the quantity of that metal necessary for realising those new prices is provided beforehand. A one-sided
observation of the results that followed upon the discovery of
fresh supplies of gold and silver, led some economists in the
17th, and particularly in the 18th century, to the false conclusion, that the prices of commodities had gone up in consequence of the increased quantity of gold and silver serving as
means of circulation. Henceforth we shall consider the value
of gold to be given, as, in fact, it is momentarily whenever we
estimate the price of a commodity.

On this supposition then, the quantity of the medium of

circulation is determined by the sum of the prices that have to be realised. If now we further suppose the price of each commodity to be given, the sum of the prices clearly depends on the mass of commodities in circulation. It requires but little racking of brains to comprehend that if one quarter of wheat cost £2, 100 quarters will cost £200, 200 quarters £400, and so on, that consequently the quantity of money that changes place with the wheat, when sold, must increase with the quantity of that wheat.

If the mass of commodities remain constant, the quantity of circulating money varies with the fluctuations in the prices of those commodities. It increases and diminishes because the sum of the prices increases or diminishes in consequence of the change of price. To produce this effect, it is by no means requisite that the prices of all commodities should rise or fall simultaneously. A rise or a fall in the prices of a number of leading articles, is sufficient in the one case to increase, in the other to diminish, the sum of the prices of all commodities, and, therefore, to put more or less money in circulation. Whether the change in the price correspond to an actual change of value in the commodities, or whether it be the result of mere fluctuations in market prices, the effect on the quantity of the medium of circulation remains the same.

Suppose the following articles to be sold or partially metamorphosed simultaneously in different localities: say, one quarter of wheat, 20 yards of linen, one Bible, and 4 gallons of brandy. If the price of each article be £2, and the sum of the prices to be realised be consequently £8, it follows that £8 in money must go into circulation. If, on the other hand, these same articles are links in the following chain of metamorphoses: 1 quarter of wheat—£2—20 yards of linen—£2—1 Bible—£2—4 gallons of brandy—£2, a chain that is already well-known to us, in that case the £2 cause the different commodities to circulate one after the other, and after realizing their prices successively, and therefore the sum of those prices, £8, they come to rest at last in the pocket of the distiller. The £2 thus make four moves. This repeated change of place of the same pieces of money corresponds to the double change in form of the commodities, to their motion in opposite directions through two stages of circulation, and to the interlacing of the metamorphoses of different commodities.[1] These antithetic and complementary phases, of which the process of metamorphosis consists, are gone through, not simultaneously, but successively. Time is therefore required for the completion of the series. Hence the velocity of the currency of money is measured by the number of moves made by a given piece of money in a given time. Suppose the circulation of the 4 articles takes a day. The sum of the prices to be realised in the day is £8, the number of moves of the two pieces of money is four, and the quantity of money circulating is £2. Hence, for a given interval of time during the process of circulation, we have the following relation: the quantity of money functioning as the circulating medium is equal to the sum of the prices of the commodities divided by the number of moves made by coins of the same denomination. This law holds generally.

The total circulation of commodities in a given country during a given period is made up on the one hand of numerous isolated and simultaneous partial metamorphoses, sales which are at the same time purchases, in which each coin changes its place only once, or makes only one move; on the other hand, of numerous distinct series of metamorphoses partly running side by side, and partly coalescing with each other, in each of which series each coin makes a number of moves, the number being greater or less according to circumstances. The total number of moves made by all the circulating coins of one denomination being given, we can arrive at the average number of moves made by a single coin of that denomination, or at the average velocity of the currency of money. The quantity of money thrown into the circulation at the beginning of each day is of course determined by the sum of the prices of all the commodities circulating simultaneously side by side. But once in circulation, coins are, so to say, made responsible for one another. If the one increase its velocity, the other either

---

[1] " Ce sont les productions qui le (l'argent) mettent en mouvement et le font circuler . . . La célérité de son mouvement (sc. de l'argent) supplée à sa quantité. Lorsqu'il en est besoin, il ne fait que glisser d'une main dans l'autre sans s'arrêter un instant." (Le Trosne l. c. pp. 915, 916.)

retards its own, or altogether falls out of circulation; for the
circulation can absorb only such a quantity of gold as when
multiplied by the mean number of moves made by one single
coin or element, is equal to the sum of the prices to be realised.   Hence if the number of moves made by the separate.
pieces increase, the total number of those pieces in circulation
diminishes.   If the number of the moves diminish, the total
number of pieces increases.   Since the quantity of money capable of being absorbed by the circulation is given for a given
mean velocity of currency, all that is necessary in order to abstract a given number of sovereigns from the circulation is to
throw the same number of one-pound notes into it, a trick well
known to all bankers.

Just as the currency of money, generally considered, is but
a reflex of the circulation of commodities, or of the antithetical
metamorphoses they undergo, so, too, the velocity of that currency reflects the rapidity with which commodities change
their forms, the continued interlacing of one series of metamorphoses with another, the hurried social interchange of
matter, the rapid disappearance of commodities from the
sphere of circulation, and the equally rapid substitution of
fresh ones in their places.   Hence, in the velocity of the currency we have the fluent unity of the antithetical and complementary phases, the unity of the conversion of the useful
aspect of commodities into their value-aspect, and their re-conversion from the latter aspect to the former, or the unity of the
two processes of sale and purchase.   On the other hand, the
retardation of the currency reflects the separation of these two
processes into isolated antithetical phases, reflects the stagnation in the change of form, and therefore, in the social interchange of matter.   The circulation itself, of course, gives no
clue to the origin of this stagnation; it merely puts in evidence
the phenomenon itself.   The general public, who, simultaneously, with the retardation of the currency, see money appear
and disappear less frequently at the periphery of circulation,
naturally attribute this retardation to a quantitive deficiency
in the circulating medium.[1].

[1] Money being . . . the common measure of buying and selling, every body who

The total quantity of money functioning during a given
period as the circulating medium, is determined, on the one
hand, by the sum of the prices of the circulating commodities,
and on the other hand, by the rapidity with which the antithetical phases of the metamorphoses follow one another. On
this rapidity depends what proportion of the sum of the prices
can, on the average, be realised by each single coin. But the
sum of the prices of the circulating commodities depends on
the quantity, as well as on the prices, of the commodities.
These three factors, however, state of prices, quantity of circulating commodities, and velocity of money-currency, are all
variable. Hence, the sum of the prices to be realised, and
consequently the quantity of the circulating medium depending on that sum, will vary with the numerous variations of
these three factors in combination. Of these variations we
shall consider those alone that have been the most important
in the history of prices.

While prices remain constant, the quantity of the circulating medium may increase owing to the number of circulating
commodities increasing, or to the velocity of currency decreasing, or to a combination of the two. On the other hand the

hath anything to sell, and cannot procure chapmen for it, is presently apt to think,
that want of money in the kingdom, or country, is the cause why his goods do not
go off; and so, want of money is the common cry; which is a great mistake. . .
What do these people want, who cry out for money? . . . The farmer complains
. . . he thinks that were more money in the country, he should have a price for his
goods. Then it seems money is not his want, but a price for his corn and cattel,
which he would sell, but cannot. . . Why cannot he get a price? . . . (1) Either
there is too much corn and cattel in the country, so that most who come to market
have need of selling, as he hath, and few of buying; or (2) There wants the usual
vent abroad by transportation. . . ; or (3) The consumption fails, as when men,
by reason of poverty, do not spend so much in their houses as formerly they did;
wherefore it is not the increase of specific money, which would at all advance the
farmer's goods, but the removal of any of these three causes, which do truly keep
down the market. . . . The merchant and shopkeeper want money in the same
manner, that is, they want a vent for the goods they deal in, by reason that the
markets fail " . . . [A nation] " never thrives better, than when riches are tost
from hand to hand." (Sir Dudley North: " Discourses upon Trade," Lond. 1691,
pp. 11-15, passim.) Herrenschwand's fanciful notions amount merely to this, that
the antagonism, which has its origin in the nature of commodities, and is reproduced in their circulation, can be removed by increasing the circulating medium.
But if, on the one hand, it is a popular delusion to ascribe stagnation in production
and circulation to insufficiency of the circulating medium, it by no means follows,
on the other hand, that an actual paucity of the medium in consequence, *e.g.*, of
bungling legislative interference with the regulation of currency, may not give rise
to such stagnation.

quantity of the circulating medium may decrease with a decreasing number of commodities, or with an increasing rapidity of their circulation.

With a general rise in the prices of commodities, the quantity of the circulating medium will remain constant, provided the number of commodities in the circulation decrease proportionally to the increase in their prices, or provided the velocity of currency increase at the same rate as prices rise, the number of commodities in circulation remaining constant. The quantity of the circulating medium may decrease, owing to the number of commodities decreasing more rapidly; or to the velocity of currency increasing more rapidly, than prices rise.

With a general fall in the prices of commodities, the quantity of the circulating medium will remain constant, provided the number of commodities increase proportionately to their fall in price, or provided the velocity of currency decrease in the same proportion. The quantity of the circulating medium will increase, provided the number of commodities increase quicker, or the rapidity of circulation decrease quicker, than the prices fall.

The variations of the different factors may mutually compensate each other, so that notwithstanding their continued instability, the sum of the prices to be realised and the quantity of money in circulation remains constant; consequently, we find, especially if we take long periods into consideration, that the deviations from the average level, of the quantity of money current in any country, are much smaller than we should at first sight expect, apart of course from excessive perturbations periodically arising from industrial and commercial crises, or, less frequently, from fluctuations in the value of money.

The law, that the quantity of the circulating medium is determined by the sum of the prices of the commodities circulating, and the average velocity of currency[1] may also be

[1] " There is a certain measure and proportion of money requisite to drive the trade of a nation, more or less than which would prejudice the same. Just as there is a certain proportion of farthings necessary in a small retail trade, to change silver money, and to even such reckonings as cannot be adjusted with the smallest silver pieces. . . . Now, as the proportion of the number of farthings requisite in commerce is to be taken from the number of people, the frequency of their

stated as follows: given the sum of the values of commodities, and the average rapidity of their metamorphoses, the quantity of precious metal current as money depends on the value of that precious metal. The erroneous opinion that it is, on the contrary, prices that are determined by the quantity of the circulating medium, and that the latter depends on the quantity of the precious metals in a country;[1] this opinion was based by those who first beheld it, on the absurd hypothesis that commodities are without a price, and money without a value, when they first enter into circulation, and that, once in the circulation, an aliquot part of the medley of commodities is exchanged for an aliquot part of the heap of precious metals.[2]

exchanges: as also, and principally, from the value of the smallest silver pieces of money; so in like manner, the proportion of money [gold and silver specie] requisite in our trade, is to be likewise taken from the frequency of commutations, and from the bigness of the payments." (William Petty. "A Treatise on Taxes and Contributions." Lond. 1662, p. 17.) The Theory of Hume was defended against the attacks of J. Steuart and others, by A. Young, in his "'Political Arithmetic," Lond. 1774, in which work there is a special chapter entitled " Prices depend on quantity of money," at p. 112, sqq. I have stated in " Critique, &c.," p. 232: " He (Adam Smith) passes over without remark the question as to the quantity of coin in circulation, and treats money quite wrongly as a mere commodity." This statement applies only in so far as Adam Smith, ex officio, treats of money. Now and then, however, as in his criticism of the earlier systems of political economy, he takes the right view. " The quantity of coin in every country is regulated by the value of the commodities which are to be circulated by it. . . . The value of the goods annually bought and sold in any country requires a certain quantity of money to circulate and distribute them to their proper consumers, and can give employment to no more. The channel of circulation necessarily draws to itself a sum sufficient to fill it, and never admits any more." (" Wealth of Nations." Bk. IV., ch. I.) In like manner, ex officio, he opens his work with an apotheosis on the division of labour. Afterwards, in the last book which treats of the sources of public revenue, he occasionally repeats the denunciations of the division of labour made by his teacher, A. Ferguson.

[1] "The prices of things will certainly rise in every nation, as the gold and silver increase amongst the people; and consequently, where the gold and silver decrease in any nation, the prices of all things must fall proportionably to such decrease of money." (Jacob Vanderlint: "Money answers all Things." Lond. 1734, p. 5.) A careful comparison of this book with Hume's "Essays," proves to my mind without doubt that Hume was acquainted with and made use of Vanderlint's work, which is certainly an important one. The opinion that prices are determined by the quantity of the circulating medium, was also held by Barbon and other much earlier writers. " No inconvenience," says Vanderlint, " can arise by an unrestrained trade, but very great advantage; since, if the cash of the nation be decreased by it, which prohibitions are designed to prevent, those nations that get the cash will certainly find everything advance in price, as the cash increases amongst them. And . . . our manufactures, and everything else, will soon become so moderate as to turn the balance of trade in our favour, and thereby fetch the money back again." (l. c., pp. 43, 44.)

[2] That the price of each single kind of commodity forms part of the sum of the

c. Coin and symbols of value.

That money takes the shape of coin, springs from its function as the circulating medium. The weight of gold represented in imagination by the prices or money-names of commodities, must confront those commodities, within the circulation, in the shape of coins or pieces of gold of a given denomination. Coining, like the establishment of a standard of prices, is the business of the State. The different national uniforms worn at home by gold and silver as coins, and doffed again in the market of the world, indicate the separation between the internal or national spheres of the circulation of commodities, and their universal sphere.

The only difference, therefore, between coin and bullion, is one of shape, and gold can at any time pass from one form to

prices of all the commodities in circulation, is a self-evident proposition. But how use-values, which are incommensurable with regard to each other, are to be exchanged, en masse, for the total sum of gold and silver in a country, is quite incomprehensible. If we start from the notion that all commodities together form one single commodity, of which each is but an aliquot part, we get the following beautiful result: The total commodity = x cwt. of gold; commodity A = an aliquot part of the total commodity = the same aliquot part of x cwt. of gold. This is stated in all seriousness by Montesquieu: " Si l'on compare la masse de l'or et de l'argent qui est dans le monde avec la somme des marchandises qui y sont, il est certain que chaque denrée ou marchandise, en particulier, pourra être comparée à une certaine portion de le masse entière. Supposons qu'il n'y ait qu'une seule denrée ou marchandise dans le monde, ou qu'il n'y ait qu'une seule qui s'achéte, et qu'elle se divise comme l'argent: Cette partie de cette marchandise repondra à une partie de la masse de l'argent; la moitié du total de l'une à la moitié du total de l'autre, &c. . . . l'établissement du prix des choses dépend toujours fondamentalement de la raison du total des choses au total des signes." (Montesquieu l. c. t III., pp. 122, 13.) As to the further development of this theory by Ricardo and his disciples, James Mill, Lord Overstone, and others, see "Critique of Political Economy," pp. 235, ff. John Stuart Mill, with his usual eclectic logic, understands how to hold at the same time the view of his father, James Mill, and the opposite view. On a comparison of the text of his compendium, "Principles of Pol. Econ.," with his preface to the first edition, in which preface he announces himself as the Adam Smith of his day — we do not know whether to admire more the simplicity of the man, or that of the public, who took him, in good faith, for the Adam Smith he announced himself to be, although he bears about as much resemblance to Adam Smith as say General Williams, of Kars, to the Duke of Wellington. The original researches of Mr. J. S. Mill, which are neither extensive nor profound, in the domain of political economy, will be found mustered in rank and file in his little work, " Some Unsettled Questions of Political Economy," which appeared in 1844. Locke asserts point blank the connexion between the absence of value in gold and silver, and the determination of their values by quantity alone, "Mankind having consented to put an imaginary value upon gold and silver . . . the intrinsik value, regarded in these metals, is nothing but the quantity." ("Some considerations," &c., 1691, Works Ed. 1777, vol. II., p. 15.)

the other.[1] But no sooner does coin leave the mint, than it immediately finds itself on the high-road to the melting pot. During their currency, coins wear away, some more, others less. Name and substance, nominal weight and real weight, begin their process of separation. Coins of the same denomination become different in value, because they are different in weight. The weight of gold fixed upon as the standard of prices, deviates from the weight that serves as the circulating medium, and the latter thereby ceases any longer to be a real equivalent of the commodities whose prices it realises. The history of coinage during the middle ages and down into the 18th century, records the ever renewed confusion arising from this cause. The natural tendency of circulation to convert coins into a mere semblance of what they profess to be, into a symbol of the weight of metal they are officially supposed to contain, is recognised by modern legislation, which fixes the loss of weight sufficient to demonetise a gold coin, or to make it no longer legal tender.

The fact that the currency of coins itself effects a separation between their nominal and their real weight, creating a distinction between them as mere pieces of metal on the one hand, and as coins with a definite function on the other—this fact implies the latent possibility of replacing metallic coins by tokens of some other material, by symbols serving the same purposes as coins. The practical difficulties in the way of coining extremely minute quantities of gold or silver, and the circumstance that at first the less precious metal is used as a measure of value instead of the more precious, copper instead

---

[1] It lies, of course, entirely beyond my purpose to take into consideration such details as the seigniorage on minting. I will, however, cite for the benefit of the romantic sycophant, Adam Müller, who admires the "generous liberality" with which the English Government coins gratuitously, the following opinion of Sir Dudley North: "Silver and gold, like other commodities, have their ebbings and flowings. Upon the arrival of quantities from Spain . . . it is carried into the Tower, and coined. Not long after there will come a demand for bullion to be exported again. If there is none, but all happens to be in coin, what then? Melt it down again; there's no loss in it, for the coining costs the owner nothing. Thus the nation has been abused, and made to pay for the twisting of straw for asses to eat. If the merchant were made to pay the price of the coinage, he would not have sent his silver to the Tower without consideration; and coined money would always keep a value above uncoined silver." (North, l. c., p. 18.) North was himself one of the foremost merchants in the reign of Charles II.

of silver, silver instead of gold, and that the less precious circulates as money until dethroned by the more precious—all these facts explain the parts historically played by silver and copper tokens as substitutes for gold coins. Silver and copper tokens take the place of gold in those regions of the circulation where coins pass from hand to hand most rapidly, and are subject to the maximum amount of wear and tear. This occurs where sales and purchases on a very small scale are continually happening. In order to prevent these satellites from establishing themselves permanently in the place of gold, positive enactments determine the extent to which they must be compulsorily received as payment instead of gold. The particular tracks pursued by the different species of coin in currency, run naturally into each other. The tokens keep company with gold, to pay fractional parts of the smallest gold coin; gold is, on the one hand, constantly pouring into retail circulation, and on the other hand is as constantly being thrown out again by being changed into tokens.[1]

The weight of metal in the silver and copper tokens is arbitrarily fixed by law. When in currency, they wear away even more rapidly than gold coins. Hence their functions are totally independent of their weight, and consequently of all value. The function of gold as coin becomes completely independent of the metallic value of that gold. Therefore things that are relatively without value, such as paper notes, can serve as coins in its place. This purely symbolic character is to a certain extent masked in metal tokens. In paper money it stands out plainly. In fact, ce n'est oue le premier pas qui coûte.

We allude here only to inconvertible paper money issued by

---

[1] If silver never exceed what is wanted for the smaller payments, it cannot be collected in sufficient quantities for the larger payments . . . the use of gold in the main payments necessarily implies also its use in the retail trade: those who have gold coin offering them for small purchases, and receiving with the commodity purchased a balance of silver in return; by which means the surplus of silver that would otherwise encumber the retail dealer, is drawn off and dispersed into general circulation. But if there is as much silver as will transact the small payments independent of gold, the retail trader must then receive silver for small purchases; and it must of necessity accumulate in his hands." (David Buchanan. "Inquiry into the Taxation and Commercial Policy of Great Britain." Edinburgh, 1844, pp. 248, 249.)

the State and having compulsory circulation. It has its immediate origin in the metallic currency. Money based upon credit implies on the other hand conditions, which from our standpoint of the simple circulation of commodities, are as yet totally unknown to us. But we may affirm this much, that just as true paper money takes its rise in the function of money as the circulating medium, so money based upon credit takes root spontaneously in the function of money as the means of payment.[1]

.The State puts in circulation bits of paper on which their various denominations, say £1, £5, &c., are printed. In so far as they actually take the place of gold to the same amount, their movement is subject to the laws that regulate the currency of money itself. A law peculiar to the circulation of paper money can spring up only from the proportion in which that paper money represents gold. Such a law exists; stated simply, it is as follows: the issue of paper money must not exceed in amount the gold (or silver as the case may be) which would actually circulate if not replaced by symbols. Now the quantity of gold·which the circulation can absorb, constantly fluctuates about a given level. Still, the mass of the circulating medium in a given country never sinks below a certain minimum easily ascertained by actual experience. The fact that this minimum mass continually undergoes changes in its constituent parts, or that the pieces of gold of which it consists are being constantly replaced by fresh ones, causes of course no change either in its amount or in the continuity of its circula-

[1] The mandarin Wan-mao-in, the Chinese Chancellor of the Exchequer, took it into his head one day to lay before the Son of Heaven a proposal that secretly aimed at converting the *assignats* of the empire into convertible bank notes. The assignats Committee, in its report of April, 1854, gives him a severe snubbing. Whether he also received the traditional drubbing with bamboos is not stated. The concluding part of the report is as follows: — "The Committee has carefully examined his proposal and finds that it is entirely in favour of the merchants, and that no advantage will result to the crown." (Arbeiten der Kaiserlich Russischen Gesandtschaft zu Peking über China. Aus dem Russischen von Dr. K. Abel und F. A. Mecklenburg. Erster Band. Berlin, 1858, pp. 47, 59.) In his evidence before the Committee of the House of Lords on the Bank Acts, a governor of the Bank of England says with regard to the abrasion of gold coins during currency: "Every year a fresh class of sovereigns becomes too light. The class which one year passes with full weight, loses enough by wear and tear to draw the scales next year against it." (House of Lords' Committee, 1848, n. 429.)

tion. It can therefore be replaced by paper symbols. If, on the other hand, all the conduits of circulation were to-day filled with paper money to the full extent of their capacity for absorbing money, they might to-morrow be overflowing in consequence of a fluctuation in the circulation of commodities. There would no longer be any standard. If the paper money exceed its proper limit, which is the amount of gold coins of the like denomination that can actually be current, it would, apart from the danger of falling into general disrepute, represent only that quantity of gold, which, in accordance with the laws of the circulation of commodities, is required, and is alone capable of being represented by paper. If the quantity of paper money issued be double what it ought to be, then, as a matter of fact, £1 would be the money-name not of $\frac{1}{4}$ of an ounce, but of $\frac{1}{8}$ of an ounce of gold. The effect would be the same as if an alteration had taken place in the function of gold as a standard of prices. Those values that were previously expressed by the price of £1 would now be expressed by the price of £2.

Paper-money is a token representing gold or money. The relation between it and the values of commodities is this, that the latter are ideally expressed in the same quantities of gold that are symbolically represented by the paper. Only in so far as paper-money represents gold, which like all other commodities has value, is it a symbol of value.[1]

Finally, some one may ask why gold is capable of being replaced by tokens that have no value? But, as we have already seen, it is capable of being so replaced only in so far as it functions exclusively as coin, or as the circulating

---

[1] The following passage from Fullarton shows the want of clearness on the part of even the best writers on money, in their comprehension of its various functions: "That, as far as concerns our domestic exchanges, all the monetary functions which are usually performed by gold and silver coins, may be performed as effectually by a circulation of inconvertible notes, having no value but that factitious and conventional value they derive from the law, is a fact which admits, I conceive, of no denial. Value of this description may be made to answer all the purposes of intrinsic value, and supersede even the necessity for a standard, provided only the quantity of issues be kept under due limitation." (Fullarton: "Regulation of Currencies," London, p. 210.) Because the commodity that serves as money is capable of being replaced in circulation by mere symbols of value, therefore its functions as a measure of value and a standard of prices are declared to be superfluous.

medium, and as nothing else. Now, money has other functions besides this one, and the isolated function of serving as the mere circulating medium is not necessarily the only one attached to gold coin, although this is the case with those abraded coins that continue to circulate. Each piece of money is a mere coin, or means of circulation, only so long as it actually circulates. But this is just the case with that minimum mass of gold, which is capable of being replaced by paper-money. That mass remains constantly within the sphere of circulation, continually functions as a circulating medium, and exists exclusively for that purpose. Its movement therefore represents nothing but the continued alternation of the inverse phases of the metamorphosis C—M—C, phases in which commodities confront their value-forms, only to disappear again immediately. The independent existence of the exchange value of a commodity is here a transient apparition, by means of which the commodity is immediately replaced by another commodity. Hence, in this process which continually makes money pass from hand to hand, the mere symbolical existence of money suffices. Its functional existence absorbs, so to say, its material existence. Being a transient and objective reflex of the prices of commodities, it serves only as a symbol of itself, and is therefore capable of being replaced by a token.[1] One thing is, however, requisite; this token must have an objective social validity of its own, and this the paper symbol acquires by its forced currency. This compulsory action of the State can take effect only within that inner sphere of circulation which is co-terminous with the territories of the community, but it is also only within that sphere that money completely responds to its function of being the circulating medium, or becomes coin.

[1] From the fact that gold and silver, so far as they are coins, or exclusively serve as the medium of circulation, become mere tokens of themselves, Nicholas Barbon deduces the right of Governments "to raise money," that is, to give to the weight of silver that is called a shilling the name of a greater weight, such as a crown; and so to pay creditors shillings, instead of crowns. "Money does wear and grow lighter by often telling over . . . It is the denomination and currency of the money that men regard in bargaining, and not the quantity of silver . . . 'Tis the public authority upon the metal that makes it money." (N. Barbon, l. c., pp. 29, 30, 25.)

SECTION 3.—MONEY.

The commodity that functions as a measure of value, and, either in its own person or by a representative, as the medium of circulation, is money. Gold (or silver) is therefore money. It functions as money, on the one hand, when it has to be present in its own golden person. It is then the money-commodity, neither merely ideal, as in its function of a measure of value, nor capable of being represented, as in its function of circulating medium. On the other hand, it also functions as money, when by virtue of its function, whether that function be performed in person or by representative, it congeals into the sole form of value, the only adequate form of existence of exchange-value, in opposition to use-value, represented by all other commodities.

a. Hoarding.

The continual movement in circuits of the two antithetical metamorphoses of commodities, or the never ceasing alternation of sale and purchase, is reflected in the restless currency of money, or in the function that money performs of a perpetuum mobile of circulation. But so soon as the series of metamorphoses is interrupted, so soon as sales are not supplemented by subsequent purchases, money ceases to be mobilised; it is transformed, as Boisguillebert says, from "meuble" into "immeuble," from movable into immovable, from coin into money.

With the very earliest development of the circulation of commodities, there is also developed the necessity, and the passionate desire, to hold fast the product of the first metamorphosis. This product is the transformed shape of the commodity, or its gold-chrysalis.[1] Commodities are thus sold not for the purpose of buying others, but in order to replace their commodity-form by their money-form. From being the mere means of effecting the circulation of commodities, this change of form becomes the end and aim. The changed form of the commodity is thus prevented from functioning as its uncondi-

[1] "Une richesse en argent n'est que . . . richesse en productions, convertie en argent." (Mercier de la Riviére, 1. c.) "Une valeur en productions n'a fait que changer de forme." (Id., p. 486.)

tionally alienable form, or as its merely transient money-form. The money becomes petrified into a hoard, and the seller becomes a hoarder of money.

In the early stages of the circulation of commodities, it is the surplus use-values alone that are converted into money. Gold and silver thus become of themselves social expressions for superfluity of wealth. This naïve form of hoarding becomes perpetuated in those communities in which the traditional mode of production is carried on for the supply of a fixed and limited circle of home wants. It is thus with the people of Asia, and particularly of the East Indies. Vanderlint, who fancies that the prices of commodities in a country are determined by the quantity of gold and silver to be found in it, asks himself why Indian commodities are so cheap. Answer: Because the Hindoos bury their money. From 1602 to 1734, he remarks, they buried 150 millions of pounds sterling of silver, which originally came from America to Europe.[1] In the 10 years from 1856 to 1866, England exported to India and China £120,000,000 in silver, which had been received in exchange for Australian gold. Most of the silver exported to China makes its way to India.

As the production of commodities further develops, every producer of commodities is compelled to make sure of the *nexus rerum* or the social pledge.[2] His wants are constantly making themselves felt, and necessitate the continual purchase of other people's commodities, while the production and sale of his own goods require time, and depend upon circumstances. In order then to be able to buy without selling, he must have sold previously without buying. This operation, conducted on a general scale, appears to imply a contradiction. But the precious metals at the sources of their production are directly exchanged for other commodities. And here we have sales (by the owners of commodities) without purchases (by the owners of gold or silver.)[3] And subsequent sales, by other

---

[1] " 'Tis by this practice they keep all their goods and manufactures at such low rates." (Vanderlint, l. c., p. 96.)

[2] "Money . . . is a pledge." (John Bellers: "Essays about the Poor, Manufacturers, Trade, Plantations, and Immorality," Lond., 1699, p. 13.)

[3] A purchase, in a "categorical" sense, implies that gold and silver are already the converted form of commodities, or the product of a sale.

producers, unfollowed by purchases, merely bring about the distribution of the newly produced precious metals among all the owners of commodities. In this way, all along the line of exchange, hoards of gold and silver of varied extent are accumulated. With the possibility of holding and storing up exchange value in the shape of a particular commodity, arises also the greed for gold. Along with the extension of circulation, increases the power of money, that absolutely social form of wealth ever ready for use. "Gold is a wonderful thing! Whoever possesses it is lord of all he wants. By means of gold one can even get souls into Paradise." (Columbus in his letter from Jamaica, 1503.) Since gold does not disclose what has been transformed into it, everything, commodity or not, is convertible into gold. Everything becomes saleable and buyable. The circulation becomes the great social retort into which everything is thrown, to come out again as a gold-crystal. Not even are the bones of saints, and still less are more delicate res sacrosanctæ extra commercium hominum able to withstand this alchemy.[1] Just as every qualitative difference between commodities is extinguished in money, so money, on its side, like the radical leveller that it is, does away with all distinctions.[2] But money itself is a commodity,

---

[1] Henry III., most Christian king of France, robbed cloisters of their relics, and turned them into money. It is well known what part the despoiling of the Delphic Temple, by the Phocians, played in the history of Greece. Temples with the ancients served as the dwellings of the gods of commodities. They were " sacred banks." With the Phœnicians, a trading people par excellence, money was the transmuted shape of everything. It was, therefore, quite in order that the virgins, who, at the feast of the Goddess of Love, gave themselves up to strangers, should offer to the goddess the piece of money they received.

[2] "Gold, yellow, glittering, precious gold!
Thus much of this, will make black white; foul, fair;
Wrong right; base, noble; old, young; coward, valiant.
. . . What this, you gods? Why, this
Will lug your priests and servants from your sides;
Pluck stout men's pillows from below their heads;
This yellow slave
Will knit and break religions; bless the accurs'd;
Make the hoar leprosy ador'd; place thieves,
And give them title, knee and approbation,
With senators on the bench; this is it,
That makes the wappen'd widow wed again:
. . . . . Come damned earth,
Thou common whore of mankind.".
(Shakespeare: Timon of Athens.)

an external object, capable of becoming the private property of any individual. Thus social power becomes the private power of private persons. The ancients therefore denounced money as subversive of the economical and moral order of things.[1] Modern society, which soon after its birth, pulled Plutus by the hair of his head from the bowels of the earth,[2] greets gold as its Holy Grail, as the glittering incarnation of the very principle of its own life.

A commodity, in its capacity of a use-value, satisfies a particular want, and is a particular element of material wealth. But the value of a commodity measures the degree of its attraction for all other elements of material wealth, and therefore measures the social wealth of its owner. To a barbarian owner of commodities, and even to a West-European peasant, value is the same as value-form, and therefore, to him the increase in his hoard of gold and silver is an increase in value. It is true that the value of money varies, at one time in consequence of a variation in its own value, at another, in consequence of a change in the value of commodities. But this, on the one hand, does not prevent 200 ounces of gold from still containing more value than 100 ounces, nor, on the other hand, does it hinder the actual metallic form of this article from continuing to be the universal equivalent form of all other commodities, and the immediate social incarnation of all human labour. The desire after hoarding is in its very nature unsatiable. In its qualitative aspect, or formally considered, money has no bounds to its efficacy, *i.e.*, it is the universal representative of material wealth, because it is directly convertible into any other commodity. But, at the same time, every actual sum of money is limited in amount, and therefore, as a

---

[1] " Οὐδὲν γὰρ ἀνθρώποισιν οἷον ἄργυρος
Κακὸν νόμισμα ἔβλαστε· τοῦτο καὶ πόλεις
Πορθεῖ, τόδ᾿ ἄνδρας ἐξανίστησίν δόμων.
Τόδ᾿ ἐκδιδάσκει καὶ παραλλάσσει φρένας
Χρηστὰς πρὸς αἰσχρὰ ἀνθρώποις ἔχειν
Καὶ παντὸς ἔργου δυσσέβειαν εἰδέναι.
(Sophocles, Antigone.)

[2] " ᾿Ελπιζούσης τῆς πλεονεξίας ἀνάξειν ἐκ τῶν μυχῶν τῆς γῆς αὐτὸν τὸν Πλούτωνα."
(Athen. Deipnos.)

means of purchasing, has only a limited efficacy. This antagonism between the quantitive limits of money and its qualitative boundlessness, continually acts as a spur to the hoarder in
his Sisyphus-like labour of accumulating. It is with him as it
is with a conqueror who sees in every new country annexed,
only a new boundary.

In order that gold may be held as money, and made to form
a hoard, it must be prevented from circulating, or from transforming itself into a means of enjoyment. The hoarder,
therefore, makes a sacrifice of the lusts of the flesh to his gold
fetish. He acts in earnest up to the Gospel of abstention. On
the other hand, he can withdraw from circulation no more than
what he has thrown into it in the shape of commodities. The
more he produces, the more he is able to sell. Hard work,
saving, and avarice, are, therefore, his three cardinal virtues,
and to sell much and buy little the sum of his political
economy.[1]

By the side of the gross form of a hoard, we find also its
æsthetic form in the possession of gold and silver articles.
This grows with the wealth of civil society. " Soyons riches ou
paraissons riches" (Diderot). In this way there is created,
on the one hand, a constantly extending market for gold and
silver, unconnected with their functions as money, and, on the
other hand, a latent source of supply, to which recourse is had
principally in times of crisis and social disturbance.

Hoarding serves various purposes in the economy of the
metallic circulation. Its first function arises out of the conditions to which the currency of gold and silver coins is subject. We have seen how, along with the continual fluctuations
in the extent and rapidity of the circulation of commodities
and in their prices, the quantity of money current unceasingly
ebbs and flows. This mass must, therefore, be capable of expansion and contraction. At one time money must be attracted
in order to act as circulating coin, at another, circulating coin
must be repelled in order to act again as more or less stagnant

---

[1] "Accrescere quanto più si può il numero de' venditori d'ogni merce, diminuere
quanto più si può il numero dei compratori, questi sono i cardini sui quali si
raggirano tutte le operazioni di economia politica." (Verri, l. c. p. 52.)

money. In order that the mass of money, actually current, may constantly saturate the absorbing power of the circulation, it is necessary that the quantity of gold and silver in a country be greater than the quantity required to function as coin. This condition is fulfilled by money taking the form of hoards. These reserves serve as conduits for the supply or withdrawal of money to or from the circulation, which in this way never overflows its banks.[1]

b. Means of Payment.

In the simple form of the circulation of commodities hitherto considered, we found a given value always presented to us in a double shape, as a commodity at one pole, as money at the opposite pole. The owners of commodities came therefore into contact as the respective representatives of what were already equivalents. But with the development of circulation, conditions arise under which the alienation of commodities becomes separated, by an interval of time, from the realisation of their prices. It will be sufficient to indicate the most simple of these conditions. One sort of article requires a longer, another a shorter time for its production. Again, the production of different commodities depends on different seasons of the year. One sort of commodity may be born on its own market place, another has to make a long journey to market. Commodity-owner No. 1, may therefore be ready to sell, before No. 2 is ready to buy. When the same transactions are continually repeated between the same persons, the conditions of sale are

---

[1] "There is required for carrying on the trade of the nation a determinate sum of specifick money, which varies, and is sometimes more, sometimes less, as the circumstances we are in require. . . . This ebbing and flowing of money supplies and accommodates itself, without any aid of Politicians. . . . The buckets work alternately; when money is scarce, bullion is coined; when bullion is scarce, money is melted." (Sir D. North, l. c., Postscript, p. 3.) John Stuart Mill, who for a long time was an official of the East India Company, confirms the fact that in India silver ornaments still continue to perform directly the functions of a hoard. The silver ornaments are brought out and coined when there is a high rate of interest, and go back again when the rate of interest falls. (J. S. Mill's Evidence. "Reports on Bank Acts," 1857, 2084.) According to a Parliamentary document of 1864, on the gold and silver import and export of India, the import of gold and silver in 1863 exceeded the export by £19,367,764. During the 8 years immediately preceding 1864, the excess of imports over exports of the precious metals amounted to £109,652,917. During this century far more than £200,000,000 has been coined in India.

regulated in accordance with the conditions of production. On the other hand, the use of a given commodity, of a house, for instance, is sold (in common parlance, let) for a definite period. Here, it is only at the end of the term that the buyer has actually received the use-value of the commodity. He therefore buys it before he pays for it. The vendor sells an existing commodity, the purchaser buys as the mere representative of money, or rather of future money. The vendor becomes a creditor, the purchaser becomes a debtor. Since the metamorphosis of commodities, or the development of their value-form, appears here under a new aspect, money also acquires a fresh function; it becomes the means of payment.

The character of creditor, or of debtor, results here from the simple circulation. The change in the form of that circulation stamps buyer and seller with this new die. At first, therefore, these new parts are just as transient and alternating as those of seller and buyer, and are in turns played by the same actors. But the opposition is not nearly so pleasant, and is far more capable of crystallization.[1] The same characters can, however, be assumed independently of the circulation of commodities. The class-struggles of the ancient world took the form chiefly of a contest between debtors and creditors, which in Rome ended in the ruin of the plebeian debtors. They were displaced by slaves. In the middle-ages the contest ended with the ruin of the feudal debtors, who lost their political power together with the economical basis on which it was established. Nevertheless, the money relation of debtor and creditor that existed at these two periods reflected only the deeper-lying antagonism between the general economical conditions of existence of the classes in question.

Let us return to the circulation of commodities. The appearance of the two equivalents, commodities and money, at the two poles of the process of sale, has ceased to be simultaneous. The money functions now, first as a measure of value

---

[1] The following shows the debtor and creditor relations existing between English traders at the beginning of the 18th century. "Such a spirit of cruelty reigns here in England among the men of trade, that is not to be met with in any other society of men, nor in any other kingdom of the world." ("An Essay on Credit and the Bankrupt Act," Lond., 1707, p. 2.)

in the determination of the price of the commodity sold; the price fixed by the contract measures the obligation of the debtor, or the sum of money that he has to pay at a fixed date. Secondly, it serves as an ideal means of purchase. Although existing only in the promise of the buyer to pay, it causes the commodity to change hands. It is not before the day fixed for payment that the means of payment actually steps into circulation, leaves the hand of the buyer for that of the seller. The circulating medium was transformed into a hoard, because the process stopped short after the first phase, because the converted shape of the commodity, viz., the money, was withdrawn from circulation. The means of payment enters the circulation, but only after the commodity has left it. The money is no longer the means that brings about the process. It only brings it to a close, by stepping in as the absolute form of existence of exchange value, or as the universal commodity. The seller turned his commodity into money, in order thereby to satisfy some want; the hoarder did the same in order to keep his commodity in its money-shape, and the debtor in order to be able to pay; if he do not pay, his goods will be sold by the sheriff. The value-form of commodities, money, is therefore now the end and aim of a sale, and that owing to a social necessity springing out of the process of circulation itself.

The buyer converts money back into commodities before he has turned commodities into money: in other words, he achieves the second metamorphosis of commodities before the first. The seller's commodity circulates, and realises its price, but only in the shape of a legal claim upon money. It is converted into a use-value before it has been converted into money. The completion of its first metamorphosis follows only at a later period.[1]

---

[1] It will be seen from the following quotation from my book which appeared in 1859, why I take no notice in the text of an opposite form: "Contrariwise, in the process M — C, the money can be alienated as a real means of purchase, and in that way, the price of the commodity can be realised before the use-value of the money is realised and the commodity actually delivered. This occurs constantly under the every-day form of pre-payments. And it is under this form, that the English government purchases opium from the ryots of India. . . . In these cases, however, the money always acts as a means of purchase. . . . Of course capital

The obligations falling due within a given period, represent the sum of the prices of the commodities, the sale of which gave rise to those obligations. The quantity of gold necessary to realise this sum, depends, in the first instance, on the rapidity of currency of the means of payment. That quantity is conditioned by two circumstances: first the relations between debtors and creditors form a sort of chain, in such a way that A, when he receives money from his debtor B, straightway hands it over to C his creditor, and so on; the second circumstance is the length of the intervals between the different due-days of the obligations. The continuous chain of payments, or retarded first metamorphoses, is essentially different from that interlacing of the series of metamorphoses which we considered on a former page. By the currency of the circulating medium, the connexion between buyers and sellers, is not merely expressed. This connexion is originated by, and exists in, the circulation alone. Contrariwise, the movement of the means of payment expresses a social relation that was in existence long before.

The fact that a number of sales take place simultaneously, and side by side, limits the extent to which coin can be replaced by the rapidity of currency. On the other hand, this fact is a new lever in economising the means of payment. In proportion as payments are concentrated at one spot, special institutions and methods are developed for their liquidation. Such in the middle ages were the *virements* at Lyons. The debts due to A from B, to B from C, to C from A, and so on, have only to be confronted with each other, in order to annul each other to a certain extent like positive and negative quantities. There thus remains only a single balance to pay. The greater the amount of the payments concentrated, the less is this balance relatively to that amount, and the less is the mass of the means of payment in circulation.

The function of money as the means of payment implies a contradiction without a terminus medius. In so far as the

also is advanced in the shape of money. . . . This point of view, however, does not fall within the horizon of simple circulation. ("Critique," &c., pp. 188.

payments balance one another, money functions only ideally as money of account, as a measure of value. In so far as actual payments have to be made, money does not serve as a circulating medium, as a mere transient agent in the interchange of products, but as the individual incarnation of social labour, as the independent form of existence of exchange value, as the universal commodity. This contradiction comes to a head in those phases of industrial and commercial crises which are known as monetary crises.[1] Such a crisis occurs only where the ever-lengthening chain of payments, and an artificial system of settling them, has been fully developed. Whenever there is a general and extensive disturbance of this mechanism, no matter what its cause, money becomes suddenly and immediately transformed, from its merely ideal shape of money of account, into hard cash. Profane commodities can no longer replace it. The use-value of commodities becomes valueless, and their value vanishes in the presence of its own independent form. On the eve of the crisis, the bourgeois, with the self-sufficiency that springs from intoxicating prosperity, declares money to be a vain imagination. Commodities alone are money. But now the cry is everywhere: money alone is a commodity! As the hart pants after fresh water, so pants his soul after money, the only wealth.[2] In a crisis, the antithesis between commodities and their value-form, money, becomes heightened into an absolute contradiction. Hence, in such events, the form under which money appears is of no importance. The money famine continues,

---

[1] The monetary crisis referred to in the text, being a phase of every crisis, must be clearly distinguished from that particular form of crisis, which also is called a monetary crisis, but which may be produced by itself as an independent phenomenon in such a way as to react only indirectly on industry and commerce. The pivot of these crises is to be found in moneyed capital, and their sphere of direct action is therefore the sphere of that capital, viz., banking, the stock exchange, and finance.

[2] "The sudden reversion from a system of credit to a system of hard cash heaps theoretical fright on top of the practical panic; and the dealers by whose agency circulation is affected, shudder before the impenetrable mystery in which their own economical relations are involved" (Karl Marx, l. c. p. 198). "The poor stand still, because the rich have no money to employ them, though they have the same land and hands to provide victuals and clothes, as ever they had; . . . which is the true Riches of a Nation, and not the money." (John Bellers: "Proposals for raising a College of Industry." Lond. 1695. p. 3.)

whether payments have to be made in gold or in credit money such as bank notes.[1]

If we now consider the sum total of the money current during a given period, we shall find that, given the rapidity of currency of the circulating medium and of the means of payment, it is equal to the sum of the prices to be realised, plus the sum of the payments falling due, minus the payments that balance each other, minus finally the numbér of circuits in which the same piece of coin serves in turn as means of circulation anJ of payment. Hence, even when prices, rapidity of currency, and the extent of the economy in payments, are given, the quantity of money current and the mass of commodities circulating during a given period, such as a day, no longer correspond. Money that represents commodities long withdrawn from circulation, continues to be current. Commodities circulate, whose equivalent in money will not appear on the scene till some future day. Moreover, the debts contracted each day, and the payments falling due on the same day, are quite incommensurable quantities.[2]

Credit-money springs directly out of the function of money as a means of payment. Certificates of the debts owing for the purchased commodities circulate for the purpose of trans-

[1] The following shows how such times are exploited by the "amis du commerce." "On one occasion (1839) an old grasping banker (in the city) in his private room raised the lid of the desk he sat over, and displayed to a friend rolls of banknotes, saying with intense glee there were £600,000 of them, they were held to make money tight, and would all be let out after three o'clock on the same day." ("The Theory of Exchanges. The Bank Charter Act of 1844." Lond. 1864. p. 81.) The *Observer*, a semi-official government organ, contained the following paragraph on 24th April, 1864: "Some very curious rumours are current of the means which have been resorted to in order to create a scarcity of Banknotes. . . . . Questionable as it would seem, to suppose that any trick of the kind would be adopted, the report has been so universal that it really deserves mention."

[2] "The amount of purchases or contracts entered upon during the course of any given day, will not affect the quantity of money afloat on that particular day, but, in the vast majority of cases, will resolve themselves into multifarious drafts upon the quantity of money which may be afloat at subsequent dates more or less distant. . . . . The bills granted or credits opened, to-day, need have no resemblance whatever, either in quantity, amount, or duration, to those granted or entered upon to-morrow or next day; nay, many of to-day's bills, and credits, when due, fall in with a mass of liabilities whose origins traverse a range of antecedent dates altogether indefinite, bills at 12, 6, 3 months or 1 often aggregating together to swell the common liabilities of one particular day. . . . " ("The Currency Theory Reviewed: a letter to the Scottish people." By a Banker in England. Edinburgh, 1845, pp. 29, 30 passim.)

ferring those debts to others. On the other hand, to the same extent as the system of credit is extended, so is the function of money as a means of payment. In that character it takes various forms peculiar to itself under which it makes itself at home in the sphere of great commercial transactions. Gold and silver coin, on the other hand, are mostly relegated to the sphere of retail trade.[1]

When the production of commodities has sufficiently extended itself, money begins to serve as the means of payment beyond the sphere of the circulation of commodities. It becomes the commodity that is the universal subject-matter of all contracts.[2] Rents, taxes, and such like payments are transformed from payments in kind into money payments. To what extent this transformation depends upon the general conditions of production, is shown, to take one example, by the fact that the Roman Empire twice failed in its attempt to levy all contributions in money. The unspeakable misery of the French agricultural population under Louis XIV., a misery so eloquently denounced by Boisguillebert, Marshal, Vauban, and others, was due not only to the weight of the taxes, but also to the conversion of taxes in kind into money taxes.[3]

[1] As an example of how little ready money is required in true commercial operations, I give below a statement by one of the largest London houses of its yearly receipts and payments. Its transactions during the year 1856, extending to many milions of pounds sterling, are here reduced to the scale of one million.

RECEIPTS.		PAYMENTS.	
Bankers' and Merchants' Bills payable after date, -	£533,596	Bills payable after date, -	£302,674
Cheques on Bankers, &c., payable on demand, -	357,715	Cheques on London Bankers,	663,672
Country Notes, - - -	9,627	Bank of England Notes, -	22,743
Bank of England Notes, -	68,554	Gold - - - - -	9,427
Gold - - -	28,089	Silver and Copper, - -	1,484
Silver and Copper, - -	1,486		
Post Office Orders, - -	933		
Total, -	£1,000,000	Total, -	£1,000,000

"Report from the Select Committee on the Bank Acts, July, 1858," p. lxxi.

[2] "The course of trade being thus turned, from exchanging of goods for goods, or delivering and taking, to selling and paying, all the bargains . . . are now stated upon the foot of a price in money." "An Essay upon Publick Credit." 3rd Ed. Lond., 1710, p. 8.)

[3] "L'argent. . . est devenu le bourreau de toutes choses." Finance is the "alambic, qui a fait évaporer une quantité effroyable de biens et de denrées pour

In Asia, on the other hand, the fact that state taxes are chiefly composed of rents payable in kind, depends on conditions of production that are reproduced with the regularity of natural phenomena. And this mode of payment tends in its turn to maintain the ancient form of production. It is one of the secrets of the conservation of the Ottoman Empire. If the foreign trade, forced upon Japan by Europeans, should lead to the substitution of money rents for rents in kind, it will be all up with the exemplary agriculture of that country. The narrow economical conditions under which that agriculture is carried on, will be swept away.

In every country, certain days of the year become by habit recognised settling days for various large and recurrent payments. These dates depend, apart from other revolutions in the wheel of reproduction, on conditions closely connected with the seasons. They also regulate the dates for payments that have no direct connexion with the circulation of commodities such as taxes, rents, and so on. The quantity of money requisite to make the payments, falling due on those dates all over the country, causes periodical, though merely superficial, perturbations in the economy of the medium of payment.[1]

From the law of the rapidity of currency of the means of payment, it follows that the quantity of the means of payment required for all periodical payments, whatever their source, is in inverse proportion to the length of their periods.[2]

---

faire ce fatal précis." "L'argent déclare la guerre à tout le genre humain." (Bois guillebert: "Dissertation sur la nature des richesses, de l'argent et des tributs." Edit. Daire. Economistes financiers. Paris, 1843, t. i., pp. 413, 419, 417.)

[1] "On Whitsuntide, 1824," says Mr. Craig before the Commons' Committee of 1826, "there was such an immense demand for notes upon the banks of Edinburgh, that by 11 o'clock they had not a note left in their custody. They sent round to all the different banks to borrow, but could not get them, and many of the transactions were adjusted by slips of paper only; yet by three o'clock the whole of the notes were returned into the banks from which they had issued! It was a mere transfer from hand to hand." Although the average effective circulation of bank-notes in Scotland is less than three millions sterling, yet on certain pay days in the year, every single note in the possession of the bankers, amounting in the whole to about £7,000,000, is called into activity. On these occasions the notes have a single and specific function to perform, and so soon as they have performed it, they flow back into the various banks from which they issued. (See John Fullarton, "Regulation of Currencies." Lond: 1844, p. 85 note.) In explanation it should be stated, that in Scotland, at the date of Fullarton's work, notes and not cheques were used to withdraw deposits.

[2] To the question. "If there were occasion to raise 40 millions p.a., whether the

The development of money into a medium of payment makes it necessary to accumulate money against the dates fixed for the payment of the sums owing. While hoarding, as a distinct mode of acquiring riches, vanishes with the progress of civil society, the formation of reserves of the means of payment grows with that progress.

c. Universal Money.

When money leaves the home sphere of circulation, it strips off the local garbs which it there assumes, of a standard of prices, of coin, of tokens, and of a symbol of value, and returns to its original form of bullion. In the trade between the markets of the world, the value of commodities is expressed so as to be universally recognised. Hence their independent value-form also, in these cases, confronts them under the shape of universal money. It is only in the markets of the world that money acquires to the full extent the character of the commodity whose bodily form is also the immediate social incarnation of human labour in the abstract. Its real mode of existence in this sphere adequately corresponds to its ideal concept.

Within the sphere of home circulation, there can be but one commodity which, by serving as a measure of value, becomes money. In the markets of the world a double measure of value holds sway, gold and silver.[1]

same 6 millions (gold) . . . would suffice for such revolutions and circulations thereof, as trade requires," Petty replies in his usual masterly manner, "I answer yes: for the expense being 40 millions, if the revolutions were in such short circles, viz., weekly, as happens among poor artizans and labourers, who receive and pay every Saturday, then $\frac{40}{52}$ parts of 1 million of money would answer these ends; but if the circles be quarterly, according to our custom of paying rent, and gathering taxes, then 10 millions were requisite. Wherefore, supposing payments in general to be of a mixed circle between one week and 13, then add 10 millions to $\frac{40}{52}$, the half of which will be 5½, so as if we have 5½ millions we have enough." (William Petty: "Political Anatomy of Ireland." 1672. Edit.: Lond. 1691, pp. 13, 14.)

[1] Hence the absurdity of every law prescribing that the banks of a country shall form reserves of that precious metal alone which circulates at home. The "pleasant difficulties" thus self-created by the Bank of England, are well known. On the subject of the great epochs in the history of the changes in the relative value of gold and silver, see Karl Marx, l. c. p. 215 sq. Sir Robert Peel, by his Bank Act of 1844, sought to tide over the difficulty, by allowing the Bank of England to issue notes against silver bullion, on condition that the reserve of silver should never exceed more than one-fourth of the reserve of gold. The value of silver being for

Money of the world serves as the universal medium of payment, as the universal means of purchasing, and as the universally recognised embodiment of all wealth. Its function as a means of payment in the settling of international balances is its chief one. Hence the watchword of the mercantilists, balance of trade.[1] Gold and silver serve as international

that purpose estimated at its price in the London market.—Note to the 4th German edition.—We find ourselves once more in a period of a marked change in the relative values of gold and silver. About 25 years ago the ratio of gold to silver was 15.5 to 1, now it is about 22 to 1, and silver is continually falling against gold. This is essentially a result of a revolution in the process of production of these two metals. Formerly gold was obtained almost exclusively by washing alluvial strata containing gold, the products of disintegration of gold-carrying rocks. But now this method is no longer sufficient and has been crowded to the rear by the mining of quartz layers containing gold, a . iod formerly consi d as secondary, although well known even to the ancients (Diodorus, III, 12-14). On the other hand, immense new silver deposits were discovered in the American Rocky Mountains, and these as well as the Mexican silver mines opened u, 1 means of railroads, which permitted the influx of modern machinery and fuel and thereby reduced the cost and increased the output of silver mining. But there is a great difference in the way in which both metals occur in the cre beds. The gold is generally solid, but scattered in minute particles through 1 c quartz layers. The whole diggings must therefore be crushed and the gold washed out or extracted by means of quicksilver. Frequently one million grams of quartz do not contain more than 1 to 3 grams of gold, and rarely more than 30 to 60 grams. Silver, on the other hand, is rarely found in the pure state, but it occurs in some ores which are easily separated from the dross and contain as much as 40 to 90% of silver. Or smaller quantities of it are found in ores like copper, lead, etc., which are themselves worth mining. This alone is sufficient to show that the work of producing gold has rather increased, while that of producing silver has certainly decreased, and this quite naturally explains the fall in the value of silver. This fall in value would express itself in a still greater fall of price, if the price of silver were not held up even now by artificial means. The silver deposits of America, however, have been made accessible only to a small extent, and there is, consequently, every prospect of a continued fall in the value of silver. This must be further promoted by the relative decrease of the demand for silver for articles of use and luxury, its displacement by plated wares, aluminum, etc. Judge, then, of the utopianism of the bimetallist illusion that a forced international quotation could raise silver to its old value of 15.5 to 1. The chances are rather that silver will lose more and more of its character as money on the world market. F. E.

[1] The opponents, themselves, of the mercantile system, a system which considered the settlement of surplus trade balances in gold and silver as the aim of international trade, entirely misconceived the functions of money of the world. I have shown by the example of Ricardo in what way their false conception of the laws that regulate the quantity of the circulating medium, is reflected in their equally false conception of the international movement in the precious metals (l. c. pp. 150 sq.). His erroneous dogma: "An unfavourable balance of trade never arises but from a redundant currency. . . . The exportation of the coin is caused by its cheapness, and is not the effect, but the cause of an unfavourable balance," already occurs in Barbon: "The Balance of Trade, if there be one, is not the cause of sending away the money out of a nation; but that proceeds from the difference of the value of bullion in every country." (N. Barbon; l. c. pp. 59, 60.) MacCulloch in "the Literature of Political Economy, a classified catalogue, Lond. 1845,"

means of purchasing chiefly and necessarily in those periods
when the customary equilibrium in the interchange of products
between different nations is suddenly disturbed. And lastly,
it serves as the universally recognised embodiment of social
wealth, whenever the question is not of buying or paying, but
of transferring wealth from one country to another, and whenever this transference in the form of commodities is rendered
impossible, either by special conjunctures in the markets, or
by the purpose itself that is intended.[1]

Just as every country needs a reserve of money for its home
circulation, so, too, it requires one for external circulation in
the markets of the world. The functions of hoards, therefore,
arise in part out of the function of money, as the medium of
the home circulation and home payments, and in part out
of its function of money of the world.[2] For this latter function, the genuine money-commodity, actual gold and silver, is
necessary. On that account, Sir James Steuart, in order to
distinguish them from their purely local substitutes, calls gold
and silver "money of the world."

The current of the stream of gold and silver is a double one.
On the one hand, it spreads itself from its sources over all the
markets of the world, in order to become absorbed, to various
extents, into the different national spheres of circulation, to
fill the conduits of currency, to replace abraded gold and silver

praises Barbon for this anticipation, but prudently passes over the naïve forms, in
which Barbon clothes the absurd suppositoin on which the "currency principle" is
based. The absence of real criticism and even of honesty, in that catalogue, cul-
minates in the sections devoted to the history of the theory of money; the reason
is that MacCulloch in this part of the work is flattering Lord Overstone whom he
calls "fecile princeps argentariorum."

[1] For instance, in subsidies, money loans for carrying on wars or for enabling
banks to resume cash payments, &c., it is the money form, and no other, of value
that may be wanted.

[2] I would desire, indeed, no more convincing evidence of the competency of the
machinery of the hoards in specie-paying countries to perform every necessary office
of international adjustment, without any sensible aid from the general circulation,
than the facility with which France, when but just recovering from the shock of a
destructive foreign invasion, completed within the space of 27 months the payment
of her forced contribution of nearly 20 millions to the allied powers, and a considerable proportion of the sum in specie, without any perceptible contraction or
derangement of her domestic currency, or even any alarming fluctuation of her
exchanges." (Fullarton, l. c., p. 134.)—Note to the 4th German edition.—A still
more convincing illustration is given by the ease with which the same France, in
1871 to 1873, was able to pay off in 30 months a war indemnity ten times larger,
and to a considerable extent also in metal money. F. E.

coins, to supply the material of articles of luxury, and to petrify into hoards.[1] This first current is started by the countries that exchange their labour, realise in commodities, for the labour embodied in the precious metals by gold and silver-producing countries. On the other hand, there is a continual flowing backwards and forwards of gold and silver between the different national spheres of circulation, a current whose motion depends on the ceaseless fluctuations in the course of exchange.[2]

Countries in which the bourgeois form of production is developed to a certain extent, limit the hoards concentrated in the strong rooms of the banks to the minimum required for the proper performance of their peculiar functions.[3] Whenever these hoards are strikingly above their average level, it is, with some exceptions, an indication of stagnation in the circulation of commodities, of an interruption in the even flow of their metamorphoses.[4]

[1] "L'argent se partage entre les nations relativement au besoin qu'elles en ont. . . . étant toujours attiré par les productions." (Le Trosne l. c., p. 916.) "The mines which are continually giving gold and silver, do give sufficient to supply such a needful balance to every nation." (J. Vanderlint, l. c., p. 40.)

[2] "Exchanges rise and fall every week, and at some particular times in the year run high against a nation, and at other times run as high on the contrary." (N. Barbon, l. c., p. 39.)

[3] These various functions are liable to come into dangerous conflict with one another whenever gold and silver have also to serve as a fund for the conversion of bank-notes.

[4] "What money is more than of absolute necessity for a Home Trade, is dead stock . . . and brings no profit to that country it's kept in, but as it is transported in trade, as well as imported." (John Bellers, Essays, p. 12.) "What if we have too much coin? We may melt down the heaviest and turn it into the splendour of plate, vessels or utensils of gold or silver; or send it out as a commodity, where the same is wanted or desired; or let it out at interest, where interest is high." (W. Petty: "Quantulumcunque," p. 39.) "Money is but the fat of the Body Politick, whereof too much doth as often hinder its agility, as too little makes it sick . . . . as fat lubricates the motion of the muscles, feeds in want of victuals, fills up the uneven cavities, and beautifies the body; so doth money in the state quicken its action, feeds from abroad in time of dearth at home; evens accounts . . and beautifies the whole; altho more especially the particular persons that have it in plenty." (W. Petty. "Political Anatomy of Ireland," p. 14.)

PART II.

THE TRANSFORMATION OF MONEY INTO CAPITAL.

CHAPTER IV.

THE GENERAL FORMULA FOR CAPITAL.

THE circulation of commodities is the starting point of capital. The production of commodities, their circulation, and that more developed form of their circulation called commerce, these form the historical groundwork from which it rises. The modern history of capital dates from the creation in the 16th century of a world-embracing commerce and a world-embracing market.

If we abstract from the material substance of the circulation of commodities, that is, from the exchange of the various use-values, and consider only the economic forms produced by this process of circulation, we find its final result to be money: this final product of the circulation of commodities is the first form in which capital appears.

As a matter of history, capital, as opposed to landed property, invariably takes the form at first of money; it appears as moneyed wealth, as the capital of the merchant and of the usurer.[1] But we have no need to refer to the origin of capital in order to discover that the first form of appearance of capital is money. We can see it daily under our very eyes.

---

[1] The contrast between the power, based on the personal relations of dominion and servitude, that is conferred by landed property, and the impersonal power that is given by money, is well expressed by the two French proverbs, "Nulle terre sans seigneur," and "L'argent n'a pas de maître."

All new capital, to commence with, comes on the stage, that is, on the market, whether of commodities, labour, or money, even in our days, in the shape of money that by a definite process has to be transformed into capital.

The first distinction we notice between money that is money only, and money that is capital, is nothing more than a difference in their form of circulation.

The simplest form of the circulation of commodities is C— M—C, the transformation of commodities into money, and the change of the money back again into commodities; or selling in order to buy. But alongside of this form we find another specifically different form: M—C—M, the transformation of money into commodities, and the change of commodities back again into money; or buying in order to sell. Money that circulates in the latter manner is thereby transformed into, becomes capital, and is already potentially capital.

Now let us examine the circuit M—C—M a little closer. It consists, like the other, of two antithetical phases. In the first phase, M—C, or the purchase, the money is changed into a commodity. In the second phase, C—M, or the sale, the commodity is changed back again into money. The combination of these two phases constitutes the single movement whereby money is exchanged for a commodity and the same commodity is again exchanged for money; whereby a commodity is bought in order to be sold, or, neglecting the distinction in form between buying and selling, whereby a commodity is bought with money, and then money is bought with a commodity.[1] The result, in which the phases of the process vanish, is the exchange of money for money, M—M. If I purchase 2000 lbs. of cotton for £100, and resell the 2000 lbs. of cotton for £110, I have, in fact, exchanged £100 for £110, money for money.

Now it is evident that the circuit M—C—M would be absurd and without meaning if the intention were to exchange by this means two equal sums of money, £100 for £100. The

---

[1] "Avec de l'argent on achète des marchandises, et avec des marchandises on achète de l'argent." (Mercier de la Raviere: "L'ordre naturel et essentiel des sociétés politiques," p. 543.)

miser's plan would be far simpler and surer; he sticks to his £100 instead of exposing it to the dangers of circulation. And yet, whether the merchant who has paid £100 for his cotton sells it for £110, or lets it go for £100, or even £50, his money has, at all events, gone through a characteristic and original movement, quite different in kind from that which it goes through in the hands of the peasant who sells corn, and with the money thus set free buys clothes. We have therefore to examine first the distinguishing characteristics of the forms of the circuits M—C—M and C—M—C, and in doing this the real difference that underlies the mere difference of form will reveal itself.

Let us see, in the first place, what the two forms have in common.

Both circuits are resolvable into the same two antithetical phases, C—M, a sale, and M—C, a purchase. In each of these phases the same material elements—a commodity, and money, and the same economical dramatis personæ, a buyer and a seller—confront one another. Each circuit is the unity of the same two antithetical phases, and in each case this unity is brought about by the intervention of three contracting parties, of whom one only sells, another only buys, while the third both buys and sells.

What, however, first and foremost distinguishes the circuit C—M—C from the circuit M—C—M, is the inverted order of succession of the two phases. The simple circulation of commodities begins with a sale and ends with a purchase, while the circulation of money as capital begins with a purchase and ends with a sale. In the one case both the starting-point and the goal are commodities, in the other they are money. In the first form the movement is brought about by the intervention of money, in the second by that of a commodity.

In the circulation C—M—C, the money is in the end converted into a commodity, that serves as a use-value; it is spent once for all. In the inverted form, M—C—M, on the contrary, the buyer lays out money in order that, as a seller, he may recover money. By the purchase of his commodity he throws money into circulation, in order to withdraw it again by the sale of the same commodity. He lets the money go, but only with the sly intention of getting it back again. The money, therefore, is not spent, it is merely advanced.[1]

In the circuit C—M—C, the same piece of money changes its place twice. The seller gets it from the buyer and pays it away to another seller. The complete circulation, which begins with the receipt, concludes with the payment, of money for commodities. It is the very contrary in the circuit M—C—M. Here it is not the piece of money that changes its place twice, but the commodity. The buyer takes it from the hands of the seller and passes it into the hands of another buyer. Just as in the simple circulation of commodities the double change of·place of the same piece of money effects its passage from one hand into another, so here the double change of place of the same commodity brings about the reflux of the money to its point of departure.

Such reflux is not dependent on the commodity being sold for more than was paid for it. This circumstance influences only the amount of the money that comes back. The reflux itself takes place, so soon as the purchased commodity is resold, in other words, so soon as the circuit M—C—M is completed. We have here, therefore, a palpable difference between the circulation of money as capital, and its circulation as mere money.

The circuit C—M—C comes completely to an end, so soon as the money brought in by the sale of one commodity is abstracted again by the purchase of another.

If, nevertheless, there follows a reflux of money to its starting point, this can only happen through a renewal or repetition of the operation. If I sell a quarter of corn for £3, and with this £3 buy clothes, the money, so far as I am concerned, is spent and done with. It belongs to the clothes merchant. If I now sell a second quarter of corn, money indeed flows back to me, not however as a sequel to the first transaction,

---

[1] "When a thing is bought in order to be sold again, the sum employed is called money advanced; when it is bought not to be sold, it may be said to be expended."— (James Steuart: "Works," &c. Edited by Gen. Sir James Steuart, his son. Lond., 1805. V. I., p. 274.)

but in consequence of its repetition. The money again leaves me, so soon as I complete this second transaction by a fresh purchase. Therefore, in the circuit C—M—C, the expenditure of money has nothing to do with its reflux. On the other hand, in M—C—M, the reflux of the money is conditioned by the very mode of its expenditure. Without this reflux, the operation fails, or the process is interrupted and incomplete, owing to the absence of its complementary and final phase, the sale.

The circuit C—M—C starts with one commodity, and finishes with another, which falls out of circulation and into consumption. Consumption, the satisfaction of wants, in one word, use-value, is its end and aim. The circuit M—C—M, on the contrary, commences with money and ends with money. Its leading motive, and the goal that attracts it, is therefore mere exchange value.

In the simple circulation of commodities, the two extremes of the circuit have the same economic form. They are both commodities, and commodities of equal value. But they are also use-values differing in their qualities, as, for example, corn and clothes. The exchange of products, of the different materials in which the labour of society is embodied, forms here the basis of the movement. It is otherwise in the circulation M—C—M, which at first sight appears purposeless, because tautological. Both extremes have the same economic form. They are both money, and therefore are not qualitatively different use-values; for money is but the converted form of commodities, in which their particular use-values vanish. To exchange £100 for cotton, and then this same cotton again for £100, is merely a roundabout way of exchanging money for money, the same for the same, and appears to be an operation just as purposeless as it is absurd.[1]

---

[1] "On n'échange pas de l'argent contre de l'argent," says Mercier de la Rivière to the Mercantilists (l. c., p. 486). In a work, which, ex professo, treats of "trade" and "speculation," occurs the following: "All trade consists in the exchange of things of different kinds; and the advantage" (to the merchant?) "arises out of this difference. To exchange a pound of bread against a pound of bread . . . . would be attended with no advantage; . . . . Hence trade is advantageously contrasted with gambling, which consists in a mere exchange of money for money." (Th. Corbet, "An Inquiry into the Causes and Modes of the Wealth of Individuals;

One sum of money is distinguishable from another only by its amount. The character and tendency of the process M—C —M, is therefore not due to any qualitative difference between its extremes, both being money, but solely to their quantitative difference. More money is withdrawn from circulation at the finish than was thrown into it at the start. The cotton that was bought for £100 is perhaps resold for £100+£10 or £110. The exact form of this process is therefore M—C—M′, where M′=M+ $\triangle$ M=the original sum advanced, plus an increment. This increment or excess over the original value I call "surplus-value." The value originally advanced, therefore, not only remains intact while in circulation, but adds to itself a surplus-value or expands itself. It is this movement that converts it into capital.

Of course it is also possible, that in C—M—C, the two extremes C—C, say corn and clothes, may represent different quantities of value. The farmer may sell his corn above its value, or may buy the clothes at less than their value. He may, on the other hand, "be done" by the clothes merchant. Yet, in the form of circulation now under consideration, such differences in value are purely accidental. The fact that the corn and the clothes are equivalents, does not deprive the process of all meaning, as it does in M—C—M. The equivalence of their values is rather a necessary condition to its normal course.

The repetition or renewal of the act of selling in order to buy, is kept within bounds by the very object it aims at, namely, consumption or the satisfaction of definite wants, an

or the principles of Trade and Speculation explained." London, 1841, p. 5.) Although Corbet does not see that M—M, the exchange of money for money, is the characteristic form of circulation, not only of merchants' capital but of all capital, yet at least he acknowledges that this form is common to gambling and to one species of trade, viz., speculation: but then comes MacCulloch and makes out, that to buy in order to sell, is to speculate, and thus the difference between Speculation and Trade vanishes. "Every transaction in which an individual buys produce in order to sell it again, is, in fact, a speculation." (MacCulloch: "A Dictionary Practical, &c., of Commerce." Lond., 1847, p. 1058.) With much more naïveté, Pinto, the Pindar of the Amsterdam Stock Exchange, remarks, "Le commerce est un jeu: (taken from Locke) et ce n'est pas avec des gueux qu'on peut gagner. Si l'on gagnait long-temps en tout avec tous, il faudrait rendre de bon accord les plus grandes parties du profit pour recommencer le jeu." (Pinto: "Traité de la Circulation et du Crédit." Amsterdam, 1771, p. 231.)

aim that lies altogether outside the sphere of circulation. But when we buy in order to sell, we, on the contrary, begin and end with the same thing, money, exchange-value; and thereby the movement becomes interminable. No doubt, M becomes M+△ M, £100 become £110. But when viewed in their qualitative aspect alone, £110 are the same as £100, namely money; and considered quantitatively, £110 is, like £100, a sum of definite and limited value. If now, the £110 be spent as money, they cease to play their part. They are no longer capital. Withdrawn from circulation, they become petrified into a hoard, and though they remained in that state till doomsday, not a single farthing would accrue to them. If, then, the expansion of value is once aimed at, there is just the same inducement to augment the value of the £110 as that of the £100; for both are but limited expressions for exchange-value, and therefore both have the same vocation to approach, by quantitative increase, as near as possible to absolute wealth. Momentarily, indeed, the value originally advanced, the £100 is distinguishable from the surplus value of £10 that is annexed to it during circulation; but the distinction vanishes immediately. At the end of the process we do not receive with one hand the original £100, and with the other, the surplus-value of £10. We simply get a value of £110, which is in exactly the same condition and fitness for commencing the expanding process, as the original £100 was. Money ends the movement only to begin it again.[1] Therefore, the final result of every separate circuit, in which a purchase and consequent sale are completed, forms of itself the starting point of a new circuit. The simple circulation of commodities—selling in order to buy—is a means of carrying out a purpose unconnected with circulation, namely, the appropriation of use-values, the satisfaction of wants. The circulation of money as capital is, on the contrary, an end in itself, for the expansion of value takes place only within this constantly

---

[1] "Capital is divisible . . . . into the original capital and the profit, the increment to the capital . . . . although in practice this profit is immediately turned into capital, and set in motion with the original." (F. Engels, "Umrisse zu einer Kritik der Nationalökonomie, in: Deutsch-Französische Jahrbücher, herausgegeben von Arnold Ruge und Karl Marx." Paris, 1844, p. 99.)

renewed movement. The circulation of capital has therefore no limits.[1] Thus the conscious representative of this movement, the possessor of money becomes a capitalist. His person, or rather his pocket, is the point from which the money starts and to which it returns. The expansion of value, which is the objective basis or main-spring of the circulation M—C—M, becomes his subjective aim, and it is only in so far as the appropriation of ever more and more wealth in the abstract becomes the sole motive of his operations, that he functions as a capitalist, that is, as capital personified and endowed with consciousness and a will. Use-values must therefore never be looked upon as the real aim of the capitalist;[2] neither must the profit on any single transaction. The restless never-ending process of profit-making alone is what he aims

[1] Aristotle opposes Œconomic to Chrematistic. He starts from the former. So far as it is the art of gaining a livelihood, it is limited to procuring those articles that are necessary to existence, and useful either to a household or the state. "True wealth (ὁ ἀληθινὸς πλοῦτος) consists of such values in use; for the quantity of possessions of this kind, capable of making life pleasant, is not unlimited. There is, however, a second mode of acquiring things, to which we may by preference and with correctness give the name of Chrematistic, and in this case, there appear to be no limits to riches and possessions. Trade (ἡ καπηλικὴ is literally retail trade, and Aristotle takes this kind because in it values in use predominate) does not in its nature belong to Chrematistic, for here the exchange has reference only to what is necessary to themselves (the buyer or seller)." Therefore, as he goes on to show, the original form of trade was barter, but with the extension of the latter, there arose the necessity for money. On the discovery of money, barter of necessity developed into καπηλικὴ into trading in commodities, and this again, in opposition to its original tendency, grew into Chrematistic, into the art of making money. Now Chrematistic is distinguishable from Œconomic in this way, that "in the case of Chrematistic, circulation is the source of riches (ποιητικὴ χρημάτων . . . . διὰ χρημάτων διαβολῆς). And it appears to revolve about money, for money is the beginning and end of this kind of exchange (τὸ γὰρ νόμισμα στοιχεῖον καὶ πέρας τῆς ἀλλαγῆς ἐστίν). Therefore also riches, such as Chrematistic strives for, are unlimited. Just as every art that is not a means to an end, but an end in itself, has no limit to its aims, because it seeks constantly to approach nearer and nearer to that end, while those arts that pursue means to an end, are not boundless, since the goal itself imposes a limit upon them, so with Chrematistic, there are no bounds to its aims, these aims being absolute wealth. Œconomic not Chrematistic has a limit . . . . the object of the former is something different from money, of the latter the augmentation of money . . . . By confounding these two forms, which overlap each other, some people have been led to look upon the preservation and increase of money ad infinitum as the end and aim of Œconomic." (Aristotles De Rep. edit. Bekker. lib. I. c. 8, 9. passim.)

[2] "Commodities (here used in the sense of use-values) are not the terminating object of the trading capitalist, money is his terminating object." (Th. Chalmers, On Pol. Econ. &c., 2nd Ed., Glasgow, 1832, p. 165, 166.)

at.[1] This boundless greed after riches, this passionate chase after exchange-value,[2] is common to the capitalist and the miser; but while the miser is merely a capitalist gone mad, the capitalist is a rational miser. The never-ending augmentation of exchange-value, which the miser strives after, by seeking to save [3] his money from circulation, is attained by the more acute capitalist, by constantly throwing it afresh into circulation.[4]

The independent form, *i. e.,* the money-form, which the value of commodities assumes in the case of simple circulation, serves only one purpose, namely, their exchange, and vanishes in the final result of the movement. On the other hand, in the circulation M—C—M, both the money and the commodity represent only different modes of existence of value itself, the money its general mode, and the commodity its particular, or, so to say, disguised mode.[5] It is constantly changing from one form to the other without thereby becoming lost, and thus assumes an automatically active character. If now we take in turn each of the two different forms which self-expanding value successively assumes in the course of its life, we then arrive at these two propositions: Capital is money: Capital is commodities.[6] In truth, however, value is here the active factor in a process, in which, while constantly assuming the form in turn of money and commodities, it at the same time changes in magnitude, differentiates itself by throwing off surplus-value from itself; the original value, in other words,

[1] "Il mercante non conta quasi per niente il lucro fatto, ma mira sempre al futuro." (A. Genovesi, Lezioni di Economia Civile 1765), Custodi's edit. of Italian Economists. Parte Moderna t. xiii. p. 139.)

[2] "The inextinguishable passion for gain, the auri sacra fames, will always lead capitalists." (MacCulloch: "The principles of Polit. Econ." London, 1830, p. 179.) This view, of course, does not prevent the same MacCulloch and others of his kidney, when in theoretical difficulties, such, for example, as the question of over-production, from transforming the same capitalist into a moral citizen, whose sole concern is for use-values, and who even developes an insatiable hunger for boots, hats, eggs, calico, and other extremely familiar sorts of use-values.

[3] Σώζειν is a characteristic Greek expression for hoarding. So in English to save has the same two meanings: sauver and épargner.

[4] "Questo infinito che le cose non hanno in progresso, hanno in giro." (Galiani.)

[5] "Ce n'est pas la matière qui fait le capital, mais la valeur de ces matières." (J. B. Say: "Traité de l'Econ. Polit." 3ème. éd. Paris, 1817, t. 1., p. 428.)

[6] "Currency (!) employed in producing articles . . . is capital." (MacLeod: "The Theory and Practice of Banking." London, 1855, v. 1., ch. i., p. 55.) "Capital is commodities." (James Mill: "Elements of Pol. Econ." Lond., 1821, p. 74.)

expands spontaneously. For the movement, in the course of which it adds surplus value, is its own movement, its expansion, therefore, is automatic expansion. Because it is value, it has acquired the occult quality of being able to add value to itself. It brings forth living offspring, or, at the least, lays golden eggs.

Value, therefore, being the active factor in such a process, and assuming at one time the form of money, at another that of commodities, but through all these changes preserving itself and expanding, it requires some independent form, by means of which its identity may at any time be established. And this form it possesses only in the shape of money. It is under the form of money that value begins and ends, and begins again, every act of its own spontaneous generation. It began by being £100, it is now £110, and so on. But the money itself is only one of the two forms of value. Unless it takes the form of some commodity, it does not become capital. There is here no antagonism, as in the case of hoarding, between the money and commodities. The capitalist knows that all commodities, however scurvy they may look, or however badly they may smell, are in faith and in truth money, inwardly circumcised Jews, and what is more, a wonderful means whereby out of money to make more money.

In simple circulation, C—M—C, the value of commodities attained at the most a form independent of their use-values, *i. e.,* the form of money; but that same value now in the circulation M—C—M, or the circulation of capital, suddenly presents itself as an independent substance, endowed with a motion of its own, passing through a life-process of its own, in which money and commodities are mere forms which it assumes and casts off in turn. Nay, more: instead of simply representing the relations of commodities, it enters now, so to say, into private relations with itself. It differentiates itself as original value from itself as surplus-value; as the father differentiates himself from himself quâ the son, yet both are one and of one age: for only by the surplus value of £10 does the £100 originally advanced become capital, and so soon as this takes place, so soon as the son, and by the son, the father, is begotten, so soon does their difference vanish, and they again become one, £110.

Value therefore now becomes value in process, money in process, and, as such, capital. It comes out of circulation, enters into it again, preserves and multiplies itself within its circuit, comes back out of it with expanded bulk, and begins the same round ever afresh.[1] M—M′, money which begets money, such is the description of Capital from the mouths of its first interpreters, the Mercantilists.

Buying in order to sell, or, more accurately, buying in order to sell dearer, M—C—M′, appears certainly to be a form peculiar to one kind of capital alone, namely, merchants′ capital. But industrial capital too is money, that is changed into commodities, and by the sale of these commodities, is reconverted into more money. The events that take place outside the sphere of circulation, in the interval between the buying and selling, do not affect the form of this movement. Lastly, in the case of interest-bearing capital, the circulation M—C—M′ appears abridged. We have its result without the intermediate stage, in the form M—M′, "en style lapidaire" so to say, money that is worth more money, value that is greater than itself.

M—C—M′ is therefore in reality the general formula of capital as it appears prima facie within the sphere of circulation.

CHAPTER V.

CONTRADICTIONS IN THE GENERAL FORMULA OF CAPITAL.

THE form which circulation takes when money becomes capital, is opposed to all the laws we have hitherto investigated bearing on the nature of commodities, value and money, and even of circulation itself. What distinguishes this form from that of the simple circulation of commodities, is the inverted

---

[1] Capital: "portion fructifiante de la richesse accumulée . . . valeur permanente, multipliante." (Sismondi: "Nouveaux principes de l'écon. polit.," t. i., p. 88, 89.)

order of succession of the two antithetical processes, sale and purchase. How can this purely formal distinction between these processes change their character as it were by magic?

But that is not all. This inversion has no existence for two out of the three persons who transact business together. As capitalist, I buy commodities from A and sell them again to B, but as a simple owner of commodities, I sell them to B and then purchase fresh ones from A. A and B see no difference between the two sets of transactions. They are merely buyers or sellers. And I on each occasion meet them as a mere owner of either money or commodities, as a buyer or a seller, and, what is more, in both sets of transactions, I am opposed to A only as a buyer and to B only as a seller, to the one only as money, to the other only as commodities, and to neither of them as capital or a capitalist, or as representative of anything that is more than money or commodities, or that can produce any effect beyond what money and commodities can. For me the purchase from A and the sale to B are part of a series. But the connexion between the two acts exists for me alone. A does not trouble himself about my transaction with B, nor does B about my business with A. And if I offered to explain to them the meritorious nature of my action in inverting the order of succession, they would probably point out to me that I was mistaken as to that order of succession, and that the whole transaction, instead of beginning with a purchase and ending with a sale, began, on the contrary, with a sale and was concluded with a purchase. In truth, my first act, the purchase, was from the standpoint of A, a sale, and my second act, the sale, was from the standpoint of B, a purchase. Not content with that, A and B would declare that the whole series was superfluous and nothing but Hokus Pokus; that for the future B would buy direct from A, and A sell direct to B. Thus the whole transaction would be reduced to a single act forming an isolated, non-complemented phase in the ordinary circulation of commodities, a mere sale from A's point of view, and from B's, a mere purchase. The inversion, therefore, of the order of succession, does not take us outside the sphere of the simple circulation of commodities, and we must rather look, whether there is in this simple circulation anything permitting an expansion of the value that enters into circulation, and, consequently, a creation of surplus-value.

Let us take the process of circulation in a form under which it presents itself as a simple and direct exchange of commodities. This is always the case when two owners of commodities buy from each other, and on the settling day the amounts mutually owing are equal and cancel each other. The money in this case is money of account and serves to express the value of the commodities by their prices, but is not, itself, in the shape of hard cash, confronted with them. So far as regards use-values, it is clear that both parties may gain some advantage. Both part with goods that, as use-values, are of no service to them, and receive others that they can make use of. And there may also be a further gain. A, who sells wine and buys corn, possibly produces more wine, with given labour time, than farmer B could, and B, on the other hand, more corn than wine-grower A could. A, therefore, may get, for the same exchange value, more corn, and B more wine, than each would respectively get without any exchange by producing his own corn and wine. With reference, therefore, to use-value, there is good ground for saying that "exchange is a transaction by which both sides gain."[1] It is otherwise with exchange value. "A man who has plenty of wine and no corn treats with a man who has plenty of corn and no wine; an exchange takes place between them of corn to the value of 50, for wine of the same value. This act produces no increase of exchange value either for the one or the other; for each of them already possessed, before the exchange, a value equal to that which he acquired by means of that operation."[2] The result is not altered by introducing money, as a medium of circulation, between the commodities, and making the sale and the purchase two distinct acts.[3] The value of a commodity is

[1] "L'échange est une transaction admirable dans laquelle les deux contractants gagnent—toujours (!)" (Destutt de Tracy: "Traité de la Volonté et de ses effets." Paris, 1826, p. 68.) This work appeared afterwards as "Traité de l'Econ. Polit.

[2] "Mercier de la Rivière," l. c. p. 544.

[3] "Que l'une de ces deux valeurs soit argent, ou qu'elles soient toutes deux marchandises usuelles, rien de plus indifférent en soi." (Mercier de la Rivière," l. c. p. 543.)

expressed in its price before it goes into circulation, and is therefore a precedent condition of circulation, not its result.[1]

Abstractedly considered, that is, apart from circumstances not immediately flowing from the laws of the simple circulation of commodities, there is in an exchange nothing (if we except the replacing of one use-value by another) but a metamorphosis, a mere change in the form of the commodity. The same exchange value, *i.e.*, the same quantity of incorporated social labour, remains throughout in the hands of the owner of the commodity first in the shape of his own commodity, then in the form of the money for which he exchanged it, and lastly, in the shape of the commodity he buys with that money. This change of form does not imply a change in the magnitude of the value. But the change, which the value of the commodity undergoes in this process, is limited to a change in its money form. This form exists first as the price of the commodity offered for sale, then as an actual sum of money, which, however, was already expressed in the price, and lastly, as the price of an equivalent commodity. This change of form no more implies, taken alone, a change in the quantity of value, than does the change of a £5 note into sovereigns, half sovereigns and shillings. So far therefore as the circulation of commodities effects a change in the form alone of their values, and is free from disturbing influences, it must be the exchange of equivalents. Little as Vulgar-Economy knows about the nature of value, yet whenever it wishes to consider the phenomena of circulation in their purity, it assumes that supply and demand are equal, which amounts to this, that their effect is nil. If therefore, as regards the use-values exchanged, both buyer and seller may possibly gain something, this is not the case as regards the exchange values. Here we must rather say, "Where equality exists there can be no gain."[2] It is true, commodities may be sold at prices deviating from their values, but these deviations are to be considered as in-

---

[1] "Ce ne sont pas les contractants qui prononcent sur valeur; elle est déridée avant la convention." ("Le Trosne," p. 906.)

[2] "Dove è egualità non è lucro." (Galiani, "Della Moneta in Custodi, Parte Moderna," t. iv. p. 244.)

fractions of the laws of the exchange of commodites,[1] which in its normal state is an exchange of equivalents, consequently, no method for increasing value.[2]

Hence, we see that behind all attempts to represent the circulation of commodities as a source of surplus-value, there lurks a *quid pro quo,* a mixing up of use-value and exchange value. For instance, Condillac says: "It is not true that on an exchange of commodities we give value for value. On the contrary, each of the two contracting parties in every case, gives a less for a greater value. . . . If we really exchanged equal values, neither party could make a profit. And yet, they both gain, or ought to gain. Why? The value of a thing consists solely in its relation to our wants. What is more to the one is less to the other, and *vice versâ.* . . . It is not to be assumed that we offer for sale articles required for our own consumption. . . . We wish to part with a useless thing, in order to get one that we need; we want to give less for more. . . . It was natural to think that, in an exchange, value was given for value, whenever each of the articles exchanged was of equal value with the same quantity of gold. . . . But there is another point to be considered in our calculation. The question is, whether we both exchange something superfluous for something necessary."[3] We see in this passage, how Condillac not only confuses use-value with exchange value, but in a really childish manner assumes, that in a society, in which the production of commodities is well developed, each producer produces his own means of subsistence, and throws into circulation only the excess over his own requirements.[4] Still, Condillac's argument is frequently used

[1] "Léchange devient désavantageux pour l'une des parties, lorsque quelque chose étrangère vient diminuer ou exagérer le prix; alors l'égalité est blessée, mais la lésion procède de cette cause et non de l'échange." ("Le Trosne," l. c. p. 904.)

[2] "L'échange est de sa nature un contrat d'égalité qui se fait de valeur pour valeur égale. Il n'est donc pas un moyen de s'enrichir, puisque l'on donne autant que l'on reçoit." ("Le Trosne," l. c. p. 903.)

[3] Condillac: "Le Commerce et le Gouvernement" (1776). Edit. Daire et Molinari in the "Mélanges d'Econ. Polit." Paris, 1847, p. 267, etc.

[4] Le Trosne, therefore, answers his friend Condillac with justice as follows: "Dans une . . . société formée il n'y a pas de surabondant en aucun genre." At the same time, in a bantering way, he remarks: "If both the persons who exchange receive more to an equal amount, and part with less to an equal amount, they both get the same." It is because Condillac has not the remotest idea of the nature of

by modern economists, more especially when the point is to show, that the exchange of commodities in its developed form, commerce, is productive of surplus-value. For instance, "Commerce . . . . adds value to products, for the same products in the hands of consumers, are worth more than in the hands of producers, and it may strictly be considered an act of production."[1] But commodities are not paid for twice over, once on account of their use-value, and again on account of their value. And though the use-value of a commodity is more servicable to the buyer than to the seller, its money form is more serviceable to the seller. Would he otherwise sell it? We might therefore just as well say that the buyer performs "strictly an act of production," by converting stockings, for example, into money.

If commodities, or commodities and money, of equal exchange-value, and consequently equivalents, are exchanged, it is plain that no one abstracts more value from, than he throws into, circulation. There is no creation of surplus-value. And, in its normal form, the circulation of commodities demands the exchange of equivalents. But in actual practice, the process does not retain its normal form. Let us, therefore, assume an exchange of non-equivalents.

In any case the market for commodities is only frequented by owners of commodities, and the power which these persons exercise over each other, is no other than the power of their commodities. The material variety of these commodities is the material incentive to the act of exchange, and makes buyers and sellers mutually dependent, because none of them possesses the object of his own wants, and each holds in his hand the object of another's wants. Besides these material differences of their use-values, there is only one other difference between commodities, namely, that between their bodily form and the form into which they are converted by sale, the difference be-

exchange value that he has been chosen by Herr Professor Wilhelm Roscher as a proper person to answer for the soundness of his own childish notions. See Roscher's "Die Grundlagen der Nationalökomonie, Dritte Auflage," 1858.

[1] S. P. Newman: "Elements of Polit. Econ." Andover and New York, 1835, p. 175.

tween commodities and money. And consequently the owners of commodities are distinguishable only as sellers, those who own commodities, and buyers, those who own money.

Suppose then, that by some inexplicable privilege, the seller is enabled to sell his commodities above their value, what is worth 100 for 110, in which case the price is nominally raised 10%. The seller therefore pockets a surplus value of 10. But after he has sold he becomes a buyer. A third owner of commodities comes to him now as seller, who in this capacity also enjoys the privilege of selling his commodities 10% too dear. Our friend gained 10 as a seller only to lose it again as a buyer.[1] The nett result is, that all owners of commodities sell their goods to one another at 10% above their value, which comes precisely to the same as if they sold them at their true value. Such a general and nominal rise of prices has the same effect as if the values had been expressed in weight of silver instead of in weight of gold. The nominal prices of commodities would rise, but the real relation between their values would remain unchanged.

Let us make the opposite assumption, that the buyer has the privilege of purchasing commodities under their value. In this case it is no longer necessary to bear in mind that he in his turn wll become a seller. He was so before he became buyer; he had already lost 10% in selling before he gained 10% as buyer.[2] Everything is just as it was.

The creation of surplus-value, and therefore the conversion of money into capital, can consequently be explained neither on the assumption that commodities are sold above their value, nor that they are bought below their value.[3]

---

[1] "By the augmentation of the nominal value of the produce. . . sellers not enriched . . . since what they gain as sellers, they precisely expend in the quality of buyers." ("The Essential Principles of the Wealth of Nations," &c., London, 1797, p. 66.)

[2] "Si l'on est forcé de donner pour 18 livres une quantité de telle production qui en valait 24, lorsqu'on employera ce même argent à acheter, on aura également pour 18 l. ce que l'on payait 24." ("Le Trosne," l. c. p. 897.)

[3] "Chaque vendeur ne peut donc parvenir à renchérir habituellement ses marchandises, qu'en se soumettant aussi à payer habituellement plus cher les marchandises des autres vendeurs; et par la même raison, chaque consommateur ne peut payer habituellement moins cher ce qu'il achète, qu'en se soumettant aussi a une diminution semblable sur le prix des choses qu il vend." (Mercier de la Raviére," l. c. p. 555.)

The problem is in no way simplified by introducing irrelevant matters after the manner of Col. Torrens: "Effectual demand consists in the power and inclination (!), on the part of consumers, to give for commodities, either by immediate or circuitous barter, some greater portion of . . . capital than their production costs." [1] In relation to circulation, producers and consumers meet only as buyers and sellers. To assert that the surplus-value acquired by the producer has its origin in the fact that consumers pay for commodities more than their value, is only to say in other words: The owner of commodities possesses, as a seller, the privilege of selling too dear. The seller has himself produced the commodities or represents their producer, but the buyer has to no less extent produced the commodities represented by his money, or represents their producer. The distinction between them is, that one buys and the other sells. The fact that the owner of the commodities, under the designation of producer, sells them over their value, and under the designation of consumer, pays too much for them, does not carry us a single step further. [2]

To be consistent therefore, the upholders of the delusion that surplus-value has its origin in a nominal rise of prices or in the privilege which the seller has of selling too dear, must assume the existence of a class that only buys and does not sell, *i.e.*, only consumes and does not produce. The existence of such a class is inexplicable from the standpoint we have so far reached, viz., that of simple circulation. But let us anticipate. The money with which such a class is constantly making purchases, must constantly flow into their pockets, without any exchange, gratis, by might or right, from the pockets of the commodity-owners themselves. To sell commodities above their value to such a class, is only to crib back again a part of the money previously given to it. [3] The towns of Asia

---

[1] R. Torrens: "An Essay on the Production of Wealth." London, 1821, p. 349.

[2] "The idea of profits being paid by the consumers, is, assuredly, very absurd. Who are the consumers?" (G. Ramsay: "An Essay on the Distribution of Wealth." Edinburgh, 1836, p. 183.)

[3] "When a man is in want of a demand, does Mr. Malthus recommend him to pay some other person to take off his goods?" is a question put by an angry disciple of Ricardo to Malthus, who, like his disciple, Parson Chalmers, economically glorifies this class of simple buyers or consumers. (See "An Inquiry into those princi-

Minor thus paid a yearly money tribute to ancient Rome. With this money Rome purchased from them commodities, and purchased them too dear. The provincials cheated the Romans, and thus got back from their conquerors, in the course of trade, a portion of the tribute. Yet, for all that, the conquered were the really cheated. Their goods were still paid for with their own money. That is not the way to get rich or to create surplus-value.

Let us therefore keep within the bounds of exchange where sellers are also buyers, and buyers, sellers. Our difficulty may perhaps have arisen from treating the actors as personifications instead of as individuals.

A may be clever enough to get the advantage of B or C without their being able to retaliate. A sells wine worth £40 to B, and obtains from him in exchange corn to the value of £50. A has converted his £40 into £50, has made more money out of less, and has converted his commodities into capital. Let us examine this a little more closely. Before the exchange we had £40 worth of wine in the hands of A, and £50 worth of corn in those of B, a total value of £90. After the exchange we have still the same total value of £90. The value in circulation has not increased by one iota, it is only distributed differently between A and B. What is a loss of value to B is surplus-value to A; what is "minus" to one is "plus" to the other. The same change would have taken place, if A, without the formality of an exchange, had directly stolen the £10 from B. The sum of the values in circulation can clearly not be augmented by any change in their distribution, any more than the quantity of the precious metals in a country by a Jew selling a Queen Ann's farthing for a guinea. The capitalist class, as a whole, in any country, cannot over-reach themselves.[1]

Turn and twist then as we may, the fact remains unaltered.

---

ples respecting the Nature of Demand and the necessity of Consumption, lately advocated by Mr. Malthus," &c. Lond., 1821, p. 55.)

[1] Destutt de Tracy, although, or perhaps because, he was a member of the Institute, held the opposite view. He says, industrial capitalists make profits because "they all sell for more than it has cost to produce. And to whom do they sell? In the first instance to one another." (l. c., p. 239.)

If equivalents are exchanged, no surplus-value results, and if non-equivalents are exchanged, still no surplus-value.[1] Circulation, or the exchange of commodities, begets no value.[2]

The reason is now therefore plain why, in analysing the standard form of capital, the form under which it determines the economical organisation of modern society, we entirely left out of consideration its most popular, and, so to say, antediluvian forms, merchants' capital and money-lenders' capital.

The circuit M—C—M', buying in order to sell dearer, is seen most clearly in genuine merchants' capital. But the movement takes place entirely within the sphere of circulation. Since, however, it is impossible, by circulation alone, to account for the conversion of money into capital, for the formation of surplus-value, it would appear, that merchants' capital is an impossibility, so long as equivalents are exchanged;[3] that, therefore, it can only have its origin in the twofold advantage gained, over both the selling and the buying producers, by the merchant who parasitically shoves himself in between them. It is in this sense that Franklin says, "war is robbery, commerce is generally cheating."[4] If the transformation of merchants' money into capital is to be explained otherwise than by the producers being simply cheated, a long series of intermediate steps would be necessary, which, at present, when

---

[1] "L'échange qui se fait de deux valeurs égales n'augmente ni ne diminue la masse des valeurs subsistantes dans la société. L'échange de deux valeurs inégales . . . ne change rien non plus à la somme des valeurs sociales, bien qu'il ajoute à la fortune de l'un ce pu'il ôte de la fortune de l'autre." J. B. Say, l. c. t. I., pp. 344, 345.) Say, not in the least troubled as to the consequences of this statement, borrows it, almost word for word, from the Physiocrats. The following example will shew how Monsieur Say turned to account the writings of the Physiocrats, in his day quite forgotten, for the purpose of expanding the "value" of his own. His most celebrated saying, "On n'achète des produits qu'avec des produits" (l. c., t. II., p. 438) runs as follows in the original physiocratic work: "Les productions ne se paient qu'avec des productions." ("Le Trosne," l. c., p. 899.)

[2] "Exchange confers no value at all upon products." (F. Wayland: "The Elements of Political Economy." Boston, 1853, p. 168.)

[3] Under the rule of invariable equivalents commerce would be impossible. (G. Opdyke: "A Treatise on Polit Economy." New York, 1851, p. 66-69.) "The difference between real value and exchange-value is based upon this fact, namely, that the value of a thing is different from the socalled equivalent given for it in trade, *i.e.*, that this equivalent is no equivalent." (F. Engels, l. c. p. 96.)

[4] Benjamin Franklin: Works, Vol. II. edit. Sparks in "Positions to be examined concerning National Wealth," p. 876.

the simple circulation of commodities forms our only assumption, are entirely wanting.

What we have said with reference to merchants' capital, applies still more to money-lenders' capital. In merchants' capital, the two extremes, the money that is thrown upon the market, and the augmented money that is withdrawn from the market, are at least connected by a purchase and a sale, in other words by the movement of the circulation. In money-lenders' capital the form M—C—M' is reduced to the two extremes without a mean, M—M', money exchanged for more money, a form that is incompatible with the nature of money, and therefore remains inexplicable from the standpoint of the circulation of commodities. Hence Aristotle: "since chrema-tistic is a double science, one part belonging to commerce, the other to economic, the latter being necessary and praiseworthy, the former based on circulation and with justice disapproved (for it is not based on Nature, but on mutual cheating), therefore the usurer is most rightly hated, because money itself is the source of his gain, and is not used for the purposes for which it was invented. For it originated for the exchange of commodities, but interest makes out of money, more money. Hence its name (τόκος interest and offspring). For the begotten are like those who beget them. But interest is money of money, so that of all modes of making a living, this is the most contrary to nature." [1]

In the course of our investigation, we shall find that both merchants' capital and interest-bearing capital are derivative forms, and at the same time it will become clear, why these two forms appear in the course of history before the modern standard form of capital.

We have shown that surplus-value cannot be created by circulation, and, therefore, that in its formation, something must take place in the background, which is not apparent in the circulation itself.[2] But can surplus-value possibly originate anywhere else than in circulation, which is the sum total

[1] Aristotle, 1. c. c. 10.
[2] Profit, in the usual condition of the market, is not made by exchanging. Had it not existed before, neither could it after that transaction." (Ramsay, 1. c., p. 184.)

of all the mutual relations of commodity-owners, as far as they are determined by their commodities? Apart from circulation, the commodity-owner is in relation only with his own commodity. So far as regards value, that relation is limited to this, that the commodity contains a quantity of his labour, that quantity being measured by a definite social standard. This quantity is expressed by the value of the commodity, and since the value is reckoned in money of account, this quantity is also expressed by the price, which we will suppose to be £10. But his labour is not represented both by the value of the commodity, and by a surplus over that value, not by a price of 10 that is also a price of 11, not by a value that is greater than itself. The commodity owner can, by his labour, create value, but not self-expanding value. He can increase the value of his commodity, by adding fresh labour, and therefore more value to the value in hand, by making, for instance, leather into boots. The same material has now more value, because it contains a greater quantity of labour. The boots have therefore more value than the leather, but the value of the leather remains what it was; it has not expanded itself, has not, during the making of the boots, annexed surplus value. It is therefore impossible that outside the sphere of circulation, a producer of commodities can, without coming into contact with other commodity owners, expand value, and consequently convert money or commodities into capital.

It is therefore impossible for capital to be produced by circulation, and it is equally impossible for it to originate apart from circulation. It must have its origin both in circulation and yet not in circulation.

We have, therefore, got a double result.

The conversion of money into capital has to be explained on the basis of the laws that regulate the exchange of commodities, in such a way that the starting point is the exchange of equivalents.[1] Our friend, Moneybags, who as yet is only an

---

[1] From the foregoing investigation, the reader will see that this statement only means that the formation of capital must be possible even though the price and value of a commodity be the same; for its formation cannot be attributed to any deviation of the one from the other. If prices actually differ from values, we must, first of

embryo capitalist, must buy his commodities at their value, must sell them at their value, and yet at the end of the process must withdraw more value from circulation than he threw into it at starting. His development into a full-grown capitalist must take place, both within the sphere of circulation and without it. These are the conditions of the problem. Hic Rhodus, hic salta!

CHAPTER VI.

THE BUYING AND SELLING OF LABOUR-POWER.

THE change of value that occurs in the case of money intended to be converted into capital, cannot take place in the money itself, since in its function of means of purchase and of payment, it does no more than realise the price of the commodity it buys or pays for; and, as hard cash, it is value petrified, never varying.[1] Just as little can it originate in the second act of circulation, the re-sale of the commodity, which does no more than transform the article from its bodily form back again into its money-form. The change must, therefore, take place in the commodity bought by the first act, M—C, but not in its value, for equivalents are exchanged, and the commodity is paid for at its full value. We are, therefore, forced to the

all, reduce the former to the latter, in other words treat the difference as accidental in order that the phenomena may be observed in their purity, and our observations not interfered with by disturbing circumstances that have nothing to do with the process in question. We know, moreover, that this reduction is no mere scientific process. The continual oscillation in prices, their rising and falling, compensate each other, and reduce themselves to an average price, which is their hidden regulator. It forms the guiding star of the merchant or the manufacturer in every undertaking that requires time. He knows that when a long period of time is taken, commodities are sold neither over nor under, but at their average price. If therefore he thought about the matter at all, he would formulate the problem of the formation of capital as follows: How can we account for the origin of capital on the supposition that prices are regulated by the average price, *i.e.,* ultimately by the value of the commodities? I say "ultimately," because average prices do not directly coincide with the values of commodities, as Adam Smith, Ricardo, and others believe.

[1] "In the form of money. . . capital is productive of no profit." (Ricardo: "Princ. of Pol. Econ." p. 267.)

conclusion that the change originates in the use-value, as such, of the commodity, *i.e.,* in its consumption. In order to be able to extract value from the consumption of a commodity, our friend, Moneybags, must be so lucky as to find, within the sphere of circulation, in the market, a commodity, whose use-value possesses the peculiar property of being a source of value, whose actual consumption, therefore, is itself an embodiment of labour, and, consequently, a creation of value. The possessor of money does find on the market such a special commodity in capacity for labour or labour-power.

By labour-power or capacity for labour is to be understood the aggregate of those mental and physical capabilities existing in a human being, which he exercises whenever he produces a use-value of any description.

But in order that our owner of money may be able to find labour-power offered for sale as a commodity, various conditions must first be fulfilled. The exchange of commodities of itself implies no other relations of dependence than those which result from its own nature. On this assumption, labour-power can appear upon the market as a commodity only if, and so far as, its possessor, the individual whose labour-power it is, offers it for sale, or sells it, as a commodity. In order that he may be able to do this, he must have it at his disposal, must be the untrammelled owner of his capacity for labour, *i.e.,* of his person.[1] He and the owner of money meet in the market, and deal with each other as on the basis of equal rights, with this difference alone, that one is buyer, the other seller; both, therefore, equal in the eyes of the law. The continuance of this relation demands that the owner of the labour-power should sell it only for a definite period, for if he were to sell it rump and stump, once for all, he would be selling himself, converting himself from a free man into a slave, from an owner of a commodity into a commodity. He must constantly look upon his labour-power as his own property, his own commodity, and this he can only do by placing it at the disposal of

[1] In encyclopædias of classical antiquities we find such nonsense as this—that in the ancient world capital was fully developed, "except that the free labourer and a system of credit was wanting." Mommsen also, in his "History of Rome," commits, in this respect, one blunder after another.

the buyer temporarily, for a definite period of time. By this means alone can he avoid renouncing his rights of ownership over it.[1]

The second essential condition to the owner of money finding labour-power in the market as a commodity is this—that the labourer instead of being in the position to sell commodities in which his labour is incorporated, must be obliged to offer for sale as a commodity that very labour-power, which exists only in his living self.

In order that a man may be able to sell commodities other than labour-power, he must of course have the means of production, as raw material, implements, &c. No boots can be made without leather. He requires also the means of subsistence. Nobody—not even "a musician of the future" can live upon future products, or upon use-values in an unfinished state; and ever since the first moment of his appearance on the world's stage, man always has been, and must still be a consumer, both before and while he is producing. In a society where all products assume the form of commodities, these commodities must be sold after they have been produced; it is only after their sale that they can serve in satisfying the requirements of their producer. The time necessary for their sale is superadded to that necessary for their production.

For the conversion of his money into capital, therefore, the owner of money must meet in the market with the free labourer, free in the double sense, that as a free man he can

---

[1] Hence legislation in various countries fixes a maximum for labour-contracts. Wherever free labour is the rule, the laws regulate the mode of terminating this contract. In some States, particularly in Mexico (before the American Civil War, also in the territories taken from Mexico, and also as a matter of fact, in the Danubian provinces till the revolution affected by Kusa), slavery is hidden under the form of *peonage*. By means of advances, repayable in labour, which are handed down from generation to generation, not only the individual labourer, but his family, become, *de facto*, the property of other persons and their families. Juarez abolished *peonage*. The so-called Emperor Maximilian re-established it by a decree, which, in the House of Representatives at Washington, was aptly denounced as a decree for the re-introduction of slavery into Mexico. "I may make over to another the use, for a limited time, of my particular bodily and mental aptitudes and capabilities; because, in consequence of this restriction, they are impressed with a character of alienation with regard to me as a whole. But by the alienation of all my labour-time and the whole of my work, I should be converting the substance itself, in other words, my general activity and reality, my person, into the property of another." (Hegel, "Philosophie des Rechts." Berlin, 1840, p. 104 § 67.)

dispose of his labour-power as his own commodity, and that on the other hand he has no other commodity for sale, is short of everything necessary for the realisation of his labour-power.

The question why this free labourer confronts him in the market, has no interest for the owner of money, who regards the labour market as a branch of the general market for commodities. And for the present it interests us just as little. We cling to the fact theoretically, as he does practically. One thing, however, is clear—nature does not produce on the one side owners of money or commodities, and on the other men possessing nothing but their own labour-power. This relation has no natural basis, neither is its socal basis one that is common to all historical periods. It is clearly th result of a past historial development, the product of many economical revolutions, of the extinction of a whole series of older forms of social production.

So, too, the economical categories, already iscussed by us, bear the stamp of history. Definite historical conditions are necessary that a product may become a commodity. It must not be produced as the immediate means of subsjstence of the producer himself. Had we gone further, and inquired under what circumstances all, or even the majority of produ ' take the form of commodities, we should have found that this (n only happen with production of a very specific kind, capitalist production. Such an inquiry, however, would have been foreign to the analysis of commodities. Production and circulation of commodities can take place, although the great mass of the objects produced are intended for the immediate requirements of their producers, are not turned into commodities, and consequently social production is not yet by a long way dominated in its length and breadth by exchange-value, the appearance of products as commodities presupposed such a development of the social division of labour, that the separation of use-value from exchange-value, a separation which first begins with barter, must already have been completed. But such a degree of development is common to many forms of society, which in other respects present the most varying historical features. On the other hand, if we consider money, its existence implies a definite stage in the exchange of commodities. The particular functions of money which it performs, either as the mere equivalent of commodities, or as means of circulation, or means of payment, as hoard or as universal money, point, according to the extent and relative preponderance of the one function or the other, to very different stages in the process of social production. Yet we know by experience that a circulation of commodities relatively primitive, suffices for the production of all these forms. Otherwise with capital. The historical conditions of its existence are by no means given with the mere circulation of money and commodities. It can spring into life, only when the owner of the means of production and subsistence meets in the market with the free labourer selling his labour-power. And this one historical condition comprises a world's history. Capital therefore, announces from its first appearance a new epoch in the process of social production.[1]

We must now examine more closely this peculiar commodity, labour-power. Like all others it has a value.[2] How is that value determined?

The value of labour-power is determined, as in the case of every other commodity, by the labour-time necessary for the production, and consequently also the reproduction, of this special article. So far as it has value, it represents no more than a definite quantity of the average labour of society incorporated in it. Labour-power exists only as a capacity, or power of the living individual. Its production consequently presupposes his existence. Given the individual, the production of labour-power consists in his reproduction of himself or his maintenance. For his maintenance he requires a given quantity of the means of subsistence. Therefore the labour-time requisite for the production of labour-power reduces itself

---

[1] The capitalist epoch is therefore characterised by this, that labour-power takes in the eyes of the labourer himself the form of a commodity which is his property; his labour consequently becomes wage labour. On the other hand, it is only from this moment that the produce of labour universally becomes a commodity.

[2] "The value or worth of a man, is as of all other things his price—that is to say, so much as would be given for the use of his power." (Th. Hobbes: "Leviathan" in Works, Ed. Molesworth. Lond. 1839-44, v. iii., p. 76.)

to that necessary for the production of those means of subsistence; in other words, the value of labour-power is the value of the means of subsistence necessary for the maintenance of the labourer. Labour-power, however, becomes a reality only by its exercise; it sets itself in action only by working. But thereby a definite quantity of human muscle, nerve, brain, &c., is wasted, and these require to be restored. This increased expenditure demands a larger income.[1] If the owner of labour-power works to-day, to-morrow he must again be able to repeat the same process in the same conditions as regards health and strength. His means of subsistence must therefore be sufficient to maintain him in his normal state as a labouring individual. His natural wants, such as food, clothing, fuel, and housing, vary according to the climatic and other physical conditions of his country. On the other hand, the number and extent of his so-called necessary wants, as also the modes of satisfying them, are themselves the product of historical development, and depend therefore to a great extent on the degree of civilisation of a country, more particularly on the conditions under which, and consequently on the habits and degree of comfort in which, the class of free labourers has been formed.[2] In contradistinction therefore to the case of other commodities, there enters into the determination of the value of labour-power a historical and moral element. Nevertheless, in a given country, at a given period, the average quantity of the means of subsistence necessary for the labourer is practically known.

The owner of labour-power is mortal. If then his appearance in the market is to be continuous, and the continuous conversion of money into capital assumes this, the seller of labour-power must perpetuate himself, "in the way that every living individual perpetuates himself, by procreation."[3] The labour-power withdrawn from the market by wear and tear and death, must be continually replaced by, at the very least, an

---

[1] Hence the Roman Villicus, as overlooker of the agricultural slaves, received "more meagre fare than working slaves, because his work was lighter." (Th. Mommsen, Röm. Geschichte, 1856, p. 810.)

[2] Compare W. H. Thornton: "Overpopulation and its Remedy," Lond., 1846.

[3] Petty.

equal amount of fresh labour-power. Hence the sum of the means of subsistence necessary for the production of labour-power must include the means necessary for the labourer's substitutes, *i.e.,* his children, in order that this race of peculiar commodity-owners may perpetuate its appearance in the market.[1]

In order to modify the human organism, so that it may acquire skill and handiness in a given branch of industry, and become labour-power of a special kind, a special education or training is requisite, and this, on its part, costs an equivalent in commodities of a greater or less amount. This amount varies according to the more or less complicated character of the labour-power. The expenses of this education (excessively small in the case of ordinary labour-power), enter pro tanto into the total value spent in its production.

The value of labour-power resolves itself into the value of a definite quantity of the means of subsistence. It therefore varies with the value of these means or with the quantity of labour requisite for their production.

Some of the means of subsistence, such as food and fuel, are consumed daily, and a fresh supply must be provided daily. Others such as clothes and furniture last for longer periods and require to be replaced only at longer intervals. One article must be bought or paid for daily, another weekly, another quarterly, and so on. But in whatever way the sum total of these outlays may be spread over the year, they must be covered by the average income, taking one day with another. If the total of the commodities required daily for the production of labour-power$=A$, and those required weekly $=B$, and those required quarterly$=C$, and so on, the daily average of these commodities$=\frac{365A+52B+4C+\&c}{365}$. Suppose that in this mass of commodities requisite for the average day there are embodied 6 hours of social labour, then there is incor-

---

[1] Its (labour's) natural price. . . . consists in such a quantity of necessaries and comforts of life, as, from the nature of the climate, and the habits of the country, are necessary to support the labourer, and to enable him to rear such a family as may preserve, in the market, an undiminished supply of labour." (R. Torrens: "An Essay on the external Corn Trade." Lond., 1815, p. 62.) The word labour is here used incorrectly for labour-power.

porated daily in labour-power half a day's average social labour, in other words, half a day's labour is requisite for the daily production of labour-power. This quantity of labour forms the value of a day's labour-power or the value of the labour-power daily reproduced. If half a day's average social labour is incorporated in three shillings, then three shillings is the price corresponding to the value of a day's labour-power. If its owner therefore offers it for sale at three shillings a day, its selling price is equal to its value, and according to our supposition, our friend Moneybags, who is intent upon converting his three shillings into capital, pays this value.

The minimum limit of the value of labour-power is determined by the value of the commodities, without the daily supply of which the labourer cannot renew his vital energy, consequently by the value of those means of subsistence that are physically indispensable. If the price of labour-power fall to this minimum, it falls below its value, since under such circumstances it can be maintained and developed only in a crippled state. But the value of every commodity is determined by the labour-time requisite to turn it out so as to be of normal quality.

It is a very cheap sort of sentimentality which declares this method of determining the value of labour-power, a method prescribed by the very nature of the case, to be a brutal method, and which wails with Rossi that, "To comprehend capacity for labour (puissance de travail) at the same time that we make abstraction from the means of subsistence of the labourers during the process of production, is to comprehend a phantom (être de raison). When we speak of labour, or capacity for labour, we speak at the same time of the labourer and his means of subsistence, of labourer and wages."[1] When we speak of capacity for labour, we do not speak of labour, any more than when we speak of capacity for digestion, we speak of digestion. The latter process requires something more than a good stomach. When we speak of capacity for labour we do not abstract from the necessary means of subsistence. On the contrary, their value is expressed in its value. If his capacity

[1] Rossi. "Cours d'Econ. Polit: "Bruxelles, 1842, p. 370.

for labour remains unsold, the labourer derives no benefit from it, but rather he will feel it to be a cruel nature-imposed necessity that this capacity has cost for its production a definite amount of the means of subsistence and that it will continue to do so for its reproduction. He will then agree with Sismondi: "that capacity for labour. . . . is nothing unless it is sold."[1]

One consequence of the peculiar nature of labour-power as a commodity is, that its use-value does not, on the conclusion of this contract between the buyer and seller, immediately pass into the hands of the former. Its value, like that of every other commodity, is already fixed before it goes into circulation, since a definite quantity of social labour has been spent upon it; but its use-value consists in the subsequent exercise of its force. The alienation of labour-power and its actual appropriation by the buyer, its employment as a use-value, are separated by an interval of time. But in those cases in which the formal alienation by sale of the use-value of a commodity, is not simultaneous with its actual delivery to the buyer, the money of the latter usually functions as means of payment.[2] In every country in which the capitalist mode of production reigns, it is the custom not to pay for labour-power before it has been exercised for the period fixed by the contract, as for example, the end of each week. In all cases, therefore, the use-value of the labour-power is advanced to the capitalist: the labourer allows the buyer to consume it before he receives payment of the price; he everywhere gives credit to the capitalist. That this credit is no mere fiction, is shown not only by the occasional loss of wages on the bankruptcy of the capitalist,[3] but also by a series of more enduring consequences.[4] Never-

---

[1] Sismondi: "Nouv. Princ. etc.," t. I. p. 112.

[2] All labour is paid after it has ceased." ("An inquiry into those Principles respecting the nature of Demand," &c., p. 104.) "Le crédit commercial a dü commencer au moment où l'ouvrier, premier artisan de la production, a pu, au moyen de ses économies, attendre le salaire de son travail jusqu, à la fin de la semaine, de la quinzaine, du mois, du trimestre, &c. (Ch. Ganilh: "Des Systèmes de l'Econ. Polit." 2éme. edit. Paris, 1821, t. I. p. 150.)

[3] "L'ouvrier prête son industrie," but adds Storch slyly: he "risks nothing" except "de perdre son salaire . . . . L'ouvrier ne transmet rien de materiel." (Storch: "Cours d'Econ. Polit. Econ." Pétersbourg, 1815, t. II., p. 37.)

[4] One example. In London there are two sorts of bakers, the "full priced," whr

theless, whether money serves as a means of purchase or as a means of payment, this makes no alteration in the nature of the exchange of commodities. The price of the labour-power is fixed by the contract, although it is not realised till later, like the rent of a house. The labour-power is sold, although it is only paid for at a later period. It will, therefore, be useful, for a clear comprehension of the relation of the parties, to assume provisionally, that the possessor of labour-power, on the occasion of each sale, immediately receives the price stipulated to be paid for it.

We now know how the value paid by the purchaser to the

sell bread at its full value, and the "undersellers," who sell it under its value. The latter class comprises more than three-fourths of the total number of bakers. (p. xxxii in the Report of H. S. Tremenheere, commissioner to examine into "the grievances complained of by the journeymen bakers," &c., Lond. 1862.) The undersellers, almost without exception, sell bread adulterated with alum, soap, pearl ashes, chalk, Derbyshire stone-dust, and such like agreeable nourishing and wholesome ingredients. (See the above cited blue book, as also the report of "the committee of 1855 on the adulteration of bread," and Dr. Hassall's "Adulterations detected," 2d Ed. Lond. 1862.) Sir John Gordon stated before the committee of 1855, that "in consequence of these adulterations, the poor man, who lives on two pounds of bread a day, does not now get one fourth part of nourishing matter, let alone the deleterious effects on his health." Tremenheere states (l. c. p. xlviii), as the reason, why a very large part of the working class, although well aware of this adulteration, nevertheless accept the alum, stone-dust, &c., as part of their purchase: that it is for them "a matter of necessity to take from their baker or from the chandler's shop, such bread as they choose to supply." As they are not paid their wages before the end of the week, they in their turn are unable "to pay for the bread consumed by their families, during the week, before the end of the week," and Tremenheere adds on the evidence of witnesses, "it is notorious that bread composed of those mixtures, is made expressly for sale in this manner." In many English and still more Scotch agricultural districts, wages are paid fortnightly and even monthly; with such long intervals between the payments, the agricultural labourer is obliged to buy on credit. . . . He must pay higher prices, and is in fact tied to the shop which gives him credit. Thus at Horningham in Wilts, for example, where the wages are monthly, the same flour that he could buy elsewhere at 1s 10d per stone, costs him 2s 4d per stone. ("Sixth Report" on "Public Health" by "The Medical Officer of the Privy Council, &c., 1864." p. 264.) "The block printers of Paisley and Kilmarnock enforced, by a strike, fortnightly, instead of monthly payment of wages." (Reports of the Inspectors of Factories for 31st Oct., 1853," p. 34.) As a further pretty result of the credit given by the workmen to the capitalist, we may refer to the method current in many English coal mines, where the labourer is not paid till the end of the month, and in the meantime, receives sums on account from the capitalist, often in goods for which the miner is obliged to pay more than the market price (Truck-system). "It is a common practice with the coal masters to pay once a month, and advance cash to their workmen at the end of each intermediate week. The cash is given in the shop" (*i. e.*, the Tommy shop which belongs to the master); "the men take it on one side and lay it out on the other." (Children's Employment Commission, III, Report, London, 1864, p. 38, n. 192.)

possessor of this peculiar commodity, labour-power, is determined. The use-value which the former gets in exchange, manifests itself only in the actual usufruct, in the consumption of the labour-power. The money owner buys everything necessary for this purpose, such as raw material, in the market, and pays for it at its full value. The consumption of labour-power is at one and the same time the production of commodities and of surplus value. The consumption of labour-power is completed, as in the case of every other commodity, outside the limits of the market or of the sphere of circulation. Accompanied by Mr. Moneybags and by the possessor of labour-power, we therefore take leave for a time of this noisy sphere, where everything takes place on the surface and in view of all men, and follow them both into the hidden abode of production, on whose threshold there stares us in the face "No admittance except on business." Here we shall see, not only how capital produces, but how capital is produced. We shall at last force the secret of profit making.

This sphere that we are deserting, within whose boundaries the sale and purchase of labour-power goes on, is in fact a very Eden of the innate rights of man. There alone rule Freedom, Equality, Property and Bentham. Freedom, because both buyer and seller of a commodity, say of labour-power, are constrained only by their own free will. They contract as free agents, and the agreement they come to, is but the form in which they give legal expression to their common will. Equality, because each enters into relation with the other, as with a simple owner of commodities, and they exchange equivalent for equivalent. Property, because each disposes only of what is his own. And Bentham, because each looks only to himself. The only force that brings them together and puts them in relation with each other, is the selfishness, the gain and the private interests of each. Each looks to himself only, and no one troubles himself about the rest, and just because they do so, do they all, in accordance with the pre-established harmony of things, or under the auspices of an all-shrewd providence, work together to their mutual advantage, for the common weal and in the interest of all.

On leaving this sphere of simple circulation or of exchange of commodities, which furnishes the "Free-trader Vulgaris" with his views and ideas, and with the standard by which he judges a society based on capital and wages, we think we can perceive a change in the physiognomy of our dramatis personæ. He, who before was the money owner, now strides, in front as capitalist; the possessor of labour-power follows as his labourer. The one with an air of importance, smirking, intent on business; the other, timid and holding back, like one who is bringing his own hide to market and has nothing to expect but— a hiding.

PART III.

THE PRODUCTION OF ABSOLUTE SURPLUS-VALUE.

CHAPTER VII.

THE LABOUR-PROCESS AND THE PROCESS OF PRODUCING SURPLUS-VALUE.

SECTION 1.—THE LABOUR-PROCESS OR THE PRODUCTION OF USE-VALUES.

THE capitalist buys labour-power in order to use it; and labour-power in use is lab   itself.   The purchaser of labour-power consumes it by setting the seller of it to work.   By working, the latter becomes actually, what before he only was potentially, labour-power in action, a labourer.   In order that his labour may reappear in a commodity, he must, before all things, expend it on something useful, on something capable of satisfying a want of some sort.   Hence, what the capitalist sets the labourer to produce, is a particular use-value, a specified article.   The fact that the production of use-values, or goods, is carried on under the control of a capitalist and on his behalf, does not alter the general character of that production.   We shall, therefore, in the first place, have to consider the labour-process independently of the particular form it assumes under given social conditions.

Labour is, in the first place, a process in which both man and Nature participate, and in which man of his own accord starts, regulates, and controls the material re-actions between himself and Nature.   He opposes himself to Nature as one of her own forces, setting in motion arms and legs, head and hands, the natural forces of his body, in order to appropriate Nature's productions in a form adapted to his own wants. By thus acting on the external world and changing it, he at the same time changes his own nature. He develops his slumbering powers and compels them to act in obedience to his sway. We are not now dealing with those primitive instinctive forms of labour that remind us of the mere animal. An immeasurable interval of time separates the state of things in which a man brings his labour-power to market for sale as a commodity, from that state in which human labour was still in its first instinctive stage. We presuppose labour in a form that stamps it as exclusively human. A spider conducts operations that resemble those of a weaver, and a bee puts to shame many an architect in the construction of her cells. But what distinguishes the worst architect from the best of bees is this, that the architect raises his structure in imagination before he erects it in reality. At the end of every labour-process, we get a result that already existed in the imagination of the labourer at its commencement. He not only effects a change of form in the material on which he works, but he also realises a purpose of his own that gives the law to his modus operandi, and to which he must subordinate his will. And this subordination is no mere momentary act. Besides the exertion of the bodily organs, the process demands that, during the whole operation, the workman's will be steadily in consonance with his purpose. This means close attention. The less he is attracted by the nature of the work, and the mode in which it is carried on, and the less, therefore, he enjoys it as something which gives play to his bodily and mental powers, the more close his attention is forced to be.

The elementary factors of the labour-process are 1, the personal activity of man, *i.e.*, work itself, 2, the subject of that work, and 3, its instruments.

The soil (and this, economically speaking, includes water) in the virgin state in which it supplies[1] man with necessaries

[1] "The earth's spontaneous productions being in small quantity, and quite independent of man, appear, as it were, to be furnished by Nature, in the same way as a

or the means of subsistence ready to hand, exists independently of him, and is the universal subject of human labour. All those things which labour merely separates from immediate connection with their environment, are subjects of labour spontaneously provided by Nature. Such are fish which we catch and take from their element, water, timber which we fell in the virgin forest, and ores which we extract from their veins. If, on the other hand, the subject of labour has, so to say, been filtered through previous labour, we call it raw material; such is ore already extracted and ready for washing. All raw material is the subject of labour, but not every subject of labour is raw material; it can only become so. after it has undergone some alteration by means of labour.

An instrument of labour is a thing, or a complex of things, which the labourer interposes between himself and the subject of his labour, and which serves as the conductor of his activity. He makes use of the mechanical, physical, and chemical properties of some substances in order to make other substances subservient to his aims.[1] Leaving out of consideration such ready-made means of subsistence as fruits, in gathering which a man's own limbs serve as the instruments of his labour, the first thing of which the labourer possesses himself is not the subject of labour but its instrument. Thus Nature becomes one of the organs of his activity, one that he annexes to his own bodily organs, adding stature to himself in spite of the Bible. As the earth is his original larder, so too it is his original tool house. It supplies him, for instance, with stones for throwing, grinding, pressing, cutting, &c. The earth itself is an instrument of labour, but when used as such in agriculture implies a whole series of other instruments and a comparatively high development of labour.[2] No sooner does

small sum is given to a young man, in order to put him in a way of industry, and of making his fortune." (James Steuart: "Principles of Polit. Econ." edit. Dublin, 1770, v. I. p. 116.)

[1] "Reason is just as cunning as she is powerful. Her cunning consists principally in her mediating activity, which, by causing objects to act and re-act on each other in accordance with their own nature, in this way, without any direct interference in the process, carries out reason's intentions." (Hegel: "Encyklopädie, Erster Theil. Die Logik." Berlin, 1840, p. 382.)

[2] In his otherwise miserable work ("Théorie de l'Econ. Polit." Paris, 1819), Ganilh enumerates in a striking manner in opposition to the "Physiocrats" the

labour undergo the least development, than it requires specially
prepared instruments.   Thus in the oldest caves we find stone
implements and weapons.   In the earliest period of human
history domesticated animals, *i.e.*, animals which have been
bred for the purpose, and have undergone modifications by
means of labour, play the chief part as instruments of labour
along with specially prepared stones, wood, bones, and shells.[1]
The use and fabrication of instruments of labour, although
existing in the germ among certain species of animals, is
specifically characteristic of the human labour-process, and
Franklin therefore defines man as a tool-making animal.
Relics of by-gone instruments of labour possess the same importance for the investigation of extinct economical forms of
society, as do fossil bones for the determination of extinct
species of animals.   It is not the articles made, but how they
are made, and by what instruments, that enables us to distinguish different economical epochs.[2]   Instruments of labour
not only supply a standard of the degree of development to
which human labour has attained, but they are also indicators
of the social conditions under which that labour is carried on.
Among the instruments of labour, those of a mechanical nature,
which, taken as a whole, we may call the bone and muscles of
production, offer much more decided characteristics of a given
epoch of production, than those which, like pipes, tubs, baskets,
jars, &c., serve only to hold the materials for labour, which
latter class, we may in a general way, call the vascular system
of production.   The latter first begins to play an important
part in the chemical industries.

   In a wider sense we may include among the instruments of

----

long series of previous processes necessary before agriculture properly so called
can commence.
   [1] Turgot in his "Reflexions sur la Formation et la Distribution des Richesses"
(1766) brings well into prominence the importance of domesticated animals to
early civilisation.
   [2] The least important commodities of all for the technological comparison of
different epochs of production are articles of luxury, in the strict meaning of the
term.   However little our written histories up to this time notice the development of
material production, which is the basis of all social life, and therefore of all real
history, yet prehistoric times have been classified in accordance with the results,
not of so called historical, but of materialistic investigations.   These periods have
been divided, to correspond with the materials from which their implements and
weapons are made, viz., into the stone, the bronze, and the iron ages.

labour, in addition to those things that are used for directly transferring labour to its subject, and which therefore, in one way or another, serve as conductors of activity, all such objects as are necessary for carrying on the labour-process. These do not enter directly into the process, but without them it is either impossible for it to take place at all, or possible only to a partial extent. Once more we find the earth to be a universal instrument of this sort, for it furnishes a locus standi to the labourer and a field of employment for his activity. Among instruments that are the result of previous labour and also belong to this class, we find workshops, canals, roads, and so forth.

In the labour-process, therefore, man's activity, with the help of the instruments of labour, effects an alteration, designed from the commencement, in the material worked upon. The process disappears in the product; the latter is a use-value, Nature's material adapted by a change of form to the wants of man. Labour has incorporated itself with its subject: the former is materialised, the latter transformed. That which in the labourer appeared as movement, now appears in the product as a fixed quality without motion. The blacksmith forges and the product is a forging.

If we examine the whole process from the point of view of its result, the product, it is plain that both the instruments and the subject of labour, are means of production,[1] and that the labour itself is productive labour.[2]

Though a use-value, in the form of a product, issues from the labour-process, yet other use-values, products of previous labour, enter into it as means of production. The same use-value is both the product of a previous process, and a means of production in a later process. Products are therefore not only results, but also essential conditions of labour.

With the exception of the extractive industries, in which

[1] It appears paradoxical to assert, that uncaught fish, for instance, are a means of production in the fishing industry. But hitherto no one has discovered the art of catching fish in waters that contain none.

[2] This method of determining from the standpoint of the labour-process alone, what is productive labour, is by no means directly applicable to the case of the capitalist process of production.

the material for labour is provided immediately by nature,
such as mining, hunting, fishing, and agriculture (so far as the
latter is confined to breaking up virgin soil), all branches of
industry manipulate raw material, objects already filtered
through labour, already products of labour. Such is seed in
agriculture. Animals and plants, which we are accustomed to
consider as products of nature, are in their present form, not
only products of, say last year's labour, but the result of a
gradual transformation, continued through many generations,
under man's superintendence, and by means of his labour.
But in the great majority of cases, instruments of labour show
even to the most superficial observer, traces of the labour of
past ages.

Raw material may either form the principal substance of a
product, or it may enter into its formation only as an accessory. An accessory may be consumed by the instruments of
labour, as coal under a boiler, oil by a wheel, hay by draft-
horses, or it may be mixed with the raw material in order to
produce some modification thereof, as chlorine into unbleached
linen, coal with iron, dye-stuff with wool, or again, it may help
to carry on the work itself, as in the case of the materials used
for heating and lighting workshops. The distinction between
principal substance and accessory vanishes in the true chemical
industries, because there none of the raw material reappears, in
its original composition, in the substance of the product.[1]

Every object possesses various properties, and is thus capable
of being applied to different uses. One and the same product
may therefore serve as raw material in very different processes.
Corn, for example, is a raw material for millers, starch-manu-
facturers, distillers, and cattle-breeders. It also enters as raw
material into its own production in the shape of seed: coal, too,
is at the same time the product of, and a means of production
in, coal-mining.

Again, a particular product may be used in one and the same
process, both as an instrument of labour and as raw material.
Take, for instance, the fattening of cattle, where the animal is

---

[1] Storch calls true raw materials "matières," and accessory material "matériaux:"
Cherbuliez describes accessories as "matières instrumentales."

the raw material, and at the same time an instrument for the production of manure.

A product, though ready for immediate consumption, may yet serve as raw material for a further product, as grapes when they become the raw material for wine. On the other hand, labour may give us its product in such a form, that we can use it only as raw material, as is the case with cotton, thread, and yarn. Such a raw material, though itself a product, may have to go through a whole series of different processes: in each of these in turn, it serves, with constantly varying form, as raw material, until the last process of the series leaves it a perfect product, ready for individual consumption, or for use as an instrument of labour.

Hence we see, that whether a use-value is to be regarded as raw material, as instrument of labour, or as product, this is determined entirely by its function in the labour process, by the position it there occupies: as this varies, so does its character.

Whenever therefore a product enters as a means of production into a new labour-process, it thereby loses its character of product, and becomes a mere factor in the process. A spinner treats spindles only as implements for spinning, and flax only as the material that he spins. Of course it is impossible to spin without material and spindles; and therefore the existence of these things as products, at the commencement of the spinning operation, must be presumed: but in the process itself, the fact that they are products of previous labour, is a matter of utter indifference; just as in the digestive process, it is of no importance whatever, that bread is the produce of the previous labour of the farmer, the miller, and the baker. On the contrary, it is generally by their imperfections as products, that the means of production in any process assert themselves in their character as products. A blunt knife or weak thread forcibly remind us of Mr. A., the cutler, or Mr. B., the spinner. In the finished product the labour by means of which it has acquired its useful qualities is not palpable, has apparently vanished.

A machine which does not serve the purposes of labour, is useless. In addition, it falls a prey to the destructive influence

of natural forces. Iron rusts and wood rots. Yarn with which
we neither weave nor knit, is cotton wasted. Living labour
must seize upon these things and rouse them from their death-
sleep, change them from mere possible use-values into real and
effective ones. Bathed in the fire of labour, appropriated as
part and parcel of labour's organism, and, as it were, made
alive for the performance of their functions in the process, they
are in truth consumed, but consumed with a purpose, as elementary constituents of new use-values, of new products, ever
ready as means of subsistence for individual consumption, or
as means of production for some new labour-process.

If then, on the one hand, finished products are not only
results, but also necessary conditions, of the labour-process, on
the other hand, their assumption into that process, their contact with living labour, is the sole means by which they can be
made to retain their character of use-values, and be utilised.

Labour uses up its material factors, its subject and its instruments, consumes them, and is therefore a process of consumption. Such productive consumption is distinguished
from individual consumption by this, that the latter uses up
products, as means of subsistence for the living individual; the
former, as means whereby alone, labour, the labour-power of
the living individual, is enabled to act. The product, therefore, of individual consumption, is the consumer himself; the
result of productive consumption. is a product distinct from
the consumer.

In so far then, as its instruments and subjects are themselves
products, labour consumes products in order to create products,
or in other words, consumes one set of products by turning
them into means of production for another set. But, just as
in the beginning, the only participators in the labour-process
were man and the earth, which latter exists independently of
man, so even now we still employ in the process many means
of production, provided directly by nature, that do not represent any combination of natural substances with human labour.

The labour process, resolved as above into its simple elementary factors, is human action with a view to the production of use-values, appropriation of natural substances to hu-

man requirements; it is the necessary condition for effecting exchange of matter between man and Nature; it is the everlasting nature-imposed condition of human existence, and therefore is independent of every social phase of that existence, or rather, is common to every such phase. It was, therefore, not necessary to represent our labourer in connexion with other labourers; man a 1 his labour on one side, Nature and its materials on the other, sufficed. As the taste of the porridge does not tell you who grew the oats, no more does this simple process tell you of itself what are the social conditions under which it is taking place, whether under the slave-owner's brutal lash, or the anxious eye of the capitalist, whether Cincinnatus carries it on in tilling his modest farm or a savage in killing wild animals with stones.[1]

Let us now return to our would-be capitalist. We left him just after he had purchased, in the open market, all the necessary factors of the labour-process; its objective factors, the means of production, as well as its subjective factor, labourpower. With the keen eye of an expert, he had selected the means of production and the kind of labour-power best adapted to his particular trade, be it spinning, bootmaking, or any other kind. He then proceeds to consume the commodity, the labour-power that he has just bought, by causing the labourer, the impersonation of that labour-power, to consume the means of production by his labour. The general character of the labour-process is evidently not changed by the fact, that the labourer works for the capitalist instead of for himself; moreover, the particular methods and operations employed in bootmaking or spinning are not immediately changed by the intervention of the capitalist. He must begin by taking the labourpower as he finds it in the market, and consequently be satisfied with labour of such a kind as would be found in the period immediately preceding the rise of the capitalists. Changes in

---

[1] By a wonderful feat of logical acumen, Colonel Torrens has discovered in this stone of the savage the origin of capital. "In the first stone which he [the savage] flings at the wild animal he pursues, in the stick that he seizes to strike down the fruit which hangs above his reach, we see the appropriation of one article for the purpose of aiding in the acquisition of another, and thus discover the origin of capital. (R. Torrens: "An Essay on the Production of Wealth," &c., pp. 70-71.)

the methods of production by the subordination of labour to capital, can take place only at a later period, and therefore will have to be treated of in a later chapter.

The labour-process, turned into the process by which the capitalist consumes labour-power, exhibits two characteristic phenomena. First, the labourer works under the control of the capitalist to whom his labour belongs; the capitalist taking good care that the work is done in a proper manner, and that the means of production are used with intelligence, so that there is no unnecessary waste of raw material, and no wear and tear of the implements beyond what is necessarily caused by the work.

Secondly, the product is the property of the capitalist and not that of the labourer, its immediate producer. Suppose that a capitalist pays for a day's labour-power at its value; then the right to use that power for a day belongs to him, just as much as the right to use any other commodity, such as a horse that he has hired for the day. To the purchaser of a commodity belongs its use, and the seller of labour-power, by giving his labour, does no more, in reality, than part with the use-value that he has sold. From the instant he steps into the workshop, the use-value of his labour-power, and therefore also its use, which is labour, belongs to the capitalist. By the purchase of labour-power, the capitalist incorporates labour, as a living ferment, with the lifeless constituents of the product. From his point of view, the labour-process is nothing more than the consumption of the commodity purchased, *i.e.,* of labour-power; but this consumption cannot be effected except by supplying the labour-power with the means of production. The labour-process is a process between things that the capitalist has purchased, things that have become his property. The product of this process also belongs, therefore, to him, just as much as does the wine which is the product of a process of fermentation completed in his cellar.[1]

[1] "Products are appropriated before they are converted into capital; this conversion does not secure them from such appropriation." (Cherbuliez: "Riche ou Pauvre," edit. Paris, 1841, pp. 53, 54.) "The Proletarian, by selling his labour for a definite quantity of the necessaries of life, renounces all claim to a share in the product. The mode of appropriation of the products remains the same as

SECTION 2.—THE PRODUCTION OF SURPLUS-VALUE.

The product appropriated by the capitalist is a use-value, as yarn, for example, or boots. But, although boots are, in one sense, the basis of all social progress, and our capitalist is a decided "progressist," yet he does not manufacture boots for their own sake. Use-value is, by no means, the thing "qu'on aime pour lui-même" in the production of commodities. Use-values are only produced by capitalists, because, and in so far as, they are the material substratum, the depositaries of exchange-value. Our capitalist has two objects in view: in the first place, he wants to produce a use-value that has a value in exchange, that is to say, an article destined to be sold, a commodity; and secondly, he desires to produce a commodity whose value shall be greater than the sum of the values of the commodities used in its production, that is, of the means of production and the labour-power, that he purchased with his good money in the open market. His aim is to produce not only a use-value, but a commodity also; not only use-value, but value; not only value, but at the same time surplus-value.

It must be borne in mind, that we are now dealing with the production of commodities, and that, up to this point, we have only considered one aspect of the process. Just as commodities are, at the same time, use-values and values, so the process of producing them must be a labour-process, and at the same time, a process of creating value.[1]

before; it is no way altered by the bargain we have mentioned. The product belongs exclusively to the capitalist, who supplied the raw material and the necessaries of life; and this is a rigorous consequence of the law of appropriation, a law whose fundamental principle was the very opposite, namely, that every labourer has an exclusive right to the ownership of what he produces." (l. c. p. 58.) "When the labourers receive wages for their labour . . . . the capitalist is then the owner not of the capital only" (he means the means of production) "but of the labour also. If what is paid as wages is included, as it commonly is, in the term capital, it is absurd to talk of labour separately from capital. The word capital as thus employed includes labour and capital both." (James Mill: "Elements of Pol. Econ.," &c., Ed. 1821, pp. 70, 71.)

[1] As has been stated in a previous note, the English language has two different expressions for these two different aspects of labour; in the Simple Labour-process, the process of producing Use-Values, it is *Work*; in the process of creation of Value, it is *Labour*, taking the term in its strictly economical sense.—Ed.

Let us now examine production as a creation of value.

We know that the value of each commodity is determined by the quantity of labour expended on and materialised in it, by the working-time necessary, under given social conditions, for its production. This rule also holds good in the case of the product that accrued to our capitalist, as the result of the labour-process carried on for him. Assuming this product to be 10 lbs. of yarn, our first step is to calculate the quantity of labour realised in it.

For spinning the yarn, raw material is required; suppose in this case 10 lbs. of cotton. We have no need at present to investigate the value of this cotton, for our capitalist has, we will assume, bought it at its full value, say of ten shillings. In this price the labour required for the production of the cotton is already expressed in terms of the average labour of society. We will further assume that the wear and tear of the spindle, which, for our present purpose, may represent all other instruments of labour employed, amounts to the value of 2s. If, then, twenty-four hours' labour, or two working days, are required to produce the quantity of gold represented by twelve shillings, we have here, to begin with, two days' labour already incorporated in the yarn.

We must not let ourselves be misled by the circumstance that the cotton has taken a new shape while the substance of the spindle has to a certain extent been used up. By the general law of value, if the value of 40 lbs. of yarn=the value of 40 lbs. of cotton+the value of a whole spindle, *i.e.*, if the same working time is required to produce the commodities on either side of this equation, then 10 lbs. of yarn are an equivalent for 10 lbs. of cotton, together with one-fourth of a spindle. In the case we are considering the same working time is materialised in the 10 lbs. of yarn on the one hand, and in the 10 lbs. of cotton and the fraction of a spindle on the other. Therefore, whether value appears in cotton, in a spindle, or in yarn, makes no difference in the amount of that value. The spindle and cotton, instead of resting quietly side by side, join together in the process, their forms are altered, and they are turned into yarn; but their value is no more affected by this fact than it would be if they had been simply exchanged for their equivalent in yarn.

The labour required for the production of the cotton, the raw material of the yarn, is part of the labour necessary to produce the yarn, and is therefore contained in the yarn. The same applies to the labour embodied in the spindle, without whose wear and tear the cotton could not be spun.

Hence, in determining the value of the yarn, or the labour-time required for its production, all the special processes carried on at various times and in different places, which were necessary, first to produce the cotton and the wasted portion of the spindle, and then with the cotton and spindle to spin the yarn, may together be looked on as different and successive phases of one and the same process. The whole of the labour in the yarn is past labour; and it is a matter of no importance that the operations necessary for the production of its constituent elements were carried on at times which, referred to the present, are more remote than the final operation of spinning. If a definite quantity of labour, say thirty days, is requisite to build a house, the total amount of labour incorporated in it is not altered by the fact that the work of the last day is done twenty-nine days later than that of the first. Therefore the labour contained in the raw material and the instruments of labour can be treated just as if it were labour expended in an earlier stage of the spinning process, before the labour of actual spinning commenced.

The values of the means of production, *i.e.,* the cotton and the spindle, which values are expressed in the price of twelve shillings, are therefore constituent parts of the value of the yarn, or, in other words, of the value of the product.

Two conditions must nevertheless be fulfilled. First, the cotton and spindle must concur in the production of a use-value; they must in the present case become yarn. Value is independent of the particular use-value by which it is borne, but it must be embodied in a use-value of some kind. Secondly, the time occupied in the labor of production must not exceed the time really necessary under the given social conditions of the case. Therefore, if no more than 1 lb. of cotton be requisite to spin 1 lb. of yarn, care must be taken that no more than this weight of cotton is consumed in the production of 1 lb. of yarn; and similarly with regard to the spindle. Though the capitalist have a hobby, and use a gold instead of a steel spindle, yet the only labour that counts for anything in the value of the yarn is that which would be required to produce a steel spindle, because no more is necessary under the given social conditions.

We now know what portion of the value of the yarn is owing to the cotton and the spindle. It amounts to twelve shillings or the value of two days' work. The next point for our consideration is, what portion of the value of the yarn is added to the cotton by the labour of the spinner.

We have now to consider this labour under a very different aspect from that which it had during the labour-process; there, we viewed it solely as that particular kind of human activity which changes cotton into yarn; there, the more the labour was suited to the work, the better the yarn, other circumstances remaining the same. The labour of the spinner was then viewed as specifically different from other kinds of productive labour, different on the one hand in its special aim, viz., spinning, different, on the other hand, in the special character of its operations, in the special nature of its means of production and in the special use-value of its product. For the operation of spinning, cotton and spindles are a necessity, but for making rifled cannon they would be of no use whatever. Here, on the contrary, where we consider the labour of the spinner only so far as it is value-creating, *i.e.,* a source of value, his labour differs in no respect from the labour of the man who bores cannon, or (what here more nearly concerns us), from the labour of the cotton-planter and spindle-maker incorporated in the means of production. It is solely by reason of this identity, that cotton planting, spindle making and spinning, are capable of forming the component parts, differing only quantitatively from each other, of one whole, namely, the value of the yarn. Here, we have nothing more to do with the quality, the nature and the specific character of the labour, but merely with its quantity. And this simply requires to be calculated. We proceed upon the assumption that spinning is simple, unskilled labour, the average labour of a given state of society. Hereafter we shall see that the contrary assumption would make no difference.

While the labourer is at work, his labour constantly undergoes a transformation: from being motion, it becomes an object without motion; from being the labourer working, it becomes the thing produced. At the end of one hour's spinning, that act is represented by a definite quantity of yarn; in other words, a definite quantity of labour, namely that of one hour, has become embodied in the cotton. We say labour, *i.e.*, the expenditure of his vital force by the spinner, and not spinning labour, because the special work of spinning counts here, only so far as it is the expenditure of labour-power in general, and not in so far as it is the specific work of the spinner.

In the process we are now considering it is of extreme importance, that no more time be consumed in the work of transforming the cotton into yarn than is necessary under the given social conditions. If under normal, *i.e.*, average social conditions of production, *a* pounds of cotton ought to be made into *b* pounds of yarn by one hour's labour, then a day's labour does not count as 12 hours' labour unless 12 *a* pounds of cotton have been made into 12 *b* pounds of yarn; for in the creation of value, the time that is socially necessary alone counts.

Not only the labour, but also the raw material and the product now appear in quite a new light, very different from that in which we viewed them in the labour-process pure and simple. The raw material serves now merely as an absorbent of a definite quantity of labour. By this absorption it is in fact changed into yarn, because it is spun, because labour-power in the form of spinning is added to it; but the product, the yarn, is now nothing more than a measure of the labour absorbed by the cotton. If in one hour $1\frac{2}{3}$ lbs. of cotton can be spun into $1\frac{2}{3}$ lbs. of yarn, then 10 lbs. of yarn indicate the absorption of 6 hours' labour. Definite quantities of product, these quantities being determined by experience, now represent nothing but definite quantities of labour, definite masses of crystallized labour-time. They are nothing more than the materialisation of so many hours or so many days of social labour.

We are here no more concerned about the facts, that the labour is the specific work of spinning, that its subject is cotton and its product yarn, than we are about the fact that the subject itself is already a product and therefore raw material. If the spinner, instead of spinning, were working in a coal mine, the subject of his labour, the coal, would be supplied by Nature; nevertheless, a definite quantity of extracted coal, a hundred weight, for example, would represent a definite quantity of absorbed labour.

We assumed, on the occasion of its sale, that the value of a day's labour-power is three shillings, and that six hours' labour are incorporated in that sum; and consequently that this amount of labour is requisite to produce the necessaries of life daily required on an average by the labourer. If now our spinner by working for one hour, can convert $1\frac{2}{3}$ lbs. of cotton into $1\frac{2}{3}$ lbs. of yarn,[1] it follows that in six hours he will convert 10 lbs. of cotton into 10 lbs. of yarn. Hence, during the spinning process, the cotton absorbs six hours' labour. The same quantity of labour is also embodied in a piece of gold of the value of three shillings. Consequently by the mere labour of spinning, a value of three shillings is added to the cotton.

Let us now consider the total value of the product, the 10 lbs. of yarn. Two and a half days' labour have been embodied in it, of which two days were contained in the cotton and in the substance of the spindle worn away, and half a day was absorbed during the process of spinning. This two and a half days' labour is also represented by a piece of gold of the value of fifteen shillings. Hence, fifteen shillings is an adequate price for the 10 lbs. of yarn, or the price of one pound is eighteen-pence.

Our capitalist stares in astonishment. The value of the product is exactly equal to the value of the capital advanced. The value so advanced has not expanded, no surplus-value has been created, and consequently money has not been converted into capital. The price of the yarn is fifteen shillings, and

[1] These figures are quite arbitrary.

fifteen shillings were spent in the open market upon the constituent elements of the product, or, what amounts to the same thing, upon the factors of the labour-process; ten shillings were paid for the cotton, two shillings for the substance of the spindle worn away, and three shillings for the labour-power. The swollen value of the yarn is of no avail, for it is merely the sum of the values formerly existing in the cotton, the spindle, and the labour-power; out of such a simple addition of existing values, no surplus-value can possibly arise.[1] These separate values are now all concentrated in one thing; but so they were also in the sum of fifteen shillings, before it was split up into three parts, by the purchase of the commodities.

There is in reality nothing very strange in this result. The value of one pound of yarn being eighteenpence, if our capitalist buys 10 lbs. of yarn in the market, he must pay fifteen shillings for them. It is clear that, whether a man buys his house ready built, or gets it built for him, in neither case will the mode of acquisition increase the amount of money laid out on the house.

Our capitalist, who is at home in his vulgar economy, exclaims: "Oh! but I advanced my money for the express purpose of making more money." The way to Hell is paved with good intentions, and he might just as easily have intended to make money, without producing at all.[2] He threatens all sorts of things. He won't be caught napping again. In future he will buy the commodities in the market, instead of manufacturing them himself. But if all his brother capitalists were to do the same, where would he find his commodities in the market? And his money he cannot eat. He tries persuasion.

[1] This is the fundamental proposition on which is based the doctrine of the Physiocrats as to the unproductiveness of all labour that is not agriculture: it is irrefutable for the orthodox economist. "Cette façon d'imputer à une seule chose la valeur de plusieurs autres" (par exemple au lin la consommation du tisserand), "d'appliquer, pour ainsi dire, couche sur couche, plusieurs valeurs sur une seule, fait que celle-ci grossit d'autant . . . . Le terme d'addition peint très-bien la manière dont se forme le prix des ouvrages de main-d'œuvre; ce prix n'est qu'un total de plusieurs valeurs consommées et additionées ensemble; or, additionner n'est pas multiplier." ("Mercier de la Rivière," l. c., p. 599.)

[2] Thus from 1844-47 he withdrew part of his capital from productive employment, in order to throw it away in railway speculations; and so also, during the American Civil War, he closed his factory, and turned his work-people into the streets, in order to gamble on the Liverpool cotton exchange.

"Consider my abstinence; I might have played ducks and drakes with the 15 shillings; but instead of that I consumed it productively, and made yarn with it." Very well, and by way of reward he is now in possession of good yarn instead of a bad conscience; and as for playing the part of a miser, it would never do for him to relapse into such bad ways as that; we have seen before to what results such asceticism leads. Besides, where nothing is, the king has lost his rights: whatever may be the merit of his abstinence, there is nothing wherewith specially to remunerate it, because the value of the product is merely the sum of the values of the commodities that were thrown into the process of production. Let him therefore console himself with the reflection that virtue is its own reward. But no, he becomes importunate. He says: "The yarn is of no use to me: I produced it for sale." In that case let him sell it, or, still better, let him for the future produce only things for satisfying his personal wants, a remedy that his physician M'Culloch has already prescribed as infallible against an epidemic of over-production. He now gets obstinate. "Can the labourer," he asks, "merely with his arms and legs, produce commodities out of nothing? Did I not supply him with the materials, by means of which, and in which alone, his labour could be embodied? And as the greater part of society consists of such ne'er-do-weels, have I not rendered society incalculable service by my instruments of production, my cotton and my spindle, and not only society, but the labourer also, whom in addition I have provided with the necessaries of life? And am I to be allowed nothing in return for all this service?" Well, but has not the labourer rendered him the equivalent service of changing his cotton and spindle into yarn? Moreover, there is here no question of service.[1] A service is nothing more than the useful effect of

---

[1] Extol thyself, put on finery and adorn thyself . . . but whoever takes more or better than he gives, that is usury, and is not service, but wrong done to his neighbour, as when one steals and robs. All is not service and benefit to a neighbour that is called service and benefit. For an adulteress and adulterer do one another great service and pleasure. A horseman does an incendiary a great service, by helping him to rob on the highway, and pillage land and houses. The papists do ours a great service in that they don't drown, burn, murder all of them, or let them all rot in prison; but let some live, and only drive them out,

a use-value, be it of a commodity, or be it of labour.[1] But here we are dealing with exchange-value. The capitalist paid to the labourer a value of 3 shillings, and the labourer gave him back an exact equivalent in the value of 3 shillings, added by him to the cotton: he gave him value for value. Our friend, up to this time so purse-proud, suddenly assumes the modest demeanour of his own workman, and exclaims: "Have I myself not worked? Have I not performed the labour of superintendence and of overlooking the spinner? And does not this labour, too, create value?" His overlooker and his manager try to hide their smiles. Meanwhile, after a hearty laugh, he re-assumes his usual mien. Though he chanted to us the whole creed of the economists, in reality, he says, he would not give a brass farthing for it. He leaves this and all such like subterfuges and juggling tricks to the professors of political economy, who are paid for it. He himself is a practical man; and though he does not always consider what he says outside his business, yet in his business he knows what he is about.

Let us examine the matter more closely. The value of a day's labour-power amounts to 3 shillings, because on our assumption half a day's labour is embodied in that quantity of labour-power, *i.e.,* because the means of subsistence that are daily required for the production of labour-power, cost half a day's labour. But the past labour that is embodied in the labour-power, and the living labour that it can call into action; the daily cost of maintaining it, and its daily expenditure in work, are two totally different things. The former determines the exchange-value of the labour-power, the latter is its use-value. The fact that half a day's labour is necessary to keep the labourer alive during 24 hours, does not in any way prevent him from working a whole day. Therefore, the value of labour-power, and the value which that labour-power creates

or take from them what they have. The devil himself does his servants inestimable service . . . To sum up, the world is full of great, excellent, and daily service and benefit." (Martin Luther: "An die Pfarherrn, wider den Wucher zu predigen," Wittenberg, 1540.)

[1] In "Critique of Pol. Ec.," p. 34, I make the following remark on this point—"It is not difficult to understand what 'service' the category 'service' must render to a class of economists like J. B. Say and F. Bastiat.'"

in the labour process, are two entirely different magnitudes; and this difference of the two values was what the capitalist had in view, when he was purchasing the labour-power. The useful qualities that labour-power possesses, and by virtue of which it makes yarn or boots, were to him nothing more than a conditio sine qua non; for in order to create value, labour must be expended in a useful manner. What really influenced him was the specific use-value which this commodity possesses of being *a source not only of value, but of more value than it has itself.* This is the special service that the capitalist expects from labour-power, and in this transaction he acts in accordance with the "eternal laws" of the exchange of commodities. The seller of labour-power, like the seller of any other commodity, realises its exchange-value, and parts with its use-value. He cannot take the one without giving the other. The use-value of labour-power, or in other words, labour, belongs just as little to its seller, as the use-value of oil after it has been sold belongs to the dealer who has sold it. The owner of the money has paid the value of a day's labour-power; his, therefore, is the use of it for a day; a day's labour belongs to him. The circumstance, that on the one hand the daily sustenance of labour-power costs only half a day's labour, while on the other hand the very same labour-power can work during a whole day, that consequently the value which its use during one day creates, is double what he pays for that use, this circumstance is, without doubt, a piece of good luck for the buyer, but by no means an injury to the seller.

Our capitalist foresaw this state of things, and that was the cause of his laughter. The labourer therefore finds, in the workshop, the means of production necessary for working, not only during six, but during twelve hours. Just as during the six hours' process our 10 lbs. of cotton absorbed six hours' labour, and became 10 lbs. of yarn, so now, 20 lbs. of cotton will absorb 12 hours' labour and be changed into 20 lbs. of yarn. Let us now examine the product of this prolonged process. There is now materialised in this 20 lbs. of yarn the labour of five days, of which four days are due to the cotton and the lost steel of the spindle, the remaining day having been absorbed by the cotton during the spinning process. Expressed in gold, the labour of five days is thirty shillings. This is therefore the price of the 20 lbs. of yarn, giving, as before, eighteenpence as the price of a pound. But the sum of the values of the commodities that entered into the process amounts to 27 shillings. The value of the yarn is 30 shillings. Therefore the value of the product is $\frac{1}{9}$ greater than the value advanced for its production; 27 shillings have been transformed into 30 shillings; a surplus-value of 3 shillings has been created. The trick has at last succeeded; money has been converted into capital.

Every condition of the problem is satisfied, while the laws that regulate the exchange of commodities, have been in no way violated. Equivalent has been exchanged for equivalent. For the capitalist as buyer paid for each commodity, for the cotton, the spindle and the labour-power, its full value. He then did what is done by every purchaser of commodities; he consumed their use-value. The consumption of the labour-power, which was also the process of producing commodities, resulted in 20 lbs. of yarn, having a value of 30 shillings. The capitalist, formerly a buyer, now returns to market as a seller, of commodities. He sells his yarn at eighteenpence a pound, which is its exact value. Yet for all that he withdraws 3 shillings more from circulation than he originally threw into it. This metamorphosis, this conversion of money into capital, takes place both within the sphere of circulation and also outside it; within the circulation, because conditioned by the purchase of the labour-power in the market; outside the circulation, because what is done within it is only a stepping-stone to the production of surplus-value, a process which is entirely confined to the sphere of production. Thus "tout est pour le mieux dans le meilleur des mondes possibles."

By turning his money into commodities that serve as the material elements of a new product, and as factors in the labour-process, by incorporating living labour with their dead substance, the capitalist at the same time converts value, *i.e.,* past, materialised, and dead labour into capital, into value big with value, a live monster that is fruitful and multiplies.

If we now compare the two processes of producing value and of creating surplus-value, we see that the latter is nothing but the continuation of the former beyond a definite point. If on the one hand the process be not carried beyond the point, where the value paid by the capitalist for the labour-power is replaced by an exact equivalent, it is simply a process of producing value; if, on the other hand, it be continued beyond that point, it becomes a process of creating surplus-value.

If we proceed further, and compare the process of producing value with the labour-process, pure and simple, we find that the latter consists of the useful labour, the work, that produces use-values. Here we contemplate the labour as producing a particular article; we view it under its qualitative aspect alone, with regard to its end and aim. But viewed as a value-creating process, the same labour-process presents itself under its quantitative aspect alone. Here it is a question merely of the time occupied by the labourer in doing the work; of the period during which the labour-power is usefully expended. Here, the commodities that take part in the process, do not count any longer as necessary adjuncts of labour-power in the production of a definite, useful object. They count merely as depositaries of so much absorbed or materialised labour; that labour, whether previously embodied in the means of production, or incorporated in them for the first time during the process by the action of labour-power, counts in either case only according to its duration; it amounts to so many hours or days as the case may be.

Moreover, only so much of the time spent in the production of any article is counted, as, under the given social conditions, is necessary. The consequences of this are various. In the first place, it becomes necessary that the labour should be carried on under normal conditions. If a self-acting mule is the implement in general use for spinning, it would be absurd to supply the spinner with a distaff and spinning wheel. The cotton too must not be such rubbish as to cause extra waste in being worked, but must be of suitable quality. Otherwise the spinner would be found to spend more time in producing a pound of yarn than is socially necessary, in which case the excess of time would create neither value nor money. But whether the material factors of the process are of normal quality or not, depends not upon the labourer, but entirely upon the capitalist. Then again, the labour-power itself must be of average efficacy. In the trade in which it is being employed, it must possess the average skill, handiness and quickness prevalent in that trade, and our capitalist took good care to buy labour-power of such normal goodness. This power must be applied with the average amount of exertion and with the usual degree of intensity; and the capitalist is as careful to see that this is done, as that his workmen are not idle for a single moment. He has bought the use of the labour-power for a definite period, and he insists upon his rights. He has no intention of being robbed. Lastly, and for this purpose our friend has a penal code of his own, all wasteful consumption of raw material or instruments of labour is strictly forbidden, because what is so wasted, represents labour superfluously expended, labour that does not count in the product or enter into its value.[1]

We now see, that the difference between labour, considered on the one hand as producing utilities, and on the other hand,

[1] This is one of the circumstances that makes production by slave labour such a costly process. The labourer here is, to use a striking expression of the ancients, distinguishable only as *instrumentum vocale*, from an animal as *instrumentum semi-vocale*, and from an implement as *instrumentum mutum*. But he himself takes care to let both beast and implement feel that he is none of them, but is a man. He convinces himself with immense satisfaction, that he is a different being, by treating the one unmercifully and damaging the other con amore. Hence the principle, universally applied in this method of production, only to employ the rudest and heaviest implements and such as are difficult to damage owing to their sheer clumsiness. In the slave-states bordering on the Gulf of Mexico, down to the date of the civil war, ploughs constructed on old Chinese models, which turned up the soil like a hog or a mole, instead of making furrows, were alone to be found. Conf. J. C. Cairns. "The Slave Power," London, 1862, p. 46-49. In his "Sea Board Slave States," Olmsted tells us: "I am here shown tools that no man in his senses, with us, would allow a labourer, for whom he was paying wages, to be incumbered with; and the excessive weight and clumsiness of which, I would judge, would make work at least ten per cent greater than with those ordinarily used with us. And I am assured that, in the careless and clumsy way they must be used by the slaves, anything lighter or less rude could not be furnished them with good economy, and that such tools as we constantly give our labourers and find our profit in giving them, would not last out a day in a Virginia cornfield—much lighter and more free from stones though it be than ours. So, too, when I ask why mules are so universally substituted for horses on the farm, the first reason given, and confessedly the most conclusive one, is that horses cannot bear the treatment that they always must get from the negroes; horses are always soon foundered or crippled by them,

as creating value, a difference which we discovered by our analysis of a commodity, resolves itself into a distinction between two aspects of the process of production.

The process of production, considered on the one hand as the unity of the labour-process and the process of creating value, is production of commodities; considered on the other hand as the unity of the labour-process and the process of producing surplus-value, it is the capitalist process of production, or capitalist production of commodities.

We stated, on a previous page, that in the creation of surplus-value it does not in the least matter, whether the labour appropriated by the capitalist be simple unskilled labour of average quality or more complicated skilled labour. All labour of a higher or more complicated character than average labour is expenditure of labour-power of a more costly kind, labour-power whose production has cost more time and labour, and which therefore has a higher value, than unskilled or simple labour-power. This power being of higher value, its consumption is labour of a higher class, labour that creates in equal times proportionally higher values than unskilled labour does. Whatever difference in skill there may be between the labour of a spinner and that of a jeweller, the portion of his labour by which the jeweller merely replaces the value of his own labour-power, does not in any way differ in quality from the additional portion by which he creates surplus-value. In the making of jewellery, just as in spinning, the surplus-value results only from a quantitative excess of labour, from a lengthening-out of one and the same labour-process, in the one case, of the process of making jewels, in the other of the process of making yarn.[1]

---

while mules will bear cudgelling, or lose a meal or two now and then, and not be materially injured, and they do not take cold or get sick, if neglected or overworked. But I do not need to go further than the window of the room in which I am writing, to see at almost any time, treatment of cattle that would ensure the immediate discharge of the driver by almost any farmer owning them in the North."

[1] The distinction between skilled and unskilled labour rests in part on pure illusion, or, to say the least, on distinctions that have long since ceased to be real, and that survive only by virtue of a traditional convention; in part on the helpless condition of some groups of the working-class, a condition that prevents them from exacting equally with the rest the value of their labour-power. Accidental circumstances here play so great a part, that these two forms of labour sometimes

But on the other hand, in every process of creating value, the reduction of skilled labour to average social labour, *e.g.*, one day of skilled to six days of unskilled labour, is unavoidable.[1] We therefore save ourselves a superfluous operation, and simplify our analysis, by the assumption, that the labour of the workman employed by the capitalist is unskilled average labour.

CHAPTER VIII.

CONSTANT CAPITAL AND VARIABLE CAPITAL.

THE various factors of the labour-process play different parts in forming the value of the product.

The labourer adds fresh value to the subject of his labour by expending upon it a given amount of additional labour, no matter what the specific character and utility of that labour may be. On the other hand, the values of the means of production used up in the process are preserved, and present

change places. Where, for instance, the physique of the working-class has deteriorated, and is, relatively speaking, exhausted, which is the case in all countries with a well developed capitalist production, the lower forms of labour which demand great expenditure of muscle, are in general considered as skilled, compared with much more delicate forms of labour; the latter sink down to the level of unskilled labour. Take as an example the labour of a bricklayer, which in England occupies a much higher level than that of a damask-weaver. Again, although the labour of a fustian cutter demands great bodily exertion, and is at the same time unhealthy, yet it counts only as unskilled labour. And then, we must not forget, that the so-called skilled labour does not occupy a large space in the field of national labour. Laing estimates that in England (and Wales) the livelihood of 11,300,000 people depends on unskilled labour. If from the total population of 18,000,000 living at the time when he wrote, we deduct 1,000,000 for the "genteel population," and 1,500,000 for paupers, vagrants, criminals, prostitutes, &c., and 4,650,000 who compose the middle-class, there remain the above mentioned 11,000,000. But in his middle-class he includes people that live on the interest of small investments, officials, men of letters, artists, schoolmasters and the like, and in order to swell the number he also includes in these 4,650,000 the better paid portion of the factory operatives! The bricklayers, too, figure amongst them. (S. Laing: "National Distress," &c., London, 1844.) "The great class who have nothing to give for food but ordinary labour, are the great bulk of the people." (James Mill, in art: "Colony," Supplement to the Encyclop. Brit., 1831.)

[1] "Where reference is made to labour as a measure of value, it necessarily implies labour of one particular kind . . . the proportion which the other kinds bear to it being easily ascertained." ("Outlines of Pol. Econ.," Lond., 1832, pp. 22 and 23.)

themselves afresh as constituent parts of the value of the product; the values of the cotton and the spindle, for instance, reappear again in the value of the yarn. The value of the means of production is therefore preserved, by being transferred to the product. This transfer takes place during the conversion of those means into a product, or in other words, during the labour-process. It is brought about by labour; but how?

The labourer does not perform two operations at once, one in order to add value to the cotton, the other in order to preserve the value of the means of production, or, in what amounts to the same thing, to transfer to the yarn, to the product, the value of the cotton on which he works, and part of the value of the spindle with which he works. But, by the very act of adding new value, he preserves their former values. Since, however, the addition of new value to the subject of his labour, and the preservation of its former value, are two entirely distinct results, produced simultaneously by the labourer, during one operation, it is plain that this twofold nature of the result can be explained only by the twofold nature of his labour; at one and the same time, it must in one character create value, and in another character preserve or transfer value.

Now, in what manner does every labourer add new labour and consequently new value? Evidently, only by labouring productively in a particular way; the spinner by spinning, the weaver by weaving, the smith by forging. But, while thus incorporating labour generally, that is value, it is by the particular form alone of the labour, by the spinning, the weaving and the forging respectively, that the means of production, the cotton and spindle, the yarn and loom, and the iron and anvil become constituent elements of the product, of a new use-value.[1] Each use-value disappears, but only to re-appear under a new form in a new use-value. Now, we saw, when we were considering the process of creating value, that, if a use-value be effectively consumed in the production of a new use-value, the quantity of labour expended in the production

---

[1] "Labour gives a new creation for one extinguished." ("An essay on the Polit. Econ. of Nations," London, 1821, p. 13.)

of the consumed article, forms a portion of the quantity of labour necessary to produce the new use-value; this portion is therefore labour transferred from the means of production to the new product. Hence, the labourer preserves the values of the consumed means of production, or transfers them as portions of its value to the product, not by virtue of his additional labour, abstractedly considered, but by virtue of the particular useful character of that labour, by virtue of its special productive form. In so far then as labour is such specific productive activity, in so far as it is spinning, weaving, or forging, it raises, by mere contact, the means of production from the dead, makes them living factors of the labour-process, and combines with them to form the new products.

If the special productive labour of the workman were not spinning, he could not convert the cotton into yarn, and therefore could not transfer the values of the cotton and spindle to the yarn. Suppose the same workman were to change his occupation to that of a joiner, he would still by a day's labour add value to the material he works upon. Consequently, we see, first, that the addition of new value takes place not by virtue of his labour being spinning in particular, or joinering in particular, but because it is labour in the abstract, a portion of the total labour of society; and we see next, that the value added is of a given definite amount, not because his labour has a special utility, but because it is exerted for a definite time. On the one hand, then, it is by virtue of its general character, as being expenditure of human labour-power in the abstract, that spinning adds new value to the values of the cotton and the spindle; and on the other hand, it is by virtue of its special character, as being a concrete, useful process, that the same labour of spinning both transfers the values of the means of production to the product, and preserves them in the product. Hence at one and the same time there is produced a twofold result.

By the simple addition of a certain quantity of labour, new value is added, and by the quality of this added labour, the original values of the means of production are preserved in the product. This twofold effect, resulting from the twofold character of labour, may be traced in various phenomena.

Let us assume, that some invention enables the spinner to spin as much cotton in 6 hours as he was able to spin before in 36 hours. His labour is now six times as effective as it was, for the purposes of useful production. The product of 6 hours' work has increased sixfold, from 6 lbs. to 36 lbs. But now the 36 lbs. of cotton absorb only the same amount of labour as formerly did the 6 lbs. One-sixth as much new labour is absorbed by each pound of cotton, and consequently, the value added by the labour to each pound is only one-sixth of what it formerly was. On the other hand, in the product, in the 36 lbs. of yarn, the value transferred from the cotton is six times as great as before. By the 6 hours' spinning, the value of the raw material preserved and transferred to the product is six times as great as before, although the new value added by the labour of the spinner to each pound of the very same raw material is one-sixth what it was formerly. This shows that the two properties of labour, by virtue of which it is enabled in one case to preserve value, and in the other to create value, are essentially different. On the one hand, the longer the time necessary to spin a given weight of cotton into yarn, the greater is the new value added to the material; on the other hand, the greater the weight of the cotton spun in a given time, the greater is the value preserved, by being transferred from it to the product.

Let us now assume, that the productiveness of the spinner's labour, instead of varying, remains constant, that he therefore requires the same time as he formerly did, to convert one pound of cotton into yarn, but that the exchange value of the cotton varies, either by rising to six times its former value or falling to one-sixth of that value. In both these cases, the spinner puts the same quantity of labour into a pound of cotton, and therefore adds as much value, as he did before the change in the value: he also produces a given weight of yarn in the same time as he did before. Nevertheless, the value that he transfers from the cotton to the yarn is either one-sixth of what it was before the variation, or, as the case may be, six times as much as before. The same result occurs when the value of the instruments of labour rises or falls, while their useful efficacy in the process remains unaltered.

Again, if the technical conditions of the spinning process remain unchanged, and no change of value takes place in the means of production, the spinner continues to consume in equal working-times equal quantities of raw material, and equal quantities of machinery of unvarying value. The value that he preserves in the product is directly proportional to the new value that he adds to the product. In two weeks he incorporates twice as much labour, and therefore twice as much value, as in one week, and during the same time he consumes twice as much material, and wears out twice as much machinery, of double the value in each case; he therefore preserves, in the product of two weeks, twice as much value as in the product of one week. So long as the conditions of production remain the same, the more value the labourer adds by fresh labour, the more value he transfers and preserves; but he does so merely because this addition of new value takes place under conditions that have not varied and are independent of his own labour. Of course, it may be said in one sense, that the labourer preserves old value always in proportion to the quantity of new value that he adds. Whether the value of cotton rise from one shilling to two shillings, or fall to sixpence, the workman invariably preserves in the product of one hour only one half as much value as he preserves in two hours. In like manner, if the productiveness of his own labour varies by rising or falling, he will in one hour spin either more or less cotton, as the case may be, than he did before, and will consequently preserve in the product of one hour, more or less value of cotton; but, all the same, he will preserve by two hours' labour twice as much value as he will by one.

Value exists only in articles of utility, in objects: we leave out of consideration its purely symbolical representation by tokens. (Man himself, viewed as the impersonation of labour-power, is a natural object, a thing, although a living conscious thing, and labour is the manifestation of this power residing in him.) If therefore an article loses it utility, it also loses its value. The reason why means of production do not lose their value, at the same time that they lose their use-value, is this: they lose in the labour-process the original form of their use-value, only to assume in the product the form of a new use-value. But, however important it may be to value, that it should have some object of utility to embody itself in, yet it is a matter of complete indifference what particular object serves this purpose; this we saw when treating of the metamorphosis of commodities. Hence it follows that in the labour-process the means of production transfer their value to the product only so far as along with their use-value they lose also their exchange value. They give up to the product that value alone which they themselves lose as means of production. But in this respect the material factors of the labour-process do not all behave alike.

The coal burnt under the boiler vanishes without leaving a trace; so, too, the tallow with which the axles of wheels are greased. Dye stuffs and other auxiliary substances also vanish but re-appear as properties of the product. Raw material forms the substance of the product, but only after it has changed its form. Hence raw material and auxiliary substances lost the characteristic form with which they are clothed on entering the labour-process. It is otherwise with the instruments of labour. Tools, machines, workshops, and vessels, are of use in the labour-process, only so long as they retain their original shape, and are ready each morning to renew the process with their shape unchanged. And just as during their lifetime, that is to say, during the continued labour-process in which they serve, they retain their shape independent of the product, so, too, they do after their death. The corpses of machines, tools, workshops, &c., are always separate and distinct from the product they helped to turn out. If we now consider the case of any instrument of labour during the whole period of its service, from the day of its entry into the workshop, till the day of its banishment into the lumber room, we find that during this period its use-value has been completely consumed, and therefore its exchange value completely transferred to the product. For instance, if a spinning machine lasts for 10 years, it is plain that during that working period

its total value is gradually transferred to the product of the
10 years.   The lifetime of an instrument of labour, therefore,
is spent in the repetition of a greater or less number of similar
operations.   Its life may be compared with that of a human
being.   Every day brings a man 24 hours nearer to his grave:
but how many days he has still to travel on that road, no man
can tell accurately by merely looking at him.   This difficulty,
however, does not prevent life insurance offices from drawing,
by means of the theory of averages, very accurate, and at the
same time very profitable conclusions. . So it is with the instruments of labour.   It is known by experience how long on the
average a machine of a particular kind will last.   Suppose its
use-value in the labour-process to last only six days.   Then,
on the average, it loses each day one-sixth of its use-value, and
therefore parts with one-sixth of its value to the daily product.
The wear and tear of all instruments, their daily loss of use-
value, and the corresponding quantity of value they part with
to the product, are accordingly calculated upon this basis.

It is thus strikingly clear, that means of production never
transfer more value to the product than they themselves lose
during the labour-process by the destruction of their own use-
value.   If such an instrument has no value to lose, if, in other
words, it is not the product of human labour, it transfers no
value to the product.   It helps to create use-value without contributing to the formation of exchange value.   In this class
are included all means of production supplied by Nature without human assistance, such as land, wind, water, metals in
situ, and timber in virgin forests.

Yet another interesting phenomenon here presents itself.
Suppose a machine to be worth £1000, and to wear out in 1000
days.   Then one thousandth part of the value of the machine
is daily transferred to the day's product.   At the same time,
though with diminishing vitality, the machine as a whole continues to take part in the labour-process.   Thus it appears
that one factor of the labour-process, a means of production,
continually enters as a whole into that process, while it enters
into the process of the formation of value by fractions only.
The difference between the two processes is here reflected in

their material factors, by the same instrument of production taking part as a whole in the labour-process, while at the same time as an element in the formation of value, it enters only by fractions.[1]

On the other hand, a means of production may take part as a whole in the formation of value, while into the labour-process it enters only bit by bit. Suppose that in spinning cotton, the waste for every 115 lbs. used amounts to 15 lbs., which is converted, not into yarn, but into "devil's dust." Now, although this 15 lbs. of cotton never becomes a constituent element of the yarn, yet assuming this amount of waste to be normal and inevitable under average conditions of spinning, its value is just as surely transferred to the value of the yarn, as is the value of the 100 lbs. that form the substance of the yarn. The use-value of 15 lbs. of cotton must vanish into dust, before 100 lbs. of yarn can be made. The destruction of this cotton is therefore a necessary condition in the production of the yarn. And because it is a necessary condition, and for no other reason, the value of that cotton is transferred to the product. The same holds good for every kind of refuse resulting from a labour-process, so far at least as such refuse cannot be further employed as a means in the production of new and independent

---

[1] The subject of repairs of the implements of labour does not concern us here. A machine that is undergoing repair, no longer plays the part of an instrument, but that of a subject of labour. Work is no longer done with it, but upon it. It is quite permissible for our purpose to assume, that the labour expended on the repairs of instruments is included in the labour necessary for their original production. But in the text we deal with that wear and tear, which no doctor can cure, and which little by little brings about death, with "that kind of wear which cannot be repaired from time to time, and which, in the case of a knife, would ultimately reduce it to a state in which the cutler would say of it, it is not worth a new blade." We have shewn in the text, that a machine takes part in every labour-process as an integral machine, but that into the simultaneous process of creating value it enters only bit by bit. How great then is the confusion of ideas exhibited in the following extract! "Mr. Ricardo says a portion of the labour of the engineer in making [stocking] machines" is contained for example in the value of a pair of stockings. "Yet the total labour, that produced each single pair of stockings . . . . includes the whole labour of the engineer, not a portion; for one machine makes many pairs, and none of those pairs could have been done without any part of the machine." ("Obs. on certain verbal disputes in Pol. Econ. particularly relating to value," p. 54.) The author, an uncommonly self-satisfied wiseacre, is right in his confusion and therefore in his contention, to this extent only, that neither Ricardo nor any other economist, before or since him, has accurately distinguished the two aspects of labour, and still less, therefore, the part played by it under each of these aspects in the formation of value.

use-values. Such an employment of refuse may be seen in the large machine works at Manchester, where mountains of iron turnings are carted away to the foundry in the evening, in order the next morning to re-appear in the workshops as solid masses of iron.

We have seen that the means of production transfer value to the new product, so far only as during the labour-process they lose value in the shape of their old use-value. The maximum loss of value that they can suffer in the process, is plainly limited by the amount of the original value with which they came into the process, or in other words, by the labour-time necessary for their production. Therefore the means of production can never add more value to the product than they themselves possess independently of the process in which they assist. However useful a given kind of raw material, or a machine, or other means of production may be, though it may cost £150, or, say, 500 days' labour, yet it cannot, under any circumstances, add to the value of the product more than £150. Its value is determined not by the labour-process into which it enters as a means of production, but by that out of which it has issued as a product. In the labour-process it only serves as a mere use-value, a thing with useful properties, and could not, therefore, transfer any value to the product, unless it possessed such value previously.[1]

---

[1] From this we may judge of the absurdity of J. B. Say, who pretends to account for surplus-value (Interest, Profit, Rent), by the "services productifs" which the means of production, soil, instruments, and raw material, render in the labour-process by means of their use-values. Mr. Wm. Roscher who seldom loses an occasion of registering, in black and white, ingenious apologetic fancies, records the following specimen:—"J. B. Say (Traité, t. 1. ch. 4) very truly remarks: the value produced by an oil mill, after deduction of all costs, is something new, something quite different from the labour by which the oil mill itself was erected." (l. c., p. 82, note.) Very true, Mr. Professor! the oil produced by the oil mill is indeed something very different from the labour expended in constructing the mill! By value, Mr. Roscher understands such stuff as "oil," because oil has value, notwithstanding that "Nature" produces petroleum, though relatively "in small quantities," a fact to which he seems to refer in his further observation: "It (Nature) produces scarcely any exchange value." Mr. Roscher's "Nature" and the exchange value it produces are rather like the foolish virgin who admitted indeed that she had had a child, but "it was such a little one." This "savant sérieux" in continuation remarks: "Ricardo's school is in the habit of including capital as accumulated labour under the head of labour. This is unskilful work, because, indeed, the owner of capital, after all, does something more than the merely creating and preserving of the same: namely, the abstention from the enjoyment of it, for which he demands, *e.g.*, interest." (l. c.)

While productive labour is changing the means of production into constituent elements of a new product, their value undergoes a metempsychosis. It deserts the consumed body, to occupy the newly created one. But this transmigration takes place, as it were, behind the back of the labourer. He is unable to add new labour, to create new value, without at the same time preserving old values, and this, because the labour he adds must be of a specific useful kind; and he cannot do work of a useful kind, without employing products as the means of production of a new product, and thereby transferring their value to the new product. The property therefore which labour-power in action, living labour, possesses of preserving value, at the same time that it adds it, is a gift of Nature which costs the labourer nothing, but which is very advantageous to the capitalist inasmuch as it preserves the existing value of his capital.[1] So long as trade is good, the capitalist is too much absorbed in money-grubbing to take notice of this gratuitous gift of labour. A violent interruption of the labour-process by a crisis, makes him sensitively aware of it.[2]

As regards the means of production, what is really consumed is their use-value, and the consumption of this use-value by labour results in the product. There is no consumption of

How very "skilful" is this "anatomico-physiological method" of political economy, which, "indeed," converts a mere desire "after all" into a source of value.

[1] "Of all the instruments of the farmers' trade, the labour of man . . . is that on which he is most to rely for the repayment of his capital. The other two . . . the working stock of the cattle and the . . . carts, ploughs, spades, and so forth, without a given portion of the first, are nothing at all." (Edmund Burke: "Thoughts and Details on Scarcity, originally presented to the Right Hon. W. Pitt, in the month of November 1795," Edit. London, 1800, p. 10.)

[2] In "The Times" of 26th November, 1862, a manufacturer, whose mill employed 800 hands, and consumed, on the average, 150 bales of East Indian, or 130 bales of American cotton, complains, in doleful manner, of the standing expenses of his factory when not working. He estimates them at £6,000 a year. Among them are a number of items that do not concern us here, such as rent, rates, and taxes, insurance, salaries of the manager, book-keeper, engineer, and others. Then he reckons £150 for coal used to heat the mill occasionally, and run the engine now and then. Besides this, he includes the wages of the people employed at odd times to keep the machinery in working order. Lastly, he puts down £1,200 for depreciation of machinery, because "the weather and the natural principle of decay do not suspend their operations because the steam-engine ceases to revolve." He says, emphatically, he does not estimate his depreciation at more than the small sum of £1,200, because his machinery is already nearly worn out.

their value,[1] and it would therefore be inaccurate to say that
it is reproduced. It is rather preserved; not by reason of any
operation it undergoes itself in the process; but because the
article in which it originally exists, vanishes, it is true, but
vanishes into some other article. Hence, in the value of the
product, there is a re-appearance of the value of the means of
production, but there is, strictly speaking, no reproduction of
that value. That which is produced is a new use-value in
which the old exchange-value re-appears.[2]

It is otherwise with the subjective factor of the labour-process, with labour-power in action. While the labourer, by
virtue of his labour being of a specialised kind that has a
special object, preserves and transfers to the product the value
of the means of production, he at the same time, by the mere
act of working, creates each instant an additional or new value.
Suppose the process of production to be stopped just when the
workman has produced an equivalent for the value of his own
labour-power, when, for example, by six hours' labour, he has
added a value of three shillings. This value is the surplus, of
the total value of the product, over the portion of its value
that is due to the means of production. It is the only original
bit of value formed during this process, the only portion of the
value of the product created by this process. Of course, we
do not forget that this new value only replaces the money
advanced by the capitalist in the purchase of the labour-power,

[1] "Productive consumption . . . where the consumption of a commodity is a part
of the process of production. . . . In these instances there is no consumption of
value." (S. P. Newman, l. c. p. 296.)

[2] In an American compendium that has gone through, perhaps, 20 editions, this
passage occurs: "It matters not in what form capital re-appears;" then after a
lengthy enumeration of all the possible ingredients of production whose value re-
appears in the product, the passage concludes thus: "The various kinds of food,
clothing, and shelter, necessary for the existence and comfort of the human being,
are also changed. They are consumed from time to time, and their value re-appears
in that new vigour imparted to his body and mind, forming fresh capital, to be employed again in the work of production." (F. Wayland, l. c. pp. 31, 32.) Without
noticing any other oddities, it suffices to observe, that what re-appears in the fresh
vigour, is not the bread's price, but its blood-forming substances. What, on the
other hand, re-appears in the value of that vigour, is not the means of subsistence,
but their value. The same necessaries of life, at half the price, would form just as
much muscle and bone, just as much vigour, but not vigour of the same value. This
confusion of "value" and "vigour" coupled with our author's pharisaical indefinite-
ness, mark an attempt, futile for all that, to thrash out an explanation of surplus-
value from a mere re-appearance of pre-existing values.

and spent by the labourer on the necessaries of life. With
regard to the money spent, the new value is merely a reproduction; but, nevertheless, it is an actual, and not, as in the
case of the value of the means of production, only an apparent,
reproduction. The substitution of one value for another, is
here effected by the creation of new value.

We know, however, from what has gone before, that the
labour-process may continue beyond the time necessary to reproduce and incorporate in the product a mere equivalent for
the value of the labour-power. Instead of the six hours that
are sufficient for the latter purpose, the process may continue
for twelve hours. The action of labour-power, therefore, not
only reproduces its own value, but produces value over and
above it. This surplus-value is the difference between the
value of the product and the value of the elements consumed
in the formation of that product, in other words, of the means
of production and the labour-power.

By our explanation of the different parts played by the various factors of the labour-process in the formation of the product's value, we have, in fact, disclosed the characters of the
different functions allotted to the different elements of capital
in the process of expanding its own value. The surplus of the
total value of the product, over the sum of the values of its
constituent factors, is the surplus of the expanded capital over
the capital originally advanced. The means of production on
the one hand, labour-power on the other, are merely the different modes of existence which the value of the original capital
assumed when from being money it was transformed into the
various factors of the labour-process. That part of capital
then, which is represented by the means of production, by the
raw material, auxiliary material and the instruments of labour,
does not, in the process of production, undergo any quantitative
alteration of value. I therefore call it the constant part of
capital, or, more shortly, *constant capital*.

On the other hand, that part of capital, represented by
labour-power, does, in the process of production, undergo an
alteration of value. It both reproduces the equivalent of its
own value, and also produces an excess, a surplus-value, which

may itself vary, may be more or less according to circumstances. This part of capital is continually being transformed from a constant into a variable magnitude. I therefore call it the variable part of capital, or, shortly, *variable capital.* The same elements of capital which, from the point of view of the labour-process, present themselves respectively as the objective and subjective factors, as means of production and labour-power, present themselves, from the point of view of the process of creating surplus-value, as constant and variable capital.

The definition of constant capital given above by no means excludes the possibility of a change of value in its elements. Suppose the price of cotton to be one day sixpence a pound, and the next day, in consequence of a failure of the cotton crop, a shilling a pound. Each pound of the cotton bought at sixpence, and worked up after the rise in value, transfers to the product a value of one shilling; and the cotton already spun before the rise, and perhaps circulating in the markets as yarn, likewise transfers to the product twice its original value. It is plain, however, that these changes of value are independent of the increment or surplus-value added to the value of the cotton by the spinning itself. If the old cotton had never been spun, it could, after the rise, be resold at a shilling a pound instead of at sixpence. Further, the fewer the processes the cotton has gone through, the more certain is this result. We therefore find that speculators make it a rule when such sudden changes in value occur to speculate in that material on which the least possible quantity of labour has been spent: to speculate, therefore, in yarn rather than in cloth, in cotton itself, rather than in yarn. The change of value in the case we have been considering, originates, not in the process in which the cotton plays the part of a means of production, and in which it therefore functions as constant capital, but in the process in which the cotton itself is produced. The value of a commodity, it is true, is determined by the quantity of labour contained in it, but this quantity is itself limited by social conditions. If the time socially necessary for the production of any commodity alters—and a given weight of cotton represents, after a bad harvest, more labour than after a good one—all previously existing commodities of the same class are affected, because they are, as it were, only individuals of the species,[1] and their value at any given time is measured by the labour socially necessary, *i.e.*, by the labour necessary for their production under the then existing social conditions.

As the value of the raw material may change, so, too, may that of the instruments of labour, of the machinery, &c., employed in the process; and consequently that portion of the value of the product transferred to it from them, may also change. If in consequence of a new invention, machinery of a particular kind can be produced by a diminished expenditure of labour, the old machinery becomes depreciated more or less and consequently transfers so much less value to the product. But here again, the change in value originates outside the process in which the machine is acting as a means of production. Once engaged in this process, the machine cannot transfer more value than it possesses apart from the process.

Just as a change in the value of the means of production, even after they have commenced to take a part in the labour process, does not alter their character as constant capital, so, too, a change in the proportion of constant to variable capital does not affect the respective functions of these two kinds of capital. The technical conditions of the labour process may be revolutionised to such an extent, that where formerly ten men using ten implements of small value worked up a relatively small quantity of raw material, one man may now, with the aid of one expensive machine, work up one hundred times as much raw material. In the latter case we have an enormous increase in the constant capital, that is represented by the total value of the means of production used, and at the same time a great reduction in the variable capital, invested in labour-power. Such a revolution, however, alters only the quantitave relation between the constant and the variable capital, or the proportions in which the total capital is split up into its constant and variable constituents; it has not in the least degree affected the essential difference between the two.

[1] "Toutes les productions d'un même genre ne forment proprement qu'une masse, dont le prix se détermine en général et sans égard aux circonstances particulières." (Le Trosne, l. c., p. 893.)

CHAPTER IX.

THE RATE OF SURPLUS-VALUE.

SECTION 1.—THE DEGREE OF EXPLOITATION OF LABOUR-POWER.

THE surplus-value generated in the process of production by C, the capital advanced, or in other words, the self-expansion of the value of the capital C, presents itself for our consideration, in the first place, as a surplus, as the amount by which the value of the product exceeds the value of its constituent element.

The capital C is made up of two components, one, the sum of money c laid out upon the means of production, and the other, the sum of money v expended upon the labour-power; c represents the portion that has become constant capital, and v the portion that has become variable capital. At first then, C=c+v: for example, if £500 is the capital advanced, its components may be such that the £500=£410 const.+£90 var. When the process of production is finished, we get a commodity whose value=(c+v)+s, where s is the surplus-value; or taking our former figures, the value of this commodity may be (£410 const.+£90 var.)+£90 surpl. The original capital has now changed from C to C', from £500 to £590. The difference is s or a surplus value of £90. Since the value of the constituent elements of the product is equal to the value of the advanced capital, it is mere tautology to say, that the excess of the value of the product over the value of its constituent elements, is equal to the expansion of the capital advanced or to the surplus-value produced.

Nevertheless, we must examine this tautology a little more closely. The two things compared are, the value of the product, and the value of its constituents consumed in the process of production. Now we have seen how that portion of the constant capital which consists of the instruments of labour, transfers to the product only a fraction of its value, while the remainder of that value continues to reside in those instru-

ments.   Since this remainder plays no part in the formation of
value, we may at present leave it on one side.   To introduce it
into the calculation would make no difference.   For instance,
taking our former example, c=£410: suppose this sum to consist of £312 value of raw material, £44 value of auxiliary
material, and £54 value of the machinery worn away in the
process; and suppose that the total' value of the machinery
employed is £1,054.   Out of this latter sum, then, we reckon
as advanced for the purpose of turning out the product, the
sum of £54 alone, which the machinery loses by wear and
tear in the process; for this is all it parts with to the product.
Now if we also reckon the remaining £1,000, which still continues in the machinery, as transferred to the product, we
ought also to reckon it as part of the value advanced, and thus
make it appear on both sides of our calculation.[1]   We should,
in this way, get £1,500 on one side and £1,590 on the other.
The difference of these two sums, or the surplus-value, would
still be £90.   Throughout this Book therefore, by constant
capital advanced for the production of value, we always mean,
unless the context is repugnant thereto, the value of the means
of production actually consumed in the process, and that value
alone.

This being so, let us return to the formula C=c+v, which
we saw transformed into C′=(c+v)+s,   C becoming C′.
We know that the value of the constant capital is transferred to, and merely re-appears in the product.   The
new value actually created in the process, the value produced, or value-product, is therefore not the same as the value
of the product; it is not, as it would at first sight appear
(c+v)+s or £410 const.+£90 var.+£90 surpl.; but v+s
or £90 var.+£90 surpl. not £590 but £180.   If c=o, or in
other words, if there were branches of industry in which the
capitalist could dispense with all means of production made
by previous labour, whether they be raw material, auxiliary
material, or instruments of labour, employing only labour-

---

[1] "If we reckon the value of the fixed capital employed as a part of the advances,
we must reckon the remaining value of such capital at the end of the year as a part
of the annual returns."   (Malthus, "Princ. of Pol. Econ." 2nd ed., Lond., 1836, p.
269.)

power and materials supplied by Nature, in that case, there would be no constant capital to transfer to the product. This component of the value of the product, *i.e.*, the £410 in our example, would be eliminated, but the sum of £180, the amount of new value created, or the value produced, which contains £90 of surplus-value, would remain just as great as if c represented the highest value imaginable. We should have $C = (0 + v) = v$ or C' the expanded capital $= v + s$ and therefore $C' - C = s$ as before. On the other hand, if $s = 0$, or in other words, if the labour-power, whose value is advanced in the form of variable capital, were to produce only its equivalent, we should have $C = c + v$ or C' the value of the product $= (c + v) + 0$ or $C = C'$. The capital advanced would, in this case, not have expanded its value.

From what has gone before, we know that surplus-value is purely the result of a variation in the value of v, of that portion of the capital which is transformed into labour-power; consequently, $v + s = v + v'$ or v plus an increment of v. But the fact that it is v alone that varies, and the conditions of that variation, are obscured by the circumstance that in consequence of the increase in the variable component of the capital, there is also an increase in the sum total of the advanced capital. It was originally £500 and becomes £590. Therefore in order that our investigation may lead to accurate results, we must make abstraction from that portion of the value of the product, in which constant capital alone appears, and consequently must equate the constant capital to zero or make $c = 0$. This is merely an application of a mathematical rule, employed whenever we operate with constant and variable magnitudes, related to each other by the symbols of addition and subtraction only.

A further difficulty is caused by the original form of the variable capital. In our example, $C' = £410$ const. $+ £90$ var $+ £90$ surpl.; but £90 is a given and therefore a constant quantity; hence it appears absurd to treat it as variable. But in fact, the term £90 var. is here merely a symbol to show that this value undergoes a process. The portion of the capital invested in the purchase of labour-power is a definite quantity of materialised labour, a constant value like the value of the labour-power purchased. But in the process of production the place of the £90 is taken by the labour-power in action, dead labour is replaced by living labour, something stagnant by something flowing, a constant by a variable. The result is the reproduction of v plus an increment of v. From the point of view, then, of capitalist production, the whole process appears as the spontaneous variation of the originally constant value, which is transformed into labour-power. Both the process and its result, appear to be owing to this value. If, therefore, such expressions as "£90 variable capital," or "so much self-expanding value," appear contradictory, this is only because they bring to the surface a contradiction immanent in capitalist production.

At first sight it appears a strange proceeding, to equate the constant capital to zero. Yet it is what we do every day. If, for example, we wish to calculate the amount of England's profits from the cotton industry, we first of all deduct the sums paid for cotton to the United States, India, Egypt and other countries; in other words, the value of the capital that merely re-appears in the value of the product, is put=0.

Of course the ratio of surplus-value not only to that portion of the capital from which it immediately springs, and whose change of value it represents, but also to the sum total of the capital advanced is economically of very great importance. We shall, therefore, in the third book, treat of this ratio exhaustively. In order to enable one portion of a capital to expand its value by being converted into labour-power, it is necessary that another portion be converted into means of production. In order that variable capital may perform its function, constant capital must be advanced in proper proportion, a proportion given by the special technical conditions of each labour-process. The circumstance, however, that retorts and other vessels, are necessary to a chemical process, does not compel the chemist to notice them in the result of his analysis. If we look at the means of production, in their relation to the creation of value, and to the variation in the quantity of value, apart from anything else, they appear simply as the material in which labour-power, the value-creator, incorporates itself. Neither the nature, nor the value of this material is of any importance. The only requisite is that there be a sufficient supply to absorb the labour expended in the process of production. That supply once given, the material may rise or fall in value, or even be, as land and the sea, without any value in itself; but this will have no influence on the creation of value or on the variation in the quantity of value.[1]

In the first place then we equate the constant capital to zero. The capital advanced is consequently reduced from c+v to v, and instead of the value of the product (c+v)+s we have now the value produced (v+s). Given the new value produced = £180, which sum consequently represents the whole labour expended during the process, then subtracting from it £90 the value of the variable capital, we have remaining £90, the amount of the surplus-value. This sum of £90 or s expresses the absolute quantity of surplus-value produced. The relative quantity produced, or the increase per cent of the variable capital, is determined, it is plain, by the ratio of the surplus-value to the variable capital, or is expressed by $\frac{s}{v}$. In our example this ratio is $\frac{90}{90}$, which gives an increase of 100%. This relative increase in the value of the variable capital, or the relative magnitude of the surplus-value, I call, "The rate of surplus-value."[2]

We have seen that the labourer, during one portion of the labour-process, produces only the value of his labour-power, that is, the value of his means of subsistence. Now since his work forms part of a system, based on the social division of labour, he does not directly produce the actual necessaries which he himself consumes; he produces instead a particular commodity, yarn for example, whose value is equal to the value of those necessaries or of the money with which they

---

[1] What Lucretius says is self-evident; "nil posse creari de nihilo," out of nothing, nothing can be created. Creation of value is transformation of labour-power into labour. Labour-power itself is energy transferred to a human organism by means of nourishing matter.

[2] In the same way that the English use the terms "rate of profit," "rate of interest." We shall see, in Book III., that the rate of profit is no mystery, so soon as we know the laws of surplus-value. If we reverse the process, we cannot comprehend either the one or the other.

can be bought. The portion of his day's labour devoted to this purpose, will be greater or less, in proportion to the value of the necessaries that he daily requires on an average, or, what amounts to the same thing, in proportion to the labour-time required on an average to produce them. If the value of those necessaries represents on an average the expenditure of six hours' labour, the workman must on an average work for six hours to produce that value. If instead of working for the capitalist, he worked independently on his own account, he would, other things being equal, still be obliged to labour for the same number of hours, in order to produce the value of his labour-power, and thereby to gain the means of subsistence necessary for his conservation or continued reproduction. But as we have seen, during that portion of his day's labour in which he produces the value of his labour-power, say three shillings, he produces only an equivalent for the value of his labour-power already advanced by the capitalist; the new value created only replaces the variable capital advanced. It is owing to this fact, that the production of the new value of three shillings takes the semblance of a mere reproduction. That portion of the working day, then, during which this re-production takes place, I call *"necessary"* labour-time, and the labour expended during that time I call *"necessary"* labour.[1] Necessary, as regards the labourer, because independent of the particular social form of his labour; necessary, as regards capital, and the world of capitalists, because on the continued existence of the labourer depends their existence also.

During the second period of the labour-process, that in which his labour is no longer necessary labour, the workman, it is true, labours, expends labour-power; but his labour, being no longer necessary labour, he creates no value for himself. He creates surplus-value which, for the capitalist, has all the charms of a creation out of nothing. This portion of the

---

[1] In this work, we have, up to now, employe l the term "necessary labour-time," to designate the time i :cessary under given social conditions for the production of any commodity. Henceforward we use it to desi-nate also the time necessary for the production of the p^ cular commodity labour-power. The use of one and the same technical term in different senses is inconvenient, but in no science can it be altogether avoided. Compare, for instance, the higher with the lower branches of mathematics.

working day, I name surplus labour-time, and to the labour
expended during that time, I give the name of surplus-labour.
It is every bit as important, for a correct understanding of
surplus-value, to conceive it as a mere congelation of surplus-
labour-time, as nothing but materialised surplus-labour, as it
is, for a proper comprehension of value, to conceive it as a mere
congelation of so many hours of labour, as nothing but materialised labour. The essential difference between the various
economic forms of society, between, for instance, a society
based on slave labour, and one based on wage labour, lies only
in the mode in which this surplus-labour is in each case extracted from the actual producer, the labourer.[1]

Since, on the one hand, the values of the variable capital
and of the labour-power purchased by that capital are equal,
and the value of this labour-power determines the necessary
portion of the working day; and since, on the other hand, the
surplus-value is determined by the surplus portion of the
working day, it follows that surplus-value bears the same ratio
to variable capital, that surplus-labour does to necessary labour,
or in other words, the rate of surplus-value $\frac{s}{v} = \frac{\text{surplus labor}}{\text{necessary labor}}$
Both ratios, $\frac{s}{v}$ and $\frac{\text{surplus labor}}{\text{necessary labor}}$ express the same thing in different ways; in the one case by reference to materialised, incor-
porated labour, in the other by reference to living, fluent
labour.

The rate of surplus-value is therefore an exact expression
for the degree of exploitation of labour-power by capital, or of
the labourer by the capitalist.[2]

---

[1] Herr Wilhelm Thucydides Roscher has found a mare's nest. He has made the
important discovery that if, on the one hand, the formation of surplus-value, or
surplus-produce, and the consequent accumulation of capital, is now-a-days due to
the thrift of the capitalist, on the other hand, in the lowest stages of civilisation it
is the strong who compel the weak to economise (l. c. p. 78). To economise what?
Labour? Or superfluous wealth that does not exist? What is it that makes such
men as Roscher account for the origin of surplus-value, by a mere rechauffé of the
more or less plausible excuses by the capitalist, for his appropriation of surplus-
value? It is, besides their real ignorance, their apologetic dread of a scientific
analysis of value and surplus-value, and of obtaining a result, possibly not altogether palatable to the powers that be.

[2] Although the rate of surplus-value is an exact expression for the degree of exploitation of labour-power, it is, in no sense, an expression for the absolute amount
of exploitation. For example, if the necessary labour=5 hours and the surplus-la-
bour=5 hours, the degree of exploitation is 100%. The amount of exploitation is

We assumed in our example, that the value of the product
=£410 const.+£90 var.+£90 surpl., and that the capital
advanced=£500. Since the surplus-value=£90, and the advanced capital=£500, we should, according to the usual way
of reckoning, get as the rate of surplus value (generally confounded with rate of profits) 18%, a rate so low as possibly
to cause a pleasant surprise to Mr. Carey and other harmon-
isers. But in truth, the rate of surplus-value is not equal
to $\frac{s}{C}$ or $\frac{s}{c+v}$ but to $\frac{s}{v}$: thus it is not $\frac{90}{500}$ but $\frac{90}{90}$ or 100%, which
is more than five times the apparent degree of exploitation.
Although, in the case we have supposed, we are ignorant of
the actual length of the working day, and of the duration in
days or weeks of the labour-process, as also of the number of
labourers employed, yet the rate of surplus-value $\frac{s}{v}$ accurately
discloses to us, by means of its equivalent expression, $\frac{\text{surplus labor}}{\text{necessary labor}}$
the relation between the two parts of the working day. This
relation is here one of equality, the rate being 100%. Hence,
it is plain, the labourer, in our example, works one half of the
day for himself, the other half for the capitalist.

The method of calculating the rate of surplus value is therefore, shortly, as follows. We take the total value of the product and put the constant capital which merely re-appears in it,
equal to zero. What remains, is the only value that has, in
the process of producing the commodity, been actually created.
If the amount of surplus-value be given, we have only to deduct
it from this remainder, to find the variable capital. And *vice
versa,* if the latter be given, and we require to find the surplus-
value. If both be given, we have only to perform the concluding operation, viz., to calculate $\frac{s}{v}$, the ratio of the surplus-
value to the variable capital.

Though the method is so simple, yet it may not be amiss, by
means of a few examples, to exercise the reader in the application of the novel principles underlying it.

First we will take the case of a spinning mill containing

here measured by 5 hours. If, on the other hand, the necessary labour=6 hours
and the surplus-labour=6 hours, the degree of exploitation remains, as before,
100%, while the actual amount of exploitation has increased 20%, namely from five
hours to six.

10,000 mule spindles, spinning No. 32 yarn from American cotton, and producing 1 lb. of yarn weekly per spindle. We assume the waste to be 6% : under these circumstances 10,600 lbs. of cotton are consumed weekly, of which 600 lbs. go to waste. The price of the cotton in April, 1871, was 7¾d. per lb.; the raw material therefore costs in round numbers £342. The 10,000 spindles, including preparation-machinery, and motive power, cost, we will assume, £1 per spindle, amounting to a total of £10,000. The wear and tear we put at 10%, or £1000 yearly=£20 weekly. The rent of the building we suppose to be £300 a year or £6 a week. Coal consumed (for 100 horse-power indicated, at 4 lbs. of coal per horse-power per hour during 60 hours, and inclusive of that consumed in heating the mill), 11 tons a week at 8s. 6d. a ton, amounts to about £4½ a week : gas, £1 a week, oil, &c., £4½ a week. Total cost of the above auxiliary materials, £10 weekly. Therefore the constant portion of the value of the week's product is £378. Wages amount to £52 a week. The price of the yarn is 12¼d. per lb., which gives for the value of 10,000 lbs. the sum of £510. The surplus value is therefore in this case £510—£430=£80. We put the constant part of the value of the product=0, as it plays no part in the creation of value. There remains £132 as the weekly value created, which=£52 var.+ £80 surpl. The rate of surplus-value is therefore $\frac{80}{52}$ = $153\frac{11}{13}$%. In a working day of   hours with average labour the result is: necessary labour=$3\frac{31}{33}$hours and surplus-labour =$6\frac{2}{33}$.[1]

One more example. Jacob gives the following calculation for the year 1815. Owing to the previous adjustment of several items it is very imperfect; nevertheless for our purpose it is sufficient. In it he assumes the price of wheat to be 8s. a quarter, and the average yield per acre to be 22 bushels.

[1] The above data, which may be relied upon, were given me by a Manchester spinner. In England the horse-power of an engine was formerly calculated from the diameter of its cylinder, now the actual horse-power shown by the indicator is taken.

Value Produced Per Acre.

Seed, ...	£1	9	0	Tithes, Rates, and Taxes, ..	£1	1	0
Manure, ...	2	10	0	Rent, ...	1	8	0
Wages, ...	3	10	0	Farmer's Profit and Interest,.	1	2	0
Total, ..	£7	9	0	Total, ..	£3	11	0

Assuming that the price of the product is the same as its value, we here find the surplus-value distributed under the various heads of profit, interest, rent, etc. We have nothing to do with these in detail; we simply add them together, and the sum is a surplus-value of £3 11s. 0d. The sum of £3 19s. 0d., paid for seed and manure, is constant capital, and we put it equal to zero. There is left the sum of £3 10s. 0d., which is the variable capital advanced: and we see that a new value of £3 10s. 0d.+£3 11s. 0d. has been produced in its place. Therefore $\frac{s}{v} = \frac{£3 \ 11s. \ 0d.}{£3 \ 10s. \ 0d.}$, giving a rate of surplus-value of more than 100%. The labourer employs more than one-half of his working day in producing the surplus-value, which different persons, under different pretexts, share amongst themselves.[1]

SECTION 2.—THE REPRESENTATION OF THE COMPONENTS OF THE VALUE OF THE PRODUCT BY CORRESPONDING PRO-PORTIONAL PARTS OF THE PRODUCT ITSELF.

Let us now return to the example by which we were shown how the capitalist converts money into capital.

The product of a working day of 12 hours is 20 lbs. of yarn, having a value of 30s. No less than $\frac{8}{10}$ths of this value, or 24s., is due to mere re-appearance in it, of the value of the

[1] The calculations given in the test are intended merely as illustrations. We have in fact assumed that prices=values. We shall, however, see in Volume III., that even in the case of average prices the assumption cannot be made in this very sim-ple manner.

means of production (20 lbs. of cotton, value 20s., and spindle worn away, 4s.): it is therefore constant capital. The remaining $\frac{2}{10}$ ths or 6s. is the new value created during the spinning process: of this one half replaces the value of the day's labour-power, or the variable capital, the remaining half constitutes a surplus-value of 3s. The total value then of the 20 lbs. of yarn is made up as follows:

30s. value of yarn=24 const.+3s. var.+3s. surpl.

Since the whole of the value is contained in the 20 lbs. of yarn produced, it follows that the various component parts of this value, can be represented as being contained respectively in corresponding parts of the product.

If the value of 30s. is contained in 20 lbs. of yarn, then $\frac{8}{10}$ ths of this value, or the 24s. that form its constant part, is contained in $\frac{8}{10}$ ths of the product or in 16 lbs. of yarn. Of the latter $13\frac{1}{3}$ lbs. represent the value of the raw material, the 20s. worth of cotton spun, and $2\frac{2}{3}$ lbs. represent the 4s. worth of spindle, &c., worn away in the process.

Hence the whole of the cotton used up in spinning the 20 lbs. of yarn, is represented by $13\frac{1}{3}$ lbs. of yarn. This latter weight of yarn contains, it is true, by weight, no more than $13\frac{1}{3}$ lbs. of cotton, worth $13\frac{1}{3}$ shillings; but the $6\frac{2}{3}$ shillings additional value contained in it, are the equivalent for the cotton consumed in spinning the remaining $6\frac{2}{3}$ lbs. of yarn. The effect is the same as if these $6\frac{2}{3}$ lbs. of yarn contained no cotton at all, and the whole 20 lbs. of cotton were concentrated in the $13\frac{1}{3}$ lbs. of yarn. The latter weight, on the other hand, does not contain an atom either of the value of the auxiliary materials and implements, or of the value newly created in the process.

In the same way, the $2\frac{2}{3}$ lbs. of yarn, in which the 4s., the remainder of the constant capital, is embodied, represents nothing but the value of the auxiliary materials and instruments of labour consumed in producing the 20 lbs. of yarn.

We have, therefore, arrived at this result: although eighttenths of the product, or 16 lbs. of yarn, is, in its character of an article of utility, just as much the fabric of the spinner's labour, as the remainder of the same product, yet when viewed in this connexion, it does not contain, and has not absorbed any labour expended during the process of spinning. It is just as if the cotton had converted itself into yarn, without help; as if the shape it had assumed was mere trickery and deceit: for so soon as our capitalist sells it for 24s., and with the money replaces his means of production, it becomes evident that this 16 lbs. of yarn is nothing more than so much cotton and spindle-waste in disguise.

On the other hand, the remaining $\frac{2}{10}$ths of the product, or 4 lbs. of yarn, represent nothing but the new value of 6s., created during the 12 hours' spinning process. All the value transferred to those 4 lbs., from the raw material and instruments of labour consumed, was, so to say, intercepted in order to be incorporated in the 16 lbs. first spun. In this case, it is as if the spinner had spun 4 lbs. of yarn out of air, or, as if he had spun them with the aid of cotton and spindles, that, being the spontaneous gift of Nature, transferred no value to the product.

Of this 4 lbs. of yarn, in which the whole of the value newly created during the process, is condensed, one half represents the equivalent for the value of the labour consumed, or the 3s. variable capital, the other half represents the 3s. surplus-value.

Since 12 working hours of the spinner are embodied in 6s., it follows that in yarn of the value of 30s., there must be embodied 60 working hours. And this quantity of labour-time does in fact exist in the 20 lbs. of yarn; for in $\frac{8}{10}$ths or 16 lbs. there are materialised the 48 hours of labour expended, before the commencement of the spinning process, on the means of production; and in the remaining $\frac{2}{10}$ths or 4 lbs. there are materialised the 12 hours' work done during the process itself.

On a former page we saw that the value of the yarn is equal to the sum of the new value created during the production of that yarn plus the value previously existing in the means of production.

It has now been shown how the various component parts of the value of the product, parts that differ functionally from each other, may be represented by corresponding proportional parts of the product itself.

To split up in this manner the product into different parts, of which one represents only the labour previously spent on the means of production, or the constant capital, another, only the necessary labour spent during the process of production, or the variable capital, and another and last part, only the surplus-labour expended during the same process, or the surplus-value; to do this, is, as will be seen later on from its application to complicated and hitherto unsolved problems, no less important than it is simple.

In the preceding investigation we have treated the total product as the final result, ready for use, of a working day of 12 hours. We can however follow this total product through all the stages of its production; and in this way we shall arrive at the same result as before, if we represent the partial products, given off at the different stages, as functionally different parts of the final or total product.

The spinner produces in 12 hours 20 lbs. of yarn, or in 1 hour 1⅔ lbs.; consequently he produces in 8 hours 13⅓ lbs., or a partial product equal in value to all the cotton that is spun in a whole day. In like manner the partial product of the next period of 1 hour and 36 minutes, is 2⅔ lbs. of yarn: this represents the value of the instruments of labour that are consumed in 12 hours. In the following hour and 12 minutes, the spinner produces 2 lbs. of yarn worth 3 shillings, a value equal to the whole value he creates in his 6 hours necessary labour. Finally, in the last hour and 12 minutes he produces another 2 lbs. of yarn, whose value is equal to the surplus-value, created by his surplus-labour during half a day. This method of calculation serves the English manufacturer for everyday use; it shows, he will say, that in the first 8 hours, or ⅔ of the working day, he gets back the value of his cotton; and so on for the remaining hours. It is also a perfectly correct method: being in fact the first method given above with this difference, that instead of being applied to space, in which the different parts of the completed product lie side by side, it deals with time, in which those parts are successively produced. But it can also be accompanied by very barbarian notions, more especially in the heads of those who are as much interested, practically, in the process of making value beget value, as they are in misunderstanding that process theoreti-cally. Such people may get the notion into their heads, that one spinner, for example, produces or replaces in the first 8 hours of his working day the *value* of the cotton; in the following hour and 36 minutes the *value* of the instruments of labour worn away; in the next hour and 12 minutes the *value* of the wages; and that he devotes to the production of surplus-value for the manufacturer, only that well known "last hour." In this way the poor spinner is made to perform the two-fold miracle not only of producing cotton, spindles, steam-engine, coal, oil, &c., at the same time that he spins with them, but also of turning one working day into five; for in, the example we are considering, the production of the raw material and in-struments of labour demands four working days of twelve hours each, and their conversion into yarn requires another such day. That the love of lucre induces an easy belief in such miracles, and that sycophant doctrinaires are never wanting to prove them, is vouched for by the following inci-dent of historical celebrity.

SECTION 3.—SENIOR'S "LAST HOUR."

One fine morning, in the year 1836, Nassau W. Senior, who may be called the bel-esprit of English economists, well known, alike for his economical "science," and for his beautiful style, was summoned from Oxford to Manchester, to learn in the latter place the political economy that he taught in the former. The manufacturers elected him as their champion, not only against the newly passed Factory Act, but against the still more menacing Ten-hours' agitation. With their usual prac-tical acuteness, they had found out that the learned Professor "wanted a good deal of finishing;" it was this discovery that caused them to write for him. On his side the Professor has embodied the lecture he received from the Manchester manu-facturers, in a ·pamphlet, entitled: "Letters on the Factory Act, as it affects the cotton manufacture." London, 1837. Here we find, amongst others, the following edifying passage: "Under the present law, no mill in which persons under 18 years of age are employed, ... can be worked more than 11½ hours a day, that is 12 hours for 5 days in the week, and nine on Saturday.

"Now the following analysis (!) will show that in a mill so worked, the whole net profit is derived *from the last hour.* I will suppose a manufacturer to invest £100,000 :—£80,000 in his mill and machinery, and £20,000 in raw material and wages. The annual return of that mill, supposing the capital to be turned once a year, and gross profits to be 15 per cent., ought to be goods worth £115,000. . . . . . Of this £115,000, each of the twenty-three half-hours of work produces 5-115ths or one twenty-third. Of these 23-23rds (constituting the whole £115,000) twenty, that is to say £100,000 out of the £115,000, simply replace the capital;—one twenty-third (or £5000 out of the £115,000) makes up for the deterioration of the mill and machinery. The remaining 2-23rds, that is, the last two of the twenty-three half-hours of every day, produce the net profit of 10 per cent. If, therefore (prices remaining the same), the factory could be kept at work thirteen hours instead of eleven and a half, with an addition of about £2600 to the circulating capital, the net profit would be more than doubled. On the other hand, if the hours of working were reduced by one hour per day (prices remaining the same), the *net* profit would be destroyed—if they were reduced by one hour and a half, even the *gross* profit would be destroyed."[1]

---

[1] Senior, l. c., p. 12, 13. We let pass such extraordinary notions as are of no importance for our purpose; for instance, the assertion, that manufacturers reckon as part of their profit, gross or net, the amount required to make good wear and tear of machinery, or in other words, to replace a part of the capital. So, too, we pass over any question as to the accuracy of his figures. Leonard Horner has shown in "A Letter to Mr. Senior," &c., London, 1837, that they are worth no more than the so-called "Analysis." Leonard Horner was one of the Factory Inquiry Commissioners in 1833, and Inspector, or rather Censor of Factories till 1859. He rendered undying service to the English working class. He carried on a life-long contest, not only with the embittered manufacturers, but also with the Cabinet, to whom the number of votes given by the masters in the Lower House, was a matter of far greater importance than the number of hours worked by the "hands" in the mills.

Apart from errors in principle, Senior's statement is confused. What he really intended to say was this: The manufacturer employs the workman for 11½ hours or for 23 half-hours daily. As the working day, so, too, the working year, may be conceived to consist of 11½ hours or 23 half-hours, but each multiplied by the number of working days in the year. On this supposition, the 23 half-hours yield an annual product of £115,000; one half-hour yields $\frac{1}{23}$ × £115,000; 20 half-hours yield $\frac{20}{23}$ × £115,000; =£100,000, *i.e.*, they replace no more than the capital ad-

And the professor calls this an "analysis!" If, giving credence to the out-cries of the manufacturers, he believed that the workmen spend the best part of the day in the production, *i. e.,* the reproduction or replacement of the value of the buildings, machinery, cotton, coal, &c., then his analysis was superfluous. His answer would simply have been:—Gentlemen! if you work your mills for 10 hours instead of 11½, then, other things being equal, the daily consumption of cotton, machinery, &c., will decrease in proportion. You gain just as much as you lose. Your work-people will in future spend one hour and a half less time in producing or replacing the capital that has been advanced.—If, on the other hand, he did not believe them without further inquiry, but, as being an expert in such matters, deemed an analy is necessary, then he ought, in a question that is concerned exclusively with the relations of net profit to the length of the working day, before all things to have asked the manufacturers, to be careful not to lump together machinery, workshops, raw material, and labour, but to be good enough to place the constant capital, invested in buildings, machinery, raw material, &c., on one ide of the account, and the capital advanced in wages on the other side. If the professor then found, that in accordance with the calculation of the manufacturers, the workman reproduced or replaced his wages in 2 half-hours, in that case, he should have continued his analysis thus:

According to your figures, the workman in the last hour but one produces his wages, and in the last hour your surplus-value or net profit. Now, since in equal periods he produces equal values, the produce of the last hour but one, must have the same value as that of the last hour. Further, it is only while he labours that he produces any value at all, and the amount of his labour is measured by his labour-time. This you say, amounts to 11½ hours a day. He employs one portion of these 11½ hours, in producing or replacing his wages, and

vanced. There remain 3 half-hours, which yield $\frac{3}{23} \times £115,000 = £15,000$ or the gross profit. Of these 3 half-hours, one yields $\frac{1}{23} \times £115,000 = £5000$; *i. e.,* it makes up for the wear and tear of the machinery; the remaining 2 half-hours, *i.e.,* the last hour, yield $\frac{2}{23} \times £115,000 = £10,000$ or the net profit. In the text Senior converts the last $\frac{2}{23}$ of the product into portions of the working day itself.

the remaining portion in producing your net profit. Beyond this he does absolutely nothing. But since, on your assumption, his wages, and the surplus-value he yields, are of equal value, it is clear that he produces his wages in $5\frac{3}{4}$ hours, and your net profit in the other $5\frac{3}{4}$ hours. Again, since the value of the yarn produced in 2 hours, is equal to the sum of the values of his wages and of your net profit, the measure of the value of this yarn must be $11\frac{1}{2}$ working hours, of which $5\frac{3}{4}$ hours measure the value of the yarn produced in the last hour but one, and $5\frac{3}{4}$, the value of the yarn produced in the last hour. We now come to a ticklish point; therefore, attention! The last working hour but one is, like the first, an ordinary working hour, neither more nor less. How then can the spinner produce in one hour, in the shape of yarn, a value that embodies $5\frac{3}{4}$ hours labour? The truth is that he performs no such miracle. The use-value produced by him in one hour, is a definite quantity of yarn. The value of this yarn is measured by $5\frac{3}{4}$ working hours, of which $4\frac{3}{4}$ were, without any assistance from him, previously embodied in the means of production, in the cotton, the machinery, and so on; the remaining one hour is added by him. Therefore since his wages are produced in $5\frac{3}{4}$ hours, and the yarn produced in one hour also contains $5\frac{3}{4}$ hours' work, there is no witchcraft in the result, that the value created by his $5\frac{3}{4}$ hours' spinning, is equal to the value of the product spun in one hour. You are altogether on the wrong track, if you think that he loses a single moment of his working day, in reproducing or replacing the values of the cotton, the machinery, and so on. On the contrary, it is because his labour converts the cotton and spindles into yarn, because he spins, that the values of the cotton and spindles go over to the yarn of their own accord. This result is owing to the quality of his labour, not to its quantity. It is true, he will in one hour tranfer to the yarn more value, in the shape of cotton, than he will in half an hour; but that is only because in one hour he spins up more cotton than in half an hour. You see then, your assertion, that the workman produces, in the last hour but one, the value of his wages, and in the last hour your net profit, amounts to no more than this, that in the yarn produced by him in 2 working hours, whether they are the 2 first or the 2 last hours of the working day, in that yarn, there are incorporated $11\frac{1}{2}$ working hours, or just a whole day's work, *i. e.*, two hours of his own work and $9\frac{1}{2}$ hours of other people's. And my assertion that, in the first $5\frac{3}{4}$ hours, he produces his wages, and in the last $5\frac{3}{4}$ hours your net profit, amounts only to this, that you pay him for the former, but not for the latter. In speaking of payment of labour, instead of payment of labour-power, I only talk your own slang. Now, gentlemen, if you compare the working time you pay for, with that which you do not pay for, you will find that they are to one another, as half a day is to half a day; this gives a rate of 100%, and a very pretty percentage it is. Further, there is not the least doubt, that if you make your "hands" toil for 13 hours instead of $11\frac{1}{2}$, and, as may be expected from you, treat the work done in that extra one hour and a half, as pure surplus-labour, then the latter will be increased from $5\frac{3}{4}$ hours' labour to $7\frac{1}{4}$ hours' labour, and the rate of surplus-value from 100%, to $126\frac{2}{23}$%. So that you are altogether too sanguine. in expecting that by such an addition of $1\frac{1}{2}$ hours to the working day, the rate will rise from 100% to 200% and more, in other words that it will be "more than doubled." On the other hand—man's heart is a wonderful thing, especially when carried in the purse—you take too pessimistic a view, when you fear, that with a reduction of the hours of labour from $11\frac{1}{2}$ to 10, the whole of your net profit will go to the dogs. Not at all. All other conditions remaining the same, the surplus-labour will fall from $5\frac{3}{4}$ hours to $4\frac{3}{4}$ hours, a period that still gives a very profitable rate of surplus-value, namely $82\frac{14}{32}$%. But this dreadful "last hour," about which you have invented more stories than have the millenarians about the day of judgment, is "all bosh." If it goes, it will cost neither you, your net profit, nor the boys and girls whom you employ, their "purity of mind."[1] Whenever *your* "last hour" strikes in

[1] If, on the one hand, Senior proved that the net profit of the manufacturer, the existence of the English cotton industry, and England's command of the markets of the world, depend on "the last working hour," on the other hand, Dr. Andrew Ure showed, that if children and young persons under 18 years of age, instead of being kept the full 12 hours in the warm and pure moral atmosphere of the factory,

earnest, think on the Oxford Professor. And now, gentleman, "farewell, and may we meet again in yonder better world, but not before."

Senior invented the battle cry of the "last hour" in 1836.[1]

are turned out an hour sooner into the heartless and frivolous outer world, they will be deprived, by idleness and vice, of all hope of salvation for their souls. Since 1848, the factory inspectors have never tired of twitting the masters with this "last," this "fatal hour." Thus Mr. Howell in his report of the 31st May, 1855: "Had the following ingenious calculation (he quotes Senior) been correct, every cotton factory in the United Kingdom would have been working at a loss since the year 1850." (Reports of the Insp. of Fact. for the half-year, ending 30th April, 1855, pp. 19, 20.) In the year 1848, after the passing of the 10 hour's bill, the masters of some flax spinning mills, scattered, few and far between, over the country on the borders of Dorset and Somerset, foisted a petition against the bill on to the shoulders of a few of their work people. One of the clauses of this petition is as follows: "Your petitioners, as parents, conceive that an additional hour of leisure will . tend more to demoralise the children than otherwise, believing that idleness is the parent of vice." On this the factory report of 31st Oct., 1848, says: The atmosphere of the flax mills, in which the children of these virtuous and tender parents work, is so loaded with dust and fibre from the raw material, that it is exceptionally unpleasant to stand even 10 minutes in the spinning rooms: for you are unable to do so without the most painful sensation, owing to the eyes, the ears, the nostrils, and mouth, being immediately filled by the clouds of flax dust from which there is no escape. The labour itself, owing to the feverish haste of the machinery, demands unceasing application of skill and movement, under the control of a watchfulness that never tires, and it seems somewhat hard, to let parents apply the term "idling" to their own children, who, after allowing for meal times, are fettered for 10 whole hours to such an occupation, in such an atmosphere. . . . These children work longer than the labourers in the neighbouring villages. . . . . . Such cruel talk about "idleness and vice" ought to be branded as the purest cant, and the most shameless hypocrisy. . . . . . That portion of the public, who, about 12 years ago, were struck by the assurance with which, under the sanction of high authority, it was publicly and most earnestly proclaimed, that the whole net profit of the manufacturer flows from the labour of the last hour, and that, therefore, the reduction of the working day by one hour, would destroy his net profit; that portion of the public, we say, will hardly believe its own eyes, when it now finds, that the original discovery of the virtues of "the last hour" has since been so far improved, as to include morals as well as profit; so that, if the duration of the labour of children, is reduced to a full 10 hours, their morals, together with the net profits of their employers, will vanish, both being dependent on this last, this fatal hour. (See Repts., Insp. of Fact., for 31st Oct., 1848, p. 101.) The same report then gives some examples of the morality and virtue of these same pure-minded manufacturers, of the tricks, the artifices, the cajoling, the threats, and the falsifications, they made use of, in order, first, to compel a few defenceless workmen to sign petitions of such a kind, and then to impose them upon Parliament as the petitions of a whole branch of industry, or a whole country. It is highly characteristic of the present status of so called economical science, that neither Senior himself, who, at a later period, to his honour be it said, energetically supported the factory legislation, nor his opponents, from first to last, have ever been able to explain the false conclusions of the "original discovery." They appeal to actual experience, but the why and wherefore remains a mystery.

[1] Nevertheless, the learned professor was not without some benefit from his journey to Manchester. In the "Letters on the Factory Act," he makes the whole net gains including "profit" and "interest," and even "something more," depend upon

In the London Economist of the 15th April, 1848, the same cry was again raised by James Wilson, an economical mandarin of high standing: this time in opposition to the 10 hours' bill.

SECTION 4.—SURPLUS PRODUCE.

The portion of the product that represents the surplus-value, (one-tenth of the 20 lbs., or 2 lbs. of yarn, in the example given in Sec. 2,) we call "surplus-produce." Just as the rate of surplus-value is determined by its relation, not to the sum total of the capital, but to its variable part; in like manner, the relative quantity of surplus-produce is determined by the ratio that this produce bears, not to the remaining part of the total product, but to that part of it in which is incorporated the necessary labour. Since the production of surplus-value is the chief end and aim of capitalist production, it is clear, that the greatness of a man's or a nation's wealth should be measured, not by the absolute quantity produced, but by the relative magnitude of the surplus-produce.[1]

The sum of the necessary labour and the surplus-labour, *i.e.*, of the periods of time during which the workman replaces the

a single unpaid hour's work of the labourer. One year previously, in his "Outlines of Political Economy," written for the instruction of Oxford students and cultivated Philistines, he had also "discovered, in opposition to Ricardo's determination of value by labour, that profit is derived from the labour of the capitalist, and interest from his asceticism, in other words, from his "abstinence." The dodge was an old one, but the word "abstinence" was new. Herr Roscher translates it rightly by "Enthaltung." Some of his countrymen, the Browns, Jones, and Robinsons, of Germany, not so well versed in Latin as he, have, monk-like, rendered it by "Entsagung" (renunciation).

[1] "To an individual with a capital of £20,000, whose profits were £2,000 per annum, it would be a mattter quite indifferent whether his capital would employ a 100 or 1,000 men, whether the commodity produced sold for £10,000 or £20,000, provided, in all cases, his profit were not diminished below £2,000. Is not the real interest of the nation similar? Provided its net real income, its rent and profits, be the same, it is of no importance whether the nation consists of 10 or of 12 millions of inhabitants." (Ric. l. c., p. 416.) Long before Ricardo, Arthur Young, a fanatical upholder of surplus produce, for the rest, a rambling uncritical writer, whose reputation is in the inverse ratio of his merit, says, "Of what use, in a modern kingdom, would be a whole province thus divided, [in the old Roman manner, by small independent peasants], however well cultivated, except for the mere purpose of breeding men, which taken singly is a most useless purpose?" (Arthur Young: Political Arithmetic, &c. London, 1774, p. 47.)

Very curious is "the strong inclination . . . to represent net wealth as beneficial to the labouring class . . . . though it is evidently not on account of being net." (Th. Hopkins, On Rent of Land, &c. London, 1823, p. 126.)

value of his labour-power, and produces the surplus-value, this sum constitutes the actual time during which he works, *i.e.,* the working day.

CHAPTER X.

THE WORKING DAY.

SECTION 1—THE LIMITS OF THE WORKING DAY.

WE started with the supposition that labour-power is bought and sold at its value. Its value, like that of all other commodities, is determined by the working time necessary to its production. If the production of the average daily means of subsistence of the labourer takes up 6 hours, he must work, on the average, 6 hours every day, to produce his daily labour-power, or to reproduce the value received as the result of its sale. The necessary part of his working day amounts to 6 hours, and is, therefore, *cœteris paribus,* a given quantity. But with this, the extent of the working day itself is not yet given.

Let us assume that the line A B represents the length of the necessary working time, say 6 hours. If the labour be prolonged 1, 3, or 6 hours beyond A B, we have 3 other lines: Working day I. Working day II. Working day III. A————B——C. A————B——C. A————B————C. representing 3 different working days of 7, 9, and 12 hours. The extension B C of the line A B represents the length of the surplus labour. As the working day is A B + B C or A C, it varies with the variable quantity B C. Since A B is constant, the ratio of B C to A B can always be calculated. In working day I. it is $\frac{1}{6}$, in working day II, $\frac{3}{6}$ in working day III, $\frac{6}{6}$ of A B. Since, further the ratio $\frac{\text{surplus working time}}{\text{necessary working time}}$ determines the rate of the surplus-value, the latter is given by the ratio of B C to A B. It amounts in the 3 different working days respectively to $16\frac{2}{3}$, 50 and 100 per cent. On the other hand, the rate of surplus-value alone would not give us the extent of the working day. If this rate *e.g.,* were 100 per cent., the working day might be of 8, 10, 12, or more hours. It would indicate that the 2 constituent parts of the working day, necessary-labour and surplus-labour time, were equal in extent, but not how long each of these two constituent parts was.

The working day is thus not a constant, but a variable quantity. One of its parts, certainly, is determined by the working time required for the reproduction of the labour-power of the labourer himself. But its total amount varies with the duration of the surplus-labour. The working day is, therefore, determinable, but is, *per se,* indeterminate.[1]

Although the working day is not a fixed, but a fluent quantity, it can, on the other hand, only vary within certain limits. The minimum limit is, however, not determinable; of course, if we make the extension line BC or the surplus-labour=0, we have a minimum limit, *i.e.,* the part of the day which the labourer must necessarily work for his own maintenance. On the basis of capitalist production, however, this necessary labour can form a part only of the working day; the working day itself can never be reduced to this minimum. On the other hand, the working day has a maximum limit. It cannot be prolonged beyond a certain point. This maximum limit is conditioned by two things. First, by the physical bounds of labour-power. Within the 24 hours of the natural day a man can expend only a definite quantity of his vital force, A horse, in like manner, can only work from day to day, 8 hours. During part of the day this force must rest, sleep; during another part the man has to satisfy other physical needs, to feed, wash, and clothe himself. Besides these purely physical limitations, the extension of the working day encounters moral ones. The labourer needs time for satisfying his intellectual and social wants, the extent and number of which are conditioned by the general state of social advancement. The variation of the working day fluctuates, therefore, within physical and social bounds. But both these limiting condi-

[1] "A day's labour is vague, it may be long or short." ("An Essay on Trade and Commerce, containing observations on taxes," &c. London, 1770. p. 73.)

tions are of a very elastic nature, and allow the greatest lati-
tude. So we find working days of 8, 10, 12, 14, 16, 18 hours,
i.e., of the most different lengths.

The capitalist has bought the labour-power at its day-rate.
To him its use-value belongs during one working day. He
has thus acquired the right to make the labourer work for him
during one day. But what is a working day? [1]

At all even , less than a natural day. By how much?
The capitalist has his own views of this *ultima Thule,* the
necessary limit of the working day. As capitalist, he is only
capital personified. His soul is the soul of capital. But
capital has one single life impulse, the tendency to create
value and surplus-value, to make its constant factor, the means
of production, absorb the greatest possible amount of surplus-
labour. [2]

Capital is dead labour, that vampire-like, only lives by
sucking living labour, and lives the more, the more labour it
sucks. The time during which the labourer works, is the time
during which the capitalist consumes the labour-power he has
purchased of him. [3]

If the labourer consumes his disposable time for himself, he
robs the capitalist. [4]

The capitalist then takes his stand on the law of the exchange of commodities. He, like all other buyers, seeks to get
the greatest possible benefit out of the use-value of his commodity. Suddenly the voice of the labourer, which had been

[1] This question is far more important than the celebrated question of Sir Robert
Peel to the Birmingham Chamber of Commerce: What is a pound? A question
that could only have been proposed, because Peel was as much in the dark as to the
nature of money as the "little shilling men" of Birmingham.

[2] It is the aim of the capitalist to obtain with his expended capital the greatest
possible quantity of labour (d'obetnir du capital dépensé la plus forte somme de
travail possible). J. G. Courcelle-Seneuil . . Traité théorique et pratique des entre-
prises industrielles. 2nd ed. Paris, 1857, p. 63.

[3] "An hour's labour lost in a day is a prodigious injury to a commercial State.
. . . There is a very great consumption of luxuries among the labouring poor of
this kingdom: particularly among the manufacturing populace, by which they also
consume their time, the most fatal of consumptions." An Essay on Trade and
Commerce, &c., p. 47 and 153.

[4] "Si le manouvrier libre prend un instant de repos, l'économie sordide qui le suit
des yeux avec inquiétude prétend qu'il la vole." N. Linguet. "Théorie des loix
civiles, &c. London, 1767," t. II., p. 466.

stifled in the storm and stress of the process of production, rises:

The commodity that I have sold to you differs from the crowd of other commodities, in that its use creates value, and a value greater than its own. That is why you bought it. That which on your side appears a spontaneous expansion of capital, is on mine extra expenditure of labour-power. You and I know on the market only one law, that of the exchange of commodities. And the consumption of the commodity belongs not to the seller who parts with it, but to the buyer, who acquires it. To you, therefore, belongs the use of my daily labour-power. But by means of the price that you pay for it each day, I must be able to reproduce it daily, and to sell it again. Apart from natural exhaustion through age, &c., I must be able on the morrow to work with the same normal amount of force, health and freshness as to-day. You preach to me constantly the gospel of "saving" and "abstinence." Good! I will, like a sensible saving owner, husband my sole wealth, labour-power, and abstain from all foolish waste of it. I will each day spend, set in motion, put into action only as much of it as is compatible with its normal duration, and healthy development. By an unlimited extension of the working day, you may in one day use up a quantity of labour-power greater than I can restore in three. What you gain in labour I lose in substance. The use of my labour-power and the spoliation of it are quite different things. If the average time that (doing a reasonable amount of work) an average labourer can live, is 30 years, the value of my labour-power, which you pay me from day to day is $\frac{1}{365 \times 30}$ or $\frac{1}{10950}$ of its total value. But if you consume it in ten years, you pay me daily $\frac{1}{10950}$ instead of $\frac{1}{3650}$ of its total value, *i.e.*, only $\frac{1}{3}$ of its daily value, and you rob me, therefore, every day of $\frac{2}{3}$ of the value of my commodity. You pay me for one day's labour-power, whilst you use that of 3 days. That is against our contract and the law of exchanges. I demand, therefor, a working day of normal length, and I demand it without any appeal to your heart, for in money matters sentiment is out of place. You may be a model citizen, perhaps a member of the Society for the Prevention of Cruelty to Animals, and in the odour of sanctity to boot; but the thing that you represent face to face with me has no heart in its breast. That which seems to throb there is my own heart-beating. I demand the normal working day because I, like every other seller, demand the value of my commodity.[1]

We see then, that, apart from extremely elastic bounds, the nature of the exchange of commodities itself imposes no limit to the working day, no limit to surplus-labour. The capitalist maintains his rights as a purchaser when he tries to make the working day as long as possible, and to make, whenever possible, two working days out of one. On the other hand, the peculiar nature of the commodity sold implies a limit to its consumption by the purchaser, and the labourer maintains his right as seller when he wishes to reduce the working day to one of definite normal duration. There is here, therefore, an antinomy, right against right, both equally bearing the seal of the law of exchanges. Between equal rights force decides. Hence is it that in the history of capitalist production, the determination of what is a working day, presents itself as the result of a struggle, a struggle between collective capital, *i.e.,* the class of capitalists, and collective labour, *i.e.,* the working class.

SECTION 2.—THE GREED FOR SURPLUS LABOR. MANUFAC- TURER AND BOYARD.

Capital has not invented surplus-labour. Wherever a part of society possesses the monopoly of the means of production, the labourer free or not free, must add to the working time necessary for his own maintenance an extra working time in order to produce the means of subsistence for the owners of the means of production,[2] whether this proprietor be the Athenian

---

[1] During the great strike of the London builders, 1860-61, for the reduction of the working day to 9 hours, their Committee published a manifesto that contained, to some extent, the plea of our workers. The manifesto alludes, not without irony, to the fact, that the greatest profit-monger amongst the building masters, a certain Sir M. Peto, was in the odour of sanctity. (This same Peto, after 1867, came to an end à la Strousberg.)

[2] "Those who labour . . . . in reality feed both the pensioners . . . [called the rich] and themselves." (Edmund Burke, l. c., p. 2.)

καλὸς κἀγαθός, Etruscan theocrat, civis Romanus, Norman baron, American slave owner, Wallachian Boyard, modern landlord or capitalist.[1] It is, however, clear that in any given economic formation of society, where not the exchange value but the use-value of the product predominates, surplus-labour will be limited by a given set of wants which may be greater or less, and that here no boundless thirst for surplus-labour arises from the nature of the production itself. Hence in antiquity overwork becomes horrible only when the object is to obtain exchange value in its specific independent money-form; in the production of gold and silver. Compulsory working to death is here the recognized form of over-work. Only read Diodorus Siculus.[2] Still these are exceptions in antiquity. But as soon as people, whose production still moves within the lower forms of slave-labour, corvée-labour, &c., are drawn into the whirlpool of an international market dominated by the capitalistic mode of production, the sale of their products for export becoming their principal interest, the civilized horrors of over-work are grafted on the barbaric horrors of slavery, serfdom, &c. Hence the negro labour in the Southern States of the American Union preserved something of a patriarchal character, so long as production was chiefly directed to immediate local consumption. But in proportion, as the export of cotton became of vital interest to these states, the over-working of the negro and sometimes the using up of his life in 7 years' of labour became a factor in a calculated and calculating system. It was no longer a question of obtaining from him a certain quantity of useful products. It was now a question of production of surplus-labour itself. So was it also with the corvée, *e.g.,* in the Danubian Principalities (now Roumania).

---

[1] Niebuhr in his "Roman History" says very naïvely: "It is evident that works like the Etruscan, which, in their ruins astound us, presuppose in little (!) states lords and vassals." Sismondi says far more to the purpose that "Brussels lace" presupposes wage-lords and wage-slaves.

[2] "One cannot see these unfortunates (in the gold mines between Egypt, Ethiopia, and Arabia) who cannot even have their bodies clean, or their nakedness clothed, without pitying their miserable lot. There is no indulgence, no forbearance for the sick, the feeble, the aged, for woman's weakness. All must, forced by blows, work on until death puts an end to their sufferings and their distress." ("Diod. Sic. Bibl. Hist." lib. 3, c. 13.)

The comparison of the greed for surplus-labour in the Danubian Principalities with the same greed in English factories has special interest, because surplus-labour, in the corvée has an independent and palpable form.

Suppose the working day consists of 6 hours of necessary labour, and 6 hours of surplus-labour. Then the free labourer gives the capitalist every week 6 × 6 or 36 hours of surplus-labour. It is the same as if he worked 3 days in the week for himself, and 3 days in the week gratis for the capitalist. But this is not evident on the surface. Surplus-labour and necessary labour glide one into the other. I can, therefore, express the same relationship by saying, *e.g.*, that the labourer in every minute works 30 seconds for himself, and 30 for the capitalist, etc. It is otherwise with the corvée. The necessary labour which the Wallachian peasant does for his own maintenance is distinctly marked off from his surplus-labour on behalf of the Boyard. The one he does on his own field, the other on the seignorial estate. Both parts of the labour-time exist, therefore, independently, side by side one with the other. In the corvée the surplus-labour is accurately marked off from the necessary labour. This, however, can make no difference with regard to the quantitative relation of surplus-labour to necessary labour. Three days' surplus-labour in the week remain three days that yield no equivalent to the labourer himself, whether it be called corvée or wage-labour. But in the capitalist the greed for surplus-labour appears in the straining after an unlimited extension of the working day, in the Boyard more simply in a direct hunting after days of corvée.[1]

In the Danubian Principalities the corvée was mixed up with rents in kind and other appurtenances of bondage, but it formed the most important tribute paid to the ruling class. Where this was the case, the corvée rarely arose from serfdom; serfdom much more frequently on the other hand took origin from the corvée.[2] This is what took place in the Roumanian

---

[1] That which follows refers to the situation in the Roumanian provinces before the change effected since the Crimean war.

[2] This holds likewise for Germany, and especially for Prussia east of the Elbe. In the 15th century the German peasant was nearly everywhere a man, who, whilst subject to certain rents paid in produce and labour was otherwise at least practically

Provinces. Their original mode of production was based on community of the soil, but not in the Slavonic or Indian form. Part of the land was cultivated in severalty as freehold by the members of the community, another part—*ager publicus*—was cultivated by them in common. The products of this common labour served partly as a reserve fund against bad harvests and other accidents, partly as a public store for providing the costs of war, religion, and other common expenses. In course of time military and clerical dignitaries usurped, along with the common land, the labour spent upon it. The labour of the free peasants on their common land was transformed into corvée for the thieves of the common land. This corvée soon developed into a servile relationship existing in point of fact, not in point of law, until Russia, the liberator of the world, made it legal under pretence of abolishing serfdom. The code of the corvée, which the Russian General Kisseleff proclaimed in 1831, was of course dictated by the Boyards themselves. Thus Russia conquered with one blow the magnates of the Danubian provinces, and the applause of liberal crétins throughout Europe.

According to the "Réglement organique," as this code of the corvée is called, every Wallachian peasant owes to the so-called landlord, besides a mass of detailed payments in kind: (1), 12 days of general labour; (2), one day of field labour; (3), one day of wood carrying. In all, 14 days in the year. With deep insight into political economy, however, the working day is not taken in its ordinary sense, but as the working day necessary to the production of an average daily product; and that average daily product is determined in so crafty a way that no Cyclops would be done with it in 24 hours. In dry words, the Réglement itself declares with true Russian irony that by 12 working days one must understand the product of the manual labour of 36 days, by 1 day of field labour 3 days, and by 1 day

free. The German colonists in Brandenburg, Pomerania, Silesia, and Eastern Prussia, were even legally acknowledged as free men. The victory of the nobility in the peasants' war put an end to that. Not only were the conquered South German peasants again enslaved. From the middle of the 16th century the peasants of Eastern Prussia, Brandenburg, Pomerania, and Silesia, and soon after the free peasants of Schleswig-Holstein were degraded to the condition of serfs. (Maurer, Fronhöfe iv. vol.,—Meitzen, der Boden des preussischen Staats.—Hansen, Leibeigenschaft in Schleswig-Holstein.—ED.)

of wood carrying in like manner three times as much. In all, 42 corvée days. To this had to be added the so-called jobagie, service due to the lord for extraordinary occasions. In proportion to the size of its population, every village has to furnish annually a definite contingent to the jobagie. This additional corvée is estimated at 14 days for each Wallachian peasant Thus the prescribed corvée amounts to 56 working days yearly. But the agricultural year in Wallachia numbers in consequence of the severe climate only 210 days, of which 40 for Sundays and holidays, 30 on an average for bad weather, together 70 days, do not count. 140 working days remain. The ratio of the corvée to the necessary labour $\frac{56}{84}$ or $66\frac{2}{3}\%$ gives a much smaller rate of surplus-value than that which regulates the labour of the English agricultural of factory labourer. This is, however, only the legally prescribed corvée. And in a spirit yet more "liberal" than the English Factory Acts, the "Réglement organique" has known how to facilitate its own evasion. After it has made 56 days out of 12, the nominal days work of each of the 56 corvée days is again so arranged that a portion of it must fall on the ensuing day. In one day, *e.g.,* must be weeded an extent of land, which, for this work, especially in maize plantations, needs twice as much time. The legal day's work for some kinds of agricultural labour is interpretable in such a way that the day begins in May and ends in October. In Moldavia conditions are still harder. "The corvée days of the 'Réglement organique,'" cried a Boyard, drunk with victory, "amount to 365 days in the year." [1]

If the Réglement organique of the Danubian provinces was a positive expression of the greed for surplus-labour which every paragraph legalised, the English Factory Acts are the negative expression of the same greed. These acts curb the passion of capital for a limitless draining of labour-power, by forcibly limiting the working day by state regulations, made by a state that is ruled by capitalist and landlord. Apart from the working-class movement that daily grew more threatening, the limiting of factory labour was dictated by the same neces-

---

[1] Further details are to be found in E. Regnault's "Histoire politique et sociale des Principautés Danubiennes." Paris, 1855.

sity which spread guano over the English fields. The same blind eagerness for plunder that in the one case exhausted the soil, had, in the other, torn up by the roots the living force of the nation. Periodical epidemics speak on this point as clearly as the diminishing military standard in Germany and France.[1]

The Factory Act of 1850 now in force (1867) allows for the average working-day 10 hours, *i.e.,* for the first 5 days 12 hours from 6 a.m. to 6 p.m., including $\frac{1}{2}$ an hour for breakfast, and an hour for dinner, and thus leaving $10\frac{1}{2}$ working hours, and 8 hours for Saturday, from 6 a.m. to 2 p.m., of which $\frac{1}{2}$ an hour is subtracted for breakfast. 60 working hours are left, $10\frac{1}{2}$ for each of the first 5 days, $7\frac{1}{2}$ for the last.[2] Certain guardians of these laws are appointed, Factory Inspectors, directly under the Home Secretary, whose reports are published half-yearly by order of Parliament. They give regular and official statistics of the capitalistic greed for surplus-labour.

Let us listen, for a moment, to the Factory Inspectors.[3]

[1] "In general and within certain limits, exceeding the medium size of their kind, is evidence of the prosperity of organic beings. As to man, his bodily height lessens if his due growth is interfered with, either by physical or social conditions. In all European countries in which the conscription holds, since its introduction, the medium height of adult men, and generally their fitness for military service, has diminished. Before the revolution (1789), the minimum for the infantry in France was 165 centimetres; in 1818 (law of March 10th), 157; by the law of 1852, 156 c. m.; on the average in France more than half are rejected on account of deficient height or bodily weakness. The military standard in Saxony was in 1780, 178 c. m. It is now 155. In Prussia it is 157. According to the statement of Dr. Meyer in the Bavarian Gazette, May 9th, 1862, the result of an average of 9 years is, that in Prussia out of 1000 conscripts 716 were unfit for military service, 317 because of deficiency in height, and 399 because of bodily defects. . . . Berlin in 1858, could not provide its contingent of recruits; it was 156 men short." J. von Liebig: "Die Chemie in ihrer Anwendung auf Agrikultur und Physiologie, 1863," 7th Ed., vol 1., pp. 117, 118.

[2] The history of the Factory Act of 1850 will be found in the course of this chapter.

[3] I only touch here and there on the period from the beginning of modern industry in England to 1845. For this period I refer the reader to "Die Lage der arbeitenden Klasse in England, von Friedrich Engels, Leipzig, 1845." How completely Engels understood the nature of the capitalist mode of production is shown by the Factory Reports, Reports on Mines, &c., that have appeared since 1845, and how wonderfully he painted the circumstances in detail is seen on the most superficial comparison of his work with the official reports of the Children's Employment Commission, published 18 to 20 years later (1863-1867). These deal especially with the branches of industry in which the Factory Acts had not, up to 1862, been introduced, in fact are not yet introduced. Here, then, little or no alteration had been enforced, by authority, in the conditions painted by Engels. I borrow my examples

"The fraudulent millowner begins work at a quarter of an hour (sometimes more, sometimes less) before 6 a.m., and leaves off a quarter of an hour (sometimes more, sometimes less) after 6 p.m. He takes 5 minutes from the beginning and from the end of the half hour nominally allowed for breakfast, and 10 minutes at the beginning and end of the hour nominally allowed for dinner. He works for a quarter of an hour (sometimes more, sometimes less after 2 p.m. on Saturday. Thus his gain is

Before 6 a. m.	15	minutes.
After 6 p. m.	15	"
At breakfast time	10	"
At dinner time	20	"
	60	"

Five days—300 minutes.

On Saturday before 6 a. m.	15	minutes.
At breakfast time	10	"
After 2 p. m.	15	"
	40	minutes.
Total weekly	340	minutes.

Or 5 hours and 40 minutes weekly, which multiplied by 50 working weeks in the year (allowing two for holidays and occasional stoppages) is equal to 27 working days." [1]

"Five minutes a day's increased work, multiplied by 50 weeks, are equal to two and a half days of produce in the year." [2]

"An additional hour a day gained by small instalments before 6 a.m., after 6 p.m., and at the beginning and end of the

chiefly from the free trade period after 1848, that age of paradise, of which the commercial travellers for the great firm of free trade, blatant as ignorant, tell such fabulous tales. For the rest England figures here in the forground because she is the classic representative of capitalist production, and she alone has a continuous set of official statistics of the things we are considering.

[1] Suggestions, &c. by Mr. L. Horner, Inspector of Factories in: Factory Regulations Act. Ordered by the House of Commons to be printed, 9th August, 1859; p. 4, 5.

[2] Reports of the Inspector of Factories for the half year, October, 1856, p. 35.

times nominally fixed for meals, is nearly equivalent to work-ing 13 months in the year."[1]

Crises during which production is interrupted and the fac-tories work "short time," *i.e.,* for only a part of the week, naturally do not affect the tendency to extend the working day. The less business there is, the more profit has to be made on the business done. The less time spent in work, the more of that time has to be turned into surplus labour-time.

Thus the Factory Inspector's report on the period of the crisis from 1857 to 1858:

"It may seem inconsistent that there should be any over-working at a time when trade is so bad; but that very bad-ness leads to the transgression by unscrupulous men, they get the extra profit of it. . . . . In the last half year, says Leonard Horner, 122 mills in my district have been given up; 143 were found standing," yet, overwork is continued beyond the legal hours.[2]

"For a great part of the time," says Mr. Howell, "owing to the depression of trade, many factories were altogether closed, and a still greater number were working short time. I continue, however, to receive about the usual number of complaints that half, or three-quarters of an hour in the day, are snatched from the workers by encroaching upon the times professedly allowed for rest and refreshment."[3] The same phenomenon was repro-duced on a smaller scale during the frightful cotton-crisis from 1861 to 1865.[4] "It is sometimes advanced by way of excuse, when persons are found at work in a factory, either at a meal hour, or at some illegal time, that they will not leave the mill at the appointed hour, and that compulsion is necessary to force them to cease work [cleaning their machinery, &c.], especially on Saturday afternoons. But, if the hands remain in a factory after the machinery has ceased to revolve . . . they would not have been so employed if sufficient time had been set apart

---

[1] Reports, &c., 30th April, 1858, p. 9.
[2] Reports, &c., l. c., p. 43.
[3] Reports, &c., l. c., p. 25.
[4] Reports, &c., for the half year ending 30th April, 1861. See Appendix No. 2; Reports, &c., 31st October, 1862, p. 7, 52, 53. The violations of the Acts became more numerous during the last half year 1863. Cf. Reports, &c., ending 31st October, 1863, p. 7.

specially for cleaning, &c., either before 6 a.m. [*sic!*] or before 2 p. m. on Saturday afternoons."[1]

"The profit to be gained by it (over-working in violation of the Act) appears to be, to many, a greater temptation than they can resist; they calculate upon the chance of not being found out; and when they see the small amount of penalty and costs, which those who have been convicted have had to pay, they find that if they should be detected there will still be a considerable balance of gain. . . .[2] In cases where the additional time is gained by a multiplication of small thefts in the course of the day, there are insuperable difficulties to the inspectors making out a case."[3]

These "small thefts" of capital from the labourer's meal and recreation time, the factory inspectors also designate as "petty pilfering of minutes,"[4] "snatching a few minutes,"[5] or, as the labourers technically called them, "nibbling and cribbling at meal times."[6]

It is evident that in this atmosphere the formation of surplus-value by surplus-labour, is not secret. "If you allow me," said a highly respectable master to me, "to work only ten minutes in the day over-time, you put one thousand a year in my pocket."[7] "Moments are the elements of profit."[8]

---

[1] Reports, &c., October 31st, 1860, p. 23. With what fanaticism, according to the evidence of manufacturers given in courts of law, their hands set themselves against every interruption in factory labour, the following curious circumstance shows. In the beginning of June, 1836, information reached the magistrates of Dewsbury (Yorkshire) that the owners of 8 large mills in the neighbourhood of Batley had violated the Factory Acts. Some of these gentlemen were accused of having kept at work 5 boys between 12 and 15 years of age, from 6 a.m. on Friday to 4 p.m. on the following Saturday, not allowing them any respite except for meals and one hour for sleep at midnight. And these children had to do this ceaseless labour of 30 hours in the "shoddy-hole," as the hole is called, in which the woolen rags are pulled in pieces, and where a dense atmosphere of dust, shreds, &c., forces even the adult workman to cover his mouth continually with handkerchiefs for the protection of his lungs! The accused gentlemen affirm in lieu of taking an oath—as quakers they were too scrupulously religious to take an oath—that they had, in their great compassion for the unhappy children, allowed them four hours for sleep, but the obstinate children absolutely would not go to bed. The quaker gentlemen were mulcted in £20. Dryden anticipated these gentry:

"Fox full fraught in seeming sanctity,
That feared an oath, but like the devil would lie,
That look'd like Lent, and had the holy leer,
And durst not sin! before he said his prayer!"

[2] Rep., 31st Oct., 1856, p. 34.   [4] l. c. p., p. 48.   [6] l. c., p. 48.
[3] l. c., p. 35.   [5] l. c., p. 48.   [7] l. c., p. 48.
[8] Report of the Insp., &c., 30th April, 1860, p. 56.

Nothing is from this point of view more characteristic than the designation of the workers who work full time as "full-timers," and the children under 13 who are only allowed to work 6 hours as "half-timers." The worker is here nothing more than personified labour-time. All individual distinctions are merged in those of "full-timers" and "half-timers."[1]

SECTION 3.—BRANCHES OF ENGLISH INDUSTRY WITHOUT LEGAL LIMITS TO EXPLOITATION.

We have hitherto considered the tendency to the extension of the working day, the were-wolf's hunger for surplus-labour in a department where the monstrous exactions, not surpassed, says an English bourgeois economist, by the cruelties of the Spaniards to the American red-skins,[2] caused capital at last to be bound by the chains of legal regulations. Now, let us cast a glance at certain branches of production in which the exploitation of labour is either free from fetters to this day, or was so yesterday.

Mr. Broughton Charlton, county magistrate, declared as chairman of a meeting held at the Assembly Rooms, Nottingham, on the 14th of January, 1860, "that there was an amount of privation and suffering among that portion of the population connected with the lace trade, unknown in other parts of the kingdom, indeed, in the civilized world . . . Children of nine or ten years are dragged from their squalid beds at two, three, or four o'clock in the morning and compelled to work for a bare subsistence until ten, eleven, or twelve at night, their limbs wearing away, their frames dwindling, their faces whitening, and their humanity absolutely sinking into a stone-like torpor, utterly horrible to contemplate . . . . . We are not surprised that Mr. Mallett, or any other manufacturer, should stand forward and protest against discussion . . . . . The

---

[1] This is the official expression both in the factories and in the reports.

[2] "The cupidity of mill-owners whose cruelties in the pursuit of gain have hardly been exceeded by those perpetrated by the Spaniards in the conquest of America in the pursuit of gold." John Wade, History of the Middle and Working Classes, 3rd Ed. London, 1835, p. 114. The theoretical part of this book, a kind of hand-book of Political Economy, is, considering the time of its publication, original in some parts, *e.g.*, on commercial crises. The historical part is, to a great extent, a shameless plagiarism of Sir F. M. Eden's "History of the Poor," London, 1799.

system, as the Rev. Montagu Valpy describes it, is one of unmitigated slavery, socially, physically, morally, and spiritually. . . . . What can be thought of a town which holds a public meeting to petition that the period of labour for men shall be diminished to eighteen hours a day ? . . . . . We declaim against the Virginian and Carolina cotton-planters. Is their black-market, their lash, and their barter of human flesh more detestable than this slow sacrifice of humanity which takes place in order that veils and collars may be fabricated for the benefit of capitalists ?"[1]

The potteries of Staffordshire have, during the last 22 years, been the subject of three parliamentary inquiries. The result is embodied in Mr. Scriven's Report of 1841 to the "Children's Employment Commissioners," in the report of Dr. Greenhow of 1860 published by order of the medical officer of the Privy Council (Public Health, 3rd Report, 112-113), lastly, in the report of Mr. Longe of 1862 in the "First Report of the Children's Employment Commission, of the 13th June, 1863." For my purpose it is enough to take, from the reports of 1860 and 1863, some depositions of the exploited children themselves. From the children we may form an opinion as to the adults, especially the girls and women, and that in a branch of industry by the side of which cotton-spinning appears an agreeable and healthful occupation.[2]

William Wood, 9 years old, was 7 years and 10 months when he began to work. He "ran moulds" (carried ready-moulded articles into the drying room, afterwards bringing back the empty mould) from the beginning. He came to work every day in the week at 6 a.m., and left off about 9 p.m. "I work till 9 o'clock at night six days in the week. I have done so seven or eight weeks." Fifteen hours of labour for a child of 7 years old ! J. Murray, 12 years of age, says: "I turn jigger, and run moulds. I come at 6. Sometimes I come at 4. I worked all last night, till 6 o'clock this morning. I have not been in bed since the night before last. There were eight or nine other boys working last night. All but one have come this

---

[1] "Daily Telegraph," 17th January, 1860.
[2] Cf. F. Engels' Lage, etc., p. 249-51.

morning. I get 3 shillings and sixpence. I do not get any
more for working at night. I worked two nights last week."
Fernyhough, a boy of ten: "I have not always an hour (for
dinner). I have only half an hour sometimes; on Thursday,
Friday, and Saturday."[1]

Dr. Greenhow states that the average duration of life in the
pottery districts of Stoke-on-Trent, and Wolstanton is extraordinarily short. Although in the district of Stoke, only
36.6% and in Wolstanton only 30.4% of the adult male
population above 20 are employed in the potteries, among the
men of that age in the first district more than half, in the
second, nearly ⅔ of the whole deaths are the result of pulmonary diseases among the potters. Dr. Boothroyd, a medical
practitioner at Hanley, says: "Each successive generation of
potters is more dwarfed and less robust than the preceding
one." In like manner another doctor, Mr. M'Bean: "Since he
began to practise among the potters 25 years ago, he has observed a marked degeneration especially shown in diminution
of stature and breadth." These statements are taken from the
report of Dr. Greenhow in 1860.[2]

From the report of the Commissioners in 1863, the following: Dr. J. T. Arledge, senior physician of the North Staffordshire Infirmary, says: "The potters as a class, both men
and women, represent a degenerated population, both physically and morally. They are, as a rule, stunted in growth,
ill-shaped, and frequently ill-formed in the chest; they become
prematurely old, and are certainly short-lived; they are
phlegmatic and bloodless, and exhibit their debility of constitution by obstinate attacks of dyspepsia, and disorders of the
liver and kidneys, and by rheumatism. But of all diseases
they are especially prone to chest-disease, to pneumonia,
phthisis, bronchitis, and asthma. One form would appear peculiar to them, and is known as potter's asthma, or potter's
consumption. Scrofula attacking the glands, or bones, or other
parts of the body, is a disease of two-thirds or more of the

[1] Children's Employment Commission. First report, etc., 1863. Evidence, p. 16,
19, 18.
[2] Public Health, 3rd report, etc., p. 102, 104, 105.

potters . . . . . That the 'degenerescence' of the population of this district is not even greater than it is, is due to the constant recruiting from the adjacent country, and intermarriages with more healthy races."[1]

Mr. Charles Parsons, late house surgeon of the same institution, writes in a letter to Commissioner Longe, amongst other things: "I can only speak from personal observation and not from statistical data(but I do not hesitate to assert that my indignation has been aroused again and again at the sight of poor children whose health has been sacrificed to gratify the avarice of either parents or employers." He enumerates the causes of the diseases of the potters, and sums them up in the phrase, "long hours." The report of the Commission trusts that "a manufacture which has assumed so prominent a place in the whole world, will not long be subject to the remark that its great success is accompanied with the physical deterioration, wide-spread bodily suffering, and early death of the work-people . . by whose labour and skill such great results have been achieved."[2] And all that holds of the potteries in England is true of those in Scotland.[3]

The manufacture of lucifer matches dates from 1833, from the discovery of the method of applying phosphorus to the match itself. Since 1845 this manufacture has rapidly developed in England, and has extended especially amongst the thickly populated parts of London as well as in Manchester, Birmingham, Liverpool, Bristol, Norwich, Newcastle and Glasgow. With it has spread the form of lockjaw, which a Vienna physician in 1845 discovered to be a disease peculiar to lucifer-matchmakers. Half the workers are children under thirteen, and young persons under eighteen. The manufacture is on account of its unhealthiness and unpleasantness in such bad odour that only the most miserable part of the labouring class, half-starved widows and so forth, deliver up their children to it, "the ragged, half-starved, untaught children."[4]

Of the witnesses that Commissioner White examined

[1] Child. Empl. Comm. I. Report, p. 24.
[2] Children's Employment Commission, p. 22, and xi.
[3] l. c. p. xlvii.
[4] l. c. p. liv.

(1863), 270 were under 18, 50 under 10, 10 only 8, and 5 only 6 years old. A range of the working day from 12 to 14 or 15 hours, night-labour, irregular meal times, meals for the most part taken in the very workrooms that are pestilent with phosphorus. Dante would have found the worst horrors of his Inferno surpassed in this manufacture.

In the manufacture of paper-hangings the coarser sorts are printed by machine; the finer by hand (block-printing). The most active business months are from the beginning of October to the end of April. During this time the work goes on fast and furious without intermission from 6 a.m. to 10 p.m. or further into the night.

J. Leach deposes: "Last winter six out of nineteen girls were away from ill-health at one time from over-work. I have to bawl at them to keep them awake." W. Duffy: "I have seen when the children could none of them keep their eyes open for the work; indeed, none of us could." J. Lightbourne: "Am 13 . . . We worked last winter till 9 (evening), and the winter before till 10. I used to cry with sore feet every night last winter." G. Apsden: "That boy of mine . . . when he was 7 years old I used to carry him on my back to and fro through the snow, and he used to have 16 hours a day . . . I have often knelt down to feed him as he stood by the machine, for he could not leave it or stop." Smith, the managing partner of a Manchester factory: "We (he means his "hands" who work for "us")work on, with no stoppage for meals, so that the day's work of 10½ hours is finished by 4.30. p.m., and all after that is overtime."[1] (Does this Mr. Smith take no meals himself during 10½ hours?) "We (this same Smith) seldom leave off working before 6 p.m. (he means leave off the consumption of 'our' labour-power machines), so that we (iterum Crispinus) are really working overtime the whole year round . . . . . For all these, children and adults alike (152

---

[1] This is not to be taken in the same sense as our surplus-labour time. These gentlemen consider 10½ hours of labour as the normal working day, which includes of course the normal surplus-labour. After this begins "overtime" which is paid a little better. It will be seen later that the labour expended during the so-called normal day is paid below its value, so that the overtime is simply a capitalist trick in order to extort more surplus-labor, which it would still be, even if the labour-power expended during the normal working day were properly paid.

children and young persons and 140 adults), the average work for the last 18 months has been at the very least 7 days, 5 hours, or 78½ hours a week. For the six weeks ending May 2nd this year (1862), the average was higher—8 days or 84 hours a week." Still this same Mr. Smith, who is so extremely devoted to the *pluralis majestatis,* adds with a smile, "Machine work is not great." So the employers in the block-printing say: "Hand labour is more healthy than machine-work." On the whole, manufacturers declare with indignation against the proposal "to stop the machines at least during meal times.' A clause, says Mr. Otley, manager of a wall-paper factory in the Borough, "which allowed work between, say 6 a.m. and 9 p.m. . . . would suit us (!) very well, but the factory hours, 6 a.m. to 6 p.m., are not suitable. Our machine is always stopped for dinner. (What generosity!) There is no waste of paper and colour to speak of. But," he adds sympathetically, "I can understand the loss of time not being liked.' The report of the Commission opines with naïveté that the fear of some "leading firms" of losing time, *i.e.,* the time for appropriating the labour of others, and thence losing profit is not a sufficient reason for allowing children under 13, and young persons under 18, working 12 to 16 hours per day, to lose their dinner, nor for giving it to them as coal and water are supplied to the steam-engine, soap to wool, oil to the wheel—as merely auxiliary material to the instruments of labour, during the process of production itself.[1]

No branch of industry in England (we do not take into account the making of bread by machinery recently introduced) has preserved up to the present day a method of production so archaic, so—as we see from the poets of the Roman Empire—pre-christian, as baking. But capital, as was said earlier, is at first indifferent as to the technical character of the labour-process; it begins by taking it just as it finds it.

The incredible adulteration of bread, especially in London, was first revealed by the House of Commons Committee "on the adulteration of articles of food" (1855-56), and Dr.

[1] l. c. Evidence, p. 123, 124, 125, 140, and 54.

Hassall's work, "Adulterations detected."[1] The consequence of these revelations was the Act of August 6th, 1860, "for preventing the adulteration of articles of food and drink," an inoperative law, as it naturally shows the tenderest consideration for every free-trader who determines by the buying or selling of adulterated commodities "to turn an honest penny."[2] The Committee itself formulated more or less naïvely its conviction that free-trade meant essentially trade with adulterated, or as the English ingeniously put it, "sophisticated" goods. In fact this kind of sophistry knows better than Protagoras how to make white black, and black white, and better than the Eleatics how to demonstrate *ad oculos* that everything is only appearance.[3]

At all events the committee had directed the attention of the public to its "daily bread," and therefore to the baking trade. At the same time in public meetings and in petitions to Parliament rose the cry of the London journeymen bakers against their over-work, &c. The cry was so urgent that Mr. H. S. Tremenheere, also a member of the Commission of 1863 several times mentioned, was appointed Royal Commissioner of Inquiry. His report,[4] together with the evidence given, roused not the heart of the public but its stomach. Englishmen, always well up in the Bible, knew well enough that man, unless by elective grace a capitalist, or landlord, or sinecurist,

---

[1] Alum finely powdered, or mixed with salt, is a normal article of commerce bearing the significant name of "bakers' stuff."

[2] Soot is a well-known and very energetic form of carbon, and forms a manure that capitalistic chimney-sweeps sell to English farmers. Now in 1862 the British juryman had in a law-suit to decide whether soot, with which, unknown to the buyer 90% of dust and sand are mixed, is genuine soot in the commercial sense or adulterated soot in the legal sense. The "amis du commerce" decided it to be genuine commercial soot, and non-suited the plaintiff farmer, who had in addition to pay the costs of the suit.

[3] The French chemist, Chevallier, in his treatise on the "sophistications" of commodities, enumerates for many of the 600 or more articles which he passes in review, 10, 20, 30 different methods of adulteration. He adds that he does not know all the methods, and does not mention all that he knows. He gives 6 kinds of adulteration of sugar, 9 of olive oil, 10 of butter, 12 of salt, 19 of milk, 20 of bread, 23 of brandy, 24 of meal, 28 of chocolate, 30 of wine, 32 of coffee, etc. Even God Almighty does not escape this fate. See Ronard de Card, on the falsifications of the materials of the Sacrament. (De la falsification des substances sacramentelles, Paris, 1856.)

[4] "Report, &c., relating to the grievances complained of by the journeymen bakers &c., London, 1862," and "Second Report &c., London, 1863."

is commanded to eat his bread in the sweat of his brow, but they did not know that he had to eat daily in his bread a certain quantity of human perspiration mixed with the discharge of abcesses, cobwebs, dead black-beetles, and putrid German yeast, without counting alum, sand, and other agreeable mineral ingredients. Without any regard to his holiness, Freetrade, the free baking-trade was therefore placed under the supervision of the State inspectors (Close of th₃ Parliamentary session of 1863), and by the same Act of Parliament, work from 9 in the evening to 5 in the morning was forbidden for journeymen bakers under 18. The last clausₑ speaks volumes as to the over-work in this old-fashioned, homely line of business.

"The work of a London journeyman baker begins, as a rule, at about eleven at night. At that hour he 'makes the dough,' —a laborious process, which lasts from half-an-hour to three quarters of an hour, according to the size of the batch or the labour bestowed upon it. He then lies down upon the kneading-board, which is also the covering of the trough in which the dough is 'made;' and with a sack under him, and another rolled up as a pillow, he sleeps for about a couple of hours. He is then engaged in a rapid and continuous labour for about five hours—throwing out the dough, 'scaling it off,' moulding it, putting it into the oven, preparing and baking rolls and fancy bread, taking the batch bread out of the oven, and up into the shop, &c., &c. The temperature of a bakehouse ranges from about 75 to upwards of 90 degrees, and in the smaller bakehouses approximates usually to the higher rather than to the lower degree of heat. When the business of making the bread, rolls, &c., is over, that of its distribution begins, and a considerable proportion of the journeymen in the trade, after working hard in the manner described during the night, are upon their legs for many hours during the day, carrying baskets, or wheeling hand-carts, and sometimes again in the bakehouse, leaving off work at various hours between 1 and 6 p.m. according to the season of the year, or the amount and nature of their master's business; while others are again engaged in the bakehouse in 'bringing out' more batches until late in the afternoon.[1] . . . During what is called 'the London season,' the operatives belonging to the 'full-priced' bakers at the West End of the town, generally begin work at 11 p.m., and are engaged in making the bread, with one or two short (sometimes very short) intervals of rest, up to 8 o'clock the next morning. They are then engaged all day long, up to 4, 5, 6, and as late as 7 o'clock in the evening carrying out bread, or sometimes in the afternoon in the bakehouse again, assisting in the biscuit-baking. They may have, after they have done their work, sometimes five or six, sometimes only four or five hours' sleep before they begin again. On Fridays they always begin sooner, some about ten o'clock, and continue in some cases, at work, either in making or delivering the bread up to 8 p.m. on Saturday night, but more generally up to 4 or 5 o'clock, Sunday morning. On Sundays the men must attend twice or three times during the day for an hour or two to make preparations for the next day's bread. . . . . The men employed by the underselling masters (who sell their bread under the 'full price,' and who, as already pointed out, comprise three-fourths of the London bakers) have not only to work on the average longer hours, but their work is almost entirely confined to the bakehouse. The underselling masters generally sell their bread . . . . in the shop. If they send it out, which is not common, except as supplying chandlers' shops, they usually employ other hands for that purpose. It is not their practice to deliver bread from house to house. Towards the end of the week. . . . . the men begin on Thursday night at 10 o'clock, and continue on with only slight intermission until late on Saturday evening."[2]

Even the bourgeois intellect understands the position of the "underselling" masters. "The unpaid labour of the men was made the source whereby the competition was carried on."[3] And the "full-priced" baker denounces his underselling competitors to the Commission of Inquiry as thieves of foreign labour and adulterators. "They only exist now by first defrauding the public, and next getting 18 hours work out of their men for 12 hours' wages."[4]

[1] l. c. First Report, &c., p. vi.
[2] l. c. p. lxxi.   [3] George Read, The History of Baking, London, 1848, p. 16.
[4] Report (First) &c. Evidence of the "full-priced" baker Cheeseman, p. 108.

The adulteration of bread and the formation of a class of bakers that sells the bread below the full price, date from the beginning of the 18th century, from the time when the corporate character of the trade was lost, and the capitalist in the form of the miller or flour-factor, rises behind the nominal master baker.[1] Thus was laid the foundation of capitalistic production in this trade, of the unlimited extension of the working day and of night labour, although the latter only since 1824 gained a serious footing, even in London.[2]

After what has just been said, it will be understood that the Report of the Commission classes journeymen bakers among the short-lived labourers, who, having by good luck escaped the normal decimation of the children of the working-class, rarely reach the age of 42. Nevertheless, the baking trade is always overwhelmed with applicants. The sources of the supply of these labour-powers to London are Scotland, the western agricultural districts of England, and Germany.

In the years 1858-60, the journeymen bakers in Ireland organized at their own expense great meetings to agitate against night and Sunday work. The public—*e.g.*, at the Dublin meeting in May, 1860—took their part with Irish warmth. As a result of this movement, day labor alone was successfully established in Wexford, Kilkenny, Clonmel, Waterford, &c. "In Limerick, where the grievances of the journeymen are demonstrated to be excessive, the movement has been defeated by the opposition of the master bakers, the miller bakers being the greatest opponents. The example of Limerick led to a retrogression in Ennis and Tipperary. In Cork, where the strongest possible demonstration of feeling took place, the masters, by exercising their power of turning the men out of employment, have defeated the movement. In Dublin, the master bakers have offered the most determined opposition to

---

[1] George Read, l. c. At the end of the 17th and the beginning of the 18th centuries the factors (agents) that crowded into every possible trade were still denounced as "public nuisances." Thus the Grand Jury at the quarter session of the Justices of the Peace for the County of Somerset, addressed a presentment to the Lower House which, among other things, states, "that these factors of Blackwell Hall are a Public Nuisance and Prejudice to the Clothing Trade, and ought to be put down as a Nuisance." The case of our English Wool, &c., London, 1685, p. 6, 7.

[2] First Report, &c.

the movement, and by discountenancing as much as possible the journeymen promoting it, have succeeded in leading the men into acquiescence in Sunday work and night work, contrary to the convictions of the men."[1]

The Committee of the English Government, which Government, in Ireland, is armed to the teeth, and generally knows how to show it, remonstrates in mild, though funereal, tones with the implacable master bakers of Dublin, Limerick, Cork, &c.: "The Committee believe that the hours of labour are limited by natural laws, which cannot be violated with impunity. That for master bakers to induce their workmen, by the fear of losing employment, to violate their religious convictions and their better feelings, to disobey the laws of the land, and to disregard public opinion (this all refers to Sunday labour), is calculated to provoke ill-feeling between workmen and masters, . . . and affords an example dangerous to religion, morality, and social order. . . . The Committee believe that any constant work beyond 12 hours a-day encroaches on the domestic and private life of the working man, and so leads to disastrous moral results, interfering with each man's home, and the discharge of his family duties as a son, a brother, a husband, a father. That work beyond 12 hours has a tendency to undermine the health of the working man, and so leads to premature old age and death, to the great injury of families of working men, thus deprived of the care and support of the head of the family when most required."[2]

So far, we have dealt with Ireland. On the other side of the channel, in Scotland, the agricultural labourer, the ploughman, protests against his 13-14 hours' work in the most inclement climate, with 4 hours' additional work on Sunday (in this land of Sabbatarians!),[3] whilst, at the same time, three railway men are standing before a London coroner's jury—a guard, an engine-driver, a signalman. A tremendous railway accident has hurried hundreds of passengers into another world. The negligence of the employés is the cause of the

[1] Report of Committee on the Baking Trade in Ireland for 1861.
[2] l. c.
[3] Public meeting of agricultural labourers at Lasswade, near Edinburgh, January 5th, 1866. (See "Workman's Advocate," January 13th, 1866.) The formation

misfortune. They declare with one voice before the jury that ten or twelve years before, their labour only lasted eight hours a-day. During the last five or six years it had been screwed up to 14, 18, and 20 hours, and under a specially severe pressure of holiday-makers, at times of excursion trains, it often lasted for 40 or 50 hours without a break. They were ordinary men, not Cyclops. At a certain point their labour-power failed. Torpor seized them. Their brain ceased to think, their eyes to see. The thoroughly "respectable" British jurymen answered by a verdict that sent them to the next assizes on a charge of manslaughter, and, in a gentle "rider" to their verdict, expressed the pious hope that the capitalistic magnates of the railways would, in future, be more extravagant in the purchase of a sufficient quantity of labour-power, and more "abstemious," more "self-denying," more "thrifty," in the draining of paid labour-power.[1]

From the motley crowd of labourers of all callings, ages,

since the close of 1865 of a Trades' Union among the agricultural labourers at first in Scotland is a historic event. In one of the most oppressed agricultural districts of England, Buckinghamshire, the labourers, in March, 1867, made a great strike for the raising of their weekly wage from 9-10 shillings to 12 shillings. (It will be seen from the preceding passage that the movement of the English agricultural proletariat entirely crushed since the suppression of its violent manifestations after 1830, and especially since the introduction of the new Poor Laws, begins again in the sixties, until it becomes finally epoch-making in 1872. I return to this in the 2nd volume, as well as to the blue books that have appeared since 1867 on the position of the English land labourers. Addendum to the 3rd ed.)

[1] "Reynolds' Newspaper," January, 1866.—Every week this same paper has, under the sensational headings, "Fearful and fatal accidents," "Appalling tragedies," &c., a whole list of fresh railway catastrophes. On these an employé on the North Staffordshire line comments: "Everyone knows the consequences that may occur if the driver and fireman of a locomotive engine are not continually on the look-out. How can that be expected from a man who has been at such work for 29 or 30 hours, exposed to the weather, and without rest. The following is an example which is of very frequent occurrence:—One fireman commenced work on the Monday morning at a very early hour. When he had finished what is called a day's work, he had been on duty 14 hours 50 minutes. Before he had time to get his tea, he was again called on for duty. . . . The next time he finished he had been on duty 14 hours 25 minutes, making a total of 29 hours 15 minutes without intermission. The rest of the week's work was made up as follows:—Wednesday, 15 hours; Thursday, 15 hours 35 minutes; Friday, 14½ hours; Saturday, 14 hours 10 minutes, making a total for the week of 88 hours 40 minutes. Now, sir, fancy his astonishment on being paid 6¼ days for the whole. Thinking it was a mistake, he applied to the time-keeper, . . . and inquired what they considered a day's work, and was told 13 hours for a good man (*i.e.*, 78 hours. . . . He then asked for what he had made over and above the 78 hours per week, but was refused. However, he was at last told they would give him another quarter, *i.e.*, 10d." l. c., 4th February, 1866.

sexes, that press on us more busily than the souls of the slain on Ulysses, on whom—without referring to the blue books under their arms—we see at a glance the mark of over-work, let us take two more figures whose striking contrast proves that before capital all men are alike—a milliner and a blacksmith.

In the last week of June, 1863, all the London daily papers published a paragraph with the "sensational" heading "Death from simple over-work." It dealt with the death of the milliner, Mary Anne Walkley, 20 years of age, employed in a highly-respectable dressmaking establishment, exploited by a lady with the pleasant name of Elise. The old, often-told story,[1] was once more recounted. This girl worked, on an average, $16\frac{1}{2}$ hours, during the season often 30 hours, without a break, whilst her failing labour-power was revived by occasional supplies of sherry, port, or coffee. It was just now the height of the season. It was necessary to conjure up in the twinkling of an eye the gorgeous dresses for the noble ladies bidden to the ball in honour of the newly-imported Princess of Wales. Mary Anne Walkley had worked without intermission for $26\frac{1}{2}$ hours, with 60 other girls, 30 in one room, that only afforded $\frac{1}{3}$ of the cubic feet of air required for them. At night, they slept in pairs in one of the stifling holes into which the bedroom was divided by partitions of board.[2] And this was one of the best

---

[1] Cf. F. Engels. l. c., pp. 253, 154.

[2] Dr. Letheby, Consulting Physician of the Board of Health, declared: "The minimum of air for each adult ought to be in a sleeping room 300, and in a dwelling room 500 cubic feet." Dr. Richardson, Senior Physician to one of the London Hospitals: "Wit! needlewomen of all kinds, including milliners, dressmakers, and ordinary sempstresses, there are three miseries—over-work, deficient air, and either deficient food or deficient digestion. . . . Needlework, in the main, . . . is infinitely better adapted to women than to men. But the mischiefs of the trade, in the metropolis especially, are that it is monopolised by some twenty-six capitalists, who, under the advantages that spring from capital, can bring in capital to force economy out of labour. This power tells throughout the whole class. If a dressmaker can get a little circle of customers, such is the competition that, in her home, she must work to the death to hold together, and this same over-work she must of necessity inflict on any who may assist her. If she fail, or do not try independently, she must join an establishment, where her labour is not less, but where her money is safe. Placed thus, she becomes a mere slave, tossed about with the variations of society. Now at home, in one room, starving, or near to it, then engaged 15, 16, aye, even 18 hours out of the 24, in an air that is scarcely tolerable, and on food which, even if it be good, cannot be digested in the absence of pure

millinery establishments in London. Mary Anne Walkley fell
ill on the Friday, died on Sunday, without, to the astonishment of Madame Elise, having previously completed the work
in hand. The doctor, Mr. Keys, called too late to the deathbed, duly bore witness before the coroner's jury that "Mary
Anne Walkley had died from long hours of work in an over-
crowded workroom, and a too small and badly-ventilated bedroom." In order to give the doctor a lesson in good manners,
the coroner's jury thereupon brought in a verdict that "the
deceased had died of apoplexy, but there was reason to fear
that her death had been accelerated by over-work in an over-
crowded workroom, &c." "Our white slaves," cried the "Morning Star," the organ of the free-traders, Cobden and Bright,
"our white slaves, who are toiled into the grave, for the most
part silently pine and die."[1]

"It is not in dressmakers' rooms that working to death is
the order of the day, but in a thousand other places; in every
place I had almost said, where 'a thriving business' has to be
done. . . . We will take the blacksmith as a type. If
the poets were true, there is no man so hearty, so merry, as
the blacksmith; he rises early and strikes his sparks before
the sun; he eats and drinks and sleeps as no other man.
Working in moderation, he is, in fact, in one of the best of

air. On these victims, consumption, which is purely a disease of bad air, feeds."
Dr. Richardson: "Work and Overwork," in "Social Science Review," 18th July,
1863.

[1] "Morning Star," 23rd June, 1863.—The "Times" made use of the circumstance
to defend the American slave owners against Bright, &c. "Very many of us think,"
says a leader of July 2nd, 1868, "that, while we work our own young women to
death, using the scourge of starvation, instead of the crack of the whip, as the
instrument of compulsion, we have scarcely a right to hound on fire and slaughter
against families who were born slave owners, and who, at least, feed their slaves
well, and work them lightly." In the same manner, the "Standard," a Tory organ,
fell foul of the Rev. Newman Hall: "He excommunicated the slave owners, but
prays with the fine folk who, without remorse, make the omnibus drivers and conductors of London, &c., work 16 hours a-day for the wages of a dog." Finally,
spake the oracle, Thomas Carlyle, of whom I wrote, in 1850, "Zum Teufel ist der
Genius, der Kultus ist geblieben." In a short parable, he reduces the one great
event of contemporary history, the American civil war, to this level, that the Peter
of the North wants to break the head of the Paul of the South with all his might,
because the Peter of the North hires his labour by the day, and the Paul of the
South hires his by the life. ("Macmillan's Magazine." Ilias Americana in nuce.
August, 1863.) Thus, the bubble of Tory sympathy for the urban workers—by no
means for the rural—has burst at last. The sum of all is—slavery!

human positions, physically speaking. But we follow him into the city or town, and we see the stress of work on that strong man, and what then is his position in the death-rate of his country. In Marylebone, blacksmiths die at the rate of 31 per thousand per annum, or 11 above the mean of the male adults of the country in its entirety. The occupation, instinctive almost as a portion of human art, unobjectionable as a branch of human industry, is made by mere excess of work, the destroyer of the man. He can strike so many blows per day, walk so many steps, breathe so many breaths, produce so much work, and live an average, say of fifty years; he is made to strike so many more blows, to walk so many more steps, to breathe so many more breaths per day, and to increase altogether a fourth of his life. He meets the effort; the result is, that producing for a limited time a fourth more work, he dies at 37 for 50."[1]

SECTION 4.—DAY AND NIGHT WORK.   THE RELAY SYSTEM.

Constant capital, the means of production, considered from the standpoint of the creation of surplus-value, only exist to absorb labour, and with every drop of labour a proportional quantity of surplus-labour. While they fail to do this, their mere existence causes a relative loss to the capitalist, for they represent during the time they lie fallow, a useless advance of capital. And this loss becomes positive and absolute as soon as the intermission of their employment necessitates additional outlay at the recommencement of work. The prolongation of the working day beyond the limits of the natural day, into the night, only acts as a palliative. It quenches only in a slight degree the vampire thirst for the living blood of labour. To appropriate labour during all the 24 hours of the day is, therefore, the inherent tendency of capitalist production. But as it is physically impossible to exploit the same individual labour-power constantly during the night as well as the day, to overcome this physical hindrance, an alternation becomes necessary between the workpeople whose powers are exhausted by day,

---

[1] Dr. Richardson, l. c.

and those who are used up by night. This alternation may be effected in various ways; *e.g.,* it may be so arranged that part of the workers are one week employed on day work, the next week on night work. It is well-known that this relay system, this alternation of two sets of workers, held full sway in the full-blooded youth-time of the English cotton manufacture, and that at the present time it still flourishes, among others, in the cotton spinning of the Moscow district. This 24 hours' process of production exists to-day as a system in many of the branches of industry of Great Britain that are still "free," in the blast-furnaces, forges, plate-rolling mills, and other metallurgical establishments in England, Wales, and Scotland. The working time here includes, besides the 24 hours of the 6 working days, a great part also of the 24 hours of Sunday. The workers consist of men and women, adults and children of both sexes. The ages of the children and young persons run through all intermediate grades, from 8 (in some cases from 6) to 18.[1]

In some branches of industry, the girls and women work through the night together with the males.[2]

Placing on one side the generally injurious influence of night-labour,[3] the duration of the process of production, un-

---

[1] Children's Employment Commissio.. Third Report. Lond .:, 1864, p. iv., v., vi.

[2] "Both in Staffordshire and in South Wale 'oung girls an' women are employed on the pit banks and on the coke heaps, not only y day but also by night. This practice has been often noticed in Reports presente o Parliament, as being attended with great and notorious evils. These females er loyed with the men, hardly distinguished from them in their dress, and b grimed with dirt and smoke, are exposed to the deterioration of character, arising from the loss of self-respect, which can hardly fail to follow from their unfeminine occupation." (l. c. 194., p. xxvi. Cf. Fourth Report (1865), 61, p. xiii.) It is the same in glass-works.

[3] A steel manufacturer who employs children in night labour remarked: "It seems but natural that boys who work at night cann t leep and get proper rest by day, but will be running about." (l. c. Fourth Report, 63, p. xiii.) On the importance of sunlight f.r the maintenance and growth of t' body, a physician writes: "Light also acts up i the tissues of the body directly in hardening them and supporting their elasticity. The muscles of animals, when they are deprived of a proper amount of light, become soft and inelastic, the nervous power loses its tone from defective stimulation, and the elaboration of all growth seems to be perverted. . . . In the case of children, constant access to plenty of light during the day, and to the direct rays of the sun for a part of it, is most essential to health. Light assists in the elaboration of good plastic blood, and hardens the fibre after it has been laid down. It also acts as a stimulus upon the organs of sight, and by this means brings about more activity in the various cerebral functions." Dr. W. Strange, Senior Physician of the Worcester General Hospital, from

broken during the 24 hours, offers very welcome opportunities of exceeding the limits of the normal working day, *e.g.,* in the branches of industry already mentioned, which are of an exceedingly fatiguing nature; the official working day means for each worker usually 12 hours by night or day. But the over-work beyond this amount is in many cases, to use the words of the English official report, "truly fearful."[1]

"It is impossible," the report continues, "for any mind to realise the amount of work described in the following passages as being performed by boys of from 9 to 12 years of age . . . . without coming irresistibly to the conclusion that such abuses of the power of parents and of employers can no longer be allowed to exist."[2]

"The practice of boys working at all by day and night turns either in the usual course of things, or at pressing times, seems inevitably to open the door to their not unfrequently working unduly long hours. These hours are, indeed, in some cases, not only cruelly but even incredibly long for children. Amongst a number of boys it will, of course, not unfrequently happen that one or more are from some cause absent. When this happens, their place is made up by one or more boys, who work in the other turn. That this is a well understood system is plain . . . from the answer of the manager of some large rolling-mills, who, when I asked him how the place of the boys absent from their turn was made up, 'I daresay, sir, you know that as well as I do,' and admitted, the fact."[3]

"At a rolling-mill where the proper hours were from 6 a.m. to $5\frac{1}{2}$ p.m., a boy worked about four nights every week till $8\frac{1}{2}$ p.m. at least . . . and this for six months. Another, at 9 years old, sometimes made three 12-hour shifts running, and,

whose work on "Health" (1864) this passage is taken, writes in a letter to Mr. White, one of the commissioners: "I have had opportunities formerly, when in Lancashire, of observing the effects of night-work upon children, and I have no hesitation in saying, contrary to what *some* employers were fond of asserting, those children who were subjected to it soon suffered in their health." (l. c. 284, p. 55.) That such a question should furnish the material of serious controversy, shows plainly how capitalist production acts on the brain-functions of capitalists and their retainers.

[1] l. c. 57, p. xii.   [2] l. c. Fourth Report (1865), 58, p. xii.   [3] l. c.

when 10, has made two days and two nights running." A
third, "now 10 . . . worked from 6 a.m. till 12 p.m. three
nights, and till 9 p.m. the other nights." "Another, now 13,
. . . worked from 6 p.m. till 12 noon next day, for a week
together, and sometimes for three shifts together, *e.g.,* from
Monday morning till Tuesday night." "Another, now 12, has
worked in an iron foundry at Stavely from 6 a.m. till 12 p.m.
for a fortnight on end; could not do it any more." "George
Allinsworth, age 9, came here as cellar-boy last Friday; next
morning we had to begin at 3, so I stopped here all night.
Live five miles off. Slept on the floor of the furnace, over
head, with an apron under me, and a bit of a jacket over me.
The two other days I have been here at 6 a.m. Aye! it *is* hot
in here. Before I came here I was nearly a year at the same
work at some works in the country. Began there, too, at 3 on
Saturday morning—always did, but was very gain [near]
home, and could sleep at home. Other days I began at 6 in the
morning, and gi'en over at 6 or 7 in the evening," &c.[1]

[1] l. c., p. xiii. The degree of culture of these "labour-powers" must naturally be
such as appears in the following dialogues with one of the commissioners: Jere-
miah Haynes, age 12—"Four times four is 8; 4 fours are 16. A king is him that
s all m ney and ld. We have a King (told it is a Queen), they call her
th. Princess Alexandria. Told that she married the Queen's son. The Queen's
son the incess Alexandria. A Princess is a man." William Turner, age 12—
"Don't live in England. Think it *is* a country, but didn't know before." John
Morris, age 14—"Have heard say that God made the world, and that all the people
was drownde' but one; heard say that one was a little bird." William Smith, age
15—"God i .de man, man made woman." Edward Taylor, age 15—"Do not know
of London." Henry Matthewman, age 17—"Had been to chapel, but missed a good
many times lately. One name that they preached about was Jesus Christ, but I
cannot say any ', and I cannot tell anything about him. He was not killed,
but died like other people. He was not the same as other people in some ways,
because he was religious in some ways, and others isn't." (l. c. p. xv.) "The
devil is a good person. I don't know where he lives." "Christ was a wicked
man." "This girl spelt God as dog, and did not know the name of the queen."
("Ch. Employment Comm. V. Report, 1866," p. 55, n. 278.) The same system
obtains in the glass and paper works as in the metallurgical, already cited. In the
paper factories, where the paper is made by machinery, night-work is the rule for
all processes, except rag-sorting. In some cases night-work, by relays, is carried
on incessantly through the whole week, usually from Sunday night until midnight
of the following Saturday. Those who are on day-work work 5 days of 12, and 1
day of 18 hours; those on night-work 5 nights of 12, and 1 of 6 hours in each
week. In other cases each set works 24 hours consecutively on alternate days, one
set working 6 hours on Monday, and 18 on Saturday to make up the 24 hours. In
other cases an intermediate system prevails, by which all employed on the paper-
making machinery work 15 or 16 hours every day in the week. This system, says
Commissioner Lord, "seems to combine all the evils of both the 12 hours' and the 24

Let us now hear how capital itself regards this 24 hours' system. The extreme forms of the system, its abuse in the "cruel and incredible" extension of the working day are naturally passed over in silence. Capital only speaks of the system in its "normal" form.

Messrs. Naylor & Vickers, steel manufacturers, who employ between 600 and 700 persons, among whom only 10 per cent. are under 18, and of those, only 20 boys under 18 work in night sets thus express themselves: "The boys do not suffer from the heat. The temperature is probably from 86° to 90°. . . . . At the forges and in the rolling-mills the hands work night and day, in relays, but all the other parts of the work are day work, *i.e.,* from 6 a.m. to 6 p.m. In the forge the hours are from 12 to 12. Some of the hands always work in the night, without any alternation of day and night work. . . . . . We do not find any difference in the health of those who work regularly by night and those who work by day, and probably people can sleep better if they have the same period of rest than if it is changed. . . . . About 20 of the boys under the age of 18 work in the night sets. . . . . . We could not well do without lads under 18 working by night. The objection would be in the increase in the cost of production. . . . . Skilled hands and the heads in every department are difficult to get, but of the lads we could get any number. . . . . . But from the small proportion of boys that we employ the subject (*i.e.,* of restrictions on night work) is of little importance or interest to us."[1]

Mr. J. Ellis, one of the firm of Messrs. John Brown & Co., steel and iron works, employing about 3000 men and boys, part

hours' relays." Children under 13, young persons under 18, and women, work under this night system. Sometimes under the 12 hours' system they are obliged, on account of the non-appearance of those that ought to relieve them, to work a double turn of 24 hours. The evidence proves that boys and girls very often work overtime, which, not unfrequently, extends to 24 or even 36 hours of uninterrupted toil. In the continuous and unvarying process of glazing are found girls of 12 who work the whole month 14 hours a day, "without any regular relief or cessation beyond 2 or, at most, 3 breaks of half-an-hour each for meals." In some mills, where regular night-work has been entirely given up, over-work goes on to a terrible extent, "and that often in the dirtiest, and in the hottest, and in the most monotonous of the various processes." ("Ch. Employment Comm. Report IV., 1865," p. xxxviii. and xxxix.) [1] Fourth Report, &c., 1865, 79, p. xvi.

of whose operations, namely, iron and heavier steel work, goes on night and day by relays states "that in the heavier steel work one or two boys are employed to a score or two men." Their concern employs upwards of 500 boys under 18 of whom about ⅓ or 170 are under the age of 13. With reference to the proposed alteration of the law, Mr. Ellis says: "I do not think it would be very objectionable to require that no person under the age of 18 should work more than 12 hours in the 24. But we do not think that any line could be drawn over the age of 12, at which boys could be dispensed with for night work. But we would sooner be prevented from employing boys under the age of 13, or even so high as 14, at all, than not be allowed to employ boys that we do have at night. Those boys who work in the day sets must take their turn in the night sets also, because the men could not work in the night sets only; it would ruin their health. . . . . We think, however, that night work in alternate weeks is no harm. (Messrs. Naylor & Vickers, on the other hand, in conformity with the interest of their business, considered that periodically changed night-labour might possibly do more harm than continual night-labour.) We find the men who do it, as well as the others who do other work only by day. . . . . . Our objections to not allowing boys under 18 to work at night, would be on account of the increase of expense, but this is the only reason. (What cynical naïveté!) We think that the increase would be more than the trade, with due regard to its being successfully carried out, could fairly bear. (What mealy-mouthed phraseology!) Labour is scarce here, and might fall short if there were such a regulation." (*i.e.,* Ellis Brown & Co. might fall into the fatal perplexity of being obliged to pay labour-power its full value.)'

The "Cyclops Steel and Iron Works," of Messrs. Cammel & Co., are conducted on the same large scale as those of the above mentioned John Brown & Co. The managing director had handed in his evidence to the Government Commissioner, Mr. White, in writing. Later he found it convenient to suppress the MS. when it had been returned to him for revision. Mr. White, however, has a good memory. He remembered quite

¹ l. c. 80, p. xvi.

clearly that for the Messrs. Cyclops the forbidding of the night-labour of children and young persons "would be impossible, it would be tantamount to stopping their works," and yet their business employs little more than 6% of boys under 18, and less than 1% under 13.[1]

On the same subject Mr. E. F. Sanderson, of the firm of Sanderson, Bros., & Co., steel rolling-mills and forges, Attercliffe, says: "Great difficulty would be caused by preventing boys under 18 from working at night. The chief would be the increase of cost from employing men instead of boys. I cannot say what this would be, but probably it would not be enough to enable the manufacturers to raise the price of steel, and consequently it would fall on them, as of course the men (what queer-headed folk!) would refuse to pay it." Mr. Sanderson does not know how much he pays the children, but "perhaps the younger boys get from 4s. to 5s. a week. . . . The boys' work is of a kind for which the strength of the boys is generally ('generally,' of course not always) quite sufficient, and consequently there would be no gain in the greater strength of the men to counterbalance the loss, or it would be only in the few cases in which the metal is heavy. The men would not like so well not to have boys under them, as men would be less obedient. Besides, boys must begin young to learn the trade. Leaving day work alone open to boys would not answer this purpose." And why not? Why could not boys learn their handicraft in the day-time? Your reason? "Owing to the men working days and nights in alternate weeks, the men would be separated half the time from their boys, and would lose half the profit which they make from them. The training which they give to an apprentice is considered as part of the return for the boys' labour, and thus enables the men to get it at a cheaper rate. Each man would want half of this profit." In other words, Messrs. Sanderson would have to pay part of the wages of the adult men out of their own pockets instead of by the night work of the boys. Messrs. Sanderson's profit would thus fall to some extent, and this is the good Sanderson-

---

[1] l. c. 82, p. xvii.

ian reason why boys cannot learn their handicraft in the day.[1] In addition to this, it would throw night labour on those who worked instead of the boys, which they would not be able to stand. The difficulties in fact would be so great that they would very likely lead to the giving up of night work altogether, and "as far as the work itself is concerned," says E. F. Sanderson, "this would suit as well, but—" But Messrs. Sanderson have something else to make besides steel. Steelmaking is simply a pretext for surplus-value making. The smelting furnaces, rolling-mills, &c., the buildings, machinery, iron, coal, &c. have something more to do than transform themselves into steel. They are there to absorb surplus-labour, and naturally absorb more in 24 hours than in 12. In fact they give, by grace of God and law, the Sandersons a cheque on the working time of a certain number of hands for all the 24 hours of the day, and they lose their character as capital, are therefore a pure loss for the Sandersons, as soon as their function of absorbing labour is interrupted. "But then there would be the loss from so much expensive machinery, lying idle half the time, and to get through the amount of work which we are able to do on the present system, we should have to double our premises and plant, which would double the outlay." But why should these Sandersons pretend to a privilege not enjoyed by the other capitalists who only work during the day, and whose buildings, machinery, raw material, therefore lie "idle" during the night? E. F. Sanderson answers in the name of all the Sandersons: "It is true that there is this loss from machinery lying idle in those manufactories in which work only goes on by day. But the use of furnaces would involve a further loss in our case. If they were kept up there would be a waste of fuel (instead of, as now, a waste of the living substance of the workers), and if they were not, there would be loss of time in laying the fires and getting the heat up (whilst the loss of sleeping time, even to children of 8, is a gain of working time for the Sanderson tribe), and the furnaces themselves

[1] In our reflecting and reasoning age a man is not worth much who cannot give a good reason for everything, no matter how bad or how crazy. Everything in the world that has been done wrong has been done wrong for the very best of reasons. (Hegel, l. c., p. 249.)

would suffer from the changes of temperature." (Whilst those same furnaces suffer nothing from the day and night changes of labour.)[1]

SECTION 5.—THE STRUGGLE FOR A NORMAL WORKING DAY. COMPULSORY LAWS FOR THE EXTENSION OF THE WORKING DAY FROM THE MIDDLE OF THE 14TH TO THE END OF THE 17TH CENTURY.

"What is a working day? What is the length of time during which capital may consume the labour-power whose daily value it buys? How far may the working day be extended beyond the working time necessary for the reproduction of labour-power itself?" It has been seen that to these questions capital replies: the working day contains the full 24 hours, with the deduction of the few hours of repose without which labour-power absolutely refuses its services again.

---

[1] l. c. 85, p. xvii. To similar tender scruples of the glass manufacturers that regular meal times for the children are impossible because as a consequence a certain quantity of heat, radiated by the furnaces, wou i be "a pure loss" or "wasted," Commissioner White makes answer. His answer is unlike that o. Ur Seni r, &c., and their puny German plagiarists à la Roscher who are touche . b th "abstinence," "self-denial," "saving," of the capitalists in the expenditure of their gold, and by their Timur-Tamerlanish prodigality of human life! "A certain amount of heat beyond what is usual at present might also be going to waste, if meal times were secured in these cases, but it seems likely not equal in money-value to the waste of animal power now going on in glass-hou s throughout the kingdom from growing boys not having enough quiet time to e t their meals at ease, with a little rest afterwards for digestion." (l. c., p. xlv.) And this in the year of progress 1865! Without considering the expenditure of strength in lifting and carrying, such a child, in the sheds where bottle and flint glass are made, walks during the performance of his work 15–20 miles in every 6 hours! And the work often lasts 14 or 15 hours! In many of these glass works, as in the Moscow spinning mills, the system of 6 hours' relays is in force. "During the working part of the week six hours is the utmost unbroken period ever attained at any one time for rest, and out of this has to come the time spent in coming and going to and from work, washing, dressing, and meals, leaving a very short period indeed for rest, and none for fresh air and play, unless at the expense of the sleep necessary for young boys, especially at such hot and fatiguing work. . . . Even the short sleep is obviously liable to be broken by a boy having to wake himself if it is night, or by the noise, if it is day." Mr. White gives cases where a boy worked 36 consecutive hours; others where boys of 12 drudged on until 2 in the morning, and then slept in the works till 5 a.m. (3 hours!) only to resume their work. "The amount of work," say Tremenheere and Tufnell, who drafted the general report, "done by boys, youths, girls, and women, in the course of their daily or nightly spell of labour, is certainly extraordinary." (l. c., xliii. and xliv.) Meanwhile, late by night perhaps, self-denying Mr. Glass-Capital, primed with port-wine, reels out of his club homeward droning out idiotically, "Britons never, never shall be slaves!"

Hence it is self-evident that the labourer is nothing else, his whole life through, than labour-power, that therefore all his disposable time is by nature and law labour-time, to be devoted to the self-expansion of capital. Time for education, for intellectual development, for the fulfilling of social functions and for social intercourse, for the free-play of his bodily and mental activity, even the rest time of Sunday (and that in a country of Sabbatarians!)[1]—moonshine! But in its blind unrestrainable passion, its were-wolf hunger for surplus-labour, capital oversteps not only the moral, but even the merely physical maximum bounds of the working day. It usurps the time for growth, development, and healthy maintenance of the body. It steals the time required for the consumption of fresh air and sunlight. It higgles over a meal-time, incorporating it where possible with the process of production itself, so that food is given to the labourer as to a mere means of production, as coal is supplied to the boiler, grease and oil to the machinery. It reduces the sound sleep needed for the restoration, reparation, refreshment of the bodily powers to just so many hours of torpor as the revival of an organism, absolutely exhausted, renders essential. It is not the normal maintenance of the labour-power which is to determine the limits of the working day; it is the greatest possible daily expenditure of labour-power, no matter how diseased, compulsory, and painful it may be, which is to determine the limits of the labourers' period of repose. Capital cares nothing for the length of life of labour-power. All that concerns it is simply and solely the maximum of labour-power, that can be rendered fluent in a

---

[1] In England even now occasionally in rural districts a labourer is condemned to imprisonment for desecrating the Sabbath, by working in his front garden. The same labourer is punished for breach of contract if he remains away from his metal, paper, or glass works on the Sunday, even if it be from a religious whim. The orthodox Parliament will hear nothing of Sabbath-breaking if it occurs in the process of expanding capital. A memorial (August 1863), in which the London day-labourers in fish and poultry shops asked for the abolition of Sunday labour, states that their work lasts for the first 6 days of the week on an average 15 hours a-day, and on Sunday 8–10 hours. From this same memorial we learn also that the delicate gourmands among the aristocratic hypocrites of Exeter Hall, especially encourage this "Sunday labour." These "holy ones," so zealous *in cute curanda*, show their Christianity by the humility with which they bear the over-work, the privations, and the hunger of others. *Obsequium ventris istis (the labourers) perniciosius est.*

working day. It attains this end by shortening the extent of the labourer's life, as a greedy farmer snatches increased produce from the soil by robbing it of its fertility.

The capitalistic mode of production (essentially the production of surplus value, the absorption of surplus-labour), produces thus, with the extension of the working day, not only the deterioration of human labour-power by robbing it of its normal, moral and physical, conditions of development and function. It produces also the premature exhaustion and death of this labour-power itself.[1] It extends the labourer's time of production during a given period by shortening his actual life-time.

But the value of the labour-power includes the value of the commodities necessary for the reproduction of the worker, or for the keeping up of the working class. If then the unnatural extension of the working day, that capital necessarily strives after in its unmeasured passion for self-expansion, shortens the length of life of the individual labourer, and therefor the duration of his labour-power, the forces used up have to be replaced at a more rapid rate and the sum of the expenses for the reproduction of labour-power will be greater; just as in a machine the part of its value to be reproduced every day is greater the more rapidly the machine is worn out. It would seem therefore that the interest of capital itself points in the direction of a normal working day.

The slave-owner buys his labourer as he buys his horse. If he loses his slave, he loses capital that can only be restored by new outlay in the slave-mart. But "the rice-grounds of Georgia, or the swamps of the Mississippi may be fatally injurious to the human constitution; but the waste of human life which the cultivation of these districts necessitates, is not so great that it cannot be repaired from the teeming preserves of Virginia and Kentucky. Considerations of economy, moreover, which, under a natural system, afford some security for humane treatment by identifying the master's interest with

[1] "We have given in our previous reports the statements of several experienced manufacturers to the effect that over-hours. . . . certainly tend prematurely to exhaust the working power of the men." (l. c. 64, p. xiii.)

the slave's preservation, when once trading in slaves is practised, become reasons for racking to the uttermost the toil of
the slave; for, when his place can at once be supplied from foreign preserves, the duration of his life becomes a matter of less
moment than its productiveness while it lasts. It is accordingly a maxim of slave management, in slave-importing countries, that the most effective economy is that which takes out
of the human chattel in the shortest space ? time the utmost
amount of exertion it is capable of p tting forth. It is in
tropical culture, where annual profits often equal the whole
capital of plantations, that negro life is most recklessly sacrificed. It is the agriculture of the West Indies, which has
been for centuries prolific of fabulous wealth, that has engulfed
millions of the African race. It is in Cuba, at this day, whose
revenues are reckoned by millions, and whose planters are
princes, that we see in the servile class, the coarsest fare, the
most exhausting and unremitting toil, and even the absolute
destruction of a portion of its numbers every year."[1]

Mutato nomine de te fabula narratur. For slave-trade
read labour-market for Kentucky and Virginia Ireland and
the agricultu: l districts of England, Scotland, and Wales,
for Afric , Germany. We heard how over-wor'. thinned the
ranks of the baker, in London. Nevertheless the London
labour-market is always over-stocked with German and other
candidates for death in the bakeries. Pottery, as we saw, is
one of the shortest-lived industries. Is there any want here-
fore of potters? Josiah Wedgwood, the inventor of modern
pottery, himself originally a common workman, said in 1785
before the House of Commons that the whole trade employed
from 15,000 to 20,000 people.[2] In the year 1861 the population alone of the town centres of this industry in Great Britain
numbered 101,302. "The cotton trade has existed for ninety
years. . . . . It has existed for three generations of the English
race, and I believe I may safely say that during that period it
has destroyed nine generations of factory operatives."[3]

---

[1] Cairnes, "The Slave Power," p. 110, 111.
[2] John Ward: "History of the Borough of Stoke-upon-Trent," London, 1843,
p. 42.
[3] Ferrand's Speech in the House of Commons, 27th April, 1863.

No doubt in certain epochs of feverish activity the labour-market shows significant gaps. In 1834, *e.g.* But then the manufacturers proposed to the Poor Law Commissioners that they should send the "surplus-population" of the agricultural districts to the north, with the explanation "that the manufacturers would absorb and use it up."[1] "Agents were appointed with the consent of the Poor Law Commissioners. . . . An office was set up in Manchester, to which lists were sent of those workpeople in the agricultural districts wanting employment, and their names were registered in books. The manufacturers attended at these offices, and selected such persons as they chose; when they had selected such persons as their 'wants required,' they gave instructions to have them forwarded to Manchester, and they were sent, ticketed like bales of goods, by canals, or with carriers, others tramping on the road, and many of them were found on the way lost and half-starved. This system had grown up into a regular trade. This House will hardly believe it, but I tell them, that this traffic in human flesh was as well kept up, they were in effect as regularly sold to these [Manchester] manufacturers as slaves are sold to the cotton-grower in the United States. . . . . In 1860, 'the cotton trade was at its zenith.' . . . . The manufacturers again found that they were short of hands. . . . They applied to the 'flesh agents,' as they are called. Those agents sent to the southern downs of England, to the pastures of Dorsetshire, to the glades of Devonshire, to the people tending kine in Wiltshire, but they sought in vain. The surplus-population was 'absorbed.' " The "Bury Guardian," said, on the completion of the French treaty, that "10,000 additional hands could be absorbed by Lancashire, and that 30,000 or 40,000 will be needed." After the "flesh agents and sub-agents" had in vain sought through the agricultural districts, "a deputation came up to London, and waited on the right hon. gentleman. [Mr. Villiers, President of the Poor Law Board] with a view of obtaining poor children from certain union houses for the mills of Lancashire."[2]

---

[1] "Those were the very words used by the cotton manufacturers," l. c.

[2] l. c. Mr. Villiers, despite the best of intentions on his part, was "legally"

What experience shows to the capitalist generally is a constant excess of population, *i.e.*, an excess in relation to the
momentary requirements of surplus labour absorbing capital,
although this excess is made up of generations of human beings
stunted, short-lived, swiftly replacing each other, plucked, so
to say, before maturity.[1] And, indeed, experience shows to

obliged to refuse the requests of the manufacturers. These gentlemen, however,
attained their end through the obliging nature of local poor law boards. Mr. A.
Redgrave, Inspector of Factories, asserts that this time the system under which
orphans and pauper children were treated "legally" as apprentices "was not accompanied with the old abuses" (on these "abuses" see Engels, l. c.), although in one
case there certainly was "abuse of this system in respect to a number of girls and
young women brought from the agricultural districts of Scotland into Lancashire
and Cheshire." Under this system the manufacturer entered into a contract with
the workhouse authorities for a certain period. He fed, clothed, and lodged the
children, and gave them a small allowance of money. A remark of Mr. Redgrave
to be quoted directly seems strange, especially if we consider that even among the
years of prosperity of the English cotton trade, the year 1860 stands unparalleled,
and that, besides, wages were exceptionally high. For this extraordinary demand
for work had to contend with the depopulation of Ireland, with unexampled emigration from the English and Scotch agricultural districts to Australia and America,
with an actual diminution of the population in some of the English agricultural
districts, in consequence partly of an actual breakdown of the vital force of the
labourers, partly of the already effected dispersion of the disposable population
through the dealers in human flesh. Despite all this Mr. Redgrave says: "This
kind of labour, however, would only be sought after when none other could be
procured, for it is a high-priced labour. The ordinary wages of a boy of 13 would
be about 4s. per week, but to lodge, to clothe, to feed, and to provide medical
attendance and proper superintendence for 50 or 100 of these boys, and to set
aside some remuneration for them, could not be accomplished for 4s. a-head per
week." (Report of the Inspector of Factories for 30th April, 1860, p. 27.) Mr.
Redgrave forgets to tell us how the labourer himself can do all this for his children out of their 4s. a-week wages, when the manufacturer cannot do it for the
50 or 100 children lodged, boarded, superintended all together. To guard against
false conclusions from the text, I ought here to remark that the English cotton
industry, since it was placed under the Factory Act of 1850 with its regulations of
labour-time, &c., must be regarded as the model industry of England. The English
cotton operative is in every respect better off than his continental companion in
misery. "The Prussian factory operative labours at least ten hours per week more
than his English competitor, and if employed at his own loom in his own house,
his labour is not restricted to even those additional hours." ("Rep. of Insp. of
Fact.," Oct. 1853, p. 103.) Redgrave, the Factory Inspector mentioned above, after
the Industrial Exhibition in 1851, travelled on the Continent, especially in France
and Germany, for the purpose of inquiring into the conditions of the factories.
Of the Prussian operative he says: "He receives a remuneration sufficient to procure the simple fare, and to supply the slender comforts, to which he has been
accustomed. . . . he lives upon his coarse fare, and works hard, wherein his
position is subordinate to that of the English operative." ("Rep. of Insp. of Fact.,"
31st Oct., 1853, p. 85.)

[1] The overworked "die off with strange rapidity; but the places of those who
perish are instantly filled, and a frequent change of persons makes no alteration
in the scene." ("England and America." London, 1833, vol. I, p. 55. By E. G.
Wakefield.)

the intelligent observer with what swiftness and grip the capitalist mode of production, dating, historically speaking, only from yesterday, has seized the vital power of the people by the very root—show how the degeneration of the industrial population is only retarded by the constant absorption of primitive and physically uncorrupted elements from the country— shows how even the country labourers, in spite of fresh air and the principle of natural selection, that works so powerfully amongst them, and only permits the survival of the strongest, are already beginning to die off.[1] Capital that has such good reasons for denying the sufferings of the legions of workers that surround it, is in practice moved as much and as little by the sight of the coming degradation and final depopulation of the human race, as by the probable fall of the earth into the sun. In every stock-jobbing swindle every one knows that some time or other the crash must come, but every one hopes that it may fall on the head of his neighbour, after he himself has caught the shower of gold and placed it in safety. *Après moi le déluge!* is the watchword of every capitalist and of every capitalist nation. Hence Capital is reckless of the health or length of life of the labourer, unless under compulsion from society.[2] To the outcry as to the physical and mental degradation, the premature death, the torture of overwork, it answers: Ought these to trouble us since they in-

---

[1] See "Public Health. Sixth Report of the Medical Officer of the Privy Council, 1863." Published in London 1864. This report deals especially with the agricultural labourers. "Sutherland . . . is commonly represented as a highly improved county . . . but . . . recent inquiry has discovered that even there, in districts once famous for fine men and gallant soldiers, the inhabitants have degenerated into a meagre and stunted race. In the healthiest situations, on hill sides fronting the sea, the faces of their famished children are as pale as they could be in the foul atmosphere of a London alley." (W. T. Thornton. "Overpopulation and its remedy." l. c., p. 74, 75.) They resemble in fact the 30,000 "gallant Highlanders" whom Glasgow pigs together in its wynds and closes, with prostitutes and thieves.

[2] "But though the health of a population is so important a fact of the national capital, we are afraid it must be said that the class of employers of labour have not been the most forward to guard and cherish this treasure. . . . The consideration of the health of the operatives was forced upon the millowners. ("Times," November 5th, 1861.) "The men of the West Riding became the clothiers of mankind . . . the health of the workpeople was sacrificed, and the race in a few generations must have degenerated. But a reaction set in. Lord Shaftesbury's Bill limited the hours of children's labour," &c. ("Report of the Registrar-General," for October, 1861.)

crease our profits? But looking at things as a whole, all this does not, indeed, depend on the good or ill will of the individual capitalist. Free competition brings out the inherent laws of capitalist production, in the shape of external coercive laws having power over every individual capitalist.[1]

The establishment of a normal working day is the result of centuries of struggle between capitalist and labourer. The history of this struggle shows two opposed tendencies. Compare, *e.g.*, the English factory legislation of our time with the English Labour Statutes from the 14th century to well into the middle of the 18th.[2] Whilst the modern Factory Acts compulsorily shortened the working-day, the earlier statutes tried to lengthen it by compulsion. Of course the pretensions of capital in embryo—when, beginning to grow, it secures the right of absorbing a *quantum sufficit* of surplus-labour, not merely by the force of economic relations, but by the help of the State—appear very modest when put face to face with the concessions that, growling and struggling, it has to make in its adult condition. It takes centuries ere the "free" labourer, thanks to the development of capitalistic production, agrees, *i.e.*, is compelled by social conditions, to sell the whole of his active life, his very capacity for work, for the price of the necessaries of life, his birthright for a mess of pottage. Hence it is natural that the lengthening of the working day, which

[1] We, therefore, find, *e.g.*, that in the beginning of 1863, 26 firms owning extensive potteries in Staffordshire, amongst others, Josiah Wedgwood, & Sons' petition in a memorial for "some legislative enactment." Competition with other capitalists permits them no voluntary limitation of working-time for children, &c. " Much as we deplore the evils before mentioned, it would not be possible to prevent them by any scheme of agreement between the manufacturers. . . . Taking all these points into consideration, we have come to the conviction that some legislative enactment is wanted." ("Children's Employment Comm." Rep. 1., 1863, p. 322.) Most recently a much more striking example offers. The rise in the price of cotton during a period of feverish activity, had induced the manufacturers in Blackburn to shorten, by mutual consent, the working-time in their mills during a certain fixed period. This period terminated about the end of November, 1871. Meanwhile, the wealthier manufacturers, who combined spinning with weaving, used the diminution of production resulting from this agreement, to extend their own business and thus to make great profits at the expense of the small employers. The latter thereupon turned in their extremity to the operatives, urged them earnestly to agitate for the 9 hours' system, and promised contributions in money to this end.

[2] The Labour Statutes, the like of which were enacted at the same time in France, the Netherlands, and elsewhere, were first formally repealed in England in 1813, long after the changes in methods of production had rendered them obsolete.

capital from the middle of the 14th to the end of the 17th century, tries to impose by State-measures on adult labourers, approximately coincides with the shortening of the working day which, in the second half of the 19th century, has here and there been effected by the State to prevent the coining of children's blood into capital. That which to-day, *e.g.*, in the State of Massachusetts, until recently the freest State of the North-American Republic, has been proclaimed as the statutory limit of the labour of children under 12, was in England, even in the middle of the 17th century, the normal working-day of able-bodied artizans, robust labourers, athletic blacksmiths.[1]

The first "Statute of Labourers" (23 Edward III., 1349) found its immediate pretext (not its cause, for legislation of this kind lasts centuries after the pretext for it has disappeared) in the great plague that decimated the people, so that, as a Tory writer says, "The difficulty of getting men to work on reasonable terms (*i.e.*, at a price that left their employers a reasonable quantity of surplus-labour) grew to such a height as to be quite intolerable."[2] Reasonable wages were, therefore, fixed by law as well as the limits of the working day. The latter point, the only one that here interests us, is repeated in the Statute of 1496 (Henry VIII.). The working day for all artificers and field labourers from March to September ought, according to this statute (which, however, could not be enforced), to last from 5 in the morning to between 7 and 8

---

[1] "No child under 12 years of age shall be employed in any manufacturing establishment more than 10 hours in one day." General Statutes of Massachusetts, 63, ch. 12. (The various Statutes were passed between 1836 and 1858.) "Labour performed during a period of 10 hours on any day in all cotton, woollen, silk, paper, glass, and flax factories, or in manufactories of iron and brass, shall be considered a legal day's labour. And be it enacted, that hereafter no minor engaged in any factory shall be holden or required to work more than 10 hours in any day, or 60 hours in any week; and that hereafter no minor shall be admitted as a worker under the age of 10 years in any factory within this State." State of New Jersey. An Act to limit the hours of labour, &c., 61 and 62. (Law of 11th March, 1855.) "No minor who has attained the age of 12 years, and is under the age of 15 years, shall be employed in any manufacturing establishment more than 11 hours in any one day, nor before 5 o'clock in the morning, nor after 7.30 in the evening." ("Revised Statutes of the State of Rhode Island," &c., ch. 39, § 23, 1st July, 1857.)

[2] "Sophisms of Free Trade." 7th Ed. London, 1850, p. 205. 9th Ed., p. 253. This same Tory, moreover, admits that "Acts of Parliament regulating wages, but against the labourer and in favour of the master, lasted for the long period of 464 years. Population grew. These laws were then found, and really became, unnecessary and burdensome." (l. c., p. 206.)

in the evening. But the meal times consist of 1 hour for breakfast, 1½ hours for dinner, and ½ an hour for "noon-meate," *i.e.*, exactly twice as much as under the factory acts now in force.[1] In winter, work was to last from 5 in the morning until dark, with the same intervals. A statute of Elizabeth of 1562 leaves the length of the working day for all labourers "hired for daily or weekly wage" untouched, but aims at limiting the intervals to 2½ hours in the summer, or to 2 in the winter. Dinner is only to last 1 hour, and the "afternoon-sleep of half an hour" is only allowed between the middle of May and the middle of August. For every hour of absence 1d. is to be subtracted from the wage. In practice, however, the conditions were much more favourable to the labourers than in the statute-book. William Petty, the father of political economy, and to some extent the founder of Statistics, says in a work that he published in the last third of the 17th century: "Labouring-men (then meaning field-labourers) work 10 hours per diem, and make 20 meals per week, viz., 3 a day for working days, and 2 on Sundays; whereby it is plain, that if they could fast on Fryday nights, and dine in one hour and a half, whereas they take two, from eleven to one; thereby this working $\frac{1}{20}$ more, and spending $\frac{1}{20}$ less, the above-mentioned (tax) might be raised."[2] Was not Dr. Andrew Ure right in crying down the 12 hours' bill of 1833 as a retrogression to the times of the dark ages? It is true, these regulations contained in the statute mentioned by Petty, apply also to apprentices. But the condition of child-labour, even at the end of the 17th century, is seen from the following complaint: "'Tis not their practice (in Germany) as with us in this king-

---

[1] In reference to this statute, J. Wade with truth remarks: "From the statement above (*i. e.*, with regard to the statute) it appears that in 1496 the diet was considered equivalent to one third of the income of an artificer and one-half the income of a labourer, which indicates a greater degree of independence among the working classes than prevails at present; for the board, both of labourers and artificers, would now be reckoned at a much higher proportion of their wages." (J. Wade, "History of the Middle and Working Classes," p. 24, 25, and 577.) The opinion that this difference is due to the difference in the price-relations between food and clothing then and now is refuted by the most cursory glance at "Chronicon Pretiosum, &c." By Bishop Fleetwood. 1st Ed., London, 1707; 2d Ed., London, 1745.

[2] W. Petty, "Political Anatomy of Ireland. Verbum Sapienti," 1762, Ed. 1691, p. 10.

dom, to bind an apprentice for seven years; three or four is
their common standard: and the reason is, because they are
educated from their cradle to something of employment, which
renders them the more apt and docile, and consequently the more
capable of attaining to a ripeness and quicker proficiency in
business. Whereas our youth, here in England, being bred to
nothing before they come to be apprentices, make a very slow
progress and require much longer time wherein to reach the
perfection of accomplished artists."[1]

Still, during the greater part of the 18th century, up to the
epoch of Modern Industry and machinism, capital in England
had not succeeded in seizing for itself, by the payment of the
weekly value of labour-power, the whole week of the labourer
with the exception, however, of the agricultural labourers.
The fact that they could live for a whole week on the wage of
four days, did not appear to the labourers a sufficient reason
that they should work the other two days for the capitalist.
One party of English economists, in the interest of capital, denounces this obstinacy in the most violent manner, another

---

[1] "A Discourse on the necessity of encouraging Mechanick Industry," London,
1689, p. 13. Macaulay, who has falsified English history in the interest of the
Whigs and the bourgeoisie, declares as follows: "The practice of setting children
prematurely to work . . . prevailed in the 17th century to an extent which,
when compared with the extent of the manufacturing system, seems almost incredible. At Norwich, the chief seat of the clothing trade, a little creature of six years
old was thought fit for labour. Several writers of that time, and among them some
who were considered as eminently benevolent, mention with exultation the fact
that in that single city, boys and girls of very tender age create wealth exceeding
what was necessary for their own subsistence by twelve thousand pounds a year.
The more carefully we examine the history of the past, the more reason shall we
find to dissent from those who imagine that our age has been fruitful of new
social evils. . . . That which is new is the intelligence and the humanity which
remedies them." ("History of England," vol. I., p. 419.) Macaulay might have
reported further that "extremely well-disposed" *amis du commerce* in the 17th
century, narrate with "exultation" how in a poorhouse in Holland a child of four
was employed, and that this example of *"vertu mise en pratique"* passes muster in
all the humanitarian works, *à la* Macaulay, to the time of Adam Smith. It is
true that with the substitution of manufacture for handicrafts, traces of the exploitation of children begin to appear. This exploitation existed always to a certain
extent among peasants, and was the more developed, the heavier the yoke pressing
on the husbandman. The tendency of capital is there unmistakably; but the facts
themselves are still as isolated as the phenomena of two-headed children. Hence
they were noted "with exultation" as especially worthy of remark and as wonders
by the far-seeing *"amis du commerce,"* and recommended as models for their own
time and for posterity. This same Scotch sycophant and fine talker, Macaulay,
says: "We hear to-day only of retrogression and see only progress." What eyes,
and especially what ears!

party defends the labourers. Let us listen, *e.g.*, to the contest between Postlethwayt whose Dictionary of Trade then had the same reputation as the kindred works of M'Culloch and M'Gregor to-day, and the author (already quoted) of the "Essay on Trade and Commerce."[1]

Postlethwayt says among other things: "We cannot put an end to those few observations, without noticing that trite remark in the mouth of too many; that if the industrious poor can obtain enough to maintain themselves in five days, they will not work the whole six. Whence they infer the necessity of even the necessaries of life being made dear by taxes, or any other means, to compel the working artizan and manufacturer to labour the whole six days in the week, without ceasing. I must beg leave to differ in sentiment from those great politicians, who contend for the perpetual slavery of the working people of this kingdom; they forget the vulgar adage, all work and no play. Have not the English boasted of the ingenuity and dexterity of her working artists and manufacturers which have heretofore given credit and reputation to British wares in general? What has this been owing to? To nothing more probably than the relaxation of the working people in their own way. Were they obliged to toil the year round, the whole six days in the week, in a repetition of the same work, might it not blunt their ingenuity, and render them stupid instead of alert and dexterous; and might not our workmen lose their reputation instead of maintaining it by such eternal slavery? .... And what sort of workmanship could we expect from such hard-driven animals? .... Many of them will execute as much work in four days as a Frenchman will in

---

[1] Among the accusers of the workpeople, the most angry is the anonymous author quoted in the text of "An Essay on trade and commerce, containing observations on Taxation, &c., London, 1770." He had already dealt with this subject in his earlier work: "Considerations on Taxes." London, 1765. On the same side follows Polonius Arthur Young, the unutterable statistical prattler. Among the defenders of the working classes the foremost are: Jacob Vanderlint, in: "Money answers all things." London, 1734; the Rev. Nathaniel Forster, D.D.; in "An Enquiry into the Causes of the Present Price of Provisions," London, 1766; Dr. Price, and especially Postlethwayt, as well in the supplement to his "Universal Dictionary of Trade and Commerce," as in his "Great Britain's Commercial Interest explained and improved." 2nd Edition, 1755. The facts themselves are confirmed by many other writers of the time, among others by Josiah Tucker.

five or six. But if Englishmen are to be eternal drudges, 'tis
to be feared they will degenerate below the Frenchmen. As
our people are famed for bravery in war, do we not say that it
is owing to good English roast beef and pudding in their
bellies, as well as their constitutional spirit of liberty? And
why may not the superior ingenuity and dexterity of our
artists and manufactures, be owing to that freedom and liberty
to direct themselves in their own way, and I hope we shall
never have them deprived of such privileges and that good
living from whence their ingenuity no less than their courage
may proceed."[1] Thereupon the author of the "Essay on Trade
and Commerce" replies: "If the making of every seventh
day an holiday is supposed to be of divine institution, as it
implies the appropriating the other six days to labour" (he
means capital as we shall soon see) "surely it will not be
thought cruel to enforce it. . . . . That mankind in
general, are naturally inclined to ease and indolence, we fatally
experience to be true, from the conduct of our manufacturing
populace, who do not labour, upon an average, above four days
in a week, unless provisions happen to be very dear. . . . .
Put all the necessaries of the poor under one denomination;
for instance, call them all wheat, or suppose that . . . . the
bushel of wheat shall cost five shillings and that he (a manufacturer) earns a shilling by his labour, he then would be
obliged to work five days only in a week. If the bushel of
wheat should cost but four shillings, he would be obliged to
work but four days; but as wages in this kingdom are much
higher in proportion to the price of necessaries. . . . the
manufacturer, who labours four days, has a surplus of money
to live idle with the rest of the week . . . . I hope I
have said enough to make it appear that the moderate labour
of six days in a week is no slavery. Our labouring people do
this, and to all appearance are the happiest of all our labouring poor,[2] but the Dutch do this in manufactures, and appear
to be a very happy people. The French do so, when holidays

---

[1] Postlethwayt, 1. c., "First Preliminary Discourse," p. 14.

[2] "An Essay," &c. He himself relates on p. 96 wherein the "happiness" of the
English agricultural labour already in 1770 consisted. "Their powers are always
upon the stretch, they cannot live cheaper than they do, nor work harder."

do not intervene.[1] But our populace have adopted a notion, that as Englishmen they enjoy a birthright privilege of being more free and independent than in any country in Europe. Now this idea, as far as it may affect the bravery of our troops, may be of some use; but the less the manufacturing poor have of it, certainly the better for themselves and for the State. The labouring people should never think themselves independent of their superiors. . . . . It is extremely dangerous to encourage mobs in a commercial state like ours, where, perhaps, seven parts out of eight of the whole, are people with little or no property. The cure will not be perfect, till our manufacturing poor are contented to labour six days for the same sum which they now earn in four days."[2] To this end, and for "extirpating idleness, debauchery and excess," promoting a spirit of industry, "lowering the price of labour in our manufactories, and easing the lands of the heavy burden of poor's rates," our "faithful Eckart" of capital proposes this approved device: to shut up such labourers as become dependent on public support, in a word, paupers, in "an *ideal workhouse.*" Such ideal workhouse must be made a "House of Terror," and not an asylum for the poor, "where they are to be plentifully fed, warmly and decently clothed, and where they do but little work."[3] In this "House of Terror," this "ideal workhouse, the poor shall work 14 hours in a day, allowing proper time for meals, in such manner that there shall remain 12 hours of neat-labour."[4]

Twelve working hours daily in the Ideal Workhouse, in the "House of Terror" of 1770! 63 years later, in 1833, when the English Parliament reduced the working day for children of 13 to 18, in four branches of industry to 12 full hours, the judgment day of English Industry had dawned! In 1852,

---

[1] Protestantism, by changing almost all the traditional holidays into workdays, plays an important part in the genesis of capital.

[2] "An Essay," &c., p. 15, 41, 96, 97, 55, 57, 69.—Jacob Vanderlint, as early as 1734, declared that the secret of the out-cry of the capitalists as to the laziness of the working people was simply that they claimed for the same wages 6 days' labour instead of 4.

[3] l. c. p. 242.

[4] l. c. "The French," he says, "laugh at our enthusiastic ideas of liberty." l. c. p. 78.

when Louis Bonaparte sought to secure his position with the bourgeoisie by tampering with the legal working day, the French people cried out with one voice "the law that limits the working day to 12 hours is the one good that has remained to us of the legislation of the Republic!"[1]. At Zürich the work of children over 10, is limited to 12 hours; in Aargau in 1862, the work of children between 13 and 16, was reduced from 12½ to 12 hours; in Austria in 1860, for children between 14 and 16, the same reduction was made.[2] "What a progress," since 1770! Macaulay would shout with exultation!

The "House of Terror" for paupers of which the capitalistic soul of 1770 only dreamed, was realized a few years later in the shape of a gigantic "Workhouse" for the industrial worker himself. It is called the Factory. And the ideal this time fades before the reality.

SECTION 6.—THE STRUGGLE FOR THE NORMAL WORKING DAY. COMPULSORY LIMITATION BY LAW OF THE WORKING TIME. THE ENGLISH FACTORY ACTS, 1833 TO 1864.

After capital had taken centuries in extending the working-day to its normal maximum limit, and then beyond this to the limit of the natural day of 12 hours,[3] there followed on the birth of machinism and modern industry in the last third of

[1] "They especially objected to work beyond the 12 hours per day, because the law which fixed those hours, is the only good which remains to them of the legislation of the Republic." ("Rep. of Insp. of Fact.," 31st October, 1856, p. 80.) The French Twelve hours' Bill of September 5th, 1850, a bourgeois edition of the decree of the Provisional Government of March 2nd, 1848, holds in all workshops without exceptions. Before this law the working day in France was without definite limit. It lasted in the factories 14, 15, or more hours. See "Des classes ouvrières en France pendant l'année 1848. Par M. Blanqui." M. Blanqui the economist, not the Revolutionist, had been entrusted by the Government with an inquiry into the condition of the working class.

[2] Belgium is the model bourgeois state in regard to the regulation of the working day. Lord Howard of Welden, English Plenipotentiary at Brussels, reports to the Foreign Office, May 12th, 1862: "M. Rogier, the minister, informed me that children's labour is limited neither by a general law nor by any local regulations; that the Government, during the last three years, intended in every session to propose a bill on the subject, but always found an insuperable obstacle in the jealous opposition to any legislation in contradiction with the principle of perfect freedom of labour."

[3] "It is certainly much to be regretted that any class of persons should toil 12 hours a day, which, including the time for their meals and for going to and returning from their work, amounts, in fact, to 14 of the 24 hours. . . . Without

the 18th century, a violent encroachment like that of an avalanche in its intensity and extent. All bounds of morals and nature, age and sex, day and night, were broken down. Even the ideas of day and night, of rustic simplicity in the old statutes, became so confused that an English judge, as late as 1860, needed a quite Talmudic sagacity to explain "judicially" what was day and what was night.[1] Capital celebrated its orgies.

As soon as the working class, stunned at first by the noise and turmoil of the new system of production, recovered, in some measure, its senses, its resistance began, and first in the native land of machinism, in England. For 30 years, however, the concessions conquered by the workpeople were purely nominal. Parliament passed 5 Labour Laws between 1802 and 1833, but was shrewd enough not to vote a penny for their carrying out, for the requisite officials, &c.[2]

They remained a dead letter. "The fact is, that prior to the Act of 1833, young persons and children were worked all night, all day, or both *ad libitum.*"[3]

A normal working day for modern industry only dates from the Factory Act of 1833, which included cotton, wool, flax, and silk factories. Nothing is more characteristic of the spirit of

entering into the question of health, no one will hesitate, I think, to admit that, *in a moral point of view,* so entire an absorption of the time of the working classes, without intermission, from the early age of 13, and in trades not subject to restriction, much younger, must be extremely prejudicial, and is an evil greatly to be deplored . . . . For the sake, therefore, of public morals, of bringing up an orderly population, and of giving the great body of the people a reasonable enjoyment of life, it is much to be desired that in all trades some portion of every working day should be reserved for rest and leisure." (Leonard Horner in Reports of Insp. of Fact., Dec., 1841.)

[1] See "Judgment of Mr. J. H. Otwey, Belfast. Hilary Sessions, County Antrim, 1860."

[2] It is very characteristic of the régime of Louis Philippe, the bourgeois king, that the one Factory Act passed during his reign, that of March 22nd, 1841, was never put in force. And this law only dealt with child-labour. It fixed 8 hours a day for children between 8 and 12, 12 hours for children between 12 and 16, &c., with many exceptions which allow night-work even for children 8 years old. The supervision and enforcement of this law are, in a country where every mouse is under police administration, left to the good-will of the *amis du commerce.* Only since 1853, in one single department—the Département du Nord—has a paid government inspector been appointed. Not less characteristic of the development of French society, generally, is the fact, that Louis Philippe's law stood solitary among the all-embracing mass of French laws, till the Revolution of 1848.

[3] "Report of Insp. of Fact.," 30th April, 1860, p. 50.

capital than the history of the English Factory Acts from **1833** to 1864.

The Act of 1833 declares the ordinary factory working day to be from half-past five in the morning to half-past eight in the evening, and within these limits, a period of 15 hours, it is lawful to employ young persons (*i.e.*, persons between 13 and 18 years of age), at any time of the day, provided no one individual young person should work more than 12 hours in any one day, except in certain cases especially provided for. The 6th section of the Act provided: "That there shall be allowed in the course of every day not less than one and a half hours for meals to every such person restricted as hereinbefore provided." The employment of children under 9, with exceptions mentioned later, was forbidden; the work of children between 9 and 13 was limited to 8 hours a day, night work, *i.e.*, according to this Act, work between 8.30 p.m. and 5.30 a.m., was forbidden for all persons between 9 and 18.

The law-makers were so far from wishing to trench on the freedom of capital to exploit adult labour-power, or, as they called it, "the freedom of labour," that they created a special system in order to prevent the Factory Acts from having a consequence so outrageous.

"The great evil of the factory system as at present conducted," says the first report of the Central Board of the Commission of June 28th, 1833, "has appeared to us to be that it entails the necessity of continuing the labour of children to the utmost length of that of the adults. The only remedy for this evil, short of the limitation of the labour of adults, which would, in our opinion, create an evil greater than that which is sought to be remedied, appears to be the plan of working double sets of children." . . . Under the name of System of Relays, this "plan" was therefore carried out, so that, *e.g.*, from 5.30 a.m. until 1.30 in the afternoon, one set of children between 9 and 13, and from 1.30 p.m. to 8.30 in the evening another set were "put to," &c.

In order to reward the manufacturers for having, in the most barefaced way, ignored all the Acts as to children's labour passed during the last twenty-two years, the bill was yet further gilded for them. Parliament decreed that after March 1st, 1834, no child under 11, after March 1st, 1835, no child under 12, and after March 1st, 1836, no child under 13, was to work more than eight hours in a factory. This "liberalism," so full consideration for "capital," was the more noteworthy as, Dr. Farre, Sir A. Carlisle, Sir B. Brodie, Sir C. Bell, Mr. Guthrie, &c., in a word, the most distinguished physicians and surgeons in London, had declared in their evidene before the House of Commons, that there was danger in delay. Dr. Farre expressed himself still more coarsely. "Legislation is necessary for the prevention of death, in any form in which it can be prematurely inflicted, and certainly this (*i.e.,* the factory method) must be viewed as a most cruel mode of inflicting it."

That same "reformed" Parliament, which in its delicate consideration for the manufacturers, condemned children under 13, for years to come, to 72 hours of work per week in the Factory Hell, on the other hand, in the Emancipation Act, which also administered freedom drop by drop, forbade the planters, from the outset, to work any negro slave more than 45 hours a week.

But in no wise conciliated capital now began a noisy agitation that went on for several years. It turned chiefly on the age of those who, under the name of children, were limited to 8 hours work, and were subject to a certain amount of compulsory education. According to capitalistic anthropology, the age of childhood ended at 10, or at the outside, at 11. The more nearly the time approached for the coming into full force of the Factory Act, the fatal year 1836, the more wildly raged the mob of manufacturers. They managed, in fact, to intimidate the government to such an extent that in 1835 it proposed to lower the limit of the age of childhood from 13 to 12. In the meantime the pressure from without grew more threatening. Courage failed the House of Commons. It refused to throw children of 13 under the Juggernaut Car of capital for more than 8 hours a day, and the Act of 1833 came into full operation. It remained unaltered until June, 1844.

In the ten years during which it regulated factory work,

first in part, and then entirely, the official reports of the factory inspectors teem with complaints as to the impossibility of putting the Act into force.   As the law of 1833 left it optional with the lords of capital during the 15 hours, from 5.30 a.m. to 8.30 p.m., to make every "young person," and "every child" begin, break off, resume, or end his 12 or 8 hours at any moment théy liked, and also permitted them to assign to different persons different times for meals, these gentlemen soon discovered a new "system of relays," by which the labour-horses were not changed at fixed stations, but wer· constantly re-harnessed at changing stations.   We do not pausc longer ⸳ . the beauty of this system, as we shall have to return to it later. But this much is clear at the first glance: that this system annulled the whole Factory Act, not only in the spirit, but in the letter.   How could factory inspectors, with this complex book-keeping in respect to each individual child or young person, enforce the legally determined work time and the granting of the legal meal-times?   In a great many of the factories, the old brutalities soon blossomed out agai un-punished.   In an interview with the Home Secretary (1844), the factory inspectors demonstrated the impossibility of any control under the newly invented relay system.[1]   In the mean-time, however, circumstances had greatly changed.   The fac-tory hands, especially since 1838, had made the Ten Hours' Bill their economical, as they had made the Charter theiʀ political, election-cry.   Some of the manufacturers, even, who had managed their factories in conformity with the Act of 1833, overwhelmed Parliament with memorials on the im-moral competitión of their false brethren whom greater impu-dence, or more fortunate local circumstances, enabled to break the law.   Moreover, however much the individual manufac-turer might give the rein to his old lust for gain, the spokes-men and political leaders of the manufacturing class ordered a change of front and of speech towards the workpeople.   They had entered upon the contest for the repeal of the Corn Laws, and needed the workers to help them to victory.   They prom-ised, therefore, not only a double-sized loaf of bread, but the

[1] "Rept. of Insp. of Fact.," 31st October, 1849, p. 6.

enactment of the Ten Hours' Bill in the Free Trade millenium.[1] Thus they still less dared to oppose a measure intended only to make the law of 1833 a reality. Threatened in their holiest interest, the rent of land, the Tories thundered with philanthropic indignation against the "nefarious practices"[2] of their foes.

This was the origin of the additional Factory Act of June 7th, 1844. It came into effect on September 10th, 1844. It places under protection a new category of workers, viz., the women over 18. They were placed in every respect on the same footing as the young persons, their work time limited to twelve hours, their night-labour forbidden, &c. For the first time, legislation saw itself compelled to control directly and officially the labour of adults. In the Factory Report of 1844, 1845, it is said with irony: "No instances have come to my knowledge of adult women having expressed any regret at their *rights* being thus far interfered with."[3] The working time of children under 13 was reduced to 6½, and in certain circumstances to 7 hours a-day.[4]

To get rid of the abuses of the "spurious relay-system," the law established besides others the following important regulations:—"That the hours of work of children and young persons shall be reckoned from the time when any child or young person shall begin to work in the morning." So that if A, *e.g.*, begins work at 8 in the morning, and B at 10, B's workday must nevertheless end at the same hour as A's. "The time shall be regulated by a public clock," for example, the nearest railway clock, by which the factory clock is to be set. The occupier is to hang up a "legible" printed notice stating the hours for the beginning and ending of work and the times allowed for the several meals. Children beginning work before 12 noon may not be again employed after 1 p.m. The afternoon shift must therefore consist of other children than

---

[1] "Rept. of Insp. of Fact.," 31st October, 1848, p. 98.

[2] Leonard Horner uses the expression "nefarious practices" in his official reports. ("Report of Insp. of Fact.," 31st October, 1859, p. 7.)

[3] "Rept.," &c., 30th Sept., 1844, p. 15.

[4] The Act allows children to be employed for 10 hours if they do not work day after day, but only on alternate days. In the main this clause remained inoperative.

those employed in the morning. Of the hour and a half for meal times, "one hour thereof at the least shall be given before three of the clocl. in the afternoon. . . . and at the same period of the day. No child or young person shall be employed more than five hours before 1 p.m. without an interval for meal time of at least 30 minutes. No child or young person [or female] shall be employed or allowed to remain in any room in which any manufacturing process is then [*i.e.,* at meal times] carri·l on," &c.

I. ht: been seen that these minutiæ, which, with military uniformity, regulate by stroke of the clock the times, limits, pauses of the work, were not at all the products of Parliamentary fancy. They developed gradually out of circumstances as natural laws of the modern mode of production. Their formulation, official recognition, and proclamation by the State, were the result of a long struggle of classes. One of tLeir first consequences was that in practice the working day of the adult males in factories became subject to the same limitations, since in most processes of production the co-operation of the children, young persons, and women is indispensable. On the whole, therefore, during the period from 1844 to 1847, the 12 hours' working day became general and uniform in all branches of industry under the Factory Act.

The manufacturers, however, did not allow this "progress" without a compensating "retrogression." At their instigation the House of Commons reduced the minimum age for exploitable children from 9 to 8, in order to assure that additional supply of factory children which is due to capitalists, according to divine and human law.[1]

The years 1846-47 are epoch-making in the economic history of England. The Repeal of the Corn Laws, and of the duties on cotton and other raw material; free trade proclaimed as the guiding star of legislation; in a word, the arrival of the millenium. On the other hand, in the same years, the Chartist movement and the 10 hours' agitation reached their highest

[1] "As a reduction in their hours of work would cause a larger number (of children) to be employed, it was thought that the additional supply of children from 8 to 9 years of age would meet the increased demand" (l. c., p. 13.)

point. They found allies in the Tories panting for revenge. Despite the fanatical opposition of the army of perjured Free-traders, with Bright and Cobden at their head, the Ten Hours' Bill, struggled for so long, went through Parliament.

The new Factory Act of June 8th, 1847, enacted that on July 1st, 1847, there should be a preliminary shortening of the working day for "young persons" (from 13 to 18), and all females ⸜ 11 hours, but that on May 1st, 1848, there should be a definite limitation of the working day to 10 hours. In other respects, the Act only amended and completed the Acts of 1833 and 1844.

Capital now entered upon a preliminary campaign in order to hinder the Act from coming into full force on May 1st, 1848. And the workers themselves, under the pretence that they had been taught by experience, were to help in the destruction of their own work. The moment was cleverly chosen. "It must be remembered, too, that there has been more than two years of great suffering (in consequence of the terrible crisis of 1846-47) among the factory operatives, from many mills having worked short time, and many being altogether closed. A considerable number of the operatives must therefore be i ⸗ very narrow circumstances; many, it is to be feared, in debt; so that it might fairly have been presumed that at the present time they would prefer working the longer time, in order to make up for past losses, perhaps to pay off debts, or get their furniture out of pawn, or replace that sold, or to get a new supply of clothes for themselves and their families."[1]

The manufacturers tried to aggravate the natural effect of these circumstances by a general reduction of wages by 10%. This was done, so to say, to celebrate the inauguration of the new Free Trade era. Then followed a further reduction of $8\frac{1}{3}\%$ as soon as the working day was shortened to 11, and a reduction of double that amount as soon as it was finally shortened to 10 hours. Wherever, therefore, circumstances allowed it, a reduction of wages of at least 25% took place.[2]

---

[1] "Rep. of Insp. of Fact.," 31st Oct., 1848, p. 16.

[2] "I found that men who had been getting 10s. a week, had had 1s. taken off for a reduction in the rate of 10 per cent, and 1s. 6d. off the remaining 9s. for the re-

Under such favourably prepared conditions the agitation among the factory workers for the repeal of the Act of 1847 was begun. Neither lies, bribery, nor threats were spared in this attempt. But all was in vain. Concerning the half-dozen petitions in which workpeople were made to complain of "their oppression by the Act," the petitioners themselves declared under oral examination, that their signatures had been extorted from them. "They felt themselves oppressed, but not exactly by the Factory Act."[1] But if the manufacturers did not succeed in making the workpeople speak as they wished, they themselves shrieked all the louder in press and Parliament in the name of the workpeople. They denounced the Factory Inspectors as a kind of revolutionary commissioners like those of the French National Convention ruthlessly sacrificing the unhappy factory workers to their humanitarian crotchet. This manœuvre also failed. Factory Inspector Leonard Horner conducted in his own person, and through his sub-inspectors, many examinations of witnesses in the factories of Lancashire. About 70% of the workpeople examined declared in favour of 10 hours, a much smaller percentage in favour of 11, and an altogether insignificant minority for the old 12 hours.[2]

Another "friendly" dodge was to make the adult males work 12 to 15 hours, and then to blazon abroad this fact as the best proof of what the proletariat desired in its heart of hearts. But the "ruthless" Factory Inspector Leonard Horner was again to the fore. The majority of the "over-timers" declared: "They would much prefer working ten hours for less wages, but that they had no choice; that so many were out of employment (so many spinners getting very low wages by having to work as piecers, being unable to do better), that if they refused to work the longer time, others would im-

duction in time, together 2s. 6d., and notwithstanding this, many of them said they would rather work 10 hours." l. c.

[1] " 'Though I signed it [the petition], I said at the time I was putting my hand to a wrong thing.' 'Then why did you put your hand to it?' 'Because I should have been turned off if I had refused.' Whence it would appear that this petitioner felt himself 'oppressed,' but not exactly by the Factory Act." l. c. p. 102.

[2] l. c. p. 17, l. c. In Mr. Horner's district 10,270 adult male labourers were thus examined in 101 factories. Their evidence is to be found in the appendix to the Factory Reports for the half-year ending October 1848. These examinations furnish valuable material in other connexions also.

mediately get their places, so that it was a question with them of agreeing to work the long time, or of being thrown out of employment altogether."[1]

The preliminary campaign of capital thus came to grief, and the Ten Hours' Act came into force May 1st, 1848. But meanwhile the fiasco of the Chartist party whose leaders were imprisoned, and whose organisation was dismembered, had shaken the confidence of the English working class in its own strength. Soon after this the June insurrections in Paris and its bloody suppression united, in England as on the Continent, all fractions of the ruling classes, landlords and capitalists, stock-exchange wolves and shop-keepers. Protectionists and Free-traders, government and opposition, priests and free-thinkers, young whores and old nuns, under the common cry for the salvation of Property, Religion, the Family and Society. The working class was everywhere proclaimed, placed under a ban, under a virtual law of suspects. The manufacturers had no need any longer to restrain themselves. They broke out in open revolt not only against the Ten Hours' Act, but against th whole of the legislation that since 1833 had aimed at restricting in some measure the "free" exploitation of labour-power. It was a pro-slavery rebellion in miniature, carried on for over two years with a cynical recklessness, a terrorist energy all the cheaper because the rebel capitalist risked nothing except the skin of his "hands."

To understand that which follows we must remember that the Factory Acts of 1833, 1844, and 1847 were all three in force so far as the one did not amend th other: that not one of these limited the working day of th male worker over 18, and that since 1833 the 15 hours from 5.30 a.m. to 8.30 p.m. had remained the legal "day," within the limits of which at first the 12, and later t e 10 hours' labour of young persons and women had to be performed under the prescribed conditions.

The manufacturers began by here and there discharging a

---

[1] l. c. See the evidence collected l Leonard Horner himself, Nos. 69, 70, 71, 72, 92, 93, and that collected by Sub-Inspector A., Nos. 51, 52, 58, 59, 62, 70, of the Appendix. One manufacturer, too, tells the plain truth. See No. 14, and No. 265, l. c.

part of, in many cases half of, the young persons and women employed by them, and then, for the adult males, restoring the almost obsolete night-work. The Ten Hours' Act, they cried, leaves no other alternative.[1]

Their second step dealt with the legal pauses for meals. Let us hear the Factory Inspectors. "Since the restriction of the hours of work to ten, the factory occupiers maintain, although they have not yet practically gone the whole length, that supposing the hours of work to be from 9 a.m. to 7 p.m., they fulfil the provisions of the statutes by allowing an hour before 9 a.m. and half-an-hour after 7 p.m. [for meals]. In some cases they now allow an hour, or half an hour for dinner, insisting at the same time, that they are not bound to allow any part of the hour and a half in the course of the factory working-day."[2] The manufacturers maintained therefore that the scrupulously strict provisions of the Acts of 1844 with regard to meal times only gave the operatives permission to eat and drink before coming into, and after leaving the factory— *i.e.,* at home. And why should not the workpeople eat their dinner before 9 in the morning? The crown lawyers, however, decided that the prescribed meal times "must be in the interval during the working hours, and that it will not be lawful to work for 10 hours continuously, from 9 a.m. to 7 p.m., without any interval."[3]

After these pleasant demonstrations, Capital preluded its revolt by a step which agreed with the letter of the law of 1844, and was therefore legal.

The Act of 1844 certainly prohibited the employment after 1 p.m. of such children, from 8 to 13, as had been employed before noon. But it did not regulate in any way the $6\frac{1}{2}$ hours' work of the children whose work-time began at 12 midday or later. Children of 8 might, if they began work at noon, be employed from 12 to 1, 1 hour; from 2 to 4 in the afternoon, 2 hours; from 5 to 8:30 in the evening, $3\frac{1}{2}$ hours; in all, the legal $6\frac{1}{2}$ hours. Or better still. In order to make their work

---

[1] Reports, &c., for 31st October, 1848, p. 133, 134.
[2] Reports, &c., for 30th April, 1848, p. 47.
[3] Reports, &c., for 31st October, 1848, p. 130.

coincide with that of the adult male labourers up to 8.30 p.m., the manufacturers only had to give them no work till 2 in the afternoon; they could then keep them in the factory without intermission till 8.30 in the evening. "And it is now expressly admitted that the practice exists in England from the desire of mill-owners to have their machinery at work for more than 10 hours a-day, to keep the children at work with male adults after all the young persons and women have left, and until 8.30 p.m., if the factory-owners choose."[1] Workmen and factory inspectors protested on hygienic and moral grounds, but Capital answered:

> "My deeds upon my head! I crave the law,
> The penalty and forfeit of my bond."

In fact, according to statistics laid before the House of Commons on July 26th, 1850, in spite of all protests, on July 15th, 1850, 3,742 children were subjected to this "practice" in 257 factories.[2] Still this was not enough. The lynx eye of Capital discovered that the Act of 1844 did not allow 5 hours' work before mid-day without a pause of at least 30 minutes for refreshment, but prescribed nothing of the kind for work after mid-day. Therefore, it claimed and obtained the enjoyment not only of making children of 8 drudge without intermission from 2 to 8.30 p.m., but also of making them hunger during that time.

> "Ay, his heart,
> So says the bond."[3]

This Shylock-clinging to the letter of the law of 1844, so far as it regulated children's labour, was but to lead up to an open

---

[1] Reports, &c., 1 c., p. 142.

[2] Reports, &c., for 31st October, 1850, pp. 5, 6.

[3] The nature of capital remains the same in its developed as in its undeveloped form. In the code which the influence of the slave-owners, shortly before the outbreak of the American civil war, imposed on the territory of New Mexico, it is said that the labourer, in as much as the capitalist has bought his labour-power, "is his (the capitalist's) money." The same view was current among the Roman patricians. The money they had advanced to the plebeian debtor had been transformed *via* the means of subsistence into the flesh and blood of the debtor. This "flesh and blood" were, therefore, "their money." Hence, the Shylock-law of the Ten Tables. Linguet's hypothesis that the patrician creditors from time to time prepared, beyond the Tiber, banquets of debtors' flesh, may remain as undecided as that of Daumer on the Christian Eucharist.

revolt against the same law, so far as it regulated the labour of "young persons and women." It will be remembered that the abolition of the "false relay system" was the chief aim and object of that law. The masters began their revolt with the simple declaration that the sections of the Act of 1844 which prohibited the *ad libitum* use of young persons and women in such short fractions of the day of 15 hours as the employer chose, were "comparatively harmless" so long as the worktime was fixed at 12 hours. But under the Ten Hours' Act they were a "grievous hardship."[1] They informed the inspectors in the coolest manner that they should place themselves above the letter of the law, and re-introduce the old system on their own account.[2] They were acting in the interests of the ill-advised operatives themselves, "in order to be able to pay them higher wages." "This was the only possible plan by which to maintain, under the Ten Hours' Act, the industrial supremacy of Great Britain." "Perhaps it may be a little difficult to detect irregularities under the relay system; but what of that? Is the great manufacturing interest of this country to be treated as a secondary matter in order to save same little trouble to Inspectors and Sub-Inspectors of Factories?"[3]

All these shifts naturally were of no avail. The Factory Inspectors appealed to the Law Courts. But soon such a cloud of dust in the way of petitions from the masters overwhelmed the Home Secretary, Sir George Grey, that in a circular of August 5th, 1848, he recommends the inspectors not "to lay informations against mill-owners for a breach of the letter of the Act, or for employment of young persons by relays in cases in which there is no reason to believe that such young persons have been actually employed for a longer period than that sanctioned by law." Hereupon, Factory Inspector J. Stuart allowed the so-called relay system during the 15 hours of the factory day throughout Scotland, where it soon flourished again as of old. The English Factory Inspectors, on the other hand,

[1] Reports, &c., for 30th April, 1848, p. 28.
[2] Thus, among others, Philanthropist Ashworth to Leonard Horner, in a disgusting Quaker letter. (Reports, &c., April, 1849, p. 4.)
[3] l. c., p. 140.

declared that the Home Secretary had no power dictatorially to suspend the law, and continued their legal proceedings against the pro-slavery rebellion.

But what was the good of summoning the capitalists when the Courts, in this case the country magistrates—Cobbett's "Great Unpaid"—acquitted them? In these tribunals, the masters sat in judgment on themselves. An example. One Eskrigge, cotton-spinner, of the firm of Kershaw, Leese, & Co., had laid before the Factory Inspector of his district the scheme of a relay system intended for his mill. Receiving a refusal, he at first kept quiet. A few months later, an individual named Robinson, also a cotton-spinner, and if not his Man Friday, at all events related to Eskrigge, appeared before the borough magistrates of Stockport on a charge of introducing the identical plan of relays invented by Eskrigge. Four Justices sat, among them three cotton-spinners, at their head this same inevitable Eskrigge. Eskrigge acquitted Robinson, and now was of opinion that what was right for Robinson was fair for Eskrigge. Supported by his own legal decision, he introduced the system at once into his own factory.[1] Of course, the composition of this tribunal was in itself a violation of the law.[2] These judicial farces, exclaims Inspector Howell, urgently call for a remedy—either that the law should be so altered as to be made to conform to these decisions, or that it should be administered by a less fallible tribunal, whose decisions would conform to the law. . . . when these cases are brought forward. I long for a stipendiary magistrate."[3]

The Crown lawyers declared the masters' interpretation of the Act of 1848 absurd. But the Saviours of Society would not allow themselves to be turned from their purpose. Leonard Horner reports, "Having endeavoured to enforce the Act . . . by ten prosecutions in seven magisterial divisions, and having been supported by the magistrates in one case only. . . . I

---

[1] Reports, &c., for 30th April, 1849, pp. 21, 22. Cf. like examples ibid. pp. 4, 5.

[2] By I. and II. Will. IV., ch. 24, s. 10, known as Sir John Hobhouse's Factory Act, it was forbidden to any owner of a cotton spinning or weaving mill, or the father, son, or brother of such owner, to act as Justice of the Peace in any inquiries that concerned the Factory Act.

[3] l. c.

considered it useless to prosecute more for this evasion of the law. That part of the Act of 1848 which was framed for securing uniformity in the hours of work, . . . is thus no longer in force in my district (Lancashire). Neither have the sub-inspectors or myself any means of satisfying ourselves, when we inspect a mill working by shifts, that the young persons and women are not working more than 10 hours a-day. . . . In a return of the 30th April, . . . of mill-owners working by shifts, the number amounts to 114, and has been for some time rapidly increasing. In general, the time of working the mill is extended to $13\frac{1}{2}$ hours, from 6 a.m. to $7\frac{1}{2}$ p.m., . . . in some instances it amounts to 15 hours, from $5\frac{1}{2}$ a.m. to $8\frac{1}{2}$ p. m."[1] Already, in December, 1848, Leonard Horner had a list of 65 manufacturers and 29 overlookers who unanimously declared that no system of supervision could, under this relay system, prevent enormous overwork.[2] Now, the same children and young persons were shifted from the spinning-room to the weaving-room, now, during 15 hours, from one factory to another.[3] How was it possible to control a system which, "under the guise of relays, is some one of the many plans for shuffling 'the hands' about in endless variety, and shifting the hours of work and of rest for different individuals throughout the day, so that you may never have one complete set of hands working together in the same room at the same time."[4]

But altogether independently of actual overwork, this so-called relay-system was an offspring of capitalistic fantasy such as Fourier, in his humorous sketches of "Courtes Séances," has never surpassed, except that the "attraction of labour" was changed into the attraction of capital. Look, for example, at those schemes of the masters which the "respectable" press praised as models of "what a reasonable degree of care and method can accomplish." The *personnel* of the work-people was sometimes divided into from 12 to 14 categories, which themselves constantly changed and rechanged their con-

[1] Reports, &c., for 30th April, 1849, p. 5.
[2] Reports, &c., for 31st October, 1849, p. 6.
[3] Reports, &c., for 30th April, 1849, p. 21.
[4] Reports, &c., for 1st October, 1848, p. 95.

stituent parts. During the 15 hours of the factory day, capital dragged in the labourer now for 30 minutes, now for an hour, and then pushed him out again, to drag him into the factory and to thrust him out afresh, hounding him hither and thither, in scattered shreds of time, without ever losing hold of him until the full 10 hours' work was done. As on the stage, the same persons had to appear in turns in the different scenes of the different acts. But as an actor during the whole course of the play belongs to the stage, so the operatives, during 15 hours, belonged to the factory, without reckoning the time for going and coming. Thus the hours of rest were turned into hours of enforced idleness, which drove the youths to the pot-house, and the girls to the brothel. At every new trick that the capitalist, from day to day, hit upon for keeping his machinery going 12 or 15 hours without increasing the number of his hands, the worker had to swallow his meals now in this fragment of time, now in that. At the time of the 10 hours' agitation, the masters cried out that the working mob petitioned in the hope of obtaining 12 hours' wages for 10 hours' work. Now they reversed the medal. They paid 10 hours' wages for 12 or 15 hours' lordship over labour-power.[1] This was the gist of the matter, this the masters' interpretation of the 10 hours' law! These were the same unctuous free-traders, perspiring with the love of humanity, who for full 10 years, during the Anti-Corn Law agitation, had preached to the operatives, by a reckoning of pounds, shillings and pence, that with free importation of corn, and with the means possessed by English industry, 10 hours' labour would be quite enough to enrich the capitalist.[2] This revolt of capital, after two years, was at last crowned with victory by a decision of one of the four highest Courts of Justice in England, the Court of Exchequer, which in a case brought before it on February 8th, 1850, decided that the manufacturers were

[1] See Reports, &c., for 30th April, 1849, p. 6, and the detailed explanation of the "shifting system," by Factory Inspectors Howell and Saunders, in "Reports, &c., for 31st October, 1848." See also the petition to the Queen from the clergy of Ashton and vicinity, in the spring of 1849, against the "shift system."

[2] Cf. for example, "The Factory Question and the Ten Hours' Bill." By R. H. Greg. 1837.

certainly acting against the sense of the Act of 1844, but that
this Act itself contained certain words that rendered it meaningless. "By this decision, the Ten Hours' Act was aboli-
ished."[1] A crowd of masters, who until then had been afraid
of using the relay-system for young persons and women, now
took it up heart and soul.[2]

But on this apparently decisive victory of capital, followed
at once a revulsion. The workpeople had hitherto offered a
passive, although inflexible and unremitting resistance. They
now protested in Lancashire and Yorkshire in threatening
meetings. The pretended Ten Hours' Act, was thus simple
humbug, parliamentary cheating, had never existed! The
Factory Inspectors urgently warned the Government that the
antagonism of classes had arrived at an incredible tension.
Some of the masters themselves murmured: "On account of
the contradictory decisions of the magistrates, a condition of
things altogether abnormal and anarchial obtains. One law
holds in Yorkshire, another in Lancashire; one law in one
parish of Lancashire, another in its immediate neighborhood.
The manufacturer in large towns could evade the law, the
manufacturer in country districts could not find the people
necessary for the relay-system, still less for the shifting of
hands from one factory to another," &c. And the first birthright of capital is equal exploitation of labour-power by all
capitalists.

Under these circumstances a compromise between masters
and men was effected that received the seal of Parliament in
the additional Factory Act of August 5th, 1850. The working day for "young persons and women," was raised from 10
to 10½ hours for the first five days of the week, and was
shortened to 7½ on the Saturday. The work was to go on between 6 a.m. and 6 p.m.,[3] with pauses of not less than 1½ hours
for meal-times, these meal-times to be allowed at one and the

---

[1] F. Engels: "The English Ten Hours' Bill." (In the "Neue Rheinische Zeitung,
Politisch-œkonomische Revue." Edited by K. Marx. April number, 1850, p. 13.)
The same "high" Court of Justice discovered, during the American Civil War, a
verbal ambiguity which exactly reversed the meaning of the law against the arming
of pirate ships.

[2] Rep., &c., for 30th April, 1850.

[3] In winter, from 7 a.m. to 7 p.m. may be substituted.

same time for all, and conformably to the conditions of 1844.
By this an end was put to the relay-system once for all.[1] For
children's labour, the Act of 1844 remained in force.

One set of masters, this time as before, secured to itself
special seigneurial rights over the children of the proletariat.
These were the silk manufacturers. In 1833 they had howled
out in threatening fashion, "if the liberty of working children
of any age for 10 hours a day were taken away, it would stop
their works."[2] It would be impossible for them to buy a sufficient number of children over 13. They extorted the privilege
they desired. The pretext was shown on subsequent investigation to be a deliberate lie.[3] It did not, however, prevent them,
during 10 years, from spinning silk 10 hours a day out of the
blood of little children who had to be placed upon stools for
the performance of their work.[4] The Act of 1844 certainly
"robbed" them of the "liberty" of employing children under
11 longer than 6½ hours a day. But it secured to them, on the
other hand, the privilege of working children between 11 and
13, 10 hours a day, and of annulling in their case the education made compulsory for all other factory children. This
time the pretext was "the delicate texture of the fabric in
which they were employed, requiring a lightness of touch, only
to be acquired by their early introduction to these factories."[5]
The children were slaughtered out-and-out for the sake of their
delicate fingers, as in Southern Russia the horned cattle for the
sake of their hide and tallow. At length, in 1850, the privilege
granted in 1844 was limited to the departments of silk-twist-
ing and silk-winding. But here, to make amends to capital
bereft of its "freedom," the work time for children from 11
to 13 was raised from 10 to 10½ hours. Pretext: "Labour in
silk mills was lighter than in mills for other fabrics, and less
likely in other respects also to be prejudicial to health."[6]
Official medical inquiries proved afterwards that, on the con-

---

[1] "The present law (of 1850) was a compromise whereby the employed surrendered
the benefit of the Ten Hours' Act for the advantage of one uniform period for the
commencement and termination of the labour of those whose labour is restricted."
(Reports, &c., for 30th April, 1852, p. 14.)

[2] Reports, &c., for Sept., 1844, p. 13.   [3] l. c.   [4] l. c.

[5] l. c.

[6] Reports, &c., for 31st Oct., 1861, p. 26.

trary, "the average death-rate is exceedingly high in the silk districts, and amongst the female part of the population is higher even than it is in the cotton districts of Lancashire."[1] Despite the protests of the Factory Inspector, renewed every 6 months, the mischief continues to this hour.[2]

The Act of 1850 changed the 15 hours' time from 6 a.m. to 8:30 p.m., into the 12 hours from 6 a.m. to 6 p.m. for "young persons and women" only. It did not, therefore, affect children who could always be employed for half an hour before and 2½ hours after this period, provided the whole of their labour did not exceed 6½ hours. Whilst the bill was under discussion, the Factory Inspectors laid before Parliament statistics of the infamous abuses due to this anomaly. To no purpose. In the background lurked the intention of screwing up, during prosperous years, the working day of adult males

[1] l. c., p. 27. On the whole the working population, subject to the Factory Act, has greatly improved physically. All medical testimony agrees on this point, and personal observation at different times has convinced me of it. Nevertheless, and exclusive of the terrible death-rate of children in the first years of their life, the official reports of Dr. Greenhow show the unfavourable health condition of the manufacturing districts as compared with "agricultural districts of normal health." As evidence, take the following table from his 1861 report:—

Percentage of Adult Males engaged in manufactures.	Death-rate from Pulmonary Affections per 100,000 Males.	Name of District.	Death-rate from Pulmonary Affections per 100,000 Females.	Percentage of Adult Females engaged in manufactures.	Kind of Female Occupation.
14.9	598	Wigan	644	18.0	Cotton
42.6	708	Blackburn	734	34.9	Do.
37.3	547	Halifax	564	20.4	Worsted
41.9	611	Bradford	603	30.0	Do.
31.0	691	Macclesfield	804	26.0	Silk
14.9	588	Leek	705	17.2	Do.
36.6	721	Stoke-upon-Trent	665	19.3	Earthenware
30.4	726	Woolstanton	727	13.9	Do.
	305	Eight healthy agricultural districts	340		

[2] It is well-known with what reluctance the English "free traders" gave up the protective duty on the silk manufacture. Instead of the protection against French importation, the absence of protection to English factory children now serves their turn.

to 15 hours by the aid of the children. The experience of the three following years showed that such an attempt must come to grief against the resistance of the adult male operatives. The Act of 1850 was therefore finally completed in 1853 by forbidding the "employment of children in the morning before and in the evening after young persons and women." Henceforth with a few exceptions the Factory Act of 1850 regulated the working day of all workers in the branches of industry that come under it.[1] Since the passing of the first Factory Act half a century had elapsed.[2]

Factory legislation for the first time went beyond its original sphere in the "Printworks' Acts of 1845." The displeasure with which capital received this new "extravagance" speaks through every line of the Act. It limits the working day for children from 8 to 13, and for women to 16 hours, between 6 a.m. and 10 p.m., without any legal pause for meal times. It allows males over 13 to be worked at will day and night.[3] It is a Parliamentary abortion.[4]

However, the principle had triumphed with its victory in those great branches of industry which form the most characteristic creation of the modern mode of production. Their wonderful development from 1853 to 1860, hand-in-hand with the physical and moral regeneration of the factory workers,

---

[1] During 1859 and 1860, the zenith years of the English cotton industry, some manufacturers tried, by the decoy bait of higher wages for over-time, to reconcile the adult male operatives to an extension of the working day. The hand-mule spinners and self-actor minders put an end to the experiment by a petition to their employers in which they say, "Plainly speaking, our lives are to us a burthen; and, while we are confined to the mills *nearly two days a week more* than the other operatives of the country, we feel like helots in the land, and that we are perpetuating a system injurious to ourselves and future generations. . . . This, therefore, is to give you most respectful notice that when we commence work again after the Christmas and New Years' holidays, we shall work 60 hours per week, and no more, or from six to six, with one hour and a half out." (Reports, &c., for 30th April, 1860, p. 30.)

[2] On the means that the wording of this Act afforded for its violation cf. the Parliamentary Return "Factory Regulations Act" (6th August, 1859), and in it Leonard Horner's "Suggestions for amending the Factory Acts to enable the Inspectors to prevent illegal working, now become very prevalent."

[3] "Children of the age of 8 years and upwards, have, indeed, been employed from 6 a.m. to 9 p.m. during the last half year in my district." (Reports, &c., for 31st October, 1857, p. 39.)

[4] "The Printworks' Act is admitted to be a failure, both with reference to its educational and protective provisions." (Reports, &c., for 31st October, 1862, p. 52.)

struck the most purblind. The masters from whom the legal limitation and regulation had been wrung step by step after a civil war of half a century, themselves referred ostentatiously to the contrast with the branches of exploitation still "free."[1] The Pharisees of "political econom," now proclaimed the discernment of the necessity of a legally fixed working day as a characteristic new discovery of their "science."[2] It will be easily understood that after the factory magnates had resigned themselves and become reconciled to the inevitable, the power of resistance of capital gradually weakened, whilst at the same time the power of attack of the working class grew with the number of its allies in the classes f society not immediately interested in the question. Hence the comparatively rapid advance since 1860.

The dye-works and bleach-works all came under the Factory Act of 1850 in 1860;[3] lace and stocking manufacturers in 1861.

In consequence of the first report of the Commission on the employment of children (1863), the same fate was shared by the manufacturers of all earthenwares (not merely pottery), lucifer-matches, percussion-caps, cartridges, carpets, fustian-

---

[1] Thus, *e.g.*, E. Potter in a letter to the "Times" of March 24th, 1863. The "Times" reminded him of the manufacturers' revolt against the Ten Hours' Bill.

[2] Thus, among others, Mr. W. Newmarch, collaborator and editor of Tooke's "History of Prices." Is it a scientific advance to make cowardly concessions to public opinion?

[3] The Act passed in 1860, determined that, in regard to dye and bleach-works, the working day should be fixed on August 1st, 1861, provisionally at 12 hours, and definitely on August 1st, 1862, at 10 hours, *i.e.*, at 10½ hours for ordinary days, and 7½ for Saturday. Now, when the fatal year, 1862, came, the old farce was repeated. Besides, the manufacturers petitioned Parliament to allow the employment of young persons and women for 12 hours during one year longer. "In the existing condition of the trade (the time of the cotton famine), it was greatly to the advantage of the operatives to work 12 hours per day, and make wages when they could." A bill to this effect had been brought in, "and it was mainly due to the action of the operative bleachers in Scotland that e bill was abandoned." (Reports, &c., for 31st October, 1862, p. 14-15.) Thus efea d by the very work-people, in whose name it pretended to speak, Capital iscovered, with the help of lawyer spectacles, that the Act of 1860, drawn up, like all the Acts of Parliament for the "protection of labour," in equivocal phrases, gave them a pretext to exclude from its working the calenderers and finishers. English jurisprudence, ever the faithful servant of capital, sanctioned in the Court of Common Pleas this piece of pettifogging. "The operatives have been greatly disappointed . . . they have complained of overwork, and it is greatly to be regretted that the clear intention of the legislature should have failed by reason of a faulty definition." (l. c., p. 18.)

cutting, and many processes included under the name of "finishing." In the year 1863 bleaching in the open air[1] and baking were placed under special Acts, by which, in the former, the labour of young persons and women during the night-time (from 8 in the evening to 6 in the morning), and in the latter, the employment of journeymen bakers under 18, between 9 in the evening and 5 in the morning were forbidden. We shall return to the later proposals of the same Commission, which threatened to deprive of their "freedom" all the important branches of English Industry, with the exception of agriculture, mines, and the means of transport.[2]

[1] The "open-air bleachers" had evaded the law of 1860, by means of the lie that no women worked at it in the night. The lie was exposed by the Factory Inspectors, and at the same time Parliament was, by petitions from the operatives, bereft of its notions as to the cool meadow-fragrance, in which bleaching in the open-air was reported to take place. In this aerial bleaching. drying-rooms were used at temperatures of from 90° to 100° Fahrenheit, in which the work was done for the most part by girls. "Cooling" is the technical expression for their occasional escape from the drying-rooms into the fresh air. "Fifteen girls in stoves. Heat from 80° to 90° for linens, and 100' and upwards for cambrics. Twelve girls ironing and doing up in a small room about 10 feet square, in the centre of which is a close stove. The girls stand round the stove, which throws out a terrific heat, and dries the cambrics rapidly for the ironers. The hours of work for these hands are unlimited. If busy, they work till 9 or 12 at night for successive nights." (Reports, &c., for 31st October, 1862, p. 56.) A medical man states: "No special hours are allowed for cooling, but if the temperature gets too high, or the workers' hands get soiled from erspiration, they are allowed to go out for a few minutes. . . . My experience, which is considerable, in treating the diseases of stove workers, compels me to express the opinion that their sanitary condition is by no means so high as that of the operatives in a spinning factory (and Capital, in its memorials to Parliament, had painted them as floridly healthy, after the manner of Rubens). The diseases most observable amongst them are phthisis, bronchitis, irregularity of uterine functions, hysteria in its most aggravated forms, and rheumatism. All of these, I believe, are either directly or indirectly induced by the impure, overheated air of the apartments in which the hands are employed, and the want of sufficient comfortable clothing to protect them from the cold, damp atmosphere, in winter, when going to their homes." (l. c., p. 56-57.) The Factory Inspectors remarked on the supplementary law of 1860, torn from these open-air bleachers: "The Act has not only failed to afford that protection to the workers which it appears to offer, but contains a clause . . . apparently so worded that, unless persons are detected working after 8 o'clock at night they appear to come under no protective provisions at all, and if they do so work, the mode of proof is so doubtful that a conviction can scarcely follow." (l. c., p. 52.) "To all intents and purposes, therefore, as an Act for any benevolent or educational purpose, it is a failure; since it can scarcely be called benevolent to permit, which is tantamount to compelling, women and children to work 14 hours a day with or without meals, as the case may be, and perhaps for longer hours than these, without limit as to age, without reference to sex, and without regard to the social habits of the families of the neighbourhood, in which such works (bleaching and dyeing) are situated." (Reports, &c., for 30th April, 1863, p. 40.)

[2] Note to the 2nd Ed. Since 1866, when I wrote the above passages, a re-action has again set in.

SECTION 7.—THE STRUGGLE FOR THE NORMAL WORKING-DAY.
RE-ACTION OF THE ENGLISH ACTS ON OTHER COUNTRIES.

The reader will bear in mind that the production of surplus value, or the extraction of surplus-labour, is the specific end and aim, the sum and substance, of capitalist production quite apart from any changes in the mode of production, which may arise from the subordination of labour to capital. He will remember that as far as we have at present gone, only the independent labourer, and therefore only the labourer legally qualified to act for himself, enters as a vendor of a commodity 'into a contract with the capitalist. If, therefore, in our historical sketch, modern industry, on the one hand; the labour of those who are physically and legally minors, on the other, play important parts, the former was to us only a special department, and the latter only a specially striking example of labour exploitation. Without, however, anticipating the subsequent development of our inquiry, from the mere connexion of the historic facts before us, it follows:

First. The passion of capital for an unlimited and reckless extension of the working day, is first gratified in the industries earliest revolutionised by water-power, steam, and machinery, in those first creations of the modern mode of production, cotton, wool, flax, and silk spinning, and weaving. The changes in the material mode of production, and the corresponding changes in the social relations of the producers[1] gave rise first to an extravagance beyond all bounds, and then in opposition to this, called forth a control on the part of Society which legally limits, regulates, and makes uniform the working day and its pauses. This control appears, therefore, during the first half of the nineteenth century simply as exceptional legislation.[2] As soon as this primitive dominion of

---

[1] "The conduct of each of these classes (capitalists and workmen) has been the result of the relative situation in which they have been placed." (Reports, &c., for 31st October, 1848, p. 113.)

[2] "The employments, placed under restriction, were connected with the manufacture of textile fabrics by the aid of steam or water-power. There were two conditions to which an employment must be subject to cause it to be inspected, viz., the use of steam or water-power, and the manufacture of certain specified fibres." (Reports, &c., for 31st October, 1864, p. 8.)

the new mode of production was conquered, it was found that, in the meantime, not only had many other branches of production been made to adopt the same factory system, but that manufacturers with more or less obsolete methods, such as potteries, glass-making, &c., that old-fashioned handicrafts, like baking, and, finally, even that the so-called domestic industries such as nail-making,[1] had long since fallen as completely under capitalist exploitation as the factories themselves. Legislation was, therefore, compelled to gradually get rid of its exceptional character, or where, as in England, it proceeds after the manner of the Roman Casuists, to declare any house in which work was done to be a factory.[2]

Second. The history of the regulation of the working day in certain branches of production, and the struggle still going on in others in regard to this regulation, prove conclusively that the isolated labourer, the labourer as "free" vendor of his labour-power, when capitalist production has once attained a certain stage, succumbs without any power of resistance. The creation of a normal working day is, therefore, the product of a protracted civil war, more or less dissembled, between the capitalist class and the working class. As the contest takes place in the arena of modern industry, it first breaks out in the home of that industry—England.[3] The English factory workers were the champions, not only of the English, but of the modern working-class generally, as their theorists were the first to throw down the gauntlet to the theory of capital.[4]

---

[1] On the condition of so-called domestic industries, specially valuable materials are to be found in the latest reports of the Children's Employment Commission.

[2] "The Acts of last Session (1864) . . . embrace a diversity of occupations, the customs in which differ greatly, and the use of mechanical power to give motion to machinery is no longer one of the elements necessary, as formerly, to constitute, in legal phrase, a 'Factory.'" (Reports, &c., for 31st October, 1864, p. 8.)

[3] Belgium, the paradise of Continental Liberalism, shows no trace of this movement. Even in the coal and metal mines, labourers of both sexes, and all ages, are consumed in perfect "freedom," at any period, and through any length of time. Of every 1000 persons employed there, 733 are men, 88 women, 135 boys, and 44 girls under 16; in the blast-furnaces, &c., of every 1000, 688 are men, 149 women, 98 boys, and 85 girls under 16. Add to this the low wages for the enormous exploitation of mature and immature labour-power. The average daily pay for a man is 2s. 8d., for a woman, 1s. 8d., for a boy, 1s. 2½d. As a result, Belgium had in 1863, as compared with 1850, nearly doubled both the amount and the value of its exports of coal, iron, &c.

[4] Robert Owen, soon after 1810, not only maintained the necessity of a limitation

Hence, the philosopher of the Factory, Ure, denounces as an ineffable disgrace to the English working-class that they inscribed "the slavery of the Factory Acts" on the banner which they bore against capital, manfully striving for "perfect freedom of labour."[1]

France limps slowly behind England. The February revolution was necessary to bring into the world the 12 hours' law,[2] which is much more deficient than its English original. For all that, the French revolutionary method has its special advantages. It once for all commands the same limit to the working-day in all shops and factories without distinction, whilst English legislation reluctantly yields to the pressure of circumstances, now on this point or on that, and is getting lost in a hopelessly bewildering tangle of contradictory enactments.[3] On the other hand, the French law proclaims as a principle that which in England was only won in the name of children, minors, and women, and has been only recently for the first time claimed as a general right.[4]

of the working day in theory, but actually introduced the 10 hours' day into his factory at New Lanark. This was laughed at as a communistic Utopia; so were his "Combination of children's education with productive labour," and the Co-operative Societies of working-men, first called into being by him. To-day, the first Utopia is a Factory Act, the second figures as an official phrase in all Factory Acts, the third is already being used as a cloak for reactionary humbug.

[1] Ure: "French translation, Philosophie des Manufactures." Paris, 1836, Vol. II., p. 39, 40, 67, 77, &c.

[2] In the Compte Rendu of the International Statistical Congress at Paris, 1855, it is stated: "The French law, which limits the length of daily labour in factories and workshops to 12 hours, does not confine this work to definite fixed hours. For children's labour only the work-time is prescribed as between 5 a. m. and 9 p. m. Therefore, some of the masters use the right which this fatal silence gives them to keep their works going, without intermission, day in, day out, possibly with the exception of Sunday. For this purpose they use two different sets of workers, of whom neither is in the workshop more than 12 hours at a time, but the work of the establishment lasts day and night. The law is satisfied, but is humanity?" Besides "the destructive influence of night labour on the human organism," stress is also laid upon "the fatal influence of the association of the two sexes by night in the same badly-lighted workshops."

[3] "For instance, there is within my district one occupier who, within the same curtilage, is at the same time a bleacher and dyer under the Bleaching and Dyeing Works Act, a printer under the Print Works Act, and a finisher under the Factory Act." (Report of Mr. Baker, in Reports, &c., for Octobre 31st, 1861, p. 20.) After enumerating the different provisions of these Acts, and the complications arising from them, Mr. Baker says: "It will hence appear that it must be very difficult to secure the execution of these three Acts of Parliament where the occupier chooses to evade the law." But what is assured to the lawyers by this is lawsuits.

[4] Thus the Factory Inspectors at last venture to say: "These objections (of

In the United States of North America, every independent movement of the workers was paralysed so long as slavery disfigured a part of the Republic. Labour cannot emancipate itself in the white skin where in the black it is branded. But out of the death of slavery a new life at once arose. The first fruit of the Civil War was the eight hours' agitation, that ran with the seven-leagued boots of the locomotive from the Atlantic to the Pacific, from New England to California. The General Congress of Labour at Baltimore (August 16th, 1866) declared: "The first and great necessity of the present, to free the labour of this country from capitalistic slavery, is the passing of a law by which eight hours shall be the normal working-day in all States of the American Union. We are resolved to put forth all our strength until this glorious result is attained."[1] At the same time, the Congress of the International Working Men's Association at Geneva, on the proposition of the London General Council, resolved that "the limitation of the working-day is a preliminary condition without which all further attempts at improvement and emancipation must prove abortive. . . . the Congress proposes eight hours as the legal limit of the working-day."

Thus the movement of the working-class on both sides of the Atlantic, that had grown instinctively out of the conditions of production themselves, endorsed the words of the English Factory Inspector, R. J. Saunders: "Further steps towards a reformation of society can never be carried out with any hope of success, unless the hours of labour be limited, and the prescribed limit strictly enforced."[2]

It must be acknowledged that our labourer comes out of the

capital to the legal limitation of the working-day) must succumb before the broad principle of the rights of labour. . . . There is a time when the master's right in his workman's labour ceases, and his time becomes his own, even if there were no exhaustion in the question." (Reports, &c., for 31st Oct., 1862, p. 54.)

[1] "We, the workers of Dunkirk, declare that the length of time of labour required under the present system is too great, and that, far from leaving the worker time for rest and education, it plunges him into a condition of servitude but little better than slavery. That is why we decide that 8 hours are enough for a working-day, and ought to be legally recognized as enough; why we call to our help that powerful lever, the press; . . . and why we shall consider all those that refuse us this help as enemies of the reform of labour and of the rights of the labourer." (Resolution of the Working Men of Dunkirk, New York State, 1866.)

[2] Reports, &c., for Oct., 1848, p. 112.

process of production other than he entered. In the market he stood as owner of the commodity "labour-power" face to face with other owners of commodities, dealer against dealer. The contract by which he sold to the capitalist his labour-power proved, so to say, in black and white that he disposed of himself freely. The bargain concluded, it is discovered that he was no "free agent," that the time for which he is free to sell his labour-power is the time for which he is forced to sell it,[1] that in fact the vampire will not lose its hold on him "so long as there is a muscle, a nerve, a drop of blood to be exploited."[2] For "protection" against "the serpent of their agonies," the labourers must put their heads together, and, as a class, compel the passing of a law, an all-powerful social barrier that shall prevent the very workers from selling, by voluntary contract with capital, themselves and their families into slavery and death.[3] In place of the pompous catalogue of the "inalienable rights of man" comes the modest Magna Charta of a legally limited working-day, which shall make clear "when the time which the worker sells is ended, and when his own begins."[4] Quantum mutatus ab illo!

[1] "The proceedings (the manœuvres of capital, *e.g.*, from 1848–50) have afforded, moreover, incontrovertible proof of the fallacy of the assertion so often advanced, that operatives need no protection, but may be considered as free agents in the disposal of the only property which they possess—the labour of their hands and the sweat of their brows." (Reports, &c., for April 30th, 1850, p. 45.) "Free labour (if so it may be termed) even in a free country, requires the strong arm of the law to protect it." (Reports, &c., for October 31st, 1864, p. 34.) "To permit, which is tantamount to compelling . . . to work 14 hours a day with or without meals," &c. (Repts., &c., for April 30th, 1863, p. 40.)　　[2] Friedrich Engels, l. c., p. 5.
[3] The 10 Hours' Act has, in the branches of industry that come under it, "put an end to the premature decrepitude of the former long-hour workers." (Reports, &c., for 31st Oct., 1859, p. 47.) "Capital (in factories) can never be employed in keeping the machinery in motion beyond a limited time, without certain injury to the health and morals of the labourers employed; and they are not in a position to protect themselves." (l. c., p. 8.)
[4] "A still greater boon is the distinction at last made clear between the worker's own time and his master's. The worker knows now when that which he sells is ended, and when his own begins; and by possessing a sure foreknowledge of this, is enabled to pre-arrange his own minutes for his own purposes." (l. c., p. 52.) "By making them masters of their own time (the Factory Acts) have given them a moral energy which is directing them to the eventual possession of political power" (l. c., p. 47). With suppressed irony, and in very well weighed words, the Factory Inspectors hint that the actual law also frees the capitalist from some of the brutality natural to a man who is a mere embodiment of capital, and that it has. given him time for little "culture." Formerly the master had no time for anything but money; the servant had no time for anything but labour" (l. c., p. 48).

CHAPTER XI.

RATE AND MASS OF SURPLUS-VALUE.

In this chapter, as hitherto, the value of labour-power, and therefore the part of the working-day necessary for the reproduction or maintenance of that labour-power, are supposed to be given constant magnitudes.

This premised with the rate, the mass is at the same time given of the surplus-value that the individual labourer furnishes to the capitalist in a definite period of time. If, *e.g.,* the necessary labour amounts to 6 hours daily, expressed in a quantum of gold=3 shillings, then 3s. is the daily value of one labour-power or the value of the capital advanced in the buying of one labour-power. If, further, the rate of surplus-value be=100%, this variable capital of 3s. produces a mass of surplus-value of 3s., or the labourer supplies daily a mass of surplus-labour equal to 6 hours.

But the variable capital of a capitalist is the expression in money of the total value of all the labour-powers that he employs simultaneously. Its value is, therefore, equal to the average value of one labour-power, multiplied by the number of labour-powers employed. With a given value of labour-power, therefore, the magnitude of the variable capital varies directly as the number of labourers employed simultaneously. If the daily value of one labour-power=3s., then a capital of 300s. must be advanced in order to exploit daily 100 labour-powers, of n times 3s., in order to exploit daily n labour-powers.

In the same way, if a variable capital of 3s., being the daily value of one labour-power, produce a daily surplus-value of 3s., a variable capital of 300s. will produce a daily surplus-value of 300s., and one of n times 3s. a daily surplus-value of $n \times 3s.$ The mass of the surplus-value produced is therefore equal to the surplus-value which the working-day of one labourer supplies multiplied by the number of labourers employed. But as further the mass of surplus-value which a single labourer produces, the value of labour-power being given, is determined by the rate of the surplus-value, this law follows: the mass of the surplus-value produced is equal to the amount of the variable capital advanced, multiplied by the rate of surplus-value; in other words: it is determined by the compound ratio between the number of labour-powers exploited simultaneously by the same capitalist and the degree of exploitation of each individual labour-power.

Let the mass of the surplus-value be S, the surplus-value supplied by the individual labourer in the average day s, the variable capital daily advanced in the purchase of one individual labour-power v, the sum total of the variable capital V, the value of an average labour-power P, its degree of exploitation $\frac{a' \text{ (surplus-labor)}}{a \text{ (necessary-labor)}}$ and the number of labourers employed n; we have:

$$S = \begin{cases} \dfrac{s}{v} \times V \\ P \times \dfrac{\acute{a}}{a} \times n \end{cases}$$

It is always supposed, not only that the value of an average labour-power is constant, but that the labourers employed by a capitalist are reduced to average labourers. There are exceptional cases in which the surplus-value produced does not increase in proportion to the number of labourers exploited, but then the value of the labour-power does not remain constant.

In the production of a definite mass of surplus-value, therefore, the decrease of one factor may be compensated by the increase of the other. If the variable capital diminishes, and at the same time the rate of surplus-value increases in the same ratio, the mass of surplus-value produced remains unaltered. If on our earlier assumption the capitalist must advance 300s., in order to exploit 100 labourers a day, and if the rate of surplus-value amounts to 50%, this variable capital of 300s. yields a surplus-value of 150s. or of 100×3 working hours. If the rate of surplus-value doubles, or the working day, instead of being extended from 6 to 9, is extended from 6 to 12 hours and at the same time variable capital is lessened by half, and reduced to 150s., it yields also a surplus-value of 150s. or 50×6 working hours. Diminution of the variable capital may therefore be compensated by a proportionate rise in the degree of exploitation of labour-power, or the decrease in the number of the labourers employed by a proportionate extension of the working-day. Within certain limits therefore the supply of labour exploitable by capital is independent of the supply of labourers.[1] On the contrary, a fall in the rate of surplus-value leaves unaltered the mass of the surplus-value produced, if the amount of the variable capital, or number of the labourers employed, increases in the same proportion.

Nevertheless, the compensation of a decrease in the number of labourers employed, or of the amount of variable capital advanced, by a rise in the rate of surplus-value, or by the lengthening of the working-day, has impassable limits. Whatever the value of labour-power may be, whether the working time necessary for the maintenance of the labourer is 2 or 10 hours, the total value that a labourer can produce, day in, day out, is always less than the value in which 24 hours of labour are embodied, less than 12s., if 12s. is the money expression for 24 hours of realized labour. In our former assumption, according to which 6 working hours are daily necessary in order to reproduce the labour-power itself or to replace the value of the capital advanced in its purchase, a variable capital of 1500s., that employs 500 labourers at a rate of surplus-value of 100% with a 12 hours' working-day, produces daily a surplus-value of 1500s. or of 6×500 working hours. A capital of 300s. that employs 100 labourers a day with a rate of surplus-value of 200% or with a working-day of 18 hours, produces only a mass of surplus-value of 600s. or 12×100 working hours; and its total value-product, the equivalent of the variable capital advanced plus the surplus-value, can, day in, day out, never reach the sum of 1200s. or 24×100 working hours.

[1] This elementary law appears to be unknown to the vulgar economists, who, upsidedown Archimedes, in the determination of the market-price of labour by supply and demand, imagine they have found the fulcrum by means of which, not to move the world, but to stop its motion.

The absolute limit of the average working-day—this being by Nature always less than 24 hours—sets an absolute limit to the compensation of a reduction of variable capital by a higher rate of surplus-value, or of the decrease of the number of labourers exploited by a higher degree of exploitation of labour-power. This palpable law is of importance for the clearing up of many phenomena, arising from a tendency (to be worked out later on) of capital to reduce as much as possible the number of labourers employed by it, or its variable constituent transformed into labour-power, in contradiction to its other tendency to produce the greatest possible mass of surplus-value. On the other hand, if the mass of labour-power employed, or the amount of variable capital, increases, but not in proportion to the fall in the rate of surplus-value, the mass of the surplus-value produced, falls.

A third law results from the determination, of the mass of the surplus-value produced, by the two factors: rate of surplus-value and amount of variable capital advanced. The rate of surplus-value, or the degree of exploitation of labour-power, and the value of labour-power, or the amount of necessary working time being given, it is self-evident that the greater the variable capital, the greater would be the mass of the value produced and of the surplus-value. If the limit of the working-day is given, and also the limit of its necessary constituent, the mass of value and surplus-value that an individual capitalist produces, is clearly exclusively dependent on the mass of labour that he sets in motion. But this, under the conditions supposed above, depends on the mass of labour-power, or the number of labourers whom he exploits, and this number in its turn is determined by the amount of the variable capital advanced. With a given rate of surplus-value, and a given value of labour-power, therefore, the masses of surplus-value produced vary directly as the amounts of the variable capitals advanced. Now we know that the capitalist divides his capital into two parts. One part he lays out in means of production. This is the constant part of his capital. The other part he lays out in living labour-power. This part forms his variable capital. On the basis of the same mode of social production, the division of capital into constant and variable differs in different branches of production, and within the same branch of production, too, this relation changes with changes in the technical conditions and in the social combinations of the processes of production. But in whatever proportion a given capital breaks up into a constant and a variable part, whether the latter is to the former as $1:2$ or $1:10$ or $1:x$, the law just laid down is not affected by this. For, according to our previous analysis, the value of the constant capital reappears in the value of the product, but does not enter into the newly produc d value, the newly created value-product. To employ 1000 spinners, more raw material, spindles, &c., are, f course, required, than to employ 100. The value of these additional means of production however may rise fall, remai unaltered, be large or small; it has no influence on the process of creation of surplus-value by means of the labour-power tha put them in motion. The law demonstrated above now, therefore, takes this form: the masses of value and of surplus-value produced by different capitals—the value of labour-power being given and its degree of exploitation being equal—vary directly as the amounts of the variable constituents of these capitals, *i.e.*, as their constituents transformed into living labour-power.

This law clearly contradicts all experience based on appearance. Every one knows that a cotton spinner, who, reckoning the percentage on the whole of his applied capital, employs much constant and little variable capital, does not, on account of this, pocket less profit or surplus-value than a baker, who relatively sets in motion much variable and little constant capital. For the solution of this apparent contradiction, many intermediate terms are as yet wanted, as from the standpoint of elementary algebra many intermediate terms are wanted to understand that $\frac{0}{0}$ may represent an actual magnitude. Classical economy, although not formulating the law, holds instinctively to it, because it is a necessary consequence of the general law of value. It tries to rescue the law from collision with contradictory phenomena by a violent abstraction. It will be seen later[1] how the school of Ricardo has come to grief over

[1] Further particulars will be found in "Theories of Surplus-Value," edited by Karl Kautsky.

this stumbling-block. Vulgar economy which, indeed, "has really learnt nothing," here as everywhere sticks to appearances in opposition to the law which regulates and explains them. In opposition to Spinoza, it believes that "ignorance is a sufficient reason."

The labour which is set in motion by the total capital of a society, day in, day out, may be regarded as a single collective working-day. If, *e.g.*, the number of labourers is a million, and the average working-day of a labourer is 10 hours, the social working-day consists of ten million hours. With a given length of this working-day, whether its limits are fixed physically or socially, the mass of surplus-value can only be increased by increasing the number of labourers, *i.e.*, of the labouring population. The growth of population here forms the mathematical limit to the production of surplus-value by the total social capital. On the contrary, with a given amount of population, this limit is formed by the possible lengthening of the working-day.[1] It will, however, be seen in the following chapter that this law only holds for the form of surplus-value dealt with up to the present.

From the treatment of the production of surplus-value, so far, it follows that not every sum of money, or of value, is at pleasure transformable into capital. To effect this transformation, in fact, a certain minimum of money or of exchange-value must be presupposed in the hands of the individual possessor of money or commodities. The minimum of variable capital is the cost price of a single labour-power, employed the whole year through, day in, day out, for the production of surplus-value. If this labourer were in possession of his own means of production, and were satisfied to live as a labourer, he need not work beyond the time necessary for the reproduction of his means of subsistence, say 8 hours a day. He would, besides, only require the means of production sufficient for 8 working hours. The capitalist, on the other hand, who makes

---

[1] "The labour, that is the economic time, of society, is a given portion, say ten hours a day of a million of people, or ten million hours. . . . Capital has its boundary of increase. This boundary may, at any given period, be attained in the actual extent of economic time employed." ("An Essay on the Political Economy of Nations." London, 1821, pp. 47, 49.)

him do, besides these 8 hours, say 4 hours' surplus-labour, requires an additional sum of money for furnishing the additional means of production.   On our supposition, however, he
would have to employ two labourers in order to live, on the
surplus-value appropriated daily, as well as, and no better than
a labourer, *i.e.*, to be able to satisfy his necessary wants.   In
this case the mere maintenance of life would be the end of his
production, not the increase of wealth; but this latter is implied in capitalist production.   That he may live only twice
as well as an ordinary labourer, and besides turn half of the
surplus-value produced into capital, he would have to raise,
with the number of labourers, the minimum of the capital advanced 8 times.   Of course he can, like his labourer, take to
work himself, participate directly in the process of production,
but he is then only a hybrid between capitalist and labourer, a
"small master."   A certain stage of capitalist production necessitates that the capitalist be able to devote the whole of the
time during which he functions as a capitalist, *i.e.*, as personified capital, to the appropriation and therefore control of the
labour of others, and to the selling of the products of this labour.[1]   The guilds of the middle ages therefore tried to
prevent by force the transformation of the master of a trade
into a capitalist, by limiting the number of labourers that could
be employed by one master within a very small maximum.
The possessor of money or commodities actually turns into a
capitalist in such cases only where the minimum sum advanced
for production greatly exceeds the maximum of the middle
ages.   Here, as in natural science, is shown the correctness of

---

[1] "The farmer cannot rely on his own labour, and if he does, I will maintain that
he is a loser by it.   His employment should be a general attention to the whole: his
thresher must be watched, or he will soon lose his wages in corn not threshed out;
his mowers, reapers, &c., must be looked after; he must constantly go round his
fences; he must see there is no neglect; which would be the case if he was confined
to any one spot."   ("An Inquiry into the connection between the Price of Provisions
and the Size of Farms, &c.   By a Farmer."   London, 1773, p. 12.)   This book is
very interesting.   In it the genesis of the "capitalist farmer" or "merchant farmer,"
as he is explicitly called, may be studied, and his self-glorification at the expense
of the small farmer who has only to do with bare subsistence, be noted.   "The class
of capitalists are from the first partially, and they become ultimately completely,
discharged from the necessity of the manual labour."   ("Text-book of Lectures on
the Political Economy of Nations.   By the Rev. Richard Jones."   Hertford, 1852.
Lecture III. p. 39.)

the law discovered by Hegel (in his "Logic"), that merely quantitative differences beyond a certain point pass into qualitative changes.[1]

The minimum of the sum of value that the individual possessor of money or commodities must command, in order to metamorphose himself into ⸱ capitalist, changes with the different stages of development of capitalist production, and is at given stages different ⸱n different spheres of produⱯtion, according to their special and technical conditions. Certain spheres of production demand, even at the very outset of capitalist production, a minimum of capital that is not as yet found in the hands of single individuals. This gives rise partly to state subsidies to private persons, as in France in the time of Colbert, and as in many German states up to our own epoch; partly to the formation of societies with legal monopoly for the exploitation of certain branches of industry and commerce, the fore-runners of our own modern joint-stock companies.[2]

Within the process of production, as we have seen, capital acquired the command over labour, i. e., over functioning labouring-power or the labourer himself. Personified capital, the capitalist takes care that the labourer does his work regularly and with the proper degree of intensity.

Capital further developed into a coercive relation, which compels the working class to do more work than the narrow round of its own life-wants prescribes. As a producer of the activity of others, as a pumper-out of surplus-labour and exploiter of labour-power, it surpasses in energy, disregard of

[1] The molecular theory of modern chemistry first scientifically worked out by Laurent and Gerhardt rests on no other law. (Addition to 3rd Edition.) For the explanation of this statement, which is not very clear to non-chemists, we remark that the author speaks here of the homologous series of carbon compounds, first so named by C. Gerhardt in 1843, each series of which has its own general algebraic formula. Thus the series of paraffins: $Cn\ H^2n+^2$, that of the normal alcohols: $Cn\ H^2n+^2O$; of the normal fatty acids: $Cn\ H^2n\ O^2$ and many others. In the above examples, by the simply quantitative addition of $C\ H^2$ to the molecular formula, a qualitatively different body is each time formed. On the share (overestimated by Marx) of Laurent and Gerhardt in the determination of this important fact see Kopp, "Entwicklung der Chemie." München, 1873, pp. 709, 716, and Schorlemmer, "Rise and Progress of Organic Chemistry." London, 1879, p. 54.—Ed.

[2] Martin Luther calls these kinds of institutions: "The Company Monopolia."

bounds, recklessness and efficiency, all earlier-systems of production based on directly compulsory labour.

At first, capital subordinates labour on the basis of the technical conditions in which it historically finds it. It does not, therefore, change immediately the mode of production. The production of surplus-value—in the form hitherto considered by us—by means of simple extension of the working-day, proved, therefore, to be independent of any change in the mode of production itself. It was not less active in the old-fashioned bakeries than in the modern cotton factories.

If we consider the process of production from the point of view of the simple labour-process, the labourer stands in relation to the means of production, not in their quality as capital, but as the mere means and material of his own intelligent productive activity. In tanning, *e. g.*, he deals with the skins as his simple object of labour. It is not the capitalist whose skin he tans. But it is different as soon as we deal with the process of production from the point of view of the process of creation of surplus-value. The means of production are at once changed into means for the absorption of the labour of others. It is now no longer the labourer that employes the means of production, but the means of production that employ the labourer. Instead of being consumed by him as material elements of his productive activity, they consume him as the ferment necessary to their own life-process, and the life-process of capital consists only in its movement as value constantly expanding, constantly multiplying itself. Furnaces and workshops that stand idle by night, and absorb no living labour, are "a mere loss" to the capitalist. Hence, furnaces and workshops constitute lawful claims upon the night-labour of the workpeople. The simple transformation of money into the material factors of the process of production, into means of production, transforms the latter into a title and a right to the labour and surplus-labour of others. An example will show, in conclusion, how this sophistication, peculiar to and characteristic of capitalist production, this complete inversion of the relation between dead and living labour, between value and

the force that creates value, mirrors itself in the consciousness
of capitalists. During the revolt of the English factory lords
between 1848 and 1850, "the head of one of the oldest and
most respectable houses in the West of Scotland, Messrs. Carlile Sons & Co., of the linen and cotton thread factory at Paisley, a company which has now existed for about a century,
which was in operation in 1752, and four generations of the
same family have conducted it" . . . this "very intelligent gentleman" then wrote a letter [1] in the "Glasgow Daily
Mail" of April 25th, 1849, with the title, "The relay system,"
in which among other things the following grotesquely naïve
passage occurs: "Let us now . . . see what evils will
attend the limiting to 10 hours the working of the factory.
. . . They amount to the most serious damage to the millowner's prospects and property. If he (*i. e.,* his "hands")
worked 12 hours before, and is limited to 10, then every 12
machines or spindles in his establishment shrink to 10, and
should the works be disposed of, they will be valued only as 10,
so that a sixth part would thus be deducted from the value of
every factory in the country." [2]

To this West of Scotland bourgeois brain, inheriting the
accumulated capitalistic qualities of "four generations," the
value of the means of production, spindles, &c. is so inseparably mixed up with their property, as capital, to expand their
own value, and to swallow up daily a definite quantity of the
unpaid labour of others, that the head of the firm of Carlile &
Co. actually imagines that if he sells his factory, not only will
the value of the spindles be paid to him, but, in addition, their
power of annexing surplus-value, not only the labour which is
embodied in them, and is necessary to the production of spindles of this kind, but also the surplus-labour which they help

---

[1] Reports of Insp. of Fact., April 30th, 1849, p. 59.

[2] l. c., p. 60. Factory Inspector Stuart, himself a Scotchman, and in contrast to
the English Factory Inspectors, quite taken captive by the capitalistic method of
thinking, remarks expressly on this letter which he incorporates in his report that it
is "the most useful of the communications which any of the factory-owners working
with relays have given to those engaged in the same trade, and which is the most
calculated to remove the prejudices of such of them as have scruples respecting any
change of the arrangement of the hours of work."

to pump out daily from the brave Scots of Paisley, and for that very reason he thinks that with the shortening of the working-day by 2 hours, the selling-price of 12 spinning machines dwindles to that of 10!

PART IV.

PRODUCTION OF RELATIVE SURPLUS-VALUE.

CHAPTER XII.

THE CONCEPT OF RELATIVE SURPLUS-VALUE.

THAT portion of the working-day which merely produces an equivalent for the value paid by the capitalist for his labour-power, has, up to this point, been treated by us as a constant magnitude; and such in fact it is, under given conditions of production and at a given stage in the economical development of society. Beyond this, his necessary labour-time, the labourer, we saw, could continue to work for 2, 3, 4, 6, &c., hours. The rate of surplus-value and the length of the working day depended on the magnitude of this prolongation. Though the necessary labour-time was constant, we saw, on the other hand, that the total working-day was variable. Now suppose we have a working-day whose length, and whose apportionment between necessary labour and surplus-labour, are given. Let the whole line a c, a———————b——c, represent, for example, a working-day of 12 hours; the portion of a b 10 hours of necessary labour, and the portion b c 2 hours of surplus-labour. How now can the production of surplus-value be increased, *i.e.*, how can the surplus-labour be prolonged, without, or independently of, any prolongation of a c?

Although the lengh of a c is given, b c appears to be capable of prolongation, if not by extension beyond its end c, which is also the end of the working day a c, yet, at all events, by pushing back its starting point b in the direction of a. Assume that b'—b in the line, a b' b c is equal to half of b c

a————b'—b——c

or to one hour's labour-time. If now, in a c, the working day of 12 hours, we move the point b to b', b c becomes b' c; the surplus-labour increases by one-half, from 2 hours to 3 hours, although the working day remains as before at 12 hours. This extension of the surplus labour-time from b c to b' c, from 2 hours to 3 hours, is, however, evidently impossible, without a simultaneous contraction of the necessary labour-time from a b into a b', from 10 hours to 9 hours. The prolongation of the surplus-labour would correspond to a shortening of the necessary labour; or a portion of the labour-time previously consumed, in reality, for the labourer's own benefit, would be converted into labour-time for the benefit of the capitalist. There would be an alteration, not in the length of the working day, but in its division into necessary labour-time and surplus labour-time.

On the other hand, it is evident that the duration of the surplus-labour is given, when the length of the working day, and the value of labour-power, are given. The value of labour-power, *i.e.*, the labour-time requisite to produce labour-power, determines the labour-time necessary for the reproduction of that value. If one working hour be embodied in sixpence, and the value of a day's labour-power be five shillings, the labourer must work 10 hours a day, in order to replace the value paid by capital for his labour-power, or to produce an equivalent for the value of his daily necessary means of subsistence. Given the value of these means of subsistence, the value of his labour-power is given; [1] and given the value of his labour-power, the duration of his necessary labour-time is given. The duration of the surplus-labour, how-

[1] The value of his average daily wages is determined by what the labourer requires "so as to live, labour, and generate." (Wm. Petty: "Political Anatomy of Ireland," 1672, p. 64.) "The price of Labour is always constituted of the price of necessaries . . . whenever . . . the labouring man's wages will not, suitably to his low rank and station, as a labouring man, support such a family as is often the lot of many of them to have," he does not receive proper wages. (J. Vanderlint, l. c. p. 15.) "Le simple ouvrier, qui n'a que ses bras et son industrie, n'a rien qu'autant qu'il parvient à vendre à d'autres sa peine. . . . En tout genre de travail il doit arriver, et il arrive en effet, que le salaire de l'ouvrier se borne à ce qui lui est nécessaire pour lui procurer sa substance." (Turgot, Réflexions, &c., Oeuvres ed. Daire t. I. p. 10). "The price of the necessaries of life is, in fact, the cost of producing labour." (Malthus, Inquiry into, &c., Rent, London, 1815, p. 48 note).

ever, is arrived at, by subtracting the necessary labour-time from the total working day. Ten hours subtracted from twelve, leave two, and it is not easy to see, how, under the given conditions, the surplus-labour can possibly be prolonged beyond two hours. No doubt, the capitalist can, instead of five shillings, pay the labourer four shillings and sixpence or even less. For the reproduction of this value of four shillings and sixpence, nine hours labour-time would suffice; and consequently three hours of surplus-labour, instead of two, would accrue to the capitalist, and the surplus-value would rise from one shilling to eighteenpence. This result, however, would be obtained only by lowering the wages of the labourer below the value of his labour-power. With the four shillings and sixpence which he produces in nine hours, he commands one-tenth less of the necessaries of life than before, and consequently the proper reproduction of his labour-power is crippled. The surplus-labour would in this case be prolonged only by an overstepping of its normal limits; its domain would be extended only by a usurpation of part of the domain of necessary labour-time. Despite the important part which this method plays in actual practice, we are excluded from considering it in this place, by our assumption, that all commodities, including labour-power, are bought and sold at their full value. Granted this, it follows that the labour-time necessary for the production of labour-power, or for the reproduction of its value, cannot be lessened by a fall in the labourer's wages below the value of his labour-power, but only by a fall in this value itself. Given the length of the working day, the prolongation of the surplus-labour must of necessity originate in the curtailment of the necessary labour-time; the latter cannot arise from the former. In the example we have taken, it is necessary that the value of labour-power should actually fall by one-tenth, in order that the necessary labour-time may be diminished by one-tenth, *i.e.,,* from ten hours to nine, and in order that the surplus-labour may consequently be prolonged from two hours to three.

Such a fall in the value of labour-power implies, however, that the same necessaries of life which were formerly produced in ten hours, can now be produced in nine hours. But this is impossible without an increase in the productiveness of labour. For example, suppose a shoemaker, with given tools, makes in one working day of twelve hours, one pair of boots. If he must make two pairs in the same time, the productiveness of his labour must be doubled; and this cannot be done, except by an alteration in his tools or in his mode of working, or in both. Hence, the conditions of production, *i.e.*, his mode of production, and the labour-process itself, must be revolutionised. By increase in the productiveness of labour, we mean, generally, an alteration in the labour-process, of such a kind as to shorten the labour-time socially necessary for the production of a commodity, and to endow a given quantity of labour with the power of producing a greater quantity of use-value.[1] Hitherto in treating of surplus-value, arising from a simple prolongation of the working day, we have assumed the mode of production to be given and invariable. But when surplus-value has to be produced by the conversion of necessary labour into surplus-labour, it by no means suffices for capital to take over the labour-process in the form under which it has been historically handed down, and then simply to prolong the duration of that process. The technical and social conditions of the process, and consequently the very mode of production must be revolutionised, before the productiveness of labour can be increased. By that means alone can the value of labour-power be made to sink, and the portion of the working day necessary for the reproduction of that value, be shortened.

The surplus-value produced by prolongation of the working day, I call *absolute surplus-value*. On the other hand, the surplus-value arising from the curtailment of the necessary labour-time, and from the corresponding alteration in the respective lengths of the two components of the working day, I call *relative surplus-value*.

---

[1] "Quando si perfezionano le arti, che non è altro che la scoperta di nuove vie, onde si possa compiere una manufattura con meno gente o (che è lo stesso) in minor tempo di prima." (Galiani l. c. p. 159.) "L'économie sur les frais de production ne peut donc être autre chose que l'économie sur la quantité de travail employé pour produire." (Sismondi, Études t. I. p. 22.)

In order to effect a fall in the value of labour-power, the increase in the productiveness of labour must seize upon those branches of industry, whose products determine the value of labour-power, and consequently either belong to the class of customary means of subsistence, or are capable of supplying the place of those means. But the value of a commodity is determined, not only by the quantity of labour which the labourer directly bestows upon that commodity, but also by the labour contained in the means of production. For instance, the value of a pair of boots depends, not only on the cobbler's labour, but also on the value of the leather, wax, thread, &c. Hence, a fall in the value of labour-power is also brought about by an increase in the productiveness of labour, and by a corresponding cheapening of commodities in those industries which supply the instruments of labour and the raw material, that form the material elements of the constant capital required for producing the necessaries of life. But an increase in the productiveness of labour in those branches of industry which supply neither the necessaries of life, nor the means of production for such necessaries, leaves the value of labour-power undisturbed.

The cheapened commodity, of course, causes only a pro tanto fall in the value of labour-power, a fall proportional to the extent of that commodity's employment in the reproduction of labour-power. Shirts, for instance, are a necessary means of subsistence, but are only one out of many. The totality of the necessaries of life consists, however, of various commodities, each the product of a distinct industry; and the value of each of those commodities enters as a component part into the value of labour-power. This latter value decreases with the decrease of the labour-time necessary for its reproduction; the total decrease being the sum of all the different curtailments of labour-time effected in those various and distinct industries. This general result is treated, here, as if it were the immediate result directly aimed at in each individual case. Whenever an individual capitalist cheapens shirts, for instance, by increasing the productiveness of labour, he by no means necessarily aims at reducing the value of labour-power

and shortening, pro tanto, the necessary labour-time. But it
is only in so far as he ultimately contributes to this result,
that he assists in raising the general rate of surplus-value.[1]
The general and necessary tendencies of capital must be distinguished from their forms of manifestation.

It is not our intention to consider, here, the way in which
the laws, immanent in capitalist production, manifest themselves in the movements of individual masses of capital, where
they assert themselves as coercive laws of competition, and are
brought home to the mind and consciousness of the individual
capitalist as the directing motives of his operations. But this
much is clear; a scientific analysis of competition is not possible, before we have a conception of the inner nature of capital,
just as the apparent motions of the heavenly bodies are not
intelligible to any but him, who is acquainted with their real
motions, motions which are not directly perceptible by the
senses. Nevertheless, for the better comprehension of the
production of relative surplus-value, we may add the following remarks, in which we assume nothing more than the results we have already obtained.

If one hour's labour is embodied in sixpence, a value of six
shillings will be produced in a working day of 12 hours.
Suppose, that with the prevailing productiveness of labour, 12
articles are produced in these 12 hours. Let the value of the
means of production used in each article be sixpence. Under
these circumstances, each article costs one shilling: sixpence
for the value of the means of production, and sixpence for the
value newly added in working with those means. Now let
some one capitalist contrive to double the productiveness of
labour, and to produce in the working day of 12 hours, 24 instead of 12 such articles. The value of the means of production remaining the same, the value of each article will fall to
ninepence, made up of sixpence for the value of the means of
production and threepence for the value newly added by the
labour. Despite the doubled productiveness of labour, the

---

[1] "Let us suppose . . . the products . . . of the manufacturer are doubled
by improvement in machinery . . . he will be able to clothe his workmen by
means of a smaller proportion of the entire return . . . and thus his profit will
be raised. But in no other way will it be influenced." (Ramsay, l. c. p. 168, 169.)

day's labour creates, as before, a new value of six shillings **and** no more, which, however, is now spread over twice as many articles. Of this value each article now has embodied in it $\frac{1}{24}$th, instead of $\frac{1}{12}$th, threepence instead of sixpence; or, what amounts to the same thing, only half an hour's instead of a whole hour's labour-time, is now added to the means of production while they are being transformed into each article. The individual value of these articles is now below their social value; in other words, they have cost less labour-time than the great bulk of the same article produced under the average social conditions. Each article costs, on an average, one shilling, and represents 2 hours of social labour; but under the altered mode of production it costs only nine epence, or contains only $1\frac{1}{2}$ hours' labour. The real value of a commodity is, however, not its individual value but its social value; that is to say, the real value is not measured by the labour-time that the article in each individual case costs the producer, but by the labour-time socially required for its production. If therefore, the capitalist who applies the new method, sells his commodity at its social value of one shilling, he sells it for threepence above its individual value, and thus realises an extra surplus-value of threepence. On the other hand, the working day of 12 hours is, as regards him, now represented by 24 articles instead of 12. Hence, in order to get rid of the product of one working day, the demand must be double what it was, *i.e.,* the market must become twice as extensive. Other things being equal, his commodities can command a more extended market only by a diminution of their prices. He will therefore sell them above their individual but under their social value, say at tenpence each. By this means he still squeezes an extra surplus-value of one penny out of each. This augmentation of surplus-value is pocketed by him, whether his commodities belong or not to the class of necessary means of subsistence that participate in determining the general value of labour-power. Hence, independently of this latter circumstance, there is a motive for each individual capitalist to cheapen his commodities, by increasing the productiveness of labour.

Nevertheless, even in this case, the increased production of surplus-value arises from the curtailment of the necessary labour-time, and from the corresponding prolongation of the surplus-labour.[1] Let the necessary labour-time amount to 10 hours, the value of a day's labour-power to five shillings, the surplus labour-time to 2 hours, and the daily surplus-value to one shilling. But the capitalist now produces 24 articles, which he sells at tenpence a-piece, making twenty shillings in all. Since the value of the means of production is twelve shillings, $14\frac{2}{5}$ of these articles merely replace the constant capital advanced. The labour of the 12 hours' working day is represented by the remaining $9\frac{3}{5}$ articles. Since the price of the labour power is five shillings, 6 articles represent the necessary labour-time, and $3\frac{3}{5}$ articles the surplus-labour. The ratio of the necessary labour to the surplus-labour, which under average social conditions was $5:1$, is now only $5:3$. The same result may be arrived at in the following way. The value of the product of the working day of 12 hours is twenty shillings. Of this sum, twelve shillings belong to the value of the means of production, a value that merely re-appears. There remain eight shillings, which are the expression in money, of the value newly created during the working day. This sum is greater than the sum in which average social labour of the same kind is expressed: twelve hours of the latter labour are expressed by six shillings only. The exceptionally productive labour operates as intensified labour; it creates in equal periods of time greater values than average social labour of the same kind. (See Ch. I. Sect. 1. p. 45.) But our capitalist still continues to pay as before only five shillings as the value of a day's labour-power. Hence, instead of 10 hours, the labourer need now work only $7\frac{1}{2}$ hours, in order to re-produce this value. His surplus-labour is, therefore, increased $2\frac{1}{2}$ hours, and the surplus-value he produces

---

[1] "A man's profit does not depend upon his command of the produce of other men's labour, but upon his command of labour itself. If he can sell his goods at a higher price, while his workmen's wages remain unaltered, he is clearly benefited. . . . A smaller proportion of what he produces is sufficient to put that labour into motion, and a larger proportion consequently remains for himself." ("Outlines of Pol. Econ." London, 1832, pp. 49, 50.)

grows from one, into three shillings. Hence, the capitalist who applies the improved method of production appropriates to surplus-labour a greater portion of the working day, than the other capitalists in the same trade. He does individually, what the whole body of capitalists engaged in producing relative surplus-value, do collectively. On the other hand, however, this extra surplus-value vanishes, so soon as the new method of production has become general and has consequently caused the difference between the individual value of the cheapened commodity and its social value to vanish. The law of the determination of value by labour-time, a law which brings under its sway the individual capitalist who applies the new method of production, by compelling him to sell his goods under their social value, this same law, acting as a coercive law of competition, forces his competitors to adopt the new method.[1] The general rate of surplus-value is, therefore, ultimately affected by the whole process, only when the increase in the productiveness of labour, has seized upon those branches of production that are connected with, and has cheapened those commodities that form part of, the necessary means of subsistence, and are therefore elements of the value of labour-power.

The value of commodities is in inverse ratio to the productiveness of labour. And so, too, is the value of labour-power, because it depends on the values of commodities. Relative surplus-value is, on the contrary, directly proportional to that productiveness. It rises with rising and falls with falling productiveness. The value of money being assumed to be constant, an average social working day of 12 hours always produces the same new value, six shillings, no matter how this sum may be apportioned between surplus-value and wages. But if, in consequence of increased productiveness, the value of the necessaries of life fall, and the value of a day's labour-

---

[1] "If my neighbour by doing much with little labour, can sell cheap, I must contrive to sell as cheap as he. So that every art, trade, or engine, doing work with labour of fewer hands, and consequently cheaper, begets in others a kind of necessity and emulation, either of using the same art, trade, or engine, or of inventing something like it, that every man may be upon the square, that no man may be able to undersell his neighbour." ("The Advantages of the East India Trade to England." London, 1720, p. 67.)

power be thereby reduced from five shillings to three, the surplus-value increases from one shilling to three. Ten hours were necessary for the reproduction of the value of the labourpower; now only six are required. Four hours have been set free, and can be annexed to the domain of surplus-labour. Hence there is immanent in capital an inclination and constant tendency, to heighten the productiveness of labour, in order to cheapen commodities, and by such cheapening to cheapen the labourer himself.[1]

The value of a commodity is, in itself, of no interest to the capitalist. What alone interests him, is the surplus-value that dwells in it, and is realisable by sale. Realisation of the surplus-value necessarily carries with it the refunding of the value that was advanced. Now, since relative surplus-value increases in direct proportion to the development of the productiveness of labour, while, on the other hand, the value of commodities diminishes in the same proportion; since one and the same process cheapens commodities, and augments the surplus-value contained in them; we have here the solution of the riddle: why does the capitalist, whose sole concern is the production of exchange-value, continually strive to depress the exchange-value of commodities? A riddle with which Quesnay, one of the founders of political economy, tormented his opponents, and to which they could give him no answer. "You acknowledge," he says, "that the more expenses and the cost of labour can, in the manufacture of industrial products, be reduced without injury to production, the more advantageous is such reduction, because it diminishes the price of the finished article. And yet, you believe that the production of wealth, which arises from the labour of the workpeople, con-

---

[1] "In whatever proportion the expenses of a labourer are diminished, in the same proportion will his wages be diminished, if the restraints upon industry are at the same time taken off." ("Considerations concerning taking off of the Bounty on Corn Exported," &c., Lond., 1753, p. 7.) "The interest of trade requires, that corn and all provisions should be as cheap as possible; for whatever makes them dear, must make labour dear also . . . in all countries where industry is not restrained the price of provisions must affect the price of labour. .This will always be diminished when the necessaries of life grow cheaper." (l. c. p. 3.) "Wages are decreased in the same proportion as the powers of production increase. Machinery, it is true, cheapens the necessaries of life, but it also cheapens the labourer." ("A Prize Essay on the Comparative Merits of Competition and Co-operation." London, 1834, p. 27.)

sists in the augmentation of the exchange-value of their products."[1]

The shortening of the working day is, therefore, by no means what is aimed at, in capitalist production, when labour is economised by increasing its productiveness.[2] It is only the shortening of the labour-time, necessary for the production of a definite quantity of commodities, that is aimed at. The fact that the workman, when the productiveness of his labour has been increased, produces, say 10 times as many commodities as before, and thus spends one-tenth as much labour-time on each, by no means prevents him from continuing to work 12 hours as before, nor from producing in those 12 hours 1200 articles instead of 120. Nay, more, his working day may be prolonged at the same time, so as to make him produce, say 1400 articles in 14 hours. In the treatises, therefore, of economists of the stamp of MacCulloch, Ure, Senior, and tutti quanti, we may read upon one page, that the labourer owes a debt of gratitude to capital for developing his productiveness, because the necessary labour-time is thereby shortened, and on the next page, that he must prove his gratitude by working in future for 15 hours instead of 10. The object of all development of the productiveness of labour, within the limits of capitalist production, is to shorten that part of the working day, during which the workman must labour for his own benefit, and by that very shortening, to lengthen the other part of the day, during which he is at liberty to work gratis for the capitalist. How far this result is also attainable, without cheapening commodities, will appear from an examination of

[1] "Ils conviennent que plus on peut, sans préjudice, épargner de frais ou de travaux dispendieux dans la fabrication des ouvrages des artisans, plus cette épargne est profitable par la diminution des prix de ces ouvrages. Cependant ils croient que la production de richesse qui résulte des travaux des artisans consiste dans l'augmentation de la valeur vénale de leurs ouvrages." (Quesnay: "Dialogues sur le Commerce et sur les Travaux des artisans," pp. 188, 189.)

[2] "Ces spéculateurs si économes du travail des ouvriers qu'il faudrait qu'ils payassent." (J. N. Bidaut: "Du Monopole qui s'établit dans les arts industriels et le commerce." Paris, 1828, p. 13.) "The employer will be always on the stretch to economise time and labour." (Dugald Stewart: Works ed. by Sir W. Hamilton. Edinburgh, v. viii., 1855. Lecture on Polit. Econ., p. 318.) "Their (the capitalists') interest is that the productive powers of the labourers they employ should be the greatest possible. On promoting that power their attention is fixed and almost exclusively fixed." (R. Jones: l. c. Lecture III.)

the particular modes of producing relative surplus-value, to which examination we now proceed.

CHAPTER XIII.

CO-OPERATION.

CAPITALIST production only then really begins, as we have already seen, when each individual capital employs simultaneously a comparatively large number of labourers; when consequently the labour-process is carried on on an extensive scale and yields, relatively, large quantities of products. A greater number of labourers working together, at the same time, in one place (or, if you will, in the same field of labour), in order to produce the same sort of commodity under the mastership of one capitalist, constitutes, both historically and logically, the starting point of capitalist production. With regard to the mode of production itself, manufacture, in its strict meaning, is hardly to be distinguished, in its earliest stages, from the handicraft trades of the guilds, otherwise than by the greater number of workmen simultaneously employed by one and the same individual capital. The workshop of the mediæval master handicraftsman is simply enlarged.

At first, therefore, the difference is purely quantitative. We have shown that the surplus-value produced by a given capital is equal to the surplus-value produced by each workman multiplied by the number of workmen simultaneously employed. The number of workmen in itself does not affect, either the rate of surplus-value, or the degree of exploitation of labour-power. If a working day of 12 hours be embodied in six shillings, 1200 such days will be embodied in 1200 times 6 shillings. In one case 12×1200 working hours, and in the other 12 such hours are incorporated in the product. In the production of value a number of workmen rank merely as so many individual workmen; and it therefore makes no difference in the value produced whether the 1200 men work separately or united under the control of one capitalist.

Nevertheless, within certain limits, a modification takes place. The labour realised in value, is labour of an average social quality; is consequently the expenditure of average labour-power. Any average magnitude, however, is merely the average of a number of separate magnitudes all of one kind, but differing as to quantity. In every industry, each individual labourer, be he Peter or Paul, differs from the average labourer. These individual differences, or "errors" as they are called in mathematics, compensate one another, and vanish, whenever a certain minimum number of workmen are employed together. The celebrated sophist and syco-phant, Edmund Burke, goes so far as to make the following assertion, based on his practical observations as a farmer; viz., that "in so small a platoon" as that of five farm labour-ers, all individual differences in the labour vanish, and that consequently any given five adult farm labourers taken to-gether, will in the same time do as much work as any other five.[1] But, however that may be, it is clear, that the collec-tive working day of a large number of workmen simultane-ously employed, divided by the number of these workmen, gives one day of average social labour. For example, let the working day of each individual be 12 hours. Then the collect-ive working day of 12 men simultaneously employed, consists of 144 hours; and although the labour of each of the dozen men may deviate more or less from average social labour, each of them requiring a different time for the same operation, yet since the working day of each is one-twelfth of the collective working day of 144 hours, it possesses the qualities of an aver-age social working day. From the point of view, however, of the capitalist who employs these 12 men, the working day is that of the whole dozen. Each individual man's day is

[1] "Unquestionably, there is a good deal of difference between the value of one man's labour and that of another from strength, dexterity, and honest application. But I am quite sure, from my best observation, that any given five men will, in their total, afford a proportion of labour equal to any other five within the periods of life I have stated; that is, that among such five men there will be one possessing all the qualifications of a good workman, one bad, and the other three middling, and ap-proximating to the first and the last. So that in so small a platoon as that of even five, you will find the full complement of all that five men can earn." (E. Burke, l. c. p. 15, 16). Compare Quételet on the average individual.

an aliquot part of the collective working day, no matter whether the 12 men assist one another in their work, or whether the connexion between their operations consists merely in the fact, that the men are all working for the same capitalist. But if the 12 men are employed in six pairs, by as many different small masters, it will be quite a matter of chance, whether each of these masters produces the same value, and consequently whether he realises the general rate of surplus-value. Deviations would occur in individual cases. If one workman required considerably more time for the production of a commodity than is socially necessary, the duration of the necessary labour-time would, in his case, sensibly deviate from the labour-time socially necessary on an average; and consequently his labour would not count as average labour, nor his labour-power as average labour-power. It would either be not saleable at all, or only at something below the average value of labour-power. A fixed minimum of efficiency in all labour is therefore assumed, and we shall see, later on, that capitalist production provides the means of fixing this minimum. Nevertheless, this minimum deviates from the average, although on the other hand the capitalist has to pay the average value of labour-power. Of the six small masters, one would therefore squeeze out more than the average rate of surplus-value, another less. The inequalities would be compensated for the society at large, but not for the individual masters. Thus the laws of the production of value are only fully realised for the individual producer, when he produces as a capitalist, and employes a number of workmen together, whose labour, by its collective nature, is at once stamped as average social labour.[1]

Even without an alteration in the system of working, the simultaneous employment of a large number of labourers effects a revolution in the material conditions of the labour-process. The buildings in which they work, the store-houses

[1] Professor Roscher claims to have discovered that one needlewoman employed by Mrs. Roscher during two days, does more work than two needlewomen employed together during one day. The learned professor should not study the capitalist process of production in the nursery, nor under circumstances where the principal personage, the capitalist, is wanting.

for the raw material, the implements and utensils used simultaneously or in turns by the workmen; in short, a portion of the means of production, are now consumed in common. On the one hand, the exchange-value of these means of production is not increased; for the exchange value of a commodity is not raised by its use-value being consumed more thoroughly and to greater advantage. On the other hand, they are used in common, and therefore on a larger scale than before. A room where twenty weavers work at twenty looms must be larger than the room of a single weaver with two assistants. But it costs less labour to build one workshop for twenty persons than to build ten to accommodate two weavers each; thus the value of the means of production that are concentrated for use in common on a large scale does not increase in direct proportion to the expansion and to the increased useful effect of those means. When consumed in common, they give up a smaller part of their value to each single product; partly because the total value they part with is spread over a greater quantity of products, and partly because their value, though absolutely greater, is, having regard to their sphere of action in the process, relatively less than the value of isolated means of production. Owing to this, the value of a part of the constant capital falls, and in proportion to the magnitude of the fall, the total value of the commodity also falls. The effect is the same as if the means of production had cost less. The economy in their application is entirely owing to their being consumed in common by a large number of workmen. Moreover, this character of being necessary conditions of social labour, a character that distinguishes them from the dispersed and relatively more costly means of production of isolated, independent labourers, or small masters, is acquired even when the numerous workmen assembled together do not assist one another, but merely work side by side. A portion of the instruments of labour acquires this social character before the labour-process itself does so.

Economy in the use of the means of production has to be considered under two aspects. First, as cheapening commodities, and thereby bringing about a fall in the value of labour-

power. Secondly, as altering the ratio of the surplus-value to
the total capital advanced, *i.e.,* to the sum of the values of the
constant and variable capital. The latter aspect will not be
considered until we come to the third volume, to which, with
the object of treating them in their proper connexion, we also
relegate many other points that relate to the present question.
The march of our analysis compels this splitting up of the
subject matter, a splitting up that is quite in keeping with the
spirit of capitalist production. For since, in this mode of production, the workman finds the instruments of labour existing
independently of him as another man's property, economy in
their use appears, with regard to him, to be a distinct operation,
one that does not concern him, and which, therefore, has no
connexion with the methods by which his own personal productiveness is increased.

When numerous labourers work together side by side,
whether in one and the same process, or in different but connected processes, they are said to co-operate, or to work in co-
operation.[1]

Just as the offensive power of a squadron of cavalry, or the
defensive power of a regiment of infantry, is essentially different from the sum of the offensive or defensive powers of the
individual cavalry or infantry soldiers taken separately, so
the sum total of the mechanical forces exerted by isolated
workmen differs from the social force that is developed, when
many hands take part simultaneously in one and the same undivided operation, such as raising a heavy weight, turning a
winch, or removing an obstacle.[2] In such cases the effect of
the combined labour could either not be produced at all by
isolated individual labour, or it could only be produced by a
great expenditure of time, or on a very dwarfed scale. Not
only have we here an increase in the productive power of the

---

[1] "Concours de forces." (Destutt de Tracy, l. c., p. 78.)

[2] "There are numerous operations of so simple a kind as not to admit a division
into parts, which cannot be performed without the co-operation of many pairs of
hands. I would instance the lifting of a large tree on to a wain . . . everything, in short, which cannot be done unless a great many pairs of hands help each
other in the same undivided employment and at the same time" (E. G. Wakefield:
"A View of the Art of Colonisation." London: 1849, p. 168).

individual, by means of co-operation, but the creation of a new power, namely, the collective power of masses.[1]

Apart from the new power that arises from the fusion of many forces into one single force, mere social contact begets in most industries an emulation and a stimulation of the animal spirits that heighten the efficiency of each individual workman. Hence it is that a dozen persons working together will, in their collective working-day of 144 hours, produce far more than twelve isolated men each working 12 hours, or than one man who works twelve days in succession.[2] The reason of this is that a man is, if not as Aristotle contends, a political,[3] at all events a social animal.

Although a number of man may be occupied together at the same time on the same, or the same kind of work, yet the labour of each, as a part of the collective labour, may correspond to a distinct phase of the labour-process, through all whose phases, in consequence of co-operation, the subject of their labour passes with greater speed. For instance, if a dozen masons place themselves in a row, so as to pass stones from the foot of a ladder to its summit, each of them does the same thing; nevertheless, their separate acts form connected parts of one total operation; they are particular phases, which must be gone through by each stone; and the stones are thus carried up quicker by the 24 hands of the row of men than they could be if each man went separately up and down the

---

[1] "As one man cannot, and ten men must strain to lift a tun of weight, yet 100 men can do it only by the strength of a finger of each of them." (John Bellers: "Proposals for raising a College of Industry." London, 1696, p. 21.)

[2] "There is also" (when the same number of men are employed by one farmer on 300 acres, instead of by ten farmers with 30 acres a piece) "an advantage in the proportion of servants, which will not so easily be understood but by practical men; for it is natural to say, as 1 is to 4, so are 3: to 12; but this will not hold good in practice; for in harvest time and many other operations which require that kind of despatch by the throwing many hands together, the work is better and more expeditiously done; f. i. in harvest, 2 drivers, 2 loaders, 2 pitchers, 2 rakers, and the rest at the rick, or in the barn, will despatch double the work that the same number of hands would do if divided into different gangs on different farms." ("An Inquiry into the connection between the present Price of Provisions and the Size of Farms." By a Farmer. London, 1773, pp. 7, 8.)

[3] Strictly, Aristotle's definition is that man is by nature a town-citizen. This is quite as characteristic of ancient classical society as Franklin's definition of man, as a tool-making animal, is characteristic of Yankeedom.

ladder with his burden.[1] The object is carried over the same distance in a shorter time. Again, a combination of labour occurs whenever a building, for instance, is taken in hand on different sides simultaneously; although here also the co-operating masons are doing the same, or the same kind of work. The 12 masons, in their collective working day of 144 hours, make much more progress with the building than one mason could make working for 12 days, or 144 hours. The reason is, that a body of men working in concert has hands and eyes both before and behind, and is, to a certain degree, omni-present. The various parts of the work progress simultaneously.

In the above instances we have laid stress upon the point that the men do the same, or the same kind of work, because this, the most simple form of labour in common, plays a great part in co-operation, even in its most fully developed stage. If the work be complicated, then the mere number of the men who co-operate allows of the various operations being apportioned to different hands, and, consequently, of being carried on simultaneously. The time necessary for the completion of the whole work is thereby shortened.[2]

In many industries, there are critical periods, determined by the nature of the process, during which certain definite results must be obtained. For instance, if a flock of sheep has to be shorn, or a field of wheat to be cut and harvested, the quantity and quality of the product depends on the work being begun and ended within a certain time. In these cases, the time that ought to be taken by the process is prescribed, just as it

---

[1] On, doit encore remarquer que cette division partielle de travail peut se faire quand même les ouvriers sont occupés d'une même besogne. Des maçons par exemple, occupés à faire passer de mains en mains des briques à un échafaudage supérieur, font tous la même besogne, et pourtant il existe parmi eux une espèce de division de travail, qui consiste en ce que chacun d'eux fait passer la brique par un espace donné, et que tous ensemble la font parvenir beaucoup plus promptement á l'endroit marqué qu'ils ne le feraient si chacun d'eux portait sa brique séparément jusqu 'à l'échafaudage supérieur," (F. Skarbek: "Théorie des richesses sociales." Paris, 1829. t. I. pp. 97, 98.)

[2] "Est-il question d'exécuter un travail compliqué, plusieurs choses doivent être faites simultanément. L'un en fait une pendant que l'autre en fait une autre, et tous contribuent à l'effet qu'un seul homme n'aurait pu produire. L'un rame pendant que l'autre tient le gouvernail, et qu'un troisième jette le filet ou harponne le poisson, et la pêche a un succès impossible sans ce concours." (Destutt de Tracy, l. c.)

is in herring fishing. A single person cannot carve a working day of more than, say 12 hours, out of the natural day, but 100 men co-operating extend the working day to 1,200 hours. The shortness of the time allowed for the work is compensated for by the large mass of labour thrown upon the field of production at the decisive moment. The completion of the task within the proper time depends on the simultaneous application of numerous combined working days; the amount of useful effect depends on the number of labourers; this number, however, is always smaller than the number of isolated labourers required to do the same amount of work in the same period.[1] It is owing to the absence of this kind of co-operation that, in the western part of the United States, quantities of corn, and in those parts of East India where English rule has destroyed the old communities, quantities of cotton, are yearly wasted.[2]

On the one hand, co-operation allows of the work being carried on over an extended space; it is consequently imperatively called for in certain undertakings, such as draining, constructing dykes, irrigation works, and the making of canals, roads and railways. On the other hand, while extending the scale of production, it renders possible a relative contraction of the arena. This contraction of arena simultaneous with, and arising from, extension of scale, whereby a number of useless expenses are cut down, is owing to the conglomeration of labourers, to the aggregation of various processes, and to the concentration of the means of production.[3]

---

[1] "The doing of it (agricultural work) at the critical juncture is of so much the greater consequence." ("An Inquiry into the Connection between the Present Price," &c., p. 9.) "In agriculture, there is no more important factor than that of time." (Liebig: "Ueber Theorie und Praxis in der Landwirthschaft." 1856. p. 23.)

[2] "The next evil is one which one would scarcely expect to find in a country which exports more labour than any other in the world, with the exception, perhaps, of China and England—the impossibility of procuring a sufficient number of hands to clean the cotton. The consequence of this is that large quantities of the crop are left unpicked, while another portion is gathered from the ground when it has fallen, and is of course discoloured and partially rotted, so that for want of labour at the proper season the cultivator is actually forced to submit to the loss of a large part of that crop for which England is so anxiously looking." (Bengal Hurkaru. Bi-Monthly Overland Summary of News, 22nd July, 1861.)

[3] In the progress of culture "all, and perhaps more than all, the capital and labour which once loosely occupied 500 acres, are now concentrated for the more complete tillage of 100." Although "relatively to the amount of capital and labour employed,

The combined working day produces, relatively to an equal sum of isolated working-days, a greater quantity of use-values, and, consequently, diminishes the labour-time necessary for the production of a given useful effect. Whether the combined working-day, in a given case, acquires this increased productive power, because it heightens the mechanical force of labour, or extends its sphere of action over a greater space, or contracts the field of production relatively to the scale of production, or at the critical moment sets large masses of labour to work, or excites emulation between individuals and raises their animal spirits, or impresses on the similar operations carried on by a number of men the stamp of continuity and many-sidedness, or performs simultaneously different operations, or economises the means of production by use in common, or lends to individual labour the character of average social labour—which ever of these be the cause of the increase, the special productive power of the combined working day is, under all circumstances, the social productive power of labour, or the productive power of social labour. This power is due to co-operation itself. When the labourer co-operates systematically with others, he strips off the fetters of his individuality, and develops the capabilities of his species.[1]

As a general rule, labourers cannot co-operate without being brought together: their assemblage in one place is a necessary condition of their co-operation. Hence wage labourers cannot co-operate, unless they are employed simultaneously by the same capital, the same capitalist, and unless therefore their labour-powers are bought simultaneously by him. The total value of these labour-powers, or the amount of the wages of these labourers for a day, or a week, as the case may be, must be ready in the pocket of the capitalist, before the workmen are assembled for the process of production. The payment of

space is concentrated, it is an enlarged sphere of production, as compared to the sphere of production formerly occupied or worked upon by one single independent agent of production." (R. Jones: "An Essay on the Distribution of Wealth," part I. On Rent. London, 1831, p. 191.)

[1] "La forza di ciascuno uomo è minima, ma la riünione delle minime forze forma una forza totale maggiore anche della somma delle forze medesime fino a che le forze per essere riunite possono diminuere il tempo ed accrescere lo spazio della loro azione." (G. R. Carli, Note to P. Verri, l. c. t., xv. p. 196.)

300 workmen at once, though only for one day, requires ⅼ greater outlay of capital, than does the payment of a smaller number of men, week by week, during a whole year. Hence the number of the labourers that co-operate, or the scale of co-operation, depends, in the first instance, on the amount of capital that the individual capitalist can spare for the purchase of labour-power; in other words, on the extent to which a single capitalist has command over the means of subsistence of a number of labourers.

And as with the variable, so it is with the constant capital. For example, the outlay on raw material is 30 times as great, for the capitalist who employs 300 men, as it is for each of the 30 capitalists who employ 10 men. The value and quantity of the instruments of labour used in common do not, it is true, increase at the same rate as the number of workmen, but they do increase very considerably. Hence, concentration of large masses of the means of production in the hands of individual capitalists, is a material condition for the co-operation of wage-labourers, and the extent of the co-operation or the scale of production, depends on the extent of this concentration.

We saw in a former chapter, that a certain minimum amount of capital was necessary, in order that the number of labourers simultaneously employed, and, consequently, the amount of surplus-value produced, might suffice to liberate the employer himself from manual labour, to convert him from a small master into a capitalist, and thus formally to establish capitalist production. We now see that a certain minimum amount is a necessary condition for the conversion of numerous isolated and independent processes into one combined social process.

We also saw that at first, the subjection of labour to capital was only a formal result of the fact, that the labourer, instead of working for himself, works for and consequently under the capitalist. By the co-operation of numerous wage-labourers, the sway of capital developes into a requisite for carrying on the labour-process itself, into a real requisite of production. That a capitalist should command on the field of production, is now as indispensable as that a general should command on the field of battle.

All combined labour on a large scale requires, more or less, a directing authority, in order to secure the harmonious working of the individual activities, and to perform the general functions that have their origin in the action of the combined organism, as distinguished from the action of its separate organs. A single violin player is his own conductor; an orchestra requires a separate one. The work of directing, superintending, and adjusting, becomes one of the functions of capital, from the moment that the labour under the control of capital, becomes co-operative. Once a function of capital, it acquires special characteristics.

The directing motive, the end and aim of capitalist production, is to extract the greatest possible amount of surplus-value,[1] and consequently to exploit labour-power to the greatest possible extent. As the number of the co-operating labourers increases, so too does their resistance to the domination of capital, and with it, the necessity for capital to overcome this resistance by counter-pressure. The control exercised by the capitalist is not only a special function, due to the nature of the social labour-process, and peculiar to that process, but it is, at the same time, a function of the exploitation of a social labour-process, and is consequently rooted in the unavoidable antagonism between the exploiter and the living and labouring raw material he exploits.

Again, in proportion to the increasing mass of the means of production, now no longer the property of the labourer, but of the capitalist, the necessity increases for some effective control over the proper application of those means.[2] More-

---

[1] "Profits . . . is the sole end of trade." (J. Vanderlint, l. c., p. 11.)

[2] That Philistine paper, the *Spectator*, states that after the introduction of a sort of partnership between capitalist and workmen in the "Wirework Company of Manchester," "the first result was a sudden decrease in waste, the men not seeing why they should waste their own property any more than any other master's, and waste is, perhaps, next to bad debts, the greatest source of manufacturing loss." The same paper finds that the main defect in the Rochdale co-operative experiments is this: "They showed that associations of workmen could manage shops, mills, and almost all forms of industry with success, and they immediately improved the condition of the men; but then they did not leave a clear place for masters." Quelle horreur!

over, the co-operation of wage labourers is entirely brought about by the capital that employs them. Their union into one single productive body and the establishment of a connexion between their individual functions, are matters foreign and external to them, are not their own act, but the act of the capital that brings and keeps them together. Hence the connexion existing between their various labours appears to them, ideally, in the shape of a preconceived plan of the capitalist, and practically in the shape of the authority of the same capitalist, in the shape of the powerful will of another, who subjects their activity to his aims. If, then, the control of the capitalist is in substance twofold by reason of the twofold nature of the process of production itself,—which, on the one hand, is a social process for producing use-values, on the other, a process for creating surplus-value—in form that control is despotic. As co-operation extends its scale, this despotism takes forms peculiar to itself. Just as at first the capitalist is relieved from actual labour so soon as his capital has reached that minimum amount with which capitalist production, as such begins, so now, he hands over the work of direct and constant supervision of the individual workmen, and groups of workmen, to a special kind of wage labourer. An industrial army of workmen, under the command of a capitalist, requires, like a real army, officers (managers), and sergeants (foremen, overlookers), who, while the work is being done, command in the name of the capitalist. The work of supervision becomes their established and exclusive function. When comparing the mode of production of isolated peasants and artizans with production by slave labour the political economist counts this labour of superintendence among the *faux frais* of production.[1] But, when considering the capitalist mode of production, he, on the contrary, treats the work of control made necessary by the co-operative character of the labour process as identical with the different work of control, necessitated by the capitalist

---

[1] Professor Cairns, after stating that the superintendence of labour is a leading feature of production by slaves in the Southern States of North America, continues: "The peasant proprietor (of the North), appropriating the whole produce of his toil, needs no other stimulus to exertion. Superintendence is here completely dispensed with." (Cairnes, l. c., pp. 48, 49.)

character of that process and the antagonism of interests between capitalist and labourer.[1] It is not because he is a leader of industry that a man is a capitalist; on the contrary, he is a leader of industry because he is a capitalist. The leadership of industry is an attribute of capital, just as in feudal times the functions of general and judge were attributes of landed property.[2]

The labourer is the owner of his labour-power until he has done bargaining for its sale with the capitalist; and he can sell no more than what he has—*i.e.,* his individual, isolated labour-power. This state of things is in no way altered by the fact that the capitalist, instead of buying the labour-power of one man, buys that of 100, and enters into separate contracts with 100 unconnected men instead of with one. He is at liberty to set the 100 men to work, without letting them co-operate. He pays them the value of 100 independent labour-powers, but he does not pay for the combined labour-power of the hundred. Being independent of each other, the labourers are isolated persons, who enter into relations with the capitalist, but not with one another. This co-operation begins only with the labour process, but they have then ceased to belong to themselves. On entering that process, they become incorporated with capital. As co-operators, as members of a working organism, they are but special modes of existence of capital. Hence, the productive power developed by the labourer when working in co-operation, is the productive power of capital. This power is developed gratuitously, whenever the workmen are placed under given conditions, and it is capital that places them under such conditions. Because this power costs capital nothing, and because, on the other hand, the labourer himself does not develop it before his labour belongs to capital, it appears as a power with which capital

[1] Sir James Steuart, a writer altogether remarkable for his quick eye for the characteristic social distinctions between different modes of production, says: "Why do large undertakings in the manufacturing way ruin private industry, but by coming nearer to the simplicity of slaves?" ("Prin. of Pol. Econ.," London, 1767, v. I., p. 167, 168.)

[2] Auguste Comte and his school might therefore have shown that feudal lords are an eternal necessity in the same way that they have done in the case of the lords of capital.

368 Capitalist Production.

is endowed by Nature—a productive power that is immanent in capital.

The colossal effects of simple co-operation are to be seen in the gigantic structures of the ancient Asiatics, Egyptians, Etruscans, &c. "It has happened in times past that these Oriental States, after supplying the expenses of their civil and military establishments, have found themselves in possession of a surplus which they could apply to works of magnificence or utility, and in the construction of these their command over the hands and arms of almost the entire non-agricultural population has produced stupendous monuments which still indicate their power. The teeming valley of the Nile . . . produced food for a swarming non-agricultural population, and this food, belonging to the monarch and the priesthood, afforded the means of erecting the mighty monuments which filled the land. . . . In moving the colossal statues and vast masses of which the transport creates wonder, human labour almost alone, was prodigally used, . . . The number of the labourers and the concentration of their efforts sufficed. We see mighty coral reefs rising from the depths of the ocean into islands and firm land, yet each individual depositor is puny, weak, and contemptible. The non-agricultural labourers of an Asiatic monarchy have little but their individual bodily exertions to bring to the task, but their number is their strength, and the power of directing these masses gave rise to the palaces and temples, the pyramids, and the armies of gigantic statues of which the remains astonish and perplex us. It is that confinement of the revenues which feed them, to one or a few hands, which makes such undertakings possible."[1] This power of Asiatic and Egyptian kings, Etruscan theocrats, &c., has in modern society been transferred to the capitalist, whether he be an isolated, or as in joint stock companies, a collective capitalist.

Co-operation, such as we find it at the dawn of human development, among races who live by the chase,[2] or say, in

---

[1] R. Jones. "Text-book of Lectures," &c., pp. 77, 78. The ancient Assyrian, Egyptian, and other collections in London, and in other European capitals, make us eye-witnesses of the modes of carrying on that co-operative labour.

[2] Linguet is probably right, when in his "Theorie des Lois Civiles," he declares

the agriculture of Indian communities, is based, on the one hand, on ownership in common of the means of production, and on the other hand, on the fact, that in those cases, each individual has no more torn himself off from the navel-string of his tribe or community, than each bee has freed itself from connexion with the hive. Such co-operation is distinguished from capitalistic co-operation by both of the above characteristics. The sporadic application of co-operation on a large scale in ancient times, in the middle ages, and in modern colonies, reposes on relations of dominion and servitude, principally on slavery. The capitalistic form, on the contrary, presupposes from first to last, the free wage labourer, who sells his labour-power to capital. Historically, however, this form is developed in opposition to peasant agriculture and to the carrying on of independent handicrafts whether in guilds or not.[1] From the standpoint of these, capitalistic co-operation does not manifest itself as a particular historical form of co-operation, but co-operation itself appears to be a historical form peculiar to, and specifically distinguishing, the capitalist process of production.

Just as the social productive power of labour that is developed by co-operation, appears to be the productive power of capital, so co-operation itself, contrasted with the process of production carried on by isolated independent labourers, or even by small employers, appears to be a specific form of the capitalist process of production. It is the first change experienced by the actual labour-process, when subjected to capital. This change takes place spontaneously. The simultaneous employment of a large number of wage-labourers, in one and the same process, which is a necessary condition of this change, also forms the starting point of capitalist production. This point coincides with the birth of capital itself. If then, on the

hunting to be the first form of co-operation, and man-hunting (war) one of the earliest forms of hunting.

[1] Peasant agriculture on a small scale, and the carrying on of independent handicrafts, which together form the basis of the feudal mode of production, and after the dissolution of that system, continue side by side with the capitalist mode, also form the economic foundation of the classical communities at their best, after the primitive form of ownership of land in common had disappeared, and before slavery had seized on production in earnest.

one hand, the capitalist mode of production presents itself to us historically, as a necessary condition to the transformation of the labour-process into a social process, so, on the other hand, this social form of the labour-process presents itself, as a method employed by capital for the more profitable exploitation of labour, by increasing that labour's productiveness.

In the elementary form, under which we have hitherto viewed it, co-operation is a necessary concomitant of all production on a large scale, but it does not, in itself, represent a fixed form characteristic of a particular epoch in the development of the capitalist mode of production. At the most it appears to do so, and that only approximately, in the handicraft-like beginnings of manufacture,[1] and in that kind of agriculture on a large scale, which corresponds to the epoch of manufacture, and is distinguished from peasant agriculture, mainly by the number of the labourers simultaneously employed, and by the mass of the means of production concentrated for their use. Simple co-operation is always the prevailing form, in those branches of production in which capital operates on a large scale, and division of labour and machinery play but a subordinate part.

Co-operation ever constitutes the fundamental form of the capitalist mode of production; nevertheless, the elementary form of co-operation continues to subsist as a particular form of capitalist production side by side with the more developed forms of that mode of production.

CHAPTER XIV.

DIVISION OF LABOUR AND MANUFACTURE.

SECTION 1.—TWOFOLD ORIGIN OF MANUFACTURE.

THAT co-operation which is based on division of labour, assumes its typical form in the manufacture, and is the prevalent

[1] "Whether the united skill, industry, and emulation of many together on the same work be not the way to advance it? And whether it had been otherwise possible for England, to have carried on her Woollen Manufacture to so great a perfection?" (Berkeley. "The Querist." London, 1750, p. 56, par. 521.)

characteristic form of the capitalist process of production throughout the manufacturing period properly so called. That period, roughly speaking, extends from the middle of the 16th to the last third of the 18th century.

Manufacture takes its rise in two ways:—

(1) By the assemblage, in one workshop under the control of a single capitalist, of labourers belonging to various independent handicrafts, but through whose hands a given article must pass on its way to completion. A carriage, for example, was formerly the product of the labour of a great number of independent artificers, such as wheelwrights, harness-makers, tailors, locksmiths, upholsterers, turners, fringe-makers, glaziers, painters, polishers, gilders, &c. In the manufacture of carriages, however, all these different artificers are assembled in one building, where they work into one another's hands. It is true that a carriage cannot be gilt before it has been made. But if a number of carriages are being made simultaneously, some may be in the hands of the gilders while others are going through an earlier process. So far, we are still in the domain of simple co-operation, which finds its materials ready to hand in the shape of men and things. But very soon an important change takes place. The tailor, the locksmith, and the other artificers, being now exclusively occupied in carriage-making, each gradually loses, through want of practice, the ability to carry on, to its full extent, his old handicraft. But, on the other hand, his activity now confined in one groove, assumes the form best adapted to the narrowed sphere of action. At first, carriage manufacture is a combination of various independent handicrafts. By degrees, it becomes the splitting up of carriage making into its various detail processes, each of which crystallizes into the exclusive function of a particular workman, the manufacture, as a whole, being carried on by the men in conjunction. In the same way, cloth manufacture, as also a whole series of other manufactures, arose by combining different handicrafts together under the control of a single capitalist.[1]

---

[1] To give a more modern instance: The silk spinning and weaving of Lyons and Nimes "est toute patriarcale; elle emploie beaucoup de femmes et d'enfants, mais

(2.) Manufacture also arises in a way exactly the reverse of this—namely, by one capitalist employing simultaneously in one workshop a number of artificers, who all do the same, or the same kind of work, such as making paper, type, or needles. This is co-operation in its most elementary form. Each of these artificers (with the help, perhaps, of one or two apprentices), makes the entire commodity, and he consequently performs in succession all the operations necessary for its production. He still works in his old handicraft-like way. But very soon external circumstances cause a different use to be made of the concentration of the workmen on one spot, and of the simultaneousness of their work. An increased quantity of the article has perhaps to be delivered within a given time. The work is therefore re-distributed. Instead of each man being allowed to perform all the various operations in succession, these operations are changed into disconnected, isolated ones, carried on side by side; each is assigned to a different artificer, and the whole of them together are performed simultaneously by the co-operating workmen. This accidental repartition gets repeated, developes advantages of its own, and gradually ossifies into a systematic division of labour. The commodity, from being the individual product of an independent artificer, becomes the social product of a union of artificers, each of whom performs one, and only one, of the constituent partial operations. The same operations which, in the case of a papermaker belonging to a German Guild, merged one into the other as the successive acts of one artificer, became in the Dutch paper manufacture so many partial operations carried on side by side by numerous co-operating labourers. The needlemaker of the Nuremberg Guild was the corner-

sans les épuiser ni les corrompre; elle les laisse dans leur belles vallées de la Drôme, du Var, de l'Isère, de Vaucluse, pour y élever des vers et dévider leurs cocons; jamais elle n'entre dans une véritable fabrique. Pour être aussi bien observé . . . le principe de la division du travail s'y revêt d'un caractère spécial. Il y a bien des dévideuses, des moulineurs, des teinturiers, des encolleurs, puis des tisserands; mais ils ne sont pas réunis dans un même établissement, ne dépendent pas d'un même maître; tous ils sont indépendants." (A. Blanqui: "Cours d'Econ. Industrielle." Recueilli par A. Blaise. Paris, 1838-39, pp. 79). Since Blanqui wrote this, the various independent labourers have, to some extent, been united in factories. [And since Marx wrote the above, the powerloom has invaded these factories, and is now —1886—rapidly superseding the handloom. ED.]

stone on which the English needle manufacture was raised. But while in Nuremberg that single artificer performed a series of perhaps 20 operations one after another, in England it was not long before there were 20 needlemakers side by side, each performing one alone of those 20 operations; and in consequence of further experience, each of those 20 operations was again split up, isolated, and made the exclusive function of a separate workman.

The mode in which manufacture arises, its growth out of handicrafts, is therefore twofold. On the one hand, it arises from the union of various independent handicrafts, which become stripped of their independence and specialised to such an extent as to be reduced to mere supplementary partial processes in the production of one particular commodity. On the other hand, it arises from the co-operation of artificers of one handicraft; it splits up that particular handicraft into its various detail operations, isolating, and making these operations independent of one another up to the point where each becomes the exclusive function of a particular labourer. On the one hand, therefore, manufacture either introduces division of labour into a process of production, or further developes that division; on the other hand, it unites together handicrafts that were formerly separate. But whatever may have been its particular starting point, its final form is invariably the same—a productive mechanism whose parts are human beings.

For a proper understanding of the division of labour in manufacture, it is essential that the following points be firmly grasped. First, the decomposition of a process of production into its various successive steps coincides, here, strictly with the resolution of a handicraft into its successive manual operations. Whether complex or simple, each operation has to be done by hand, retains the character of a handicraft, and is therefore dependent on the strength, skill, quickness, and sureness, of the individual workman in handling his tools. The handicraft continues to be the basis. This narrow technical basis excludes a really scientific analysis of any definite process of industrial production, since it is still a condition that each detail process gone through by the product must be capable of being done by hand and of forming, in its way, a separate handicraft. It is just because handicraft skill continues, in this way, to be the foundation of the process of production, that each workman becomes exclusively assigned to a partial function, and that for the rest of his life, his labour-power is turned into the organ of this detail function.

Secondly, this division of labour is a particular sort of co-operation, and many of its disadvantages spring from the general character of co-operation, and not from this particular form of it.

SECTION 2.—THE DETAIL LABOURER AND HIS IMPLEMENTS.

If we now go more into detail, it is, in the first place, clear that a labourer who all his life performs one and the same simple operation, converts his whole body into the automatic, specialised implement of that operation. Consequently, he takes less time in doing it, than the artificer who performs a whole series of operations in succession. But the collective labourer, who constitutes the living mechanism of manufacture, is made up solely of such specialised detail labourers. Hence, in comparison with the independent handicraft, more is produced in a given time, or the productive power of labour is increased.[1] Moreover, when once this fractional work is established as the exclusive function of one person, the methods it employs become perfected. The workman's continued repetition of the same simple act, and the concentration of his attention on it, teach him by experience how to attain the desired effect with the minimum of exertion. But since there are always several generations of labourers living at one time, and working together at the manufacture of a given article, the technical skill, the tricks of the trade thus acquired, become established, and are accumulated and handed down.[2] Manufacture, in fact, produces the skill of the detail labourer,

---

[1] "The more any manufacture of much variety shall be distributed and assigned to different artists, the same must needs be better done and with greater expedition, with less loss of time and labour." ("The Advantages of the East India Trade," Lond., 1720. p. 71.)

[2] "Easy labour is transmitted skill." (Th. Hodgskin, l. c. p. 125.)

by reproducing, and systematically driving to an extreme within the workshop, the naturally developed differentiation of trades, which it found ready to hand in society at large. On the other hand, the conversion of fractional work into the life-calling of one man, corresponds to the tendency shown by earlier societies, to make trades hereditary; either to petrify them into castes, or whenever definite historical conditions beget in the individual a tendency to vary in a manner incompatible with the nature of castes, to ossify them into guilds. Castes and guilds arise from the action of the same natural law, that regulates the differentiation of plants and animals into species and varieties, except that, when a certain degree of development has been reached, the heredity of castes and the exclusiveness of guilds are ordained as a law of society.[1] "The muslins of Dakka in fineness, the calicoes and other piece goods of Coromandel in brilliant and durable colours, have never been surpassed. Yet they are produced without capital, machinery, division of labour, or any of those means which give such facilities to the manufacturing interest of Europe. The weaver is merely a detached individual, working a web when ordered of a customer, and with a loom of the rudest construction, consisting sometimes of a few branches or bars of wood, put roughly together. There is even no expedient for rolling up the warp; the loom must therefore be kept stretched to its full length, and becomes so inconveniently large, that it cannot be contained within the hut of the manufacturer, who is therefore compelled to ply his trade in the open air, where it is interrupted by every vicissitude of the weather."[2] It is only the special skill accumulated from generation to genera-

---

[1] "The arts also have . . . in Egypt reached the requisite degree of perfection. For it is the only country where artificers may not in any way meddle with the affairs of another class of citizens, but must follow that calling alone which by law is hereditary in their clan . . . In other countries it is found that tradesmen divide their attention between too many objects. At one time they try agriculture, at another they take to commerce, at another they busy themselves with two or three occupations at once. In free countries, they mostly frequent the assemblies of the people. . . . In Egypt, on the contrary, every artificer is severely punished if he meddles with affairs of State, or carries on several trades at once. Thus there is nothing to disturb their application to their calling. . . . Moreover, since they inherit from their forefathers numerous rules, they are eager to discover fresh advantages." (Diodorus Siculus: Bibl. Hist. 1. 1. c. 74.)

[2] Historical and descriptive account of Brit. India, &c., by Hugh Murray and

tion, and transmitted from father to son, that gives to the Hindoo, as it does to the spider, this proficiency. And yet the work of such a Hindoo weaver is very complicated, compared with that of a manufacturing labourer.

An artificer, who performs one after another the various fractional operations in the production of a finished article, must at one time change his place, at another his tools. The transition from one operation to another interrupts the flow of his labour, and creates, so to say, gaps in his working day. These gaps close up so soon as he is tied to one and the same operation all day long; they vanish in proportion as the changes in his work diminish. The resulting increased productive power is owing either to an increased expenditure of labour-power in a given time—*i.e.*, to increased intensity of labour—or to a decrease in the amount of labour-power unproductively consumed. The extra expenditure of power, demanded by every transition from rest to motion, is made up for by prolonging the duration of the normal velocity when once acquired. On the other hand, constant labour of one uniform kind disturbs the intensity and flow of a man's animal spirits, which find recreation and delight in mere change of activity.

The productiveness of labour depends not only on the proficiency of the workman, but on the perfection of his tools. Tools of the same kind, such as knives, drills, gimlets, hammers, &c. may be employed in different processes; and the same tool may serve various purposes in a single process. But so soon as the different operations of a labour-process are disconnected the one from the other, and each fractional operation acquires in the hands of the detail labourer a suitable and peculiar form, alterations become necessary in the implements that previously served more than one purpose. The direction taken by this change is determined by the difficulties experienced in consequence of the unchanged form of the implement. Manufacture is characterized by the differentiation of

James Wilson, &c., Edinburgh 1832. v. II. p. 449. The Indian loom is upright, *i. e.*, the warp is stretched vertically.

the instruments of labour—a differentiation whereby implements of a given sort acquire fixed shapes, adapted to each particular application, and by the specialisation of those instruments, giving to each special instrument its full play only in the hands of a specific detail labourer. In Birmingham alone 500 varieties of hammers are produced, and not only is each adapted to one particular process, but several varieties often serve exclusively for the different operations in one and the same process. The manufacturing period simplifies, improves, and multiplies the implements of labour, by adapting them to the exclusively special functions of each detail labourer.[1] It thus creates at the same time one of the material conditions for the existence of machinery, which consists of a combination of simple instruments.

The detail labourer and his implements are the simplest elements of manufacture. Let us now turn to its aspect as a whole.

SECTION 3.—THE TWO FUNDAMENTAL FORMS OF MANUFACTURE: HETEROGENEOUS MANUFACTURE, SERIAL MANUFACTURE.

The organisation of manufacture has two fundamental forms, which, in spite of occasional blending, are essentially different in kind, and, moreover, play very distinct parts in the subsequent transformation of manufacture into modern industry carried on by machinery. This double character arises from the nature of the article produced. This article either results from the mere mechanical fitting together of partial products made independently, or owes its completed shape to a series of connected processes and manipulations.

A locomotive, for instance, consists of more than 5000 independent parts. It cannot, however, serve as an example of

---

[1] Darwin in his epoch-making work on the origin of species, remarks, with reference to the natural organs of plants and animals, "So long as one and the same organ has different kinds of work to perform, a ground for its changeability may possibly be found in this, that natural selection preserves or suppresses each small variation of form less carefully than if that organ were destined for one special purpose alone. Thus, knives that are adapted to cut all sorts of things, may, on the whole, be of one shape; but an implement destined to be used exclusively in one way must have a different shape for every different use."

the first kind of genuine manufacture, for it is a structure produced by modern mechanical industry. But a watch can; and William Petty used it to illustrate the division of labour in manufacture. Formerly the individual work of a Nuremberg artificer, the watch has been transformed into the social product of an immense number of detail labourers, such as mainspring makers, dial makers, spiral spring makers, jewelled hole makers, ruby lever makers, hand makers, case makers, screw makers, gilders, with numerous sub-divisions, such as wheel makers (brass and steel separate), pin makers, movement makers, acheveur de pignon (fixes the wheels on the axles, polishes the facets, &c.), pivot makers, planteur de finissage (puts the wheels and springs in the works), finisseur de barillet (cuts teeth in the wheels, makes the holes of the right size, &c.), escapement makers, cylinder makers for cylinder escapement, escapement wheel makers, balance wheel makers, raquette makers (apparatus for regulating the watch), the planteur d'échappement (escapement maker proper); then the repasseur de barrillet (finishes the box for the spring, &c.), steel polishers, wheel polishers, screw polishers, figure painters, dial enamellers (melt the enamel on the copper), fabricant de pendants (makes the ring by which the case is hung), finisseur de charnière (puts the brass hinge in the cover, &c.) faiseur de secret (puts in the springs that open the case), graveur, ciseleur, polisseur de boîte, &c., &c., and last of all the repasseur, who fits together the whole watch and hands it over in a going state. Only a few parts of the watch pass through several hands; and all these membra disjecta come together for the first time in the hand that binds them into one mechanical whole. This external relation between the finished product, and its various and diverse elements makes it, as well in this case as in the case of all similar finished articles, a matter of chance whether the detail labourers are brought together in one workshop or not. The detail operations may further be carried on like so many independent handicrafts, as they are in the Cantons of Vaud and Neufchâtel; while in Geneva there exist large watch manufactories where the detail labourers directly co-operate under the control of a single capitalist.

And even in the latter case the dial, the springs, and the case, are seldom made in the factory itself. To carry on the trade as a manufacture, with concentration of workmen, is, in the watch trade, profitable only under exceptional conditions, because competition is greater between the labourers who desire to work at home, and because the splitting up of the work into a number of heterogeneous processes, permits but little use of the instruments of labour in common, and the capitalist, by scattering the work, saves the outlay on workshops, &c.[1] Nevertheless the position of this detail labourer who, though he works at home, does so for a capitalist (manufacturer, établisseur), is very different from that of the independent artificer, who works for his own customers.[2]

The second kind of manufacture, its perfected form, produces articles that go through connected phases of development, through a series of processes step by step, like the wire in the manufacture of needles, which passes through the hands of 72 and sometimes even 92 different detail workmen.

In so far as such a manufacture, when first started, combines scattered handicrafts, it lessens the space by which the various phases of production are separated from each other. The time taken in passing from one stage to another is shortened, so is the labour that effectuates this passage.[3] In comparison with a handicraft, productive power is gained, and

---

[1] In the year 1854 Geneva produced 80,000 watches, which is not one-fifth of the production in the Canton of Neufchâtel. La Chaux-de-Fond alone, which we may look upon as a huge watch manufactory, produces yearly twice as many as Geneva. From 1850-61 Geneva produced 750,000 watches. See "Report from Geneva on the Watch Trade" in "Reports by H. M.'s Secretaries of Embassy and Legation on the Manufactures, Commerce, &c., No. 6, 1863." The want of connexion alone, between the processes into which the production of articles that merely consist of parts fitted together is split up, makes it very difficult to convert such a manufacture into a branch of modern industry carried on by machinery; but in the case of a watch there are two other impediments in addition, the minuteness and delicacy of its parts, and its character as an article of luxury. Hence their variety, which is such, that in the best London houses scarcely a dozen watches are made alike in the course of a year. The watch manufactory of Messrs. Vacheron & Constantin, in which machinery has been employed with success, produces at the most three or four different varieties of size and form.

[2] In watchmaking, that classical example of heterogeneous manufacture, we may study with great accuracy the above mentioned differentiation and specialisation of the instruments of labour caused by the sub-division of handicrafts.

[3] "In so close a cohabitation of the people, the carriage must needs be less." ("The Advantages of the East India Trade," p. 106.)

this gain is owing to the general co-operative character of manufacture. On the other hand, division of labour, which is the distinguishing principle of manufacture, requires the isolation of the various stages of production and their independence of each other. The establishment and maintenance of a connexion between the isolated functions necessitates the incessant transport of the article from one hand to another, and from one process to another. From the standpoint of modern mechanical industry, this necessity stands forth as a characteristic and costly disadvantage, and cne that is immanent in the principle of manufacture.[1]

If we confine our attention to some particular lot of raw materials, of rags, for instance, in paper manufacture, or of wire in needle manufacture, we perceive that it passes in succession through a series of stages in the hands of the various detail workmen until completion. On the other hand, if we look at the workshop as a whole, we see the raw material in all the stages of its production at the same time. The collective labourer, with one set of his many hands armed with one kind of tools, draws the wire with another set, armed with different tools, he, at the same time, straightens it, with another, he cuts it, with another forms it and so on. The different detail processes which were successive in time, have become simultaneous, go on side by side in space. Hence, production of greater quantum of finished commodities in a given time.[2] This simultaneity, it is true, is due to the general co-operative form of the process as a whole; but Manufacture not only finds the conditions for co-operation really to hand, it also, to some extent, creates them by the sub-division of handicraft labour. On the other hand, it

---

[1] "The isolation of the different stages of manufacture, consequent upon the employment of manual labour, adds immensely to the cost of production, the loss mainly arising from the mere removals from one process to another." ("The Industry of Nations." Lond., 1855. Part II., p. 200.)

[2] "It (the division of labour) produces also an economy of time by separating the work into its different branches, all of which may be carried on into execution at the same moment. . . . By carrying on all the different processes at once, which an individual must have executed separately, it becomes possible to produce a multitude of pins completely finished in the same time as a single pin might have been either cut or pointed." (Dugald Stewart, l. c., p. 319.)

accomplishes this social organisation of the labour-process only by riveting each labourer to a single fractional detail.

Since the fractional product of each detail labourer is, at the same time, only a particular stage in the development of one and the same finished article, each labourer, or each group of labourers, prepares the raw material for another labourer or group. The result of the labour of the one is the starting point for the labour of the other. The one workman therefore gives occupation directly to the other. The labour-time necessary in each partial process, for attaining the desired effect, is learnt by experience; and the mechanism of Manufacture, as a whole, is based on the assumption that a given result will be obtained in a given time. It is only on this assumption that the various supplementary labour-processes can proceed uninterruptedly, simultaneously, and side by side. It is clear that this direct dependence of the operations, and therefore of the labourers, on each other, compels each one of them to spend on his work no more than the necessary time, and thus a continuity, uniformity, regularity, order,[1] and even intensity of labour, of quite a different kind, is begotten than is to be found in an independent handicraft or even in simple co-operation. The rule that the labour-time expended on a commodity should not exceed that which is socially necessary for its production, appears, in the production of commodities generally, to be established by the mere effect of competition; since, to express ourselves superficially, each single producer is obliged to sell his commodity at its market price. In Manufacture, on the contrary, the turning out of a given quantum of product in a given time is a technical law of the process of production itself.[2]

Different operations take, however, unequal periods, and yield therefore, in equal times unequal quantities of fractional products. If, therefore the same labourer has, day after day,

---

[1] "The more variety of artists to every manufacture . . . the greater the order and regularity of every work, the same must needs be done in less time, the labour must be less." ("The Advantages," &c., p. 68.)

[2] Nevertheless, the manufacturing system, in many branches of industry, attains this result but very imperfectly, because it knows not how to control with certainty the general chemical and physical conditions of the process of production.

to perform the same operation, there must be a different number of labourers for each operation; for instance, in type manufacture, there are four founders and two breakers to one rubber: the founder casts 2,000 type an hour, the breaker breaks up 4,000, and the rubber polishes 8,000. Here we have again the principle of co-operation in its simplest form, the simultaneous employment of many doing the same thing; only now, this principle is the expression of an organic relation. The division of labour, as carried out in the Manufacture, not only simplifies and multiplies the qualitatively different parts of the social collective labourer, but also creates a fixed mathematical relation or ratio which regulates the quantitative extent of those parts—*i.e.*, the relative number of labourers, or the relative size of the group of labourers, for each detail operation. It developes, along with the qualitative sub-division of the social labour process, a quantitative rule and proportionality for that process.

When once the most fitting proportion has been experimentally established for the numbers of the detail labourers in the various groups when producing on a given scale, that scale can be extended only by employing a multiple of each particular group.[1] There is this to boot, that the same individual can do certain kinds of work just as well on a large as on a small scale; for instance, the labour of superintendence, the carriage of the fractional product from one stage to the next, &c. The isolation of such functions, their allotment to a particular labourer, does not become advantageous till after an increase in the number of labourers employed; but this increase must affect every group proportionally.

The isolated group of labourers to whom any particular detail function is assigned, is made up of homogeneous elements, and is one of the constituent parts of the total mechanism. In many manufactures, however, the group itself

---

[1] "When (from the peculiar nature of the produce of each manufactory), the number of processes into which it is most advantageous to divide it is ascertained, as well as the number of individuals to be employed, then all other manufactories which do not employ a direct multiple of this number will produce the article at a greater cost. . . . Hence arises one of the causes of the great size of manufacturing establishments." (C. Babbage. "On the Economy of Machinery," 1st ed. London, 1832. Ch. xxi., p. 172-173.)

is an organised body of labour, the total mechanism being a repetition or multiplication of these elementary organisms. Take, for instance, the manufacture of glass bottles. It may be resolved into three essentially different stages. First, the preliminary stage, consisting of the preparation of the components of the glass, mixing the sand and lime, &c., and melting them into a fluid mass of glass.[1] Various detail labourers are employed in this first stage, and also in the final one of removing the bottles from the drying furnace, sorting and packing them, &c. In the middle, between these two stages, comes the glass melting proper, the manipulation of the fluid mass. At each mouth of the furnace, there works a group, called "the hole," consisting of one bottlemaker or finisher, one blower, one gatherer, one putter-up or whetter-off, and one taker-in. These five detail workers are so many special organs of a single working organism that acts only as a whole, and therefore can operate only by the direct co-operation of the whole five. The whole body is paralysed if but one of its members be wanting. But a glass furnace has several openings (in England from 4 to 6), each of which contains an earthenware melting-pot full of molten glass, and employs a similar five-membered group of workers. The organisation of each group is based on division of labour, but the bond between the different groups is simple co-operation, which, by using in common one of the means of production the furnace, causes it to be more economically consumed. Such a furnace, with its 4-6 groups, constitutes a glass house; and a glass manufactory comprises a number of such glass houses, together with the apparatus and workmen requisite for the preparatory and final stages.

Finally, just as Manufacture arises in part from the combination of various handicrafts, so, too, it developes into a combination of various manufactures. The larger English glass manufacturers, for instance, make their own earthenware melting-pots, because, on the quality of these depends, to a great extent, the success or failure of the process. The manu-

---

[1] In England, the melting-furnace is distinct from the glass-furnace in which the glass is manipulated. In Belgium, one and the same furnace serves for both processes.

facture of one of the means of production is here united with that of the product. On the other hand, the manufacture of the product may be united with other manufactures, of which that product is the raw material, or with the products of which it is itself subsequently mixed. Thus, we find the manufacture of flint glass combined with that of glass cutting and brass founding; the latter for the metal settings of various articles of glass. The various manufactures so combined form more or less separate departments of a larger manufacture, but are at the same time independent processes, each with its own division of labour. In spite of the many advantages offered by this combination of manufactures, it never grows into a complete technical system on its own foundation. That happens only on its transformation into an industry carried on by machinery.

Early in the manufacturing period, the principle of lessening the necessary labour-time in the production of commodities,[1] was accepted and formulated: and the use of machines, especially for certain simple first processes that have to be conducted on a very large scale, and with the application of great force, sprang up here and there. Thus, at an early period in paper manufacture, the tearing up of the rags was done by paper mills; and in metal works, the pounding of the ores was effected by stamping mills.[2] The Roman Empire had handed down the elementary form of all machinery in the water-wheel.[3]

The handicraft period bequeathed to us the great inventions of the compass, of gunpowder, of type-printing, and of the automatic clock. But, on the whole, machinery played that subordinate part which Adam Smith assigns to it in comparision with division of labour.[4] The sporadic use of machinery

[1] This can be seen from W. Petty, John Bellers, Andrew Yarranton, "The Advantages of the East India Trade," and J. Vanderlint, not to mention others.

[2] Towards the end of the 16th century, mortars and sieves were still used in France for pounding and washing ores.

[3] The whole history of the development of machinery can be traced in the history of the corn mill. The factory in England is still a "mill." In German technological works of the first decade of this century, the term "Mühle" is still found in use, not only for all machinery driven by the forces of Nature, but also for all manufactures where apparatus in the nature of machinery is applied.

[4] As will be seen more in detail in "Theories of Surplus-Value," Adam Smith has

in the 17th century was of the greatest importance, because it supplied the great mathematicians of that time with a practical basis and stimulant to the creation of the science of mechanics.

The collective labourer, formed by the combination of a number of detail labourers, is the mechanism specially characteristic of the manufacturing period. The various operations that are performed in turns by the producer of a commodity, and coalesce one with another during the progress of production, lay claim to him in various ways. In one operation he must exert more strength, in another more skill, in another more attention; and the same individual does not possess all these qualities in an equal degree. After Manufacture has once separated, made independent, and isolated the various operations, the labourers are divided, classified, and grouped according to their predominating qualities. If their natural endowments are, on the one hand, the foundation on which the division of labour is built up, on the other hand, Manufacture, once introduced, developes in them new powers that are by nature fitted only for limited and special functions. The collective labourer now possesses, in an equal degree of excellence, all the qualities requisite for production, and expends them in the most economical manner, by exclusively employing all his organs, consisting of particular labourers, or groups of labourers, in performing their special functions.[1] The one-sidedness and the deficiencies of the detail labourer become perfections when he is a part of the collective labourer.[2] The habit of doing only one thing converts him into a never

not established a single new proposition relating to division of labour. What, however, characterises him as the political economist par excellence of the period of Manufacture, is the stress he lays on division of labour. The subordinate part which he assigns to machinery gave occasion in the early days of modern mechanical industry to the polemic of Lauderdale, and, at a later period, to that of Ure. A. Smith also confounds differentiation of the instruments of labour, in which the detail labourers themselves took an active part, with the invention of machinery; in this latter, it is not the workmen in manufactories, but learned men, handicraftsmen, and even peasants (Brindley), who play a part.

[1] "The master manufacturer, by dividing the work to be executed into different processes, each requiring different degrees of skill or of force, can purchase exactly that precise quantity of both which is necessary for each process; whereas, if the whole work were executed by one workman, that person must possess sufficient skill to perform the most difficult, and sufficient strength to execute the most laborious of the operations into which the article is divided." (Ch. Babbage. l. c., ch. xviii.)

[2] For instance, abnormal development of some muscles, curvature of bones, &c.

failing instrument, while his connexion with the whole me-chanism compels him to work with the regularity of the parts of a machine.[1]

Since the collective labourer has functions, both simple and complex, both high and low, his members, the individual labour-powers, require different degrees of training, and must therefore have different values. Manufacture, therefore, de-velopes a hierarchy of labour-powers, to which there corres-ponds a scale of wages. If, on the one hand, the individual laborers are appropriated and annexed for life by a limited function; on the other hand, the various operations of the hierarchy are parcelled out among the laboures according to both their natural and their acquired capabilities.[2] Every process of production, however, requires certain simple manip-ulations, which every man is capable of doing. They too are now severed from their connexion with more pregnant mo-ments of activity, and ossified into exclusive functions of spec-ially appointed labourers. Hence, Manufacture begets, in every handicraft that it seizes upon, a class of so-called unskilled labourers, a class which handicraft industry strictly excluded. If it developes a one-sided specialty into a perfection, at the expense of the whole of a man's working capacity, it also begins to make a specialty of the absence of all development. Alongside of the hierarchic gradation there steps the sim-ple separation of the labourers into skilled and unskilled. For the latter, the cost of apprenticeship vanishes; for the former, it diminishes, compared with that of artificers, in

---

[1] The question put by one of the Inquiry Commissioners, How the young persons are kept steadily to their work, is very correctly answered by Mr. Wm. Marshall, the general manager of a glass manufactory: "They cannot well neglect their work; when they once begin, they must go on; they are just the same as parts of a machine." ("Children's Empl. Comm.," 4th Rep., 1865, p. 247.)

[2] Dr. Ure, in his apotheosis of Modern Mechanical Industry, brings out the peculiar character of manufacture more sharply than previous economists, who had not his polemical interest in the matters, and more sharply even than his contemporaries—Babbage, *e.g.*, who, though much his superior as a mathematician and mechanician, treated mechanical industry from the standpoint of manufacture alone. Ure says, "This appropriation . . . to each, a workman of appropriate value and cost was naturally assigned, forms the very essence of division of labour." On the other hand, he describes this division as "adaptation of labour to the different talents of men," and lastly, characterises the whole manufacturing system as "a system for the division or gradation of labour," as "the division of labour into degrees of skill," &c. (Ure, l. c. pp. 19-23 passim.)

consequence of the functions being simplified.
cases the value of labour-power falls.[1] An exception to
law holds good whenever the decomposition of the labour-
process begets new and comprehensive functions, that either
had no plac: at all, or only a very modest one, in handicrafts.
The fall i.. he value of labour-power. caused by the disappearance of diminution of the expense of apprenticeship, implies a direct increase of surplus-value for the benefit of
capital; for everything that shortens the necessary labour-
time required for the reproduction of labour-power, extends
the domain of surplus-labour.

SECTION 4.—DIVISION OF LABOUR IN MANUFACTURE, AND DIVISION OF LABOUR IN SOCIETY.

We first considered the origin of Manufacture, then its
simple elements, then the detail labourer and his implements,
and finally, the totality of the mechanism. We shall now
lightly touch upon the relation between the division of labour
in manufacture, and the social division of labour, which forms
the foundation of all production of commodities.

If we keep labour alone in view, we may designate the
separation of social production into its main division or
genera—viz., agriculture, industries, etc., as division of labour
in general, and the splitting up of these families into species
and sub-species, as division of labour in particular, and the
division of labour within the workshop as division of labour in
singular or in detail.[2]

[1] "Each handicraftsman being . . . enabled to perfect himself by practice in
one point, became . . . a cheaper workman." (Ure, l. c., p. 19.)
[1] "Division of labour proceeds from the separation of professions the most widely
different to that division, where several labourers divide between them the preparation
of one and the same product, as in manufacture." (Storch: "Cours d'Econ. Pol.
Paris Edn." t. I., p. 173.) ˙ "Nous rencontrons chez les peuples parvenus à un certain
degré de civilisation trois genres de divisions d'industrie: la première, que nous
nommerons générale, amène la distinction des producteurs en agriculteurs, manu-
facturiers et commerçans, elle se rapporte aux trois principales branches d'industrie
nationale; la seconde, qu'on pourrait appeler spéciale, est la division de chaque genre
d'industrie en espèces . . . la troisième division d'industrie, celle enfin qu'on
devrait qualifier de division de la besogne ou de travail proprement dit, est celle qui
s'établit dans les arts et les métiers séparés . . . qui s'etablit dans la plupart des
manufactures et des ateliers." (Skarbek. l. c. pp. 84, 85.)

Division of labour in a society, and the corresponding tying down of individuals to a particular calling, developes itself, just as does the division of labour in manufacture, from opposite starting points. Within a family,[1] and after further development within a tribe, there springs up naturally a division of labour, caused by differences of sex and age, a division that is consequently based on a purely physiological foundation, which division enlarges its materials by the expansion of the community, by the increase of population, and more especially, by the conflicts between different tribes, and the subjugation of one tribe by another. On the other hand, as I have before remarked, the exchange of products springs up at the points where different families, tribes, communities, come in contact; for, in the beginning of civilisation, it is not private individuals but families, tribes, &c., that meet on an independent footing. Different communities find different means of production and different means of subsistence in their natural environment. Hence, their modes of production, and of living, and their products are different. It is this spontaneously developed difference which, when different communities come in contact, calls forth the mutual exchange of products, and the consequent gradual conversion of those products into commodities. Exchange does not create the differences between the spheres of production, but brings such as are already different into relation, and thus converts them into more or less interdependent branches of the collective production of an enlarged society. In the latter case, the social division of labour arises from the exchange between spheres of production, that are originally distinct and independent of one another. In the former, where the physiological division of labour is the starting point, the particular organs of a compact whole grow loose, and break off, principally owing to the exchange of commodities with foreign communities, and then isolate themselves so

[1] Note to the third edition. Subsequent very searching study of the primitive condition of man, led the author to the conclusion, that it was not the family that originally developed into the tribe, but that, on the contrary, the tribe was the primitive and spontaneously developed form of human association, on the basis of blood relationship, and that out of the first incipient loosening of the tribal bonds, the many and various forms of the family were afterwards developed. (Ed. 3rd ed.)

far, that the sole bond, still connecting the various kinds of work, is the exchange of the products as commodities. In the one case, it is the making dependent what was before independent; in the other case, the making independent what was before dependent.

The foundation of every division of labour that is well developed, and brought about by the exchange of commodities, is the separation between town and country.[1] It may be said, that the whole economical history of society is summed up in the movement of this antithesis. We pass it over, however, for the present.

Just as a certain number of simultaneously employed labourers are the material pre-requisites for division of labour in manufacture, so are the number and density of the population, which here correspond to the agglomeration in one workshop, a necessary condition for the division of labour in society.[2] Nevertheless, this density is more or less relative. A relatively thinly populated country, with well-developed means of communication, has a denser population than a more numerously populated country, with badly-developed means of communication; and in this sense the Northern States of the American Union, for instance, are more thickly populated than India.[3]

Since the production and the circulation of commodities are the general pre-requisites of the capitalist mode of production, division of labour in manufacture demands, that division of labour in society at large should previously have attained a

[1] Sir James Steuart is the economist who has handled this subject best. How little his book, which appeared ten years before the "Wealth of Nations," is known, even at the present time, may be judged from the fact that the admirers of Malthus do not even know that the first edition of the latter's work on population contains, except in the purely declamatory part, very little but extracts from Steuart, and in a less degree, from Wallace and Townsend.

[2] "There is a certain density of population which is convenient, both for social intercourse, and for that combination of powers by which the produce of labour is increased." (James Mill, l. c. p. 50.) "As the number of labourers increases, the productive power of society augments in the compound ratio of that increase, multiplied by the effects of the division of labour." (Th. Hodgskin, l. c. pp. 125, 126.)

[3] In consequence of the great demand for cotton after 1861, the production of cotton, in some thickly populated districts of India, was extended at the expense of rice cultivation. In consequence there arose local famines, the defective means of communication not permitting the failure of rice in one district to be compensated by importation from another.

certain degree of development. Inversely, the former division reacts upon and developes and multiplies the latter. Simultaneously, with the differentiation of the instruments of labour, the industries that produce these instruments, become more and more differentiated.[1] If the manufacturing system seize upon an industry, which, previously, was carried on in connexion with others, either as a chief or as a subordinate industry, and by one producer, these industries immediately separate their connexion, and become independent. If it seize upon a particular stage in the production of a commodity, the other stages of its production become converted into so many independent industries. It has already been stated, that where the finished article consists merely of a number of parts fitted together, the detail operations may re-establish themselves as genuine and separate handicrafts. In order to carry out more perfectly the division of labour in manufacture, a single branch of production is, according to the varieties of its raw material, or the various forms that one and the same raw material may assume, split up into numerous, and to some extent, entirely new manufactures. Accordingly, in France alone, the first half of the 18th century, over 100 different kinds of silk stuffs were woven, and in Avignon, it was law, that " every apprentice should devote himself to only one sort of fabrication, and should not learn the preparation of several kinds of stuff at once." The territorial division of labour, which confines special branches of production to special districts of a country, acquires fresh stimulus from the manufacturing system, which exploits every special advantage.[2] The Colonial system and the opening out of the markets of the world, both of which are included in the general conditions of existence of the manufacturing period, furnish rich material for developing the division of labour in society. It is not the place, here, to go on to

---

[1] Thus, the fabrication of shuttles formed, as early as the 17th century, a special branch of industry in Holland.

[2] "Whether the woollen manufacture of England is not divided into several parts or branches appropriated to particular places, where they are only or principally manufactured; fine cloths in Somersetshire coarse in Yorkshire, long ells at Exeter, soies at Sudbury, crapes at Norwich, linseys at Kendal, blankets at Whitney, and so forth." (Berkeley: "The Querist," 1750, p. 520.)

show how division of labour seizes upon, not only the economical, but every other sphere of society, and everywhere lays the foundation of that all engrossing system of specialising and sorting men, that development in a man of one single faculty at the expense of all other faculties, which caused A. Ferguson, the master of Adam Smith, to exclaim: " We make a nation of Helots, and have no fi e itizens."[1]

But, in spite of the numberous analogies and links connecting them, division of labour in the interior of a society, and that in the interior of a workshop, differ not only in degree, but also in kind. The analogy appears most indisputable where there is an invisible bond uniting the various branches of trade. For instance the cattle breeder produces hides, the tanner makes the hides into leather, and the shoemaker, the leather into boots. Here the thing produced by each of them is but a step towards the final form, which is the product of all their labours combined. There are, besides, all the various industries that supply the cattle-breeder, the tanner, and the shoemaker with the means of production. Now it is quite possible to imagine, with Adam Smith, that the difference between the above social division of labour, and the division in manufacture, is merely subjective, exists merely for the observer, who, in a manufacture, can see with one glance, all the numerous operations being performed on one spot, while in the instance given above, the spreading out of the work over great areas, and the great number of people employed in each branch of labour, obscure the connexion.[2] But what is

[1] A. Ferguson: "History of Civil Society." Edinburgh, 1767; Part iv. sect. ii., p. 285.

[2] In manufacture proper, he says, the division of labour appears to be greater, because "those employed in every different branch of the work can often be collected into the same workhouse, and placed at once under the view of the spectator. In those great manufactures, (!) on the contrary, which are destined to supply the great wants of the great body of the people, every different branch of the work employs so great a number of workmen, that it is impossible to collect them all into the same workhouse . . . the division is not near so obvious." (A. Smith: "Wealth of Nations," bk. i. ch. i.) The celebrated passage in the same chapter that begins with the words, "Observe the accommodation of the most common artificer or day labourer in a civilized and thriving country," &c., and then proceeds to depict what an enormous number and variety of industries contribute to the satisfaction of the wants of an ordinary labourer, is copied almost word for word from B. de Mandeville's Remarks to his "Fable of the Bees, or Private Vices, Publick Benefits." (First ed., without the remarks, 1706; with the remarks, 1714.)

it that forms the bond between the independent labours of the cattle-breeder, the tanner, and the shoemaker? It is the fact that their respective products are commodities. What, on the other hand, characterises division of labour in manufactures? The fact that the detail labourer produces no commodities.[1] It is only the common product of all the detail labourers that becomes a commodity.[2] Division of labour in a society is brought about by the purchase and sale of the products of different branches of industry, while the connexion between the detail operations in a workshop, are due to the sale of the labour-power of several workmen to one capitalist, who applies it as combined labour-power. The division of labour in the workshop implies concentration of the means of production in the hands of one capitalist; the division of labour in society implies their dispersion among many independent producers of commodities. While within the workshop, the iron law of proportionality subjects definite numbers of workmen to definite functions, in the society outside the workshop, chance and caprice have full play in distributing the producers and their means of production among the various branches of industry. The different spheres of production, it is true, constantly tend to an equilibrium: for, on the one hand, while each producer of a commodity is bound to produce a use-value, to satisfy a particular social want, and while

[1] "There is no longer anything which we can call the natural reward of individual labour. Each labourer produces only some part of a whole, and each part, having no value or utility in itself, there is nothing on which the labourer can seize, and say: It is my product, this I will keep to myself." ("Labour Defended against the Claims of Capital." Lond., 1825, p. 25.) The author of this admirable work is the Th. Hodgskin I have already cited.

[2] This distinction between division of labour in society and in manufacture, was practically illustrated to the Yankees. One of the new taxes devised at Washington during the civil war, was the duty of 6% "on all industrial products." Question: What is an industrial product? Answer of the legislature: A thing is produced "when it is made," and it is made when it is ready for sale. Now, for one example out of many. The New York and Philadelphia manufacturers had previously been in the habit of "making" umbrellas, with all their belongings. But since an umbrella is a *mixtum compositum* of very heterogeneous parts, by degrees these parts became the products of various separate industries, carried on independently in different places. They entered as separate commodities into the umbrella manufactory, where they were fitted together. The Yankees have given to articles thus fitted together, the name of "assembled articles," a name they deserve, for being an assemblage of taxes. Thus the umbrella "assembles," first, 6% on the price of each of its elements, and a further 6% on its own total price.

the extent of these wants differs quantitatively, still there exists an inner relation which settles their proportions into a regular system, and that system one of spontaneous growth; and, on the other hand, the law of the value of commodities ultimately determines how much of its disposable working-time society can expend on each particular class of commodities. But this constant tendency to equilibrium, of the various spheres of production, is exercised, only in the shape of a reaction against the constant upsetting of this equilibrium. The *a priori* system on which the division of labour, within the workshop, is regularly carried out, becomes in the division of labour within the society, an *a posteriori,* nature-imposed necessity, controlling the lawless caprice of the producers, and perceptible in the barometrical fluctuations of the market prices. Division of labour within the workshop implies the undisputed authority of the capitalist over men, that are but parts of a mechanism that belongs to him. The division of labour within the society brings into contact independent commodity-producers, who acknowledge no other authority but that of competition, of the coercion exerted by the pressure of their mutual interests; just as in the animal kingdom, the *bellum omnium contra omnes* more or less preserves the conditions of existence of every species. The same bourgeois mind which praises division of labour in the workshop, life-long annexation of the labourer to a partial operation, and his complete subjection to capital, as being an organisation of labour that increases its productiveness—that same bourgeois mind denounces with equal vigour every conscious attempt to socially control and regulate the process of production, as an inroad upon such sacred things as the rights of property, freedom and unrestricted play for the bent of the individual capitalist. It is very characteristic that the enthusiastic apologists of the factory system have nothing more damning to urge against a general organization of the labour of society, than that it would turn all society into one immense factory.

If, in a society with capitalist production, anarchy in the social division of labour and despotism in that of the workshop are mutual conditions the one of the other, we find, on the con-

trary, in those earlier forms of society in which the separation
of trades has been spontaneously developed, then crystallized,
and finally made permanent by law, on the one hand, a specimen of the organization of the labour of society, in accordance
with an approved and authoritative plan, and on the other,
the entire exclusion of division of labour in the workshop,
or at all events a mere dwarflike or sporadic and accidental
development of the same.[1]

Those small and extremely ancient Indian communities,
some of which have continued down to this day, are based on
possession in common of the land, on the blending of agriculture and handicrafts, and on an unalterable division of labour,
which serves, whenever a new community is started, as a plan
and scheme ready cut and dried. Occupying areas of from
100 up to several thousand acres, each forms a compact whole
producing all it requires. The chief part of the products is
destined for direct use by the community itself, and does not
take the form of a commodity. Hence, production here is
independent of that division of labour brought about, in Indian
society as a whole, by means of the exchange of commodities.
It is the surplus alone that becomes a commodity, and a portion
of even that, not until it has reached the hands of the State,
into whose hands from time immemorial a certain quantity of
these products has found its way in the shape of rent in kind.
The constitution of these communities varies in different parts
of India. In those of the simplest form, the land is tilled in
common, and the produce divided among the members. At
the same time, spinning and weaving are carried on in each
family as subsidiary industries. Side by side with the masses
thus occupied with one and the same work, we find the "chief
inhabitant," who is judge, police, and tax-gatherer in one; the
bookkeeper who keeps the accounts of the tillage and registers
everything relating thereto; another official, who prosecutes

---

[1] "On peut . . . établir en règle générale, que moins l'autorite préside à la
division du travail dans l'intérieur de la société, plus la division du travail se
développe dans l'intérieur de l'atelier, ét plus elle y est soumise à l'autorité d'un
seul. Ainsi l'autorité dans l'atelier et celle dans la société, par rapport à la division
dutravail, sont en raison inverse l'une de l'autre." (Karl Marx, "Misère," &c., pp.
130-131.)

criminals, protects strangers travelling through, and escorts them to the next village; the boundary man, who guards the boundaries against neighbouring communities; the water-over-seer, who distributes the water from the common tanks for irrigation; the Brahmin, who conducts the religious services; the schoolmaster, who on the sand teaches the children reading and writing; the calendar-Brahmin, or astrologer, who makes known the lucky or unlucky days for seed-time and harvest, and for every other kind of agricultural work; a smith and a carpenter, who make and repair all the agricultural imple-ments; the potter, who makes all the pottery of the village; the barber, the washerman, who washes clothes, the silversmith, here and there the poet, who in some communities replaces the silversmith, in others the schoolmaster. This dozen of indi-viduals is maintained at the expense of the whole community. If the population increases, a new community is founded, on the pattern of the old one, on unoccupied land. The whole mechanism discloses a systematic division of labour; but a division like that in manufactures is impossible, since the smith and the carpenter, &c., find an unchanging market, and at the most there occur, according to the sizes of the villages, two or three of each, instead of one.[1] The law that regulates the division of labour in the community acts with the irresisti-ble authority of a law of Nature, at the same time that each individual artificer, the smith, the carpenter, and so on, con-ducts in his workshop all the operations of his handicraft in the traditional way, but independently, and without recogniz-ing any authority over him. The simplicity of the organisa-tion for production in these self-sufficing communities that constantly reproduce themselves in the same form, and when accidentally destroyed, spring up again on the spot and with the same name[2]—this simplicity supplies the key to the secret

[1] Lieut.-Col. Mark Wilks: "Historical Sketches of the South of India." Lond., 1810-17, v. I., pp. 118-20. A good description of the various forms of the Indian communities is to be found in George Campbell's "Modern India." Lond., 1852.

[2] "Under this simple form . . . the inhabitants of the country have lived from time immemorial. The boundaries of the villages have been but seldom altered; and though the villages themselves have been sometimes injured, and even desolated by war, famine, and disease, the same name, the same limits, the same interests, and even the same families, have continued for ages. The inhabitants give themselves

of the unchangeableness of Asiatic societies, an unchangeableness in such striking contrast with the constant dissolution and refounding of Asiatic States, and the never-ceasing changes of dynasty. The structure of the economical elements of society remains untouched by the storm-clouds of the political sky.

The rules of the guilds, as I have said before, by limiting most strictly the number of apprentices and journeymen that a single master could employ, prevented him from becoming a capitalist. Moreover, he could not employ his journeymen in any other handicraft than the one in which he was a master. The guilds zealously repelled every encroachment by the capital of merchants, the only form of free capital with which they came in contact. A merchant could buy every kind of commodity, but labour as a commodity he could not buy. He existed only on sufferance, as a dealer in the products of the handicrafts. If circumstances called for a further division of labour, the existing guilds split themselves up into varieties, or founded new guilds by the side of the old ones; all this, however, without concentrating various handicrafts in a single workshop. Hence, the guild organization, however much it may have contributed by separating, isolating, and perfecting the handicrafts, to create the material conditions for the existence of manufacture, excluded division of labour in the workshop. On the whole, the labourer and his means of production remained closely united, like the snail with its shell, and thus there was wanting the principal basis of manufacture, the separation of the labourer from his means of production, and the conversion of these means into capital.

While division of labour in society at large, whether such division be brought about or not by exchange of commodities, is common to economical formations of society the most diverse, division of labour in the workshop, as practised by manufacture, is a special creation of the capitalist mode of production alone.

no trouble about the breaking up and division of kingdoms; while the village remains entire, they care not to what power it is transferred, or to what sovereign it devolves; its internal economy remains unchanged." (Th. Stamford Raffles, late Lieut. Gov. of Java: "The History of Java." Lond., 1817, Vol. I., p. 285.)

SECTION 5.—THE CAPITALISTIC CHARACTER OF MANUFACTURE.

An increased number of labourers under the control of one capitalist is the natural starting-point, as well of co-operation generally, as of manufacture in particular. But the division of labour in the manufacture makes this increase in the number of workmen a technical necessity. The minimum number that any given capitalist is bound to employ is here prescribed by the previously established division of labour. On the other hand, the advantages of further division are obtainable only by adding to the number of workmen, and this can be done only by adding multiples of the various detail groups. But an increase in the variable component of the capital employed necessitates an increase in its constant component, too, in the workshops, implements, &c., and, in particular, in the raw material, the call for which grows quicker than the number of workmen. The quantity of it consumed in a given time, by a given amount of labour, increases in the same ratio as does the productive power of that labour in consequence of its division. Hence, it is a law, based on the very nature of manufacture, that the minimum amount of capital, which is bound to be in the hands of each capitalist, must keep increasing; in other words, that the transformation into capital of the social means of production and subsistence must keep extending.[1]

In manufacture, as well as in simple co-operation, the collective working organism is a form of existence of capital. The mechanism that is made up of numerous individual detail labourers belongs to the capitalist. Hence, the productive power resulting from a combination of labourers appears to be the productive power of capital. Manufacture proper not only

---

[1] "It is not sufficient that the capital" (the writer should have said the necessary means of subsistence and of production) "required for the sub-division of handicrafts should be in readiness in the society: it must also be accumulated in the hands of the employers in sufficiently large quantities to enable them to conduct their operations on a large scale. . . . The more the division increases, the more does the constant employment of a given number of labourers require greater outlay of capital in tools, raw material, &c.," (Storch: Cours d'Econ. Polit. Paris Ed., t. I. pp. 250, 251.) "La concentration des instruments de production et la division du travail sont aussi inséparables l'une de l'autre que le sont, dans le régime politique, la concentration des pouvoirs publics et la division des intérêts privés." (Karl Marx. l. c., p. 134.)

subjects the previously independent workman to the discipline and command of capital, but, in addition, creates a hierarchic gradation of the workmen themselves. While simple co-operation leaves the mode of working by the individual for the most part unchanged, manufacture thoroughly revolutionises it, and seizes labour-power by its very roots. It converts the labourer into a crippled monstrosity, by forcing his detail dexterity at the expense of a world of productive capabilities and instincts; just as in the States of La Plata they butcher a whole beast for the sake of his hide or his tallow. Not only is the detail work distributed to the different individuals, but the individual himself is made the automatic motor of a fractional operation,[1] and the absurd fable of Menenius Agrippa, which makes man a mere fragment of his own body, becomes realised.[2] If, at first, the workman sells his labour-power to capital, because the material means of producing a commodity fail him, now his very labour-power refuses its services unless it has been sold to capital. Its functions can be exercised only in an environment that exists in the workshop of the capitalist after the sale. By nature unfitted to make anything independently, the manufacturing labourer developes productive activity as a mere appendage of the capitalist's workshop.[3] As the chosen people bore in their features the sign manual of Jehovah, so division of labour brands the manufacturing workman as the property of capital.

The knowledge, the judgment, and the will, which, though in ever so small a degree, are practised by the independent peasant or handicraftsman, in the same way as the savage makes the whole art of war consist in the exercise of his personal cunning—these faculties are now required only for the workshop as a whole. Intelligence in production expands in

---

[1] Dugald Stewart calls manufacturing labourers "living automatons . . . employed in the details of the work." (l. c., p. 318.)

[2] In corals, each individual is, in fact, the stomach of the whole group; but it supplies the group with nourishment, instead of, like the Roman patrician, withdrawing it.

[3] "L'ouvrier qui porte dans ses bras tout un métier, peut aller partout exercer son industrie et trouver des moyens de subsister: l'autre (the manufacturing labourer) n'est qu'un accessoire qui, séparé de ses confrères, n'a plus ni capacité, ni indépendance, et qui se trouve forcé d'accepter la loi qu'on juge à propos de lui imposer." (Storch. l. c. Petersb. edit., 1815, t. I., p. 204.)

one direction, because it vanishes in many others. What is lost by the detail labourers, is concentrated in the capital that employs them.[1] It is a result of the division of labour in manufactures, that the labourer is brought face to face with the intellectual potencies of the material process of production, as the property of another, and as a ruling power. This separation begins in simple co-operation, where the capitalist represents to the single workman, the oneness and the will of the associated labour. It is developed in manufacture which cuts down the labourer into a detail labourer. It is completed in modern industry, which makes science a productive force distinct from labour and presses it into the service of capital.[2]

In manufacture, in order to make the collective labourer, and through him capital, rich in social productive power, each labourer must be made poor in individual productive powers. "Ignorance is the mother of industry as well as of superstition. Reflection and fancy are subject to err; but a habit of moving the hand or the foot is independent of either. Manufactures, accordingly, prosper most where the mind is least consulted, and where the workshop may . . . be considered as an engine, the parts of which are men."[3] As a matter of fact, some few manufacturers in the middle of the 18th century preferred, for certain operations that were trade secrets, to employ half-idiotic persons.[4]

"The understandings of the greater part of men," says Adam Smith, "are necessarily formed by their ordinary employments. The man whose whole life is spent in performing a few simple operations . . . has no occasion to exert his understanding. . . . . He generally becomes as stupid and ignorant as it is

[1] A. Ferguson, l. c., p. 281: "The former may have gained what the other has lost."

[2] "The man of knowledge and the productive labourer come to be widely divided from each other, and knowledge, instead of remaining the handmaid of labour in the hand of the labourer to increase his productive powers . . . has almost everywhere arrayed itself against labour . . . systematically deluding and leading them (the labourers) astray in order to render their muscular powers entirely mechanical and obedient." (W. Thompson: "An Inquiry into the Principles of the Distribution of Wealth. London, 1824," p. 274.)

[3] A. Ferguson, l. c., p. 280.

[4] J. D. Tuckett: "A History of the Past and Present State of the Labouring Population." Lond., 1846.

possible for a human creature to become." After describing
the stupidity of the detail labourer he goes on: "The uniformity of his stationary life naturally corrupts the courage of
his mind. . . . . It corrupts even the activity of his body and
renders him incapable of exerting his strength with vigour and
perseverance in any other employments than that to which
he has been bred. His dexterity at his own particular trade
seems in this manner to be acquired at the expense of his intellectual, social, and martial virtues. But in every improved
and civilised society, this is the state into which the labouring
poor, that is, the great body of the people, must necessarily
fall."[1] For preventing the complete deterioration of the great
mass of the people by division of labour, A. Smith commends
education of the people by the State, but prudently, and in
homœopathic doses. G. Garnier, his French translator and
commentator, who, under the first French Empire, quite naturally developed into a senator, quite as naturally opposes him
on this point. Education of the masses, he urges, violates the
first law of the division of labour, and with it "our whole
social system would be proscribed." "Like all other divisions
of labour," he says, "that between hand labour and head labour [2] is more pronounced and decided in proportion as society
(he rightly uses this word, for capital, landed property and
their State) becomes richer. This division of labour, like
every other, is an effect of past, and a cause of future progress
. . . . ought the government then to work in opposition to this
division of labour, and to hinder its natural course? Ought it
to expend a part of the public money in the attempt to con-

---

[1] A. Smith: Wealth of Nations, Bk. V., ch. I., art. II. Being a pupil of A. Ferguson who showed the disadvantageous effects of division of labour, Adam Smith was
perfectly clear on this point. In the introduction to his work, where he *ex professo* praises division of labour, he indicates only in a cursory manner that it is the
source of social inequalities. It is not till the 5th Book, on the Revenue of the
State, that he reproduces Ferguson. In my "Misère de la Philosophie," I have
sufficiently explained the historical connection between Ferguson, A. Smith,
Lemontey, and Say, as regards their criticisms of Division of Labour, and have
shown, for the first time, that Division of Labour as practised in manufactures, is
a specific form of the capitalist mode of production.

[2] Ferguson had already said, l. c. p. 281: "And thinking itself, in this age of
separations, may become a peculiar craft."

found and blend together two classes of labour, which are striving after division and separation ?"[1]

Some crippling of body and mind is inseparable even from division of labour in society as a whole. Since, however, manufacture carries this social separation of branches of labour much further, and also, by its peculiar division, attacks the individual at the very roots of his life, it is the first to afford the materials for, and to give a start to, industrial pathology.[2]

"To subdivide a man is to execute him, if he deserves the sentence, to assassinate him if he does not. . . . The subdivision of labour is the assassination of a people."[3]

Co-operation based on division of labour, in other words, manufacture, commences as a spontaneous formation. So soon as it attains some consistence and extension, it becomes the recognised methodical and systematic form of capitalist production. History shows how the division of labour peculiar to manufacture, strictly so called, acquires the best adapted form at first by experience, as it were behind the backs of the actors, and then, like the guild handicrafts, strives to hold fast that form when once found, and here and there succeeds in keeping it for centuries. Any alteration in this form, except in trivial matters, is solely owing to a revolution in the instruments of labour. Modern manufacture wherever it arises—I do not here allude to modern industry based on machinery—either finds the disjecta membra poetæ ready to hand, and only wait-

---

[1] G. Garnier, vol. V. of his translation of A. Smith, pp. 4–5.

[2] Ramazzini, professor of practical medicine at Padua, published in 1713 his work "De morbis artificum," which was translated into French 1781, reprinted in 1841 in the "Encyclopédie des Sciences Médicales. 7me Dis. Auteurs Classiques." The period of Modern Mechanical Industry has, of course, very much enlarged his catalogue of labour's diseases. See "Hygiène physique et morale de l'ouvrier dans les grandes villes en général et dans la ville de Lyon en particulier. Par le Dr. A. L. Fonterel, Paris, 1858," and "Die Krankheiten, welche verschiednen Ständen, Altern und Geschlechtern eigenthümlich sind. 6 Vols. Ulm, 1860," and others. In 1854 the Society of Arts appointed a Commission of Inquiry into industrial pathology. The list of documents collected by this commission is to be seen in the catalogue of the "Twickenham Economic Museum." Very important are the official "Reports on Public Health." See also Eduard Reich, M.D. "Ueber die Entartung des Menschen," Erlangen, 1868.

[3] (D. Urquhart: Familiar Words. Lond., 1855, p. 119.) Hegel held very heretical views on division of labour. In his Rechtsphilosophie he says: "By well educated men we understand in the first instance, those who can do everything that others do."

ing to be collected together, as is the case in the manufacture
of clothes in large towns, or it can easily apply the principle
of division, simply by exclusively assigning the various ope a-
tions of a handicraft (such as bookbinding) to particular men.
In such cases, a week's experience is enough to determine the
proportion between the numbers of the hands necessary for the
various functions.[1]

By decomposition of handicrafts, by specialisation of the instruments of labour, by the formation of detail labourers, and
by grouping and combining th : latter into a single mechanism,
division of labour in manufacture creates a qualitative gradation, and a quantitative proportion in the social proces: of
production; it consequently creates a definite organization of
the labour of society, and thereby developes at the same time
new productive forces in the society. In its specific capitalist
form—and under the given conditions, it could take no other
form than a capitalistic one—manufacture is but a particular
method of begetting relative surplus-value, or of augmenting
at the expense of the labourer the self-expansion of capital—
usually called social wealth, "Wealth of Nations," &c. It increases the social productive power of labour, not only for the
benefit of the capitalist instead of for that of the labourer, but
it does this by crippling the individual labourers. It creates
new conditions for the lordship of capital over labour. If,
therefore, on the one hand, it presents itself historically as a
progress and as a necessary phase in the economic development of society, on the other hand it is a refined and civilised
method of exploitation.

Political economy, which as an independent science, first
sprang into being during the period of manufacture, views
the social division of labour only from the standpoint of manufacture,[2] and sees in it only the means of producing more commodities with a given quantity of labour, and, consequently,

---

[1] The simple belief in the inventive genius exercised a priori by the individual
capitalist in division of labour, exists now-a-days only among German professors,
of the stamp of Herr Roscher, who, to recompense the capitalist from whose
Jovian head division of labour sprang ready formed, dedicates to him "various
wages" (diverse Arbeitslöhne). The more or less extensive application of division
of labour depends on length of purse, not on greatness of genius.

[2] The older writers, like Petty and the anonymous author of "Advantages of the

of cheapening commodities and hurrying on the accumulation of capital. In most striking contrast with this accentuation of quantity and exchange-value, is the attitude of the writers of classical antiquity, who hold exclusively by quality and use-value.[1] In consequence of the separation of the social branches of production, commodities are better made, the various bents and talents of men select a suitable field,[2] and without some restraint no important results can be obtained anywhere.[3] Hence both product and producer are improved by division of labour. If the growth of the quantity produced is occasionally mentioned, this is only done with reference to the greater abundance of use values. There is not a word alluding to exchange-value or to the cheapening of commodities. This aspect, from the standpoint of use-value alone, is taken as well by Plato,[4] who treats division of labour as the foundation on

East India Trade," bring out the capitalist character of division of labour as applied in manufacture more than A. Smith does.

[1] Amongst the moderns may be excepted a few writers of- the 18th century, like Beccaria and James Harris, who with regard to division of labour almost entirely follow the ancients. Thus, Beccaria: "Ciascuno prova coll' esperienza, che applicando la mano e l'ingegno sempre allo stesso genere di opere e di produtte, egli più facili, più abbondanti e migliori ne traca risultati, di quello che se ciascuno isolatamente le cose tutte a se necessarie soltanto facesse. . . . Dividendosi in tal maniera per la comune e privati utilità gli uomini in varie classi e condizioni." (Cesare Beccaria: "Elementi di Econ. Pubblica," ed. Custodi, Parte Moderna, t. xi., p. 28.) James Harris, afterwards Earl of Malmesbury, celebrated for the "Diaries" of his embassy at St. Petersburg, says in a note to his "Dialogue Concerning Happiness," Lond., 1741, reprinted afterwards in "Three Treatises, &c., 3 Ed., Lond., 1772:" "The whole argument to prove society natural (*i.e.*, by division of employments). . . . is taken from the second book of Plato's Republic."

[2] Thus, in the Odyssey xiv., 228, "῞Αλλος γὰρ τ' ἄλλοισιν ἀνὴρ ἐπιτέρπεται ἔργοις," and Archilochus in Sextus Empiricus, " "Αλλος ἄλλῳ ἐπ' ἔργῳ καρδίην ἰαίνεται."

[3] "Πολλ' ἠπίστατο ἔργα, κακῶς δ'ἠπίστατο πάντα." Every Athenian considered himself superior as a producer of commodities to a Spartan; for the latter in time of war had men enough at his disposal but could not command money, as Thucydides makes Pericles say in the speech inciting the Athenians to the Peloponnesian war: "Σώμασί τε ἑτοιμότεροι οἱ αὐτουργοὶ τῶν ἀνθρώπων ἢ χρήμασι πολεμεῖν." (Thuc: l.I.c. 41.) Nevertheless, even with regard to material production, αὐταρκεία, as opposed to division of labour remained their ideal, " παρ' ὧν γὰρ τὸ εὖ, παρὰ τούτων καὶ τὸ αὔταρκες." It should be mentioned here that at the date of the fall of the 30 Tyrants there were still not 5000 Athenians without landed property.

[4] With Plato, division of labour within the community is a development from the multifarious requirements, and the limited capacities of individuals. The main point with him is, that the labourer must adapt himself to the work, not the work to the labourer; which latter is unavoidable, if he carries on several trades at once, thus making one or the other of them subordinate. "Οὐ γὰρ ἐθέλει τὸ πραττόμενον τὴν τοῦ πράττοντος σχολὴν περιμένειν, ἀλλ' ἀνάγκη τὸν πράττοντα τῷ πραττομένῳ ἐπακολουθεῖν μὴ ἐν παρέργου μέρει.—Ἀνάγκη.—Ἐκ δὴ τούτων πλείω τε ἕκαστα

which the division of society into classes is based, as by Xeno-phon,[1] who with characteristic bourgeois instinct, approaches more nearly to division of labour within the workshop. Plato's Republic, in so far as division of labour is treated in it, as the formative principle of the State, is merely the Athenian ideali-sation of the Egyptian system of castes, Egypt having served as the model of an industrial country to many of his contem-poraries also, amongst others to Isocrates,[2] and it continued to have this importance to the Greeks of the Roman Empire.[3]

During the manufacturing period proper, *i.e.*, the period

γίγνεται καὶ κάλλιον καὶ ῥᾷον, ὅταν εἷς ἕν κατὰ φύσιν καὶ ἐν καιρῷ σχολὴν τῶν ἄλλων ἄγων κράττῃ" (Rep. l. 2. Ed. Baiter, Orelli, &c.). So in Thucydides l. c. c., 42: "Seafaring is an art like any other, and cannot, as circumstances require, be carried on as a subsidiary occupation; nay, other subsidiary occupations cannot be carried on alongside of this one." If the work, says Plato, has to wait for the labourer, the critical point in the process is missed and the article spoiled, ἔργου καιρὸν διόλλυται. The same Platonic idea is found recurring in the protest of the English bleachers against the cause in the Factory Act that provides fixed meal times for all oper-atives. Their business cannot wait the convenience of the workmen, for "in the various operations of singeing, washing, bleaching, mangling, calendering, and dyeing, none of them can be stopped at a given moment without risk of damage . . . . to enforce the same dinner hour for all the work-people might occasion-ally subject valuable goods to the risk of danger by incomplete operations." Le platonisme où va-t-il se nicher!

[1] Xenophon says, it is not only an honour to receive food from the table of the King of Persia, but such food is much more tasty than other food. "And there is nothing wonderful in this, for as the other arts are brought to special perfection in the great towns, so the royal food is prepared in a special way. For in the small towns the same man makes bedsteads, doors, ploughs and tables: often, too, he builds houses into the bargain, and is quite content if he finds custom sufficient for his sustenance. It is altogether impossible for a man who does so many things to do them all well. But in the great towns, where each man can find many buyers, one trade is sufficient to maintain the man who carries it on. Nay, there is often not even need of one complete trade, but one man makes shoes for men, another for women. Here and there one man gets a living by sewing, another by cutting out shoes; one does nothing but cut out clothes, another nothing but sew the pieces together. It follows necessarily then, that he who does the simplest kind of work, undoubted-ly does it better than any one else. So it is with the art of cooking." (Xen. Cyrop. l. viii., c. 2.) Xenophon here lays stress exclusively upon the excellence to be attained in use-value, although he well knows that the gradations of the di-vision of labour depend on the extent of the market.

[2] He (Busiris) divided them all into special castes. . . . . commanded that the same individuals should always carry on the same trade, for he knew that they who change their occupations become skilled in none; but that those who constantly stick to one occupation bring it to the highest perfection. In truth, we shall also find that in relation to the arts and handicrafts, they have outstripped their rivals more than a master does a bungler; and the contrivances for maintaining the mon-archy and the other institutions, of their State are so admirable that the most celebrated philosophers who treat of this subject praise the constitution of the Egyptian State above all others. (Isocrates, Busiris, c. 8.)

[3] Cf. Diodorus Siculus.

during which manufacture is the predominant form taken by
capitalist production, many obstacles are opposed to the full
development of the peculiar tendencies of manufacture. Although manufacture creates, as we have already seen, a simple
separation of the labourers into skilled and unskilled, simultaneously with their hierarchic arrangement in classes, yet the
number of the unskilled labourers, owing to the preponderating
influence of the skilled, remains very limited. Although it
adapts the detail operations to the various degrees of maturity,
strength, and development of the living instruments of labour,
thus conducing to exploitation of women and children, yet this
tendency as a whole is wrecked on the habits and the resistance
of the male labourers. Although the splitting up of handicrafts lowers the cost of forming the workman, and thereby
lowers his value, yet for the more difficult detail work, a longer
apprenticeship is necessary, and, even where it would be superfluous, is jealously insisted upon by the workmen. In England, for instance, we find the laws of apprenticeship, with the
seven years' probation, in full force down to the end of the
manufacturing period; and they are not thrown on one side till
the advent of Modern Industry. Since handicraft skill is the
foundation of manufacture, and since the mechanism of manufacture as a whole possesses no framework, apart from the labourers themselves, capital is constantly compelled to wrestle
with the insubordination of the workmen. "By the infirmity
of human nature," says friend Ure, "it happens that the more
skilful the workman, the more self-willed and intractable he is
apt to become, and of course the less fit a component of a mechanical system in which . . . he may do great damage to the
whole."[1] Hence throughout the whole manufacturing period
there runs the complaint of want of discipline among the workmen.[2] And had we not the testimony of contemporary writers,
the simple facts that, during the period between the 16th century and the epoch of Modern Industry, capital failed to become the master of the whole disposable working-time of the

---

[1] Ure, l. c., p. 20.
[2] This is more the case in England than in France, and more in France than in
Holland.

manufacturing labourers, that manufactures are short-lived, and change their locality from one country to another with the emigrating or immigrating workmen, these facts would speak volumes. "Order must in one way or another be established," exclaims in 1770 the oft-cited author of the "Essay on Trade and Commerce." "Order," re-echoes Dr. Andrew Ure 66 years later, "Order" was wanting in manufacture based on "the scholastic dogma of division of labour," and "Arkwright created order."

At the same time manufacture was unable, either to seize upon the production of society to its full extent, or to revolutionise that production to its very core. It towered up as an economical work of art, on the broad foundation of the town handicrafts, and of the rural domestic industries. At a given stage in its development, the narrow technical basis on which manufacture rested, came into conflict with requirements of production that were created by manufacture itself.

One of its most finished creations was the workshop for the production of the instruments of labour themselves, including especially the complicated mechanical apparatus then already employed. A machine-factory, says Ure, "displayed the division of labour in manifold gradations—the file, the drill, the lathe, having each its different workman in the order of skill." (p. 21.) This workshop, the product of the division of labour in manufacture, produced in its turn—machines. It is they that sweep away the handicraftsman's work as the regulating principle of social production. Thus, on the one hand, the technical reason for the life-long annexation of the workman to a detail function is removed. On the other hand, the fetters that this same principle laid on the dominion of capital, fall away.

CHAPTER XV.

MACHINERY AND MODERN INDUSTRY.

SECTION 1.—THE DEVELOPMENT OF MACHINERY.

JOHN STUART MILL says in his Principles of Political Economy: "It is questionable if all the mechanical inventions yet made have lightened the day's toil of any human being."[1] That is, however, by no means the aim of the capitalistic application of machinery. Like every other increase in the productiveness of labour, machinery is intended to cheapen commodities, and, by shortening that portion of the working-day, in which the labourer works for himself, to lengthen the other portion that he gives, without an equivalent, to the capitalist. In short, it is a means for producing surplus-value.

In manufacture, the revolution in the mode of production begins with the labour-power, in modern industry it begins with the instruments of labour. Our first inquiry then is, how the instruments of labour are converted from tools into machines, or what is the difference between a machine and the implements of a handicraft? We are only concerned here with striking and general characteristics; for epochs in the history of society are no more separated from each other by hard and fast lines of demarcation, than are geological epochs.

Mathematicians and mechanicians, and in this they are followed by a few English economists, call a tool a simple machine, and a machine a complex tool. They see no essential difference between them, and even give the name of machine to the simple mechanical powers, the lever, the inclined plane, the screw, the wedge, &c.[2] As a matter of fact, every machine is a combination of those simple powers, no matter how they

---

[1] Mill should have said, "of any human being not fed by other people's labour," for, without doubt, machinery has greatly increased the number of well-to-do idlers.

[2] See, for instance, Hutton: "Course of Mathematics."

may be disguised. From the economical standpoint this explanation is worth nothing, because the historical element is wanting. Another explanation of the difference between tool and machine is that in the case of a tool, man is the motive power, while the motive power of a machine is something different from man, is, for instance, an animal, water, wind, and so on.[1] According to this, a plough drawn by oxen, which is a contrivance common to the most different epochs, would be a machine, while Claussen's circular loom, which, worked by a single labourer, weaves 96,000 picks per minute, would be a mere tool. Nay, this very loom, though a tool when worked by hand, would, if worked by steam, be a machine. And since the application of animal power is one of man's earliest inventions, production by machinery would have preceded production by handicrafts. When in 1735, John Wyatt brought out his spinning machine, and began the industrial revolution of the 18th century, not a word did he say about an ass driving it instead of a man, and yet this part fell to the ass. He described it as a machine "to spin without fingers."[2]

[1] "From this point of view we may draw a sharp line of distinction between a tool and a machine: spades, hammers, chisels, &c., combinations of levers and of screws, in all of which, no matter how complicated they may be in other respects, man is the motive power, ... all this falls under the idea of a tool; but the plough, which is drawn by animal power, and windmills, &c., must be classed among machines." (Wilhelm Schulz: "Die Bewegung der Produktion. Zürich, 1843," p. 38.) In many respects a book to be recommended.

[2] Before his time, spinning machines, although very imperfect ones, had already been used, and Italy was probably the country of their first appearance. A critical history of technology would show how little any of the inventions of the 18th century are the work of a single individual. Hitherto there is no such book. Darwin has interested us in the history of Nature's Technology, *i.e.*, in the formation of the organs of plants and animals, which organs serve as instruments of production for sustaining life. Does not the history of the productive organs of man, of organs that are the material basis of all social organisation, deserve equal attention? And would not such a history be easier to compile since, as Vico says, human history differs from natural history in this, that we have made the former, but not the latter? Technology discloses man's mode of dealing with Nature, the process of production by which he sustains his life, and thereby also lays bare the mode of formation of his social relations, and of the mental conceptions that flow from them. Every history of religion even, that fails to take account of this material basis, is uncritical. It is, in reality, much easier to discover by analysis the earthly core of the misty creations of religion, than, conversely, it is, to develop from the actual relations of life the corresponding celestialised forms of those relations. The latter method is the only materialistic, and therefore the only scientific one. The weak points in the abstract materialism of natural science, a materialism that excludes history and its process, are at once evident from the abstract and ideological

All fully developed machinery consists of three essentially different parts, the motor mechanism, the transmitting mechanism, and finally the tool or working machine. The motor mechanism is that which puts the whole in motion. It either generates its own motive power, like the steam engine, the caloric engine, the electro-magnetic machine, &c., or it receives its impulse from some already existing natural force, like the water-wheel from a head of water, the wind-mill from wind, &c. The transmitting mechanism, composed of fly-wheels, shafting, toothed wheels, pullies, straps, ropes, bands, pinions, and gearing of the most varied kinds, regulates the motion, changes its form where necessary, as for instance, from linear to circular, and divides and distributes it among the working machines. These two first parts of the whole mechanism are there, solely for putting the working machines in motion, by means of which motion the subject of labour is seized upon and modified as desired. The tool or working-machine is that part of the machinery with which the industrial revolution of the 18th century started. And to this day it constantly serves as such a starting point, whenever a handicraft, or a manufacture, is turned into an industry carried on by machinery.

On a closer examination of the working-machine proper, we find in it, as a general rule, though often, no doubt, under very altered forms, the apparatus and tools used by the handicraftsman or manufacturing workman; with this difference, that instead of being human implements, they are the implements of a mechanism, or mechanical implements. Either the entire machine is only a more or less altered mechanical edition of the old handicraft tool, as, for instance, the power-loom;[1] or the working parts fitted in the frame of the machine are old acquaintances, as spindles are in a mule, needles in a stocking-loom, saws in a sawing machine, and knives in a chopping machine. The distinction between these tools and the body proper of the machine, exists from their very birth; for they

conceptions of its spokesmen, whenever they venture beyond the bounds of their own speciality.

[1] Especially in the original form of the power-loom, we recognise, at the first glance, the ancient loom. In its modern form, the power-loom has undergone essential alterations.

continue for the most part to be produced by handicraft, or by manufacture, and are afterwards fitted into the body of the machine, which is the product of machinery.[1] The machine proper is therefore a mechanism that, after being set in motion, performs with its tools the same operations that were formerly done by the workman with similar tools. Whether the motive power is derived from man, or from some other machine, makes no difference in this respect. From the moment that the tool proper is taken from man, and fitted into a mechanism, a machine takes the place of a mere implement. The difference strikes one at once, even in those cases where man himself continues to be the prime mover. The number of implements that he himself can use simultaneously, is limited by the number of his own natural instruments of production, by the number of his bodily organs. In Germany, they tried at first to make one spinner work two spinning wheels, that is, to work simultaneously with both hands and both feet. This was too difficult. Later, a treddle.spinning wheel with two spindles was invented, but adepts in spinning, who could spin two threads at once, were almost as scarce as two-headed men. The Jenny, on the other hand, even at its very birth, spun with 12-18 spindles, and the stocking-loom knits with many thousand needles at once. The number of tools that a machine can bring into play simultaneously, is from the very first emancipated from the organic limits that hedge in the tools of a handicraftsman.

In many manual implements the distinction between man as mere motive power, and man as the workman or operator properly so-called, is brought into striking contrast. For instance, the foot is merely the prime mover of the spinning wheel, while the hand, working with the spindle, and drawing and twisting, performs the real operation of spinning. It is this last part of the handicraftsman's implement that is first

---

[1] It is only during the last 15 years (*i.e.*, since about 1850), that a constantly increasing portion of these machine tools have been made in England by machinery, and that not by the same manufacturers who make the machines. Instances of machines for the fabrication of these mechanical tools are, the automatic bobbin-making engine, the card-setting engine, shuttle-making machines, and machines for forging mule and throstle spindles.

seized upon by the industrial revolution, leaving to the workman, in addition to his new labour of watching the machine
with his eyes and correcting its mistakes with his hands, the
merely mechanical part of being the moving power. On the
other hand, implements, in regard to which man has always
acted as a simple motive power, as, for instance, by turning the
crank of a mill,[1] by pumping, by moving up and down the arm
of a bellows, by pounding with a mortar, &c., such implements
soon call for the application of animals, water,[2] and wind as
motive powers. Here and there, long before the period of
manufacture, and also, to some extent, during that period,
these implements pass over into machines, but without creating any revolution in the mode of production. It becomes
evident, in the period of Modern Industry, that these implements, even under their form of manual tools, are already
machines. For instance, the pumps with which the Dutch, in
1836–7, emptied the Lake of Harlem, were constructed on the
principle of ordinary pumps; the only difference being, that
their pistons were driven by cyclopean steam-engines, instead
of by men. The common and very imperfect bellows of the
blacksmith is, in England, occasionally converted into a blow-
ing-engine, by connecting its arm with a steam-engine. The
steam-engine itself, such as it was at its invention, during the
manufacturing period at the close of the 17th century, and
such as it continued to be down to 1780,[3] did not give rise to
any industrial revolution. It was, on the contrary, the inven-

---

[1] Moses says: "Thou shalt not muzzle the ox that treads the corn." The Christian
philanthropists of Germany, on the contrary, fastened a wooden board round the
necks of the serfs, whom they used as a motive power for grinding, in order to
prevent them from putting flour into their mouths with their hands.

[2] It was partly the want of streams with a good fall on them, and partly their
battles with superabundance of water in other respects, that compelled the Dutch to
resort to wind as a motive power. The windmill itself they got from Germany,
where its invention was the origin of a pretty squabble between the nobles, the
priests, and the emperor, as to which of those three the wind "belonged." The air
makes bondage, was the cry in Germany, at the same time that the wind was making
Holland free. What it reduced to bondage in this case, was not the Dutchman, but
the land for the Dutchman. In 1836, 12,000 windmills of 6000 horse-power were
still employed in Holland, to prevent two-thirds of the land from being reconverted
into morasses.

[3] It was, indeed, very much improved by Watt's first so-called single acting engine; but, in this form, it continued to be a mere machine for raising water, and
the liquor from salt mines.

tion of machines that made a revolution in the form of steam-engines necessary. As soon as man, instead of working with an implement on the subject of his labour, becomes merely the motive power of an implement-machine, it is a mere accident that motive power takes the disguise of human muscle; and it may equally well take the form of wind, water or steam. Of course, this does not prevent such a change of form from producing great technical alterations in the mechanism that was originally constructed to be driven by man alone. Nowadays, all machines that have their way to make, such as sewing machines, bread-making machines, &c., are, unless from their very nature their use on a small scale is excluded, constructed to be driven both by human and by purely mechanical motive power.

The machine, which is the starting point of the industrial revolution, supersedes the workman, who handles a single tool, by a mechanism operating with a number of similar tools, and set in motion by a single motive power, whatever the form of that power may be.[1] Here we have the machine, but only as an elementary factor of production by machinery.

Increase in the size of the machine, and in the number of its working tools, calls for a more massive mechanism to drive it; and this mechanism requires, in order to overcome its resistance, a mightier moving power than that of man, apart from the fact that man is a very imperfect instrument for producing uniform continued motion. But assuming that he is acting simply as a motor, that a machine has taken the place of his tool, it is evident that he can be replaced by natural forces. Of all the great motors handed down from the manufacturing period, horse-power is the worst, partly because a horse has a head of his own, partly because he is costly, and the extent to which he is applicable in factories is very restricted.[2] Never-

---

[1] "The union of all these simple instruments, set in motion by a single motor, constitutes a machine." (Babbage, l. c.)

[2] In January, 1861, John C. Morton read before the Society of Arts a paper on "The forces employed in agriculture." He there states: "Every improvement that furthers the uniformity of the land makes the steam-engine more and more applicable to the production of pure mechanical force. . . . Horse-power is requisite wherever crooked fences and other obstructions prevent uniform action. These obstructions are vanishing day by day. For operations that demand more exercise

theless the horse was extensively used during the infancy of Modern Industry. This is proved, as well by the complaints of contemporary agriculturists, as by the term "horse-power," which has survived to this day as an expression for mechanical force.

Wind was too inconstant and uncontrollable, and besides, in England, the birthplace of Modern Industry, the use of water-power preponderated even during the manufacturing period. In the 17th century attempts had already been made to turn two pairs of millstones with a single water-wheel. But the increased size of the gearing was too much for the water-power, which had now become insufficient, and this was one of the circumstances that led to a more accurate investigation of the laws of friction. In the same way the irregularity caused by the motive power in mills that were put in motion by pushing and pulling a lever, led to the theory, and the application, of the fly-wheel, which afterwards plays so important a part in Modern Industry.[1] In this way, during the manufacturing period, were developed the first scientific and technical elements of Modern Mechanical Industry. Arkwright's throstle-spinning mill was from the very first turned by water. But for all that, the use of water, as the predominant motive power, was beset with difficulties. It could not be increased at will, it failed at certain seasons of the year, and, above all, it was essentially local.[2] Not till the invention of Watt's second and so called double-acting steam-engine, was a

of will than actual force, the only power applicable is that controlled every instant by the human mind—in other words, man-power." Mr. Morton then reduces steam-power, horse-power, and man-power, to the unit in general use for steam-engines, namely, the force required to raise 33,000 lbs. one foot in one minute, and reckons the cost of one horse-power from a steam-engine to be 3d., and from a horse to be 5½d. per hour. Further, if a horse must fully maintain its health, it can work no more than 8 hours a day. Three at the least out of every seven horses used on tillage land during the year can be dispensed with, by using steam-power, at an expense not greater than that which, the horses dispensed with, would cost during the 3 or 4 months in which alone they can be used effectively. Lastly, steam-power, in those agricultural operations in which it can be employed, improves, in comparison with horse-power, the quality of the work. To do the work of a steam-engine would require 66 men, at a total cost of 15s. an hour, and to do the work of a horse, 32 men, at a total cost of 8s. an hour.

[1] Faulhebr, 1625; De Cous, 1688.

[2] The modern turbine frees the industrial exploitation of water-power from many of its former fetters.

prime mover found, that begot its own force by the consumption of coal and water, whose power was entirely under man's control, that was mobile and a means of locomotion, that was urban and not, like the water-wheel, rural, that permitted production to be concentrated in towns instead of, like the water-wheels, being scattered up and down the country,[1] that was of universal technical application, and, relatively speaking, little affected in its choice of residence by local circumstances. The greatness of Watt's genius showed itself in the specification of the patent that he took out in April, 1784. In that specification his steam-engine is described, not as an invention for a specific purpose, but as an agent universally applicable in Mechanical Industry. In it he points out applications, many of which, as for instance, the steam-hammer, were not introduced till half a century later. Nevertheless he doubted the use of steam-engines in navigation. His successors, Boulton and Watt, sent to the exhibition of 1851 steam-engines of colossal size for ocean steamers.

As soon as tools had been converted from being manual implements of man into implements of a mechanical apparatus, of a machine, the motive mechanism also acquired an independent form, entirely emancipated from the restraints of human strength. Thereupon the individual machine, that we have hitherto been considering, sinks into a mere factor in production by machinery. One motive mechanism was now able to drive many machines at once. The motive mechanism grows with the number of the machines that are turned simultaneously, and the transmitting mechanism becomes a wide-spreading apparatus.

We now proceed to distinguish the co-operation of a number

---

[1] "In the early days of textile manufactures, the locality of the factory depended upon the existence of a stream having a sufficient fall to turn a water-wheel; and, although the establishment of the water-mills was the commencement of the breaking up of the domestic system of manufacture, yet the mills necessarily situated upon streams, and frequently at considerable distances the one from the other, formed part of a rural, rather than an urban system; and it was not until the introduction of the steam-power as a substitute for the stream that factories were congregated in towns, and localities where the coal and water required for the production of steam were found in sufficient quantities. The steam-engine is the parent of manufacturing towns." (A. Redgrave in "Reports of the Insp. of Fact. 30th April, 1866," p. 36.)

of machines of one kind from a complex system of machinery. In the one case, the product is entirely made by a single machine, which performs all the various operations previously done by one handicraftsman with his tool; as, for instance, by a weaver with his loom; or by several handicraftsmen success- ively, either separately or as members of a system of Manu- facture.[1] For example, in the manufacture of envelopes, one man folded the paper with the folder, another laid on the gum, a third turned the flap over, on which the device is impressed, a fourth embossed the device, and so on; and for each of these operations the envelope had to change hands. One single envelope machine now performs all these operations at once, and makes more than 3000 envelopes in an hour. In the Lon- don exhibition of 1862, there was an American machine for making paper cornets. It cut the paper, pasted, folded, and finished 300 in a minute. Here, the whole process, which, when carried on as Manufacture, was split up into, and carried out by, a series of operations, is completed by a single machine, working a combination of various tools. Now, whether such a machine be merely a reproduction of a complicated manual implement, or a combination of various simple implements specialised by Manufacture, in either case, in the factory, *i.e.*, in the workshop in which machinery alone is used, we meet again with simple co-operation; and, leaving the workman out of consideration for the moment, this co-operation presents itself to us, in the first instance, as the conglomeration in one place of similar and simultaneously acting machines.' Thus, a weaving factory is constituted of a number of power-looms, working side by side, and a sewing factory of a number of sewing machines all in the same building. But there is here a technical oneness in the whole system, owing to all the ma-

---

[1] From the standpoint of division of labour in Manufacture, weaving was not simple, but on the contrary, complicated manual labour; and consequently the power-loom is a machine that does very complicated work. It is altogether errone- ous to suppose that modern machinery originally appropriated these operations alone, which division of labour had simplified. Spinning and weaving were, during the manufacturing period, split up into new species, and the implements were modified and improved; but the labour itself was in no way divided, and it retained its handi- craft character. It is not the labour, but the instrument of labour, that serves as the starting-point of the machine.

chines receiving their impulse simultaneously, and in an equal degree, from the pulsations of the common prime mover, by the intermediary of the transmitting mechanism; and this mechanism, to a certain extent, is also common to them all, since only particular ramifications of it branch off to each machine. Just as a number of tools, then, form the organs of a machine, so a number of machines of one kind constitute the organs of the motive mechanism.

A real machinery system, however, does not take the place of these independent machines, until the subject of labour goes through a connected series of detail processes, that are carried out by a chain of machines of various kinds, the one supplementing the other. Here we have again the co-operation by division of labour that characterises Manufacture; only now, it is a combination of detail machines. The special tools of the various detail workmen, such as those of the beaters, combers, spinners, &c., in the woollen manufacture, are now transformed into the tools of specialised machines, each machine constituting a special organ, with a special function, in the system. In those branches of industry in which the machinery system is first introduced, Manufacture itself furnishes, in a general way, the natural basis for the division, and consequent organisation, of the process of production.[1] Nevertheless an essential difference at once manifests itself. In Manufacture it is the workmen who. with their manual implements, must,

---

[1] Before the epoch of Mechanical Industry, the wool manufacture was the predominating manufacture in England. Hence it was in this industry that, in the first half of the 18th century, the most experiments were made. Cotton, which required less careful preparation for its treatment by machinery, derived the benefit of the experience gained on wool, just as afterwards the manipulation of wool by machinery was developed on the lines of cotton-spinning and weaving by machinery. It was only during the 10 years immediately preceding 1866, that isolated details of the wool manufacture, such as wool-combing, were incorporated in the factory system. "The application of power to the process of combing wool . . . . extensively in operation since the introduction of the combing machine, especially Lister's . . . undoubtedly had the effect of throwing a very large number of men out of work. Wool was formerly combed by hand, most frequently in the cottage of the comber. It is now very generally combed in the factory, and hand-labour is superseded, except in some particular kinds of work, in which hand-combed wool is still preferred. Many of the hand-combers found employment in the factories, but the produce of the hand-combers bears so small a proportion to that of the machine, that the employment of a very large number of combers has passed away." (Rep. of Insp. of Fact. for 31st Oct., 1856, p. 16.)

either singly or in groups, carry on each particular detail process. If, on the one hand, the workman becomes adapted to the process, on the other, the process was previously made suitable to the workman. This subjective principle of the division of labour no longer exists in production by machinery. Here, the process as a whole is examined objectively, in itself, that is to say, without regard to the question of its execution by human hands, it is analysed into its constituent phases; and the problem, how to execute each detail process, and bind them all into a whole, is solved by the aid of machines, chemistry, &c.[1] But, of course, in this case also, theory must be perfected by accumulated experience on a large scale. Each detail machine supplies raw material to the machine next in order; and since they are all working at the same time, the product is always going through the various stages of its fabrication, and is also constantly in a state of transition, from one phase to another. Just as in Manufacture, the direct co-operation of the detail labourers establishes a numerical proportion between the special groups, so in an organised system of machinery, where one detail machine is constantly kept employed by another, a fixed relation is established between their numbers, their size, and their speed. The collective machine, now an organised system of various kinds of single machines, and of groups of single machines, becomes more and more perfect, the more the process as a whole becomes a continuous one, *i.e.,* the less the raw material is interrupted in its passage from its first phase to its last; in other words, the more its passage from one phase to another is effected, not by the hand of man, but by the machinery itself. In Manufacture the isolation of each detail process is a condition imposed by the nature of division of labour, but in the fully developed factory the continuity of those processes is, on the contrary, imperative.

A system of machinery, whether it reposes on the mere co-operation of similar machines, as in weaving, or on a combination of different machines, as in spinning, constitutes in itself

---

[1] "The principle of the factory system, then, is to substitute . . . the partition of a process into its essential constituents, for the division or graduation of labour among artisans." (Andrew Ure: "The Philosophy of Manufactures." Lond., 1835, p. 20.)

a huge automaton, whenever it is driven by a self-acting prime mover. But although the factory as a whole be driven by its steam-engine, yet either some of the individual machines may require the aid of the workman for some of their movements (such aid was necessary for the running in of the mule carriage, before the invention of the self-acting mule, and is still necessary in fine-spinning mills); or, to enable a machine to do its work, certain parts of it may require to be handled by the workman like a manual tool; this was the case in machine-makers' workshops, before the conversion of the slide rest into a self-actor. As soon as a machine executes, without man's help, all the movements requisite to elaborate the raw material, needing only attendance from him, we have an automatic system of machinery, and one that is susceptible of constant improvement in its details. Such improvements as the apparatus that stops a drawing frame, whenever a sliver breaks, and the self-acting stop, that stops the power-loom so soon as the shuttle bobbin is emptied of weft, are quite modern inventions. As an example, both of continuity of production, and of the carrying out of the automatic principle, we may take a modern paper mill. In the paper industry generally, we may advantageously study in detail not only the distinctions between modes of production based on different means of production, but also the connexion of the social conditions of production with those modes: for the old German paper-making furnishes us with a sample of handicraft production; that of Holland in the 17th and of France in the 18th century with a sample of manufacturing in the strict sense; and that of modern England with a sample of automatic fabrication of this article. Besides these, there still exist, in India and China, two distinct antique Asiatic forms of the same industry.

An organised system of machines, to which motion is communicated by the transmitting mechanism from a central automaton, is the most developed form of production by machinery. Here we have, in the place of the isolated machine, a mechanical monster whose body fills whole factories, and whose demon power, at first veiled under the slow and measured motions of his giant limbs, at length breaks out into the fast and furious whirl of his countless working organs.

There were mules and steam-engines before there were any labourers whose exclusive occupation it was to make mules and steam-engines; just as men wore clothes before there were such people as tailors. The inventions of Vaucanson, Arkwright, Watt, and others, were, however, practicable, only because those inventors found, ready to hand, a considerable number of skilled mechanical workmen, placed at their disposal by the manufacturing period. Some of these workmen were independent handicraftmen of various trades, others were grouped together in manufactures, in which, as before-mentioned, division of labour was strictly carried out. As inventions increased in number, and the demand for the newly discovered machines grew larger, the machine-making industry split up, more and more, into numerous independent branches, and division of labour in these manufactures was more and more developed. Here, then, we see in Manufacture the immediate technical foundation of Modern Industry. Manufacture produced the machinery, by means of which Modern Industry abolished the handicraft and manufacturing systems in those spheres of production that it first seized upon. The factory system was therefore raised, in the natural course of things, on an inadequate foundation. When the system attained to a certain degree of development, it had to root up this ready-made foundation, which in the meantime had been elaborated on the old lines, and to build up for itself a basis that should correspond to its methods of production. Just as the individual machine retains a dwarfish character, so long as it is worked by the power of man alone, and just as no system of machinery could be properly developed before the steam engine took the place of the earlier motive powers, animals, wind, and even water; so, too, Modern Industry was crippled in its complete development, so long as its characteristic instrument of production, the machine, owed its existence to personal strength and personal skill, and depended on the muscular development, the keenness of sight, and the cunning of hand, with which the detail workmen in manufactures and the manual labourers in handicrafts, wielded their dwarfish implements. Thus, apart from the dearness of the machines made in this way, a circumstance that is ever present to the mind of the capitalist, the expansion of industries carried on by means of machinery, and the invasion by machinery of fresh branches of production, were dependent on the growth of a class of workmen, who, owing to the almost artistic nature of their employment, could increase their numbers only gradually, and not by leaps and bounds. But besides this, at a certain stage of its development, Modern Industry became .technologically incompatible with the basis furnished for it by handicraft and Manufacture. The increasing size of the prime movers, of the transmitting mechanism, and of the machines proper, the greater complication, multiformity and regularity of the details of these machines, as they more and more departed from the model of those originally made by manual labour, and acquired a form, untrammelled except by the conditions under which they worked,[1] the perfecting of the automatic system, and the use, every day more avoidable, of a more refractory material, such as iron instead of wood—the solution of all these problems, which sprang up by the force of circumstances, everywhere met with a stumbling-block in the personal restrictions which even the collective labourer of Manufacture could not break through, except to a limited extent. Such machines as the modern hydraulic press, the modern powerloom, and the modern carding engine, could never have been furnished by Manufacture.

A radical change in the mode of production in one sphere of industry involves a similar change in other spheres. This

---

[1] The powerloom was at first made chiefly of wood; in its improved modern form ft is made of iron. To what an extent the old forms of the instruments of pro. duction influenced their new forms at first starting, is shown by, amongst other things, the most superficial comparison of the present powerloom with the old one, of the modern blowing apparatus of a blast-furnace with the first inefficient mechanical reproduction of the ordinary bellows, and perhaps more strikingly than in any other way, by the attempts before the invention of the present locomotive, to construct a locomotive that actually had two feet, which after the fashion of a horse, it raised alternately from the ground. It is only after considerable development of the science of mechanics,. and accumulated practical experience, that the form of a machine becomes settled entirely in accordance with mechanical principles, and emancipated from the traditional form of the tool that gave rise to it.

happens at first in such branches of industry as are connected together by being separate phases of a process, and yet are isolated by the social division of labour, in such a way, that each of them produces an independent commodity. Thus spinning by machinery made weaving by machinery a necessity, and both together made the mechanical and chemical revolution that took place in bleaching, printing, and dyeing, imperative. So too, on the other hand, the revolution in cotton-spinning called forth the invention of the gin, for separating the seeds from the cotton fibre; it was only by means of this invention, that the production of cotton became possible on the enormous scale at present required.[1] But more especially, the revolution in the modes of production of industry and agriculture made necessary a revolution in the general conditions of the social process of production, *i.e.,* in the means of communication and of transport. In a society whose pivot, to use an expression of Fourier, was agriculture on a small scale, with its subsidiary domestic industries, and the urban handicrafts, the means of communication and transport were so utterly inadequate to the productive requirements of the manufacturing period, with its extended division of social labour, its concentration of the instruments of labour, and of the workmen, and its colonial markets, that they became in fact revolutionised. In the same way the means of communication and transport handed down from the manufacturing period soon became unbearable trammels on Modern Industry, with its feverish haste of production, its enormous extent, its constant flinging of capital and labour from one sphere of production into another, and its newly-created connexions with the markets of the whole world. Hence, apart from the radical changes introduced in the construction of sailing vessels, the means of communication and transport became gradually adapted to the modes of production of mechanical industry, by the creation of a system of river steamers, railways, ocean steamers, and

---

[1] Eli Whitney's cotton gin had until very recent times undergone less essential changes than any other machine of the 18th century. It is only during the last decade (*i.e., since* 1856) that another American, Mr. Emery, of Albany, New York, has rendered Whitney's gin antiquated by an improvement as simple as it is effective.

telegraphs. But the huge masses of iron that had now to be forged, to be welded, to be cut, to be bored, and to be shaped, demanded, on their part, cyclopean machines, for the construction of which the methods of the manufacturing period were utterly inadequate.

Modern Industry had therefore itself to take in hand the machine, its characteristic instrument of production, and to construct machines by machines. It was not till it did this, that it built up for itself a fitting technical foundation, and stood on its own feet. Machinery, simultaneously with the increasing use of it, in the first decades of this century, appropriated, by degrees, the fabrication of machines proper. But it was only during the decade preceding 1866, that the construction of railways and ocean steamers on a stupendous scale called into existence the cyclopean machines now employed in the construction of prime movers.

The most essential condition to the production of machines by machines was a prime mover capable of exerting any amount of force, and yet under perfect control. Such a condition was already supplied by the steam-engine. But at the same time it was necessary to produce the geometrically accurate straight lines, planes, circles, cylinders, cones, and spheres, required in the detail parts of the machines. This problem Henry Maudsley solved in the first decade of this century by the invention of the slide rest, a tool that was soon made automatic, and in a modified form was applied to other constructive machines besides the lathe, for which it was originally intended. This mechanical appliance replaces, not some particular tool, but the hand itself, which produces a given form by holding and guiding the cutting tool along the iron or other material operated upon. Thus it became possible to produce the forms of the individual parts of machinery "with a degree of ease, accuracy, and speed, that no accumulated experience of the hand of the most skilled workman could give."[1]

---

[1] "The Industry of Nations, Lond., 1855," Part II., p. 239. This work also remarks: "Simple and outwardly unimportant as this appendage to lathes may appear, it is not, we believe, averring too much to state, that its influence in improving and extending the use of machinery has been as great as that produced by Watt's improvements of the steam-engine itself. Its introduction went at once to perfect all machinery, to cheapen it, and to stimulate invention and improvement."

If we now fix our attention on that portion of the machinery employed in the construction of machines, which constitutes the operating tool, we find the manual implements reappearing, but on a cyclopean scale. The operating part of the boring machine is an immense drill driven by a steam-engine; without this machine, on the other hand, the cylinders of large steam-engines and of hydaulic presses could not be made. The mechanical lathe is only a cyclopean reproduction of the ordinary foot-lathe; the planing machine, an iron carpenter, that works on iron with the same tools that the human carpenter employs on wood; the instrument that, on the London wharves, cuts the veneers, is a gigantic razor; the tool of the shearing machine, which shears iron as easily as a tailor's scissors cut cloth, is a monster pair of scissors; and the steam hammer works with an ordinary hammer head, but of such a weight that not Thor himself could wield it.[1] These steam hammers are an invention of Nasmyth, and there is one that weighs over 6 tons and strikes with a vertical fall of 7 feet, on an anvil weighing 36 tons. It is mere child's play for it to crush a block of granite into powder, yet it is no less capable of driving, with a succession of light taps, a nail into a piece of soft wood.[2]

The implements of labour, in the form of machinery, necessitate the substitution of natural forces for human force, and the conscious application of science, instead of rule of thumb. In Manufacture, the organisation of the social labour-process is purely subjective; it is a combination of detail labourers; in its machinery system, Modern Industry has a productive organism that is purely objective, in which the labourer becomes a mere appendage to an already existing material condition of production. In simple co-operation, and even in that founded on division of labour, the suppression of the isolated, by the collective, workman still appears to be more or less accidental. Machinery, with a few exceptions to be mentioned later, oper-

[1] One of these machines, used for forging paddle-wheel shafts in London, is called "Thor." It forges a shaft of 16½ tons with as much ease as a blacksmith forges a horse-shoe.

[2] Wood working machines that are also capable of being employed on a small scale are mostly American inventions.

ates only by means of associated labour, or labour in common. Hence, the co-operative character of the labour-process is, in the latter case, a technical necessity dictated by the instrument of labour itself.

SECTION 2.—THE VALUE TRANSFERRED BY MACHINERY TO THE PRODUCT.

We saw that the productive forces resulting from co-operation and division of labour cost capital nothing. They are natural forces of social labour. So also physical forces, like steam, water, &c., when appropriated to productive processes, cost nothing. But just as a man requires lungs to breathe with, so he requires something that is work of man's hand, in order to consume physical forces productively. A water-wheel is necessary to exploit the force of water, and a steam engine to exploit the elasticity of steam. Once discovered, the law of the deviation of the magnetic needle in the field of an electric current, or the law of magnetisation of iron, around which an electric current circulates, cost never a penny.[1] But the exploitation of these laws for the purposes of telegraphy, &c., necessitates a costly and expensive apparatus. The tool, as we have seen, is not exterminated by the machine. From being a dwarf implement of the human organism, it expands and multiplies into the implement of mechanism created by man. Capital now sets the labourer to work, not with a manual tool, but with a machine which itself handles the tools. Although, therefore, it is clear at the first glance that, by incorporating both stupendous physical forces, and the natural sciences, with the process of production, Modern Industry raises the productiveness of labour to an extraordinary degree, it is by no means equally clear, that this increased productive force is not, on the other hand, purchased by an increased expenditure of

---

[1] Science, generally speaking, costs the capitalist nothing, a fact that by no means hinders him from exploiting it. The science of others is as much annexed by capital as the labour of others. Capitalistic appropriation and personal appropriation, whether of science or of material wealth, are, however, totally different things. Dr. Ure himself deplores the gross ignorance of mechanical science existing among his dear machinery-exploiting manufacturers, and Liebig can a tale unfold about the astounding ignorance of chemistry displayed by English chemical manufacturers.

labour. Machinery, like every other component of constant capital, creates no new value, but yields up its own value to the product that it serves to beget. In so far as the machine has value, and, in consequence, parts with value to the product, it forms an element in the value of that product. Instead of being cheapened, the product is made dearer in proportion to the value of the machine. And it is clear as noon-day, that machines and systems of machinery, the characteristic instruments of labour of Modern Industry, are incomparably more loaded with value than the implements used in handicrafts and manufactures.

In the first place, it must be observed that the machinery, while always entering as a whole into the labour-process, enters into the value-begetting process only by bits. It never adds more value than it loses, on an average, by wear and tear. Hence there is a great difference between the value of a machine, and the value transferred in a given time by that machine to the product. The longer the life of the machine in the labour-process, the greater is that difference. It is true, no doubt, as we have already seen, that every instrument of labour enters as a whole into the labour-process, and only piecemeal, proportionally to its average daily loss by wear and tear, into the value-begetting process. But this difference between the instrument as a whole and its daily wear and tear, is much greater in a machine than in a tool, because the machine, being made from more durable material, has a longer life; because its employment, being regulated by strictly scientific laws, allows of greater economy in the wear and tear of its parts, and in the materials it consumes; and lastly, because its field of production is incomparably larger than that of a tool. After making allowance, both in the case of the machine and of the tool, for their average daily cost, that is for the value they transmit to the product by their average daily wear and tear, and for their consumption of auxiliary substances, such as oil, coal, and so on, they each do their work gratuitously, just like the forces furnished by nature without the help of man. The greater the productive power of the machinery compared with that of the tool, the greater is the extent of its gratuitous service com-

pared with that of the tool. In Modern Industry man succeeded for the first time in making the product of his past
labour work on a large scale gratuitously, like the forces of
nature.[1]

In treating of Co-operation and Manufacture, it was shown
that certain general factors of production, such as buildings,
are, in comparison with the scattered means of production of
the isolated workman, economised by being consumed in common, and that they therefore make the product cheaper. In a
system of machinery, not only is the framework of the machine
consumed in common by its numerous operating implements,
but the prime mover, together with a part of the transmitting
mechanism, is consumed in common by the numerous operative
machines.

Given the difference between the value of the machinery,
and the value transferred by it in a day to the product, the
extent to which this latter value makes the product dearer,
depends in the first instance, upon the size of the product; so
to say, upon its area. Mr. Baynes, of Blackburn, in a lecture
published in 1858, estimates that "each real mechanical horse-
power[2] will drive 450 self-acting mule spindles, with pre-

---

[1] Ricardo lays such stress on this effect of machinery (of which, in other connexions, he takes no more notice than he does of the general distinction between the
labour-process and the process of creating surplus-value), that he occasionally loses
sight of the value given up by machines to the product, and puts machines on the
same footing as natural forces. Thus "Adam Smith nowhere undervalues the services which the natural agents and machinery perform for us, but he very justly distinguishes the nature of the value which they add to commodities . . . as they
perform their work gratuitously, the assistance which they afford us, adds nothing
to value in exchange." (Ric. l. c., p. 336, 337.) This observation of Ricardo is of
course correct in so far as it is directed against J. B. Say, who imagines that
machines render the "service" of creating value which forms a part of "profits."

[2] A horse-power is equal to a force of 33,000 foot-pounds per minute, *i.e.*, to a
force that raises 33,000 pounds one foot in a minute, or one pound 33,000 feet.
This is the horse-power meant in the text. In ordinary language, and also here and
there in quotations in this work, a distinction is drawn between the "nominal" and
the "commercial" or "indicated" horse-power of the same engine. The old or
nominal horse-power is calculated exclusively from the length of piston-stroke, and
the diameter of the cylinder, and leaves pressure of steam and piston speed out of
consideration. It expresses practically this: This engine would be one of 50
horse-power, if it were driven with the same low pressure of steam, and the same
slow piston speed, as in the days of Boulton and Watt. But the two latter factors
have increased enormously since those days. In order to measure the mechanical
force exerted to-day by an engine, an indicator has been invented which shows the
pressure of the steam in the cylinder. The piston speed is easily ascertained. Thus

paration, or 200 throstle spindles, or 15 looms for 40 inch cloth with the appliances for warping, sizing, &c." In the first case, it is the day's produce of 450 mule spindles, in the second, of 200 throstle spindles, in the third, of 15 power-looms, over which the daily cost of one horse-power, and the wear and tear of the machinery set in motion by that power, are spread; so that only a very minute value is transferred by such wear and tear to a pound of yarn or a yard of cloth. The same is the case with the steam-hammer mentioned above. Since its daily wear and tear, its coal-consumption, &c., are spread over the stupendous masses of iron hammered by it in a day, only a small value is added to a hundredweight of iron; but that value would be very great, if the cyclopean instrument were employed in driving in nails.

Given a machine's capacity for work, that is, the number of its operating tools, or, where it is a question of force, their mass, the amount of its product will depend on the velocity of its working parts, on the speed, for instance, of the spindles, or on the number of blows given by the hammer in a minute. Many of these colossal hammers strike seventy times in a minute, and Ryder's patent machine for forging spindles with small hammers gives as many as 700 strokes per minute.

Given the rate at which machinery transfers its value to the product, the amount of value so transferred depends on the total value of the machinery.[1] The less labour it contains, the less value it imparts to the product. The less value it gives up, so much the more productive it is, and so much the more

the "indicated" or "commercial" horse-power of an engine is expressed by a mathematical formula, involving diameter of cylinder, length of stroke, piston speed, and steam pressure, simultaneously, and showing what multiple of 33,000 pounds is really raised by the engine in a minute. Hence, one "nominal" horse-power may exert three, four, or even five "indicated" or "real" horse-powers. This observation is made for the purpose of explaining various citations in the subsequent pages.—(The editor.)

[1] The reader who is imbued with capitalist notions will naturally miss here the "interest" that the machine, in proportion to its capital value, adds to the product. It is, however, easily seen that since a machine no more creates new value than any other part of constant capital, it cannot add any value under the name of "interest." It is also evident that here, where we are treating of the production of surplus value, we cannot assume *a priori* the existence of any part of that value under the name of interest. The capitalist mode of calculating, which appears, *primâ facie*, absurd, and repugnant to the laws of the creation of value, will be explained in the third book of this work.

its services approximate to those of natural forces. But the production of machinery by machinery lessens its value rela-tively to its extension and efficacy.

An analysis and comparison of the prices of commodities produced by handicrafts or manufacturers, and of the prices of the same commodities produced by machinery, shows generally that, in the product of machinery, the value due to the instruments of labour, increases relatively, but decreases absolutely. In other words, its absolute amount decreases, but its amount, relatively to the total value of the product, of a pound of yarn, for instance, increases.[1]

It is evident that whenever it costs as much labour to produce a machine as is saved by the employment of that machine, there is nothing but a transposition of labour; consequently the total labour required to produce a commodity is not lessened or the productiveness of labour is not increased. It is clear, however, that the difference between the labour a machine costs, and the labour it saves, in other words, that the degree of its productiveness does not depend on the difference between its own value and the value of the implement it replaces. As long as the labour spent on a machine, and consequently the portion of its value added to the product, remains

[1] This portion of value which is added by the machinery, decreases both absolutely and relatively, when the machinery does away with horses and other animals that are employed as mere moving forces, and not as machines for changing the form of matter. It may here be incidentally observed, that Descartes, in defining animals as mere machines, saw with eyes of the manufacturing period, while to eyes of the middle ages, animals were assistants to man, as they were later to Von Haller in his "Restauration der Staatswissenschaften." That Descartes, like Bacon, anticipated an alteration in the form of production, and the practical subjugation of Nature by Man, as a result of the altered methods of thought, is plain from his "Discours de la Méthode." He there says: "Il est possible (by the methods he introduced in philosophy) de parvenir à des connaissances fort utiles à la vie, et qu'au lieu de cette philosophie spéculative qu'on enseigne dans les écoles, on en peut trouver une pratique, par laquelle, connaissant la force et les actions du feu, de l'eau, de l'air, des astres, et de tous les autres corps qui nous environnent, aussi distinctement que nous connaissons les divers métiers de nos artisans, nous les pourrious employer en même façon à tous les usages auxquels ils sont propres, et ainsi nous rendre comme maitres et possesseurs de la nature" and thus "contribuer au perfectionnement de la vie humaine." In the preface to Sir Dudley North's "Discourses upon Trade" (1691) it is stated, that Descartes' method had begun to free political economy from the old fables and superstitious notions of gold, trade, &c. On the whole, however, the early English economists sided with Bacon and Hobbes as their philosophers; while, at a later period, the philosopher κατ' ἐξοχὴν of political economy in England, France, and Italy, was Locke.

smaller than the value added by the workman to the product with his tool, there is always a difference of labour saved in favour of the machine. The productiveness of a machine is therefore measured by the human labour-power it replaces. According to Mr. Baynes, $2\frac{1}{2}$ operatives are required for the 450 mule spindles, inclusive of preparation machinery,[1] that are driven by one-horse power; each self-acting mule spindle, working ten hours, produces 13 ounces of yarn (average number or thickness); consequently $2\frac{1}{2}$ operatives spin weekly $365\frac{5}{8}$ lbs. of yarn. Hence, leaving waste on one side, 366 lbs. of cotton absorb, during their conversion into yarn, only 150 hours' labour, or fifteen days' labour of ten hours each. But with a spinning-wheel, supposing the hand-spinner to produce thirteen ounces of yarn in sixty hours, the same weight of cotton would absorb 2700 days' labour of ten hours each, or 27,000 hours' labour.[2] Where block printing, the old method of printing calico by hand, has been superseded by machine printing, a single machine prints, with the aid of one man or boy, as much calico of four colours in one hour, as it formerly took 200 men to do.[3] Before Eli Whitney invented the cotton-gin in 1793, the separation of the seed from a pound of cotton cost an average day's labour. By means of his invention one negress was enabled to clean 100 lbs. daily; and since then, the efficacy of the gin has been considerably increased. A pound of cotton wool, previously costing 50 cents to produce, included after that invention more unpaid labour, and was consequently sold with greater profit, at 10 cents. In India they employ for separating the wool from the seed, an instrument, half machine, half tool, called a churka; with this one

---

[1] According to the annual report (1863) of the Essen chamber of commerce, there was produced in 1862, at the cast-steel works of Krupp, with its 161 furnaces, thirty-two steam-engines (in the year 1800 this was about the number of all the steam-engines working in Manchester), and fourteen steam-hammers (representing in all 1236 horse-power), forty-nine forges, 203 tool-machines, and about 2400 workmen—thirteen million pounds of cast steel. Here there are not two workmen to each horse-power.

[2] Babbage estimates that in Java the spinning labour alone adds 117% to the value of the cotton. At the same period (1832) the total value added to the cotton by machinery and labour in the fine spinning-industry, amounted to about 33% of the value of the cotton. ("On the Economy of Machinery," pp. 204-205.)

[3] Machine printing also economises colour.

man and a woman can clean 28 lbs. daily. With the churka invented some years ago by Dr. Forbes, one man and a boy produce 250 pounds daily. If oxen, steam, or water, be used for driving it, only a few boys and girls as feeders are required. Sixteen of these machines driven by oxen do as much work in a day as formerly 750 people did on an average.[1]

As already stated, a steam-plough does as much work in one hour at a cost of threepence, as 66 men at a cost of 15 shillings. I return to this example in order to clear up an erroneous notion. The 15 shillings are by no means the expression in money of all the labour expended in one hour by the 66 men. If the ratio of surplus labour to necessary labour were 100%, these 66 men would produce in one hour a value of 30 shillings, although their wages, 15 shillings, represent only their labour for half an hour. Suppose, then, a machine cost as much as the wages for a year of the 150 men it displaces, say £3000; this £3000 is by no means the expression in money of the labour added to the object produced by these 150 men before the introduction of the machine, but only of that portion of their year's labour which was expended for themselves and represented by their wages. On the other hand, the £3000, the money value of the machine, expresses all the labour expended on its production, no matter in what proportion this labour constitutes wages for the workman, and surplus-value for the capitalist. Therefore, though a machine cost as much as the labour-power displaced by its cost, yet the labour materalised in it is even then much less than the living labour it replaces.[2]

The use of machinery for the exclusive purpose of cheapening the product, is limited in this way, that less labour must be expended in producing the machinery than is displaced by the employment of that machinery. For the capitalist, however, this use is still more limited. Instead of paying for the labour, he only pays the value of the labour-power employed;

---

[1] See paper read by Dr. Watson, Reporter on Products to the Government of India, before the Society of Arts, 17th April, 1860.

[2] "These mute agents (machines) are always the produce of much less labour than that which they displace, even when they are of the same money value." (Ricardo, l. c., p. 40.)

therefore, the limit to his using a machine is fixed by the difference between the value of the machine and the value of the labour-power replaced by it. Since the division of the day's work into necessary and surplus-labour differs in different countries, and even in the same country at different periods, or in different branches of industry; and further, since the actual wage of the labourer at one time sinks below the value of his labour-power, at another rises above it, it is possible for the difference between the price of the machinery to vary very much, although the difference between the quantity of labour requisite to produce the machine and the total quantity replaced by it, remain constant.[1] But it is the former difference alone that determines the cost, to the capitalist, of producing a commodity, and, through the pressure of competition, influences his action. Hence the invention now-a-days of machines in England that are employed only in North America; just as in the sixteenth and seventeenth centuries, machines were invented in Germany to be used only in Holland, and just as many a French invention of the eighteenth century was exploited in England alone. In the older countries, machinery, when employed in some branches of industry, creates such a redundancy of labour in other branches that in these latter the fall of wages below the value of labour-power impedes the use of machinery, and, from the standpoint of the capitalist, whose profit comes, not from a diminution of the labour employed, but of the labour paid for, renders that use surperfluous and often impossible. In some branches of the woollen manufacture in England the employment of children has during recent years been considerably diminished, and in some cases has been entirely abolished. Why? Because the Factory Acts made two sets of children necessary, one working six hours, the other four, or each working five hours. But the parents refuse to sell the "half-timers" cheaper than the "full-timers." Hence the substitution of machinery for the "half-timers."[2] Before the labour of women and of children

---

[1] Hence in a communistic society there would be a very different scope for the employment of machinery than there can be in a bourgeois society.

[2] "Employers of labour would not unnecessarily retain two sets of children under thirteen. . . . In fact one class of manufacturers, the spinners of woollen yarn,

under 10 years of age was forbidden in mines, capitalists considered the employment of naked women and girls, often in company with men, so far sanctioned by their moral code, and especially by their ledgers, that it was only after the passing of the Act that they had recourse to machinery. The Yankees have invented a stone-breaking machine. The English do not make use of it, because the "wretch" [1] who does this work gets paid for such a small portion of his labour, that machinery would increase the cost of production to the capitalist.[2] In England women are still occasionally used instead of horses for hauling canal boats,[3] because the labour required to produce horses and machines is an accurately known quantity, while that required to maintain the women of the surplus population is below all calculation. Hence nowhere do we find a more shameful squandering of human labour-power for the most despicable purposes than in England, the land of machinery.

SECTION 3.—THE APPROXIMATE EFFECTS OF MACHINERY ON THE WORKMAN.

The starting point of Modern Industry is, as we have shown, the revolution in the instruments of labour, and this revolution attains its most highly developed form in the organised system of machinery in a factory. Before we inquire how human material is incorporated with this objective organism, let us consider some general effects of this revolution on the labourer himself.

now rarely employ children under thirteen years of age, *i.e.*, half-timers. They have introduced improved and new machinery of various kinds, which altogether supersedes the employment of children (*i.e.*, under 13 years); f.i., I will mention one process as an illustration of this diminution in the number of children, wherein by the addition of an apparatus, called a piecing machine, to existing machines, the work of six or four half-times, according to the peculiarity of each machine, can be performed by one young person (over 13 years) . . . the half-time system 'stimulated' the invention of the piecing machine." (Reports of Insp. of Fact. for 31st Oct., 1858.)

[1] "Wretch" is the recognized term in English political economy for the agricultural labourer.

[2] "Machinery . . . can frequently not be employed until labour (he means wages) rises." (Ricardo, l. c., p. 579.)

[3] See "Report of the Social Science Congress, at Edinburgh." Oct., 1863.

a. Appropriation of supplementary Labour-power by Capital. The Employment of Women and Children.

In so far as machinery dispenses with muscular power, it becomes a means of employing labourers of slight muscular strength, and those whose bodily development is incomplete, but whose limbs are all the more supple. The labour of women and children was, therefore, the first thing sought for by capitalists who used machinery. That mighty substitute for labour and labourers was forthwith changed into a means for increasing the number of wage-labourers by enrolling, under the direct sway of capital, every member of the workman's family, without distinction of age or sex. Compulsory work for the capitalist usurped the place, not only of the children's play, but also of free labour at home within moderate limits for the support of the family.[1]

The value of labour-power was determined, not only by the labour-time necessary to maintain the individual adult laborer, but also by that necessary to maintain his family. Machinery, by throwing every member of that family on to the labour market, spreads the value of the man's labour-power over his whole family. It thus depreciates his labour-power. To purchase the labour-power of a family of four workers may, perhaps, cost more than it formerly did to purchase the labour-power of the head of the family, but, in return, four days' labour takes the place of one, and their price falls in proportion to the excess of the surplus-labour of four over the surplus-labour of one. In order that the family may live, four people must now, not only labour, but expend

[1] Dr. Edward Smith, during the cotton crisis caused by the American Civil War, was sent by the English Government to Lancashire, Cheshire, and other places, to report on the sanitary condition of the cotton operatives. He reported, that from a hygienic point of view, and apart from the banishment of the operatives from the factory atmosphere, the crisis had several advantages. The women now had sufficient leisure to give their infants the breast, instead of poisoning them with "Godfrey's cordial." They had time to learn to cook. Unfortunately the acquisition of this art occurred at a time when they had nothing to cook. But from this we see how capital, for the purposes of its self-expansion, has usurped the labour necessary in the home of the family. This crisis was also utilised to teach sewing to the daughters of the workmen in sewing schools. An American revolution and a universal crisis in order that the working girls, who spin for the whole world, might learn to sew!

surplus-labor for the capitalist. Thus we see, that machinery, while augmenting the human material that forms the principal object of capital's exploiting power,[1] at the same time raises the degree of exploitation.

Machinery also revolutionises out and out the contract between the labourer and the capitalist, which formally fixes their mutual relations. Taking the exchange of commodities as our basis, our first assumption was that capitalist and labourer met as free persons, as independent owners of commodities; the one possessing money and means of production, the other labour-power. But now the capitalist buys children and young persons under age. Previously, the workman sold his own labour power, which he disposed of nominally as a free agent. Now he sells wife and child. He has become a slave dealer.[2] The demand for children's labour often resembles in form the inquiries for negro slaves, such as were formerly to be read among the advertisements in American

---

[1] "The numerical increase of labourers has been great, through the growing substitution of female for male, and above all, of childish for adult labour. Three girls of 13, at wages of from 6 shillings to 8 shillings a week, have replaced the one man of mature age, of wages varying from 18 shillings to 45 shillings." (Th. de Quincey: "The Logic of Political Econ., London, 1845." Note to p. 147.) Since certain family functions, such as nursing and suckling children, cannot be entirely suppressed, the mothers confiscated by capital, must try substitutes of some sort. Domestic work, such as sewing and mending, must be replaced by the purchase of ready-made articles. Hence, the diminished expenditure of labour in the house is accompanied by an increased expenditure of money. The cost of keeping the family increases, and balances the greater income. In addition to this, economy and judgment in the consumption and preparation of the means of subsistence becomes impossible. Abundant material relating to these facts, which are concealed by official political economy, is to be found in the Reports of the Inspectors of Factories, of the Children's Employment Commission, and more especially in the Reports on Public Health.

[2] In striking contrast with the great fact, that the shortening of the hours of labour of women and children in English factories was exacted from capital by the male operatives, we find in the latest reports of the Children's Employment Commission traits of the operative parents in relation to the traffic in children, that are truly revolting and thoroughly like slave-dealing. But the Pharisee of a capitalist, as may be seen from the same reports, denounces this brutality which he himself creates, perpetuates, and exploits, and which he moreover baptizes "Freedom of labour." "Infant labour has been called into aid . . . even to work for their own daily bread. Without strength to endure such disproportionate toil, without instruction to guide their future life, they have been thrown into a situation physically and morally polluted. The Jewish historian has remarked upon the overthrow of Jerusalem by Titus that it was no wonder it should have been destroyed, with such a signal destruction, when an inhuman mother sacrificed her own offspring to satisfy the cravings of absolute hunger." ("Public Economy Concentrated." Carlisle, 1833, p. 56.)

journals. "My attention," says an English factory inspector, "was drawn to an advertisement in the local paper of one of the most important manufacturing towns of my district, of which the following is a copy: Wanted, 12 to 20 young persons, not younger than what can pass for 13 years. Wages, 4 shillings a week. Apply &c."[1] The phase "what can pass for 13 years," has reference to the fact, that by the Factory Act, children under 13 years may work only 6 hours. A surgeon official appointed must certify their age. The manufacturer, therefore, asks for children who look as if they were already 13 years old. The decrease, often by leaps and bounds in the number of children under 13 years employed in factories, a decrease that is shown in an astonishing manner by the English statistics of the last 20 years, was for the most part, according to the evidence of the factory inspectors themselves, the work of the certifying surgeons, who overstated the age of the children, agreeably to the capitalist's greed for exploitation, and the sordid trafficking needs of the parents. In the notorious district of Bethnal Green, a public market is held every Monday and Tuesday morning, where children of both sexes from 9 years of age upwards, hire themselves out to the silk manufacturers. "The usual terms are 1s. 8d. a week (this belongs to the parents) and '2d. for myself and tea.' The contract is binding only for the week. The scene and language while this market is going on are quite disgraceful."[2] It has also occurred in England, that women have taken "children from the workhouse and let any one have them out for 2s. 6d. a week."[3] In spite of legislation, the number of boys sold in Great Britain by their parents to act as live chimney-sweeping machines (althought there exist plenty of machines to replace them) exceeds 2000.[4] The revolution effected by machinery in the judicial relations between the buyer and the seller of labour-power, causing the transaction as a whole to

[1] A. Redgrave in "Reports of Insp. of Fact. for 31st October, 1858," pp. 40, 41.

[2] Children's Employment Commission, Fifth Report, London, 1866, p. 81, n. 31. Note to the 4th edition: The silk industry of Bethnal Green is now almost ruined.—Ed.

[3] Children's Employment Commission, Third Report, London, 1864, p. 53, n. 15.

[4] l. c., Fifth Report, p. 22, n. 137.

lose the appearance of a contract between free persons, afforded the English Parliament an excuse, founded on judicial principles, for the interference of the state with factories. Whenever the law limits the labour of children to 6 hours in industries not before interfered with, the complaints of the manufacturers are always renewed. They allege that numbers of the parents withdraw their children from the industry brought under the act, in order to sell them where "freedom of labour" still rules *i.e.*, where children under 13 years are compelled to work like grown-up people, and therefore can be got rid of at a higher price. But since capital is by nature a leveller, since it exacts in every sphere of production equality in the conditions of the exploitation of labour, the limitation by law of children's labour, in one branch of industry, becomes the cause of its limitation in others.

We have already alluded to the physical deterioration as well of the children and young persons as of the women, whom machinery, first directly in the factories that shoot up on its bases, and then indirectly in all the remaining branches of industry, subjects to the exploitation of capital. In this place, therefore, we dwell only on one point, the enormous mortality, during the first few years of their life, of the children of the operatives. In sixteen of the registration districts into which England is divided, there are, for every 100,000 children alive under the age of one year, only 9000 death in the year on an average (in one district only 7047); in 24 districts the deaths are over 10,000, but under 11,000; in 39 districts over 11,000, but under 12,000; in 48 districts over 12,000, but under 13,000; in 22 districts over 20,000; in 25 districts over 21,000; in 17 over 22,000; in 11 over 23,000; in Hoo, Wolverhampton, Ashton-under-Lyne, and Preston, over 24,000; in Nottingham, Stockport, and Bradford, over 25,000; in Wisbeach, 26,000; and in Manchester, 26,125.[1] As was shown by an official medical inquiry in the year 1861, the high death-rates are, apart from local causes, principally due to the employment of the mothers away from their homes, and to the neglect and maltreatment consequent on her absence, such as,

[1] Sixth Report on Public Health. Lond., 1864, p. 34.

amongst others, insufficient nourishment, unsuitable food, and dosing with opiates; beside this, there arises an unnatural estrangement between mother and child, and as a consequence intentional starving and poisoning of the children.[1] In those agricultural districts, "where a minimum in the employment of women exists, the death-rate is on the other hand very low."[2] The Inquiry-Commission of 1861 led, however, to the unexpected result, that in some purely agricultural districts bordering on the North Sea, the death-rate of children under one year old almost equalled that of the worst factory districts. Dr. Julian Hunter was therefore commissioned to investigate this phenomenon on the spot. His report is incorporated with the "Sixth Report on Public Health."[3] Up to that time it was supposed, that the children were decimated by malaria, and other diseases peculiar to low-lying and marshy districts. But the inquiry showed the very opposite, namely, that the same cause which drove away malaria, the conversion of the land, from a morass in winter and a scanty pasture in summer, into fruitful corn land, created the exceptional death-rate of the infants.[4] The 70 medical men, whom Dr. Hunter examined in that district, were "wonderfully in accord" on this point. In fact, the revolution in the mode of cultivation had led to the introduction of the industrial system. Married women, who work in gangs along with boys and girls, are, for a stipulated sum of money, placed at the disposal of the farmer, by a man called "the undertaker," who contracts for the whole gang. "These gangs will sometimes travel many miles from their own village; they are to be met morning and evening on the roads, dressed in short petticoats, with suitable coats and boots, and sometimes trousers, looking wonderfully strong and healthy, but tainted with a customary immorality,

---

[1] "It (the inquiry of 1861) . . . showed, moreover, that while, with the described circumstances, infants perish under the neglect and mismanagement which their mothers' occupations imply, the mothers become to a grievous extent denaturalized towards their offspring—commonly not troubling themselves much at the death, and even sometimes . . . taking direct measures to insure it." (l. c.)

[2] l. c., p. 454.

[3] l. c., p. 454—463. " Report by Dr. Henry Julian Hunter on the excessive mortality of infants in some rural districts of England."

[4] l. c., p. 35 and pp. 455, 456.

and heedless of the fatal results which their love of this busy and independent life is bringing on their unfortunate offspring who are pining at home."[1] Every phenomenon of the factory districts is here reproduced, including, but to a greater extent, ill-disguised infanticide, and dosing children with opiates.[2] "My knowledge of such evils," says Dr. Simon, the medical officer of the Privy Council and editor in chief of the Reports on Public Health, "may excuse the profound misgiving with which I regard any large industrial employment of adult women."[3] "Happy indeed," exclaims Mr. Baker, the factory inspector, in his official report, "happy indeed will it be for the manufacturing districts of England, when every married woman having a family is prohibited from working in any textile works at all."[4]

The moral degradation caused by the capitalistic exploitation of women and children has been so exhaustively depicted by F. Engels in his "Lage der Arbeitenden Klasse Englands," and other writers, that I need only mention the subject in this place. But the intellectual desolation, artificially produced by converting immature human beings into mere machines for the fabrication of surplus-value, a state of mind clearly distinguishable from that natural ignorance which keeps the mind fallow without destroying its capacity for development, its natural fertility, this desolation finally compelled even the English Parliament to make elementary education a compulsory condition to the "productive" employment of children under 14 years, in every industry subject to the Factory Acts. The spirit of capitalist production stands out clearly in the ludicrous wording of the so-called education clauses in the Factory Acts, in the absence of an administrative machinery, an absence that again makes the compulsion illusory, in the

[1] l. c., p. 456.

[2] In the agricultural as well as in the factory districts the consumption of opium among the grown-up labourers, both male and female, is extending daily. "To push the sale of opiate . . . is the great aim of some enterprising wholesale merchants. By druggists it is considered the leading article." (l. c., p. 459.) Infants that take opiates "shrank up into little old men," or "wizzened like little monkeys," (l. c., p. 460.) We here see how India and China avenged themselves on England.

[3] l. c., p. 37.

[4] "Rep. of Insp. of Fact. for 31st Oct., 1862," p. 59. Mr. Baker was formerly a doctor.

opposition of the manufacturers themselves to these education clauses, and in the tricks and dodges they put in practice for evading them. "For this the legislature is alone to blame, by having passed a delusive law, which, while it would seem to provide that the children employed in factories shall be *educated,* contains no enactment by which that professed end can be secured. It provides nothing more than that the children shall on certain days of the week, and for a certain number of hours (three) in each day, be inclosed within the four walls of a place called a school, and that the employer of the child shall receive weekly a certificate to that effect signed by a person designated by the subscriber as a schoolmaster or schoolmistress."[1] Previous to the passing of the amended Factory Act, 1844, it happened, not unfrequently, that the certificate of attendance at school were signed by the schoolmaster or schoolmistress with a cross, as they themselves were unable to write. "On one occasion, on visiting a place called a school, from which certificates of school attendance had issued, I was so struck with the ignorance of the master, that I said to him: "Pray, sir, can you read?" His reply was: "Aye, summat!" and as a justification of his right to grant certificates, he added: "At any rate, I am before my scholars." The inspectors, when the Bill of 1844 was in preparation, did not fail to represent the disgraceful state of the places called schools, certificates from which they were obliged to admit as a compliance with the laws, but they were successful only in obtaining thus much, that since the passing of the Act of 1844, the figures in the school certificate must be filled up in the handwriting of the schoolmaster, who must also sign his Christian and surname in full."[2] Sir John Kincaid, factory inspector for Scotland, relates experiences of the same kind. "The first school we visited was kept by a Mrs. Ann Killin. Upon asking her to spell her name, she straightway made a mistake, by beginning with the letter C, but correcting herself immediately, she said her name began with a K. On looking at her signature, however, in the school certificate books, I

---

[1] Leonard Horner in "Reports of Insp. of Fact. for 30th June, 1857," p. 17.
[2] L. Horner in "Rep. of Insp. of Fact. for 31st Oct., 1855," pp. 18, 19.

noticed that she spelt it in various ways, while her hand-writing left no doubt as to her unfitness to teach. She herself also acknowledged that she could not keep the register . . . . In a second school I found the schoolroom 15 feet long, and 10 feet wide, and counted in this space 75 children, who were gabbling something unintelligible."[1] But it is not only in the miserable places above referred to that the children obtained certificates of school attendance without having received instruction of any value, for in many schools where there is a competent teacher, his efforts are of little avail from the distracting crowd of children of all ages, from infants of 3 years old and upwards; his livelihood, miserable at the best, depending on the pence received from the greatest number of children whom it is possible to cram into the space. To this is to be added scanty school furniture, deficiency of books, and other materials for teaching, and the depressing effect upon the poor children themselves of a close, noisome atmosphere. I have been in many schools, where I have seen rows of children doing absolutely nothing; and this is certified as school attendance, and, in statistical returns, such children are set down as being educated."[2] In Scotland the manufacturers try all they can to do without the children that are obliged to attend school. "It requires no further argument to prove that the educational clauses of the Factory Act, being held in such disfavour among mill owners tend in a great measure to exclude that class of children alike from the employment and the benefit of education contemplated by this Act."[3] Horribly grotesque does this appear in print works, which are regulated by a special Act. By that Act, "every child, before being employed in a print work must have attended school for at least 30 days, and not less than 150 hours, during the six months immediately preceding such first day of employment, and during the continuance of its employment in the print works, it must attend for a like period of 30 days, and 150 hours during every successive period of six months. . . . The

[1] Sir John Kincaid in "Rep. of Insp. of Fact. for 31st Oct., 1858," pp. 31, 32.
[2] L. Horner in "Reports, &c., for 31st Oct., 1857," pp. 17, 18.
[3] Sir J. Kincaid in "Reports, &c., 31st Oct., 1856," p. 66.

attendance at school must be between 8 a.m. and 6 p.m. No attendance of less than 2½ hours, nor more than 5 hours on any one day, shall be reckoned as part of the 150 hours. Under ordinary circumstances the children attend school morning and afternoon for 30 days, for at least 5 hours each day, and upon the expiration of the 30 days, the statutory total of 150 hours having been attained, having, in their language, made up their book, they return to the print work, where they continue until the six months have expired, when another instalment of school attendance becomes due, and they again seek the school until the book is again made up. . . . . Many boys having attended school for the required number of hours, when they return to school after the expiration of their six months' work in the print work, are in the same condition as when they first attended school as print-work boys, that they have lost all they gained by their previous school attendance. . . . In other print works the children's attendance at school is made to depend altogether upon the exigencies of the work in the establishment. The requisite number of hours is made up each six months, by instalments consisting of from 3 to five hours at a time, spreading over, perhaps, the whole six months. . . . For instance, the attendance on one day might be from 8 to 11 a.m., on another day from 1 p.m. to 4 p.m., and the child might not appear at school again for several days, when it would attend from 3 p.m. to 6 p.m.; then it might attend for 3 or 4 days consecutively, or for a week, then it would not appear in school for 3 weeks or a month, after that upon some odd days at some odd hours when the operative who employed it chose to spare it; and thus the child was, as it were, buffeted from school to work, from work to school, until the tale of 150 hours was told."[1]

---

[1] A. Redgrave in "Rep. of Insp. of Fact., 31st Oct., 1857," pp. 41-42. In those industries where the Factory Act proper (not the Print Works Act referred to in the text) has been in force for some time, the obstacles in the way of the education clauses have, in recent years, been overcome. In industries not under the Act, the views of Mr. J. Geddes, a glass manufacturer, still extensively prevail. He informed Mr. White, one of the Inquiry Commissioners: "As far as I can see, the greater amount of education which a part of the working class has enjoyed for some years past is an evil. It is dangerous, because it makes them independent." (Children's Empl. Comm., Fourth Report, Lond., 1865, p. 253.)

By the excessive addition of women and children to the ranks of the workers, machinery at last breaks down the resistance which the male operatives in the manufacturing period continued to oppose to the despotism of capital.[1]

b. *Prolongation of the working-day.*

If machinery be the most powerful means for increasing the productiveness of labour—*i.e.,* for shortening the working time required in the production of a commodity, it becomes in the hands of capital the most powerful means, in those industries first invaded by it, for lengthening the working day beyond all bounds set by human nature. It creates, on the one hand, new conditions by which capital is enabled to give free scope to this its constant tendency, and on the other hand, new motives with which to whet capital's appetite for the labour of others.

In the first place, in form of machinery, the implements of labour become automatic, things moving and working independent of the workman. They are thenceforth an industrial *perpetuum mobile,* that would go on producing forever, did it not meet with certain natural obstructions in the weak bodies and the strong wills of its human attendants. The automaton, as capital, and because it is capital, is endowed, in the person of the capitalist, with intelligence and will; it is therefore animated by the longing to reduce to a minimum the resistance offered by that repellant yet elastic natural barrier, man.[2] This resistance is moreover lessened by the apparent lightness of machine work, and by the more pliant and docile character of the women and children employed on it.[3]

---

[1] "Mr. E., a manufacturer . . . informed me that he employed females exclusively at his power-looms . . . gives a decided preference to married females, especially those who have families at home dependent on them for support; they are attentive, docile, more so than unmarried females, and are compelled to use their utmost exertions to procure the necessaries of life. Thus are the virtues, the peculiar virtues of the female character to be perverted to her injury—thus all that is most dutiful and tender in her nature is made a means of her bondage and suffering." (Ten Hours' Factory Bill. The Speech of Lord Ashley, March 15th, Lond., 1844, p. 20.)

[2] "Since the general introduction of machinery, human nature has been forced far beyond its average strength." (Rob. Owen: "Observations on the effects of the manufacturing system, 2nd Ed., Lond., 1817.")

[3] The English, who have a tendency to look upon the earliest form of appearance

The productiveness of machinery is, as we saw, inversely proportional to the value transferred by it to the product. The longer the life of the machine, the greater is the mass of the products over which the value transmitted by the machine is spread, and the less is the portion of that value added to each single commodity. The active lifetime of a machine is, however, clearly dependent on the length of the working day, or on the duration of the daily labour-process multiplied by the number of days for which the process is carried on.

The wear and tear of a machine is not exactly proportional to its working time. And even if it were so, a machine working 16 hours daily for $7\frac{1}{2}$ years, covers as long a working period as, and transmits to the total product no more value than, the same machine would if it worked only 8 hours daily for 15 years. But in the first case the value of the machine would be reproduced twice as quickly as in the latter, and the capitalist would, by this use of the machine, absorb in $7\frac{1}{2}$ years as much surplus-value as in the second case he would in 15.

The material wear and tear of a machine is of two kinds. The one arises from use, as coins wear away by circulating, the other from non-use, as a sword rusts when left in its scabbard. The latter kind is due to the elements. The former is more or less directly proportional, the latter to a certain extent inversely proportional, to the use of the machine.[1]

---

of a thing as the cause of its existence, are in the habit of attributing the long hours of work in factories to the extensive kidnapping of children, practised by capitalists in the infancy of the factory system, on workhouses and orphanages, by means of which robbery, unresisting material for exploitation was procured. Thus, for instance, Fielden, himself a manufacturer, says: "It is evident that the long hours of work were brought about by the circumstance of so great a number of destitute children being supplied from different parts of the country, that the masters were independent of the hands, and that having once established the custom by means of the miserable materials they had procured in this way, they could impose it on their neighbours with the greater facility." (J. Fielden: "The Curse of the Factory System. Lond., 1836," p. 11.) With reference to the labour of women, Saunders, the Factory inspector, says in his report of 1844: "Amongst the female operatives there are some women who, for many weeks in succession, except for a few days, are employed from 6 a. m. till midnight, with less than 2 hours for meals, so that on 5 days of the week they have only 6 hours left out of the 24, for going to and from their homes and resting in bed."

[1] Occasion . . . injury to the delicate moving parts of metallic mechanism by inaction." (Ure, l. c., p. 28.)

But in addition to the material wear and tear, a machine also undergoes, what we may call a moral depreciation. It loses exchange-value, either by machines of the same sort being produced cheaper than it, or by better machines entering into competition with it.[1] In both cases, be the machine ever so young and full of life, its value is no longer determined by the labour actually materialised in it, but by the labour-time requisite to reproduce either it or the better machine. It has, therefore, lost value more or less. The shorter the period taken to reproduce its total value, the less is the danger of moral depreciation; and the longer the working day, the shorter is that period. When machinery is first introduced into an industry, new methods of reproducing it more cheaply follow blow upon blow,[2] and so do improvements, that not only affect individual parts and details of the machine, but its entire build. It is, therefore, in the early days of the life of machinery that this special incentive to the prolongation of the working day makes itself felt most acutely.[3]

Given the length of the working day, all other circumstances remaining the same, the exploitation of double the number of workmen demands, not only a doubling of that part of constant capital which is invested in machinery and buildings, but also of that part which is laid out in raw material and auxiliary substances. The lengthening of the working day, on the other hand, allows of production on an extended scale without any alteration in the amount of capital laid out on machinery and

[1] The "Manchester Spinner" (*Times,* 26th Nov. 1862) before referred to says in relation to this subject: "It (namely, the "allowance for deterioration of machinery") is also intended to cover the loss which is constantly arising from the superseding of machines before they are worn out, by others of a new and better construction."

[2] "It has been estimated, roughly, that the first individual of a newly-invented machine will cost about five times as much as the construction of the second." (Babbage, l. c., p. 211.)

[3] "The improvements which took place not long ago in frames for making patent net was so great that a machine in good repair which had cost £1,200, sold a few years after for £60 . . . improvements succeeded each other so rapidly, that machines which had never been finished were abandoned in the hands of their makers, because new improvements had superseded their utility." (Babbage, l. c., p. 233.) In these stormy, go-ahead times, therefore, the tulle manufacturers soon extended the working day, by means of double sets of hands, from the original 8 hours to 24.

buildings.[1] Not only is there, therefore, an increase of surplus-value, but the outlay necessary to obtain it diminishes. It is true that this takes place, more or less, with every lengthening of the working day; but in the case under consideration, the change is more marked, because the capital converted into the instruments of labour preponderates to a greater degree.[2] The development of the factory system fixes a constantly increasing portion of the capital in a form, in which, on the one hand, its value is capable of continual self-expansion, and in which, on the other hand, it loses both use-value and exchange-value whenever it loses contact with living labour. "When a labourer," said Mr. Ashworth, a cotton magnate, to Professor Nassau W. Senior, "lays down his spade, he renders useless, for that period, a capital worth eighteenpence. When one of our people leaves the mill, he renders useless a capital that has cost £100,000."[3] Only fancy! making "useless" for a single moment, a capital that has cost £100,000! It is, in truth, monstrous, that a single one of our people should ever leave the factory! The increased use of our machinery, as Senior after the instruction he received from Ashworth clearly perceives, makes a constantly increasing lengthening of the working day "desirable."[4]

Machinery produces relative surplus-value; not only by directly depreciating the value of labour-power, and by in-

---

[1] "It is self-evident, that, amid the ebbings and flowings of the markets and the alternate expansions and contractions of demand, occasions will constantly recur, in which the manufacturer may employ additional floating capital without employing additional fixed capital . . . if additional quantities of raw material can be worked up without incurring an additional expense for buildings and machinery." (R. Torrens: "On Wages and Combinations. London, 1834," p. 63.)

[2] This circumstance is mentioned only for the sake of completeness, for I shall not consider the rate of profit, *i.e.*, the ratio of the surplus-value to the total capital advanced, until I come to the third book.

[3] Senior, "Letters on the Factory Act. London, 1837," p. 13, 14.

[4] "The great proportion of fixed to circulating capital . . . makes long hours of work desirable." With the increased use of machinery, &c., "the motives to long hours of work will become greater, as the only means by which a large proportion of fixed capital can be made profitable." (l. c., pp. 11–13.) "There are certain expenses upon a mill which go on in the same proportion whether the mill be running short or full time, as, for instance, rent, rates, and taxes, insurance against fire, wages of several permanent servants, deterioration of machinery, with various other charges upon a manufacturing establishment, the proportion of which to profits increases as the production decreases. ("Rep. of Insp. of Fact. for 31st Oct., 1862," p. 19.)

directly cheapening the same through cheapening the commodities that enter into its reproduction, but also, when it is first introduced sporadically into an industry, by converting the labour employed by the owner of that machinery, into labour of a higher degree and greater efficacy, by raising the social value of the article produced above its individual value, and thus enabling the capitalist to replace the value of a day's labour-power by a smaller portion of the value of the day's product. During this transition period, when the use of machinery is a sort of monopoly, the profits are therefore exceptional, and the capitalist endeavours to exploit thoroughly "the sunny time of this his first love," by prolonging the working day as much as possible. The magnitude of the profit whets his appetite for more profit.

As the use of machinery becomes more general in a particular industry, the social value of the product sinks down to its individual value, and the law that surplus-value does not arise from the labour-power that has been replaced by the machinery, but from the labour-power actually employed in working with the machinery, asserts itself. Surplus-value arises from the variable capital alone, and we saw that the amount of surplus-value depends on two factors, *viz.*, the rate of surplus-value and the number of the workmen simultaneously employed. Given the length of the working day, the rate of surplus-value is determined by the relative duration of the necessary labour and of the surplus-labour in a day. The number of the labourers simultaneously employed depends, on its side, on the ratio of the variable to the constant capital. Now, however much the use of machinery may increase the surplus-labour at the expense of the necessary labour by heightening the productiveness of labour, it is clear that it attains this result, only by diminishing the number of workmen employed by a given amount of capital. It converts what was formerly variable capital, invested in labour-power, into machinery, which, being constant capital, does not produce surplus-value. It is impossible, for instance, to squeeze as much surplus-value out of 2 as out of 24 labourers. If each of these 24 men gives only one hour of surplus-labour in 12, the

24 men give together 24 hours of surplus-labour, while 24 hours is the total labour of the two men. Hence, the application of machinery to the production of surplus-value implies a contradiction which is immanent in it, since, of the two factors of the surplus-value created by a given amount of capital, one, the rate of surplus-value cannot be increased, except by diminishing the other, the number of workmen. This contradiction comes to light, as soon as by the general employment of machinery in a given industry, the value of the machine-produced commodity regulates the value of all commodities of the same sort; and it is this contradiction, that in its turn, drives the capitalist, without his being conscious of the fact,[1] to excessive lengthening of the working day, in order that he may compensate the decrease in the relative number of labourers exploited, by an increase not only of the relative, but of the absolute surplus-labour.

If, then, the capitalistic employment of machinery, on the one hand, supplies new and powerful motives to an excessive lengthening of the working day, and radically changes, as well the methods of labour, as also the character of the social working organism, in such a manner as to break down all opposition to this tendency, on the other hand it produces, partly by opening out to the capitalist new strata of the working class, previously inaccessible to him, partly by setting free the labourers it supplants, a surplus working population,[2] which is compelled to submit to the dictation of capital. Hence that remarkable phenomenon in the history of Modern Industry, that machinery sweeps away every moral and natural restriction on the length of the working day. Hence, too, the economical paradox, that the most powerful instrument for shortening labour-time, becomes the most unfailing means for placing every moment of the labourer's time and that of his family, at the disposal of the capitalist for the purpose of expanding the value of his capital. "If," dreamed Aristotle,

[1] Why it is, that the capitalist, and also the political economists who are imbued with his views, are unconscious of this immanent contradiction, will appear from the first part of the third volume.

[2] It is one of the greatest merits of Ricardo to have seen in machinery not only the means of producing commodities, but of creating a "redundant population."

the greatest thinker of antiquity, "if every tool, when summoned, or even of its own accord, could do the work that befits
it, just as the creations of Dædalus moved of themselves, or the
tripods of Hephæstos went of their own accord to their sacred
work, if the weavers' shuttles were to weave of themselves,
then there would be no need either of apprentices for the
master workers, or of slaves for the lords."[1] And Antipatros,
a Greek poet of the time of Cicero, hailed the invention of the
water-wheel for grinding corn, an invention that is the elementary form of all machinery, as the giver of freedom to
female slaves, and the bringer back of the golden age.[2] Oh!
those heathens! They understood, as the learned Bastiat, and
before him the still wiser MacCulloch have discovered, nothing
of political economy and Christianity. They did not, for
example, comprehend that machinery is the surest means of
lengthening the working day. They perhaps excused the
slavery of one on the ground that it was a means to the full
development of another. But to preach slavery of the masses,
in order that a few crude and half-educated parvenus, might
become "eminent spinners," "extensive sausage-makers," and
"influential shoe-black dealers," to do this, they lacked the
bump of Christianity.

[1] F. Biese. "Die Philosophie des Aristoteles," Vol. 2. Berlin, 1842, p. 408.

[2] I give below the translation of this poem by Stolberg, because it brings into relief,
quite in the spirit of former quotations referring to division of labour, the antithesis
between the views of the ancients and the moderns. "Spare the hand that grinds
the corn, Oh, miller girls, and softly sleep. Let Chanticleer announce the morn in
vain! Deo has commanded the work of the girls to be done by the Nymphs, and now
they skip lightly over the wheels, so that the shaken axles revolve with their spokes
and pull round the load of the revolving stones. Let us live the life of our fathers,
and let us rest from work and enjoy the gifts that the Goddess sends us."

> "Schonet der mahlenden Hand, o Müllerinnen und schlafet
> Sanft! es verkünde der Hahn euch den Morgen umsonst!
> Dāo hat die Arbeit der Mädchen den Nymphen befohlen,
> Und itzt hüpfen sie leicht über die Räder dahin,
> Dass die erschütterten Achsen mit ihren Speichen sich wälzen,
> Und im Kreise die Last drehen des wälzenden Steins.
> Lasst uns leben das Leben der Väter, und lasst uns der Gaben
> Arbeitslos uns freun, welche die Göttin uns schenkt."

(Gedichte aus dem Griechischen übersetzt von Christian Graf zu Stolberg, Hamburg, 1782.)

c. Intensification of Labour.

The immoderate lengthening of the working day, produced by machinery in the hands of capital, leads to a reaction on the part of society, the very sources of whose life are menaced; and, thence, to a normal working day whose length is fixed by law. Thenceforth a phenomenon that we have already met with, namely, the intensification of labour, develops into great importance. Our analysis of absolute surplus-value had reference primarily to the extension or duration of the labour, its intensity being assumed as given. We now proceed to con-sider the substitution of a more intensified labour for labour of more extensive duration, and the degree of the former.

It is self-evident, that in proportion as the use of machinery spreads, and the experience of a special class of workmen habituated to machinery accumulates, the rapidity and inten-sity of labour increase as a natural consequence. Thus in England, during half a century, lengthening of the working day went hand in hand with increasing intensity of factory labour. Nevertheless the reader will clearly see, that where we have labour, not carried on by fits and starts, but repeated day after day with unvarying uniformity, a point must inevit-ably be reached, where extension of the working day and in-tensity of the labour mutually exclude one another, in such a way that lengthening of the working day becomes compatible only with a lower degree of intensity, and, a higher degree of intensity, only with a shortening of the working day. So soon as the gradually surging revolt of the working class compelled Parliament to shorten compulsorily the hours of labour, and to begin by imposing a normal working day on factories proper, so soon consequently as an increased production of surplus value by the prolongation of the working day was once for all put a stop to, from that moment capital threw itself with all its might into the production of relative surplus-value, by hastening on the further improvement of machinery. At the same time a change took place in the nature of relative surplus-value. Generally speaking, the mode of producing relative surplus-value consists in raising the productive power of the workman, so as to enable him to produce more in a given time with the same expenditure of labour. Labour-time continues to transmit as before the same value to the total product, but this unchanged amount of exchange value is spread over more use-values; hence the value of each single commodity sinks. Otherwise, however, so soon as the compulsory shortening of the hours of labour takes place. The immense impetus it gives to the development of productive power, and to economy in the means of production, imposes on the workman increased expenditure of labour in a given .time, heightened tension of labour-power, and closer filling up of the pores of the working day, or condensation of labour to a degree that is attainable only within the limits of the shortened working day. This condensation of a greater mass of labour into a given period thenceforward counts for what it really is, a greater quantity of labour. In addition to a measure of its extension, *i.e.,* duration, labour now acquires a measure of its intensity or of the degree of its condensation or density.[1] The denser hour of the ten hours' working-day contains more labour, *i.e.,* expended labour-power, than the more porous hour of the twelve hours' working-day. The product therefore of one of the former hours has as much or more value than has the product of $1\frac{1}{5}$ of the latter hours. Apart from the increased yield of relative surplus-value through the heightened productiveness of labour, the same mass of value is now produced for the capitalist, say, by $3\frac{1}{3}$ hours of surplus labour, and $6\frac{2}{3}$ hours of necessary labour, as was previously produced by four hours of surplus labour and eight hours of necessary labour.

We now come to the question: How is the labour intensified?

The first effect of shortening the working day results from the self-evident law, that the efficiency of labour-power is in an inverse ratio to the duration of its expenditure. Hence, within certain limits what is lost by shortening the duration is gained by the increasing tension of labour-power. That the

---

[1] There are, of course, always differences in the intensities of the labour in various industries. But these differences are, as Adam Smith has shown, compensated to a partial extent by minor circumstances, peculiar to each sort of labour. Labour-time, as a measure of value, is not, however, affected in this case, except in so far as the duration of labour, and the degree of its intensity, are two antithetical and mutually exclusive expressions for one and the same quantity of labour.

workman moreover really does expend more labour-power, is ensured by the mode in which the capitalist pays him.[1] In those industries, such as potteries, where machinery plays little or no part, the introduction of the Factory Acts has strikingly shown that the mere shortening of the working-day increases to a wonderful degree the regularity, uniformity, order, continuity, and energy of the labour.[2] It seemed, however, doubtful whether this effect was produced in the factory proper, where the dependence of the workman on the continuous and uniform motion of the machinery had already created the strictest discipline. Hence, when in 1844 the reduction of the working-day to less than twelve hours was being debated, the masters almost unanimously declared "that their overlookers in the different rooms took good care that the hands lost no time," that the "extent of vigilance and attention on the part of the workmen was hardly capable of being increased," and therefore, that the speed of the machinery and other conditions remaining unaltered, "to expect in a well-managed factory any important result from increased attention of the workmen was an absurdity."[3] This assertion was contradicted by experiments. Mr. Robert Gardner reduced the hours of labour in his two large factories at Preston, on and after the 20th April, 1844, from twelve to eleven hours a day. The result of about a year's working was that "the same amount of product for the same cost was received, and the workpeople as a whole earned in eleven hours as much wages as they did before in twelve."[4] I pass over the experiments made in the spinning and carding rooms, because they were accompanied by an increase of 2% in the speed of the machines. But in the weaving department, where, moreover, many sorts of figured fancy articles were woven, there was not the slightest alteration in the conditions of the work. The result was: "From 6th January to 20th April, 1844, with a twelve hours' day, average weekly wages of each hand 10s. 1½d., from 20th April to 29th June, 1844, with

[1] Especially by piece-work, a form we shall investigate in Part VI. of this book.
[2] See "Rep. of Insp. of Fact. for 31st October, 1865."
[3] Rep. of Insp. of Fact. for 1844 and the quarter ending 30th April 1845, pp. 20–21.
[4] l. c., p. 19. Since the wages for piece-work were unaltered, the weekly wages depended on the quantity produced.

day of eleven hours, average weekly wages 10s. 3½d."[1] Here we have more produced in eleven hours than previously in twelve, and entirely in consequence of more steady application and economy of time by the workpeople. While they got the same wages and gained one hour of spare time, the capitalist got the same amount produced and saved the cost of coal, gas, and other such items, for one hour. Similar experiments, and with the like success, were carried out in the mills of Messrs. Horrocks and Jacson.[2]

The shortening of the hours of labour creates, to begin with, the subjective conditions for the condensation of labour, by enabling the workman to exert more strength in a given time. So soon as that shortening becomes compulsory, machinery becomes in the hands of capital the objective means, systematically employed for squeezing out more labour in a given time. This is effected in two ways: by increasing the speed of the machinery, and by giving the workman more machinery to tend. Improved construction of the machinery is necessary, partly because without it greater pressure cannot be put on the workman, and partly because the shortened hours of labour force the capitalist to exercise the strictest watch over the cost of production. The improvements in the steam-engine have increased the piston speed, and at the same time have made it possible, by means of a greater economy of power, to drive with the same or even a smaller consumption of coal more machinery with the same engine. The improvements in the transmitting mechanism have lessened friction, and, what so strikingly distinguishes modern from the older machinery, have reduced the diameter and weight of the shafting to a constantly decreasing minimum. Finally, the improvements in the operative machines have, while reducing their size, increased their speed and efficiency, as in the modern power-loom; or, while increasing the size of their frame-work, have also increased the extent and number of their working parts,

---

[1] l. c., p. 22.

[2] The moral element played an important part in the above experiments. The workpeople told the factory inspector: "We work with more spirit, we have the reward ever before us of getting away sooner at night, and one active and cheerful spirit pervades the whole mill, from the youngest piecer to the oldest hand, and we can greatly help each other" (l. c.)

as in spinning mules, or have added to the speed of these working parts by imperceptible alterations of detail, such as those which ten years ago increased the speed of the spindles in self-acting mules by one-fifth.

The reduction of the working day to 12 hours dates in England from 1832. In 1836 a manufacturer stated: "The labour now undergone in the factories is much greater than it used to be . . . compared with thirty or forty years ago . . . owing to the greater attention and activity required by the greatly increased speed which is given to the machinery."[1] In the year 1844, Lord Ashley, now Lord Shaftesbury, made in the House of Commons the following statements, supported by documentary evidence:

"The labour performed by those engaged in the processes of manufacture, is three times as great as in the beginning of such operations. Machinery has executed, no doubt, the work that would demand the sinews of millions of men; but it has also prodigiously multiplied the labour of those who are governed by its fearful movements . . . In 1815, the labour of following a pair of mules spinning cotton of No. 40—reckoning 12 hours to the working-day—involved a necessity of walking 8 miles. In 1832, the distance travelled in following a pair of mules, spinning cotton yarn of the same number, was 20 miles, and frequently more. In 1835" (query—1815 or 1825 ?) "the spinner put up daily, on each of these mules, 820 stretches, making a total of 1,640 stretches in the course of the day. In 1832, the spinner put up on each mule 2,200 stretches, making a total of 4,400. In 1844, 2,400 stretches, making a total of 4,800; and in some cases the amount of labour required is even still greater . . . I have another document sent to me in 1842, stating that the labour is progressively increasing—increasing not only because the distance to be travelled is greater, but because the quantity of goods produced is multiplied, while the hands are fewer in proportion than before; and, moreover, because an inferior species of cotton is now often spun, which it is more difficult to work . . . In the carding-room there has also been a great increase of labour.

[1] John Fielden, l. c., p. 32.

One person there does the work formerly divided between two. In the weaving-room, where a vast number of persons are employed, and principally females . . . the labour has increased within the last few years fully 10 per cent, owing to the increased speed of the machinery in spinning. In 1838, the number of hanks spun per week was 18,000, in 1843 it amounted to 21,000. In 1819 the number of picks in power-loom-weaving per minute was 60—in 1842 it was 140, showing a vast increase of labour."[1]

In the face of this remarkable intensity of labour which had already been reached in 1844 under the Twelve Hours' Act, there appeared to be a justification for the assertion made at that time by the English manufacturers, that any further progress in that direction was impossible, and therefore that every further reduction of the hours of labour meant a lessened production. The apparent correctness of their reasons will be best shown by the following contemporary statement by Leonard Horner, the factory inspector, their ever watchful censor.

"Now, as the quantity produced must, in the main, be regulated by the speed of the machinery, it must be the interest of the mill owner to drive it at the utmost rate of speed consistent with these following conditions, viz., the preservation of the machinery from too rapid deterioration; the preservation of the quality of the article manufactured; and the capability of the workman to follow the motion without a greater exertion than he can sustain for a constancy. One of the most important problems, therefore, which the owner of a factory has to solve is to find out the maximum speed at which he can run, with a due regard to the above conditions. It frequently happens that he finds he has gone too fast, that breakages and bad work more than counterbalance the increased speed, and that he is obliged to slacken his pace. I therefore concluded, that as an active and intelligent millowner would find out the safe maximum, it would not be possible to produce as much in eleven hours as in twelve. I further assumed that the operative paid by piece work, would exert himself to the utmost

---

[1] Lord Ashley, l. c., p. 6–9, passim.

consistent with the power of continuing at the same rate."[1] Horner, therefore, came to the conclusion that a reduction of the working hours below twelve would necessarily diminish production.[2] He himself, ten years later, cites his opinion of 1845 in proof of how much he under-estimated in that year the elasticity of machinery, and of man's labour-power, both of which are simultaneously stretched to an extreme by the compulsory shortening of the working day.

We now come to the period that follows the introduction of the Ten Hours' Act in 1847 into the English cotton, woollen, silk, and flax mills.

"The speed of the spindles has increased upon throstles 500, and upon mules 1000 revolutions a minute, *i.e.,* the speed of the throstle spindle, which in 1839 was 4500 times a minute, is now (1862) 5000; and of the mule spindle, that was 5000, is now 6000 times a minute, amounting in the former case to one-tenth, and in the second case to one-fifth addition increase."[3] James Nasmyth, the eminent civil engineer of Patricroft, near Manchester, explained in a letter to Leonard Horner, written in 1852, the nature of the improvements in the steam-engine that had been made between the years 1848 and 1852. After remarking that the horse-power of steam-engines, being always estimated in the official returns according to the power of similar engines in 1828,[4] is only nominal, and can serve only as an index of their real power, he goes on to say: "I am confident that from the same weight of steam-engine machinery, we are now obtaining at least 50 per cent. more duty or work performed on the average, and that in many cases the identical steam-engines which in the days of the restricted speed of 220 feet per minute, yielded 50 horse-

[1] Rep. of Insp. of Fact. for Quarter ending 30th September, 1844, and from 1st October, 1844, to 30th April, 1845. p. 20.

[2] l. c., p. 22.

[3] "Rep. of Insp. of Fact. for 31st October, 1862," p. 62.

[4] This was altered in the "Parliamentary Return" of 1862. In it the actual horse-power of the modern steam-engines and water-wheels appears in place of the nominal. The doubling spindles, too, are no longer included in the spinning spindles (as was the case in the "Returns" of 1839, 1850, and 1856); further, in the case of woollen mills, the number of "gigs" is added, a distinction made between jute and hemp mills on the one hand and flax mills on the other, and finally stocking-weaving is for the first time inserted in the report.

power, are now yielding upwards of 100." . . . . "The modern steam-engine of 100 horse-power is capable of being driven at a much greater force than formerly, arising from improvements in its construction, the capacity and construction of the boilers, &c." . . . "Although the same number of hands are employed in proportion to the horse-power as at former periods, there are fewer hands employed in proportion to the machinery."[1] "In the year 1850, the factories of the United Kingdom employed 134,217 nominal horse-power to give motion to 25,638,716 spindles and 301,445 looms. The number of spindles and looms in 1856 was respectively 33,503,580 of the former, and 369,205 of the latter, which, reckoning the force of the nominal horse-power required to be the same as in 1850, would require a force equal to 175,000 horses, but the actual power given in the return for 1856 is 161,435, less by above 10,000 horses than, calculating upon the basis of the return of 1850, the factories ought to have required in 1856."[2] "The facts thus brought out by the Return (of 1856) appear to be that the factory system is increasing rapidly; that although the same number of hands are employed in proportion to the horse-power as at former periods, there are fewer hands employed in proportion to the machinery; that the steam-engine is enabled to drive an increased weight of machinery by economy of force and other methods, and that an increased quantity of work can be turned off by improvements in machinery, and in methods of manufacture, by increase of speed of the machinery, and by a variety of other causes."[3]

"The great improvements made in machines of every kind have raised their productive power very much. Without any doubt, the shortening of the hours of labour . . . . gave the impulse to these improvements. The latter, combined with the more intense strain on the workman, have had the effect, that at least as much is produced in the shortened (by two hours or one-sixth) working-day as was previously produced during the longer one."[4]

[1] "Rep. of Insp. of Fact. for 31st October, 1856," pp. 13–14, 20 and 1852, p. 23.
[2] l. c., p. 14–15. [3] l. c., p. 20.
[4] Reports, &c., for 31st October, 1858, p. 9–10. Compare Reports, &c., for 30th April, 1860, p. 30, seqq.

One fact is sufficient to show how greatly the wealth of the manufacturers increased along with the more intense exploitation of labour-power. From 1838 to 1850, the average proportional increase in English cotton and other factories was 32%, while from 1850 to 1856 it amounted to 86%.

But however great the progress of English industry had been during the 8 years from 1848 to 1856 under the influence of a working-day of 10 hours, it was far surpassed during the next period of 6 years from 1856 to 1862. In silk factories, for instance, there were in 1856, spindles 1,093,799; in 1862, 1,388,544; in 1856, looms 9,260; in 1862, 10,709. But the number of operatives was, in 1856, 56,131; in 1862, 52,429. The increase in the spindles was therefore 26.9% and in the looms 15.6%, while the number of the operatives decreased 7%. In the year 1850 there were employed in worsted mills 875,830 spindles; in 1856, 1,324,549 (increase 51.2%), and in 1862, 1,289,172 (decrease 2.7%). But if we deduct the doubling spindles that figure in the numbers for 1856, but not in those for 1862, it will be found that after 1856 the number of spindles remained nearly stationary. On the other hand, after 1850, the speed of the spindles and looms was in many cases doubled. The number of power-looms in worsted mills was in 1850, 32,617; in 1856, 38,956; in 1862, 43,048. The number of the operatives was, in 1850, 79,737; in 1856, 87,-794; in 1862, 86,063; included in these, however, the children under 14 years of age were, in 1850, 9,956; in 1856, 11,228; in 1862, 13,178. In spite, therefore, of the greatly increased number of looms in 1862, compared with 1856, the total number of the workpeople employed decreased, and that of the children exploited increased.[1]

On the 27th of April, 1863, Mr. Ferrand said in the House of Commons: "I have been informed by delegates from 16 districts of Lancashire and Cheshire, in whose behalf I speak, that the work in the factories is, in consequence of the improvements in machinery, constantly on the increase. Instead of as formerly one person with two helps tenting two looms, one person now tents three looms without helps, and it is no un-

---

[1] "Report of Insp. of Fact. for 31st Oct., 1862," pp. 100 and 130.

common thing for one person to tent four. Twelve hours' work, as is evident from the facts adduced, is now compressed into less than 10 hours. It is therefore self-evident, to what an enormous extent the toil of the factory operative has increased during the last 10 years."[1]

Although, therefore, the Factory Inspectors unceasingly and with justice, commend the results of the Acts of 1844 and 1850, yet they admit that the shortening of the hours of labour has already called forth such an intensification of the labour as is injurious to the health of the workman and to his capacity for work. "In most of the cotton, worsted, and silk mills, an exhausting state of excitement necessary to enable the workers satisfactorily to mind the machinery, the motion of which has been greatly accelerated within the last few years, seems to me not unlikely to be one of the causes of that excess of mortality from lung disease, which Dr. Greenhow has pointed out in his recent report on this subject."[2] There cannot be the slightest doubt that the tendency that urges capital as soon as a prolongation of the hours of labour is once for all forbidden, to compensate itself, by a systematic heightening of the intensity of labour, and to convert every improvement in machinery into a more perfect means of exhausting the workman, must soon lead to a state of things in which a reduction of the hours of labour will again be inevitable.[3] On the other hand, the rapid advance of English industry between 1848 and the present time, under the influence of a day of 10 hours, surpasses the advance made between 1833 and 1847, when the day was 12 hours long, by far more than the latter surpasses the advance

---

[1] On 2 modern power-looms a weaver now makes in a week of 60 hours 26 pieces of certain quality, length, and breadth; while on the old power-looms he could make no more than 4 such pieces. The cost of weaving a piece of such cloth had already soon after 1850 fallen from 2s. 9d. to 5⅛d.

"Thirty years ago (1841) one spinner with three piecers was not required to attend to more than one pair of mules with 300–324 spindles. At the present time (1871) he has to mind with the help of 5 piecers 2200 spindles, and produces not less than seven times as much yarn as in 1841." (Alex. Redgrave, Factory Inspector—in the Journal of Arts, 5th January, 1872.)

[2] Rep. of Insp. of Fact. for 31st Oct. 1861, pp. 25, 26.

[3] The agitation for a working day of 8 hours has now (1867) begun in Lancashire among the factory operatives.

made during the half century after the first introduction of the factory system, when the working day was without limits.[1]

SECTION IV.—THE FACTORY.

At the commencement of this chapter we considered that which we may call the body of the factory, *i. e.*, machinery organised into a system. We there saw how machinery, by

[1] The following few figures indicate the increase in the "factories" of the United Kingdom since 1848:

	Quantity Exported, 1848.	Quantity Exported, 1851.	Quantity Exported, 1860.	Quantity Exported, 1865.
COTTON.				
Cotton yarn....	lbs. 135,831,162	lbs. 143,966,106	lbs. 197,343,655	lbs. 103,751,455
Sewing thread.	lbs.	lbs. 4,392,176	lbs. 6,297,554	lbs. 4,648,611
Cotton cloth...	yds 1,091,373,930	yds 1,543,161,789	yds 2,776,218,427	yds 2,015,237,851
FLAX & HEMP.				
Yarn	lbs. 11,722,182	lbs. 18,841,326	lbs. 31,210,612	lbs. 36,777,334
Cloth	yds. 88,901,519	yds. 129,106,753	yds. 143,996,773	yds. 247,012,529
SILK.				
Yarn	lbs. 466,825	lbs. 462,513	lbs. 897,402	yds. 812.589
Cloth	yds.	yds. 1,181,455	yds. 1,307,293	yds. 2,869,837
WOOL.				
Woollen and Worsted yarns	lbs.	lbs. 14,670,880	lbs. 27,533,968	lbs. 31,669,267
Cloth	yds.	yds. 241,120,973	yds. 190,381,537	yds. 278,837,438

	Value Exported, 1848.	Value Exported, 1851.	Value Exported, 1860.	Value Exported, 1865.
	£	£	£	£
COTTON.				
Yarn	5,927,831	6,634,026	9,870,875	10,351,04
Cloth	16,753,369	23,454,810	42,141,505	46,903,796
FLAX & HEMP.				
Yarn	493,449	951,426	1,801,272	2,505,497
Cloth	2,802,789	4,107,396	4,804,803	9,155,318
SILK.				
Yarn		195,380	918,342	768,067
Cloth	77,789	1,130,398	1,587,303	1,409,221
WOOL.				
Yarn	776,975	1,484,544	3,843,450	5,424,017
Cloth	5,733,828	8,377,183	12,156,998	20,102,259

annexing the labour of women and children, augments the number of human beings who form the material for capitalistic exploitation, how it confiscates the whole of the workman's disposable time, by immoderate extension of the hours of labour, and how finally its progress, which allows of enormous increase of production in shorter and shorter periods, serves as a means of systematically getting more work done in a shorter time, or in exploiting labour-power more intensely. We now turn to the factory as a whole, and that in its most perfect form.

Dr. Ure, the Pindar of the automatic factory, describes it, on the one hand as "Combined co-operation of many orders of workpeople, adult and young, in tending with assiduous skill, a system of productive machines, continuously impelled by a central power" (the prime mover); on the other hand, as "a vast automaton, composed of various mechanical and intellectual organs, acting in uninterrupted concert for the production of a common object, all of them being subordinate to a self-regulated moving force." These two descriptions are far from being identical. In one, the collective labourer, or social body of labour, appears as the dominant subject and the mechanical automaton as the object; in the other, the automaton itself is the subject, and the workmen are merely conscious organs, co-ordinate with the unconscious organs of the automaton, and together with them, subordinated to the central moving-power. The first description is applicable to every possible employment of machinery on a large scale, the second is characteristic of its use by capital, and therefore of the modern factory system. Ure prefers therefore, to describe the central machine, from which the motion comes, not only as an

See the Bluebooks "Statistical Abstract of the United Kingdom, Nos. 8 and 13." Lond., 1861 and 1866. In Lancashire the number of mills increased only 4 per cent. between 1839 and 1850; 19 per cent. between 1850 and 1856; and 33 per cent. between 1856 and 1862; while the persons employed in them during each of the above periods of 11 years increased absolutely, but diminished relatively. (See "Rep. of Insp. of Fact., for 31st Oct., 1862," p. 63.) The cotton trade preponderates in Lancashire. We may form an idea of the stupendous nature of the cotton trade in that district, when we consider that, of the gross number of textile factories in the United Kingdom, it absorbs 45.2 per cent., of the spindles 83.3 per cent., of the power-looms 81.4 per cent., of the mechanical horse-power 72.6 per cent., and of the total number of persons employed 58.2 per cent. (l. c., p. 62–63.)

automaton, but as an autocrat. "In these spacious halls the benignant power of steam summons around him his myriads of willing menials."[1]

Along with the tool, the skill of the workman in handling it passes over to the machine. The capabilities of the tool are emancipated from the restraints that are inseparable from human labour-power. Thereby the technical foundation on which is based the division of labour in Manufacture, is swept away. Hence, in the place of the hierarchy of specialised workmen that characterises manufacture, there steps, in the automatic factory, a tendency to equalise and reduce to one and the same level every kind of work that has to be done by the minders of the machines;[2] in the place of the artificially produced differentiations of the detail workmen, step the natural differences of age and sex.

So far as division of labour re-appears in the factory, it is primarily a distribution of the workmen among the specialised machines; and of masses of workmen, not however organised into groups, among the various departments of the factory, in each of which they work at a number of similar machines placed together; their co-operation, therefore, is only simple. The organised group, peculiar to manufacture, is replaced by the connexion between the head workman and his few assistants. The essential division is, into workmen who are actually employed on the machines (among whom are included a few who look after the engine), and into mere attendants (almost exclusively children) of these workmen. Among the attendants are reckoned more or less all "Feeders" who supply the machines with the material to be worked. In addition to these two principal classes, there is a numerically unimportant class of persons, whose occupation it is to look after the whole of the machinery and repair it from time to time; such as engineers, mechanics, joiners, &c. This is a superior class of workmen, some of them scientifically educated, others brought up to a trade; it is distinct from the factory operative class,

---

[1] Ure, l. c., p. 18.
[2] Ure, l. c., p. 31. See Karl Marx, Poverty of Philosophy, p. 122.

and merely aggregated to it.[1] This division of labour is purely technical.

To work at a machine, the workman should be taught from childhood, in order that he may learn to adapt his own movements to the uniform and unceasing motion of an automaton. When the machinery, as a whole, forms a system of manifold machines, working simultaneously and in concert, the co-operation based upon it, requires the distribution of various groups of workmen among the different kinds of machines. But the employment of machinery does away with the necessity of crystallizing this distribution after the manner of Manufacture, by the constant annexation of a particular man to a particular function.[2] Since the motion of the whole system does not proceed from the workman, but from the machinery, a change of persons can take place at any time without an interruption of the work. The most striking proof of this is afforded by the *relays system,* put into operation by the manufacturers during their revolt from 1848–1850. Lastly, the quickness with which machine work is learnt by young people, does away with the necessity of bringing up for exclusive employment by machinery, a special class of operatives.[3] With

---

[1] It looks very like intentional misleading by statistics (which misleading it would be possible to prove in detail in other cases too), when the English factory legislation excludes from its operation the class of labourers last mentioned in the text, while the parliamentary returns expressly include in the category of factory operatives, not only engineers, mechanics, &c., but also managers, salesmen, messengers, warehousemen, packers, &c., in short everybody, except the owner of the factory himself.

[2] Ure grants this. He says, "in case of need," the workmen can be moved at the will of the manager from one machine to another, and he triumphantly exclaims: "Such a change is in flat contradiction with the old routine, that divides the labour, and to one workman assigns the task of fashioning the head of a needle, to another the sharpening of the point." He had much better have asked himself, why this "old routine" is departed from in the automatic factory, only "in case of need."

[3] When distress is very great, as, for instance, during the American civil war, the factory operative is now and then set by the Bourgeois to do the roughest of work, such as road-making, &c. The English "ateliers nationaux" of 1862 and the following years, established for the benefit of the destitute cotton operatives, differ from the French of 1848 in this, that in the latter the workmen had to do unproductive work at the expense of the state; in the former they had to do productive municipal work to the advantage of the bourgeois, and that, too, cheaper than the regular workmen, with whom they were thus thrown into competition. "The physical appearance of the cotton operatives is unquestionably improved. This I attribute . . . as to the men, to outdoor labour on public works." ("Rep. of Insp. of Fact.," 31st Oct., 1865, p. 59.) The writer here alludes to the Preston factory operatives, who were employed on Preston Moor.

regard to the work of the mere attendants, it can, to some extent, be replaced in the mill by machines,[1] and owing to its extreme simplicity, it allows of a rapid and constant change of the individuals burdened with this drudgery.

Although then, technically speaking, the old system of division of labour is thrown overboard by machinery, it hangs on in the factory, as a traditional habit handed down from Manufacture, and is afterwards systematically re-moulded and established in a more hideous form by capital, as a means of exploiting labour-power. The life-long speciality of handling one and the same tool, now becomes the life-long speciality of serving one and the same machine. Machinery is put to a wrong use, with the object of transforming the workman, from his very childhood, into a part of a detail-machine.[2] In this way, not only are the expenses of his re-production considerably lessened, but at the same time his helpless dependence upon the factory as a whole, and therefore upon the capitalist, is rendered complete. Here as everywhere else, we must distinguish between the increased productiveness due to the development of the social process of production, and that due to the capitalist exploitation of that process. In handicrafts and manufacture, the workman makes use of a tool, in the factory, the machine makes use of him. There the movements of the instrument of labour proceed from him, here it is the movements of the machine that he must follow. In manufacture the workmen are parts of a living mechanism. In the factory we have a lifeless mechanism independent of the work-

[1] An example: The various mechanical apparatus introduced since the Act of 1844 into woollen mills, for replacing the labour of children. So soon as it shall happen that the children of the manufacturers themselves have to go through a course of schooling as helpers in the mill, this almost unexplored territory of mechanics will soon make remarkable progress. "Of machinery, perhaps self-acting mules are as dangerous as any other kind. Most of the accidents from them happen to little children, from their creeping under the mules to sweep the floor whilst the mules are in motion. Several 'minders' have been fined for this offence, but without much general benefit. If machine makers would only invent a self-sweeper, by whose use the necessity for these little children to creep under the machinery might be prevented, it would be a happy addition to our protective measures." ("Reports of Insp. of Fact." for 31st Oct., 1866, p. 63.)

[2] So much then for Proudhon's wonderful idea: he "construes" machinery not as a synthesis of instruments of labour, but as a synthesis of detail operations for the benefit of the labourer himself.

man, who becomes its mere living appendage. "The miserable routine of endless drudgery and toil in which the same mechanical process is gone through over and over again, is like the labour of Sisyphus. The burden of labour, like the rock, keeps ever falling back on the worn-out labourer."[1] At the same time that factory work exhausts the nervous system to the uttermost, it does away with the many-sided play of the muscles, and confiscates every atom of freedom, both in bodily and intellectual activity.[2] The lightening of the labour, even, becomes a sort of torture, since the machine does not free the labourer from work, but deprives the work of all interest. Every kind of capitalist production in so far as it is not only a labour-process, but also a process of creating surplus-value, has this in common, that it is not the workman that employs the instruments of labour, but the instruments of labour that employ the workman. But it is only in the factory system that this inversion for the first time acquires technical and palpable reality. By means of its conversion into an automaton, the instrument of labour confronts the labourer, during the labour-process, in the shape of capital, of dead labour, that dominates, and pumps dry, living labour-power. The separation of the intellectual powers of production from the manual labour, and the conversion of those powers into the might of capital over labour, is, as we have already shown, finally completed by modern industry erected on the foundation of machinery. The special skill of each individual insignificant factory operative vanishes as an infinitesimal quantity before the science, the gigantic physical forces, and the mass of labour that are embodied in the factory mechanism and, together with that mechanism, constitute the power of the "master." This "master," therefore, in whose brain the machinery and his monopoly of it are inseparably united,

---

[1] F. Engels, l. c. p. 217. Even an ordinary and optimist freetrader, like Mr. Molinari, goes so far as to say "Un homme s'use plus vite en surveillant, quinze heures par jour, l'évolution uniforme d'un mécanisme, qu'en exerçant, dans le même espace de temps, sa force physique. Ce travail de surveillance qui servirait peut-être d'utile gymnastique à l'intelligence, s'il n'était pas trop prolongé, détruit à la longue, par son excès, et l'intelligence, et le corps même." (G. de Molinari: Études Economiques." Paris 1846.)

[2] F. Engels, l. c. p. 216.

whenever he falls out with his "hands," contemptuously tells them: "The factory operatives should keep in wholesome remembrance the fact that theirs is really a low species of skilled labour; and that there is none which is more easily acquired, or of its quality more amply remunerated, or which by a short training of the least expert can be more quickly, as well as abundantly, acquired. . . . The master's machinery really plays a far more important part in the business of production than the labour and the skill of the operative, which six months' education can teach, and a common labourer can learn."[1] The technical subordination of the workman to the uniform motion of the instruments of labour, and the peculiar composition of the body of workpeople, consisting as it does of individuals of both sexes and of all ages, give rise to a barrack discipline, which is elaborated into a complete system in the factory, and which fully developes the before mentioned labour of overlooking, thereby dividing the workpeople into operatives and overlookers, into private soldiers and sergeants of an industrial army. "The main difficulty [in the automatic factory] . . . lay . . . above all in training human beings to renounce their desultory habits of work, and to identify themselves with the unvarying regularity of the complex automaton. To devise and administer a successful code of factory discipline, suited to the necessities of factory diligence, was the Herculean enterprise, the noble achievement of Arkwright! Even at the present day, when the system is perfectly organised and its labour lightened to the utmost, it is found nearly impossible to convert persons past the age of puberty, into useful factory hands."[2] The factory code in which capital formulates, like a private legislator, and at his own good will, his autocracy over his workpeople, unaccompanied by that division of responsibility, in other matters so much approved

---

[1] "The Master Spinners' and Manufacturers' Defence Fund. Report of the Committee." Manchester, 1854, p. 17. We shall see hereafter that the "master" can sing quite another song, when he is threatened with the loss of his "living" automaton.

[2] Ure, l. c. p. 15. Whoever knows the life history of Arkwright, will never dub this barber-genius "noble." Of all the great inventors of the 18th century, he was incontestably the greatest thiever of other people's inventions and the meanest fellow.

of by the bourgeoisie, and unaccompanied by the still more approved representative system, this code is but the capitalistic caricature of that social regulation of the labour-process which becomes requisite in co-operation on a great scale, and in the employment in common, of instruments of labour and especially of machinery. The place of the slave driver's lash is taken by the overlooker's book of penalties. All punishments naturally resolve themselves into fines and deductions from wages, and the law-giving talent of the factory Lycurgus so arranges matters, that a violation of his laws is, if possible, more profitable to him than the keeping of them.[1]

[1] "The slavery in which the bourgeoisie has bound the proletariat, comes nowhere more plainly into daylight than in the factory system. In it all freedom comes to an end both at law and in fact. The workman must be in the factory at half past five. If he come a few minutes late, he is punished; if he come 10 minutes late, he is not allowed to enter until after breakfast, and thus loses a quarter of a day's wage. He must eat, drink and sleep at word of command. . . . The despotic bell calls him from his bed, calls him from breakfast and dinner. And how does he fare in the mill? There the master is the absolute law-giver. He makes what regulations he pleases; he alters and makes additions to his code at pleasure; and if he insert the veriest nonsense, the courts say to the workman: Since you have entered into this contract voluntarily, you must now carry it out. . . . These workmen are condemned to live, from their ninth year till their death, under this mental and bodily torture." (F. Engels l. c. p. 217, sq.) What, "the courts say," I will illustrate by two examples. One occurs at Sheffield at the end of 1866. In that town a workman had engaged himself for 2 years in a steelworks. In consequence of a quarrel with his employer he left the works, and declared that under no circumstances would he work for that master any more. He was prosecuted for breach of contract, and condemned to two months' imprisonment. (If the master break the contract, he can be proceeded against only in a civil action, and risks nothing but money damages). After the workman has served his two months, the master invites him to return to the works, pursuant to the contract. Workman says; no: he has already been punished for the breach. The master prosecutes again, the court condemns again, although one of the judges, Mr. Shee, publicly denounces this as a legal monstrosity, by which a man can periodically, as long as he lives, be punished over and over again for the same offence or crime. This judgment was given not by the "Great Unpaid," the provincial Dogberries, but by one of the highest courts of justice in London. Note to the 4th German edition.—This has now been abolished. With the exception of a few cases, for instance in public gas works, the English laborer has been placed on an equity with the employers in cases of contract breaking, and can be proceeded against only by the civil courts. F. E. —.
The second case occurs in Wiltshire at the end of November 1863. About 30 power-loom weavers, in the employment of one Harrup, à cloth manufacturer at Leower's Mill, Westbury Leigh, struck work because master Harrup indulged in the agreeable habit of making deductions from their wages for being late in the morning; 6d. for 2 minutes; 1s. for 3 minutes, and 1s. 6d. for ten minutes. This is at the rate of 9s. per hour, and £4 10s. 0d. per diem; while the wages of the weavers on the average of a year, never exceed 10s. to 12s. weekly. Harrup also appointed a boy to announce the starting time by a whistle, which he often did before six o'clock in the morning: and if the hands were not all there at the moment the whistle ceased, the doors were closed, and those hands who were outside were

We shall here merely allude to the material conditions under which factory labour is carried on. Every organ of sense is injured in an equal degree by artificial elevation of the temperature, by the dust-laden atmosphere, by the deafening noise, not to mention danger to life and limb among the thickly crowded machinery, which, with the regularity of the seasons, issues its list of the killed and wounded in the industrial battle.[1] Economy of the social means of production, matured

fined: and as there was no clock on the premises, the unfortunate hands were at the mercy of the young Harrup-inspired time-keeper. The hands on strike, mothers of families as well as girls, offered to resume work if the time-keeper were replaced by a clock, and a more reasonable scale of fines were introduced. Harrup summoned 19 women and girls before the magistrates for breach of contract. To the utter indignation of all present, they were each mulcted in a fine of 6d. and 2s. 6d. for costs. Harrup was followed from the court by a crowd of people who hissed him.—A favourite operation with manufacturers is to punish the workpeople by deductions made from their wages on account of faults in the material worked on. This method gave rise in 1866 to a general strike in the English pottery districts. The reports of the Ch. Empl. Com. (1863-1866), give cases where the worker not only receives no wages, but becomes, by means of his labour, and of the penal regulations, the debtor to boot, of his worthy master. The late cotton crisis also furnished edifying examples of the sagacity shown by the factory autocrats in making deductions from wages. Mr. R. Baker, the Inspector of Factories, says, "I have myself had lately to direct prosecutions against one cotton mill occupier for having in those pinching and painful times deducted 10d. a piece from some of the young workers employed by him, for the surgeon's certificate (for which he himself had only paid 6d.), when only allowed by the law to deduct 3d., and by custom nothing at all . . . . And I have been informed of another, who, in order to keep without the law, but to attain the same object, charges the poor children who work for him a shilling each, as a fee for learning them the art and mystery of cotton spinning, so soon as they are declared by the surgeon fit and proper persons for that occupation. There may therefore be undercurrent causes for such extraordinary exhibitions as strikes, not only wherever they arise, but particularly at such times as the present, which without explanation, render them inexplicable to the public understanding." He alludes here to a strike of power-loom weavers at Darwin, June, 1863. ("Reports of Insp. of Fact. for 30 April, 1863," pp. 50-51.) The reports always go beyond their official dates.

[1] The protection afforded by the Factory Acts against dangerous machinery has had a beneficial effect. "But . . . there are other sources of accident which did not exist twenty years since; one especially, viz., the increased speed on the machinery. Wheels, rollers, spindles and shuttles are now propelled at increased and increasing rates; fingers must be quicker and defter in their movements to take up the broken thread, for, if placed with hesitation or carelessness, they are sacrificed. . . . A large number of accidents are caused by the eagerness of the workpeople to get through their work expeditiously. It must be remembered that it is of the highest importance to manufacturers that their machinery should be in motion, *i.e.*, producing yarns and goods. Every minute's stoppage is not only a loss of power, but of production, and the workpeople are urged by the overlookers, who are interested in the quantity of work turned off, to keep the machinery in motion; and it is no less important to those of the operatives who are paid by the weight or piece that the machines should be kept in motion. Consequently, although it is strictly forbidden in many, nay in most factories, that machinery should be clean-

and forced as in a hothouse by the factory system, is turned, in the hands of capital into systematic robbery of what is necessary for the life of the workman while he is at work, robbery of space, light, air, and of protection to his person against the dangerous and unwholesome accompaniments of the productive process, not to mention the robbery of appliances for the comfort of the workman.[1] Is Fourier wrong when he calls factories "tempered bagnos ?"[2]

Section 5.—The Strife Between Workman and Machine.

The contest between the capitalist and the wage-labourer dates back to the very origin of capital. It raged on throughout the whole manufacturing period.[3] But only since the

ed while in motion, it is nevertheless the constant practice in most if not in all, that the workpeople do, unreproved, pick out waste, wipe rollers and wheels, &c., while their frames are in motion. Thus from this cause only, 906 accidents have occurred during the six months. . . . . Although a great deal of cleaning is constantly going on day by day, yet Saturday is generally the day set apart for the thorough cleaning of the machinery, and a great deal of this is done while the machinery is in motion." Since cleaning is not paid for, the workpeople seek to get done with it as speedily as possible. Hence "the number of accidents which occur on Fridays, and especially on Saturdays, is much larger than on any other day. On the former the excess is nearly 12 per cent. over the average number of the four first days of the week, and on the latter day the excess is 25 per cent. over the average of the preceding five days; or, if the number of working-hours on Saturday being taken into account—7½ hours on Saturday as compared with 10½ on other days—there is an excess of 65 per cent. on Saturdays over the average of the other five days." ("Rep. of Insp. of Fact., 31st Oct., 1866," p. 9, 15, 16, 17.)

[1] In Part I. of Book III. I shall give an account of a recent campaign by the English manufacturers against the Clauses in the Factory Acts that protect the "hands" against dangerous machinery. For the present, let this one quotation from the official report of Leonard Horner suffice: "I have heard some millowners speak with inexcusable levity of some of the accidents; such, for instance, as the loss of a finger being a trifling matter. A working-man's living and prospects depend so much upon his fingers, that any loss of them is a very serious matter to him. When I have heard such inconsiderate remarks made, I have usually put this question: Suppose you were in want of an additional workman, and two were to apply, both equally well qualified in other respects, but one had lost a thumb or a forefinger, which would you engage? There never was a hesitation as to the answer." . . . . The manufacturers have "mistaken prejudices against what they have heard represented as a pseudo-philanthropic legislation." ("Rep. of Insp. of Fact., 31st Oct., 1855." These manufacturers are clever folk, and not without reason were they enthusiastic for the slave-holder's rebellion.

[2] In those factories that have been longest subject to the Factory Acts, with their compulsory limitation of the hours of labour, and other regulations, many of the older abuses have vanished. The very improvement of the machinery demands to a certain extent "improved construction of the buildings," and this is an advantage to the workpeople. (See "Rep. of Insp. of Fact. for 31st Oct., 1863," p. 109.)

[3] See amongst others, John Houghton: "Husbandry and Trade improved. Lon-

introduction of machinery has the workman fought against the instrument of labour itself, the material embodiment of capital. He revolts against this particular form of the means of production, as being the material basis of the capitalist mode of production.

In the 17th century nearly all Europe experienced revolts of the workpeople against the ribbon-loom, a machine for weaving ribbons and trimmings, called in Germany Bandmühle, Schnurmühle, and Mühlenstuhl. These machines were invented in Germany. Abbé Lancellotti, in a work that appeared in Venice in 1636, but which was written in 1579, says as follows: "Anthony Müller of Danzig, saw about 50 years ago in that town, a very ingenious machine, which weaves 4 to 6 pieces at once. But the Mayor being apprehensive that this invention might throw a large number of workmen on the streets, caused the inventor to be secretly strangled or drowned." In Leyden, this machine was not used till 1629; there the riots of the ribbon-weavers at length compelled the Town Council to prohibit it. "In hac urbe," says Boxhorn (Inst. Pol., 1663), referring to the introduction of this machine in Leyden, "ante hos viginti circiter annos instrumentum quidam invenerunt textorium, quo solus plus panni et facilius conficere poterat, quam plures aequali tempore. Hinc turbæ ortæ et querulæ textorum, tandemque usus hujus instrumenti a magistratu prohibitus est." After making various decrees more or less prohibitive against this loom in 1632, 1639, &c., the States General of Holland at length permitted it to be used, under certain conditions, by the decree of the 15th December, 1661. It was also prohibited in Cologne in 1676, at the same time that its introduction into England was causing disturbances among the workpeople. By an imperial Edict of 19th Feb., 1685, its use was forbidden throughout all Germany.

don, 1727." "The Advantages of the East India Trade, 1720." John Bellers, l. c. The masters and their workmen are, unhappily, in a perpetual war with each other. The invariable object of the former is to get their work done as cheaply as possible; and they do not fail to employ every artifice to this purpose, whilst the latter are equally attentive to every occasion of distressing their masters into a compliance with higher demands." ("An Inquiry into the Causes of the Present High Prices of Provisions," p. 61-62. Author, the Rev. Nathaniel Forster, quite on the side of the workmen.)

In Hamburg it was burnt in public by order of the Senate. The Emperor Charles VI., on 9th Feb., 1719, renewed the edict of 1685, and not till 1765 was its use openly allowed in the Electorate of Saxony. This machine, which shook Europe to its foundations, was in fact the precursor of the mule and the power-loom, and of the industrial revolution of the 18th century. It enabled a totally inexperienced boy, to set the whole loom with all its shuttles in motion, by simply moving a rod backwards and forwards, and in its improved form produced from 40 to 50 pieces at once.

About 1630, a wind-sawmill, erected near London by a Dutchman, succumbed to the excesses of the populace. Even as late as the beginning of the 18th century, sawmills driven by water overcame the opposition of the people, supported as it was by parliament, only with great difficulty. No sooner had Everet in 1758 erected the first wool-shearing machine that was driven by water-power, than it was set on fire by 100,000 people who had been thrown out of work. Fifty thousand workpeople, who had previously lived by carding wool, petitioned parliament against Arkwright's scribbling mills and carding engines. The enormous destruction of machinery that occurred in the English manufacturing districts during the first 15 years of this century, chiefly caused by the employment of the power-loom, and known as the Luddite movement, gave the anti-jacobin governments of a Sidmouth, a Castlereagh, and the like, a pretext for the most re-actionary and forcible measures. It took both time and experience before the workpeople learnt to distinguish between machinery and its employment by capital, and to direct their attacks, not against the material instruments of production, but against the mode in which they are used.[1]

The contests about wages in Manufacture, presuppose manufacture, and are in no sense directed against its existence. The opposition against the establishment of new manufactures, proceeds from the guilds and privileged towns, not from the work-

[1] In old-fashioned manufactures the revolts of the workpeople against machinery, even to this day, occasionally assume a savage character as in the case of the Sheffield file cutters in 1865.

people. Hence the writers of the manufacturing period treat the division of labour chiefly as a means of virtually supplying a deficiency of labourers, and not as a means of actually displacing those in work. This distinction is self-evident. If it be said that 100 millions of people would be required in England to spin with the old spinning-wheel the cotton that is now spun with mules by 500,000 people, this does not mean that the mules took the place of those millions who never existed. It means only this, that many millions of workpeople would be required to replace the spinning machinery. If, on the other hand, we say, that in England the power-loom threw 800,000 weavers on the streets, we do not refer to existing machinery, that would have to be replaced by a definite number of workpeople, but to a number of weavers in existence who were actually replaced or displaced by the looms. During the manufacturing period, handicraft labour, altered though it was by division of labour, was yet the basis. The demands of the new colonial markets could not be satisfied owing to the relatively small number of town operatives handed down from the middle ages, and the manufactures proper opened out new fields of production to the rural population, driven from the land by the dissolution of the feudal system. At that time, therefore, division of labour and co-operation in the workshops, were viewed more from the positive aspect, that they made the workpeople more productive.[1] Long before the period of Modern Industry, co-operation and the concentration of the instruments of labour in the hands of a few, gave rise, in numerous countries where these methods were applied in agri-

---

[1] Sir James Stewart also understands machinery quite in this sense. "Je considère donc les machines comme des moyens d'augmenter (virtuellement) le nombre des gens industrieux qu'on n'est pas obligé de nourrir. . . . En quoi l'effet d'une machine diffère-t-il de celui de nouveaux habitants?" (French trans. t. I., l. I., ch. XIX.) More naïve is Petty, who says, it replaces "Polygamy." The above point of view is, at the most, admissible only for some parts of the United States. On the other hand, "machinery can seldom be used with success to abridge the labour of an individual; more time would be lost in its construction than could be saved by its application. It is only useful when it acts on great masses, when a single machine can assist the work of thousands. It is accordingly in the most populous countries, where there are most idle men, that it is most abundant. . . . It is not called into use by a scarcity of men, but by the facility with which they can be brought to work in masses." (Piercy Ravenstone: "Thoughts on the Funding System and its Effects." London, 1824, p. 15.)

culture, to great, sudden and forcible revolutions in the modes of production, and consequentially, in the conditions of exist- ence, and the means of employment of the rural populations. But this contest at first takes place more between the large and the small landed proprietors, than between capital and wage-labour; on the other hand, when the labourers are dis- placed by the instruments of labour, by sheep, horses, &c., in this case force is directly resorted to in the first instance as the prelude to the industrial revolution. The labourers are first driven from the land, and then come the sheep. Land grab- bing on a great scale, such as was perpetrated in England, is the first step in creating a field for the establishment of agri- culture on a great scale.[1]   Hence this subversion of agriculture puts on, at first, more the appearance of a political revolution.

The instrument of labour, when it takes the form of a machine, immediately becomes a competitor of the workman himself.[2]   The self-expansion of capital by means of machinery is thenceforward directly proportional to the number of the workpeople, whose means of livelihood have been destroyed by that machinery. The whole system of capitalist production is based on the fact that the workman sells his labour-power as a commodity. Division of labour specialises this labour-power, by reducing it to skill in handling a particular tool. So soon as the handling of this tool becomes the work of a machine, then, with the use-value, the exchange-value too, of the work- man's labour-power vanishes; the workman becomes unsale- able, like paper money thrown out of currency by legal enact- ment. That portion of the working class, thus by machinery rendered superfluous, *i.e.*, no longer immediately necessary for the self-expansion of capital, either goes to the wall in the unequal contest of the old handicrafts and manufactures with machinery, or else floods all the more easily accessible branches of industry, swamps the labour market, and sinks the price of labour-power below its value. It is impressed upon the work-

---

[1] Note to the 4th German edition.—This applies also to Germany. Wherever agriculture on a large scale exists in Germany, that is, particularly in the East, it was made possible through the "trapping of peasants" in vogue since the 16th century, and more particularly since 1648. F. E.—

[2] "Machinery and labour are in constant competition." Ricardo, l. c., p. 479.

people, as a great consolation, first, that their sufferings are only temporary ("a temporary inconvenience"), secondly, that machinery acquires the mastery over the whole of a given field of production, only by degrees, so that the extent and intensity of its destructive effect is diminished. The first consolation neutralizes the second. When machinery seizes on an industry by degrees, it produces chronic misery among the operatives who compete with it. Where the transition is rapid, the effect is acute and felt by great masses. History discloses no tragedy more horrible than the gradual extinction of the English hand-loom weavers, an extinction that was spread over several decades, and finally sealed in 1838. Many of them died of starvation, many with families vegetated for a long time on $2\frac{1}{2}$ d. a day.[1] On the other hand, the English cotton machinery produced an acute effect in India. The Governor General reported 1834-35. "The misery hardly finds a parallel in the history of commerce. The bones of the cotton-weavers are bleaching the plains of India." No doubt, in turning them out of this "temporal" world, the machinery caused them no more than "a temporary inconvenience." For the rest, since machinery is continually seizing upon new fields of production, its temporary effect is really permanent. Hence, the character of independance and estrangement which the capitalist mode of production as a whole gives to the instruments of labour and to the product, as against the workman, is devel-

---

[1] The competition between hand-weaving and power-weaving in England, before the passing of the Poor Law of 1833, was prolonged by supplementing the wages, which had fallen considerably below the minimum, with parish relief. "The Rev. Mr. Turner was, in 1827, rector of Wilmslow, in Cheshire, a manufacturing district. The questions of the Committee of Emigration, and Mr. Turner's answers, show how the competition of human labour is maintained against machinery.' Question: Has not the use of the power-loom superseded the use of the hand-loom? Answer: Undoubtedly; it would have superseded them much more than it has done, if the hand-loom weavers were not enabled to submit to a reduction of wages. Question: 'But in submitting he has accepted wages which are insufficient to support him, and looks to parochial contribution as the remainder of his support? Answer: Yes, and in fact the competition between the hand-loom and the power-loom is maintained out of the poor-rates. Thus degrading pauperism or expatriation, is the benefit which the industrious receive from the introduction of machinery, to be reduced from the respectable and in some degree independent mechanic, to the cringing wretch who lives on the debasing bread of charity. This they call a tempory inconvenience." ("A Prize Essay on the comparative merits of Competition and Co-operation." Lond., 1834, p. 29.)

oped by means of machinery into a thorough antagonism.[1] Therefore, it is with the advent of machinery, that the workman for the first time brutally revolts against the instruments of labour.

The instrument of labour strikes down the labourer. This direct antagonism between the two comes out most strongly, whenever newly introduced machinery competes with handicrafts or manufactures, handed down from former times. But even in Modern Industry the continual improvement of machinery, and the development of the automatic system, has an analogous effect. "The object of improved machinery is to diminish manual labour, to provide for the performance of a process or the completion of a link in a manufacture by the aid of an iron instead of the human apparatus."[2] "The adaptation of power to machinery heretofore moved by hand, is almost of daily occurrence . . . the minor improvements in machinery having for their object economy of power, the production of better work, the turning off more work in the same time, or in supplying the place of a child, a female, or a man, are constant, and although sometimes apparently of no great moment, have somewhat important results."[3] "Whenever a process requires peculiar dexterity and steadiness of hand, it is withdrawn, as soon as possible, from the cunning workman, who is prone to irregularities of many kinds, and it is placed in charge of a peculiar mechanism, so self-regulating that a child can superintend it."[4] "On the automatic plan

---

[1] "The same cause which may increase the revenue of the country" (*i.e.*, as Ricardo explains in the same passage, the revenues of landlords and capitalists, whose wealth, from the economical point of view, forms the Wealth of the Nation), "may at the same time render the population redundant and deteriorate the condition of the labourer." (Ricardo, l. c., p. 469.) "The constant aim and the tendency of every improvement in machinery is, in fact, to do away entirely with the labour of man, or to lessen its price by substituting the labour of women and children for that of grown up men, or of unskilled for that of skilled workmen." (Ure, l. c., t. I., p. 35).

[2] "Rep. Insp. Fact. for 31st October, 1858," p. 43.

[3] "Rep. Insp. Fact. for 31st October, 1856," p. 15.

[4] Ure, l. c., p. 19. "The great advantage of the machinery employed in brickmaking consists in this, that the employer is made entirely independent of skilled labourers." ("Ch. Empl. Comm. V. Report," Lond., 1866, p. 180, n. 46.) Mr. A. Sturrock, superintendent of the machine department of the Great Northern Railway, says, with regard to the building of locomotives, &c.: "Expensive English workmen are being less used every day. The production of the workshops of England is

skilled labour gets progressively superseded."[1] "The effect of improvements in machinery, not merely in superseding the necessity for the employment of the same quantity of adult labour as before, in order to produce a given result, but in substituting one description of human labour for another, the less skilled for the more skilled, juvenile for adult, female for male, causes a fresh disturbance in the rate of wages."[2] "The effect of substituting the self-acting mule for the common mule, is to discharge the greater part of the men spinners, and to retain adolescents and children."[3] The extraordinary power of expansion of the factory system owing to accumulated practical experience, to the mechanical means at hand, and to constant technical progress, was proved to us by the giant strides of that system under the pressure of a shortened working day. But who, in 1860, the Zenith year of the English cotton industry, would have dreamt of the galloping improvements in machinery, and the corresponding displacement of working people, called into being during the following 3 years, under the stimulus of the American Civil War? A couple of examples from the Reports of the Inspectors of Factories will suffice on this point. A Manchester manufacturer states: "We formerly had 75 carding engines, now we have 12, doing the same quantity of work. . . . We are doing with fewer hands by 14, at a saving in wages of £10 a-week. Our estimated saving in waste is about 10% in the quantity of cotton consumed." "In another fine spinning mill in Manchester, I was informed that through increased speed and the adoption of some self-acting processes, a reduction had been made, in number, for a fourth in one department, and of above half in another, and that the introduction of the combing machine in place of the second carding, had considerably reduced the number of hands formerly employed in the carding room." Another spinning mill is estimated to effect a saving of labour of 10%. The Messrs.

being increased by the use of improved tools and these tools are again served by a low class of labour . . . Formerly their skilled labour necessarily produced all the parts of engines. Now the parts of engines are produced by labour with less skill, but with good tools. By tools, I mean engineer's machinery, lathes, planing machines, drills, and so on. ("Royal Com. on Railways." Lond., 1867, Minutes of Evidence, n. 17,862 and 17,863.)

[1] Ure, l. c., p. 20.   [2] Ure, l. c., p. 321.   [3] Ure, l. c. p. 23.

Gilmour, spinners at Manchester, state: "In our blowing-room department we consider our expense with new machinery is fully one-third less in wages and hands . . . in the jack-frame and drawing-frame room, about one-third less in expense, and likewise one-third less in hands; in the spinning-room about one-third less in expenses. But this is not all; when our yarn goes to the manufacturers, it is so much better by the application of our new machinery, that they will produce a greater quantity of cloth, and cheaper than from the yarn produced by old machinery."[1] Mr. Redgrave further remarks in the same Report: "The reduction of hands against increased production is, in fact, constantly taking place; in woollen mills the reduction commenced some time since, and is continuing; a few days since, the master of a school in the neighbourhood of Rochdale said to me, that the great falling off in the girls' school is not only caused by the distress, but by the changes of machinery in the woollen mills, in consequence of which a reduction of 70 short-timers had taken place."[2]

The following table shows the total result of the mechanical improvements in the English cotton industry due to the American civil war.

NUMBER OF FACTORIES.

	1858	1861	1868
England and Wales	2,046	2,715	2,405
Scotland	152	163	131
Ireland	12	9	13
United Kingdom	2,210	2,887	2,549

NUMBER OF POWER-LOOMS.

	1858	1861	1868
England and Wales	275,590	368,125	344,719
Scotland	21,624	30,110	31,864
Ireland	1,633	1,757	2,746
United Kingdom	298,847	399,992	379,329

[1] "Rep. Insp. Fact., 31st Oct., 1863," pp. 108, 109.

[2] l. c., p. 109. The rapid improvement of machinery, during the crisis, allowed the English manufacturers, immediately after the termination of the American civil war, and almost in no time, to glut the markets of the world again. Cloth, during the last six months of 1866, was almost unsaleable. Thereupon began the consignment of goods to India and China, thus naturally making the glut more intense. At the beginning of 1867 the manufacturers resorted to their usual way out of the difficulty,

NUMBER OF SPINDLES.

	1858	1861	1868
England and Wales............	25,818,576	28,352,152	30,478,228
Scotland	2,041,129	1,915,398	1,397,546
Ireland	150,512	119,944	124,240
United Kingdom	28,010,217	30,387,494	32,000,014

NUMBER OF PERSONS EMPLOYED.

	1858	1861	1868
England and Wales.............	341,170	407,598	357,052
Scotland	34,698	41,237	39,809
Ireland	3,345	2,734	4,203
United Kingdom	379,213	451,569	401,064

Hence, between 1861 and 1868, 338 cotton factories disappeared, in other words more productive machinery on a larger scale was concentrated in the hands of a smaller number of capitalists. The number of power-looms decreased by 20,663; but since their product increased in the same period, an improved loom must have yielded more than an old one. Lastly the number of spindles increased by 1,612,541, while the number of operatives decreased by 50,505. The "temporary" misery, inflicted on the workpeople by the cotton-crisis, was heightened, and from being temporary made permanent, by the rapid and persistent progress of machinery.

But machinery not only acts as a competitor who gets the better of the workman, and is constantly on the point of making him superfluous. It is also a power inimical to him, and as such capital proclaims it from the roof tops and as such makes use of it. It is the most powerful weapon for repressing strikes, those periodical revolts of the working class against the autocracy of capital.[1] According to Gaskell, the steam

---

viz., reducing wages 5 per cent. The workpeople resisted, and said that the only remedy was to work short time, 4 days a-week; and their theory was the correct one. After holding out for some time, the self-elected captains of industry had to make up their minds to short time, with reduced wages in some places, and in others without.

[1] "The relation of master and man in the blown-flint bottle trades amounts to a chronic strike." Hence the impetus given to the manufacture of pressed glass, in which the chief operations are done by machinery. One firm in Newcastle, who formerly produced 350,000 lbs. of blown-flint glass, now produces in its place 3,000,500 lbs. of pressed glass. ("Ch. Empl. Comm., Fourth Rep.," 1865, pp. 262, 263.)

engine was from the very first an antagonist of human power, an antagonist that enabled the capitalist to tread under foot the growing claims of the workmen, who threatened the newly born factory system with a crisis.[1] It would be possible to write quite a history of the inventions, made since 1830, for the sole purpose of supplying capital with weapons against the revolts of the working class. At the head of these in importance, stands the self-acting mule, because it opened up a new epoch in the automatic system.[2]

Nasmyth, the inventor of the steam hammer, gives the following evidence before the Trades Union Commission, with regard to the improvements made by him in machinery and introduced in consequence of the wide-spread and long strikes of the engineers in 1851. "The characteristic feature of our modern mechanical improvements, is the introduction of self-acting tool machinery. What every mechanical workman has now to do, and what every boy can do, is not to work himself but to superintend the beautiful labour of the machine. The whole class of workmen that depend exclusively on their skill, is now done away with. Formerly, I employed four boys to every mechanic. Thanks to these new mechanical combinations, I have reduced the number of grown-up men from 1500 to 750. The result was a considerable increase in my profits."

Ure says of a machine used in calico printing: "At length capitalists sought deliverance from this intolerable bondage" [namely the, in their eyes, burdensome terms of their contracts with the workmen] "in the resources of science, and were speedily re-instated in their legitimate rule, that of the head over the inferior members." Speaking of an invention for dressing warps: "Then the combined malcontents, who fancied themselves impregnably intrenched behind the old lines of division of labour, found their flanks turned and their defences rendered useless by the new mechanical tactics, and were obliged to surrender at discretion." With regard to the in-

---

[1] Gaskell. "The Manufacturing Population of England, London, 1833," pp. 3, 4.

[2] W. Fairbairn discovered several very important applications of machinery to the construction of machines, in consequence of strikes in his own workshops.

vention of the self-acting mule, he says: "A creation destined to restore order among the industrious classes. . . . This invention confirms the great doctrine already propounded, that when capital enlists science into her service, the refractory hand of labour will always be taught docility."[1]   Although Ure's work appeared 30 years ago, at a time when the factory system was comparatively but little developed, it still perfectly expresses the spirit of the factory, not only by its undisguised cynicism, but also by the naïveté with which it blurts out the stupid contradictions of the capitalist brain.   For instance, after propounding the "doctrine" stated above, that capital, with the aid of science taken into its pay, always reduces the refractory hand of labour to docility, he grows indignant because "it (physico-mechanical science) has been accused of lending itself to the rich capitalist as an instrument for harrassing the poor."   After preaching a long sermon to show how advantageous the rapid development of machinery is to the working classes, he warns them, that by their obstinacy and their strikes they hasten that development.   "Violent revulsions of this nature," he says, "display short-sighted man in the contemptible character of a self-tormentor."   A few pages before he states the contrary.   "Had it not been for the violent collisions and interruptions resulting from erroneous views among the factory operatives, the factory system would have been developed still more rapidly and beneficially for all concerned."   Then he exclaims again: "Fortunately for the state of society in the cotton districts of Great Britain, the improvements in machinery are gradual."   "It" (improvement in machinery) "is said to lower the rate of earnings of adults by displacing a portion of them, and thus rendering their number superabundant as compared with the demand for their labour.   It certainly augments the demand for the labour of children and increases the rate of *their* wages."   On the other hand, this same dispenser of consolation defends the lowness of the children's wages on the ground that it prevents parents from sending their children at too early an age into the factory.   The whole of his book is a vindication ˆ a

[1] Ure, l. c., pp. 368-370.

working day of unrestricted length; that Parliament should forbid children of 13 years to be exhausted by working 12 hours a day, reminds his liberal soul of the darkest days of the middle ages. This does not prevent him from calling upon the factory operatives to thank Providence, who by means of machinery has given them the leisure to think of their "immortal interests."[1]

SECTION 6.—THE THEORY OF COMPENSATION AS REGARDS THE WORKPEOPLE DISPLACED BY MACHINERY.

James Mill, MacCulloch, Torrens, Senior, John Stuart Mill, and a whole series besides, of bourgeois political economists, insist that all machinery that displaces workmen, simultaneously and necessarily sets free an amount of capital adequate to employ the same identical workmen.[2]

Suppose a capitalist to employ 100 workmen, at £30 a year each, in a carpet factory. The variable capital annually laid out amounts, therefore, to £3000. Suppose, also, that he discharges 50 of his workmen, and employs the remaining 50 with machinery that costs him £1500. To simplify matters, we take no account of buildings, coal, &c. Further suppose that the raw material annually consumed costs £3000, both before and after the change.[3] Is any capital set free by this metamorphosis? Before the change, the total sum of £6000 consisted half of constant, and half of variable capital. After the change it consists of £4500 constant (£3000 raw material and £1500 machinery), and £1500 variable capital. The variable capital, instead of being one half, is only one quarter, of the total capital. Instead of being set free, a part of the capital is here locked up in such a way as to cease to be exchanged against labour-power: variable has been changed into constant capital. Other things remaining unchanged, the capital of £6000, can, in future, employ no more than 50 men.

---

[1] Ure, l. c. pp. 368, 7, 370, 280, 321, 281, 370, 475.

[2] Ricardo originally was also of this opinion, but afterwards expressly disclaimed it, with the scientific impartiality and love of truth characteristic of him. See l. c. ch. xxxi. "On Machinery."

[3] *Nota bene.* My illustration is entirely on the lines of those given by the above-named economists.

With each improvement in the machinery, it will employ fewer. If the newly introduced machinery had cost less than did the labour-power and implements displaced by it, if, for instance, instead of costing £1500, it had cost only £1000, a variable capital of £1000 would have been converted into constant capital, and locked up; and a capital of £500 would have been set free. The latter sum, supposing wages unchanged, would form a fund sufficient to employ about 16 out of the 50 men discharged; nay, less than 16, for, in order to be employed as capital, a part of this £500 must now become constant capital, thus leaving only the remainder to be laid out in labour-power.

But, suppose, besides, that the making of the new machinery affords employment to a greater number of mechanics, can that be called compensation to the carpet makers, thrown on the streets? At the best, its construction employs fewer men than its employment displaces. The sum of £1500 that formerly represented the wages of the discharged carpet-makers, now represents in the shape of machinery: (1) the value of the means of production used in the construction of that machinery, (2) the wages of the mechanics employed in its construction, and (3) the surplus-value falling to the share of their "master." Further, the machinery need not be re-newed till it is worn out. Hence, in order to keep the in-creased number of mechanics in constant employment, one carpet manufacturer after another must displace workmen by machines.

As a matter of fact, the apologists do not mean this sort of setting free. They have in their minds the means of sub-sistence of the liberated workpeople. It cannot be denied, in the above instance, that the machinery not only liberates 50 men, thus placing them at others' disposal, but, at the same time, it withdraws from their consumption, and sets free, means of subsistence to the value of £1500. The simple fact, by no means a new one, that machinery cuts off the workmen from their means of subsistence is, therefore, in economical parlance tantamount to this, that machinery liberates means of subsistence for the workman, or converts those means into capital for his employment. The mode of expression, you see, is everything. Nominibus mollire licet mala.

This theory implies that the £1500 worth of means of subsistence was capital that was being expanded by the labour of the 50 men discharged. That, consequently, this capital falls out of employment so soon as they commence their forced holidays, and never rests till it has found a fresh investment, where it can again be productively consumed by these same 50 men. That sooner or later, therefore, the capital and the workmen must come together again, and that, then, the compensation is complete. That the sufferings of the workmen displaced by machinery are therefore as transient as are the riches of this world.

In relation to the discharged workmen, the £1500 worth of means of subsistence never was capital. What really confronted them as capital, was the sum of £1500, afterwards laid out in machinery. On looking closer it will be seen that this sum represented part of the carpets produced in a year by the 50 discharged men, which part they received as wages from their employer in money instead of in kind. With the carpets in the form of money, they bought means of subsistence to the value of £1500. These means, therefore, were to them, not capital, but commodities, and they, as regards these commodities, were not wage-labourers, but buyers. The circumstance that they were "freed" by the machinery, from the means of purchase, changed them from buyers into non-buyers. Hence a lessened demand for those commodities—voilà tout. If this diminution be not compensated by an increase from some other quarter, the market price of the commodities falls. If this state of things lasts for some time, and extends, there follows a discharge of workmen employed in the production of these commodities. Some of the capital that was previously devoted to production of necessary means of subsistence, has to become reproduced in another form. While prices fall, and capital is being displaced, the labourers employed in the production of necessary means of subsistence are in their turn "freed" from a part of their wages. Instead, therefore, of proving that, when machinery frees the workman from his means of subsistence, it simultaneously converts those means into capital for his further employment, our apologists, with their cut-and-dried law of supply and demand, prove, on the contrary, that machinery throws workmen on the streets not only in that branch of production n which it is introduced, but also in those branches in which it is not introduced.

The real facts, which are travestied by the optimism of economists, are as follows: The labourers, when driven out of the workshop by the machinery, are thrown upon the labour market, and there add to the number of workmen at the disposal of the capitalists. In Part VII. of this book it will be seen that this effect of machinery, which, as we have seen, is represented to be a compensation to the working class, is on the contrary a most frightful scourge. For the present I will only say this: The labourers that are thrown out of work in any branch of industry, can no doubt seek for employment in some other branch. If they find it, and thus renew the bond between them and the means of subsistence, this takes place only by the intermediary of a new and additional capital that is seeking investment; not at all by the intermediary of the capital that formerly employed them and was afterwards converted into machinery. And even should they find employment, what a poor look-out is theirs! Crippled as they are by division of labour, these poor devils are worth so little outside their old trade, that they cannot find admission into any industries, except a few of inferior kind, that are over-supplied with underpaid workmen.[1] Further, every branch of industry attracts each year a new stream of men, who furnish a contingent from which to fill up vacancies, and to draw a supply for expansion. So soon as machinery sets free a part of the workmen employed in a given branch of industry, the reserve

---

[1] A disciple of Ricardo, in answer to the insipidities of J. B. Say, remarks on this point: "Where division of labour is well developed, the skill of the labourer is available only in that particular branch in which it has been acquired; he himself is a sort of machine. It does not therefore help matters one jot, to repeat in parrot fashion, that things have a tendency to find their level. On looking around us we cannot but see, that they are unable to find their level for a long time; and that when they do find it, the level is always lower than at the commencement of the process." ("An Inquiry into those Principles respecting the Nature of Demand," &c. Lond. 1821, p. 72.)

men are also diverted into new channels of employment, and become absorbed in other branches; meanwhile the original victims, during the period of transition, for the most part starve and perish.

It is an undoubted fact that machinery, as such, is not responsible for "setting free" the workman from the means of subsistence. It cheapens and increases production in that branch which it seizes on, and at first makes no change in the mass of the means of subsistence produced in other branches. Hence, after its introduction, the society possesses as much, if not more, of the necessaries of life than before, for the labourers thrown out of work; and that quite apart from the enormous share of the annual produce wasted by the non-workers. And this is the point relied on by our apologists! The contradictions and antagonisms inseparable from the capitalist employment of machinery, do not exist, they say, since they do not arise out of machinery, as such, but out of its capitalist employment! Since therefore machinery, considered alone, shortens the hours of labour, but, when in the service of capital, lengthens them; since in itself it lightens labour, but when employed by capital, heightens the intensity of labour; since in itself it is a victory of man over the forces of nature, but in the hands of capital, makes man the slave of those forces; since in itself it increases the wealth of the producers, but in the hands of capital, makes them paupers— for all these reasons and others besides, says the bourgeois economist without more ado, it is clear as noonday that all these contradictions are a mere semblance of the reality, and that, as a matter of fact, they have neither an actual nor a theoretical existence. Thus he saves himself from all further puzzling of the brain, and what is more, implicitly declares his opponent to be stupid enough to contend against, not the capitalistic employment of machinery, but machinery itself.

No doubt he is far from denying that temporary inconvenience may result from the capitalist use of machinery. But where is the medal without its reverse! Any employment of machinery, except by capital, is to him an impossibility. Exploitation of the workman by the machine is therefore, with

him, identical with exploitation of the machine by the workman. Whoever, therefore, exposes the real state of things in
the capitalistic employment of machinery, is against its employment in any way, and is an enemy of social progress![1]
Exactly the reasoning of the celebrated Bill Sykes. "Gentlemen of the jury, no doubt the throat of this commercial
traveller has been cut. But that is not my fault, it is the fault
of the knife! Must we, for such a temporary inconvenience,
abolish the use of the knife? Only consider! where would
agriculture and trade be without the knife? Is it not as
salutary in surgery, as it is knowing in anatomy? And in
addition a willing help at the festive board? If you abolish
the knife—you hurl us back into the depths of barbarism."[2]

Although machinery necessarily throws men out of work in
those industries into which it is introduced, yet it may, notwithstanding this, bring about an increase of employment in
other industries. This effect, however, has nothing in common
with the so-called theory of compensation. Since every article
produced by a machine is cheaper than a similar article produced by hand, we deduce the following infallible law: If the
total quantity of the article produced by machinery, be equal
to the total quantity of the article previously produced by a
handicraft or by manufacture, and now made by machinery,
then the total labour expended is diminished. The new labour
spent on the instruments of labour, on the machinery, on the
coal, and so on, must necessarily be less than the labour displaced by the use of the machinery; otherwise the product of
the machine would be as dear, or dearer, than the product of
the manual labour. But, as a matter of fact, the total quantity
of the article produced by machinery with a diminished num-

---

[1] MacCulloch, amongst others, is a past master in this pretentious cretinism.
"If," he says, with the affected naïveté of a child of 8 years, "if it be advantageous,
to develope the skill of the workman more and more, so that he is capable of producing, with the same or with a less quantity of labour, a constantly increasing quantity
of commodities, it must also be advantageous, that he should avail himself of the help
of such machinery as will assist him most effectively in the attainment of this result."
(MacCulloch: "Princ. of Pol. Econ.," Lond. 1830, p. 166.)

[2] "The inventor of the spinning machine has ruined India, a fact, however, that
touches us but little." A. Thiers: De la propriété.—M. Thiers here confounds the
spinning machine with the power-loom, "a fact, however, that touches us but
little."

ber of workmen, instead of remaining equal to, by far exceeds
the total quantity of the hand-made article that has been displaced. Suppose that 400,000 yards of cloth have been produced on power-looms by fewer weavers than could weave
100,000 yards by hand. In the quadrupled product there lies
four times as much raw material. Hence the production of
raw material must be quadrupled. But as regards the instruments of labour, such as buildings, coal, machinery, and so on,
it is different; the limit up to which the additional labour
required for their production can increase, varies with the
difference between the quantity of the machine-made article,
and the quantity of the same article that the same number of
workmen could make by hand.

Hence, as the use of machinery extends in a given industry,
the immediate effect is to increase production in the other industries that furnish the first with means of production. How
far employment is thereby found for an increased number of
men, depends, given the length of the working-day and the
intensity of labour, on the composition of the capital employed,
i.e., on the ratio of its constant to its variable component.
This ratio, in its turn, varies considerably with the extent to
which machinery has already seized on, or is then seizing on,
those trades. The number of the men condemned to work in
coal and metal mines increased enormously owing to the
progress of the English factory system; but during the last
few decades this increase of number has been less rapid, owing
to the use of new machinery in mining.[1] A new type of
workman springs into life along with the machine, namely, its
maker. We have already learnt that machinery has possessed
itself even of this branch of production on a scale that grows
greater every day.[2] As to raw material,[3] there is not the

[1] According to the census of 1861 (Vol. II., Lond., 1863), the number of people
employed in coal mines in England and Wales, amounted to 246,613, of which 73,545
were under, and 173,067 were over 20 years. Of those under 20, 835 were between
5 and 10 years, 30,701 between 10 and 15 years, 42,010 between 15 and 19 years.
The number employed in iron, copper, lead, tin, and other mines of every description, was 319,222.

[2] In England and Wales, in 1861, there were employed in making machinery,
60,807 persons, including the masters and their clerks, &c., also all agents and
business people connected with this industry, but excluding the makers of small
machines, such as sewing machines, &c., as also the makers of the operative parts
of machines, such as spindles. The total number of civil engineers amounted to
3329.

[3] Since iron is one of the most important raw materials, let me here state that, in

least doubt that the rapid strides of cotton spinning, not only pushed on with tropical luxuriance the growth of cotton in the United States, and with it the African slave trade, but also made the breeding of slaves the chief business of the border slave-states. When, in 1790, the first census of slaves was taken in the United States, their number was 697,000; in 1861 it had nearly reached four millions. On the other hand, it is no less certain that the rise of the English woollen factories, together with the gradual conversion of arable land into sheep-pasture, brought about the superfluity of agricultural labourers that led to their being driven in masses into the towns. Ireland, having during the last twenty years reduced its population by nearly one half, is at this moment undergoing the process of still further reducing the number of its inhabitants, so as exactly to suit the requirements of its landlords and of the English woollen manufacturers.

When machinery is applied to any of the preliminary or intermediate stages through which the subject of labour has to pass on its way to completion, there is an increased yield of material in those stages, and simultaneously an increased demand for labour in the handicrafts or manufactures supplied by the produce of the machines. Spinning by machinery, for example, supplied yarn so cheaply and so abundantly that the hand-loom weavers were, at first, about to work full time without increased outlay. Their earnings accordingly rose.[1] Hence a flow of people into the cotton-weaving trade, till at length the 800,000 weavers, called into existence by the Jenny, the throstle and the mule, were overwhelmed by the power-loom. So also, owing to the abundance of clothing materials produced by machinery, the number of tailors, seamstresses and needle-women, went on increasing until the appearance of the sewing machine.

1861, there were in England and Wales 125,771 operative iron founders, of whom 123,430 were males, 2341 females. Of the former 30,810 were under, and 92,620 over 20 years.

[1] "A family of four grown up persons, with two children as winders, earned at the end of the last, and the beginning of the present century, by ten hours' daily labour, £4 a week. If the work was very pressing, they could earn more . . . Before that they had always suffered from a deficient supply of yarn." (Gaskell, l. c., pp. 25-27.)

In proportion as machinery, with the aid of a relatively small number of workpeople, increases the mass of raw materials, intermediate products, instruments of labour, &c., the working-up of these raw materials and intermediate products becomes split up into numberless branches; social production increases in diversity. The factory system carries the social division of labour immeasurably further than does manufacture, for it increases the productiveness of the industries it seizes upon, in a far higher degree.

The immediate result of machinery is to augment surplus-value and the mass of products in which surplus-value is embodied. And, as the substances consumed by the capitalists and their dependants become more plentiful, so too do these orders of society. Their growing wealth, and the relatively diminished number of workmen required to produce the necessaries of life beget, simultaneously with the rise of new and luxurious wants, the means of satisfying those wants. A larger portion of the produce of society is changed into surplus produce, and a larger part of the surplus produce is supplied for consumption in a multiplicity of refined shapes. In other words, the production of luxuries increases.[1] The refined and varied forms of the products are also due to new relations with the markets of the world, relations that are created by Modern Industry. Not only are greater quantities of foreign articles of luxury exchanged for home products, but a greater mass of foreign raw materials, ingredients, and intermediate products, are used as means of production in the home industries. Owing to these relations with the markets of the world the demand for labour increases in the carrying trades, which split up into numerous varieties.[2]

The increase of the means of production and subsistence, accompanied by a relative diminution in the number of labourers, causes an increased demand for labour in making canals, docks, tunnels, bridges, and so on, works that can only

---

[1] F. Engels in "Lage, &c.," points out the miserable condition of a large number of those who work on these very articles of luxury. See also numerous instances in the "Reports of the Children's Employment Commission."

[2] In 1861, in England and Wales, there were 94,665 sailors in the merchant service.

bear fruit in the far future. Entirely new branches of production, creating new fields of labour, are also formed, as the
direct result either of machinery or of the general industrial
changes brought about by it. But the place occupied by these
branches in the general production is, even in the most developed countries, far from important. The number of
labourers that find employment in them is directly proportional to the demand, created by those industries, for the
crudest form of manual labour. The chief industries of this
kind are, at present, gas works, telegraphs, photography,
steam navigation, and railways. According to the census of
1861 for England and Wales, we find in the gas industry
(gasworks, production of mechanical apparatus, servants of
the gas companies &c.), 15,211 persons; in telegraphy, 2399;
in photography, 2366; steam navigation, 3570; and in railways, 70,599, of whom the unskilled "navvies," more or less
permanently employed, and the whole administrative and commercial staff, make up about 28,000. The total number of
persons, therefore, employed in these five new industries
amounts to 94,145.

Lastly, the extraordinary productiveness of modern industry, accompanied as it is by both a more extensive and a
more intense exploitation of labour-power in all other spheres
of production, allows of the unproductive employment of a
larger and larger part of the working class, and the consequent
reproduction, on a constantly extending scale, of the ancient
domestic slaves under the name of a servant class, including
men-servants, women-servants, lackeys, &c. According to the
census of 1861, the population of England and Wales was
20,066,244; of these, 9,776,259 males, and 10,289,965 female.
If we deduct from this population all who are too old or too
young for work, all unproductive women, young persons and
children, the "ideological" classes, such as government officials,
priests, lawyers, soldiers, &c.; further, all who have no occupation but to consume the labour of others in the form of
rent, interest, &c.; and, lastly, paupers, vagabonds, and
criminals, there remain in round numbers eight millions of
the two sexes of every age, including in that number every

capitalist who is in any way engaged in industry, commerce, or finance. Among these, 8 millions are:

	PERSONS.
Agricultural labourers (including shepherds, farm servants, and maidservants living in the houses of farmers),	1,098,261
All who are employed in cotton, woollen, worsted, flax, hemp, silk, and jute factories, in stocking making and lace making by machinery, . . .	642,607[1]
All who are employed in coal mines and metal mines, ...	565,835
All who are employed in metal works (blast-furnaces, rolling mills, &c.), and metal manufactures of every kind,	396,998[2]
The servant class, ...	1,208,648[3]

All the persons employed in textile factories and in mines, taken together, number 1,208,442; those employed in textile factories and metal industries, taken together, number 1,039,605; in both cases less than the number of modern domestic slaves. What a splendid result of the capitalist exploitation of machinery!

SECTION 7.—REPULSION AND ATTRACTION OF WORKPEOPLE BY THE FACTORY SYSTEM. CRISIS IN THE COTTON TRADE.

All political economists of any standing admit that the introduction of new machinery has a baneful effect on the workmen in the old handicrafts and manufactures with which this machinery at first competes. Almost all of them bemoan the slavery of the factory operative. And what is the great trump-card that they play? That machinery, after the

---

[1] Of these only 177,596 are males above 13 years of age.

[2] Of these, 30,501 are females.

[3] Of these, 137,447 males. None are included in the 1,208,648 who do not serve in private houses. Between 1861 and 1870 the number of male servants nearly doubled itself. It increased to 267,671. In the year 1847 there were 2694 gamekeepers (for the landlords' preserves), in 1869 there were 4921. The young servant girls in the houses of the London lower middle class are in common parlance called "slaveys."

horrors of the period of introduction and development have subsided, instead of diminishing, in the long run increases the number of the slaves of labour! Yes, political economy revels in the hideous theory, hideous to every "philanthropist" who believes in the eternal nature-ordained necessity for capitalist production, that after a period of growth and transition, even its crowning success, the factory system based on machinery, grinds down more workpeople than on its first introduction it throws on the streets.[1]

It is true that in some cases, as we saw from instances of English worsted and silk factories, an extraordinary extension of the factory system may, at a certain stage of its development, be accompanied not only by a relative, but by an absolute decrease in the number of operatives employed. In the year 1860, when a special census of all the factories in the United Kingdom was taken by order of Parliament, the factories in those parts of Lancashire, Cheshire, and Yorkshire, included in the district of Mr. Baker, the factory inspector, numbered 652; 570 of these contained 85,622 power-looms, 6,819,146 spindles (exclusive of doubling spindles), employed 27,439 horse-power (steam), and 1390 (water), and 94,119 persons. In the year 1865, the same factories contained, looms 95,163, spindles 7,025,031, had a steam-power of 28,925 horses, and a water-power of 1445 horses, and employed 88,913 persons. Between 1860 and 1865, therefore,

---

[1] Ganilh, on the contrary, considers the final result of the factory system to be an absolutely less number of operatives, at whose expense an increased number of "gens honnêtes" live and develop their well-known "perfectibilité perfectible." Little as he understands the movement of production, at least he feels, that machinery must needs be a very fatal institution, if its introduction converts busy workmen into paupers, and its development calls more slaves of labour into existence than it has suppressed. It is not possible to bring out the cretinism of his standpoint, except by his own words: "Les classes condamnées à produire et à consommer diminuent, et les classes qui dirigent le travail, qui soulagent, consolent, et éclairent toute la population, se multiplient. . . . et s'approprient tous les bienfaits qui résultent de la diminution des frais du travail, de l'abondance des productions, et du bon marché des consommations. Dans cette direction, l'espèce humaine s'élève aux plus hautes conceptions du génie, pénètre dans les profondeurs mystèrieuses de la religion, établit les principes salutaires de la morale (which consists in 's'approprier tous les bienfaits,' &c.), les lois tutélaires de la liberté (liberty of 'les classes condamnées à produire?') et du pouvoir, de l'obéissance et de la justice, du devoir et de l'humanité." For this twaddle see "Des Systèmes d'Economie Politique, &c., Par M. Ch. Ganilh." 2ème ed., Paris, 1821, t. II., p. 224, and see p. 212.

the increase in looms was 11%, in spindles 3%, and in engine-power 3%, while the number of persons employed decreased 5½%.[1]   Between 1852 and 1862, considerable extension of the English woollen manufacture took place, while the number of hands employed in it remained almost stationary, showing how greatly the introduction of new machines had superseded the labour of preceding periods.[2]   In certain cases, the increase in the number of hands employed is only apparent; that is, it is not due to the extension of the factories already established, but to the gradual annexation of connected trades; for instance, the increase in power-looms, and in the hands employed by them between 1838 and 1856, was, in the cotton trade, simply owing to the extension of this branch of industry; but in the other trades to the application of steam-power to the carpet-loom, to the ribbon-loom, and to the linen-loom, which previously had been worked by the power of men.[3]   Hence the increase of the hands in these latter trades was merely a symptom of a diminution in the total number employed.   Finally, we have considered this question entirely apart from the fact, that everywhere, except in the metal industries, young persons (under 18), and women and children form the preponderating element in the class of factory hands.

Nevertheless, in spite of the mass of hands actually displaced and virtually replaced by machinery, we can understand how the factory operatives, through the building of more mills and the extension of old ones in a given industry, may become more numerous than the manufacturing work-

[1] "Reports of Insp. of Fact., 31 Oct., 1865," p. 58, sq. At the same time, however, means of employment for an increased number of hands was ready in 110 new mills with 11,625 looms, 628,756 spindles and 2695 total horse-power of steam and water (l c.).

[2] "Reports, &c., for 31 Oct., 1862," p. 79. At the end of 1871, Mr. A. Redgrave, the factory inspector, in a lecture given at Bradford, in the New Mechanics' Institution, said: "What has struck me for some time past is the altered appearance of the woollen factories. Formerly they were filled with women and children, now machinery seems to do all the work. At my asking for an explanation of this from a manufacturer, he gave me the following: 'Under the old system I employed 63 persons; after the introduction of improved machinery I reduced my hands to 33, and lately, in consequence of new and extensive alterations, I have been in a position to reduce those 33 to 13.'"

[3] See "Reports, &c., 31 Oct., 1856," p. 16.

men and handicraftsmen that have been displaced. Suppose, for example, that in the old mode of production, a capital of £500 is employed weekly, two-fifths being constant and three-fifths variable capital, *i.e.*, £200 being laid out in means of production, and £300, say £1 per man, in labour-power. On the introduction of machinery the composition of this capital becomes altered. We will suppose it to consist of four-fifths constant and one-fifth variable, which means that only £100 is now laid out in labour-power. Consequently, two-thirds of the workmen are discharged. If now the business extends, and the total capital employed grows to £1500 under unchanged conditions, the number of operatives employed will increase to 300, just as many as before the introduction of the machinery. If the capital further grows to £2000, 400 men will be employed, or one-third more than under the old system. Their numbers have, in point of fact, increased by 100, but relatively, *i.e.*, in proportion to the total capital advanced, they have diminished by 800, for the £2000 capital would, in the old state of things, have employed 1200 instead of 400 men. Hence, a relative decrease in the number of hands is consistent with an actual increase. We assumed above that while the total capital increases, its composition remains the same, because the conditions of production remain constant. But we have already seen that, with every advance in the use of machinery, the constant component of capital, that part which consists of machinery, raw material, &c., increases, while the variable component, the part laid out in labour-power, decreases. We also know that in no other system of production is improvement so continuous, and the composition of the capital employed so constantly changing as in the factory system. These changes are, however, continually interrupted by periods of rest, during which there is a mere quantitative extension of the factories on the existing technical basis. During such periods the operatives increase in number. Thus, in 1835, the total number of operatives in the cotton, woollen, worsted, flax, and silk factories in the United Kingdom was only 354,684; while in 1861 the number of the power-loom weavers alone (of both sexes and of all ages, from eight years upwards), amounted to 230,654. Certainly, this growth appears less important when we consider that in 1838 the hand-loom weavers with their families still numbered 800,000,[1] not to mention those thrown out of work in Asia, and on the Continent of Europe.

In the few remarks I have still to make on this point, I shall refer to some actually existing relations, the existence of which our theoretical investigation has not yet disclosed.

So long as, in a given branch of industry, the factory system extends itself at the expense of the old handicrafts or of manufacture, the result is as sure as is the result of an encounter between any army furnished with breach-loaders, and one armed with bows and arrows. This first period, during which machinery conquers its field of action, is of decisive importance owing to the extraordinary profits that it helps to produce. These profits not only form a source of accelerated accumulation, but also attract into the favoured sphere of production a large part of the additional social capital that is being constantly created, and is ever on the look-out for new investments. The special advantages of this first period of fast and furious activity are felt in every branch of production that machinery invades. So soon, however, as the factory system has gained a certain breadth of footing and a definite degree of maturity, and, especially, so soon as its technical basis, machinery, is itself produced by machinery; so soon as coal mining and iron mining, the metal industries, and the means of transport have been revolutionised; so soon, in short, as the general conditions requisite for production by the modern industrial system have been established, this mode of production acquires an elasticity, a capacity for sudden extension by leaps and bounds that finds no hindrance except in the supply of raw material and in the disposal of the produce. On the one hand, the immediate effect of machinery is

[1] "The sufferings of the hand-loom weavers were the subject of an inquiry by a Royal Commission, but although their distress was acknowledged and lamented, the amelioration of their condition was left, and probably necessarily so, to the chances and changes of time, which it may now be hoped" [20 years later!] "have *nearly* obliterated those miseries, and not improbably by the present great extension of the power-loom." ("Rep. Insp. of Fct., 31 Oct., 1856," p. 15.)

to increase the supply of raw material in the same way, for example, as the cotton gin augmented the production of cotton.[1] On the other hand, the cheapness of the articles produced by machinery, and the improved means of transport and communication furnish the weapons for conquering foreign markets. By ruining handicraft production in other countries, machinery forcibly converts them into fields for the supply of its raw material. In this way East India was compelled to produce cotton, wool, hemp, jute, and indigo for Great Britain.[2] By constantly making a part of the hands "supernumerary," modern industry, in all countries where it has taken root, gives a spur to emigration and to the colonization of foreign lands, which are thereby converted into settlements for growing the raw material of the mother country; just as Australia, for example, was converted into a colony for growing wool.[3] A new and international division of labour, a division suited to the requirements of the chief centres of modern industry springs up, and converts one part of the globe into a chiefly agricultural field of production, for supplying the other part which remains a chiefly industrial field. This evolution hangs together with radical changes in agriculture which we need not here further inquire into.[4]

[1] Other ways in which machinery affects the production of raw material will be mentioned in the third book.

[2] EXPORT OF COTTON FROM INDIA TO GREAT BRITAIN.

1846.—34,540,143 lbs.   1860.—204,141,168 lbs.   1865.—445,947,600 lbs.

[3] EXPORT OF WOOL FROM INDIA TO GREAT BRITAIN.

1846.—4,570,581 lbs.   1860.—20,214,173 lbs.   1865.—20,679,111 lbs.

EXPORT OF WOOL FROM THE CAPE TO GREAT BRITAIN.

—2,958,457 lbs.   1860.—16,574,345 lbs.   1865.—29,920,623 lbs.

EXPORT OF WOOL FROM AUSTRALIA TO GREAT BRITAIN.

1846.—21,789,346 lbs.   1860.—59,166,616 lbs.   1865.—109,734,261 lbs.

[4] The economical development of the United States is itself a product of European, more especially of English modern industry. In their present form (1866) the States must still be considered a European colony. [Note to the 4th German edition.—Since then the United States has developed into the second industrial country of the world, without thereby losing its colonial character entirely. F. E.]

EXPORT OF COTTON FROM THE UNITED STATES TO GREAT BRITAIN.

1846.—401,949,893 lbs.   1852.—765,630,543 lbs.   1859.—961,707,264 lbs.   1860.—1,115,890,608 lbs.

On the motion of Mr. Gladstone, the House of Commons ordered, on the 17th February, 1867, a return of the total quantities of grain, corn, and flour, of all sorts, imported into, and exported from, the United Kingdom, between the years 1831 and 1866. I give below a summary of the result. The flour is given in quarters of corn.

QUINQUENNIAL PERIODS AND THE YEAR 1866.

ANNUAL AVERAGE.	1831-1835.	1836-1840.	1841-1845.	1846-1850.
Import (Qrs.) - -	1,096,373	2,389,729	2,843,865	8,776,552
Export " - -	225,363	251,770	139,056	155,461
Excess of Import over export - -	871,110	2,137,959	2,704,809	8,621,091
POPULATION.				
Yearly average in each period, - -	24,621,107	25,929,507	27,262,569	27,797,598
Average quantity of corn, &c., in qrs., consumed annually per head over and above the home produce consumed, - - - -	0·036	0·082	0·099	0·310

EXPORT OF CORN, &C., FROM THE UNITED STATES TO GREAT BRITAIN.

	1850.		1862.
Wheat, cwts.	16,202,312	... ...	41,033,503
Barley, "	3,669,653	... ...	6,624,800
Oats, "	3,174,801	... ...	4,426,994
Rye, "	388,749	... ...	7,108
Flour, "	3,819,440	... ...	7,207,113
Buckwheat, cwts.	1054	... ...	19,571
Maize, cwts.	5,473,161	... ...	11,694,818
Bere or Bigg (a sort of Barley), cwts.	2039		7675
Peas, cwts.	811,620	... ...	1,024,722
Beans, "	1,822,972	... ...	2,037,137
Total exports, ...	34,365,801	... ...	74,083,351

QUINQUENNIAL PERIODS, &c.—(CONTINUED.)

ANNUAL AVERAGE.	1851-1855.	1856-1860.	1861-1865.	1866.
Import (Qrs.) - -	8,345,237	10,912,612	15,009,871	16,457,340
Export " - -	307,491	341,150	302,754	216,218
Excess of Import over export - -	8,037,746	10,572,462	14,707,117	16,241,122
POPULATION.				
Yearly average in each period, - -	27,572,923	28,391,544	29,381,460	29,935,404
Average quantity of corn, &c., in qrs., consumed annually per head over and above the home produce consumed, - - - -	0·291	0·372	0·543	0·543

The enormous power, inherent in the factory system, of expanding by jumps, and the dependence of that system on the
markets of the world, necessarily beget feverish production,
followed by over-filling of the markets, whereupon contraction
of the markets brings on crippling of production. The life of
modern industry becomes a series of periods of moderate
activity, prosperity, over-production, crisis and stagnation.
The uncertainty and instability to which machinery subjects
the employment, and consequently the conditions of existence,
of the operatives become normal, owing to these periodic
changes of the industrial cycle. Except in the periods of prosperity, there rages between the capitalists the most furious
combat for the share of each in the markets. This share is
directly proportional to the cheapness of the product. Besides
the rivalry that this struggle begets in the application of
improved machinery for replacing labour-power, and of new
methods of production, there also comes a time in every industrial cycle, when a forcible reduction of wages beneath the

value of labour-power, is attempted for the purpose of cheapening commodities.[1]

A necessary condition, therefore, to the growth of the number of factory hands, is a proportionally much more rapid growth of the amount of capital invested in mills. This growth, however, is conditioned by the ebb and flow of the industrial cycle. It is, besides, constantly interrupted by the technical progress that at one time virtually supplies the place of new workmen, at another, actually displaces old ones. This qualitative change in mechanical industry continually discharges hands from the factory, or shuts its doors against the fresh stream of recruits, while the purely quantitative extension of the factories absorbs not only the men thrown out of work, but also fresh contingents. The workpeople are thus continually both repelled and attracted, hustled from pillar to post, while, at the same time, constant changes take place in the sex, age, and skill of the levies.

The lot of the factory operatives will be best depicted by taking a rapid survey of the course of the English cotton industry.

From 1770 to 1815 this trade was depressed or stagnant for

[1] In an appeal made in July, 1866, to the Trade Societies of England, by the shoemakers of Leicester, who had been thrown on the streets by a lock-out, it is stated: "Twenty years ago the Leicester shoe trade was revolutionised by the introduction of riveting in the place of stitching. At that time good wages could be earned. Great competition was shown between the different firms as to which could turn out the neatest article. Shortly afterwards, however, a worse kind of competition sprang up, namely, that of underselling one another in the market. The injurious consequences soon manifested themselves in reductions of wages, and so sweepingly quick was the fall in the price of labour, that many firms now pay only one half of the original wages. And yet, though wages sink lower and lower, profits appear, with each alteration in the scale of wages, to increase." Even bad times are utilized by the manufacturers, for making exceptional profits by excessive lowering of wages, *i.e.*, by a direct robbery of the labourer's means of subsistence. One example (it has reference to the crisis in the Coventry silk weaving): "From information I have received from manufacturers as well as workmen, there seems to be no doubt that wages have been reduced to a greater extent than either the competition of the foreign producers, or other circumstances have rendered necessary . . . the majority of weavers are working at a reduction of 30 to 40 per cent. in their wages. A piece of ribbon for making which the weaver got 6s. or 7s. five years back, now only brings them 3s. 3d. or 3s. 6d.; other work is now priced at 2s. and 2s. 3d. which was formerly priced at 4s. and 4s. 3d. The reduction in wage seems to have been carried to a greater extent than is necessary for increasing demand. Indeed, the reduction in the cost of weaving, in the case of many descriptions of ribbons, has not been accompanied by any corresponding reduction in the selling price of the manufactured article." (Mr. F. D. Longe's Report. "Ch. Emp. Com., V. Rep., 1866," p. 114, 1.)

5 years only. During this period of 45 years the English manufacturers had a monopoly of machinery and of the markets of the world. From 1815 to 1821 depression; 1822 and 1823 prosperity; 1824 abolition of the laws against Trades' Unions, great extension of factories everywhere; 1825 crisis; 1826 great misery and riots among the factory operatives; 1827 slight improvement; 1828 great increase in power-looms, and in exports; 1829 exports, especially to India, surpass all former years; 1830 glutted markets, great distress; 1831 to 1833 continued depression, the monopoly of the trade with India and China withdrawn from the East India Company; 1834 great increase of factories and machinery, shortness of hands. The new poor law furthers the migration of agricultural labourers into the factory districts. The country districts swept of children. White slave trade; 1835 great prosperity, contemporaneous starvation of the handloom weavers; 1836 great prosperity; 1837 and 1838 depression and crisis; 1839 revival; 1840 great depression, riots, calling out of the military; 1841 and 1842 frightful suffering among the factory operatives; 1842 the manufacturers lock the hands out of the factories in order to enforce the repeal of the Corn Laws. The operatives stream in thousands into the towns of Lancashire and Yorkshire, are driven back by the military, and their leaders brought to trial at Lancaster; 1843 great misery; 1844 revival; 1845 great prosperity; 1846 continued improvement at first, then reaction. Repeal of the Corn Laws; 1847 crisis, general reduction of wages by 10 and more per cent. in honour of the "big loaf;" 1848 continued depression; Manchester under military protection; 1849 revival; 1850 prosperity; 1851 falling prices, low wages, frequent strikes; 1852 improvement begins, strikes continue, the manufacturers threaten to import foreign hands; 1853 increasing exports. Strike for 8 months, and great misery at Preston; 1854 prosperity, glutted markets; 1855 news of failures stream in from the United States, Canada, and the Eastern markets; 1856 great prosperity; 1857 crisis; 1858 improvement; 1859 great prosperity, increase in factories; 1860 Zenith of the English cotton trade, the Indian, Australian, and other mark-

ets so glutted with goods that even in 1863 they had not absorbed the whole lot; the French Treaty of Commerce, enormous growth of factories and machinery; 1861 prosperity continues for a time, reaction, the American civil war, cotton famine; 1862 to 1863 complete collapse.

The history of the cotton famine is too characteristic to dispense with dwelling upon it for a moment. From the indications as to the condition of the markets of the world in 1860 and 1861, we see that the cotton famine came in the nick of time for the manufacturers, and was to some extent advantageous to them, a fact that was acknowledged in the reports of the Manchester Chamber of Commerce, proclaimed in Parliament by Palmerston and Derby, and confirmed by events.[1] No doubt, among the 2887 cotton mills in the United Kingdom in 1861, there were many of small size. According to the report of Mr. A. Redgrave, out of the 2109 mills included in his district, 392 or 19% employed less than ten horse-power each; 345, or 16% employed 10 H. P., and less than 20 H. P.; while 1372 employed upwards of 20 H. P.[2] The majority of the small mills were weaving sheds, built during the period of prosperity after 1858, for the most part by speculators, of whom one supplied the yarn, another the machinery, a third the buildings, and were worked by men who had been overlookers, or by other persons of small means. These small manufacturers mostly went to the wall. The same fate would have overtaken them in the commercial crisis that was staved off only by the cotton famine. Although they formed one-third of the total number of manufacturers, yet their mills absorbed a much smaller part of the capital invested in the cotton trade. As to the extent of the stoppage, it appears from authentic estimates, that in October 1862, 60.3% of the spindles, and 58% of the looms were standing. This refers to the cotton trade as a whole, and, of course, requires considerable modification for individual districts. Only very few mills worked full time (60 hours a week), the remainder worked at intervals. Even in those few cases where full time was worked, and at the customary rate of piece-wage, the weekly

[1] Conf. Reports of Insp. of Fact. 31st October, 1862, p. 30. [2] l. c., p. 19.

wages of the operatives necessarily shrank, owing to good cotton being replaced by bad, Sea Island by Egyptian (in fine spinning mills), American and Egyptian by Surat, and pure cotton by mixing of waste and Surat. The shorter fibre of the Surat cotton and its dirty condition, the greater fragility of the thread, the substitution of all sorts of heavy ingredients for flour in sizing the warps, all these lessened the speed of the machinery, or the number of looms that could be superintended by one weaver, increased the labour caused by defects in the machinery, and reduced the piece-wage by reducing the mass of the product turned off. Where Surat cotton was used the loss to the operatives when on full time, amounted to 20, 30, and more per cent. But besides this, the majority of the manufacturers reduced the rate of piece-wage by 5, $7\frac{1}{2}$, and 10 per cent. We can therefore conceive the situation of those hands who were employed for only 3, $3\frac{1}{2}$ or 4 days a week, of for only 6 hours a day. Even in 1863, after a comparative improvement had set in, the weekly wages of spinners and of weavers were 3s. 4d., 3s. 10d., 4s. 6d. and 5s. 1d.[1] Even in this miserable state of things, however, the inventive spirit of the master never stood still, but was exercised in making deductions from wages. These were to some extent inflicted as a penalty for defects in the finished article that were really due to his bad cotton and to his unsuitable machinery. Moreover, where the manufacturer owned the cottages of the workpeople, he paid himself his rents by deducting the amount from these miserable wages. Mr. Redgrave tells us of self-acting minders (operatives who manage a pair of self-acting mules) "earning at the end of a fortnight's full work 8s. 11d., and that from this sum was deduced the rent of the house, the manufacturer, however, returning half the rent as a gift. The minders took away the sum of 6s. 11d. In many places the self-acting minders ranged from 5s. to 9s. per week, and the weavers from 2s. to 6s. ptr week, during the latter part of 1862."[2] Even when working short time the rent was frequently deducted from the wages of the operatives.[3] No

[1] "Rep. Insp. of Fact., 31st October, 1865," pp. 41-45.
[2] "Rep. Insp. of Fact., 31st October, 1863."   [3] l. c., p. 51.

wonder that in some parts of Lancashire a kind of famine fever broke out. But more characteristic than all this, was the revolution that took place in the process of production at the expense of the workpeople. Experimenta in corpore vili, like those of anatomists on frogs, were formally made. "Although," says Mr. Redgrave, "I have given the actual earnings of the operatives in the several mills, it does not follow that they earn the same amount week by week. The operatives are subject to great fluctuation from the constant experimentalizing of the manufacturers . . . . the earnings of the operatives rise and fall with the quality of the cotton mixings; sometimes they have been within 15 per cent. of former earnings, and then, in a week or two, they have fallen off from 50 to 60 per cent."[1] These experiments were not made solely at the expense of the workman's means of subsistence. His five senses also had to pay the penalty. "The people who are employed in making up Surat cotton complain very much. They inform me, on opening the bales of cotton there is an intolerable smell, which causes sickness . . . . In the mixing, scribbling and carding rooms, the dust and dirt which are disengaged, irritate the air passages, and give rise to cough and difficulty of breathing. A disease of the skin, no doubt from the irritation of the dirt contained in the Surat cotton, also prevails . . . The fibre being so short, a great amount of size, both animal and vegetable, is used . . . . Bronchitis is more prevalent owing to the dust. Inflammatory sore throat is common, from the same cause. Sickness and dyspepsia are produced by the frequent breaking of the weft, when the weaver sucks the weft through the eye of the shuttle." On the other hand, the substitutes for flour were a Fortunatus' purse to the manufacturers, by increasing the weight of the yarn. They caused "15 lbs. of raw material to weigh 26 lbs. after it was woven."[2] In the Report of Inspectors of Factories for 30th April, 1864, we read as follows: "The trade is availing itself of this resource at present to an extent which is even discreditable. I have heard on good authority of a cloth weighing 8 lbs. which was made of $5\frac{1}{2}$ lbs. cotton and $2\frac{3}{4}$ lbs.

[1] l. c., pp. 50-51.   [2] l. c., pp. 62-63.

size; and of another cloth weighing 5¼ lbs., of which 2 lbs. was size. These were ordinary export shirtings. In cloths of other descriptions, as much as 50 per cent. size is sometimes added; so that a manufacturer may, and does truly boast, that he is getting rich by selling cloth for less money per pound than he paid for the mere yarn of which they are composed."[1] But the workpeople had to suffer, not only from the experiments of the manufacturers inside the mills, and of the municipalities outside, not only from reduced wages and absence of work, from want and from charity, and from the eulogistic speeches of lords and commons. "Unfortunate females who, in consequence of the cotton famine, were at its commencement thrown out of employment, and have thereby become outcasts of society; and now though trade has revived, and work is plentiful, continue members of that unfortunate class, and are likely to continue so. There are also in the borough more youthful prostitutes than I have known for the last 25 years."[2]

We find then, in the first 45 years of the English cotton trade, from 1770 to 1815, only 5 years of crisis and stagnation; but this was the period of monopoly. The second period from 1815 to 1863 counts, during its 48 years, only 20 years of revival and prosperity against 28 of depression and stagnation. Between 1815 and 1830 the competition with the continent of Europe and with the United States sets in. After 1833, the extension of the Asiatic markets is enforced by "destruction of the human race" (the wholesale extinction of Indian handloom weavers). After the repeal of the Corn Laws, from 1846 to 1863, there are 8 years of moderate activity and prosperity against 9 years of depression and stagnation. The condition of the adult male operatives, even during the years of prosperity, may be judged from the note subjoined.[3]

[1] Rep. &c. 30th April, 1864, p. 27.
[2] From a letter of Mr. Harris, Chief Constable of Bolton, in Rep. of Insp. of Fact., 31st October, 1865, pp. 61-62.
[3] In an appeal, dated 1863, of the factory operatives of Lancashire, &c., for the purpose of forming a society for organised emigration, we find the following: "That a large emigration of factory workers is now absolutely essential to raise them

SECTION 8.—REVOLUTION EFFECTED IN MANUFACTURE, HANDICRAFTS. AND DOMESTIC INDUSTRY BY MODERN INDUSTRY.

a. Overthrow of Co-operation based on Handicraft and on the Division of Labour.

We have seen how machinery does away with co-operation based on handicrafts, and with manufacture based on the division of handicraft labour. An example of the first sort is the mowing-machine; it replaces co-operation between mowers. A striking example of the second kind, is the needle-making machine. According to Adam Smith, 10 men, in his day, made in co-operation, over 48,000 needles a-day. On the other hand, a single needle-machine makes 145,000 in a working day of 11 hours. One woman or one girl superintends four such machines, and so produces near upon 600,000 needles in a day, and upwards of 3,000,000 in a week.[1] A single machine, when it takes the place of co-operation or of manufacture, may itself serve as the basis of an industry of a

from their present prostrate condition, few will deny; but to show that a continuous stream of emigration is at all times demanded, and, without which it is impossible for them to maintain their position in ordinary times, we beg to call attention to the subjoined facts:—In 1814 the official value of cotton goods exported was £17,665,378, whilst the real marketable value was £20,070,824. In 1858 the official value of cotton goods exported, was £182,221,681; but the real or marketable value was only £43,001,322, being a ten-fold quantity sold for little more than double the former price. To produce results so disadvantageous to the country generally, and to the factory workers in particular, several causes have co-operated, which, had circumstances permitted, we should have brought more prominently under your notice; suffice it for the present to say that the most obvious one is the constant redundancy of labour, without which a trade so ruinous in its effects never could have been carried on, and which requires a constantly extending market to save it from annihilation. Our cotton mills may be brought to a stand by the periodical stagnations of trade, which, under present arrangements, are as inevitable as death itself; but the human mind is constantly at work, and although we believe we are under the mark in stating that six millions of persons have left these shores during the last 25 years, yet, from the natural increase of population, and the displacement of labour to cheapen production, a large percentage of the male adults in the most prosperous times find it impossible to obtain work in factories on any conditions whatever." ("Reports of Insp. of Fact., 30th April, 1863," pp. 51-52. We shall, in a later chapter, see how our friends, the manufacturers, endeavored, during the catastrophe in the cotton trade, to prevent by every means, including State interference, the emigration of the operatives.

[1] "Ch. Empl. Comm. IV. Report, 1864," p. 108, n. 447.

handicraft character. Still, such a return to handicrafts
is but a transition to the factory system, which, as a rule,
makes its appearance so soon as the human muscles are replaced, for the purpose of driving the machines, by a mechanical motive power, such as steam or water. Here and
there, but in any case only for a time, an industry may be
carried on, on a small scale, by means of mechanical power.
This is effected by hiring steam power, as is done in some
of the Birmingham trades, or by the use of small caloric-
engines, as in some branches of weaving.[1] In the Coventry
silk weaving industry the experiment of "cottage factories"
was tried. In the centre of a square surrounded by rows of
cottages, an engine-house was built and the engine connected
by shafts with the looms in the cottages. In all cases the
power was hired at so much per loom. The rent was payable weekly, whether the looms worked or not. Each cottage
held from 2 to 6 looms; some belonged to the weaver, some
were bought on credit, some were hired. The struggle between these cottage factories and the factory proper, lasted
over 12 years. It ended with the complete ruin of the 300
cottage-factories.[2] Wherever the nature of the process did
not involve production on a large scale, the new industries
that have sprung up in the last few decades, such as envelope
making, steel-pen making, &c., have, as a general rule, first
passed through the handicraft stage, and then the manufacturing stage, as short phases of transition to the factory stage.
The transition is very difficult in those cases where the production of the article by manufacture consists, not of a series
of graduated processes, but of a great number of disconnected ones. This circumstance formed a great hindrance to
the establishment of steel-pen factories. Nevertheless, about
15 years ago, a machine was invented that automatically performed 6 separate operations at once. The first steel-pens
were supplied by the handicraft system, in the year 1820, at
£7 4s, the gross; in 1830 they were supplied by manufacture

---

[1] In the United States the restoration in this way, of handicrafts based on
machinery is frequent; and therefore, when the inevitable transition to the factory
system shall take place, the ensuing concentration will, compared with Europe and
even with England, stride on in seven-league boots.

[2] See "Rep. of Insp. of Fact., 31st Oct., 1865," p. 64.

at 8s., and to-day the factory system supplies them to the trade at from 2s. to 6d. the gross.[1]

b. Re-action of the Factory System on Manufacture and Domestic Industries.

Along with the development of the factory system and of the revolution in agriculture that accompanies it, production in all the other branches of industry not only extends, but alters its character. The principle, carried out in the factory system, of analysing the process of production into its constituent phases, and of solving the problems thus proposed by the application of mechanics, of chemistry, and of the whole range of the natural sciences, becomes the determining principle everywhere. Hence, machinery squeezes itself into the manufacturing industries first for one detail process, then for another. Thus the solid crystal of their organisation, based on the old division of labour, becomes dissolved, and makes way for constant changes. Independently of this, a radical change takes place in the composition of the collective labourer, a change of the persons working in combination. In contrast with the manufacturing period, the division of labour is thenceforth based, wherever possible, on the employment of women, of children of all ages, and of unskilled labourers, in one word, on cheap labour, as it is characteristically called in England. This is the case not only with all production on a large scale, whether employing machinery or not, but also with the so-called domestic industry, whether carried on in the houses of the workpeople or in small workshops. This modern so-called domestic industry has nothing, except the name, in common with the old-fashioned domestic industry, the existence of which presupposes independent urban handicrafts, independent peasant farming, and above all, a dwelling-house for the labourer and his family. That old-fash-

[1] Mr. Gillott erected in Birmingham the first steel-pen factory on a large scale. It produced, so early as 1851, over 180,000,000 of pens yearly, and consumed 120 tons of steel. Birmingham has the monopoly of this industry in the United Kingdom, and at present produces thousands of millions of steel pens. According to the Census of 1861, the number of persons employed was 1428, of whom 1268 were females from 5 years of age upwards.

ioned industry has now been converted into an outside department of the factory, the manufactory, or the warehouse. Besides the factory operatives, the manufacturing workmen and the handicraftsmen, whom it concentrates in large masses at one spot, and directly commands, capital also sets in motion, by means of invisible threads, another army; that of the workers in the domestic industries, who dwell in the large towns and are also scattered over the face of the country. An example: The shirt factory of Messrs. Tille at Londonderry, which employs 1000 operatives in the factory itself, and 9000 people spread up and down the country and working in their own houses.[1]

The exploitation of cheap and immature labour-power is carried out in a more shameless manner in modern Manufacture than in the factory proper. This is because the technical foundation of the factory system, namely, the substitution of machines for muscular power, and the light character of the labour, is almost entirely absent in Manufacture, and at the same time women and over-young children are subjected, in a most unconscionable way, to the influence of poisonous or injurious substances. This exploitation is more shameless in the so-called domestic industry than in manufactures, and that because the power of resistance in the labourers decreases with their dissemination; because a whole series of plundering parasites insinuate themselves between the employer and the workman; because a domestic industry has always to compete, either with the factory system, or with manufacturing in the same branch of production; because poverty robs the workman of the conditions most essential to his labour, of space, light and ventilation; because employment becomes more and more irregular; and, finally, because in these the last resorts of the masses made "redundant" by Modern Industry and Agriculture, competition for work attains its maximum. Economy in the means of production, first systematically carried out in the factory system, and there, from the very beginning, coincident with the most reckless squandering of labour-power, and robbery of the con-

[1] Ch. Empl. Comm., II. Rep. 1864, p. LXVIII., n. 415.

ditions normally requisite for labour—this economy now shows its antagonistic and murderous side more and more in a given branch of industry, the less the social productive power of labour and the technical basis for a combination of processes are developed in that branch.

c. Modern Manufacture.

I now proceed, by a few examples, to illustrate the principles laid down above. As a matter of fact, the reader is already familiar with numerous instances given in the chapter on the working day. In the hardware manufactures of Birmingham and the neighborhood, there are employed, mostly in very heavy work, 30,000 children and young persons, besides 10,000 women. There they are to be seen in the unwholesome brass-foundries, button factories, enamelling, galvanizing, and lackering works.[1] Owing to the excessive labour of their workpeople, both adult and non-adult, certain London houses where newspapers and books are printed have got the ill-omened name of "slaughter-houses."[2] Similar excesses are practised in bookbinding, where the victims are chiefly women, girls, and children; young persons have to do heavy work in rope-walks and night-work in salt mines, candle manufactories, and chemical works; young people are worked to death at turning the looms in silk weaving, when it is not carried on by machinery.[3] One of the most shameful, the most dirty, and the worst paid kinds of labour, and one on which women and young girls are by preference employed, is the sorting of rags. It is well known that Great Britain, apart from its own immense store of rags, is the emporium for the rag trade of the whole world. They flow in from Japan, from the most remote States of South America, and from the Canary Islands. But the chief sources of their supply are Germany, France, Russia, Italy, Egypt, Turkey, Belgium, and Holland. They are used for manure, for mak-

---

[1] And now forsooth children are employed at file-cutting in Sheffield.

[2] Ch. Empl. Comm. V. Rep. 1866, p. 3, n. 24, p. 6, n. 55, 56, p. 7, n. 59, 60.

[3] L. c. pp. 114, 115, n. 6, 7. The commissioner justly remarks that though as a rule machines take the place of men, here literally young persons replace machines.

ing bed-flocks, for shoddy, and they serve as the raw material of paper. The rag-sorters are the medium for the spread of small-pox and other infectious diseases, and they themselves are the first victims.[1] A classical example of over-work, of hard and inappropriate labour, and of its brutalising effects on the workman from his childhood upwards, is afforded not only by coal-mining and miners generally, but also by tile and brick making, in which industry the recently invented machinery is, in England, used only here and there. Between May and September the work lasts from 5 in the morning till 8 in the evening, and where the drying is done in the open air, it often lasts from 4 in the morning till 9 in the evening. Work from 5 in the morning till 7 in the evening is considered "reduced" and "moderate." Both boys and girls of 6 and even of 4 years of age are employed. They work for the same number of hours, often longer, than the adults. The work is hard and the summer heat increases the exhaustion. In a certain tile field at Mosley, *e.g.,* a young woman, 24 years of age, was in the habit of making 2000 tiles a day, with the assistance of 2 little girls, who carried the clay for her, and stacked the tiles. These girls carried daily 10 tons up the slippery sides of the clay pits, from a depth of 30 feet, and then for a distance of 210 feet. "It is impossible for a child to pass through the purgatory of a tile-field without great moral degradation . . . the low language, which they are accustomed to hear from their tenderest years, the filthy, indecent, and shameless habits, amidst which, unknowing, and half wild, they grow up, make them in after life lawless, abandoned, dissolute. . . . A frightful source of demoralization is the mode of living. Each moulder, who is always a skilled labourer, and the chief of a group, supplies his 7 subordinates with board and lodging in his cottage. Whether members of his family or not, the men, boys, and girls all sleep in the cottage, which contains generally two, exceptionally 3 rooms, all on the ground floor, and badly ventilated. These people are so exhausted after the day's work,

---

[1] See the Report on the rag trade, and numerous details in Public Health, VIII. Rep. Lond. 1866, app. pp. 196, 208.

that neither the rules of health, of cleanliness, nor of decency are in the least observed. Many of these cottages are models of untidiness, dirt, and dust. . . . The greatest evil of the system that employs young girls on this sort of work, consists in this, that, as a rule, it chains them fast from childhood for the whole of their after-life to the most abandoned rabble. They become rough, foul-mouthed boys, before Nature has taught them that they are women. Clothed in a few dirty rags, the legs naked far above the knees, hair and face besmeared with dirt, they learn to treat all feelings of decency and of shame with contempt. During meal-times they lie at full length in the fields, or watch the boys bathing in a neighboring canal. Their heavy day's work at length completed, they put on better clothes, and accompany the men to the public houses." That excessive insobriety is prevalent from childhood upwards among the whole of this class, is only natural. "The worst is that the brickmakers despair of themselves. You might as well, said one of the better kind to a chaplain of Southallfield, try to raise and improve the devil as a brickie, sir!"[1]

As to the manner in which capital effects an economy in the requisites of labour, in modern Manufacture (in which I include all workshops of larger size, except factories proper), official and most ample material bearing on it is to be found in the Public Health Reports IV. (1863) and VI. (1864). The description of the workshops, more especially those of the London printers and tailors, surpasses the most loathsome phantasies of our romance writers. The effect on the health of the workpeople is self-evident. Dr. Simon, the chief medical officer of the Privy Council and the official editor of the "Public Health Report," says: "In my fourth Report (1863) I showed, how it is practically impossible for the workpeople to insist upon that which is their first sanitary right, viz., the right that, no matter what the work for which their employer brings them together, the labour, so far as it depends upon him, should be freed from all avoidably un-

---

[1] Ch. Empl. Comm. V. Rep., 1866, xvi., n. 96, 97, and p. 130, n. 39, 61. See also III. Rep., 1864, p. 48, 56.

wholesome conditions.   I pointed out, that while the workpeople are practically incapable of doing themselves this sanitary justice, they are unable to obtain any effective support
from the paid adminstrations of the sanitary police.   .   .
The life of myriads of workmen and workwomen is now uselessly tortured and shortened by the never-ending physical
suffering that their mere occupation begets."[1]   In illustration
of the way in which the workrooms influence the state of
health, Dr. Simon gives the following table of mortality.[2]

Number of persons of all ages employed in the respective industries.	Industries compared as regards health.	Death rate per 100,000 men in the respective industries between the stated ages.		
		Age 25-35.	Age 35-45.	Age 45-55.
958,265	Agriculture in England & Wales	743	805	1,145
22,301 men 12,379 women	London tailors	958	1,262	2,093
13,803	London printers	894	1,747	2,367

d. Modern Domestic Industry.

I now come to the so-called domestic industry.   In order to
get an idea of the horrors of this sphere, in which capital
conducts its exploitation in the background of modern mechanical industry, one must go to the apparently quiet idyllic
trade of nail-making,[3] carried on in a few remote villages of
England.   In this place, however, it will be enough to give a

[1] Public Health. Sixth Rep. Lond. 1864, p. 31.
[2] l. c., p. 30.   Dr. Simon remarks that the mortality among the London tailors and
printers between the ages of 25 and 35 is in fact much greater, because the employers in London obtain from the country a great number of young people up to 30
years of age, as "apprentices" and "improvers," who come for the purpose of being
perfected in their trade.   These figure in the census as Londoners, they swell out
the number of heads on which the London death-rate is calculated, without adding
proportionally to the number of deaths in that place.   The greater part of them
in fact return to the country, and especially in cases of severe illness.   (l. c.)
[3] I allude here to hammered nails, as distinguished from nails cut out and made
by machinery.   See Child. Empl. Comm., Third Rep. p. xi, p. xix, n. 125-180, p.
53, n. 11, p. 114, n. 487. p. 137, n. 674.

few examples from those branches of the lace-making and straw-plaiting industries that are not yet carried on by the aid of machinery, and that as yet do not compete with branches carried on in factories or in manufactories.

Of the 150,000 persons employed in England in the production of lace, about 10,000 fall under the authority of the Factory Act, 1861. Almost the whole of the remaining 140,-000 are women, young persons, and children of both sexes, the male sex, however, being weakly represented. The state of health of this cheap material for exploitation will be seen from the following table, computed by Dr. Trueman, physician to the Nottingham General Dispensary. Out of 686 female patients who were lace makers, most of them between the ages of 17 and 24, the number of consumptive ones were:

1852.—1 in 45.	1855.—1 in 18.	1858.—1 in 15.
1853.—1 in 28.	1856.—1 in 15.	1859.—1 in 9.
1854.—1 in 17.	1857.—1 in 13.	1860.—1 in 8.
	1861.—1 in 8.[1]	

This progress in the rate of consumption ought to suffice for the most optimist of progressists, and for the biggest hawker of lies among the Free Trade bagmen of Germany.

The Factory Act of 1861 regulates the actual making of the lace, so far as it is done by machinery, and this is the rule in England. The branches that we are now about to examine, solely with regard to those of the workpeople who work at home, and not those who work in manufactories or warehouses, fall into two divisions, viz., (1), finishing; (2), mending. The former gives the finishing touches to the machine-made lace, and includes numerous sub-divisions.

The lace finishing is done either in what are called "Mistresses' Houses," or by women in their own houses, with or without the help of their children. The women who keep the "Mistresses' Houses" are themselves poor. The workroom is in a private house. The mistresses take orders from manufacturers, or from warehousemen, and employ as many women, girls, and young children as the size of their rooms and the fluctuating demand of the business will allow. The number of the workwomen employed in these workrooms varies from 20 to 40 in some, and from 10 to 20 in others. The average age at which the children commence work is six years, but in many cases it is below five. The usual working hours are from 8 in the morning till eight in the evening, with 1½ hours for meals, which are taken at irregular intervals, and often in the foul workrooms. When business is brisk, the labour frequently lasts from 8 or even 6 o'clock in the morning till 10, 11, or 12 o'clock at night. In English barracks the regulation space allotted to each soldier is 500-600 cubic feet, and in the military hospitals 1200 cubic feet. But in those finishing styes there are but 67 to 100 cubic feet to each person. At the same time the oxygen of the air is consumed by gas-lights. In order to keep the lace clean, and although the floor is tiled or flagged, the children are often compelled, even in winter, to pull off their shoes. "It is not at all uncommon in Nottingham to find 14 to 20 children huddled together in a small room, of, perhaps, not more than 12 feet square, and employed for 15 hours out of the 24, at work that of itself is exhausting, from its weariness and monotony, and is besides carried on under every possible unwholesome condition. . . . Even the very youngest children work with a strained attention and a rapidity that is astonishing, hardly ever giving their fingers rest or slowering their motion. If a question be asked them, they never raise their eyes from their work for fear of losing a single moment." The "long stick" is used by the mistresses as a stimulant more and more as the working hours are prolonged. "The children gradually tire and becomes as restless as birds towards the end of their long detention at an occupation that is monotonous, eye-straining, and exhausting from the uniformity in the posture of the body. Their work is like slavery."[1] When women and their children work at home, which now-a-days means in a hired room, often in a garret, the state of things is, if possible, still worse. This sort of work is giving out within a circle of 80 miles radius from Not-

[1] Ch. Empl. Comm., II. Rep., 1864, pp. xix., xx., xxi.

tingham. On leaving the warehouses at 9 or 10 o'clock at night, the children are often given a bundle of lace to take home with them and finish. The Pharisee of a capitalist represented by one of his servants, accompanies this action, of course, with the unctuous phrase: "That's for mother," yet he knows well enough that the poor children must sit up and help.[1]

Pillow lace making is chiefly carried on in England in two agricultural districts one, the Honiton lace district, extending from 20 to 30 miles along the south coast of Devonshire, and including a few places in North Devon; the other comprising a great part of the counties of Buckingham, Bedford, and Northampton, and also the adjoining portions of Oxfordshire and Huntingdonshire. The cottages of the agricultural labourers are the places where the work is usually carried on. Many manufacturers employ upwards of 3000 of these lace makers, who are chiefly children and young persons of the female sex exclusively. The state of things described as incidental to lace finishing is here repeated, save that instead of the "mistresses' houses," we find what are called "lace schools," kept by poor women in their cottages. From their fifth year and often earlier, until their twelfth or fifteenth year, the children work in these schools; during the first year the very young ones work from four to eight hours, and later on, from six in the morning till eight and ten o'clock at night. "The rooms are generally the ordinary living rooms of small cottages, the chimney stopped up to keep out draughts, the inmates kept warm by their own animal heat alone, and this frequently in winter. In other cases, these so-called school-rooms are like small store-rooms without fire-places. . . . The overcrowding in these dens and the consequent vitiation of the air are often extreme. Added to this is the injurious effect of drains, privies, decomposing substances, and other filth usual in the purileus of the smaller cottages." With regard to space: "In one lace school 18 girls and a mistress, 35 cubic feet to each person; in another, where the smell was unbearable, 18 persons and 24½ cubic feet per head. In this

[1] l. c., pp. xxi., xxvi.

industry are to be found employed children of 2 and 2½ years."[1]

Where lace-making ends in the counties of Buckingham and Bedford, straw-plaiting begins, and extends over a large part of Hertfordshire and the westerly and northerly parts of Essex. In 1861, there were 40,043 persons employed in straw-plaiting and straw-hat making; of these 3815 were males of all ages, the rest females, of whom 14,913, including about 7000 children, were under 20 years of age. In the place of the lace-schools we find here the "straw-plait schools." The children commence their instruction in straw-plaiting generally in their 4th, often between their 3rd and 4th year. Education, of course, they get none. The children themselves call the elementary schools, "natural schools," to distinguish them from these blood-sucking institutions, in which they are kept at work simply to get through the task, generally 30 .yards daily, prescribed by their half-starved mothers. These same mothers often make them work at home, after school is over, till 10, 11, and 12 o'clock at night. The straw cuts their mouths, with which they constantly moisten it, and their fingers. Dr. Ballard gives it as the general opinion of the whole body of medical officers in London, that 300 cubic feet is the minimum space proper for each person in a bedroom or work-room. But in the straw-plait schools space is more sparingly allotted than in the lace-schools, "12⅔, 17, 18½ and below 22 cubic feet for each person." The smaller of these numbers, says one of the commissioners, Mr. White, represents less space than the half of what a child would occupy if packed in a box measuring 3 feet in each direction. Thus do the children enjoy life till the age of 12 or 14. The wretched half-starved parents think of nothing but getting as much as possible out of their children. The latter, as soon as they are grown up, do not care a farthing, and naturally so, for their parents, and leave them. "It is no wonder that ignorance and vice abound in a population so brought up. . . . Their morality is at the lowest ebb, . . . a great number of the women have il-

[1] l. c., pp. xxix., xxx.

legitimate children, and that at such an immature age that even those most conversant with criminal statistics are astounded."[1] And the native land of these model families is the pattern Christian country of Europe so says at least Count Montalembert, certainly a competent authority on Christianity!

Wages in the above industries, miserable as they are (the maximum wages of a child in the straw-plait schools rising in rare cases to 3 shillings, are reduced far below their nominal amount by the prevalence of the truck system everywhere, but especially in the lace districts.[2]

e. *Passage of modern Manufacture, and Domestic Industry into Modern Mechanical Industry. The hastening of this revolution by the application of the Factory Acts to those Industries.*

The cheapening of labour-power, by sheer abuse of the labour of women and children, by sheer robbery of every normal condition requisite for working and living, and by the sheer brutality of over-work and night-work, meets at last with natural obstacles that cannot be overstepped. So also, when based on these methods, do the cheapening of commodities and capitalist exploitation in general. So soon as this point is at last reached—and it takes many years—the hour has struck for the introduction of machinery, and for the thenceforth rapid conversion of the scattered domestic industries and also of manufactures into factory industries.

An example, on the most colossal scale, of this movement is afforded by the production of wearing apparel. This industry, according to the classification of the Childrens' Employment Commission, comprises straw-hat makers, ladies'-hat makers, cap-makers, tailors, milliners and dressmakers, shirtmakers, corset-makers, glove-makers, shoemakers, besides many minor branches, such as the making of neck-ties, collars, &c. In 1861, the number of females employed in these industries, in England and Wales, amounted to 586,299, of

---

[1] l. c. pp. xl, xli.
[2] Child, Empl. Comm. I. Rep. 1863, p. 185.

these 115,242 at the least were under 20, and 16,650 under 15 years of age. The number of these workwomen in the United Kingdom in 1861, was 750,334. The number of males employed in England and Wales, in hat-making, shoe-making, glove-making and tailoring was 437,969; of these 14,964 under 15 years, 89,285 between 15 and 20, and 333,117 over 20 years. Many of the smaller branches are not included in these figures. But take the figures as they stand; we then have for England and Wales alone, according to the census of 1861, a total of 1,024,277 persons, about as many as are absorbed by agriculture and cattle breeding. We begin to understand what becomes of the immense quantities of goods conjured up by the magic of machinery, and of the enormous masses of workpeople, which that machinery sets free.

The production of wearing apparel is carried on partly in manufactories in whose workrooms there is but a reproduction of that division of labour, the membra disjecta of which were found ready to hand; partly by small master-handicraftsmen; these, however, do not, as formerly, work for individual consumers, but for manufactories and warehouses, and to such an extent that often whole towns and stretches of country carry on certain branches, such as shoe-making, as a specialty; finally, on a very great scale by the so-called domestic workers, who form an external department of the manufactories, warehouses, and even of the workshops of the smaller masters.[1]

The raw material, &c., is supplied by mechanical industry, the mass of cheap human material (taillable à merci et miséricorde) is composed of the individuals "liberated" by mechanical industry and improved agriculture. The manufactures of this class owed their origin chiefly to the capitalist's need of having at hand an army ready equipped to meet any increase of demand.[2] These manufactures, nevertheless, allowed the scattered handicrafts and domestic industries to

---

[1] In England millinery and dressmaking are for the most part carried on, on the premises of the employer, partly by workwomen who live there, partly by women who live off the premises.

[2] Mr. White, a commissioner, visited a military clothing manufactory that employed 1000 to 1200 persons, almost all females, and a shoe manufactory with 1300 persons; of these nearly one half were children and young persons.

continue to exist as a broad foundation. The great production of surplus-value in these branches of labour, and the pro-. gressive cheapening of their articles, were and are chiefly due to the minimum wages paid, no more than requisite for a miserable vegetation, and to the extension of working time up to the maximum endurable by the human organism. It was in fact by the cheapness of the human sweat and the human blood, which were converted into commodities, that the markets were constantly being extended, and continue daily to be extended; more especially was this the case with England's colonial markets, where, besides, English tastes and habits prevail. At last the critical point was reached. The basis of the old method, sheer brutality in the exploitation of the workpeople, accompanied more or less by a systematic division of labour, no longer sufficed for the extending markets and for the still more rapidly extending competition of the capitalists. The hour struck for the advent of machinery. The decisively revolutionary machine, the machine which attacks in an equal degree the whole of the numberless branches of this sphere of production, dressmaking, tailoring, shoe-making, sewing, hat-making, and many others, is the sewing-machine.

Its immediate effect on the workpeople is like that of all machinery, which, since the rise of modern industry, has seized upon new branches of trade. Children of too tender an age are sent adrift. The wage of the machine hands rises compared with that of the house-workers, many of whom belong to the poorest of the poor. That of the better situated handicraftsmen, with whom the machine competes, sinks. The new machine hands are exclusively girls and young women. With the help of mechanical force, they destroy the monopoly that male labour had of the heavier work, and they drive off from the lighter work numbers of old women and very young children. The overpowering competition crushes the weakest of the manual labourers. The fearful increase in death from starvation during the last 10 years in London runs parallel with the extension of machine sewing.[1]

[1] An instance: The weekly report of deaths by the Registrar General dated 26th

The new workwomen turn the machine by hand and foot, or by hand alone, sometimes sitting, sometimes standing, according to the weight, size and special make of the machine, and expend a great deal of labour-power. Their occupation is unwholesome, owing to the long hours, although in most cases they are not so long as under the old system. Wherever the sewing machine locates itself in narrow and already over-crowded workrooms, it adds to the unwholesome influences. "The effect," says Mr. Lord, "on entering low-ceiled workrooms in which 30 to 40 machine hands are working is unbearable. . . . The heat, partly due to the gas stoves used for warming the irons, is horrible. . . . Even when moderate hours of work, *i.e.*, from 8 in the morning till 6 in the evening, prevail in such places, yet 3 or 4 persons fall into a swoon regularly every day."[1]

The revolution in the industrial methods which is the necessary result of the revolution in the instruments of production, is effected by a medley of transition forms. These forms vary according to the extent to which the sewing machine has become prevalent in one branch of industry or the other, to the time during which it has been in operation, to the previous condition of the workpeople, to the preponderance of manufacture, of handicrafts or of domestic industry, to the rent of the workrooms, &c.[2] In dressmaking, for instance, where the labour for the most part was already organised, chiefly by simple co-operation, the sewing machine at first formed merely a new factor in that manufacturing industry. In tailoring, shirtmaking, shoemaking, &c., all the forms are intermingled. Here the factory system proper. There middlemen receive the raw material from the capitalist *en chef*, and group around their sewing machines, in "chambers" and "garrets," from 10 to 50 or more workwomen. Finally, as is

Feb., 1864, contains 5 cases of death from starvation. On the same day the "Times" reports another case. Six victims of starvation in one week!

[1] Child. Empl. Comm., Second Rep., 1864, p. lxvii. n. 406–9, p. 84, n. 124, p. lxxiii., n. 441, p. 66, n. 6, p. 84, n. 126, p. 78, n. 76, n. 69, p. lxxii., n. 483.

[2] "The rental of premises required for workrooms seems the element which ultimately determines the point; and consequently it is in the metropolis, that the old system of giving work out to small employers and families has been longest retained, and earliest returned to." (l. c. p. 83, n. 123.) The concluding statement in this quotation refers exclusively to shoemaking.

always the case with machinery when not organised into a system, and when it can also be used in dwarfish proportions, handicraftsmen and domestic workers, along with their families, or with a little extra labour from without, makes use of their own sewing machines.[1] The system actually prevalent in England is, that the capitalist concentrates a large number of machines on his premises, and then distributes the produce of those machines for further manipulation amongst the domestic workers.[2] The variety of the transition forms, however, does not conceal the tendency to conversion into the factory system proper. This tendency is nurtured by the very nature of the sewing machine, the manifold uses of which push on the concentration, under one roof, and one management, of previously separated branches of a trade. It is also favoured by the circumstance that preparatory needlework, and certain other operations, are most conveniently done on the premises where the machine is at work; as well as by the inevitable expropriation of the hand sewers, and of the domestic workers who work with their own machines. This fate has already in part overtaken them. The constantly increasing amount of capital invested in sewing machines,[3] gives the spur to the production of, and gluts the markets with, machine-made articles, thereby giving the signal to the domestic workers for the sale of their machines. The overproduction of sewing machines themselves, causes their producers, in bad want of a sale, to let them out for so much a week, thus crushing by their deadly competition the small owners of machines.[4] Constant changes in the construction of the machines, and their ever-increasing cheapness, depreciate day by day the older makes, and allow of their being sold in great numbers, at absurd prices, to large capitalists, who alone can thus employ them at a profit. Finally, the substitution of the steam-engine for man gives in this, as in all similar revolutions, the finishing blow. At first, the use of

---

[1] In glove-making and other industries where the condition of the workpeople is hardly distinguishable from that of paupers, this does not occur.

[2] l. c. p. 2, n. 122.

[3] In the wholesale boot and shoe trade of Leicester alone, there were in 1864, 800 sewing machines already in use.

[4] l. c. p. 84, n. 124.

steam power meets with mere technical difficulties, such as unsteadiness in the machines, difficulty in controlling their speed, rapid wear and tear of the lighter machines, &c., all of which are soon overcome by experience.[1] If, on the one hand, the concentration of many machines in large manufactories leads to the use of steam power, on the other hand, the competition of steam with human muscles hastens on the concentration of workpeople and machines in large factories. Thus England is at present experiencing, not only in the colossal industry of making wearing apparel, but in most of the other trades mentioned above, the conversion of manufacture, of handicrafts, and of domestic work into the factory system, after each of those forms of production, totally changed and disorganized under the influence of modern industry, has long ago reproduced, and even overdone, all the horrors of the factory system, without participating in any of the elements of social progress it contains.[2]

This industrial revolution which takes place spontaneously, is artificially helped on by the extension of the Factory Acts to all industries in which women, young persons and children are employed. The compulsory regulation of the working day as regards its length, pauses, beginning and end, the system of relays of children, the exclusion of all children under a certain age, &c., necessitates on the one hand more machinery[3] and the substitution of steam as a motive power in the place

[1] Instances: The Army Clothing Depot at Pimlico, London, the Shirt factory of Tillie and Henderson at Londonderry, and the clothes factory of Messrs. Tait at Limerick which employs about 1200 hands.

[2] "Tendency to factory system" (l. c. p. lxvii.). "The whole employment is at this time in a state of transition, and is undergoing the same change as that effected in the lace trade, weaving, &c." (l. c. n. 405.) "A complete revolution" (l. c. p. xlvi. n. 318). At the date of the Child. Empl. Comm. of 1840, stocking making was still done by manual labour. Since 1846 various sorts of machines have been introduced, which are now driven by steam. The total number of persons of both sexes and of all ages from 3 years upwards, employed in stocking making in England, was in 1862 about 129,000. Of these only 4063 were, according to the Parliamentary Return of the 11th February, 1862, working under the Factory Acts.

[3] Thus, *e.g.*, in the earthenware trade, Messrs. Cochrane, of the Britain Pottery, Glasgow, report: "To keep up our quantity we have gone extensively into machines wrought by unskilled labour, and every day convinces us that we can produce a greater quantity than by the old method." ("Rep. of Insp. of Fact., 31st Oct., 1865," p. 13.) "The effect of the Fact. Acts is to force on the further introduction of machinery" (l. c., p. 13-14).

of muscles.[1] On the other hand, in order to make up for the loss of time, an expansion occurs of the means of production used in common, of the furnaces, buildings, &c.; in one word, greater concentration of the means of production and a correspondingly greater concourse of workpeople. The chief objection, repeatedly and passionately urged on behalf of each manufacture threatened with the Factory Act, is in fact this, that in order to continue the business on the old scale a greater outlay of capital will be necessary. But as regards labour in the so-called domestic industries and the intermediate forms between them and Manufacture, so soon as limits are put to the working day and to the employment of children, those industries go to the wall. Unlimited exploitation of cheap labour-power is the sole foundation of their power to compete.

One of the essential conditions for the existence of the factory system, especially when the length of the working day is fixed, is certainty in the result, *i.e.,* the production in a given time of a given quantity of commodities, or of a given useful effect. The statutory pauses in the working day, moreover, imply the assumption that periodical and sudden cessation of the work does no harm to the article undergoing the process of production. This certainty in the result, and this possibility of interrupting the work are, of course, easier to be attained in the purely mechanical industries than in those in which chemical and physical processes play a part; as, for instance, in the earthenware trade, in bleaching, dyeing, baking, and in most of the metal industries. Wherever there is a working day without restriction as to length, wherever there is night work and unrestricted waste of human life, there the slightest obstacle presented by the nature of the work to a change for the better is soon looked upon as an everlasting barrier erected by Nature. No poison kills vermin with more certainty than the Factory Act removes such everlasting barriers. No one made a greater outcry over "impossibilities" than our friends the earthenwares manufacturers. In 1864, however, they

---

[1] Thus, after the extension of the Factory Act to the potteries, great increase of power-jiggers in place of hand-moved jiggers.

were brought under the Act, and within sixteen months every "impossibility" had vanished. "The improved method," called forth by the Act, "of making slip by pressure instead of by evaporation, the newly-constructed stoves for drying the ware in its green state, &c., are each events of great importances in the pottery art, and mark an advance which the preceding century could not rival. . . . It has even considerably reduced the temperature of the stoves themselves with a considerable saving of fuel, and with a readier effect on the ware."[1]   In spite of every prophecy, the cost price of earthenware did not rise, but the quantity produced did, and to such an extent that the export for the twelve months, ending December, 1865, exceeded in value by £138,628 the average of the preceding three years.   In the manufacture of matches it was thought to be an indispensable requirement, that boys, even while bolting their dinner, should go on dipping the matches in melted phosphorus, the poisonous vapour from which rose into their faces.   The Factory Act (1864) made the saving of time a necessity, and so forced into existence a dipping machine, the vapour from which could not come in contact with the workers.[2]   So, at the present time, in those branches of the lace manufacture not yet subject to the Factory Act, it is maintained that the meal times cannot be regular owing to the different periods required by the various kinds of lace for drying, which periods vary from three minutes up to an hour and more.   To this the Children's Employment Commissioners answer: "The circumstances of this case are precisely analogous to that of the paper-stainers, dealt with in our first report.   Some of the principal manufacturers in the trade urged that in consequence of the nature of the materials used, and their various processes, they would be unable, without serious loss, to stop for meal times at any given moment.   But it was seen from the evidence that, by due care and previous arrangement, the apprehended difficulty

---

[1] "Report of Insp. of Fact., 31st Oct., 1865," pp. 96 and 127.

[2] The introduction of this and other machinery into match-making caused in one department alone 230 young persons to be replaced by 32 boys and girls of 14 to 17 years of age. This saving in labour was carried still further in 1865, by the employment of steam power.

would be got over; and accordingly, by clause 6 of section 6 of the Factory Acts Extension Act, passed during this Session of Parliament, an interval of eighteen months is given to them from the passing of the Act before they are required to conform to the meal hours, specified by the Factory Acts."[1] Hardly had the Act been passed when our friends the manufacturers found out: "The inconveniences we expected to arise from the introduction of the Factory Acts into our branch of manufacture, I am happy to say, have not arisen. We do not find the production at all interfered with; in short, we produce more in the same time."[2] It is evident that the English legislature, which certainly no one will venture to reproach with being overdosed with genius, has been led by experience to the conclusion that a simple compulsory law is sufficient to enact away all the so-called impediments, opposed by the nature of the process, to the restriction and regulation of the working day. Hence, on the introduction of the Factory Act into a given industry, a period varying from six to eighteen months is fixed within which it is incumbent on the manufacturers to remove all technical impediments to the working of the Act. Mirabeau's "Impossible! ne me dites jamaisce bête de mot!" is particularly applicable to modern technology. But though the Factory Acts thus artificially ripen the material elements necessary for the conversion of the manufacturing system into the factory system, yet at the same time, owing to the necessity they impose for greater outlay of capital, they hasten on the decline of the small masters, and the concentration of capital.[3]

Besides the purely technical impediments that are removable by technical means, the irregular habits of the work-

---

[1] "Ch. Empl. Comm., II. Rep., 1864," p. ix., n. 50.

[2] "Rep. of Insp. of Fact., 31st Oct. 1865," p. 22.

[3] "But it must be borne in mind that those improvements, though carried out fully in some establishments, are by no means general, and are not capable of being trought into use in many of the old manufactories without an expenditure of capital beyond the means of many of the present occupiers." "I cannot but rejoice," writes Sub-Insp. May, "that notwithstanding the temporary disorganization which inevitably follows the introduction of such a measure (as the Factory Act Extension Act), and is, indeed, directly indicative of the evils which it was intended to remedy, &c." (Rep. of Insp. of Fact., 31st Oct., 1865.)

people themselves obstruct the regulation of the hours of labour. This is especially the case where piece wage predominates, and where loss of time in one part of the day or week can be made good by subsequent overtime, or by night work, a process which brutalises the adult workman, and ruins his wife and children.[1] Although this absence of regularity in the expenditure of labour-power is a natural and rude reaction against the tedium of monotonous drudgery, it originates, also, to a much greater degree from anarchy in production, anarchy that in its turn pre-supposes unbridled exploitation of labour-power by the capitalist. Besides the general periodic changes of the industrial cycle, and the special fluctuations in the markets to which each industry is subject, we may also reckon what is called "the season," dependent either on the periodicity of favourable seasons of the year for navigation; or on fashion, and the sudden placing of large orders that have to be executed in the shortest possible time. The habit of giving such orders becomes more frequent with the extension of railways and telegraphs. "The extension of the railway system throughout the country has tended very much to encourage giving short notice. Purchasers now come up from Glasgow, Manchester, and Edinburgh once every fortnight or so to the wholesale city warehouses which we supply, and give small orders requiring immediate execution, instead of buying from stock as they used to do. Years ago we were always able to work in the slack times, so as to meet the demand of the next season, but now no one can say beforehand what will be the demand then."[2]

---

[1] With blast furnaces, for instance, "work towards the end of the week being generally much increased in duration in consequence of the habit of the men of idling on Monday and occasionally during a part or the whole of Tuesday also." (Child. Empl. Comm., III. Rep., p. vi.) "The little masters generally have very irregular hours. They lose two or three days, and then work all night to make it up. . . . They always employ their own children, if they have any." (l. c., p. vii.) "The want of regularity in coming to work, encouraged by the possibility and practice of making up for this by working longer hours." (l. c., p. xviii.) "In Birmingham . . . . an enormous amount of time is lost . . . . idling part of the time, slaving the rest." (l. c., p. xi.)

[2] "Child Empl. Comm., IV. Rep. p. xxxii.," "The extension of the railway system is said to have contributed greatly to this custom of giving sudden orders, and the consequent hurry, neglect of meal times, and late hours of the workpeople." (l. c., p. xxxi.)

In those factories and manufactories that are not yet subject to the Factory Acts, the most fearful overwork prevails periodically during what is called the season, in consequence of sudden orders. In the outside department of the factory, of the manufactory, and of the warehouse, the so-called domestic workers, whose employment is at the best irregular, are entirely dependent for their raw material and their orders on the caprice of the capitalist, who, in this industry, is not hampered by any regard for depreciation of his buildings and machinery, and risks nothing by a stoppage of work, but the skin of the worker himself. Here then he sets himself systematically to work to form an industrial reserve force that shall be ready at a moment's notice; during one part of the year he decimates this force by the most inhuman toil, during the other part, he lets it starve for want of work. "The employers avail themselves of the habitual irregularity in the home-work, when any extra work is wanted at a push, so that the work goes on till 11, and 12 p.m. or 2 a.m., or as the usual phrase is, "all hours," and that in localities where "the stench is enough to knock you down, you go to the door, perhaps, and open it, but shudder to go further."[1] "They are curious men," said one of the witnesses, a shoemaker, speaking of the masters, "they think it does a boy no harm to work too hard for half the year, if he is nearly idle for the other half."[2]

In the same way as technical impediments, so too, those "usages which have grown with the growth of trade" were and still are proclaimed by interested capitalists as obstacles due to the nature of the work. This was a favorite cry of the cotton lords at the time they were first threatened with the Factory Acts. Although their industry more than any other depends on navigation, yet experience has given them the lie. Since then, every pretended obstruction to business has been treated by the Factory inspectors as a mere sham.[3] The

---

[1] Ch. Empl. Comm. IV. Rep. p. xxxv. n. 235, 237.
[2] Ch. Empl. Comm. IV. Rep. p. 127, n. 56.
[3] "With respect to the loss of trade by non-completion of shipping orders in time, I remember that this was the pet argument of the factory masters in 1832 and 1833. Nothing that can be advanced now on this subject, could have the force that it had

thoroughly conscientious investigations of the Children's Employment Commission prove that the effect of the regulation of tho hours of work, in some industries, was to spread the mass of labour previously employed more evenly over the whole year;[1] that this regulation was the first rational bridle on the murderous, meaningless caprices of fashion,[2] caprices that consort so badly with the system of modern industry; that the development of ocean navigation and of the means of communication generally, has swept away the technical basis on which season-work was really supported,[3] and that all other so-called unconquerable difficulties vanish before larger buildings, additional machinery, increase in the number of workpeople employed,[4] and the alterations caused by all these in the mode of conducting the wholesale trade.[5] But for all that, capital never becomes reconciled to such changes —and this is admitted over and over again by its own representatives—except "under the pressure of a General Act of

then, before steam had halved all distances and established new regulations for transit. It quite failed at that time of proof when put to the test, and again it will certainly fail should it have to be tried." (Reports of Insp. of Fact., 31 Oct., 1862, pp. 54, 55.

[1] Ch. Empl. Comm. IV. Rep. p. xviii. n. 118.

[2] John Bellers remarked as far back as 1699: "The uncertainty of fashions does increase necessitous poor. It has two great mischiefs in it. 1st, The journeymen are miserable in winter for want of work, the mercers and master weavers not daring to lay out their stocks to keep the journeymen employed before the spring comes, and they know what the fashion will then be: 2ndly, in the spring the journeymen are not sufficient, but the master-weavers must draw in many prentices, that they may supply the trade of the kingdom in a quarter or half a year, which robs the plough of hands, drains the country of labourers, and in a great part stocks the city with beggars, and starves some in winter that are ashamed to beg." (Essays about the Poor, Manufactures, &c., p. 9.)

[3] Ch. Empl. Comm. V. Rep. p. 171, n. 34.

[4] The evidence of some Bradford export-houses is as follows: "Under these circumstances, it seems clear that no boys need be worked longer than from 8 a.m. to 7 or 7.30 p.m., in making up. It is merely a question of extra hands and extra outlay. If some masters were not so greedy, the boys would not work late; an extra machine costs only £16 or £18; much of such overtime as does occur is to be referred to an insufficiency of appliances, and a want of space." Ch. Empl. Comm. V. Rep. p. 171, n. 31, 36, 38.

[5] l. c. A London manufacturer, who in other respects looks upon the compulsory regulation of the hours of labour as a protection for the workpeople against the manufacturers, and for the manufacturers themselves against the wholesale trade, states: "The pressure in our business is caused by the shippers, who want, *e.g.*, to send the goods by sailing vessel so as to reach their destination at a given season, and at the same time want to pocket the difference in freight between a sailing vessel and a steamship, or who select the earlier of two steamships in order to be in the foreign market before their competitors."

Parliament"[1] for the compulsory regulation of the hours of labour.

SECTION 9.——THE FACTORY ACTS. SANITARY AND EDUCATION CLAUSES OF THE SAME. THEIR GENERAL EXTENSION IN ENGLAND.

Factory legislation, that first conscious and methodical reaction of society against the spontaneously developed form of the process of production, is, as we have seen, just as much the necessary product of modern industry as cotton yarn, self-actors, and the electric telegraph. Before passing to the consideration of the extension of that legislation in England, we shall shortly notice certain clauses contained in the Factory Acts, and not relating to the hours of work.

Apart from their wording, which makes it easy for the capitalist to evade them, the sanitary clauses are extremely meagre, and, in fact, limited to provisions for whitewashing the walls, for insuring cleanliness in some other matters, for ventilation, and for protection against dangerous machinery. In the third book we shall return again to the fanatical opposition of the masters to those clauses which imposed upon them a slight expenditure on appliances for protecting the limbs of their workpeople, an opposition that throws a fresh and glaring light on the free trade dogma, according to which, in a society with conflicting interests, each individual necessarily furthers the common weal by seeking nothing but his own personal advantage! One example is enough. The reader knows that during the last 20 years, the flax industry has very much extended, and that, with that extension, the number of scutching mills in Ireland has increased. In 1864 there were in that country 1800 of these mills. Regularly in autumn and winter women and "young persons," the wives, sons, and daughters of the neighboring small farmers, a class of people totally unaccustomed to machinery, are taken from field labour to feed the rollers of the scutching

---

[1] "This could be obviated," says a manufacturer, "at the expense of an enlargement of the works under the pressure of a General Act of Parliament." l. c. p. x. n. 38.

mills with flax. The accidents, both as regards number and kind, are wholly unexampled in the history of machinery. In one scutching mill, at Kildinan, near Cork, there occurred between 1852 and 1856, six fatal accidents and sixty mutilations; every one of which might have been prevented by the simplest appliances, at the cost of a few shillings. Dr. W. White, the certifying surgeon for factories at Downpatrick, states in his official report, dated the 15th December, 1865; "The serious accidents at the scutching mills are of the most fearful nature. In many cases a quarter of the body is torn from the trunk, and either involves death, or a future of wretched incapacity and suffering. The increase of mills in the country will, of course, extend these dreadful results, and it will be a great boon if they are brought under the legislature. I am convinced that by proper supervision of scutching mills a vast sacrifice of life and limb would be averted."[1]

What could possibly show better the character of the capitalist mode of production, than the necessity that exists for forcing upon it, by Acts of Parliament, the simplest appliances for maintaining cleanliness and health? In the potteries the Factory Act of 1864 "has whitewashed and cleansed upwards of 200 workshops, after a period of abstinence from any such cleaning, in many cases of 20 years, and in some, entirely," (this is the " abstinence " of the capitalist!) " in which were employed 27,800 artisans, hitherto breathing through protracted days and often nights of labour, a mephitic atmosphere, and which rendered an otherwise comparatively innocuous occupation, pregnant with disease and death, The Act has improved the ventilation very much."[2] At the same time, this portion of the Act strikingly shows that the capitalist mode of production, owing to its very nature, excludes all rational improvement beyond a certain point. It has been stated over and over again that the English doctors are unanimous in declaring that where the work is continuous, 500 cubic feet is the very least space that should be allowed

---

[1] l. c. p. xv. n. 72. sqq.
[2] Rep. Insp. Fact., 31st October, 1865, p. 127.

for each person. Now, if the Factory Acts, owing to their compulsory provisions, indirectly hasten on the conversion of small workshops into factories, thus indirectly attacking the proprietary rights of the smaller capitalists, and assuring a monopoly to the great ones, so, if it were made obligatory to provide the proper space for each workman in every workshop, thousands of small employers would, at one full swoop, be expropriated directly! The very root of the capitalist mode of production, *i.e.*, the self-expansion of all capital, large or small, by means of the "free" purchase and consumption of labour-power, would be attacked. Factory legislation is therefore brought to a dead-lock before these 500 cubic feet of breathing space. The sanitary officers, the industrial inquiry commissioners, the factory inspectors, all harp, over and over again, upon the necessity for those 500 cubic feet, and upon the impossibility of wringing them out of capital. They thus, in fact, declare that consumption and other lung diseases among the workpeople are necessary conditions to the existence of capital.[1]

Paltry as the education clauses of the Act appear on the whole, yet they proclaim elementary education to be an indispensable condition to the employment of children.[2] The success of those clauses proved for the first time the possibility of combining education and gymnastics[3] with manual

---

[1] It has been found out by experiment, that with each respiration of average intensity made by a healthy average individual, about 25 cubic inches of air are consumed, and that about 20 respirations are made in each minute. Hence the air inhaled in 24 hours by each individual is about 720,000 cubic inches, or 416 cubic feet. It is clear, however, that air which has been once breathed, can no longer serve for the same process until it has been purified in the great workshop of Nature. According to the experiments of Valentin and Brunner, it appears that a healthy man gives off about 1300 cubic inches of carbonic acid per hour; this would give about 8 ounces of solid carbon thrown off from the lungs in 24 hours. "Every man should have at least 800 cubic feet." (Huxley.)

[2] According to the English Factory Act, parents cannot send their children under 14 years of age into Factories under the control of the Act, unless at the same time they allow them to receive elementary education. The manufacturer is responsible for compliance with the Act. "Factory education is compulsory, and it is a condition of labour." (Rep. Insp. Fact. 31st Oct., 1863, p. 111.

[3] On the very advantageous results of combining gymnastics (and drilling in the case of boys) with compulsory education for factory children and pauper scholars, see the speech of N. W. Senior at the seventh annual congress of "The National Association for the Promotion of Social Science," in "Report of Proceedings, &c., Lond. 1863," p. 63, 64, also the Rep. Insp. Fact., 31st Oct., 1865, p. 118, 119, 120, 126 sqq.

labour, and, consequently, of combining manual labour with education and gymnastics. The factory inspectors soon found out by questioning the schoolmasters, that the factory children, although receiving only one half the education of the regular day scholars, yet learnt quite as much and often more. "This can be accounted for by the simple fact that, with only being at school for one half of the day, they are always fresh, and nearly always ready and willing to receive instruction. The system on which they work, half manual labour, and half school, renders each employment a rest and a relief to the other; consequently, both are far more congenial to the child, than would be the case were he kept constantly at one. It is quite clear that a boy who has been at school all the morning, cannot (in hot weather particularly) cope with one who comes fresh and bright from his work."[1] Further information on this point will be found in Senior's speech at the Social Science Congress at Edinburgh in 1863. He there shows, amongst other things, how the monotonous and uselessly long school hours of the children of the upper and middle classes, uselessly add to the labour of the teacher, "while he not only fruitlessly, but absolutely injuriously, wastes the time, health, and energy of the children."[2] From the Factory system budded, as Robert Owen has shown us in detail, the germ of the education of the future, an education that will, in the case of every child over a given age, combine productive

[1] Rep. Insp. Fact. 31st Oct. 1865, p. 118. A silk manufacturer naïvely states to the Children's Employment Commissioners: "I am quite sure that the true secret of producing efficient workpeople is to be found in uniting education and labour from a period of childhood. Of course the occupation must not be too severe, nor irksome, or unhealthy. But of the advantage of the union I have no doubt. I wish my own children could have some work as well as play to give variety to their schooling." (Ch. Empl. Comm. V. Rep. p. 82. n. 36.)

[2] Senior, l. c. p. 66. How Modern Industry, when it has attained to a certain pitch, is capable, by the revolution it effects in the mode of production and in the social conditions of production, of also revolutionizing people's minds, is strikingly shown by a comparison of Senior's speech in 1863, with his philippic against the Factory Act of 1833; or by a comparison, of the views of the congress above referred to, with the fact that in certain country districts of England poor parents are forbidden, on pain of death by starvation, to educate their children. Thus, *e.g.*, Mr. Snell reports it to be a common occurrence in Somersetshire that, when a poor person claims parish relief, he is compelled to take his children from school. Mr. Wollarton, the clergyman at Feltham, also tells of cases where all relief was denied to certain families "because they were sending their children to school!"

labour with instruction and gymnastics, not only as one of the methods of adding to the efficiency of production, but as the only method of producing fully developed human beings.

Modern Industry, as we have seen, sweeps away by technical means the manufacturing division of labour, under which each man is bound hand and foot for life to a single detail-operation. At the same time, the capitalistic form of that industry reproduces this same division of labour in a still more monstrous shape; in the factory proper, by converting the workman into a living appendage of the machine; and everywhere outside the Factory, partly by the sporadic use of machinery and machine workers,[1] partly by re-establishing the divisions of labour on a fresh basis by the general introduction of the labour of women and children, and of cheap unskilled labour.

The antagonism between the manufacturing division of labour and the methods of Modern Industry makes itself forcibly felt. It manifests itself, amongst other ways, in the frightful fact that a great part of the children employed in modern factories and manufactures, are from their earliest years riveted to the most simple manipulations, and exploited for years, without being taught a single sort of work that would afterwards make them of use, even in the same manufactory or factory. In the English letter press printing trade, for example, there existed formerly a system, corresponding to that in the old manufactures and handicrafts, of advancing the apprentices from easy to more and more difficult work. They went through a course of teaching till they were finished printers. To be able to read and write was for every one of

---

[1] Wherever handicraft-machines, driven by men, compete directly or indirectly with more developed machines driven by mechanical power, a great change takes place with regard to the labourer who drives the machine. At first the steam-engine replaces this labourer, afterwards he must replace the steam-engine. Consequently the tension and the amount of labour-power expended become monstrous, and especially so in the case of the children who are condemned to this torture. Thus Mr. Longe, one of the commissioners, found in Coventry and the neighbourhood boys of from 10 to 15 years employed in driving the ribbon looms, not to mention younger children who had to drive smaller machines. "It is extraordinarily fatiguing work. The boy is a mere substitute for steam-power." (Ch. Empl. Comm. V. Rep. 1866, p. 114, n. 6.) As to the fatal consequences of "this system of slavery," as the official report styles it, see l. c. p. 114 sqq.

them a requirement of their trade. All this was changed by the printing machine. It employs two sort of labourers, one grown up, tenters, the other, boys mostly from 11 to 17 years of age whose sole business is either to spread the sheets of paper under the machine, or to take from it the printed sheets. They perform this weary task, in London especially, for 14, 15, and 16 hours at a stretch, during several days in the week, and frequently for 36 hours, with only 2 hours' rest for meals and sleep![1] A great part of them cannot read, and they are, as a rule, utter savages and very extraordinary creatures. " To qualify them for the work which they have to do, they require no intellectual training; there is little room in it for skill, and less for judgment; their wages, though rather high for boys, do not increase proportionately as they grow up, and the majority of them cannot look for advancement to the better paid and more responsible post of machine minder, because while each machine has but one minder, it has at least two, and often four boys attached to it."[2] As soon as they get too old for such child's work, that is about 17 at the latest, they are discharged from the printing establishments. They become recruits of crime. Several attempts to procure them employment elsewhere, were rendered of no avail by their ignorance and brutality, and by their mental and bodily degradation.

As with the division of labour in the interior of the manufacturing workshops, so it is with the division of labour in the interior of society. So long as handicraft and manufacture form the general groundwork of social production, the subjection of the producer to one branch exclusively, the breaking up of the multifariousness of his employment,[3] is a necessary step in the development. On that ground-work each separate

---

[1] l. c. p. 3, n. 24.

[2] l. c. p. 7, n. 60.

[3] "In some parts of the Highlands of Scotland, not many years ago, every peasant, according to the Statistical Account, made his own shoes of leather tanned by himself. Many a shepherd and cottar too, with his wife and children, appeared at Church in clothes which had been touched by no hands but their own, since they were shorn from the sheep and sown in the flaxfield. In the preparation of these, it is added, scarcely a single article had been purchased, except the awl, needle, thimble, and a very few parts of the iron-work employed in the weaving. The dyes, too, were chiefly extracted by the women from trees, shrubs and herbs." (Dugald Stewart's Works. Hamilton's Ed., Vol. viii., p. 327-328.)

branch of production acquires empirically the form that is technically suited to it, slowly perfects it, and, so soon as a given degree of maturity has been reached, rapidly crystallizes that form. The only thing, that here and there causes a change, besides new raw material supplied by commerce, is the gradual alteration of the instruments of labour. But their form, too, once definitely settled by experience, petrifies, as is proved by their being in many cases handed down in the same form by one generation to another during thousands of years. A characteristic feature is, that, even down into the eighteenth century, the different trades were called " mysteries " (mystères)[1]; into their secrets none but those duly initiated could penetrate. Modern Industry rent the veil that concealed from men their own social process of production, and that turned the various, spontaneously divided branches of production into so many riddles, not only to outsiders, but even to the initiated. The principle which it pursued, of resolving each process into its constituent movements, without any regard to their possible execution by the hand of man, created the new modern science of technology. The varied, apparently unconnected, and petrified forms of the industrial processes now resolved themselves into so many conscious and systematic applications of natural science to the attainment of given useful effects. Technology also discovered the few main fundamental forms of motion, which, despite the diversity of the instruments used, are necessarily taken by every productive action of the human body; just as the science of mechanics sees in the most complicated machinery nothing but the continual repetition of the simple mechanical powers.

Modern Industry never looks upon and treats the existing form of a process as final. The technical basis of that industry is therefore revolutionary, while all earlier modes of production were essentially conservative.[2] By means of machinery,

---

[1] In the celebrated "Livre des métiers" of Etienne Boileau, we find it prescribed that a journeyman on being admitted among the masters had to swear "to love his brethren with brotherly love, to support them in their respective trades, not wilfully to betray the secrets of the trade, and besides, in the interests of all, not to recommend his own wares by calling the attention of the buyer to defects in the articles made by others."

[2] "The bourgeoisie cannot exist without continually revolutionizing the instru-

chemical processes and other methods, it is continually causing changes not only in the technical basis of production, but also in the functions of the labourer, and in the social combinations of the labour-process. At the same time, it thereby also revolutionizes the division of labour within the society, and incessantly launches masses of capital and of workpeople from one branch of production to another. But if Modern Industry, by its very nature, therefore necessitates variation of labour, fluency of function, universal mobility of the labourer, on the other hand, in its capitalistic form, it reproduces the old division of labour with its ossified particularisations. We have seen how this absolute contradiction between the technical necessities of Modern Industry, and the social character inherent in its capitalistic form, dispels all fixity and security in the situation of the labourer; how it constantly threatens, by taking away the instruments of labour, to snatch from his hands his means of subsistence,[1] and, by suppressing his detail-function, to make him superfluous. We have seen, too, how this antagonism vents its rage in the creation of that monstrosity, an industrial reserve army, kept in misery in order to be always at the disposal of capital; in the incessant human sacrifices from among the working class, in the most reckless squandering of labour-power, and in the devastation caused by a social anarchy which turns every economical progress into a social calamity. This is the negative side. But if, on the one hand, variation of work at present imposes itself after the manner of an overpowering natural law, and with the blindly destructive action of a natural law that meets with resist-

ments of production, and thereby the relations of production and all the social relations. Conservation, in an unaltered form, of the old modes of production was on the contrary the first condition of existence for all earlier industrial classes. Constant revolution in production, uninterrupted disturbance of all social conditions, everlasting uncertainty and agitation, distinguish the bourgeois epoch from all earlier ones. All fixed, fast-frozen relations, with their train of ancient and venerable prejudices and opinions, are swept away, all new formed ones become antiquated before they can ossify. All that is solid melts into air, all that is holy is profaned, and man is at last compelled to face with sober senses his real conditions of life, and his relations with his kind. (F. Engels and Karl Marx: Manifest der Kommunistischen Partei. Lond, 1848, p. 5.)

[1] "You take my life
When you do take the means whereby I live." SHAKESPEARE.

ance,[1] at all points, Modern Industry, on the other hand, through its catastrophes imposes the necessity of recognising, as a fundamental law of production, variation of work, consequently fitness of the labourer for varied work, consequently the greatest possible development of his varied aptitudes. It becomes a question of life and death for society to adapt the mode of production to the normal functioning of this law, Modern Industry, indeed, compels society, under penalty of death, to replace the detail-worker of to-day, crippled by life-long repetition of one and the same trivial operation, and thus reduced to the mere fragment of a man, by the fully developed individual, fit for a variety of labours, ready to face any change of production, and to whom the different social functions he performs, are but so many modes of giving free scope to his own natural and acquired powers.

One step already spontaneously taken towards effecting this revolution is the establishment of technical and agricultural schools, and of "écoles d'enseignement professionnel," in which the children of the working-men receive some little instruction in technology and in the practical handling of the various implements of labour. Though the Factory Act, that first and meagre concession wrung from capital, is limited to combining elementary education with work in the factory, there can be no doubt that when the working class comes into power, as inevitably it must, technical instruction, both theoretical and practical, will take its proper place in the working-class schools. There is also no doubt that such revolutionary ferments, the final result of which is the abolition of the old division of labour, are diametrically opposed to the capitalisti form of production, and to the economic status of the labourer corresponding to that form. But the historical development of

---

[1] A French workman, on his return from San-Francisco, writes as follows: "I never could have believed, that I was capable of working at the various occupations I was employed on in California. I was firmly convinced that I was fit for nothing but letter-press printing. . . . Once in the midst of this world of adventurers, who change their occupation as often as they do their shirt, egad, I did as the others. As mining did not turn out remunerative enough, I left it for the town, where in succession I became typographer, slater, plumber, &c. In consequence of thus finding out that I am fit for any sort of work, I feel less of a mollusk and more of a man." (A. Courbon. De l'enseignement professionnel, 2ème ed. p. 50.)

the antagonisms, immanent in a given form of production, is
the only way in which that form of production can be dissolved
and a new form established. "Ne sutor ultra crepidam"—
this nec plus ultra of handicraft wisdom became sheer nonsense, from the moment the watchmaker Watt invented the
steam-engine, the barber Arkwright, the throstle, and the work-
ing-jeweller, Fulton, the steamship.[1]

So long as Factory legislation is confined to regulating the
labour in factories, manufactories, &c., it is regarded as a
mere interference with the exploiting rights of capital. But
when it comes to regulating the so-called "home-labour,"[2] it is
immediately viewed as a direct attack on the patria potestas,
on parental authority. The tender-hearted English Parliament long affected to shrink from taking this step. The force
of facts, however compelled it at last to acknowledge that
modern industry, in overturning the economical foundation on
which was based the traditional family, and the family labour
corresponding to it, had also unloosened all traditional family
ties. The rights of the children had to be proclaimed. The
final report of the Ch. Empl. Comm. of 1866, states: "It is
unhappily, to a painful degree, apparent throughout the whole
of the evidence, that against no persons do the children of both
sexes so much require protection as against their parents."
The system of unlimited exploitation of children's labour in
general and the so-called home-labour in particular is "maintained only because the parents are able, without check or control, to exercise this arbitrary and mischievous power over their
young and tender offspring. . . . . Parents must not
possess the absolute power of making their children mere 'ma-

---

[1] John Bellers, a very phenomenon in the history of political economy, saw most
clearly at the end of the 17th century, the necessity for abolishing the present system
of education and division of labour, which beget hypertrophy and atrophy at the
two opposite extremities of society. Amongst other things he says this: "An idle
learning being little better than the learning of idleness . . . Bodily labour,
it's a primitive institution of God . . . Labour being as proper for the bodies'
health as eating is for its living; for what pains a man saves by ease, he will find
in disease. . . . . Labour adds oyl to the lamp of life, when thinking inflames
it . . . . A childish silly employ" (a warning this, by presentiment, against the
Basedows and their modern imitators) "leaves the children's minds silly." (Proposals for raising a college of industry of all useful trades and husbandry. Lond.,
1696, p. 12, 14, 18.)

[2] This sort of labour goes on mostly in small workshops, as we have seen in the

chines to earn so much weekly wage.' . . . . The children and young persons, therefore, in all such cases may justifiably claim from the legislature, as a natural right, that an exemption should be secured to them, from what destroys prematurely their physical strength, and lowers them in the scale of intellectual and moral beings."[1] It was not, however, the misuse of parental authority that created the capitalistic exploitation, whether direct or indirect, of children's labour; but, on the contrary, it was the capitalistic mode of exploitation which, by sweeping away the economical basis of parental authority, made its exercise degenerate into a mischievous misuse of power. However terrible and disgusting the dissolution, under the capitalist system, of the old family ties may appear, nevertheless, modern industry, by assigning as it does an important part in the process of production, outside the domestic sphere, to women, to young persons, and to children of both sexes, creates a new economical foundation for a higher form of the family and of the relations between the sexes. It is, of course, just as absurd to hold the Teutonic-christian form of the family to be absolute and final as it would be to apply that character to the ancient Roman, the ancient Greek, or the Eastern forms which, moreover, taken together form a series in historic development. Moreover, it is obvious that the fact of the collective working group being composed of individuals of both sexes and all ages, must necessarily, under suitable conditions, become a source of humane development; although in its spontaneously developed, brutal, capitalistic form, where the labourer exists for the process of production, and not the process of production for the labourer, that fact is a pestiferous source of corruption and slavery.[2]

The necessity for a generalization of the Factory Acts, for transforming them from an exceptional law relating to mechanical spinning and weaving—those first creations of ma-

lace-making and straw-plaiting trades, and as could be shown more in detail from the metal trades of Sheffield, Birmingham, &c.

[1] Ch. Empl. Comm., V. Rep., p. xxv., n. 162, and II. Rep., p. xxxviii., n. 285, 289, p. xxv., xxvi., n. 191.

[2] "Factory labour may be as pure and as excellent as domestic labour, and perhaps more so." (Rep. Insp. Fact., 31st October, 1865, p. 127.)

chinery—into a law affecting social production as a whole, arose, as we have seen, from the mode in which Modern Industry was historically developed.   In the rear of that industry, the traditional form of manufacture, of handicraft, and of domestic industry, is entirely revolutionised; manufactures are constantly passing into the factory system, and handicrafts into manufactures; and lastly, the spheres of handicraft and of the domestic industries become, in a, comparatively speaking, wonderfully short time, dens of misery in which capitalistic exploitation obtains free play for the wildest excesses. There are two circumstances that finally turn the scale: first, the constantly recurring experience that capital, so soon as it finds itself subject to legal control at one point, compensates itself all the more recklessly at other points;[1] secondly, the cry of the capitalists for equality in the conditions of competition, *i.e.*, for equal restraint on all exploitation of labour.[2]   On this point let us listen to two heart-broken cries.   Messrs. Cooksley of Bristol, nail and chain, &c., manufacturers, spontaneously introduced the regulations of the Factory Act into their business.   "As the old irregular system prevails in neighbouring works, the Messrs. Cooksley are subject to the disadvantage of having their boys enticed to continue their labour elsewhere after 6 p.m.   'This,' they naturally say, 'is an unjustice and loss to us, as it exhausts a portion of the boy's strength, of which we ought to have the full benefit.'"[3]   Mr. J. Simpson (paper box and bagmaker, London) states before the commissioners of the Ch. Empl. Comm.:   "He would sign any petition for it" (legislative interference) . . . .   "As it was, he always felt restless at night, when he had closed his place, lest others should be working later than him and getting away his orders."[4]   Summarising, the Ch. Empl. Comm. says: "It would be unjust to the larger employers that their factories should be placed under regulation, while the hours of labour in the smaller places in their own branch of business were under no legislative restriction.   And to the injustice arising

---

[1] Rep. Insp. of Fact., 31st October, 1865, p, 27-32.
[2] Numerous instances will he found in Rep. of Insp. of Fact.
[3] Ch. Empl. Comm., V. Rep., p. x., n. 35.
[4] Ch. Empl. Comm., V. Rep., p. ix., n. 28.

from the unfair conditions of competition, in regard to hours, that would be created if the smaller places of work were exempt, would be added the disadvantage to the larger manufacturers, of finding their supply of juvenile and female labour drawn off to the places of work exempt from legislation. Further, a stimulus would be given to the multiplication of the smaller places of work, which are almost invariably the least favourable to the health, comfort, education, and general improvement of the people."[1]

In its final report the Commission proposes to subject to the Factory Act more than 1,400,000 children, young persons, and women, of which number about one half are exploited in small industries and by the so-called home-work.[2] It says, "But if it should seem fit to Parliament to place the whole of that large number of children, young persons and females under the protective legislation above adverted to. . . . it cannot be doubted that such legislation would have a most beneficent effect, not only upon the young and the feeble, who are its more immediate objects, but upon the still larger body of adult workers, who would in all these employments, both directly and indirectly, come immediately under its influence. It would enforce upon them regular and moderate hours; it would lead to their places of work being kept in a healthy and cleanly state; it would therefore husband and improve that store of physical strength on which their own well-being and that of the country so much depends; it would save the rising generation from that over-exertion at an early age which undermines their constitutions and leads to premature decay;

---

[1] l. c., p. xxv., n. 165-167. As to the advantages of large scale, compared with small scale, industries, see Ch. Empl. Comm., III. Rep., p. 13, n. 144, p. 25, n. 121, p. 26, n. 125, p. 27, n. 140, &c.

[2] The trades proposed to be brought under the Act were the following: Lacemaking, stocking-weaving, straw-plaiting, the manufacture of wearing apparel with its numerous subdivisions, artificial flower-making, shoemaking, hat-making, glovemaking, tailoring, all metal works, from blast furnaces down to needleworks, &c., paper-mills, glass-works, tobacco factories, india-rubber works, braid-making (for weaving), hand-carpet-making, umbrella and parasol making, the manufacture of spindles and spools, letter-press printing, book-binding, manufacture of stationery (including paper bags, cards, coloured paper, &c.,) rope-making, manufacture of jet ornaments, brick-making, silk manufacture by hand, Coventry weaving, salt works, tallow chandlers, cement works, sugar refineries, biscuit-making, various industries connected with timber, and other mixed trades.

finally, it would ensure them—at least up to the age of 13—
the opportunity of receiving the elements of education, and
would put an end to that utter ignorance . . . . so faithfully
exhibited in the Reports of our Assistant Commissioners, and
which cannot be regarded without the deepest pain, and a profound sense of national degradation." [1]

The Tory Cabinet announced in the speech from the
Throne, on February 5, 1867, that it had formulated the
recommendations[2] of the Industrial Commission of Inquiry in
"Bills." A new experiment of 20 years' duration at the expense of the working class had been necessary to accomplish
so much. As early as 1840, a Commission of Parliament had
been appointed to inquire into the conditions of child labor.
Its report, as Senior remarks, disclosed "the most frightful
picture of avarice, selfishness and cruelty on the part of
masters and of parents, and of juvenile and infantile misery,
degradation and destruction ever presented. . . . It may
be supposed that it describes the horrors of a past age. But
there is unhappily evidence that those horrors continue as intense as they were. A pamphlet published by Hardwicke
about 2 years ago states that the abuses complained of in
1842, are in full bloom at the present day. It is a strange
proof of the general neglect of the morals and health of the
children of the working class, that this report lay unnoticed
for 20 years, during which the children, 'bred up without the
remotest sign of comprehension as to what is meant by the
term morals, who had neither knowledge, nor religion, nor
natural affection,' were allowed to become the parents of the
present generation."[3]

The social conditions having undergone a change, Parliament could not venture to shelve the demands of the Com-

---

[1] l. c. p. xxv. n. 169.

[2] The Factory Acts Extension Act was passed on August 12, 1867. It regulated
all metal foundries, forges, and manufactures, including machine shops, furthermore
glass, paper, gutta-percha, caoutchouc, tobacco manufactures, printing shops, book
binderies, and finally all workshops employing more than 50 persons.—The Hours of
Labor Regulation Act was passed on August 17, 1867, and regulates the smaller
workshops and the so-called house work.—I revert to these laws, and to the new
Mining Act of 1872 in volume II.

[3] Senior, Social Science Congress, pp. 55–58.

mission of 1862, as it had done those of the Commission of 1840. Hence in 1864, when the Commission had not yet published more than a part of its reports, the earthenware industries (including the potteries, makers of paper-hangings, matches, cartridges, and caps, and fustian cutters were made subject to the Acts in force in the textile industries. In the speech from the Throne, on 5th February, 1867, the Tory Cabinet of the day announced the introduction of Bills, founded on the final recommendations of the Commission, which had completed its labours in 1866.

On the 15th August, 1867, the Factory Acts Extension Act, and on the 21st August, the Workshops' Regulation Act received the Royal Assent; the former Act having reference to large industries, the latter to small.

The former applies to blast-furnaces, iron and copper mills, foundries, machine shops, metal manufactories, gutta-percha works, paper mills, glass works, tobacco manufactories, letter-press printing (including newspapers) book-binding, in short to all industrial establishments of the above kind, in which 50 individuals or more are occupied simultaneously, and for not less than 100 days during the year.

To give an idea of the extent of the sphere embraced by the Workshops' Regulation Act in its application, we cite from its interpretation clause, the following passages:

"*Handicraft* shall mean any manual labour exercised by way of trade, or for purposes of gain, or incidental to, the making any article or part of an article, or in, or incidental to, the altering, repairing, ornamenting, finishing, or otherwise adapting for sale any article."

"'*Workshop* shall mean any room or place whatever in the open air or under cover, in which any handicraft is carried on by any child, young person, or woman, and to which and over which the person by whom such child, young person, or woman is employed, has the right of access and control."

"*Employed* shall mean occupied in any handicraft, whether for wages or not, under a master or under a parent as herein defined."

"*Parent* shall mean parent, guardian, or person, having

the custody of, or control over, any . . . child or young person."

Clause 7, which imposes a penalty for employment of children, young persons, and women, contrary to the provisions of the Act, subjects to fines, not only the occupier of the workshops, whether parent or not, but even "the parent of, or the person deriving any direct benefit from the labour of, or having the control over, the child, young person or woman."

The Factory Acts Extension Act, which affects the large establishments, derogates from the Factory Act by a crowd of vicious exceptions and cowardly compromises with the masters.

The Workshops' Regulation Act, wretched in all its details, remained a dead letter in the hands of the municipal and local authorities who were charged with its execution. When, in 1871, Parliament withdrew from them this power, in order to confer it on the Factory Inspectors, to whose province it thus added by a single stroke more than one hundred thousand workshops, and three hundred brickworks, care was taken at the same time not to add more than eight assistants to their already undermanned staff.[1]

What strikes us, then, in the English legislation of 1867, is, on the one hand, the necessity imposed on the parliament of the ruling classes, of adopting in principle measures so extraordinary, and on so great a scale, against the excesses of capitalistic exploitation; and on the other hand, the hesitation, the repugnance, and the bad faith, with which it lent itself to the task of carrying those measures into practice.

The Inquiry Commission of 1862 also proposed a new regulation of the mining industry, an industry distinguished from others by the exceptional characteristic that the interests of landlord and capitalist there join hands. The antagonism of these two interests had been favourable to Factory legislation, while on the other hand the absence of that antagonism is sufficient to explain the delays and chicanery of the legislation on mines.

[1] The "personnel" of this staff consisted of 2 inspectors, 2 assistant inspectors and 41 sub-inspectors. Eight additional sub-inspectors were appointed in 1871. The total cost of administering the Acts in England, Scotland, and Ireland amounted for the year 1871-72 to no more than £25,347, inclusive of the law expenses incurred by prosecutions of offending masters.

The Inquiry Commission of 1840 had made revelations so terrible, so shocking, and creating such a scandal all over Europe, that to salve its conscience Parliament passed the Mining Act of 1842, in which it limited itself to forbidding the employment underground in mines of children under 10 years of age and females.

Then another Act, The Mines' Inspecting Act of 1860, provides that mines shall be inspected by public officers nominated specially for that purpose, and that boys between the ages of 10 and 12 years shall not be employed, unless they have a school certificate, or go to school for a certain number of hours. This Act was a complete dead letter owing to the ridiculously small number of inspectors, the meagreness of their powers, and other causes that will become apparent as we proceed.

One of the most recent blue books on mines is the "Report from the Select Committee on Mines, together with &c. Evidence, 23rd July, 1866." This Report is the work of a Parliamentary Committee selected from members of the House of Commons, and authorised to summon and examine witnesses. It is a thick folio volume in which the Report itself occupies only five lines to this effect: that the committee has nothing to say, and that more witnesses must be examined!

The mode of examining the witnesses reminds one of the cross-examination of witnesses in English courts of justice, where the advocate tries, by means of impudent, unexpected, equivocal and involved questions, put without connection, to intimidate, surprise, and confound the witness, and to give a forced meaning to the answers extorted from him. In this inquiry the members of the committee themselves are the cross-examiners, and among them are to be found both mine owners and mine exploiters; the witnesses are mostly working coal-miners. The whole farce is too characteristic of the spirit of capital, not to call for a few extracts from this Report. For the sake of conciseness I have classified them. I may also add that every question and its answer are numbered in the English Blue Books.

I. EMPLOYMENT IN MINES OF BOYS OF 10 YEARS AND UP-
WARDS.—In the mines the work, inclusive of going and returning, usually lasts 14 or 15 hours, sometimes even from 3,
4, and 5 o'clock a.m., till 5 and 6 o'clock p.m., (n. 6., 452, 83).
The adults work in two shifts, of eight hours each; but there
is no alteration with the boys, on account of the expense
(n. 80, 203, 204.) The younger boys are chiefly employed in
opening and shutting the ventilating doors in the various parts
of the mine; the older ones are employed on heavier work, in
carrying coal, &c. (n. 122, 739, 1747). They work these long
hours underground until their 18th or 22nd year, when they
are put to miners work proper. (n. 161.) Children and
young persons are at present worse treated, and harder worked
than at any previous period (n. 1663—1667). And now
Hussey Vivian (himself an exploiter of mines) asks: "Would
not the opinion of the workman depend upon the poverty of
the workman's family?" Mr. Bruce: "Do you not think it
would be a very hard case, where a parent had been injured,
or where he was sickly, or where a father was dead, and there
was only a mother, to prevent a child between 12 and 14
earning 1s. 7d. a day for the good of the family? . . .
You must lay down a general rule? . . . Are you prepared to recommend legislation which would prevent the employment of children under 12 and 14, whatever the state of
their parents might be?" "Yes." (ns. 107-110). Vivian:
"Supposing that an enactment were passed preventing the employment of children under the age of 14, would it not be
probable that . . . the parents of children would seek
employment for their children in other directions, for instance,
in manufacture?" "Not generally I think," (n. 174). Kinnaird: "Some of the boys are keepers of doors?" "Yes." "Is
there not generally a very great draught every time you open
a door or close it?" "Yes, generally there is." "It sounds
a very easy thing, but it is in fact rather a painful one?"
"He is imprisoned there just the same as if he was in a cell
of a gaol." Bourgeois Vivian: "Whenever a boy is furnished
with a lamp cannot he read?" "Yes, he can read, if he finds
himself in candles . . . I suppose he would be found

fault with if he were discovered reading; he is there to mind
his business, he has a duty to perform, and he has to attend
to it in the first place, and I do not think it would be allowed
down the pit." (ns. 139, 141, 143, 158, 160.)

II. EDUCATION.—The working miners want a law for the
compulsory education of their children, as in factories. They
declare the clauses of the Act of 1860, which require a school
certificate to be obtained before employing boys of 10 and 12
years of age, to be quite illusory. The examination of
the witnesses on this subject is truly droll. "Is it (the Act)
required more against the masters or against the parents?"
"It is required against both I think." "You cannot say
whether it is required against one more than against the
other?" "No; I can hardly answer that question." (ns. 115,
116.) "Does there appear to be any desire on the part of the
employers that the boys should have such hours as to enable
them to go to school?" "No; the hours are never shortened
for that purpose." (n. 137.) Mr. Kinnaird: "Should you say
that the colliers generally improve their education; have you
any instances of men who have, since they began to work,
greatly improved their education, or do they not rather go
back, and lose any advantage that they may have gained?"
"They generally become worse: they do not improve; they
acquire bad habits; they get on to drinking and gambling and
such like, and they go completely to wreck," (n. 211). "Do
they make any attempt of the kind (for providing instruction)
by having schools at night?" "There are few collieries where
night schools are held, and perhaps at those collieries a few
boys do go to those schools; but they are so physically exhausted that it is to no purpose that they go there." (n. 454.)
"You are then," concludes the bourgeois, "against education?"
"Most certainly not; but," &c. (n. 443.) "But are they (the
employers) not compelled to demand them" (school certificates)? "By law they are; but I am not aware that they are
demanded by the employers." "Then it is your opinion, that
this provision of the Act as to requiring certificates, is not generally carried out in the collieries?" "It is not carried out."
(ns. 443, 444.) "Do the men take a great interest in this

question" (of education) ? "The majority of them do." (n. 717.) "Are they very anxious to see the law enforced?" "The majority are." (n. 718.) "Do you think that in this country any law that you pass . . . can really be effectual unless the population themselves assist in putting it into operation?" "Many a man might wish to object to employing a boy, but he would perhaps become marked by it." (n. 720.) "Marked by whom?" "By his employers." (n. 721.) "Do you think that the employers would find any fault with a man who obeyed the law. . . . ?" "I believe they would." (n. 722.) "Have you ever heard of any workman objecting to employ a boy between 10 and 12, who could not write or read?" "It is not left to men's option." (n. 123.) "Would you call for the interference of Parliament?" "I think that if anything effectual is to be done in the education of the colliers' children, it will have to be made compulsory by Act of Parliament." (n. 1634.) "Would you lay that obligation upon the colliers only, of all the work people of Great Britain?" "I came to speak for the colliers." (n. 1636.) "Why should you distinguish them (colliery boys) from other boys?" "Because I think they are an exception to the rule." (n. 1638.) "In what respect?" "In a physical respect." (n. 1639.) "Why should education be more valuable to them than to other classes of lads?" "I do not know that it is more valuable; but through the over-exertion in mines there is less chance for the boys that are employed there to get education, either at Sunday schools, or at day schools." (n. 1640.) "It is impossible to look at a question of this sort absolutely by itself?" (n. 1644.) "Is there a sufficiency of schools?"—"No." . . . (n. 1646.) "If the state were to require that every child should be sent to school, would there be schools for the children to go to?" "No; but I think if the circumstances were to spring up, the schools would be forthcoming." (n. 1647.) "Some of them (the boys) cannot read and write at all, I suppose?" "The majority cannot. . . . The majority of the men themselves cannot." (ns. 705, 725.)

III. EMPLOYMENT OF WOMEN.—Since 1842 women are no

more employed underground, but are occupied on the surface in loading the coal, &c., in drawing the tubs to the canals and railway waggons, in sorting, &c. Their numbers have considerably increased during the last three or four years. (n. 1727.) They are mostly the wives, daughters, and widows of the working miners, and their ages range from 12 to 50 or 60 years. (ns. 645, 1779.) "What is the feeling among the working miners as to the employment of women?" "I think they generally condemn it." (n. 648.) "What objection do you see to it?" "I think it is degrading to the sex." (n. 649.) "There is a peculiarity of dress?" "Yes . . . it is rather a man's dress, and I believe in some cases, it drowns all sense of decency." "Do the women smoke?" "Some do." "And I suppose it is very dirty work?" "Very dirty." "They get black and grimy?" "As black as those who are down the mines . . . I believe that a woman having children, (and there are plenty on the banks that have) cannot do her duty to her children." (ns. 650-654, 701.) "Do you think that those widows could get employment anywhere else, which would bring them in as much wages as that (from 8s. to 10s. a week)?" "I cannot speak to that." (n. 709.) "You would still be prepared, would you," (flint-hearted fellow!) "to prevent their obtaining a livelihood by these means?" "I would." (n. 710.) "What is the general feeling in the district . . . as to the employment of women?" "The feeling is that it is degrading; and we wish as miners to have more respect to the fair sex than to see them placed on the pit bank. . . . Some part of the work is very hard; some of these girls have raised as much as 10 tons of stuff a day." (ns. 1715, 1717.) "Do you think that the women employed about the collieries are less moral than the women employed in the factories?" " . . the percentage of bad ones may be a little more . . . than with the girls in the factories." (n. 1237.) "But you are not quite satisfied with the state of morality in the factories?" "No." (n. 1733.) "Would you prohibit the employment of women in factories also?" "No, I would not." (n. 1734.) "Why not?" "I think it a more honourable occupation for them in the mills." (n. 1735.) "Still it is injurious to their morality, you think?" "Not so much as working on the pit bank; but it is more on the social position I take it; I do not take it on its moral ground alone. The degradation, in its social bearing on the girls, is deplorable in the extreme. When these 400 or 500 girls become colliers' wives, the men suffer greatly from this degradation, and it causes them to leave their homes and drink." (n. 1736.) "You would be obliged to stop the employment of women in the ironworks as well, would you not, if you stopped it in the collieries?" "I cannot speak for any other trade." (n. 1737.) "Can you see any difference in the circumstances of women employed in iron-works, and the circumstances of women employed above ground in collieries?" "I have not ascertained anything as to that." (n. 1740.) "Can you see anything that makes a distinction between one class and the other?" "I have not ascertained that, but I know from house to house visitation, that it is a deplorable state of things in our district. . . ." (n. 1741.) "Would you interfere in every case with the employment of women where that employment was degrading?" "It would become injurious, I think, in this way: the best feelings of Englishmen have been gained from the instruction of a mother . . . " (n. 1750.) "That equally applies to agricultural employments, does it not?" "Yes, but that is only for two seasons, and we have work all the four seasons." (n. 1751.) "They often work day and night, wet through to the skin, their constitution undermined and their health ruined." "You have not inquired into that subject perhaps?" "I have certainly taken note of it as I have gone along, and certainly I have seen nothing parallel to the effects of the employment of women on the pit bank. . . . It is the work of a man . . . a strong man." (ns. 1753, 1793, 1794.) "Your feeling upon the whole subject is that the better class of colliers who desire to raise themselves and humanise themselves, instead of deriving help from the women, are pulled down by them?" "Yes." (n. 1808.) After some further crooked questions from these bourgeois, the secret of their "sympathy" for widows, poor families, &c., comes out at last. "The coal proprietor appoints certain gentlemen to take the oversight of the workings, and it is their policy, in order to receive approbation, to place things on the most economical basis they can, and these girls are employed at from 1s. up to 1s. 6d. a day, where a man at the rate of 2s. 6d. a day would have to be employed." (n. 1816.)

IV. CORONER'S INQUESTS.—"With regard to coroner's inquests in your district, have the workmen confidence in the proceedings at these inquests when accidents occur?" "No; they have not." (n. 360.) "Why not?" "Chiefly because the men who are generally chosen, are men who know nothing about mines and such like." "Are not workmen summoned at all upon the juries?" "Never but as witnesses to my knowledge." "Who are the people who are generally summoned upon these juries?" "Generally tradesmen in the neighborhood . . . from their circumstances they are sometimes liable to be influenced by their employers . . . the owners of the works. They are generally men who have no knowledge, and can scarcely understand the witnesses who are called before them, and the terms which are used and such like." "Would you have the jury composed of persons who had been employed in mining?" "Yes, partly . . . they (the workmen) think that the verdict is not in accordance with the evidence given generally. "(ns. 361, 364, 366, 368, 371, 375.) "One great object in summoning a jury is to have an impartial one, is it not?" "Yes, I should think so." "Do you think that the juries would be impartial if they were composed to a considerable extent of workmen?" "I cannot see any motive which the workmen would have to act partially . . . they necessarily have a better knowledge of the operations in connection with the mine." "You do not think there would be a tendency on the part of the workmen to return unfairly severe verdicts?" "No, I think not." (ns. 378, 379, 380.)

V. FALSE WEIGHTS AND MEASURES.—The workmen demand to be paid weekly instead of fortnightly, and by weight instead of by cubical contents of the tubs; they also demand protection against the use of false weights, &c. (n. 1071.) "If the tubs were fraudulently increased, a man could discontinue working by giving 14 days' notice?" "But if he goes to another place, there is the same thing going on there." (n. 1071.) "But he can leave that place where the wrong has been committed?" "It is general; wherever he goes, he has to submit to it." (n. 1072.) "Could a man leave by giving 14 days' notice?" "Yes," (n. 1073.) And yet they are not satisfied!

VI. INSPECTION OF MINES.—Casualties from explosions are not the only things the workmen suffer from. (n. 234, sqq.) "Our men complained very much of the bad ventilation of the collieries . . . the ventilation is so bad in general that the men can scarcely breathe; they are quite unfit for employment of any kind after they have been for a length of time in connection with their work; indeed, just at the part of the mine where I am working, men have been obliged to leave their employment and come home in consequence of that . . . some of them have been out of work for weeks just in consequence of the bad state of the ventilation where there is not explosive gas . . . there is plenty of air generally in the main courses, yet pains are not taken to get air into the workings where men are working." "Why do you not apply to the inspector?" "To tell the truth there are many men who are timid on that point; there have been cases of men being sacrificed and losing their employment in consequence of applying to the inspector." "Why; is he a marked man for having complained?" "Yes." "And he finds it difficult to get employment in another mine?" "Yes." "Do you think the mines in your neighborhood are sufficiently inspected to insure a compliance with the provisions of the Act?" "No; they are not inspected at all . . . the inspector has been down just once in the pit, and it has been going seven years. . . . In the district to which I belong there are not a sufficient number of inspectors. We have one old man more than 70 years of age to inspect more than 130 collieries." "You wish to have a class of sub-inspectors?" "Yes." (ns. 234, 241, 251, 254, 274, 275, 554, 276, 293.) "But do you think it would be possible for government to maintain such an army of inspectors as would be necessary to do all that you want them to do, without information from the men ?" "No, I should think it would be next to impossible." . . . "It would be desirable the inspectors should come oftener ?" "Yes, and without being sent for." (n. 280, 277.) "Do you not think that the effect of having these inspectors examining the collieries so frequently would be to shift the responsibility (!) of supplying proper ventilation from the owners of the collieries to the Government officials ?" "No, I do not think that, I think that they should make it their business to enforce the Acts which are already in existence." (n. 285.) "When you speak of sub-inspectors, do you mean men at a less salary, and of an inferior stamp to the present inspectors ?" "I would not have them inferior, if you could get them otherwise." (n. 294.) "Do you merely want more inspectors, or do you want a lower class of men as an inspector ?" "A man who would knock about, and see that things are kept right; a man who would not be afraid of himself." (n. 295.) "If you obtained your wish in getting an inferior class of inspectors appointed, do you think there would be no danger from want of skill, &c. ?" "I think not, I think that the Government would see after that, and have proper men in that position." (n. 297.) This kind of examination becomes at last too much even for the chairman of the committee, and he interrupts with the observation: "You want a class of men who would look into all the details of the mine, and would go into all the holes and corners, and go into the real facts . . . they would report to the chief inspector, who would then bring his scientific knowledge to bear on the facts they have stated ?" (ns. 298, 299.) "Would it not entail very great expense if all these old workings were kept ventilated ?" "Yes, expense might be incurred, but life would be at the same time protected." (n. 531.) A working miner objects to the 17th section of the Act of 1860; he says, "At the present time, if the inspector of mines finds a part of the mine unfit to work in, he has to report it to the mine owner and the Home Secretary. After doing that, there is given to the owner 20 days to look over the matter; at the end of 20 days he has the power to refuse making any alteration in the mine; but, when he refuses, the mine owner writes to the Home Secretary, at the same time nominating five engineers, and from those five engineers named by the mine owner himself, the Home Secretary appoints one, I think, as arbitrator, or appoints arbitrators from them; now we think in that case the mine owner virtually appoints his own arbitrator." (n. 581.) Bourgeois examiner, himself a mine owner: "But . . . is this a merely speculative objection?" (n. 586.) "Then you have a very poor opinion of the integrity of mining engineers?" "It is most certainly unjust and inequitable." (n. 588.) "Do not mining engineers possess a sort of public character, and do not you think that they are above making such a partial decision as you apprehend?" "I do not wish to answer such a question as that with respect to the personal character of those men. I believe that in many cases they would act very partially indeed, and that it ought not to be in their hands to do so, where men's lives are at stake." (n. 589.) This same bourgeois is not ashamed to put this question: "Do you not think that the mine owner also suffers loss from an explosion?" Finally, "Are not you workmen in Lancashire able to take care of your own interests without calling in the Government to help you?" "No." (n. 1042.)

In the year 1865 there were 3217 coal mines in Great Britain, and 12 inspectors. A Yorkshire mine owner himself calculates ("Times," 26th January, 1867), that putting on one side their office work, which absorbs all their time, each mine can be visited but once in ten years by an inspector. No wonder that explosions have increased progressively, both in number and extent (sometimes with a loss of 200-300 men), during the last ten years.

The very defective Act, passed in 1872, is the first that regulates the hours of labour of the children employed in mines, and makes exploiters and owners, to a certain extent, responsible for so-called accidents.

The Royal Commission appointed in 1867, to inquire into the employment in agriculture of children, young persons, and women, has published some very important reports. Several attempts to apply the principles of the Factory Acts, but in a modified form, to agriculture have been made, but have so far resulted in complete failure. All that I wish to draw attention to here is the existence of an irresistible tendency towards the general application of those principles.

If the general extension of factory legislation to all trades for the purpose of protecting the working class both in mind and body has become inevitable, on the other hand, as we have already pointed out, that extension hastens on the general conversion of numerous isolated small industries into a few combined industries carried on upon a large scale; it therefore accelerates the concentration of capital and the exclusive predominance of the factory system. It destroys both the ancient and the transitional forms, behind which the dominion of capital is still in part concealed, and replaces them by the direct and open sway of capital; but thereby it also generalises the direct opposition to this sway. While in each individual workshop it enforces uniformity, regularity, order, and economy, it increases by the immense spur which the limitation and regulation of the working day give to technical improvement, the anarchy and the catastrophes of capitalist production as a whole, the intensity of labour, and the competition of machinery with the labourer. By the destruction of petty and domestic industries it destroys the last resort of the "redundant population," and with it the sole remaining safety-valve of the whole social mechanism. By maturing the material conditions, and the combination on a social scale of the processes of production, it matures the contradictions and antagonisms of the capitalist form of production, and thereby provides, along with the elements for the formation of a new society, the forces for exploding the old one.[1]

[1] Robert Owen, the father of Co-operative Factories and Stores, but who, as before remarked, in no way shared the illusions of his followers with regard to the bearing of these isolated elements of transformation, not only practically made the factory system the sole foundation of his experiments, but also declared that system to be theoretically the starting point of the social revolution. Herr Vissering, Professor of Political Economy in the University of Leyden, appears to have a suspicion of this when, in his "Handboek van Praktische Staatshuishoudkunde, 1860-62," which reproduces all the platitudes of vulgar economy, he strongly supports handicrafts against the factory system. [Note to the 4th German edition.—The new juristic abortion created by English legislation in the mutually contradictory Factory Acts,

SECTION 10.—MODERN INDUSTRY AND AGRICULTURE.

The revolution called forth by modern industry in agriculture, and in the social relations of agricultural producers, will be investigated later on. In this place we shall merely indicate a few results by way of anticipation. If the use of machinery in agriculture is for the most part free from the injurious physical effect it has on the factory operative,[1] its action in superseding the labourers is more intense, and finds less resistance, as we shall see later in detail. In the counties of Cambridge and Suffolk, for example, the area of cultivated land has extended very much within the last 20 years (up to 1868), while in the same period the rural population has diminished, not only relatively, but absolutely. In the United States it is as yet only virtually that agricultural machines

Fatcory Extension Act, and Workshop Act, became finally unbearable, and in consequence, the Factory and Workshops Act of 1878 made this entire legislation into a new code. Of course, we cannot give an exhaustive critique of the present industrial code of England in this place. The following notes may suffice; The Act comprizes (1) Textile mills. Here everything remains about as it was. Working time allowed for children over 10 years, 5½ hours per day, or 6 hours per day and Saturday off. For young persons and women, 10 hours on 5 days, and no more than 6½ hours on Saturday. (2) Other than textile mills. Here the rules are more nearly approximated to those of class (1), but still many of them permit exceptions favoring the capitalist, which may even be extended in special cases by the permission of the Minister of the Interior. (3) Workshops, defined about the same as in the former act. So far as children, young persons, or women are employed in them, workshops are placed in about the same class with other than textile mills, but again with special favors. (4) Workshops, in which no children or young persons, but only persons of both sexes over 18 years are employed. This class enjoys still other favors. (5) Domestic Workshops, in which only members of the family are employed in the home of the family. Here the rules are still more elastic, with the additional restriction that the inspector must not enter rooms serving at the same time as homes without the permission of the Minister or the Judge. Finally, the unconditional surrender of straw plating, lace making, glove making to the family circle. Yet, with all its shortcomings, this law, and the factory laws of the Swiss Confederation passed March 23, 1877, are by far the best on this subject. A comparison of these two codes is particularly interesting, because it reveals the advantages and disadvantages of the two different methods of legislation, the English, "historical" method interfering from case to case, and the continental, more generalising method built upon the traditions of the French revolution. Unfortunately, the English code is still largely a dead letter on account of the lack of inspectors.—F. E.]

[1] A detailed description of the machinery employed in English agriculture is found in "The Agricultural Implements and Machines of England," by Dr. W. Hamm. Second edition, 1856. In a sketch of the evolution of English agriculture Mr. Hamm follows too narrowly the ideas of Mr. Leonce de Lavergne.—[Note to the 4th German edition. —This is now obsolete, of course.—F. E.]

replace labourers; in other words, they allow of the cultivation by the farmer of a larger surface, but do not actually
expel the labourers employed. In 1861 the number of persons occupied in England and Wales in the manufacture of
agricultural machines was 1034, whilst the number of agricultural labourers employed in the use of agricultural machines and steam engines did not exceed 1205.

In the sphere of agriculture, modern industry has a more
revolutionary effect than elsewhere, for this reason, that it
annihilates the peasant, that bulwark of the old society, and
replaces him by the wage labourer. Thus the desire for social
changes, and the class antagonisms are brought to the same
level in the country as in the towns. The irrational, old fashioned methods of agriculture are replaced by scientific ones.
Capitalist production completely tears asunder the old bond
of union which held together agriculture and manufacture in
their infancy. But at the same time it creates the material
conditions for a higher synthesis in the future, viz., the union
of agriculture and industry on the basis of the more perfected
forms they have each acquired during their temporary separation. Capitalist production, by collecting the population in
great centres, and causing an ever increasing preponderance
of town population, on the one hand concentrates the historical
motive-power of society; on the other hand, it disturbs the circulation of matter between man and the soil, *i.e.,* prevents the
return to the soil of its elements consumed by man in the form
of food and clothing; it therefore violates the conditions necessary to lasting fertility of the soil. By this action it destroys
at the same time the health of the town labourer and the intellectual life of the rural labourer.[1] But while upsetting the
naturally grown conditions for the maintenance of that circulation of matter, it imperiously calls for its restoration as a

[1] "You divide the people into two hostile camps of clownish boors and emascu-
lated dwarfs. Good heavens! a nation divided into agricultural and commercial
interests, calling itself sane; nay, styling itself enlightened and civilized, not only
in spite of, but in consequence of this monstrous and unnatural division." (David
Urquhart, l. c., p. 119.) This passage shows, at one and the same time, the
strength and the weakness of that kind of criticism which knows how to judge and
condemn the present, but not how to comprehend it.

system, as a regulating law of social production, and under a form appropriate to the full development of the human race. In agriculture as in manufacture, the transformation of production under the sway of capital, means, at the same time, the martyrdom of the producer; the instrument of labour becomes the means of enslaving, exploiting, and impoverishing the labourer; the social combination and organization of labour-processes is turned into an organised mode of crushing out the workman's individual vitality, freedom, and independence. The dispersion of the rural labourers over larger areas breaks their power of resistance while concentration increases that of the town operatives. In modern agriculture, as in the urban industries, the increased productiveness and quantity of the labour set in motion are bought at the cost of laying waste and consuming by disease labour-power itself. Moreover, all progress in capitalistic agriculture is a progress in the art, not only of robbing the labourer, but of robbing the soil; all progress in increasing the fertility of the soil for a given time, is a progress towards ruining the lasting sources of that fertility. The more a country starts its development on the foundation of modern industry, like the United States, for example, the more rapid is this process of destruction.[1]

[1] See Liebig: "Die Chemie in ihrer Anwendung auf Agricultur und Physiologie, 7. Auflage, 1862," and especially the "Einleitung in die Naturgesetze des Feldbaus," in the 1st Volume. To have developed from the point of view of natural science, the negative, *i.e.*, destructive side of modern agriculture, is one of Liebig's immortal merits. His summary, too, of the history of agriculture, although not free from gross errors, contains flashes of light. It is, however, to be regretted that he ventures on such hap-hazard assertions as the following: "By greater pulverising and more frequent ploughing, the circulation of air in the interior of porous soil is aided, and the surface exposed to the action of the atmosphere is increased and renewed; but it is easily seen that the increased yield of the land cannot be proportional to the labour spent on that land, but increases in a much smaller proportion. This law," adds Liebig, "was first enunciated by John Stuart Mill in his 'Principles of Pol. Econ.', Vol I., p. 17, as follows: 'That the produce of land increases, *cæteris paribus*, in a diminishing ratio to the increase of the labourers employed" (Mill here introduces in an erroneous form the law enunciated by Ricardo's school, for since the 'decrease of the labourers employed,' kept even pace in England with the advance of agriculture, the law discovered in, and applied to, England, could have no application to that country, at all events), "is the universal law of agricultural industry.' This is very remarkable, since Mill was ignorant of the reason for this law." (Liebig, l. c., Bd. I., p. 143 and Note.) Apart from Liebig's wrong interpretation of the word "labour," by which word he understands something quite different from what political economy does, it is, in any case, "very remarkable" that he should

Capitalist production, therefore, developes technology, and the combining together of various processes into a social whole, only by sapping the original sources of all wealth—the soil and the labourer.

make Mr. John Stuart Mill the first propounder of a theory which was first published by James Anderson in A. Smith's days, and was repeated in various works down to the beginning of the 19th century; a theory which Malthus, that master in plagiarism (the whole of his population theory is a shameless plagiarism), appropriated to himself in 1815; which West developed at the same time as, and independently of, Anderson; which in the year 1817 was connected by Ricardo with the general theory of value, then made the round of the world as Ricardo's theory, and in 1820 was vulgarised by James Mill, the father of John Stuart Mill; and which, finally, was reproduced by John Stuart Mill and others, as a dogma already quite common-place, and known to every school-boy. It cannot be denied that John Stuart Mill owes his, at all events, "remarkable" authority almost entirely to such *quid-pro-quos.*

PART V.

THE PRODUCTION OF ABSOLUTE AND OF RELATIVE SURPLUS-VALUE.

CHAPTER XVI.

ABSOLUTE AND RELATIVE SURPLUS-VALUE.

IN considering the labour-process, we began (see Chapter VII.) by treating it in the abstract, apart from its historical forms, as a process between man and nature. We there stated, p. 201: "If we examine the whole labour-process, from the point of view of its result, it is plain that both the instruments and the subject of labour are means of production, and that the labour itself is productive labour." And in Note 2, same page, we further added: "This method of determining, from the standpoint of the labour-process alone, what is productive labour, is by no means directly applicable to the case of the capitalist process of production." We now proceed to the further development of this subject.

So far as the labour-process is purely individual, one and the same labourer unites in himself all the functions, that later on become separated. When an individual appropriates natural objects for his livelihood, no one controls him but himself. Afterwards he is controlled by others. A single man cannot operate upon nature without calling his own muscles into play under the control of his own brain. As in the natural body head and hand wait upon each other, so the labour-process unites the labour of the hand with that of the head. Later on they part company and even become deadly foes. The product

557

ceases to be the direct product of the individual, and becomes a social product, produced in common by a collective labourer, *i.e.,* by a combination of workmen, each of whom takes only a part, greater or less, in the manipulation of the subject of their labour. As the co-operative character of the labour-process becomes more and more marked, so, as a necessary consequence, does our notion of productive labour, and of its agent the productive labourer, become extended. In order to labour productively, it is no longer necessary for you to do manual work yourself; enough, if you are an organ of the collective labourer, and perform one of its subordinate functions. The first definition given above of productive labour, a definition deduced from the very nature of the production of material objects, still remains correct for the collective labourer, considered as a whole. But it no longer holds good for each member taken individually.

On the other hand, however, our notion of productive labour becomes narrowed. Capitalist production is not merely the production of commodities, it is essentially the production of surplus-value. The labourer produces, not for himself, but for capital. It no longer suffices, therefore, that he should simply produce. He must produce surplus-value. That labourer alone is productive, who produces surplus-value for the capitalist, and thus works for the self-expansion of capital. If we may take an example from outside the sphere of production of material objects, a schoolmaster is a productive labourer, when, in addition to belabouring the heads of his scholars, he works like a horse to enrich the school proprietor. That the latter has laid out his capital in a teaching factory, instead of in a sausage factory, does not alter the relation. Hence the notion of a productive labourer implies not merely a relation between work and useful effect, between labourer and product of labour, but also a specific, social relation of production, a relation that has sprung up historically and stamps the labourer as the direct means of creating surplus-value. To be a productive labourer is, therefore, not a piece of luck, but a misfortune. In Book IV. which treats of the history of the theory, it will be more clearly seen, that the production of surplus-value has at all times been made, by classical political economists, the distinguishing characteristic of the productive labourer. Hence their definition of a productive labourer changes with their comprehension of the nature of surplus-value. Thus the Physiocrats insist that only agricultural labour is productive, since that alone, they say, yields a surplus-value. And they say so because, with them, surplus-value has no existence except in the form of rent.

The prolongation of the working day beyond the point at which the labourer would have produced just an equivalent for the value of his labour-power, and the appropriation of that surplus-labour by capital, this is production of absolute surplus-value. It forms the general groundwork of the capitalist system, and the starting point for the production of relative surplus-value. The latter presupposes that the working day is already divided into two parts, necessary labour, and surplus-labour. In order to prolong the surplus-labour, the necessary labour is shortened by methods whereby the equivalent for the wages is produced in less time. The production of absolute surplus-value turns exclusively upon the length of the working day; the production of relative surplus-value, revolutionises out and out the technical processes of labour, and the composition of society. It therefore presupposes a specific mode, the capitalist mode of production, a mode which, along with its methods, means, and conditions, arises and developes itself spontaneously on the foundation afforded by the formal subjection of labour to capital In the course of this development, the formal subjection is replaced by the real subjection of labour to capital.

It will suffice merely to refer to certain intermediate forms, in which surplus-labour is not extorted by direct compulsion from the producer, nor the producer himself yet formally subjected to capital In such forms capital has not yet acquired the direct control of the labour-process. By the side of independent producers who carry on their handicrafts and agriculture in the traditional old-fashioned way, there stands the usurer or the merchant, with his usurer's capital or merchant's capital, feeding on them like a parasite. The predominance, in a society, of this form of exploitation excludes the capitalist mode of production; to which mode, however, this form may serve as a transition, as it did towards the close of the Middle Ages. Finally, as is shown by modern "domestic industry," some intermediate forms are here and there reproduced in the background of Modern Industry, though their physiognomy is totally changed.

If, on the one hand, the mere formal subjection of labour to capital suffices for the production of absolute surplus-value, if, *e.g.,* it is sufficient that handicraftsmen who previously worked on their own account, or as apprentices of a master, should become wage labourers under the direct control of a capitalist; so, on the other hand, we have seen, how the methods of producing relative surplus-value, are, at the same time, methods of producing absolute surplus-value. Nay, more, the excessive prolongation of the working day turned out to be the peculiar product of Modern Industry. Generally speaking, the specifically capitalist mode of production ceases to be a mere means of producing relative surplus-value, so soon as that mode has conquered an entire branch of production; and still more so, so soon as it has conquered all the important branches. It then becomes the general, socially predominant form of production. As a special method of producing relative surplus-value, it remains effective only, first, in so far as it seizes upon industries that previously were only formally subject to capital, that is, so far as it is propagandist; secondly, in so far as the industries that have been taken over by it, continue to be revolutionized by changes in the methods of production.

From one standpoint, any distinction between absolute and relative surplus-value appears illusory. Relative surplus-value is absolute, since it compels the absolute prolongation of the working day beyond the labour-time necessary to the existence of the labourer himself Absolute surplus-value is relative, since it makes necessary such a development of the productiveness of labour, as will allow of the necessary labour-time being confined to a portion of the working day. But if we keep in mind the behaviour of surplus-value, this appearance of identity vanishes. Once the capitalist mode of production established and become general, the difference between absolute and relative surplus-value makes itself felt, whenever there is a question of raising the rate of surplus-value. Assuming that labour-power is paid for at its value, we are confronted by this alternative: given the productiveness of labour and its normal intensity, the rate of surplus-value can be raised only by the actual prolongation of the working day; on the other hand, given the length of the working day, that rise can be effected only by a change in the relative magnitudes of the components of the working day, viz., necessary labour and surplus-labour; a change, which, if the wages are not to fall below the value of labour-power, presupposes a change either in the productiveness or in the intensity of the labour.

If the labourer wants all his time to produce the necessary means of subsistence for himself and his race, he has no time left in which to work gratis for others. Without a certain degree of productiveness in his labour, he has no such superfluous time at his disposal; without such superfluous time, no surplus-labour, and therefore no capitalists, no slave-owners, no feudal lords, in one word, no class of large proprietors.[1]

Thus we may say that surplus-value rests on a natural basis; but this is permissible only in the very general sense, that there is no natural obstacle absolutely preventing one man from disburdening himself of the labour requisite for his own existence, and burdening another with it, any more, for instance, than unconquerable natural obstacles prevent one man from eating the flesh of another.[2] No mystical ideas must in any way be connected, as sometimes happens, with this historically developed productiveness of labour. It is only after men have raised themselves above the rank of animals, when therefore their labour has been to some extent socialised, that a state of things arises in which the surplus-labour of the one becomes a condition of existence for the other. At the

---

[1] "The very existence of the master-capitalists, as a distinct class, is dependent on the productiveness of industry." (Ramsay, l. c. p. 206.) "If each man's labour were but enough to produce his own food, there could be no property." (Ravenstone, l. c. p. 14, 15).

[2] According to a recent calculation, there are yet at least 4,000,000 cannibals in those parts of the earth which have already been explored.

dawn of civilisation the productiveness acquired by labour is small, but so too are the wants which develop with and by the means of satisfying them. Further, at that early period, the portion of society that lives on the labour of others is infinitely small compared with the mass of direct producers Along with the progress in the productiveness of labour, that small portion of society increases both absolutely and relatively.[1] Besides, capital with its accompanying relations springs up from an economic soil that is the product of a long process of development. The productiveness of labour that serves as its foundation and starting point, is a gift, not of nature, but of a history embracing thousands of centuries.

Apart from the degree of development, greater or less, in the form of social production, the productiveness of labour is fettered by physical conditions. These are all referable to the constitution of man himself (race, &c.), and to surrounding nature. The external physical conditions-fall into two great economical classes, (1) Natural wealth in means of subsistence, *i.e.*, a fruitful soil, waters teeming with fish, &c., and (2), natural wealth in the instruments of labour, such as waterfalls, navigable rivers, wood, metal, coal, &c. At the dawn of civilisation, it is the first class that turns the scale; at a higher stage of development, it is the second. Compare, for example, England with India, or in ancient times, Athens and Corinth with the shores of the Black Sea.

The fewer the number of natural wants imperatively calling for satisfaction, and the greater the natural fertility of the soil and the favourableness of the climate, so much less is the labour-time necessary for the maintenance and reproduction of the producer. So much greater therefore can be the excess of his labour for others over his labour for himself. Diodorus long ago remarked this in relation to the ancient Egyptians. "It is altogether incredible how little trouble and expense the bringing up of their children causes them. They cook for them the first simple food at hand; they also give them the

---

[1] "Among the wild Indians in America, almost everything is the labourer's, 99 parts of a hundred are to be put upon the account of labour. In England, perhaps, the labourer has not ⅔." (The Advantages of the East India Trade, &c. p. 73.)

lower part of the papyrus stem to eat, so far as it can be roasted in the fire, and the roots and stalks of marsh plants, some raw, some boiled and roasted. Most of the children go without shoes and unclothed, for the air is so mild. Hence a child, until he is grown up, costs his parents not more, on the whole, than twenty drachmas. It is this, chiefly, which explains why the population of Egypt is so numerous, and, therefore, why so many great works can be undertaken."[1] Nevertheless the grand structures of ancient Egypt are less due to the extent of its population than to the large proportion of it that was freely disposable. Just as the individual labourer can do more surplus-labour in proportion as his necessary labour-time is less, so with regard to the working population. The smaller the part of it which is required for the production of the necessary means of subsistence, so much the greater is the part that can be set to do other work.

Capitalist production once assumed then, all other circumstances remaining the same, and given the length of the working day, the quantity of surplus-labour will vary with the physical conditions of labour, especially with the fertility of the soil. But it by no means follows from this that the most fruitful soil is the most fitted for the growth of the capitalist mode of production. This mode is based on the dominion of man over nature. Where nature is too lavish, she "keeps him in hand, like a child in leading-strings." She does not impose upon him any necessity to develop himself.[2] It is not the tropics with their luxuriant vegetation, but the temperate zone, that is the mother country of capital. It is not the mere fertility of the soil, but the differentiation of the soil, the

---

[1] Diodorus, l. c. l. I. c. 80.

[2] "The first (natural wealth) as it is most noble and advantageous, so doth it make the people careless, proud, and given to all excesses; whereas the second enforceth vigilancy, literature, arts and policy." (England's Treasure by Foreign Trade. Or the Balance of our Foreign Trade is the Rule of our Treasure. Written by Thomas Mun of London, merchant, and now published for the common good by his son John Mun. London, 1669, p. 181, 182.) "Nor can I conceive a greater curse upon a body of people, than to be thrown upon a spot of land, where the productions for subsistence and food were, in great measure, spontaneous, and the climate required or admitted little care for raiment and covering . . . there may be an extreme on the other side. A soil incapable of produce by labour is quite as bad as a soil that produces plentifully without any labour." (An Inquiry into the present High Price of Provisions. Lond., 1767. p. 10.)

variety of its natural products, the changes of the seasons, which form the physical basis for the social division of labour, and which, by changes in the natural surroundings, spur man on to the multiplication of his wants, his capabilities, his means and modes of labour. It is the necessity of bringing a natural force under the control of society, of economising, of appropriating or subduing it on a large scale by the work of man's hand, that first plays the decisive part in the history of industry. Examples are, the irrigation works in Egypt,[1] Lombardy, Holland, or India and Persia where irrigation by means of artificial canals, not only supplies the soil with the water indispensable to it, but also carries down to it, in the shape of sediment from the hills, mineral fertilizers. The secret of the flourishing state of industry in Spain and Sicily under the dominion of the Arabs lay in their irrigation works.[2]

Favourable natural conditions alone, gave us only the possibility, never the reality, of surplus-labour, nor, consequently, of surplus-value and a surplus-product. The result of difference in the natural conditions of labour is this, that the same quantity of labour satisfies, in different countries, a different mass of requirements,[3] consequently, that under circumstances

---

[1] The necessity for predicting the rise and fall of the Nile created Egyptian astronomy, and with it the dominion of the priests, as directors of agriculture. "Le solstice est le moment de l'année où commence la crue du Nil, et celui que les Egyptiens ont dû observer avec le plus d'attention . . . C'était cette année tropique qu'il leur importait de marquer pour se diriger dans leurs opérations agricoles. Ils durent donc chercher dans le ciel un signe apparent de son retour." (Cuvier: Discours sur les révolutions du globe, ed. Hoefer. Paris, 1863, p. 141.)

[2] One of the material bases of the power of the state over the small disconnected producing organisms in India, was the regulation of the water supply. The Mahometan rulers of India understood this better than their English successors. It is enough to recall to mind the famine of 1866, which cost the lives of more than a million Hindoos in the district of Orissa, in the Bengal presidency.

[3] There are no two countries which furnish an equal number of the necessaries of life in equal plenty, and with the same quantity of labour. Men's wants increase or diminish with the severity or temperateness of the climate they live in; consequently, the proportion of trade which the inhabitants of different countries are obliged to carry on through necessity cannot be the same, nor is it practicable to ascertain the degree of variation farther than by the degrees of Heat and Cold; from whence one may make this general conclusion, that the quantity of labour required for a certain number of people is greatest in cold climates, and least in hot ones; for in the former men not only want more clothes, but the earth more cultivating than the latter." (An Essay on the Governing Causes of the Natural Rate of Interest. Lond. 1750. p. 60.) The author of this epoch-making anonymous work is J. Massey. Hume took his theory of interest from it.

in other respects analogous, the necessary labour-time is different. These conditions affect surplus-labour only as natural
limits, *i.e.*, by fixing the points at which labour for others can
begin. In proportion as industry advances, these natural
limits recede. In the midst of our West European society,
where the labourer purchases the right to work for his own
livelihood only by paying for it in surplus-labour, the idea
easily takes root that it is an inherent quality of human
labour to furnish a surplus-product.[1] But consider, for example, an inhabitant of the eastern islands of the Asiatic
Archipelago, where sago grows wild in the forests. "When
the inhabitants have convinced themselves, by boring a hole
in the tree, that the pith is ripe, the trunk is cut down and
divided into several pieces, the pith is extracted, mixed with
water and filtered: it is then quite fit for use as sago. One
tree commonly yields 300 lbs., and occasionally 500 to 600
lbs. There, then, people go into the forests, and cut bread
for themselves, just as with us they cut firewood."[2] Suppose now such an eastern bread-cutter requires 12 working
hours a week for the satisfaction of all his wants. Nature's
direct gift to him is plenty of leisure time. Before he can
apply this leisure time productively for himself, a whole series
of historical events is required; before he spends it in surplus-
labour for strangers, compulsion is necessary. If capitalist
production were introduced, the honest fellow would perhaps
have to work six days a week, in order to appropriate to himself the product of one working day The bounty of Nature
does not explain why he would then have to work 6 days a
week, or why he must furnish 5 days of surplus-labour. It
explains only why his necessary labour-time would be limited
to one day a week. But in no case would his surplus-product arise from some occult quality inherent in human labour.

Thus, not only does the historically developed social productiveness of labour, but also its natural productiveness, appear to be productiveness of the capital with which that labour
is incorporated.

[1] "Chaque travail doit (this appears also to be part of the droits et devoirs du
citoyen) laisser un excédant." Proudhon.
[2] F. Shouw: "Die Erde, die Pflanze und der Mensch. 2 Ed. Leipz. 1854, p. 148.

Ricardo never concerns himself about the origin of surplus-value. He treats it as a thing inherent in the capitalist mode of production, which mode, in his eyes, is the natural form of social production. Whenever he discusses the productiveness of labour, he seeks in it, not the cause of surplus-value, but the cause that determines the magnitude of that value. On the other hand, his school has openly proclaimed the productiveness of labour to be the originating cause of profit (read: Surplus-value). This at all events is a progress as against the mercantilists who, on their side, derived the excess of the price over the cost of production of the product, from the act of exchange, from the product being sold above its value. Nevertheless, Ricardo's school simply shirked the problem, they did not solve it. In fact these bourgeois economists instinctively saw, and rightly so, that it is very dangerous to stir too deeply the burning question of the origin of surplus-value. But what are we to think of John Stuart Mill, who, half a century after Ricardo, solemnly claims superiority over the mercantilists, by clumsily repeating the wretched evasions of Ricardo's earliest vulgarisers?

Mill says: "The cause of profit is that labour produces more than is required for its support." So far, nothing but the old story; but Mill wishing to add something of his own, proceeds: "To vary the form of the theorem; the reason why capital yields a profit, is because food, clothing, materials and tools, last longer than the time which was required to produce them." He here confounds the duration of labour-time with the duration of its products. According to this view, a baker whose product lasts only a day, could never extract from his workpeople the same profit, as a machine maker whose products endures for 20 years and more. Of course it is very true, that if a bird's nest did not last longer than the time it takes in building, birds would have to do without nests.

This fundamental truth once established, Mill establishes his own superiority over the mercantilists. "We thus see," he proceeds, "that profit arises, not from the incident of exchange, but from the productive power of labour; and the general profit of the country is always what the productive power of labour makes it, whether any exchange takes place or not. If there were no division of employments, there would be no buying or selling, but there would still be profit." For Mill then, exchange, buying and selling, those general conditions of capitalist production, are but an incident, and there would always be profits even without the purchase and sale of labour-power!

"If," he continues, "the labourers of the country collectively produce twenty per cent more than their wages, profits will be twenty per cent, whatever prices may or may not be." This is, on the one hand, a rare bit of tautology; for if labourers produce a surplus-value of 20% for the capitalist, his profit will be to the total wages of the labourers as 20 : 100. On the other hand, it is absolutely false to say that "profits will be 20%." They will always be less, because they are calculated upon the *sum total* of the capital advanced. If, for example, the capitalist have advanced £500, of which £400 is laid out in means of production and £100 in wages, and if the rate of surplus-value be 20%, the rate of profit will be 20 : 500, *i.e.,* 4% and not 20%.

Then follows a splendid example of Mill's method of handling the different historical forms of social production: "I assume, throughout, the state of things which, where the labourers and capitalists are separate classes, prevails, with few exceptions, universally; namely, that the capitalist advances the whole expenses, including the entire remuneration of the labourer." Strange optical illusion to see everywhere a state of things which as yet exist only exceptionally on our earth. But let us finish—Mill is willing to concede, "that he should do so is not a matter of inherent necessity." On the contrary: "the labourer might wait, until the production is complete, for all that part of his wages which exceeds mere necessaries; and even for the whole, if he has funds in hand sufficient for his temporary support. But in the latter case, the labourer is to that extent really a capitalist in the concern, by supplying a portion of the funds necessary for carrying it on." Mill might have gone further and have added, that the labourer who advances to himself not only the necessaries of life but also the means of production, **is in** reality nothing but his own wage-labourer. He might also have said that the American peasant proprietor is but a serf who does enforced labour for himself instead of for his lord.

After thus proving clearly, that even if capitalist production had no existence, still it would always exist, Mill is consistent enough to show, on the contrary, that it has no existence, even when it does exist. "And even in the former case" (when the workman is a wage labourer to whom the capitalist advances all the necessaries of life, he the labourer), "may be looked upon in the same light," *i.e.,* as a capitalist, "since, contributing his labour at less than the market price, (!) he may be regarded as lending the difference (?) to his employer and receiving it back with interest, &c."[1] In reality, the labourer advances his labour gratuitously to the capitalist during, say one week, in order to receive the market price at the end of the week, &c., and it is this which, according to Mill, transforms him into a capitalist. On the level plain, simple mounds look like hills; and the imbecile flatness of the present bourgeoisie is to be measured by the altitude of its great intellects.

CHAPTER XVII.

CHANGES OF MAGNITUDE IN THE PRICE OF LABOUR-POWER AND IN SURPLUS-VALUE.

THE value of labour-power is determined by the value of the necessaries of life habitually required by the average labourer. The quantity of these necessaries is known at any given epoch of a given society, and can therefore be treated as a constant magnitude. What changes, is the value of this quantity. There are, besides, two other factors that enter into the determination of the value of labour-power. One, the expenses

---

[1] J. St. Mill. Principles of Pol. Econ. Lond. 1868, p. 252–53 passim.

of developing that power, which expenses vary with the mode of production; the other, its natural diversity, the difference between the labour-power of men and women, of children and adults. The employment of these different sorts of labour power, an employment which is, in its turn, made necessary by the mode of production, makes a great difference in the cost of maintaining the family of the labourer, and in the value of the labour-power of the adult male. Both these factors, however, are excluded in the following investigation.[1]

I assume (1) that commodities are sold at their value; (2) that the price of labour-power rises occasionally above its value, but never sinks below it.

On this assumption we have seen that the relative magnitudes of surplus-value and of price of labour-power are determined by three circumstances; (1) the length of the working day, or the extensive magnitude of labour; (2) the normal intensity of labour, its intensive magnitude, whereby a given quantity of labour is expended in a given time; (3) the productiveness of labour, whereby the same quantum of labour yields, in a given time, a greater or less quantum of product, dependent on the degree of development in the conditions of production. Very different combinations are clearly possible, according as one of the three factors is constant and two variable, or two constant and one variable, or lastly, all three simultaneously variable. And the number of these combinations is augmented by the fact that, when these factors simultaneously vary, the amount and direction of their respective variations may differ. In what follows the chief combinations alone are considered.

I. *Length of the working day and intensity of labour constant.*
Productiveness of labour variable.

On these assumptions the value of labour-power, and the magnitude of surplus-value, are determined by three laws.

(1.) A working day of given length always creates the same amount of value, no matter how the productiveness of labour,

---

[1] The case considered at pages 347–350 is here of course omitted. (Note by editor of third edition.)

and, with it, the mass of the product, and the price of each single commodity produced, may vary.

If the value created by a working day of 12 hours be, say, six shillings, then, although the mass of the articles produced varies with the productiveness of labour, the only result is that the value represented by six shillings is spread over a greater or less number of articles.

(2.) Surplus-value and the value of labour-power vary in opposite directions. A variation in the productiveness of labour, its increase or diminution, causes a variation in the opposite direction in the value of labour-power, and in the same direction in surplus-value.

The value created by a working day of 12 hours is a constant quantity, say, six shillings. This constant quantity is the sum of the surplus-value plus the value of the labour-power, which latter value the labourer replaces by an equivalent. It is self-evident, that if a constant quantity consist of two parts, neither of them can increase without the other diminishing. Let the two parts at starting be equal; 3 shillings value of labour-power, 3 shillings surplus-value. Then the value of the labour-power cannot rise from three shillings to four, without the surplus-value falling from three shillings to two; and the surplus-value cannot rise from three shillings to four, without the value of labour-power falling from three shillings to two. Under these circumstances, therefore, no change can take place in the absolute magnitude, either of the surplus-value, or of the value of labour-power, without a simultaneous change in their relative magnitudes, *i.e.,* relatively to each other. It is impossible for them to rise or fall simultaneously.

Further, the value of labour-power cannot fall, and consequently surplus-value cannot rise, without a rise in the productiveness of labour. For instance, in the above case, the value of the labour-power cannot sink from three shillings to two, unless an increase in the productiveness of labour makes it possible to produce in 4 hours the same quantity of necessaries as previously required 6 hours to produce. On the other hand, the value of the labour-power cannot rise

from three shillings to four, without a decrease in the productiveness of labour, whereby eight hours become requisite
to produce the same quantity of necessaries, for the production
of which six hours previously sufficed. It follows from this,
that an increase in the productiveness of labour causes a fall
in the value of labour-power and a consequent rise in surplus-
value, while, on the other hand, a decrease in such productiveness causes a rise in the value of labour-power, and a fall in
surplus-value.

In formulating this law, Ricardo overlooked one circumstance; although a change in the magnitude of the surplus-
value or surplus-labour causes a change in the opposite direction in the magnitude of the value of labour-power, or in
the quantity of necessary labour, it by no means follows that
they vary in the same proportion. They do increase or
diminish by the same quantity. But their proportional increase or diminution depends on their original magnitudes
before the change in the productiveness of labour took place.
If the value of the labour-power be 4 shillings, or the necessary labour-time 8 hours, and the surplus- value be 2 shillings,
or the surplus-labour 4 hours, and if, in consequence of an
increase in the productiveness of labour, the value of the
labour-power fall to 3 shillings, or the necessary labour to 6
hours, the surplus-value will rise to 3 shillngs, or the surplus-
labour to 6 hours. The same quantity, 1 shilling or 2 hours, is
added in one case and subtracted in the other. But the proportional change of magnitude is different in each case. While
the value of the labour-power falls from 4 shillings to 3, *i.e.,* by
$\frac{1}{4}$ or 25%, the surplus-value rises from 2 shillings to 3, *i.e.,*
by $\frac{1}{2}$ or 50%. It therefore follows that the proportional increase of diminution in surplus-value, consequent on a given
change in the productiveness of labour, depends on the original
magnitude of that portion of the working day which embodies
itself in surplus-value; the smaller that portion, the greater
is the proportional change; the greater that portion, the less
is the proportional change.

(3.) Increase or diminution in surplus-value is always con-

sequent on, and never the cause of, the corresponding diminution or increase in the value of labour-power.[1]

Since the working-day is constant in magnitude, and is
represented by a value of constant magnitude, since, to every
variation in the magnitude of surplus-value, there corresponds
an inverse variation in the value of labour-power, and since
the value of labour-power cannot change, except in consequence
of a change in the productiveness of labour, it clearly follows,
under these conditions, that every change of magnitude in surplus-value arises from an inverse change of magnitude in the
value of labour-power. If, then, as we have already seen,
there can be no change of absolute magnitude in the value of
labour-power, and in surplus-value, unaccompanied by a
change in their relative magnitudes, so now it follows that no
change in their relative magnitudes is possible, without a
previous change in the absolute magnitude of the value of
labour-power.

According to the third law, a change in the magnitude of
surplus-value, presupposes a movement in the value of labour-
power, which movement is brought about by a variation in the
productiveness of labour. The limit of this change is given
by the altered value of labour-power. Nevertheless, even
when circumstances allow the law to operate, subsidiary movements may occur. For example: if in consequence of the
increased productiveness of labour, the value of labour-power
fall from 4 shillings to 3, or the necessary labour-time from
8 hours to 6, the price of labour-power may possibly not fall
below 3s. 8d., 3s. 6d., or 3s. 2d., and the surplus-value consequently not rise above 3s. 4d., 3c. 6d., or 3s. 10d. The
amount of this fall, the lowest limit of which is 3 shillings
(the new value of labour-power), depends on the relative

---

[1] To this third law MacCulloch has made, amongst others, this absurd addition,
that a rise in surplus value unaccompanied by a fall in the value of labour-power,
can occur through the abolition of taxes payable by the capitalist. The abolition
of such taxes makes no change whatever in the quantity of surplus-value that the
capitalist extorts at first-hand from the labourer. It alters only the proportion in
which that surplus-value is divided between himself and third persons. It consequently makes no alteration whatever in the relation between surplus-value and value
of labour-power. MacCulloch's exception therefore proves only his misapprehension
of the rule, a misfortune that as oftens happens to him in the vulgarisation of
Ricardo, as it does to J. B. Say in the vulgarisation of Adam Smith.

weight, which the pressure of capital on the one side, and the resistance of the labourer on the other, throws into the scale.

The value of labour-power is determined by the value of a given quantity of necessaries. It is the value and not the mass of these necessaries that varies with the productiveness of labour. It is, however, possible that, owing to an increase of productiveness, both the labourer, and the capitalist may simultaneously be able to appropriate a greater quantity of these necessaries, without any change in the price of labour-power or in surplus-value. If the value of labour-power be 3 shillings, and the necessary labour-time amount to 6 hours, if the surplus-value likewise be 3 shillings, and the surplus-labour 6 hours, then if the productiveness of labour were doubled without altering the ratio of necessary labour to surplus-labour, there would be no change of magnitude in surplus-value and price of labour-power. The only result would be that each of them would represent twice as many use-values as before; these use-values being twice as cheap as before. Although labour-power would be unchanged in price, it would be above its value. If, however, the prices of labour-power had fallen, not to 1s. 6d., the lowest possible point consistent with its new value, but to 2s. 10d. or 2s. 6d., still this lower price would represent an increased mass of necessaries. In this way it is possible with an increasing productiveness of labour, for the price of labour-power to keep on falling, and yet this fall to be accompanied by a constant growth in the mass of the labourer's means of subsistence. But even in such case, the fall in the value of labour-power would cause a corresponding rise of surplus-value, and thus the abyss between the labourer's position and that of the capitalist would keep widening.[1]

Ricardo was the first who accurately formulated the three laws we have above stated. But he falls into the following errors: (1) he looks upon the special conditions under which

[1] "When an alteration takes place in the productiveness of industry, and that either more or less is produced by a given quantity of labour and capital, the proportion of wages may obviously vary, whilst the quantity, which that proportion represents, remains the same, or the quantity may vary, whilst the proportion remains the same." ("Outlines of Political Economy," &c., p. 67.)

these laws hold good as the general and sole conditions of capitalist production. He knows no change, either in the length of the working day, or in the intensity of labour; consequently with him there can be only one variable factor, viz., the productiveness of labour; (2), and this error vitiates his analysis much more than (1), he has not, any more than have the other economists, investigated surplus-value as such, *i.e.*, independently of its particular forms, such a profit, rent, &c. He therefore confounds together the laws of the rate of surplus-value and the laws of the rate of profit. The rate of profit is, as we have already said, the ratio of the surplus-value to the total capital advanced; the rate of surplus-value is the ratio of the surplus-value to the variable part of that capital. Assume that a capital (C) of £500 is made up of raw material, instruments of labour, &c. (c) to the amount of £400; and of wages (v) to the amount of £100; and further, that the surplus-value (s)=£100. Then we have rate of surplus-value $\frac{s}{v} = \frac{£100}{£100} = 100\%$. But the rate of profit $\frac{s}{C} = \frac{£100}{£500} = 20\%$. It is, besides, obvious that the rate of profit may depend on circumstances that in no way affect the rate of surplus-value. I shall show in Book III. that, with a given rate of surplus-value, we may have any number of rates of profit, and that various rates of surplus-value may, under given conditions, express themselves in a single rate of profit.

II. *Working-day constant. Productiveness of labour constant. Intensity of labour variable.*

Increased intensity of labour means increased expenditure of labour in a given time. Hence a working-day of more intense labour is embodied in more products than is one of less intense labour, the length of each day being the same. Increased productiveness of labour also, it is true, will supply more products in a given working-day. But in this latter case, the value of each single product falls, for it costs less labour than before; in the former case, that value remains unchanged, for each article costs the same labour as before. Here we have an increase in the number of products, unaccompanied by a fall in their individual prices: as their number increases, so does the sum of their prices. But in the case of increased productiveness, a given value is spread over a greater mass of products. Hence the length of the working-day being constant, a day's labour of increased intensity will be incorporated in an increased value, and, the value of money remaining unchanged, in more money. The value created varies with the extent to which the intensity of labour deviates from its normal intensity in the society. A given working-day, therefore, no longer creates a constant, but a variable value; in a day of 12 hours of ordinary intensity, the value created is, say 6 shillings, but with increased intensity, the value created may be 7, 8, or more shillings. It is clear that, if the value created by a day's labour increases from, say, 6 to 8 shillings, then the two parts into which this value is divided, viz., price of labour-power and surplus-value, may both of them increase simultaneously, and either equally or unequally. They may both simultaneously increase from 3 shillings to 4. Here, the rise in the price of labour-power does not necessarily imply that the price has risen above the value of labour-power. On the contrary, the rise in price may be accompanied by a fall in value. This occurs whenever the rise in the price of labour-power does not compensate for its increased wear and tear.

We know that, with transitory exceptions, a change in the productiveness of labour does not cause any change in the value of labour-power, nor consequently in the magnitude of surplus-value, unless the products of the industries affected are articles habitually consumed by the laborers. In the present case this condition no longer applies. For when the variation is either in the duration or in the intensity of labour, there is always a corresponding change in the magnitude of the value created, independently of the nature of the article in which that value is embodied.

If the intensity of labour were to increase simultaneously and equally in every branch of industry, then the new and higher degree of intensity would become the normal degree for the society, and would therefore cease to be taken account of. But still, even then, the intensity of labour would be different in different countries, and would modify the international ap plication of the law of value. The more intense working day of one nation would be represented by a greater sum of money than would the less intense day of another nation.[1]

III. *Productiveness and Intensity of Labour constant. Length of the working-day variable.*

The working-day may vary in two ways. It may be made either longer or shorter. From our present data, and within the limits of the assumptions made on p. 569 we obtain the following laws:

(1.) The working-day creates a greater or less amount of value in proportion to its length—thus, a variable and not a constant quantity of value.

(2.) Every change in the relation between the magnitudes of surplus value and of the value of labour-power arises from a change in the absolute magnitude of the surplus-labour, and consequently of the surplus-value.

(3.) The absolute value of labour-power can change only in consequence of the reaction exercised by the prolongation of surplus-value upon the wear and tear of labour-power. Every change in this absolute value is therefore the effect, but never the cause, of a change in the magnitude of surplus-value.

We begin with the case in which the working-day is short-ened.

(1). A shortening of the working-day under the conditions given above, leaves the value of labour-power, and with it, the necessary labour-time, unaltered. It reduces the surplus-labour and surplus-value. Along with the absolute magnitude of the latter, its relative magnitude also falls, *i.e.,* its magni-tude relatively to the value of labour-power whose magni-tude remains unaltered. Only by lowering the price of la-

---

[1] "All things being equal, the English manufacturer can turn out a considerably larger amount of work in a given time than a foreign manufacturer, so much as to counterbalance the difference of the working-days, between 60 hours a week here, and 72 or 80 elsewhere." (Rep. of Insp. of Fact. for 31st Oct. 1855, p. 65.) The most infallible means for reducing this qualitative difference between the English and Continental working hour would be a law shortening quantitatively the length of the working-day in Continental factories.

bour-power below its value could the capitalist save himself harmless.

All the usual arguments against the shortening of the working-day, assume that it takes place under the conditions we have here supposed to exist; but in reality the very contrary is the case: a change in the productiveness and intensity of labour either precedes, or immediately follows, a shortening of the working-day.[1]

(2). Lengthening of the working-day. Let the necessary labour-time be 6 hours, or the value of labour-power 3 shillings; also let the surplus-labour be 6 hours or the surplus-value 3 shillings. The whole working-day then amounts to 12 hours and is embodied in a value of 6 shillings. If, now, the working-day be lengthened by 2 hours and the price of labour-power remain unaltered, the surplus-value increases both absolutely and relatively. Although there is no absolute change in the value of labour-power, it suffers a relative fall. Under the conditions assumed in I. there could not be a change of relative magnitude in the value of labour-power without a change in its absolute magnitude. Here, on the contrary, the change of relative magnitude in the value of labour-power is the result of the change of absolute magnitude in surplus-value.

Since the value in which a day's labour is embodied, increases with the length of that day, it is evident that the surplus-value and the price of labour-power may simultaneously increase, either by equal or unequal quantities. This simultaneous increase is therefore possible in two cases, one, the actual lengthening of the working-day, the other, an increase in the intensity of labour unaccompanied by such lengthening.

When the working-day is prolonged, the price of labour power may fall below its value, although that price be nominally unchanged or even rise. The value of a day's labour-power, is, as will be remembered, estimated from its normal average duration, or from the normal duration of life among

---

[1] "There are compensating circumstances . . . which the working of the Ten Hours' Act has brought to light." (Rep. of Insp. of Fact. for 1st Dec. 1848, p. 7.)

the labourers, and from corresponding normal transformations of organised bodily matter into motion,[2] in conformity with the nature of man. Up to a certain point, the increased wear and tear of labour-power, inseparable from a lengthened working-day, may be compensated by higher wages. But beyond this point the wear and tear increases in geometrical progression, and every condition suitable for the normal reproduction and functioning of labour-power is suppressed. The price of labour-power and the degree of its exploitation cease to be commensurable quantities.

IV.—*Simultaneous variations in the duration, productiveness, and intensity of labour.*

It is obvious that a large number of combinations are here possible. Any two of the factors may vary and the third remain constant, or all three may vary at once. They may vary either in the same or in different degrees, in the same or in opposite directions, with the result that the variations counteract one another, either wholly or in part. Nevertheless the analysis of every possible case is easy in view of the results given in I., II., and III. The effect of every possible combination may be found by treating each factor in turn as variable, and the other two constant for the time being. We shall, therefore, notice, and that briefly, but two important cases.

(1). *Diminishing productiveness of labour with a simultaneous lengthening of the working-day.*

In speaking of diminishing productiveness of labour, we here refer to diminution in those industries whose products determine the value of labour-power; such a diminution, for example, as results from decreasing fertility of the soil, and from the corresponding dearness of its products. Take the

---

[2] "The amount of labour which a man had undergone in the course of 24 hours might be approximately arrived at by an examination of the chymical changes which had taken place in his body, changed forms in matter indicating the anterior exercise of dynamic force." (Grove: "On the Correlation of Physical Forces.")

working-day at 12 hours and the value created by it at 6 shillings, of which one half replaces the value of the labour-power, the other forms the surplus-value. Suppose, in consequence of the increased dearness of the products of the soil, that the value of labour-power rises from 3 shillings to 4, and therefore the necessary labour-time from 6 hours to 8. If there be no change in the length of the working-day, the surplus-labour would fall from 6 hours to 4, the surplus-value from 3 shillings to 2. If the day be lengthened by 2 hours, *i.e.*, from 12 hours to 14, the surplus-labour remains at 6 hours, the surplus-value at 3 shillings, but the surplus-value decreases compared with the value of labour-power, as measured by the necessary labour-time. If the day be lengthened by 4 hours, viz., from 12 hours to 16, the proportional magnitudes of surplus-value and value of labour-power, of surplus-labour and necessary labour, continue unchanged, but the absolute magnitude of surplus-value rises from 3 shillings to 4, that of the surplus-labour from 6 hours to 8, an increment of $33\frac{1}{3}\%$. Therefore, with diminishing productiveness of labour and a simultaneous lengthening of the working-day, the absolute magnitude of surplus-value may continue unaltered, at the same time that its relative magnitude diminishes; its relative magnitude may continue unchanged, at the same time that its absolute magnitude increases; and, provided the lengthening of the day be sufficient, both may increase.

In the period between 1799 and 1815 the increasing price of provisions led in England to a nominal rise in wages, although the real wages, expressed in the necessaries of life, fell. From this fact West and Ricardo drew the conclusion, that the diminution in the productiveness of agricultural labour had brought about a fall in the rate of surplus-value, and they made this assumption of a fact that existed only in their imaginations, the starting-point of important investigations into the relative magnitudes of wages, profits, and rent. But, as a matter of fact, surplus-value had at that time, thanks to the increased intensity of labour, and to the prolongation of the working-day, increased both in absolute and relative magnitude. This was the period in which the right to prolong the hours of labour to an outrageous extent was established;[1] the period that was especially characterised by an accelerated accumulation of capital here, by pauperism there.[2]

(2) *Increasing intensity and productiveness of labour with simultaneous shortening of the working-day.*

Increased productiveness and greater intensity of labour, both have a like effect. They both augment the mass of articles produced in a given time. Both, therefore, shorten that portion of the working-day which the labourer needs to produce his means of subsistence or their equivalent. The minimum length of the working-day is fixed by this necessary but contractile portion of it. If the whole working-day were to shrink to the length of this portion, surplus-labour would vanish, a consummation utterly impossible under the régime of capital. Only by suppressing the capitalist form of production could the length of the working-day be reduced to

---

[1] "Corn and labour rarely march quite abreast; but there is an obvious limit beyond which they cannot be separated. With regard to the unusual exertions made by the labouring classes in periods of dearness, which produce the fall of wages noticed in the evidence" (namely, before the Parliamentary Committee of Inquiry, 1814-15), "they are most meritorious in the individuals, and certainly favour the growth of capital. But no man of humanity could wish to see them constant and unremitted. They are most admirable as a temporary relief; but if they were constantly in action, effects of a similar kind would result from them, as from the population of a country being pushed to the very extreme limits of its food." (Malthus: "Inquiry into the Nature and Progress of Rent," Lond., 1815, p. 48, note.) All honour to Malthus that he lays stress on the lengthening of the hours of labour, a fact to which he elsewhere in his pamphlet draws attention, while Ricardo and others, in face of the most notorious facts, make invariability in the length of the working-day the ground-work of all their investigations. But the conservative interests, which Malthus served, prevented him from seeing that an unlimited prolongation of the working-day, combined with an extraordinary development of machinery, and the exploitation of women and children, must inevitably have made a great portion of the working class "supernumerary," particularly whenever the war should have ceased, and the monopoly of England in the markets of the world should have come to an end. It was, of course, far more convenient, and much more in conformity with the interests of the ruling classes, whom Malthus adored like a true priest, to explain this "over-population" by the eternal laws of Nature, rather than by the historical laws of capitalist production.

[2] "A principal cause of the increase of capital, during the war, proceeded from the greater exertions, and perhaps the greater privations of the labouring classes, the most numerous in every society. More women and children were compelled by necessitous circumstances, to enter upon laborious occupations, and former workmen were, from the same cause, obliged to devote a greater portion of their time to increase production." (Essays on Pol. Econ., in which are illustrated the principal causes of the present national distress. Lond., 1830, p. 248.)

the necessary labour-time. But, even in that case, the latter would extend its limits. On the one hand, because the notion of "means of subsistence" would considerably expand, and the labourer would lay claim to an altogether different standard of life. On the other hand, because a part of what is now surplus-labour, would then count as necessary labour; I mean the labour of forming a fund for reserve and accumulation.

The more the productiveness of labour increases, the more can the working-day be shortened; and the more the working-day is shortened, the more can the intensity of labour increase. From a social point of view, the productiveness increases in the same ratio as the economy of labour, which, in its turn, includes not only economy of the means of production, but also the avoidance of all useless labour. The capitalist mode of production, while on the one hand, enforcing economy in each individual business, on the other hand, begets, by its anarchical system of competition, the most outrageous squandering of labour-power and of the social means of production, not to mention the creation of a vast number of employments, at present indispensable, but in themselves superfluous.

The intensity and productiveness of labour being given, the time which society is bound to devote to material production is shorter, and as a consequence, the time at its disposal for the free development, intellectual and social, of the individual is greater, in proportion as the work is more and more evenly divided among all the able-bodied members of society, and as a particular class is more and more deprived of the power to shift the natural burden of labour from its own shoulders to those of another layer of society. In this direction, the shortening of the working-day finds at last a limit in the generalisation of labour. In capitalist society spare time is acquired for one class by converting the whole life-time of the masses into labour-time.

CHAPTER XVIII.

VARIOUS FORMULÆ FOR THE RATE OF SURPLUS-VALUE.

WE have seen that the rate of surplus-value is represented by the following formulæ.

$$\text{I.} \quad \frac{\text{Surplus-value}}{\text{Variable Capital}} \left(\frac{s}{v} \right) = \frac{\text{Surplus-value}}{\text{Value of labour-power}} = \frac{\text{Surplus-labour}}{\text{Necessary labour}}$$

The two first of these formulæ represent, as a ratio of values, that which, in the third, is represented as a ratio of the times during which those values are produced. These formulæ, supplementary the one to the other, are rigorously definite and correct. We therefore find them substantially, but not consciously, worked out in classical political economy. There we meet with the following derivative formulæ.

$$\text{II.} \quad \frac{\text{Surplus-labour}}{\text{Working-day}} = \frac{\text{Surplus-value}}{\text{Value of the Product}} = \frac{\text{Surplus-product}}{\text{Total Product}}$$

One and the same ratio is here expressed as a ratio of labour-times, of the values in which those labour-times are embodied, and of the products in which those values exist. It is of course understood that, by "Value of the Product," is meant only the value newly created in a working-day, the constant part of the value of the product being excluded.

In all of these formulæ (II.), the actual degree of exploitation of labour, or the rate of surplus-value, is falsely expressed. Let the working-day be 12 hours. Then, making the same assumptions as in former instances, the real degree of exploitation of labour will be represented in the following proportions.

$$\frac{6 \text{ hours surplus-labour}}{6 \text{ hours necessary labour}} = \frac{\text{Surplus-value of 3 sh.}}{\text{Variable Capital of 3 sh.}} = 100 \%$$

From formulæ II. we get very differently,

$$\frac{6 \text{ hours surplus-labour}}{\text{Working-day of 12 hours}} = \frac{\text{Surplus-value of 3 sh.}}{\text{Value created of 6 sh.}} = 50 \%$$

These derivative formulæ express, in reality, only the proportion in which the working-day, or the value produced by it, is divided between capitalist and labourer. If they are to be treated as direct expressions of the degree of self-expansion of capital, the following erroneous law would hold good: Surplus-labour or surplus-value can never reach 100%.[1] Since the surplus-labour is only an aliquot part of the working-day, or since surplus-value is only an aliquot part of the value created, the surplus-labour must necessarily be always less than the working-day, or the surplus-value always less than the total value created. In order, however, to attain the ratio of 100:100 they must be equal. In order that the surplus-labour may absorb the whole day (*i. e.*, an average day of any week or year), the necessary labour must sink to zero. But if the necessary labour vanish, so too does the surplus-labour, since it is only a function of the former. The ratio $\frac{\text{Surplus-labour}}{\text{Working-day}}$ or $\frac{\text{Surplus-value}}{\text{Value created}}$ can therefore never reach the limit of $\frac{100}{100}$, still less rise to $\frac{100 + x}{100}$. But not so the rate of surplus-value, the real degree of exploitation of labour. Take, *e.g.*, the estimate of L. de Lavergne, according to which the English agricultural labourer gets only $\frac{1}{4}$, the capitalist (farmer) on the other hand $\frac{3}{4}$ of the product[2] or of its value, apart from the question of how the booty is subsequently divided between the

---

[1] Thus, *e.g.*, in "Dritter Brief an v. Kirchmann von Rodbertus. Widerlegung der Ricardo'schen Theorie von der Grundrente und Begründung einer neuen Rententheorie. Berlin, 1851." I shall return to this letter later on; in spite of its erroneous theory of rent, it sees through the nature of capitalist production.

Note by the Editor of the 3rd Edition. It may be seen from this how favourably Marx judged his predecessors, whenever he found in them real progress, or new and sound ideas. The subsequent publication of Rodbertus' letters to Rud. Meyer has . shown that the above acknowledgment by Marx wants restricting to some extent. In those letters this passage occurs: "Capital must be rescued not only from labour, but from itself, and that will be best effected, by treating the acts of the industrial capitalist as economical and political functions, that have been delegated to him with his capital, and by treating his profit as a form of salary, because we still know no other social organisation. But salaries may be regulated, and may also be reduced if they take too much from wages. The irruption of Marx into Society, as I may call his book, must be warded off. . . . Altogether, Marx's book is not so much an investigation into capital, as a polemic against the present form of capital, a form which he confounds with the concept itself of capital." (Briefe, &c., von Dr. Rodbertus-Jagetzow, herausgg. von Dr. Rud. Meyer, Berlin, 1881, I. Bd. p. 111., 48. Brief von Rodbertus.). To such ideological commonplaces did the bold attack by Rodbertus in his "social letters" finally dwindle down.

[2] That part of the product which merely replaces the constant capital advanced, is of course left out in this caluclation. Mr. L. de Lavergne, a blind admirer of England, is inclined to estimate the share of the capitalist too low, rather than too high.

capitalist, the landlord and others. According to this, the surplus-labour of the English agricultural labourer is to his necessary labour as 3:1, which gives a rate of exploitation of 300%.

The favourite method of treating the working-day as constant in magnitude became, through the use of the formulæ II., a fixed usage, because in them surplus-labour is always compared with a working-day of given length. The same holds good when the repartition of the value produced is exclusively kept in sight. The working-day that has already been realised in a given value, must necessarily be a day of given length.

The habit of representing surplus-value and value of labour-power as fractions of the value created—a habit that originates in the capitalist mode of production itself, and whose import will hereafter be disclosed—conceals the very transaction that characterises capital, namely the exchange of variable capital for living labour-power, and the consequent exclusion of the labourer from the product. Instead of the real fact, we have the false semblance of an association, in which labourer and capitalist divide the product in proportion to the different elements which they respectively contribute towards its formation.[1]

Moreover, the formulæ II. can at any time be reconverted into formulæ I. If, for instance, we have $\frac{\text{Surplus-labour of 6 hours}}{\text{Working-day of 12 hours}}$ the necessary labour-time being 12 hours less the surplus-labour of 6 hours, we get the following result,

$$\frac{\text{Surplus-labour of 6 hours}}{\text{Necessary-labour of 6 hours}} = \frac{100}{100}$$

There is a third formula which I have occasionally already anticipated; it is

$$\text{III.} \quad \frac{\text{Surplus-value}}{\text{Value of labour-power}} = \frac{\text{Surplus-labour}}{\text{Necessary labour}} = \frac{\text{Unpaid labour}}{\text{Paid labour}}$$

After the investigations we have given above, it is no longer possible to be misled, by the formula $\frac{\text{Unpaid labour}}{\text{Paid labour}}$, into con-

[1] All well-developed forms of capitalist production being forms of co-operation, nothing is, of course, easier, than to make abstraction from their antagonistic char-

cluding, that the capitalist pays for labour and not for labour-power. This formula is only a popular expression for $\frac{\text{Surplus-labour}}{\text{Necessary labour}}$. The capitalist pays the value, so far as price co-incides with value, of the labour-power, and receives in ex-change the disposal of the living labour-power itself. His usufruct is spread over two periods. During one the labourer produces a value that is only equal to the value of his labour-power: he produces its equivalent. Thus the capitalist re-ceives in return for his advance of the price of the labour pow-er, a product of the same price. It is the same as if he had bought the product ready made in the market. During the other period, the period of surplus-labour, the usufruct of the labour-power creates a value for the capitalist, that costs him no equivalent.[1] This expenditure of labour-power comes to him gratis. In this sense it is that surplus-labour can be called unpaid labour.

Capital, therefore, is not only, as Adam Smith says, the command over labour. It is essentially the command over un-paid labour. All surplus-value, whatever particular form (profit, interest, or rent), it may subsequently crystallise into, is in substance the materialisation of unpaid labour. The se-cret of the self-expansion of capital resolves itself into having the disposal of a definite quantity of other people's unpaid labour.

acter, and to transform them by a word into some form of free association, as is done by A. de Laborde in "De l'Esprit de l'Association dans tous les intérêts de la communauté." Paris 1818. H. Carey, the Yankee, occasionally performs this con-juring trick with like success, even with the relations resulting from slavery.

[1] Although the Physiocrats could not penetrate the mystery of surplus-value, yet this much was clear to them, viz., that it is "une richesse indépendante et disponible qu'il (the possessor) n'a point achetée et qu'il vend." (Turgot: "Réflexions sur la Formation et la Distribution des Richesses," p. 11.)

PART VI.

WAGES.

CHAPTER XIX.

ON the surface of bourgeois society the wage of the labourer appears as the price of labour, a certain quantity of money that is paid for a certain quantity of labour. Thus people speak of the value of labour and call its expression in money its necessary or natural price. On the other hand they speak of the market prices of labour, *i.e.*, prices oscillating above or below its natural price.

But what is the value of a commodity? The objective form of the social labour expended in its production. And how do we measure the quantity of this value? By the quantity of the labour contained in it. How then is the value, *e.g.*, of a 12 hours' working day to be determined? By the 12 working hours contained in a working day of 12 hours, which is an absurd tautology.[1]

---

[1] "Mr. Ricardo, ingeniously enough, avoids a difficulty which, on a first view, threatens to encumber his doctrine, that value depends on the quantity of labour employed in production. If this principle is rigidly adhered to, it follows that the value of labour depends on the quantity of labour employed in producing it—which is evidently absurd. By a dexterous turn, therefore, Mr. Ricardo makes the value of labour depend on the quantity of labour required to produce wages; or, to give him the benefit f his own language, he maintains, that the value of labour is to be estimated by the quantity of labour required to produce wages; by which he means the quantity of labour required to produce the money or commodities given to the labourer. This is similar to saying, that the value of cloth is estimated, not by the quantity of labour bestowed on its production, but by the quantity of labour bestowed on the production of the silver, for which the cloth is exchanged." (A. Critical Discourse on the Nature, &c., of Value, p. 50, 51.)

In order to be sold as a commodity in the market, labour must at all events exist before it is sold. But could the labourer give it an independent objective existence, he would sell a commodity and not labour.[1]

Apart from these contradictions, a direct exchange of money, *i.e.,* of realized labour, with living labour would either do away with the law of value which only begins to develop itself freely on the basis of capitalist production, or do away with capitalist production itself, which rests directly on wage-labour. The working day of 12 hours embodies itself, *e.g.,* in a money value of 6s. Either equivalents are exchanged, and then the labourer receives 6s. for 12 hours' labour; the price of his labour would be equal to the price of his product. In this case he produces no surplus-value, for the buyer of his labour, the 6s. are not transformed into capital, the basis of capitalist production varishes. But it is on this very basis that he sells his labour and that his labour is wage-labour. Or else he receives for 12 hours' labour less than 6s., *i.e.,* less than 12 hours' labour. Twelve hours labour are exchanged against 10, 6, &c., hours' labour. This equalisation of unequal quantities not nerely does way with the determination of value. Such a self-destructive contradiction cannot be in any way even enunciated or formulated as a law.[2]

It is of no avail to deduce the exchange of more labour against less, from their difference of form, the one being realized, the other living.[3] This is the more absurd as the

---

[1] "If you call labour a commodity, it is not like a commodity which is first produced in order to exchange, and then brought to market where it must exchange with other commodities according to the respective quantities of each which there may be in the market at the time; labour is created the moment it is brought to market; nay, it is brought to market before it is created." (Observations on some Verbal Disputes, etc., pp. 75, 76.)

[2] "Treating labour as a commodity, and capital, the produce of labour, as another, then, if the values of these two commodities were regulated by equal quantities of labour, a given amount of labour would . . . exchange for that quantity of capital which had been produced by the same amount of labour; antecedent labour would . . . exchange for the same amount as present labour. But the value of labour in relation to other commodities . . . is determined not by equal quantities of labour." (E. G. Wakefield in his edition of Adam Smith's "Wealth of Nations," vol. i., London, 1836, p. 231, note.)

[3] "Il a fallu convenir (a new edition of the contrat sociall) que toutes les fois qu'il échangerait du travail fait contre du travail à faire, le dernier (le capitaliste) aurait une valeur supérieure au premier" (le travailleur). Simonde (*i.e.,* Sismondi), "De la Richesse Commerciale," Genève, 1803, t. 1, p. 37

value of a commodity is determined not by the quantity of labour actually realized in it, but by the quantity of living labour necessary for its production. A commodity represents, say 6 working hours. If an invention is made by which it can be produced in 3 hours, the value, even of the commodity already produced, falls by half. It represents now 3 hours of social labour instead of the 6 formerly necessary. It is the quantity of labour required for its production, not the realized form of that labour, by which the amount of the value of a commodity is determined.

That which comes directly face to face with the possessor of money on the market, is in fact not labour, but the labourer. What the latter sells is his labour-power. As soon as his labour actually begins, it has already ceased to belong to him; it can therefore no longer be sold by him. Labour is the substance, and the immanent measure of value, but *has itself no value.*[1]

In the expression "value of labour," the idea of value is not only completely obliterated, but actually reversed. It is an expression as imaginary as the value of the earth. These imaginary expressions, arise, however, from the relations of production themselves. They are categories for the phenomenal forms of essential relations. That in their appearance things often represent themselves in inverted form is pretty well known in every science except political economy.[2]

---

[1] "Labour the exclusive standard of value . . . the greater of all wealth, no commodity." Th. Hodgskin, l. c. p. 186.

[2] On the other hand, the attempt to explain such expressions as merely poetic license only shows the impotence of the analysis. Hence, in answer to Proudhon's phrase; "Le travail est dit valoir, non pas en tant que marchandise lui même, mais en vue des valeurs qu'on suppose, renfermées puissanciellement en lui. La valeur du travail est une expression figurée," &c., I have remarked: "Dans le travail-marchandise qui est d'une réalité effrayant, il (Proudhon) ne voit qu'une ellipse grammaticale. Donc, toute la société actuelle fondée sur le travail-marchandise, est désormais fondée sur une license poétique, sur une expression figurée. La société veut-elle 'éliminer tous les inconvénients,' qui la travaillent, eh bien! qu'elle élimine les termes malsonnants, qu'elle change de langage, et pour cela elle n'a qu' à s'adresser à l'Académie pour lui demander une nouvelle édition de son dictionnaire." (Karl Marx. "Misère de la Philosophie," p. 34, 35.) It is naturally still more convenient to understand by value nothing at all. Then one can without difficulty subsume everything under this category. Thus, *e.g.*, J. B. Say; what is "valeur?" Answer: "C'est ce qu'une chose vaut," and what is "prix?" Answer; "La valeur d'une chose exprimée en monnaie." And why has "le travail de la terre . . .

Classical political economy borrowed from every-day life the category "price of labour" without further criticism, and then simply asked the question, how is this price determined? It soon recognized that the change in the relations of demand and supply explained in regard to the price of labour, as of all other commodities, nothing except its changes, *i.e.*, the oscillations of the market price above or below a certain mean. If demand and supply balance, the oscillation of prices ceases, all other conditions remaining the same. But then demand and supply also cease to explain anything. The price of labour, at the moment when demand and supply are in equilibrium, is its natural price, determined independently of the relation of demand and supply. And how this price is determined, is just the question. Or a larger period of oscillations in the market-price is taken, *e.g.*, a year, and they are found to cancel one the other, leaving a mean average quantity, a relatively constant magnitude. This had naturally to be determined otherwise than by its own compensating variations. This price which always finally predominates over the accidental market-prices of labour and regulates them, this "necessary price" (physiocrats) or "natural price" of labour (Adam Smith) can, as with all other commodities, be nothing else than its value expressed in money. In this way political economy expected to penetrate athwart the accidental prices of labour, to the value of labour. As with other commodities, this value was determined by the cost of production. But what is the cost of production—of the labourer, *i.e.*, the cost of producing or reproducing the labourer himself? This question unconsciously substituted itself in political economy for the original one; for the search after the cost of production of labour as such turned in a circle and never left the spot. What economists therefore call value of labour, is in fact the value of labour-power, as it exists in the personality of the labourer, which is as different from its function, labour, as a machine is from the work it performs. Occupied with the difference between

une valeur? Parce qu'on y met un prix." Therefore value is what a thing is worth, and the land has its "value," because its value is "expressed in money." This is, anyhow, a very simple way of explaining the why and the wherefore of things.

the market-price of labour and its-so-called value, with the relation of this value to the rate of profit, and to the values of the commodities produced by means of labour, &c., they never discovered that the course of the analysis had led not only from the market prices of labour to its presumed value, but had led to the resolution of this value of labour itself into the value of labour-power. Classical economy never arrived at a consciousness of the results of its own analysis; it accepted uncritically the categories "value of labour," "natural price of labour," &c., as final and as adequate expressions for the value-relation under consideration, and was thus led, as will be seen later, into inextricable confusion and contradiction, while it offered to the vulgar economists a secure basis of operations for their shallowness, which on principle worships appearances only.

Let us next see how value (and price) of labour-power, present themselves in this transformed condition as wages.

We know that the daily value of labour-power is calculated upon a certain length of the labourer's life, to which, again, corresponds a certain length of working-day. Assume the habitual working-day as 12 hours, the daily value of labour-power as 3s., the expression in money of a value that embodies 6 hours of labour. If the labourer receives 3s., then he receives the value of his labour-power functioning through 12 hours. If, now, this value of a day's labour-power is expressed as the value of a day's labour itself, we have the formula: Twelve hours' labour has a value of 3s. The value of labour-power thus determines the value of labour, or, expressed in money, its necessary price. If, on the other hand, the price of labour-power differs from its value, in like manner the price of labour differs from its so-called value.

As the value of labour is only an irrational expression for the value of labour-power, it follows, of course, that the value of labour must always be less than the value it produces, for the capitalist always makes labour-power work longer than is necessary for the reproduction of its own value. In the above example, the value of the labour-power that functions through 12 hours is 3s., a value for the reproduction of which 6 hours are required. The value which the labour-power produces is, on the other hand, 6s., because it, in fact, functions during 12 hours, and the value it produces depends, not on its own value, but on the length of time it is in action. Thus, we have a result absurd at first sight—that labour which creates a value of 6s. possesses a value of 3s.[1]

We see, further: The value of 3s. by which a part only of the working day—*i.e.,* 6 hours' labour—is paid for, appears as the value or price of the whole working-day of 12 hours, which thus includes 6 hours unpaid for. The wage-form thus extinguishes every trace of the division of the working-day into necessary labour and surplus-labour, into paid and unpaid labour. All labour appears as paid labour. In the corvée, the labour of the worker for himself, and his compulsory labour for his lord, differ in space and time in the clearest possible way. In slave-labour, even that part of the working-day in which the slave is only replacing the value of his own means of existence, in which, therefore, in fact, he works for himself alone, appears as labour for his master. All the slave's labour appears as unpaid labour.[2] In wage-labour, on the contrary, even surplus labour, or unpaid labour, appears as paid. There the property-relation conceals the labour of the slave for himself; here the money-relation conceals the unrequited labour of the wage-labourer.

Hence, we may understand the decisive importance of the transformation of value and price of labour-power into the form of wages, or into the value and price of labour itself. This phenomenal form, which makes the actual relation invisible, and, indeed, shows the direct opposite of that relation, forms the basis of all the juridicial notions of both labourer and capitalist, of all the mystifications of the capitalistic mode of

[1] Cf. Zur Kritik der Politischen Œkonomie, p. 40, where I state that, in the portion of that work that deals with Capital, this problem will be solved: "How does production, on the basis of exchange-value determined simply by labour-time, lead to the result that the exchange-value of labour is less than the exchange-value of its product?"

[2] The "Morning Star," a London free-trade organ, naïf to silliness, protested again and again during the American civil war, with all the moral indignation of which man is capable, that the negro in the "Confederate States" worked absolutely for nothing. It should have compared the daily cost of such a negro with that of the free workman in the East end of London.

production, of all its illusions as to liberty, of all the apologetic shifts of the vulgar economists.

If history took a long time to get at the bottom of the mystery of wages, nothing, on the other hand, is more easy to understand than the necessity, the *raison d'être,* of this phenomenon.

The exchange between capital and labour at first presents itself to the mind in the same guise as the buying and selling of all other commodities. The buyer gives a certain sum of money, the seller an article of a nature different from money. The jurist's consciousness recognises in this, at most, a material difference, expressed in the juridically equivalent formalæ: "Do ut des, do ut facias, facio ut des, facio ut facias."

Further. Exchange-value and use-value, being intrinsically incommensurable magnitudes, the expressions "value of labour," "price of labour," do not seem more irrational than the expressions "value of cotton," "price of cotton." Moreover, the labourer is paid after he has given his labour. In its function of means of payment, money realises subsequently the value or price of the article supplied—*i.e.,* in this particular case, the value or price of the labour supplied. Finally, the use-value supplied by the labourer to the capitalist is not, in fact, his labour-power, but its function, some definite useful labour, the work of tailoring, shoemaking, spinning, &c. That this same labour is, on the other hand, the universal value-creating element, and thus possesses a property by which it differs from all other commodities, is beyond the cognisance of the ordinary mind.

Let us put ourselves in the place of the labourer who receives for 12 hours' labour, say the value produced by 6 hours' labour, say 3s. For him, in fact, his 12 hours' labour is the means of buying the 3s. The value of his labour-power may vary, with the value of his usual means of subsistence, from 3 to 4 shillings, or from 3 to 2 shillings; or, if the value of his labour-power remains constant, its price may, in consequence of changing relations of demand and supply, rise to 4s. or fall to 2s. He always gives 12 hours of labour. Every change in the amount of the equivalent that he receives appears to him, therefore, necessarily as a change in the value or price of his 12 hours' work. This circumstance misled Adam Smith, who treated the working-day as a constant quantity,[1] to the assertion that the value of labour is constant, although the value of the means of subsistence may vary, and the same working-day, therefore, may represent itself in more, or less money for the labourer.

Let us consider, on the other hand, the capitalist. He wishes to receive as much labour as possible for as little money as possible. Practically, therefore, the only thing that interests him is the difference between the price of labour-power and the value which its function creates. But, then, he tries to buy all commodities as cheaply as possible, and always accounts for his profit by simple cheating, by buying under, and selling over the value. Hence, he never comes to see that, if such a thing as the value of labour really existed, and be really paid this value no capital would exist, his money would not be turned into capital.

Moreover, the actual movement of wages presents phenomena which seem to prove that not the value of labour-power is paid, but the value of its function, of labour itself. We may reduce these phenomena to two great classes: (1.) Change of wages with the changing length of the working-day. One might as well conclude that not the value of a machine is paid, but that of its working, because it costs more to hire a machine for a week than for a day. (2.) The individual difference in the wages of different labourers who do the same kind of work. We find this individual difference, but are not deceived by it, in the system of slavery, where, frankly and openly, without any circumlocution, labour-power itself is sold. Only, in the slave system, the advantage of a labour-power above the average, and the disadvantage of a labour-power below the average, affects the slave-owner; in the wage-labour system it affects the labourer himself, because his labour-power is, in the one case, sold by himself, in the other, by a third person.

[1] Adam Smith only accidentally alludes to the variation of the working-day when he is referring to piece-wages.

For the rest, in respect to the phenomenal form, "value and price of labour," or "wages," as contrasted with the essential relation manifested therein, viz., the value and price of labour-power, the same difference holds that holds in respect to all phenomena and their hidden substratum. The former appear directly and spontaneously as current modes of thought; the latter must first be discovered by science. Classical political economy nearly touches the true relation of things, without, however, consciously formulating it. This it cannot so long as it sticks in its bourgeois skin.

CHAPTER XX.

TIME-WAGES.

WAGES themselves again take many forms, a fact not recognizable in the ordinary economical treatises which, exclusively interested in the material side of the question, neglect every difference of form. An exposition of all these forms however, belongs to the special study of wage-labour, not therefore to this work. Still the two fundamental forms must be briefly worked out here.

The sale of labour-power, as will be remembered, takes place for a definite period of time. The converted form under which the daily, weekly, &c., value of labour-power presents itself, is hence that of time-wages, therefore day-wages, &c.

Next it is to be noted that the laws set forth, in the 17th chapter, on the changes in the relative magnitudes of price of labour-power and surplus-value, pass by a simple transformation of form, into laws of wages. Similarly the distinction between the exchange-value of labour-power, and the sum of the necessaries of life into which this value is converted, now reappears as the distinction between nominal and real wages. It would be useless to repeat here, with regard to the phenomenal form, what has been already worked out in the substantial form. We limit ourselves therefore to a few points characteristic of time-wages.

The sum of money[1] which the labourer receives for his daily or weekly labour, forms the amount of his nominal wages, or of his wages estimated in value. But it is clear that according to the length of the working-day, that is, according to the amount of actual labour daily supplied, the same daily or weekly wage may represent very different prices of labour, *i.e.,* very different sums of money for the same quantity of labour.[2] We must, therefore, in considering time-wages, again distinguish between the sum total of the daily or weekly wages, &c., and the price of labour. How then to find this price, *i.e.,* the money-value of a given quantity of labour? The average price of labour is found, when the average daily value of the labour-power is divided by the average number of hours in the working-day. If, *e.g.,* the daily value of labour-power is 3 shillings, the value of the product of 6 working hours, and if the working-day is 12 hours, the price of 1 working hour is $\frac{3}{12}$ shillings=3d. The price of the working hour thus found serves as the unit measure for the price of labour.

It follows therefore that the daily and weekly wages, &c., may remain the same, although the price of labour falls constantly. If, *e.g.,* the habitual working-day is 10 hours and the daily value of the labour-power 3s., the price of the working hour is $3\frac{3}{5}$d. It falls to 3d. as soon as the working-day rises to 12 hours, to $2\frac{2}{5}$ d. as soon as it rises to 15 hours. Daily or weekly wages remain, despite all this, unchanged. On the contrary, the daily or weekly wages may rise, although the price of labour remains constant or even falls. If, *e.g.,* the working day is 10 hours, and the daily value of labour-power 3 shillings, the price of one working hour is $3\frac{3}{5}$ d. If the labourer in consequence of increase of trade works 12 hours, the price of labour remaining the same, his daily wage

---

[1] The value of money itself is here always supposed constant.

[2] "The price of labour is the sum paid for a given quantity of labour." (Sir Edward West, "Price of Corn and Wages of Labour." London, 1836, p. 67). West is the author of the anonymous "Essay on the Application of Capital to Land. By a Fellow of the University College of Oxford, London, 1815." An epoch making work in the history of political economy.

now rises to 3 shillings $7\frac{1}{5}$ d. without any variation in the price of labour. The same result might follow if, instead of the extensive amount of labour, its intensive amount increased.[1] The rise of the nominal daily or weekly wages may therefore be accompanied by a price of labour that remains stationary or falls. The same holds as to the income of the labourer's family, as soon as the quantity of labour expended by the head of the family is increased by the labour of the members of his family. There are, therefore, methods of lowering the price of labour independent of the reduction of the nominal daily or weekly wages.[2]

As a general law it follows that, given the amount of daily, weekly labour, &c., the daily or weekly wages depend on the price of labour which, itself varies either with the value of labour-power, or with the difference between its price and its value. Given, on the other hand, the price of labour, the daily or weekly wages depend on the quantity of the daily or weekly labour.

The unit measure for time-wages, the price of the working-hour, is the quotient of the value of a day's labour-power, divided by the number of hours of the average working-day. Let the latter be 12 hours, and the daily value of labour-power 3 shillings, the value of the product of 6 hours of labour. Under these circumstances the price of a working-hour is 3d.,

---

[1] "The wages of labour depend upon the price of labour and the quantity of labour performed. . . . An increase in the wages of labour does not necessarily imply an enhancement of the price of labour. From fuller employment, and greater exertions, the wages of labour may be considerably increased, while the price of labour may continue the same." West, l. c. pp. 67, 68, 112. The main question: "How is the price of labour determined?" West, however, dismisses with mere banalities.

[2] This is perceived by the fanatical representative of the industrial bourgeoisie of the 18th century, the author of the "Essay on Trade and Commerce" often quoted by us, although he puts the matter in a confused way: "It is the quantity of labour and not the price of it (he means by this the nominal daily or weekly wages) that is determined by the price of provisions and other necessaries: reduce the price of necessaries very low, and of course you reduce the quantity of labour in proportion. Master manufacturers know that there are various ways of raising and felling the price of labour, besides that of altering its nominal amount." (l. c. pp. 48, 61.) In his "Three Lectures on the rate of Wages," London, 1830, in which N. W. Senior uses West's work without mentioning it, he says: "The labourer is principally interested in the amount of wages," (p. 14), that is to say the labourer is principally interested in what he receives, the nominal sum of his wages, not in that which he gives, the amount of labour!

the value produced in it is 6d. If the labourer is now employed less than 12 hours (or less than 6 days in the week), *e.g.*, only 6 or 8 hours, he receives, with this price of labour, only 2s. or 1s. 6d. a day.[1] As on our hypothesis he must work on the average 6 hours daily, in order to produce a day's wage corresponding merely to the value of his labour-power, as according to the same hypothesis he works only half of every hour for himself, and half for the capitalist, it is clear that he cannot obtain for himself the value of the product of 6 hours if he is employed less than 12 hours. In previous chapters we saw the destructive consequences of over-work; here we find the sources of the sufferings that result to the labourer from his insufficient employment.

If the hour's wage is fixed so that the capitalist does not bind himself to pay a day's or a week's wage, but only to pay wages for the hours during which he chooses to employ the labourer, he can employ him for a shorter time than that which is originally the basis of the calculation of the hour-wage, of the unit-measure of the price of labour. Since this unit is determined by the ratio $\frac{\text{daily value of labour-power}}{\text{working-day of a given number of hours,}}$ it, of course, loses all the meaning as soon as the working day ceases to contain a definite number of hours. The connexion between the paid and the unpaid labour is destroyed. The capitalist can now wring from the labourer a certain quantity of surplus-labour without allowing him the labour-time necessary for his own subsistence. He can annihilate all regularity of employment, and according to his own convenience, caprice, and the interest of the moment, make the most enormous over-work alternate with relative or absolute cessation of work. He can, under the pretence of paying "the normal price of labour," abnormally lengthen the working-day without any corresponding compensation to the labourer. Hence

---

[1] The effect of such an abnormal lessening of employment is quite different from that of a general reduction of the working-day, enforced by law. The former has nothing to do with the absolute length of the working-day, and may occur just as well in a working-day of 15, as of 6 hours. The normal price of labour is in the first case calculated on the labourer working 15 hours, in the second case in his working 6 hours a day on the average. The result is therefore the same if he in the one case is employed only for 7½, in the other only for 3 hours.

the perfectly rational revolt in 1860 of the London labourers, employed in the building trades, against the attempt of the capitalists to impose on them this sort of wage by the hour. The legal limitation of the working-day puts an end to such mischief, although not, of course, to the diminution of employment caused by the competition of machinery, by changes in the quality of the labourers employed, and by crisis partial or general.

With an increasing daily or weekly wage the price of labour may remain nominally constant, and yet may fall below its normal level. This occurs every time that, the price of labour (reckoned per working hour) remaining constant, the working-day is prolonged beyond its customary length. If in the fraction: $\frac{\text{daily value of labour-power}}{\text{working day}}$ the denominator increases, the numerator increases yet more rapidly. The value of labour-power, as dependent on its wear and tear, increases with the duration of its functioning, and in more rapid proportion than the increase of that duration. In many branches of industry where time-wage is the general rule without legal limits to the working-time, the habit has, therefore, spontaneously grown up of regarding the working-day as normal only up to a certain point, *e.g.,* up to the expiration of the tenth hour ("normal working-day," "the day's work," "the regular hours of work"). Beyond this limit the working-time is over-time, and is, taking the hour as unit-measure, paid better ("extra pay"), although often in a proportion ridiculously small.[1] The normal working-day exists here as a fraction of the actual working-day, and the latter, often during the whole year, lasts longer than the former.[2] The increase in the price of labour with the extension of the working-day beyond a certain normal

---

[1] "The rate of payment for overtime (in lace-making) is so small, from ½d. and ¾d. to 2d. per hour, that it stands in painful contrast to the amount of injury produced to the health and stamina of the workpeople. . . The small amount thus earned is also often obliged to be spent in extra nourishment." ("Child Emp. Com., II. Rep.," p. xvi., n. 117.)

[2] *E.g.,* in paper-staining before the recent introduction into this trade of the Factory Act. "We work on with no stoppage for meals, so that the day's work of 10½ hours is finished by 4.30 p.m., and all after that is overtime, and we seldom leave off working before 6 p.m., so that we are really working overtime the whole year round." (Mr. Smith's "Evidence in Child Emp. Com., I. Rep.," p. 125.)

limit, takes such a shape in various British industries that the low price of labour during the so-called normal time compels the labourer to work during the better paid over-time, if he wishes to obtain a sufficient wage at all.[1] Legal limitation of the working-day puts an end to these amenities.[2]

It is a fact generally known that, the longer the working-days, in any branch of industry, the lower are the wages.[3] A. Redgrave, factory-inspector, illustrates this by a comparative review of the 20 years from 1839-1859, according to which wages rose in the factories under the 10 hours' law, whilst they fell in the factories in which the work lasted 14 to 15 hours daily.[4]

From the law: "the price of labour being given, the daily or weekly wage depends on the quantity of labour expended," it follows, first of all, that, the lower the price of labour, the greater must be the quantity of labour, or the longer must be

---

[1] *E.g.*, in the Scotch bleaching-works. "In some parts of Scotland this trade [before the introduction of the Factory Act in 1862] was carried on by a system of overtime, *i.e.*, ten hours a day were the regular hours of work, for which a nominal wage of 1s. 2d. per day was paid to a man, there being every day overtime for three or four hours, paid at the rate of 3d. per hour. The effect of this system . . . a man could not earn more than 8s. per week when working the ordinary hours . . . without overtime they could not earn a fair day's wages." ("Rept. of Insp. of Factories," April 30th, 1863, p. 10.) "The higher wages, for getting adult males to work longer hours, are a temptation too strong to be resisted." ("Rept. of Insp. of Fact.," April 30th, 1848, p. 5.) The bookbinding trade in the city of London employs very many young girls from 14 to 15 years old, and that under indentures which prescribe certain definite hours of labour. Nevertheless, they work in the last week of each month until 10, 11, 12, or 1 o'clock at night, along with the older labourers, in a very mixed company. "The masters tempt them by extra pay and supper," which they eat in neighboring public-houses. The great debauchery thus produced among these 'young immortals' ("Children's Employment Comm., V. Rept.," p. 44, n. 191) is compensated by the fact that among the rest many Bibles and religious books are bound by them.

[2] *See* "Reports of Insp. of Fact.," 30th April, 1863, l. c. With very accurate appreciation of the state of things, the London labourers employed in the building trades declared, during the great strike and lockout of 1860, that they would only accept wages by the hour under two conditions (1) that, with the price of the working-hour, a normal working-day of 9 and 10 hours respectively should be fixed, and that the price of the hour for the 10 hours' working-day should be higher than that for the hour of the 9 hours' working-day; (2) that every hour beyond the normal working-day should be reckoned as overtime and proportionally more highly paid.

[3] "It is a very notable thing, too, that where long hours are the rule, small wages are also so." ("Report of Insp. of Fact.," 31st Oct., 1863, p. 9.) "The work which obtains the scanty pittance of food, is, for the most part, excessively prolonged." ("Public Health, Sixth Report," 1864, p. 15.)

[4] "Reports of Inspectors of Fact.," 30th April, 1860, pp. 31, 32.

the working-day for the labourer to secure even a miserable average-wage. The lowness of the price of labour acts here as a stimulus to the extension of the labour-time.[1]

On the other hand, the extension of the working-time produces, in its turn, a fall in the price of labour, and with this a fall in the day's or week's wages.

The determination of the price of labour by:

$$\frac{\text{daily value of labour-power}}{\text{working-day of a given number of hours,}}$$

shows that a mere prolongation of the working-day lowers the price of labour, if no compensation steps in. But the same circumstances which allow the capitalist in the long run to prolong the working-day, also allow him first, and compel him finally, to nominally lower the price of labour, until the total price of the increased number of hours is lowered, and, therefore, the daily or weekly wage. Reference to two circumstances is sufficient here. If one man does the work of $1\frac{1}{2}$ or 2 men, the supply of labour increases, although the supply of labour-power on the market remains constant. The competition thus created between the labourers allows the capitalist to beat down the price of labour, whilst the falling price of labour allows him, on the other hand, to screw up still further the working-time.[2] Soon, however, this command over abnormal quantities of unpaid labour, *i.e.,* quantities in excess of the average social amount, becomes a source of competition amongst the capitalists themselves. A part of the price of the commodity consists of the price of labour. The unpaid part of the labour-price need not be reckoned in the price of the

[1] The hand-nail makers in England, *e.g.,* have, on account of the low price of labour, to work 15 hours a day in order to hammer out their miserable weekly wage. "It's a great many hours in a day (6 a.m. to 8 p.m.), and he has to work hard all the time to get 11d. or 1s., and there is the wear of the tools, the cost o'f firing, and something for waste iron to go out of this, which takes off altogether $2\frac{1}{2}$d. or 3d." ("Children's Employment Com., III. Report," p. 136, n. 671.) The women earn by the same working-time a week's wage of only 5 shillings (l. c., p. 137, n. 674.

[2] If a factory-hand, *e.g.,* refused to work the customary long hours, "he would very shortly be replaced by somebody who would work any length of time, and thus be thrown out of employment." ("Report of Inspectors of Fact.," 31st Oct., 1848. Evidence, p. 39, n. 58.) "If one man performs the work of two . . . the rate of profits will generally be raised . . . in consequence of the additional supply of labour having diminished its price." (Senior, l. c., p. 14.)

commodity. It may be presented to the buyer. This is the first step to which competition leads. The second step to which it drives, is to exclude also from the selling-price of the commodity, at least a part of the abnormal surplus-value created by the extension of the working-day. In this way an abnormally low selling-price of the commodity arises, at first sporadically, and becomes fixed by degrees; a lower selling price which henceforward becomes the constant basis of a miserable wage for an excessive working-time, as originally it was the product of these very circumstances. This movement is simply indicated here, as the analysis of competition does not belong to this part of our subject. Nevertheless, the capitalist may, for a moment, speak for himself. "In Birmingham there is so much competition of masters one against another, that many are obliged to do things as employers that they would otherwise be ashamed of; and yet no more money is made, but only the public gets the benefit."[1] The reader will remember the two sorts of London bakers, of whom one sold the bread at its full price (the "full-priced" bakers), the other below its normal price ("the underpriced," "the undersellers"). The "full-priced" denounced their rivals before the Parliamentary Committee of Inquiry: "They only exist now by first defrauding the public, and next getting 18 hours' work out of their men for 12 hours' wages. . . . The unpaid labour of the men was made . . . the source whereby the competition was carried on, and continues so to this day. . . . The competition among the master bakers is the cause of the difficulty in getting rid of night-work. An underseller, who sells his bread below the cost price according to the price of flour, must make it up by getting more out of the labour of the men. . . . If I got only 12 hours' work out of my men, and my neighbour got 18 or 20, he must beat me in the selling price. If the men could insist on payment for over-work, this would be set right. . . . . A large number of those employed by the undersellers are foreigners,

---

[1] "Children's Employment Com., III. Rep.," Evidence, p. 66, n. 22.

and youths, who are obliged to accept almost any wages they can obtain."[1]

This jeremiad is also interesting because it shows, how the appearance only of the relations of production mirrors itself in the brain of the capitalist. The capitalist does not know that the normal price of labour also includes a definite quantity of unpaid labour, and that this very unpaid labour is the normal source of his gain. The category, surplus-labour-time, does not exist at all for him, since it is included in the normal working-day, which he thinks he has paid for in the day's wages. But overtime does exist for him, the prolongation of the working day beyond the limits corresponding with the usual price of labour. Face to face with his underselling competitor, he even insists upon extra pay for this overtime. He again does not know that this extra pay includes unpaid labour, just as well as does the price of the customary hour of labour. For example, the price of one hour of the 12 hours' working-day is 3d., say the value-product of half a working-hour, whilst the price of the overtime working-hour is 4d., or the value-product of $\frac{2}{3}$ of a working-hour. In the first case the capitalist appropriates to himself one-half, in the second, one-third of the working-hours without paying for it.

CHAPTER XXI.

PIECE-WAGES.

WAGES by the piece are nothing else than a converted form of wages by time, just as wages by time are a converted form of the value or price of labour-power.

In piece-wages it seems at first sight as if the use-value

---

[1] "Report, &c., relative to the Grievances complained of by the Journeymen Bakers." Lond. 1862, p. 411, and ib. Evidence, notes 479, 359, 27. Anyhow the full-priced also, as was mentioned above, and as their spokesman, Bennett, himself admits, make their men "generally begin work at 11 p.m. . . . up to 8 o'clock the next morning . . . they are then engaged all day long . . . as late as 7 o'clock in the evening." (l. c., p. 22.)

bought from the labourer was, not the function of his labour-power, living labour, but labour already realised in the product, and as if the price of this labour was determined, not as with time-wages, by the fraction, $\frac{\text{daily value of labor power}}{\text{working day of given number of hours}}$ but by the capacity for work of the producer.[1]

The confidence that trusts in this appearance ought to receive a first severe shock from the fact that both forms of wages exist side by side, simultaneously, in the same branches of industry; *e.g.,* "the compositors of London, as a general rule, work by the piece, time-work being the exception, while those in the country work by the day, the exception being work by the piece. The shipwrights of the port of London work by the job or piece, while those of all other parts work by the day."[2]

In the same saddlery shops of London, often for the same work, piece-wages are paid to the French, time-wages to the English. In the regular factories in which throughout piece-wages predominate, particular kinds of work are unsuitable to this form of wage, and are therefore paid by time.[3] But it is moreover self-evident that the difference of form in the payment of wages alters in no way their essential nature,

[1] "The system of piece-work illustrates an epoch in the history of the working man; it is halfway between the position of the mere day labourer depending upon the will of the capitalist and the co-operative artisan, who in the not distant future promises to combine the artizan and the capitalist in his own person. Piece-workers are in fact their own masters' even whilst working upon the capital of the employer." (John Watts: "Trade Societies and Strikes, Machinery and Co-operative Societies." Manchester, 1865, p. 52, 53.) I quote this little work because it is a very sink of all long-ago-rotten, apologetic commonplaces. This same Mr. Watts earlier traded in Owenism and published in 1842 another pamphlet: "Facts and Fictions of Political Economists," in which among other things he declares that "property is robbery." That is long ago.

[2] T. J. Dunning: "Trade's Unions and Strikes," Lond. 1860. p. 22.

[3] How the existence, side by side and simultaneously, of these two forms of wage favours the masters' cheating: "A factory employs 400 people, the half of which work by the piece, and have a direct interest in working longer hours. The other 200 are paid by the day, work equally long with the others, and get no more money for their overtime. . . . The work of these 200 people for half an hour a day is equal to one person's work for 50 hours, or ⅚ of one person's labour in a week, and is a positive gain to the employer." ("Reports of Insp. of Fact., 31st Oct., 1860," p. 9.) "Overworking to a very considerable extent still prevails; and, in most instances, with that security against detection and punishment which the law itself affords. I have in many former reports shown . . . the injury to workpeople who are not employed on piece-work, but receive weekly wages." Leonard Horner in "Reports of Insp. of Fact." 30th April, 1859, pp. 8, 9.)

although the one form may be more favorable to the development of capitalist production than the other.

Let the ordinary working day contain 12 hours of which 6 are paid, 6 unpaid. Let its value-product be 6 shillings, that of one hour's labour therefore 6d. Let us suppose that, as the result of experience, a labourer who works with the average amount of intensity and skill, who, therefore, gives in fact only the time socially necessary to the production of an article, supplies in 12 hours 24 pieces, either distinct products or measurable parts of a continuous whole. Then the value of these 24 pieces, after subtraction of the portion of constant capital contained in them, is 6 shillings, and the value of a single piece 3d. The labourer receives 1½d. per piece, and thus earns in 12 hours 3 shillings. Just as, with time-wages, it does not matter whether we assume that the labourer works 6 hours for himself and 6 hours for the capitalist, or half of every hour for himself, and the other half for the capitalist, so here it does not matter whether we say that each individual piece is half paid, and half unpaid for, or that the price of 12 pieces is the equivalent only of the value of the labour-power, whilst in the other 12 pieces surplus-value is incorporated.

The form of piece-wages is just as irrational as that of time-wages. Whilst in our example two pieces of a commodity, after subtraction of the value of the means of production consumed in them, are worth 6d. as being the product of one hour, the labourer receives for them a price of 3d. Piece-wages do not, in fact, distinctly express any relation of value. It is not, therefore, a question of measuring the value of the piece by the working time incorporated in it, but on the contrary of measuring the working-time the labourer has expended, by the number of pieces he has produced. In time-wages the labour is measured by its immediate duration, in piece-wages by the quantity of products in which the labour has embodied itself during a given time.[1] The price of labour-time itself is finally determined by the equation; value of a day's labour=daily

---

[1] "Le salaire peut se mesurer de deux manières: ou sur la durée du travail, ou sur son produit." ("Abrégé élémentaire des principes de l'Economie Politique." Paris 1796, p. 32.) The author of this anonymous work: G. Garnier.

value of labour-power. Piece-wage is, therefore, only a modified form of time-wage.

Let us now consider a little more closely the characteristic peculiarities of piece-wages.

The quality of the labour is here controlled by the work itself, which must be of average perfection if the piece-price is to be paid in full. Piece-wages become, from this point of view, the most fruitful source of reductions of wages and capitalistic cheating.

They furnish to the capitalist an exact measure for the intensity of labour. Only the working-time which is embodied in a quantum of commodities determined beforehand and experimentally fixed, counts as socially necessary working time, and is paid as such. In the larger workshops of the London tailors, therefore, a certain piece of work, a waistcoat *e.g.,* is called an hour, or half an hour, the hour at 6d. By practise it is known how much is the average product of one hour. With new fashions, repairs, etc., a contest arises between master and labourer, whether a particular piece of work is one hour, and so on, until here also experience decides. Similarly in the London furniture workshops, etc. If the labourer does not possess the average capacity, if he cannot in consequence supply a certain minimum of work per day, he is dismissed.[1]

Since the quality and intensity of the work are here controlled by the form of wage itself, superintendence of labour becomes in great part superfluous. Piece-wages therefore lay the foundation of the modern "domestic labour," described above, as well as of a hierarchically organised system of exploitation and oppression. The latter has two fundamental forms. On the one hand piece-wages facilitate the interposition of parasites between the capitalist and the wage-labourer, the "sub-letting of labour." The gain of these middle-men comes

---

[1] "So much weight of cotton is delivered to him [the spinner], and he has to return by a certain time, in lieu of it, a given weight of twist or yarn, of a certain degree of fineness, and he is paid so much per pound for all that he so returns. If his work is defective in quality, the penalty falls on him, if less in quantity than the minimum fixed for a given time, he is dismissed and an abler operative procured." (Ure l. c. p. 317.)

entirely from the difference between the labour price which the capitalist pays, and the part of that price which they actually allow to reach the labourer.[1] In England this system is characteristically called the "Sweating system." On the other hand piece-wage allows the capitalist to make a contract for so much per piece with the head labourer—in manufactures with the chief of some group, in mines with the extractor of the coal, in the factory with the actual machine-worker—at a price for which the head labourer himself undertakes the enlisting and payment of his assistant workpeople. The exploitation of the labourer by capital is here effected through the exploitation of the labourer by the labourer.[2]

Given piece-wage, it is naturally the personal interest of the labourer to strain his labour-power as intensely as possible; this enables the capitalist to raise more easily the normal degree of intensity of labour.[3] It is moreover now the personal interest of the labourer to lengthen the working day, since with it his daily or weekly wages rise.[4] This gradually brings

[1] "It is when work passes through several hands, each of which is to take its share of profits, while only the last does the work, that the pay which reaches the work-woman is miserably disproportioned." (Child Emp. Com. II. Report, p. lxx, n. 424.)

[2] Even Watts, the apologetic, remarks: "It would be a great improvement to the system of piece-work, if all the men employed on a job were partners in the contract, each according to his abilities, instead of one man being interested in overworking his fellows for his own benefit." (l. c. p. 53.) On the vileness of this system, cf. Child. Emp. Com. Rep. III. p. 66, n. 22, p. 11, n. 124, p. xi. n. 13, 53, 59, etc.

[3] This spontaneous result is often artificially helped along, e.g., in the Engineering Trade of London, a customary trick is "the selecting of a man who possesses superior physical strength and quickness, as the principal of several workmen, and paying him an additional rate, by the quarter or otherwise, with the understanding that he is to exert himself to the utmost to induce the others, who are only paid the ordinary wages, to keep up to him. . . . Without any comment this will go far to explain many of the complaints of stinting the action, superior skill, and working-power, made by the employers against the men" (in Trades-Unions. Dunning, l. c. pp. 22, 23). As the author is himself a labourer and secretary of a Trade's Union, this might be taken for exaggeration. But the reader may compare the "highly respectable" Cyclopædia of Agriculture of J. Ch. Morton, Art. "Labourer," where this method is recommended to the farmers as an approved one.

[4] "All those who are paid by piece-work . . . profit by the transgression of the legal limits of work. This observation as to the willingness to work overtime is especially applicable to the women employed as weavers and reelers." (Rept. of Insp. of Fact., 30th April, 1858, p. 9). "This system (piece-work), so advantageous to the employer . . . tends directly to encourage the young potter greatly to overwork himself during the four or five years during which he is employed in the piece-work system, but at low wages. . . . This is . . . another great cause

on a reaction like that already described in time-wages, without reckoning that the prolongation of the working day, even if the piece-wage remains constant, includes of necessity a fall in the price of the labour.

In time-wages, with few exceptions, the same wage holds for the same kind of work, whilst in piece-wages, though the price of the working time is measured by a certain quantity of product, the day's or week's wage will vary with the individual differences of the labourers, of whom one supplies in a given time the minimum of product only, another the average, a third more than the average. With regard to actual receipts there is, therefore, great variety according to the different skill, strength, energy, staying-power, etc., of the individual labourers.[1] Of course this does not alter the general relations between capital and wage-labour. First, the individual differences balance one another in the workshop as a whole, which thus supplies in a given working-time the average product, and the total wages paid will be the average wages of that particular branch of industry. Second, the proportion between wages and surplus-value remains unaltered, since the mass of surplus-labour supplied by each particular labourer corresponds with the wage received by him. But the wider scope that piece-wage gives to individuality, tends to develop on the one hand that individuality, and with it the sense of liberty, independence, and self-control of the labourers, on the other, their competition one with another. Piece-work has, therefore, a tendency, while raising individual wages above the average, to lower this average itself. But where a particular rate of piece-wage has for a long time been fixed by tradition, and its lowering, therefore, presented especial difficulties, the masters, in such exceptional cases, sometimes had recourse to its compulsory transformation into time-wages. Hence, *e.g.*, in 1860 a great strike among the ribbon-weavers

to which the bad constitutions of the potters are to be attributed." (Child Empl. Com. I. Rept., p. xiii.)

[1] "Where the work in any trade is paid for by the piece at so much per job . . . wages may very materially differ in amount. . . . But in work by the day there is generally an uniform rate . . . recognized by both employer and employed as the standard of wages for the general run of workmen in the trade." (Dunning, l. c. p. 17.)

of Coventry.[1] Piece-wage is finally one of the chief supports of the hour-system described in the preceding chapter.[2]

From what has been shown so far, it follows that piece-wage is the form of wages most in harmony with the capitalist mode of production. Although by no means new—it figures side by side with time-wages officially in the French and English labour statutes of the 14th century—it only conquers a larger field for action during the period of Manufacture, properly so-called. In the stormy youth of Modern Industry, especially from 1797 to 1815, it served as a lever for the lengthening of the working day, and the lowering of wages. Very important materials for the fluctuation of wages during that period are to be found in the Blue-books: "Report and Evidence from the Select Committee on Petitions respecting the Corn Laws," (Parliamentary Session of 1813-14), and "Report from the Lords' Committee, on the state of the Growth, Commerce, and Consumption of Grain, and all Laws relating thereto," (Session of 1814-15). Here we find documentary evidence of the constant lowering of the price of labour from the beginning of the Anti-Jacobin War. In the weaving industry, *e.g.*, piece-wages had fallen so low that in

[1] "Le travail des Compagnons-artisans sera réglé à la journée ou à la pièce . . . Ces maîtres-artisans savent à peu près combien d'ouvrage un compagnon-artisan peut faire par jour dans chaque métier, et les payent souvent à proportion de l'ouvrage qu'ils font; ainsi ces compagnons travaillent autant qu'ils peuvent, pour leur propre intérêt, sans autre inspection." (Cantillon, Essai sur la Nature du Commerce en général, Amst. Ed., 1756, pp. 185 and 202. The first edition appeared in 1755.) Cantillon, from whom Quesnay, Sir James Steuart & A. Smith have largely drawn, already here represents piece-wage as simply a modified form of time-wage. The French edition of Cantillon professes in its title to be a translation from the English, but the English edition: "The analysis of Trade, Commerce, etc., by Philip Cantillon, late of the city of London, Merchant," is not only of later date (1759), but proves by its contents that it is a later and revised edition; *e.g.*, in the French edition, Hume is not yet mentioned, whilst in the English, on the other hand, Petty hardly figures any longer. The English edition is theoretically less important, but it contains numerous details referring specifically to English commerce, bullion trade, etc., that are wanting in the French text. The words on the title-page of the English edition, according to which the work is "Taken chiefly from the manuscript of a very ingenious gentleman, deceased, and adapted, etc," seem, therefore, a pure fiction, very customary at that time.

[2] "Combien de fois n'avons-nous pas vu, dans certains ateliers, embaucher beaucoup plus d'ouvriers que ne le demandait le travail à mettre en main? Souvent, dans la prévision d'un travail aléatoire, quelquefois même imaginaire, on admet des ouvriers: comme on les paie aux pièces, on se dit qu'on ne court aucun risque, parceque toutes les pertes de temps seront à la charge des inoccupés." (H. Grégoir: "Les Typographes devant le Tribunal correctionnel de Bruxelles," Bruxelles, 1865, p. 9.)

spite of the very great lengthening of the working day, the daily wages were then lower than before. "The real earnings of the cotton weaver are now far less than they were; his superiority over the common labourer, which at first was very great, has now almost entirely ceased. Indeed . . . the difference in the wages of skilful and common labour is far less now than at any former period."[1] How little the increased intensity and extension of labour through piece-wages benefited the agricultural proletariat, the following passage borrowed from a work on the side of the landlords and farmers shows: "By far the greater part of agricultural operations is done by people, who are hired for the day or on piece-work. Their weekly wages are about 12s., and although it may be assumed that a man earns on piece-work under the greater stimulus to labour, 1s. or perhaps 2s. more than on weekly wages, yet it is found, on calculating his total income, that his loss of employment, during the year, outweighs this gain . . . Further, it will generally be found that the wages of these men bear a certain proportion to the price of the necessary means of subsistence, so that a man with two children is able to bring up his family without recourse to parish relief."[2] Malthus at that time remarked with reference to the facts published by Parliament: "I confess that I see, with misgiving, the great extension of the practice of piece-wage. Really hard work during 12 or 14 hours of the day, or for any longer time, is too much for any human being."[3]

In the workshops under the Factory Acts, piece-wage becomes the general rule, because capital can there only increase the efficacy of the working day by intensifying labour.[4]

With the changing productiveness of labour the same quantum of product represents a varying working time. Therefore, piece-wage also varies, for it is the money expression of a determined working time. In our example above, 24 pieces were produced in 12 hours, whilst the value of the product

[1] Remarks on the Commercial Policy of Great Britain, London, 1815.
[2] A defence on the Land-owners and Farmers of Great Britain, 1814, pp. 4, 5.
[3] Malthus, Inquiry into the Nature and Progress of Rent, Lond., 1815.
[4] "Those who are paid by piece-work . . . constitute probably four-fifths of the workers in the factories." "Report of Insp. of Fact., 30th April, 1858."

of the 12 hours was 6s., the daily value of the labour-power 3s., the price of the labour-hour 3d., and the wage for one piece 1½d. In one piece half-an-hour's labour was absorbed. If the same working day now supplies, in consequence of the doubled productiveness of labour, 48 pieces instead of 24, and all other circumstances remain unchanged, then the piece-wage falls from 1½d. to ¾d., as every piece now only represents ¼, instead of ½ of a working hour. 24 by 1½d. =3s., and in like manner 48 by ¾d.=3s. In other words, piece-wage is lowered in the same proportion as the number of the pieces produced in the same time rises,[1] and therefore as the working time spent on the same piece falls. This change in piece-wage, so far purely nominal, leads to constant battles between capitalist and labour. Either because the capitalist uses it as a pretext for actually lowering the price of labour, or because increased productive power of labour is accompanied by an increased intensity of the same. Or because the labourer takes seriously the appearance of piece-wages, viz., that his product is paid for, and not his labour-power, and therefore revolts against a lowering of wages, unaccompanied by a lowering in the selling price of the commodity. "The operatives . . . . carefully watch the price of the raw material and the price of manufactured goods, and are thus enabled to form an accurate estimate of their master's profits."[2]

The capitalist rightly knocks on the head such pretensions as gross errors as to the nature of wage-labour.[3] He cries out against this usurping attempt to lay taxes on the advance of

[1] "The productive power of his spinning-machine is accurately measured, and the rate of pay for work done with it decreases with, though not *as*, the increase of its productive power." (Ure, l. c., p. 317.) This last apologetic phrase Ure himself again cancels. The lengthening of the mule causes some increase of labour, he admits. The labour does therefore not diminish in the same ratio as its productivity increases. Further: "By this increase the productive power of the machine will be augmented one-fifth. When this event happens the spinner will not be paid at the same rate for work done as he was before, but as that rate will not be diminished in the ratio of one-fifth, the improvement will augment his money earnings for any given number of hours' work," but "the foregoing statement requires a certain modification. . . . The spinner has to pay something additional for juvenile aid out of his additional sixpence, accompanied by displacing a portion of adults" (l. c. p. 321), which has in no way a tendency to raise wages.

[2] H. Fawcett: "The Economic Position of the British Labourer. Cambridge and London, 1865," p. 178.

[3] In the *London Standard* of October 26, 1861, there is a report of proceedings

industry, and declares roundly that the productiveness of labour does not concern the labourer at all.[1]

CHAPTER XXII.

NATIONAL DIFFERENCES OF WAGES.

In the 17th chapter we were occupied with the manifold combinations which may bring about a change in magnitude of the value of labour-power—this magnitude being considered either absolutely or relatively, *i.e.*, as compared with surplus-value; whilst on the other hand, the quantum of the means of subsistence in which the price of labour is realised might again undergo fluctuations independent of, or different from, the changes of this price.[2] As has been already said, the simple translation of the value or respectively of the price of labour-power into the exoteric form of wages transforms all these laws into laws of the fluctuations of wages. That which appears in these fluctuations of wages within a single country as a series of varying combinations, may appear in different countries as contemporaneous difference of national wages. In the comparison of the wages in different nations, we must therefore take into account all the factors that determine

of the firm of John Bright & Co., before the Rochdale magistrates "to prosecute for intimidation the agents of the Carpet Weavers Trades' Union. Bright's partners had introduced new machinery which would turn out 240 yards of carpet in the time and with the labour (!) previously required to produce 160 yards. The work-men had no claim whatever to share in the profits made by the investment of their employer's capital in mechanical improvements. Accordingly, Messrs. Bright pro-posed to lower the rate of pay from 1½d. per yard to 1d., leaving the earnings of the men exactly the same as before for the same labour. But there was a nominal reduction, of which the operatives, it is asserted, had not fair warning before hand."

[1] "Trades' Unions, in their desire to maintain wages, endeavour to share in the benefits of improved machinery. (*Quelle horreur!*) . . . the demanding higher wages, because labour is abbreviated, is in other words the endeavour to establish a duty on mechanical improvements." ("On Combination of Trades, new ed., London, 1834," p. 42.)

[2] "It is not accurate to say that wages" (he deals here with their money expres-sion) "are increased, because they purchase more of a cheaper article." (David Buchanan in his edition of Adam Smith's "Wealth," &c., 1814, Vol. I., p. 417. Note.)

changes in the amount of the value of labour-power; the price and the extent of the prime necessaries of life as naturally and historically developed, the cost of training the labourers, the part played by the labour of women and children, the productiveness of labour, its extensive and intensive magnitude. Even the most superficial comparison requires the reduction first of the average day-wage for the same trades, in different countries, to a uniform working day. After this reduction to the same terms of the day-wages, time-wage must again be translated into piece-wage, as the latter only can be a measure both of the productivity and the intensity of labour.

In every country there is a certain average intensity of labour, below which the labour for the production of a commodity requires more than the socially necessary time, and therefore does not reckon as labour of normal quality. Only a degree of intensity above the national average affects, in a given country, the measure of value of the mere duration of the working time. This is not the case on the universal market, whose integral parts are the individual countries. The average intensity of labour changes from country to country; here it is greater, there less. These national averages form a scale, whose unit of measure is the average unit of universal labour. The more intense national labour, therefore, as compared with the less intense, produces in the same time more value, which expresses itself in more money.

But the law of value in its international application is yet more modified by this, that on the world-market the more productive national labour reckons also as the more intense, so long as the more productive nation is not compelled by competition to lower the selling price of its commodities to the level of their value.

In proportion as capitalist production is developed in a country, in the same proportion do the national intensity and productivity of labour there rise above the international level.[1] The different quantities of commodities of the same kind, produced in different countries in the same working time, have,

[1] We shall inquire, in another place, what circumstances in relation to productivity may modify this law for individual branches of industry.

therefore, unequal international values, which are expressed in different prices, *i.e.,* in sums of money varying according to international values. The relative value of money will, therefore, be less in the nation with more developed capitalist mode of production than in the nation with less developed. It follows, then, that the nominal wages, the equivalent of labour-power expressed in money, will also be higher in the first nation than in the second; which does not at all prove that this holds also for the real wages, *i.e.,* for the means of subsistence placed at the disposal of the labourer.

But even apart from these relative differences of the value of money in different countries, it will be found, frequently, that the daily or weekly, &c., wage in the first nation is higher than in the second, whilst the relative price of labour, *i.e.,* the price of labour as compared both with surplus-value and with the value of the product, stands higher in the second than in the first.[1]

J. W. Cowell, member of the Factory Commission of 1833, after careful investigation of the spinning trade, came to the conclusion that, " in England wages are virtually lower to the capitalist, though higher to the operative than on the Continent of Europe." (Ure, p. 314.) The English Factory Inspector, Alexander Redgrave, in his Report of Oct. 31st, 1866, proves by comparative statistics with Continental states, that in spite of lower wages and much longer working-time, Continental labour is, in proportion to the product, dearer than English. An English manager of a cotton factory in Olden-

---

[1] James Anderson remarks in his polemic against Adam Smith: "It deserves, likewise, to be remarked, that although the apparent price of labour is usually lower in poor countries, where the produce of the soil, and grain in general, is cheap; yet it is in fact for the most part really higher than in other countries. For it is not the wages that is given to the labourer per day that constitutes the real price of labour, although it is its apparent price. The real price is that which a certain quantity of work performed actually costs the employer; and considered in this light, labour is in almost all cases cheaper in rich countries than in those that are poorer, although the price of grain, and other provisions, is usually much lower in the last than in the first. . . . Labour estimated by the day, is much lower in Scotland than in England. . . . Labour by the piece is generally cheaper in England." (James Anderson, Observations on the means of exciting a spirit of National Industry, &c., Edin. 1777, pp. 350, 351). On the contrary, lowness of wages produces, in its turn, dearness of labour. "Labour being dearer in Ireland than it is in England . . . because the wages are so much lower." (N. 2079 in Royal Commission on Railways, Minutes, 1867.)

burg, declares that the working-time there lasted from 5.30 a.m. to 8 p.m., Saturdays included, and that the workpeople there, when under English overlookers, did not supply during this time quite so much product as the English in 10 hours, but under German overlookers much less. Wages are much lower than in England, in many cases 50%, but the number of hands in proportion to the machinery was much greater, in certain departments in the proportion of 5:3.—Mr. Redgrave gives very full details as to the Russian cotton factories. The data were given him by an English manager until recently employed there. On this Russian soil, so fruitful of all infamies, the old horrors of the early days of English factories are in full swing. The managers are, of course, English, as the native Russian capitalist is of no use in factory business. Despite all over-work, continued day and night, despite the most shameful under-payment of the workpeople, Russian manufacture manages to vegetate only by prohibition of foreign competition. I give, in conclusion, a comparative table of Mr. Redgrave's, on the average number of spindles per factory and per spinner in the different countries of Europe. He, himself, remarks that he had collected these figures a few years ago, and that since that time the size of the factories and the number of spindles per labourer in England has increased. He supposes, however, an approximately equal progress in the Continental countries mentioned, so that the numbers given would still have their value for purposes of comparison.

Average Number of Spindles per Factory.

England, average of spindles per factory	12,600
France, " " "	1,500
Prussia, " " "	1,500
Belgium, " " "	4,000
Saxony, " " "	4,500
Austria, " " "	7,000
Switzerland " " "	8,000

AVERAGE NUMBER OF PERSONS EMPLOYED TO SPINDLES.

France,	one person to	14	spindles
Russia,	"	28	"
Prussia,	"	37	"
Bavaria,	"	46	"
Austria,	"	49	"
Belgium,	"	50	"
Saxony,	"	50	"
Switzerland,	"	55	"
Smaller States of Germany,		55	"
Great Britain,	"	74	"

" This comparison," says Mr. Redgrave, " is yet more unfavourable to Great Britain, inasmuch as there is so large a number of factories in which weaving by power is carried on in conjunction with spinning [whilst in the table the weavers are not deducted], and the factories abroad are chiefly spinning factories; if it were possible to compare like with like, strictly, I could find many cotton spinning factories in my district in which mules containing 2,200 spindles are minded by one man (the " minder ") and two assistants only, turning off daily 220 lbs. of yarn, measuring 400 miles in length." (Reports of Insp. of Fact., 31st Oct., 1866, p. 31-33, passim.)

It is well known that in Eastern Europe as well as in Asia, English companies have undertaken the construction of railways, and have, in making them, employed side by side with the native labourers, a certain number of English workingmen. Compelled by practical necessity, they thus have had to take into account the national difference in the intensity of labour, but this has brought them no loss. Their experience shows that even if the height of wages corresponds more or less with the average intensity of labour, the relative price of labour varies generally in the inverse direction.

[1] "Essay on the Rate of Wages, with an Examination of the Differences in the Conditions of the Labouring Population throughout the World," Philadelphia, 1835.

In an " Essay on the Rate of Wages,"[1] one of his first economic writings, H. Carey tries to prove that the wages of the
different nations are directly proportional to the degree of
productiveness of the national working days, in order to draw
from this international relation, the conclusion that wages
everywhere rise and fall in proportion to the productiveness
of labour. The whole of our analysis of the production of
surplus value shows the absurdity of this conclusion, even if
Carey himself had proved his premises, instead of, after his
usual uncritical and superficial fashion, shuffling to and fro a
confused mass of statistical materials. The best of it is that
he does not assert that things actually are as they ought to be
according to his theory. For State intervention has falsified
the natural economic relations. The different natio..al wages
must be reckoned, therefore, as if that part of each that goes to
the State in the form of taxes, came to the labourer himself.
Ought not Mr. Carey to consider further whether those " State
expenses " are not the " natural " fruits of capitalistic development? The reasoning is quite worthy of the man who first
declared the relations of capitalist production to be eternal laws
of nature and reason, whose free, harmonious working is only
disturbed by the intervention of the State, in order afterwards to discover that the diabolical influen e of England on
the world-market · (an influence which, it appears, does not
spring from the natural laws of capitalist production) necessitates State intervention, *i.e.,* the protection of those laws of
nature and reason by the State, *alias* the System of Protection.
He discovered further, that the theorems of Ricardo and others, in which existing social antagonisms and contradictions
are formulated, are not the ideal product of the real economic
movement, but on the contrary, that the real antagonisms of
capitalist production in England and elsewhere are the result
of the theories of Ricardo and others! Finally, he discovered
that it is, in the last resort, commerce that destroys the inborn
beauties and harmonies of the capitalist mode of production.
A step further, and he will, perhaps, discover that the one
evil in capitalist production is capital itself. Only a man

with such atrocious want of the critical faculty and such spurious erudition deserved, in spite of his Protectionist heresy, to become the secret source of the harmonious wisdom of a Bastiat, and of all the other Free Trade optimists of to-day.

PART VII.

THE ACCUMULATION OF CAPITAL.

THE conversion of a sum of money into means of production and labour-power, is the first step taken by the quantum of value that is going to function as capital. This conversion takes place in the market, within the sphere of circulation. The second step, the process of production, is complete so soon as the means of production have been converted into commodities whose value exceeds that of their component parts, and, therefore, contains the capital originally advanced, plus a surplus-value. These commodities must then be thrown into circulation. They must be sold, their value realised in money, this money afresh converted into capital, and so over and over again. This circular movement, in which the same phases are continually gone through in succession, forms the circulation of capital.

The first condition of accumulation is that the capitalist must have contrived to sell his commodities, and to reconvert into capital the greater part of the money so received. In the following pages we shall assume that capital circulates in its normal way. The detailed analysis of the process will be found in Book II.

The capitalist who produces surplus-value—*i.e.*, who extracts unpaid labour directly from the labourers, and fixes it in commodities, is, indeed the first appropriator, but by no means the ultimate owner, of thi surplus value. He has to share it with capitalists, with landowners, &c., who fulfill other functions in the comple of social production. Surplus-value, therefore, splits up into various parts. Its fragments fall to various categories of persons, and take various forms, independent the one of the other, such as profit, interest, merchants' profit, rent, &c. It is only in Book III. that we can take in hand these modified forms of surplus-value.

On the one hand, then, we assume that the Capitalist sells at their value the commodities he has produced, without concerning ourselves either about the new forms that capital assumes while in the sphere of circulation, or about the concrete conditions of reproduction hidden under these forms. On the other hand, we treat the capitalist producer as owner of the entire surplus-value, or, better perhaps, as the representative of all the sharers with him in the booty. We, therefore, first of all consider accumulation from an abstract point of view—*i.e.,* as a mere phase in the actual process of production.

So far as accumulation takes place, the capitalist must have succeeded in selling his commodities, and in reconverting the sale-money into capital. Moreover, the breaking-up of surplus-value into fragments neither alters its nature nor the conditions under which it becomes an element of accumulation. Whatever be the proportion of surplus-value which the industrial capitalist retains for himself, or yields up to others, he is the one who, in the first instance, appropriates it. We, therefore, assume no more than what actually takes place. On the other hand, the simple fundamental form of the process of accumulation is obscured by the incident of the circulation which brings it about, and by the splitting up of surplus-value. An exact analysis of the process, therefore, demands that we should, for a time, disregard all phenomena that hide the play of its inner mechanism.

CHAPTER XXIII.

SIMPLE REPRODUCTION.

WHATEVER the form of the process of production in a society, it must be a continuous process, must continue to go periodically through the same phases. A society can no more cease

to produce than it can cease to consume. ' When viewed, therefore, as a connected whole, and as flowing on with incessant
renewal, every social process of production is, at the same time,
a process of reproduction.

The conditions of production are also those of reproduction.
No society can go on producing, in other words, no society can
reproduce, unless it constantly reconverts a part of its products
into means of production, or elements of fresh products.   All
other circumstances remaining the same, the only mode by
which it can reproduce its wealth, and maintain it at one level,
is by replacing the means of production—*i.e.,* the instruments
of labour, the raw material, and the auxiliary substances consumed in the course of the year—by an equal quantity of the
same kind of articles; these must be separated from the mass
of the yearly products, and thrown afresh into the process of
production.   Hence, a definite portion of each year's product
belongs to the domain of production.   Destined for productive
consumption from the very first, this portion exists, for the
most part, in the shape of articles totally unfitted for individual consumption.

If production be capitalistic in form, so, too, will be reproduction.   Just as in the former the labour-process figures but
as a means towards the self-expansion of capital, so in the latter it figures but as a means of reproducing as capital—*i.e.,* as
self-expanding value,—the value advanced.   It is only because his money constantly functions as capital that the
economical guise of a capitalist attaches to a man.   If, for
instance, a sum of £100 has this year been converted into capital, and produced a surplus-value of £20, it must continue during next year, and subsequent years, to repeat the same operation.   As a periodic increment of the capital advanced, or
periodic fruit of capital in process, surplus-value acquires the
form of a revenue flowing out of capital.[1]

[1] "Mais ces riches, qui consomment les produits du travail des autres, ne peuvent les obtenir que par des échanges [purchases of commodities.].   S'ils donnent cependant leur richesse acquise et accumulée en retour contre ces produits nouveaux
qui sont l'objet de leur fantaisie, ils semblent exposés à épuiser bientôt leur fonds de
réserve; ils ne travaillent point, avons-nous dit, et ils ne peuvent même travailler;
on croirait donc que chaque jour doit voir diminuer leurs vieilles richesses, et que
lorsqu'il ne leur en restera plus, rien ne sera offert en échange aux ouvriers qui

If this revenue serve the capitalist only as a fund to provide for his consumption, and be spent as periodically as it is gained, then, cæteris paribus, simple reproduction will take place. And although this reproduction is a mere repetition of the process of production on the old scale, yet this mere repetition, or continuity, gives a new character to the process, or, rather, causes the disappearance of some apparent characteristics which it possessed as an isolated discontinuous process.

The purchase of labour-power for a fixed period is the prelude to the process of production; and this prelude is constantly repeated when the stipulated term comes to an end, when a definite period of producti n, such as a week or a month, has elapsed. But the labourer is not paid until after he has expended his labour-power, and realised in commodities not only its value, but surplus-value. He has, therefore, produced not only surplus-value, which we for the present regard as a fund to meet the private consumption of the capitalist, but he has also produced, before it flows back to him in the shape of wages, the fund out of which he himself is paid, the variable capital; and his employment lasts only so long as he continues to reproduce this fund. Hence, that formula of the economists, referred to in Chapter XVIII., which represents wages as a share in the product itself.[1] What flows back to the labourer in the shape of wages is a portion of the product that is continuously reproduced by him. The capitalist, it is true, pays him in money, but this money is merely the transmuted form of the product of his labour. While he is converting a portion of the means of production into products, a portion of his former product is being turned into money. It is his labour of last week, or of last year, that pays for his labour-power this week or this year. The illusion begotten by

travaillent exclusivement pour eux. . . . Mais dans l'ordre social, la richesse a acquis la propriété de se reproduire par le travail d'autrui, et sans que son propriétaire y concoure. La richesse, comme le travail, et par le travail, donne un fruit annuel qui peut être détruit chaque année sans que le riche en devienne plus pauvre. Ce fruit est le *revenu* qui naît du *capital.*" (Sismondi: Nouv. Princ. d'Econ. Pol. Paris, 1819. t. I. pp. 81-82.)

[1] "Wages as well as profits are to be considered, each of them, as really a portion of the finished product." (Ramsay, l.c., p. 142.) "The share of the product which comes to the labourer in the form of wages." (J. Mill, Elements, &c. Translated by Parissot. Paris, 1823. p. 34.)

the intervention of money vanishes immediately, if, instead of taking a single capitalist and a single labourer, we take the class of capitalists and the class of labourers as a whole. The capitalist class is constantly giving to the labouring class order-notes, in the form of money, on a portion of the commodities produced by the latter and appropriated by the former. The labourers give these order-notes back just as constantly to the capitalist class, and in this way get their share of their own product. The transaction is veiled by the commodity-form of the product and the money-form of the commodity.

Variable capital is therefore only a particular historical form of appearance of the fund for providing the necessaries of life, or the labour-fund which the labourer requires for the maintenance of himself and family, and which, whatever be the system of social production, he must himself produce and reproduce. If the labour-fund constantly flows to him in the form of money that pays for his labour, it is because the product he has created moves constantly away from him in the form of capital. But all this does not alter the fact, that it is the labourer's own labour, realised in a product, which is advanced to him by the capitalist.[1] Let us take a peasant liable to do compulsory service for his lord. He works on his own land, with his own means of production, for, say, 3 days a week. The 3 other days he does forced work on the lord's domain. He constantly reproduces his own labour-fund, which never, in his case, takes the form of a money payment for his labour, advanced by another person. But in return, his unpaid forced labour for the lord, on its side, never acquires the character of voluntary paid labour. If one fine morning the lord appropriates to himself the land, the cattle, the seed, in a word, the means of production of this peasant, the latter will thenceforth be obliged to sell his labour-power to the lord. He will, cæteris paribus, labour 6 days a week as before, 3 for himself, 3 for his lord, who thenceforth becomes a wages-paying capitalist. As before, he will use up the means of production

---

[1] "When capital is employed in advancing to the workmen his wages, it adds nothing to the funds for the maintenance of labour." (Cazenove in note to his edition of Malthus, Definitions in Pol. Econ. London, 1853, p. 22.)

as means of production, and transfer their value to the product. As before, a definite portion of the product will be devoted to reproduction. But from the moment that the forced labour is changed into wage-labour, from that moment the labour-fund, which the peasant himself continues as before to produce and reproduce, takes the form of a capital advanced in the form of wages by the lord. The bourgeois economist whose narrow mind is unable to separate the form of appearance from the thing that appears, shuts his eyes to the fact, that it is but here and there on the face of the earth, that even now-a-days the labour-fund crops up in the form of capital.[1]

Variable capital, it is true, only then loses its character of a value advanced out of the capitalist's funds,[2] when we view the process of capitalist production in the flow of its constant renewal. But that process must have had a beginning of some kind. From our present stand-point it therefore seems likely that the capitalist, once upon a time, became possessed of money, by some accumulation that took place independently of the unpaid labour of others, and that this was, therefore, how he was enabled to frequent the market as a buyer of labour-power. However this may be, the mere continuity of the process, the simple reproduction, brings about some other wonderful changes, which affect not only the variable, but the total capital.

If a capital of £1000 beget yearly a surplus-value of £200, and if this surplus-value be consumed every year, it is clear that at the end of 5 years the surplus-value consumed will amount to 5×£200 or the £1000 originally advanced. If only a part, say one half, were consumed, the same result would follow at the end of 10 years, since 10×£100=£1000. General Rule: The value of the capital advanced divided by the surplus-value annually consumed, gives the number of years, or reproduction periods, at the expiration of which the

[1] "The wages of labour are advanced by capitalists in the case of less than one fourth of the labourers of the earth." (Rich. Jones: Textbook of Lectures on the Pol. Econ. of Nations. Hertford, 1852, p. 16.)

[2] "Though the manufacturer" (*i.e.* the labourer) "has his wages advanced to him by his master, he in reality costs him no expense, the value of these wages being generally reserved, together with a profit, in the improved value of the subject upon which his labour is bestowed." (A. Smith l. c. Book II. ch. III. p. 311.)

capital originally advanced has been consumed by the capitalist and has disappeared. The capitalist thinks, that he is consuming the produce of the unpaid labour of others, *i.e.*, the surplus-value, and is keeping intact his original capital; but what he thinks cannot alter facts. After the lapse of a certain number of years the capital value he then possesses is equal to the sum total of the surplus-value appropriated by him during those years, and the total value he has consumed is equal to that of his original capital. It is true, he has in hand a capital whose amount has not changed, and of which a part, *viz.*, the buildings, machinery, &c., were already there when the work of his business began. But what we have to do with here, is not the material elements, but the value, of that capital. When a person gets through all his property, by taking upon himself debts equal to the value of that property, it is clear that his property represents nothing but the sum total of his debts. And so it is with the capitalist; when he has consumed the equivalent of his original capital, the value of his present capital represents nothing but the total amount of the surplus-value appropriated by him without payment. Not a single atom of the value of his old capital continues to exist.

Apart then from all accumulation, the mere continuity of the process of production, in other words simple reproduction, sooner or later, and of necessity, converts every capital into accumulated capital, or capitalised surplus-value. Even if that capital was originally acquired by the personal labour of its employer, it sooner or later becomes value appropriated without an equivalent, the unpaid labour of others materialised either in money or in some other object. We saw in chapter VI. that in order to convert money into capital something more is required than the production and circulation of commodities. We saw that on the one side the possessor of value or money, on the other, the possessor of the value-creating substance; on the one side, the possessor of the means of production and subsistence, on the other, the possessor of nothing but labour-power, must confront one another as buyer and seller. The separation of labour from its product, of subjective labour-power from the objective conditions of labour, was therefore the real foundation in fact, and the starting point of capitalist production.

But that which at first was but a starting point, becomes, by the mere continuity of the process, by simple reproduction, the peculiar result, constantly renewed and perpetuated, of capitalist production. On the one hand, the process of production incessantly converts material wealth into capital, into means of creating more wealth and means of enjoyment for the capitalist. On the other hand the labourer, on quitting the process, is what he was on entering it, a source of wealth, but devoid of all means of making that wealth his own. Since, before entering on the process, his own labour has already been alienated from himself by the sale of his labour-power, has been appropriated by the capitalist and incorporated with capital, it must, during the process, be realised in a product that does not belong to him. Since the process of production is also the process by which the capitalist consumes labour-power, the product of the labourer is incessantly converted, not only into commodities, but into capital, into value that sucks up the value-creating power, into means of subsistence that buy the person of the labourer, into means of production that command the producers.[1] The labourer therefore constantly produces material, objective wealth, but in the form of capital, of an alien power that dominates and exploits him; and the capitalist as constantly produces labour-power, but in the form of a subjective source of wealth, separated from the objects in and by which it can alone be realised; in short he produces the labourer, but as a wage-labourer.[2] This incessant reproduction, this perpetuation of the labourer, is the sine quâ non of capitalist production.

The labourer consumes in a twofold way. While producing

[1] "This is a remarkably peculiar property of productive labour. Whatever is productively consumed is capital, and it becomes capital by consumption." (James Mill l. c. p. 242.) James Mill, however, never got on the track of this "remarkably peculiar property."

"It is true indeed, that the first introducing a manufacture employs many poor, but they cease not to be so, and the continuance of it makes many." (Reasons for a limited Exportation of Wool. London, 1677, p. 19.) "The farmer now absurdly asserts, that he keeps the poor. They are indeed kept in misery." (Reasons for the late increase of the Poor Rates; or a comparative view of the prices of labour and provisions. London, 1777, p. 37.)

he consumes by his labour the means of production, and con-. verts them into products with a higher value than that of the capital advanced. This is his productive consumption. It is at the same time consumption of his labour-power by the capitalist who bought it. On the other hand, the labourer turns the money paid to him for his labour-power, into means of subsistence: this is his individual consumption. The labourer's productive consumption, and his individual consumption, are therefore totally distinct. In the former, he acts as the motive power of capital, and belongs to the capitalist. In the latter, he belongs to himself, and performs his necessary vital functions outside the process of production. The result of the one is, that the capitalist lives; of the other, that the labourer lives.

When treating of the working-day, we saw that the labourer is often compelled to make his individual consumption a mere incident of production. In such a case, he supplies himself with necessaries in order to maintain his labour-power, just as coal and water are supplied to the steam engine and oil to the wheel. His means of consumption, in that case, are the mere means of consumption required by a means of production; his individual consumption is directly productive consumption. This, however, appears to be an abuse not essentially appertaining to capitalist production.[1]

The matter takes quite another aspect, when we contemplate, not the single capitalist, and the single labourer, but the capitalist class and the labouring class, not an isolated process of production, but capitalist production in full swing, and on its actual social scale. By converting part of his capital into labour-power, the capitalist augments the value of his entire capital. He kills two birds with one stone. He profits, not only by what he receives from, but by what he gives to, the labourer. The capital given in exchange for labour-power is converted into necessaries, by the consumption of which the muscles, nerves, bones, and brains of existing labourers are reproduced, and new labourers are begotten. Within the lim-

---

[1] Rossi would not declaim so emphatically against this, had he really penetrated the secret of "productive consumption."

its of what is strictly necessary, the individual consumption of the working class is, therefore, the reconversion of the means of subsistence given by capital in exchange for labour-power, into fresh labour-power at the disposal of capital for exploitation. It is the production and reproduction of that means of production so indispensible to the capitalist: the labourer himself. The individual consumption of the labourer, whether it proceed within the workshop or outside it, whether it be part of the process of production or not, forms therefore a factor of the production and reproduction of capital; just as cleaning machinery does, whether it be done while the machinery is working or while it is standing. The fact that the labourer consumes his means of subsistence for his own purposes, and not to please the capitalist, has no bearing on the matter. The consumption of food by a beast of burden is none the less a necessary factor in the process of production, because the beast enjoys what it eats. The maintenance and reproduction of the working-class is, and must ever be, a necessary condition to the reproduction of capital. But the capitalist may safely leave its fulfillment to the labourer's instincts of self-preservation and of propagation. All the capitalist cares for, is to reduce the labourer's individual consumption as far as possible to what is strictly necessary, and he is far away from imitating those brutal South Americans, who force their labourers to take the more substantial, rather than the less substantial, kind of food.[1]

Hence both the capitalist and his ideological representative, the political economist, consider that part alone of the labourer's individual consumption to be productive, which is requisite for the perpetuation of the class, and which therefore must take place in order that the capitalist may have labour-power to consume; what the labourer consumes for his own pleasure

[1] "The labourers in the mines of S. America, whose daily task (the heaviest perhaps in the world) consists in bringing to the surface on their shoulders a load of metal weighing from 180 to 200 pounds, from a depth of 450 feet, live on bread and beans only; they themselves would prefer the bread alone for food, but their masters, who have found out that the men cannot work so hard on bread, treat them like horses, and compel them to eat beans; beans, however, are relatively much richer in bone-earth (phosphate of lime) than is bread" (Liebig, l. c., vol. 1, p. 194, note).

beyond that part, is unproductive consumption.[1] If the accumulation of capital were to cause a rise of wages and an increase in the labourer's consumption, unaccompanied by increase in the consumption of labour-power by capital, the additional capital would be consumed unproductively.[2] In reality, the individual consumption of the labourer is unproductive as regards himself, for it reproduces nothing but the needy individual; it is productive to the capitalist and the State, since it is the production of the power that creates their wealth.[3]

From a social point of view, therefore, the working-class, even when not directly engaged in the labour-process, is just as much an appendage of capital as the ordinary instruments of labour. Even its individual consumption is, within certain limits, a mere factor in the process of production. That process, however, takes good care to prevent these self-conscious instruments from leaving it in the lurch, for it removes their product, as fast as it is made, from their pole to the opposite pole of capital. Individual consumption provides, on the one hand, the means for their maintenance and reproduction: on the other hand, it secures by the annihilation of the necessaries of life, the continued reappearance of the workman in the labour-market. The Roman slave was held by fetters: the wage-labourer is bound to his owner by invisible threads. The appearance of independence is kept up by means of a constant change of employers, and by the fictio juris of a contract.

In former times, capital resorted to legislation, whenever necessary, to enforce its proprietary rights over the free labourer. For instance, down to 1815, the emigration of mechanics employed in machine making was, in England, forbidden, under grievous pains and penalties.

---

[1] James Mill, l. c., p. 238.

[2] "If the price of labour should rise so high that, notwithstanding the increase of capital, no more could be employed, I should say that such increase of capital would be still unproductively consumed." (Ricardo, l. c., p. 163.)

[3] "The only productive consumption, properly so-called, is the consumption or destruction of wealth" (he alludes to the means of production) "by capitalists with a view to reproduction . . . . The workman . . . . is a productive consumer to the person who employs him, and to the State, but not, strictly speaking, to himself." (Malthus' Definitions, &c., p. 30.)

The reproduction of the working class carries with it the accumulation of skill, that is handed down from one generation to another.[1] To what extent the capitalist reckons the existence of such a skilled class among the factors of production that belong to him by right, and to what extent he actually regards it as the reality of his variable capital, is seen so soon as a crisis threatens him with its loss In consequence of the civil war in the United States and of the accompanying cotton famine, the majority of the cotton operatives in Lancashire were, as is well known, thrown out of work. Both from the working-class itself, and from other ranks of society, there arose a cry for State aid, or for voluntary national subscriptions, in order to enable the "superfluous" hands to emigrate to the colonies or to the United States. Thereupon, the "Times" published on the 24th March, 1863, a letter from Edmund Potter, a former president of the Manchester Chamber of Commerce. This letter was rightly called in the House of Commons, the manufacturers' manifesto.[2] We cull here a few characteristic passages, in which the proprietary rights of capital over labour-power are unblushingly asserted.

"He" (the man out of work) "may be told the supply of cotton-workers is too large . . . . and . . . . must . . . . in fact be reduced by a third, perhaps, and that then there will be a healthy demand for the remaining two-thirds . . . . Public opinion . . . . urges emigration . . . . The master cannot willingly see his labour supply being removed; he may think, and perhaps justly, that it is both wrong and unsound . . . . But if the public funds are to be devoted to assist emigration, he has a right to be heard, and perhaps to protest." Mr. Potter then shows how useful the cotton trade is, how the "trade has undoubtedly drawn the surplus-population from Ireland and from the agricultural districts," how immense is its extent, how in the year 1860 it yielded $\frac{5}{13}$ ths of the total

---

[1] "The only thing, of which one can say, that it is stored up and prepared beforehand, is the skill of the labourer . . . . The accumulation and storage of skilled labour, that most important operation, is, as regards the great mass of labourers, accomplished without any capital whatever." (Tho. Hodgskin: Labour Defended, &c., p. 13.)

[2] "That letter might be looked upon as the manifesto of the manufacturers." (Ferrand: Motion on the Cotton Famine, H. o. C., 27th April, 1863.)

English exports, how, after a few years, it will again expand by the extension of the market, particularly of the Indian market, and by calling forth a plentiful supply of cotton at 6d. per lb. He then continues: "Some time . . . , one, two, or three years, it may be, will produce the quantity . . . . The question I would put then is this—Is the trade worth retaining? Is it worth while to keep the machinery (he means the living labour machines) in order, and is it not the greatest folly to think of parting with that? I think it is. I allow that the workers are not a property, not the property of Lancashire and the masters; but they are the strength of both; they are the mental and trained power which cannot be replaced for a generation; the mere machinery which they work might much of it be beneficially replaced, nay improved, in a twelve-month.[1] Encourage or allow (!) the working-power to emigrate, and what of the capitalist? . . . . Take away the cream of the workers, and fixed capital will depreciate in a great degree, and the floating will not subject itself to a struggle with the short supply of inferior labour. . . . . We are told the workers wish it" (emigration). "Very natural it is that they should do so . . . . Reduce, compress the cotton trade by taking away its working power and reducing their wages expenditure, say one-fifth, or five millions, and what then would happen to the class above, the small shopkeepers; and what of the rents, the cottage rents . . . . Trace out the effects upward to the small farmer, the better householder, and . . . . the landowner, and say if there could be any suggestion more suicidal to all classes of the country than by enfeebling a nation by exporting the best of its manufacturing population, and destroying the value of some of its most

---

[1] It will not be forgotten that this same capital sings quite another song, under ordinary circumstances, when there is a question of reducing wages. Then the masters exclaim with one voice: "The factory operatives should keep in wholesome remembrance the fact that theirs is really a low species of skilled labour; and that there is none which is more easily acquired, or of its quality more amply remunerated, or which, by a short training of the least expert, can be more quickly, as well as abundantly, acquired . . . . The master's machinery" (which we now learn can be replaced with advantage in 12 months) "really plays a far more important part in the business of production than the labour and skill of the operative" (who cannot now be replaced under 30 years), "which six months' education can teach, and a common labourer can learn." (See ante, p. 423.)

productive capital and enrichment . . . . I advise a loan
(of five or six millions sterling), . . . extending it may be
over two or three years, administered by special commissioners added to the Boards of Guardians in the cotton districts,
under special legislative regulations, enforcing some occupation or labour, as a means of keeping up at least the moral
standard of the recipients of the loan . . . . can anything be
worse for landowners or masters than parting with the best of
the workers, and demoralising and disappointing the rest by
an extended depletive emigration, a depletion of capital and
value in an entire province ?"

Potter, the chosen mouthpiece of the manufacturers, distinguishes two sorts of "machinery," each of which belongs to the
capitalist, and of which one stands in his factory, the other at
night-time and on Sundays is housed outside the factory, in
cottages. The one is inanimate, the other living. The inanimate machinery not only wears out and depreciates from day
to day, but a great part of it becomes so quickly super-annu-
ated, by constant technical progress, that it can be replaced
with advantage by new machinery after a few months. The
living machinery, on the contrary, gets better the longer it
lasts, and in proportion as the skill, handed from one generation to another, accumulates. The "Times" answered the
cotton lord as follows :

"Mr. Edmund Potter is so impressed with the exceptional
and supreme importance of the cotton masters that, in order
to preserve this class and perpetuate their profession, he would
keep half a million of the labouring class confined in a great
moral workhouse against their will. 'Is the trade worth retaining ?' asks Mr. Potter. 'Certainly by all honest means it
is,' we answer. 'Is it worth while keeping the machinery in
order ?' again asks Mr. Potter. Here we hesitate. By the
'machinery' Mr. Potter means the human machinery, for he
goes on to protest that he does not mean to use them as an
absolute property. We must confess that we do not think it
'worth while,' or even possible, to keep the human machinery
in order—that is to shut it up and keep it oiled till it is
wanted. Human machinery *will* rust under inaction, oil and

rub it as you may. Moreover, the human machinery will, as we have just seen, get the steam up of its own accord, and burst or run a muck in our great towns. It might, as Mr. Potter says, require some time to reproduce the workers, but, having machinists and capitalists at hand, we could always find thrifty, hard, industrious men wherewith to improvise more master manufacturers than we can ever want. Mr. Potter talks of the trade reviving 'in one, two, or three years,' and he asks us not 'to encourage or allow (!) the working power to emigrate.' He says that it is very natural the workers should wish to emigrate; but he thinks that in spite of their desire, the nation ought to keep this half million of workers with their 700,000 dependents, shut up in the cotton districts; and as a necessary consequence, he must of course think that the nation ought to keep down their discontent by force, and sustain them by alms—and upon the chance that the cotton masters may some day want them . . . The time is come when the great public opinion of these islands must operate to save this 'working power' from those who would deal with it as they would deal with iron, and coal, and cotton."

The "Times' " article was only a jeu d'esprit. The "great public opinion" was, in fact, of Mr. Potter's opinion, that the factory operatives are part of the movable fittings of a factory. Their emigration was prevented.[1] They were locked up in that "moral workhouse," the cotton districts, and they form, as before, "the strength" of the cotton manufacturers of Lancashire.

Capitalist production, therefore, of itself reproduces the separation between labour-power and the means of labour. It thereby reproduces and perpetuates the condition for exploiting the labourer. It incessantly forces him to sell his labour-

---

[1] Parliament did not vote a single farthing in aid of emigration, but simply passed some Acts empowering the municipal corporations to keep the operatives in a half-starved state, *i.e.*, to exploit them at less than the normal wages. On the other hand, when 3 years later, the cattle disease broke out, Parliament broke wildly through its usages and voted, straight off, millions for indemnifying the millionaire landlords, whose farmers in any event came off without loss, owing to the rise in the price of meat. The bull-like bellow of the landed proprietors at the opening of Parliament, in 1866, showed that a man can worship the cow Sabala without being a Hindoo, and can change himself into an ox without being a Jupiter.

power in order to live, and enables the capitalist to purchase labour-power in order that he may enrich himself.[1] It is no longer a mere accident, that capitalist and labourer confront each other in the market as buyer and seller. It is the process itself that incessantly hurls back the labourer on to the market as a vendor of his labour-power, and that incessantly converts his own product into a means by which another man can purchase him. In reality, the labourer belongs to capital before he has sold himself to capital. His economical bondage[2] is both brought about and concealed by the periodic sale of himself, by his change of masters, and by the oscillations in the market price of labour-power.[3]

Capitalist production, therefore, under its aspect of a continuous connected process, of a process of reproduction, produces not only commodities, not only surplus-value, but it also produces and reproduces the capitalist relation; on the one side the capitalist, on the other the wage-labourer.[4]

[1] "L'ouvrier demandait de la subsistence pour vivre, le chef demandait du travail pour gagner." (Sismondi, l. c., p. 91.)

[2] A boorishly clumsy form of this bondage exists in the county of Durham. This is one of the few counties, in which circumstances do not secure to the farmer undisputed proprietary rights over the agricultural labourer. The mining industry allows the latter some choice. In this county, the farmer, contrary to the custom elsewhere, rents only such farms as have on them labourers' cottages. The rent of the cottage is a part of the wages. These cottages are known as "hinds' houses." They are let to the labourers in consideration of certain feudal services, under a contract called "bondage," which, amongst other things, binds the labourer during the time he is employed elsewhere, to leave some one, say his daughter, &c., to supply his place. The labourer himself is called a "bondsman." The relationship here set up also shows how individual consumption by the labourer becomes consumption on behalf of capital—or productive consumption—from quite a new point of view: "It is curious to observe that the very dung of the hind and bondsman is the perquisite of the calculating lord . . . and the lord will allow no privy but his own to exist in the neighbourhood, and will rather give a bit of manure here and there for a garden than bate any part of his seigneurial right." (Public Health, Report VII., 1864, p. 188.)

[3] It will not be forgotten, that, with respect to the labour of children, &c., even the formality of a voluntary sale disappears.

[4] "Capital pre-supposes wage-labour, and wage-labour pre-supposes capital. One is a necessary condition to the existence of the other; they mutually call each other into existence. Does an operative in a cotton-factory produce nothing but cotton goods? No, he produces capital. He produces values that give fresh command over his labour, and that, by means of such command, create fresh values." (Karl Marx: Lohnarbeit und Kapital, in the Neue Rheinische Zeitung, No. 266, 7th April, 1849.) The articles published under the above title in the N. Rh. Z. are parts of some lectures given by me on that subject, in 1847, in the German "Arbeiter-Verein" at Brussels, the publication of which was interrupted by the revolution of February.

CHAPTER XXIV.

CONVERSION OF SURPLUS-VALUE INTO CAPITAL.

SECTION I.——CAPITALIST PRODUCTION ON A PROGRESSIVELY
   INCREASING SCALE.   TRANSITION OF THE LAWS OF PROP-
   ERTY THAT CHARACTERISE PRODUCTION OF COMMODITIES
   INTO LAWS OF CAPITALIST APPROPRIATION.

HITHERTO we have investigated how surplus-value emanates
from capital; we have now to see how capital arises from
surplus-value.   Employing surplus-value as capital, reconverting it into capital, is called accumulation of capital.[1]

First let us consider this transaction from the standpoint of
the individual capitalist.   Suppose a spinner to have advanced
a capital of £10,000, of which four-fifths (£8000) are laid out
in cotton, machinery, &c., and one-fifth (£2000) in wages.
Let him produce 240,000 lbs. of yarn annually, having a value
of £12,000.   The rate of surplus-value being 100%, the surplus-value lies in the surplus or net product of 40,000 lbs. of
yarn, one sixth of the gross product, with a value of £2000
which will be realized by a sale.   £2000 is £2000.   We can
neither see nor smell in this sum of money a trace of surplus-
value.   When we know that a given value is surplus-value, we
know how its owner came by it; but that does not alter the
nature either of value or of money.

In order to convert this additional sum of £2000 into capital, the master spinner will, all circumstances remaining as
before, advance four-fifths of it (£1600) in the purchase of
cotton, &c., and one-fifth (£400) in the purchase of additional
spinners, who will find in the market the necessaries of life
whose value the master has advanced to them.   Then the new

---

[1] "Accumulation of capital; the employment of a portion of revenue as capital."
(Malthus: Definitions, &c., ed. Cazenove p. 11.)   "Conversion of revenue into capital.".   Malthus: Princ. of Pol. Econ., 2nd Ed., Lond., 1836, p. 319.)

capital of £2000 functions in the spinning mill, and brings in, in its turn, a surplus-value of £400.

The capital-value was originally advanced in the money form. The surplus-value on the contrary is, originally, the value of a definite portion of the gross product. If this gross product be sold, converted into money, the capital-value regains its original form. From this moment the capital-value and the surplus-value are both of them sums of money, and their reconversion into capital takes place in precisely the same way. The one, as well as the other, is laid out by the capitalist in the purchase of commodities that place him in a position to begin afresh the fabrication of his goods, and this time, on an extended scale. But in order to be able to buy those commodities, he must find them ready in the market.

His own yarns circulate, only because he brings his annual product to market, as all other capitalists likewise do with their commodities. But these commodities, before coming to market, were part of the general annual product, part of the total mass of objects of every kind, into which the sum of the individual capitals, *i.e.,* the total capital of society, had been converted in the course of the year, and of which each capitalist had in hand only an aliquot part. The transactions in the market effectuate only the interchange of the individual components of this annual product, transfer them from one hand to another, but can neither augment the total annual production, nor alter the nature of the objects produced. Hence the use that can be made of the total annual product, depends entirely upon its own composition, but in no way upon circulation.

The annual production must in the first place furnish all those objects (use-values) from which the material components of capital, used up in the course of the year, have to be replaced. Deducting these there remains the net or surplus-product, in which the surplus-value lies. And of what does this surplus-product consist? Only of things destined to satisfy the wants and desires of the capitalist class, things which, consequently, enter into the consumption fund of the capitalists? Were that the case, the cup of surplus-value would be drained to the very dregs, and nothing but simple reproduction would ever take place.

To accumulate it is necessary to convert a portion of the surplus-product into capital. But we cannot, except by a miracle, convert into capital anything but such articles as can be employed in the labour-process (*i.e.,* means of production), and such further articles as are suitable for the sustenance of the labourer, (*i.e.,* means of subsistence.) Consequently, a part of the annual surplus-labour must have been applied to the production of additional means of production and subsistence, over and above the quantity of these things required to replace the capital advanced. In one word, surplus-value is convertible into capital solely because the surplus-product, whose value it is, already comprises the material elements of new capital.[1]

Now in order to allow of these elements actually functioning as capital, the capitalist class requires additional labour. If the exploitation of the labourers already employed do not increase, either extensively or intensively, then additional labour-power must be found. For this the mechanism of capitalist production provides beforehand, by converting the working class into a class dependent on wages, a class whose ordinary wages suffice, not only for its maintenance, but for its increase. It is only necessary for capital to incorporate this additional labour-power, annually supplied by the working class in the shape of labourers of all ages, with the surplus means of production comprised in the annual produce, and the conversion of surplus-value into capital is complete. From a concrete point of view, accumulation resolves itself into the reproduction of capital on a progressively increasing scale. The circle in which simple reproduction moves, alters

---

[1] We here take no account of export trade, by means of which a nation can change articles of luxury either into means of production or means of subsistence, and *vice versâ*. In order to examine the object of our investigation in its integrity, free from all disturbing subsidiary circumstances, we must treat the whole world as one nation, and assume that capitalist production is everywhere established and has possessed itself of every branch of industry.

its form, and, to use Sismondi's expression, changes into a spiral.[1]

Let us now return to our illustration. It is the old story: Abraham begat Isaac, Isaac begat Jacob, and so on. The original capital of £10,000 brings in a surplus-value of £2000, which is capitalised. The new capital of £2000 brings in a surplus-value of £400, and this, too, is capitalised, converted into a second additional capital, which, in its turn, produces a further surplus-value of £80. And so the ball rolls on.

We here leave out of consideration the portion of the surplus-value consumed by the capitalist. Just as little does it concern us, for the moment, whether the additional capital is joined on to the original capital, or is separated from it to function independently; whether the same capitalist, who accumulated it, employs it, or whether he hands it over to another. This only we must not forget, that by the side of the newly-formed capital, the original capital continues to reproduce itself, and to produce surplus-value, and that this is also true of all accumulated capital, and the additional capital engendered by it.

The original capital was formed by the advance of £10,000. How did the owner become possessed of it? "By his own labour and that of his forefathers," answer unanimously the spokesmen of political economy.[2] And, in fact, their supposition appears the only one consonant with the laws of the production of commodities.

But it is quite otherwise with regard to the additional capital of £2000. How that originated we know perfectly well. There is not one single atom of its value that does not owe its existence to unpaid labour. The means of production, with which the additional labour-power is incorporated, as well as the necessaries with which the labourers are sustained, are nothing but component parts of the surplus product, of the tribute annually exacted from the working class by the capi-

---

[1] Sismondi's analysis of accumulation suffers from the great defect, that he contents himself, to too great an extent, with the phrase "conversion of revenue into capital," without fathoming the material conditions of this operation.

[2] "Le travail primitif auquel son capital a dû sa naissance." Sismondi, l. c., ed. Paris, t. I., p. 109.

talist class. Though the latter with a portion of that tribute purchases the additional labour-power even at its full price, so that equivalent is exchanged for equivalent, yet the transaction is for all that only the old dodge of every conquerer who buys commodities from the conquered with the money he has robbed them of.

If the additional capital employs the person who produced it, this producer must not only continue to augment the value of the original capital, but must buy back the fruits of his previous labour with more labour than they cost. When viewed as a transaction between the capitalist class and the working class, it makes no difference that additional labourers are employed by means of the unpaid labour of the previously employed labourers. The capitalist may even convert the additional capital into a machine that throws the producers of that capital out of work, and that replaces them by a few children. In every case the working class creates by the surplus-labour of one year the capital destined to employ additional labour in the following year.[1] And this is what is called: creating capital out of capital.

The accumulation of the first additional capital of £2000 presupposes a value of £10,000 belonging to the capitalist by virtue of his "primitive labour," and advanced by him. The second additional capital of £400 presupposes, on the contrary, only the previous accumulation of the £2000, of which the £400 is the surplus-value capitalised. The ownership of past unpaid labour is thenceforth the sole condition for the appropriation of living unpaid labour on a constantly increasing scale. The more the capitalist has accumulated, the more is he able to accumulate.

In so far as the surplus-value, of which the additional capital, No. 1, consists, is the result of the purchase of labour-power with part of the original capital, a purchase that conformed to the laws of the exchange of commodities, and that, from a legal stand-point, presupposes nothing beyond the free disposal, on the part of the labourer, of his own capacities, and

---

[1] "Labour creates capital before capital employs labour." E. G. Wakefield, England and America. Lond., 1833, Vol. II., p. 110.

on the part of the owner of money or commodities, of the values that belong to him; in so far as the additional capital, No. 2, &c., is the mere result of No. 1, and, therefore, a consequence of the above condition; in so far as each single transaction invariably conforms to the laws of the exchange of commodities, the capitalist buying labour-power, the labourer selling it, and we will assume at its real value; in so far as all this is true, it is evident that the laws of appropriation or of private property, laws that are based on the production and circulation of commodities, become by their own inner and inexorable dialectic changed into their very opposite.[1] The exchange of equivalents, the original operation with which we started, has now become turned round in such a way that there is only an apparent exchange. This is owing to the fact, first, that the capital which is exchanged for labour-power is itself but a portion of the product of others' labour appropriated without an equivalent; and, secondly, that this capital must not only be replaced by its producer, but replaced together with an added surplus. The relation of exchange subsisting between capitalist and labourer becomes a mere semblance appertaining to the process of circulation, a mere form, foreign to the real nature of the transaction, and only mystify it. The ever repeated purchase and sale of labour-power is now the mere form; what really takes place is this—the capitalist again and again appropriates, without equivalent, a portion of the previously materialised labour of others, and exchanges it for a greater quantity of living labour. At first the rights of property seemed to us to be based on a man's own labour. At least, some such assumption was necessary since only commodity owners with equal rights confronted each other, and the sole means by which a man could become possessed of the commodities of others, was by alienating his own commodities; and these could be replaced by labour alone. Now, however,

---

[1] Just as at a given stage in its development, commodity production necessarily passes into capitalistic commodity production (in fact, it is only on the basis of capitalistic production that products take the general and predominant form of commodities), so the laws of property that are based on commodity production, necessarily turn into the laws of capitalist appropriation. We may well, therefore, feel astonished at the cleverness of Proudhon, who would abolish capitalistic property by enforcing the eternal laws of property that are based on commodity production!

property turns out to be the right, on the part of the capitalist, to appropriate the unpaid labour of others or its product and to be the impossibility, on the part of the labourer, of appropriating his own product. The separation of property from labour has become the necessary consequence of a law that apparently originated in their identity.[1]

No matter how severely the capitalist mode of appropriation may seem to slap the face of the fundamental laws of the production of commodities, it does not arise from a violation, but from an application of these laws. A brief retrospect upon the succession of phases, whose climax the capitalist accumulation is, may serve once more to make this clear.

We have seen, in the first place, that the original transformation of a certain quantity of values into capital proceeded strictly according to the laws of exchange. One of the contracting parties sells his labour-power, the other buys it. The first receives the exchange-value of his commodity, while its use-value, labour, passes into the possession of the other. This second party then converts means of production belonging to him into a new product belonging to him by right through the instrumentality of labour also belonging to him.

The value of this product comprizes, in the first place, the value of the consumed means of production. Useful labour cannot consume these means of production without transferring their value to the new product. But in order to be saleable labour-power must be able to furnish useful labour in that line of industry in which it is to be employed.

The value of the new product comprizes, furthermore, the equivalent of the value of labour-power and a surplus-value. It does so for the reason that the labour-power sold for a certain length of time, such as a day, a week, etc., has less value than is produced by its employment during that time. The labourer, however, has received the exchange-value of his la-

---

[1] The property of the capitalist in the product of the labour of others "is a strict consequence of the law of appropriation, the fundamental principle of which was, on the contrary, the exclusive title of every labourer to the product of his own labour." (Cherbuliez, Riche ou Pauvre. Paris, 1841, p. 58, where, however, the dialectical reversal is not properly developed.)

bour-power and given up its use-value in return, as happens in every sale and purchase.

The fact that this particular commodity labour-power has the peculiar use-value of supplying labour and creating value cannot affect the general law of the production of commodities. Hence, if the sum of values advanced in wages is not merely reproduced in the product, but also increased by a surplus-value, this is not due to an advantage gained over the seller, who received the value of his commodity, but simply to the consumption of this commodity by the buyer.

The law of exchange requires quality only for the exchange-values of the commodities passed from hand to hand. But it requires at the outset a disparity of their use-values, and has nothing to do with their consumption, which does not begin until after the trade has been made.

The original transformation of money into capital proceeds, therefore, in strict compliance with the economic laws of the production of commodities and with the property right derived therefrom. Nevertheless it has the following results:

(1) That the product belongs to the capitalist, not to the labourer;

(2) That the value of this product comprizes a surplus-value over and above the value of the advanced capital. This surplus-value has cost the labourer labour, but the capitalist nothing, yet it becomes the lawful property of the capitalist;

(3) That the labourer has reproduced his labour-power and can sell it once more, if he finds a buyer for it.

Simple reproduction is but a periodical repetition of this first operation. Money is thereby transformed again and again into capital. The general law is not violated thereby, but rather finds an opportunity to manifest itself permanently. "Several successive exchanges have merely made of the last a representative of the first." (Sismondi, l. c., p. 70.)

Nevertheless we have seen that this simple reproduction suffices to impregnate this first operation, so far as it was considered an isolated transaction, with a totally different character. "Of those, who divide the national revenue among themselves, some (the labourers) acquire each year a new title to it by new labour, while others (the capitalists) have previously acquired a permanent title to it by primitive work." (Sismondi, l. c., p. 111.) The domain of labour is evidently not the only one in which primogeniture accomplishes wonders.

It does not alter matters any, if simple reproduction is replaced by reproduction on an enlarged scale, by accumulation. In the first instance the capitalist consumes the entire surplus-value, in the second he demonstrates his civic virtue by consuming only a part of it and converting the remainder into money.

The surplus-value is his property, it has never belonged to anybody else. If he advances it to production, he makes advances 'rom his own funds just as he did on the day when he first came n the market. That this fund in the present case comes from the unpaid labour of his labourers, does not alter the matter in the least. If labourer B is employed with surplus-values produced by labourer A, then, in the first place, A supplied this surplus-value without having the just price of his commodity reduced by one farthing, and, in the second place, this transaction is none of B's concern. What B demands and has a right to demand is that the capitalist should pay him the value of his labour-power. "Both sides are gainers; the labourer, by having the fruit of his labour advanced to him" (that is, the fruit of the unpaid labour of others) "before he has performed any labour" (that is, before his own labour has borne any fruit); "the master, because the labour of this labourer was worth more than his wages" (that is, produced a value greater than that of his wages). (Sismondi, l. c., p. 135.)

True, the matter assumes an entirely different aspect when we look upon capitalist production in the uninterrupted flow of its reproduction, and when we consider the capitalist class as a whole and its antagonist, the working class, instead of the individual capitalist and the individual labourer. But in so doing we should be applying a standard which is totally foreign to the production of commodities.

In the production of commodities only sellers and buyers, independent of one another, meet. Their mutual relations cease with the termination of their mutual contract. If the transaction is repeated, it is done by a new contract, which has nothing to do with the former one, and only an accident brings the same seller once more together with the same buyer.

Hence, if the production of commodities, or a transaction belonging to it, is to be judged by its own economic laws, we must consider each act of exchange by itself, outside of all connection with the act of exchange preceding it and following it. And since purchases and sales are transacted between in-dividuals, it will not do to seek therein relations between entire classes of society.

No matter how long may be the series of periodical repro-ductions and former accumulations through which the capital now invested may have passed, it always retains its primal virginity. So long as the laws of exchange are observed in every act of exchange, individually considered, the mode of appropriation may be completely revolutionised without in the least affecting the property right bestowed by the produc-tion of commodities. The same right remains in force, whether it be at a time when the product belonged to the pro-ducer, and when this producer, exchanging equivalent for equivalent, could enrich himself only by his own labour, or whether it be under capitalism, where the social wealth be-comes in an ever increasing degree the property of those, who are in a position to appropriate to themselves again and again the unpaid labour of others.

This result becomes inevitable, as soon as labour-power is sold as a commodity by the "free" labourer himself. It is from that time on that the production of commodities becomes universal and a typical form of production. Henceforth every product is intended at the outset for sale, and all pro-duced wealth passes through the circulation. The produc-tion of commodities does not impose itself upon the whole society, until wage-labour becomes its basis. And only then does it unfold all its powers. To say that the intervention of wage labour adulterates the production of commodities means to say that the production of commodities must not develop, if it wishes to remain unadulterated. To the same extent that it continues to develop by its own inherent laws into a capitalist production, the property laws of the production of commodities are converted into the laws of capitalistic appropriation.[1]

We have seen that even in the case of simple reproduction, all capital, whatever its original source, becomes converted into accumulated capital, capitalised surplus-value. But in the flood of production all the capital originally advanced becomes a vanishing quantity (*magnitudo evanescens*, in the mathematical sense), compared with the directly accumulated capital, *i.e.*, with the surplus-value or surplus product that is reconverted into capital, whether it function in the hands of its accumulator, or in those of others. Hence, political economy describes capital in general as "accumulated wealth" (converted surplus-value or revenue), "that is employed over again in the production of surplus-value,"[2] and the capitalist as "the owner of surplus-value."[3] It is merely another way of expressing the same thing to say that all existing capital is accumulated or capitalised interest, for interest is a mere fragment of surplus-value.[4]

SECTION 2.—ERRONEOUS CONCEPTION BY POLITICAL ECONOMY OF REPRODUCTION ON A PROGRESSIVELY IN-CREASING SCALE.

Before we further investigate accumulation or the reconversion of surplus-value into capital, we must brush on one side an ambiguity introduced by the classical economists.

[1] Admire, therefore, the craftiness of Proudhon who wishes to abolish capitalist property by enforcing against it—the eternal property laws of the production of commodities.

[2] "Capital, viz., accumulated wealth employed with a view to profit." (Malthus, l. c.) "Capital . . . . consists of wealth saved from revenue, and used with a view to profit." (R. Jones: An Introductory Lecture on Polit. Econ., Lond., 1833, p. 16.)

[3] "The possessors of surplus produce or capital." (The Source and Remedy of the National Difficulties. A Letter to Lord John Russell. Lond., 1821.)

[4] "Capital, with compound interest on every portion of capital saved, is so all engrossing that all the wealth in the world from which income is derived, has long ago become the interest on capital." (*London Economist, 19th July, 1859.*)

Just as little as the commodities that the capitalist buys with a part of the surplus-value for his own consumption, serve the purpose of production and of creation of value, so little is the labour that he buys for the satisfaction of his natural and social requirements, productive labour. Instead of converting surplus-value into capital, he, on the contrary, by the purchase of those commodities and that labour, consumes or expends it as revenue. In the face of the habitual mode of life of the old feudal nobility, which, as Hegel rightly says, "consists in consuming what is in hand," and more especially displays itself in the luxury of personal retainers, it was extremely important for bourgeois economy to promulgate the doctrine that accumulation of capital is the first duty of every citizen, and to preach without ceasing, that a man cannot accumulate, if he eats up all his revenue, instead of spending a good part of it in the acquisition of additional productive labourers, who bring in more than they cost. On the other hand the economists had to contend against the popular prejudice, that confuses capitalist production with hoarding,[1] and fancies that accumulated wealth is either wealth that is rescued from being destroyed in its existing form, *i.e.*, from being consumed, or wealth that is withdrawn from circulation. Exclusion of money from circulation would also exclude absolutely its self-expansion as capital, while accumulation of a hoard in the shape of commodities would be sheer tomfoolery.[2] The accumulation of commodities in great masses is the result either of overproduction or of a stoppage of circulation.[3] It is true that the popular mind is impressed by the sight, on the one hand, of the mass of goods that are stored up for gradual consumption by the rich,[4] and on the other hand, by the for-

[1] "No political economist of the present day can by saving mean mere hoarding: and beyond this contracted and insufficient proceeding, no use of the term in reference to the national wealth can well be imagined, but that which must arise from a different application of what is saved, founded upon a real distinction between the different kinds of labour maintained by it." (Malthus, l. c., p. 38, 39.)

[2] Thus for instance, Balzac, who so thoroughly studied every shade of avarice, represents the old usurer Gobsec as in his second childhood when he begins to heap up a hoard of commodities.

[3] "Accumulation of stocks . . . non-exchange . . . over-production." (Th. Corbet l. c., p. 14.)

[4] In this sense Necker speaks of the "objets de faste et de somptuosité," of which

mation of reserve stocks; the latter, a phenomenon that is common to all modes of production, and on which we shall dwell for a moment, when we come to analyse circulation. Classical economy is therefore quite right, when it maintains that the consumption of surplus-products by productive, instead of by unproductive labourers, is a characteristic feature of the process of accumulation. But at this point the mistakes also begin. Adam Smith has made it the fashion, to represent accumulation as nothing more than consumption of surplus-products by productive labourers, which amounts to saying, that the capitalising of surplus-value consists in merely turning surplus-value into labour-power. Let us see what Ricardo *e.g.*, says: "It must be understood that all the productions of a country are consumed; but it makes the greatest difference imaginable whether they are consumed by those who reproduce, or by those who do not reproduce another value. When we say that revenue is saved, and added to capital, what we mean is, that the portion of revenue, so said to be added to capital, is consumed by productive instead of unproductive labourers. There can be no greater error than in supposing that capital is increased by non-consumption." [1] There can be no greater error than that which Ricardo and all subsequent economists repeat after A. Smith, viz., that "the part of revenue, of which it is said, it has been added to capital, is consumed by productive labourers." According to this, all surplus-value that is changed into capital becomes variable capital. So far from this being the case, the surplus-value, like the original capital, divides itself into constant capital and variable capital, into means of production and labour-power. Labour-power is the form under which variable capital exists during the process of production. In this process the labour-power is itself consumed by the capitalist while the means of production are consumed by the labour-power in the exercise of its function, labour. At the same time, the money paid for the purchase of the labour-power, is converted into necessaries,

"le temps a grossi l'accumulation," and which "les lois de propriété ont rassemblés dans une seule classe de la société." (Oeuvres de M. Necker, Paris and Lausanne, 1789, t. ii. p. 291.)

[1] Ricardo, l. c., p. 163, note.

that are consumed, not by "productive labour," but by the "productive labourer." Adam Smith, by a fundamentally perverted analysis, arrives at the absurd conclusion, that even though each individual capital is divided into a constant and a variable part, the capital of society resolves itself only into variable capital, *i.e.*, is laid out exclusively in payment of wages. For instance, suppose a cloth manufacturer converts £2000 into capital. One portion he lays out in buying weavers, the other in woollen yarn, machinery, &c. But the people, from whom he buys the yarn and the machinery, pay for labour with a part of the purchase money, and so on until the whole £2000 are spent in the payment of wages, *i.e.*, until the entire product represented by the £2000 has been consumed by productive labourers. It is evident that the whole gist of this argument lies in the words "and so on," which send us from pillar to post. In truth, Adam Smith breaks his investigation off, just where its difficulties begin.[1]

The annual process of reproduction is easily understood, so long as we keep in view merely the sum total of the year's production. But every single component of this product must be brought into the market as a commodity, and there the difficulty begins. The movements of the individual capitals, and of the personal revenues, cross and intermingle and are lost in the general change of places, in the circulation of the wealth of society; this dazes the sight, and propounds very complicated problems for solution. In the third part of Book II. I shall give the analysis of the real bearings of the facts. It is one of the great merits of the Physiocrats, that in their *Tableau économique* they were the first to attempt to depict the annual production in the shape in which it is presented to us after passing through the process of circulation.[2]

[1] In spite of his "Logic," John St. Mill never detects even such faulty analysis as this when made by his predecessors, an analysis which, even from the bourgeois standpoint of the science, cries out for rectification. In every case he registers with the dogmatism of a disciple, the confusion of his master's thoughts. So here: "The capital itself in the long run becomes entirely wages, and when replaced by the sale of produce becomes wages again."

[2] In his description of the process of reproduction, and of accumulation, Adam Smith, in many ways, not only made no advance, but even lost considerable ground, compared with his predecessors, especially the Physiocrats. Connected with the

For the rest, it is a matter of course, that political economy, acting in the interests of the capitalist class, has not failed to exploit the doctrine of Adam Smith, viz., that the whole of that part of the surplus product which is converted into capital, is consumed by the working class.

SECTION 3.—SEPARATION OF SURPLUS-VALUE INTO CAPITAL' AND REVENUE. THE ABSTINENCE THEORY.

In the last preceding chapter, we treated surplus-value (or the surplus product) solely as a fund for supplying the individual consumption of the capitalist. In this chapter we have, so far treated it solely as a fund for accumulation. It is, however, neither the one nor the other, but is both together. One portion is consumed by the capitalist as revenue,[1] the other is employed as capital, is accumulated.

Given the mass of surplus-value, then, the larger the one of these parts, the smaller is the other. Cæteris paribus, the ratio of these parts determines the magnitude of the accumulation. But it is by the owner of the surplus-value, by the capitalist alone, that the division is made. It is his deliberate act. That part of the tribute exacted by him which he accumulates, is said to be saved by him, because he does not eat it, *i.e.*, because he performs the function of a capitalist, and enriches himself.

Except as personified capital, the capitalist has no historical value, and no right to that historical existence, which, to use an expression of the witty Lichnowsky, "hasn't got no date,"

---

illusion mentioned in the text, is the really wonderful dogma, left by him as an inheritance to political economy, the dogma, that the price of commodities is made up of wages, profit (interest) and rent, *i.e.*, of wages and surplus-value. Starting from this basis, Storch naïvely confesses, "Il est impossible de résoudre le prix nécessaire dans ses éléments les plus simples." (Storch, l. c. Petersb. Edit. 1815, t. i. p. 140, note.) A fine science of economy this, which declares it impossible to resolve the price of a commodity into its simplest elements! This point will be further investigated in the seventh part of Book iii.

[1] The reader will notice, that the word revenue is used in a double sense: first, to designate surplus-value so far as it is the fruit periodically yielded by capital; secondly, to designate the part of that fruit which is periodically consumed by the capitalist, or added to the fund that supplies his private consumption. I have retained this double meaning because it harmonises with the language of the English and French economists.

And so far only is the necessity for his own transitory existence implied in the transitory necessity for the capitalist mode of production. But, so far as he is personified capital, it is not values in use and the enjoyment of them, but exchange-value and its augmentation, that spur him into action. Fanatically bent on making value expand itself, he ruthlessly forces the human race to produce for production's sake; he thus forces the development of the productive powers of society, and creates those material conditions, which alone can form the real basis of a higher form of society, a society in which the full and free development of every individual forms the ruling principle. Only as personified capital is the capitalist respectable. As such, he shares with the miser the passion for wealth as wealth. But that which in the miser is a mere idiosyncrasy, is, in the capitalist, the effect of the social mechanism, of which he is but one of the wheels. Moreover, the development of capitalist production makes it constantly necessary to keep increasing the amount of the capital laid out in a given industrial undertaking, and competition makes the immanent laws of capitalist production to be felt by each individual capitalist, as external coercive laws. It compels him to keep constantly extending his capital, in order to preserve it, but extend it he cannot, except by means of progressive accumulation.

So far, therefore, as his actions are a mere function of capital—endowed as capital is, in his person, with consciousness and a will—his own private consumption is a robbery perpetrated on accumulation, just as in book-keeping by double entry, the private expenditure of the capitalist is placed on the debtor side of his account against his capital. To accumulate, is to conquer the world of social wealth, to increase the mass of human beings exploited by him, and thus to extend both the direct and the indirect sway of the capitalist.[1]

[1] Taking the usurer, that old-fashioned but ever renewed specimen of the capitalist for his text, Luther shows very aptly that the love of power is an element in the desire to get rich. "The heathen were able, by the light of reason, to conclude that a usurer is a double-dyed thief and murderer. We Christians, however, hold them in such honour, that we fairly worship them for the sake of their money . . . .

But original sin is at work everywhere. As capitalist production, accumulation, and wealth, become developed, the capitalist ceases to be the mere incarnation of capital. He has a fellow-feeling for his own Adam, and his education gradually enables him to smile at the rage for asceticism, as a mere prejudice of the old-fashioned miser. While the capitalist of the classical type brands individual consumption as a sin against his function, and as "abstinence" from accumulating, the modernised capitalist is capable of looking upon accumulation as "abstinence" from pleasure.

> " Two souls, alas, do dwell within his breast;
> The one is ever parting from the other." [1]

At the historical dawn of capitalist production,—and every capitalist upstart has personally to go through this historical stage—avarice, and desire to get rich, are the ruling passions.

Whoever eats up, robs, and steals the nourishment of another, that man commits as great a murder (so far as in him lies) as he who starves a man or utterly undoes him. Such does a usurer, and sits the while safe on his stool, when he ought rather to be hanging on the gallows, and be eaten by as many ravens as he has stolen guilders, if only there were so much flesh on him, that so many ravens could stick their beaks in and share it. Meanwhile, we hang the small thieves . . . Little thieves are put in the stocks, great thieves go flaunting in gold and silk . . . . Therefore is there, on this earth, no greater enemy of man (after the devil) than a gripe-money, and usurer, for he wants to be God over all men. Turks, soldiers, and tyrants are also bad men, yet must they let the people live, and confess that they are bad, and enemies, and do, nay, must, now and then show pity to some. But a usurer and money-glutton, such a one would have the whole world perish of hunger and thirst, misery and want, so far as in him lies, so that he may have a'l to himself, and every one may receive from him as from a G l, and be his serf 'Jr ever. To wear fine cloaks, golden chains, rings, to wipe his mouth, to be deemed a.J taken for a worthy, pious man . . . Usury is a great huge monster, like ; were-wolf, who lays waste all, more than any Cacus, Gerion or Antus. And ; :t decks himself out, and would be thought pious, so that people may not see where the oxen have gone, that he drags backwards into his den. But Hercules shall hear the cry of the oxen and of his prisoners, and shall seek Cacus even in cliffs and among rocks, ; d shall set the oxen loose again from the villain. For Cacus means the villain that is a pious usurer, and steals, robs, eats everything. And will not own that he has done it, and thinks no one will find him out, because the oxen, drawn backwards into his den, make it seem, from their foot-prints, that they have been let out. So the usurer would deceive the world, as though he were of use and gave the world oxen, while he, however, rends, and eats all alone . . . And since we break on the wheel, and behead highwaymen, murderers and housebreakers, how much more ought we to break on the wheel and kill, . . . hunt down, curse and behead all usurers." (Martin Luther, l. c.)

[1] See Goethe's Faust.

But the progress of capitalist production not only creates a world of delights; it lays open, in speculation and the credit system, a thousand sources of sudden enrichment. When a certain stage of development has been reached, a conventional degree of prodigality, which is also an exhibition of wealth, and consequently a source of credit, becomes a business necessity to the "unfortunate" capitalist. Luxury enters into capital's expenses of representation. Moreover, the capitalist gets rich, not like the miser, in proportion to his personal labour and restricted consumption, but at the same rate as he squeezes out the labour-power of others, and enforces on the labourer abstinence from all life's enjoyments. Although, therefore, the prodigality of the capitalist never possesses the bonâ-fide character of the open-handed feudal lord's prodigality, but, on the contrary, has always lurking behind it the most sordid avarice and the most anxious calculation, yet his expenditure grows with his accumulation, without the one necessarily restricting the other. But along with this growth, there is at the same time developed in his breast, a Faustian conflict between the passion for accumulation, and the desire for enjoyment.

Dr. Aikin says in a work published in 1795: "The trade of Manchester may be divided into four periods. First, when manufacturers were obliged to work hard for their livelihood." They enriched themselves chiefly by robbing the parents, whose children were bound as apprentices to them: the parents paid a high premium, while the apprentices were starved. On the other hand, the average profits were low, and to accumulate, extreme parsimony was requisite. They lived like misers, and were far from consuming even the interest on their capital. "The second period, when they had begun to acquire little fortunes, but worked as hard as before,"—for direct exploitation of labour costs labour, as every slave-driver knows —"and lived in as plain a manner as before. . . . The third, when luxury began, and the trade was pushed by sending out riders for orders into every market town in the Kingdom. . . . It is probable that few or no capitals of £3000 to £4000 acquired by trade existed here before 1690.

However, about that time, or a little later, the traders had got money beforehand, and began to build modern brick houses, instead of those of wood and plaster." Even in the early part of the 18th century, a Manchester manufacturer, who placed a pint of foreign wine before his guests, exposed himself to the remarks and headshakings of all his neighbors. Before the rise of machinery, a manufacturer's evening expenditure at the public-house where they all met, never exceeded sixpence for a glass of punch, and a penny for a screw of tobacco. It was not till 1758, and this marks an epoch, that a person actually engaged in business was seen with an equipage of his own. "The fourth period," the last 30 years of the 18th century, "is that in which expense and luxury have made great progress, and was supported by a trade extended by means of riders and factors through every part of Europe."[1] What would the good Dr. Aikin say if he could rise from his grave and see the Manchester of to-day?

Accumulate, accumulate! That is Moses and the prophets! "Industry furnishes the material which saving accumulates."[2] Therefore, save, save, *i.e.,* reconvert the greatest possible portion of surplus-value, or surplus-product into capital! Accumulation for accumulation's sake, production for production's sake: by this formula classical economy expressed the historical mission of the bourgeoisie, and did not for a single instant deceive itself over the birth-throes of wealth.[3] But what avails lamentation in the face of historical necessity? If to classical economy, the proletarian is but a machine for the production of surplus-value; on the other hand, the capitalist is in its eyes only a machine for the conversion of this surplus-value into additional capital. Political economy takes the historical function of the capitalist in bitter earnest. In order to charm out of his bosom the awful conflict between

[1] Dr. Aikin: Description of the country from 30 to 40 miles round Manchester. Lond., 1795, p. 182, sqq.

[2] A. Smith: l. c., bk. iii., ch. iii.

[3] Even J. B. Say says: "Les épargnes des riches se font aux dépens des pauvres." "The Roman proletarian lived almost entirely at the expense of society. . . . . It can almost be said that modern society lives at the expense of the proletarians, on what it keeps out of the remuneration of labour." (Sismondi: Etudes, &c., t. i, p. 24.)

the desire for enjoyment and the chase after riches, Malthus, about the year 1820, advocated a division of labour, which assigns to the capitalist actually engaged in production, the business of accumulating, and to the other sharers in surplus-value, to the landlords, the place-men, the beneficed clergy, &c., the business of spending. It is of the highest importance, he says, "to keep separate the passion for expenditure and the passion for accumulation."[1] The capitalists having long been good livers and men of the world, uttered loud cries. What, exclaimed one of their spokesmen, a disciple of Ricardo, Mr. Malthus preaches high rents, heavy taxes, &c., so that the pressure of the spur may constantly be kept on the industrious by unproductive consumers! By all means, production, production on a constantly increasing scale, runs the shibboleth; but "production will, by such a process, be far more curbed in than spurred on. Nor is it quite fair thus to maintain in idleness a number of persons, only to pinch others, who are likely, from their characters, if you can force them to work, to work with success."[2] Unfair as he finds it to spur on the industrial capitalist, by depriving his bread of its butter, yet he thinks it necessary to reduce the labourer's wages to a minimum "to keep him industrious." Nor does he for a moment conceal the fact, that the appropriation of unpaid labour is the secret of surplus-value. "Increased demand on the part of the labourers means nothing more than their willingness to take less of their own product for themselves, and leave a greater part of it to their employer; and if it be said, that this begets glut, by lessening consumption" (on the part of the labourers), "I can only reply that glut is synonymous with large profits."[3]

The learned disputation, how the booty pumped out of the labourer may be divided, with most advantage to accumulation, between the industrial capitalist and the rich idler, was hushed in face of the revolution of July. Shortly afterwards, the town proletariat at Lyons sounded the tocsin of

[1] Malthus, l. c., p. 319, 320.
[2] An Inquiry into those Principles respecting the Nature of Demand, &c., p. 67.
[3] l. c., p. 50.

revolution, and the country proletariat in England began to set fire to farmyards and cornstacks. On this side of the Channel Owenism began to spread; on the other side, St. Simonism and Fourierism. The hour of vulgar economy had struck. Exactly a year before Nassau W. Senior discovered at Manchester, that the profit (including interest) of capital is the product of the last hour of the twelve, he had announced to the world another discovery. "I substitute," he proudly says, "for the word capital, considered as an instrument of production, the word abstinence."[1] An unparalleled sample this, of the discoveries of vulgar economy! It substitutes for an economic category, a sycophantic phrase —*volià tout.* "When the savage," says Senior, "makes bows, he exercises an industry, but he does not practice abstinence." This explains how and why, in the earlier states of society, the implements of labour were fabricated without abstinence on the part of the capitalist. "The more society progresses, the more abstinence is demanded,"[2] namely, from those who ply the industry of appropriating the fruits of others' industry. All the conditions for carrying on the labour-process are suddenly converted into so many acts of abstinence on the part of the capitalist. If the corn is not all eaten, but part of it also sown—abstinence of the capitalist. If the wine gets time to mature—abstinence of the capitalist.[3] The

---

[1] (Senior, Principes fondamentaux de l'Econ. Pol. trad. Arrivabeue. Paris, 1836, p. 308). This was rather too much for the adherents of the old classical school. "Mr. Senior has substituted for it" (the expression, labour and profit) "the expression Labour and Abstinence. He who converts his revenue abstains from the enjoyment which its expenditure would afford him. 'It is not the capital, but the use of the capital productively, which is the cause of profits." (John Cazenove, l. c. p. 130, Note.) John St. Mill, on the contrary, accepts on the one hand Ricardo's theory of profit, and annexes on the other hand Senior's "remuneration of abstinence." He is as much at home in absurd contradictions, as he feels at sea in the Hegelian contradiction, the source of all dialectic. It has never occurred to the vulgar economist to make the simple reflexion, that every human action may be viewed, as "abstinence" from its opposite. Eating is abstinence from fasting, walking, abstinence from standing still, working, abstinence from idling, idling abstinence from working, &c. These gentlemen would do well, to ponder, once in a way, over Spinoza's: "Determinatio est Negatio."

[2] Senior, l. c. p. 342.

[3] "No one . . . will sow his wheat, for instance, and allow it to remain a twelve-month in the ground, or leave his wine in a cellar for years, instead of consuming these things or their equivalent at once . . . unless he expects to acquire additional value, &c." (Scrope, Polit. Econ. edit. by A. Potter, New York, 1841, p. 133-134.)

capitalist robs his own self, whenever he "lends (!) the instruments of production to the labourer," that is, whenever by incorporating labour-power with them, he uses them to extract surplus-value out of that labour-power, instead of eating them up, steam-engines, cotton, railways, manure, horses, and all; or as the vulgar economist childishly puts it, instead of dissipating "their value" in luxuries and other articles of consumption.[1] How the capitalist as a class are to perform that feat, is a secret that vulgar economy has hitherto obstinately refused to divulge. Enough, that the world still jogs on, solely through the self-chastisement of this modern penitent of Vishnu, the capitalist. Not only accumulation, but the simple "conservation of a capital requires a constant effort to resist the temptation of consuming it."[2] The simple dictates of humanity therefore plainly enjoin the release of the capitalist from this martyrdom and temptation, in the same way that the Georgian slave-owner was lately delivered, by the abolition of slavery, from the painful dilemma, whether to squander the surplus-product lashed out of his niggers, entirely in champagne, or whether to reconvert a part of it, into more niggers and more land.

In economic forms of society of the most different kinds, there occurs, not only simple reproduction, but, in varying degrees, reproduction on a progressively increasing scale. By degrees more is produced and more consumed, and consequently more products have to be converted into means of production. This process, however, does not present itself as accumulation of capital, nor as the function of a capitalist, so long as the labourer's means of production, and with them, his product and means of subsistence, do not confront him in the shape of capital.[3] Richard Jones, who died a few years ago, and was the successor of Malthus in the chair of po-

---

[1] "La privation que s'impose le capitaliste, en prêtant (this euphemism used, for the purpose of identifying, according to the approved method of vulgar economy, the labourer who is exploited, with the industrial capitalist who exploits, and to whom other capitalists lend money) ses instruments de production au travailleur, au lieu d'en consacrer la valeur à son propre usage, en la transforment en objets d'utilité ou d'agrément." (G. de Molinari, l. c. p. 49.)

[2] "La conservation d'un capital exige . . . un effort constant pour résister à la tentation de le consommer." (Courcelles-Seneuil, l. c. p. 57.)

[3] "The particular classes of income which yield the most abundantly to the prog-

litical economy at Haileybury College, discusses this point well in the light of two important facts. Since the great mass of the Hindoo population are peasants cultivating their land themselves, their products, their instruments of labour and means of subsistence never take "the shape of a fund saved from revenue, which fund has, therefore, gone through a previous process of accumulation." [1] On the other hand, the non-agricultural labourers in those provinces where the English rule has least disturbed the old system, are directly employed by the magnates, to whom a portion of the agricultural surplus-product is rendered in the shape of tribute or rent. One portion of this product is consumed by the magnates in kind, another is converted, for their use, by the labourers, into articles of luxury and such like things; while the rest forms the wages of the labourers, who own their implements of labour. Here, production and reproduction on a progressively increasing scale, go on their way without any intervention from that queer saint, that knight of the woeful countenance, the capitalist "abstainer."'

SECTION 4.—CIRCUMSTANCES THAT, INDEPENDENTLY OF THE DIVISION OF SURPLUS-VALUE INTO CAPITAL AND REVENUE, DETERMINE THE AMOUNT OF ACCUMULATION. DEGREE OF EXPLOITATION OF LABOUR-POWER. PRODUCTIVITY OF LABOUR. GROWING DIFFERENCE IN AMOUNT BETWEEN CAPITAL EMPLOYED AND CAPITAL CONSUMED. MAGNITUDE OF CAPITAL ADVANCED.

The proportion in which surplus-value breaks up into capital and revenue being given, the magnitude of the capital accumulated clearly depends on the absolute magnitude of the surplus-value. Suppose that 80 per cent. were capitalised

---

ress of national capital, change at different stages of their progress, and are, therefore, entirely different in nations occupying different positions in that progress . . . Profits . . . unimportant source of accumulation, compared with wages and rents, in the earlier stages of society . . . When a considerable advance in the powers of national industry has actually taken place, profits rise into comparative importance as a source of accumulation." (Richard Jones. Textbook, &c., p. 16. 21.)

[1] l. c. p. 36, sq.—Note to the 4th German edition.—This must be a mistake. This passage has not been located. F. E.—

and 20 per cent. eaten up, the accumulated capital will be £2,400 or £1,200, according as the total surplus-value has amounted to £3,000 or £1,500. Hence all the circumstances that determine the mass of surplus-value, operate to determine the magnitude of the accumulation. We sum them up once again, but only in so far as they afford new points of view in regard to accumulation.

It will be remembered that the rate of surplus-value depends, in the first place, on the degree of exploitation of labour-power. Political economy values this fact so highly, that it occasionally identifies the acceleration of accumulation due to increased productiveness of labour, with its acceleration dut to increased exploitation of the labourer.[1] In the chapters on the production of surplus-value it was constantly presupposed that wages are at least equal to the value of labour-power. Forcible reduction of wages below this value plays, however, in practice too important a part, for us not to pause upon it for a moment. It, in fact, transforms, within certain limits, the labourer's necessary consumption-fund into a fund for the accumulation of capital.

"Wages," says John Stuart Mill, "have no productive power; they are the price of productive-power. Wages do not contribute, along with labour, to the production of commodities, no more than the price of tools contributes along with the tools themselves. If labour could be had without purchase, wages might be dispensed with."[2] But if the labourers could live on air they could not be bought at any price. The zero of their cost is therefore a limit in a mathematical sense, always beyond reach, although we can always

---

[1] "Ricardo says: 'In different stages of society the accumulation of capital or of the means of employing" (*i.e.*, exploiting) "labour is more or less rapid, and must in all cases depend on the productive powers of labour. The productive powers of labour are generally greatest where there is an abundance of fertile land.' If, in the first sentence, the productive powers of labour mean the smallness of that aliquot part of any produce that goes to those whose manual labor produced it, the sentence is nearly identical, because the remaining aliquot part is the fund whence capital can, if the *owner pleases*, be accumulated. But then this does not generally happen, where there is most fertile land." ("Observations on certain verbal disputes, &c.," pp. 74, 75.)

[2] J. Stuart Mill: "Essays on some unsettled questions of Political Economy Lond., 1849," p. 90.

approximate more and more nearly to it. The constant tendency of capital is to force the cost of labour back towards this zero. A writer of the 18th century, often quoted already, the author of the "Essay on Trade and Commerce," only betrays the innermost secret soul of English capitalism, when he declares the historic mission of England to be the forcing down of English wages to the level of the French and the Dutch.[1] With other things he says naïvely: "But if our poor" (technical term for labourers) "will live luxuriously . . . then labour must, of course, be dear. . . . When it is considered what luxuries the manufacturing populace consume, such as brandy, gin, tea, sugar, foreign fruit, strong beer, printed linens, snuff, tobacco, &c."[2] He quotes the work of a Northamptonshire manufacturer, who, with eyes squinting heavenward, moans: "Labour is one-third cheaper in France than in England; for their poor work hard, and fare hard, as to their food and clothing. Their chief diet is bread, fruit, herbs, roots, and dried fish; for they very seldom eat flesh; and when wheat is dear, they eat very little bread."[3] "To which may be added," our essayist goes on, "that their drink is either water or other small liquors, so that they spend very little money. . . . These things are very difficult to be brought about; but they are not impracticable, since they have been effected both in France and in Holland."[4] Twenty

---

[1] "An Essay on Trade and Commerce, Lond., 1770," p. 44. The "Times" of December, 1866, and January, 1867, in like manner published certain outpourings of the heart of the English mineowner, in which the happy lot of the Belgian miners was pictured, who asked and received no more than was strictly necessary for them to live for their "masters." The Belgian labourers have to suffer much, but to figure in the "Times" as model labourers! In the beginning of February, 1867, came the answer: strike of the Belgian miners at Marchienne, put down by powder and lead.

[2] l. c., pp. 44, 46.

[3] The Northamptonshire manufacturer commits a pious fraud, pardonable in one whose heart is so full. He nominally compares the life of the English and French manufacturing labourer, but in the words just quoted he is painting, as he himself confesses in his confused way, the French agricultural labourers.

[4] l. c., p. 70, 71. Note to the 3rd edition: Today, thanks to the competition on the world-market, established since then, we have advanced much further. "If China," says Mr. Stapleton, M. P., to his constituents, "should become a great manufacturing country, I do not see how the manufacturing population of Europe could sustain the contest without descending to the level of their competitors." ("Times," Sept. 9, 1873, p. 8.) The wished-for goal of English capital is no longer Continental wages but Chinese.

years later, an American humbug, the baronised Yankee, Benjamin Thompson (*alias* Count Rumford) followed the same line of philanthropy to the great satisfaction of God and man. His "Essays" are a cookery book with receipts of all kinds for replacing by some succedaneum the ordinary dear food of the labourer. The following is a particularly successful receipt of this wonderful philosopher: "5 lbs. of barley meal, 7½d.; 5 lbs. of Indian corn, 6¼d.; 3d. worth of red herring, 1d. salt, 1d. vinegar, 2d. pepper and sweet herbs, in all 20¾d.; make a soup for 64 men, and at the medium price of barley and of Indian corn . . . this soup may be provided at ¼d, the portion of 20 ounces."[1] With the advance of capitalistic production, the adulteration of food rendered Thompson's ideal superfluous.[2] At the end of the 18th and during the first ten years of the 19th century, the English farmers and landlords enforced the absolute minimum of wage, by paying the agricultural labourers less than the minimum in the form of wages, and the remainder in the shape of parochial relief. An example of the waggish way in which the English Dogberries acted in their "legal" fixing of a wages tariff: "The squires of Norfolk had dined, says Mr. Burke, when they fixed the rate of wages; the squires of Berks evidently thought the labourers ought not to do so, when they fixed the rate of wages at Speenhamland, 1795. . . . There they decide that 'income (weekly) should be 3s. for a

---

[1] Benjamin Thompson: Essays, Political, Economical, and Philosophical, &c., 3 vols., Lond., 1796-1802, vol. i., p. 288. In his "The State of the Poor, or an History of the Labouring Classes in England, &c.," Sir F. M. Eden strongly recommends the Rumfordian beggar-soup to workhouse overseers, and reproachfully warns the English labourers that "many poor people, particularly in Scotland, live, and that very comfortably, for months together, upon oat-meal and barley-meal, mixed with only water and salt." (l. c., vol. i., book i., ch. 2., p. 503.) The same sort of hints in the 19th century. "The most wholesome mixtures of flour having been refused (by the English agricultural labourer) . . . . in Scotland, where education is better, this prejudice is, probably, unknown." (Charles H. Parry, M.D.: The question of the necessity of the existing Corn Laws considered. London, 1816, p. 69.) This same Parry, however, complains that the English labourer is now (1815) in a much worse condition than in Eden's time (1787).

[2] From the reports of the last Parliamentary Commission on adulteration of means of subsistence, it will be seen that the adulteration even of medicines is the rule, not the exception of England. E.g., the examination of 34 specimens of opium, purchased of as many different chemists in London, showed that 31 were adulterated with poppy heads, wheat-flour, gum, clay, sand, &c. Several did not contain an atom of morphia.

man,' when the gallon or half-peck loaf of 8 lbs. 11 oz. is
at 1s., and increase regularly till bread is 1s. 5d.; when it is
above that sum, decrease regularly till it be at 2s., and then
his food *should be* ⅕th less."[1] Before the Committee of Inquiry of the House of Lords, 1814, a certain A. Bennett, a
large farmer, magistrate, poor-law guardian, and wage-regu-
lator, was asked: "Has any proportion of the value of daily
labour been made up to the labourers out of the poors' rate?"
Answer: "Yes, it has; the weekly income of every family is
made up to the gallon loaf (8 lbs. 11 oz.), and 3d. per head!
. . . The gallon loaf per week is what we suppose sufficient for the maintenance of every person in the family for
the week; and the 3d. is for clothes, and if the parish think
proper to find clothes, the 3d. is deducted. This practice goes
through all the western part of Wiltshire, and, I believe,
throughout the country."[2] "For years," exclaims a bourgeois
author of that time, "they (the farmers) have degraded a respectable class of their countrymen, by forcing them to have
recourse to the workhouse . . . the farmer, while increasing his own gains, has prevented any accumulation on the
part of his labouring dependants."[3] The part played in our
days by the direct robbery from the labourer's necessary consumption-fund in the formation of surplus-value, and, therefore, of the accumulation fund of capital, the so-called domestic industry has served to show. (Ch. xv., sect. 8, d.)
Further facts on this subject will be given later.

Although in all branches of Industry that part of the
constant capital consisting of instruments of labour must be
sufficient for a certain number of labourers (determined by
the magnitude of the undertaking), it by no means always
necessarily increases in the same proportion as the quantity
of labour employed. In a factory, suppose that 100 labourers

---

[1] G. B. Newnham (barrister-at-law): "A Review of the Evidence before the Committee of the two Houses of Parliament on the Corn Laws. Lond., 1815," p. 28,
note.

[2] l. c., pp. 19, 20.

[3] C. H. Parry, l. c., pp. 77, 69. The landlords, on their side, not only "indemnified" themselves for the Anti-jacobin war, which they waged in the name of England, but enriched themselves enormously. Their rents doubled, trebled, quadrupled,
"and in one instance, increased sixfold in eighteen years." (l. c., pp. 100, 101.)

working 8 hours a day yield 800 working-hours. If the capitalist wishes to raise this sum by one half, he can employ 50 more workers; but then he must also advance more capital, not merely for wages, but for instruments of labour. But he might also let the 100 labourers work 12 hours instead of 8, and then the instruments of labour already on hand would be enough. These would them simply be more rapidly consumed. Thus additional labour, begotten of the greater tension of labour-power, can augment surplus-product and surplus-value (*i.e.*, the subject matter of accumulation), without corresponding augmentation in the constant part of capital.

In the extractive industries, mines, &c., the raw materials form no part of the capital advanced. The subject of labour is in this case not a product of previous labour, but is furnished by Nature gratis, as in the case of metals, minerals, coal, stone, &c. In these cases the constant capital consists almost exclusively of instruments of labour, which can very well absorb an increased quantity of labour (day and night shifts of labourers, *e.g.*). All other things being equal, the mass and value of the product will rise in direct proportion to the labour expended. As on the first day of production, the original produce-formers, now turned into the creators of the material elements of capital—man and Nature—still work together. Thanks to the elasticity of labour-power, the domain of accumulation has extended without any previous enlargement of constant capital.

In agriculture the land under cultivation cannot be increased without the advance of more seed and manure. But this advance once made, the purely mechanical working of the soil itself produces a marvellous effect on the amount of the product. A greater quantity of labour, done by the same number of labourers as before, thus increases the fertility, without requiring any new advance in the instruments of labour. It is once again the direct action of man on Nature which becomes an immediate source of greater accumulation, without the intervention of any new capital.

Finally, in what is called manufacturing industry, every additional expenditure of labour presupposes a corresponding additional expenditure of raw materials, but not necessarily of instruments of labour. And as extractive industry and agriculture supply manufacturing industry with its raw materials and those of its instruments of labour, the additional product the former have created without additional advance of capital, tells also in favour of the latter.

General result: by incorporating with itself the two primary creators of wealth, labour-power and the land, capital acquires a power of expansion that permits it to augment the elements of its accumulation beyond the limits apparently fixed by its own magnitude, or by the value and the mass of the means of production, already produced, in which it has its being.

Another important factor in the accumulation of capital is the degree of productivity of social labour.

With the productive power of labour increases the mass of the products, in which a certain value, and therefore, a surplus-value of a given magnitude, is embodied. The rate of surplus-value remaining the same or e·en falling, so long as it only falls more slowly, than the productive power of labour rises, the mass of the surplus-product increases. The division of this product into revenue and additional capital remaining the same, the consumption of the capitalist may, therefore, increase without any decrease in the fund of accumulation. The relative magnitude of the accumulation fund may even increase at the expense of the consumption fund, whilst the cheapening of commodities places at the disposal of the capitalist as many means of enjoyment as formerly, or even more than formerly. But hand-in-hand with the increasing productivity of labour, goes, as we have seen, the cheapening of the labourer, therefore a higher rate of surplus-value, even when the real wages are rising. The latter never rise proportionally to the productive power of labour. The same value in variable capital therefore sets in movement more labour-power, and, therefore, more labour. The same value in constant capital is embodied in more means of production, *i.e.*, in more instruments of labour, materials of labour and auxiliary materials; it therefore also supplies more elements for the production both of use-value and of value, and with these more absorbers of labour. The value of the additional capital, therefore, remaining the same or even diminishing, accelerated accumulation still takes place. Not only does the scale of reproduction materially extend, but the production of surplus-value increases more rapidly than the value of the additional capital.

The development of the productive power of labour reacts also on the original capital already engaged in the process of production. A part of the functioning constant capital consists of instruments of labour such as machinery, &c., which are not consumed, and therefore not reproduced, or replaced by new ones of the same kind, until after long periods of time. But every year a part of these instruments of labour perishes or reaches the limit of its productive function. It reaches, therefore, in that year, the time for its periodical reproduction, for its replacement by new ones of the same kind. If the productiveness of labour has, during the using up of these instruments of labour, increased (and it developes continually with the uninterrupted advance of science and technology), more efficient and (considering their increased efficiency), cheaper machines, tools, apparatus, &c., replace the old. The old capital is reproduced in a more productive form, apart from the constant detail improvements in the instruments of labour already in use. The other part of the constant capital, raw material and auxiliary substances, is constantly reproduced in less than a year; those produced by agriculture, for the most part annually. Every introduction of improved methods, therefore, works almost simultaneously on the new capital and on that already in action. Every advance in Chemistry not only multiplies the number of useful materials and the useful applications of those already known, thus extending with the growth of capital its sphere of investment. It teaches at the same time how to throw the excrements of the processes of production and consumption back again into the circle of the process of reproduction, and thus, without any previous outlay of capital, creates new matter for capital. Like the increased exploitation of natural wealth by the mere increase in the tension of labour-power, science and technology give capital a power of expansion independent of the given magnitude of the capital actually functioning. They react at the same time on that part of the original capital which has entered upon its stage of renewal. This, in passing into its new shape, incorporates gratis the social advance made while its old shape was being used up. Of course, this development of productive power is accompanied by a partial depreciation of functioning capital. So far as this depreciation makes itself acutely felt in competition, the burden falls on the labourer, in the increased exploitation of whom the capitalist looks for his indemnification.

Labour transmits to its product the value of the means of production consumed by it. On the other hand, the value and mass of the means of production set in motion by a given quantity of labour increase as the labour becomes more productive. Though the same quantity f labour adds always to its products only the same sum of new value, still the old capital-value, transmitted by the labour to the products, increases with the growing productivity of labour.

An English and Chinese spinner, *e.g.,* may work the same number of hours with the same intensity; then they will both in a week create equal values. But in spite of this equality, an immense difference ill obtain between the value of the week's product of the Englishman, who works with a mighty automaton, and that of the Chinaman, who has but a spinning wheel. In the same time as the Chinaman spins one pound of cotton, the Englishman spins several hundreds of pounds. A sum, many hundred times as great, of old values swells the value of his product, in which those reappear in a new, useful form, and can thus function anew as capital. "In 1782," as Frederick Engels teaches us, "all the wool crop in England of the three preceding years, lay untouched for want of labourers, and so it must have lain, if newly invented machinery had not come to its aid and spun it."[1] Labour embodied in the form of machinery of course did not directly force into life a single man, but it made it possible for a smaller number of labourers, with the addition of relatively less living labour,

[1] Frederick Engels, "Lage der arbeitenden Klasse in England," o. 20.

not only to consume the wool productively, and put into it new value, but to preserve in the form of yarn, &c., its old value. At the same time, it caused and stimulated increased reproduction of wool. It is the natural property of living labour, to transmit old value, whilst it creates new. Hence, with the increase in efficacy, extent and value of its means of production, consequently with the accumulation that accompanies the development of its productive power, labour keeps up and eternises an always increasing capital-value in a form ever new.[1] This natural power of labour takes the

---

[1] Classic economy has, on account of a deficient analysis of the labour-process, and of the process of creating value, never properly grasped this weighty element of reproduction, as may be seen in Ricardo; he says, *e.g.*, whatever the change in productive power, "a million men always produce in manufactures the same value." This is accurate, if the extension and degree of intensity of their labour are given. But it does not prevent (this Ricardo overlooks in certain conclusions he draws) a million men with different powers of productivity in their labour, turning into products very different masses of the means of production, and therefore preserving in their products very different masses of value; in consequence of which the values of the products yielded may vary considerably. Ricardo has, it may be noted in passing, tried in vain to make clear to J. B. Say, by that very example, the difference between use-value (which he here calls wealth or material riches) and exchange-value. Say answers: "Quant à la difficulté qu'élève Mr. Ricardo en disant que, par des procédés mieux entendus, un million de personnes peuvent produire deux fois, trois fois autant de richesses, sans produire plus de valeurs, cette difficulté n'est pas une lorsque l'on considère, ainsi qu'on le doit, la production comme un échange dans lequel on donne les services productifs de son travail, de sa terre, et de ses capitaux, pour obtenir des produits. C'est par le moyen de ces services productifs, que nous acquérons tous les produits qui sont au monde. Or . . . . nous sommes d'autant plus riches nos services productifs ont d'autant plus de valeur qu'ils obtiennent dans l'échange appelé production une plus grande quantité de choses utiles." (J. B. Say; "Lettres à M. Malthus, Paris, 1820," pp. 168, 169.) The "difficulté"—it exists for him, not for Ricardo—that Say means to clear up is this: Why does not the exchange-value of the use-values increase, when their quantity increases in consequence of increased productive power of labour? Answer; the difficulty is met by calling use-value, exchange-value, if you please. Exchange-value is a thing that is connected one way or another with exchange. If therefore production is called an exchange of labour and means of production against the product, it is clear as day that you obtain more exchange-value in proportion as the production yields more use-value. In other words, the more use-values, *e.g.*, stockings, a working day yields to the stocking-manufacturer, the richer is he in stockings. Suddenly, however, Say recollects that "with a greater quantity" of stockings their "price" (which of course has nothing to do with their exchange-value!) falls "parce que la concurrence les (les producteurs) oblige à donner les produits pour ce qu'ils leur coûtent." But whence does the profit come, if the capitalist sells the commodities at cost price? Never mind! Say declares that, in consequence of increased productivity, every one now receives in return for a given equivalent two pairs of stockings instead of one as before. The result he arrives at, is precisely that proposition of Ricardo that he aimed at disproving. After this mighty effort of thought, he triumphantly apostrophises Malthus in the words: "Telle est, monsieur, la doctrine bien liée, sans laquelle il est impossible, je le déclare, d'expliquer les plus grandes

appearance of an intrinsic property of capital, in which it is incorporated, just as the productive forces of social labour take the appearance of inherent properties of capital, and as the constant appropriation of surplus-labour by the capitalists, takes that of a constant self-expansion of capital.

With the increase of capital, the difference between the capital employed and the capital consumed increases. In other words, there is increase in the value and the material mass of the instruments of labour, such as buildings, machinery, drain-pipes, working-cattle, apparatus of every kind that function for a longer or shorter time in processes of production constantly repeated, or that serve for the attainment of particular useful effects, whilst they themselves only gradually wear out, therefore only lose their value piecemeal, therefore transfer that value of the product only bit by bit. In the same proportion as these instruments of labour serve as product-formers without adding value to the product, *i.e.*, in the same proportion as they are wholly employed but only partly consumed, they perform, as we saw earlier, the same gratuitous service as the natural forces, water, steam, air, electricity, etc. This gratuitous service of past labour, when seized and filled with a soul by living labour, increases with the advancing stages of accumulation.

Since past labour always disguises itself as capital, *i.e.*, since the passive of the labour of A, B, C, etc., takes the form of the active of the non-labourer X, bourgeois and political economists are full of praises of the services of dead and gone labour, which, according to the Scotch genius M'Culloch, ought to receive a special remuneration in the shape of in-

difficultés de l'économie politique, et notamment, comment il se peut qu'une nation soit plus riche lorsque ses produits diminuent de valeur, quoique la richesse soit de la valeur." (l. c. p. 170.) An English economist remarks upon the conjuring tricks of the same nature that appear in Say's "Lettres": "Those affected ways of talking make up in general that which M. Say is pleased to call his doctrine and which he earnestly urges Malthus to teach at Hertford, as it is already taught 'dans plusieurs parties de l'Europe.' He says, 'Si vous trouvez une physionomie de paradoxe à toutes ces propositions, voyez les choses qu'elles expriment, et j'ose croire qu'elles vous paraîtront fort simples et fort raisonnables.' Doubtless, and in consequence of the same process, they will appear everything else, except original." (An Inquiry into those Principles respecting the Nature of Demand, &c., p. 116, 110.)

terest, profit, etc.[1] The powerful and ever-increasing assistance given by past labour to the living labour process under the form of means of production, is therefore, attributed to that form of past labour in which it is alienated, as unpaid labour, from the worker himself, *i.e.,* to its capitalistic form. The practical agents of capitalistic production and their pettifogging ideologists are as unable to think of the means of production as separate from the antagonistic social mask they wear to-day, as a slave-owner to think of the worker himself as distinct from his character as a slave.

With a given degree of exploitation of labour-power, the mass of the surplus-value produced is determined by the number of workers simultaneously exploited; and this corresponds, although in varying proportions, with the magnitude of the capital. The more, therefore, capital increases by means of successive accumulations, the more does the sum of the value increase that is divided into consumption-fund and accumulation-fund. The capitalist can therefore, live a more jolly life, and at the same time show more "abstinence." And, finally, all the springs of production act with greater elasticity, the more its scale extends with the mass of the capital advanced.

SECTION 5.—THE SO-CALLED LABOUR FUND.

It has been shown in the course of this inquiry that capital is not a fixed magnitude, but is a part of social wealth, elastic and constantly fluctuating with the division of fresh surplus-value into revenue and additional capital. It has been seen further that, even with a given magnitude of functioning capital, the labour-power, the science, and the land (by which are to be understood, economically, all conditions of labour furnished by Nature independently of man), embodied in it, from elastic powers of capital, allowing it, within certain limits, a field of action independent of its own magnitude. In this inquiry we have neglected all effects of the process of circulation, effects which may produce very different degrees

---

[1] M'Culloch took out a patent for "wages of past labour," long before Senior did for "wages of abstinence."

of efficiency in the same mass of capital. And as we presupposed the limits set by capitalist production, that is to say, pre-supposed the process of social production in a form developed by purely spontaneous growth, we neglected any more rational combination, directly and systematically practicable with the means of production, and the mass of labour-power at present disposable. Classical economy always loved to conceive social capital as a fixed magnitude of a fixed degree of efficiency. But this prejudice was first established as a dogma by the arch-Philistine, Jeremy Bentham, that insipid, pedantic, leather-tongued oracle of the ordinary bourgeois intelligence of the 19th century.[1] Bentham is among philosophers what Martin Tupper is among poets. Both could only have been manufactured in England.[2] In the light of his dogma the commonest phenomena of the process of production, as, *e.g.,* its sudden expansions and contractions, nay, even accumulation itself, become perfectly inconceivable.[3]   The

[1] Compare among others, Jeremy Bentham: "Théorie des Peines et des Récompenses, traduct. d'Et. Dumont, 3ème édit. Paris, 1826," p. II., L. IV., ch. II.

[2] Bentham is a purely English phenomenon. Not even excepting our philosopher, Christian Wolf, in no time and in no country has the most homespun common-place ever strutted about in so self-satisfied a way. The principle of utility was no discovery of Bentham. He simply reproduced in his dull way what Helvetius and other Frenchmen had said with esprit in the 18th century. To know what is useful for a dog, one must study dog-nature. This nature itself is not to ᵇe deduced from the principle of utility. Applying this to man, he that would criticise all human acts, movements, relations, etc., by the principle of utility, must first deal with human nature in general, and then with human nature as modified in each historical epoch. Bentham makes short work of it. With the dryest naïveté he takes the modern shopkeeper, especially the English shopkeeper, as he normal man. Whatever is useful to this queer normal man, and to his world, is absolutely useful. This yard-measure, then, he applies to past, present, and future. The Christian religion, *e.g.,* is "useful," because it forbids in the name of religion the same faults that the penal code condemns in the name of the law. Artistic criticism is "harmful," because it disturbs worthy people in their enjoyment of Martin Tupper, etc. With such rubbish has the brave fellow, with his motto, "null adies sine lineâ," piled up mountains of books. Had I the courage of my friend, Heinrich Heine, I should call Mr. Jeremy a genius in the way of bourgeois stupidity.

[3] "Political economists are too apt to consider a certain quantity of capital and a certain number of labourers as productive instruments of uniform power, or operating with a certain uniform intensity . . . Those . . . who maintain . . . that commodities are the sole agents of production . . . prove that production could never be enlarged, for it requires as an indispensable condition to such an enlargement that food, raw materials, and tools should be previously augmented; which is in fact maintaining that no increase of production can take place without a previous increase, or, in other words, that an increase is impossible." (S. Bailey: "Money and its vicissitudes," pp. 26 and 70.) Bailey criticises the dogma mainly from the point of view of the process of circulation.

dogma was used by Bentham himself, as well as by Malthus, James Mill, M'Culloch, etc., for an apologetic purpose, and especially in order to represent one part of capital, namely, variable capital, or that part convertible into labour-power, as a fixed magnitude. The material of variable capital, *i.e.,* the mass of the means of subsistence it represents for the labourer, or the so-called labour fund, was fabled as a separate part of social wealth, fixed by natural laws and unchangeable. To set in motion the part of social wealth which is to function as constant capital, or, to express it in a material form, as means of production, a definite mass of living labour is required. This mass is given technologically. But neither is the number of labourers required to render fluid this mass of labour-power given (it changes with the degree of exploitation of the individual labour-power), nor is the price of this labour-power given, but only its minimum limit, which is moreover very variable. The facts that lie at the bottom of this dogma are these: on the one hand, the labourer has no right to interfere in the division of social wealth into means of enjoyment for the non-labourer and means of production.[1] On the other hand, only in favourable and exceptional cases, has he the power to enlarge the so-called labour-fund at the expense of the "revenue" of the wealthy.

What silly tautology results from the attempt to represent the capitalistic limits of the labour-fund as its natural and social limits may be seen, *e.g.,* in Professor Fawcett.[2] "The circulating capital of a country," he says, "is its wage-fund. Hence, if we desire to calculate the average money wages received by each labourer, we have simply to divide the amount

---

[1] John Stuart Mill, in his "Principles of Political Economy," says: "The really exhausting and the really repulsive labours instead of being better paid than others, are almost invariably paid the worst of all . . . The more revolting the occupation, the more certain it is to receive the minimum of remuneration . . . The hardships and the earnings, instead of being directly proportional, as in any just arrangements of society they would be, are generally in an inverse ratio to one another." To avoid misunderstanding, let me say that although men like John Stuart Mill are to blame for the contradiction between their traditional economic dogmas and their modern tendencies, it would be very wrong to class them with the herd of vulgar economic apologists.

[2] H. Fawcett, Professor of Political Economy at Cambridge. "The Economic Position of the British Labourer." London, 1865, p. 120.

of this capital by the number of the labouring population."[1]
That is to say we first add together the individual wages
actually paid, and then we affirm that the sum thus obtained,
forms the total value of the "labour-fund" determined and
vouchsafed to us by God and Nature.   Lastly, we divide the
sum thus obtained by the number of labourers to find out
again how much may come to each on the average.   An uncommonly knowing dodge this.   It did not prevent Mr. Fawcett saying in the same breath: "The aggregate wealth which
is annually saved in England, is divided into two portions;
one portion is employed as capital to maintain our industry,
and the other portion is exported to foreign countries.   .   .   .
Only a portion, and perhaps, not a large portion of the
wealth which is annually saved in this country, is invested
in our own industry."[2]

The greater part of the yearly accruing surplus-product,
embezzled, because abstracted without return of an equivalent,
from the English labourer, is thus used as capital, not in
England, but in foreign countries.   But with the additional
capital thus exported, a part of the "labour-fund" invented by
God and Bentham is also exported.[3]

[1] I must here remind the reader that the categories, "variable and constant capital,"
were first used by me.   Political Economy since the time of Adam Smith has con-
fusedly mixed up the essential distinctions involved in these categories, with the
mere formal differences, arising out of the process of circulation, of fixed and
circulating capital.   For further details on this point, see Book II., Part II.

[2] Fawcett, l. c. pp. 122, 123.

[3] It might be said that not only capital, but also labourers, in the shape of emigrants, are annually exported from England.   In the text, however, there is no question of the peculium of the emigrants, who are in great part not labourers.   The
sons of farmers make up a great part of them.   The additional capital annually transported abroad to be put out at interest is in much greater proportion to the annual
accumulation than the yearly emigration is to the yearly increase of population.

CHAPTER XXV.

THE GENERAL LAW OF CAPITALIST ACCUMULATION.

SECTION 1.—THE INCREASED DEMAND FOR LABOUR-POWER THAT ACCOMPANIES ACCUMULATION, THE COMPOSITION OF CAPITAL REMAINING THE SAME.

IN this chapter we consider the influence of the growth of capital on the lot of the labouring class. The most important factor in this inquiry, is the composition of capital and the changes it undergoes in the course of the process of accumulation.

The composition of capital is to be understood in a two-fold sense. On the side of value, it is determined by the proportion in which it is divided into constant capital or value of the means of production, and variable capital or value of labour-power, the sum total of wages. On the side of material, as it functions in the process of production, all capital is divided into means of production and living labour-power. This latter composition is determined by the relation between the mass of the means of production employed, on the one hand, and the mass of labour necessary for their employment on the other. I call the former the *value-composition,* the latter the *technical composition* of capital. Between the two there is a strict correlation. To express this, I call the value-composition of capital, in so far as it is determined by its technical composition and mirrors the changes of the latter, the *organic composition* of capital. Wherever I refer to the composition of capital, without further qualification, its organic composition is always understood.

The many individual capitals invested in a particular branch of production have, one with another, more or less different compositions. The average of their individual compositions gives us the composition of the total capital in this branch of production. Lastly, the average of these averages, in all branches of production, gives us the composition of the total social capital of a country, and with this alone are we, in the last resort, concerned in the following investigation.

Growth of capital involves growth of its variable constituent or of the part invested in labour-power. A part of the surplus-value turned into additional capital must always be re-transformed into variable capital, or additional labour-fund. If we suppose that, all other circumstances remaining the same, the composition of capital also remains constant (*i.e.*, that a definite mass of means of production constantly needs the same mass of labour-power to set in motion,) then the demand for labour and the subsistence-fund of the labourers clearly increase in the same proportion as the capital, and the more rapidly, the more rapidly the capital increases. Since the capital produces yearly a surplus-value, of which one part is yearly added to the original capital; since this increment itself grows yearly along with the augmentation of the capital already functioning; since lastly, under special stimulus to enrichment, such as the opening of new markets, or of new spheres for the outlay of capital in consequence of newly developed social wants, &c., the scale of accumulation may be suddenly extended, merely by a change in the division of the surplus-value or surplus-product into capital and revenue, the requirements of accumulating capital may exceed the increase of labour-power or of the number of labourers; the demand for labourers may exceed the supply, and, therefore, wages may rise. This must, indeed, ultimately be the case if the conditions supposed above continue. For since in each year more labourers are employed than in its predecessor, sooner or later a point must be reached, at which the requirements of accumulation begin to surpass the customary supply of labour, and, therefore, a rise of wages takes place. A lamentation on this score was heard in England during the whole of the fifteenth, and the first half of the eighteenth centuries. The more or less favourable circumstances in which the wage-working class supports and multiplies itself, in no way alter the fundamental character of capitalist production. As simple reproduction constantly reproduces the capital-relation itself, *i.e.*, the relation of capitalists on the one hand, and wage-workers on the other, so reproduction on a progressive scale, *i.e.*, accumulation, reproduces the capital relation on a progressive scale, more capitalists or larger capitalists at this pole, more wage-workers at that. The re-production of a mass of labour-power, which must incessantly re-incorporate itself with capital for that capital's self-expansion; which cannot get free from capital, and whose enslavement to capital is only concealed by the variety of individual capitalists to whom it sells itself, this reproduction of labour-power forms, in fact, an essential of the reproduction of capital itself. Accumulation of capital is, therefore, increase of the proletariat.[1]

Classical economy grasped this fact so thoroughly that Adam Smith, Ricardo, &c., as mentioned earlier, inaccurately identified accumulation with the consumption, by the productive labourers, of all the capitalised part of the surplus-product, or with its transformation into additional wage-labourers. As early as 1696 John Bellers says: "For if one had a hundred thousand acres of land and as many pounds of money, and as many cattle, without a labourer, what would the rich man be, but a labourer? And as the labourers make men rich, so the more labourers, there will be the more rich men . . . the labour of the poor being the mines of the rich."[2] So also Bernard de Mandeville at the beginning of the eighteenth century: "It would be easier, where property

---

[1] Karl Marx, l. c. "A égalité d'oppression des masses, plus un pays a de prolétaires et plus il est riche." (Colins. L'Economie politique, Source des Révolutions et des Utopies prétendues Socialistes. Paris, 1857, t. III. p. 331.) Our "proletarian" is economically none other than the wage-labourer, who produces and increases capital, and is thrown out on the streets, as soon as he is superfluous for the needs of aggrandisement of "Monsieur capital," as Pecqueur calls this person. "The sickly proletarian of the primitive forest," is a pretty Roscherian fancy. The primitive forester is owner of the primitive forest, and uses the primitive forest as his property with the freedom of an orang-utang. He is not, therefore, a proletarian. This would only be the case, if the primitive forest exploited him, instead of being exploited by him. As far as his health is concerned, such a man would well bear comparison, not only with the modern proletarian, but also with the syphilitic and scrofulous upper classes. But, no doubt, Herr Wilhelm Roscher, by "primitive forest" means his native heath of Luneburg.

[2] John Bellers, l. c. p. 2.

is well secured, to live without money than without poor; for who would do the work? . . . As they [the poor] ought to be kept from starving, so they should receive nothing worth saving. If here and there one of the lowest class by uncommon industry, and pinching his belly, lifts himself above the condition he was brought up in, nobody ought to hinder him; nay, it is undeniably the wisest course for every person in the society, and for every private family to be frugal; but it is the interest of all rich nations, that the greatest part of the poor should almost never be idle, and yet continually spend what they get. . . . Those that get their living by their daily labour . . . have nothing to stir them up to be serviceable but their wants which it is prudence to relieve, but folly to cure. The only thing then that can render the labouring man industrious, is a moderate quantity of money, for as too little will, according as his temper is, either dispirit or make him desperate, so too much will make him insolent and lazy. . . . From what has been said, it is manifest, that, in a free nation, where slaves are not allowed of, the surest wealth consists in a multitude of laborious poor; for besides, that they are the never-failing nursery of fleets and armies, without them there could be no enjoyment, and no product of any country could be valuable. To make the society" [which of course consists of non-workers] "happy and people easier under the meanest circumstances, it is requisite that great numbers of them should be ignorant as well as poor; knowledge both enlarges and multiplies our desires, and the fewer things a man wishes for, the more easily his necessities may be supplied."[1] What Mandeville, an honest, clearheaded man, had not yet seen, is that the mechanism of the process of accumulation itself increases, along with the capital, the mass of "labouring poor," *i.e.*, the wage-labourers, who turn their labour-power into an increasing power of self-ex-

---

[1] Bernard de Mandeville: "The Fable of the Bees," 5th edition, London, 1728. Remarks, pp. 212, 213, 328. "Temperate living and constant employment is the direct road, for the poor, to rational happiness" [by which he most probably means long working days and little means of subsistence], "and to riches and strength for the state" (viz., for the landlords, capitalists, and their political dignitaries and agents). (An Essay on Trade and Commerce, London, 1170, p. 54.)

pansion of the growing capital, and even by doing so must eternize their dependent relation on their own product, as personified in the capitalists. In reference to this relation of dependence, Sir F. M. Eden in his "The State of the Poor, an History of the Labouring Classes in England," says "the natural produce of our soil is certainly not fully adequate to our subsistence; we can neither be clothed, lodged nor fed but in consequence of some previous labour. A portion at least of the society must be indefatigably employed. . . . There are others who, though they 'neither toil nor spin,' can yet command the produce of industry, but who owe their exemption from labour solely to civilisation and order. . . . They are peculiarly the creatures of civil institutions,[1] which have recognised that individuals may acquire property by various other means besides the exertion of labour. . . . Persons of independent fortune . . . owe their superior advantages by no means to any superior abilities of their own, but almost entirely . . . to the industry of others. It is not the possession of land, or of money, but the command of labour which distinguishes the opulent from the labouring part of the community. . . . This [scheme approved by Eden] would give the people of property sufficient (but by no means too much) influence and authority over those who . . . work for them; and it would place such labourers, not in an abject or servile condition, but in such a state of easy and liberal dependence as all who know human nature, and its history, will allow to be necessary for their own comfort."[2] Sir F. M. Eden, it may be remarked in passing, is the only disciple of Adam Smith during the eighteenth century that produced any work of importance.[3]

---

[1] Eden should have asked, whose creatures then are "the civil institutions?" From his standpoint of juridical illusion, he does not regard the law as a product of the material relations of production, but conversely the relations of production as products of the law. Linguet overthrew Montesquieu's illusory "Esprit des lois" with one word; "L'esprit des lois, c'est la propriété."

[2] Eden l. c. Vol. I, book I. chapter I. pp. 1, 2, and preface, p. xx.

[3] If the reader reminds me of Malthus, whose "Essay on Population" appeared in 1798, I remind him that this work in its first form is nothing more than a schoolboyish, superficial plagiary of De Foe, Sir James Steuart, Townsend, Franklin, Wallace, &c., and does not contain a single sentence thought out by himself. The great sensation this pamphlet caused, was due solely to party interest. The French

Under the conditions of accumulation supposed thus far, which conditions are those most favourable to the labourers, their relation of dependence upon capital takes on a form endurable, or, as Edén says: "easy and liberal." Instead of becoming more intensive with the growth of capital, this relation

Revolution had found passionate defenders in the United Kingdom; the "principle of population," slowly worked-out in the eighteenth century, and then, in the midst of a great social crisis, proclaimed with drums and trumpets as the infallible antidote to the teachings of Condorcet, &c., was greeted with jubilance by the English oligarchy as the great destroyer of all hankerings after human development. Malthus, hugely astonished at his success, gave himself to stuffing into his book materials superficially compiled, and adding to it new matter, not discovered but annexed by him. Note further: Although Malthus was a parson of the English State Church, he had taken the monastic vow of celibacy—one of the conditions of holding a Fellowship in Protestant Cambridge University: "Socios collegiorum maritos esse non permittimus, sed statim postquam quis uxorem duxerit, socius collegii desinat esse." (Reports of Cambridge University Commission, p. 172.) This circumstance favourably distinguishes Malthus from the other Protestant parsons, who have shuffled off the command enjoining celibacy of the priesthood and have taken, "Be fruitful and multiply," as their special Biblical mission in such a degree that they generally contribute to the increase of population to a really unbecoming extent, whilst they preach at the same time to the labourers the "principle of population." It is characteristic that the economic fall of man, the Adam's apple, the urgent appetite, "the checks which tend to blunt the shafts of Cupid," as Parson Townsend waggishly puts it, that this delicate question was and is monopolised by the Reverends of Protestant Theology, or rather of the Protestant Church. With the exception of the Venetian monk, Ortes, an original and clever writer, most of the population-theory teachers are Protestant parsons. For instance, Bruckner, "Théorie du Système animal," Leyden, 1767, in which the whole subject of the modern population theory in exhausted, and to which the passing quarrel between Quesnay and his pupil, the elder Mirabeau, furnished ideas on the same topic; then Parson Wallace, Parson Townsend, Parson Malthus and his pupil, the arch-Parson Thomas Chalmers, to say nothing of lesser reverend scribblers in this line. Originally, political economy was studied by philosophers like Hobbes, Locke, Hume; by business men and statesmen, like Thomas More, Temple, Sully, De Witt, North, Law, Vanderlint, Cantillon, Franklin; and especially, and with the greatest success, by medical men like Petty, Barbon, Mandeville, Quesnay. Even in the middle of the eighteenth century, the Rev. Mr. Tucker, a notable economist of his time, excused himself for meddling with the things of Mammon. Later on, and in truth with this very "principle of population," struck the hour of the Protestant parsons. Petty, who regarded the population as the basis of wealth, and was, like Adam Smith, an outspoken foe to parsons, says, as if he had a presentiment of their bungling interference, "that Religion best flourishes when the Priests are most mortified, as was before said of the Law, which best flourisheth when lawyers have least to do." He advises the Protestant priests, therefore if they once for all, will not follow the Apostle Paul and "mortify" themselves by celibacy, "not to breed more Churchmen than the Benefices, as they now stand shared out, will receive, that is to say, if there be places for about twelve thousand in England and Wales, it will not be safe to breed up 24,000 ministers, for then the twelve thousand which are unprovided for, will seek ways how to get themselves a livelihood, which they cannot do more easily then by persuading the people that the twelve thousand incumbents do poison or starve their souls, and misguide them in their way to Heaven." (Petty; "A Treatise on Taxes and Contributions, London, 1667," p. 57.) Adam Smith's position with the Protestant priesthood of

of dependence only becomes more extensive, *i.e.,* the sphere of capital's exploitation and rule merely extends with its own dimensions and the number of its subjects. A larger part of their own surplus-product, always increasing and continually transformed into additional capital, comes back to them in the shape of means of payment, so that they can extend the circle of their enjoyments; can make some additions to their consumption-fund of clothes, furniture, &c., and can lay by small reserve-funds of money. But just as little as better clothing, food, and treatment, and a larger peculium, do away with the exploitation of the slave, so little do they set aside that of the wage-worker. A rise in the price of labour, as a consequence of accumulation of capital, only means, in fact, that the length and weight of the golden chain the wage-worker has already forged for himself, allow of a relaxation of the tension of it. In the controversies on this subject the chief fact has generally

his time is shown by the following. In "A Letter to A. Smith, L.L.D. On the Life, Death and Philosophy of his Friend, David Hume. By one of the People called Christians, 4th Edition, Oxford, 1784," Dr. Horne, Bishop of Norwich, reproves Adam Smith, because in a published letter to Mr. Strahan, he "embalmed his friend David" (sc. Hume); because he told the world how "Hume amused himself on his deathbed with Lucian and Whist," and because he even had the impudence to write of Hume: "I have always considered him, both in his life-time and since his death, as approaching as nearly to the idea of a perfectly wise and virtuous man, as, perhaps, the nature of human frailty will permit." The bishop cries out, in a passion: "Is it right in you, Sir, to hold up to our view as 'perfectly wise and virtuous,' the *character* and *conduct* of one, who seems to have been possessed with an incurable antipathy to all that is called *Religion;* and who strained every nerve to explode, suppress and extirpate the spirit of it among men, that it's very name, if he could effect it, might no more be had in remembrance?" (l. c. p. 8). "But let not the lovers of truth be discouraged. Atheism cannot be of long continuance." (p. 17.) Adam Smith, "had the atrocious wickedness to propagate atheism through the land (viz. by his "Theory of moral sentiments.") Upon the whole, Doctor, your meaning is good; but I think you will not succeed this time. You would persuade us, by the example of *David Hume, Esq.,* that atheism is the only cordial for low spirits, and the proper antidote against the fear of death . . . You may smile over *Babylon* in ruins and congratulate the hardened *Pharaoh* on his overthrow in the Red Sea." (l. c. pp. 21, 22.) One orthodox individual, amongst Adam Smith's college friends, writes after his death: "Smith's well-placed affection for Hume . . . hindered him from being a Christian . . . When he met with honest men whom he liked . . . he would believe almost anything they said. Had he been a friend of the worthy ingenious Horrox he would have believed that the moon sometimes disappeared in a clear sky without the interposition of a cloud. . . . He approached to republicanism in his political principles." (The Bee. By James Anderson, 18 Vols., Vol. 3, pp. 165, 164, Edinburgh, 1791-93.) Parson Thomas Chalmers has his suspicions as to Adam Smith having invented the category of "unproductive labourers," solely for the Protestant parsons, in spite of their blessed work in the vineyard of the Lord.

been overlooked, viz., the *differentia specifica* of capitalistic production. Labour-power is sold to-day, not with a view of satisfying, by its service or by its product, the personal needs of the buyer. His aim is augmentation of his capital, production of commodities containing more labour than he pays for, containing therefore a portion of value that costs him nothing, and that is nevertheless realised when the commodities are sold. Production of surplus-value is the absolute law of this mode of production. Labour-power is only saleable so far as it preserves the means of production in their capacity of capital, reproduces its own value as capital, and yields in unpaid labour a source of additional capital.[1] The conditions of its sale, whether more or less favourable to the labourer, include therefore the necessity of its constant re-selling, and the constantly extended reproduction of all wealth in the shape of capital. Wages, as we have seen, by their very nature, always imply the performance of a certain quantity of unpaid labour on the part of the labourer. Altogether, irrespective of the case of a rise of wages with a falling price of labour, &c., such an increase only means at best a quantitative diminution of the unpaid labour that the worker has to supply. This diminution can never reach the point at which it would threaten the system itself. Apart from violent conflicts as to the rate of wages (and Adam Smith has already shown that in such a conflict, taken on the whole, the master is always master), a rise in the price of labour resulting from accumulation of capital implies the following alternative:

Either the price of labour keeps on rising, because its rise does not interfere with the progress of accumulation. In this there is nothing wonderful, for, says Adam Smith, "after these (profits) are diminished, stock may not only continue to increase, but to increase much faster than before. . . . A great stock, though with small profits, generally increases

---

[1] "The limit, however, to the employment of both the operative and the labourer is the same; namely, the possibility of the employer realising a *profit* on the produce of their industry. If the rate of wages is such as to reduce the master's gains below the average profit of capital, he will cease to employ them, or he will only employ them on condition of submission to a reduction of wages." (John Wade, l. c., p. 241.)

faster than a small stock with great profits." (l. c. ii., p. 189.) In this case it is evident that a diminution in the unpaid labour in no way interferes with the extension of the domain of capital.—Or, on the other hand, accumulation slackens in consequence of the rise in the price of labour, because the stimulus of gain is blunted. The rate of accumulation lessens; but with its lessening, the primary cause of that lessening vanishes, *i.e.,* the disproportion between capital and exploitable labour-power. The mechanism of the process of capitalist production removes the very obstacles that it temporarily creates. The price of labour falls again to a level corresponding with the needs of the self-expansion of capital, whether the level be below, the same as, or above the one which was normal before the rise of wages took place. We see thus: In the first case, it is not the diminished rate either of the absolute, or of the proportional, increase in labour-power, or labouring population, which causes capital to be in excess, but conversely the excess of capital that makes exploitable labour-power insufficient. In the second case, it is not the increased rate either of the absolute, or of the proportional, increase in labour-power, or labouring population, that makes capital insufficient; but, conversely, the relative diminution of capital that causes the exploitable labour-power, or rather its price, to be in excess. It is these absolute movements of the accumulation of capital which are reflected as relative movements of the mass of exploitable labour-power, and therefore seem produced by the latter's own independent movement. To put it mathematically: the rate of accumulation is the independent not the dependent, variable; the rate of wages, the dependent, not the independent, variable. Thus, when the industrial cycle is in the phase of crisis, a general fall in the price of commodities is expressed as a rise in the value of money, and, in the phase of prosperity, a general rise in the price of commodities, as a fall in the value of money. The so-called currency school concludes from this that with high prices too little, with low prices too much money is in circulation. Their ignorance and complete misunderstanding of facts[1] are worthily paralleled by the economists, who interpret the above phenomena of accumulation by saying that there are now too few, now too many wage labourers.

The law of capitalist production, that is at the bottom of the pretended "natural law of population," reduces itself simply to this: The correlation between accumulation of capital and rate of wages is nothing else than the correlation between the unpaid labour transformed into capital, and the additional paid labour necessary for the setting in motion of this additional capital. It is therefore in no way a relation between two magnitudes, independent one of the other: on the one hand, the magnitude of the capital; on the other, the number of the labouring population; it is rather, at bottom, only the relation between the unpaid and the paid labour of the same labouring population. If the quantity of unpaid labour supplied by the working-class, and accumulated by the capitalist class, increases so rapidly that its conversion into capital requires an extraordinary addition of paid labour, then wages rise, and, all other circumstances remaining equal, the unpaid labour diminishes in proportion. But as soon as this diminution touches the point at which the surplus-labour that nourishes capital is no longer supplied in normal quantity, a reaction sets in: a smaller part of revenue is capitalised, accumulation lags, and the movement of rise in wages receives a check. The rise of wages therefore is confined within limits that not only leave intact the foundations of the capitalistic system, but also secure its reproduction on a progressive scale. The law of capitalistic accumulation, metamorphosed by economists into a pretended law of nature, in reality merely states that the very nature of accumulation excludes every diminution in the degree of exploitation of labour, and every rise in the price of labour, which could seriously imperil the continual reproduction, on an ever enlarging scale, of the capitalistic relation. It cannot be otherwise in a mode of production in which the labourer exists to satisfy the needs of self-expansion of existing values, instead of on the contrary, ma-

[1] Cf. Karl Marx: *Zur Kritik der Politischen Oekonomie,* pp. 166, seq.

terial wealth existing to satisfy the needs of development on the part of the labourer. As, in religion, man is governed by the products of his own brain, so in capitalistic production, he is governed by the products of his own hand.[1]

SECTION 2.——RELATIVE DIMINUTION OF THE VARIABLE PART OF CAPITAL SIMULTANEOUSLY WITH THE PROGRESS OF AC' CUMULATION AND OF THE CONCENTRATION THAT AC- COMPANIES IT.

According to the economists themselves, it is neither the actual extent of social wealth, nor the magnitude of the capital already functioning, that lead to a rise of wages, but only the constant growth of accumulation and the degree of rapidity of that growth. (Adam Smith, Book I., chapter 8.) So far, we have only considered one special phase of this process, that in which the increase of capital occurs along with a constant technical composition of capital. But the process goes beyond this phase.

Once given the general basis of the capitalistic system, then, in the course of accumulation, a point is reached at which the development of the productivity of social labour becomes the most powerful lever of accumulation. "The same cause," says Adam Smith, "which raises the wages of labour, the increase of stock, tends to increase its productive powers, and to make a smaller quantity of labour produce a greater quantity of work."

Apart from natural conditions, such as fertility of the soil, &c., and from the skill of independent and isolated producers (shown rather qualitatively in the goodness than quantitatively in the mass of their products), the degree of productivity of labour, in a given society, is expressed in the relative extent of the means of production that one labourer, during a given

---

[1] "If we now return to our first inquiry, wherein it was shown that capital itself is only the result of human labour . . . . . it seems quite incomprehensible that man can have fallen under the denomination of capital, his own product; can be subordinated to it; and as in reality this is beyond dispute the case, involuntarily the question arises: How has the labourer been able to pass from being master of capital—as its creator—to being its slave?" (Von Thünen. "Der isolirte Staat." Part ii., Section ii. Rostock, 1863, pp. 5, 6.) It is Thünen's merit to have asked this question. His answer is simply childish.

time, with the same tension of labour-power, turns into products. The mass of the means of production which he thus transforms, increases with the productiveness of his labour. But those means of production play a double part. The increase of some is a consequence, that of the others a condition of the increasing productivity of labour. *E.g.,* with the division of labour in manufacture, and with the use of machinery, more raw material is worked up in the same time, and, therefore, a greater mass of raw material and auxiliary substances enter into the labour-process. That is the consequence of the increasing productivity of labour. On the other hand, the mass of machinery, beasts of burden, mineral manures, drainpipes, &c., is a condition of the increasing productivity of labour. So also is it with the means of production concentrated in buildings, furnaces, means of transport, &c. But whether condition or consequence, the growing extent of the means of production, as compared with the labour-power incorporated with them, is an expression of the growing productiveness of labour. The increase of the latter appears, therefore, in the diminution of the mass of labour in proportion to the mass of means of production moved by it, or in the diminution of the subjective factor of the labour process as compared with the objective factor.

This change in the technical composition of capital, this growth in the mass of means of production, as compared with the mass of the labour-power that vivifies them, is reflected again in its value-composition, by the increase of the constant constituent of capital at the expense of its variable constituent. There may be, *e.g.,* originally 50 per cent. of a capital laid out in means of production, and 50 per cent. in the labour-power; later on, with the development of the productivity of labour, 80 per cent. in means of production, 20 per cent. in labour-power, and so on. This law of the progressive increase in constant capital, in proportion to the variable, is confirmed at every step (as already shown) by the comparative analysis of the prices of commodities, whether we compare different economic epochs or different nations in the same epoch. The relative magnitude of the element of price, which represents the value of the means of production only, or the constant part of capital consumed, is in direct, the relative magnitude of the other element of price that pays labour (the variable part of capital) is in inverse proportion to the advance of accumulation.

This diminution in the variable part of capital as compared with the constant, or the altered value-composition of the capital, however, only shows approximately the change in the composition of its material constituents. If, *e.g.,* the capital-value employed to-day in spinning is $\frac{7}{8}$ constant and $\frac{1}{8}$ variable, whilst at the beginning of the 18th century it was $\frac{1}{2}$ constant and $\frac{1}{2}$ variable, on the other hand, the mass of raw material, instruments of labour, &c., that a certain quantity of spinning labour consumes productively to-day, is many hundred times greater than at the beginning of the 18th century. The reason is simply that, with the increasing productivity of labour, not only does the mass of the means of production consumed by it increase, but their value compared with their mass diminishes. Their value therefore rises absolutely, but not in proportion to their mass. The increase of the difference between constant and variable capital is, therefore, much less than that of the difference between the mass of the means of production into which the constant, and the mass of the labour-power into which the variable, capital is converted. The former difference increases with the latter, but in a smaller degree.

But, if the progress of accumulation lessens the relative magnitude of the variable part of capital, it by no means, in doing this, excludes the possibility of a rise in its absolute magnitude. Suppose that a capital-value at first is divided into 50 per cent. of constant and 50 per cent. of variable capital; later into 80 per cent. of constant and 20 per cent. of variable. If in the meantime the original capital, say £6,000, has increased to £18,000, its variable constituent has also increased. It was £3,000, it is now £3,600. But whereas formerly an increase of capital by 20 per cent. would have sufficed to raise the demand for labour 20 per cent., now this latter rise requires a tripling of the original capital.

In Part IV. it was shown, how the development of the productiveness of social labour presupposes co-operation on a large scale; how it is only upon this supposition that division and combination of labour can be organised, and the means of production economised by concentration on a vast scale; how instruments of labour which, from their very nature, are only fit for use in common, such as a system of machinery, can be called into being; how huge natural forces can be pressed into the service of production; and how the transformation can be effected of the process of production into a technological application of science. On the basis of the production of commodities, where the means of production are the property of private persons, and where the artisan therefore either produces commodities, isolated from and independent of others, or sells his labour-power as a commodity, because he lacks the means for independent industry, co-operation on a large scale can realise itself only in the increase of individual capitals, only in proportion as the means of social production and the means of subsistence are transformed into the private property of capitalists. The basis of the production of commodities can admit of production on a large scale in the capitalistic form alone. A certain accumulation of capital, in the hands of individual producers of commodities, forms therefore the necessary preliminary of the specifically capitalistic mode of production. We had, therefore, to assume that this occurs during the transition from handicraft to capitalistic industry. It may be called primitive accumulation, because it is the historic basis, instead of the historic result of specifically capitalist production. How it itself originates, we need not here inquire as yet. It is enough that it forms the starting-point. But all methods for raising the social productive power of labour that are developed on this basis, are at the same times methods for the increased production of surplus-value or surplus-product. which in its turn is the formative element of accumulation. They are, therefore, at the same time methods of the production of capital by capital, or methods of its accelerated accumulation. The continual re-transformation of surplus-value into capital now appears in the shape of the increasing magnitude of the capital that enters into the process of production. This in turn is the basis of an extended scale of production, of the methods for raising the productive power of labour that accompany it, and of accelerated production of surplus-value. If, therefore, a certain degree of accumulation of capital appears as a condition of the specifically capitalist mode of production, the latter causes conversely an accelerated accumulation of capital. With the accumulation of capital, therefore, the specifically capitalistic mode of production developes, and with the capitalist mode of production the accumulation of capital. Both these economic factors bring about, in the compound ratio of the impluses they reciprocally give one another, that change in the technical composition of capital by which the variable constituent becomes always smaller and smaller as compared with the constant.

Every individual capital is a larger or smaller concentration of means of production, with a corresponding command over a larger or smaller labour-army. Every accumulation becomes the means of new accumulation. With the increasing mass of wealth which functions as capital, accumulation increases the concentration of that wealth in the hands of individual capitalists, and thereby widens the basis of production on a large scale and of the specific methods of capitalist production. The growth of social capital is effected by the growth of many individual capitals. All other circumstances remaining the same, individual capitals, and with them the concentration of the means of production, increases in such proportion as they form aliquot parts of the total social capital. At the same time portions of the original capitals disengage themselves and function as new independent capitals. Besides other causes, the division of property, within capitalist families, plays a great part in this. With the accumulation of capital, therefore, the number of capitalists grows to a greater or less extent. Two points characterise this kind of concentration which grows directly out of, or rather is identical with, accumulation. First: The increasing concentration of the social means of production in the hands of individual capitalists is.

other things remaining equal, limited by the degree of increase of social wealth. Second: The part of social capital domiciled in each particular sphere of production is divided among many capitalists who face one another as independent commodity-producers competing with each other. Accumulation and the concentration accompanying it are, therefore, not only scattered over many points, but the increase of each functioning capital is thwarted by the formation of new and the subdivision of old capitals. Accumulation, therefore, presents itself on the one hand as increasing concentration of the means of production, and of the command over labour; on the other, as repulsion of many individual capitals one from another.

This splitting-up of the total social capital into many individual capitals or the repulsion of its fractions one from another, is counteracted by their attraction. This last does not mean that simple concentration of the means of production and of the command over labour, which is identical with accumulation. It is concentration of capitals already formed, destruction of their individual independence, expropriation of capitalist by capitalist, transformation of many small into few large capitals. This process differs·from the former in this, that it only presupposes a change in the distribution of capital already to hand, and functioning; its field of action is therefore not limited by the absolute growth of social wealth, by the absolute limits of accumulation. Capital grows in one place to a huge mass in a single hand, because it has in another place been lost by many. This is centralisation proper, as distinct from accumulation and concentration.

The laws of this centralisation of capitals, or of the attraction of capital by capital, cannot be developed here. A brief hint at a few facts must suffice. The battle of competition is fought by cheapening of commodities. The cheapness of commodities depends, *cæteris paribus,* on the productiveness of labour, and this again on the scale of production. Therefore, the larger capitals beat the smaller. It will further be remembered that, with the development of the capitalist mode of production, there is an increase in the minimum amount of individual capital necessary to carry on a business under its normal conditions. The smaller capitals, therefore, crowd into spheres of production which Modern Industry has only sporadically or incompletely got hold of. Here competition rages in direct proportion to the number, and in inverse proportion to the magnitudes, of the antagonistic capitals. It always ends in the ruin of many small capitalists, whose capitals partly pass into the hand of their conquerors, partly vanish. Apart from this, with capitalist production an altogether new force comes into play—the credit system.

In its beginnings, the credit system sneaks in as a modest helper of accumulation and draws by invisible threads the money resources scattered all over the surface of society into the hands of individual or associated capitalists. But soon it becomes a new and formidable weapon in the competitive struggle, and finally it transforms itself into an immense social mechanism for the centralisation of capitals.

Competition and credit, the two most powerful levers of centralization, develop in proportion as capitalist production and accumulation do. At the same time the progress of accumulation increases the matter subject to centralisation, that is, the individual capitals, while the expansion of capitalist production creates the social demand here, the technical requirements there, for those gigantic industrial enterprises, which depend for their realisation on a previous centralisation of capitals. Nowadays, then, the mutual attraction of individual capitals and the tendency to centralisation are stronger than ever before. However, while the relative expansion and energy of the centralisation movement is determined to a certain degree by the superiority of the economic mechanism, yet the progress of centralisation is by no means dependent upon the positive growth of the volume of social capital. This is the particular distinction between centralisation and concentration, the latter being but another expression for reproduction on an enlarged scale. Centralisation may take place by a mere change in the distribution of already existing capitals, a simple change in the quantitative arrangement of the components of social capital. Capital may in that case accumulate in one hand in large masses by withdrawing it from many individual hands. Centralisation in a certain line of industry would have reached its extreme limit, if all the individual capitals invested in it would have been amalgamated into one single capital.[1]

This limit would not be reached in any particular society until the entire social capital would be united, either in the hands of one single capitalist, or in those of one single corporation.

Centralisation supplements the work of accumulation, by enabling the industrial capitalists to expand the scale of their operations. The economic result remains the same, whether this consummation is brought about by accumulation or centralisation, whether centralisation is accomplished by the violent means of annexation, by which some capitals become such overwhelming centers of gravitation for others as to break their individual cohesion and attracting the scattered fragments, or whether the amalgamation of a number of capitals, which already exist or are in process of formation, proceeds by the smoother road of forming stock companies. The increased volume of industrial establishments forms everywhere the point of departure for a more comprehensive organisation of the co-operative labor of many, for a wider development of their material powers, that is, for the progressive transformation of isolated processes of production carried on in accustomed ways into socially combined and scientifically managed processes of production.

It is evident, however, that accumulation, the gradual propagation of· capital by a reproduction passing from a circular into a spiral form, is a very slow process as compared with centralisation, which needs but to alter the quantitative grouping of the integral parts of social capital. The world would still be without railroads, if it had been obliged to wait until accumulation should have enabled a few individual capitals to undertake the construction of a railroad. Centralisation, on the other hand, accomplished this by a turn of the

[1] Note to the 4th German edition—The latest English and American "trusts" are aiming to accomplish this by trying to unite at least all the large establishments of a certain line of industry into one great stock company with a practical monopoly.— F. E.

hand through stock companies. Centralisation, by thus ac-
celerating and intensifying the effects of accumulation, extends and hastens at the same time the revolutions in the
technical composition of capital, which increase its constant
part at the expense of its variable part and thereby reduce
the relative demand for labor.

The masses of capital amalgamated over night by centralisation reproduce and augment themselves like the others, only
faster, and thus become new and powerful levers of social accumulation. Hence, if the progress of social accumulation
is mentioned nowadays, it comprizes as a matter of course the
effects of centralisation. The additional capitals formed in
the course of normal accumulation (see chapter XXIV, 1.)
serve mainly as vehicles for the exploitation of new inventions and discoveries, or of industrial improvements in general. However, the old capital likewise arrives in due time
at the moment when it must renew its head and limbs, when
it casts off its old skin and is likewise born again in its perfected industrial form, in which a smaller quantity of labor
suffices to set in motion a larger quantity of machinery and
raw materials. The absolute decrease of the demand for
labor necessarily following therefrom will naturally be so
much greater, the more these capitals going through the process of rejuvenation have become accumulated in masses by
means of the movement of centralisation.

On the one hand, therefore, the additional capital formed
in the course of accumulation attracts fewer and fewer labourers in proportion to its magnitude. On the other hand,
the old capital periodically reproduced with change of composition, repels more and more of the labourers formerly employed by it.

SECTION 3.—PROGRESSIVE PRODUCTION OF A RELATIVE SUR-
PLUS-POPULATION OR INDUSTRIAL RESERVE ARMY.

The accumulation of capital, though originally appearing as
its quantitative extension only, is effected, as we have seen,
under a progressive qualitative change in its composition,

under a constant increase of its constant, at the expense of its variable constitutent.[1]

The specifically capitalist mode of production, the development of the productive power of labour corresponding to it, and the change thence resulting in the organic composition of capital, do not merely keep pace with the advance of accumulation, or with the growth of social wealth. They develop at a much quicker rate, because mere accumulation, the absolute increase of the total social capital, is accompanied by the centralisation of the individual capitals of which that total is made up; and because the change in the technological composition of the additional capital goes hand in hand with a similar change in the technological composition of the original capital. With the advance of accumulation, therefore, the proportion of constant to variable capital changes. If it was originally say 1:1, it now becomes successively 2:1, 3:1, 4:1, 5:1, 7:1, &c., so that, as the capital increases, instead of $\frac{1}{2}$ of its total value, only $\frac{1}{3}$, $\frac{1}{4}$, $\frac{1}{5}$, $\frac{1}{6}$, $\frac{1}{8}$, &c., is transformed into labour-power, and, on the other hand, $\frac{2}{3}$, $\frac{3}{4}$, $\frac{4}{5}$, $\frac{5}{6}$, $\frac{7}{8}$ into means of production. Since the demand for labour is determined not by the amount of capital as a whole, but by its variable constituent alone, that demand falls progressively with the increase of the total capital, instead of, as previously assumed, rising in proportion to it. It falls relatively to the magnitude of the total capital, and at an accelerated rate, as this magnitude increases. With the growth of the total capital, its variable constituent or the labour incorporated in it, also does increase, but in a constantly diminishing proportion. The intermediate pauses are shortened, in which accumulation works as simple extension of production, on a given technical basis. It is not merely that an accelerated accumulation of total capital, accelerated in a constantly growing progression, is needed to absorb an additional number of labourers, or even, on account of the constant metamorphosis

---

[1] Note to the 3rd edition. In Marx's copy there is here the marginal note: "Here note for working out later; if the extension is only quantitative, then for a greater and a smaller capital in the same branch of business the profits are as the magnitudes of the capitals advanced. If the quantitative extension induces qualitative change, then the rate of profit on the larger capital rises simultaneously."

of old capital, to keep employed those already functioning. In its turn, this increasing accumulation and centralisation becomes a source of new changes in the composition of capital, of a more accelerated diminution of its variable, as compared with its constant constituent. This accelerated relative diminution of the variable constituent, that goes along with the accelerated increase of the total capital, and moves more rapidly than this increase, takes the inverse form, at the other pole, of an apparently absolute increase of the labouring population, an increase always moving more rapidly than that of the variable capital or the means of employment. But in fact, it is capitalistic accumulation itself that constantly produces, and produces in the direct ratio of its own energy and extent, a relatively redundant population of labourers, *i.e.*, a population of greater extent than suffices for the average needs of the self-expansion of capital, and therefore a surplus-population.

Considering the social capital in its totality, the movement of its accumulation now causes periodical changes, affecting it more or less as a whole, now distributes its various phases simultaneously over the different spheres of production. In some spheres a change in the composition of capital occurs without increase of its absolute magnitude, as a consequence of simple centralisation; in others the absolute growth of capital is connected with absolute diminution of its variable constituent, or of the labour-power absorbed by it; in others again, capital continues growing for a time on its given technical basis, and attracts additional labour-power in proportion to its increase, while at other times it undergoes organic change, and lessens its variable constituent; in all spheres, the increase of the variable part of capital, and therefore of the number of labourers employed by it, is always connected with violent fluctuations and transitory production of surplus-population, whether this takes the more striking form of the repulsion of labourers already employed, or the less evident but not less real form of the more difficult absorption of the additional labouring population through the usual chan-

nels.[1] With the magnitude of social capital already functioning, and the degree of its increase, with the extension of the
scale of production, and the mass of the labourers set in motion, with the development of the productiveness of their
labour, with the greater breadth and fulness of all sources of
wealth, there is also an extension of the scale on which greater
attraction of. labourers by capital is accompanied by their
greater repulsion; the rapidity of the change in the organic
composition of capital, and in its technical form increases,
and an increasing number of spheres of production becomes
involved in this change, now simultaneously, now alternately.
The labouring population therefore produces, along with the
accumulation of capital produced by it, the means by which
itself is made relatively superfluous, is turned into a relative
surplus population; and it does this to an always increasing
extent.[2] This is a law of population peculiar to the capitalist

[1] The census of England and Wales shows: all persons employed in agriculture
(landlords, farmers, gardeners, shepherds, &c., included): 1851, 2,011,447: 1861,
1,924,110. Fall, 87,337. Worsted manufacture: 1851, 102,714 persons: 1861,
79,242. Silk weaving: 1851, 111,940: 1861, 101,678. Calico-printing: 1851,
12,098: 1861, 12,556. A small rise that, in the face of the enormous
extension of this industry and implying a great fall proportionally in the
number of labourers employed. Hat-making: 1851, 15,957: 1861, 13,814. Straw-
hat and bonnet-making: 1851, 20,393: 1861, 18,176. Malting: 1851, 10,566: 1861,
10,677. Chandlery, 1851, 4949: 1861, 4686. This fall is due, besides other causes,
to the increase in lighting by gas. Comb-making: 1851, 2,038: 1861, 1,478. Sawyers:
1851, 30,552: 1861, 31,647—a mall rise in consequence of the increase of sewing-
machines. Nail-making. 1851, 26,940: 1861, 26,130—fall in consequence of the
competition of machinery. Tin and copper-mining: 1851, 31,360: 1861, 32,041. On
the other hand: Cotton-spinning and weaving: 1851, 371,777: 1861, 456,646. Coal-
mining: 1851, 183,389: 1861, 246, 613. "The increase of labourers is generally
greatest, since 1851, in such branches of industry in which machinery has not up
to the present been empl yed with success." (Census of England and Wales for
1862. Vol. III. London, 1863, p. 36.)

[2] The law of the progressive decrease of the relative size of the variable capital,
and of its effects on the condition of the wage-working class, has been more intui-
tively felt than actuall, comprehended b, some xcellent economists of the classic
school. The greatest hon r in this respect is ue to John Barton, although he,
like all the others, jumbles together e constant with the fixed capital and the
circulating with the variable cap'tal. He says: "The dem nd for labour depends on
the increase of circulating, an t of fixeu capital. Were it true that the proportion between these two sorts f capital i the same at all times, and in all circumstances, then, indeed, it follows that th number of labourers employed is in proportion to the wealth of the state. But uch a proposition has not the semblance of
probability. As arts are cultivated, and civilization is extended, fixed capital bears
a larger and larger proportion to circulating capital. The amount of fixed capital
employed in the production of a piece of British muslin is at least a hundred,
probably a thousand times greater than that employed in a similar piece of Indian

mode of production; and in fact every special historic mode of production has its own special laws of population, historically valid within its limits alone. An abstract law of population exists for plants and animals only, and only in so far as man has not interfered with them.

But if a surplus labouring population is a necessary product of accumulation or of the development of wealth on a capitalist basis, this surplus population becomes, conversely, the lever of capitalistic accumulation, nay, a condition of existence of the capitalist mode of production. It forms a disposable industrial reserve army, that belongs to capital quite as absolutely as if the latter had bred it at its own cost. Independently of the limits of the actual increase of population, it creates, for the changing needs of the self-expansion of capital, a mass of human material always ready for exploitation. With accumulation, and the development of the productiveness of labour that accompanies it, the power of sudden expansion of capital grows also; it grows, not merely because the elasticity of the capital already functioning increases, not merely because the absolute wealth of society expands, of which capital only forms an elastic part, not merely because credit, under every special stimulus, at once places an unusual part of this wealth at the disposal of production in the form of additional capital; it grows, also, because the technical conditions of the process of production themselves— machinery, means of transport, &c.—now admit of the rapid

muslin. And the proportion of circulating capital is a hundred or thousand times less . . . the whole of the annual savings, added to the fixed capital, would have no effect in increasing the demand for labour." (John Barton. "Observations on the Circumstances which Influence the Condition of the Labouring Classes of Society." London, 1817, pp. 16, 17.) "The same cause which may increase the net revenue of the country may at the same time render the population redundant, and deteriorate the condition of the labourer." (Ricardo, l. c., p. 469.) With increase of capital, "the demand [for labour] will be in a diminishing ratio." (ibid. p. 480, Note.) "The amount of capital devoted to the maintenance of labour may vary, independently of any changes in the whole amount of capital. . . . Great fluctuations in the amount of employment, and great suffering may become more frequent as capital itself becomes more plentiful." (Richard Jones. "An Introductory Lecture on Pol. Econ., Lond. 1833," p. 13.) "Demand [for labour] will rise . . . not in proportion to the accumulation of the general capital. . . . Every augmentation, therefore, in the national stock destined for reproduction, comes, in the progress of society, to have less and less influence upon the condition of the labourer." (Ramsay, l. c., pp. 90, 91.)

est transformation of masses of surplus product into additional means of production. The mass of social wealth, overflowing with the advance of accumulation, and transformable into additional capital, thrusts itself frantically into old branches of production, whose market suddenly expands, or into newly formed branches, such as railways, &c., the need for which grows out of the development of the old ones. In all such cases, there must be the possibility of throwing great masses of men suddenly on the decisive points without injury to the scale of production in other spheres. Over-population supplies these masses. The course characteristic of modern industry, viz., a decennial cycle (interrupted by smaller oscillations), of periods of average activity, production at high pressure, crisis and stagnation, depends on the constant formation, the greater or less absorption, and the re-formation of the industrial reserve army of surplus population. In their turn, the varying phases of the industrial cycle recruit the surplus population, and become one of the most energetic agents of its reproduction. This peculiar course of modern industry, which occurs in no earlier period of human history, was also impossible in the childhood of capitalist production. The composition of capital changed but very slowly. With its accumulation, therefore, there kept pace, on the whole, a corresponding growth in the demand for labour. Slow as was the advance of accumulation compared with that of more modern times, it found a check in the natural limits of the exploitable labouring population, limits which could only be got rid of by forcible means to be mentioned later. The expansion by fits and starts of the scale of production is the preliminary to its equally sudden contraction; the latter again evokes the former, but the former is impossible without disposable human material, without an increase in the number of labourers independently of the absolute growth of the population. This increase is effected by the simple process that constantly "sets free" a part of the labourers; by methods which lessen the number of labourers employed in proportion to the increased production. The whole form of the movement of modern industry depends, therefore, upon the constant

transformation of a part of the labouring population into unemployed or half-employed hands. The superficiality of Political Economy shows itself in the fact that it looks upon
the expansion and contraction of credit, which is a mere symptom of the periodic changes of the industrial cycle, as their
cause. As the heavenly bodies, once thrown into a certain
definite motion, always repeat this, so is it with social production as soon as it is once thrown into this movement of
alternate expansion and contraction. Effects, in their turn,
become causes, and the varying accidents of the whole process,
which always reproduces its own conditions, take on the form
of periodicity. When this periodicity is once consolidated,
even Political Economy then sees that the production of a
relative surplus population—*i.e.,* surplus with regard to the
average needs of the self-expansion of capital—is a necessary
condition of modern industry.

"Suppose," says H. Marivale, formerly Professor of Political Economy at Oxford, subsequently employed in the English Colonial Office, "suppose that, on the occasion of some
of these crises, the nation were to rouse itself to the effort of
getting rid by emigration of some hundreds of thousands of
superfluous arms, what would be the consequence? That, at
the first returning demand for labour, there would be a deficiency. However rapid reproduction may be, it takes, at all
events, the space of a generation to replace the loss of adult
labour. Now, the profits of our manufacturers depend mainly
on the power of making use of the prosperous moment when
demand is brisk, and thus compensating themselves for the
interval during which it is slack. This power is secured to
them only by the command of machinery and of manual labour. They must have hands ready by them, they must be
able to increase the activity of their operations when required,
and to slacken it again, according to the state of the market,
or they cannot possibly maintain the pre-eminence in the race
of competition on which the wealth of the country is founded."[1] Even Malthus recognises over-population as a necessity of modern industry, though, after his narrow fashion, he

[1] H. Merivale: Lectures on Colonization and Colonies, 1841." Vol. I., p. 146.

explains it by the absolute over-growth of the labouring population, not by their becoming relatively supernumerary. He says: "Prudential habits with regard to marriage, carried to a considerable extent among the labouring class of a country mainly depending upon manufactures and commerce, might injure it. . . . From the nature of a population, an increase of labourers cannot be brought into market in consequence of a particular demand till after the lapse of 16 or 18 years, and the conversion of revenue into capital, by saving, may take place much more rapidly; a country is always liable to an increase in the quantity of the funds for the maintenance of labour faster than the increase of population." [1] After Political Economy has thus demonstrated the constant production of a relative surplus-population of labourers to be a necessity of capitalistic accumulation, she very aptly, in the guise of an old maid, puts in the mouth of her "beau ideal" of a capitalist the following words addressed to those supernumeraries thrown on the streets by their own creation of additional capital:—"We manufacturers do what we can for you, whilst we are increasing that capital on which you must subsist, and you must do the rest by accommodating your numbers to the means of subsistence." [2]

Capitalist production can by no means content itself with the quantity of disposable labour-power which the natural increase of population yields. It requires for its free play an industrial reserve army independent of these natural limits.

Up to this point it has been assumed that the increase or diminution of the variable capital corresponds rigidly with the increase or diminution of the number of labourers employed.

The number of labourers commanded by capital may remain the same, or even fall, while the variable capital increases. This is the case if the individual labourer yields more labour,

---

[1] Malthus. "Principles of Political Economy," pp. 254, 319, 320. In this work, Malthus finally discovers, with the help of Sismondi, the beautiful Trinity of capitalistic production: over-production, over-population, over-consumption—three very delicate monsters, indeed. Cf. F. Engels. "Umrisse zu einer Kritik der National-Oekonomie," l. c., p. 107, et seq.

[2] Harriet Martineau. "The Manchester Strike," 1842, p. 101.

and therefore his wages increase and this although the price of labour remains the same or even falls, only more slowly than the mass of labour rises. Increase of variable capital, in this case, becomes an index of more labour, but not of more labourers employed. It is the absolute interest of every capitalist to press a given quantity of labour out of a smaller, rather than a greater number of labourers, if the cost is about the same. In the latter case, the outlay of constant capital increases in proportion to the mass of labour set in action; in the former that increase is much smaller. The more extended the scale of production, the stronger this motive. Its force increases with the accumulation of capital.

We have seen that the development of the capitalist mode of production and of the productive power of labour—at once the cause and effect of accumulation—enables the capitalist, with the same outlay of variable capital, to set in action more labour by greater exploitation (extensive or intensive) of each individual labour-power. We have further seen that the capitalist buys with the same capital a greater mass of labour-power, as he progressively replaces skilled labourers by less skilled, mature labour-power by immature, male by female, that of adults by that of young persons or children.

On the one hand, therefore, with the progress of accumulation, a larger variable capital sets more labour in action without enlisting more labourers; on the other, a variable capital of the same magnitude sets in action more labour with the same mass of labour-power; and, finally, a greater number of inferior labour-power by displacement of higher.

The production of a relative surplus-population, or the setting free of labourers, goes on therefore yet more rapidly than the technical revolution of the process of production that accompanies, and is accelerated by, the advances of accumulation; and more rapidly than the corresponding diminution of the variable part of capital as compared with the constant. If the means of production, as they increase in extent and effective power, become to a less extent means of employment of labourers, this state of things is again modified by the fact that in proportion as the productiveness of labour increases, capital increases its supply of labour more quickly than its demand for labourers. The over-work of the employed part of the working class swells the ranks of the reserve, whilst conversely the greater pressure that the latter by its competition exerts on the former, forces these to submit to over-work and to subjugation under the dictates of capital. The condemnation of one part of the working-class to enforced idleness by the over-work of the other part, and the converse, becomes a means of enriching the individual capitalists,[1] and accelerates at the same time the production of the industrial reserve army on a scale corresponding with the advance of social accumulation. How important is this element in the formation of the relative surplus-population, is shown by the example of England. Her technical means for saving labour are colossal. Nevertheless, if to-morrow morning labour generally were reduced to a rational amount, and proportioned to the different sections of the working-class according to age and sex, the working population to hand would be absolutely insufficient for the carrying on of national production on its present scale. The great majority of the labourers now "unproductive" would have to be turned into "productive" ones.

---

[1] Even in the cotton famine of 1863 we find, in a pamphlet of the operative cotton-spinners of Blackburn, fierce denunciations of overwork, which, in consequence of the Factory Acts, of course only affected adult male labourers. "The adult operatives at this mill have been asked to work from 12 to 13 hours per day, while there are hundreds who are compelled to be idle who would willingly work partial time, in order to maintain their families and save their brethren from a premature grave through being overworked . . . We," it goes on to say, "would ask if the practice of working overtime by a number of hands, is likely to create a good feeling between masters and servants. Those who are worked overtime feel the injustice equally with those who are condemned to forced idleness. There is in the district almost sufficient work to give to all partial employment if fairly distributed. We are only asking what is right in requesting the masters generally to pursue a system of short hours, particularly until a better state of things begins to dawn upon us, rather than to work a portion of the hands overtime, while others, for want of work, are compelled to exist upon charity." (Reports of Insp. of Fact., Oct. 31, 1863, p. 8.) The author of the "Essay on Trade and Commerce" grasps the effect of a relative surplus-population on the employed labourers with his usual unerring bourgeois instinct. "Another cause of idleness in this kingdom is the want of a sufficient number of labouring hands . . . . Whenever from an extraordinary demand for manufacturers, labour grows scarce, the labourers feel their own consequence, and will make their masters feel it likewise—it is amazing; but so depraved are the dispositions of these people, that in such cases a set of workmen have combined to distress the employer, by idling a whole day together." (Essay, &c., pp. 27, 28.) The fellows in fact were hankering after a rise in wages.

Taking them as a whole, the general movements of wages are exclusively regulated by the expansion and contraction of the industrial reserve army, and these again correspond to the periodic changes of the industrial cycle. They are, therefore, not determined by the variations of the absolute number of the working population, but by the varying proportions in which the working class is divided into active and reserve army, by the increase of diminution in the relative amount of the surplus-population, by the extent to which it is now absorbed, now set free. For Modern Industry with its decennial cycles and periodic phases, which, moreover, as accumulation advances, are complicated by irregular oscillations following each other more and more quickly, that would indeed be a beautiful law, which pretends to make the action of capital dependent on the absolute variation of the population, instead of regulating the demand and supply of labour by the alternate expansion and contraction of capital, the labour-market now appearing relatively under-full, because capital is expanding, now again over-full, because it is contracting. Yet this is the dogma of the economists. According to them, wages rise in consequence of accumulation of capital. The higher wages stimulate the working population to more rapid multiplication, and this goes on until the labour-market becomes too full, and therefore capital, relatively to the supply of labour, becomes insufficient. Wages fall, and now we have the reverse of the modal. The working population is little by little decimated as the result of the fall in wages, so that capital is again in excess relatively to them, or, as others explain it, falling wages and the corresponding increase in the exploitation of the labourer again accelerates accumulation, whilst, at the same time, the lower wages hold the increase of the working-class in check. Then comes again the time, when the supply of labour is less than the demand, wages rise, and so on. A beautiful mode of motion this for developed capitalist production! Before, in consequence of the rise of wages, any positive increase of the population really fit for work could occur, the time would have been passed again and again, during which the industrial campaign must have been carried through, the battle fought and won.

Between 1849 and 1859, a rise of wages practically insignificant, though accompanied by falling prices of corn, took place in the English agricultural districts. In Wiltshire, *e.g.,* the weekly wages rose from 7s. to 8s.; in Dorsetshire from 7s. or 8s., to 9s., &c. This was the result of an unusual exodus of the agricultural surplus-population caused by the demands of war, the vast extension of railroads, factories, mines, &c. The lower the wages, the higher is the proportion in which ever so insignificant a rise of them expresses itself. If the weekly wage, *e.g.,* is 20s. and it rises to 22s., that is a rise of 10 per cent.; but if it is only 7s. and it rises to 9s., that is a rise of $28\frac{4}{7}$ per cent., which sounds very fine. Everywhere the farmers were howling, and the "London Economist," with reference to these starvation-wages, prattled quite seriously of "a general and substantial advance."[1] What did the farmers do now? Did they wait until, in consequence of this brilliant remuneration, the agricultural labourers, had so increased and multiplied that their wages must fall again, as prescribed by the dogmatic economic brain? They introduced more machinery, and in a moment the labourers were redundant again in a proportion satisfactory even to the farmers. There was now "more capital" laid out in agriculture than before, and in a more productive form. With this the demand for labour fell, not only relatively, but absolutely.

The above economic fiction confuses the laws that regulate the general movement of wages, or the ratio between the working-class—*i.e.,* the total labour-power—and the total social capital, with the laws that distribute the working population over the different spheres of production. If, *e.g.,* in consequence of favourable circumstances, accumulation in a particular sphere of production becomes especially active, and profits in it, being greater than the average profits, attract additional capital, of course the demand for labour rises and wages also rise. The higher wages draw a larger part of the working population into the more favoured sphere, until it is

[1] Economist. Jan. 21. 1860.

glutted with labour-power, and wages at length fall again to their average level or below it, if the pressure is too great. Then, not only does the immigration of labourers into the branch of industry in question cease; it gives place to their emigration. Here the political economist thinks he sees the why and wherefore of an absolute increase of workers accompanying an increase of wages, and of a diminution of wages accompanying an absolute increase of labourers. But he sees really only the local oscillation of the labour-market in a particular sphere of production—he sees only the phenomena accompanying the distribution of the working population into the different spheres of outlay of capital, according to its varying needs.

The industrial reserve army, during the periods of stagnation and average prosperity, weighs down the active labour-army; during the periods of over-production and paroxysm, it holds its pretensions in check. Relative surplus-population is therefore the pivot upon which the law of demand and supply of labour works. It confines the field of action of this law within the limits absolutely convenient to the activity of exploitation and to the domination of capital.

This is the place to return to one of the grand exploits of economic apologetics. It will be remembered that if through the introduction of new, or the extension of old, machinery, a portion of variable capital is transformed into constant, the economic apologist interprets this operation which "fixes" capital and by that very act set labourers "free," in exactly the opposite way, pretending that it sets free capital for the labourers. Only now can one fully understand the effrontery of these apologists. What are set free are not only the labourers immediately turned out by the machines, but also their future substitutes in the rising generation, and the additional contingent, that with the usual extension of trade on the old basis would be regularly absorbed. They are now all "set free," and every new bit of capital looking out for employment can dispose of them. Whether it attracts them or others, the effect on the general labour demand will be nil, if this capital is just sufficient to take out of the market as many labourers as the machines threw upon it. If it employs a smaller number, that of the supernumeraries increases; if it employs a greater, the general demand for labour only increases to the extent of the excess of the employed over those "set free." The impulse that additional capital, seeking an outlet, would otherwise have given to the general demand for labour, is therefore in every case neutralised to the extent of the labourers thrown out of employment by the machine. That is to say, the mechanism of capitalistic production so manages matters that the absolute increase of capital is accompanied by no corresponding rise in the general demand for labour. And this the apologist calls a compensation for the misery, the sufferings, the possible death of the displaced labourers during the transition period that banishes them into the industrial reserve army! The demand for labour is not identical with increase of capital, nor supply of labour with increase of the working class. It is not a case of two independent forces working on one another. Les dés sont pipés. Capital works on both sides at the same time. If its accumulation, on the one hand, increases the demand for labour, it increases on the other the supply of labourers by the "setting free" of them, whilst at the same time the pressure of the unemployed compels those that are employed to furnish more labour, and therefore makes the supply of labour, to a certain extent, independent of the supply of labourers. The action of the law of supply and demand of labour on this basis completes the despotism of capital. As soon, therefore, as the labourers learn the secret, how it comes to pass that in the same measure as they work more, as they produce more wealth for others, and as the productive power of their labour increases, so in the same measure even their function as a means of the self-expansion of capital becomes more and more precarious for them; as soon as they discover that the degree of intensity of the competition among themselves depends wholly on the pressure of the relative surplus-population; as soon as, by Trades' Unions, &c., they try to organise a regular co-operation between employed and unemployed in order to destroy or to weaken the ruinous effects of this natural law

of capitalistic production on their class, so soon capital and its
sycophant, political economy, cry out at the infringement of
the "eternal" and so to say "sacred" law of supply and demand. Every combination of employed and unemployed disturbs the "harmonious" action of this law. But, on the other
hand, as soon as (in the colonies, *e.g.*,) adverse circumstances
prevent the creation of an industrial reserve army and, with
it, the absolute dependence of the working class upon the
capitalist class, capital, along with its commonplace Sancho
Panza, rebels against the "sacred" law of supply and demand,
and tries to check its inconvenient action by forcible means
and State interference.

SECTION 4.—DIFFERENT FORMS OF THE RELATIVE SURPLUS-
    POPULATION. THE GENERAL LAW OF CAPITALISTIC AC-
    CUMULATION.

The relative surplus population exists in every possible
form. Every labourer belongs to it during the time when he
is only partially employed or wholly unemployed. Not taking into account the great periodically recurring forms that
the changing phases of the industrial cycle impress on it, now
an acute form during the crisis, then again a chronic form
during dull times—it has always three forms, the floating,
the latent, the stagnant.

In the centres of modern industry—factories, manufactur
ers, ironworks, mines, &c.—the labourers are sometimes repelled, sometimes attracted again in greater masses, the number of those employed increasing on the whole, although in a
constantly decreasing proportion to the scale of production.
Here the surplus population exists in the floating form.

In the automatic factories, as in all the great workshops,
where machinery enters as a factor, or where only the modern
divisions of labour is carried out, large numbers of boys are
employed up to the age of maturity. When this term is
once reached, only a very small number continue to find employment in the same branches of industry, whilst the majority are regularly discharged. This majority forms an ele-

ment of the floating surplus-population, growing with the extension of those branches of industry. Part of them emigrates, following in fact capital that has emigrated. One consequence is that the female population grows more rapidly than the male, *teste* England. That the natural increase of the number of labourers does not satisfy the requirements of the accumulation of capital, and yet all the time is in excess of them, is a contradiction inherent to the movement of capital itself. It wants larger numbers of youthful labourers, a smaller number of adults. The contradiction is not more glaring than that other one that there is a complaint of the want of hands, while at the same time many thousands are out of work, because the division of labour chains them to a particular branch of industry.[1]

The consumption of labour-power by capital is, besides, so rapid that the labourer, half-way through his life, has already more or less completely lived himself out. He falls into the ranks of the supernumeraries, or is thrust down from a higher to a lower step in the scale. It is precisely among the work-people of modern industry that we meet with the shortest duration of life. Dr. Lee, Medical Officer of Health for Manchester, stated "that the average age at death of the Manchester . . . upper middle class was 38 years, while the average age at death of the labouring class was 17; while at Liverpool those figures were represented as 35 against 15. It thus appeared that the well-to-do classes had a lease of life which was more than double the value of that which fell to the lot of the less favoured citizens." [2] In order to conform to these circumstances, the absolute increase of this section of the proletariat must take places under conditions that shall swell their numbers, although the individual elements are

---

[1] Whilst during the last six months of 1866, 80-90,000 working people in London were thrown out of work, the Factory Report for that same half year says: "It does not appear absolutely true to say that demand will always produce supply just at the moment when it is needed. It has not done so with labour, for much machinery has been idle last year for want of hands." (Rep. of Insp. of Fact., 31st Oct., 1866, p. 81.)

[2] Opening address to the Sanitary Conference, Birmingham, January 15th, 1875, by J. Chamberlain, Mayor of the town, now (1883) President of the Board of Trade.

used up rapidly. Hence, rapid renewal of the generations of labourers (this law does not hold for the other classes of the population). This social need is met by early marriages, a necessary consequence of the conditions in which the labourers of modern industry live, and by the premium that the exploitation of children sets on their production.

As soon as capitalist production takes possession of agriculture, and in proportion to the extent to which it does so, the demand for an agricultural labouring population falls absolutely, while the accumulation of the capital employed in agriculture advances, without this repulsion being, as in non-agricultural industries, compensated by a greater attraction. Part of the agricultural population is therefore constantly on the point of passing over into an urban or manufacturing proletariat, and on the look-out for circumstances favourable to this transformation. (Manufacture is used here in the sense of all non-agricultural industries).[1] This source of relative surplus-population is thus constantly flowing. But the constant flow towards the towns presupposes, in the country itself, a constant latent surplus-population, the extent of which becomes evident only when its channels of outlet open to exceptional width. The agricultural labourer is therefore reduced to the minimum of wages, and always stands with one foot already in the swamp of pauperism.

The third category of the relative surplus-population, the stagnant, forms a part of the active labour army, but with extremely irregular employment. Hence it furnishes to capital an inexhaustible reservoir of disposable labour-power. Its conditions of life sink below the average normal level of the working class; this makes it at once the broad basis of special branches of capitalist exploitation. It is character-

[1] 781 Towns given in the census for 1861 for England and Wales "contained 10,960,998 inhabitants, while the villages and country parishes contained 9,105,226. In 1851, 580 towns were distinguished, and the population in them and in the surrounding country was nearly equal. But while in the subsequent ten years the population in the villages and the country increased half a million, the population in the 580 towns increased by a million and a half (1,554,067). The increase of the population of the country parishes is 6.5 per cent., and of the towns 17.3 per cent. The difference in the rates of increase is due to the migration from country to town. Three-fourths of the total increase of population has taken place in the towns. (Census, &c., pp. 11 and 12.)

ized by maximum of working time, and minimum of wages. We have learnt to know its chief form under the rubric of "domestic industry." It recruits itself constantly from the supernumerary forces of modern industry and agriculture, and specially from those decaying branches of industry where handicraft is yielding to manufacture, manufacture to machinery. Its extent grows, as with the extent and energy of accumulation, the creation of a surplus popul tion advances. But it forms at the same time a self-reproducing and self-perpetuating element of the working class, taking a proportionally greater part in the general increase of thaι class than the other elements. In fact, not onιy the number of births and deaths, but the absoluιe size   the ιamilies stand in inverse proportion to the height of wages,   therefor to the ιmount of means of subsistence of which the differ t categories of labourers dispose. This law of ·apιtꞌ listic society would sound absurd to savages, or eveι civilized colonists. It calls to mind the boundlᵉss reproduction of animals individually weak and constantly hunted down.[1]

The lowest sediment of the relative surplus-population finally dwells in the sphere of pauperism. Exclusive of vagabonds, criminals, prostitutes, in a word, the "dangerous" classes, this layer of society consists of three categories. First, those able to work. One need only glance superficially at the statistics of English pauperism to find that the quantity of paupers increases with every crisis, and diminishes with every revival of trade. Second, orphans and pauper children. These are ca didates for the industrial reserve-army, and are, in times of great prosperity, as 1860, *e.g.*, speedily and in large numbers enrolled in the active army of labourers. Third, the demoralized and ragged, and those unable to work, chꞌefly people who succumb to their incapacity

---

[1] Poverty seems favourable to generation." (A. Smith.) This is even a specially wise arrangement of God, according to the gallant and witty Abbé Galiᴀni. "Iddio fa che gli uomini che esercitano mestieri di prima utilità nascono abbondanteᴍ mente." (Galiani, l. c., p. 78.) "Misery up to the extreme point of famine and pestilence, instead of checking, tends to increase population." (S. Laing: National Distress, 1844, p. 69.) After Laing has illustrated this by statistics, he continues: "If the people were all in easy circumstances, the world would soon be depopulated."

for adaptation, due to the division of labour; people who have passed the normal age of the labourer; the victims of industry, whose number increases with the increase of dangerous machinery, of mines, chemical works, &c., the mutilated, the sickly, the widows, &c. Pauperism is the hospital of the active labour-army and the dead weight of the industrial reserve-army. Its production is included in that of the relative surplus-population, its necessity in theirs; along with the surplus-population, pauperism forms a condition of capitalist production, and of the capitalist development of wealth. It enters into the *faux frais* of capitalist production; but capital knows how to throw these, for the most part, from its own shoulders on to those of the working-class and the lower middle class.

The greater the social wealth, the functioning capital, the extent and energy of its growth, and, therefore, also the absolute mass of the proletariat and the productiveness of its labour, the greater is the industrial reserve-army. The same causes which develop the expansive power of capital, developes also the labour-power at its disposal. The relative mass of the industrial reserve-army increases therefore with the potential energy of wealth. But the greater this reserve-army in proportion to the active labour-army, the greater is the mass of a consolidated surplus-population, whose misery is in inverse ratio to its torment of labour. The more extensive, finally, the lazurus-layers of the working-class, and the industrial reserve-army, the greater is official pauperism. *This is the absolute general law of capitalist accumulation.* Like all other laws it is modified in its working by many circumstances, the analysis of which does not concern us here.

The folly is now patent of the economic wisdom that preaches to the labourers the accommodation of their number to the requirements of capital. The mechanism of capitalist production and accumulation constantly effects this adjustment. The first word of this adaptation is the creation of a relative surplus-population, or industrial reserve-army. Its last word is the misery of constantly extending strata of the active army of labour, and the dead weight of pauperism.

The law by which a constantly increasing quantity of means of production, thanks to the advance in the productiveness of social labour, may be set in movement by a progressively diminishing expenditure of human power, this law, in a capitalist society—where the labourer does not employ the means of production, but the means of production employ the labourer—undergoes a complete inversion and is expressed thus: the higher the productiveness of labour, the greater is the pressure of the labourers on the means of employment, the more precarious, therefore, becomes their condition of existence, viz., the sale of their own labour-power for the increasing of another's wealth, or for the self-expansion of capital. The fact that the means of production, and the productiveness of labour, increase more rapidly than the productive population, expresses itself, therefore, capitalistically in the inverse form that the labouring population always increases more rapidly than the conditions under which capital can employ this increase for its own self-expansion.

We saw in Part IV., when analysing the production of relative surplus-value: within the capitalist system all methods for raising the social productiveness of labour are brought about at the cost of the individual labourer; all means for the development of production transform themselves into means of domination over, and exploitation of, the producers; they mutilate the labourer into a fragment of a man, degrade him to the level of an appendage of a machine, destroy every remnant of charm in his work and turn it into a hated toil; they estrange from him the intellectual potentialities of the labour-process in the same proportion as science is incorporated in it as an independant power; they distort the conditions under which he works, subject him during the labour-process to a despotism the more hateful for its meanness; they transform his life-time into working-time, and drag his wife and child beneath the wheels of the Juggernaut of capital, But all methods for the production of surplus value are at the same time methods of accumulation; and every extension of accumulation becomes again a means for the development of those methods. It follows therefore that in proportion as capital accumulates, the lot of the labourer, be his payment high or low, must grow worse. The law, finally, that always equilibrates the relative surplus-population, or industrial reserve army, to the extent and energy of accumulation, this law rivets the labourer to capital more firmly than the wedges of Vulcan did Prometheus to the rock. It establishes an accumulation of misery, corresponding with accumulation of capital. Accumulation of wealth at one pole is, therefore, at the same time accumulation of misery, agony of toil, slavery, ignorance, brutality, mental degradation, at the opposite pole, *i.e.,* on the side of the class that produces its own product in the form of capital.

This antagonistic character of capitalistic accumulation[1] is enunciated in various forms by political economists, although by them it is confounded with phenomena, certainly to some extent analogous, but nevertheless essentially distinct, and belonging to precapitalistic modes of production.

The Venetian monk Ortes, one of the great economic writers of the 18th century, regards the antagonism of capitalist production as a general natural law of social wealth. "In the economy of a nation, advantages and evils always balance one another (il bene ed il male economico in una nazione sempre all, istessa misura): the abundance of wealth with some people, is always equal to the want of it with others (la copia dei beni in alcuni sempre eguale alla mancanza di essi in altri): the great riches of a small number are always accompanied by the absolute privation of the first necessaries of life for many others. The wealth of a nation corresponds with its population, and its misery corresponds with its wealth. Diligence in some compels idleness in others. The poor and idle are a necessary consequence of the rich and active," &c.[2] In a

---

[1] "De jour en jour il devient donc plus clair que les rapports de production dans lesquels se meut la bourgeoisie n'ont pas un caractère un, uncaractère simple, mais un caractère de duplicité; que dans les mêmes rapports dans lesquels se produit la richesse, la misère se produit aussi; que dans les mêmes rapports dans lesquels il y a développement des forces productives, il y a une force productive de répression; que ces rapports ne produisent la richesse bourgeoise, c'est-à-dire la richesse de la classe bourgeoise, qu'en anéantissant continuellement la richesse des membres intégrants de cette classe et en produisant un prolétariat toujours croissant." (Karl Marx: Misère de la Philosophie, p. 116.)

[2] G. Ortes: Della Economia Nazionale libri sei, 1777, in Custodi, Parte Moderna.

thoroughly brutal way about 10 years after Ortes, the Church of England parson, Townsend, glorified misery as a necessary condition of wealth. "Legal constraint (to labour) is attended with too much trouble, violence, and noise, . . . whereas hunger is not only a peaceable, silent, unremitted pressure, but at the most natural motive to industry and labour, it calls forth the most powerful exertions." Everything therefore depends upon making hunger permanent among the working class, and for this, according to Townsend, the principle of population, especially active among the poor, provides. "It seems to be a law of nature that the poor should be to a certain degree improvident." [*i.e.,* so improvident as to be born *without* a silver spoon in the mouth], "that there may always be some to fulfil the most servile, the most sordid, and the most ignoble offices in the community. The stock of human happiness is thereby much increased, whilst the more delicate are not only relieved from drudgery . . . but are left at liberty without interruption to pursue those callings which are suited to their various dispositions . . . it [the Poor Law] tends to destroy the harmony and beauty, the symmetry and order of that system which God and Nature have established in the world."[1] If the Venetian monk found in the fatal destiny that makes misery eternal, the *raison d'être* of Christian charity, celibacy, monasteries and holy houses, the Protestant prebendary finds in it a pretext for condemning the laws in virtue of which the poor possessed a right to a miserable relief.

t. xxi. pp. 6, 9, 22, 25, etc. Ortes says, l. c., p. 32: "In luoco di progettar sistemi inutili per la felicità de'popoli, mi limiterò a investigare la ragione della loro infelicità."

[1] A Dissertation on the Poor Laws. By a Well-wisher of Mankind. (The Rev. J. Townsend) 1786, republished Lond. 1817, pp. 15, 39, 41. This "delicate" parson, from whose work just quoted, as well as from his "Journey through Spain," Malthus often copies whole pages himself borrowed the greater part of his doctrine from Sir James Steuart, whom he however alters in the borrowing. *E.g.,* when Steuart says: "Here, in slavery, was a forcible method of making mankind diligent," [for the non-workers] . . . "Men were then forced to work" [*i.e.* to work gratis for others], "because they were slaves of others; men are now forced to work" [*i.e.,* to work gratis for non-workers] because they are the slaves of their necessities," he does not thence conclude, like the fat holder of benefices, that the wage-labourer must always go fasting. He wishes, on the contrary, to increase their wants and to make the increasing number of their wants a stimulus to their labour for the "more delicate."

"The progress of social wealth," says Storch, "begets this useful class of society . . . which performs the most wearisome, the vilest, the most disgusting functions, which takes, in a word, on its shoulders all that is disagreeable and servile in life, and procures thus for other classes leisure, serenity of mind and conventional [c'est bon!] dignity of character." [1] Storch asks himself in what then really consist the progress of this capitalistic civilization with its misery and its degradation of the masses, as compared with barbarism. He finds but one answer: security!

"Thanks to the advance of industry and science," says Sismondi, "every labourer can produce every day much more than his consumption requires. But at the same time, whilst his labour produces wealth, that wealth would, were he called on to consume it himself, make him less fit for labour." According to him, "men," [*i.e.*, non-workers] "would probably prefer to do without all artistic perfection, and all the enjoyments that manufacturers procure for us, if it were necessary that all should buy them by constant toil like that of the labourer. . . . Exertion to-day is separated from its recompense; it is not the same man that first works, and then reposes; but it is because the one works that the other rests. . . . The indefinite multiplication of the productive powers of labour can then only have for result the increase of luxury and enjoyment of the idle rich." [2]

Finally Destutt de Tracy, the fish-blooded bourgeois doctrinaire, blurts out brutally: "In poor nations the people are comfortable, in rich nations they are generally poor." [3]

SECTION 5.—ILLUSTRATIONS OF THE GENERAL LAW OF CAPITALIST ACCUMULATION.

(a.) *England from* 1846-1866.

No period of modern society is so favourable for the study of capitalist accumulation as the period of the last 20 years.

---

[1] Storch, l. c. t. iii., p. 223.

[2] Sismondi l. c. pp. 79, 80, 85.

[3] Destutt de Tracy, l. c. p. 231: "Les nations pauvres, c'est là où le peuple est à son aise; et les nations riches, c'est là où il est ordinairement pauvre."

It is as if this period had found Fortunatus' purse. But of all countries England again furnishes the classical example, because it holds the foremost place in the world-market, because capitalist production is here alone completely developed, and lastly, because the introduction of the Free Trade millennium since 1846 has cut off the last retreat of vulgar economy. The titanic advance of production—the latter half of the 20 years period again far surpassing the former—has been already pointed out sufficiently in Part IV.

Although the absolute increase of the English population in the last half century was very great, the relative increase or rate of growth fell constantly, as the following table borrowed from the census shows.

Annual increase per cent. of the population of England and Wales in decimal numbers:

1811-1821	1.533 per cent.
1821-1831	1.446 „
1831-1841	1.326 „
1841-1851	1.216 „
1851-1861	1.141 „

Let us now, on the other hand, consider the increase of wealth. Here the movement of profit, rent of land, &c., that come under the income tax, furnishes the surest basis. The increase of profits liable to income tax (farmers and some other categories not included) in Great Britain from 1853 to 1864 amounted to 50.47% or 4.58% as the annual average,[1] that of the population during the same period to about 1.2%. The augmentation of the rent of land subject to taxation (including houses, railways, mines, fisheries, &c.), amounted for 1853 to 1864 to 38% or 3$\frac{5}{11}$% annually. . Under this head the following categories show the greatest increase:

Houses, 38.60%	3.50%
Quarries, 84.76%	7.70%
Mines, 68.85%	6.26%

[1] Tenth Report of the Commissioners of H.M. Inland Revenue. Lond. 1866, p. 38.

Iron-works, 39.92%   3.63%
Fisheries, 57.37%   5.21%
Gasworks, 126.02%   11.45%
Railways, 83.29%   7.57%[1]

If we compare the years from 1853 to 1864 in three sets of **four** consecutive years each, the rate of augmentation of the income increases constantly. It is, *e.g.*, for that arising from profits between 1853 to 1857, 1.73% yearly; 1857-1861, 2.74%, and for 1861-64, 9.30% yearly. The sum of the incomes of the United Kingdom that come under the income tax was in 1856 £307,068,898; in 1859, £328,127,416; in 1862, £351,745,241; in 1863, £359,142,897; in 1864, £362,462,279; in 1865, £385,530,020.[2]

The accumulaton of capital was attended at the same time by its concentration and centralisation. Although no official statistics of agriculture existed for England (they did for Ireland), they were voluntarily given in 10 counties. These statistics gave the result that from 1851 to 1861 the number of farms of less than 100 acres had fallen from 31,583 to 26,597, so that 5016 had been thrown together into larger farms.[3] From 1815 to 1825 no personal estate of more than £1,000,000 came under the succession duty; from 1825 to 1855, however, 8 did; and 4 from 1856 to June, 1859, *i.e.*, in 4½ years.[4] The centralisation will, however, be best seen from a short analysis of the Income Tax Schedule D (profits, exclusive of farms, &c.), in the years 1864 and 1865. I note beforehand that incomes from this source pay income tax on everything over £60. These incomes liable to taxation in England,

---

[1] Ibidem.

[2] These figures are sufficient for comparison, but, taken absolutely, are false, since, perhaps, £100,000,000 of income are annually not declared. The complaints of the Inland Revenue Commissioners of systematic fraud, especially on the part of the commercial and industrial classes, are repeated in each of their reports. So *e.g.*, "A Joint-stock company returns £6000 as assessable profits, the surveyor raises the amount to £88,000, and upon that sum duty is ultimately paid. Another company which returns £190,000 is finally compelled to admit that the true return should be £250,000." (Ibid., p. 42.)

[3] Census, &c., l. c., p. 29. John Bright's assertion that 150 landlords own half of England, and 12 half the Scotch soil, has never been refuted.

[4] Fourth Report, &c., of Inland Revenue. Lond., 1860, p. 17.

Wales, and Scotland, amounted in 1864 to £95,844,222, in
1865 to £105,435,579.[1] The number of persons taxed were
in 1864, 308,416, out of a population of 23,891,009; in 1865,
332,431 out of a population of 24,127,003. The following
table shows the distribution of these incomes in the two years:

YEAR ENDING APRIL 5TH, 1864.   YEAR ENDING APRIL 5TH, 1865.

INCOME FROM PROFITS.	PERSONS.	INCOME FROM PROFITS.	PERSONS.
Total Income £95,844,222	308,416	Total Income £105,435,738	332,431
of these 57,028,289	23,334	of these 64,554,297	24,265
„ 36,415,225	3,619	„ 42,535,576	4,021
„ 22,809,781	832	„ 27,555,313	973
„ 8,744,762	91	„ 11,077,238	107

In 1855 there were produced in the United Kingdom 61,-
453,079 tons of coal, of value £16,113,167; in 1864, 92,787,-
873 tons, of value £23,197,968; in 1855, 3,218,154 tons of
pig-iron, of value £8,045,385; 1864, 4,767,951 tons, of value
£11,919,877. In 1854 the length of the railroads worked in
the United Kingdom was 8054 miles, with a paid-up capital
of £286,068,794; in 1864 the length was 12,789 miles, with
capital paid up of £425,719,613. In 1854 the total sum of
the exports and imports of the United Kingdom was £268,-
210,145; in 1865, £489,923,285. The following table shows
the movement of the exports:

1846	£58,842,377
1849	63,596,052
1856	115,826,948
1860	135,842,817
1865	165,862,402
1866	188,917,563[2]

[1] These are the net incomes after certain legally authorized abatements.
[2] At this moment, March, 1867, the Indian and Chinese market is again over-
stocked by the consignments of the British cotton manufacturers. In 1866 a re-

After these few examples one understands the cry of triumph of the Registrar-General of the British people: "Rapidly as the population has increased, it has not kept pace with the progress of industry and wealth." [1]

Let us turn now to the direct agents of this industry, or the producers of this wealth, to the working cass. "It is one of the most melancholy features in the social state of this country," says Gladstone, "that while there was a decrease in the consuming powers of the people, and while there was an increase in the privations and distress of the labouring class and operatives, there was at the same time a constant accumulation of wealth in the upper classes, and a constant increase of capital." [2] Thus spake this unctuous minister in the House of Commons on February 13th, 1843. On April 16th, 1863, 20 years later, in the speech in which he introduced his Budget: "From 1842 to 1852 the taxable income of the country increased by 6 per cent. . . . . In the 8 years from 1853 to 1861 it had increased from the basis taken in 1853 by 20 per cent! The fact is so astonishing as to be almost incredible . . . . this intoxicating augmentation of wealth and power . . . . entirely confined to classes of property . . . . must be of indirect benefit to the labouring population, because it cheapens the commodities of general consumption. While the rich have been growing richer, the poor have been growing less poor. At any-rate, whether the extremes of poverty are less, I do not presume to say." [3] How lame an anti-climax! If the working-class has remained "poor," only "less poor" in proportion as it produces for the wealthy class "an intoxicating aug-

---

duction in wages of 5 per cent. took place amongst the cotton operatives. In 1867, as consequence of a similar operation, there was a strike of 20,000 men at Preston. Note to the 4th German edition.—This was a prelude to the crisis, which broke out soon afterwards.—F. E.

[1] Census, &c., 1. c., p. 11.

[2] Gladstone in the House of Commons, Feb. 13th, 1843. "Times," Feb. 14th, 1843. —"It is one of the most melancholy features in the social state of this country that we see, beyond the possibility of denial, that while there is at this moment a decrease in the consuming powers of the people, an increase of the pressure of privations and distress; there is at the same time a constant accumulation of wealth in the upper classes, an increase of the luxuriousness of their habits, and of their means of enjoyment." (Hansard, 13th Feb.)

[3] Gladstone in the House of Commons, April 16th, 1863. "Morning Star," April 17th.

mentation of wealth and power," then it has remained relatively just as poor. If the extremes of poverty have not lessened, they have increased, because the extremes of wealth have. As to the cheapening of the means of subsistence, the official statistics, *e.g.,* the accounts of the London Orphan Asylum, show an increase in price of 20% for the average of the three years 1860-1862, compared with 1851-1853. In the following three years, 1863-1865, there was a progressive rise in the price of meat, butter, milk, sugar, salt, coals, and a number of other necessary means of subsistence.[1] Gladstone's next Budget speech of April 7th, 1864, is a Pindaric dithyrambus on the advance of surplus-value-making and the happiness of the people tempered by "poverty." He speaks of masses "on the border" of pauperism, of branches of trade in which "wages have not increased," and finally sums up the happiness of the working class in the words: "human life is but, in nine cases out of ten, a struggle for existence." [2] Professor Fawcett, not bound like Gladstone by official considerations, declares roundly: "I do not, of course, deny that money wages have been augmented by this increase of capital (in the last ten years), but this apparent advantage is to a great extent lost, because many of the necessaries of life are becoming dearer" (he believes because of the fall in value of the precious metals) . . . . "the rich grow rapidly richer, whilst there is no perceptible advance in the comfort enjoyed by the indus-

---

[1] See the official accounts in the Blue Book: "Miscellaneous statistics of the United Kingdom," Part vi., London, 1866, pp. 260-273, passim. Instead of the statistics of orphan asylums, &c., the declamations of the ministerial journals in recommending dowries for the Royal children might also serve. The greater dearness of the means of subsistence is never forgotten there.

[2] Gladstone, House of Commons, 7th April, 1864.—"The Hansard version runs: "Again, and yet more at large—what is human life, but, in the majority of cases, a struggle for existence." The continual crying contradictions in Gladstone's Budget speeches of 1863 and 1864 were characterised by an English writer by the following quotation from Molière:

"Voilà l'homme en effet. Il va du blanc au noir,
Il condamne au matin ses sentiments du soir.
Importun à tout autre, à soi-même incommode,
Il change à tout moment d'esprit comme de mode."

(The Theory of Exchanges, &c., London, 1864, p. 135.)

trial classes . . . . They (the labourers) become almost the slaves of the tradesman, to whom they owe money."[1]

In the chapters on the "working day" and "machinery," the reader has seen under what circumstances the British working-class created an "intoxicating augmentation of wealth and power" for the propertied classes. There we were chiefly concerned with the social functioning of the labourer. But for a full elucidation of the law of accumulation, his condition outside the workshop must also be looked at, his condition as to food and dwelling. The limits of this book compel us to concern ourselves chiefly with the worst paid part of the industrial proletariat, and with the agricultural labourers, who together form the majority of the working-class.

But first, one word on official pauperism, or on that part of the working-class which has forfeited its condition of existence (the sale of labour-power), and vegetates upon public alms. The official list of paupers numbered in England[2] 851,369 persons; in 1856, 977,767; in 1865, 971,433. In consequence of the cotton famine, it grew in the years 1863 and 1864 to 1,079,382 and 1,014,978. The crisis of 1866, which fell most heavily on London, created in this centre of the world-market, more populous than the kingdom of Scotland, an increase of pauperism for the year 1866 of 19.5% compared with 1865, and of 24.4% compared with 1864, and a still greater increase for the first months of 1867 as compared with 1866. From the analysis of the statistics of pauperism, two points are to be taken. On the one hand, the fluctuation up and down of the number of paupers, reflects the periodic changes of the industrial cycle. On the other, the official statistics become more and more misleading as to the actual extent of pauperism in proportion as, with the accumulation of capital, the class-struggle, and, therefore, the class-consciousness of the working-men, develope. *E.g.,* the barbarity in the treatment of the paupers, at which the English Press (*The Times, Pall Mall Gazette,* etc.) have cried out so loudly during the last

---

[1] H. Fawcett, l. c., pp. 67-82. As to the increasing dependence of labourers on the retail shopkeepers, this is the consequence of the frequent oscillations and interruptions of their employment.

[2] Wales here is always included in England.

two years, is of ancient date. F. Engels showed in 1844 exactly the same horrors, exactly the same transient canting outcries of "sensational literature." But frightful increase of "deaths by starvation" in London during the last ten years proves beyond doubt the growing horror in which the working-people hold the slavery of the workhouse, that place of punishment for misery.[1]

(b). *The badly paid Strata of the British Industrial Class.*

During the Cotton famine of 1862, Dr. Smith was charged by the Privy Council with an inquiry into the conditions of nourishment of the distressed operatives in Lancashire and Cheshire. His observations during many preceding years had led him to the conclusion that "to avert starvation diseases," the daily food of an average woman ought to contain at least 3,900 grains of carbon with 180 grains of nitrogen; the daily food of an average man, at least 4,300 grains of carbon with 200 grains of nitrogen; for women, about the same quantity of nutritive elements as are contained in 2 lbs of good wheaten bread, for men 1-9 more; for the weekly average of adult men and women, at least 28,600 grains of carbon and 1,330 grains of nitrogen. His calculation was practically confirmed in a surprising manner by its agreement with the miserable quantity of nourishment to which want had forced down the consumption of the cotton operatives. This was, in December, 1862, 29,211 grains of carbon, and 1,295 grains of nitrogen weekly.

In the year 1863, the Privy Council ordered an inquiry into the state of distress of the worst-nourished part of the English working-class. Dr. Simon, medical officer to the Privy Council, chose for this work the above-mentioned Dr. Smith. His inquiry ranges on the one hand over the agricultural labourers, on the other, over silk-weavers, needle-women, kid-glovers,

---

[1] A peculiar light is thrown on the advance made since the time of Adam Smith, by the fact that by him the word "workhouse" is still occasionally used as synonymous with "manufactory;" *e.g.*, the opening of his chapter on the division of labour; "those employed in every different branch of the work can often be collected into the same workhouse."

stocking-weavers, glove-weavers, and shoe-makers. The latter categories are, with the exception of the stocking-weavers, exclusively town-dwellers. It was made a rule in the inquiry to select in each category the most healthy families, and those comparatively in the best circumstances.

As a general result it was found that "in only one of the examined classes of in-door operatives did the average nitrogen-supply just exceed, while in another it nearly reached, the estimated standard of bare sufficiency [*i.e.,* sufficient to avert starvation diseases], and that in two classes there was defect—in one a very large defect—of both nitrogen and carbon. Moreover, as regards the examined families of the agricultural population, it appeared that more than a fifth were with less than the estimated sufficiency of carbonaceous food, that more than one third were with less than the estimated sufficiency of nitrogeneous food, and that in three counties (Berkshire, Oxfordshire, and Somersetshire), insufficiency of nitrogenous food was the average local diet."[1] Among the Agricultural labourers, those of England, the wealthiest part of the United Kingdom, were the worst fed.[2] The insufficiency of food among the agricultural labourers, fell, as a rule, chiefly on the women and children, for "the man must eat to do his work." Still greater penury ravaged the town-workers examined. "They are so ill fed that assuredly among them there must be many cases of severe and injurious privation."[3] ("Privation" of the capitalist all this! *i.e.,* "abstinence" from paying for the means of subsistence absolutely necessary for the mere vegetation of his hands.")

The following table shows the conditions of nourishment of the above-named categories of purely town-dwelling workpeople, as compared with the minimum assumed by Dr. Smith, and with the food-allowance of the cotton operatives during the time of their greatest distress:

[1] Public Health. Sixth Report, 1864, p. 13.
[2] l. c. p. 17.
[3] l. c. p. 13.

BOTH SEXES.	AVERAGE WEEKLY CARBON.	AVERAGE WEEKLY NITROGEN.
Five in-door occupations - - -	28,876 grains	1,192 grains
Unemployed Lancashire Operatives	28,211 „	1,295 „
Minimum quantity to be allowed to the Lancashire Operatives, equal number of males and females, - - - - -	28,600 „	1,330 „ [1]

One half, or $\frac{60}{125}$ of the industrial labour categories investi-gated, had absolutely no beer, 28% no milk. The weekly aver-age of the liquid means of nourishment in the families varied from seven ounces in the needle-women to 24¾ ounces in the stocking-makers. The majority of those who did not obtain milk were needle-women in London. The quantity of bread-stuffs consumed weekly varied from 7¾lbs for the needle-women to 11½ lbs for the shoemakers, and gave a total average of 9.9 lbs. per adult weekly. Sugar (treacle, etc.) varied from 4 ounces weekly for the kid-glovers to 11 ounces for the stocking-makers; and the total average per week for all categories was 8 ounces per adult weekly. Total weekly average of butter (fat, etc.) 5 ounces per adult. The weekly average of meat (bacon, etc.) varied from 7¼ ounces for the silk-weavers, to 18¼ ounces for the kid-glovers; total average for the differ-ent categories 13.6 ounces. The weekly cost of food per adult, gave the following average figures; silk-weavers 2s 2½d., needle-women 2s. 7d., kid-glovers 2s. 9½d., shoemakers 2s 7¾d., stocking weavers 2s. 6¼d. For the silk-weavers of Maccles-field the average was only 1s. 8½d. The worst categories were the needle-women, silk-weavers and kid-glovers.[2] Of these facts, Dr. Simon in his General Health Report says: "That cases are innumerable in which defective diet is the cause or the aggravator of disease, can be affirmed by any one who is conversant with poor law medical practice, or with the wards

[1] l. c., Appendix p. 232.
[2] l. c. pp. 232, 233.

and out-patient rooms of hospitals. . . . Yet in this point of view, there is, in my opinion, a very important sanitary context to be added. It must be remembered that privation of food is very reluctantly borne, and that as a rule great poorness of diet will only come when other privations have preceded it. Long before insufficiency of diet is a matter of hygienic concern, long before the physiologist would think of counting the grains of nitrogen and carbon which intervene between life and starvation, the household will have been utterly destitute of material comfort; clothing and fuel will have been even scantier than food—against inclemencies of weather there will have been no adequate protection—dwelling space will have been stinted to the degree in which overcrowding produces or increases disease; of household utensils and furniture there will have been scarcely any—even cleanliness will have been found costly or difficult, and if there still be self-respectful endeavours to maintain it, every such endeavour will represent additional pangs of hunger. The home, too, will be where shelter can be cheapest bought; in quarters where commonly there is least fruit of sanitary supervision, least drainage, least scavenging, least suppression of public nuisances, least or worst water supply, and, if in town, least light and air. Such are the sanitary dangers to which poverty is almost certainly exposed, when it is poverty enough to imply scantiness of food. And while the sum of them is of terrible magnitude against life, the mere scantiness of food is in itself of very serious moment. . . . . . These are painful reflections, especially when it is remembered that the poverty to which they advert is not the deserved poverty of idleness. In all cases it is the poverty of working populations. Indeed, as regards the indoor operatives, the work which obtains the scanty pittance of food, is for the most part excessively prolonged. Yet evidently it is only in a qualified sense that the work can be deemed self-supporting. . . . . And on a very large scale the nominal self-support can be only a circuit, longer or shorter, to pauperism."[1]

The intimate connexion between the pangs of hunger of the

[1] l. c. pp. 14, 15.

most industrious layers of the working class, and the extravagant consumption, coarse or refined, of the rich, for which capitalist accumulation is the basis, reveals itself only when the economic laws are known. It is otherwise with the "housing of the poor." Every unprejudiced observer sees that the greater the centralisation of the means of production, the greater is the corresponding heaping together of the labourers, within a given space; that therefore the swifter capitalistic accumulation, the more miserable are the dwellings of the working-people. "Improvements" of towns, accompanying the increase of wealth, by the demolition of badly built quarters, the erection of palaces for banks, warehouses, &c., the widening of streets for business traffic, for the carriages of luxury, and for the introduction of tramways, &c., drive away the poor into even worse and more crowded hiding places. On the other hand, every one knows that the dearness of dwellings is in inverse ratio to their excellence, and that the mines of misery are exploited by house speculators with more profit or less cost than ever were the mines of Potosi. The antagonistic character of capitalist accumulation, and therefore of the capitalistic relations of property generally,[1] is here so evident, that even the official English reports on this subject teem with heterodox onslaughts on "property and its rights." With the development of industry, with the accumulation of capital, with the growth and "improvement of towns, the evil makes such progress that the mere fear of contagious diseases which do not spare even "respectability," brought into existence from 1847 to 1864 no less than 10 Acts of Parliament on sanitation, and that the frightened bourgeois in some towns, as Liverpool, Glasgow, &c., took strenuous measures through their municipalities. Nevertheless Dr. Simon, in his report of 1865, says: "Speaking generally it may be said that the evils are uncontrolled in England." By order of the Privy Council in 1864, an inquiry was made into the conditions of the housing of the

---

[1] "In no particular have the rights of *persons* been so avowedly and shamefully sacrificed to the rights of *property* as in regard to the lodging of the labouring class. Every large town may be looked upon as a place of human sacrifice, a shrine where thousands pass yearly through the fire as offerings to the moloch of avarice." S. Laing, l. c. p. 150.

agricultural labourers, in 1865 of the poorer classes in the towns. The results of the admirable work of Dr. Julian Hunter are to be found in the seventh (1865) and eighth (1866) reports on "Public Health." To the agricultural labourers, I shall come later. On the condition of town dwellings, I quote, as preliminary, a general remark of Dr. Simon. "Although my official point of view," he says, "is one exclusively physical, common humanity requires that the other aspect of this evil should not be ignored. . . . In its higher degrees it [*i.e.,* overcrowding] almost necessarily involves such negation of all delicacy, such unclean confusion of bodies and bodily functions, such exposure of animal and sexual nakedness, as is rather bestial than human., To be subject to these influences is a degradation which must become deeper and deeper for those on whom it continues to work. To children who are born under its curse, it must often be a very baptism into infamy. And beyond all measure hopeless is the wish that persons thus circumstanced should ever in other respects aspire to that atmosphere of civilization which has its essence in physical and moral cleanliness."[1]

London takes the first place in overcrowded habitations, absolutely unfit for human beings. "He feels clear," says Dr. Hunter, "on two points; first, that there are about 20 large colonies in London, of about 10,000 persons each, whose miserable condition exceeds almost anything he has seen elsewhere in England, and is almost entirely the result of their bad house accommodation; and second, that the crowded and delapidated condition of the houses of these colonies is much worse than was the case 20 years ago."[2] "It is not too much to say that life in parts of London and Newcastle is infernal."[3]

Further, the better-off part of the working class, together

---

[1] Public Health, eighth report, 1865, p. 14, note.

[2] l. c. p. 89. With reference to the children in these colonies, Dr. Hunter says: "People are not now alive to tell us how children were brought up before this age of dense agglomerations of poor began, and he would be a rash prophet who should tell us what future behaviour is to be expected from the present growth of children, who, under circumstances probably never before paralleled in this country, are now completing their education for future practice, as "dangerous classes" by sitting up half the night with persons of every age, half naked, drunken, obscene, and quarrelsome." (l. c. p. 56.)

[3] l. c. p. 62.

with the small shopkeepers and other elements of the lower
middle class, falls in London more and more under the curse
of these vile conditions of dwelling, in proportion as "improvements," and with them the demolition of old streets and houses,
advance, as factories and the afflux of human beings grow in
the metropolis, and finally as house rents rise with the ground
rents. "Rents have become so heavy that few labouring men
can afford more than one room."[1] There is almost no house-
property in London that is not overburdened with a number of
middlemen. For the price of land in London is always very
high in comparison with its yearly revenue, and therefore
every buyer speculates on getting rid of it again at a jury
price (the expropriation valuation fixed by jurymen), or on
pocketing an extraordinary increase of value arising from the
neighbourhood of some large establishment. As a consequence
of this there is a regular trade in the purchase of "fag-ends of
leases." Gentlemen in this business may be fairly expected
to do as they do—get all they can from the tenants while they
have them, and leave as little as they can for their successors."[2]

The rents are weekly, and these gentlemen run no risk. In
consequence of the making of railroads in the City, "the
spectacle has lately been seen in the East of London of a
number of families wandering about some Saturday night with
their scanty worldly goods on their backs, without any resting
place but the workhouse."[3] The workhouses are already over-
crowded, and the "improvements" already sanctioned by Parliament are only just begun. If labourers are driven away by
the demolition of their old houses, they do not leave their old
parish, or at most they settle down on its borders, as near as
they can get to it. "They try, of course, to remain as near as
possible to their workshops. The inhabitants do not go beyond
the same or the next parish, parting their two-room tenements
into single rooms, and crowding even those. . . . Even at
an advanced rent, the people who are displaced will hardly be
able to get an accommodation so good as the meagre one they

---

[1] Report of the Officer of Health of St. Martins-in-the-Fields, 1865.
[2] Public Health, eighth report, 1865, p. 91.
[3] l. c. p. 88.

have left. . . . Half the workmen . . . of the
Strand . . . walked two miles to their work."[1] This
same Strand, a main thoroughfare which gives strangers an
imposing idea of the wealth of London, may serve as an example of the packing together of human beings in that own. In
one of its parishes, the Officer of Health reckoned 581 persons
per acre, although half the width of the Thames was reckoned
in. It will be self-understood that every sanitary measure,
which, as has been the case hitherto in London, hunts the labourers from one quarter, by demolishing uninhabitable
houses, serves only to crowd them together yet more closely in
another. "Either," says Dr. Hunter, 'the whole proceeding
will of necessity stop as an absurdity, or the public compassion (!) be effectually aroused to the obligation which may
now be without exaggeration called national, of supplying
cover to those who by reason of their having no capital, cannot provide it for themselves, though they can by periodical
payments reward those who will provide it for them."[2] Admire this capitalistic justice! The owner of and, of houses,
the business man, when expropriated by "improvements" such
as railroads, the building of new streets, &c., not only receives
full indemnity. He must, according to law, human and divine, be comforted for his enforced "abstinence" over and
above this by a thumping profit. The labourer, with his wife
and child and chattels, is thrown out into the street, and—
if he crowds in too large numbers towards quarters of the
town where the vestries insist on decency, he is prosecuted in
the name of sanitation!

Except London, there was at the beginning of the 19th
century no single town in England of 100,000 inhabitants.
Only five had more than 50,000. Now there are 28 towns
with more than 50,000 inhabitants. "The result of this
change is not only that the class of town people is enormously
increased, but the old close-packed little towns are now centres,
built round on every side, open nowhere to air, and being no
longer agreeable to the rich are abandoned by them for the
pleasanter outskirts. The successors of these rich are occupy-

ing the larger houses at the rate of a family to each room
[. . . and find accommodation for two or three lodgers
. . .] and a population, for which the houses were not
intended, and quite unfit, has been created, whose surroundings are truly degrading to the adults and ruinous to the children."[1] The more rapidly capital accumulates in an industrial or commercial town, the more rapidly flows the stream
of exploitable human material, the more miserable are the improvised dwellings of the labourers.

Newcastle-on-Tyne, as the centre of a coal and iron district
of growing productiveness, takes the next place after London
in the housing inferno. Not less than 34,000 persons live
there in single rooms. Because of their absolute danger to
the community, houses in great numbers have lately been destroyed by the authorities in Newcastle and Gateshead. The
building of new houses progresses very slowly, business very
quickly. The town was, therefore, in 1865, more full than
ever. Scarcely a room was to let. Dr. Embleton, of the Newcastle Fever Hospital, says: "There can be little doubt that
the great cause of the continuance and spread of the typhus has
been the overcrowding of human beings, and the uncleanliness
of their dwellings. The rooms, in which labourers in many
cases live, are situated in confined and unwholesome yards or
courts, and for space, light, air, and cleanliness, are models of
insufficiency and insalubrity, and a disgrace to any civilised
community; in them men, women, and children lie at night
huddled together; and as regards the men, the night-shift succeed the day-shift, and the day-shift the night-shift in unbroken series for some time together, the beds having scarcely
time to cool; the whole house badly supplied with water, and
worse with privies; dirty, unventilated, and pestiferous."[2]
The price per week of such lodgings ranges from 8d. to 3s.
"The town of Newcastle-on-Tyne," says Dr. Hunter, "contains
a sample of the finest tribe of our countrymen, often sunk by
external circumstances of house and street into an almost savage degradation."[3]

---

[1] 55 and 56.   [2] l. c. p. 149.   [3] l. c. p. 51

As result of the ebbing and flowing of capital and labour, the state of the dwellings of an industrial town may to-day be bearable, to-morrow hideous. Or the ædileship of the town may have pulled itself together for the removal of the most shocking abuses. To-morrow, like a swarm of locusts, come crowding in masses of ragged Irishmen or decayed English agricultural labourers. They are stowed away in cellars and lofts, or the hitherto respectable labourer's dwelling is transformed int a lodging-house, whose *personnel* changes as quickly as the billets in the 30 years' war. Example: Bradford (Yorkshire). There the municipal philistine was just busied with urba improvements. Besides, there were still in Bradford, i. 1861, 1751 uninhabited houses. But now comes that revive' of trade which the mildly liberal Mr. Forster, the negro's friend, recently crowed over with so much grace. With the revival of trade came of course an overflow from the waves of the ever fluctuating "reserve-army" or "relative surplus population." The frightful cellar habitations and rooms registered in the list,[1] which Dr. Hunter obtained from the agent of an Insurance Company, were for the most part inhabited by well-paid labourers. They declared that they would willingly pay for better dwellings if they were to be had. Meanwhile, they become degraded, they fall ill, one and

[1] COLLECTING AGENTS' LIST (BRADFORD).

Houses.

Vulcan Street, No. 122	1 room	16 persons
Lumley Street, No. 13	1 "	11 "
Bower Street, No. 41	1 "	11 "
Portland Street, No. 112	1 "	10 "
Hardy Street, No. 17	1 "	10 "
North Street, No. 18	1 "	16 "
North Street, No. 17	1 "	13 "
Wymer Street, No. 191	1 "	8 adults
Jowett Street, No. 56	1 "	12 persons
George Street, No. 150	1 "	3 families
Rifle Court Marygate, No. 11	1 room	11 persons
Marshall Street, No. 28	1 "	10 "
Marshall Street, No. 28	3 "	3 families
George Street, No. 128	1 "	18 persons
George Street, No. 130	1 "	16 "
Edward Street, No. 4	1 "	17 "
George Street, No. 49	1	2 families
York Street, No. 34	1 "	2 "
Salt Pie Street (bottom)	2 "	26 persons

all, whilst the mildly liberal Forster, M.P., sheds tears over the blessings of free-trade, and the profits of the eminent men of Bradford who deal in worsted. In the Report of September, 1865, Dr. Bell, one of the poor law doctors of Bradford, ascribes the frightful mortality of fever-patients in his district to the nature of their dwellings. "In one small cellar measuring 1500 cubic feet . . . there are ten persons. . . . Vincent Street, Green Aire Place, and the Leys include 223 houses having 1450 inhabitants, 435 beds, and 36 privies. . . . The beds—and in that term I include any roll of dirty old rags, or an armful of shavings—have an average of 3.3 person to each, many have 5 and 6 persons to each, and some people, I am told, are absolutely without beds; they sleep in their ordinary clothes, on the bare boards—young men and women, married and unmarried, all together. I need scarcely add that many of these dwellings are dark, damp, dirty, stinking holes, utterly unfit for human habitations; they are the centres from which disease and death are distributed amongst those in better circumstances, who have allowed them to fester in our midst."[1]

Bristol takes the third place after London in the misery of its dwellings. "Bristol, where the blankest poverty and domestic misery abound in the wealthiest town of Europe."[2]

c. *The Nomad Population.*

We turn now to a class of people whose origin is agricultural, but whose occupation is in great part industrial. They are the light infantry of capital, thrown by it, according to its needs, now to this point, now to that. When they are not on the march, they "camp." Nomad labour is used for various

Cellars.

Regent Square	1 cellar	8 persons
Acre Street	1 "	7 "
33 Roberts Court	1 "	7 "
Back Pratt Street, used as a brazier's shop.	1 "	7 "
27 Ebenezer Street	1 "	6 " l. c. p. iii.

[1] l. c. p. 114.
[2] l. c. p. 50.

operation of building and draining, brick-making, lime-burning, railway-making, &c. A flying column of pestilence, it carries into the places in whose neighbourhood it pitches its camp, small-pox, typhus, cholera, scarlet fever, &c.[1] In undertakings that involve much capital outlay, such as railways, &c., the contractor himself generally provides his army with wooden huts and the like, thus improvising villages without any sanitary provisions, outside the control of the local boards, very profitable to the contractor, who exploits the labourers ir two-fold fashion—as soldiers of industry and as tenants. According as the wooden hut contains 1, 2, or 3 holes, its inhabitant, navvy, or whatever he may be, has to pay 1, 3, or 4 shillings weekly.[2] One example will suffice. In September, 1864, Dr. Simon reports that the Chairman of the Nuisances Removal Committee of the parish of Sevenoaks sent the following denunciation to Sir George Grey, Home Secretary :— "Small-pox cases were rarely heard of in this parish until about twelve months ago. Shortly before that time, the works for a railway from Lewisham to Tunbridge were commenced here, and, in addition to the principal works being in the immediate neighbourhood of this town, here was also established the depôt for the whole of the works, so that a large number of persons was of necessity employed here. As cottage accommodation could not be obtained for them all, huts were built in several places along the line of the works by the contractor, Mr. Jay, for their especial occupation. These huts possessed no ventilation nor drainage, and, besides, were necessarily overcrowded, because each occupant had to accommodate lodgers, whatever the number in his own family might be, although there were only two rooms to each tenement. The consequences were, according to the medical report we received, that in the night-time these poor people were compelled to endure all the horror of suffocation to avoid the pestiferous smells arising from the filthy, stagnant water, and the privies close under the windows. Complaints were at length made to the Nuisances Removal Committee by a medical gentleman who had occasion to visit these huts, and he spoke

[1] Public Health. Seventh Report. 1864, p. 18.　　　　[2] l. c. p. 165.

of their condition as dwellings in the most severe terms, and he expressed his fears that some very serious consequences might ensue, unless some sanitary measures were adopted. About a year ago, Mr. Jay promised to appropriate a hut, to which persons in his employ, who were suffering from contagious diseases, might at once be removed. He repeated that promise on the 23rd July last, but although since the date of the last promise there have been several cases of small-pox in his huts, and two deaths from the same disease, yet he has taken no steps whatever to carry out his promise. On the 9th September instant, Mr. Kelson, surgeon, reported to me further cases of small-pox in the same huts, and he described their condition as most disgraceful. I should add, for your (the Home Secretary's information that) an isolated house, called the Pest-house, which is set apart for parishioners who might be suffering from infectious diseases, has been continually occupied by such patients for many months past, and is also now occupied; that in one family five children died from small-pox and fever; that from the 1st April to the 1st September this year, a period of five months, there have been no fewer than ten deaths from small-pox in the parish, four of them being in the huts already referred to; that it is impossible to ascertain the exact number of persons who have suffered from that disease, although they are known to be many, from the fact of the families keeping it as private as possible."[1]

The labourers in coal and other mines belong to the best paid categories of the British proletariat. The price at which they buy their wages was shown on an earlier page.[2] Here I merely cast a hurried glance over the conditions of their dwell-

---

[1] l. c., p. 18, Note.—The Relieving Officer of the Chapel-en-le-Frith Union reported to the Registrar-General as follows:—"At Doveholes, a number of small excavations have been made into a large hillock of lime ashes (the refuse of lime-kilns), and which are used as dwellings, and occupied by labourers and others employed in the construction of a railway now in course of construction through that neighbourhood. The excavations are small and damp, and have no drains or privies about them, and not the slightest means of ventilation except up a hole pulled through the top, and used for a chimney. In consequence of this defect, small-pox has been raging for some time, and some deaths [amongst the troglodytes] have been caused by them." (l. c., note 2.)

[2] The details given at the end of Part IV. refer especially to the labourers in coal mines. On the still worse condition in metal mines, see the very conscientious Report of the Royal Commission of 1864.

ings. As a rule, the exploiter of a mine, whether its owner or his tenant, builds a number of cottages for his hands. They receive cottages and coal for firing "for nothing"—*i.e.,* these form part of their wages, paid in kind. Those who are not lodged in this way receive in compensation £4 per annum. The mining districts attract with rapidity a large population, made up of the miners themselves, and the artisans, shop-keepers, &c., that group themselves around them. The ground-rents are high, as they are generally where population is dense. The master tries, therefore, to run up, within the smallest space possible at the mouth of the pit, just so many cottages as are necessary to pack together his hands and their families. If new mines are opened in the neighbourhood, or old ones are again set working, the pressure increases. In the construction of the cottages, only one point of view is of moment, the "abstinence" of the capitalist from all expenditure that is not absolutely unavoidable. "The lodging which is obtained by the pitmen and other labourers connected with the collieries of Northumberland and Durha ," says Dr. Julian Hunter, "is perhaps, on the whole, the worst and the dearest of which any large specimens can be found in England, the similar parishes of Monmouthshire excepted. . . . The extreme badness is in the high number of men found in one room, in the smallness of the ground-plot on which a great number of houses are thrust, the want of water, the absence of privies, and the frequent placing of one house on the top of another, or distribution into flats, . . . the lessee acts as if the whole colony were encamped, not resident."[1]

"In pursuance of my instructions," says Dr. Stevens, "I visited most of the large colliery villages in the Durham Union. . . . With very few exceptions, the general statement that no means are taken to secure the health of the inhabitants would be true of all of them. . . . All colliers are bound ['bound,' an expression which, like bondage, dates from the age of serfdom] to the colliery lessee or owner for twelve months. . . . If the colliers express discontent, or in any way annoy the 'viewer,' a mark or memorandum is

---

[1] l. c., pp. 180, 182.

made against their names, and, at the annual 'binding,' such men are turned off. . . . It appears to me that no part of the 'truck system' could be worse than what obtains in these densely-populated districts. The collier is bound to take as part of his hiring a house surrounded with pestiferous influences; he cannot help himself, and it appears doubtful whether anyone else can help him except his proprietor (he is, to all intents and purposes, a serf), and his proprietor first consults his balance-sheet, and the result is tolerably certain. The collier is also often supplied with water by the proprietor, which, whether it be good or bad, he has to pay for, or rather he suffers a deduction for from his wages."[1]

In conflict with "public opinion," or even with the Officers of Health, capital makes no difficulty about "justifying" the conditions partly dangerous, partly degrading, to which it confines the working and domestic life of the labourer, on the ground that they are necessary for profit. It is the same thing when capital "abstains" from protective measures against dangerous machinery in the factory, from appliances for ventilation and for safety in mines, &c. It is the same here with the housing of the miners. Dr. Simon, medical officer of the Privy Council, in his official Report says: "In apology for the wretched household accommodation . . . it is alleged that mines are commonly worked on lease; that the duration of the lessee's interest (which in collieries is commonly for 21 years), is not so long that he should deem it worth his while to create good accommodation for his labourers, and for the tradespeople and others whom the work attracts; that even if he were disposed to act liberally in the matter, this disposition would commonly be defeated by his landlord's tendency to fix on him, as ground rent, an exorbitant additional charge for the privilege of having on the surface of the ground the decent and comfortable village which the labourers of the subterranean property ought to inhabit, and that prohibitory price (if not actual prohibition) equally excludes others who might desire to build. It would be foreign to the purpose of this report to enter upon any discussion of the merits of the

[1] l. c., pp. 515, 517.

above apology. Nor here is it even needful to consider where it would be that, if decent accommodation were provided, the cost . . . would eventually fall—whether on landlord, or lessee, or labourer, or public. But in presence of such shameful facts as are vouched for in the annexed reports [those of Dr. Hunter, Dr. Stevens, &c.] a remedy may well be claimed. . . . Claims of landlordship are being so used as to do great public wrong. The landlord in his capacity of mine-owner invites an industrial colony to labour on his estate, and then in his capacity of surface-owner makes it impossible that the labourers whom he collects, should find proper lodging where they must live. The lessee [the capitalist exploiter] meanwhile has no pecuniary motive for resisting that division of the bargain; well knowing that if its latter conditions be exorbitant, the consequences fall, not on him, that his labourers on whom they fall have not education enough to know the value of their sanitary rights, that neither obscenest lodging nor foulest drinking water will be appreciable inducements towards a 'strike.' "[1]

(d). Effect of Crises on the best paid part of the Working Class.

Before I turn to the regular agricultural labourers, I may be allowed to show, by one example, how industrial revulsions affect even the best-paid, the aristocracy, of the working-class. It will be remembered that the year 1857 brought one of the great crises with which the industrial cycle periodically ends. The next termination of the cycle was due in 1866. Already discounted in the regular factory districts by the cotton famine, which threw much capital from its wonted sphere into the great centres of the money-market, the crisis assumed, at this time, an especially financial character. Its outbreak in 1866 was signalised by the failure of a gigantic London Bank, immediately followed by the collapse of countless swindling companies. One of the great London branches of industry involved in the catastrophe was iron shipbuilding. The mag-

[1] l. c., p. 16.

nates of this trade had not only over-produced beyond all measure during the overtrading time, but they had, besides, engaged in enormous contracts on the speculation that credit would be forthcoming to an equivalent extent. Now, a terrible reaction set in, that even at this hour (the end of March, 1867) continues in this and other London industries.[1] To show the condition of the labourers, I quote the following from the circumstantial report of a correspondent of the "Morning Star," who, at the end of 1866, and beginning of 1867, visited the chief centres of distress: "In the East End districts of Poplar, Millwall, Greenwich, Deptford, Limehouse and Canning Town, at least 15,000 workmen and their families were in a state of utter destitution, and 3000 skilled mechanics were breaking stones in the workhouse yard (after distress of over half a year's duration). . . . I had great difficulty in reaching the workhouse door, for a hungry crowd besieged it. . . . They were waiting for their tickets, but the time had not yet arrived for the distribution. The yard was a great square place with an open shed running all round it, and several large heaps of snow covered the paving-stones in the middle. In the middle, also, were little wicker-fenced spaces, like sheep pens, where in finer weather the men worked; but on the day of my visit the pens were so snowed up that nobody could sit in them. Men were busy, however, in the open shed breaking paving-stones into macadam. Each man had a big paving-stone for a seat, and he chipped away at the rime-covered granite with a big hammer until he had broken up, and think! five bushels of it, and then he had done his day's work, and got his day's pay—threepence and an allow-

---

[1] "Wholesale starvation of the London Poor. . . . Within the last few days the walls of London have been placarded with large posters, bearing the following remarkable announcement:—'Fat oxen! Starving men! The fat oxen from their palace of glass have gone to feed the rich in their luxurious abode, while the starving men are left to rot and die in their wrecked dens.' The placards bearing these ominous words are put up at certain intervals. No sooner has one set been defaced or covered over, than a fresh set is placarded in the former, or some equally public place. . . . This . . . reminds one of the secret revolutionary associations which prepared the French people for the events of 1789. . . . . . At this moment, while English workmen with their wives and children are dying of cold and hunger, there are millions of English gold—the produce of English labour—being invested in Russian, Spanish, Italian, and other foreign enterprises."—"Reynolds' Newspaper," January 20th, 1867.

ance of food. In another part of the yard was a rickety little wooden house, and when we opened the door of it, we found it filled with men who were huddled together shoulder to shoulder, for the warmth of one another's bodies and breath. They were picking oakum and disputing the while as to which could work the longest on a given quantity of food—for endurance was the point of honour. Seven thousand . . . in this one workhouse . . . were recipients of relief . . . many hundreds of them . . . it appeared, were, six or eight months ago, earning the highest wages paid to artisans. . . . Their number would be more than doubled by the count of those who, having exhausted all their savings, still refuse to apply to the parish, because they have a little left to pawn. Leaving the workhouse, I took a walk through the streets, mostly of little one-storey houses, that abound in the neighbourhood of Poplar. My guide was a member of the Committee of the Unemployed. . . . My first call was on an ironworker who had been seven and twenty weeks out of employment. I found the man with his family sitting in a little back room. The room was not bare of furniture, and there was a fire in it. This was necessary to keep the naked feet of the young children from getting frost bitten, for it was a bitterly cold day. On a tray in front of the fire lay a quantity of oakum, which the wife and children were picking in return for their allowance from the parish. The man worked in the stone yard of the workhouse for a certain ratio of food, and three pence per day. He had now come home to dinner quite hungry, as he told us with a melancholy smile, and his dinner consisted of a couple of slices of bread and dripping, and a cup of milkless tea. . . . The next door at which we knocked was opened by a middle-aged woman, who, without saying a word, led us into a little back parlour, in which sat all her family, silent and fixedly staring at a rapidly dying fire. Such desolation, such hopelessness was about these people and their little room, as I should not care to witness again. 'Nothing have they done, sir,' said the woman, pointing to her boys, 'for six and twenty weeks; and all our money gone— all the twenty pounds that me and father saved when times

were better, thinking it would yield a little to keep us when
we got past work. Look at it,' she said, almost fiercely, bringing out a bank book with all its well-kept entries of money
paid in, and money taken out, so that we could see how the
little fortune had begun with the first five shilling deposit,
and had grown by little and little to be twenty pounds, and
how it had melted down again till the sum in hand got from
pounds to shillings, and the last entry made the book as worth-
less as a blank sheet. This family received relief from the
workhouse, and it furnished them with just one scanty meal
per day. . . . Our next visit was to an iron labourer's
wife, whose husband had worked in the yards. We found her
ill from want of food, lying on a mattress in her clothes, and
just covered with a strip of carpet, for all the bedding had been
pawned. Two wretched children were tending her, themselves
looking as much in need of nursing as their mother. Nineteen
weeks of enforced idleness had brought them to this pass, and
while the mother told the history of that bitter past, she
moaned as if all her faith in a future that should atone for it
were dead. . . . On getting outside a young fellow came
running after us, and asked us to step inside his house and see
if anything could be done for him. A young wife, two pretty
children, a cluster of pawn-tickets, and a bare room were all
he had to show."

On the after pains of the crisis of 1866, the following extract
from a Tory newspaper. It must not be forgotten that the
East-end of London, which is here dealt with, is not only the
seat of the iron shipbuilding mentioned above, but also of
a so-called "home-industry" always underpaid. "A frightful
spectacle was to be seen yesterday in one part of the metropolis. Although the unemployed thousands of the East End
did not parade with their black flags *en masse,* the human
torrent was imposing enough. Let us remember what these
people suffer. They are dying of hunger. That is the simple
and terrible fact. There are 40,000 of them. . . . In
our presence, in one quarter of this wonderful metropolis, are
packed—next door to the most enormous accumulation of
wealth the world ever saw—cheek by jowel with this are

40,000 helpless, starving people. These thousands are now breaking in upon the other quarters, always half-starving, they cry their misery in our ears, they cry to Heaven, they tell us from their miserable dwellings, that it is impossible for them to find work, and useless for them to beg. The local ratepayers themselves are driven by the parochial charges to the verge of pauperism."—("Standard," 5th April, 1866.)

As it is the fashion amongst English capitalists to quote Belgium as the Paradise of the labourer becauses "freedom of labour," or what is the same thing, "freedom of capital," is there limited neither by the despotism of Trade's Unions, nor by Factory Acts, a word or two on the "happiness" of the Belgian labourer. Assuredly no one was more thoroughly initiated in the mysteries of this happiness than the late M. Ducpétiaux, inspector-general of Belgian prisons and charitable institutions, and member of the central commission of Belgian statistics. Let us take his work: "Budgets économiques des classes ouvrières de la Belgique, Bruxelles, 1855." Here we find among other matters, a normal Belgian labourer's family, whose yearly income and expenditure he calculates on very exact data, and whose conditions of nourishment are then compared with those of the soldier, sailor, and prisoner. The family "consists of father, mother, and four children." Of these 6 persons "four may be usefully employed the whole year through." It is assumed that "there is no sick person nor one incapable of work, among them," nor are there "expenses for religious, moral, and intellectual purposes, except a very small sum for church sittings," nor "contributions to savings banks or benefit societies," nor "expenses due to luxury or the result of improvidence." The father and eldest son, however, allow themselves "the use of tobacco," and on Sundays "go to the *cabaret*," for which a whole 86 centimes a week are reckoned. "From a general compilation of wages allowed to the labourers in different trades, it follows that the highest average of daily wage is 1 franc 56c., for men, 89 centimes for women, 56 centimes for boys, and 55 centimes for girls. Calculated at this rate, the resource of the family would amount, at the maximum, to 1068 francs a-year.

. . . In the family . . . taken as typical we have calculated all possible resources. But in ascribing wages to the mother of the family we *raise the question of the direction of the household.* How will its internal economy be cared for? Who will look after the young children? Who will get ready the meals, do the washing and mending? This is the dilemma incessantly presented to the labourers."

According to this the budget of the family is:

The father 300 working days at fr. 1·56 ... fr. 468
  „ mother „   „   „   „   89 ... „ 267
  „ boy „   „   „   „   56 ... „ 168
  „ girl „   „   „   „   55 ... „ 165

Total fr. 1,068

The annual expenditure of the family would cause a deficit upon the hypothesis that the labourer has the food of:

The man of war's man fr. 1828 .. .. Deficit fr. 760
  „ soldier   „ 1473 .. .. „   „ 405
  „ prisoner   „ 1112 .. .. „   „ 44

"We see that few labouring families can reach, we will not say the average of the sailor or soldier, but even that of the prisoner. The general average (of the cost of each prisoner in the different prisons during the period 1847-1849), has been 63 centimes for all prisons. This figure, compared with that of the daily maintenance of the labourer, shows a difference of 13 centimes. It must be remarked further, that if in the prisons it is necessary to set down in the account the expenses of administration and surveillance on the other hand, the prisoners have not to pay for their lodging; that the purchases they make at the canteens are not included in the expenses of maintenance, and that these expenses are greatly lowered in consequence of the large number of persons that make up the establishments, and of contracting for or buying wholesale, the food and other things that enter into their consumption. . . . How comes it, however, that a great number, we might say, a great majority, of labourers, live in a more economical way? It is . . . by adopting expedients, the secret of which only the labourer knows; by reducing his daily rations; by substituting rye-bread for wheat; by eating less meat, or even none at all, and the same with butter and condiments; by contenting themselves with one or two rooms where the family is crammed together, where boys and girls sleep side by side, often on the same pallet; by economy of clothing, washing, decency; by giving up the Sunday diversions; by, in short, resigning themselves to the most painful privations. Once arrived at this extreme limit, the least rise in the price of food, stoppage of work, illness, increases the labourer's distress and determines his complete ruin; debts accumulate, credit fails, the most necessary clothes and furniture are pawned, and finally, the family asks to be enrolled on the list of paupers." (Ducpétiaux, l. c., pp. 151, 154, 155.) In fact, in this "Paradise of capitalists" there follows, on the smallest change in the price of the most essential means of subsistence, a change in the number of deaths and crimes! (See Manifesto of the Maatschappij: De Vlamingen Vooruit! Brussels, 1860, pp. 15, 16.) In all Belgium are 930,000 families, of whom, according to the official statistics, 90,000 are wealthy and on the list of voters =450,000 persons; 390,000 families of the lower middle-class in towns and villages, the greater part of them constantly sinking into the proletariat,=1,950,000 persons. Finally, 450,000 working-class families=2,250,000 persons of whom the model ones enjoy the happiness depicted by Ducpétiaux. Of the 450,000 working-class families, over 200,000 are on the pauper list.

(e.) *The British Agricultural Proletariat.*

Nowhere does the antagonistic character of capitalistic production and accumulation assert itself more brutally than in the progress of English agriculture (including cattle-breeding) and the retrogression of the English agricultural labourer. Before I turn to his present situation, a rapid retrospect:

Modern agriculture dates in England from the middle of the 18th century, although the revolution in landed property, from which the changed mode of production starts as a basis, has a much earlier date.

If we take the statements of Arthur Young, a careful observer, though a superficial thinker, as to the agricultural labourer of 1771, the latter plays a very pitiable part compared with his predecessor of the end of the 14th century, "when the labourer . . . could live in plenty, and accumulate wealth,"[1] not to speak of the 15th century, "the golden age of the English labourer in town and country." We need not, however, go back so far. In a very instructive work of the year 1777 we read: "The great farmer is nearly mounted to a level with him [the genttleman]; while the poor labourer is depressed almost to the earth. His unfortunate situation will fully appear, by taking a comparative view of it, only forty years ago, and at present. . . . Landlord and tenant . . . have both gone hand in hand in keeping the labourer down."[2] It is then proved in detail that the real agricultural wages between 1737 and 1777 fell nearly $\frac{1}{4}$ or 25 per cent. "Modern policy," says Dr. Richard Price also, "is, indeed, more favourable to the higher classes of people; and the consequences may in time prove that the whole kingdom will consist of only gentry and beggars, or of grandees and slaves."[3]

Nevertheless, the position of the English agricultural labourer from 1770 to 1780, with regard to his food and dwell-

---

[1] James E. Thorold Rogers. (Prof. of Polit. Econ. in the University of Oxford.) A History of Agriculture and Prices in England. Oxford, 1866, v. I., p. 690. This work, the fruit of patient and diligent labour, contains in the two volumes that have so far appeared, only the period 1259 to 1400. The second volume contains simply statistics. It is the first authentic "History of Prices" of the time that we possess.

[2] Reasons for the late increase of the Poor-Rates, or a comparative view of the price of labour and provisions. Lond., 1777, pp. 5, 11.

[3] Dr. Richard Price: Observations on Reversionary Payments, 6th Ed. By W. Morgan, Lond., 1803, v. II., pp. 158, 159. Price remarks on p. 159: "The nominal price of day-labour is at present no more than about four times, or, at most, five times higher than it was in the year 1514. But the price of corn is seven times, and of flesh-meat and raiment about fifteen times higher. So far, therefore, has the price of labour been even from advancing in proportion to the increase in the expenses of living, that it does not appear that it bears now half the proportion to those expenses that it did bear."

ing, as well as to his self-respect, amusements, &c., is an ideal never attained again since that time. His average wage expressed in pints of what was from 1770 to 1771, 90 pints, in Eden's time (1797) only 65, in 1808 but 60.[1]

The state of the agricultural labourer at the end of the Anti-Jacobin war, during which landed proprietors, farmers, manufacturers, merchants, bankers, stockbrokers, army-contractors, &c., enriched themselves so extraordinarily, has been already indicated above. The nominal wages rose in consequence partly of the bank-note depreciation, partly of a rise in the price of the primary means of subsistence independent of this depreciation. But the actual wage-variation can be evidenced in a very simple way, without entering into details that are here unnecessary. The Poor Law and its administration were in 1795 and 1814 the same. It will be remembered how this law was carried out in the country districts: in the form of alms the parish made up the nominal wage to the nominal sum required for the simple vegetation of the labourer. The ratio between the wages paid by the farmer, and the wage-deficit made good by the parish, shows us two things. First, the falling of wages below their minimum; second, the degree in which the agricultural labourer was a compound of wage-labourer and pauper, or the degree in which he had been turned into a serf of his parish. Let us take one county that represents the average condition of things in all counties. In Northamptonshire, in 1795, the average weekly wage was 7s. 6d.; the total yearly expenditure of a family of 6 persons, £36 12s. 5d.; their total income, £29 18s.; deficit made good by the parish, £6 14s. 5d. In 1814, in the same county, the weekly wage was 12s. 2d.; the total yearly expenditure of a family of 5 persons, £54 18s. 4d.; their total income, £36 2s.; deficit made good by the parish, £18 16s. 4d.[2] In 1795 the deficit was less than ¼ the wage, in 1814, more than half. It is self-evident that, under these circumstances, the meagre comforts that Eden still found in the cottage of the agricultural labourer, had van-

---

[1] Barton, l. c., p. 26. For the end of the 18th century cf. Eden, l. c.

[2] Parry, l. c., p. 86.

ished by 1814.[1] Of all the animals kept by the farmer, the labourer, the *instrumentum vocale,* was, thenceforth, the most oppressed, the worst nourished, the most brutally treated.

The same state of things went on quietly until "the Swing riots, in 1830, revealed to us [*i.e.,* the ruling classes] by the light of blazing corn-stacks, that misery and black mutinous discontent smouldered quite as fiercely under the surface of agricultural as of manufacturing England."[2] At this time, Sadler, in the House of Commons, christened the agricultural labourers "white slaves," and a Bishop echoed the epithet in the Upper House. The most notable political economist of that period—E. G. Wakefield—says: "The peasant of the South of England . . . is not a freeman, nor is he a slave; he is a pauper."[3]

The time just before the repeal of the Corn Laws threw new light on the condition of the agricultural labourers. On the one hand, it was to the interest of the middle-class agitators to prove how little the Corn Laws protected the actual producers of the corn. On the other hand, the industrial bourgeoisie foamed with sullen rage at the denunciations of the factory system by the landed aristocracy, at the pretended sympathy with the woes of the factory operatives, of those utterly corrupt, heartless, and genteel loafers, and at their "diplomatic zeal" for factory legislation. It is an old English proverb that "when thieves fall out, honest men come by their own," and, in fact, the noisy, passionate quarrel between the two fractions of the ruling class about the question, which of the two exploited the labourers the more shamefully, was on each hand the midwife of the truth. Earl Shaftesbury, then Lord Ashley, was commander-in-chief in the aristocratic, philanthropic, anti-factory campaign. He was, therefore, in 1845, a favourite subject in the revelations of the "Morning Chronicle" on the condition of the agricultural labourers. This journal, then the most important Liberal organ, sent special commissioners into the agricultural districts, who did not content themselves with mere general descriptions and

[1] id., p. 213.   [2] S. Laing. l. c., p. 62.
[3] England and America. Lond., 1833. Vol. I., p. 47.

statistics, but published the names both of the labouring families examined and of their landlords. The following list gives the wages paid in three villages in the neighborhood of Blanford, Wimbourne, and Poole. The villages are the property of Mr. G. Bankes and of the Earl of Shaftesbury. It will be noted that, just like Bankes, this "low church pope," this head of English pietists, pockets a great part of the miserable wages of the labourers under the pretext of house-rent:—

FIRST VILLAGE.

(*a*) Children.	(*b*) Number of Members in Family.	(*c*) Weekly Wage of the Men.	(*d*) Weekly Wage of the Children.	(*e*) Weekly Income of the Whole Family.	(*f*) Weekly Rent.	(*g*) Total weekly wage after deduction of Rent.	(*h*) Weekly Income per head.
		s. d.		s. d.	s. d.	s. d.	s. d.
2	4	8 0	—	8 0	2 0	6 0	1 6
3	5	8 0	—	8 0	1 6	6 6	1 3½
2	4	8 0	—	8 0	1 0	7 0	1 9
2	4	8 0	—	8 0	1 0	7 0	1 9
6	8	7 0	1 -, 1 6,	10 6	2 0	8 6	1 0¼
3	5	7 0	1 -, 2 -	7 0	1 4	5 8	1 1¼

SECOND VILLAGE.

		s. d.		s. d.	s. d.	s. d.	s. d.
6	8	7 0	1 -, 1 6,	10 0	1 6	8 6	1 0¼
6	8	7 0	1 ., 1 6,	7 0	1 3½	5 8½	0 8½
8	10	7 0	—	7 0	1 3½	5 8½	0 7
4	6	7 0	—	7 0	1 6½	5 5½	0 11
3	5	7 0	—	7 0	1 6½	5 5¼	1 1

THIRD VILLAGE.

(*a*) Children.	(*b*) Number of Members in Family.	(*c*) Weekly Wage of the Men.		(*d*) Weekly Wage of the Children.	(*e*) Weekly Income of the Whole Family.		(*f*) Weekly Rent		(*g*) Total weekly wage after deduction of Rent.		(*h*) Weekly Income per head.	
		s.	d.		s.	d.	s.	d.	s.	d.	s.	d.
4	6	7	0	—	7	0	1	0	6	0	1	0
3	5	7	0	1 -, 2 -,	11	6	0	10	10	8	2	1½
0	2	5	0	1 -, 2 6,	5	0	1	0	4	0	2	0 [1]

The repeal of the Corn Laws gave a marvellous impulse to English agriculture.[2] Drainage on the most extensive scale, new methods of stall-feeding, and of the artificial cultivation of green crops, introduction of mechanical manuring apparatus, new treatment of clay soils, increased use of mineral manures, employment of the steam-engine, and of all kinds of new machinery, more intensive cultivation generally, characterised this epoch. Mr. Pusey, Chairman of the Royal Agricultural Society, declares that the (relative) expenses of farming have been reduced nearly one-half by the introduction of new machinery. On the other hand, the actual return of the soil rose rapidly. Greater outlay of capital per acre, and, as a consequence, more rapid concentration of farms, were essential conditions of the new method.[3] At the same

---

[1] London Economist, March 29th, 1845, p. 290.

[2] The landed aristocracy advanced themselves to this end, of course per Parliament, funds from the State Treasury, at a very low rate of interest, which the farmers have to make good at a much higher rate.

[3] The decrease of the middle-class farmers can be seen especially in the census category: "Farmer's son, grandson, brother, nephew, daughter, grand-daughter, sister, niece"; in a word, the members of his own family, employed by the farmer. This category numbered, in 1851, 216,851 persons; in 1861, only 176,151. From 1851 to 1871, the farms under 20 acres fell by more than 900 in number; those between 50 and 75 acres fell from 8,253 to 6,370; the same thing occurred with all other farms under 100 acres. On the other hand, during the same twenty years, the number of large farms increased; those of 300-500 acres rose from 7,771 to 8,410, those of more than 500 acres from 2.755 to 3,914, those of more than 1,000 acres from 492 to 582.

time, the area under cultivation increased, from 1846 to 1856, by 464,119 acres, without reckoning the great area in the Eastern Counties which was transformed from rabbit warrens and poor pastures into magnificent cornfields It has already been seen that, at the same time, the total number of persons employed in agriculture fell. As fa as the actual agricultural labourers of both sexes and of all ages are concerned, their number fell from 1,241,396, in 1851, to ,163,-217 in 1861.[1] If the English Registrar-General therefore, rightly remarks: "The increase of farmers and farm-labourers, since 1801, bears no kind of proportion . . . to the increase of agricultural produce,"[2] this disproportion obtains much more for the last period, when a positive decrease of the agricultural population went hand in hand with increase of the area under cultivation, with more intensive cultivation, unheard-of accumulation of the capital incorporated with the soil, and devoted to its working, an augmentation in the products of the soil without parallel in the history of English agriculture, plethoric rent-rolls of landlords, and growing wealth of the capitalist farmers. If we take this, together with the swift, unbroken extension of the markets, viz., the towns, and the reign of Free Trade, then the agricultural laborer was at last, *post tot discrimina rerum,* placed in circumstances that ought, *secundum artem,* to have made him drunk with happiness.

But Professor Rogers comes to the conclusion that the lot of the English agricultural labourer of to-day, not to speak of his predecessor in the last half on the 14th and in the 15th century, but only compared with his predecessor from 1770 to 1780, has changed for the worse to an extraordinary extent, that "the peasant has again become a serf," and a serf worse fed and worse clothed.[3] Dr. Julian Hunter, in his epoch-making report on the dwellings of the agricultural labourers, says: "The cost of the hind" (a name for the agricultural labourer, inherited from time of serfdom) "is fixed at the

---

[1] The number of shepherds increased from 12,517 to 25,559.

[2] Census. l. c., p. 36.

[3] Rogers. l. c. p. 693, p. 10. Mr. Rogers belongs to the Liberal School, is a personal friend of Cobden and Bright, and therefore no laudator temporis acti.

lowest possible amount on which he can live . . . the supplies of wages and shelter are not calculated on the profit to be derived from him. He is a zero in farming calculations.[1] . . . The means [of subsistence] being always supposed to be a fixed quantity.[2] As to any further reduction of his income, he may say, *nihil habeo nihil curo.* He has no fears for the future, because he has now only the spare supply necessary to keep him. He has reached the zero from which are dated the calculations of the farmer. Come what will, he has no share either in prosperity or adversity."[3]

In the year 1863, an official inquiry took place into the conditions of nourishment and labour of the criminals condemned to transportation and penal servitude. The results are recorded in two voluminous blue books. Among other things it is said: "From an elaborate comparison between the diet of convicts in the convict prisons in England, and that of paupers in workhouses and of free labourers in the same country . . . it certainly appears that the former are much better fed than either of the two other classes,"[4] whilst "the amount of labour required from an ordinary convict under penal servitude is about one half of what would be done by an ordinary day labourer."[5] A few characteristic depositions of witnesses: John Smith, governor of the Edinburgh prison, deposes: No. 5056. "The diet of the English prisons [is] superior to that of ordinary labourers in England." No. 50. "It is the fact . . . that the ordinary agricultural labourers in Scotland very seldom get any meat at all." Answer No. 3047. "Is there anything that you are aware of to account for the necessity of feeding them very much better than ordinary labourers?—Certainly not." No. 3048. "Do you think that further experiments ought to be made in order

---

[1] Public Health. Seventh Report, 1864, p. 242. It is therefore nothing unusual either for the landlord to raise a labourer's rent as soon as he hears that he is earning a little more, or for the farmer to lower the wage of the labourer, "because his wife has found a tade," l. c.

[2] l. c. p. 135. [3] l. c. p. 134.

[4] Report of the Commissioners . . . . relating to transportation and penal servitude, Lond. 1863, pp. 42, 50.

[5] l. c. p. 77. Memorandum by the Lord Chief Justice.

to ascertain whether a dietary might not be hit upon for prisoners employed on public works nearly approaching to the dietary of free labourers?[1] . . . "He [the agricultural labourer] might say: 'I work hard, and have not enough to eat, and when in prison I did not work harder where I had plenty to eat, and therefore it is better for me to be in prison again than here.'"[2] From the tables appended to the first volume of the Report I have compiled the annexed comparative summary.

WEEKLY AMOUNT OF NUTRIMENT.

	Quantity of Nitrogenous Ingredients.	Quantity of Non-Nitrogenous Ingredients.	Quantity of Mineral Matter.	Total.
	Ounces	*Ounces*	*Ounces*	*Ounces*
Portland (convict	28·95	150·06	4·68	183.69
Sailor in the Navy	29·03	152·91	4:52	187·06
Soldier	25·55	114·49	3·94	143.98
Working Coachmaker	24·53	162·06	4·23	190:82
Compositor	21·24	100·83	3·12	125:19
Agricultural labourer	17:73	118·06	3·29	139·08[3]

The general result of the inquiry by the medical commission of 1863, on the food of the lowest fed classes, is already known to the reader. He will remember that the diet of a great part of the agricultural labourer's families is below the minimum necessary "to arrest starvation diseases." This is especially the case in all the purely rural districts of Cornwall, Devon, Somerset, Wilts, Stafford, Oxford, Berks, and Herts. "The nourishment obtained by the labourer himself," says Dr. E. Smith, "is larger than the average quantity indicates, since he eats a larger share . . . necessary to enable him to per-

[1] l. c. Vol. II. Minutes of Evidence.
[2] l. c. Vol. I. Appendix p. 280.
[3] l. c. pp. 274, 275.

form his labour . . . of food than the other members of the family, including in the poorer districts nearly all the meat and bacon. . . . The quantity of food obtained by the wife and also by the children at the period of rapid growth, is in many cases, in almost every county, deficient, and particularly in nitrogen."[1] The male and female servants living with the farmers themselves are sufficiently nourished. Their number fell from 288,277 in 1851, to 204,962 in 1861. "The labour of women in the fields," says Dr. Smith, "whatever may be its disadvantages, . . . is under present circumstances of great advantage to the family, since it adds that amount of income which . . . provides shoes and clothing and pays the rent, and thus enables the family to be better fed."[2] One of the most remarkable results of the inquiry was that the agricultural labourer of England, as compared with other parts of the United Kingdom, "is considerably the worst fed," as the appended table shows:

Quantities of Carbon and Nitrogen weekly consumed by an average agricultural adult.

	Carbon, grains.	Nitrogen, grains.
England	46·673	1·594
Wales	48·354	2·031
Scotland	48·980	2·348
Ireland	43·366	2·434.[3]

[1] Public Health, Sixth Report, 1863, pp. 238, 249, 261, 262.
[2] l. c. p. 262.
[3] l. c. p. 17. The English agricultural labourer receives only ¼ as much milk and ½ as much bread as the Irish. Arthur Young in his "Tour through Ireland," at the beginning of this century, already noticed the better nourishment of the latter. The reason is simply this, that poor Irish farmer is incomparably more humane than the rich English. As regards Wales, that which is said in the text holds only for the south-west. All the doctors there agree that the increase of the deathrate through tuberculosis, scrofula, etc., increases in intensity with the deterioration of the physical condition of the population, and all ascribe this deterioration to poverty. "His (the farm labourer's) keep is reckoned at about five pence a day, but in many districts it was said to be of much less cost to the farmer," [himself very poor]. . . . "A morsel of the salt meat or bacon, . . . salted and dried to the texture of mahogany, and hardly worth the difficult process of assimilation . . . . is used to flavour a large quantity of broth or gruel, of meal and leeks, and day after day this is the labourer's dinner." The advance of industry resulted for him, in this harsh and damp climate, in "the abandonment of the solid homespun clothing in favour of the cheap and so-called cotton goods," and of stronger

"To the insufficient quantity and miserable quality of the house accommodation generally had," says Dr. Simon, in his official Health Report, "by our agricultural labourers, almost every page of Dr. Hunter's report bears testimony. And gradually, for many years past, the state of the labourer in these respects has been deteriorating, house-room being now greatly more difficult for him to find, and, when found, greatly less suitable to his needs than, perhaps, for centuries had been the case. Especially within the last twenty or thirty years, the evil has been in very rapid increase, and the household circumstances of the labourer are now in the highest degree deplorable. Except in so far as they whom his labour enriches, see fit to treat him with a kind of pitiful indulgence, he is quite peculiarly helpless in the matter. Whether he shall find house-room on the land which he contributes to till, whether the house-room which he gets shall be human or swineish,

drinks for so-called tea. "The agriculturist, after several hours' exposure to wind and rain, gains his cottage to sit by a fire of peat or of balls of clay and small coal kneaded together, from which volumes of carbonic and sulphurous acids are poured forth. His walls are of mud and stones, his floor the bare earth which was there before the hut was built, his roof a mass of loose and sodden thatch. Every crevice is stopped to maintain warmth, and in an atmosphere of diabolic odour, with a mud floor, with his only clothes drying on his back, he often sups and sleeps with his wife and children. Obstetricians who have passed parts of the night in such cabins have described how they found their feet sinking in the mud of the floor, and they were forced (easy task) to drill a hole through the wall to effect a little private respiration. It was attested by numerous witnesses in various grades of life, that to these insanitary influences, and many more, the underfed peasant was nightly exposed, and of the result, a debilitated and scrofulous people, there was no want of evidence. . . . . The statements of the relieving officers of Carmarthenshire and Cardiganshire show in a striking way the same state of things. There is besides "a plague more horrible still, the great number of idiots." Now a word on the climatic conditions. "A strong south-west wind blows over the whole country for 8 or 9 months in the year, bringing with it torrents of rain, which discharge principally upon the western slopes of the hills. Trees are rare, except in sheltered places, and where not protected, are blown out of all shape. The cottages generally crouch under some bank, or often in a ravine or quarry, and none but the smallest sheep and native cattle can live on the pastures. . . . . The young people migrate to the eastern mining districts of Glamorgan and Monmouth. Carmarthenshire is the breeding ground of the mining population and their hospital. The population can therefore barely maintain its numbers." Thus in Cardiganshire:

	1851.	1861.
Males	45,155	44,446
Females	52,459	52,955
	97,614	97,401

Dr. Hunter's Report in Public Health, Seventh Report. 1864. pp. 498-502 passim.

whether he shall have the little space of garden that so vastly
lessens the pressure of his poverty—all this does not depend
on his willingness and ability to pay reasonable rent for the
decent accommodation he requires, but depends on the use
which others may see fit to make of their 'right to do as they
will with their own.' However large may be a farm, there
is no law that a certain proportion of labourers' dwellings
(much less of decent dwellings) shall be upon it; nor does any
law reserve for the labourer ever so little right in that soil to
which his industry is as needful as sun and rain. . . . An
extraneous element weighs the balance heavily against him
. . . the influence of the Poor Law in its provisions concerning settlement and chargeability.[1] Under this influence,
each parish has a pecuniary interest in reducing to a minimum
the number of its resident labourers:—for, unhappily, agricultural labour instead of implying a safe and permanent independence for the hard-working labourer and his family, implies for the most part only a longer or shorter circuit to
eventual pauperism—a pauperism which, during the whole circuit, is so near, that any illness or temporary failure of occupation necessitates immediate recourse to parochial relief—
and thus all residence of agricultural population in a parish is
glaringly an addition to its poor rates. . . . Large proprietors[2] . . . have but to resolve that there shall be no
labourers' dwellings on their estates, and their estates will
thenceforth be virtually free from half their responsibility for
the poor. How far it has been intended, in the English constitution and law, that this kind of unconditional property in
land should be acquirable, and that a landlord, 'doing as he
wills with his own,' should be able to treat the cultivators
of the soil as aliens, whom he may expel from his territory, is
a question which I do not pretend to discuss. . . . For
that (power) of eviction . . . does not exist only in

---

[1] In 1865 this law was improved to some extent. It will soon be learnt from
experience that tinkering of this sort is of no use.

[2] In order to understand that which follows, we must remember that "Close
Villages" are those whose owners are one or two large landlords. "Open villages,"
those whose soil belongs to many smaller landlords. It is in the latter that building
speculators can build cottages and lodging-houses.

theory. On a very large scale it prevails in practice—prevails
. . . as a main governing condition in the household circumstances of agricultural labour. . . . As regards the
extent of the evil, it may suffice to refer to the evidence which
Dr. Hunter has compiled from the last census, that destruction of houses, notwithstanding increased local demands for
them, had, during the last ten years, been in progress in 821
separate parishes or townships of England, so that irrespec-
tively of persons who had been forced to become non-resident
(that is in the parishes in which they work), these parishes
and townships were receiving in 1861, as compared with 1851,
a population 5⅓ per cent. greater, into house-room 4½ per
cent. less. . . . When the process of depopulation has
completed itself, the result, says Dr. Hunter, is a show-
village where the cottages have been reduced to a few, and
where none but persons who are needed as shepherds, gardeners, or game-keepers, are allowed to live; regular servants who
receive the good treatment usual to their class.[1] But the land
requires cultivation, and it will be found that the labourers
employed upon it are not the tenants of the owner, but that
they come from a neighboring open village, perhaps three
miles off, where a numerous small proprietary had received
them when their cottages were destroyed in the close villages
around. Where things are tending to the above result, often
the cottages which stand, testify, in their unrepaired and
wretched condition, to the extinction to which they are doomed.
They are seen standing in the various stages of natural decay.
While the shelter holds together, the labourer is permitted to
rent it, and glad enough he will often be to do so, even at the
price of decent lodging. But no repair, no improvement shall
it receive, except such as its penniless occupants can supply.
And when at last it becomes quite uninhabitable—uninhabit-

---

[1] A show village of this kind looks very nice, but is as unreal as the villages that
Catherine II. saw on her journey to the Crimea. In recent times the shepherd also
has often been banished from the show villages; *e.g.*, near Market Harboro' is a
sheep-farm of about 500 acres, which only employs the labour of one man. To
reduce the long trudges over these wide plains, the beautiful pastures of Leicester and
Northampton, the shepherd used to get a cottage on the farm. Now they give him
a thirteenth shilling a week for lodging, that he must find far away in an open
village.

able even to the humblest standard of serfdom—it will be
but one more destroyed cottage, and future poor-rates will be
somewhat lightened. While great owners are thus escaping
from poor-rates through the depopulation of lands over which
they have control, the nearest town or open village receive the
evicted labourers: the nearest, I say, but this "nearest" may
mean three or four miles distant from the farm where the labourer has his daily toil. To that daily toil there will then
have to be added, as though it were nothing, the daily need of
walking six or eight miles for power of earning his bread.
And whatever farm-work is done by his wife and children, is
done at the same disadvantage. Nor is this nearly all the toil
which the distance occasions him. In the open village, cot-
tage-speculators buy scraps of land, which they throng as
densely as they can with the cheapest of all possible hovels.
And into those wretched habitations (which, even if they ad-
join the open country, have some of the worst features of the
worst town residences) crowd the agricultural labourers of
England.[1] . . . Nor on the other hand must it be supposed that even when the labourer is housed upon the lands
which he cultivates, his household circumstances are generally
such as his life of productive industry would seem to deserve.
Even on princely estates . . . his cottage . . . may

---

[1] "The labourers' houses (in the open villages, which, of course, are always over-
crowded) are usually in rows, built with their backs against the extreme edge of the
plot of land which the builder could call his, and on this account are not allowed
light and air, except from the front." (Dr. Hunter's Report, l. c. ,p. 135.) Very
often the beerseller or grocer of the village is at the same time the letter of its
houses. In this case the agricultural labourer finds in him a second master, besides
the farmer. He must be his customer as well as his tenant. "The hind with his
10s. a week, minus a rent of £4 a year . . . . is obliged to buy at the seller's
own terms, his modicum of tea, sugar, flour, soap, candles, and beer." (l. c., p.
132.) These open villages form, in fact, the "penal settlements" of the English
agricultural proletariat. Many of the cottages are simply lodging-houses, through
which all the rabble of the neighbourhood passes. The country labourer and his
family who had often, in a way truly wonderful, preserved, under the foulest conditions, a thoroughness and purity of character, go, in these, utterly to the devil.
it is, of course, the fashion amongst the aristocratic shylocks to shrug their shoulders
pharisaically at the building speculators, the small landlords, and the open villages.
They know well enough that their "close villages" and "show villages" are the birth-
places of the open villages, and could not exist without them. "The labourers
. . . . were it not for the small owners, would, for by far the most part, have
to sleep under the trees of the farms on which they work." (l. c., p. 135.) The
system of "open" and "closed" villages obtains in all the Midland counties and
throughout the East of England.

be of the meanest description. There are landlords who deem any sty good enough for their labourer and his family, and who yet do not disdain to drive with him the hardest possible bargain for rent.[1] It may be but a ruinous one-bed-roomed hut, having no fire-grate, no privy, no opening window, no water supply but the ditch, no garden—but the labourer is helpless against the wrong. . . . And the Nuisances Removal Acts . . . are . . . a mere dead letter . . . in great part dependent for their working on such cottage owners as the one from whom his (the labourer's) hovel is rented. . . . From brighter, but exceptional scenes, it is requisite in the interests of justice, that attention should again be drawn to the overwhelming preponderance of facts which are a reproach to the civilization of England. Lamentable indeed, must be the case, when, notwithstanding all that is evident with regard to the quality of the present accommodation, it is the common conclusion of competent observers that even the general badness of dwellings is an, evil infinitely less urgent than their mere numerical insufficiency. For years the overcrowding of rural labourer's dwellings has been a matter of deep concern, not only to persons who care for sanitary good, but to persons who care for decent and moral life. For again and again in phrases so uniform that they seem stereotyped, reporters on the spread of epidemic disease in rural districts, have insisted on the extreme importance of that over-crowding, as an influence which renders it a quite hopeless task, to attempt the limiting of any infection which is introduced. And again and again it has been pointed out that, notwithstanding the many salubrious influences which there are in country life, the crowding which

---

[1] "The employer . . . . is . . . . directly or indirectly securing to himself the profit on a man employed at 10s. a week, and receiving from this poor hind £4 or £5 annual rent for houses not worth £20 in a really free market, but maintained at their artificial value by the power of the owner to say 'Use my house, or go seek a hiring elsewhere, without a character from me.' . . . . Does a man wish to better himself, to go as a plate-layer on the railway, or to begin quarry-work, the same power is ready with 'Work for me at this low rate of wages, or begone at a week's notice; take your pig with you, and get what you can for the potatoes growing in your garden.' Should his interest appear to be better served by it, an enhanced rent is sometimes preferred in these cases by the owner (*i.e.* the farmer) as the penalty for leaving his service." (Dr. Hunter, l. c., p. 132.)

so favours the extension of contagious disease, also favours the origination of disease which is not contagious. And those who have denounced the over-crowded state of our rural population have not been silent as to a further mischief. Even where their primary concern has been only with the injury to health, often almost perforce they have referred to other relations on the subject. In showing how frequently it happens that adult persons of both sexes, married and unmarried, are huddled together in single small sleeping rooms, their reports have carried the conviction that, under the circumstances they describe, decency must always be outraged, and morality almost of necessity must suffer.[1] Thus, for instance, in the appendix of my last annual report, Dr. Ord, reporting on an outbreak of fever at Wing, in Buckinghamshire, mentions how a young man who had come thither from Wingrave with fever, "in the first days of his illness slept in a room with nine other persons. Within a fortnight several of these persons were attacked, and in the course of a few weeks five out of the nine had fever, and one died." . . . From Dr. Harvey, of St. George's Hospital, who, on private professional business, visited Wing during the time of the epidemic, I received information exactly in the sense of the above report. . . . "A young woman having fever, lay at night in a room occupied by her father and mother, her bastard child, two young men (her brothers), and her two sisters, each with a bastard child—10 persons in all. A few weeks ago 13 persons slept in it."[2]

Dr. Hunter investigated 5,375 cottages of agricultural labourers, not only in the purely agricultural districts, but in all counties of England. Of these, 2,195 had only one bed-

---

[1] "New married couples are no edifying study for grown-up brothers and sisters; and though instances must not be recorded, sufficient data are remembered to warrant the remark, that great depression and sometimes death are the lot of the female participator in the offence of incest." (Dr. Hunter, l. c., p. 137.) A member of the rural police who had for many years been a detective in the worst quarters of London, says of the girls of his village: "their boldness and shamelessness I never saw equalled during some years of police life and detective duty in the worst parts of London. . . . . They live like pigs, great boys and girls, mothers and fathers, all sleeping in one room, in many instances." (Child. Empl. Com. Sixth Report, 1867, p. 77 sq. 155.)

[2] Public Health. Seventh Report, 1864, pp. 9. 14 passim.

room (often at the same time used as living-room), 2,930 only two, and 250, more than two. I will give a few specimens culled from a dozen counties.

(1.) BEDFORDSHIRE.

Wrestlingworth. Bedrooms about 12 feet long and 10 broad, although many are smaller than this. The small, one-storied cots are often divided by partitions into two bedrooms, one bed frequently in a kitchen, 5 feet 6 inches in height. Rent, £3 a year. The tenants have to make their own privies, the landlord only supplies a hole. As soon as one has made a privy, it is made use of by the whole neighborhood. One house, belonging to a family called Richardson, was of quite unapproachable beauty. "Its plaster walls bulged very like a lady's dress in a curtsey. One gable end was convex, the other concave, and on this last, unfortunately, stood the chimney, a curved tube of clay and wood like an elephant's trunk. A long stick served as prop to prevent the chimney from falling. The doorway and window were rhomboidal." Of 17 houses visited, only 4 had more than one bedroom, and those four overcrowded. The cots with one bedroom sheltered 3 adults and 3 children, a married couple with 6 children, &c.

Dunton. High rents, from £4 to £5; weekly wages of the man, 10s. They hope to pay the rent by the straw-plaiting of the family. The higher the rent, the greater the number that must work together to pay it. Six adults, living with 4 children in one sleeping apartment, pay £3 10s. for it. The cheapest house in Dunton, 15 feet long externally, 10 broad, let for £3. Only one of the houses investigated had 2 bedrooms. A little outside the village, a house whose "tenants dunged against the house-side," the lower 9 inches of the door eaten away through sheer rottenness; the doorway, a single opening closed at night by a few bricks, ingeniously pushed up after shutting and covered with some matting. Half a window, with glass and frame, had gone the way of all flesh. Here, without furniture, huddled together, were 3 adults and 5 children. Dunton is not worse than the rest of Biggleswade Union.

(2.) Berkshire.

Beenham. In June, 1864, a man, his wife and 4 children lived in a cot (one-storied cottage). A daughter came home from service with scarlet fever. She died. One child sickened and died. The mother and one child were down with typhus when Dr. Hunter was called in. The father and one child slept outside, but the difficulty of securing isolation was seen here, for in the crowded market of the miserable village lay the linen of the fever stricken household, waiting for the wash. The rent of H.'s house, 1s. a week; one bedroom for man, wife, and 6 children. One house let for 8d. a-week, 14 feet 6 inches long, 7 feet broad; kitchen, 6 feet high; the bedroom without window, fire-place, door, or opening, except into the lobby; no garden. A man lived here for a little while, with two grown-up daughters and one grown-up son; father and son slept on the bed, the girls in the passage. Each of the latter had a child while the family was living here, but one went to the workhouse for her confinement and then came home.

(3.) Buckinghamshire.

30 cottages—on 1,000 acres of land—contained here about 130-140 persons. The parish of *Bradenham* comprises 1,000 acres; it numbered, in 1851, 36 houses and a population of 84 males and 54 females. This inequality of the sexes was partly remedied in 1861, when they numbered 98 males and 87 females; increase in 10 years of 14 men and 33 women. Meanwhile, the number of houses was one less.

Winslow. Great part of this newly built in good style; demand for houses appears very marked, since very miserable cots let at 1s. to 1s. 3d. per week.

Water Eaton. Here the landlords, in view of the increasing population, have destroyed about 20 per cent. of the existing houses. A poor labourer, who had to go about 4 miles to his work, answered the question, whether he could not find a cot nearer: "No; they know better than to take a man in with my large family."

Tinker's End, near Winslow. A bedroom in which were 4 adults and 4 children; 11 feet long, 9 feet broad, 6 feet 5 inches high at its highest part; another 11 feet 3 inches by 9 feet, 5 feet 10 inches high, sheltered 6 persons. Each of these families had less space than is considered necessary for a convict. No house had more than one bedroom, not one of them a back-door; water very scarce; weekly rent from 1s. 4d. to 2s. In 16 of the houses visited, only 1 man that earned 10s. a week. The quantity of air for each person under the circumstances just described corresponds to that which he would have if he were shut up in a box of 4 feet measuring each way, the whole night. But then, the ancient dens afforded a certain amount of unintentional ventilation.

(4.) CAMBRIDGESHIRE.

Gamblingay belongs to several landlords. It contains the wretchedest cots to be found anywhere. Much straw-plaiting. "A deadly lassitude, a hopeless surrendering up to filth," reigns in Gamblingay. The neglect in its centre, becomes mortification at its extremities, north and south, where the houses are rotting to pieces. The absentee landlords bleed this poor rookery too freely. The rents are very high; 8 or 9 persons packed in one sleeping apartment, in 2 cases 6 adults, each with 1 or 2 children in one small bedroom.

(5.) ESSEX.

In this county, diminutions in the number of persons and of cottages go, in many parishes, hand in hand. In not less than 22 parishes, however, the destruction of houses has not prevented increase of population, or has not brought about that expulsion which, under the name "migration to towns," generally occurs. In Fingringhoe, a parish of 3443 acres, were in 1851, 145 houses; in 1861, only 110. But the people did not wish to go away, and managed even to increase under these circumstances. In 1851, 252 persons inhabited 61 houses, but in 1861, 262 persons were squeezed into 49 houses. In Basilden, in 1851, 157 persons lived on 1827 acres, in 35 houses; at the end of ten years, 180 persons in 27 houses. In the parishes of Fingringhoe, South Farnbridge, Widford, Basilden, and Ramsden Crags, in 1851, 1392 persons were living on 8449 acres in 316 houses; in 1861, on the same area, 1473 persons in 249 houses.

(6.) HEREFORDSHIRE.

This little county has suffered more from the "eviction-spirit" than any other in England. At Nadby, over-crowded cottages generally, with only 2 bedrooms, belonging for the most part to the farmers. They easily let them for £3 or £4 a-year, and paid a weekly wage of 9s.

(7.) HUNTINGDON.

Hartford had, in 1851, 87 houses; shortly after this, 19 cottages were destroyed in this small parish of 1720 acres; population in 1831, 452; in 1852, 832; and in 1861, 341. 14 cottages, each with 1 bedroom, were visited. In one, a married couple, 3 grown-up sons, 1 grown-up daughter, 4 children—in all 10; in another, 3 adults, 6 children. One of these rooms, in which 8 people slept, was 12 feet 10 inches long, 12 feet 2 inches broad, 6 feet 9 inches high: the average, without making any deduction for projections into the apartment, gave about 130 cubic feet per head. In the 14 sleeping rooms, 34 adults and 33 children. These cottages are seldom provided with gardens, but many of the inmates are able to farm small allotments at 10s. or 12s. per rood. These allotments are at a distance from the houses, which are without privies. The family "must either go to the allotment to deposit their ordures," or, as happens in this place, saving your presence, "use a closet with a trough set like a drawer in a chest of drawers, and drawn out weekly and conveyed to the allotment to be emptied where its contents were wanted." In Japan, the circle of life-conditions moves more decently than this.

(8.) LINCOLNSHIRE.

Langtoft. A man lives here, in Wright's house, with his wife, her mother, and 5 children; the house has a front kitchen, scullery, bedroom over the front kitchen; front kitchen and bedroom, 12 feet 2 inches by 9 feet 5 inches; the whole ground floor, 21 feet 2 inches by 9 feet 5 inches. The bedroom is a garret; the walls run together into the roof like a sugar-loaf, a dormer-window opening in front. "Why did he live here? On account of the garden? No; it is very small. Rent? High, 1s. 3d. per week. Near his work? No; 6 miles away, so that he walks daily, to and fro, 12 miles. He lived there, because it was a tenantable cot," and because he wanted to have a cot for himself alone, anywhere, at any price, and in any conditions. The following are the statistics of 12 houses in Langtoft, with 12 bedrooms, 38 adults. and 36 children.

TWELVE HOUSES IN LANGTOFT.

Houses.	Bedrooms.	Adults.	Children.	Number of persons.	Houses.	Bedrooms.	Adults.	Children.	Number of persons.
No. 1.	1	3	5	8	No. 7.	1	3	3	6
„ 2.	1	4	3	7	„ 8.	1	3	2	5
„ 3.	1	4	4	8	„ 9.	1	2	0	2
„ 4.	1	5	4	9	„ 10.	1	2	3	5
„ 5.	1	2	2	4	„ 11.	1	3	3	6
„ 6.	1	5	3	8	„ 12.	1	2	4	6

(9.) KENT.

Kennington, very seriously over-populated in 1859, when diphtheria appeared, and the parish doctor instituted a medical inquiry into the condition of the poorer classes. He found that in this locality, where much labour is employed, various cots had been destroyed and no new ones built. In one district stood four houses, named birdcages; each had 4 rooms of the following dimensions in feet and inches:

Kitchen: 9 ft. 5 by 8 ft. 11 by 6 ft. 6.
Scullery: 8 ft. 6 by 4 ft. 6 by 6 ft. 6.
Bedroom: 8 ft. 5 by 5 ft. 10 by 6 ft. 3.
Bedroom: 8 ft. 3 by 8 ft. 4 by 6 ft. 3.

(10.) NORTHAMPTONSHIRE.

Brinworth, Pickford and *Floore:* in these villages in the winter 20—30 men were lounging about the streets from want of work. The farmers do not always till sufficiently the corn and turnip lands, and the landlord has found it best to throw all his farms together into 2 or 3. Hence want of employment. Whilst on one side of the wall, the land calls for labour, on the other side the defrauded labourers are casting at it longing glances. Feverishly overworked in summer, and half-starved in winter, it is no wonder if they say in their peculiar dialect, "the parson and gentlefolk seem frit to death at them."

At Floore, instances, in one bedroom of the smallest size, of couples with 4, 5, 6 children; 3 adults with 5 children; a couple with grandfather and 6 children down with scarlet fever, &c.; in two houses with two bedrooms, two families of 8 and 9 adults respectively.

(11.) WILTSHIRE.

Stratton. 31 houses visited, 8 with only one bedroom. Pentill, in the same parish: a cot let at 1s. 3d. weekly with 4 adults and 4 children, had nothing good about it, except the walls, from the floor of rough-hewn pieces of stones to the roof of worn-out thatch.

(12.) WORCESTERSHIRE.

House-destruction here not quite so excessive; yet from 1851 to 1861, the number of inhabitants to each house on the average, has risen from 4:2 to 4·6.

Badsey. Many cots and little gardens here. Some of the farmers declare that the cots are "a great nuisance here, because they bring the poor." On the statement of one gentleman: "The poor are none the better for them; if you build 500 they will let fast enough, in fact, the more you build, the more they want," (according to him the houses give birth to the inhabitants, who then by a law of Nature press on "the means of housing"). Dr. Hunter remarks: "Now these poor must come from somewhere, and as there is no particular attraction, such as doles, at Badsey, it must be repulsion from some other unfit place, which will send them here. If each could find an allotment near his work, he would not prefer Badsey, where he pays for his scrap of ground twice as much as the farmer pays for his."

The continual emigration to the towns, the continual formation of surplus-population in the country through the concentration of farms, conversion of arable land into pasture, machinery, &c., and the continual eviction of the agricultural population by the destruction of their cottages, go hand in hand. The more empty the district is of men, the greater is its "relative surplus-population," the greater is their pressure on the means of employment, the greater is the absolute excess of the agricultural population over the means for housing it, the greater, therefore, in the villages is the local surplus-population and the most pestilential packing together of human beings. The packing together of knots of men in scattered little villages and small country towns corresponds to the forcible draining of men from the surface of the land. The continuous superseding of the agricultural labourers, in spite of their diminishing number and the increasing mass of their products, gives birth to their pauperism. Their pauperism is ultimately a motive to their eviction and the chief source of their miserable housing which breaks down their last power of resistance, and makes them mere slaves of the landed proprietors and the farmers.[1] Thus the minimum of wages becomes a law of Nature to them. On the other hand, the land, in spite of its constant "relative surplus-population," is at the same time under-populated. This is seen, not only locally at the points where the efflux of men to towns, mines, railroad-making, &c., is most marked. It is to be seen everywhere, in harvest-time as well as in spring and summer, at those frequently recurring times when English agriculture, so careful and intensive, wants extra hands. There are always too many agricultural labourers for the ordinary, and always too few for the exceptional or temporary needs of the cultivation of the soil.[2] Hence we find in the official documents contradictory complaints from the same places of deficiency and excess of labour simultaneously. The temporary or local want of labour brings about no rise in wages, but a forcing of the women and children into the fields, and exploitation at an age constantly lowered. As soon as the exploitation of the

[1] "The heaven-born employment of the hind gives dignity even to this position. He is not a slave, but a soldier of peace, and deserves his place in married men's quarters to be provided by the landlord, who has claimed a power of enforced labour similar to that the country demands of the soldier. He no more receives market price for his work than does the soldier. Like the soldier he is caught young, ignorant, knowing only his own trade, and his own locality. Early marriage and the operation of the various laws of settlement affect the one as enlistment and the Mutiny Act affect the other." (Dr. Hunter, l. c., p. 132.) Sometimes an exceptionally soft-hearted landlord relents at the solitude he has created. "It is a melancholy thing to stand alone in one's country," said Lord Leicester, when complimented on the completion of Hookham. "I look around and not a house is to be seen but mine. I am the giant of Giant Castle, and have eat up all my neighbours."

[2] A similar movement is seen during the last ten years in France; in proportion as capitalist production there takes possession of agriculture, it drives the "surplus" agricultural population into the towns. Here also we find deterioration in the housing and other conditions at the source of the surplus-population. On the special "prolétariat foncier," to which this system of parcelling out the land has given rise, see, among others, the work of Colins, already quoted, and Karl Marx "Der Achtzehnte Brumaire des Louis Bonaparte." 2nd edition. Hamburg, 1869, pp. 56, &c. In 1846, the town population in France was represented by 24.42, the agricultural by 75.58; in 1861, the town by 28.86, the agricultural by 71.4 per cent. During the last 5 years, the diminution of the agricultural percentage of the population has been yet more marked. As early as 1846, Pierre Dupont in his "Ouvriers" sang:

Mal vêtus, logés dans des trous,
Sous les combles, dans les décombres,
Nous vivons avec les hiboux
Et les larrons, amis des ombres.

women and children takes place on a larger scale, it becomes
in turn a new means of making a surplus-population of the
male agricultural labourer and of keeping down his wage. In
the east of England thrives a beautiful fruit of this vicious
circle—the so-called gang-system, to which I must briefly return here.[1]

The gang-system obtains almost exclusively in the counties
of Lincoln, Huntingdon, Cambridge, Norfolk, Suffolk, and
Nottingham, here and there in the neighbouring counties of
Northampton, Bedford, and Rutland. Lincolnshire will serve
us as an example. A large part of this country is new land,
marsh formerly, or even, as in others of the eastern counties
just named, won lately from the sea. The steam-engine has
worked wonders in the way of drainage. What were once
fens and sandbanks, bear now a luxuriant sea of corn and the
highest of rents. The same thing holds of the alluvial lands
won by human endeavor, as in the island of Axholme and
other parishes on the banks of the Trent. In proportion as
the new farms arose, not only were no new cottages built: old
ones were demolished, and the supply of labour had to come
from open villages, miles away, by long roads that wound
along the sides of the hills. There alone had the population
formerly found shelter from the incessant floods of the winter-
time. The labourers that dwell on the farms of 400—1000
acres (they are called "confined labourers") are solely employed on such kinds of agricultural work as is permanent,
difficult, and carried on by aid of horses. For every 100
acres there is, on an average, scarcely one cottage. A fen
farmer, *e.g.*, gave evidence before the Commission of Inquiry: "I farm 320 acres, all arable land. I have not one
cottage on my farm. I have only one labourer on my farm
now. I have four horsemen lodging about. We get light
work done by gangs."[2] The soil requires much light field
labour, such as weeding, hoeing, certain processes of manuring, removing of stones, &c. This is done by the gangs, or organised bands that dwell in the open villages.

[1] "Sixth and last Report of the Children's Employment Commission," published
at the end of March, 1867. It deals solely with the agricultural.
[2] "Child. Empl. Comm., VI. Report." Evidence 173, p. 37.

The gang consists of 10 to 40 or 50 persons, women, young persons of both sexes (13-18 years of age, although the boys are for the most part eliminated at the age of 13), and children of both sexes (6-13 years of age). At the head is the gang-master, always an ordinary agricultural labourer, generally what is called a bad lot, a scapegrace, unsteady, drunken, but with a dash of enterprise and *savior faire*. He is the recruiting-sergeant for the gang, which works under him, not under the farmer. He generally arranges with the latter for piece-work, and his income, which on the average is not very much above that of an ordinary agricultural labourer,[1] depends almost entirely upon the dexterity with which he manages to extract within the shortest time the greatest possible amount of labour from his gang. The farmers have discovered that women work steadily only under the direction of men, but that women and children, once set going, impetuously spend their life-force— as Fourier knew —while the adult male labourer is shrewd enough to economise his as much as he can. The gang-master goes from one farm to another, and thus employs his gang from 6 to 8 months in the year. Employment by him is, therefore, much more lucrative and more certain for the labouring families, than employment by the individual farmer, who only employs children occasionally. This circumstance so completely rivets his influence in the open villages that children are generally only to be hired through his instrumentality. The lending out of these individually, independently of the gang, is his second trade.

The "drawbacks" of the system are the over-work of the children and young persons, the enormous marches that they make daily to and from the farms, 5, 6, and sometimes 7 miles distant, finally, the demoralisation of the gang. Although the gangmaster, who, in some districts is called "the driver," is armed with a long stick, he uses it but seldom, and complaints of brutal treatment are exceptional. He is a democratic emperor, or a kind of Pied Piper of Hamelin. He must there-

---

[1] Some gangmasters, however, have worked themselves up to the position of farmers of 500 acres, or proprietors of whole rows of houses.

fore be popular with his subjects, and he binds them to himself by the charms of the gipsy life under his direction.
Coarse freedom, a noisy jollity, and obscenest impudence give
attractions to the gang. Generally the gangmaster pays up
in a public house; then he returns home at the head of the
procession reeling drunk, propped up right and left by a
stalwart virago, while children and young persons bring up
the rear, boisterous, and singing chaffing and bawdy songs.
On the return journey what Fourier calls "phanerogamie," is
the order of the day. The getting with child of girls of 13
and 14 by their male companions of the same age, is common.
The open villages which supply the contingent of the gang,
become Sodoms and Gomorrahs,[1] and have twice as high a
rate of illegitimate births as the rest of the kingdom. The
moral character of girls bred in these schools, when married
women, was shown above. Their children, when opium does
not give them the finishing stroke, are born recruits of the
gang.

The gang in its classical form just described, is called the
public, common, or tramping gang. For there are also private
gangs. These are made up in the same way as the common
gang, but count fewer members, and work, not under a gang-
master, but under some old farm servant, whom the farmer
does not know how to employ in any better way. The gipsy
fun has vanished here, but according to all witnesses, the payment and treatment of the children is worse.

The gang-system, which during the last years has steadily
increased,[2] clearly does not exist for the sake of the gang-
master. It exists for the enrichment of the large farmers,[3]
and indirectly of the landlords.[4] For the farmer there is no

---

[1] "Half the girls of Ludford have been ruined by going out" (in gangs). l. c.
p. 6, § 32.

[2] "They (gangs) have greatly increased of late years. In some places they are
said to have been introduced at comparatively late dates; in others where gangs
. . . . have been known for many years . . . . more and younger children
are employed in them." (l. c., p. 79, § 174.)

[3] "Small farmers never employ gangs." "It is not on poor land, but on land
which affords rent of from 40 to 50 shillings, that women and children are employed in the greatest numbers." (l. c., pp. 17, 14.)

[4] To one of these gentlemen the taste of his rent was so grateful that he in-
dignantly declared to the Commission of Inquiry that the whole hubbub was only

more ingenious method of keeping his labourers well below
the normal level, and yet of always having an extra hand
ready for extra work, of extracting the greatest possible
amount of labour with the least possible amount of money,[1]
and of making adult male labour "redundant." From the
exposition already made, it will be understood why, on the
one hand, a greater or less lack of employment for the
agricultural labourer is admitted, while on the other, the
gang-system is at the same time declared "necessary" on account of the want of adult male labour and its migration to
the towns.[2] The cleanly weeded land, and the uncleanly human weeds, of Lincolnshire, are pole and counterpole of
capitalistic production.[3]

due to the name of the system. If instead of "gang" it were called "the Agricultural Juvenile Industrial Self-supporting Association," everything would be all right.

[1] "Gang work is cheaper than other work; that is why they are employed," says a
former gangmaster (l. c., p. 17, § 14). "The gang-system is decidedly the cheapest for the farmer, and decidedly the worst for the children," says a farmer. (l. c.,
p. 16, § 3.)

[2] "Undoubtedly much of the work now done by children in gangs used to be done
by men and women. More men are out of work now where children and women
are employed than formerly." (l. c., p. 43, n. 202.) On the other hand, "the
labour question in some agricultural districts, particularly the arable, is becoming so
serious in consequence of emigration, and the facility afforded by railways for getting to large towns that I (the "I" is the steward of a great lord) think the services
of children are most indispensable." (l. c., p. 80, n. 180.) For the "labour question" in English agricultural districts, differently from the rest of the civilised
world, means the landlords' and farmers' question, viz., how it is possible, despite
an always increasing exodus of the agricultural folk, to keep up a sufficient relative
surplus-population in the country, and by means of it keep the wages of the agricultural labourer at a minimum?

[3] The "Public Health Report," where in dealing with the subject of children's
mortality, the gang-system is treated in passing, remains unknown to the press, and,
therefore, to the English public. On the other hand, the last report of the "Child.
Empl. Comm." afforded the press sensational copy always welcome. Whilst the
Liberal press asked how the fine gentlemen and ladies, and the well-paid clergy of
the State Church, with whom Lincolnshire swarms, could allow such a system to
arise on their estates, under their very eyes, they who send out expressly missions
to the Antipodes, "for the improvement of the morals of South Sea Islanders"—the
more refined press confined itself to reflections on the coarse degradation of the agricultural population who are capable of selling their children into such slavery!
Under the accursed conditions to which these "delicate" people condemn the agricultural labourer, it would not be surprising if he ate his own children. What is
really wonderful is the healthy integrity of character, he has, in great part, retained.
The official reports prove that the parents, even in the gang districts, loathe the
gang-system. "There is much in the evidence that show that the parents of the
children would, in many instances, be glad to be aided by the requirements of a legal
obligation, to resist the pressure and the temptations to which they are often subject. They are liable to be urged at times by the parish officers, at times by em

(f.) IRELAND.

In concluding this section, we must travel for a moment to Ireland. First, the main facts of the case.

The population of Ireland had, in 1841, reached 8,222,664; in 1851, it had dwindled to 6,623,985; in 1861, to 5,850,309; in 1866, to 5½ millions, nearly to its level in 1801. The diminution began with the famine year, 1846, so that Ireland, in less than twenty years, lost more than $\frac{5}{16}$ ths of its people.[1]

Table A.

LIVE STOCK.

| Year. | HORSES. | | CATTLE. | | |
	Total Number.	Decrease.	Total Number.	Decrease.	Increase.
1860	619,811		3,606,374		
1861	614,232	5,993	3,471,688	138,316	
1862	602,894	11,338	3,254,890	216,798	
1863	579,978	22,916	3,144,231	110,695	
1864	562,158	17,820	3,262,294		118,063
1865	547,867	14,291	3,493,414		231,120

ployers, under threats of being themselves discharged, to be taken to work at an age when . . . school attendance . . . would be manifestly to their greater advantage. . . . . All that time and strength wasted; all the suffering from extra and unprofitable fatigue produced to the labourer and to his children; every instance in which the parent may have traced the moral ruin of his child to the undermining of delicacy by the overcrowding of cottages, or to the contaminating influences of the public gang, must have been so many incentives to feelings in the minds of the labouring poor which can be well understood, and which it would be needless to particularise. They must be conscious that much bodily and mental pain has thus been inflicted upon them from causes for which they were in no way answerable; to which, had it been in their power, they would have in no way consented; and against which they were powerless to struggle." (l. c., p. xx., § 82, and xxiii., n. 96.)

[1] Population of Ireland, 1801, 5,319.867 persons; 1811, 6,084,996; 1821, 6,869,544; 1831, 7,828,347; 1841, 8.222.664.

Its total emigration from May, 1851, to July, 1865, numbered 1,591,487: the emigration during the years 1861-1865 was more than half-a-million. The number of inhabited houses fell, from 1851-1861, by 52,990. From 1851-1861, the number of holdings of 15 to 30 acres increased 61,000, that of holdings over 30 acres, 109,000, whilst the total number of all farms fell 120,000, a fall, therefore, solely due to the suppression of farms under 15 acres—*i.e.,* to their central-isation.

Year.	SHEEP.			PIGS.		
	Total Number.	Decrease.	Increase.	Total Number.	Decrease.	Increase.
1860	3,542,080			1,271,072		
1861	3,556,050		13,970	1,102,042	169,030	
1862	3,456,132	99,918		1,154,324		52,282
1863	3,308,204	147,982		1,067,458	86,866	
1864	3,366,941		58,737	1,058,480	8,978	
1865	3,688,742		321,801	1,299,893		241,413

The decrease of the population was naturally accompanied by a decrease in the mass of products. For our purpose, it suffices to consider the 5 years from 1861-1865 during which over half-a-million emigrated, and the absolute number of people sank by more than $\frac{1}{3}$ of a million.

From the above tables it results:—

HORSES.	CATTLE.	SHEEP.	PIGS.
Absolute Decrease.	Absolute Decrease.	Absolute Increase.	Absolute Increase.
72,358	116,626	146,608	28,819 [1]

- The result would be found yet more unfavourable if we went further back.

Let us now turn to agriculture, which yields the means of subsistence for cattle and for men. In the following table is calculated the decrease or increase for each separate year, as compared with its immediate predecessor. The Cereal Crops include wheat, oats, barley, rye, beans and peas; the Green Crops, potatoes, turnips, mangolds, beet-root, cabbages, carrots, parsnips, vetches, &c.

Table B.

INCREASE OR DECREASE IN THE AREA UNDER CROPS AND GRASS IN ACERAGE.

Year.	Cereal Crops. Decrease.	Green Crops. Decrease.	Increase.	Grass and Clover. Decrease.	Increase.	Flax. Decrease.	Increase.	Total Cultivated Land. Decrease.	Increase.
	Acres.	Acres.	Acres	Acres	Acres	Acres	Acres.	Acres	Acres.
1861	15,701	36,974		47,969			19,271	81,873	
1862	72,734	74,785			6,623		2,055	138,841	
1863	144,719	19,358			7,724		63,922	92,431	
1864	122,437	2,317			47,486		87,761		10,493
1855	72,450		25,241		68,970	50,159		28,218	
1861-65	438,041	107,984			89,834		199,850	330,860	

In the year 1865, 127,470 additional acres came under the heading "grass land," chiefly because the area under the heading of "bog and waste unoccupied," decreased by 101,543 acres. If we compare 1865 with 1864, there is a decrease in cereals of 246,667 qrs., of which 48,999 were wheat, 160,605 oats, 29,892 barley, &c.: the decrease in potatoes was 446,398 tons, although the area of their cultivation increased in 1865.

From the movement of population and the agricultural produce of Ireland, we pass to the movement in the purse of its

Thus: Sheep in 1865, 3,688,742, but in 1856, 3,694,294. Pigs in 1865, 1,299,893, but in 1858, 1,409,883.

Table C.

INCREASE OR DECREASE IN THE AREA UNDER CULTIVATION, PRODUCT PER ACRE, AND TOTAL PRODUCT OF 1865 COMPARED WITH 1864.

Product	Acres of Cultivated Land. 1864.	Acres of Cultivated Land. 1865.	Increase or Decrease, 1865.	Product per Acre, 1864.	Product per Acre, 1865.	Increase or Decrease 1865	Total Product. 1864.	Total Product. 1865.	Increase or Decrease, 1865.
Wheat,.........	276,483	266,989	9,494	Wheat, cwt., 13·3	13·0	0·3	Qrs. 875,782	Qrs. 826,783	48,999 qs.
Oats,...........	1,814,886	1,745,228	69,658	Oats, ,, 12·1	12·3	0·2	7,826,332 ,,	7,659,727 ,,	166,605 ,,
Barley,.........	172,700	177,102	4,402	Barley, ,, 15·9	14·9	1·0	761,909 ,,	732,017 ,,	29,892 ,,
Bere,.......... ⎱ Rye,........... ⎰	8,894	10,091	1,197	Bere, ,, 16·4 / 8·5 Rye, ,, 14·8 / 10·4		1·6 / 1·9	15,160 ,, / 12,680 ,,	18,989 ,, / 18,364 ,,	5,684 qs.
Potatoes,.......	1,039,724	1,066,260	26,536	Potatoes, tons, 4·1	3·6	0·5	4,312,388 ts.	3,865,990 ts.	446,398 ts.
Turnips,........	337,355	334,212	3,143	Turnips, ,, 10·3	9·9	0·4	3,467,659 ,,	3,301,683 ,,	165,976 ,,
Mangold-wurzel	14,073	14,889	816	Mangold-wurzel ,, 10·5	13·3	2·8	147,284 ,,	191,987 ,,	44,653 ts.
Cabbages,......	31,821	33,622	1,801	Cabbages, ,, 9·3	10·4	1·1	297,375 ,,	350,252 ,,	52,877 ,,
Flax,..........	301,693	251,433	50,260	Flax st. (14 lb.) 34·2	25·2	9·0	64,506 st.	39,561 st.	24,945 st.
Hay,...........	1,609,569	1,678,493	68,924	Hay, tons, 1·6	1·8	0·2	2,607,153 ts.	3,068,707 ts.	461,554 ,,

[1] The data of the text are put together from the materials of the "Agricultural Statistics, Ireland, General Abstracts, Dublin," for the years 1860, *et seq.*, and "Agricultural Statistics, Ireland, Tables showing the estimated average produce, &c., Dublin, 1866." These statistics are official, and laid before Parliament annually. [Note to 2nd edition. The official statistics for the year 1872 show, as compared with 1871, a decrease in area under cultivation of 134,915 acres. An increase occurred in the cultivation of green crops, turnips, mangold-wurzel, and the like; a decrease in the area under cultivation for wheat of 16,000 acres: oats, 14,000; barley and rye, 4,000; potatoes, 66,632; flax, 34,667; grass, clover, vetches, rape-seed, 30,000. The soil under cultivation for wheat shows for the last 5 years the following stages of decrease:—1868, 285,000 acres; 1869, 280,000; 1870, 259,000; 1871, 244,000; 1872, 228,000. For 1872 we find, in round numbers, an increase of 2,600 horses, 80,000 horned cattle, 68,609 sheep, and a decrease of 236,000 pigs.]

landlords, larger farmers, and industrial capitalists. It is reflected in the rise and fall of the Income-tax. It may be remembered that Schedule D (profits with the exception of those of farmers), includes also the so-called, "professional" profits—*i.e.,* the incomes of lawyers, doctors, &c.; and the Schedules C. and E., in which no special details are given, include the incomes of employés, officers, State sinecurists, State fundholders, &c.

Table. D.

THE INCOME-TAX ON THE SUBJOINED INCOMES IN
POUNDS STERLING.

	1860.	1861.	1862.	1863.	1864	1865.
SCHEDULE A.						
Rent of Land	13,893,829	13,003,554	13,398,938	13,494,091	13,470,700	13,801,616
SCHEDULE B.						
Farmrs'. Pfts.	2,765,387	2,773,644	2,937,899	2,938,823	2,930,874	2,946,072
SCHEDULE D.						
Industrial, &c. Profits	4,891,652	4,836,203	4,858.800	4,846,497	4,546,147	4,850,199
Total Schedls. A. to E....	22,962,885	22,998,394	23,597,574	23,658,631	23,236,298	23,930,340[1]

Under Schedule D. the average annual increase of income from 1853-1864 was only 0·93; whilst, in the same period, in Great Britain, it was 4·58. Table E, p. 772, shows the distribution of the profits (with the exception of those of farmers) for the years 1864 and 1865.

England, a country with fully developed capitalist production, and pre-eminently industrial, would have bled to death with such a drain of population as Ireland has suffered. But Ireland is at present only an agricultural district of England, marked off by a wide channel from the country to which it yields corn, wool, cattle, industrial and military recruits.

[1] Tenth Report of the Commissioners of Inland Revenue. Lond. 1866.

Table E.

SCHEDULE D. INCOME FROM PROFITS (OVER £60) IN IRELAND.

	1864. £.		1865. £.	
Total yearly income of	4,368,610 divided among	17,467 persons.	4,669,979 divided among	18,081 persons.
Yearly income over £60 and under £100	238,626	„ 5,015 „	222,575	„ 4,703 „
Of the yearly total income	1,979,066	„ 11,321 „	2,028,471	„ 12,184 „
Remainder of the total yearly income	2,150,818	„ 1,131 „	2,418,933	„ 1,194 „
Of these.........	1,083,906	„ 910 „	1,097,937	„ 1,044 „
	1,066,912	„ 121 „	1,320,996	„ 186 „
	430,535	„ 105 „	584,458	„ 122 „
	646,377	„ 26 „	736,448	„ 28 „
	262,610	„ 3 „	264,528	„ 3 „[1]

The depopulation of Ireland has thrown much of the land out of cultivation, has greatly diminished the produce of the soil,[2] and, in spite of the greater area devoted to cattle breeding, has brought about, in some of its branches, an absolute diminution, in others, an advance scarcely worthy of mention, and constantly interrupted by retrogressions. Nevertheless, with the fall in numbers of the population, rents and farmers' profits rose, although the latter not as steadily as the former.

---

[1] The total yearly income under Schedule D. is different in this style from that which appears in the preceding ones, because of certain deductions allowed by law.

[2] If the product also diminishes relatively per acre, it must not be forgotten that for a century and a half England has indirectly exported the soil of Ireland, without as much as allowing its cultivators the means for making up the constituents of the soil that had been exhausted.

The reason of this is easily comprehensible. On the one hand, with the throwing of small holdings into large ones, and the change of arable into pasture land, a larger part of the whole produce was transformed into surplus produce. The surplus produce increased, although the total produce, of which it formed a fraction, decreased. On the other hand, the money-value of this surplus produce increased yet more rapidly than its mass, in consequence of the rise in the English market-price of meat, wool, &c., during the last 20, and especially during the last 10, years.

The scattered means of production that serve the producers themselves as means of employment and subsistence, without expanding their own value by the incorporation of the labour of others, are no more capital than a product consumed by its own producer is a commodity. If, with the mass of the population, that of the means of production employed in agricultural also diminished, the mass of the capital employed in agriculture increased, because a part of the means of production that were formerly scattered, was concentrated and turned into capital.

The total capital of Ireland outside agriculture, employed in industry and trade, accumulated during the last two decades slowly, and with great and constantly recurring fluctuations; so much the more rapidly did the concentration of its individual constituents develop. And, however small its absolute increase, in proportion to the dwindling population it had increased largely.

Here, then, under our own eyes and on a large scale, a process is revealed, than which nothing more excellent could be wished for by orthodox economy for the support of its dogma: that misery springs from absolute surplus-population, and that equilibrium is re-established by depopulation. This is a far more important experiment than was the plague in the middle of the 14th century so belauded of Malthusians. Note further: If only the naïveté of the schoolmaster could apply, to the conditions of production and population of the nineteenth century, the standard of the 14th, this naïveté, into the bargain, overlooked the fact that whilst, after the plague and the decimation that accompanied it, followed on this side of the channel, in England, enfranchisement and enrichment of the agricultural population, on that side, in France, followed greater servitude and more misery.[1]

The Irish famine of 1846 killed more than 1,000,000 people, but it killed poor devils only. To the wealth of the country it did not the slightest damage. The exodus of the next 20 years, an exodus still constantly increasing did not, as, *e.g.,* the thirty years' war, decimate, along with the human beings, their means of production. Irish genius discovered an altogether new way of spiriting a poor people thousands of miles away from the scene of its misery. The exiles transplanted to the United States, send home sums of money every year as travelling expenses for those left behind. Every troop that emigrates one year, draws another after it the next. Thus, instead of costing Ireland anything, emigration forms one of the most lucrative branches of its export trade. Finally, it is a systematic process, which does not simply make a passing gap in the population, but sucks out of it every year more people than are replaced by the births, so that the absolute level of the population falls year by year.[2]

What were the consequences for the Irish labourers left behind and freed from the surplus-population? That the relative surplus-population is to-day as great as before 1846; that wages are just as low, that the oppression of the labourers has increased, that misery is forcing the country towards a new crisis. The facts are simple. The revolution in agriculture has kept pace with emigration. The production of relative surplus population has more than kept pace with the absolute depopulation. A glance at table C shows that the change of arable to pasture land must work yet more acutely in Ireland than in England. In England the cultivation of green crops increases with the breeding of cattle; in Ireland,

---

[1] As Ireland is regarded as the promised land of the "principle of population," A. Sadler, before the publication of his work on population, issued his famous book, "Ireland, its evils and their remedies. 2nd edition, London, 1829." Here, by comparison of the statistics of the individual provinces, and of the individual counties in each province, he proves that the misery there is not, as Malthus would have it, in proportion to the number of the population, but in inverse ratio to this.

[2] Between 1851 and 1874, the total number of emigrants amounted to 2,325,922.

it decreases. Whilst large number of acres, that were formerly tilled, lie idle or are turned permanently into grassland, a great part of the waste land and peat bogs that were unused formerly, become of service for the extension of cattle-breeding. The smaller and medium farmers—I reckon among these all who do not cultivate more than 100 acres—still make up about $\frac{8}{10}$ ths of the whole number.[1] They are, one after the other, and with a degree of force unknown before, crushed by the competition of an agriculture managed by capital, and therefore they continually furnish new recruits to the class of wage-labourers. The one great industry of Ireland, linen-manufacture, requires relatively few adult men and only employs altogether, in spite of its expansion since the price of cotton rose in 1861-1866, a comparatively insignificant part of th population. Like all the other great modern industries, it constantly produces, by incessant fluctuations, a relative surplus-population within its own sphere, even with an absolute increase in the mass of human beings absorbed by it. The misery of the agricultural population forms the pedestal for gigantic shirt-factories, whose armies of labourers are, for the most part, scattered over the country. Here, we encounter again the system described above of domestic industry, which in under-payment and over-work, possesses its own systematic means for creating supernumerary labourers. Finally, although the depopulation has not such destructive consequences as would result in a country with fully developed capitalistic production, it does not go on without constant reaction upon the home-market. The gap which emigration causes here, limits not only the local demand for labour, but also the incomes of small shopkeepers, artisans, tradespeople generally. Hence the diminution in incomes between £60 and £100 in table E.

A clear statement of the condition of the agricultural labourers in Ireland is to be found in the Reports of the Irish Poor Law Inspectors (1870).[2] Officials of a government

---

[1] According to a table in Murphy's "Ireland industrial, political and social," 1870, 94.6 per cent. of the holdings do not reach 100 acres, 5.4 exceed 100 acres.

[2] "Reports from the Poor Law Inspectors on the wages of Agricultural Labourers

which is maintained only by bayonets and by a state of siege, now open, now disguised, they have to observe all the precautions of language that their colleagues in England disdain. In spite of this, however, they do not let their government cradle itself in illusions. According to them the rate of wages in the country, still very low, has within the last 20 years risen 50-60 per cent., and stands now, on the average, at 6s. to 9s. per week. But behind this apparent rise, is hidden an actual fall in wages, for it does not correspond at all to the rise in price of the necessary means of subsistence that has taken place in the meantime. For proof, the following extract from the official accounts of an Irish workhouse.

AVERAGE WEEKLY COST PER HEAD.

Year ended	Provisions and Necessaries.	Clothing.	Total.
29th Sept. 1849	1s. 3¼d.	3d.	1s. 6¼d.
„ 1869	2s. 7¼d.	6d.	3s. 1¼d.

The price of the necessary means of subsistence is therefore fully twice, and that of clothing exactly twice, as much as they were 20 years before.

Even apart from this disproportion, the mere comparison of the rate of wages expressed in gold would give a result far from accurate. Before the famine, the great mass of agricultural wages were paid in kind, only the smallest part in money; to-day, payment in money is the rule. From this it follows that, whatever the amount of the real wage, its money rate must rise. "Previous to the famine, the labourer enjoyed his cabin . . . with a rood, or half-acre or acre

in Dublin, 1870." See also "Agricultural Labourers (Ireland) Return, etc., 4 March 1862, London 1862."

&c land, and facilities for . . . a crop of potatoes. He was able to read his pig and keep fowl. . . . But they now have to buy bread, and they have no refuse upon which they can feed a pig or fowl, and they have consequently no benefit from the sale of a pig, fowl, or eggs."[1] In fact, formerly, the agricultural labourers were but the smallest of the small farmers, and formed for the most part a kind of rearguard of the medium and large farms on which they found employment. Only since the catastrophe of 1846 have they begun to form a fraction of the class of purely wage-labourers, a special class, connected with its wage-masters only by monetary relations.

We know what were the conditions of their dwellings in 1846. Since then they have grown yet worse. A part of the agricultural labourers, which, however, grows less day by day, dwells still on the holdings of the farmers in over-crowded huts, whose hideousness far surpasses the worst that the English agricultural labourers offered us in this way. And this holds generally with the exception of certain tracts of Ulster; in the south, in the counties of Cork, Limerick, Kilkenny, &c.; in the east, in Wicklow, Wexford, &c.; in the centre of Ireland, in King's and Queen's County, Dublin, &c.; in the west, in Sligo, Roscommon, Mayo, Galway, &c. "The agricultural labourers' huts," an inspector cries out, "are a disgrace to the Christianity and to the civilisation of this country."[2] In order to increase the attractions of these holes for the labourers, the pieces of land belonging thereto from time immemorial, are systematically confiscated. "The mere sense that they exist subject to this species of ban, on the part of the landlords and their agents, has . . . given birth in the minds of the labourers to corresponding sentiments of antagonism and dissatisfaction towards those by whom they are thus led to regard themselves are being treated as . . . a proscribed race."[3]

The first act of the agricultural revolution was to sweep away the huts situated on the field of labour. This was done on the largest scale, and as if in obedience to a command from

[1] l. c. pp. 29, 1. [2] l. c. p. 12. [3] l. c. p. 12.

.on high. Thus many labourers were compelled to seek shelter in villages and towns. There they were thrown like refuse into garrets, holes, cellars and corners, in the worst back slums. Thousands of Irish families, who according to the testimony of the English, eaten up as these are with national prejudice, are notable for their rare attachment to the domestic hearth, for their gaiety and the purity of their home-life, found themselves suddenly transplanted into hotbeds of vice. The men are now obliged to seek work of the neighboring farmers and are only hired by the day, and therefore under the most precarious forms of wage. Hence "they sometimes have long distances to go to and from work, often get wet, and suffer much hardship, not unfrequently ending in sickness, disease and want."[1]

"The towns have had to receive from year to year what was deemed to be the surplus-labour of the rural division; "[2] and then people still wonder "there is still a surplus of labour in the towns and villages, and either a scarcity or a threatened scarcity in some of the country divisions."[3] The truth is that this want only becomes perceptible "in harvest-time, or during spring, or at such times as agricultural operations are carried on with activity; at other periods of the year many hands are idle;"[4] that "from the digging out of the main crop of potatoes in October until the early spring following . . . there is no employment for them;"[5] and further, that during the active times they " are subject to broken days and to all kinds of interruptions."[6]

These results of the agricultural revolution—*i.e.,* the change of arable into pasture land, the use of machinery, the most rigorous economy of labour, &c., are still further aggravated by the model landlords, who, instead of spending their rents in other countries, condescend to live in Ireland on their demesnes. In order that the law of supply and demand may not be broken, these gentlemen draw their "labour-supply . . . chiefly from their small tenants, who are obliged to attend when required to do the landlord's work, at rates of wages, in

---

[1] l. c. p. 25.   [3] l. c. p. 25.   [5] l. c. pp. 31, 32.
[2] l. c. p. 27.   [4] l. c. p. 1.   [6] l. c. p. 25.

many instances, considerably under the current rates paid to ordinary labourers, and without regard to the inconvenience or loss to the tenant of being obliged to neglect his own business at critical periods of sowing or reaping."[1]

The uncertainty and irregularity of employment, the constant return and long duration of gluts of labour, all these symptoms of a relative surplus-population, figure therefore in the reports of the Poor Law administration, as so many hardships of the agricultural proletariat. It will be remembered that we met, in the English agricultural proletariat, with a similar spectacle. But the difference is that in England, an industrial country, the industrial reserve recruits itself from the country districts, whilst in Ireland, an agricultural country, the agricultural reserve recruits itself from the towns, the cities of refuge of the expelled agricultural labourers. In the former, the supernumeraries of agriculture are transformed into factory-operatives; in the latter, those forced into the towns, whilst at the same time they press on the wages in towns, remain agricultural labourers, and are constantly sent back to the country districts in search of work.

The official inspectors sum up the material condition of the agricultural labourer as follows: "Though living with the strictest frugality, his own wages are barely sufficient to provide food for an ordinary family and pay his rent, and he depends upon other sources for the means of clothing himself, his wife, and children. . . The atmosphere of these cabins, combined with the other privations they are subjected to, has made this class particularly susceptible to low fever and pulmonary consumption."[2] After this, it is no wonder that, according to the unanimous testimony of the inspectors, a sombre discontent runs through the ranks of this class, that they long for the return of the past, loathe the present, despair of the future, give themselves up to "to the evil influence of agitators," and have only one fixed idea, to emigrate to America. This is the land of Cockaigne, into which the great Malthusian panacea, depopulation, has transformed green Erin.

What a happy life the Irish factory operative leads, one

[1] l. c. p. 30   [2] l. c. pp. 21, 13.

example will show: "On my recent visit to the North of Ireland," says the English Factory Inspector, Robert Baker, "I met with the following evidence of effort in an Irish skilled workman to afford education to his children; and I give his evidence verbatim, as I took it from his mouth. That he was a skilled factory hand, may be understood when I say that he was employed on goods for the Manchester market. 'Johnson.—I am a beetler and work from 6 in the morning till 11 at night, from Monday till Friday. Saturday we leave off at 6 p.m,. and get three hours of it (for meals and rest). I have five children in all. For this work I get 10s. 6d. a week; my wife works here also, and gets 5s. a week. The oldest girl who is 12, minds the house. She is also cook, and all the servant we have. She gets the young ones ready for school. A girl going past the house wakes me at half past five in the morning. My wife gets up and goes along with me. We get nothing (to eat) before we come to work. The child of 12 takes care of the little children all the day, and we get nothing till breakfast at eight. At eight we go home. We get tea once a week; at other times we get stirabout, sometimes of oatmeal, sometimes of Indian meal, as we are able to get it. In the winter we get a little sugar and water to our Indian meal. In the summer we get a few potatoes, planting a small patch ourselves; and when they are done we get back to stirabout. Sometimes we get a little milk as it may be. So we go on from day to day, Sunday and week day, always the same the year round. I am always very much tired when I have done at night. We may see a bit of flesh meat sometimes, but very seldom. Three of our children attend school, for whom we pay 1d. a week a head. Our rent is 9d. a week. Peat for firing costs 1s. 6d. a fortnight at the very lowest."[1] Such are Irish wages, such is Irish life!

In fact the misery of Ireland is again the topic of the day in England. At the end of 1866 and the beginning of 1867, one of the Irish land magnates, Lord Dufferin, set about its solution in the "Times." "Wie menschlich von solch grossem Herrn!"

---

[1] Rept. of Insp. of Fact. 31st Oct., 1866, p. 96.

From Table E. we saw that, during 1864, of £4,368,610 of total profits, three surplus-value makers pocketed only £262,610; that in 1865, however, out of £4,669,979 total profits, the same three virtuosi of "abstinence" pocketed £274,448; in 1864, 26 surplus-value makers reached to £646,377; in 1865, 28 surplus-value makers reached to £736,448; in 1864, 121 surplus-value makers, £1,066,912; in 1865, 186 surplus-value makers, £1,320,996; in 1864, 1131 surplus-value makers £2,150,818, nearly half of the total annual profit; in 1865, 1194 surplus-value makers £2,418,933, more than half of the total annual profit. But the lion's share, which an inconceivably small number of land magnates in England, Scotland and Ireland swallow up of the yearly national rental, is so monstrous that the wisdom of the English state does not think fit to afford the same statistical materials about the distribution of rents as about the distribution of profits. Lord Dufferin is one of those land magnates. That rent-rolls and profits can ever be "excessive," or that their plethora is in any way connected with plethora of the people's misery is, an idea as "disreputable" as "unsound." He keeps to facts. The fact is that, as the Irish population diminishes, the Irish rent-rolls swell; that depopulation benefits the landlords, therefore also benefits the soil, and, therefore the people, that were accessory of the soil. He declares, therefore, that Ireland is still over-populated, and the stream of emigration still flows too lazily. To be perfectly happy, Ireland must get rid of at least one-third of a million of labouring men. Let no man imagine that this lord, poetic into the bargain, is a physician of the school of Sangrado, who as often as he did not find his patient better, ordered phlebotomy and again phlebotomy, until the patient lost his sickness at the same time as his blood. Lord Dufferin demands a new blood-letting of one-third of a million only, instead of about two millions; in fact, without the getting rid of these, the millennium in Erin is not to be. The proof is easily given.

Centralisation has from 1851 to 1861 destroyed principally farms of the first three categories, under 1 and not over 15 acres. These above all must disappear. This gives 307,058

NUMBER AND EXTENT OF FARMS IN IRELAND IN 1864.

(1) Farms not over 1 acre.		(2) Farms over 1, not over 5 acres.		(3) Farms over 5, not over 15 acres.		(4) Farms over 15, not over 30 acres.	
No.	Acres.	No.	Acres.	No.	Acres.	No.	Acres.
48,653	25,394	82,037	288,916	176,368	1,836,310	136,578	3,051,343

(5) Farms over 30, not over 50 acres.		(6) Farms over 50, not over 100 acres.		(7) Farms over 100 acres.		(8) Total area.
No.	Acres.	No.	Acres.	No.	Acres.	Acres.
71,961	2,906,274	54,247	3,983,880	31,927	8,227,807	26,319,924[1]

"supernumerary" farmers, and reckoning the families the low average of 4 persons 1,228,232 persons. On the extravagant supposition that, after the agricultural revolution is complete, one-fourth of these are again absorbable, there remain for emigration 921,174 persons. Categories, 4, 5, 6, of over 15 and not over 100 acres, are, as was known long since in England, too small for capitalistic cultivation of corn, and for sheepbreeding are almost vanishing quantities. On the same supposition as before, therefore, there are further 788,761 persons to emigrate; total, 1,709,532. And as l'appétit vient en mangeant, Rent-roll's eyes will soon discover that Ireland, with 3½ millions, is still always miserable because she is overpopulated. Therefore her depopulation must go yet further, that thus she may fulfill her true destiny, that of an English sheep walk and cattle-pasture.[2]

---

[1] The total area includes also peat, bogs, and waste land.

[2] How the famine and its consequences have been deliberately made the most of, both by the individual landlords and by the English legislature, to forcibly carry out the agricultural revolution and to thin the population of Ireland down to the proportion satisfactory to the landlords, I shall show more fully in Vol. III. of this work, in the section on landed property. There also I return to the condition of the small farmers and the agricultural labourers. At present, only one quotation. Nassau W. Senior says, with other things, in his posthumous work, "Journals, Conversations and Essays, relating to Ireland." 2 vols. London 1868; Vol. II., p. 282. "Well," said Dr. G., "we have got our Poor Law and it is a great instrument for giving the

Like all good things in this bad world, this profitable method has its drawbacks. With the accumulation of rents in Ireland, the accumulation of the Irish in America keeps pace. The Irishman, banished by sheep and ox, reappears on the other side of the ocean as a Fenian, and face to face with the old queen of the sea rises, threatening and more threatening, the young giant Republic:

> Acerba fata Romanos agunt
> Scelusque fraternæ necis.

victory to the landlords. Another, and a still more powerful instrument is emigration . . . No friend to Ireland can wish the war to be prolonged [between the landlords and the small Celtic farmers]—still less, that it should end by the victory of the tenants. The sooner it is over—the sooner Ireland becomes a grazing country, with the comparatively thin population which a grazing country requires, the better for all classes." The English Corn Laws of 1815 secured Ireland the monopoly of the free importation of corn into Great Britain. They favoured artificially, therefore, the cultivation of corn. With the abolition of the Corn Laws in 1846, this monopoly was suddenly removed. Apart from all other circumstances, this event alone was sufficient to give a great impulse to the turning of Irish arable into pasture land, to the concentration of farms, and to the eviction of small cultivators. After the fruitfulness of the Irish soil had been praised from 1815 to 1846, and proclaimed loudly as by Nature herself destined for the cultivation of wheat, English agronomists, economists, politicians. discover suddenly that it is good for nothing but to produce forage. M. Léonce de Lavergne has hastened to repeat this on the other side of the Channel. It takes a "serious" man, à La Lavergne, to be caught by such childishness.

PART VIII.

THE SO-CALLED PRIMITIVE ACCUMULATION.

CHAPTER XXVI.

THE SECRET OF PRIMITIVE ACCUMULATION.

WE have seen how money is changed into capital; how through capital surplus-value is made, and from surplus-value more capital. But the accumulation of capital presupposes surplus-value; surplus-value presupposes capitalistic production; capitalistic production presupposes the pre-existence of considerable masses of capital and of labour-power in the hands of producers of commodities. The whole movement, therefore, seems to turn in a vicious circle, out of which we can only get by supposing a primitive accumulation (previous accumulation of Adam Smith) preceding capitalistic accumulation; an accumulation not the result of the capitalist mode of production, but its starting point.

This primitive accumulation plays in Political Economy about the same part as original sin in theology. Adam bit the apple, and thereupon sin fell on the human race. Its origin is supposed to be explained when it is told as an anecdote of the past. In times long gone by there were two sorts of people; one, the diligent, intelligent, and, above all, frugal élite; the other, lazy rascals, spending their substance, and more, in riotous living. The legend of theological original sin tells us certainly how man came to be condemned to eat his bread in the sweat of his brow; but the history of economic original sin reveals to us that there are people to whom this is by no means essential. Never mind! Thus it came to pass that the former sort accumulated wealth, and the latter sort had at last nothing to sell except their own skins. And from this original sin dates the poverty of the great majority that, despite all its labour, has up to now nothing to sell but itself, and the wealth of the few that increases constantly although they have long ceased to work. Such insipid childishness is every day preached to us in the defence of property. M. Thiers, *e.g.*, had the assurance to repeat it with all the solemnity of a statesman, to the French people, once so *spirituel*. But as soon as the question of property crops up, it becomes a sacred duty to proclaim the intellectual food of the infant as the one thing fit for all ages and for all stages of development. In actual history it is notorious that conquest, enslavement, robbery, murder, briefly force, play the great part. In the tender annals of Political Economy, the idyllic reigns from time immemorial. Right and "labour" were from all time the sole means of enrichment, the present year of course always excepted. As a matter of fact, the methods of primitive accumulation are anything but idyllic.

In themselves, money and commodities are no more capital than are the means of production and of subsistence. They want transforming into capital. But this transformation itself can only take place under certain circumstances that centre in this, *viz.*, that two very different kinds of commodity-possessors must come face to face and into contact; on the one hand, the owners of money, means of production, means of subsistence, who are eager to increase the sum of values they possess, by buying other people's labour-power; on the other hand, free labourers, the sellers of their own labour-power, and therefore the sellers of labour. Free labourers, in the double sense that neither they themselves form part and parcel of the means of production, as in the case of slaves, bondsmen, &c., nor do the means of production belong to them, as in the case of peasant-proprietors; they are, therefore, free from, unencumbered by, any means of production of their own. With this polarisation of the market for commodities, the fundamental conditions of capitalist production are given. The capitalist system presupposes the complete separation of the labourers from all property in the means by which they can realise their labour. As soon as capitalist production is once on its own legs, it not only maintains this separation, but reproduces it on a continually extending scale. The process, therefore, that clears the way for the capitalist system, can be none other than the process which takes away from the labourer the possession of his means of production; a process that transforms, on the one hand, the social means of subsistence and of production into capital, on the other, the immediate producers into wage-labourers. The so-called primitive accumulation, therefore, is nothing else than the historical process of divorcing the producer from the means of production. It appears as primitive, because it forms the pre-historic stage of capital and of the mode of production corresponding with it.

The economic structure of capitalistic society has grown out of the economic structure of feudal society. The dissolution of the latter set free the elements of the former.

The immediate producer, the labourer, could only dispose of his own person after he had ceased to be attached to the soil and ceased to be the slave, serf, or bondman of another. To become a free seller of labour-power, who carries his commodity wherever he finds a market, he must further have escaped from the regime of the guilds, their rules for apprentices and journeymen, and the impediments of their labour regulations. Hence, the historical movement which changes the producers into wage-workers, appears, on the one hand, as their emancipation from serfdom and from the fetters of the guilds, and this side alone exists for our bourgeois historians. But, on the other hand, these new freedmen became sellers of themselves only after they had been robbed of all their own means of production, and of all the guarantees of existence afforded by the old feudal arrangements. And the history of this, their expropriation, is written in the annals of mankind in letters of blood and fire.

The industrial capitalists, these new potentates, had on their part not only to displace the guild masters of handicrafts, but also the feudal lords, the possessors of the sources of wealth.

In this respect their conquest of social power appears as the fruit of a victorious struggle both against feudal lordship and its revolting prerogatives, and against the guilds and the fetters they laid on the free development of production and the free exploitation of man by man. The chevaliers d'industrie, however, only succeed in supplanting the chevaliers of the sword by making use of events of which they themselves were wholly innocent. They have risen by means as vile as those by which the Roman freed-man once on a time made himself the master of his *patronus.*

The starting-point of the development that gave rise to the wage-labourer as well as to the capitalist, was the servitude of the labourer. The advance consisted in a change of form of this servitude, in the transformation of feudal exploitation into capitalist exploitation. To understand its march, we need not go back very far. Although we come across the first beginnings of capitalist production as early as the 14th or 15th century, sporadically, in certain towns of the Mediterranean, the capitalistic era dates from the 16th century. Wherever it appears, the abolition of serfdom has been long effected, and the highest development of the middle ages, the existence of sovereign towns, has been long on the wane.

In the history of primitive accumulation, all revolutions are epoch-making that act as levers for the capitalist class in course of formation; but, above all, those moments when great masses of men are suddenly and forcibly torn from their means of subsistence, and hurled as free and "unattached" proletarians on the labour market. The expropriation of the agricultural producer, of the peasant, from the soil, is the basis of the whole process. The history of this expropriation, in different countries, assumes different aspects, and runs through its various phases in different orders of succession, and at different periods. In England alone, which we take as our example, has it the classic form.[1]

---

[1] In Italy, where capitalistic production developed earliest, the dissolution of serfdom also took place earlier than elsewhere. The serf was emancipated in that country before he had acquired any prescriptive right to the soil. His emancipation at once transformed him into a free proletarian, who, moreover, found his master ready waiting for him in the towns, for the most part handed down as legacies from

CHAPTER XXVII.

EXPROPRIATION OF THE AGRICULTURAL POPULATION FROM THE LAND.

In England, serfdom had practically disappeared in the last part of the 14th century. The immense majority of the population[1] consisted then, and to a still larger extent, in the 15th century, of free peasant proprietors, whatever was the feudal title under which their right of property was hidden. In the larger seignorial domains, the old bailiff, himself a serf, was displaced by the free farmer. The wage-labourers of agriculture consisted partly of peasants, who utilised their leisure time by working on the large estates, partly of an independent special class of wage-labourers, relatively and absolutely few in numbers. The latter also were practically at the same time peasant farmers, since, besides their wages, they had alloted to them arable land to the extent of 4 or more acres, together with their cottages. Besides they, with the rest of the peasants, enjoyed the usufruct of the common land, which gave pasture to their cattle, furnished them with timber, fire-wood, turf, &c.[2] In all countries of Europe,

the Roman time. When the revolution of the world-market, about the end of the 15th century, annihilated Northern Italy's commercial supremacy, a movement in the reverse direction set in. The labourers of the towns were driven *en masse* into the country, and gave an impulse, never before seen, to the *petite culture,* carried on in the form of gardening.

[1] "The petty proprietors who cultivated their own fields with their own hands, and enjoyed a modest competence . . . . then formed a much more important part of the nation than at present. If we may trust the best statistical writers of that age, not less than 160,000 proprietors who, with their families, must have made up more than a seventh of the whole population, derived their subsistence from little freehold estates. The average income of these small landlords . . . . was estimated at between £60 and £70 a year. It was computed that the number of persons who tilled their own land was greater than the number of those who farmed the land of others." Macaulay: History of England, 10th ed., 1854, I. p. 333,334. Even in the last third of the 17th century, ⅘ of the English people were agricultural. (l. c., p. 413.) I quote Macaulay, because as systematic falsifier of history he minimises as much as possible facts of this kind.

[2] We must never forget that even the serf was not only the owner, if but a tribute-paying owner, of the piece of land attached to his house, but also a co-possessor of the common land. "Le paysan y (in Silesia, under Frederick II.) est

feudal production is characterised by division of the soil amongst the greatest possible number of sub-feudatories. The might of the feudal lord, like that of the sovereign, depended not on the length of his rent roll, but on the number of his subjects, and the latter depended on the number of peasant proprietors.[1] Although, therefore, the English land, after the Norman conquest, was distributed in gigantic baronies, one of which often included some 900 of the old Anglo-Saxon lordships, it was bestrewn with small peasant properties, only here and there interspersed with great seignorial domains. Such conditions, together with the prosperity of the towns so characteristic of the 15th century, allowed of that wealth of the people which Chancellor Fortescue so eloquently paints in his "Laudes legum Angliæ;" but it excluded the possibility of capitalistic wealth.

The prelude of the revolution that laid the foundation of the capitalist mode of production, was played in the last third of the 15th, and the first decade of the 16th century. A mass of free proletarians was hurled on the labour-market by the breaking-up of the bands of feudal retainers, who, as Sir James Steuart well says, "everywhere uselessly filled house and castle." Although the royal power, itself a product of bourgeois development, in its strife after absolute sovereignty forcibly hastened on the dissolution of these bands of retainers, it was by no means the sole cause of it. In insolent conflict with king and parliament, the great feudal lords created an incomparably larger proletariat by the forcible driving of the peasantry from the land, to which the latter had the same feudal right as the lord himself, and by the usurpation of the common lands. The rapid rise of the Flemish wool manufactures, and the corresponding rise in the price of wool in England, gave the direct impulse to these evictions. The old nobil-

serf." Nevertheless, these serfs possess common lands. "On n' a pas pu encore engager les Silésiens au partage des communes, tandis que dans la Nouvelle Marche, il n'y a guère de village où ce partage ne soit exécuté avec le plus grand succès." (Mirabeau: De la Monarchie Prussienne. Londres, 1788, t. ii., pp. 125, 126.)

[1] Japan, with its purely feudal organisation of landed property and its developed *petite culture*, gives a much truer picture of the European middle ages than all our history books, dictated as these are, for the most part, by bourgeois prejudices. It is very convenient to be "liberal" at the expense of the middle ages.

ity had been devoured by the great feudal wars. The new nobility was the child of its time, for which money was the power of all powers. Transformation of arable land into sheep-walks was, therefore, its cry. Harrison, in his "Description of England, prefixed to Holinshed's Chronicle," describes how the expropriation of small peasants is ruining the country. "What care our great encroachers?" The dwellings of the peasants and the cottages of the labourers were razed to the ground or doomed to decay. "If," says Harrison, "the old records of euerie manour be sought . . . . it will soon appear that in some manour seventeene, eighteene, or twentie houses are shrunk . . . . that England was neuer less furnished with people than at the present. . . . Of cities and townes either utterly decaied or more than a quarter or half diminished, though some one be a little increased here or there; of townes pulled downe for sheepe-walks, and no more but the lordships now standing in them . . . . I could saie somewhat." The complaints of these old chroniclers are always exaggerated, but they reflect faithfully the impression made on contemporaries by the revolution in the conditions of production. A comparison of the writings of Chancellor Fortescue and Thomas More reveals the gulf between the 15th and 16th century. As Thornton rightly has it, the English working-class was precipitated without any transition from its golden into its iron age.

Legislation was terrified at this revolution. It did not yet stand on that height of civilisation where the "wealth of the nation" (*i.e.*, the formation of capital, and the reckless exploitation and impoverishing of the mass of the people) figure as the *ultima Thule* of all state-craft. In his history of Henry VII., Bacon says: "Inclosures at that time (1489) began to be more frequent, whereby arable land (which could not be manured without people and families) was turned into pasture, which was easily rid by a few herdsmen; and tenancies for years, lives, and at will (whereupon much of the yeomanry lived) were turned into demenses. This bred a decay of people, and (by consequence) a decay of towns, churches, tithes, and the like. . . . . In remedying of this inconvenience the king's wisdom was admirable, and the parliament at that time . . . . they took a course to take away depopulating inclosures, and depopulating pasturage." An Act of Henry VII., 1489, cap. 19, forbad the destruction of all "houses of husbandry" to which at least 20 acres of land belonged. By an Act, 25 Henry VIII., the same law was renewed. It recites, among other things, that many farms and large flocks of cattle, especially of sheep, are concentrated in the hands of a few men, whereby the rent of land has much risen and tillage has fallen off, churches and houses have been pulled down, and marvellous numbers of people have been deprived of the means wherewith to maintain themselves and their families. The Act, therefore, ordains the rebuilding of the decayed farmsteads, and fixes a proportion between corn land and pasture land, &c. An Act of 1533 recites that some owners possess 24,000 sheep, and limits the number to be owned to 2000.[1] The cry of the people and the legislation directed, for 150 years after Henry VII., against the expropriation of the small farmers and peasants, were alike fruitless. The secret of their inefficiency Bacon, without knowing it, reveals to us. "The device of King Henry VII.," says Bacon, in his "Essays, Civil and Moral," Essay 29, "was profound and admirable, in making farms and houses of husbandry of a standard; that is, maintained with such a proportion of land unto them as may breed a subject to live in convenient plenty, and no servile condition, and to keep the plough in the hands of the owners and not mere hirelings."[2] What the capital system

[1] In his "Utopia," Thomas More says, that in England "your shepe that were wont to be so meke and tame, and so smal eaters, now, as I heare saye, be become so great devourers and so wylde that they eate up, and swallow downe, the very men themselfes." "Utopia," transl. by Robinson., ed. Arber, Lond., 1869, p. 41.

[2] Bacon shows the connexion between a free, well-to-do peasantry and good infantry. "This did wonderfully concern the might and mannerhood of the kingdom to have farms as it were of a standard sufficient to maintain an able body out of penury, and did in effect amortize a great part of the lands of the kingdom unto the hold and occupation of the yeomanry or middle people, of a condition between gentlemen, and cottagers and peasants. . . . . For it hath been held by the general opinion of men of best judgment in the wars . . . . that the principal strength of an army consisteth in the infantry or foot. And to make good infantry it requireth men bred, not in a servile or indigent fashion, but in some free and plentiful manner. Therefore, if a state run most to noblemen and gentlemen, and that the husbandmen and ploughmen be but as their workfolk and labourers, or

demanded was, on the other hand, a degraded and almost
servile condition of the mass of the people, the transformation
of them into mercenaries, and of their means of labour into
capital. During this rtansformation period, legislation also
strove to retain the 4 acres of land by the cottage of the agricultural wage-labourer, and forbad him to take lodgers into
his cottage. In the reign of James I. 1627, Roger Crocker of
Front Mill, was condemned for having built a cottage on
the manor of Front Mill witho 4 acres of land attached to
the same in perpetuity. As late as Charles I.'s reign, 1638,
a royal commission was appo nted to enforce the carrying out
of the old laws, especially that referring to the 4 acres of
land. Even in Cromwell's time, the building of a house within 4 miles of London was forbidden unless it was endowed
with 4 acres of land. As late as the first half of the 18th
century complaint is made if the cottage of the agricultural
labourer has not an adjunct of one or two acres of land. Nowadays he is lucky if it is furnished with a little garden, or
if he may rent, far away from his cottage, a few roods.
"Landlords and farmers," says Dr. Hunter, "work here hand
in hand. A few acres to the cottage would make the labourers
too independent."[1]

The process of forcible expropriation of the people received
in the 16th century a new and frightful impulse from the
Reformation, and from the consequent colossal spoliation
of the church property. The Catholic church was, at the
time of the Reformation, feudal proprietor of a great part of
the English land. The suppression of the monasteries, &c.,
hurled their inmates into the proletariat. The estates of
the church were to a large extent given away to rapacious

else mere cottages (which are but hous'd beggars), you may have a good cavalry,
but never good stable bands of foot. . . . . And this is to be seen in France,
and Italy, and some other parts abroad, where in effect all is noblesse or peasantry
. . . . insomuch that they are inforced to employ mercenary bands of Switzers
and the like, for their battalions of foot; whereby also it comes to pass that those
nations have much people and few soldiers." ("The Reign of Henry VII." Verbatim reprint from Kennet's England. Ed. 1719. Lond., 1870, p. 308.)

[1] Dr. Hunter, l. c., p. 134. "The quantity of land assigned (in the old laws)
would now be judged too great for labourers, and rather as likely to convert them
into small farmers." (George Roberts: "The Social History of the People of the
Southern Counties of England in past centuries." Lond., 1856, pp. 184-185.)

royal favourites, or sold at a nominal price to speculating farmers and citizens, who drove out, *en masse,* the hereditary sub-tenants and threw their holdings into one. The legally guaranteed property of the poorer folk in a part of the church's tithes was tacitly confiscated.[1] "Pauper ubique jacet," cried Queen Elizabeth, after a journey through England. In the 43rd year of her reign the nation was obliged to recognise pauperism officially by the introduction of a poor-rate. "The authors of this law seem to have been ashamed to state the grounds of it, for [contrary to traditional usage] it has no preamble whatever."[2] By the 16th of Charles I., ch. 4, it was declared perpetual, and in fact only in 1834 did it take a new and harsher form.[3] These immediate results of the Reformation were not its most lasting ones. The property of the

[1] "The right of the poor to share in the tithe, is established by the tenour of ancient statutes." (Tuckett, l. c., Vol. II., pp. 804-805.)

[2] William Cobbett: "A History of the Protestant Reformation," § 471.

[3] The "spirit" of Protestantism may be seen from the following, among other things. In the south of England certain landed proprietors and well-to-do farmers put their heads together and propounded ten questions as to the right interpretation of the poor-law of Elizabeth. These they laid before a celebrated jurist of that time, Sergeant Snigge (later a judge under James I.) for his opinion. "Question 9—Some of the more wealthy farmers in the parish have devised a skilful mode by which all the trouble of executing this Act (the 43rd of Elizabeth) might be avoided. They have proposed that we shall erect a prison in the parish, and then give notice to the neighbourhood, that if any persons are disposed to farm the poor of this parish, they do give in sealed proposals, on a certain day, of the lowest price at which they will take them off our hands; and that they will be authorised to refuse to any one unless he be shut up in the aforesaid prison. The proposers of this plan conceive that there will be found in the adjoining counties, persons, who, being unwilling to labour and not possessing substance or credit to take a farm or ship, so as to live without labour, may be induced to make a very advantageous offer to the parish. If any of the poor perish under the contractor's care, the sin will lie at his door, as the parish will have done its duty by them. We are, however, apprehensive that the present Act (43rd of Elizabeth) will not warrant a prudential measure of this kind; but you are to learn that the rest of the freeholders of the county, and of the adjoining county of B, will very readily join in instructing their members to propose an Act to enable the parish to contract with a person to lock up and work the poor; and to declare that if any person shall refuse to be so locked up and worked, he shall be entitled to no relief. This, it is hoped, will prevent persons in distress from wanting relief, and be the means of keeping down parishes." (R. Blakey: "The History of Political Literature from the earliest Times." Lond., 1855, Vol. II., pp. 84-85.) In Scotland. the abolition of serfdom took place some centuries later than in England. Even in 1698, Fletcher of Saltoun, declared in the Scotch parliament, "The number of beggars in Scotland is reckoned at not less than 200,000. The only remedy that I, a republican on principle can suggest, is to restore the old state of serfdom, to make slaves of all those who are unable to provide for their own subsistence." Eden, l. c., Book I., ch. 1, pp. 60-61, says, "The decrease of villenage seems necessarily to have been the era of the origin of the poor. Manu-

church formed the religious bulwark of the traditional conditions of landed property. With its fall these were no longer tenable.[1]

Even in the last decade of the 17th century, the yeomanry, the class of independent peasants, were more numerous than the class of farmers. They had formed the backbone of Cromwell's strength, and, even according to the confession of Macaulay, stood in favourable contrast to the drunken squires and to their servants, the country clergy, who had to marry their master's cast-off mistresses. About 1750, the yeomanry had disappeared,[2] and so had, in the last decade of the 18th century, the last trace of the common land of the agricultural labourer. We leave on one side here the purely economic causes of the agricultural revolution. We deal only with the forcible means employed.

After the restoration of the Stuarts, the landed proprietors carried, by legal means, an act of usurpation, effected everywhere on the Continent without any legal formality. They abolished the feudal tenure of land, *i.e.*, they got rid of all its obligations to the State, "indemnified" the State by taxes on the peasantry and the rest of the mass of the people, vindicated for themselves the rights of modern private property in estates to which they had only a feudal title, and, finally, passed those laws of settlement, which, *mutatis mutandis,* had the same effect on the English agricultural labourer, as the

factures and commerce are the two parents of our national poor." Eden, like our Scotch republican on principle, errs only in this: not the abolition of villenage, but the abolition of the property of the agricultural labourer in the soil made him a proletarian, and eventually a pauper. In France, where the expropriation was effected in another way, the ordonnance of Moulins, 1571, and the Edict of 1656, correspond to the English poor-laws.

[1] Professor Rogers, although formerly Professor of Political Economy in the University of Oxford, the hotbed of Protestant orthodoxy, in his preface to the "History of Agriculture" lays stress on the fact of the pauperisation of the mass of the people by the Reformation.

[2] A letter to Sir T. C. Banbury, Bart., on the High Price of Provisions. By a Suffolk Gentleman. Ipswich, 1795, p. 4. Even the fanatical advocate of the system of large farms, the author of the "Inquiry into the connection of large farms, etc., London, 1773," p. 133, says: "I most lament the loss of our yeomanry, that set of men who really kept up the independence of this nation; and sorry I am to see their lands now in the hands of monopolizing lords, tenanted out to small farmers, who hold their leases on such conditions as to be little better than vassals ready to attend a summons on every mischievous occasion."

edict of the Tartar Boris Godunof on the Russian peasantry.

The "glorious Revolution" brought into power, along with William of Orange, the landlord and capitalist appropriators of surplus-value.[1] They inaugurated the new era by practising on a colossal scale thefts of state lands, thefts that had been hitherto managed more modestly. These estates were given away, sold at a ridiculous figure, or even annexed to private estates by direct seizure.[2] All this happened without the slightest observation of legal etiquette. The crown lands thus fraudulently appropriated, together with the robbery of the Church estates, as far as these had not been lost again during the republican revolution, form the basis of the to-day princely domains of the English oligarchy.[3] The bourgeois capitalists favoured the operation with the view, among others, to promoting free trade in land, to extending the domain of modern agriculture on the large farm-system, and to increasing their supply of the free agricultural proletarians ready to hand. Besides, the new landed aristocracy was the natural ally of the new bankocracy, of the newly-hatched *haute finance,* and of the large manufacturers, then depending on protective duties. The English bourgeoisie acted for its own interest quite as wisely as did the Swedish bourgeoisie who, reversing the process, hand in hand with their economic allies, the peasantry, helped the kings in the forcible resumption of the Crown lands from the oligarchy. This happened since 1604 under Charles X. and Charles XI.

Communal property—always distinct from the State prop-

---

[1] On the private moral character of this bourgeois hero, among other things: "The large grant of lands in Ireland to Lady Orkney, in 1695, is a public instance of the king's affection, and the lady's influence. . . . Lady Orkney's endearing offices are supposed to have been—fœda labiorum ministeria." (In the Sloane Manuscript Collection, at the British Museum, No. 4224. The Manuscript is entitled: "The charakter and behaviour of King William, Sunderland, etc., as represented in Original Letters to the Duke of Shrewsbury, from Somers Halifax, Oxford, Secretary Vernon, etc." It is full of curiosa.)

[2] "The illegal alienation of the Crown Estates, partly by sale and partly by gift, is a scandalous chapter in English history . . . a gigantic fraud on the nation." (F. W. Newman, Lectures on Political Economy. London, 1851, pp. 129, 130.) [For details as to how the present large landed proprietors of England came into their possessions see "Our Old Nobility. By Noblesse Oblige." London, 1879.—Ed.]

[3] Read *e.g.,* E. Burke's Pamphlet on the ducal house of Bedford, whose offshoot was Lord John Russell, the "tomtit of Liberalism."

erty just dealt with—was an old Teutonic institution which lived on under cover of feudalism. We have seen how the forcible usurpation of this, generally accompanied by the turning of arable into pasture land, begins at the end of the 15th and extends into the 16th century. But, at that time, the process was carried on by means of individual acts of violence against which legislation, for a hundred and fifty years, fought in vain. The advance made by the 18th century shows itself in this, that the law itself becomes now the instrument of the theft of the people's land, although the large farmers make use of their little independent methods as well.[1] The parliamentary form of the robbery is that of Acts for enclosures of Commons, in other words, decrees by which the landlords grant themselves the people's land as private property, decrees of expropriation of the people. Sir F. M. Eden refutes his own crafty special pleading, in which he tries to represent communal property as the private property of the great landlords who have taken the place of the feudal lords, when he, himself, demands a "general "Act of Parliament for the enclosure of Commons," (admitting thereby that a parliamentary *coup d'état* is necessary for its transformation into private property), and moreover calls on the legislature for the indemnification for the expropriated poor.[2]

Whilst the place of the independent yeoman was taken by tenants at will, small farmers on yearly leases, a servile rabble dependent on the pleasure of the landlords, the systematic robbery of the Communal lands helped especially, next to the theft of the State domains, to swell those large farms, that were called in the 18th century capital farms[3] or merchant farms,[4] and to "set free" the agricultural populations as proletarians for manufacturing industry.

[1] "The farmers forbid cottagers to keep any living creatures besides themselves and children, under the pretence that if they keep any beasts or poultry, they will steal from the farmers' barns for their support; they also say, keep the cottagers poor and you will keep them industrious, &c., but the real fact, I believe, is that the farmers may have the whole right of common to themselves." (A Political Inquiry into the consequences of enclosing Waste Lands. London, 1785 p. 75.)

[2] Eden, l. c. preface.

[3] "Capital Farms." Two letters on the Flour Trade and the Dearness of Corn. By a person in business. London, 1767, pp. 19, 20.

[4] "Merchant Farms." An inquiry into ... present High Prices of Provisions.

The 18th century, however, did not yet recognise as fully as the 19th, the identity between national wealth and the poverty of the people. Hence the most vigorous polemic, in the economic literature of that time, on the "enclosure of commons." From the mass of materials that lie before me, I give a few extracts that will throw a strong light on the circumstances of the time. "In several parishes of Hertfordshire," writes one indignant person, "24 farms, numbering on the average 50-150 acres, have been melted up into three farms."[1] "In Northamptonshire and Leicestershire the enclosure of common lands has taken place on a very large scale, and most of the new lordships, resulting from the enclosure, have been turned into pasturage, in consequence of which many lordships have not now 50 acres ploughed yearly, in which 1500 were ploughed formerly. The ruins of former dwelling-houses, barns, stables, &c.," are the sole traces of the former inhabitants. "An hundred houses and families have in some open field villages . . . . dwindled to eight or ten . . . . The land-holders in most parishes that have been enclosed only 15 or 20 years, are very few in comparison of the numbers who occupied them in their open-field state. It is no uncommon thing for 4 or 5 wealthy graziers to engross a large enclosed lorship which was before in the hands of 20 or 30 farmers, and as many smaller tenants and proprietors. All these are hereby thrown out of their livings with their families and many other families who were chiefly employed and supported by them."[2] It was not only the land that lay waste, but often land cultivated either in common or held under a definite rent paid to the community, that was annexed by the neighbouring landlords under pretext of enclosure. "I have here in view enclosures of open fields and lands already improved. It is acknowledged by even the writers in defence of enclosures that these diminished villages increase the monopolies of farms, raise the

London, 1767, p. 11. Note.—This excellent work, that was published anonymously, is by the Rev. Nathaniel Forster.

[1] Thomas Wright: A short address to the public on the monopoly of large farms, 1779, pp. 2, 3.

[2] Rev. Addington: Inquiry into the reasons for or against enclosing open fields. London, 1772, pp. 37, 43 passim.

prices of provisions, and produce depopulation . . . . and
even the enclosure of waste lands (as now carried on) bears
hard on the poor, by depriving them of a part of their subsistence, and only goes towards increasing farms already too
large.[1] "When," says Dr. Price, "this land gets into the
hands of a few great farmers, the consequence must be that the
little farmers" (earlier designated by him "a multitude of little proprietors and tenants, who maintain themselves and
families by the produce of the ground they occupy by sheep
kept on a common, by poultry, hogs, &c., and who therefore
have little occasion to purchase any of the means of subsistence") "will be converted into a body of men who earn their
subsistence by working for others, and who will be under a necessity of going to market for all they want . . . . There will,
perhaps, be more labour, because there will be more compulsion
to it . . . . Towns and manufacturers will increase, because
more will be driven to them in quest of places and employment.
This is the way in which the engrossing of farms naturally
operates. And this is the way in which, for many years, it
has been actually operating in this kingdom.[2]" He sums up the
effect of the enclosures thus: "Upon the whole, the circumstances of the lower ranks of men are altered in almost every
respect for the worse. From little occupiers of land, they are
reduced to the state of day-labourers and hirelings; and, at the
same time, their subsistence in that state has become more difficult."[3] In fact, usurpation of the common lands and the

---

[1] Dr. R. Price, l. c., v. ii., p. 155, Forster, Addington, Kent, Price, and James
Anderson, should be read and compared with the miserable prattle of Sycophant
MacCulloch in his catalogue: The Literature of Political Economy, London, 1845.

[2] Price, l. c., p. 147.

[3] Price, l. c., p. 159. We are reminded of ancient Rome. "The rich had got possession of the greater part of the undivided land. They trusted in the conditions
of the time, that these possessions would not be again taken from them, and bought,
therefore, some of the pieces of land lying near theirs, and belonging to the poor,
with the acquiescence of their owners, and took some by force, so that they now
were cultivating widely extended domains, instead of isolated fields. Then they
employed slaves in agriculture and cattle-breeding, because freemen would have been
taken from labour for military service. The possession of slaves brought them great
gain, inasmuch as these, on account of their immunity from military service, could
freely multiply and have a multitude of children. Thus the powerful men drew all
wealth to themselves, and all the land swarmed with slaves. The Italians, on the
other hand, were always decreasing in number, destroyed as they were by poverty,
taxes, and military service. Even when times of peace came, they were doomed to

revolution in agriculture accompanying this, told so acutely on
the agricultural labourers that, even according to Eden, between 1765 and 1780, their wages began to fall below the minimum, and to be supplemented by official poor-law relief.
Their wages, he says, "were not more than enough for the absolute necessaries of life."

Let us hear for a moment a defender of enclosures and an
opponent of Dr. Price. "Nor is it a consequence that there
must be depopulation, because men are not seen wasting their
labour in the open field . . . . If, by converting the little
farmers into a body of men who must work for others, more
labour is produced, it is an advantage which the nation" (to
which, of course, the "converted" ones do not belong) "should
wish for . . . . the produce being greater when their joint
labours are employed on one farm, there will be a surplus for
manufactures, and by this means manufactures, one of the
mines of the nation, will increase, in proportion to the quantity
of corn produced."[1]

The stoical peace of mind with which the political economist
regards the most shameless violation of the "sacred rights of
property" and the grossest acts of violence to persons, as soon
as they are necessary to lay the foundations of the capitalistic
mode of production, is shown by Sir. F. M. Eden, philanthropist and tory, to boot. The whole series of thefts, outrages,
and popular misery, that accompanied the forcible expropriation of the people, from the last third of the 15th to the end of
the 18th century, lead him merely to the comfortable conclusion: "The due proportion between arable land and pasture
had to be established. During the whole of the 14th and the
greater part of the 15th century, there was one acre of pasture

complete inactivity, because the rich were in possession of the soil, and used slaves
instead of free men in the tilling of it." (Appian: Civil Wars, I. 7.) This passage refers to the time before the Licinian rogations. Military service, which hastened to so great an extent the ruin of the Roman plebeians, was also the chief
means by which, as in a forcing-house, Charlemagne brought about the transformation of free German peasants into serfs and bondsmen.

[1] An Inquiry into the Connection between the Present Prices of Provisions, &c., p.
124, 129. To the like effect, but with an opposite tendency: "Working men are
driven from their cottages and forced into the towns to seek for employment; but
then a larger surplus is obtained, and thus capital is augmented." (The Perils of
the Nation, 2nd ed. London. 1843, p. 14.)

to 2, 3 and even 4 of arable land. About the middle of the 16th century the proportion was changed to 2 acres of pasture to 2, later on, of 2 acres of pasture to one of arable, until at last the just proportion of 3 acres of pasture to one of arable land was attained."

In the 19th century, the very memory of the connexion between the agricultural labourer and the communal property had, of course, vanished. To say nothing of more recent times, have the agricultural population received a farthing of compensation for the 3,511,770 acres of common land which between 1801 and 1831 were stolen from them and by parliamentary devices presented to the landlords by the landlords?

The last process of wholesale expropriation of the agricultural population from the soil is, finally, the so-called clearing of estates, *i.e.*, the sweeping men off them. All the English methods hitherto considered culminated in "clearing." As we saw in the picture of modern conditions given in a former chapter, where there are no more independent peasants to get rid of, the "clearing" of cottages begins; so that the agricultural labourers do not find on the soil cultivated by them even the spot necessary for their own housing. But what "clearing of estates" really and properly signifies, we learn only in the promised land of modern romance, the Highlands of Scotland. There the process is distinguished by its systematic character, by the magnitude of the scale on which it is carried out at one blow (in Ireland landlords have gone to the length of sweeping away several villages at once; in Scotland areas as large as German principalities are dealt with), finally by the peculiar form of property, under which the embezzled lands were held.

The Highland Celts were organised in clans, each of which was the owner of the land on which it was settled. The representative of the clan, its chief or "great man," was only the titular owner of this property, just as the Queen of England is the titular owner of all the national soil. When the English government succeeded in suppressing the intestine wars of these "great men," and their constant incursions into the Lowland plains, the chiefs of the clans by no means gave up their time-honoured trade as robbers; they only changed its form. On their own authority they transformed their nominal right into a right of private property, and as this brought them into collision with their clansmen, resolved to drive them out by open force. "A king of England might as well claim to drive his subjects into the sea," says Professor Newman.[1] This revolution, which began in Scotland after the last rising of the followers of the Pretender, can be followed through its first phases in the writings of Sir James Steuart[2] and James Anderson.[3] In the 18th century the hunted-out Gaels were forbidden to emigrate from the country, with a view to driving them by force to Glasgow and other manufacturing towns.[4] As an example of the method[5] obtaining in the 19th century, the "clearing" made by the Duchess of Sutherland will suffice here. This person, well instructed in economy, resolved,

---

[1] l. c., p. 132.

[2] Steuart says: "If you compare the rent of these lands" (he erroneously includes in this economic category the tribute of the taskmen to the clan-chief) "with the extent, it appears very small. If you compare it with the numbers fed upon the farm, you will find that an estate in the Highlands maintains, perhaps, ten times as many people as another of the same value in a good and fertile province." (l. c., vol. i., ch. xvi., p. 104.)

[3] James Anderson: Observations on the means of exciting a spirit of National Industry, &c. Edinburgh, 1777.

[4] In 1860 the people expropriated by force were exported to Canada under false pretences. Some fled to the mountains and neighbouring islands. They were followed by the police, came to blows with them and escaped.

[5] "In the Highlands of Scotland," says Buchanan, the commentator on Adam Smith, 1814, "the ancient state of property is daily subverted. . . . The landlord, without regard to the hereditary tenant (a category used in error here), now offers his land to the highest bidder, who, if he is an improver, instantly adopts a new system of cultivation. The land, formerly overspread with small tenants or labourers, was peopled in proportion to its produce, but under the new system of improved cultivation and increased rents, the largest possible produce is obtained at the least possible expense: and the useless hands being, with this view, removed, the population is reduced, not to what the land will maintain, but to what it will employ. The dispossessed tenants either seek a subsistence in the neighbouring towns," &c. (David Buchanan: Observations on, &c., A. Smith's Wealth of Nations. Edinburgh, 1814, vol. iv., p. 144.) "The Scotch grandees dispossessed families as they would grub up coppice-wood, and they treated villages and their people as Indians harassed with wild beasts do, in their vengeance, a jungle with tigers. . . . Man is bartered for a fleece or a carcase of mutton, nay, held cheaper. . . . Why, how much worse is it than the intention of the Moguls, who, when they had broken into the northern provinces of China, proposed in council to exterminate the inhabitants, and convert the land into pasture. This proposal many Highland proprietors have effected in their own country against their own countrymen." (George Ensor: An inquiry concerning the population of nations. Lond., 1818, pp. 215, 216.)

on entering upon her government, to effect a radical cure, and to turn the whole country, whose population had already been, by earlier processes of the like kind, reduced to 15,000, into a sheep-walk. From 1814 to 1820 these 15,000 inhabitants, about 3000 families, were systematically hunted and rooted out. All their villages were destroyed and burnt, all their fields turned into pasturage. British soldiers enforced this eviction, and came to blows with the inhabitants. One old woman was burnt to death in the flames of the hut, which she refused to leave. Thus this fine lady appropriated 794,-000 acres of land that had from time immemorial belonged to the clan. She assigned to the expelled inhabitants about 6000 acres on the sea-shore—2 acres per family. The 6000 acres had until this time lain waste, and brought in no income to their owners. The Duchess, in the nobility of her heart, actually went so far as to let these at an average ren⁺ of 2s. 6d. per acre to the clansmen, who for centuries had shed their blood for her family. The whole of the stolen clan-land she divided into 29 great sheep farms, each inhabited by a single family, for the most part imported English farm-servants. In the year 1835 the 15,000 Gaels were already replaced by 131,000 sheep. The remnant of the aborigines flung on the sea-shore, tried to live by catching fish. They became amphibious and lived, as an English author says, half on land and half on water, and withal only half on both.[1]

But the brave Gaels must expiate yet more bitterly their idolatry, romantic and of the mountains, for the "great men" of the clan. The smell of their fish rose to the noses of the great men. They scented some profit in it, and let the sea-shore to the great fishmongers of London. For the second time the Gaels were hunted out.[2]

[1] When the present Duchess of Sutherland entertained Mrs. Beecher Stowe, authoress of "Uncle Tom's Cabin," with great magnificence in London, to show her sympathy for the negro slaves of the American republic—a sympathy that she prudently forgot, with her fellow-aristocrats, during the civil war, in which every "noble" English heart beat for the slave-owner—I gave in the "New York Tribune" the facts about the Sutherland slaves. (Epitomised in part by Carey in The Slave Trade. London, 1853, p. 202, 203.) My article was reprinted in a Scotch newspaper, and led to a pretty polemic between the latter and the sycophants of the Sutherlands.

[2] Interesting details on this fish trade will be found in Mr. David Urquhart's

But, finally, part of the sheep-walks are turned into deer preserves. Every one knows that there are no real forests in England. The deer in the parks of the great are demurely domestic cattle, fat as London aldermen. Scotland is thero fore the last refuge of the "noble passion." "In the Highlands," says Somers in 1848, "new forests are springing up like mushrooms. Here, on one side of Gaick, you have the new forest of Glenfeshie; and there on the other you have the new forest of Ardverikie. In the same line you have the Black Mount, an immense waste also recently erected. From east to west—from the neighbourhood of Aberdeen to the crags of Oban—you have now a continuous line of forests; while in other parts of the Highlands there are the new forests of Loch Archaig, Glengarry, Glenmoriston, &c. Sheep were introduced into glens which had been the seats of communities of small farmers; and the latter were driven to seek subsistence on coarser and more sterile tracks of soil. Now deer are supplanting sheep; and these are once more dispossessing the small tenants, who will necessarily be driven down upon still coarser land and to more grinding penury. Deer forests[1] and the people cannot co-exist. One or other of the two must yield. Let the forests be increased in number and extent during the next quarter of a century, as they have been in the last, and the Gaels will perish from their native soil. . . . This movement among the Highland proprietors is with some a matter of ambition. . . . with some love of sport. . . . while others, of a more practical cast, follow the trade in deer with an eye solely to profit. For it is a fact, that a mountain range laid out in forest is, in many cases, more profitable to the proprietor than when let as a sheep walk. . . . The huntsman who wants a deer-forest limits his offers by no other calculation than the extent of his purse. . . . Sufferings have been inflicted in the Highlands

---

Portfolio, new series.—Nassau W. Senior, in his posthumous work, already quoted, terms "the proceedings in Sutherlandshire one of the most beneficent clearings since the memory of man." (l. c.)

[1] The deer-forests of Scotland contain not a single tree. The sheep are driven from, and then the deer driven to, the naked hills, and then it is called a deer-forest. Not even timber-planting and real forest culture.

scarcely less severe than those occasioned by the policy of the Norman kings. Deer have received extended ranges, while men have been hunted within a narrower and still narrower circle. . . . One after one the liberties of the people have been cloven down. . . . And the oppressions are daily on the increase. . . . The clearance and dispersion of the people is pursued by the proprietors as a settled principle, as an agricultural necessity, just as trees and brushwood are cleared from the wastes of America or Australia; and the operation goes on in a quiet, business-like way, &c."[1]

[1] Robert Somers: Letters from the Highlands: or the Famine of 1847. London 1848, pp. 12-. passim. These letters originally appeared in the "Times." The English economists f course explained the famine of the Gaels i 1847, by their overpopulation. At all events, they "were pressing on their food-supply." The "clearing of estates," or as it is called in Germany "Bauernlegen," occurred in Germany especially fter the 30 years' war, and led to peasant-revolts as late as 1790 in Kursachsen. It obtained especially in East Germany. In most f the Prussian provinces, Frederick II. for the first time secured right of property r the peasants. After the conquest of Silesia he forced the landlords to rebuild the huts, barns, etc., and to provide the peasants with cattle and implements. He wanted soldiers for his army and tax-payers for his treasury. For the rest, the pleasant e t at the peasant led under Frederick's system of finance and hodge-podge rule of despotism, bureaucracy and feudalism, may be seen from the following quotation from his admirer, Mirabeau: "Le lin fait donc une des grandes richesses du cultivateur dans le Nord de l'Allemagne. Malheureusement pour l'espèce humaine, ce n'est qu'une ressource contre la misère et non un moyen de bien-être. Les impôts directs, les corvées, les servitudes de tout genre, écrasent le cultivateur allemand, qui paie encore des impôts indirects dans tout ce qu'il achète . . . et poure comble de ruine, il n'ose pas vendre ses productions où et comme il le veut; il n'ose pas achter ce dont il a besoin aux marchands qui pourraient le lui livrer au meilleur prix. Toutes ces causes le ruinent insensiblement, et il se trouverait hors d'état de payer les impôts directs à l'échéance sans la filerie; elle lui offre une ressource, en occupant utilement sa femme, ses enfants, ses servants, ses valets, et lui-même; mais quelle pénible vie, même aidée de ce secours. En été, il travaille comme un forçat au labourage et à la récolte; il se couche à 9 heures et se lève à deux, pour suffire aux travaux; en hiver il devrait réparer ses forces par un plus grand repos; mais il manquera de grains pour le pain et les semailles, s'il se défait des denrées qu'il faudrait vendre pour payer les impôts. Il faut donc filer pour suppléer à ce vide . . . il faut y apporter la plus grande assiduité. Aussi le paysan se couche-t-il en hiver à minuit, une heure, et se lève à cinq ou six; ou bien il se couche à neuf, et se lève à deux, et cela tous les jours de la vie si ce n'est le dimanche. Ces excès de veille et de travail usent la nature humaine, et de là vient qu' hommes et femmes vieillissent beaucoup plûtôt dans les campagnes que dans les villes. (Mirabeau, l. c. t. III., pp. 212 sqq.)

Note to the second edition. In April 1866, 18 years after the publication of the work of Robert Somers quoted above, Professor Leone Levi gave a lecture before the Society of Arts on the transformation of sheep walks into deer-forests, in which he depicts the advance in the devastation of the Scottish Highlands. He says, with other things: "Depopulation and transformation into sheep-walks were the most convenient means for getting an income without expenditure. . . . A deer forest in place of a sheep-walk was a common change in the Highlands. The landowners turned out the sheep as they once turned out the men from their estates, and wel-

The spoliation of the churche's property, the fraudulent alienation of the State domains, the robbery of the common lands, the usurpation of feudal and clan property, and its transformation into modern private property under circumstances of reckless terrorism, were just so many idyllic methods of primitive accumulation. They conquered the field for capitalistic agriculture, made the soil part and parcel of capital, and created for the town industries the necessary supply of a "free" and outlawed proletariat.

CHAPTER XXVIII.

BLOODY LEGISLATION AGAINST THE EXPROPRIATED, FROM THE END OF THE 15TH CENTURY. FORCING DOWN OF WAGES BY ACTS OF PARLIAMENT.

THE proletariat created by the breaking up of the bands of feudal retainers and by the forcible expropriation of the peo-

comed the new tenants—the wild beasts and the feathered birds. . . . One can walk from the Earl of Dalhousie's estates in Forfarshire to John o' Groats, without ever leaving forest land. . . . In many of these woods the fox, the wild cat, the marten, the polecat, the weasel and the Alpine hare are common; whilst the rabbit, the squirrel and the rat have lately made their way into the country. Immense tracts of land, much of which is described in the statistical account of Scotland as having a pasturage in richness and extent of very superior description, are thus shut out from all cultivation and improvement, and are solely devoted to the sport of a few persons for a very brief period of the year." *The London Economist* of June 2, 1866, says, "Amongst the items of news in a Scotch paper of last week, we read. . . . 'One of the finest sheep farms in Sutherlandshire, for which a rent of £1,200 a year was recently offered, on the expiry of the existing lease this year, is to be converted into a deer forest.' Here we see the modern instincts of feudalism . . . operating pretty much as they did when the Norman Conqueror . . . destroyed 36 villages to create the New Forest. . . . Two millions of acres . . . totally laid waste, embracing within their area some of the most fertile lands of Scotland. The natural grass of Glen Tilt was among the most nutritive in the county of Perth. The deer forest of Ben Aulder was by far the best grazing ground in the wide district of Badenoch; a part of the Black Mount forest was the best pasture for black-faced sheep in Scotland. Some idea of the ground laid waste for purely sporting purposes in Scotland may be formed from the fact that it embraced an area larger than the whole county of Perth. The resources of the forest of Ben Aulder might give some idea of the loss sustained from the forced desolations. The ground would pasture 15,000 sheep, and as it was not more than one-thirtieth part of the old forest ground in Scotland . . . it might, &c., . . . All that forest land is as totally unproductive. . . . It might thus as well have been submerged under the waters of the German Ocean. . . . Such extemporized wildernesses or deserts ought to be put down by the decided interference of the Legislature."

ple from the soil, this "free" proletariat could not possibly be absorbed by the nascent manufactures as fast as it was thrown upon the world. On the other hand, these men, suddenly dragged from their wanted mode of life, could not as suddenly adapt themselves to the discipline of their new condition. They were turned *en masse* into beggars, robbers, vagabonds, partly from inclination, in most cases from stress of circumstances. Hence at the end of the 15th and during the whole of the 16th century, throughout Western Europe a bloody legislation against vagabondage. The fathers of the present working-class were chastised for their enforced transformation into vagabonds and paupers. Legislation treated them as "voluntary" criminals, and assumed that it depended on their own goodwill to go on working under the old conditions that no longer existed.

In England this legislation began under Henry VII.

Henry VIII. 1530: Beggars old and unable to work receive a beggar's licence. On the other hand, whipping and imprisonment for sturdy vagabonds. They are to be tied to the cart-tail and whipped until the blood streams from their bodies, then to swear an oath to go back to their birthplace or to where they have lived the last three years and to "put themselves to labour." What grim irony! In 27 Henry VIII. the former statute is repeated, but strengthened with new clauses. For the second arrest for vagabondage the whipping is to be repeated and half the ear sliced off; but for the third relapse the offender is to be executed as a hardened criminal and enemy of the common weal.

Edward VI.: A statute of the first year of his reign, 1547, ordains that if anyone refuses to work, he shall be condemned as a slave to the person who has denounced him as an idler. The master shall feed his slave on bread and water, weak broth and such refuse meat as he thinks fit. He has the right to force him to do any work, no matter how disgusting, with whip and chains. If the slave is absent a fortnight, he is condemned to slavery for life and is to be branded on forehead or back with the letter S; if he runs away thrice, he is to be executed as a felon. The master can sell him, bequeath him, let

him out on hire as a slave, just as any other personal chattel or
cattle. If the slaves attempt anything against the masters,
they are also to be executed. Justices of the peace, on information, are to hunt the rascals down. If it happens that a vagabond has been idling about for three days, he is to be taken to
his birthplace, branded with a redhot iron with the letter V
on the breast and be set to work, in chains, in the streets or at
some other labour. If the vagabond gives a false birthplace,
he is then to become the slave for life of this place, of its inhabitants, or its corporation, and to be branded with an S. All
persons have the right to take away the children of the vagabonds and to keep them as apprentices, the young men until the
24th year, the girls until the 20th. If they run away, they
are to become up to this age the slaves of their masters, who
can put them in irons, whip them, &c., if they like. Every
master may put an iron ring round the neck, arms or legs of his
slave, by which to know him more easily and to be more certain
of him.[1] The last part of the statute provides, that certain
poor people may be employed by a place or by persons, who are
willing to give them food and drink and to find them work.
This kind of parish-slaves was kept up in England until far
into the 19th century under the name of "roundsmen."

Elizabeth, 1572: Unlicensed beggars above 14 years of age
are to be severely flogged and branded on the left ear unless
some one will take them into service for two years; in case of a
repetition of the offence, if they are over 18, they are to be
executed, unless some one will take them into service for two
years; but for the third offence they are to be executed without
mercy as felons. Similar statutes: 18 Elizabeth, c. 13, and
another of 1597.

James I: Any one wandering about and begging is declared
a rogue and a vagabond. Justices of the peace in petty sessions are authorised to have them publicly whipped and for the
first offence to imprison them for 6 months, for the second for
2 years. Whilst in prison they are to be whipped as much

---

[1] The author of the Essay on Trade, etc., 1770, says, "In the reign of Edward VI.
indeed the English seem to have set, in good earnest, about encouraging manufactures and employing the poor. This we learn from a remarkable statute which runs
thus: 'That all vagrants shall be branded, &c.,' " l. c., p. 5.

and as often as the justices of the peace think fit . . . Incorrigible and dangerous rogues are to be branded with an R on the left shoulder and set to hard labour, and if they are caught begging again, to be executed without mercy. These statutes, legally binding until the beginning of the 18th century, were only repealed by 12 Ann, c. 23.[1]

Similar laws in France, where by the middle of the 17th century a kingdom of vagabonds (truands) was established in Paris. Even at the beginning of Louis XVI.'s reign (Ordinance of July 13th, 1777) every man in good health from 16 to 60 years of age, if without means of subsistence and not practising a trade, is to be sent to the galleys. Of the same nature are the statute of Charles V. for the Netherlands (October, 1537), the first edict of the States and Towns of Holland (March 10, 1614), the "Plakaat" of the United Provinces (June 26, 1649), &c.

Thus were the agricultural people, first forcibly expropri-

---

[1] Thomas More says in his "Utopia": "Therefore that one covetous and unsatiable cormaraunte and very plage of his native contrey maye compasse aboute and inclose many thousand akers of grounde together within one pale or hedge, the husbandmen be thrust owte of their owne, or els either by coneyne and fraude, or by violent oppression they be put besydes it, or by wrongs and iniuries thei be so weried that they be compelled to sell all: by one meanes, therfore, or by other, either by hooke or crooke they muste needes departe awaye, poore, selye, wretched soules, men, women, husbands, wiues, fatherlesse children, widowes, wofull mothers with their yonge babes, and their whole household smal in substance, and muche in numbre, as husbandrye requireth many handés. Awaye thei trudge, I say, owte of their knowen accustomed houses, fyndynge no place to reste in. All their householde stuffe, which is very little woorthe, thoughe it might well abide the sale: yet beeynge sodainely thruste owte, they be constrayned to sell it for a thing of nought. And when they haue wandered abrode tyll that be spent, what can they then els doe but steale, and then iustly pardy be hánged, or els go about beggyng. And yet then also they be caste in prison as vagabondes, because theey go aboute and worke not; whom no man wyl set a worke though thei neuer so willyngly profre themselues therto." Of these poor fugitives of whom Thomas More says that they were forced to thieve, "7200 great and petty thieves were put to death," in the reign of Henry VIII. (Hollinshed, description of England, Vol. 1., p. 186.) In Elizabeth's time, "rogues were trussed up apace, and that there was not one year commonly wherein three or four hundred were not devoured and eaten up by the gallowes." (Strype's Annals of the Reformation and Establishment of Religion, and other Various Occurrences in the Church of England during Queen Elizabeth's Happy Reign. Second ed., 1725, Vol. 2.) According to this same Strype, in Somersetshire, in one year, 40 persons were executed, 35 robbers burnt in the hand, 37 whipped, and 183 discharged as "incorrigible vagabonds." Nevertheless, he is of opinion that this large number of prisoners does not comprise even a fifth of the actual criminals, thanks to the negligence of the justices and the foolish compassion of the people; and the other counties of England were not better off in this respect than Somersetshire, while some were even worse.

ated from the soil, driven from their homes, turned into vagabonds, and then whipped, branded, tortured by laws grotesquely terrible, into the discipline necessary for the wage
system.

It is not enough that the conditions of labour are concentrated in a mass, in the shape of capital, at the one pole of
society, while at the other are grouped masses of men, who
have nothing to sell but their labour-power. Neither is it
enough that they are compelled to sell it voluntarily. The
advance of capitalist production develops a working-class,
which by education, tradition, habit, looks upon the conditions
of that mode of production as self-evident laws of nature.
The organization of the capitalist process of production, once
fully developed, breaks down all resistance. The constant
generation of a relative surplus-population keeps the law of
supply and demand of labour, and therefore keeps wages, in
a rut that corresponds with the wants of capital. The dull
compulsion of economic relations completes the subjection of
the labourer to the capitalist. Direct force, outside economic
conditions, is of course still used, but only exceptionally. In
the ordinary run of things, the labourer can be left to the
"natural laws of production," *i.e.,* to his dependence on capital,
a dependence springing from, and guaranteed in perpetuity by,
the conditions of production themselves. It is otherwise during the historic genesis of capitalist production. The bourgeoisie, at its rise, wants and uses the power of the state to
"regulate" wages, *i.e.,* to force them within the limits suitable
for surplus-value making, to lengthen the working-day and to
keep the labourer himself in the normal degree of dependence.
This is an essential element of the so-called primitive accumulation.

The class of wage-labourers, which arose in the latter half of
the 14th century, formed then and in the following century
only a very small part of the population, well protected in its
position by the independent peasant proprietary in the country and the guild-organization in the town. In country and
town master and workman stood close together socially. The
subordination of labour to capital was only formal—*i.e.,* the

mode of production itself had as yet no specific capitalistic character. Variable capital preponderated greatly over constant. The demand for wage-labour grew, therefore, rapidly with every accumulation of capital, whilst the supply of wage-labour followed but slowly. A large part of the national product, changed later into a fund of capitalist accumulation, then still entered into the consumption fund of the labourer.

Legislation on wage-labour, (from the first, aimed at the exploitation of the labourer and, as it advanced, always equally hostile to him),[1] is started in England by the Statute of Labourers, of Edward III., 1349. The ordinance of 1350 in France, issued in the name of King John, corresponds with it. English and French legislation run parallel and are identical in purport. So far as the labour-statutes aim at compulsory extension of the working-day, I do not return to them, as this point was treated earlier (Chap. X., Section 5).

The Statute of Labourers was passed at the urgent instance of the House of Commons. A Tory says naively: "Formerly the poor demanded such *high* wages as to threaten industry and wealth. Next, their wages are so *low* as to threaten industry and wealth equally and perhaps more, but in another way."[2] A tariff of wages was fixed by law for town and country, for piece-work and day-work. The agricultural labourers were to hire themselves out by the year, the town ones "in open market." It was forbidden, under pain of imprisonment, to pay higher wages than those fixed by the statute, but the taking of higher wages was more severely punished than the giving them. [So also in Sections 18 and 19 of the Staute of Apprentices of Elizabeth, ten days' imprisonment is decreed for him that pays the higher wages, but twenty-one days for him that receives them.] A statute of 1360 increased the penalties and authorised the masters to extort labour at the legal rate of wages by corporal punishment. All combina-

---

[1] "Whenever the legislature attempts to regulate the differences between masters and their workmen, its counsellors are always the masters," says A. Smith. "L'esprit des lois, c'est la propriété," says Linguet.

[2] "Sophisms of Free Trade." By a Barrister. Lond., 1850, p. 53. He adds maliciously: "We were ready enough to interfere for the employer, can nothing now be done for the employed?"

Legislation Against the Expropriated. 811

tions, contracts, oaths, &c., by which masons and carpenters reciprocally bound themselves, were declared null and void. Coalition of the labourers is treated as a heinous crime from the 14th century to 1825, the year of the repeal of tho laws against Trades' Unions. The spirit of the Statute of Labourers of 1349 and of its offshoots, comes out clearly in the fact, that indeed a maximum of wages is dictated by the State, but on no account a minimum.

In the 16th century, tho condition of the labourers had, as we know, become much worse. The money wage rose, but not in proportion to the depreciation of money and the corresponding rise in the prices of commodities. Wages, therefore, in reality fell. Nevertheless, the laws for keeping them down remained in force, together with the ear-clipping and branding of those "whom no one was willing to take into service." By the Statute of Apprentices 5 Elizabeth, c. 3, the justices of the peace were empowered to fix certain wages and to modify them according to the time of the year and the price of commodities. James I. extended these regulations of labour also to weavers, spinners, and all possible categories of workers.[1] George II. extended the laws against coalitions of labourers to manufactures. In the manufacturing period *par excellence,* the capitalist mode of production had become sufficiently strong to render legal regulation of wages as impracticable as it was unnecessary; but the ruling classes were unwilling in case of

[1] From a clause of Statute 2 James I., c. 6, wc see that certain cloth-makers took upon themselves to dictate, in their capacity of justices of the peace, the official tariff of wages in their own shops. In Germany, especially after the Thirty Years' War, statutes for keeping down wages were general. "The want of servants and labourers was very troublesome to the landed proprietors in the depopulated districts. All villagers were forbidden to let rooms to single men and women; all the latter were to be reported to the authorities and cast into prison if they were unwilling to become servants, even if they were employed at any other work, such as sowing seeds for the peasants at a daily wage, or even buying and selling corn. (Imperial privileges and sanctions for Silesia, I., 25.) For a whole century in the decrees of the small German potentates a bitter cry goes up again and again about the wicked and impertinent rabble that will not reconcile itself to its hard lot, will not be content with the legal wage; the individual landed proprietors are forbidden to pay more than the State had fixed by a tariff. And yet the conditions of service were at times better after the war than 100 years later; the farm servants of Silesia had, in 1652, meat twice a week, whilst even in our century, districts are known where they have it only three times a year. Further, wages after the war were higher than in the following century." (G. Freitag.)

necessity to be without the weapons of the old arsenal. Still, 8 George II. forbade a higher day's wage than 2s. 7½d. for journeymen tailors in and around London, except in cases of general mourning; still 13 George III., c. 68, gave the regulation of the wages of silk-weavers to the justices of the peace; still, in 1706, it required two judgments of the higher courts to decide, whether the mandates of justices of the peace as to wages held good also for non-agricultural labourers; still, in 1799, an act of Parliament ordered that the wages of the Scotch miners should continue to be regulated by a statute of Elizabeth and two Scotch acts of 1661 and 1671. How completely in the meantime circumstances had changed, is proved by an occurrence unheard-of before in the English Lower House. In that place, where for more than 400 years laws had been made for the maximum, beyond which wages absolutely must not rise, Whitbread in 1796 proposed a legal minimum wage for agricultural labourers. Pitt opposed this, but confessed that the "condition of the poor was cruel." Finally, in 1813, the laws for the regulation of wages were repealed. They were an absurd anomaly, since the capitalist regulated his factory by his private legislation, and could by the poor-rates make up the wage of the agricultural labourer to the indispensable minimum. The provisions of the labour statutes as to contracts between master and workman, as to giving notice and the like, which only allows of a civil action against the contract-breaking master, but on the contrary permit a criminal action against the contract-breaking workman, are to this hour (1873) in full force. The barbarous laws against Trades' Unions fell in 1825 before the threatening bearing of the proletariat. Despite this, they fell only in part. Certain beautiful fragments of the old statute vanished only in 1859. Finally, the act of Parliament of June 29, 1871, made a pretence of removing the last traces of this class of legislation by legal recognition of Trades Unions. But an act of Parliament of the same date (an act to amend the criminal law relating to violence, threats, and molestation), re-established, in point of fact, the former state of things in a new shape. By this Parliamentary escamotage the means which the labourers

could use in a strike or lock-out were withdrawn from the laws
common to all citizens, and placed under exceptional penal legislation, the interpretation of which fell to the masters themselves in their capacity as justices of the peace. Two years
earlier, the same House of Commons and the same Mr. Gladstone in the well-known straightforward fashion brought in a
bill for the abolition of all exceptional penal legislation against
the working-class. But this was never allowed to go beyond
the second reading, and the matter was thus protracted until
at last the "great Liberal party," by an alliance with the Tories, found courage to turn against the very proletariat that had
carried it into power. Not content with this treachery, the
"great Liberal party" allowed the English judges, ever com-
plaisant in the service of the ruling classes, to dig up again
the earlier laws against "conspiracy," and to apply them to
coalitions of labourers. We see that only against its will and
under the pressure of the masses did the English Parliament
give up the laws against Strikes and Trades' Unions, after it
had itself, for 500 years, held, with shameless egoism, the position of a permanent Trades' Union of the capitalists against
the labourers.

During the very first storms of the revolution, the French
bourgeoisie dared to take away from the workers the right of
association but just acquired. By a decree of June 14, 1791,
they declared all coalition of the workers as "an attempt
against liberty and the declaration of the rights of man," pun-
ishable by a fine of 500 livres, together with deprivation of the
rights of an active citizen for one year.[1] This law which, by
means of State compulsion, confined the struggle between capital and labour within limits comfortable for capital, has outlived revolutions and changes of dynasties. Even the Reign
of Terror left it untouched. It was but quite recently struck
out of the Penal Code. Nothing is more characteristic than
the pretext for this bourgeois coup d'état. "Granting," says
Chapelier, the reporter of the Select Committee on this law,
"that wages ought to be a little higher than they are, . . .
that they ought to be high enough for him that receives them,

---

[1] Article I. of this law runs: "L' anéantissement de toute espèce de corporations

to be free from that state of absolute dependence due to the want of the necessaries of life, and which is almost that of slavery," yet the workers must not be allowed to come to any understanding about their own interests, nor to act in common and thereby lessen their "absolute dependence, which is almost that of slavery;" because, forsooth, in doing this they injure "the freedom of their cidevant masters, the present entrepreneurs," and because a coalition against the despotism of the quondam masters of the corporations is—guess what!—is a restoration of the corporations abolished by the French constitution.[1]

CHAPTER XXIX.

GENESIS OF THE CAPITALIST FARMER.

Now that we have considered the forcible creation of a class of outlawed proletarians, the bloody discipline that turned them into wage-labourers, the disgraceful action of the state which employed the police to accelerate the accumulation of capital by increasing the degree of exploitation of labour, the question remains: whence came the capitalists originally? For the expropriation of the agricultural population creates, directly, none by great landed proprietors. As far, however, as concerns the genesis of the farmer, we can, so to say, put our hand on it, because it is a slow process evolving through many centuries. The serfs, as well as the free small proprietors, held land under very different tenures, and were therefore emancipated under very different economic conditions. In England the first form of the farmer is the bailiff, himself a

----

du même état et profession étant l'une des bases fondamentales de la constitution française, il est défendu de les rétablir de fait sous quelque prétexte et sous quelque forme que ce soit." Article IV. declares, that if "des citoyens attachés aux mêmes professions, arts et métiers prenaient des délibérations, faisaient entre eux des conventions tendantes à refuser de concert ou à n'accorder qu'à un prix déterminé le secours de leur industrie ou de leurs travaux, les dites délibérations et conventions . . . seront déclarées inconstitutionnelles, attentatoires à la liberté et à la déclaration des droits de l'homme, &c.": felony, therefore, as in the old labour-statutes. ("Revolutions de Paris." Paris, 1791, t. III., p. 523.)

[1] Buchez et Roux: "Histoire Parlementaire," t. x., p. 195.

serf. His position is similar to that of the old Roman *villicus,* only in a more limited sphere of action. During the second half of the 14th century he is replaced by a farmer, whom the landlord provides with seed, cattle and implements. His condition is not very different from that of the peasant. Only he exploits more wage-labour. Soon he becomes a métayer, a half-farmer. He advances one part of the agricultural stock, the landlord the other. The two divide the total product in proportions determined by contract. This form quickly disappears in England, to give place to the farmer proper, who makes his own capital breed by employing wage-labourers, and pays a part of the surplus product, in money or in kind, to the landlord as rent. So long, during the 15th century, as the independent peasant and the farm-labourer working for himself as well as for wages, enriched themselves by their own labour, the circumstances of the farmer, and his field of production, were equally mediocre. The agricultural revolution which commenced in the last third of the 15th century, and continued during almost the whole of the 16th (excepting, however, its last decade), enriched him just as speedily as it impoverished the mass of the agricultural people.[1]

The usurpation of the common lands allowed him to augment greatly his stock of cattle, almost without cost, whilst they yielded him a richer supply of manure for the tillage of the soil. To this, was added in the 16th century, a very important element. At that time the contracts for farms ran for a long time, often for 99 years. The progressive fall in the value of the precious metals, and therefore of money, brought the farmers golden fruit. Apart from all the other circumstances discussed above, it lowered wages. A portion of the latter was now added to the profits of the farm. The continuous rise in the price of corn, wool, meat, in a word of all agricultural produce, swelled the money capital of the farmer without any action on his part, whilst the rent he paid, (being

---

[1] Harrison in his 'Description of England,' says "although peradventure foure pounds of old rent be improved to fortie, toward the end of his term, if he have not six or seven years rent liefig by him, fiftie or a hundred pounds, yet will the farmer thinke his gaines verie small."

calculated on the old value of money) diminished in reality.[1] Thus they grew rich at the expense both of their labourers and their landlords. No wonder therefore, that England, at the end of the 16th century, had a class of capitalist farmers, rich, considering the circumstances of the time.[2]

[1] On the influence of the depreciation of money in the 16th century, on the different classes of society, see "A Compendious or Briefe Examination of Certayne Ordinary complaints of Diverse of our Countrymen in these our days." By W. S., Gentleman. (London 1581). The dialogue form of this work led people for a long time to ascribe it to Shakespeare, and even in 1751, it was published under his name. Its author is William Stafford. In one place the knight reasons as follows: Knight: "You, my neighbour, the husbandman, you Maister Mercer, and you Goodman Cooper, with other artificers, may save yourselves metely well. For as much as all things are deerer than they were, so mucu do you arise in the pryce of your wares and occupations that ye sell agayne. B t e have nothing to sell where-i, we might advance ye price there of, to countervaile those t ings that we must buy agayne." In another pla the knight asks the doctor: "I pray you, what be those sorts that ye meane. And first, those that ye thinke should have no losse thereby?—Doctor: I mean all those ha live by buying and selling, for as they buy deare, they sell thereafter. Knight: What is the next sort that ye say would win by t? Doctor. Marry, all such as have takings or fearmes in their owne manurance [cultivation] a the old rent, for where they pay after the olde rate they sell after the newe—that is, they paye for theire lande good cheape, and sell all things growing thereof deare. Knight: What sorte is that which, ye sayde should have greater losse hereby, than these men had profit? Doctor: It is all noblemen, gentlemen, and all other that live either by a stinted rent or stypend, or do not manure [cultivation] the ground, or doe occupy no buying and selling."

[2] In France, the régisseur, steward, collector of dues for the feudal lords during the earlier part of the middle ages, soon became an homme d'affaires, who by extortion, cheating, &c., swindled himself into a capitalist. These régisseurs themselves were sometimes noblemen. E. g. C'est li compte que messire Jacques de Thoraine, chevalier chastelain sor Besançon rent ès-seigneur tenant les comptes à Dijon pour monseigneur le duc et comte de Bourgoigne, des rentes appartenant à la dite chastellenie, depuis xxve jour de décembre MCCCLIX jusqu' au xxviiie jour de décembre MCCCLX. (Alexis Monteil: Histoire des Materiaux manuscrits, etc., p. 244.) Already it is evident here how in all spheres of social life the lion's share falls to the middleman. In the economic domain, *e.g.*, financiers, stock-exchange speculators, merchants, shopkeepers skim the cream; in civil matters, the lawyer fleeces his clients; in politics the representative is of more importance than the voters, the minister than the sovereign; in religion God is pushed into the background by the "Mediator," and the latter again is shoved back by the priests, the inevitable middlemen between the good shepherd and his sheep. In France, as in England, the great feudal territories were divided into inumerable small homesteads, but under conditions incomparably more unfavourable for the people. During the 14th century arose the farms or *terriers*. Their number grew constantly, far beyond 100,000. They paid rents varying from $\frac{1}{12}$ to $\frac{1}{5}$ of the product in money or in kind. These farms were fiefs, sub-fiefs, &., according to the value and extent of the domains, many of them only containing a few :cres. But these farmers had rights of jurisdiction in some degree over the dwellers on the soil; there were four grades. The oppression of the agricultural population under all these petty tyrants will be understood. Monteil says that there were once in France 160,000 judges, where today 4000 tribunals, including justices of the peace, suffice.

CHAPTER XXX.

REACTION OF THE AGRICULTURAL REVOLUTION ON INDUSTRY.
CREATION OF THE HOME MARKET FOR INDUSTRIAL CAPI-
TAL.

THE expropriation and expulsion of the agricultural population, intermittent but renewed again and again, supplied, as
we saw, the town industries with a mass of proletarians, entirely unconnected with the corporate guilds and unfettered
by them; a fortunate circumstance that makes old A. Anderson (not to be confounded with James Anderson) in his "History of Commerce," believe in the direct intervention of
Providence. We must still pause a moment on this element of
primitive accumulation. The thinning-out of the independent,
self-supporting peasants not only brought about the crowding
together of the industrial proletariat, in the way that Geoffroy
Saint Hilaire explained the condensation of cosmical matter at
one place, by its rarefaction at another.[1] In spite of the
smaller numbers of its cultivators, the soil brought forth as
much or more produce, after as before, because the revolution
in the conditions of landed property was accompanied by improved methods of culture, greater co-operation, concentration
of the means of production, &c., and because not only were
the agricultural wage-labourers put on the strain more intensely,[2] but the field of production on which they worked for
themselves, became more and more contracted. With the setting free of a part of the agricultural population, therefore,
their former means of nourishment were also set free. They
were now transformed into material elements of variable capital. The peasant, expropriated and cast adrift, must buy
their value in the form of wages, from his new master, the industrial capitalist. That which holds good of the means of
subsistence holds with the raw materials of industry dependent

[1] In his Notions de Philosophie Naturelle. Paris, 1838.
[2] A point that Sir James Stewart emphasises.

upon home agriculture. They were transformed into an element of constant capital. Suppose, *e.g.,* a part of the Westphalian peasants, who, at the time of Frederic II., all span flax, forcibly expropriated and hunted from the soil; and the other part that remained, turned into day-labourers of large farmers. At the same time arise large establishments for flax-spinning and weaving, in which the men "set free" now work for wages. The flax looks exactly as before. Not a fibre of it is changed, but a new social soul has popped into its body. It forms now a part of the constant capital of the master manufacturer. Formerly divided among a number of small producers, who cultivated it themselves and with their families spun it in retail fashion, it is now concentrated in the hand of one capitalist, who sets others to spin and weave it for him. The extra labour expended in flax-spinning realised itself formerly in extra income to numerous peasant families, or maybe, in Frederic II.'s time, in taxes pour le roi de Prusse. It realises itself now in profit for a few capitalists. The spindles and looms, formerly scattered over the face of the country, are now crowded together in a few great labour-barracks, together with the labourers and the raw material. And spindles, looms, raw material, are now transformed, from means of independent existence for the spinners and weavers, into means for commanding them and sucking out of them unpaid labour.[1] One does not perceive, when looking at the large manufactories and the large farms, that they have originated from the throwing into one of many small centres of production, and have been built up by the expropriation of many small independent producers. Nevertheless, the popular intuition was not at fault. In the time of Mirabeau, the lion of the Revolution, the great manufactories were still called manufactures réunies, workshops thrown into one, as we speak of fields thrown into one. Says Mirabeau: "We are only paying attention to the grand manufactories, in which hundreds of men work under a director and which are commonly called *manufactures ré-*

---

[1] "Je permettrai," says the capitalist, "que vous ayez l'honneur de me servir, à condition que vous me donnez le peu qui vous reste pour la peine que je prends de vous commander." (J. J. Rousseau: Discours sur l'Economie Politique.)

unies. Those where a very large number of labourers work, each separately and on his own account, are hardly considered; they are placed at an infinite distance from the others. This is a great error, as the latter alone make a really important object of national prosperity . . . The large workshop (manufacture réunie) will enrich prodigiously one or two entrepreneurs, but the labourers will only be journeymen, paid more or less, and will not have any share in the success of the undertaking. In the discrete workshop (manufacture séparée,) on the contrary, no one will become rich, but many labourers will be comfortable; the saving and the industrious will be able to amass a little capital, to put by a little for a birth of a child, for an illness, for themselves or their belongings. The number of saving and industrious labourers will increase, because they will see in good conduct, in activity, a means of essentially bettering their condition, and not of obtaining a small rise of wages that can never be of any importance for the future, and whose sole result is to place men in the position to live a little better, but only from day to day . . . The large workshops, undertakings of certain private persons who pay labourers from day to day to work for their gain, may be able to put these private individuals at their ease, but they will never be an object worth the attention of governments. Discrete workshops, for the most part combined with cultivation of small holdings, are the only free ones."[1] The expropriation and eviction of a part of the agricultural population not only set free for industrial capital, the labourers, their means of subsistence, and material for labour; it also created the home market.

In fact, the events that transformed the small peasants into wage-labourers, and their means of subsistence and of labour into material elements of capital, created, at the same time, a home-market for the latter. Formerly, the peasant family produced the means of subsistence and the raw materials, which they themselves, for the most part, consumed. These raw

---

[1] Mirabeau, l. c. t. III, pp. 20-100 passim. That Mirabeau considers the separate workshops more economic and productive than the "combined," and sees in the latter merely artificial exotics under government cultivation, is explained by the position at that time of a great part of the continental manufactures.

materials and means of subsistence have now become commodities; the large farmer sells them, he finds his market in
manufactures. Yarn, linen, coarse woollen stuffs—things
whose raw materials had been within the reach of every
peasant family, had been spun and woven by it for its own
use—were now transformed into articles of manufacture, to
which the country districts at once served for markets. The
many scattered customers, whom stray artizans until now had
found in the numerous small producers working on their own
account, concentrate themselves now into one great market
provided for by industrial capital.[1] Thus, hand in hand with
the expropriation of the self-supporting peasants, with their
separation from their means of production, goes the destruction of rural domestic industry, the process of separation between manufacture and agriculture. And only the destruction of rural domestic industry can give the internal market
of a country that extension and consistence which the capitalist
mode of production requires. Still the manufacturing period,
properly so-called, does not succeed in carrying out this transformation radically and completely. It will be remembered
that manufacture, properly so-called, conquers but partially
the domain of national production, and always rests on the
handicrafts of the town and the domestic industry of the rural
districts as its ultimate basis. If it destroys these in one form,
in particular branches, at certain points, it calls them up again
elsewhere, because it needs them for the preparation of raw
material up to a certain point. It produces, therefore, a new
class of small villagers who, while following the cultivation of
the soil as an accessory calling, find their chief occupation in
industrial labour, the products of which they sell to the manufacturers directly, or through the medium of merchants. This
is one, though not the chief, cause of a phenomenon which, at

---

[1] "Twenty pounds of wool converted unobtrusively into the yearly clothing of a
labourer's family by its own industry in the intervals of other work—this makes no
show; but bring it to market, send it to the factory, thence to the broker, thence to
the dealer, and you will have great commercial operations, and nominal capital engaged to the amount of twenty times its value. . . . The working class is thus
emerced to support a wretched factory population, a parasitical shop-keeping class,
and a fictitious commercial, monetary, and financial system. (David Urquhart, l. c.,
p. 120.)

first, puzzles the student of English history. From the last third of the 15th century he finds continually complaints, only interrupted at certain invervals, about the encroachment of capitalist farming in the country districts, and the progressive destruction of the peasantry. On the other hand, he always finds this peasantry turning up again, although in diminished number, and always under worse conditions.[1] The chief reason is: England is at one time chiefly a cultivator of corn, at another chiefly a breeder of cattle, in alternate periods, and with these the extent of peasant cultivation fluctuates. Modern Industry alone, and finally, supplies, in machinery, the lasting basis of capitalistic agriculture, expropriates radically the enormous majority of the agricultural population, and completes the separation between agriculture and rural domestic industry. whose roots—spinning and weaving—it tears up.[2] It therefore also, for the first time, conquers for industrial capital the entire home market.[3]

[1] Cromwell's time forms an exception. So long as the Republic lasted, the mass of the English people of all grades rose from the degradation into which they had sunk under the Tudors.

[2] Tuckett is aware that the modern woollen industry has sprung, with the introduction of machinery, from manufacture proper and from the destruction of rural and domestic industries. "The plough, the yoke, were 'the invention of gods, and the occupation of heroes;' are the loom, the spindle, the distaff, of less noble parentage. You sever the distaff and the plough, the spindle and the yoke, and you get factories and poorhouses, credit and panics, two hostile nations, agricultural and commercial." (David Urquhart, l. c., p. 122.) But now comes Carey, and cries out upon England, surely not with unreason, that it is trying to turn every other country into a mere agricultural nation, whose manufacturer is to be England. He pretends that in this way Turkey has been ruined, because "the owners and occupants of land have never been permitted by England to strengthen themselves by the formation of that natural alliance between the plough and the loom, the hammer and the harrow." (The Slave Trade, p. 125.) According to him, Urquhart himself is one of the chief agents in the ruin of Turkey, where he had made free trade propaganda in the English interest. The best of it is that Carey, a great Russophile by the way, wants to prevent the process of separation by that very system of protection which accelerates it.

[3] Philanthropic English economists, like Mill, Rogers, Goldwin, Smith, Fawcett, &c., and liberal manufacturers like John Bright & Co., ask the English landed proprietors, as God asked Cain after Abel, Where are our thousands of freeholders gone? But where do *you* come from, then? From the destruction of those freeholders. Why don't you ask further, where are the independent weavers, spinners, and artizans gone?

CHAPTER XXXI.

GENESIS OF THE INDUSTRIAL CAPITALIST.

THE genesis of the industrial[1] capitalist did not proceed in such a gradual way as that of the farmer. Doubtless many small guild-masters, and yet more independent small artisans, or even wage-labourers, transformed themselves into small capitalists, and (by gradually extending exploitation of wage-labour and corresponding accumulation) into full-blown capitalists. In the infancy of capitalist production, things often happened as in the infancy of mediæval towns, where the question, which of the escaped serfs should be master and which servant, was in great part decided by the earlier or later date of their flight. The snail's-pace of this method corresponded in no wise with the commercial requirements of the new world-market that the great discoveries of the end of the 15th century created. But the middle age had handed down two distinct forms of capital, which mature in the most different economic social formations, and which, before the era of the capitalist mode of production, are considered as capital quand même—usurer's capital and merchant's capital.

"At present, all the wealth of society goes first into the possession of the capitalist . . . . he pays the landowner his rent, the labourer his wages, the tax and tithe gatherer their claims, and keeps a large, indeed the largest, and a continually augmenting share, of the annual produce of labour for himself. The capitalist may now be said to be the first owner of all the wealth of the community, though no law has conferred on him the right to this property . . . . this change has been effected by the taking of interest on capital . . . . and it is not a little curious that all the lawgivers of Europe endeavoured to prevent this by statutes, viz., statutes against usury. . . . . The power of the capitalist over all the wealth of the country is a

---

[1] Industrial here in contradistinction to agricultural. In the "categoric" sense the farmer is an industrial capitalist as much as the manufacturer.

complete change in the right of property, and by what law, or series of laws, was it effected?" [1] The author should have remembered that revolutions are not made by laws.

The money capital formed by means of usury and commerce was prevented from turning into industrial capital, in the country by the feudal constitution. in the towns by the guild organization.[2] These fetters vanished with the dissolution of feudal society, with the expropriation and partial eviction of the country population. The new manufacturers were established at sea-ports, or in inland points beyond the control of the old municipalities and their guilds. Hence in England an embittered struggle of the corporate towns against these new industrial nurseries.

The discovery of gold and silver in America, the extirpation, enslavement and entombment in mines of the aboriginal population, the beginning of the conquest and looting of the East Indies, the turning of Africa into a warren for the commercial hunting of black-skins, signalised the rosy dawn of the era of capitalist production. These idyllic proceedings are the chief momenta of primitive accumulation. On their heels treads the commercial war of the European nations, with the globe for a theatre. It begins with the revolt of the Netherlands from Spain, assumes giant dimensions in England's anti-jacobin war, and is still going on in the opium wars against China, &c.

The different momenta of primitive accumulation distribute themselves now, more or less in chronological order, particularly over Spain, Portugal, Holland, France, and England. In England at the end of the 17th century, they arrive at a systematical combination, embracing the colonies, the national debt, the modern mode of taxation, and the protectionist system. These methods depend in part on brute force, *e.g.,* the colonial system. But they all employ the power of the State, the concentrated and organised force of society, to hasten,

---

[1] "The Natural and Artificial Rights of Property Contrasted." Lond., 1832, pp 98-99. Author of the anonymous work: "Th. Hodgskin."

[2] Even as late as 1794, the small cloth-makers of Leeds sent a deputation to Parliament, with a petition for a law to forbid any merchant from becoming a manufacturer. (Dr. Aikin, 1. c.)

hothouse fashion, the process of transformation of the feudal mode of production into the capitalist mode, and to shorten the transition. Force is the midwife of every old society pregnant with a new one. It is itself an economic power.

Of the Christian colonial system, W. Howitt, a man who makes a specialty of Christianity, says: "The barbarities and desperate outrages of the so-called Christian race, throughout every region of the world, and upon every people they have been able to subdue, are not to be paralleled by those of any other race, however fierce, however untaught, and however reckless of mercy and of shame, in any age of the earth." [1] The history of the colonial administration of Holland—and Holland was the head capitalistic nation of the 17th century —"is one of the most extraordinary relations of treachery, bribery, massacre, and meanness." [2] Nothing is more characteristic than their system of stealing men, to get slaves for Java. The men stealers were trained for this purpose. The thief, the interpreter, and the seller, were the chief agents in this trade, native princes the chief sellers. The young people stolen, were thrown into the secret dungeons of Celebes, until they were ready for sending to the slave-ships. An official report says: "This one town of Macassar, *e.g.*, is full of secret prisons, one more horrible than the other, crammed with unfortunates, victims of greed and tyranny fettered in chains, forcibly torn from their families." To secure Malacca, the Dutch corrupted the Portuguese governor. He let them into the town in 1641. They hurried at once to his house and assassinated him, to "abstain" from the payment of £21,875, the price of his treason. Wherever they set foot, devastation and depopulation followed. Banjuwangi, a province of Java, in 1750 numbered over 80,000 inhabitants, in 1811 only 18,-000. Sweet commerce!

[1] William Howitt: "Colonisation and Christianity: A Popular History of the Treatment of the Natives by the Europeans in all their Colonies." London, 1838, p. 9. On the treatment of the slaves there is a good compilation in Charles Comte, Traité de la Législation. 3me éd. Bruxelles, 1837. This subject one must study in detail, to see what the bourgeoisie makes of itself and of the labourer, wherever it can, without restraint, model the world after its own image.

[2] Thomas Stamford Raffles, late Lieut.-Gov. of that island: "History of Java and its dependencies." Lond., 1817

The English East India Company, as is well known, obtained, besides the political rule in India, the exclusive monopoly of the tea-trade, as well as of the Chinese trade in general, and of the transport of goods to and from Europe. But the coasting trade of India and between the islands, as well as the internal trade of India, were the monopoly of the higher employés of the company. The monopolies of salt, opium, betel and other commodities, were inexhaustible mines of wealth. The employés themselves fixed the price and plundered at will the unhappy Hindus. The Governor-General took part in this private traffic. His favourite received contracts under conditions whereby they, cleverer than the alchemists, made gold out of nothing. Great fortunes sprang up like mushrooms in a day; primitive accumulation went on without the advance of a shilling. The trial of Warren Hastings swarms with such cases. Here is an instance. A contract for opium was given to a certain Sullivan at the moment of his departure on an official mission to a part of India far removed from the opium district. Sullivan sold his contract to one Binn for £40,000; Binn sold it the same day for £60,000, and the ultimate purchaser who carried out the contract declared that after all he realised an enormous gain. According to one of the lists laid before Parliament, the Company and its employés from 1757–1766 got £6,000,000 from the Indians as gifts. Between 1769 and 1770, the English manufactured a famine by buying up all the rice and refusing to sell it again, except at fabulous prices.[1]

The treatment of the aborigines was, naturally, most frightful in plantation-colonies destined for export trade only, such as the West Indies, and in rich and well-populated countries, such as Mexico and India, that were given over to plunder. But even in the colonies properly so-called, the Christian character of primitive accumulation did not belie itself. Those sober virtuosi of Protestantism, the Puritans of New England, in 1703, by decrees of their assembly set a premium of £40 on

[1] In the year 1866 more than a million Hindus died of hunger in the province of Orissa alone. Nevertheless, the attempt was made to enrich the Indian treasury by the price at which the necessaries of life were sold to the starving people.

every Indian scalp and every captured red-skin: in **1720** a premium of £100 on every scalp; in 1744, after Massachusetts-Bay had proclaimed a certain tribe as rebels, the following prices: for a male scalp of 12 years and upwards £100 (new currency), for a male prisoner £105, for women and children prisoners £50, for scalps of women and children £50. Some decades later, the colonial system took its revenge on the descendants of the pious pilgrim fathers, who had grown seditious in the meantime. At English instigation and for English pay they were tomahawked by red-skins. The British Parliament, proclaimed blood-hounds and scalping as "means that God and Nature had given into its hand."

The colonial system ripened, like a hot-house, trade and navigation. The "societies Monopolia" of Luther were powerful levers for concentration of capital. The colonies secured a market for the budding manufactures, and, through the monopoly of the market, an increased accumulation. The treasures captured outside Europe by undisguised looting, enslavement, and murder, floated back to the mother-country and were there turned into capital. Holland, which first fully developed the colonial system, in 1648 stood already in the acme of its commercial greatness. It was "in almost exclusive possession of the East Indian trade and the commerce between the south-east and north-west of Europe. Its fisheries, marine, manufactures, surpassed those of any other country. The total capital of the Republic was probably more important than that of all the rest of Europe put together." Gülich forgets to add that by 1648, the people of Holland were more overworked, poorer and more brutally oppressed than those of all the rest of Europe put together.

To-day industrial supremacy implies commercial supremacy, In the period of manufacture properly so-called, it is, on the other hand, the commercial supremacy that gives industrial predominance. Hence the preponderant rôle that the colonial system plays at that time. It was "the strange God" who perched himself on the altar cheek by jowl with the old Gods of Europe, and one fine day with a shove and a kick chucked

them all of a heap. It proclaimed surplus-value making as
the sole end and aim of humanity.

The system of public credit, *i.e.* of national debts, whose
origin we discover in Genoa and Venice as early as the middle
ages, took possession of Europe generally during the manufacturing period. The colonial system with its maritime trade
and commercial wars served as a forcing-house for it. Thus it
first took root in Holland. National debts, *i.e.,* the alienation
of the state—whether despotic, constitutional or republican—
marked with its stamp the capitalistic era. The only part of
the so-called national wealth that actually enters into the collective possessions of modern peoples is—their national debt.[1]
Hence, as a necessary consequence, the modern doctrine that a
nation becomes the richer the more deeply it is in debt.
Public credit becomes the *credo* of capital. And with the
rise of national debt-making, want of faith in the national
debt takes the place of the blasphemy against the Holy Ghost,
which may not be forgiven.

The public debt becomes one of the most powerful levers of
primitive accumulation. As with the stroke of an enchanter's
wand, it endows barren money with the power of breeding and
thus turns it into capital, without the necessity of its exposing
itself to the troubles and risks inseparable from its employment in industry or even in usury. The state-creditors actually give nothing away, for the sum lent is transformed into
public bonds, easily negotiable, which go on functioning in
their hands just as so much hard cash would. But further,
apart from the class of lazy annuitants thus created, and from
the improvised wealth of the financiers, middlemen between
the government and the nation—as also apart from the tax-
farmers, merchants, private manufacturers, to whom a good
part of every national loan renders the service of a capital
fallen from heaven—the national debt has given rise to joint-
stock companies, to dealings in negotiable effects of all kinds,
and to agiotage, in a word to stock-exchange gambling and the
modern bankocracy.

[1] William Cobbett remarks that in England all public institutions are designated
"royal;" as compensation for this, however, there is the "national" debt.

At their birth the great banks, decorated with national titles, were only associations of private speculators, who placed themselves by the side of governments, and, thanks to the privileges they received, were in a position to advance money to the state. Hence the accumulation of the national debt has no more infallible measure than the successive rise in the stock of these banks, whose full development dates from the founding of the Bank of England in 1694. The Bank of England began with lending its money to the Government at 8% ; at the same time it was empowered by Parliament to coin money out of the same capital, by lending it again to the public in the form of bank-notes. It was allowed to use these notes for discounting bills, making advances on commodities, and for buying the precious metals. It was not long ere this credit-money, made by the bank itself, became the coin in which the Bank of England made its loans to the state, and paid, on account of the state, the interest on the public debt. It was not enough that the bank gave with one hand and took back more with the other; it remained, even whilst receiving, the eternal creditor of the nation down to the last shilling advanced. Gradually it became inevitably the receptacle of the metallic hoard of the country, and the centro of gravity of all commercial credit. What effect was produced on their contemporaries by the sudden uprising of this brood of bankocrats, financiers, rentiers, brokers, stock-jobbers, &c., is proved by the writings of that time, *e.g.,* by Bolingbroke's.[1]

With the national debt arose an international credit system, which often conceals one of the sources of primitive accumulation in this or that people. Thus the villanies of the Venetian thieving system formed one of the secret bases of the capital-wealth of Holland to whom Venice in her decadence lent large sums of money. So also was it with Holland and England. By the beginning of the 18th century the Dutch manufactures were far outstripped. Holland had ceased to be the nation preponderant in commerce and industry. One of its

---

[1] "Si les Tartares inondaient l'Europe aujourd'hui, il faudrait bien des affaires pour leur faire entendre ce que c'est qu'un financier parmi nous." Montesquieu Esprit des lois, t. iv. p. 33, ed. Londres, 1769.

main lines of business, therefore, from 1701-1776, is the lending out of enormous amounts of capital, especially to its great rival England. The same thing is going on to-day between England and the United States. A great deal of capital, which appears to-day in the United States without any certificate of birth, was yesterday, in England, the capitalised blood of children.

As the national debt finds its support in the public revenue, which must cover the yearly payments for interest, &c., the modern system of taxation was the necessary complement of the system of national loans. The loans enable the government to meet extraordinary expenses, without the tax-payers feeling it immediately, but they necessitate, as a consequence, increased taxes. On the other hand, the raising of taxation caused by the accumulation of debts contracted one after another, compels the government always to have recourse to new loans for new extraordinary expenses. Modern fiscality, whose pivot is formed by taxes on the most necessary means of subsistence (thereby increasing their price), thus contains within itself the germ of automatic progression. Over-taxation is not an incident, but rather a principle. In Holland, therefore, where this system was first inaugurated, the great patriot, De Witt, has in his "Maxims" extolled it as the best system for making the wage-labourer submissive, frugal, industrious, and overburdened with labour. The destructive influence that it exercises on the condition of the wage-labourer concerns us less however, here, than the forcible expropriation, resulting from it, of peasants, artisans, and in a word, all elements of the lower middle-class. On this there are not two opinions, even among the bourgeois economists. Its expropriating efficacy is still further heightened by the system of protection, which forms one of its integral parts.

The great part that the public debt, and the fiscal system corresponding with it, has played in the capitalisation of wealth and the expropriation of the masses, has led many writers, like Cobbett, Doubleday and others, to seek in this, incorrectly, the fundamental cause of the misery of the modern peoples.

The system of protection was an artificial means of manufacturing manufacturers, of expropriating independent labourers, of capitalising the national means of production and subsistence, of forcibly abbreviating the transition from the mediæval to the modern mode of production. The European states tore one another to pieces about the patent of this invention, and, once entered into the service of the surplus-value makers, did not merely lay under contribution in the pursuit of this purpose their own people, indirectly through protective duties, directly through export premiums. They also forcibly rooted out, in their dependent countries, all industry, as, *e.g.,* England did with the Irish woollen manufacture. On the continent of Europe, after Colbert's example, the process was much simplified. The primitive industrial capital, here, came in part directly out of the state treasury. "Why," cries Mirabeau, "why go so far to seek the cause of the manufacturing glory of Saxony before the war? 180,000,000 of debts contracted by the sovereigns!"[1]

Colonial system, public debts, heavy taxes, protection, commercial wars, &c., these children of the true manufacturing period, increase gigantically during the infancy of Modern Industry. The birth of the latter is heralded by a great slaughter of the innocents. Like the royal navy, the factories were recruited by means of the press-gang. Blasé as Sir F. M. Eden is as to the horrors of the expropriation of the agricultural population from the soil, from the last third of the 15th century to his own time; with all the self-satisfaction with which he rejoices in this process, "essential" for establishing capitalistic agriculture and "the due proportion between arable and pasture land"—he does not show, however, the same economic insight in respect to the necessity of child-stealing and child-slavery for the transformation of manufacturing exploitation into factory exploitation, and the establishment of the "true relation" between capital and labour-power. He says: "It may, perhaps, be worthy the attention of the public to consider, whether any manufacture, which, in order to be carried on successfully, requires that cottages and workhouses

[1] Mirabeau, l. c., t. vi., p. 101.

should be ransacked for poor children; that they should be employed by turns during the greater part of the night and robbed of that rest which, though indispensable to all, is most required by the young; and that numbers of both sexes, of different ages and dispositions, should be collected together in such a manner that the contagion of example cannot but lead to profligacy and debauchery; will add to the sum of individual or national felicity?"[1]

"In the counties of Derbyshire, Nottinghamshire, and more particularly in Lancashire," says Fielden, "the newly-invented machinery was used in large factories built on the sides of streams capable of turning the water-wheel. Thousands of hands were suddenly required in these places, remote from towns; and Lancashire, in particular, being, till then, comparatively thinly populated and barren, a population was all that she now wanted. The small and nimble fingers of little children being by very far the most in request, the custom instantly sprang up of procuring *apprentices* from the different parish workhouses of London, Birmingham, and elsewhere. Many, many thousands of these little, hapless creatures were sent down into the north, being from the age of 7 to the age of 13 or 14 years old. The custom was for the master to clothe his apprentices and to feed and lodge them in an "apprentice house" near the factory; overseers were appointed to see to the works, whose interest it was to work the children to the utmost, because their pay was in proportion to the quantity of work that they could exact. Cruelty was, of course, the consequence. . . In many of the manufacturing districts, but particularly, I am afraid, in the guilty county to which I belong [Lancashire], cruelties the most heart-rending were practised upon the unoffending and friendless creatures who were thus consigned to the charge of master manufacturers; they were harassed to the brink of death by excess of labour . . . were flogged, fettered and tortured in the most exquisite refinement of cruelty; . . . they were in many cases starved to the bone while flogged to their work and . . . . even in some instances . . . were driven to commit suicide . . . The

[1] Eden, l. c., Vol. I., Book II., Ch. I., p. 421.

beautiful and romantic valleys of Derbyshire, Nottingham-shire and Lancashire, secluded from the public eye, became the dismal solitudes of torture, and of many a murder. The profits of manufactures were enormous; but this only whetted the appetite that it should have satisfied, and therefore the manufacturers had recourse to an expedient that seemed to secure to them those profits without any possibility of limit; they began the practice of what is termed "night-working," that is, having tired one set of hands, by working them throughout the day, they had another set ready to go on working throughout the night; the day-set getting into the beds that the 'night-set had just quitted, and in their turn again, the night-set getting into the beds that the day-set quitted in the morning. It is a common tradition in Lanca-shire, that the beds *never get cold.*"[1]

With the development of capitalist production during the manufacturing period, the public opinion of Europe had lost the last remnant of shame and conscience. The nations bragged cynically of every infamy that served them as a means to capitalistic accumulation. Read, *e.g.,* the naïve Annals of Commerce of the worthy A. Anderson. Here it is trumpetted forth as a triumph of English statecraft that at the Peace of Utrecht, England extorted from the Spaniards by the Asiento Treaty the privilege of being allowed to ply the negro-trade, until then only carried on between Africa and the English

---

[1] John Fielden, l. c. pp. 5, 6. On the earlier infamies of the factory system, cf. Dr. Aikin (1795) l. c. p. 219, and Gisborne: Enquiry into the Duties of Men, 1795, Vol. II. When the steam-engine transplanted the factories from the country water-falls to the middle of towns, the "abstemious" surplus-value maker found the child-material ready to his hand, without being forced to seek slaves from the workhouses. When Sir R. Peel, (father of the "minister of plausibility"), brought in his bill for the protection of children, in 1815, Francis Horner, lumen of the Bullion Committee and intimate friend of Ricardo, said in the House of Commons: "It is notorious, that with a bankrupt's effects, a gang, if he might use the word, of these children had been put up to sale, and were advertised publicly as part of the property. A most atrocious instance had been brought before the Court of King's Bench two years before, in which a number of these boys, apprenticed by a parish in London to one manufacturer, had been transferred to another, and had been found by some benevolent persons in a state of absolute famine. Another case more horrible had come to his knowledge while on a [Parliamentary] Committee . . . that not many years ago, an agreement had been made between a London parish and a Lancashire manufacturer, by which it was stipulated, that with every 20 sound chil-dren one idiot should be taken."

West Indies, between Africa and Spanish America as well. England thereby acquired the right of supplying Spanish America until 1743 with 4800 negroes yearly. This threw, at the same time, an official cloak over British smuggling. Liverpool waxed fat on the slave-trade. This was its method of primitive accumulation. And, even to the present day, Liverpool "respectability" is the Pindar of the slave-trade which—compare the work of Aikin [1795] already quoted— "has coincided with that spirit of bold adventure which-has characterised the trade of Liverpool and rapidly carried it to its present state of prosperity; has occasioned vast employment for shipping and sailors, and greatly augmented the demand for the manufactures of the country" (p. 339). Liverpool employed in the slave trade, in 1730, 15 ships; in 1751, 53; in 1760, 74; in 1770, 96; and in 1792, 132.

Whilst the cotton industry introduced child-slavery in England, it gave in the United States a stimulus to the transformation of the earlier, more or less patriarchal slavery, into a system of commercial exploitation. In fact, the veiled slavery of the wage-earners in Europe needed, for its pedestal, slavery pure and simple in the new world.[1]

Tantæ molis erat, to establish the "eternal laws of Nature" of the capitalist mode of production, to complete the process of separation between labourers and conditions of labour, to transform, at one pole, the social means of production and subsistence into capital, at the opposite pole, the mass of the population into wage-labourers, into "free labouring poor," that artificial product of modern society.[2] If

---

[1] In 1790, there were in the English West Indies ten slaves for one free man, in the French fourteen for one, in the Dutch twenty-three for one. (Henry Brougham: An Inquiry into the Colonial Policy of the European Powers. Edin. 1803, vol. II. p. 74.)

[2] The phrase, "labouring poor," is found in English legislation from the moment when the class of wage-labourers becomes noticeable. This term is used in opposition, on the one hand, to the "idle poor," beggars, etc., on the other to these labourers, who, pigeons not yet plucked, are still possessors of their own means of labour. From the Statute Book it passed into political economy, and was handed down by Culpeper, J. Child, etc., to Adam Smith and Eden. After this, one can judge of the good faith of the "execrable political cant-monger," Edmund Burke, when he called the expression, "labouring poor,"—"execrable political cant." This sycophant who, in the pay of the English oligarchy, played the romantic laudator temporis acti against the French Revolution, just as, in the pay of the North Ameri-

money, according to Augier,[1] "comes into the world wi.o a congenital blood-stain on one cheek," capital comes dripping from head to foot, from every pore, with blood and dirt.[2]

CHAPTER XXXII.

HISTORICAL TENDENCY OF CAPITALIST ACCUMULATION.

WHAT does the primitive accumulation of capital, *i.e.*, its historical genesis, resolve itself into? In so far as it is not immediate transformation of slaves and serfs into wage-labourers. and therefore a mere change of form, it only means the expropriation of the immediate producers, *i.e.*, the dissolution of private property based on the labour of its owner. Private property, as the antithesis to social, collective property, exists only where the means of labour and the external conditions of labour belong to private individuals. But according as these private individuals are labourers or not labourers, private property has a different character. The numberless shades, that it at first sight presents, correspond to the intermediate stages lying between these two extremes. The private prop-

can Colonies, at the beginning of the American troubles, he had played the Liberal against the English oligarchy, was an out and out vulgar bourgeois. "The laws of commerce are the laws of Nature, and therefore the laws of God." (E. Burke, l. c., pp. 31, 32.) No wonder that, true to the laws of God and of Nature, he always sold himself in the best market. A very good portrait of this Edmund Burke, during his liberal time, is to be found in the writings of the Rev. Mr. Tucker. Tucker was a parson and a Tory, but, for the rest, an honourable man and a competent political economist. In face of the infamous cowardice of character that reigns to-day, and believes most devoutly in "the laws of commerce," it is our bounden duty again and again to brand the Burkes, who only differ from their successors in one thing—talent.

[1] Marie Augier: Du Crédit Public. Paris, 1842.

[2] "Capital is said by a Quarterly Reviewer to fly turbulence and strife, and to be timid, which is very true; but this is very incompletely stating the question. Capital eschews no profit, or very small profit, just as Nature was formerly said to abhor a vacuum. With adequate profit, capital is very bold. A certain 10 per cent. will ensure its employment anywhere; 20 per cent. certain will produce eagerness; 50 per cent., positive audacity; 100 per cent. will make it ready to trample on all human laws; 300 per cent., and there is not a crime at which it will scruple, nor a risk it will not run, even to the chance of its owner being hanged. If turbulence and strife will bring a profit, it will freely encourage both. Smuggling and the slave-trade have amply proved all that is here stated." (P. J. Dunning, l. c., p. 35.)

erty of the labourer in his means of production is the foundation of petty industry, whether agricultural, manufacturing
or both; petty industry, again, is an essential condition for the
development of social production and of the free individuality
of the labourer himself. Of course, this petty mode of production exists also under slavery, serfdom, and other states
of dependence. But it flourishes, it lets loose its whole energy,
it attains its adequate classical form, only where the labourer
is the private owner of his own means of labour set in action
by himself: the peasant of the land which he cultivates, the
artizan of the tool which he handles as a virtuoso. This mode
of production pre-supposes parcelling of the soil, and scattering of the other means of production. As it excludes the concentration of these means of production, so also it excludes co-
operation, division of labour within each separate process of
production, the control over, and the productive application
of the forces of Nature by society, and the free development
of the social productive powers. It is compatible only with
a system of production, and a society, moving within narrow
and more or less primitive bounds. To perpetuate it would
be, as Pecqueur rightly says, "to decree universal mediocrity."
At a certain stage of development it brings forth the material
agencies for its own dissolution. From that moment new forces
and new passions spring up in the bosom of society; but the
old social organization fetters them and keeps them down. It
must be annihilated; it is annihilated. Its annihilation, the
transformation of the individualised and scattered means of
production into socially concentrated ones, of the pigmy property of the many into the huge property of the few, the expropriation of the great mass of the people from the soil,
from the means of subsistence, and from the means of labour,
this fearful and painful expropriation of the mass of the people forms the prelude to the history of capital. It comprises
a series of forcible methods, of which we have passed in review only those that have been epoch-making as methods of
the primitive accumulation of capital. The expropriation of
the immediate producers was accomplished with merciless Van-
dalism, and under the stimulus of passions the most infamous,

the most sordid, the, pettiest, the most meanly odious. Self-earned private property, that is based, so to say, on the fusing together of the isolated, independent labouring-individual with the conditions of his labour, is supplanted by capitalistic private property, which rests on exploitation of the nominally free labour of others, *i.e.*, on wages-labour.[1]

As soon as this process of transformation has sufficiently decomposed the old society from top to bottom, as soon as the labourers are turned into proletarians, their means of labour into capital, as soon as the capitalist mode of production stands on its own feet, then the further socialisation of labour and further transformation of the land and other means of production into socially exploited and, therefore, common means of production, as well as the further expropriation of private proprietors, takes a new form. That which is now to be expropriated is no longer the labourer working for himself, but the capitalist exploiting many labourers. This expropriation is accomplished by the action of the immanent laws of capitalistic production itself, by the centralisation of capital. One capitalist always kills many. Hand in hand with this centralisation, or this expropriation of many capitalists by few, develop, on an ever extending scale, the co-operative form of the labour-process, the conscious technical application of science, the methodical cultivation of the soil, the transformation of the instruments of labour into instruments of labour only usable in common, the economising of all means of production by their use as the means of production of combined, socialised labour, the entanglement of all peoples in the net of the world-market, and this, the international character of the capitalistic régime. Along with the constantly diminishing number of the magnates of capital, who usurp and monopolise all advantages of this process of transformation, grows the mass of misery, oppression, slavery, degradation, exploitation; but with this too grows the revolt of the working-class, a class always increasing in numbers, and disciplined,

---

[1] "Nous sommes dans une condition tout-à-fait nouvelle de la société . . . nous tendons à séparer toute espèce de propriété d'avec toute espèce de travail." (Sismondi: Nouveaux Principes de l'Econ. Polit. t. II., p. 434.)

united, organised by the very mechanism of the process of capitalist production itself. The monopoly of capital becomes a fetter upon the mode of production, which has sprung up and flourished along with, and under it. Centralisation of the means of production and socialisation of labour at last reach a point where they become incompatible with their capitalist integument. This integument is burst asunder. The knell of capitalist private property sounds. The expropriators are expropriated.

The capitalist mode of appropriation, the result of the capitalist mode of production, produces capitalist private property. This is the first negation of individual private property, as founded on the labour of the proprietor. But capitalist production begets, with the inexorability of a law of Nature, its own negation. It is the negation of negation. This does not re-establish private property for the producer, but gives him individual property based on the acquisitions of the capitalist era: *i.e.,* on co-operation and the possession in common of the land and of the means of production.

The transformation of scattered private property, arising from individual labour, into capitalist private property is, naturally, a process, incomparably more protracted, violent, and difficult, than the transformation of capitalistic private property, already practically resting on socialised production, into socialised property. In the former case, we had the expropriation of the mass of the people by a few usurpers; in the latter, we have the expropriation of a few usurpers by the mass of the people.[1]

---

[1] The advance of industry, whose involuntary promoter is the bourgeoisie, replaces the isolation of the labourers, due to competition, by their revolutionary combination, due to association. The development of Modern Industry, therefore, cuts from under its feet, the very foundation on which the bourgeoisie produces and appropriates products. What the bourgeoisie therefore, produces, above all, are its own grave-diggers. Its fall and the victory of the proletariat are equally inevitable. . . . Of all the classes, that stand face to face with the bourgeoisie to-day, the proletariat alone is a really revolutionary class. The other classes perish and disappear in the face of Modern Industry, the proletariat is its special and essential product. . . . The lower middle-classes, the small manufacturers, the shop keepers, the artisan, the peasant, all these fight against the bourgeoisie, to save from extinction their existence as fractions of the middle-class . . . they are reactionary, for they try to roll back the wheel of history. "Karl Marx and Frederick Engels, Manifest der Kommunistischen Partei," London, 1847, pp. 911.

CHAPTER XXXIII.

THE MODERN THEORY OF COLONISATION.[1]

POLITICAL economy confuses on principle two very different kinds of private property, of which one rests on the producers' own labour, the other on the employment of the labour of others. It forgets that the latter not only is the direct anti-thesis of the former, but absolutely grows on its tomb only. In Western Europe, the home of political economy, the process of primitive accumulation is more or less accomplished. Here the capitalist régime has either directly conquered the whole domain of national production, or, where economic conditions are less developed, it, as least, indirectly controls those strata of society which, though belonging to the antiquated mode of pro-duction, continue to exist side by side with it in gradual decay. To this ready-made world of capital, the political economist applies the notions of law and of property inherited from a pre-capitalistic world with all the more anxious zeal and all the greater unction, the more loudly the facts cry out in the face of his idealogy. It is otherwise in the colonies. There the capitalist régime everywhere comes into collision with the resistance of the producer, who, as owner of his own condi-tions of labour, employs that labour to enrich himself, instead of the capitalist. The contradiction of these two diametrically opposed economic systems, manifests itself here practically in a struggle between them. Where the capitalist has at his back the power of the mother-country, he tries to clear out of his way by force, the 'modes of production and appropriation, based on the independent labour of the producer. The same interest which compels the sycophant of capital, the political economist, in the mother-country, to proclaim the theoretical

---

[1] We treat here of real Colonies, virgin soils, colonised by free immigrants. The United States are, speaking economically, still only a Colony of Europe. Besides, to this category belong also such old plantations as those in which the abolition of slavery has completely altered the earlier conditions.

identity of the capitalist mode of production with its contrary, that same interest compels him in the colonies to make a clean breast of it, and to proclaim aloud the antagonism of the two modes of production. To this end he proves how the development of the social productive power of labour, co-operation, division of labour, use of machinery on a large scale, &c., are impossible without the expropriation of the labourers, and the corresponding transformation of their means of production into capital. In the interest of the so-called national wealth, he seeks for artificial means to ensure the poverty of the people. Here his apologetic armour crumbles off, bit by bit, like rotten touchwood. It is the great merit of E. G. Wakefield to have discovered, not anything new about the Colonies,[1] but to have discovered in the Colonies the truth as to the conditions of capitalist production in the mother-country. As the system of protection at its origin[2] attempted to manufacture capitalists artificially in the mother-country, so Wakefield's colonisation theory, which England tried for a time to enforce by Acts of Parliament, attempted to effect the manufacture of wage-workers in the Colonies. This he calls "systematic colonisation."

First of all, Wakefield discovered that in the Colonies property in money, means of subsistence, machines and other means of production, does not as yet stamp a man as a capitalist if there be wanting the correlative—the wage-worker, the other man who is compelled to sell himself of his own free-will. He discovered that capital is not a thing, but a social relation between persons, established by the instrumentality of things.[3] Mr. Peel, he moans, took with him from England to Swan River, West Australia, means of subsistence and of produc-

---

[1] Wakefield's few glimpses on the subject of Modern Colonisation are fully anticipated by Mirabeau Père, the physiocrat, and even much earlier by English economists.

[2] Later, it became a temporary necessity in the international competitive struggle. But, whatever its motive, the consequences remain the same.

[3] A negro is a negro. In certain circumstances he becomes a slave. A mule is a machine for spinning cotton. Only under certain circumstances does it become capital. Outside these circumstances, it is no more capital than gold is intrinsically money, or sugar is the price of sugar. . . . Capital is a social relation of production. It is a historical relation of production. (Karl Marx, "Lohnarbeit und Kapital." N. Rh. Z. No. 266, April 7, 1849.)

tion to the amount of £50,000.   Mr. Peel had the foresight to
bring with him, besides, 3000 persons of the working-class,
men, women, and children.   Once arrived at his destination,
"Mr. Peel was left without a servant to make his bed or fetch
him water from the river."[1]   Unhappy Mr. Peel who provided for everything except the export of English modes of
production to Swan River!

For the understanding of the following discoveries of Wakefield, two preliminary remarks: We know that the means of
production and subsistence, while they remain the property of
the immediate producer, are not capital.   They become capital, only under circumstances in which they serve at the same
time as means of exploitation and subjection of the labourer.
But this capitalist soul of theirs is so intimately wedded, in
the head of the political economist, to their material substance,
that he christens them capital under all circumstances, even
when they are its exact opposite.   Thus is it with Wakefield.
Further: the splitting up of the means of production into the
individual property of many independent labourers, working
on their own account, he calls equal division of capital.   It is
with the political economist as with the feudal jurist.   The
latter stuck on to pure monetary relations the labels supplied
by feudal law.

"If," says Wakefield, "all the members of the society are
supposed to possess equal portions of capital . . .   no man
would have a motive for accumulating more capital than he
could use with his own hands.   This is to some extent the
case in new American settlements, where a passion for owning
land prevents the existence of a class of labourers for hire."[2]
So long, therefore, as the labourer can accumulate for himself—and this he can do so long as he remains possessor of
his means of production—capitalist accumulation and the capitalistic mode of production are impossible.   The class of
wage-labourers, essential to these, is wanting.   How, then, in
old Europe, was the expropriation of the labourer from his
conditions of labour, *i.e.*, the co-existence of capital and wage-

[1] E. G. Wakefield: England and America, vol. ii., p. 33.
[2] L c., p. 17.

labour, brought about? By a social contract of a quite original kind. "Mankind have adopted a . . . simple contrivance for promoting the accumulation of capital," which, of course, since the time of Adam, floated in their imagination as the sole and final end of thier existence: "they have divided themselves into owners of capital and owners of labour. . . . This division was the result of concert and combination."[1] In one word: the mass of mankind expropriated itself in honour of the "accumulation of capital." Now, one would think, that this instinct of self-denying fanaticism would give itself full fling especially in the Colonies, where alone exist the men and conditions that could turn a social contract from a dream to a reality. But why, then, should "systematic colonisation" be called in to replace its opposite, spontaneous, unregulated colonisation? But—but—"In the Northern States of the American Union, it may be doubted whether so many as a tenth of the people would fall under the description of hired labourers. . . . In England . . . the labouring class compose the bulk of the people."[2] Nay, the impulse to self-expropriation, on the part of labouring humanity, for the glory of capital, exists so little, that slavery, according to Wakefield himself, is the sole natural basis of Colonial wealth. His systematic colonisation is a mere *pis aller,* since he unfortunately has to do with free men, not with slaves. "The first Spanish settlers in Saint Domingo did not obtain labourers from Spain. But, without labourers, their capital must have perished, or, at least, must soon have been diminished to that small amount which each individual could employ with his own hands. This has actually occurred in the last Colony founded by Englishmen—the Swan River Settlement—where a great mass of capital, of seeds, implements, and cattle, has perished for want of labourers to use it, and where no settler has preserved much more capital than he can employ with his own hands."[3]

We have seen that the expropriation of the mass of the people from the soil forms the basis of the capitalist mode of production. The essence of a free colony, on the contrary, con-

[1] l. c., vol. i., p. 18.   [2] l. c., pp. 42, 43, 44.   [3] l. c., vol. ii., p. 5.

sists in this — that the bulk of the soil is still public property, and every settler on it therefore can turn part of it into his private property and individual means of production, without hindering the later settlers in the same operation.[1] This is the secret both of the prosperity of the colonies and of their inveterate vice—opposition to the establishment of capital. "Where land is very cheap and all men are free, where one who so pleases can easily obtain a piece of land for himself, not only is labour very dear, as respects the labourer's share of the produce, but the difficulty is to obtain combined labour at any price."[2]

As in the colonies the separation of the labourer from the conditions of labour and their root, the soil, does not yet exist, or only sporadically, or on too limited a scale, so neither does the separation of agriculture from industry exist, nor the destruction of the household industry of the peasantry. Whence then is to come the internal market for capital? "No part of the population of America is exclusively agricultural, excepting slaves and their employers who combine capital and labour in particular works. Free Americans, who cultivate the soil, follow many other occupations. Some portion of the furniture and tools which they use is commonly made by themselves. They frequently build their own houses, and carry to market, at whatever distance, the produce of their own industry. They are spinners and weavers; they make soap and candles, as well as, in many cases, shoes and clothes for their own use. In America the cultivation of land is often the secondary pursuit of a blacksmith, a miller or a shopkeeper."[3] With such queer people as these, where is the "field of abstinence" for the capitalists?

The great beauty of capitalist production consists in this— that it not only constantly reproduces the wage-worker as wage-worker, but produces always, in proportion to the accumulation of capital, a relative surplus population of wage-workers. Thus the law of supply and demand of labour is

---

[1] "Land, to be an element of colonization, must not only be waste, but it must be public property, liable to be converted into private property." (l. c. Vol. II., p. 125.)
[2] l. c. Vol. I. p. 247. [3] l. c. pp. 21, 22.

kept in the right rut, the oscillation of wages is penned within limits satisfactory to capitalist exploitation, and lastly, the social dependence of the labourer on the capitalist, that indispensable requisite, is secured; an unmistakeable relation of dependence, which the smug political economist, at home, in the mother country, can transmogrify into one of free contract between buyer and seller, between equally independent owners of commodities, the owner of the commodity capital and the owner of the commodity labour. But in the colonies this pretty fancy is torn asunder. The absolute population here increases much more quickly than in the mother-country, because many labourers enter this world as ready-made adults, and yet the labour market is always understocked. The law of the supply and demand of labour falls to pieces. On the one hand, the old world constantly throws in capital, thirsting after exploitation and "abstinence;" on the other, the regular reproduction of the wage-labourer as wage-labourer comes into collision with impediments the most impertinent and in part invincible. What becomes of the production of wage-labourers, supernumerary in proportion to the accumulation of capital? The wage-worker of to-day is to-morrow an independent peasant, or artisan, working for himself. He vanishes from the labour-market, but not into the workhouse. This constant transformation of the wage-labourers into independent producers, who work for themselves instead of for capital, and enrich themselves instead of the capitalist gentry, reacts in its turn very perversely on the conditions of the labour-market. Not only does the degree of exploitation of the wage-labourer remain indecently low. The wage-labourer loses into the bargain, along with the relation of dependence, also the sentiment of dependence on the abstemious capitalist. Hence all the inconveniences that our E. G. Wakefield pictures so doughtily, so eloquently, so pathetically.

The supply of wage-labour, he complains, is neither constant, nor regular, nor sufficient. "The supply of labour is always, not only small, but uncertain."[1] "Though the produce divided between the capitalist and the labourer be large the

[1] l. c., Vol. II., p. 116.

labourer takes só great a share that he soon becomes a capitalist. . . . Few, even of those whose lives are unusually
long, can accumulate great masses of wealth."[1] The labourers
most distinctly decline to allow the capitalist to abstain from
the payment of the greater part of their labour. It avails him
nothing if he is so cunning as to import from Europe, with
his own capital, his own wage-workers. They soon "cease
. . . to be labourers for hire; they . . . become independent landowners, if not competitors with their former
masters in the labour market."[2] Think of the horror! The
excellent capitalist has imported bodily from Europe, with his
own good money, his own competitors! The end of the world
has come! No wonder Wakefield laments the absence of all
dependence and of all sentiment of dependence on the part
of the wage-workers in the colonies. On account of the high
wages, says his disciple, Merivale, there is in the colonies "the
urgent desire for cheaper and more subservient labourers—
for a class to whom the capitalist might dictate terms, instead of being dictated to by them. . . . In ancient civilized countries the labourer, though free, is by law of nature
dependent on capitalists; in colonies this dependence must be
created by artificial means."[3]

What is now, according to Wakefield, the consequence of

---

[1] l. c., Vol. I., p. 131   [2] l. c., Vol. II., p. 5.

[3] Merivale, l. c., Vol. II., pp. 235-314 passim. Even the mild, free-trade, vulgar
economist, Molinari, says: "Dans les colonies où l'esclavage a été aboli sans que le
travail forcé se trouvait remplacé par une quantité équivalente de travail libre, on a
vu s'opérer la contre-partie du fait qui se réalise tous les jours sous nos yeux. On a
vu les simples travailleurs exploiter à leur tour les entrepreneurs d'industrie, exiger
d'eux des salaires hors de toute proportion avec la part légitime qui leur revenait dans
le produit. Les planteurs, ne pouvant obtenir de leurs sucres un prix suffisant pour
couvrir la hausse de salaire, ont été obligés de fournir l'excédant, d'abord sur leurs
profits, ensuite sur leurs capitaux mêmes. Une foule de planteurs ont été ruinés de la
sorte, d'autres ont fermé leurs ateliers pour échapper à une ruine imminente. . . .
Sans doute, il vaut mieux voir périr des accumulations de capitaux que des généra-
tions d'hommes [how generous of Mr. Molinari!]: mais ne vaudrait-il pas mieux que
ni les uns ni les autres périssent?" (Molinari l. c. pp. 51, 52.) Mr. Molinari, Mr.
Molinari! What then becomes of the ten commandments, of Moses and the prophets,
of the law of supply and demand, if in Europe the "entrepreneur" can cut down
the labourer's legitimate part, and in the West Indies, the labourer can cut down
the entrepreneur's? And what, if you please, is this "legitimate part," which on
your own showing the capitalist in Europe daily neglects to pay? Over yonder, in
the colonies where the labourers are so "simple" as to "exploit" the capitalist, Mr.
Molinari feels a strong itching to set the law of supply and demand, that works
elsewhere automatically, on the right road by means of the police.

this unfortunate state of things in the colonies? A "barbarising tendency of dispersion" of producers and national wealth.[1] The parcelling-out of the means of production among innumerable owners, working on their own account, annihilates, along with the centralisation of capital, all the foundations of combined labour. Every long-winded undertaking, extending over several years and demanding outlay of fixed capital, is prevented from being carried out. In Europe, capital invests without hesitating a moment, for the working-class constitutes its living appurtenance, always in excess, always at disposal. But in the colonies! Wakefield tells an extremely doleful anecdote. He was talking with some capitalists of Canada and the state of New York, where the immigrant wave often becomes stagnant and deposits a sediment of "supernumerary" labourers. "Our capital," says one of the characters in the melodrama, "was ready for many operations which require a considerable period of time for their completion; but we could not begin such operations with labour which, we knew, would soon leave us. If we had been sure of retaining the labour of such emigrants, we should have been glad to have engaged it at once, and for a high price: and we should have engaged it, even though we had been sure it would leave us, provided we had been sure of a fresh supply whenever we might need it."[2]

After Wakefield has contrasted the English capitalist agriculture and its "combined" labour with the scattered cultivation of American peasants, he unwittingly gives us a glimpse at the reverse of the medal. He depicts the mass of the American people as well-to-do, independent, enterprising and comparatively cultured, whilst "the English agricultural labourer is a miserable wretch, a pauper. . . . In what country, except North America and some new colonies, do the wages of free labour employed in agriculture, much exceed a bare subsistence for the labourer? . . . Undoubtedly, farm-horses in England, being a valuable property, are better fed than English peasants."[3] But, never mind, national

[1] Wakefield, l. c., Vol. II., p. 52.　　　　[2] l. c. pp. 191, 192.
[3] l. c., Vol. I., pp. 47, 246.

wealth is, once again, by its very nature, identical with misery of the people.

How, then, to heal the anti-capitalistic cancer of the colonies? If men were willing, at a blow, to turn all the soil from public into private property, they would destroy certainly the root of the evil, but also—the colonies. The trick is how to kill two birds with one stone. Let the Government put upon the virgin soil an artificial price, independent of the law of supply and demand, a price that compels the immigrant to work a long time for wages before he can earn enough money to buy land, and turn himself into an independent peasant.[1] The funds resulting from the sale of land at a price relatively prohibitory for the wage-workers, this fund of money extorted from the wages of labour by violation of the sacred law of supply and demand, the Government is to employ, on the other hand, in proportion as it grows, to import have-nothings from Europe into the colonies, and thus keep the wage-labour market full for the capitalists. Under these circumstances, tout sera pour le mieux dans le meilleur des mondes possibles. This is the great secret of "systematic colonisation." By this plan, Wakefield cries in triumph, "the supply of labour *must* be constant and regular, because, first, as no labourer would be able to procure land until he had worked for money, all immigrant labourers, working for a time for wages and in combination, would produce capital for the employment of more labourers; secondly, because every labourer who left off working for wages and became a landowner, would, by purchasing land, provide a fund for bringing fresh labour to the colony."[2] The price of the soil imposed by the State must, of course, be a "sufficient price"—*i.e.*, so high "as to prevent the labourers from becoming independent landown-

---

[1] "C'est, ajoutez-vous, grâce à l'appropriation du sol et des capitaux que l'homme, qui n' a que ses bras, trouve de l'occupation, et se fait un revenu . . . c'est au contraire, grâce à l'appropriation individuelle du sol qu'il se trouve des hommes n'ayant que leurs bras. . . . Quand vous mettez un homme dans le vide, vous vous emparez de l'atmosphère. Ainsi faites-vous, quand vous vous emparez du sol. . . . C'est le mettre dans le vide de richesses, pour ne le laisser vivre qu'à votre volonté." (Colins, l. c., t. III., pp. 268-271, passim.)

[2] Wakefield, l. c., Vol. II., p. 192.

ers until others had followed to take their place."[1] This "sufficient price for the land" is nothing but a euphemistic circumlocution for the ransom which the labourer pays to the capitalist for leave to retire from the wage-labour market to the land. First, he must create for the capitalist "capital," with which the latter may be able to exploit more labourers; then he must place, at his own expense, a *locum tenens* on the labour market, whom the Government forwards across the sea for the benefit of his old master, the capitalist.

It is very characteristic that the English Government for years practised this method of "primitive accumulation," prescribed by Mr. Wakefield expressly for the use of the colonies. The fiasco was, of course, as complete as that of Sir Robert Peel's Bank Act. The stream of emigration was only diverted from the English colonies to the United States. Meanwhile, the advance of capitalistic production in Europe, accompanied by increasing Government pressure, has rendered Wakefield's recipe superfluous. On the one hand, the enormous and ceaseless stream of men, year after year driven upon America, leaves behind a stationary sediment in the east of the United States, the wave of immigration from Europe throwing men on the labour market there more rapidly than the wave of emigration westwards can wash them away. On the other hand, the American Civil War brought in its train a colossal national debt, and, with it, pressure of taxes, the rise of the vilest financial aristocracy, the squandering of a huge part of the public land on speculative companies for the exploitation of railways, mines, &c., in brief, the most rapid centralisation of capital. The great republic has, therefore, ceased to be the promised land for emigrant labourers. Capitalistic production advances there with giant strides, even though the lowering of wages and the dependence of the wage-worker are yet far from being brought down to the normal European level. The shameless lavishing of uncultivated colonial land on aristicrats and capitalists by the Government, so loudly denounced even by Wakefield, has produced, especially in Australia,[2] in

[1] l. c., p. 45.

[2] As soon as Australia became her own law-giver, she passed, of course, laws

conjunction with the stream of men that the gold-diggings attract, and with the competition that the importation of English commodities causes even to the smallest artisan, an ample "relative surplus labouring population," so that almost every mail brings the Job's news of a "glut of the Australian labour-market," and prostitution in some places there flourishes as wantonly as in the London Haymarket.

However, we are not concerned here with the condition of the colonies. The only thing that interests us is the secret discovered in the new world by the political economy of the old world, and proclaimed on the house-tops: that the capitalist mode of production and accumulation, and therefore capitalist private property, have for their fundamental condition the annihilation of self-earned private property; in other words, the expropriation of the labourer.

favourable to the settlers, but the squandering of the land, already accomplished by the English Government, stands in the way. "The first and main object at which the new Land Act of 1862 aims is to give increased facilities for the settlement of the people." (The Land Law of Victoria, by the Hon. O. G. Duffy, Minister of Public Lands. Lond. 1862.)

WORKS AND AUTHORS QUOTED IN "CAPITAL"

Author.	Work.	Date.

'ABEL, K.,and Meck-
lenburg, F. A...Arbeiten der Kaiserlich Russischen
Gesandtschaft zu Pekin über China.Berlin, 1858.

ADDINGTON, Steph..Enquiry into the Reasons for or
against enclosing Open Fields....London, 1772.

" ABRÉGÉ Élémentaire des Principes
d'Économie Politique. (*See* under
Anonymous)....................

" ADVANTAGES of the East Indian
Trade. (*See* under Anonymous).

AIKIN, Dr........Description of the country from
thirty to forty miles round Man-
chester ....London, 1795.

ANONYMOUS .....ABRÉGÉ Élémentaire des Principes
de l' Économie Politique. (*See*
Garnier, G.)...................Paris, 1796.

" ADVANTAGES of the East Indian
Trade to England..............London, 1720.

" CASE, The, of our English Wool, etc.London, 1685.

" COMBINATION, On, of Trades.......London, 1834.

" CONSIDERATIONS concerning taking
off the bounty on Corn exported..London, 1753.

" CURRENCY QUESTION, The........London, 1847.

" CURRENCY QUESTION reviewed, The.
A Letter to the Scotch People. By
- a Banker in England...........London, 1845.

" DEFENCE, A, of the Landowners and
Farmers of Great Britain........London, 1814.

" DISCOURSE concerning Trade, that in
particular of the East Indies....London, 1689

" DISCOURSE, A, on the general notions of Money, Trade, and Exchange as they stand in relation to
each other. By a merchant......London, 1695.

" DISCOURSE, A, on the Necessity of
encouraging Mechanick Industry..London, 1690

" DISSERTATION, A critical, on the
Nature, Measure, and Causes of
Value, etc. (*See* Bailey S.).....London, 1825.

" DISSERTATION on the Poor Laws.
By A Well-wisher of Mankind.
(*See* Townsend) ....London, 1786 (re-
pub. 1817.)

Author.	Work.	Date.

ANONYMOUS ......EAST India Trade, The, a most profitable Trade....................London, 1696.

" ECONOMY, Public, concentrated....Carlisle, 1833.

ENQUIRY into the connection between the high price of Provisions and the size of Farms. By a Farmer...London, 1773.

" ENQUIRY into the present high price of Provisions....................London, 1767.

" ENQUIRY into the causes of the present high price of Provisions. (*See* Forster, Nathaniel)..............London, 1773.

" ENQUIRY into those principles respecting the nature of Demand as lately advocated by Mr. Malthus...London, 1821.

" ENQUIRY, A political, into the consequences of enclosing Waste Lands.London, 1785.

" ESSAY, An, on the Governing Causes of the Natural rate of Interest (*See* J. Massey)................London, 1750.

" ESSAY, a prize, on the Comparative merits of Competition and Co-operation ....London, 1834.

" ESSAY on Credit and the Bankrupt Act ....London, 1707.

ESSAY on the Political Economy of Nations ....London, 1821.

" ESSAY on Public Credit...........London, 1710.

" ESSAY on Trade and Commerce....London, 1770.

" ESSAYS on Political Economy in which are illustrated the principal causes of the present National Distress ....London, 1830.

" FARMS, Capital, Two Letters on the Flour Trade, and the dearness of Corn. By a Person in Business...London, 1767.

" INDUSTRY of Nations, The..........London, 1855.

" INQUIRY. (See Enquiry)..........

" KRANKHEITEN, Die. Welche verschiednen Ständen, Altern und Geschlechtern eigenthümlich sind..Ulm, 1860.

" LABOUR DEFENDED against Capital, by T. H. (*See* Hodgskin).......London, 1825.

" LETTER, A, to Sir J. C. Banbury, Bt., On the high Price of Provisions. By a Suffolk Gentleman....Ipswich, 1795.

" MONEY and its Vicissitudes. (*See* S. Bailey)......................London, 1837.

" OUTLINES of Political Economy....London, 1832.

" OBSERVATIONS on certain verbal disputes in Political Economy.......London, 1821.

" PERILS, The, of the Nation.......London, 1843.

" PRINCIPLES, Essential, of the Wealth of Nations....................London, 1797.

" REASONS for the late increase of the Poor Rate....................London, 1777.

Author.   *Work.*   *Date.*

ANONYMOUS ...... REASONS for a limited Exportation
        of Wool........................London, 1677.
"   REMARKS on the Commercial Policy
        of Great Britain...............London, 1815.
"   S. W. A Compendious and Briefe
        Examination of certayne ordinary
        complaints of diverse of our coun-
        trymen in these our days. (*See*
        William Stafford)..............London, 1581.
"   SOPHISMS of Free Trade. By a
        Barrister........Reprint, 1870. London, 1850.
"   SOURCE, The, and Remedies of the
        National Difficulties. A letter to
        Lord John Russell.............London, 1821.
"   THEORY, The, of the Exchanges.
        The Bank Charter Act of 1844.
        The abuse of the Metallic Principle
        to Depreciation ....London, 1864.
"   THOUGHTS, Some, on the interest of
        money in general, and particularly
        in the English Funds...........London, 1870.
APPIAN .... De bellis Civilibus................
ASHLEY, Anth., The Ten Hours' Factory Bill, Speech
Lord.   of the 15th March.............London, 1844
ARISTOTLE .... De Republica ....
AUGIER, Marie.... Du crédit public et de son Histoire
        depuis les temps anciens jus qu' à
        nos jours......................Paris, 1842.

B.

BAILEY, S........ A Critical Dissertation, etc., chiefly
        in reference to the writings of Mr.
        Ricardo ....London, 1825.
BAILEY, S........ Money and its Vicissitudes. (Pub-
        lished Anon.)..................London, 1837.
BABBAGE, Charles. On the Economy of Machinery.....London, 1832.
BACON .... Life of Henry VII. (Kennet's Eng-
        land). ....London, 1817.
"   BANK ACTS. (*See* Parliamentary
        Papers) ....
BANKER, A....... The Currency Question reviewed.
        A letter to the Scotch people by
        a Banker in England...........London, 1845.
BARBON, Nicolas.. A Discourse on coining the new
        money lighter, in answer to Mr.
        Locke's Considerations..........London, 1696.
BARTON, John.... Observations on the circumstances
        which influence the condition of the
        Labouring Classes of Society...London, 1817.
BARRISTER, A..... Sophisms of Free Trade. (*See*
        under Anonymous)..............
BECCARIA, CESARE. Elementi di Economia Pubblica.
        Custodi's ed. of Italian Economists. Milano, 1803.
BELLERS, John.... Essays about the Poor. Manufactur-

Author.	*Work.*	*Date.*

ers, Trade, Plantations, and Im-
morality. ....London, 1699.
BENGAL HURKARU. (*See* under
Newspapers) ....
BENTHAM, Jeremy.Théorie des peines et des récom-
penses (d'après des manuscrits
inédits, ed. by E. Dumont)......Londres, 1811.
BERKELEY, George.The Querist......................London, 1750.
BIDAUT, J. N.....Du Monopole qui s'établit dans les
arts industriels et le Commerce...Paris, 1828.
BIESE, F.........Die Philosophie des Aristoteles....Berlin, 1842.
BLAKEY, Robert...The History of Political Literature
from the earliest times..........London, 1855.
BLANQUI, J. A...Des Classes Ouvrières en France
pendant 1 année, 1848.
    "   Cours d'économie industrielle......Paris, 1835-39.
BOISGUILLEBERT ..Dissertation sur la nature des rich-
esses, de l'argent et des tributs.
(Ed. Daire)....................Paris, 1843.
BOXHORN ....Institutiones politicæ ....Leyden, 1663.
BOYLEAU, Etienne.Livres des métiers. (Collection de
documents inédits) ....Paris, 1835.
BROADHURST, J...Political Economy ....London, 1842.
BROUGHAM, Henry.An Inquiry into the Colonial Policy
of the European Powers..........Edinburgh, 1803.
BRUCKNER, ...Théorie du système animal........Leyden, 1767.
BUCHANAN, David.Inquiry into the Taxation and Com-
mercial Policy of Great Britain...Edinburgh, 1844.
    "   Smith's Wealth of Nations. With
notes and an additional volume...London, 1814.
BUCHEZ et ROUX..Histoire Parlementaire de la Révo-
lution Française...............Paris, 1834-38.
BURKE, Edmund..Thoughts and details on Scarcity...London, 1800.
    "   A Letter from the Right Hon. Ed.
Burke, to a noble lord, on the at-
tacks made upon him and his pen-
sion in the House of Lords by the
Duke of Bedford, etc............Philadephia, 1795
BUTLER ....Hudibras. (?)

C.

CAIRNES, J. E....The Slave Power.................London, 1862.
CAMPBELL, George.Modern India....................London, 1852.
CANTILLON, Philip.Essai sur la nature du Commerce
en général......................Amsterdam, 1756.
    "   The Analysis of Trade, Commerce,
etc. (English translation).......London, 1759.
CARD, Ronard de..Falsification des substances sacra-
mentelles ....
CAREY, H. C.....The Slave Trade.................Philadelphia, 1853.
    "   Essay on the Rate of Wages.......London, 1834.
CARLI, G. R......Notes in his edition of Verri. (*See*
Verri) ....Milano, 1803.

Author.   Work.   Date.

CAZENOVE, John...Notes in his edition of Malthus' De-
                     finitions in Political Economy....London, 1853.
                     CENSUS. (*See* Parliamentary Pa-
                     pers).............................
CHALMERS, Th....On Political Economy.............Glasgow, 1832.
CHAMBERLAIN, Jos.Speech at Sanitary Congress, Bir-
                     mingham. (*Times*, 15th Jan.,
                     1875.) ....
CHERBULIEZ, A. E.Riche ou pauvre.................Paris, 1841.
COBBETT, William.A History of the Protestant Refor-
                     mation ....Dublin, 1868.
COLINS, H........L'Économie Politique.............Paris, 1857.
    "   Combination (On) of Trades. (*See*
                     Anon.) ....London, 1834.
                     COMMISSIONS. (Children's Employ-
                     ment, on Railways, etc. (*See*
                     Parl. Papers)...................
                     CONGRESS. (International Statis-
                     tic). Compte rendu............Paris.
CONDILLAC ....Le Commerce et le Gouvernement..Paris, 1776.
                     Reprinted in:
                     Mélanges de l' Économie Politique.
                     (Ed. Daire et Molinari)........Paris, 1847.
                     CONSIDERATIONS concerning taking
                     off the Bounty on Corn exported.
                     (*See* Anonymous)..............London, 1753.
CORBET. Th.......An Inquiry into the Causes and
                     Modes of the Wealth of Individuals.London, 1841.
CORBON, C. A.....De l'enseignement professionnel....Paris, 1858.
COURCELLE - SEN-Traité théorique et pratique des en-
EUIL, J. G.....treprises industrielles............Paris, 1857.
                     CURRENCY Question, The. (*See*
                     Anon.) ....London, 1847.
                     CURRENCY Question, reviewed, The
                     (*See* Anon.)...................London, 1845.
CUVIER, J. L. C...Discours sur les Révolutions du
                     Globe. (Ed. Hoefer)...........Paris, 1863.

D.

                     DAILY TELEGRAPH. (*See* News-
                     papers).
DARWIN, Charles..Origin of Species...............London, 1859.
                     Defence, A, of the landlords and
                     farmers of Great Britain. (*See*
                     Anon.) ....London, 1814.
DE QUINCEY, Th..The Logic of Political Economy....London, 1844.
DESCARTES, René..Discours de la Méthode...........Paris, 1668.
                     DEUTSCH - FRANZÖSISCHE JAHR-
                     BÜCHER (See Marx and Ruge)....
                     DISCOURSE concerning Trade, etc.Paris, 1844.
DIODORUS SICULUS.Bibliotheca Historica...........
                     (*See* Anonymous)..............London, 1689.
                     DISCOURSE on the General Notions
                     of Money, etc. (*See* Anon.).....London, 1695.

Author.	Work.	Date.

DISCOURSE on the necessity of encouraging Mechanick Industry, (*See* Anon.) ....London, 1690.
DISSERTATION on the Poor Laws, etc. (*See* Anon.)..............London, 1786.
DUNNING, T. J....Trades' Unions and Strikes.......London, 1860.
DUPONT, Pierre...Chansons ....Paris, 1846.

E.

EAST INDIAN TRADE, etc., (*See* Anon.) ....London, 1696.
ECONOMY, Public, Concentrated, (*see* Anon.) ....Carlisle, 1833.
ECONOMIST (*see* under Newspapers).
EDEN, F. M......The State of the Poor.............London, 1797.
EMPIRICUS, Sextus.Opera ....
ENGELS, Friedrich.Lage der arbeitenden Klasse in England ....Leipzig, 1845.
"   Umrisse zu einer Kritik der Nationalœkonomie (Deutsch-Französische Jahrbücher) ....Paris, 1844.
"   Die Englische Zehn - Stunden - Bill (Neue Rheinische Zeitung April number) ....Hamburg, 1850.
ENGELS, F. & Marx,Manifest der Kommunistischen Partei ....London, 1847.
K.
ENQUIRY into, etc. (*see* under Anonymous) ....
ESSAY, etc. (*see* under Anonymous.)
ENSOR, George....An Inquiry concerning the Population of Nations.................London, 1818.

F.

FACTORY ACTS, Reports of Inspectors, (*see* Parl. Papers)..........
FARMER, A.......Enquiry into the Connection, etc., (*see* Enquiry under Anonymous)..London, 1773.
FARMS, Capital, etc., (*see* under Anonymous) ....London, 1767.
FAWCETT, Henry..The Economic Position of the British Labourer....................London, 1865.
FERGUSON, A.....A History of Civil Society, Reprinted.London, 1850.
FERRAND ....Speech in House of Commons. ` (*see* Hansard) ....
FERRIER, F. L. A..Le gouvernement considéré dans ses rapports avec le commerce.......Paris, 1822.
FIELDEN, J.......The Curse of the Factory System..London, 1836.
FLEETWOOD,Bishop.Chronicon pretiosum..............London, 1707.
FONTEROL, A. L...Hygiène physique et morale de l'ouvrier, etc....................Paris, 1858.
FORBONNAIS, V. de.Eléments du Commerce, Nouvelle Edition ....Leyde, 1766.

Author.   *Work.*   *Date.*

FORSTER, Rev. Na-An enquiry into the Causes of the
thaniel .... present high price of Provisions..London, 1773.
FRANKLIN, Benja-
min ....Works, (Edited by Sparks),......Boston, 1830-36-40
FULLARTON, John.Regulation of Currencies.........London, 1844.

G.

GALIANI, F.......Della Moneta, (Custodi Ed.)......Milano, 1803.
GANILH, Charles..Des systèmes de l'économie politique.Paris, 1821.
GARNIER, G.......Abrégé élémentaire des principes de
l'économie politique (published
anonymously) ....Paris, 1796.
GASKELL, P......The Manufacturing Population of
England ....London, 1833.
GENTLEMAN, A Suf-Letter to Sir J. C. Banbury on the
folk .... higl price of provisions.........London, 1795.
GENOVESI, A......Lezioni di Economia civile (Custodi
Ed.) ....Milano, 1803.
GISBOURNE ....Enquiry into the Duties of Man...London, 1795.
GLADSTONE, W. E.See Hansard....................
GREGOIR, H.......Les Typographes devant le Tribunal
Correctionnel de Bruxelles........Bruxelles, 1865
GREG, R. H......The Factory question and the Ten
Hours' Bill ....London, 1837.
GROVE, W. R.....On the Correlation of Physical
Forces ....London, 1846.

H.

HALLER, C. L. Von.Restauration der Staatswissenschaf-
ten ....Wintherthur, 1820-
1834.
HAMM, W........Die Landwirthschaftlichen Geräthe
und Maschinen Englands.........Braunschweig,1856.
HANSARD ....Parliamentary Debates. Speech of
Mr. Ferrand, April 27th, 1863....London, 1863.
"   Parliamentary Debates. Speech of
Mr. Gladstone on the Budget, Feb.
14th, 1843.....................London, 1843.
HANSARD ....Parliamentary Debates. Speech of
Mr. Gladstone on the Budget,
April 16th, 1863...............London, 1863.
"   Parliamentary Debates. Speech of
Mr. Gladstone, April 7th, 1864. London, 1864.
HARRIS,James,Earl
of Malmesbury..Dialogue concerning Happiness (re-
published in " Three Treatises,"
1765) ....London, 1741.
HASSALL, Dr. H. H.Adulterations detected...........London, 1857.
HEGEL, G. W. F...WERKE ....Berlin, 1832-40.
HILAIRE,GeoffroiSt.Notions de Philosophie Naturelle....Paris, 1838.
HOBBES, Th......Leviathan. (Works).............London, 1839-44
HODGSKIN, Th.....Labour Defended against Capital.
By T. H. (*See* under Anon.)....London, 1825.

Author.   *Work.*   **Date.**

HODGSKIN, Th....Natural and Artificial Rights, The,
                    of Property Contrasted. (Anony-
                    mous) ....London, 1832.
HOLLINSHED .....Description of England............
HOMER ....Iliad and Odyssey................
HOPKINS, Th......On Rent of Land.................London, 1828.
HORNE, Geo.......A Letter to Adam Smith, LL.D., On
                    the Life, Death and Philosophy of
                    his Friend, David Hume..........Oxford, 1784.
HORNER, Leonard..A Letter to Mr. Senior, etc........London, 1837.
HOUGHTON, John..Husbandry and Trade Improved...London, 1727.
HOWITT, William..Colonization and Christianity......London, 1838.
HUTTON, C.......Course of Mathematics...........Reprint,   London,
                                                            1841–43.

I.

INDUSTRY of Nations. (*See* Anony-
    mous) ....London, 1855.
INQUIRY. (*See* Enquiry under Anon.)
INTERNATIONAL Statistic Congress,
    Compte rendu...................Paris.
ISOCRATES ....Orationes et Epistolae...........

J.

JONES, Richard...An Essay on the Distribution of
                    Wealth. Part I., On Rent.......London, 1831.
    "   An Introductory Lecture on Polit-
                    ical Economy ....London, 1833.
    "   Text Book of Lectures on the Po-
                    litical Economy of Nations.......Hertford, 1852.
    "   JOURNAL of the Society of Arts.
                    (*See* under newspapers).........

K.

KRANKHEITEN, Die welche verschie-
    denen Ständen, Altern und Ge-
    schlechtern eigenthümlich sind....Ulm, 1860.

L.

LABORDE, A. de...De l'esprit de l'association dans tous
                    les interêts de la communauté....Paris, 1818.
                LABOUR defended. (*See* Hodgskin).
                LABOURERS, (Agricultural) Ireland.
                    (*See* Parliamentary Papers)......
LAING, S.........National Distress, etc.............London, 1844.
LANCELLOTTI, Abb.Farfalloni de gli Antichi Historici..Venetia, 1636.
LASSALLE, Ferdin.Die Philosophie des Herakleitos...Berlin, 1858.
LAVERGNE, Léonce
    de ....Essai sur l'économie rurale de l'An-
                    gleterre ....Paris, 1858.
LAW, J..........Considérations sur le numéraire et
                    sur le Commerce. (Ed. Daire)...Paris, 1843.

Work.   Date.

LETTER, A, to Sir J. C. Banbury,
   etc. By a Suffolk gentleman.
   (*See* Anonymous)...............Ipswich, 1795.
LE TROSNE.......De l'intérêt Social. (Ed. Daire)..Paris, 1840.
LEVI, Leone......Lecture before the Society of Arts,
   April, 1866. (*See* Newspapers)..London, 1866.
LIEBIG, J. von....Die Chemie in ihrer Anwendung auf
   Agrikultur Braunschweig,1862
   "   Ueber Theorie und Praxis in der
   Landwirthschaft Braunschweig,1856
LINGUET, N.......Théorie des loix civiles..........Londres, 1767.
LOCKE, John......Some Considerations on the Conse-
   quences of the Lowering of Inter-
   est. (Works, Vol. II.)..........London, 1777.
   LORDS (House of) Committee on
   Bank Acts. (*See* Parliamentary
   Papers) ....
LUCRETIUS ....De Rerum Naturâ...............
LUTHER, Martin...An die Pfarherrn, wider den
   Wucher zu predigen............Wittenberg, 1540.

M.

MACAULAY,Thos.B.History of England. 10th Edit....London, 1854.
MACLAREN, James.History of the Currency..........London, 1858.
MACLEOD, H. D...Theory and Practice of Banking...London, 1855.
M'CULLOCH, J. R..A Dictionary, Practical, &c., of Com-
   merce ....London, 1847.
   "   The Literature of Political Economy.London, 1845.
   "   Principles of Political Economy....London, 1830.
MALTHUS, T. R...Definitions in Political Economy...London, 1827,
   "   Inquiry into the Nature and Prog-
   ress of Rent....................London, 1815.
MALTHUS, T. R...Principles of Political Economy...London, 1836.
MANDEVILLE, B. de.Fable of the Bees................London, 1728.
MARTINEAU, Har-
   riet ....The Manchester Strike............(?) 1842.
MARX, Karl, and
Engels, F......Manifest der Kommunistischen Par-
   tei ....London, 1847
MARX, Karl, and
Ruge, A........Deutsch-französische Jahrbücher....Paris, 1844.
MARX, Karl.....Lohnarbeit und Kapital. (Neue
   Rheinische Zeitung, 7th April.)..Köln, 1849.
   "   Misère de la philosophie: Réponse
   à la philosophie de la Misère de M.
   Proudhon ....Paris, 1847.
   "   Zur Kritik der Politischen Oekon-
   omie ....Berlin, 1859.
MASSEY, J........An Essay on the Governing Causes
   of the Natural Rate of Interest.
   (Pub. Anon.)..................London, 1750.
   MASTER SPINNERS and Manufactur-
   Geschichte der Fronhöfe..........
MAURER ....Geschichte der Fronhöfe.........Erlangen, 1862

Author. *Work.* *Date.*

MAUER ....Einleitung zur Geschichte der Mark-
verfassung ....München, 1854.
MERCIER de la Ri-
vière ....(*See* Rivière.)....................
MERCHANT, A....A Discourse on the General Notions
of Money, etc. (*See* under Anony-
mous) ....London, 1695.
MERIVALE, H.....Lectures on Colonization and Colo-
nies ....London, 1841.
MILL, James......Article " Colony," Supplement of
Encyclopædia Britannica........Edinburgh, 1831.
"   Elements of Political Economy....London, 1821.
MILL, John Stuart.Essays on some Unsettled Questions
of Political Economy............London, 1844.
"   Principles of Political Economy....London, 1848.
MIRABEAU ......:.De la Monarchie Prussienne.......Lond.es, 1788.
MOLINARI, G. de..Etudes Économiques.............. Paris, 1846.
MOMMSEN, Th....Römische Geschichte............Berlin, 1856.
Money and its Vicissitudes. (*See*
S. Bailey. Pub. Anon.).........London, 1837.
MONTEIL, Alexis...Histoire des Matériaux manuscripts,
&c. ....Paris, 1835.
MONTESQUIEU ....Esprit des Lois. Œuvres.........Londres, 1767.
MORE, Thomas....Utopia ....
MORNING STAR. (*See* under News-
papers) ....
MORTON, J. C.....Article LABOURER in Cyclopædia of
Agriculture ....
Paper read before the Society of
Arts Jan. 1861 ....
MORNING STAR. (*See* under News-
papers) ....
MUN, Th.........England's Treasure by Foreign
Trade ....London, 1669.
MURPHY ....Ireland, Industrial, Political, and
Social ....London, 1870.
MURRAY, Hugh,   Historic and descriptive account of
WILSON, etc.... British India..................Edinburgh, 1832.

N.

NASMITH ..\......Speech at Trades' Union Commis-
sion, 1851....................London, 1851.
NEWMAN, S. P....Elements of Political Economy....New York, 1835.
NEWMAN, W. F...Lectures on Political Economy.....London, 1851.
NEWNHAM, G. B..A Review of the Evidence before the
Committee of the two Houses of
Parliament on the Corn Laws....London, 1815.
NEWSPAPERS .....NEWSPAPERS and journals, etc.
BENGAL HURKARU. Bi-monthly Over-
land Summary of news, July 22nd..Calcutta (?) 1861.
DAILY TELEGRAPH, Jan. 7th........London, 1860.
ECONOMIST, July 19th   London, 1859.
"   Janr., 21st...........London, 1860.
"   June, 2nd...........London, 1866.

Author.   **Work.**   **Date.**

JOURNAL of the Society of Arts....London.
  "   January, 1861...........
  "   January, 1872...........
  "   April, 1866, etc..........
MORNING STAR, April 17th........London, 1863.
  "   "   June 23rd.......London, 1863.
OBSERVER, April 24th.............London, 1864.
REVOLUTIONS DE PARIS............Paris, 1789-94.
REYNOLDS' NEWSPAPER, Jan.......London, 1860.
  "   "   Feb ......London, 1866.
  "   "   Jan. 20th..London, 1867.
SPECTATOR, June.................London, 1866 (?)
STANDARD ....London, 1865 (?)
  "   Oct. 26th...............London, 1861.
TIMES, Nov. 5th.................London, 1861.
  "   Nov. 26th.................London, 1862.
  "   Nov. 29th.................London, 1862.
  "   March 24th...............London, 1863.
  "   Sept. 9th.................London, 1873.
WORKMAN'S Advocate, Jan. 1866...London, 1866.
NIEBUHR, G. B....Römische Geschichte (reprinted)..Berlin, 1853.
NORTH, Sir Dudley.Discourses upon Trade............London, 1691.

O.

OBSERVATIONS on certain verbal dis-
     putes. (*See* Anonymous).......London, 1821.
OBSERVER. (*See* Newspapers).
OLMSTED, F......Sea board Slave States............New York, 1856.
OPDYKE, G.......A treatise on Political Economy....New York, 1851.
ORTES, G.........Della Economia libri sei (Ed. Cus-
     todi) ....Milano, 1803.
OTWAY, J. H.....Judgment of J. H. Otway, Hilary
     Sessions, Belfast................
OWEN, Robert.....Observations on the Effects of the
     Manufacturing System...........London, 1817.

P.

PAGNINI, L. A....Saggio sopra il giusto pregio delle
     cose. (Ed. Custodi)............Milano, 1803
PARLIAMENTARY   AGRICULTURAL Labourers, (Ireland)
PAPERS ....   1862 ....
     CENSUS for Great Britain, Ireland
     and Wales, 1863, etc............
     CHILDREN's Employment Commission
     Factory Regulation Acts, 1859....
     HOUSE OF COMMONS Committee,
     1826.
     HOUSE OF LORDS Committee on
     Bank Acts, 1848................
     REPORTS on Bank Acts, 1857......
     of Select Committe on Bank Acts,
     1858 ....

Author.   *Work.*   *Date.*

REPORTS of Select Committee on
    Mines, 1866....................
REPORTS of Commissioners of H. M.'s
    Inland Revenue. (Fourth & Tenth).
REPORTS of Commissioners relating
    to Transportation and Penal Servi-
    tude. (1863....................
REPORTS of Foreign Office. (How-
    ard de Welden)................
REPORTS of Ispectors of Factories..
REPORTS of Royal Commission on
    the Grievances of the Journeymen
    Bakers. (1862).. ....
REPORTS from the Poor Law Inspec-
    tors on the Wages of Agricultural
    Labourers in Dublin. (1870)....
REPORTS on Public Health.........
REPORTS of the Registrar General..
REPORTS of H. M. Secretaries of
    Embassies and Legations on Manu-
    factures. (1863)..............
STATISTICAL Abstract for or United
    Kingdom. (1861 and 1774)......
STATISTICS (Miscellaneou.) ι. the
    United Kingdom. (18 6)........
PARRY, C. H......The Question of the Necessity of the
                    Existing Corn Laws Considered...London, 1816.
PERSON in Busi-
    ness, A........Capital Farms. (*See* under Anon.). London, 1767.
PETTY, William...Political Anatomy of Ireland and
                    Verbum Sapienti...............London, 1691.
    "   Quantulumcunque concerning money. London, 1695.
    "   A Treatise on Taxes and Contribu-
                    tions ....London, 1662.
    "   Verbum Sapienti. (*See* Political
                    Anatomy of Ireland)..........
PINTO, Isaac......Traité de la Circulation et du Crédit. Amsterdam, 1771.
PLATO ....De Republica.....................
POSTLETHWAYT, M.First Preliminary Discourse.......London.
PRICE, Richard....Observations on Reversionary Pay-
                    ments ....London, 1803.
    "   Universal Dictionary of Trade and
                    Commerce ....London.
    "   Great Britain's Commercial Interest
                    Explained ....London, 1755.
PROUDHON ....Oeuvres ....Paris.

Q.

QUESNAY. Dr. F...Dialogue sur le Commerce. (Ed.
                    Daire) ....Paris, 1846.
                Maximes Générales. (Ed. Daire). Paris, 1846.

Author.	Work.	Date.

R.

RAFFLES, Th. Stam-
ford ....History of Java................. London, 1817.

RAMAZZINI ....De morbis artificum (1713). French
translation in " Encyclopédie des
Sciences Médicales." ....Paris, 1841.

RAMSAY, G.......An Essay on the Distribution of
Wealth ....Edinburgh, 1836.

RAVENSTONE, P...Thoughts on the Funding System
and its Effects................London, 1824.

READ, George ....History of Baking...............London, 1848.

REDGRAVE, A......Report of Speech in Journal of the
Society of Arts. (Jan., 1872)...

REGNAULT, E.....Histoire politique et sociale des
Principautés Danubiennes........Paris, 1855.

REICH, Eduard....Ueber die Entartung des Menschen..Erlangen, 1868.

REPORT of the Committee of the
Master Spinners and Manufactur-
ers Defence Fund...............Manchester, 1854.

REPORT of Social Science Congress,
Edinburgh, Oct., 1863............

REPORTS (Inspectors of Factories,
Health, etc. *See* under Parliamentary Papers.)................

RESOLUTION of Working Men of
Dunkirk ....New York, 1866.

REVOLUTIONS de Paris. (*See* under
Newspapers) ....

REYNOLDS' Newspapers. (*See* under
Newspapers) ....

RICARDO, David...Principles of Political Economy.... London, 1821.

RICHARDSON, B. W.Work and Overwork. (Social Science Review, July, 1863).........London, 1863.

RIVIÈRE, Mercier
de la...........(*See* Mercier)....................

RODBERTUS-JAGET-
ZOW, C.........Soziale Briefe an Kirchmann......Berlin, 1850.
Briefe, etc., Edited by Dr. R. Meyer.Berlin, 1881.

ROGERS, James E.
Thorold ....A History of Agriculture and Prices.Oxford, 1866.

ROSCHER, W......Grundlagen der Nationalœkonomie..Berlin, 1858.

ROSSI, P.........Cours d'Économie Politique.......Bruxelles, 1842.

ROUSSEAU, Jean-
Jacques ....Discours sur l'Économie Politique..Genève, 1765.

ROUX et Buchez..(*See* Buchez)....................

S.

SAINT-HILAIRE,
Geoffroi ....Notions de Philosophie Naturelle..Paris, 1838.

SAY, J. B........Lettres à M. Malthus............Paris, 1820.

"   Traité de l'Économie Politique....Paris, 1841.

SCHOUW, F.......Die Erde, die Pflanze und der Mensch.Leipzig, 1854.

SCHULZ, Wilhelm..Die Bewegung der Produktion......Zürich, 1843.

Author.	Work.	Date.
SCROPE, G. P.....	Political Economy (Edited by A. Potter)	New York, 1541.
SENIOR, William Nassau	Journals, Conversations and Essays relating to Ireland................	London, 1868.
"	Letters on the Factory Acts.......	London, 1837.
"	Principes Fondamentaux de l'Économie Politique (French translation by Arrivabene)..................	Paris, 1836.
"	Three Lectures on the Rate of Wages.	London, 1830.
SHAKESPEARE, Wm.	Works	
SISMONDI, Simonde de	Etudes d'Économie Politique.......	Paris, 1837.
"	Nouveaux Principes de l'Économie Politique	Paris, 1819.
"	De la Richesse Commerciale.......	Genève, 1803.
SKARBEK, F.......	Théorie des Richesses Sociales.....	Paris, 1829.
SMITH, Adam.....	Wealth of Nations...............	Aberdeen, 1848.
	SOCIAL SCIENCE Congress. (*See* under Report)..................	
	SOCIETY of Arts, Journal of. (*See* under Newspapers)..............	
	SOCIETY of Arts, Commission of Inquiry into Industrial Pathology..	
SOMERS, Robert...	Letters from the Highlands, on the Famine of 1847.................	London, 1848.
SOPHOCLES	Antigone	
	SPECTATOR. (See under Newspapers).	
STAFFORD, William.	A Compendius and Briefe Examination of certayne ordinary complaints of diverse of our countrymen in these our days (Publ. Anon.)..	London, 1581.
	STANDARD. (*See* under Newspapers).	
	STATISTICS. (*See* under Parliamentary Papers)................	
	STATUTES, General, of Massachusetts.	
	STATUTES, Revised of Rhode Island.	
	STATUTE, Decree of Philippe de Valois, 1346.....................	
STEUART, Sir Jas.	Principles of Political Economy...	Dublin, 1770.
"	Works	London, 1805.
STEWART, Dugald..	Works. (Edited by Sir William Hamilton)	Edinburgh, 1855.
STOLBERG, Christian	Gedichte aus dem Griechischen	Hamburg, 1782.
STORCH, H. F......	Cours d'Économie Politique.......	St.Petersburg,1815.
STRYPE	Annals of the Reformation........	London, 1725.

T.

	TIMES. (See under Newspapers)..	
THIERS, Adolphe..	De la propriété..................	Paris, 1848
THOMPSON, Benj..	Essays, Political, Economical, and Philosophical, etc.	London, 1796-1802.

Author. **Work.** **Date.**

THOMPSON, W....An Inquiry into the principles of
the distribution of Wealth.......London, 1824.
THORNTON, W. T..Over-population and its Remedy...London, 1864.
THUCIDY DES......De Bello Peloponnesiaco..........
THÜNEN, J. H. von.Der isolirte Staat................Rostock, 1863.
TOOKE, Thos......History of Prices (partly Ed. by W.
Newmarch) ....London, 1853-57.
TORRENS, R.......An Essay on the External Corn
Trade ....London, 1815.
" An Essay on the Production of
Wealth ....London, 1821.
" On Wages and Combinations......London, 1834.
TOWNSEND, W....Dissertation on the Poor Laws, etc.
(*See* under Anonymous)..)......London, 1817.
TRACY, Destutt de.Traité de la Volonté et de ses Effets.Paris, 1826.
TRADES' Union Commission........
TUCKETT, J. D....A History of the Past and Present
State of the Labouring Population..London, 1846.
TURGOT ....Réflexions sur la formation et la dis-
tribution des richesses...........Paris, 1844.

U.

URE, Andrew.....Philosophy of Manufacturs........London, 1835.
URQUHART, David.Familiar Words.................London, 1858
" Portfolio, New Series, (*see* under
Newspapers) ....

V.

VANDERLINT, Jas..Money answers all things........London, 1734.
VERRI, Pietro.....Meditazioni sulla Economia politica,
(Ed. Custodi).................Milano, 1803.
VISSERING, S.....Handboek van pratische Staatshuis-
houdkunde ....Amsterdam, 1860-
62.

W.

WADE, John......History of the Middle and Working
Classes ....London, 1833.
WAKEFIELD, E. G..England and America............London, 1833.
" Notes in his ed. of Smith's Wealth
of Nations.....................London, 1835.
" A view of the Art of Colonization..London, 1849.
WARD, John.......History of the Borough of Stoke-
upon Trent....................London, 1843.
WATSON, S.......(*See* under Society of Arts).......
WATTS, John.....Facts and Fictions of Political Econ-
omists ....Manchester, 1842.
" Trade Societies and Strikes........Manchester, 1865.
WAYLAND, F......Elements of Political Economy....London, 1856.
WEST, Edward....Price of Corn and Wages of Labour.London, 1826.
WILKS, Mark.....Historical Sketches of the South of
India ....London, 1810-17.

Author.	Work.	Date.

WORKMAN'S ADVOCATE, (*see* under Newspapers) ....

WRIGHT, Thomas.. Short Address to the Public on the Monopoly of large Farms........London, 1779.

X.

Xenophon .... Cyropædia ....

Y.

YOUNG, Arthur.... Political Arithmetic............ ....London, 1774.

INDEX.

A.

Abstinence, two kinds of, 650.
Absurdities of vulgar economy, 180, 205 note, 241 note, 249, 352, 489, 653, 654, 655, 666, 669, 701, 839, 841.
Accumulation of capital, its concept, 634; not identical with hoarding, 645; at a faster rate than increase of population increases wages, 673; means increase of proletariat, 674; means concentration of capital and labourers, 685; causes a relative overpopulation (industrial reserve army), 691; its absolute general law, 707; its general law illustrated, 711–717; degrades the labourer, 727–733; primitive, its secret, 784; promoted by public debt, 827; see also Capitalist Accumulation.
Additions to the text of the fourth German edition of "Capital," 32.
Adulteration of commodities, 194, 274, 277.
Agricultural laborers' misery in England, 719, 739–773, 779.
Agricultural revolution in England, 778, 788–805; its reaction on industry, 817.
American Civil War centralised capital, 847; stimulated improvements in cotton machinery, 473.
Animals and plants transformed by a continuous process of labor, 202.
Antagonism between capitalists and laborers, 363.
Aristotle lacked a concept of value, 69.

B.

Barter, direct, its development, 100.
Bentham's dogma of a fixed wage fund, 668.
Burke's observation of compensation of differences in co-operative labor, 354.

C.

"Capital," the Bible of the working class, 30.
Capital, first money-capital, 163; its circulation without limits, 170; contradictions in its general formula, 173; merchant's and money-lender's does not create any new value, 183; problem of its production posed, 184; its creation accomplished, 217; constant, 232; variable, 233; dead labor sucking living labor, 257; squanders labor-power, 581; means command over unpaid labor, 585; not increased by non-consumption, 646; its technical and organic composition, 672; see also Value.
Capitalist, creates no surplus-value, 638; his individual consumption robs accumulation, 649; Faustian conflict in his breast, 651; not interested in value, but in surplus-value, 351; in the labor-process, 205.
Capitalist, industrial, his genesis, 822; a lover of force, 824, 826.
Capitalist Accumulation, its phases reviewed, 640; its historical tendencies, 834–837.
Capitalist Argument, to conceal true nature of labor process, 213; against ten hours' day, 240.
Capitalist Co-operation differs from antique co-operation, 367.
Capitalist Era, its beginning, 787.
Capitalist View of production of commodities individualistic, 642.
Capitalist Production, a production of surplus-value, 558; based on man's dominion over nature, 563; begets class-struggle, 633; means anarchy in social division of labor and despotism in the workshop, 391.
Capitalists, denouncing one another, 601; preventing one another from obeying laws, 537.
Centralisation, its difference from concentration, 686.
Changes in the original plan of "Capital," 7, 8.
Child Labor in England, 268, 284–289, 510, 511.
Circulation, sweating money, 127; not a source of surplus-value, 177.
Classic Economy never understood the process of reproduction, 665, note; see also Political Economy.
Class-Struggles between creditors and debtors in antiquity, 152.
Coin as money, 140.
Colonisation, its modern theory, 838; independent labor its obstacle, 840; on a capitalist basis impossible without wage-labor, 843; uncovers secret of capitalist accumulation, 848.
Commodities, defined, 41; their fetishism, 81; their exchange, 96; explaining their own nature, 95; their relation to their owners, 97; their circulation, 106; their metamorphosis, 116; differentiated from gold, 117; in love with money, 121; their complete metamorphosis, 125.
Condition of Political Economy in 1848, 17–19.
Constant Capital, see Capital.
Co-operation, based on division of labor typical of manufacturing period, 369; implies concentration of labor and capital, 362; in antiquity, 366; of machinery, 414; under capitalism develops despotism, 364.
Co-operative Labor different in effect from individual labor, 357.
Corvée, abuse of, 261.

Cost-Price, 589.
Cotton Industry, promoted slave breeding industry, 485.
Credit-System, helps centralisation, 687; grows with national debt, 828.
Crises, cycle of, 31; see also Over-Population, Accumulation, Money, Machinery, Stock Exchange Gambling.
Crusoe, Robinson, in political economy, 88.

D.

Death from over-work, 280.
Death Rate increased by capitalist production, 282, 434, 435, 510.
Debt, Public, a lever of primitive accumulation, 827.
Degeneration of laborer, 270.
Degradation of laborer by capitalism, 727, 729, 731, 733, 736, 737, 832.
Difference between English and American edition of "Capital," 9.
Diseases caused by capitalist exploitation, 270, 510, 511, 721, 727, 729, 731.
Division of Labor, necessary for production of commodities, 49; not based on production of commodities, 49; under manufacture explained, 371; in manufacture and society compared, 385; fatal to free citizenship, 389; in guilds, 394; its stupefying effect on the laborer, 397; increases capitalist authority, 391; in Indian communities, 393; makes automaton of laborer, 396.
Domestic Industry, Modern, 509; employs women and children, 510, 511; cause of overcrowding, 512; an industrial reserve force, 524.

E.

Economy in constant capital through co-operative labor, 356.
Emigration of laborers meets opposition of masters, 629.
Engels, his additional work on "Capital," 32; his ridicule of Malthus, 696.
Epochs, Economic, distinguished by tools, 200.
Equivalent, see Value.
Exchange, illustrated, 118; a double process, 122.
Exchange Value defined and explained, 43; see also Production and Value.
Excrements of production, 663.
Experiments, made to intensify labor, 449; in labor legislation made at the expense of the laborers, 539.
Exports refute wage fund theory, 670.
Extinction of English handloom weavers, 471.

F.

Factory, modern, described, 457–466.
Factory Acts, hasten industrial revolution, 514, 519, 521, 522; circumvented, 265; a curb on the greed for surplus-labor, 263; their effect on sanitation and education in England, 526; regarded as an interference with the rights of capital, 525; hasten concentration of capital, 552.
Factory Acts Extension Acts, sphere embraced by them, 540; spoil Factory Acts, 541.

Factory System, ruining handicrafts and manufacture, 492–493; its effect on English cotton industry, 497–501; its enormous power of expansion, 495; its reactic on handicrafts, manufacture. and domestic industries, 502–505.
Family, its transformation under capitalist production, 511–514.
Farmer, Capitalist, his genesis, 814.
Force, an element in primitive accumulation, 809; the midwife of social revolution, 824.
Forecast of events by averages, 227.
Freedom, Equality, and Bentham, 195.
French revolution abolished laborer's right of association, 813.

G.

Gladstone, his contradictory speech, 716.
Gold and Silver, natural money, 102; differences in mining, 160 note; their different weight as a standard of price and medium of circulation, 141; see also Metal.
Guilds, medieval, tried to prevent trade masters from becoming capitalists, 837.

H.

Handicraft, skill an obstacle to capitalist discipline, 403; revolutionised by modern industry, see Machinery.
Hegel's dialectics inv'ted by Marx, 25, 26; law of transformation of quantity into quality, 338.
Hoarding, see Money.
Home-Market, conquered by modern industry, 821.

I.

Ideas reflexes of the real world, 91.
Industrial Reserve Army, caused by accumulation of capital, 691; a necessary condition of capitalist production, 693; a regulator of wages, 699; a check upon the emancipation of labor, 701.
Industry, Modern, revolutionises agriculture, 553, 778, 788–805; revolutionises handicrafts and manufacture, see Machinery and Accumulation; annihilates peasant, 554; breaks power of resistance of agricultural laborer, 555; increases public debts and taxation, 830.
Interest, not analyzed in volume I; see volu1e III.
International bread of "Capital," 30.
Internationalism of capitalist production, see World Market.
Invention causes more invention, 419.
Inventions of handicraft period, 382.

J.

June Insurrection in France, its effect on ruling class of England, 313.
Justice of capitalism illustrated, 725.
Justification of the phrase "value of labor," 592.

L.

Labor, the common property of commodities, 44; its twofold character, 48; simple average labor in the abstract, 51; skilled, reduced to simple average labor.

51, 52; the cause of the fetishism of commodities, 83; its social character, 84; homogeneous, the secret of social production, 85; in free communities, 90; its property transformed into capitalist property, 140; skilled and unskilled, their difference in value, 220; necessary, 240; has no value, 588; separated from property, 640; co-operative, see Co-Operation; surplus, see Surplus-Labor.

Labor Fund, its relation to capital, 622.

Labor Laws in England, from the 14th to the 17th century, 290–304; from 1833–1864. 304–330.

Labor-Power, general property of labor-process, 57; bought and sold, 185; a commodity, 186; its value determined, 189; minimum limit of its value, 192; advanced to the capitalist, 193; produces more value than it has itself, 216; its value determined by average necessities of life 568; three laws of determining its value, 569.

Labor-Process, explained, 203; a productive process, 557.

Labor Time, a standard measure of value, 45; socially necessary, 46; its assertion as a social law, 86; regulated by competition, 379.

Laborer, the free, 187; his demand for a normal use of his labor-power, 258; a specialised implement in division of labor, 372; the collective, 383; feeds himself and the capitalist, 621; his productive and individual consumption, 626–628.

Land, first used as money in the 17th century, 101.

Law, concerning issue of paper money, 143; of population explained, 681; of value in its international application, 612; of value in general, see Value.

Legislation against expropriated in England, 805–808, 810–814; in France, 808, 813.

Leisure, nature's gift to primitive man, 565.

Limits of Compensation of rate and mass of surplus-value, 333; see also Surplus-Value.

M.

Machine, collective, 415; a product of modern industry, 418.

Machinery, its difference from tools, 405; not a means of shortening labor time under capitalism, 405; uses more tools than man, 408; the starting point of industrial revolution, 410; more exact than skilled labor, 420; its giant power, 421; differences in its wear and tear, 423; its capacity for speed, 425; its productivity, 427; substituted for half-time laborers, 429; increases female and child labor, 4; develops slave trade in white children, 432; increases death rate among laborers, 434; undermines morality, 435, 436; prevents education of children, 437–439; prolongs working day, 440; its twofold wear and tear, 441; its moral depreciation, 442; increases relative surplus-value, 443; reduces variable capital relatively, 444; intensifies contradictions of capitalist production, 445; in antiquity lightened labor, 446; intensifies exploitation, 447; fought by laborers, 467; its use forbidden by law, 467–468; increases profits, 476; does not compensate working people for loss of employment, 479, 481; lowers consumption of commodities, 480; under capitalism and in a free society compared, 482; in one industry increases production in another, 484; animate and inanimate, 631.

Malthus, his queer division of labor between accumulating and spending exploiters, 653; his "Essay on Population," 675; his "Principles of Political Economy," 696.

Malthusianism exploded, 676, note.

Mandeville's Fable of the Bees, 674.

Manufacture, its twofold rise, 369, 370; its two fundamental forms, 375; its narrow technical basis, 404; modern. in operation, 506–509; ruined by machinery, see Machinery.

Mass, of profit, see Profit; of surplus-value, see Surplus-Value.

Market, see Home-Market and World-Market.

Marx's method explained by himself, 12, 15, 21, 22, 24, 25; method of quotation, 30, 33; quotation from Gladstone vindicated, 34–39.

Materialist Conception of History, 15, 22.

Means of Production, necessary for reproduction, 620; see also Constant Capital.

Mercantilists and Free Traders, their misconception of value, 70.

Metal, its weight in silver and copper arbitrarily fixed by law, 142; see also Gold, Silver, and Money.

Mill, John Stuart, his superiority over the mercantilists, 566; his misinterpretation of profits, 567; his excessive generalisations, 567; an apologist of the wage fund theory, 669.

Mind, Human, operating on materials after the fact, 87.

Mines' Inspection Act, a dead letter, 542; farce of questioning witnesses, 543–551.

Misery of British industrial proletariat, 718.

Modern Industry, see Industry, Machinery, and Accumulation.

Money, the universal equivalent, 99; its magic, 105; a measure of value, 106; wild theories of, 108; its two functions as a measure of value and a standard of price, 109; historical origin of its names, 112; its currency, 128; keeps up the continuity of circulation, 130; its change of place in simple circulation, 131; effect of its rise or fall on the prices of commodities, 132; its quantity in circulation determined by volume of production, 134; its currency a reflex of circulation of commodities, 132; its quantity determined by sum of prices and velocity of exchange, 137; mutual compensation of factors in its currency, 138; erroneous opinion concerning determination of its quantity in circulation, 139; paper, symbolising gold and silver, 144; replaced by tokens, 145; hoarding of, 146; buried by Hindoos, 147; its power, 148; bounds of its efficacy, 149; a means of payment, 151;

development of special institutions for its payment, 154; its contradictory character expressed through crises, 155; its rise as a means of credit, 156; universal, 159; reserve, 161; its transformation into capital, 163; the beginning and end of value, 172; its international value, 613; probable form of its primitive accumulation, 623.

Moore, Samuel, and Aveling, Edward, translators of the first volume of "Capital," 27, 28.

Morality, of capitalism illustrated, 265, 273, 274, 278, 279, 287, 292, 294, 302, 311, 319, 321, 389, 396, 446, 725; of working people destroyed by capitalism, 283, 432, 433, 435, 436, 501, 507, 508.

Mysteries of trades, 532.

N.

National Debt, see Debt.
Natural forces cost capital nothing, 422.
Nature, the basis of the labor-process, 199, 201, 227, 230; its two economic classes, 562; and labor-power primary wealth creators, 662.
Night Work opposed by laborers, 277.
Nomad Races the first to develop the money form, 101.

O.

Original Plan of "Capital," 7.
Over-Crowding of laborer by capitalism, 728, 729, 731.
Over-Population, Relative, caused by accumulation of capital, 691; its different forms, 703.
Over-Production, see Over-Population, Accumulation, Industrial Reserve Army, and Machinery.
Over-Time paid extra, 598.
Over-Work shortening life, 270, 272, 275, 279.

P.

Pauperism a form of relative over-population, 706.
Physiocrats, consider only agricultural labor as productive, 559; their Tableau Economique, 647.
Piece Wages, a converted form of time wages, 602; irrationality of their form, 604; their characteristic peculiarities, 605; a form of the sweating system, 606; compared with time wages, 607; in vogue since the 14th century, 608; the general rule under the Factory Acts, 609; lowered in proportion as the number of prices increases, 610; see also Wages.
Plato's Republic on division of labor, 402.
Political Economy, as a science a product of manufacturing period, 400; in antiquity dwells most on use-value and quality, 401; classic, could not explain price or value, 589, 590; stuck in its bourgeois skin, 594; its condition in 1848, 17, 19; vulgar, see Absurdities.
Precious Metals, their increase accompanied by a fall in prices, 133; see also Metal, Money, Gold, and Silver.
Price, the money-form of commodities,
107; its fluctuations explained, 111; the money-name of labor, 114; without value, 115; affected by changes in labor time, 120; of products of handicrafts and machinery compared, 426.
Productivity, its effect on value, 53; depends on proficiency of laborer and perfection of tools, 374; declared to be no concern of the laborer's, 611.
Production and Reproduction without "abstinence," 656.
Production of commodities converted into capitalist production, 643.
Production of use-value and exchange value compared, 218; see also Exchange Value and Use-Value.
Profit, according to classic economy, 525; not analyzed in volume I, see volume III.
Property, its different forms, 89.
Protective Legislation for children benefits also the adult, 538.
Protestantism changed holidays into working days, 303 note.
Public Auction of children. 433.
Public Debt, see Debt.
Public Opinion a tool of capitalists, 632.
Purchase, the second metamorphosis of commodities, 123.

Q.

Quesnay's Riddle for vulgar economists, 351.

R.

Railway System encourages short orders, 523.
Rate of Profit, not analysed in volume I; see volume III.
Rate of Surplus-Value, see Surplus-Value.
Raw Materials supplied by nature are not capital, 661.
Reception of "Capital" in Germany, 20.
Reduction of labor time under capitalism produces intensification of exploitation, 456.
Relay System, 282.
Religion a reflex of the real world, 91.
Rent, not analysed in volume I; see volume III.
Reproduction, see Capitalist Production.
Reserve Army, Industrial, created by modern industry, 533; see also Industrial Reserve Army, Accumulation, and Machinery.
Revolution, see Capitalist Production, Agricultural Revolution, Factory System, and Industry.
Ricardo, his insufficient analysis of value, 92, 566; his three laws of value, 569–573; his errors, 574.
Rodbertus, his own detractor, 583.
Roman Empire, its failure to collect all ntributions in money, 157.
Roscher's nursery economics, 355, note.
Rumford's receipts for cheap living, 659.

S.

Sale, the first metamorphosis of commodities, 119.
Schools, technical and agricultural, 534.
Self-earned Money of capitalists, 637.
Sentimentality in economics, 192.

Silver, see Gold, Metal, and Money.

Slave Labor is unpaid labor, 591.

Smith, Adam, contended that additional capital is consumed by laborer, 646; supposed that social capital was only variable capital, 647.

Social Laws, mistaken by bourgeois for natural laws, 93, 709; evolved by natural processes, 373.

Soul of Capital, surplus-value, 257.

Speculation, see Stock Exchange Gambling.

Stock Companies a means of centralisation, 68.

Stock Exchange Gambling promoted by public debt, 827.

Sunday Work, 278; double standard of justice in regard to it, 291, note.

Superintendence creates no value, 215.

Supply and Demand no explanation for value or price, 589; used and abused by capitalists, 702.

Surplus-Labor, 241; not invented by capital, 259; its intermediate forms, 559; its natural basis, 561; appears as paid labor, 591.

Surplus-Product, its concept, 635; becomes property of capitalist by virtue of laws of commodity production, 642.

Surplus-Value, absolute, its concept, 345, 559; its production, 197; the end of capitalist production, 207; its rate, 235; calculation of its rate, 242; produced only by variable capital, 237; its rate and mass, 331; its mass varies in direct proportion to the variable capital, 335; relative, its concept, 142, 345, 559; explained in detail, 347; three laws determining its magnitude, 569; its nature concealed by capitalist production, 585; converted into capital, 636; divided into capital and revenue, 648.

Survival of the Fittest among agricultural laborers of England, 296.

Symbols of money and commodities, 103.

T.

Tableau Economique, see Physiocrats.

Taxation a product of national loans, 829.

Taxes payable in kind a means of preserving the old order, 158.

Terminology of "Capital" explained, 29.

Time Wages, 594; see also Wages.

Trade Unions desire to share benefits of improved machinery, 611, note.

Traffic in human flesh, 294.

Transition from manufacture to machine production, its different forms, 517.

U.

Unemployed, parade in London, 736; see also Over-Population and Machinery.

Unproductive Laborers, their increase, 487.

Ure, denouncing law for reduction of labor time as a retrogression, 299.

Use-Value, defined and explained, 42; without exchange value, 47, 48; as quality compared to exchange-value as quantity, 52, 53; see also Value and Production.

V.

Value, its substance and form, 41–96; crystallised human labor, 45; by labor time illustrated, 47; as a relation and an equivalent, 56; equivalent form illustrated, 58; relative and absolute compared, 63; its elementary form, 71; its expanded relative form, 72; its particular equivalent form, 73; defects of its expanded form, 74; its general form, 75; interdependent development of its forms, 78; its transition from the general to the money form, 79; its creation explained, 208; how transferred to the product in production, 222; of constant capital transferred to the product, 234; represented by different parts of the product, 245; of commodities in inverse ratio to productivity, 350; surplus, see Surplus-Value; in use, see Use-Value; exchange, see Exchange Value.

Variable Capital, see Capital.

Vulgar Economy, see Absurdities.

W.

Wage Laborer, his incessant reproduction the indispensable condition of capitalist production, 625.

Wages, the price of labor-power, 586; nominal rise may be actual fall, 579; not equal to full value of product, 587; their variations, 595; lower with longer working hours, 599; compared internationally, 614, 615; do not rise or fall in proportion as productivity varies, 616; their forcible reduction a means of accumulation, 657; their general movement regulated by industrial reserve army, 699; regulated by laws of distribution of population, 700; see also Piece Wages, Time Wages, and Variable Capital.

Wage Fund, according to Bentham, 668; according to Fawcett, 669.

Water and Wind as motive powers, 411.

Watt's genius shown by proclaiming the universality of the steam engine, 412.

Wealth, National, measured by relative magnitude of surplus produce, 254; its primary creators labor-power and land, 662.

Work, unsanitary, a source of disease, 271.

Working Day, indeterminate, 256; capitalist idea of, 290; summary of its two historical stages in England, 326–330.

World-Market, 823–834.

X.

Xenophon's bourgeois instinct shown by his idea of division of labor, 402.

A CATALOG OF SELECTED
DOVER BOOKS
IN ALL FIELDS OF INTEREST

A CATALOG OF SELECTED DOVER
BOOKS IN ALL FIELDS OF INTEREST

100 BEST-LOVED POEMS, Edited by Philip Smith. "The Passionate Shepherd to His Love," "Shall I compare thee to a summer's day?" "Death, be not proud," "The Raven," "The Road Not Taken," plus works by Blake, Wordsworth, Byron, Shelley, Keats, many others. 96pp. 5³⁄₁₆ x 8¼. 0-486-28553-7

100 SMALL HOUSES OF THE THIRTIES, Brown-Blodgett Company. Exterior photographs and floor plans for 100 charming structures. Illustrations of models accompanied by descriptions of interiors, color schemes, closet space, and other amenities. 200 illustrations. 112pp. 8⅜ x 11. 0-486-44131-8

1000 TURN-OF-THE-CENTURY HOUSES: With Illustrations and Floor Plans, Herbert C. Chivers. Reproduced from a rare edition, this showcase of homes ranges from cottages and bungalows to sprawling mansions. Each house is meticulously illustrated and accompanied by complete floor plans. 256pp. 9⅜ x 12¼.
0-486-45596-3

101 GREAT AMERICAN POEMS, Edited by The American Poetry & Literacy Project. Rich treasury of verse from the 19th and 20th centuries includes works by Edgar Allan Poe, Robert Frost, Walt Whitman, Langston Hughes, Emily Dickinson, T. S. Eliot, other notables. 96pp. 5³⁄₁₆ x 8¼. 0-486-40158-8

101 GREAT SAMURAI PRINTS, Utagawa Kuniyoshi. Kuniyoshi was a master of the warrior woodblock print — and these 18th-century illustrations represent the pinnacle of his craft. Full-color portraits of renowned Japanese samurais pulse with movement, passion, and remarkably fine detail. 112pp. 8⅜ x 11. 0-486-46523-3

ABC OF BALLET, Janet Grosser. Clearly worded, abundantly illustrated little guide defines basic ballet-related terms: arabesque, battement, pas de chat, relevé, sissonne, many others. Pronunciation guide included. Excellent primer. 48pp. 4³⁄₁₆ x 5¾.
0-486-40871-X

ACCESSORIES OF DRESS: An Illustrated Encyclopedia, Katherine Lester and Bess Viola Oerke. Illustrations of hats, veils, wigs, cravats, shawls, shoes, gloves, and other accessories enhance an engaging commentary that reveals the humor and charm of the many-sided story of accessorized apparel. 644 figures and 59 plates. 608pp. 6 ⅛ x 9¼.
0-486-43378-1

ADVENTURES OF HUCKLEBERRY FINN, Mark Twain. Join Huck and Jim as their boyhood adventures along the Mississippi River lead them into a world of excitement, danger, and self-discovery. Humorous narrative, lyrical descriptions of the Mississippi valley, and memorable characters. 224pp. 5³⁄₁₆ x 8¼. 0-486-28061-6

ALICE STARMORE'S BOOK OF FAIR ISLE KNITTING, Alice Starmore. A noted designer from the region of Scotland's Fair Isle explores the history and techniques of this distinctive, stranded-color knitting style and provides copious illustrated instructions for 14 original knitwear designs. 208pp. 8⅜ x 10⅞. 0-486-47218-3

ALICE'S ADVENTURES IN WONDERLAND, Lewis Carroll. Beloved classic about a little girl lost in a topsy-turvy land and her encounters with the White Rabbit, March Hare, Mad Hatter, Cheshire Cat, and other delightfully improbable characters. 42 illustrations by Sir John Tenniel. 96pp. 5³⁄₁₆ x 8¼. 0-486-27543-4

AMERICA'S LIGHTHOUSES: An Illustrated History, Francis Ross Holland. Profusely illustrated fact-filled survey of American lighthouses since 1716. Over 200 stations — East, Gulf, and West coasts, Great Lakes, Hawaii, Alaska, Puerto Rico, the Virgin Islands, and the Mississippi and St. Lawrence Rivers. 240pp. 8 x 10¾.
0-486-25576-X

AN ENCYCLOPEDIA OF THE VIOLIN, Alberto Bachmann. Translated by Frederick H. Martens. Introduction by Eugene Ysaye. First published in 1925, this renowned reference remains unsurpassed as a source of essential information, from construction and evolution to repertoire and technique. Includes a glossary and 73 illustrations. 496pp. 6⅛ x 9¼. 0-486-46618-3

ANIMALS: 1,419 Copyright-Free Illustrations of Mammals, Birds, Fish, Insects, etc., Selected by Jim Harter. Selected for its visual impact and ease of use, this outstanding collection of wood engravings presents over 1,000 species of animals in extremely lifelike poses. Includes mammals, birds, reptiles, amphibians, fish, insects, and other invertebrates. 284pp. 9 x 12. 0-486-23766-4

THE ANNALS, Tacitus. Translated by Alfred John Church and William Jackson Brodribb. This vital chronicle of Imperial Rome, written by the era's great historian, spans A.D. 14-68 and paints incisive psychological portraits of major figures, from Tiberius to Nero. 416pp. 5³⁄₁₆ x 8¼. 0-486-45236-0

ANTIGONE, Sophocles. Filled with passionate speeches and sensitive probing of moral and philosophical issues, this powerful and often-performed Greek drama reveals the grim fate that befalls the children of Oedipus. Footnotes. 64pp. 5³⁄₁₆ x 8 ¼. 0-486-27804-2

ART DECO DECORATIVE PATTERNS IN FULL COLOR, Christian Stoll. Reprinted from a rare 1910 portfolio, 160 sensuous and exotic images depict a breathtaking array of florals, geometrics, and abstracts — all elegant in their stark simplicity. 64pp. 8⅜ x 11. 0-486-44862-2

THE ARTHUR RACKHAM TREASURY: 86 Full-Color Illustrations, Arthur Rackham, Selected and Edited by Jeff A. Menges. A stunning treasury of 86 full-page plates span the famed English artist's career, from *Rip Van Winkle* (1905) to masterworks such as *Undine, A Midsummer Night's Dream*, and *Wind in the Willows* (1939). 96pp. 8⅜ x 11.
0-486-44685-9

THE AUTHENTIC GILBERT & SULLIVAN SONGBOOK, W. S. Gilbert and A. S. Sullivan. The most comprehensive collection available, this songbook includes selections from every one of Gilbert and Sullivan's light operas. Ninety-two numbers are presented uncut and unedited, and in their original keys. 410pp. 9 x 12.
0-486-23482-7

THE AWAKENING, Kate Chopin. First published in 1899, this controversial novel of a New Orleans wife's search for love outside a stifling marriage shocked readers. Today, it remains a first-rate narrative with superb characterization. New introductory Note. 128pp. 5³⁄₁₆ x 8¼. 0-486-27786-0

BASIC DRAWING, Louis Priscilla. Beginning with perspective, this commonsense manual progresses to the figure in movement, light and shade, anatomy, drapery, composition, trees and landscape, and outdoor sketching. Black-and-white illustrations throughout. 128pp. 8⅜ x 11. 0-486-45815-6

THE BATTLES THAT CHANGED HISTORY, Fletcher Pratt. Historian profiles 16 crucial conflicts, ancient to modern, that changed the course of Western civilization. Gripping accounts of battles led by Alexander the Great, Joan of Arc, Ulysses S. Grant, other commanders. 27 maps. 352pp. 5⅜ x 8½. 0-486-41129-X

BEETHOVEN'S LETTERS, Ludwig van Beethoven. Edited by Dr. A. C. Kalischer. Features 457 letters to fellow musicians, friends, greats, patrons, and literary men. Reveals musical thoughts, quirks of personality, insights, and daily events. Includes 15 plates. 410pp. 5⅜ x 8½. 0-486-22769-3

BERNICE BOBS HER HAIR AND OTHER STORIES, F. Scott Fitzgerald. This brilliant anthology includes 6 of Fitzgerald's most popular stories: "The Diamond as Big as the Ritz," the title tale, "The Offshore Pirate," "The Ice Palace," "The Jelly Bean," and "May Day." 176pp. 5⅜ x 8½. 0-486-47049-0

BESLER'S BOOK OF FLOWERS AND PLANTS: 73 Full-Color Plates from Hortus Eystettensis, 1613, Basilius Besler. Here is a selection of magnificent plates from the *Hortus Eystettensis,* which vividly illustrated and identified the plants, flowers, and trees that thrived in the legendary German garden at Eichstätt. 80pp. 8⅜ x 11. 0-486-46005-3

THE BOOK OF KELLS, Edited by Blanche Cirker. Painstakingly reproduced from a rare facsimile edition, this volume contains full-page decorations, portraits, illustrations, plus a sampling of textual leaves with exquisite calligraphy and ornamentation. 32 full-color illustrations. 32pp. 9⅜ x 12¼. 0-486-24345-1

THE BOOK OF THE CROSSBOW: With an Additional Section on Catapults and Other Siege Engines, Ralph Payne-Gallwey. Fascinating study traces history and use of crossbow as military and sporting weapon, from Middle Ages to modern times. Also covers related weapons: balistas, catapults, Turkish bows, more. Over 240 illustrations. 400pp. 7¼ x 10⅛. 0-486-28720-3

THE BUNGALOW BOOK: Floor Plans and Photos of 112 Houses, 1910, Henry L. Wilson. Here are 112 of the most popular and economic blueprints of the early 20th century — plus an illustration or photograph of each completed house. A wonderful time capsule that still offers a wealth of valuable insights. 160pp. 8⅜ x 11. 0-486-45104-6

THE CALL OF THE WILD, Jack London. A classic novel of adventure, drawn from London's own experiences as a Klondike adventurer, relating the story of a heroic dog caught in the brutal life of the Alaska Gold Rush. Note. 64pp. 5³⁄₁₆ x 8¼. 0-486-26472-6

CANDIDE, Voltaire. Edited by Francois-Marie Arouet. One of the world's great satires since its first publication in 1759. Witty, caustic skewering of romance, science, philosophy, religion, government — nearly all human ideals and institutions. 112pp. 5³⁄₁₆ x 8¼. 0-486-26689-3

CELEBRATED IN THEIR TIME: Photographic Portraits from the George Grantham Bain Collection, Edited by Amy Pastan. With an Introduction by Michael Carlebach. Remarkable portrait gallery features 112 rare images of Albert Einstein, Charlie Chaplin, the Wright Brothers, Henry Ford, and other luminaries from the worlds of politics, art, entertainment, and industry. 128pp. 8⅜ x 11. 0-486-46754-6

CHARIOTS FOR APOLLO: The NASA History of Manned Lunar Spacecraft to 1969, Courtney G. Brooks, James M. Grimwood, and Loyd S. Swenson, Jr. This illustrated history by a trio of experts is the definitive reference on the Apollo spacecraft and lunar modules. It traces the vehicles' design, development, and operation in space. More than 100 photographs and illustrations. 576pp. 6¾ x 9¼. 0-486-46756-2

A CHRISTMAS CAROL, Charles Dickens. This engrossing tale relates Ebenezer Scrooge's ghostly journeys through Christmases past, present, and future and his ultimate transformation from a harsh and grasping old miser to a charitable and compassionate human being. 80pp. 5³⁄₁₆ x 8¼.　　　　　　0-486-26865-9

COMMON SENSE, Thomas Paine. First published in January of 1776, this highly influential landmark document clearly and persuasively argued for American separation from Great Britain and paved the way for the Declaration of Independence. 64pp. 5³⁄₁₆ x 8¼.　　　　　　0-486-29602-4

THE COMPLETE SHORT STORIES OF OSCAR WILDE, Oscar Wilde. Complete texts of "The Happy Prince and Other Tales," "A House of Pomegranates," "Lord Arthur Savile's Crime and Other Stories," "Poems in Prose," and "The Portrait of Mr. W. H." 208pp. 5³⁄₁₆ x 8¼.　　　　　　0-486-45216-6

COMPLETE SONNETS, William Shakespeare. Over 150 exquisite poems deal with love, friendship, the tyranny of time, beauty's evanescence, death, and other themes in language of remarkable power, precision, and beauty. Glossary of archaic terms. 80pp. 5³⁄₁₆ x 8¼.　　　　　　0-486-26686-9

THE COUNT OF MONTE CRISTO: Abridged Edition, Alexandre Dumas. Falscly accused of treason, Edmond Dantès is imprisoned in the bleak Chateau d'If. After a hair-raising escape, he launches an elaborate plot to extract a bitter revenge against those who betrayed him. 448pp. 5³⁄₁₆ x 8¼.　　　　　　0-486-45643-9

CRAFTSMAN BUNGALOWS: Designs from the Pacific Northwest, Yoho & Merritt. This reprint of a rare catalog, showcasing the charming simplicity and cozy style of Craftsman bungalows, is filled with photos of completed homes, plus floor plans and estimated costs. An indispensable resource for architects, historians, and illustrators. 112pp. 10 x 7.　　　　　　0-486-46875-5

CRAFTSMAN BUNGALOWS: 59 Homes from "The Craftsman," Edited by Gustav Stickley. Best and most attractive designs from Arts and Crafts Movement publication — 1903–1916 — includes sketches, photographs of homes, floor plans, descriptive text. 128pp. 8¼ x 11.　　　　　　0-486-25829-7

CRIME AND PUNISHMENT, Fyodor Dostoyevsky. Translated by Constance Garnett. Supreme masterpiece tells the story of Raskolnikov, a student tormented by his own thoughts after he murders an old woman. Overwhelmed by guilt and terror, he confesses and goes to prison. 480pp. 5³⁄₁₆ x 8¼.　　　　　　0-486-41587-2

THE DECLARATION OF INDEPENDENCE AND OTHER GREAT DOCUMENTS OF AMERICAN HISTORY: 1775-1865, Edited by John Grafton. Thirteen compelling and influential documents: Henry's "Give Me Liberty or Give Me Death," Declaration of Independence, The Constitution, Washington's First Inaugural Address, The Monroe Doctrine, The Emancipation Proclamation, Gettysburg Address, more. 64pp. 5³⁄₁₆ x 8¼.　　　　　　0-486-41124-9

THE DESERT AND THE SOWN: Travels in Palestine and Syria, Gertrude Bell. "The female Lawrence of Arabia," Gertrude Bell wrote captivating, perceptive accounts of her travels in the Middle East. This intriguing narrative, accompanied by 160 photos, traces her 1905 sojourn in Lebanon, Syria, and Palestine. 368pp. 5⅜ x 8½.　　　　　　0-486-46876-3

A DOLL'S HOUSE, Henrik Ibsen. Ibsen's best-known play displays his genius for realistic prose drama. An expression of women's rights, the play climaxes when the central character, Nora, rejects a smothering marriage and life in "a doll's house." 80pp. 5³⁄₁₆ x 8¼.　　　　　　0-486-27062-9

DOOMED SHIPS: Great Ocean Liner Disasters, William H. Miller, Jr. Nearly 200 photographs, many from private collections, highlight tales of some of the vessels whose pleasure cruises ended in catastrophe: the *Morro Castle, Normandie, Andrea Doria, Europa,* and many others. 128pp. 8⅞ x 11¾.　　　　0-486-45366-9

THE DORÉ BIBLE ILLUSTRATIONS, Gustave Doré. Detailed plates from the Bible: the Creation scenes, Adam and Eve, horrifying visions of the Flood, the battle sequences with their monumental crowds, depictions of the life of Jesus, 241 plates in all. 241pp. 9 x 12.　　　　0-486-23004-X

DRAWING DRAPERY FROM HEAD TO TOE, Cliff Young. Expert guidance on how to draw shirts, pants, skirts, gloves, hats, and coats on the human figure, including folds in relation to the body, pull and crush, action folds, creases, more. Over 200 drawings. 48pp. 8¼ x 11.　　　　0-486-45591-2

DUBLINERS, James Joyce. A fine and accessible introduction to the work of one of the 20th century's most influential writers, this collection features 15 tales, including a masterpiece of the short-story genre, "The Dead." 160pp. 5³⁄₁₆ x 8¼.
0-486-26870-5

EASY-TO-MAKE POP-UPS, Joan Irvine. Illustrated by Barbara Reid. Dozens of wonderful ideas for three-dimensional paper fun — from holiday greeting cards with moving parts to a pop-up menagerie. Easy-to-follow, illustrated instructions for more than 30 projects. 299 black-and-white illustrations. 96pp. 8⅜ x 11.
0-486-44622-0

EASY-TO-MAKE STORYBOOK DOLLS: A "Novel" Approach to Cloth Dollmaking, Sherralyn St. Clair. Favorite fictional characters come alive in this unique beginner's dollmaking guide. Includes patterns for Pollyanna, Dorothy from *The Wonderful Wizard of Oz,* Mary of *The Secret Garden,* plus easy-to-follow instructions, 263 black-and-white illustrations, and an 8-page color insert. 112pp. 8¼ x 11.　0-486-47360-0

EINSTEIN'S ESSAYS IN SCIENCE, Albert Einstein. Speeches and essays in accessible, everyday language profile influential physicists such as Niels Bohr and Isaac Newton. They also explore areas of physics to which the author made major contributions. 128pp. 5 x 8.　　　　0-486-47011-3

EL DORADO: Further Adventures of the Scarlet Pimpernel, Baroness Orczy. A popular sequel to *The Scarlet Pimpernel,* this suspenseful story recounts the Pimpernel's attempts to rescue the Dauphin from imprisonment during the French Revolution. An irresistible blend of intrigue, period detail, and vibrant characterizations. 352pp. 5³⁄₁₆ x 8¼.　　　　0-486-44026-5

ELEGANT SMALL HOMES OF THE TWENTIES: 99 Designs from a Competition, Chicago Tribune. Nearly 100 designs for five- and six-room houses feature New England and Southern colonials, Normandy cottages, stately Italianate dwellings, and other fascinating snapshots of American domestic architecture of the 1920s. 112pp. 9 x 12.　　　　0-486-46910-7

THE ELEMENTS OF STYLE: The Original Edition, William Strunk, Jr. This is the book that generations of writers have relied upon for timeless advice on grammar, diction, syntax, and other essentials. In concise terms, it identifies the principal requirements of proper style and common errors. 64pp. 5⅜ x 8½.　0-486-44798-7

THE ELUSIVE PIMPERNEL, Baroness Orczy. Robespierre's revolutionaries find their wicked schemes thwarted by the heroic Pimpernel — Sir Percival Blakeney. In this thrilling sequel, Chauvelin devises a plot to eliminate the Pimpernel and his wife. 272pp. 5³⁄₁₆ x 8¼.　　　　0-486-45464-9

AN ENCYCLOPEDIA OF BATTLES: Accounts of Over 1,560 Battles from 1479 B.C. to the Present, David Eggenberger. Essential details of every major battle in recorded history from the first battle of Megiddo in 1479 B.C. to Grenada in 1984. List of battle maps. 99 illustrations. 544pp. 6½ x 9¼. 0-486-24913-1

ENCYCLOPEDIA OF EMBROIDERY STITCHES, INCLUDING CREWEL, Marion Nichols. Precise explanations and instructions, clearly illustrated, on how to work chain, back, cross, knotted, woven stitches, and many more — 178 in all, including Cable Outline, Whipped Satin, and Eyelet Buttonhole. Over 1400 illustrations. 219pp. 8⅜ x 11¼. 0-486-22929-7

ENTER JEEVES: 15 Early Stories, P. G. Wodehouse. Splendid collection contains first 8 stories featuring Bertie Wooster, the deliciously dim aristocrat and Jeeves, his brainy, imperturbable manservant. Also, the complete Reggie Pepper (Bertie's prototype) series. 288pp. 5⅜ x 8½. 0-486-29717-9

ERIC SLOANE'S AMERICA: Paintings in Oil, Michael Wigley. With a Foreword by Mimi Sloane. Eric Sloane's evocative oils of America's landscape and material culture shimmer with immense historical and nostalgic appeal. This original hardcover collection gathers nearly a hundred of his finest paintings, with subjects ranging from New England to the American Southwest. 128pp. 10⅝ x 9.

0-486-46525-X

ETHAN FROME, Edith Wharton. Classic story of wasted lives, set against a bleak New England background. Superbly delineated characters in a hauntingly grim tale of thwarted love. Considered by many to be Wharton's masterpiece. 96pp. 5 3⁄16 x 8 ¼. 0-486-26690-7

THE EVERLASTING MAN, G. K. Chesterton. Chesterton's view of Christianity — as a blend of philosophy and mythology, satisfying intellect and spirit — applies to his brilliant book, which appeals to readers' heads as well as their hearts. 288pp. 5⅜ x 8½. 0-486-46036-3

THE FIELD AND FOREST HANDY BOOK, Daniel Beard. Written by a co-founder of the Boy Scouts, this appealing guide offers illustrated instructions for building kites, birdhouses, boats, igloos, and other fun projects, plus numerous helpful tips for campers. 448pp. 5 3⁄16 x 8¼. 0-486-46191-2

FINDING YOUR WAY WITHOUT MAP OR COMPASS, Harold Gatty. Useful, instructive manual shows would-be explorers, hikers, bikers, scouts, sailors, and survivalists how to find their way outdoors by observing animals, weather patterns, shifting sands, and other elements of nature. 288pp. 5⅜ x 8½. 0-486-40613-X

FIRST FRENCH READER: A Beginner's Dual-Language Book, Edited and Translated by Stanley Appelbaum. This anthology introduces 50 legendary writers — Voltaire, Balzac, Baudelaire, Proust, more — through passages from *The Red and the Black, Les Misérables, Madame Bovary*, and other classics. Original French text plus English translation on facing pages. 240pp. 5⅜ x 8½. 0-486-46178-5

FIRST GERMAN READER: A Beginner's Dual-Language Book, Edited by Harry Steinhauer. Specially chosen for their power to evoke German life and culture, these short, simple readings include poems, stories, essays, and anecdotes by Goethe, Hesse, Heine, Schiller, and others. 224pp. 5⅜ x 8½. 0-486-46179-3

FIRST SPANISH READER: A Beginner's Dual-Language Book, Angel Flores. Delightful stories, other material based on works of Don Juan Manuel, Luis Taboada, Ricardo Palma, other noted writers. Complete faithful English translations on facing pages. Exercises. 176pp. 5⅜ x 8½. 0-486-25810-6

Browse over 9,000 books at www.doverpublications.com

FIVE ACRES AND INDEPENDENCE, Maurice G. Kains. Great back-to-the-land classic explains basics of self-sufficient farming. The one book to get. 95 illustrations. 397pp. 5⅜ x 8½. 0-486-20974-1

FLAGG'S SMALL HOUSES: Their Economic Design and Construction, 1922, Ernest Flagg. Although most famous for his skyscrapers, Flagg was also a proponent of the well-designed single-family dwelling. His classic treatise features innovations that save space, materials, and cost. 526 illustrations. 160pp. 9⅜ x 12¼. 0-486-45197-6

FLATLAND: A Romance of Many Dimensions, Edwin A. Abbott. Classic of science (and mathematical) fiction — charmingly illustrated by the author — describes the adventures of A. Square, a resident of Flatland, in Spaceland (three dimensions), Lineland (one dimension), and Pointland (no dimensions). 96pp. 5$\frac{3}{16}$ x 8¼. 0-486-27263-X

FRANKENSTEIN, Mary Shelley. The story of Victor Frankenstein's monstrous creation and the havoc it caused has enthralled generations of readers and inspired countless writers of horror and suspense. With the author's own 1831 introduction. 176pp. 5$\frac{3}{16}$ x 8¼. 0-486-28211-2

THE GARGOYLE BOOK: 572 Examples from Gothic Architecture, Lester Burbank Bridaham. Dispelling the conventional wisdom that French Gothic architectural flourishes were born of despair or gloom, Bridaham reveals the whimsical nature of these creations and the ingenious artisans who made them. 572 illustrations. 224pp. 8⅜ x 11. 0-486-44754-5

THE GIFT OF THE MAGI AND OTHER SHORT STORIES, O. Henry. Sixteen captivating stories by one of America's most popular storytellers. Included are such classics as "The Gift of the Magi," "The Last Leaf," and "The Ransom of Red Chief." Publisher's Note. 96pp. 5$\frac{3}{16}$ x 8¼. 0-486-27061-0

THE GOETHE TREASURY: Selected Prose and Poetry, Johann Wolfgang von Goethe. Edited, Selected, and with an Introduction by Thomas Mann. In addition to his lyric poetry, Goethe wrote travel sketches, autobiographical studies, essays, letters, and proverbs in rhyme and prose. This collection presents outstanding examples from each genre. 368pp. 5⅜ x 8½. 0-486-44780-4

GREAT EXPECTATIONS, Charles Dickens. Orphaned Pip is apprenticed to the dirty work of the forge but dreams of becoming a gentleman — and one day finds himself in possession of "great expectations." Dickens' finest novel. 400pp. 5$\frac{3}{16}$ x 8¼. 0-486-41586-4

GREAT WRITERS ON THE ART OF FICTION: From Mark Twain to Joyce Carol Oates, Edited by James Daley. An indispensable source of advice and inspiration, this anthology features essays by Henry James, Kate Chopin, Willa Cather, Sinclair Lewis, Jack London, Raymond Chandler, Raymond Carver, Eudora Welty, and Kurt Vonnegut, Jr. 192pp. 5⅜ x 8½. 0-486-45128-3

HAMLET, William Shakespeare. The quintessential Shakespearean tragedy, whose highly charged confrontations and anguished soliloquies probe depths of human feeling rarely sounded in any art. Reprinted from an authoritative British edition complete with illuminating footnotes. 128pp. 5$\frac{3}{16}$ x 8¼. 0-486-27278-8

THE HAUNTED HOUSE, Charles Dickens. A Yuletide gathering in an eerie country retreat provides the backdrop for Dickens and his friends — including Elizabeth Gaskell and Wilkie Collins — who take turns spinning supernatural yarns. 144pp. 5⅜ x 8½. 0-486-46309-5